Account Number	Account Title

Liability Accounts

200	Accounts Payable
201	Notes Payable
202	Discount on Notes Payable
203	Loan Payable
204	Interest Payable
205	Vouchers Payable
206	Salaries Payable (or Wages Payable)
207	Sales Salaries Payable
208	Office Salaries Payable
209	Officers' Salaries Payable
210	Unearned Delivery Fees
211	Unearned Subscriptions
212	Unearned Ticket Fees
213	Unearned Laundry Fees
214	Unearned Management Fees
215	Unearned Rent
216	Unearned Service Fees
217	Unearned Commissions
218	Mortgage Note Payable
219	Travel Expenses Payable
220	Employees' Federal Income Taxes Payable
221	FICA Taxes Payable
222	Medical Insurance Premiums Payable
223	Employees' State Income Taxes Payable
224	Federal Unemployment Taxes Payable
225	State Unemployment Taxes Payable
226	Sales Tax Payable
227	Federal Excise Tax Payable
230	Estimated Product Warranty Payable
232	Estimated Property Taxes Payable
235	Other Liabilities
240	Commissions Payable

Stockholder's Equity Accounts

300	Capital Stock
310	Retained Earnings
320	Dividends

Revenue and Gain Accounts

400	Service Revenue
401	Ticket Revenue
402	Horse Boarding Fees Revenue
403	Concessions Revenue
404	Riding and Lesson Fees Revenue
405	Tennis Lesson Revenue
406	Campsite Rental Revenue
407	Rental Revenue

PRINCIPLES OF
FINANCIAL & MANAGERIAL
ACCOUNTING

The Irwin Series in Undergraduate Accounting

Anderson and Clancy
Cost Accounting

Bernstein
Financial Statement Analysis: Theory, Application and Interpretation
Fifth Edition

Bernstein and Maksy
Cases in Financial Statement Reporting and Analysis

Boockholdt
Accounting Information Systems
Third Edition

Danos and Imhoff
Introduction to Financial Accounting

Deakin and Maher
Cost Accounting
Third Edition

Dyckman, Dukes, and Davis
Intermediate Accounting
Revised Edition

Dyckman, Dukes, and Davis
Intermediate Accounting
Standard Edition

Edwards, Hermanson, and Maher
Principles of Financial and Managerial Accounting
Revised Edition

Engler
Managerial Accounting
Third Edition

Engler and Bernstein
Advanced Accounting
Second Edition

FASB 1992–93 Editions
  Current Text: General Standards
  Current Text: Industry Standards
  Original Pronouncements, Volumes I and II
  Statements of Financial Accounting Concepts

Ferris
Financial Accounting and Corporate Reporting: A Casebook
Third Edition

Garrison
Managerial Accounting
Sixth Edition

Griffin, Williams, Boatsman, and Vickrey
Advanced Accounting
Sixth Edition

Hay and Engstrom
Essentials of Accounting for Governmental and Not-for-Profit Organizations
Third Edition

Hay and Wilson
Accounting for Governmental and NonProfit Entities
Ninth Edition

Hendriksen and Van Breda
Accounting Theory
Fifth Edition

Hermanson and Edwards
Financial Accounting
Fifth Edition

Hermanson, Edwards, and Maher
Accounting Principles
Fifth Edition

Hermanson, Plunkett, and Turner
Computerized Accounting with Peachtree Complete III

Hermanson, Strawser, and Strawser
Auditing Theory and Practice
Sixth Edition

Hopson, Spradling, and Meyer
Income Tax Fundamentals for 1992 Tax Returns, 1993 Edition

Hoyle
Advanced Accounting
Third Edition

Hutton and Dalton
Two 1992 Individual Tax Return Practice Problems

Hutton and Dalton
1992 Tax Return Practice Problems for Corporations, S Corporations, and Partnerships

Koerber
College Accounting
Revised Edition

Larson and Miller
Fundamental Accounting Principles
Thirteenth Edition

Larson and Miller
Financial Accounting
Fifth Edition

Marshall
A Survey of Accounting: What the Numbers Mean
Second Edition

Miller and Redding
The FASB: The People, The Process, and the Politics
Second Edition

Mueller, Gernon, and Meek
Accounting: An International Perspective
Second Edition

Pratt and Kulsrud
Federal Taxation, 1993 Edition

Pratt and Kulsrud
Individual Taxation, 1993 Edition

Pratt, Burns, and Kulsrud
Corporate Partnership, Estate and Gift Taxation, 1993 Edition

Rayburn
Cost Accounting: Using a Cost Management Approach
Fifth Edition

Robertson
Auditing
Seventh Edition

Schroeder and Zlatkovich
Survey of Accounting

Short
Fundamentals of Financial Accounting
Seventh Edition

Smith and Wiggins
Readings and Problems in Accounting Information Systems

Whittington, Pany, Meigs, and Meigs
Principles of Auditing
Tenth Edition

PRINCIPLES OF FINANCIAL & MANAGERIAL ACCOUNTING

Revised Edition

JAMES DON EDWARDS, PH. D., CPA

J. M. Tull Professor of Accounting
J. M. Tull School of Accounting
University of Georgia

ROGER H. HERMANSON, PH. D., CPA

Regents Professor of Accounting
Ernst & Young–J. W. Holloway Memorial Professor
School of Accountancy
Georgia State University

MICHAEL W. MAHER, PH. D., CPA

Graduate School of Management
University of California at Davis

IRWIN
Homewood, IL 60430
Boston, MA 02116

This symbol indicates that the paper in this book is made of
recycled paper. Its fiber content exceeds the recommended
minimum of 50% waste paper fibers as specified by the EPA.

FASB Concept Statements: Copyright by Financial Accounting Standards Board,
401 Merritt 7, P.O. Box 5116, Norwalk Connecticut, 06856-5116, U.S.A.
Reprinted with permission. Copies of the complete documents are available from
the FASB.

The previous edition of this book was published under the title,
A Survey of Financial and Managerial Accounting

Senior sponsoring editor: Ron M. Regis
Editorial coordinator: Jennifer Lloyd
Marketing manager: Cindy L. Ledwith
Project editor: Karen M. Smith
Production manager: Bette K. Ittersagen
Designer: Jeanne M. Rivera
Art coordinator: Mark Malloy
Compositor: BiComp, Inc.
Typeface: 10/12 Times Roman
Printer: R. R. Donnelley & Sons Company

Library of Congress Cataloging-in-Publication Data

Edwards, James Don.
    Principles of financial and managerial accounting. — Rev. ed. /
James Don Edwards, Roger H. Hermanson, Michael W. Maher.
        p.   cm.
    Rev. and expanded ed. of: A survey of financial and managerial
accounting / James Don Edwards, Roger H. Hermanson, R. F. Salmonson.
5th ed. 1989.
    Includes index.
    ISBN 0-256-13000-0
    1. Accounting.   2. Managerial accounting.   I. Hermanson, Roger H.
II. Maher, Michael, date.   IV. Title.
HF5635.S17   1993
657—dc20   92–31865

Printed in the United States of America

1 2 3 4 5 6 7 8 9 0 DOC 0 9 8 7 6 5 4 3

PREFACE

This edition of *Principles of Financial and Managerial Accounting* has undergone substantial changes from the previous edition. The book is now a 50-50 split between financial and managerial accounting. The title of the book has changed from *A Survey of Financial and Managerial Accounting* to reflect this new emphasis and the fact that the book has been expanded from 20 chapters to 22 chapters (with two optional "appendix" chapters). Our coauthor on our *Accounting Principles* text, Michael Maher, has joined us on this text. He is a nationally renowned managerial accountant and has strengthened and expanded the managerial coverage substantially.

Numerous reviewer comments resulted in improvements in almost every chapter. The important topic of ethics has been included in every chapter throughout the text because of its recent emphasis in business.

The Accounting Education Change Commission recommends that the first course "be a rigorous course focusing on the relevance of accounting information to decision making (use) as well as its source (preparation)."[1] We believe this new edition meets this standard. This text provides both the "how" and "why" in applying accounting concepts and techniques. The use of accounting information is the focus of our business decision problem(s) included at the end of every chapter and of many of the ethics cases included in each chapter. Several ethics cases also provide students with the opportunity to confront unstructured problems having more than one defensible solution.

This text is for use in introductory accounting courses—where 22 to 24 chapters will be covered instead of the traditional 28 chapters—or in survey of accounting courses. The book is suitable whether these courses are conducted in colleges and universities or in business settings.

The Accounting Education Change Commission states that the first course in accounting ". . . should help students perform financial analysis; derive information for personal or organizational decisions; and understand business, governmental, and other organizational entities."[2] We believe our chapters on analysis of financial statements and the statement of cash flows serve to meet the first objective. Our business decision problems at the end of every chapter emphasize decision making. And our inclusion of four sets of real company financial statements—with questions, exercises, and business decision problems based on these actual financial statements—adds a

---

[1] Accounting Education Change Commission, *Position Statement No. Two* (June 1992), "The First Course In Accounting," p. 3.

[2] *Ibid.* p. 2.

"real-world" emphasis that few other texts can match. Excerpts included in some chapters from *Accounting Trends and Techniques* and in every chapter from accounting and business publications (in boxed items called "A Broader Perspective") also add to the "real-world" emphasis throughout the text.

We recognize that people taking these accounting courses seek various careers. Some may choose accounting as a profession, while others will choose another area of business or possibly a nonbusiness career. All who study from this text will find the ability to use and interpret accounting information valuable in both their careers and their personal lives.

Principles of Financial and Managerial Accounting serves as a foundation for subsequent courses in accounting and business. We assume that students using this text have a limited understanding of business concepts. Thus, when new terms and concepts are introduced they are defined, illustrated, and fully explained.

Two major reasons that previous editions of this text had such "staying power" with adopters were their readability and teachability. These two attributes combined to make it easy for students to learn from the text. With each revision, we continue to focus on improving these features even more. The result of our efforts is a text of which we are especially proud.

NEW FEATURES IN THIS EDITION

- A challenging and realistic ethics case entitled, "Ethics: A Closer Look" now appears in every chapter. In the previous edition, no ethics cases were included.
- New "real-world" questions and exercises were added to most chapters. A new "real-world" business decision case was added to several chapters.
- Appendix C at the end of the text includes excerpts from the annual reports of The Coca-Cola Company, Maytag Corporation, The Limited, Inc., and John H. Harland Company. Many of the "real-world" questions, exercises, and business decision problems are based on these excerpts.
- A current business situation or some other form of "real-world" information entitled "A Broader Perspective" was added to each chapter.
- Each chapter includes a "Self-Test," which consists of true-false and multiple-choice questions. The answers and explanations for these appear at the end of the chapter.
- The Introduction to the text provides the instructor with material to discuss on the first day of class. The Accounting Education Change Commission states that ". . . students completing the first course in accounting should have a broad view of accounting's role in satisfying society's need for information and its function in business, in government, in other organizations, and in public accounting. Students should gain an overview of the accounting profession, encompassing its history, its ethics, its public

responsibilities, and its international dimensions as well as an appreciation of the role of auditing in enhancing the credibility of publicly reported information."[3] The Introduction provides much of this material and gives the instructor the opportunity to supplement the content with his or her own perceptions. This edition contains a section at the end of the Introduction entitled, "How to Study Chapters in this Text," that should be very helpful to students.

- Former Chapter 4, on inventories, has been split into two chapters (4 and 5). Chapter 5 places emphasis on perpetual inventory procedure because this method is used increasingly as companies continue switching to computerized accounting software packages.

- An important topic in accounting today, international accounting, is now covered in an appendix to Chapter 11. We believe this coverage is the most complete of any introductory text. This appendix will assist in meeting the accreditation standards of the American Assembly of Collegiate Schools of Business regarding internationalizing the curriculum.

- The managerial chapters have been expanded to constitute half of the book and have been thoroughly modernized in accordance with the "new managerial approach." This modernization addresses the criticisms that have been made about the antiquated coverage of managerial accounting in most textbooks.

- Examples of modern, relevant topics in the managerial chapters include activity based costing, just-in-time inventory systems, managerial accounting in high-tech companies, allocation of joint-product costs, job order and process costing in service companies, effects of automation on cost-volume-profit analysis, using computer spreadsheets for cost-volume-profit analysis, distribution cost analysis, and nonfinancial performance measures.

- Special emphasis is given just-in-time production systems. The cost savings of this system are described. Also, the effects of the use of the just-in-time system on the recording of transactions are discussed and illustrated.

- Manufacturing overhead costs are assigned to production on a machine-hour basis to a greater extent to conform to modern practice.

- The chapter on short-term decision making (Chapter 19 in the previous edition) was divided into two chapters. The portion covering cost-volume-profit analysis is now Chapter 15, and the portion covering differential analysis is now Chapter 16.

- The last two chapters of the text on the analysis of financial statements and the statement of cash flows provide the student with enhanced analytical skills, as recommended by the Accounting Education Change Commission. While studying these chapters, students can refer to the financial statements of four real companies in Appendix C to use their newly acquired analytical tools on those financial statements. In fact, each of four teams of students could be assigned to apply the analytical techniques on

---

[3] *Ibid.* p. 2.

one of the real companies in Appendix C and report the results of their analysis to the class. This type of group project is strongly encouraged by the Accounting Education Change Commission.

- A uniform chart of accounts appears on the inside of the cover to the text. This uniform chart of accounts is used consistently throughout the first eight chapters. We believe students will benefit from using the same chart of accounts for all homework problems in those chapters.
- Many new illustrations were added throughout the text.

SPECIAL FEATURES THAT MAKE THIS EDITION MORE READABLE

- Introductions have been improved in many chapters. We continue to work at making the introductions both interesting to read and helpful as a preview to the chapter. Students discover in the first paragraph of each chapter what the chapter contains and how the contents fit into the accounting process that has been covered up to that point. The introductions give continuity to the text and show students how accounting concepts relate to one another.
- Each chapter contains an ethics case entitled "A Closer Look." These cases present challenging and realistic situations that are likely to occur in the careers of accounting and business graduates.
- Each chapter has a section "Understanding the Learning Objectives." These "summaries" enable the student to determine how well the learning objectives were accomplished. We were the first authors (1974) to ever include learning objectives in an accounting text. These objectives are presented at the beginning of the chapter, as marginal notes within the chapter, and in the exercises and problems at the end of the chapter.
- Improvements in the text's organization reflect feedback from adopters, suggestions by reviewers, and a serious study of the learning process itself by the authors and editors. New material is introduced only after the stage has been set by transitional paragraphs between topic headings. Transitions provide students with the reasons for proceeding to the new material, and they explain the progression of topics within the chapter.
- Without business experience, students sometimes lack a frame of reference for relating to accounting concepts and business transactions. In this edition we have sought to involve the student more in real-world business applications as we introduced and explained the material.
- Each chapter contains a business situation or "real-world" information entitled "A Broader Perspective." These situations, taken from articles in current business periodicals such as *Accounting Today, New Accountant, The Wall Street Journal, Business Week,* and *Management Accounting,* relate to material covered in that chapter or present other useful information. These real-world examples demonstrate the business relevance of accounting.
- We have retained and revised our popular "Business Decision Problems" at the end of each chapter. These problems give students an opportunity

to apply their newly learned accounting concepts to management situations in the business world. Several of these problems now deal with real companies and constitute critical thinking cases.

- Numerous illustrations adapted from *Accounting Trends and Techniques* show the frequent use of various accounting techniques in business. Scattered throughout the text, these illustrations give students real-world data to consider while learning about different accounting techniques.
- Special attention was paid to continually improve the book's teaching effectiveness. Specifically:

  Key terms are set in boldface for emphasis.

  End-of-chapter glossaries contain the page number where the new term was first introduced and defined. Students can easily flip back to the original discussion and study the term's significance in context with the chapter material.

  A description of each exercise and problem, with an indication of the learning objective(s) covered by each, appears in the left-hand margin beside each one. These descriptions let students know what they are expected to do in the problem.

  The use of learning objectives has been extended throughout each chapter.

- Appendix D reprints the codes of ethics of the American Institute of Certified Public Accountants, the Institute of Management Accountants, and the Financial Executives Institute. We believe reading this appendix will help students understand the high standards of behavior expected of accountants. We and others feel that the communication of ethical considerations to students is extremely important.

TEACHING AIDS FOR THE INSTRUCTOR— SUPPLEMENTARY MATERIAL

A package of supplemental teaching aids contains all you need to efficiently and effectively teach the course. For universities where graduate students or part-time instructors teach this course, we have an excellent instructor's resource guide (new in this edition) and a test bank to assist in the preparation of both lectures and examinations. The test bank has been carefully edited to revise and improve the questions, and it has been substantially increased in size.

Instructor's Resource Guide and Teaching Transparency Masters. This new supplement is extremely helpful to both new instructors of accounting and new adopters of our test. The pages are three-hole punched so that individual chapters or the entire manual can be carried in a notebook for easy access. The instructor's resource guide contains sample syllabi for both quarter- and semester-basis courses. New in this edition, each chapter in the Instructor's Resource Guide contains (1) a summary of major concepts that can serve as a handy lecture organizer; (2) learning objectives from the text repeated for the instructor's convenience; (3) space for the instructor's own notes; (4) an outline of the chapter with an indication of when each exercise can be worked; and (5) detailed lecture notes that also refer to specific end-of-chapter exercises illustrating these concepts. Any of these formats can serve as effective lecture notes depending on the instructor's personal preference. Each chapter also contains (6) a summary of the estimated time, learning objectives, level of difficulty, and content of each exercise and problem. This is useful in deciding which items to cover in class or to assign as homework. Finally, each chapter contains (7) teaching transparency masters that can be used in discussing important points in that chapter.

Solutions Manual.   The solutions manual contains suggested discussion points for the ethics case as well as detailed answers to the questions, exercises, problems, and business decision problems for each chapter.

Test Bank.   The test bank, *expanded and revised significantly in this edition,* contains about 3,000 questions and problems to choose from in preparing examinations. The exam book contains true-false questions, multiple-choice questions, and short problems for each chapter.

Computest 3.   This improved microcomputer version of the text bank allows editing of questions, provides up to 99 different versions of each test, and allows question selection based on type of question or level of difficulty. Computest 3 is available on 5.25″ and 3.5″ disks.

LEARNING AIDS FOR THE STUDENT— SUPPLEMENTARY MATERIAL

Study Guide.   A comprehensive Study Guide is available. The purpose of the Study Guide is to review and reinforce the concepts the student has learned in studying each chapter. Included for each chapter are learning objectives, a reference outline, chapter review, a different demonstration problem and solution than is shown in the text, matching and true-false questions, completion questions and exercises, multiple-choice questions, and solutions to all exercises and questions.

Working Papers.   Also available are Working Papers for completing assigned exercises, problems, and business decision problems. In many instances, the Working Papers are partially filled in to reduce the "pencil pushing" required to solve the problems, yet are not so complete as to reduce the learning impact. The format and spacing used in the Working Papers are generally similar to the Solutions Manual. This feature makes it easier for the grader to compare the students' solutions to the authors' solutions.

Check Figures.   A list of check figures gives key amounts for the problems and the business decision problems. Check figures are available in bulk free to adopters. Students can determine whether they are "on the right track" when working a problem by comparing their solution with the key amounts given for a particular problem.

SPECIAL FEATURES THAT MAKE THIS EDITION MORE TEACHABLE

- We have included a vast amount of resource material within the text from which the instructor may draw: a relatively large selection of end-of-chapter exercises and problems; from one to three business decision problems per chapter; and excerpts from the annual reports of four different companies that can be used throughout the course to illustrate financial reporting.
- All end-of-chapter problem materials (questions, exercises, problems, and business decision problems) have been thoroughly revised. "Real-world" questions, exercises, and business decision problems have been added to many of the chapters.
- All end-of-chapter problem material has been traced back to the chapters to ensure that nothing is asked of a student that does not appear in the book. This was a strength of the previous edition, ensuring that instructors could confidently assign problems without having to check for applicability. Also, we took notes while teaching from the text and clarified problem and exercise instructions that seemed confusing to our students.
- Demonstration problems and solutions are included for each chapter, and a different one appears for each chapter in the Study Guide and the Working Papers Manual. These demonstration problems help students to assess their own progress by showing them how problems that focus on the topic(s) covered in the chapter are worked, before the students do their assigned homework problems.
- In Chapter 4 we present two variations of the closing process: merchandise-related expense accounts are treated first as closing entries and then as adjusting entries. Instructors seem to be quite evenly split on their "favorite" procedure and can choose which method(s) to teach.

SPECIAL FEATURES OF THIS EDITION THAT HELP STUDENTS LEARN ACCOUNTING

Students often come into beginning accounting courses feeling anxious about learning the material. Recognizing this apprehension, we studied ways to make learning easier and came up with some helpful ideas on how to make this edition work even better for students. Our "study of learning" resulted in the following improvements. Specifically we:

- Organized ideas for improved flow of material. The improved introductions preview the chapter material, so students know exactly where they have been and where they are going. Transitional paragraphs are used to improve the flow and continuity of material. Carefully worded and designed headings are strategically placed in the chapters as signposts. Every chapter ends with a reference to what the next chapter covers and how it relates to the chapter just covered.
- Included examples to associate concepts with experiences. Throughout

the test we used examples taken from everyday life to relate an accounting concept being introduced or discussed to students' experiences.
- Used an informal style and the active voice. Our research showed that for an accounting principles text today, an informal writing style and the active voice are more effective for learning than the formal style and passive voice. In this edition, we use the pronoun *you* more to involve students with the text material.
- Added several new graphics. Learning is enhanced when a picture reinforces a verbal understanding of new material. Wherever possible, we have added graphic illustrations to help explain accounting concepts to students. For example, in Chapter 2 we have illustrated the steps in recording and posting the effects of a business transaction.

We are indebted to several individuals for reviewing the manuscript of this edition: Paula Morris, Kennesaw State College; David J. Evans, Johnson County Community College; and Nancy L. Saltz, Lynchburg College. In addition, we are especially indebted to colleagues and students at our respective universities for their helpful suggestions.

James Don Edwards
Roger H. Hermanson
Michael W. Maher

NOTE TO THE STUDENT

A Study Guide and a Working Papers manual are available to assist you in understanding the material in this text. Students who used these materials in the previous edition found them to be extremely helpful in maximizing their understanding and class performance. Each chapter of the Study Guide is keyed to a chapter of the text and provides learning objectives, a reference outline, a detailed chapter review, a demonstration problem and answer, matching questions concerning important new terms and concepts, completion questions and exercises, true-false questions, and multiple-choice questions. Answers to all Study Guide exercises and questions are included in the Guide to provide you with immediate feedback on your responses. Explanations are also given for the answers to many of the true-false and multiple-choice questions. The Working Papers manual includes papers to use for assigned exercises and problems. Both the Study Guide and the Working Papers booklets, published by Richard D. Irwin, Inc., are available through your college bookstore. If they are not in stock, please ask your bookstore manager to order copies for you.

J.D.E.
R.H.H.
M.W.M.

CONTENTS IN BRIEF

CONTENTS

P A R T

II

FINANCIAL ACCOUNTING: PROCESSING ACCOUNTING INFORMATION   61

PART III

FINANCIAL ACCOUNTING: ASSETS, LIABILITIES, AND STOCKHOLDERS' EQUITY   305

CHAPTER 14   PROCESS COST SYSTEMS 737

P A R T

V

MANAGERIAL ACCOUNTING: DECISION MAKING, PLANNING, AND CONTROL 775

CHAPTER 15   COST-VOLUME-PROFIT ANALYSIS 777

CHAPTER 16   SHORT-TERM DECISION MAKING:
DIFFERENTIAL ANALYSIS 809

CHAPTER 17   BUDGETING FOR PLANNING
AND CONTROL 841

CHAPTER 18   CONTROL THROUGH STANDARD COSTS 883

PART

I

FINANCIAL ACCOUNTING: THE LANGUAGE OF BUSINESS

INTRODUCTION: THE ACCOUNTING ENVIRONMENT

CHAPTER 1
ACCOUNTING AND ITS USE IN
BUSINESS DECISIONS

INTRODUCTION: THE ACCOUNTING ENVIRONMENT

LEARNING OBJECTIVES

After studying this Introduction, you should be able to:

1. Define accounting.
2. Describe the functions performed by accountants.
3. Describe employment opportunities in accounting.
4. Differentiate between financial and managerial accounting.
5. Identify several organizations that have a role in the development of financial accounting standards.

You have embarked on the challenging and rewarding study of accounting—an old and time-honored discipline. History indicates that all developed societies require certain accounting records. Record-keeping in an accounting sense is thought to have begun about 4000 B.C.

Record-keeping, control, and verification problems of the ancient world had characteristics similar to those we encounter today. For example, ancient governments also kept records of receipts and disbursements and used procedures that checked on the honesty and reliability of employees.

A study of the evolution of accounting suggests that accounting processes have developed primarily in response to business needs. Also, economic progress has affected the development of accounting processes. History shows that the higher the level of civilization, the more elaborate the accounting methods.

The emergence of double-entry bookkeeping was a crucial event in accounting history. In 1494, a Franciscan monk, Luca Pacioli, described the double-entry "Method of Venice" system in his text called *Summa de Arithmetica, Geometric, Proportion et Proportionalite* (Everything about Arithmetic, Geometry, and Proportion). Many consider Pacioli's *Summa* to be a reworked version of a manuscript that circulated among teachers and pupils of the Venetian school of commerce and arithmetic.

In accounting, the name "Luca Pacioli" will always be important for the contribution he made to accounting systems. At the age of 20, Pacioli became a tutor to three sons of a rich merchant. Later he lectured on mathematics and traveled throughout Italy. He also authored several books. Pacioli's friend Leonardo da Vinci helped prepare the drawings for one of Pacioli's books. Records indicate that Pacioli calculated the amount of bronze Leonardo needed for his large statue of the Duke. Thus, early civilizations recognized the accountant's special abilities in working with other professions to improve the overall quality of life.

Since Pacioli's days, the roles of accountants and professional accounting organizations have expanded in business and society. As professionals, accountants have a responsibility for performing public service above their commitment to personal economic gain. Complementing their obligation to society, accountants have analytical and evaluative skills needed in the solution of ever-growing world problems. The special abilities of accountants, their independence, and their high ethical standards permit them to make a significant and unique contribution to business and areas of public interest.

You will probably find that of all the business knowledge you have acquired or will learn, the study of accounting will be the most useful. Your financial and economic decisions as a student and consumer involve accounting information. When you file income tax returns, accounting information will help determine your taxes payable. Understanding the discipline of accounting will also influence many of your future professional decisions. You cannot escape the effects of accounting information on your personal and professional life.

Every profit-seeking business organization that has economic resources, such as money, machinery, and buildings, uses accounting information. For this reason, accounting is called the *language of business*. Accounting also serves as the language providing financial information about not-for-profit organizations such as governments, churches, charities, fraternities, and hospitals. However, this text concentrates on the use of accounting as it relates to the business firm.

The accounting system of a profit-seeking business is an information system designed to provide relevant financial information on the resources of a business and the effects of the use of these resources. Information is relevant if it has some impact on a decision that must be made. Companies present this relevant information in their financial statements.[1] In preparing these statements, accountants consider the types of users of the information,

---

[1] When first studying any discipline, students encounter new terms. Usually these terms are set in boldface and defined at their first occurrence. However, sometimes it is more feasible not to define a term at its first occurrence. This is true with the term *financial statements*. This term is defined later in the Introduction and set in boldface. The boldface terms are also listed and defined at the end of this Introduction, or in the case of the chapters, at the end of the chapter. After the definition of the term in the term list, a page number is given in italics indicating where the term is discussed in the chapter.

such as owners and creditors, and decisions they make that require financial information.

As a background for studying accounting, this Introduction defines accounting and lists the functions accountants perform. You will learn about the employment opportunities in accounting and be able to differentiate between financial and managerial accounting. Accounting information must conform to certain standards. This Introduction discusses several prominent organizations contributing to these standards. As you continue your study of accounting in the chapters of this text, accounting—the language of business—will also become your language. You will also realize that you are constantly exposed to accounting information in your everyday life.

ACCOUNTING DEFINED

Objective 1
Define accounting

The American Accounting Association—one of the accounting organizations discussed later in this Introduction—defines **accounting** as **"the process of identifying, measuring, and communicating economic information to permit informed judgments and decisions by the users of the information."**[2] This information is primarily financial—stated in money terms. Accounting, then, is a measurement and communication process used to report on the activities of profit-seeking business organizations and not-for-profit organizations. As a measurement and communication process for business, accounting supplies information that permits informed judgments and decisions by users of the data.

The accounting process provides financial data for a broad range of individuals whose objectives in studying the data vary widely. Bank officials, for example, may study a company's financial statements to evaluate the company's ability to repay a loan. Prospective investors may compare accounting data from several companies to decide which company represents the best investment. Accounting also supplies management with significant financial data that are useful for decision making.

Reliable information is necessary before decision makers can make a sound decision involving the allocation of scarce resources. In decision making, you always have alternatives—even if one of the alternatives is to take no action or to delay action. Accounting information is valuable because decision makers can use it to evaluate the financial consequences of each alternative. Accountants eliminate the need for a "crystal ball" to estimate the future. They can reduce uncertainty by using professional judgment to quantify the future financial impact of various alternatives.

Although accounting information plays a significant role within the organization in reducing uncertainty, it also provides financial data for persons outside the company. This information tells how a company's management

---

[2] American Accounting Association, *A Statement of Basic Accounting Theory* (Evanston, Ill., 1966), p. 1.

has discharged its responsibility for protecting and managing the company's resources. Owners have the right to know how a company is managing their investments. In fulfilling this obligation, accountants prepare financial statements such as an income statement, a statement of retained earnings, a balance sheet, and a statement of cash flows. In addition, they prepare tax returns for federal and state governments as well as fulfill other governmental filing requirements.

Accounting is often confused with bookkeeping. Bookkeeping is a mechanical process that records the routine economic activities of a business. Accounting includes bookkeeping but goes well beyond it in scope. Accountants analyze and interpret financial information, prepare financial statements, conduct audits, design accounting systems, prepare special business and financial studies, prepare forecasts and budgets, and provide tax services.

Objective 2
Describe the functions performed by accountants

Specifically the accounting process consists of the following groups of functions (Illustration 0.1):

1. Accountants *observe* many events (or activities) and *identify* and *measure* in financial terms (dollars) those events considered evidence of economic activity. (These three functions are often collectively referred to as *analyze*.) The purchase and sale of goods and services are examples of economic events.
2. Next, the economic events are *recorded, classified* into meaningful groups, and *summarized*.
3. Accountants *report* on economic events (or business activity) by preparing financial statements and special reports. Often accountants are asked to *interpret* these statements and reports for various groups such as management, investors, and creditors. Interpretation may involve determining how the business is performing compared to prior years and other similar businesses.

EMPLOYMENT OPPORTUNITIES IN ACCOUNTING

Objective 3
Describe employment opportunities in accounting

As stated earlier, accounting is an old profession. Business transactions have been recorded for centuries. However, only during the last half-century has accounting gained the same professional status as the medical and legal professions. Today, the accountants that practice their profession in the United States number well over a million. In addition, several million people hold accounting-related positions. Typically, accountants provide services in various branches of accounting. These branches include public accounting, management (industrial) accounting, governmental or other not-for-profit accounting, and higher education. The future for employment in accounting is very promising. According to the Bureau of Labor Statistics, the demand for accountants will increase by 40% over the next ten years. This

Illustration 0.1
FUNCTIONS PERFORMED BY ACCOUNTANTS

```
┌─────────────────────────────┐  ┐
│      Observe events         │  │
└─────────────────────────────┘  │
              │                   │
              ▼                   │  Observe, identify,
┌─────────────────────────────┐  │  and measure
│  Identify those events that │  │  events
│  are economic events        │  │
└─────────────────────────────┘  │
              │                   │
              ▼                   │
┌─────────────────────────────┐  │
│  Measure economic events    │  │
│  in financial terms         │  │
└─────────────────────────────┘  ┘
              │
              ▼
┌─────────────────────────────┐  ┐
│  Record measurements        │  │
└─────────────────────────────┘  │
              │                   │
              ▼                   │  Record, classify,
┌─────────────────────────────┐  │  and summarize
│  Classify measurements      │  │  measurements
└─────────────────────────────┘  │
              │                   │
              ▼                   │
┌─────────────────────────────┐  │
│  Summarize measurements     │  │
└─────────────────────────────┘  ┘
              │
              ▼
┌─────────────────────────────┐  ┐
│  Report economic events     │  │
│  in financial statements    │  │
│  and other reports          │  │  Report economic
└─────────────────────────────┘  │  events and interpret
              │                   │  financial
              ▼                   │  statements
┌─────────────────────────────┐  │
│  Interpret the contents     │  │
│  of financial statements    │  │
│  and other reports          │  │
└─────────────────────────────┘  ┘
```

increase is greater than for any other discipline.[3] You may want to consider accounting as a career.

Public Accounting

Public accounting firms offer professional accounting and related services for a fee to companies, other organizations, and individuals. An accountant may

---

[3] "Projection Puts Demand for CPAs Up 40% by 2000," *Accounting Today,* October 23, 1989, p. 14.

become a **Certified Public Accountant (CPA).** A CPA is a person who has passed an examination prepared and graded by the American Institute of Certified Public Accountants (AICPA). In addition, CPA candidates must meet other requirements, which include obtaining a state license. These requirements vary by state. A number of states require a CPA candidate to have completed certain accounting courses and earned a certain number of college credits (five years of study in an increasing number of states); worked a certain number of years in public accounting, industry, or government; and lived in that state a certain length of time before taking the CPA examination.

After a candidate passes the CPA examination, some states (called *one-tier states*) insist that the candidate meet all requirements before the state grants the CPA certificate and license to practice. Other states (called *two-tier states*) issue the CPA certificate immediately after the candidate passes the exam. However, these states issue the license to practice only after all other requirements have been met. CPAs who want to renew their license to practice must "stay current" by engaging in continuing professional education programs. They must also document this education to the State Board of Accountancy, the state CPA society, and (in the future) the American Institute of Certified Public Accountants. A person cannot claim to be a CPA and offer the services normally provided by a CPA unless that person holds an active license to practice.

Until the late 1980s, the public accounting profession in the United States consisted of the "Big-Eight" international CPA firms, several national firms, many regional firms, and numerous local firms. The Big-Eight firms included Arthur Andersen & Co.; Arthur Young & Co.; Coopers & Lybrand; Deloitte, Haskins & Sells; Ernst & Whinney; Peat Marwick & Co.; Price Waterhouse & Co.; and Touche Ross & Co. These public accounting firms provided auditing, tax, and management advisory (or consulting) services. In the late 1980s, some of the Big-Eight firms have merged with non-Big-Eight firms or other Big-Eight firms to become the "Big-Six."

In 1987, KMG Main Hurdman and Peat Marwick Mitchell became the first major merger of CPA firms forming the world's largest accounting firm at that time. Perhaps it was the successful completion of this merger that persuaded other international firms to combine their practices. In 1989 Ernst & Whinney and Arthur Young merged into Ernst & Young and moved ahead of KPMG Peat Marwick in size. Deloitte, Haskins & Sells and Touche Ross merged their two firms into a new firm called Deloitte & Touche. One of the primary motivations for those mergers was to be large enough to serve large international clients as the economy becomes more global.

Illustration 0.2 shows the ranking of the Big-Six CPA firms by approximate size of their U.S. revenues for 1990. As you can see in the illustration, the ranking would differ if the firms were ranked by number of offices, number of partners, or number of professionals.

Illustration 0.2
THE BIG-SIX CPA FIRMS—RANKED BY APPROXIMATE 1990 U.S. REVENUES*

Firm Name	Location of Headquarters	Approximate U.S. Revenues	No. of Offices	No. of Partners	No. of Professionals
Ernst & Young	New York	$2,195,000,000	123	2,054	18,653
Arthur Andersen	Chicago	1,993,000,000	82	1,268	17,740
KPMG Peat Marwick	Montvale, N.J.	1,929,000,000	132	1,900	14,400
Deloitte & Touche	Wilton, Conn.	1,900,000,000	126	1,713	15,500
Coopers & Lybrand	New York	1,250,000,000	98	1,253	16,000
Price Waterhouse	New York	1,100,000,000	115	920	9,430

* This information is based on "An Annual Survey of America's Largest Accounting Firms" reported in *Accounting Today*. The revenues for Ernst & Young, Coopers & Lybrand, and Deloitte & Touche were estimated by *Accounting Today*. Reprinted by permission from *Accounting Today*, September 24, 1990, p. 56. Copyright Lebhar-Friedman, Inc., 475 Park Avenue, New York, NY 10022.

Auditing. A business seeking a loan or attempting to have its securities traded on a stock exchange usually must provide financial statements to support its request. Users of a company's financial statements are more confident that the company is presenting its statements fairly when a CPA has audited the statements. For this reason, companies hire CPA firms to conduct an examination **(independent audit)** of their accounting and related records. **Independent auditors** of the CPA firm check some of the company's records by contacting external sources. For example, the accountant may contact a bank to verify the cash balances of the client. After completing a company audit, independent auditors are able to give an **independent auditor's opinion or report.** (For an example of an auditor's opinion, see The Coca-Cola Company annual report in Appendix C at the end of the text.) This report states whether or not the company's financial statements fairly (equitably) report the economic performance and financial condition of the business. As you will learn in the section "Management (or Industrial) Accounting," auditors *within* a business also conduct audits. However, these audits are not independent audits.

Tax Services. CPAs often provide expert advice on tax planning and the preparation of federal, state, and local tax returns. The objective in preparing tax returns is to use legal means to minimize the amount of taxes paid. Almost every major business decision has a tax impact. Tax planning helps clients know the tax effects of each financial decision.

Management Advisory (or Consulting) Services. The management advisory services area is the fastest growing service area for most large CPA firms and for many smaller CPA firms. Management frequently identifies projects for which it decides to retain the services of a CPA. For example, management may seek help in selecting new computer hardware and software. Also, the auditing services provided by CPAs often result in suggestions to clients on how to improve their operations. For example, CPAs might suggest improvements in the design and installation of an accounting system, the electronic processing of accounting data, inventory control, budgeting, or financial planning. In addition, a relatively fast-growing service area provided by CPAs is financial planning, often for the executives of audit clients.

Management (or Industrial) Accounting

In contrast to public accountants, who provide accounting services for many clients, **management accountants** provide accounting services for a single business. Some companies employ only one management accountant, while other companies employ a large number. In a company with several management accountants, the person in charge of the accounting activity is often called the **controller or chief financial officer.**

Management accountants may or may not be CPAs. If these accountants pass an examination prepared and graded by the Institute of Certified Management Accountants (ICMA) and meet certain other requirements, they become **Certified Management Accountants (CMAs).** The ICMA is an affiliate of the Institute of Management Accountants, an organization primarily consisting of management accountants employed in private industry.

Many management accountants specialize in one particular area of accounting. For example, some may specialize in measuring and controlling costs, others in budgeting—the development of plans for future operations—and still others in financial accounting and reporting. Many management accountants become specialists in the design and installation of computerized accounting systems. Other management accountants are **internal auditors** who conduct **internal audits.** Their job is to see that the company's divisions and departments follow the policies and procedures of management. This last group of management accountants may earn the designation of **Certified Internal Auditor (CIA).** The Institute of Internal Auditors (IIA) grants the CIA certificate to accountants after they have successfully completed an examination prepared and graded by the Institute and have met certain other requirements.

Governmental and Other Not-for-Profit Accounting

Many accountants, including CPAs, work in **governmental and other not-for-profit accounting.** They have essentially the same educational background and training as accountants in public accounting and management (or industrial) accounting.

Governmental agencies at the federal, state, and local levels employ governmental accountants. Often the duties of these accountants relate to tax revenues and expenditures. For example, Internal Revenue Service employees use their accounting background in reviewing tax returns and investigating tax fraud. Government agencies that regulate business activity, such as a state public service commission that regulates public utilities (e.g., telephone company, electric company, and so on) employ accountants.

BERESFORD GETS SECOND FASB TERM

Norwalk, Conn.—Dennis R. Beresford, who led the Financial Accounting Standards Board through some of its stormiest times, has been reappointed for another five years.

In his tenure at the business world's capital of accounting rule-making, Beresford has overseen the issuance of a flurry of standards—including accounting for income taxes and disclosure of financial instruments—and walked a political tightrope—buffeted by interests as diverse as the Business Roundtable to the Securities and Exchange Commission.

The appointments to FASB are made by the Financial Accounting Foundation, chaired by Price Waterhouse chief executive Shaun O'Malley, who himself was also reelected.

In other news from the foundation:

• Three new members were added to the board

of trustees to replace three who are retiring from the board.

• Paul Kolton tendered his resignation after about 13 years as the founding chairman of the Financial Accounting Standards Advisory Council, which works with FASB.

• And the FAF trustees reported that a FASB oversight committee had found that "there is strong continuing support among the FASB's constituents for private sector standard-setting and that the FASB is generally viewed as doing a reasonably good job at an extremely difficult task." The oversight committee is chaired by Deloitte & Touche chairman J. Michael Cook.

SOURCE: Rick Telberg, *Accounting Today.* Reprinted by permission from *Accounting Today,* November 25, 1991, p. 22. Copyright Lebhar-Friedman, Inc., 425 Park Avenue, New York, NY 10022.

These agencies often employ governmental accountants who can review and evaluate the utilities' financial statements and rate increase requests. Also, FBI agents trained as accountants find their accounting background useful in investigating criminals involved in illegal business activities, such as drugs or gambling.

Not-for-profit organizations such as churches, charities, fraternities, and universities need accountants to record and account for funds received and disbursed. Even though these agencies do not have a profit motive, they should operate efficiently and use resources effectively.

Higher Education

Approximately 10,000 accountants are employed in higher education. The activities of these **academic accountants** include teaching accounting courses, conducting scholarly and applied research and publishing the results, and performing service for the institution and the community. Faculty positions exist in two- and four-year colleges and in universities with graduate programs. A significant shortage of accounting faculty will probably develop due to the anticipated retirement in the late 1990s of many current faculty members. Starting salaries will continue to rise significantly because of the shortage. You may want to speak with some of your professors about the advantages and disadvantages of pursuing an accounting career in higher education.

FINANCIAL ACCOUNTING VERSUS MANAGERIAL ACCOUNTING

Objective 4
Differentiate between financial and managerial accounting

An accounting information system provides data to decision makers both outside and inside the business. Decision makers *outside* the business *are affected in some way by the performance of the business*. Decision makers *inside* the business *are responsible for the performance of the business*. For this reason, accounting is divided into two categories: financial accounting and managerial accounting. This section discusses the distinction between financial and managerial accounting.

Financial Accounting

Financial accounting information is intended primarily for external use. Managerial accounting information is intended for internal use. Stockholders and creditors are examples of people outside a company who want and need financial accounting information. These outside persons decide on matters pertaining to the entire company, such as whether to extend credit to a company or to invest in a company. Consequently, financial accounting information relates to the company as a whole. Managerial accounting, on the other hand, serves the needs of those inside the company and focuses on the parts or segments of the company.

Financial statements convey financial accounting information to external users. Management accountants in a company prepare these financial statements. Thus, management accountants must be knowledgeable concerning financial accounting and reporting. The financial statements are the representations of management, not the CPA firm that performs the audit.

Several groups of individuals are external users of accounting information. Each group has different interests in the company and wants answers to certain questions. The groups and some of their possible questions are:

1. *Owners and prospective owners.*   Has the company earned satisfactory income on its total investment? Should an investment be made in this company? Should the present investment be increased, decreased, or retained at the same level? Can the company install costly pollution control equipment and still be profitable?
2. *Creditors and lenders.*   Should a loan be granted to the company? Will the company be able to pay its debts as they become due?
3. *Employees and their unions.*   Does the company have the ability to pay increased wages? Is the company financially able to provide long-term employment for its work force?

4. *Customers*. Does the company offer useful products at fair prices? Will the company survive long enough to honor its product warranties?
5. *Governmental units*. Is the company (such as a local public utility) charging a fair rate for its services?
6. *General public*. Is the company providing useful products and gainful employment for citizens without causing serious environmental problems?

General-purpose financial statements provide much of the information needed by external users of financial accounting. These **financial statements** are formal reports providing information on a company's financial position, cash inflows and outflows, and the results of operations. Many companies publish these statements in an annual report. The **annual report** (see The Coca-Cola Company annual report in Appendix C at the end of the text) also contains the independent auditor's opinion as to the fairness of the financial statements, as well as information about the company's activities, products, and plans.

Financial accounting information is historical in nature, reporting on what has happened in the past. To facilitate comparisons between companies, this information must conform to certain accounting standards or principles called **generally accepted accounting principles (GAAP).** These generally accepted accounting principles for business or governmental organizations have been developed through accounting practice or have been established by an authoritative organization. You will learn about several of these authoritative organizations in the next major section of the chapter.

Managerial Accounting

Managerial accounting information is intended for internal use and provides special information for the managers of a company. The kind of information used by managers may range from broad, long-range planning data to detailed explanations of why actual costs varied from cost estimates.

Managerial accounting information should:

1. Relate to the part of the company for which the manager is responsible. For example, a production manager will want information on costs of production but not on advertising.
2. Involve planning for the future. For instance, a budget may be prepared that shows financial plans for the coming year.
3. Meet two tests: the accounting information must be useful (relevant) and must not cost more to gather and process than it is worth.

The purpose of managerial accounting is to generate information that a manager can use to make sound decisions. Internal management decisions can be classified into four major types:

1. *Financial decisions*—deciding what amounts of capital (funds) are needed to run the business and whether these funds are to be secured from owners or creditors. *Capital* used in this sense means *money* to be used by the company to purchase resources such as machinery and buildings and to pay expenses of conducting the business.
2. *Resource allocation decisions*—deciding how the total capital of a company is to be invested, such as the amount to be invested in machinery.
3. *Production decisions*—deciding what products are to be produced, by what means, and when.
4. *Marketing decisions*—setting selling prices and advertising budgets; determining the location of a company's markets and how to reach them.

DEVELOPMENT OF FINANCIAL ACCOUNTING STANDARDS

*Objective 5
Identify several
organizations that
have a role in the
development of
financial account-
ing standards*

Several organizations are influential in the establishment of generally accepted accounting principles (GAAP) for business or governmental organizations. These are the American Institute of Certified Public Accountants, the Financial Accounting Standards Board, the Governmental Accounting Standards Board, the Securities and Exchange Commission, the American Accounting Association, the Financial Executives Institute, and the Institute of Management Accountants. Each organization has contributed in a different way to the development of GAAP.

American Institute of Certified Public Accountants (AICPA)

The **American Institute of Certified Public Accountants (AICPA)** is a professional organization of CPAs. Many of these CPAs are in public accounting practice. Until recent years, the AICPA was the dominant organization in the development of accounting standards. In a 20-year period ending in 1959, the AICPA Committee on Accounting Procedure issued 51 *Accounting Research Bulletins* recommending certain principles or practices. From 1959 through 1973, the committee's successor, the **Accounting Principles Board (APB),** issued 31 numbered *Opinions* that CPAs generally are required to follow. Through its monthly magazine, the *Journal of Accountancy,* its research division, and its other divisions and committees, the AICPA continues to influence the development of accounting standards and practices. Two of its committees—the Accounting Standards Committee and the Auditing Standards Committee—are particularly influential in providing input to the Financial Accounting Standards Board (the current rule-making body) and to the Securities and Exchange Commission and other regulatory agencies.

Financial Accounting Standards Board (FASB)

In 1973, an independent, seven-member, full-time **Financial Accounting Standards Board (FASB)** replaced the Accounting Principles Board (APB).

The FASB has issued numerous *Statements of Financial Accounting Standards.* The old *Accounting Research Bulletins* and *Accounting Principles Board Opinions* are still effective unless specifically superceded by a Financial Accounting Standards Board Statement. The FASB is the *private sector* organization now responsible for the development of new financial accounting standards.

The Emerging Issues Task Force of the FASB interprets official pronouncements for general application by accounting practitioners. The conclusions of this task force must also be followed in filings with the Securities and Exchange Commission.

Governmental Accounting Standards Board (GASB)

In 1984, the **Governmental Accounting Standards Board (GASB)** was established with a full-time chairperson and four part-time members. The GASB issues statements on accounting and financial reporting in the governmental area. This organization is the *private sector* organization now responsible for the development of new governmental accounting concepts and standards. The GASB also has the authority to issue interpretations of these standards.

Securities and Exchange Commission (SEC)

Created under the Securities and Exchange Act of 1934, the **Securities and Exchange Commission (SEC)** is a government agency that administers a number of important acts dealing with the interstate sale of securities (stocks and bonds). The SEC has the authority to prescribe accounting and reporting practices for companies under its jurisdiction. This includes virtually every major U.S. business corporation. Instead of exercising this power, the SEC has adopted a policy of working closely with the accounting profession, especially the FASB, in the development of accounting standards. The SEC indicates to the FASB the accounting topics it believes the FASB should address.

American Accounting Association (AAA)

Consisting largely of accounting educators, the **American Accounting Association (AAA)** has sought to encourage research and study at a theoretical level into the concepts, standards, and principles of accounting. One of its quarterly magazines, *The Accounting Review,* carries many articles reporting on scholarly accounting research. Another quarterly journal, *Accounting Horizons,* reports on more practical matters directly related to accounting practice. A third journal, *Issues in Accounting Education,* contains articles relating to accounting education matters. Students may join the AAA as associate members by contacting the American Accounting Association, 5717 Bessie Drive, Sarasota, Florida 34233.

Financial Executives Institute (FEI)

The **Financial Executives Institute** is an organization established in 1931 whose members are primarily financial policy-making executives. Slightly more than 13,000 financial officers, representing approximately 7,000 companies in the United States and Canada, comprise its membership. Through its Committee on Corporate Reporting (CCR) and other means, the FEI is very effective in representing the views of the private financial sector to the FASB and to the Securities and Exchange Commission and other regulatory agencies.

Institute of Management Accountants (IMA)

The **Institute of Management Accountants** is an organization with approximately 75,000 members, consisting of management accountants in private industry and CPAs and academics who are interested in management accounting. The primary focus of the organization is on the use of management accounting information for internal decision making. However, management accountants prepare the financial statements for external users. Thus, through its Management Accounting Practices (MAP) Committee and other means, the IMA provides input on financial accounting standards to the Financial Accounting Standards Board and to the Securities and Exchange Commission and other regulatory agencies.

Other Organizations

Many other organizations such as the Financial Analysts Federation (comprised of investment advisors and investors), the Security Industry Associates (comprised of investment bankers), and CPA firms have committees or task forces that respond to Exposure Drafts of proposed FASB Statements issued by the FASB. Their reactions are in the form of written statements sent to the FASB and testimony given at FASB hearings. Many individuals also make their reactions known to the FASB in the same manner.

ETHICAL BEHAVIOR OF ACCOUNTANTS

Several accounting organizations have formulated codes of ethics that govern the behavior of their members. For instance, both the American Institute of Certified Public Accountants and the Institute of Management Accountants have formulated such codes. We have included the codes of ethics of these two organizations in Appendix D at the end of the text. By examining these codes, you will gain some understanding of the expectations that exist regarding the ethical behavior of accountants. Many business firms have also developed codes of ethics for their employees to follow.

Ethical behavior involves more than merely making sure you are not violating a code of ethics. Most of us sense what is right and wrong. Yet the

Jim Ballard is an accounting student at Midland State College. He is majoring in accounting and was planning a career in industry. Jim interviewed with eight large companies in November and December of 1992 and received several verbal offers, including one from his top choice—Moreland Industries. He accepted the offer from Moreland on February 1, 1993, and notified the other companies of this fact. Several recruiters from other companies expressed disappointment with his decision. Jim was to begin work on September 1, 1993. No formal employment contract was signed at the time of acceptance, but Jim assumed that the parties entered into a verbal contract that was binding on both parties.

On July 25, 1993, Jim received an urgent call from the recruiter at Moreland Industries stating that the company had decided to reorganize its accounting function and had to renege on its offer. To ease the pain for Jim, the company was going to send him a check for $1,000. Jim was in shock, since he was to be married on August 20 and needed a job badly. He called the recruiters at the other companies with which he had interviewed and was informed that all of their positions had been filled. He contacted other companies and the placement officer at the university and was told that it was just too late this year for him to find a job in industrial accounting.

Required
a. Did Moreland Industries behave ethically?
b. Why do you think Moreland was going to send Jim a check for $1,000?
c. What would you do if you were Jim?

"get rich quick" opportunities that arise tempt many of us. Almost any day, you can read in the newspaper about public officials and business leaders who did not "do the right thing." Greed ruled over their sense of right and wrong. These individuals followed slogans such as: "Get yours while the getting is good"; "Do unto others before they do unto you"; and "You have only done wrong if you get caught." More appropriate slogans might be: "If it seems too good to be true, it usually is"; "There are no free lunches"; and the golden rule, "Do unto others as you would have them do unto you."

An accountant's most valuable asset is his or her reputation. Those who take the *high road* of ethical behavior receive praise, honor, and are sought out for their advice and services. They also like themselves and what they represent. Occasionally, accountants do take the *low road* and suffer the consequences. They sometimes find their name in print in *The Wall Street Journal* in an unfavorable light, and former friends and colleagues look down on them. Occasionally, these individuals are removed from the profession. Fortunately, the accounting profession has many leaders who have taken the high road, gained the respect of friends and colleagues, and become role models for all of us to follow.

In each chapter in the text we have included an ethics case entitled, "A Closer Look." We think you will benefit from being exposed to the *situational ethics* contained in these cases.

HOW TO STUDY THE CHAPTERS IN THIS TEXT

The authors recommend that you proceed as follows in studying each chapter:

1. Begin each chapter by reading the Learning Objectives at the beginning of the chapter.
2. Read the section, "Understanding the Learning Objectives," at the end of the chapter for a preview of the chapter content.
3. Read the chapter content. Notice that the "Learning Objectives" appear in the margins at the appropriate places in the chapter. Each of the exercises at the end of each chapter identifies the learning objective(s) to which it pertains. If you learn best by reading about a concept and then working a short exercise that illustrates that concept, you will want to work the exercises as you read the chapter. Forms are provided in the Working Papers supplement for working these exercises.
4. Reread the section "Understanding the Learning Objectives" to determine if you have achieved each objective.
5. Study the New Terms to see if you understand each term. If you do not understand a certain term, refer back to the page indicated to read about the term in its original context.
6. Take the Self-Test and then check your answers with the correct answers at the end of the chapter.
7. Work the Demonstration Problem to further reinforce your understanding of the chapter content. Then compare your solution to the correct solution, which follows immediately.
8. Read "A Closer Look," the ethics case, and think about how you would respond to the questions asked.
9. Look over the questions at the end of the chapter and think about an answer to each one. If you cannot answer a particular question, refer back into the chapter for the needed information.
10. Work at least some of the Exercises at the end of the chapter.
11. Work any of the Problems or Business Decision Problems assigned by your instructor, using the forms provided in the Working Papers supplement.
12. Work the Study Guide for the chapter. The Study Guide is a supplement that contains for each chapter Learning Objectives; Reference Outline; Chapter Review; Demonstration Problem and Solution (different than in the text); Matching, Completion, True-False, and Multiple-Choice Questions; and Solutions to all Questions and Exercises in the Study Guide.

If you perform each of the above steps for each chapter, you should do well in the course. A knowledge of accounting will serve you well regardless of the career you decide to pursue.

UNDERSTANDING THE LEARNING OBJECTIVES

1. Define accounting.
   - Accounting is "the process of identifying, measuring, and communicating economic information to permit informed judgments and decisions by the users of the information."

2. Describe the functions performed by accountants.
   - Accountants observe many events (or activities) and identify and measure in financial terms (dollars) those events considered evidence of economic activity.
   - The economic events are recorded, classified into meaningful groups, and summarized.
   - Accountants report on economic events (or business activity) by preparing financial statements and special reports. Often accountants are asked to interpret these statements and reports for various groups such as management, investors, and creditors.

3. Describe employment opportunities in accounting.
   - An accountant may be employed in public accounting and specialize in auditing, tax, or management advisory (or consulting) services.
   - Management accountants are employed by a single company and may specialize in measuring and controlling costs, budgeting, computerized accounting systems, internal auditing, or some other function.
   - Other accountants are employed in government agencies or other not-for-profit organizations such as churches, charities, fraternities, and organizations.
   - Universities and colleges hire accountants (CPAs, CMAs, and CIAs who usually have a graduate degree) to teach accounting to students and conduct research on accounting issues.

4. Differentiate between financial and managerial accounting.
   - Financial accounting information is intended primarily for external use; it provides information for groups such as owners and prospective owners, creditors and lenders, employees and their unions, customers, governmental units, and the general public.
   - Managerial accounting information is intended for internal use; it provides special information for the managers of the company.

5. Identify several organizations that have a role in the development of financial accounting standards.
   - American Institute of Certified Public Accountants (AICPA)—made up of persons holding the CPA certificate. The Accounting Principles Board (APB) was under the AICPA.
   - Financial Accounting Standards Board (FASB)—issues FASB statements, which are the *rules* of financial accounting.

- Governmental Accounting Standards Board (GASB)—issues GASB statements, which are the *rules* of governmental accounting.
- Securities and Exchange Commission (SEC)—a government agency that has legislative authority over financial accounting standards. To date, the SEC has allowed the private sector to set the standards.
- American Accounting Association (AAA)—an organization consisting largely of accountants who teach and engage in research.
- Financial Executives Institute (FEI)—an organization whose members are primarily financial policy-making executives.
- Institute of Management Accountants (IMA)—an organization consisting of management accountants in private industry and CPAs and academics who are interested in management accounting.

NEW TERMS

Academic accountants   Accountants in the academic segment of the accounting profession who teach accounting courses, conduct scholarly and applied research and publish the results, and perform service for the institution and the community. *11*

Accounting   "The process of identifying, measuring, and communicating economic information to permit informed judgments and decisions by the users of the information." *5*

Accounting Principles Board (APB)   An organization created in 1959 by the AICPA and empowered to speak for it on matters of accounting principle; replaced in 1973 by the Financial Accounting Standards Board. *14*

American Accounting Association (AAA)   A professional organization of accountants, many of whom are college or university professors of accounting. *15*

American Institute of Certified Public Accountants (AICPA)   A professional organization of Certified Public Accountants, most of whom are in public accounting practice. *14*

Annual report   A pamphlet or document of varying length containing audited financial statements and other information about a company, distributed annually to its owners. *13*

Audit (independent)   Performed by independent auditors to determine whether the financial statements of a business fairly reflect the economic performance of the business. *9*

Audit (internal)   Performed by accounting employees of a company to determine if company policies and procedures are being followed. *10*

Certified Internal Auditor (CIA)   An accountant who has passed an examination prepared and graded by the Institute of Internal Auditors (IIA) and who has met certain other requirements. *10*

Certified Management Accountants (CMA)   Persons who have passed an examination prepared and graded by the Institute of Certified Management Accountants (ICMA), an affiliate of the Institute of Management Accountants, and who have met certain other requirements. *10*

Certified Public Accountant (CPA)   A person who has passed an examination prepared and graded by the American Institute of Certified Public Accountants (AICPA) and has an active license to practice as a CPA. *8*

Controller or chief financial officer   The executive officer in charge of a company's accounting activity. *10*

Financial accounting   Relates to the company as a whole; the process of supplying financial information to parties external to the reporting entity. *12*

Financial Accounting Standards Board (FASB)   A seven-member board of independent professionals that issues *Statements of Financial Accounting Standards*. The private sector organization now responsible for the development of new financial accounting standards. *14*

Financial Executives Institute (FEI)   An organization whose members are primarily financial policy-making executives. *16*

Financial statements   Formal reports providing information on a company's financial position, cash inflows and outflows, and the results of operations. *13*

Generally accepted accounting principles (GAAP)   Accounting standards and principles that have been developed through accounting practice or have been established by an authoritative organization. *13*

Governmental Accounting Standards Board (GASB)   The private sector organization now responsible for the development of new governmental accounting concepts and standards. *15*

Governmental and other not-for-profit accounting   Governmental accountants are employed by government agencies at the federal, state, and local levels. Other not-for-profit accountants record and account for receipts and disbursements for churches, charities, fraternities, and universities. *10*

Independent audit   See Audit (independent).

Independent auditors   Certified Public Accountants who perform an audit to determine whether or not a company's financial statements fairly (equitably) report the economic performance and financial condition of the company. *9*

Independent auditor's opinion or report   The formal written statement by a Certified Public Accountant that states whether or not the company's financial statements fairly report the economic performance and financial condition of the company. *9*

Institute of Management Accountants (IMA)   An organization consisting of management accountants in private industry and CPAs and academics who are interested in management accounting. *16*

Internal audit   See Audit (internal).

Internal auditors   Private accountants employed by a company to ensure that the policies and procedures established by the company are followed in its divisions and departments. *10*

Management accountants   Accountants who provide accounting services for a single business and are employees of that business. *10*

Managerial accounting   Relates to the process of supplying financial information for internal management use. *13*

Public accounting firms   Offer professional accounting and related services for a fee to companies, other organizations, and individuals. *7*

Securities and Exchange Commission (SEC) A governmental agency created by Congress to administer acts dealing with interstate sales of securities and having the authority to prescribe the accounting and reporting practices of firms under its jurisdiction. *15*

QUESTIONS

1. Who was the author of the first book written on double-entry bookkeeping?

2. Why should almost everyone have some knowledge of accounting?

3. What does CPA stand for? How does one become a CPA? Do all CPAs work in public accounting?

4. How favorable do employment opportunities appear in accounting?

5. Identify what is meant by CPA, CMA, and CIA. What are some of the services provided by individuals with these designations?

6. What is the primary difference between internal auditors and independent auditors?

7. What is the role of accountants employed in government?

8. What activities are required of accountants employed in higher education?

9. Describe the basic difference between financial accounting and managerial accounting.

10. Name several organizations that have played or are playing an important role in the development of accounting standards. Describe each briefly.

11. What guides the ethical behavior of accountants?

The Coca-Cola Company

12. *Real-world question*   Refer to the report of the independent auditors contained in The Coca-Cola Company annual report in Appendix C at the end of the text. Which CPA firm performed the audit? Whose responsibility are the financial statements—the company's or the auditor's?

The Coca-Cola Company

13. *Real-world question*   Referring to the same report of the independent auditors mentioned in Question 12, did the auditors examine all the evidence supporting the amounts and disclosures in all of the financial statements?

1 ACCOUNTING AND ITS USE IN BUSINESS DECISIONS

LEARNING OBJECTIVES

After studying this chapter, you should be able to:

1. Identify and describe the three basic forms of business organizations.
2. Distinguish among the three types of activities performed by business organizations.
3. Describe the content and purposes of the income statement, statement of retained earnings, and balance sheet.
4. State the basic accounting equation and describe its relationship to the balance sheet.
5. Using the underlying assumptions or concepts, analyze business transactions, and determine their effects on items in the financial statements.
6. Prepare an income statement, a statement of retained earnings, and a balance sheet.

The Introduction to this text provided a background for your study of accounting. **(If you have not read the Introduction, you should do so before reading Chapter 1.)** You can now define accounting and explain the functions performed by accountants. After reading about the employment opportunities in accounting, you may have decided to consider a career in accounting. Even if you select another profession or occupation, accounting information will be useful throughout your lifetime.

Now you are ready to learn about the forms of business organizations and the types of business activities they perform. This chapter presents three of the financial statements used by businesses. In this chapter, you will also study the accounting process (or accounting cycle) that accountants use to prepare those financial statements. This accounting process uses financial data such as the records of sales made to customers and purchases made from suppliers. In a systematic manner, these data are analyzed, recorded, classified, summarized, and finally reported in the financial statements of businesses. As you study this chapter, you will begin to understand the unique, systematic nature of accounting—the language of business.

FORMS OF BUSINESS ORGANIZATIONS

Objective 1
Identify and de-
scribe the three
basic forms of
business organiza-
tions[1]

Accountants frequently refer to a business organization as an *accounting entity* or a *business entity*. A business entity is any business organization, such as a hardware store or grocery store, that exists as an economic unit. For accounting purposes, each business organization or **entity** has an existence separate from its owner(s), creditors, employees, customers, and other businesses. This separate existence of the business organization is known as the **business entity concept.** Thus, in the accounting records of the business entity, the activities of each business should be kept separate from the activities of other businesses and from the personal financial activities of the owner(s).

Assume, for example, that you own two businesses, a physical fitness center and a horse stable. According to the business entity concept, you would consider each business as an independent business unit. Thus, you would normally keep separate accounting records for each business. Now assume your physical fitness center is unprofitable because you are not charging enough for the use of your exercise equipment. You can determine this fact because you are treating your physical fitness center and horse stable as two separate business entities. You must also keep your personal financial activities separate from your two businesses. Therefore, you cannot include the car you drive only for personal use as a business activity of your physical fitness center or your horse stable. However, the use of your truck to pick up feed for your horse stable is a business activity of your horse stable.

As you will see in the discussion that follows on the three forms of business organizations—single proprietorships, partnerships, and corporations—the business entity concept applies to all forms of businesses. Thus, for accounting purposes, all three business forms are separate from other business entities and from their owners. You will learn that corporations are also *legally* separate from their owners, while this is not true for single proprietorships and partnerships.

Single Proprietorship

A **single proprietorship** is an unincorporated business owned by an individual and often managed by that same individual. Single proprietors include physi-

---

[1] After reading a portion of text material that covers a certain learning objective, some students may want to work immediately an exercise that illustrates that material. The exercises at the end of each chapter are labeled with the learning objective to which they pertain. For instance, turn to pages 53–55 to see which learning objective(s) each exercise covers in Chapter 1.

cians, lawyers, electricians, and other people who are "in business for themselves." Many small service-type businesses and retail establishments are single proprietorships. No legal formalities are necessary to organize such businesses, and usually business operations can begin with only a limited investment.

In a single proprietorship, the owner is solely responsible for all debts of the business. For accounting purposes, however, the business is a separate entity from the owner. Thus, single proprietors must keep the financial activities of the business, such as the receipt of fees from selling services to the public, separate from their personal financial activities. For example, owners of single proprietorships should not enter the cost of a personal house or car payment in the financial records of their business.

Partnership

A **partnership** is an unincorporated business owned by two or more persons associated as partners. Often the same persons who own the business also manage the business. Many small retail establishments and professional practices, such as dentists, physicians, attorneys, and many CPA firms, are partnerships.

Partnerships begin with a verbal or written agreement. A written agreement is preferable because it provides a permanent record of the terms of the partnership. These terms include the initial investment of each partner, the duties of each partner, the means of dividing profits or losses between the partners each year, and the settlement after the death or withdrawal of a partner. Each partner may be held liable for all the debts of the partnership and for the actions of each partner within the scope of the business. However, as with the single proprietorship, for accounting purposes, the partnership is a separate business entity.

Corporation

A **corporation** is a business incorporated under the laws of one of the states and owned by a few persons or by thousands of persons. Almost all large businesses and many small businesses are incorporated.

The corporation is unique in that it is a separate legal business entity. The owners of the corporation are called **stockholders or shareholders.** They buy shares of stock, which are units of ownership, in the corporation. Should the corporation fail, the owners would only lose the amount they paid for their stock. The corporate form of business protects the personal assets of the owners from the creditors of the corporation.[2]

---

[2] When individuals seek a bank loan to finance the formation of a small corporation, the bank will often require those individuals to sign documents making them personally responsible for repaying the loan if the corporation cannot pay. In this instance, the individuals can lose their original investment plus the amount of the loan they are obligated to repay.

The stockholders do not directly manage the corporation. They elect a board of directors to represent their interests. The board of directors selects the officers of the corporation, such as the president and vice presidents, who manage the corporation for the stockholders.

Accounting is necessary for all three forms of business organizations, and each company, regardless of business form, must follow generally accepted accounting principles (GAAP). Since corporations have such an important impact on our economy, we will use them in this text to illustrate the basic accounting principles and concepts.

TYPES OF ACTIVITIES PERFORMED BY BUSINESS ORGANIZATIONS

Objective 2
Distinguish among the three types of activities performed by business organizations

The forms of business entities discussed in the previous section are classified according to the type of ownership of the business entity. Single proprietorships have one owner, partnerships have two or more owners, and corporations usually have many owners. Business entities can also be grouped by the type of business activities they perform—service companies, merchandising companies, and manufacturing companies. Any of these three types of activities can be performed by companies using any of the three forms of business organizations.

1. **Service companies** perform services for a fee. This group includes companies such as accounting firms, law firms, dry cleaning establishments, and many others. Accounting for service companies is illustrated in the early chapters of this text.
2. **Merchandising companies** purchase goods that are ready for sale and then sell them to customers. Merchandising companies include such companies as auto dealerships, clothing stores, and supermarkets. Accounting for merchandising companies is first illustrated in Chapter 4.
3. **Manufacturing companies** buy materials, convert them into products, and then sell the products to other companies or to final customers (consumers). Examples of manufacturing companies are steel mills, auto manufacturers, and clothing manufacturers.

All of these companies produce financial statements as the final end product of their accounting process. As stated in the Introduction, these financial statements provide relevant financial information both to those inside the company—management—and those outside the company—creditors, stockholders, and other interested parties. In the next section, you will learn about three common financial statements—the income statement, the statement of retained earnings, and the balance sheet. A fourth financial statement, the statement of cash flows, is discussed in Chapter 21.

A BROADER PERSPECTIVE

INTERVIEWERS SPEAK OUT

Recently, 114 interviewers with on-campus experience were asked to identify the most important attributes, characteristics and behavior which would persuade them to offer an office visit to a recruit. The chart below shows what they had to say.

Recruiters' Ten Most Important
Campus Interview
Characteristics/Behavior Items

- Oral expression during the interview.
- Quality of questions asked during the interview.
- Expression of personal and professional goals during the interview.
- Appropriate interview attire.
- Being on-time for the interview.
- Eye contact during the interview.
- Accounting GPA.
- Expression of why the firm should hire you.
- Overall GPA.
- Ability to discuss current events.

Oral Expression. Recruiters consider the ability to speak clearly, concisely and with confidence as the most important item for success in the campus interview process. They are looking for candidates with communication skills. The ability to convince the recruiter to offer you an office visit in a short period of time is crucial. Remember, most campus interviews are less than one hour.

Quality of Questions Asked. One of the worst things you can do is ask a question which could have been answered by reading the recruiting literature or job description. That would indicate that the candidate hadn't done his "homework" for the interview. Don't hesitate to ask questions, but don't ask questions just to say something.

Academic Performance. The importance of your grades should not come as a surprise. Recruiters indicated strong concerns for both overall grade-point averages and performance within the major. Granted, there isn't much you can do about your GPA as you enter your senior year, but if it is not as high as you would have liked, you should be able to explain why. It is surprising how receptive interviewers are to reasonable explanations for a "bad" semester or term.

Résumé. Not only should you look good in person, but you should look good on paper as well. Since the résumé is usually used in the initial screening process for scheduling interviews, recruiters will see you in print before they do in person. Misspellings, poor grammar and sloppy headings and margins were mentioned as turn-offs by the recruiters.

Appropriate Interview Attire. Doesn't it make sense to dress in business attire if you are interviewing for a position in business? A conservative suit (for both men and women) is acceptable. Of course, being well-groomed and neat should go without saying.

Tardiness. Simply stated, being on-time for the interview is key. If you are even slightly late, it may reflect on your interest in the position, as well as your dependability as a potential employee.

Remember, you really are trying to sell yourself. You want to show how much you know and receive a good grade for your performance.

SOURCE: Joseph M. Larkin, *New Accountant,* September 1990, p. 33. © 1990 New DuBois Corporation.

FINANCIAL STATEMENTS OF BUSINESS ORGANIZATIONS

*Objective 3
Describe the
content and pur-
poses of the in-
come statement,
statement of re-
tained earnings,
and balance sheet*

Business entities may have many objectives and goals (e.g., one of your objectives in owning a physical fitness center may be to improve *your* physi-cal fitness). However, the two primary objectives of every business are profitability and solvency. **Profitability** is the ability to generate income. **Solvency** is the ability to pay debts as they become due. Unless a business can produce satisfactory income and pay its debts as they become due, the business will not survive to realize its other objectives.

The financial statement that reflects a company's profitability is the **income statement.** The **statement of retained earnings** shows the change in retained earnings between the beginning of a period (e.g., a month or a year) and the end of that period. The **balance sheet** reflects a company's solvency. The headings and elements of each statement are similar from company to company. You have probably noticed this similarity if you have seen finan-cial statements of actual companies.

Chapter 21 thoroughly discusses and illustrates a fourth financial state-ment, the statement of cash flows. We only mention it now so you will know it exists. The **statement of cash flows** shows the cash inflows and outflows for a company over a period of time.

The Income Statement

The **income statement,** sometimes called an *earnings statement,* reports the profitability of a business organization for a *stated period of time.* In ac-counting, profitability is measured for a period of time, such as a month or year, by comparing the revenues generated with the expenses incurred to produce these revenues. **Revenues** are the inflows of assets (such as cash) resulting from the sale of products or the rendering of services to customers. Revenues are measured by the prices agreed on in the exchanges in which a business delivers goods or renders services. **Expenses** are the costs incurred to produce revenues. Expenses are measured by the assets surrendered or consumed in serving customers. If the revenues of a period exceed the expenses of the same period, **net income** results. Thus,

$$\text{Net income} = \text{Revenues} - \text{Expenses}$$

Net income is often called the *earnings* of the company. If expenses exceed revenues, the business has a **net loss,** and it has operated unprofit-ably.

In Illustration 1.1, Part A shows the income statement of Beck Company for July 1995. Beck Company is a corporation that performs delivery ser-vices. Remember that an income statement is for a specified *period* of time.

Beck's income statement for the month ended July 31, 1995, shows that the revenues (or delivery fees) generated by serving customers for July totaled $5,700. Expenses for the month amounted to $3,600. As a result of

Illustration 1.1

A. Income Statement

BECK COMPANY
Income Statement
For the Month Ended July 31, 1995

Revenues:		
Service revenue		$5,700
Expenses:		
Salaries expense	$2,600	
Rent expense	400	
Gas and oil expense	600	
Total expenses		3,600
Net income		$2,100

B. Statement of Retained Earnings

BECK COMPANY
Statement of Retained Earnings
For the Month Ended July 31, 1995

Retained earnings, July 1	$ –0–
Add: Net income for July	2,100
Retained earnings, July 31	$2,100

C. Balance Sheet

BECK COMPANY
Balance Sheet
July 31, 1995

Assets		**Liabilities and Stockholders' Equity***	
Cash	$15,500	Liabilities:	
Accounts receivable	700	Accounts payable	$ 600
Trucks.	20,000	Notes payable	6,000
Office equipment.	2,500	Total liabilities	$ 6,600
		Stockholders' equity:	
		Capital stock.	$30,000
		Retained earnings	2,100
		Total stockholders' equity	$32,100
Total assets	$38,700	Total liabilities and stockholders' equity. .	$38,700

---

* The liabilities and stockholders' equity portion of the balance sheet may be shown directly beneath the assets instead of to the right of them, as shown in the illustration. When liabilities and stockholders' equity are placed under the assets, the balance sheet is in the *vertical format* or *report form*. The vertical format is as acceptable as the *horizontal format* (or account form) used above. For an example of the vertical format, see the Solution to Demonstration Problem, page 48.

these business activities, Beck's net income for July was $2,100. The *net income* amount is determined by subtracting the company's expenses of $3,600 from its revenues of $5,700. Corporations are taxable entities, but we ignore corporate income taxes at this point.

The Statement of Retained Earnings

One of the purposes of the *statement of retained earnings* is to connect the income statement and the balance sheet. The **statement of retained earnings** explains the changes in retained earnings that occurred between two balance sheet dates. These changes usually consist of the addition of net income (or deduction of net loss) and the deduction of dividends.

Dividends are the means by which a corporation rewards its stockholders (owners) for providing it with investment funds. A **dividend** is a payment (usually of cash) to the owners of the business; it is a distribution of income to owners rather than an expense of doing business. Since dividends are not an expense, they do not appear on the income statement.

The effect of a dividend is to reduce cash and retained earnings by the amount paid out. Then, the company no longer "retains" a portion of the income (earnings) but has passed it on to the stockholders (owners). Earning a return in the form of dividends is, of course, one of the primary reasons why people invest in corporations.

The statement of retained earnings for Beck Company for July 1995 is relatively simple (Part B of Illustration 1.1). Beck was organized on June 1 and did not earn any revenues or incur any expenses during June. So Beck's beginning retained earnings balance on July 1 is zero. Beck then adds its $2,100 net income for July. Since Beck paid no dividends in July, the $2,100 would be the ending balance.

In Illustration 1.1, Part B shows first that the beginning balance in retained earnings was $-0-. This balance is added to July's net income of $2,100 from the income statement (Part A) to arrive at the ending retained earnings balance of $2,100. Next, this ending balance is carried to the balance sheet (Part C). If there had been a net loss, it would have been deducted from the beginning balance on the statement of retained earnings.

Dividends could also have affected the Retained Earnings balance. To give a more realistic illustration, assume that (1) Beck Company's net income for August was $1,500 (revenues of $5,600 less expenses of $4,100) and (2) the company declared and paid dividends of $1,000. Beck's statement of retained earnings for August is shown on the next page.

The Balance Sheet

The **balance sheet,** sometimes called the *statement of financial position,* lists the company's assets, liabilities, and stockholders' equity (including dollar amounts) *as of a specific moment in time*. The specific moment of time is the close of business on the date appearing on the balance sheet. Notice how the

BECK COMPANY
Statement of Retained Earnings
For the Month Ended August 31, 1995

Retained earnings, July 31	$2,100
Add: Net income for August	1,500
Total	$3,600
Less: Dividends	1,000
Retained earnings, August 31.	$2,600

heading of the balance sheet differs from the headings on the income statement and statement of retained earnings. A balance sheet is like a still photograph; it captures the financial position of a company at a particular *point* in time. The other two statements are for a *period* of time. As you study about the assets, liabilities, and stockholders' equity contained in a balance sheet, you will understand why this financial statement provides information about the solvency of the business.

Assets are things of value owned by the business. They are also called the *resources* of the business. Examples include cash, machines, and buildings. Assets have value because a business can use or exchange them to produce the services or products of the business. In Part C of Illustration 1.1, the assets of Beck Company, which performs delivery services, amount to $38,700. Beck's assets consist of cash, **accounts receivable** (amounts due from customers for services previously rendered or merchandise sold), trucks, and office equipment.

Liabilities are the *debts* owed by a business. Typically, a business must pay its debts by certain dates. A business incurs many of its liabilities by purchasing an item on credit. Beck's liabilities consist of **accounts payable** (amounts owed to suppliers for previous purchases) and **notes payable** (written promises to pay a specific sum of money) totaling $6,600.[3]

Beck Company is a corporation. The owners' interest in a corporation is referred to as **stockholders' equity.** Beck's stockholders' equity consists of (1) $30,000 paid for shares of capital stock and (2) retained earnings of $2,100. **Capital stock** shows the amount of the owners' investment in the corporation. **Retained earnings** generally consists of the accumulated net income of the corporation minus dividends distributed to stockholders. These items will be discussed later in the text. At this point, you should simply note that the balance sheet heading includes the name of the organization and the title and date of the statement. Note also that the dollar amount of the total assets is equal to the claims on (or interest in) those

---

[3] Most notes bear interest, but in this chapter we assume that all notes bear no interest. Interest is an amount paid by the borrower to the lender (in addition to the amount of the loan) for use of the money over time.

assets. The balance sheet shows these claims under the heading "Liabilities and Stockholders' Equity."

The income statement, statement of retained earnings, and balance sheet of Beck Company are the end products of the accounting process, which we explain in the next section. These financial statements give a picture of the solvency and profitability of the company. The accounting process details how this picture was made.

THE FINANCIAL ACCOUNTING PROCESS

Objective 4
State the basic accounting equation and describe its relationship to the balance sheet

In this section, we explain first the accounting equation—the framework for the entire accounting process. Then, we show you how to recognize a business transaction and describe underlying assumptions that accountants use to record business transactions. Next, you will learn how to analyze and record business transactions. Beck Company will be your "tour guide" as you move from transaction to transaction. Accounting—the language of business—is now also becoming part of your language.

The Accounting Equation

In the balance sheet presented in Illustration 1.1 (Part C), the total assets of Beck Company were equal to its total liabilities and stockholders' equity. This equality shows that the assets of a business are equal to its equities; that is,

$$\text{Assets} = \text{Equities}$$

Assets were defined earlier as the things of value owned by the business, or the economic resources of the business. **Equities** are all claims to, or interests in, assets. For example, assume that you purchased a new company automobile for $5,000 by investing $400 in your own corporation and borrowing $4,600 in the name of the corporation from a bank. Your equity in the automobile is $400, and the bank's equity is $4,600. You can further describe the $4,600 as a liability because the corporation owes the bank $4,600. Also, you can describe your $400 equity as *stockholders' equity* or interest in the asset. Since the owners in a corporation are stockholders, the basic **accounting equation** becomes:

$$\text{Assets (A)} = \text{Liabilities (L)} + \text{Stockholders' Equity (SE)}$$

From Beck Company's balance sheet in Illustration 1.1 (Part C), we can enter in the amount of its assets, liabilities, and stockholders' equity:

$$
\begin{array}{ccccc}
\text{A} & = & \text{L} & + & \text{SE} \\
\$38,700 & = & \$6,600 & + & \$32,100
\end{array}
$$

Remember that someone must provide assets or resources—either a creditor or a stockholder. Therefore, this equation must always be in balance.

You can also look at the right side of the above equation in another manner. The liabilities and stockholders' equity show the sources of an existing group of assets. Thus, liabilities are not only claims against assets but also sources of assets.

Either creditors or owners provide all the assets in a corporation. As a business engages in economic activity, the *dollar amounts* and *composition* of its assets, liabilities, and stockholders' equity change. **However, the equality of the basic accounting equation always holds.**

Analysis of Transactions

Objective 5
Using the underlying assumptions or concepts, analyze business transactions, and determine their effects on items in the financial statements

An accounting **transaction** is a business activity or event that must be recorded in the accounting records. For example, an exchange of cash for merchandise is evidence of a business event. An exchange takes place at an agreed price, and this price provides an objective measure of the economic activity that has occurred. For example, the objective measure of the exchange may be $5,000. These two factors—evidence and measurement—make possible the recording of a transaction. **Merely placing an order for goods is not a recordable transaction because no exchange has taken place.**

The evidence of the transaction is usually supported by a *source document*. A **source document** is any written or printed evidence of a business transaction that describes the essential facts of that transaction. Examples of source documents are receipts for cash paid or received, checks written or received, bills sent to customers for services performed or bills received from suppliers for items purchased, cash register tapes, sales tickets, and notes given or received. We handle source documents constantly in our everyday life. Each source document initiates the process of recording a transaction.

Underlying Assumptions or Concepts. In recording business transactions, accountants rely on certain underlying assumptions or concepts. Both preparers and users of financial statements must understand these assumptions.

1. **Business entity concept (or accounting entity concept).** Data gathered in an accounting system relate to a specific business unit or *entity*. The business entity concept assumes that each business has an existence separate from its owners, creditors, employees, customers, other interested parties, and other businesses.
2. **Money measurement concept.** Economic activity is initially recorded and reported in terms of a *common monetary unit of measure*—the dollar in the United States. This form of measurement is known as *money measurement*.

3. **Exchange-price (or cost) concept (principle).** Most of the amounts entered in an accounting system are the objective money prices determined in the exchange process. As a result, most assets are recorded at their acquisition cost, measured in terms of money paid. **Cost** is the sacrifice made or the resources given up, measured in money terms, to acquire some desired thing, such as a new truck (asset).

4. **Going-concern (continuity) concept.** Unless strong evidence exists to the contrary, accountants assume that the business entity will continue operations into the indefinite future. Accountants call this assumption the *going-concern or continuity* concept. Assuming that the entity will continue indefinitely allows the accountant to value long-term assets, such as land, at cost on the balance sheet since they are to be used rather than sold. Market values of these assets would only be relevant if they were for sale. Thus, subsequent increases in value are not recorded. For instance, land recorded at its cost of $100,000 in 1989 is still shown at $100,000 on the December 31, 1995, balance sheet even though its market value has risen to $300,000.

5. **Periodicity (time periods) concept.** According to the *periodicity (time periods)* concept or assumption, an entity's life can be meaningfully subdivided into time periods (such as months or years) for purposes of reporting the results of its economic activities.

Now that you understand business transactions and the five basic accounting assumptions, you are ready to follow step by step some actual business transactions. The transactions of Beck Company serve as examples. These transactions are divided into two groups: (1) transactions affecting only the balance sheet in June, and (2) transactions affecting the income statement and/or the balance sheet in July. Then, a summary of the transactions is given.

Transactions Affecting Only the Balance Sheet. Since each transaction affecting a business entity must be recorded in the accounting records, the analysis of the transaction before the actual recording of the transaction is an important part of financial accounting. An error in transaction analysis will result in an incorrect picture given in the financial statements.

To illustrate the analysis of transactions and their effects on the basic accounting equation, the activities of Beck Company that led to the statements in Illustration 1.1 are presented below. The numbers 1a, 2a, and so on refer to the summary of transactions found later in Part B of Illustration 1.2. The first set of transactions (1a–5a) occurred in June 1995. The second set (1b–6b) occurred in July 1995.

1a. Owners Invested Cash. When Beck Company was organized as a corporation on June 1, 1995, the company issued shares of capital stock for $30,000 cash to John Beck, his wife, and their son. This transaction increased assets (cash) of Beck by $30,000 and increased equities (the capital stock element of stockholders' equity) by $30,000. Consequently, the transaction yields the following basic accounting equation:

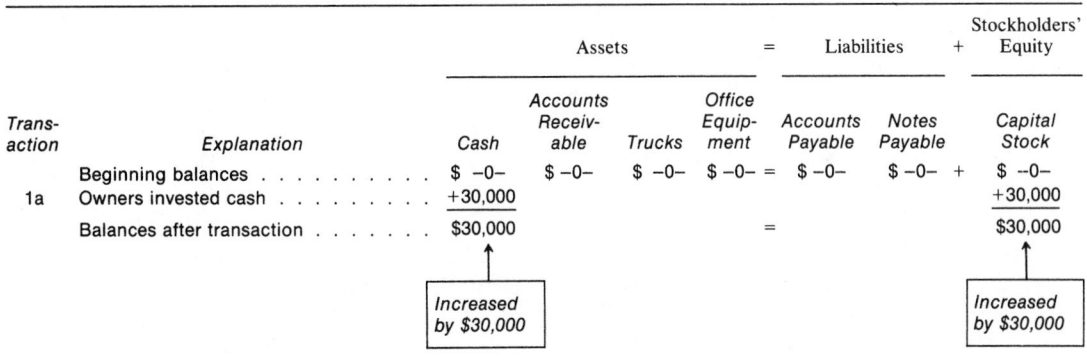

2a. Borrowed Money.   The company borrowed $6,000 from Beck's father. Beck signed the note for the company. The note bore no interest and the company promised to repay (recorded as a *note payable*) the amount borrowed within one year. After including the effects of this transaction, the basic equation is:

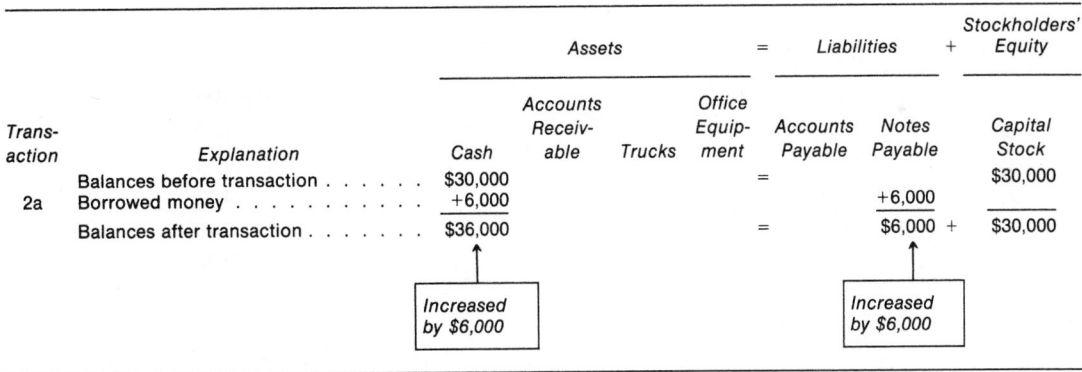

3a. Purchased Trucks and Office Equipment for Cash.   Beck bought (by paying cash) two small delivery trucks for $20,000 and office equipment for $1,500. Trucks and office equipment are assets because the company uses them to earn revenues in the future. **Note that this transaction does not change the totals in the basic equation but only changes the composition of the assets.** This transaction decreased cash and increased trucks and office equipment (assets) by the total amount of the cash decrease. Beck received two assets and gave up one asset of equal value. Total assets are still $36,000. The accounting equation now is:

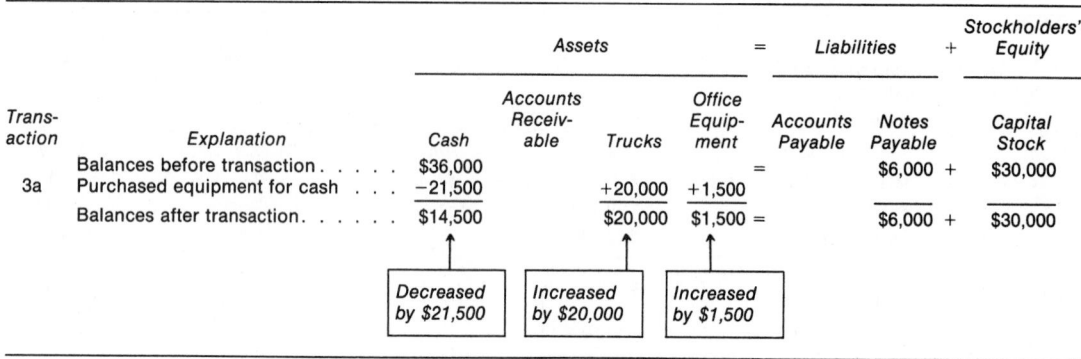

Trans-action	Explanation	Cash	Accounts Receiv-able	Trucks	Office Equip-ment	Accounts Payable	Notes Payable	Capital Stock
	Balances before transaction.	$36,000				=	$6,000 +	$30,000
3a	Purchased equipment for cash . . .	−21,500		+20,000	+1,500			
	Balances after transaction.	$14,500		$20,000	$1,500 =		$6,000 +	$30,000

Cash: Decreased by $21,500
Trucks: Increased by $20,000
Office Equipment: Increased by $1,500

4a. Purchased Office Equipment on Account (for Credit). Beck purchased $1,000 of office equipment on account, agreeing to pay within 10 days after receiving the bill. (To purchase an item ''on account'' means to buy it on credit.) This transaction increased assets in the form of office equipment and liabilities in the form of *accounts payable* by $1,000. As stated earlier, accounts payable are amounts owed to suppliers for items purchased on credit. The $1,000 increase in the assets and the liabilities is shown as follows:

| | | | Assets | | | = | Liabilities | + | Stockholders' Equity |

Trans-action	Explanation	Cash	Accounts Receiv-able	Trucks	Office Equip-ment	Accounts Payable	Notes Payable	Capital Stock
	Balances before transaction	$14,500		$20,000	$1,500 =		$6,000 +	$30,000
4a	Purchased office equipment on account				+1,000	+1,000		
	Balances after transaction	$14,500		$20,000	$2,500 =	$1,000	$6,000 +	$30,000

Office Equipment: Increased by $1,000
Accounts Payable: Increased by $1,000

5a. Paid an Account Payable. Eight days after receiving the bill, Beck paid $1,000 for the office equipment purchased on account (transaction 4a). This transaction reduced cash by $1,000 and reduced accounts payable by $1,000. Thus, the assets and liabilities both are reduced by $1,000, and the equation again balances as follows:

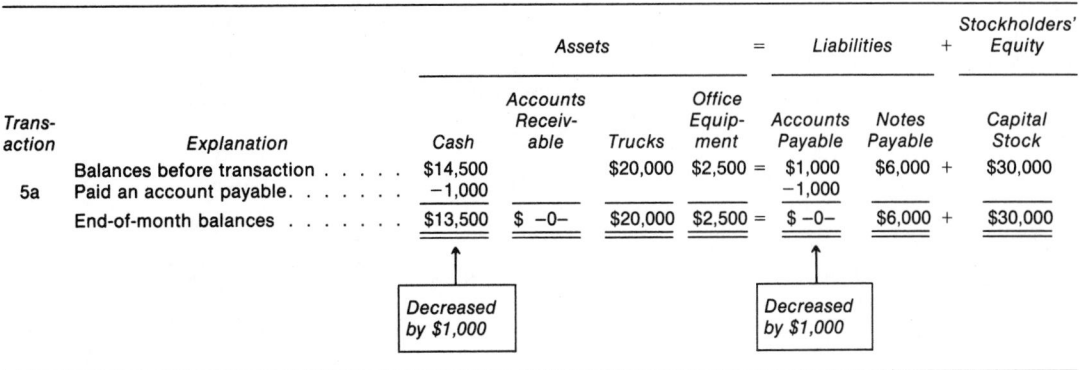

Trans-action	Explanation	Cash	Accounts Receiv-able	Trucks	Office Equip-ment	Accounts Payable	Notes Payable	Capital Stock
						=	+	
	Balances before transaction	$14,500		$20,000	$2,500 =	$1,000	$6,000 +	$30,000
5a	Paid an account payable.	−1,000				−1,000		
	End-of-month balances	$13,500	$ –0–	$20,000	$2,500 =	$ –0–	$6,000 +	$30,000

Decreased by $1,000

Decreased by $1,000

In Illustration 1.2, Part A shows a *summary of transactions* prepared in accounting equation form for June. A **summary of transactions** is a teaching tool used to show the effects of transactions on the accounting equation. Note that the stockholders' equity has remained at $30,000. This amount will change as the business begins to earn revenues and incur expenses. You can see how the totals at the bottom of Part A of Illustration 1.2 tie into the balance sheet shown in Part B. The date on the balance sheet is June 30, 1995. These totals become the beginning balances for July 1995.

Thus far, all transactions have consisted of exchanges or acquisitions of assets either by borrowing or by owner investment. This procedure was used so you could focus on the accounting equation as it relates to the balance sheet. However, people do not form a business only to *hold present assets*. Businesses are formed so *their assets can be used to generate greater amounts of assets*. Thus, a business increases its assets by providing goods or services to customers. The results of these activities are shown in the income statement. The section that follows shows more of the transactions of Beck Company as it begins its business of earning revenues and incurring expenses.

Transactions Affecting the Income Statement and/or Balance Sheet. To survive, a business must be profitable. This means that the revenues earned by providing goods and services to customers must exceed the expenses incurred.

In July 1995, Beck Company began selling services and incurring expenses. The explanations of transactions that follow will allow you to participate in this process and learn the necessary accounting procedures.

1b. Earned Service Revenue and Received Cash.   As its first transaction in July, Beck performed delivery services for customers and received $4,800 cash. This transaction increased the cash balance by $4,800. Stock-

Illustration 1.2

A. Summary of Transactions

BECK COMPANY
Summary of Transactions
Month of June 1995

Trans-action	Explanation	Cash	Accounts Receivable	Trucks	Office Equipment	Accounts Payable	Notes Payable	Capital Stock
				Assets		=	*Liabilities* +	*Stockholders' Equity*
	Beginning balances.	$ –0–	$ –0–	$ –0–	$ –0– =	$ –0–	$ –0–	$ –0–
1a	Owners invested cash.	+30,000						+30,000
		$30,000				=		$30,000
2a	Borrowed money	+6,000					+6,000	
		$36,000				=	$6,000 +	$30,000
3a	Purchased trucks and office equip-ment for cash	–21,500		+20,000	+1,500			
		$14,500		$20,000	$1,500 =		$6,000 +	$30,000
4a	Purchased office equipment on account				+1,000	+1,000		
		$14,500		$20,000	$2,500 =	$1,000	$6,000 +	$30,000
5a	Paid an account payable	–1,000				–1,000		
	End-of-month balances	$13,500	$ –0–	$20,000	$2,500 =	$ –0–	$6,000 +	$30,000

B. Balance Sheet

BECK COMPANY
Balance Sheet
June 30, 1995

Assets		*Liabilities and Stockholders' Equity*	
Cash.	$13,500	Liabilities:	
Trucks	20,000	Notes payable	$6,000
Office Equipment.	2,500	Total liabilities.	$ 6,000
		Stockholders' equity:	
		Capital Stock	30,000
		Total liabilities and stockholders'	
Total assets	$36,000	equity.	$36,000

holders' equity (in the form of retained earnings) also increased by $4,800, and the accounting equation is in balance.

The $4,800 is a revenue earned by the business and, as such, increases stockholders' equity because owners prosper when the business earns profits. Likewise, the owners would sustain any losses. If the business continues to have losses, it may fail.

The amount of retained earnings is increased by revenues and decreased by expenses and dividends. In this first chapter, all of these items are shown as immediately affecting retained earnings. In later chapters, the revenues, expenses, and dividends are kept separate from retained earnings during the accounting period and transferred to retained earnings only at the end of an accounting period.

The effects of this $4,800 transaction on the financial status of Beck are:

Trans-action	Explanation	Assets				=	Liabilities		+	Stockholders' Equity	
		Cash	Accounts Receivable	Trucks	Office Equipment		Accounts Payable	Notes Payable		Capital Stock	Retained Earnings
	Beginning balances (Illustration 1.2). . . .	$13,500	$–0–	$20,000	$2,500 =		$–0–	$6,000	+	$30,000	$ –0–
1b	Earned service revenue and received cash. . .	+4,800									+4,800 (service revenue)
	Balances after transaction	$18,300		$20,000	$2,500 =			$6,000	+	$30,000	$4,800

Cash: Increased by $4,800

Retained Earnings: Increased by $4,800

Note that the increase in stockholders' equity brought about by the revenue transaction is recorded as a separate item, "Retained Earnings." We cannot record this increase as capital stock because the Capital Stock account is increased only when the company issues shares of stock. The expectation is that revenue transactions will exceed expenses and yield net income. If net income is not distributed to stockholders, it is in fact retained. As stated above, later chapters will show that because of complexities in handling large numbers of transactions, revenues will be shown as affecting retained earnings only at the end of an accounting period. The procedure presented above is a shortcut used to explain why the accounting equation remains in balance.

2b. Service Revenue Earned on Account (for Credit).   Beck performed delivery services for a customer who agreed to pay $900 at a later date. The company granted credit rather than requiring the customer to pay cash immediately. This is called earning revenue *on account*. The transaction consists of an exchange of services for a promise by the customer to pay later. This transaction is similar to the preceding transaction in that stockholders' equity is increased because the company has earned revenues. However, the transaction differs because the company has not received cash. Instead, the company has received another asset, an *account receivable*. As noted earlier, an account receivable is the amount due from a customer for goods or services already provided. The company has a legal right to collect from the customer in the future. Accounting recognizes such claims as assets. The accounting equation, including this $900 item, is as follows:

Trans-action	Explanation	Cash	Accounts Receiv-able	Trucks	Office Equip-ment	Accounts Payable	Notes Payable	Capital Stock	Retained Earn-ings
				Assets	=	**Liabilities**	+	**Stockholders' Equity**	
	Balances before transaction	$18,300		$20,000	$2,500 =		$6,000 +	$30,000	$4,800
2b	Earned service revenue on account		+900						+900 (service revenue)
	Balances after transaction	$18,300	$900	$20,000	$2,500 =		$6,000 +	$30,000	$5,700

Increased by $900

Increased by $900

3b. Collected Cash on Accounts Receivable. Beck collected $200 on account from the customer in transaction 2b. The customer will pay the remaining $700 later. This transaction affects only the balance sheet and consists of giving up a claim on a customer in exchange for cash. The effects of the transaction are to increase cash by $200 and to decrease accounts receivable by $200. **Note that this transaction consists solely of a change in the composition of the assets.** The revenue was recorded when the company performed the services. Therefore, the revenue is not recorded again when the cash is collected.

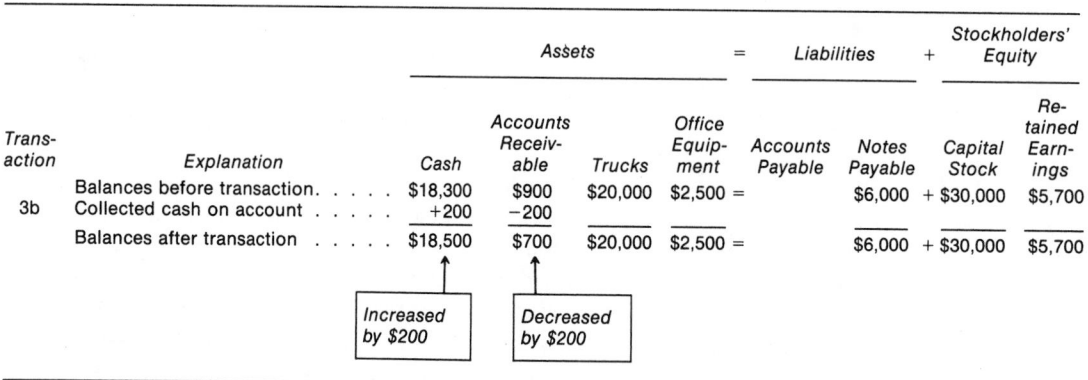

Trans-action	Explanation	Cash	Accounts Receiv-able	Trucks	Office Equip-ment	Accounts Payable	Notes Payable	Capital Stock	Retained Earn-ings
				Assets	=	**Liabilities**	+	**Stockholders' Equity**	
	Balances before transaction.	$18,300	$900	$20,000	$2,500 =		$6,000 +	$30,000	$5,700
3b	Collected cash on account	+200	−200						
	Balances after transaction	$18,500	$700	$20,000	$2,500 =		$6,000 +	$30,000	$5,700

Increased by $200

Decreased by $200

4b. Paid Salaries. Beck paid employees $2,600 in salaries. This transaction is an exchange of cash for employee services. Typically, companies pay employees for their services after they perform their work. Salaries (or wages) are costs companies incur to produce revenues, and companies consider them an expense. Thus, the accountant treats the transaction as a decrease in an asset (cash) and a decrease in stockholders' equity because the company has incurred an expense. Expense transactions reduce net income. Since net income becomes a part of the retained earnings balance, expense transactions reduce the retained earnings.

Trans-action	Explanation	Cash	Accounts Receiv-able	Trucks	Office Equip-ment	=	Accounts Payable	Notes Payable	+	Capital Stock	Re-tained Earn-ings
							Assets		**= Liabilities + Stockholders' Equity**		
	Balances before transaction	$18,500	$700	$20,000	$2,500 =			$6,000	+	$30,000	$5,700
4b	Paid salaries	−2,600									−2,600 (salaries expense)
	Balances after transaction	$15,900	$700	$20,000	$2,500 =			$6,000	+	$30,000	$3,100

Decreased by $2,600 (Cash)   Decreased by $2,600 (Retained Earnings)

5b. Paid Rent. In July, Beck paid $400 cash for office space rental. This transaction causes a decrease in cash of $400 and a decrease in the stockholders' equity of $400 because of the incurrence of rent expense.

Transaction 5b has the following effects on the amounts in the accounting equation:

Trans-action	Explanation	Cash	Accounts Receiv-able	Trucks	Office Equip-ment	Accounts Payable	Notes Payable	Capital Stock	Re-tained Earn-ings
	Balances before transaction	$15,900	$700	$20,000	$2,500 =		$6,000	+ $30,000	$3,100
5b	Paid rent	−400							−400 (rent expense)
	Balances after transaction	$15,500	$700	$20,000	$2,500 =		$6,000	+ $30,000	$2,700

Decreased by $400 (Cash)   Decreased by $400 (Retained Earnings)

ETHICS   A CLOSER LOOK

Mike Jennings was captain of the football team at Elite University. He also earned a master's degree in business administration with a concentration in accounting.

Upon graduation, Mike accepted a position with Tax Shelters, Inc., in the accounting and finance division. At first, things were going smoothly. Mike was tall, good looking, and had an outgoing personality. The president of the company took a liking to him. However, Mike was somewhat bothered when the president of the company started asking him to do some things that Mike recognized as being slightly unethical. When Mike mildly protested, the president said, "Come on, son, this is the way the business world works. You have great potential if you don't let things like this get in your way."

As time went on, the things Mike was asked to do became more unethical, and finally he was performing illegal acts. When he resisted doing some of these things, the president appealed to his "loyalty" and "being a team player" to gain his cooperation. The president also promised Mike great wealth sometime in the future. Finally, when Mike was told to falsify some financial state-ments by making improper adjusting entries and to sign some documents Mike knew to contain material errors, the president supported his "request" by stating, "You are in too deeply now to refuse to cooperate. If I go down, you are going with me." Through various company schemes, Mike had convinced some friends and relatives to invest about $10 million. Most of this would be lost if the various company schemes were discovered.

Mike could not sleep at night and began each day with a pain in his stomach and by becoming physically ill. He was under great strain and believed that he could lose his mind. He also heard that the president had a shady past and could become violent in retaliating against his enemies. If Mike "blows the whistle," he believes he will go to prison for his part in the schemes. (Note: This problem is based on an actual situation with some facts changed to protect the guilty.)

Required
a. What motivated Mike to go along with unethical and illegal actions?
b. What are Mike's options now?
c. What would you do if you were Mike?
d. What do you think the real "Mike" did?

Paying cash for other expenses, such as advertising, gas and oil, and miscel-laneous, would be recorded in the same way as transactions 4b and 5b.

6b. Received Bill for Gas and Oil Used. At the end of the month, Beck received a $600 bill for gas and oil consumed during the month. This transac-tion involves an increase in accounts payable (a liability) because Beck has not yet paid the bill and a decrease in retained earnings because Beck has incurred an expense. Beck's accounting equation now reads:

Trans-action	Explanation	Assets				=	Liabilities		+	Stockholders' Equity	
		Cash	Accounts Receiv-able	Trucks	Office Equip-ment		Accounts Payable	Notes Payable		Capital Stock	Re-tained Earn-ings
	Balances before transaction	$15,500	$700	$20,000	$2,500 =			$6,000	+	$30,000	$2,700
6b	Received bill for gas and oil used						+600				−600 (gas and oil
	End-of-month balances .	$15,500	$700	$20,000	$2,500 =		$600	$6,000	+	$30,000	$2,100 expense)

Increased by $600

Decreased by $600

Objective 6
Prepare an in-come statement, a statement of re-tained earnings, and a balance sheet.

Summary of Balance Sheet and Income Statement Transactions. Part A of Illustration 1.3 summarizes the effects of all the preceding transactions on the assets, liabilities, and stockholders' equity of Beck Company in July. The beginning balances are those shown as ending balances in Part A of Illustration 1.2. The summary shows subtotals after each transaction; these subtotals are optional and may be omitted. Note how the accounting equation remains in balance after each transaction and at the end of the month.

The ending balances in each of the columns in Part A of Illustration 1.3 are the dollar amounts in Part B and those reported earlier in the balance sheet in Part C of Illustration 1.1. The itemized data in the Retained Earnings column are the revenue and expense items in Part C of Illustration 1.3 and those reported earlier in the income statement in Part A of Illustration 1.1. The beginning balance in the Retained Earnings column ($–0–) plus net income for the month ($2,100) is equal to the ending balance in Retained Earnings ($2,100) shown earlier in Part B of Illustration 1.2.

Dividends Paid to Owners (Stockholders). Stockholders' equity is (1) increased by capital contributed by stockholders and by revenues earned through operations and (2) decreased by expenses incurred in producing revenues. The payment of cash or other assets to stockholders in the form of dividends also reduces stockholders' equity. Thus, if the owners receive a dividend in the form of cash, the effect would be to reduce cash and stock-holders' equity by that amount. This transaction would reduce the retained earnings part of stockholders' equity, and the amount of dividends is not an expense but rather a distribution of income.

Chapter 1 has introduced two important components of the accounting process—the accounting equation and the business transaction. In Chapter 2, you will learn about debits and credits and how accountants use them in recording transactions.

Illustration 1.3

A. Summary of Transactions

BECK COMPANY
Summary of Transactions
Month of July 1995

		Assets				=	Liabilities	+	Stockholders' Equity	
Trans-action	Explanation	Cash	Accounts Receiv-able	Trucks	Office Equip-ment	=	Accounts Payable	Notes Payable	Capital Stock	Re-tained Earn-ings
	Beginning balances (Illustration 1.2)	$13,500	$–0–	$20,000	$2,500 =		$–0–	$6,000 +	$30,000	$ –0–
1b	Earned service revenue and received cash . .	+4,800								+4,800 (service
		$18,300		$20,000	$2,500 =			$6,000 +	$30,000	$4,800 revenue)
2b	Earned service revenue on account.		+900							+900 (service
		$18,300	$900	$20,000	$2,500 =			$6,000 +	$30,000	$5,700 revenue)
3b	Collected cash on account	+200	–200							
		$18,500	$700	$20,000	$2,500 =			$6,000 +	$30,000	$5,700
4b	Paid salaries	–2,600								–2,600 (salaries
		$15,900	$700	$20,000	$2,500 =			$6,000 +	$30,000	$3,100 expense)
5b	Paid rent.	–400								–400 (rent
		$15,500	$700	$20,000	$2,500 =			$6,000 +	$30,000	$2,700 expense)
6b	Received bill for gas and oil used						+600			–600 (gas and oil
	End-of-month balances .	$15,500	$700	$20,000	$2,500 =		$600	$6,000 +	$30,000	$2,100 expense)

$38,700 $6,600 $32,100

B. Balance Sheet

BECK COMPANY
Balance Sheet
July 31, 1995

Assets		Liabilities and Stockholders' Equity	
Cash	$15,500	Liabilities:	
Accounts receivable. . .	700	Accounts payable . . .	$ 600
Trucks	20,000	Notes payable	6,000
Office equipment	2,500	Total liabilities	$ 6,600
		Stockholders' equity:	
		Capital stock.	$30,000
		Retained earnings . . .	2,100
		Total stockholders' equity	$32,100
Total assets.	$38,700	Total liabilities and stockholders' equity . .	$38,700

C. Income Statement

BECK COMPANY
Income Statement
For the Month Ended July 31, 1995

Revenues:		
Service revenue		$5,700
Expenses:		
Salaries expense. . . .	$2,600	
Rent expense	400	
Gas and oil expense . .	600	
Total expenses. . . .		3,600
Net income		$2,100

UNDERSTANDING THE LEARNING OBJECTIVES

1. Identify and describe the three basic forms of business organizations.
    *   A single proprietorship is an unincorporated business owned by an individual and often managed by that same individual.
    *   A partnership is an unincorporated business owned by two or more persons associated as partners and is often managed by those same persons.
    *   A corporation is a business incorporated under the laws of one of the states and owned by a few persons or by thousands of stockholders.
2. Distinguish among the three types of activities performed by business organizations.
    *   Service companies perform services for a fee.
    *   Merchandising companies purchase goods that are ready for sale and then sell them to customers.
    *   Manufacturing companies buy materials, convert them into products, and then sell the products to other companies or to final customers.
3. Describe the content and purposes of the income statement, statement of retained earnings, and balance sheet.
    *   The income statement reports the revenues and expenses of a company and shows the profitability of that business organization for a stated period of time.
    *   The statement of retained earnings shows the change in retained earnings between the beginning of the period (e.g., a month) and the end of that period.
    *   The balance sheet lists the assets, liabilities, and stockholders' equity (including dollar amounts) of a business organization at a specific moment in time.
4. State the basic accounting equation and describe its relationship to the balance sheet.
    *   The accounting equation is: Assets = Liabilities + Stockholders' Equity.
    *   The left-hand side of the equation represents the left-hand side of the balance sheet and shows things of value owned by the business.
    *   The right-hand side of the equation represents the right-hand side of the balance sheet and shows who provided the funds to acquire the things of value (assets).
5. Using the underlying assumptions or concepts, analyze business transactions and determine their effects on items in the financial statements.
    *   Some transactions only affect balance sheet items: assets (such as cash, accounts receivable, and equipment), liabilities (such as accounts payable and notes payable), and stockholders' equity (capital stock). Other transactions affect both balance sheet items and in-

income statement items (revenues and expenses and eventually retained earnings).

 • Illustration 1.3 (Part A) shows the effects of business transactions on the accounting equation.

6. Prepare an income statement, a statement of retained earnings, and a balance sheet.

 • The income statement is shown in Illustrations 1.1 (Part A) and 1.3 (Part C).

 • The statement of retained earnings is shown in Illustration 1.1 (Part B).

 • The balance sheet is shown in Illustrations 1.1 (Part C) and 1.3 (Part B).

DEMONSTRATION PROBLEM

On June 1, 1995, Rolling Hills Riding Stable, Incorporated, was organized. The following transactions occurred during June:

June 1 Shares of capital stock were issued for $20,000 cash.
      4 A horse stable and riding equipment were rented (and paid for) for the month at a cost of $1,200.
      8 Horse feed for the month was purchased on credit, $800.
     15 Boarding fees of $3,000 for June were charged to those owning horses that were boarded at the stable. (This amount is due on July 10.)
     20 Miscellaneous expenses of $600 were paid.
     29 Land was purchased from a savings and loan association by borrowing $40,000 on a note from that association. The loan is due to be repaid in five years. Interest payments are due at the end of each month beginning July 31.
     30 Salaries of $700 for the month were paid.
     30 Riding and lesson fees were billed to customers in the amount of $2,400. (They are due on July 10.)

Required:

a. Prepare a summary of the above transactions. Use columns headed Cash, Accounts Receivable, Land, Accounts Payable, Notes Payable, Capital Stock, and Retained Earnings. Determine balances after each transaction to show that the basic equation is in balance.
b. Prepare an income statement for June 1995.
c. Prepare a statement of retained earnings for June 1995.
d. Prepare a balance sheet as of June 30, 1995.

Solution to demonstration problem

a.

ROLLING HILLS RIDING STABLE, INCORPORATED
Summary of Transactions
Month of June 1995

		Assets			=	Liabilities		+	Stockholders' Equity	
Date	Explanation	Cash	Accounts Receivable	Land		Accounts Payable	Notes Payable		Capital Stock	Retained Earnings
June 1	Capital stock issued . .	$20,000			=				$20,000	
4	Rent expense	−1,200								$−1,200
		$18,800			=				$20,000	$−1,200
8	Feed expense					$+800				−800
		$18,800			=	$ 800		+	$20,000	$−2,000
15	Boarding fees		$+3,000							+3,000
		$18,800	$ 3,000		=	$ 800		+	$20,000	$ 1,000
20	Miscellaneous expenses	−600								−600
		$18,200	$ 3,000		=	$ 800		+	$20,000	$ 400
29	Purchased land by borrowing			$+40,000			$+40,000			
		$18,200	$ 3,000	$ 40,000	=	$ 800	$ 40,000	+	$20,000	$ 400
30	Salaries paid	−700								−700
		$17,500	$ 3,000	$ 40,000	=	$ 800	$ 40,000	+	$20,000	$ −300
30	Riding and lesson fees billed		+2,400							+2,400
		$17,500	$ 5,400	$ 40,000	=	$ 800	$ 40,000		$20,000	$ 2,100

b.

ROLLING HILLS RIDING STABLE, INCORPORATED
Income Statement
For the Month Ended June 30, 1995

Revenues:

Horse boarding fees revenue	$3,000	
Riding and lesson fees revenue.	2,400	
Total revenues.		$5,400

Expenses:

Rent expense	$1,200	
Feed expense	800	
Salaries expense.	700	
Miscellaneous expense.	600	
Total expenses		3,300
Net Income		$2,100

c.

ROLLING HILLS RIDING STABLE, INCORPORATED
Statement of Retained Earnings
For the Month Ended June 30, 1995

Retained earnings, June 1 . . . . $ –0–
Add: Net income for June   2,100

Total $2,100
Less: Dividends . . . .   –0–

Retained earnings, June 30 . . . . $2,100

---

d.

ROLLING HILLS RIDING STABLE, INCORPORATED
Balance Sheet
June 30, 1995
Assets

Cash $17,500
Accounts receivable   5,400
Land   40,000

Total assets $62,900

Liabilities and Stockholders' Equity

Liabilities:
  Accounts payable . . . . $ 800
  Notes payable   40,000

  Total liabilities $40,800

Stockholders' equity:
  Capital stock $20,000
  Retained earnings   2,100

  Total stockholders' equity   22,100

Total liabilities and stockholders' equity . . $62,900

NEW TERMS

Accounting equation Basically, Assets = Equities; or, Assets = Liabilities + Stockholders' Equity. *32*

Accounts payable Amounts owed to suppliers for goods or services purchased on credit. *31*

Accounts receivable Amounts due from customers for services already provided. *31*

Assets Things of value owned by the business. Examples include cash, machines, and buildings. Assets possess service potential or utility to their owners that can be measured and expressed in money terms. *31*

Balance sheet Financial statement that lists a company's assets, liabilities, and stockholders' equity (including dollar amounts) as of a specific moment in time. Also called a *statement of financial position*. *28, 30*

Business entity concept The separate existence of the business organization. *24, 33*

Capital stock The title given to an equity account showing the investment in a business corporation by its stockholders. *31*

Continuity See Going concern.

Corporation Business incorporated under the laws of one of the states and owned by a few persons or by thousands of persons. *25*

Cost Sacrifice made or the resources given up, measured in money terms, to acquire some desired thing, such as a new truck (asset). *34*

Dividend Payment (usually of cash) to the owners of the business; it is a distribution of income to owners rather than an expense of doing business. *30*

Entity A unit that is deemed to have an existence separate and apart from its owners, creditors, employees, customers, other interested parties, and other businesses, and for which accounting records are maintained. *24*

Equities Broadly speaking, all claims to, or interests in, assets; includes liabilities and stockholders' equity. *32*

Exchange-price (or cost) concept (principle) The objective money prices determined in the exchange process are used to record most assets. *34*

Expenses Costs incurred to produce revenues, measured by the assets surrendered or consumed in serving customers. *28*

Going concern (continuity) concept The assumption by the accountant that unless strong evidence exists to the contrary, a business entity will continue operations into the indefinite future. *34*

Income statement Financial statement that shows the revenues and expenses and reports the profitability of a business organization for a stated period of time. Sometimes called an *earnings statement. 28*

Liabilities Debts owed by a business—or creditors' equity. Examples: notes payable, accounts payable. *31*

Manufacturing companies Companies that buy materials, convert them into products, and then sell the products to other companies or to final customers. *26*

Merchandising companies Companies that purchase goods that are ready for sale and then sell them to customers. *26*

Money measurement concept Recording and reporting economic activity in terms of a common monetary unit of measure such as the dollar. *33*

Net income Amount by which the revenues of a period exceed the expenses of the same period. *28*

Net loss Amount by which the expenses of a period exceed the revenues of the same period. *28*

Notes payable Amounts owed to parties who loan the company money after the owner signs a written agreement (a note) for the company to repay each loan. *31*

Partnership An unincorporated business owned by two or more persons associated as partners. *25*

Periodicity (time periods concept) An assumption that an entity's life can be meaningfully subdivided into time periods (such as months or years) for purposes of reporting its economic activities. *34*

Profitability Ability to generate income. The income statement reflects a company's profitability. *28*

Retained earnings Accumulated net income less dividend distributions to stockholders. *31*

Revenues   Inflows of assets (such as cash) resulting from the sale of products or the rendering of services to customers. *28*

Service companies   Companies (such as accounting firms, law firms, or dry cleaning establishments) that perform services for a fee. *26*

Single proprietorship   An unincorporated business owned by an individual and often managed by that same individual. *24*

Solvency   Ability to pay debts as they become due. The balance sheet reflects a company's solvency. *28*

Source document   Any written or printed evidence of a business transaction that describes the essential facts of that transaction, such as receipts for cash paid or received. *33*

Statement of cash flows   Shows cash inflows and outflows for a company over a period of time. *28*

Statement of retained earnings   Statement used to explain the changes in retained earnings that occurred between two balance sheet dates. *28, 30*

Stockholders' equity   The owners' interest in a corporation. *31*

Stockholders or shareholders   Owners of a corporation; they buy shares of stock, which are units of ownership, in the corporation. *25*

Summary of transactions   Teaching tool used in chapter to show the effects of transactions on the accounting equation. *37*

Transaction   A business activity or event that must be recorded in the accounting records. *33*

SELF-TEST

True-False

Indicate whether each of the following statements is true or false.

1. The three forms of business organizations are single proprietorship, partnership, and trust.

2. The three types of business activity are service, merchandising, and manufacturing.

3. The income statement shows the profitability of the company and is dated as of a particular date, such as December 31, 1995.

4. The statement of retained earnings shows both the net income for the period and the beginning and ending balances of retained earnings.

5. The balance sheet contains the same major headings as appear in the accounting equation.

Multiple-Choice

Select the best answer for each of the following questions.

1. The ending balance in retained earnings is shown in the:
    a. Income statement.
    b. Statement of retained earnings.
    c. Balance sheet.
    d. Both *(b)* and *(c)*.

2. Which of the following is *not* a correct form of the accounting equation?

a. Assets = Equities.
b. Assets = Liabilities + Stockholders' Equity.
c. Assets − Liabilities = Stockholders' Equity.
d. Assets + Stockholders' Equity = Liabilities.

3. Which of the following is *not* one of the five underlying assumptions or concepts mentioned in the chapter?
   a. Exchange-price concept.
   b. Inflation accounting concept.
   c. Business entity concept.
   d. Going-concern concept.

4. When the stockholders invest cash in the business, what is the effect?
   a. Liabilities increase and stockholders' equity increases.
   b. Both assets and liabilities increase.
   c. Both assets and stockholders' equity increase.
   d. None of the above.

5. When services are performed on account, what is the effect?
   a. Both cash and retained earnings decrease.
   b. Both cash and retained earnings increase.
   c. Both accounts receivable and retained earnings increase.
   d. Accounts payable increases and retained earnings decreases.

Now turn to page 60 to check your answers.

QUESTIONS

1. Accounting has often been called the language of business. In what respects would you agree with this description? How might you argue that this description is deficient?

2. Define asset, liability, and stockholders' equity.

3. How do liabilities and stockholders' equity differ? How are they similar?

4. How do accounts payable and notes payable differ? How are they similar?

5. Define revenues. How are revenues measured?

6. Define expenses. How are expenses measured?

7. What is a balance sheet? On what aspect of a business does the balance sheet provide information?

8. What is an income statement? On what aspect of a business does this statement provide information?

9. What information does the statement of retained earnings provide?

10. What is a transaction? What use does the accountant make of transactions? Why?

11. What is the accounting equation? Why must it always balance?

12. Give an example from your personal life that you believe illustrates your use of accounting information in reaching a decision.

13. You have been elected to the governing board of your church. At the first meeting you attend, mention is made of building a new church. What accounting information would the board need in deciding whether or not to go ahead?

14. A company purchased equipment for $1,000 cash. The vendor stated that the equipment was worth $1,200. At what amount should the equipment be recorded?

15. What is meant by money measurement?

16. Of what significance is the exchange-price (or cost) concept? How is the cost to acquire an asset determined?

17. What effect does the going-concern (continuity) concept have on amounts at which long-term assets are carried on the balance sheet?

18. Of what importance is the periodicity (time periods) concept to the preparation of financial statements?

19. Describe a transaction that would:

   a. Increase both an asset and capital stock.

   b. Increase both an asset and a liability.

   c. Increase one asset and decrease another asset.

   d. Decrease both a liability and an asset.

   e. Increase both an asset and retained earnings.

   f. Decrease both an asset and retained earnings.

   g. Increase a liability and decrease retained earnings.

   h. Decrease both an asset and retained earnings.

20. Identify the causes of increases and decreases in stockholders' equity.

21. *Real-world question*   Refer to "A Broader Perspective" on page 27. When you go for a job interview, what are some of the factors that will help you obtain the position?

MAYTAG
CORPORATION

22. *Real-world question*   Refer to the financial statements of Maytag Corporation in Appendix C at the end of the text. What were the net income amounts in 1989, 1990, and 1991?

MAYTAG
CORPORATION

23. *Real-world question*   Referring to the financial statements of The Limited, Inc., in Appendix C at the end of the text, has net income increased or decreased over the period 1989–91?

EXERCISES

Matching
(L.O. 1, 2)

1–1. Match the descriptions in Column B with the appropriate terms in Column A.

Column A	Column B
1. Corporation.	a. An unincorporated business owned by an individual.
2. Merchandising company.	b. The form of organization used by most large businesses.
3. Partnership.	c. Buys raw materials and converts them into finished products.
4. Manufacturing company.	d. Buys goods in their finished form and sells them to customers in that same form.
5. Service company.	e. An unincorporated business with more than one owner.
6. Single proprietorship.	f. Performs services for a fee.

Compute net
income and
revenue
(L.O. 3)

1–2. Assume that retained earnings increased by $28,800 from July 1, 1994, to June 30, 1995. A cash dividend of $2,400 was declared and paid during the year.

a. Compute the net income for the year.

b. Assume expenses for the year were $72,000. Compute the revenue for the year.

Compute retained
earnings
(L.O. 3, 4)

1–3. On December 31, 1994, Stiner Company had assets of $270,000, liabilities of $195,000, and capital stock of $60,000. During 1995, Stiner earned revenues of $90,000 and incurred expenses of $67,500. Dividends declared and paid amounted to $3,000.

a. Compute the company's retained earnings on December 31, 1994.

b. Compute the company's retained earnings on December 31, 1995.

Compute retained
earnings and total
assets at
beginning of year
(L.O. 3, 4)

1–4. At the start of the year, a company had liabilities of $54,000 and capital stock of $150,000. At the end of the year, retained earnings amounted to $135,000. Net income for the year was $45,000, and $15,000 of dividends were declared and paid. Compute retained earnings and total assets at the beginning of the year.

Analyze
transactions
(L.O. 4, 5)

1–5. For each event below, determine if it has an effect on the basic elements of the accounting equation. For the events that do have an effect, present an analysis of the transaction showing its two sides or dual nature.

a. Purchased equipment for cash, $2,500.

b. Purchased a truck for $18,000, payment to be made later in the month.

c. Paid $500 for the current month's utilities.

d. Paid for the truck purchased in (b).

e. Employed Joseph Carcello as a salesperson at $1,200 per month. He is to start work next week.

f. Signed an agreement with a bank in which the bank agreed to lend the company up to $135,000 any time within the next two years.

Indicate effect of
transactions on
items in the
accounting
equation
(L.O. 4, 5)

1–6. Ruiz Company, engaged in a service business, completed the following selected transactions during July 1995:

a. Purchased office equipment on account.

b. Paid an account payable.

c. Earned service revenue on account.

d. Borrowed money by signing a note at the bank.

e. Paid salaries for month to employees.

f. Received cash on account from a charge customer.

g. Received gas and oil bill for month.

h. Purchased delivery truck for cash.

i. Declared and paid a cash dividend.

Using a tabular form similar to Illustration 1.3 (Part A), indicate the effect of each transaction on the accounting equation using (+) for increase and (−) for decrease. No dollar amounts are needed, and you need not fill in the Explanation column.

Determine effect
of transactions on
stockholders'
equity
(L.O. 5)

1–7. Indicate the amount of change (if any) in the stockholders' equity balance based on each of the following transactions:

a. The owner invested $60,000 cash in the business by purchasing capital stock.

b. Land costing $10,000 was purchased by paying cash.

c. The company performed services for a customer who agreed to pay $16,000 in one month.

d. Paid salaries for the month, $14,400.

e. Paid $5,000 on an account payable.

Analyze
transactions
(L.O. 5)

1–8. Give examples of transactions that would have the following effects on the items in a firm's financial statements:

a. Increase cash; decrease some other asset.

b. Decrease cash; increase some other asset.

c. Increase an asset; increase a liability.

d. Increase retained earnings; decrease an asset.

e. Increase an asset other than cash; increase retained earnings.

f. Decrease an asset; decrease a liability.

Identify
transactions that
increase expenses
(L.O. 5)

1–9. Which of the following transactions results in a decrease in retained earnings? Why?

a. Employees were paid $20,000 for services received during the month.

b. $100,000 was paid to acquire land.

c. Paid a $10,000 note payable. No interest was involved.

d. Paid a $50 account payable.

Compute net
income
(L.O. 6)

1–10. Selected data for Boardman Company for 1995 are as follows (including all income statement data):

Revenue from services rendered on account	$244,000
Revenue from services rendered for cash	72,000
Cash collected from customers on account	201,600
Stockholders' equity, January 1, 1995.	384,000
Expenses incurred on account	144,000
Expenses incurred for cash	96,000
Dividends declared and paid	24,000
Capital stock issued for cash.	48,000
Stockholders' equity, December 31, 1995	484,000

Compute net income for 1995.

Prepare income statement (L.O. 6)

1–11. Assume that the following items were included in the Retained Earnings column in the summary of transactions for Foster Company for July 1995:

Salaries expense	$240,000
Service revenue	480,000
Gas and oil expense	54,000
Rent expense	96,000
Dividends paid	60,000

Prepare an income statement for July 1995.

Prepare statement of retained earnings (L.O. 6)

1–12. Given the following facts, prepare a statement of retained earnings for Rubin Company for August 1995:

Balance in retained earnings at end of July, $84,000.
Dividends paid in August, $28,800.
Net income for August, $36,000.

Prepare balance sheet (L.O. 6)

1–13. The column totals of a summary of transactions for Hardy Company as of December 31, 1995, were as follows (listed in alphabetical order):

Accounts payable	$ 45,000
Accounts receivable	90,000
Capital stock	150,000
Cash	60,000
Land	240,000
Notes payable	30,000
Retained earnings	?

Prepare a balance sheet.

PROBLEMS

1–1. Wilson Company completed the following transactions in September 1995:

Sept. 1 The company was organized and received $40,000 cash from the issuance of capital stock.

  5 The company bought equipment for cash at a cost of $10,800.

  7 The company performed services for a customer who agreed to pay $4,000 in one week.

  14 The company received the $4,000 from the transaction of September 7.

  20 Equipment that cost $1,600 was acquired today; payment was postponed until September 28.

  28 $1,200 was paid on the liability incurred on September 20.

  30 Employee services for the month, $1,400, were paid.

  30 Placed an order for new equipment advertised at $10,000.

Required:

Prepare a summary of transactions (see Part A of Illustration 1.3) for the company for the above transactions. Use money columns headed Cash, Accounts Receivable, Equipment, Accounts Payable, Capital Stock, and Retained Earnings. Determine balances after each transaction to show that the basic accounting equation balances.

1–2. Landis Company completed the following transactions in June 1995:

June 1 The company was organized and received $100,000 cash from the issuance of capital stock.

  4 The company paid $48,000 cash for equipment.

  7 The company borrowed $9,000 from its bank on a note.

  9 Cash received for services performed to date was $4,500.

  12 Costs of operating the business so far this month were paid in cash, $3,150.

  18 Services performed for a customer who agreed to pay within a month amounted to $5,400.

  25 The company paid $4,065 on its loan from the bank, including $4,050 of principal and $15 of interest. (The principal is the amount of the loan. Interest is an expense, which reduces stockholders' equity.)

  30 Miscellaneous expenses incurred in operating the business from June 13 to date were $3,825 and were paid in cash.

  30 An order was received from a customer for services to be performed tomorrow, which will be billed at $3,000.

Required:

a. Prepare a summary of transactions (see Part A of Illustration 1.3). Include money columns for Cash, Accounts Receivable, Equipment, Notes Payable, Capital Stock, and Retained Earnings. Determine balances after each transaction to show that the basic accounting equation balances.

b. Prepare a balance sheet as of June 30, 1995.

1–3. The following transactions are for Sanchez Company:

May 1 Paid May rent on the parking structure, $80,000.

  8 Received cash for eight days' parking services, $38,720.

15   Received cash for a week's parking services, $48,320.
15   Salaries paid for first half of May, $19,200.
17   Received cash for shares of capital stock issued, $40,000.
19   Paid advertising expenses for May, $6,400.
22   Received cash for a week's parking services, $63,360.
31   Salaries paid for last half of May, $24,000.
31   Cash received for nine days' parking services, $56,320.
31   Purchased motorized sweeper to clean parking structure, $48,000 cash.

Required:

By analyzing these transactions, prepare an income statement for the month of May 1995.

Prepare income
statement
(L.O. 6)

1–4. Following are summarized transaction data for Kelley Company for the year ending June 30, 1995. The company owns and operates an apartment building.

Rent revenue from building owned	$123,030
Building repairs	2,870
Building cleaning, labor cost.	3,185
Property taxes on the building	3,605
Insurance on the building	1,225
Commissions paid to rental agent	5,250
Legal and accounting fees (for preparation of tenant leases)	1,260
Utilities expense.	8,225
Cost of new awnings installed	2,800

Of the $123,030 of rent revenue above, $3,500 was not collected in cash until July 5, 1995.

Required:

Prepare an income statement for the year ended June 30, 1995.

Prepare summary
of transactions,
income statement,
statement of
retained earnings,
and balance sheet
(L.O. 4–6)

1–5. The following data are for Indiana Corporation:

INDIANA CORPORATION
Balance Sheet
October 1, 1995
Assets

Cash	$224,000
Accounts receivable	18,000
Total assets	$242,000

Liabilities and Stockholders' Equity

Accounts payable	$ 54,000
Capital stock.	152,000
Retained earnings	36,000
Total liabilities and stockholders' equity	$242,000

The summarized transactions for October 1995 are as follows:

Oct. 1 The accounts payable owed as of October 1 ($54,000) were paid.
   1 The company paid rent for the premises for October, $19,200.
   7 The company received cash of $4,200 for parking by daily customers during the week.
   10 The company collected $14,400 of the accounts receivable in the balance sheet at October 1.
   14 Cash receipts for the week from daily customers were $6,600.
   15 Parking revenue earned but not yet collected from fleet customers was $3,000.
   16 The company paid salaries of $2,400 for the period October 1–15.
   19 The company paid advertising expenses of $1,200 for October.
   21 Cash receipts for the week from daily customers were $7,200.
   24 The company incurred miscellaneous expenses of $840, which will be due November 10.
   31 Cash receipts for the last 10 days of the month from daily customers were $8,400.
   31 The company paid salaries of $3,000 for the period October 16–31.
   31 Billings to monthly customers totaled $21,600 for October.
   31 Paid cash dividends of $24,000.

Required:

a. Prepare a summary of transactions (see Part A of Illustration 1.3) using column headings as given in the above balance sheet. Determine balances after each transaction.
b. Prepare an income statement for October 1995.
c. Prepare a statement of retained earnings for October 1995.
d. Prepare a balance sheet as of October 31, 1995.

State causes of balance sheet changes (L.O. 3, 6)

1–6. Given below are balance sheets for May and June 1995, and the income statement for June, of Dunwoody Company (common practice is to show the most recent period first):

DUNWOODY COMPANY
Comparative Balance Sheets

	June 30, 1995	May 31, 1995
Assets		
Cash	$ 84,000	$120,000
Accounts receivable	48,000	–0–
Land	72,000	72,000
Total assets	$204,000	$192,000
Liabilities and Stockholders' Equity		
Liabilities	$ 24,000	$ 48,000
Capital stock	120,000	120,000
Retained earnings	60,000	24,000
Total liabilities and stockholders' equity	$204,000	$192,000

DUNWOODY COMPANY
Income Statement
For the Month Ended June 30, 1995

Revenues:

Service revenue		$192,000

Expenses:

Salaries expense	$96,000	
Supplies bought and used	48,000	144,000
Net income.		$ 48,000

A cash dividend of $12,000 was declared and paid in June.

Required:

State the probable causes of the changes in each of the balance sheet accounts from May 31 to June 30, 1995.

BUSINESS DECISION PROBLEMS

Identify
information
needed to make
decision
(L.O. 3)

1–1. Upon graduation from high school, Mark Wexler went to work for a builder of houses and small apartment buildings. During the next six years, Mark earned a reputation as an excellent employee—hardworking, dedicated, and dependable—in the light construction industry. He could handle almost any job requiring carpentry, electrical, or plumbing skills.

Mark then decided to go into business for himself under the name of Mark's Fix-It Shop, Inc. He invested cash, some power tools, and a used truck in his business. He completed many repair and remodeling jobs for both homeowners and apartment owners. The demand for his services was so large that he had more work than he could handle. He operated out of his garage, which he had converted into a shop, adding several new pieces of power woodworking equipment.

Now two years after going into business for himself, Mark is faced with a decision of whether to continue in his own business or to accept a position as construction supervisor for a home builder. He has been offered an annual salary of $42,000 and a package of "fringe benefits" (medical and hospitalization insurance, pension contribution, vacation and sick pay, and life insurance) worth approximately $8,000 per year. The offer is attractive to Mark. But he dislikes giving up his business since he has thoroughly enjoyed "being his own boss," even though it has led to an average workweek well in excess of the standard 40 hours.

Required:

Suppose Mark comes to you for assistance in gathering the information needed to help him make a decision. He brings along the accounting records that have been maintained for his business by an experienced accountant. Using logic and your own life experiences, indicate the nature of the information Mark needs if he is to make an informed decision. Pay particular attention to the information likely to be found in the accounting records for Mark's business that would be useful. Does the accounting information available enter directly into the decision? Explain.

Prepare income statement and balance sheet; judge profitability of company (L.O. 6)

1–2. The Miami Moon Drive-In Theater, Inc., opened for business on June 1, 1995. Analysis of the transactions for June 1995 discloses the following:

Ticket revenue	$142,000
Rent expense for premises and equipment	18,000
Film rental expense paid	35,600
Revenue received from operators of candy and popcorn concessions	20,000
Advertising expense.	16,800
Salaries expense	31,200
Utilities expense	10,000

Asset and liability amounts as of June 30 that the accountant calculated include the following:

Cash	$200,000
Land	32,000
Accounts payable	41,600

The balance in the Capital Stock account on June 1 was $140,000.

Required:

a. Prepare an income statement for June 1995.
b. Prepare a balance sheet as of June 30, 1995.
c. Did June seem to be a profitable month for this company?

ANSWERS TO SELF-TEST

True-False

1. *False.* Corporation, not trust, is the third form.
2. *True.* The accounting for all three of these will be covered in this text.
3. *False.* The income statement is dated using a period of time, such as "For the Year

Ended December 31, 1995."

4. *True.* In addition, the statement of retained earnings shows dividends declared.
5. *True.* Both show assets, liabilities, and stockholders' equity.

Multiple-Choice

1. *d.* The ending balance in retained earnings is shown in both the statement of retained earnings and in the balance sheet.
2. *d.* This form of the equation would not balance.
3. *b.* The inflation accounting concept was not one of the ones discussed. The other

two were the money measurement concept and the periodicity concept.

4. *c.* When the stockholders invest cash, assets and stockholders' equity increase.
5. *c.* The performance of services on account increases both accounts receivable and retained earnings.

II FINANCIAL ACCOUNTING: PROCESSING ACCOUNTING INFORMATION

2 RECORDING BUSINESS TRANSACTIONS

LEARNING OBJECTIVES

After studying this chapter, you should be able to:

1. Use the account as the basic classifying and storage unit for accounting information.
2. Express the effects of business transactions in terms of debits and credits to different types of accounts.
3. Record the effects of business transactions in a journal.
4. Post journal entries to the accounts in the ledger.
5. Prepare a trial balance to test the equality of debits and credits in the journalizing and posting process.

In Chapter 1, you learned that accountants classify business organizations according to the form of ownership of the business entity and by the type of business activities the business entity performs. The three forms of business organizations are single proprietorships, partnerships, and corporations. These organizations may perform three types of business activities— service, merchandising, and manufacturing. The three financial statements illustrated in Chapter 1 are the income statement, the statement of retained earnings, and the balance sheet. These statements are the end products of the financial accounting process (or cycle), which has the accounting equation as its foundation.

The raw data of accounting are the business transactions. The transactions in Chapter 1 were recorded as increases or decreases in the assets, liabilities, and stockholders' equity items of the accounting equation. This procedure showed you how the various transactions affected the items in the accounting equation. When working through these sample transactions, you probably noticed that listing all transactions as increases or decreases in the transactions summary columns would be too cumbersome in practice. Most businesses, even small ones, enter into many transactions every day. Chapter 2 teaches you how business transactions are actually recorded in the accounting process.

To understand the dual procedure of recording business transactions with debits and credits, you will use some new tools. You begin with the T-account, which classifies and summarizes the measurements of business activity. Then you learn how to use the journal and ledger. You will follow a company through its various business transactions using these tools. Like accountants, you will use a trial balance to check the equality of your recorded debits and credits. This is the double-entry accounting system that the Franciscan monk, Luca Pacioli, described centuries ago.

THE ACCOUNT AND RULES OF DEBIT AND CREDIT

A business may engage in thousands of transactions during a year. The data in these transactions must be classified and summarized before becoming useful information.

Steps in Recording Business Transactions

Illustration 2.1 shows the steps used in recording and posting the effects of a business transaction. Source documents provide the evidence that a business transaction occurred. These source documents include such items as bills received from suppliers for goods or services received, bills sent to customers for goods sold or services performed, and cash register tapes. The information in the source document serves as the basis for preparing a journal entry. Then that information is posted (transferred) to accounts in the ledger.

You can see from Illustration 2.1 that first the journal entry is prepared and then it is posted to the accounts in the ledger. However, before you can record the journal entry, you must understand the rules of debit and credit. To teach you these rules, we must temporarily skip the journal entry step and study the nature of an account.

Illustration 2.1
THE STEPS IN RECORDING AND POSTING THE EFFECTS OF A BUSINESS TRANSACTION

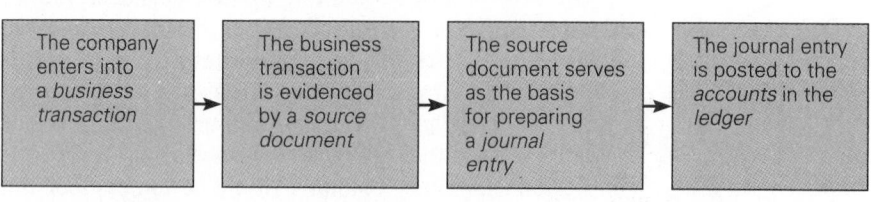

The company enters into a *business transaction* → The business transaction is evidenced by a *source document* → The source document serves as the basis for preparing a *journal entry* → The journal entry is posted to the *accounts* in the ledger

The Account

Fortunately, most business transactions are repetitive in nature. This characteristic makes the task of accountants somewhat easier because they can classify the transactions into groups having common characteristics. For example, a company may have thousands of receipts or payments of cash during a year. As a result, a part of every cash transaction can be recorded and summarized in a single place called an *account*.

An **account** is a part of the accounting system used to classify and summarize the increases, decreases, and balances of each asset, liability, stockholders' equity item, dividends, revenue, and expense. Accounts are set up for each different type of business element, such as cash, accounts receivable, and accounts payable. Every business has a *Cash account* in its accounting system because knowledge of the amount of cash on hand is useful information.

Accountants may differ on the account title (or name) they give for the same item. For example, one accountant might name an account Notes Payable and another might call it Loans Payable. Both account titles refer to the amounts borrowed by the company. The account title should be logical to help the accountant group similar transactions into the same account. Once you give an account a title, you must use that same title for that account throughout the accounting records.

The number of accounts in a company's accounting system depends on the information needs of those interested in the business. **The main requirement is that each account provides useful information.** Thus, one account may be set up for all cash rather than having a separate account for each form of cash (coins on hand, currency on hand, and deposits in banks). The amount of cash is useful information; the form of cash often is not.

The T-Account

To understand how the increases and decreases in an account are recorded, texts use the **T-account,** which looks like a capital letter T. The title (name) of the item accounted for, such as cash, is written across the top of the T. Increases are recorded on one side of the vertical line of the T and decreases on the other side. A T-account appears as follows:

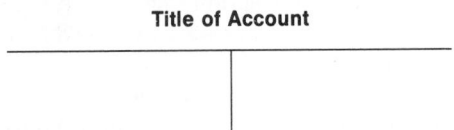

Title of Account

In Chapter 1, you saw that each business transaction affects at least two items. For example, if you—an owner—invest cash in the company, the company's assets increase and its stockholders' equity increases. This result was illustrated in the summary of transactions schedule in Chapter 1, Illustration 1.3. In the following sections, we will use debits and credits and the double-entry procedure to explain how to record the increases and decreases caused by business transactions.

Debits and Credits

Objective 2
Express the effects of business transactions in terms of debits and credits to different types of accounts

Accountants use the term **debit** instead of saying ''place an entry on the left side of the T-account.'' They use the term **credit** for ''place an entry on the right side of the T-account.'' **Debit** (abbreviated Dr.) simply means left side; **credit** (abbreviated Cr.) means right side.[1] Thus, a debit entry is an entry on the left side of an account, while a credit entry is an entry on the right side of an account. **For any account, the left side is the debit side, and the right side is the credit side, as shown below:**

Any Account

Left, or debit, side	Right, or credit, side

Double-Entry Procedure

Once a business event is recognized as a business transaction, it is analyzed to determine its increase or decrease effects on the assets, liabilities, stockholders' equity, dividends, revenues, or expenses of the business. These increase or decrease effects are then translated into debits and credits.

In each business transaction that is recorded, the total dollar amount of debits must equal the total dollar amount of credits. When we debit one account (or accounts) for $100, we must credit another account (or accounts) for a total of $100. The accounting requirement that each transaction be recorded by an entry that has equal debits and credits is called **double-entry procedure,** or duality. This double-entry procedure keeps the accounting equation in balance.

The dual recording process produces two sets of accounts—those with debit balances and those with credit balances. The totals of these two groups of accounts must be equal. Then, some assurance exists that the arithmetic part of the transaction recording process has been properly carried out. Now let us actually learn how to record business transactions in T-accounts using debits and credits.

Recording Changes in Assets, Liabilities, and Stockholders' Equity. From Chapter 1, you know that the foundation of the accounting process is the following basic accounting equation:

$$Assets = Liabilities + Stockholders' \ Equity$$

---

[1] The abbreviations ''*Dr.*'' and ''*Cr.*'' are based on the Latin words ''*debere*'' and ''*credere.*'' A synonym for *debit* an account is *charge* an account.

Recording transactions into the T-accounts is easier when you think first of the equal sign in the accounting equation. Then, remembering the equation, remember also that assets, which are on the left side of the equal sign, are increased on the left side of the T-accounts. Now, again remembering the equation, remember also that liabilities and stockholders' equity, to the right of the equal sign, are increased on the right side of the T-accounts. You already know that the left side of the T-account is the debit side and the right side is the credit side. So you should be able to fill in the rest of the rules of increases and decreases by deduction, such as:

Assets		=	**Liabilities**		+	**Stockholders' Equity**	
Debit for increases	Credit for decreases		Debit for decreases	Credit for increases		Debit for decreases	Credit for increases

To summarize:

1. Assets are *increased* by debits (left side) of the T-account and *decreased* by credits (right side) of the T-account.
2. Liabilities and stockholders' equity are *decreased* by debits (left side) of the T-account and *increased* by credits (right side) of the T-account.

Applying these two rules keeps the accounting equation in balance. Now we will apply the debit and credit rules for assets, liabilities, and stockholders' equity to business transactions.

Assume a corporation issues shares of its capital stock for $10,000 (Transaction 1). The company records the receipt of $10,000 as follows (the figure in parentheses refers to the number of the transaction and ties the two sides of the transaction together):

(Dr.)	**Cash**	*(Cr.)*	*(Dr.)*	**Capital Stock**	*(Cr.)*
(1)	10,000			(1)	10,000

The transaction involves first an increase in the asset, cash, which is recorded on the left side of the Cash account. Then, the transaction involves an increase in stockholders' equity, which is recorded on the right side of the Capital Stock account.

Assume the company borrowed $5,000 from a bank on a note (Transaction 2). As explained in Chapter 1, a **note** is an unconditional written promise to pay to another party (in this case the bank) the amount owed either when demanded or at a specified date, usually with interest at a specified rate. We record this transaction as follows:

(Dr.)	**Cash**	*(Cr.)*	*(Dr.)*	**Notes Payable**	*(Cr.)*
(1)	10,000			(2)	5,000
(2)	5,000				

Note that liabilities, in this case Notes Payable, are increased by an entry on the right (credit) side of the account.

Recording Changes in Revenues and Expenses. In Chapter 1, we recorded the revenues and expenses directly in the Retained Earnings account. However, this procedure is not done in practice because of the volume of revenue and expense transactions. Instead, the expense accounts are treated as if they were subclassifications of the debit side of the Retained Earnings account, and the revenue accounts as if they were subclassifications of the credit side. Since the amounts of revenues and expenses are needed to prepare the income statement, a separate account is kept for each revenue and expense. The recording rules for revenues and expenses are:

a. Record increases in revenues on the right (credit) side of the T-account and decreases on the left (debit) side. The reasoning behind this rule is that revenues increase retained earnings, and, as explained earlier, increases in retained earnings are recorded on the right side.
b. Record increases in expenses on the left (debit) side of the T-account and decreases on the right (credit) side. The reasoning behind this rule is that expenses decrease retained earnings, and, as explained earlier, decreases in retained earnings are recorded on the left side.

To illustrate these rules, assume a company received $1,000 cash from a customer for services rendered (Transaction 3). The Cash account, an asset, is increased on the left (debit) side of the T-account; and the Service Revenue account, an increase in retained earnings, is increased on the right (credit) side.

(Dr.)	**Cash**	*(Cr.)*	*(Dr.)*	**Service Revenue**	*(Cr.)*
(1)	10,000			(3)	1,000
(2)	5,000				
(3)	1,000				

Now assume a company paid $600 in salaries to employees (Transaction 4). The Cash account, an asset, is decreased on the right (credit) side of the T-account; and the Salaries Expense account, a decrease in retained earnings, is increased on the left (debit) side.[2]

(Dr.)	**Cash**	*(Cr.)*		*(Dr.)*	**Salaries Expense**	*(Cr.)*
(1)	10,000	(4)	600	(4)	600	
(2)	5,000					
(3)	1,000					

Recording Changes in Dividends. Since dividends decrease retained earnings, increases are shown on the left side of the Dividends account and

---

[2] Certain deductions are normally taken out of employees' pay for social security taxes, federal and state withholding, and so on. Those deductions will be ignored here.

decreases on the right side. Thus, the payment of a $2,000 cash dividend is recorded (Transaction 5) as follows:

(Dr.)	**Cash**		*(Cr.)*	*(Dr.)*	**Dividends**[3]	*(Cr.)*
(1)	10,000	(4)	600	(5)	2,000	
(2)	5,000	(5)	2,000			
(3)	1,000					

At the end of the accounting period, any balances in the expense, revenue, and Dividends accounts are transferred to the Retained Earnings account. This transfer occurs only after the information in the expense and revenue accounts has been used to prepare the income statement. This step is discussed and illustrated in Chapter 4.

Determining the Balance of an Account

To determine the balance of any T-account, total the debits to the account, total the credits to the account, and subtract the smaller sum from the larger. If the sum of the debits exceeds the sum of the credits, the account has a **debit balance.** For example, the Cash account shown below uses the information from the preceding transactions. The account has a debit balance of $13,400, computed as total debits of $16,000 less total credits of $2,600.

(Dr.)	**Cash**		*(Cr.)*
(1)	10,000	(3)	600
(2)	5,000	(5)	2,000
(4)	1,000		
	16,000		2,600
Dr. bal.	13,400		

If, on the other hand, the sum of the credits exceeds the sum of the debits, the account will have a **credit balance.** For instance, assume that a company has an Accounts Payable account with a total of $10,000 in debits and $13,000 in credits. The account will have a credit balance of $3,000, as shown in the following T-account:

(Dr.)	**Accounts Payable**	*(Cr.)*
	10,000	7,000
		6,000
	10,000	13,000
	Cr. bal.	3,000

---

[3] As we illustrate later in the text, dividends can be debited directly to the Retained Earnings account rather than to a Dividends account.

Normal Balances. Since asset, expense, and Dividend accounts are increased by debits, they *normally* have debit (or left-side) balances. Conversely, liability, Capital Stock, Retained Earnings, and revenue accounts are increased by credits and *normally* have credit (or right-side) balances.

The following diagram shows the normal balances of the seven types of accounts that we have used:

	Normal Balances	
Types of Accounts	*Debit*	*Credit*
Assets	X	
Liabilities		X
Stockholders' equity:		
Capital Stock		X
Retained Earnings. . . .		X
Dividends.	X	
Expenses.	X	
Revenues.		X

Rules of Debit and Credit Summarized

At this point you are ready for a summary of the rules of debit and credit. At first, it may be necessary to memorize these rules. Later, as you proceed in your study of accounting, the rules will become automatic. Then, you will no longer ask yourself, "Is this increase or decrease a debit or credit?"

As stated earlier, asset accounts are increased on the debit side, while liability and stockholders' equity accounts are increased on the credit side. When the account balances are totaled, they will conform to the following two independent equations:

$$\text{Assets} = \text{Liabilities} + \text{Stockholders' Equity}$$
$$\text{Debits} = \text{Credits}$$

The arrangement of these two formulas gives the first three rules of debit and credit:

1. Increases in asset accounts are debits; decreases are credits.
2. Decreases in liability accounts are debits; increases are credits.
3. Decreases in stockholders' equity accounts are debits; increases are credits.

The debit and credit rules for expense and Dividends accounts and for revenue accounts follow logically if you remember that expenses and dividends are decreases in stockholders' equity and revenues are increases in stockholders' equity. Since stockholders' equity accounts decrease on the debit side, expense and Dividend accounts increase on the debit side. Since stockholders' equity accounts increase on the credit side, revenue accounts increase on the credit side. Debit and credit rules 4, 5, and 6 are:

4. Decreases in revenue accounts are debits; increases are credits.
5. Increases in expense accounts are debits; decreases are credits.
6. Increases in Dividends accounts are debits; decreases are credits.

Illustration 2.2 shows these six rules of debit and credit. Note first the treatment of expense and Dividends accounts as if they were subclassifications of the debit side of the Retained Earnings account. Then, note the treatment of the revenue accounts as if they were subclassifications of the credit side of the Retained Earnings account.

THE JOURNAL

Objective 3
Record the effects
of business trans-
actions in
a journal

In explaining the rules of debit and credit, we recorded transactions directly in the accounts. Each ledger (general ledger) account shows only the increases and decreases in that account. Thus, all the effects of a single business transaction would not appear in any one account. For example, the Cash account contains only data on changes in cash and does not show how the cash was generated or how it was spent. To have a permanent record of an entire transaction, the accountant uses a book or record known as a *journal.*

A **journal** is a chronological (arranged in order of time) record of business transactions. A *journal entry* is the recording of a business transaction

Illustration 2.2
RULES OF DEBIT AND CREDIT

Assets = Liabilities + Stockholders' Equity					
Asset Accounts =		**Liability Accounts** +		**Stockholders' Equity Account(s) (Capital Stock and Retained Earnings)**	
Debit*	Credit	Debit	Credit*	Debit	Credit*
+ Debit for increase	− Credit for decrease	− Debit for decrease	+ Credit for increase	− Debit for decrease	+ Credit for increase

Debits	**Credits**
1. Increase assets.	1. Decrease assets.
2. Decrease liabilities.	2. Increase liabilities.
3. Decrease stockholders' equity.	3. Increase stockholders' equity.
4. Decrease revenues.	4. Increase revenues.
5. Increase expenses.	5. Decrease expenses.
6. Increase dividends.	6. Decrease dividends.

Expense Accounts and Dividends Account		**Revenue Accounts**	
Debit*	Credit	Debit	Credit*
+ Debit for increase	− Credit for decrease	− Debit for decrease	+ Credit for increase

* Normal balance.

in the journal. A **journal entry** shows all the effects of a business transaction as expressed in terms of debit(s) and credit(s) and may include an explanation of the transaction. **A transaction is entered in a journal before it is entered in ledger accounts.** Because each transaction is initially recorded in a journal rather than directly in the ledger, a journal is called a *book of original entry*.

The General Journal

A business usually has more than one journal. Appendix B at the end of the text describes several special journals. In this chapter, we use the basic form of a journal, which is the general journal. As shown in Illustration 2.3, a general journal contains the following columns:

1. *Date column.* The first column on each journal page is for the date. When entering the first journal entry on a page, this column is used for the year, month, and day (number). For all other journal entries on a page, only the day of the month is entered, until the month changes.
2. *Account titles and explanation column.* The first line of an entry shows the account debited. The second line shows the account credited. Notice that the credit account title is indented to the right. For instance, Illustration 2.3 first shows the debit to the Cash account and then shows the credit to the Capital Stock account. Any necessary explanation of a transaction appears on the line(s) below the credit entry and is indented halfway between the accounts debited and credited. A journal entry explanation should be complete enough to describe fully the transaction and prove the entry's accuracy, and yet be concise. If a journal entry is self-explanatory, the explanation may be omitted.
3. *Posting reference column.* This column shows the account number of the debited or credited account. For instance, in Illustration 2.3, the

Illustration 2.3
GENERAL JOURNAL

SPEEDY DELIVERY COMPANY
GENERAL JOURNAL

Page 1

Date		Account Titles and Explanation	Post. Ref.	Debit	Credit
1995					
Nov.	28	Cash	100	5 0 0 0 0	
		Capital Stock	300		5 0 0 0 0
		Stockholders invested $50,000 cash in the business.			

number 100 in the first entry means that the Cash account number is 100. No number appears in this column until the information is posted to the appropriate ledger account. Posting is discussed later in the chapter.
4. *Debit column.*   In the debit column, the amount of the debit is placed on the same line as the title of the account debited.
5. *Credit column.*   In the credit column, the amount of the credit is placed on the same line as the title of the account credited.

Functions and Advantages of a Journal

A summary of the functions and advantages of using a journal follows.

The journal—
1. Records transactions in chronological order.
2. Shows the analysis of each transaction in terms of debit and credit.
3. Supplies an explanation of each transaction when necessary.
4. Serves as a source for future reference to accounting transactions.
5. Eliminates the need for lengthy explanations from the accounts.
6. Makes possible posting to the ledger at convenient times.
7. Assists in maintaining the ledger in balance because the debit(s) must always equal the credit(s) in each journal entry.
8. Aids in tracing errors when the ledger is not in balance.

THE LEDGER

A **ledger** (general ledger) is the complete collection of all the accounts of a company. The ledger may be in loose-leaf form, in a bound volume, or in a computer memory.

Accounts are classified into two general groups: (1) *balance sheet accounts* (assets, liabilities, and stockholders' equity) and (2) *income statement accounts* (revenues and expenses). The terms *real accounts* and *permanent accounts* also refer to balance sheet accounts. Balance sheet accounts are called **real accounts** because they are *not* subclassifications or subdivisions of any other account. They are called **permanent accounts** because their balances are not transferred (or closed) to any other account at the end of the accounting period. Income statement accounts and the Dividends account are also called **nominal accounts** because they are merely subclassifications of the stockholders' equity accounts. *Nominal* literally means "in name only." Nominal accounts are also called **temporary accounts** because they temporarily contain the revenue, expense, and dividend information that is transferred (or closed) to the Retained Earnings account at the end of the accounting period.

The **chart of accounts** is a complete listing of account titles and account numbers of all the accounts in the ledger. The chart of accounts can be compared to a table of contents. The groups of accounts usually appear in the following order: assets, liabilities, stockholders' equity, dividends, revenues, and expenses.

Individual accounts are arranged in sequence in the ledger. Each account typically has an identification number and a title to help locate accounts when recording data. For example, a company might number asset accounts 100–199; liability accounts, 200–299; stockholders' equity accounts and Dividends account, 300–399; revenue accounts, 400–499; and expense accounts, 500–599. We use this numbering system in this text. *The uniform chart of accounts used in the first eight chapters appears on the inside cover of the text.* **Companies may use other numbering systems.** For instance, sometimes a company numbers its accounts in sequence starting with 1, 2, and so on. **The important idea is that companies use some numbering system.**

Now that you understand how to record debits and credits in an account and how all accounts together form a ledger, you are ready to study the accounting process in operation. To illustrate the accounting process, we use Speedy Delivery Company as our example.

THE ACCOUNTING PROCESS IN OPERATION

Speedy Delivery Company is a small corporation. The accounting process used by this company is similar to that of any small company. The ledger accounts used for the Speedy Delivery Company are shown at the top of the next page.

Notice that a gap is left between account numbers (100, 103, 107, and so on). These gaps provide flexibility in later adding new accounts between the existing accounts. Other Speedy Delivery Company accounts are introduced in the next chapter.

The Recording of Transactions and Their Effects on the Accounts

First, a transaction must be "journalized." **Journalizing** is the process of entering the effects of a transaction in a journal. Then, the information is transferred, or posted, to the proper accounts in the ledger. **Posting** is the process of recording in the ledger accounts the information contained in the journal. Posting is explained in more detail later in the chapter.

In the following example, notice that each business transaction affects two or more accounts in the ledger. Also note that the transaction date in both the general journal and the general ledger accounts is the same. In the ledger accounts, the date used is the date that the transaction was recorded in the general journal, even if the entry is not posted until several days later. Our example shows that the journal entries are posted to T-accounts. In practice, journal entries are normally posted to three-column ledger accounts, as you will see later in the chapter.

Accountants use the *accrual basis of accounting*. Under the **accrual basis of accounting,** revenues are recognized when the company makes a

	Acct. No.	Account Title	Description
Assets	100	Cash	Bank deposits and cash on hand.
	103	Accounts Receivable	Amounts owed to the company by customers.
	107	Supplies on Hand	Items such as paper, envelopes, writing materials, rope, and other materials used in performing services for customers or in doing administrative and clerical office work.
	108	Prepaid Insurance	Insurance policy premium paid in advance of the periods for which the insurance coverage applies.
	112	Prepaid Rent	Rent paid in advance of the periods for which the rent payment applies.
	150	Trucks	Trucks used to perform delivery services for customers.
Liabilities	200	Accounts Payable	Amounts owed to creditors for items purchased from them.
	210	Unearned Delivery Fees	Amounts received from customers before the services have been performed for the customers.
Stockholders' equity	300	Capital Stock	The stockholders' investment in the business.
	310	Retained Earnings	The earnings retained in the business.
Dividends	320	Dividends	The amount of dividends declared to stockholders.
Revenues	400	Service Revenue	Amounts earned by performing delivery services for customers.
Expenses	505	Advertising Expense	The cost of advertising incurred in the current period.
	506	Gas and Oil Expense	The cost of gas and oil used in trucks in the current period.
	507	Salaries Expense	The amount of salaries incurred in the current period.
	511	Utilities Expense	The cost of utilities incurred in the current period.

sale or performs a service, regardless of when the company receives the cash. Expenses are recognized as incurred, whether or not the company has paid out cash. Chapter 3 discusses the accrual basis of accounting in more detail.

In the Speedy Delivery Company example that follows, Transaction 1 increases (debits) Cash and increases (credits) Capital Stock by $50,000. First, the transaction is recorded in the general journal, then the entry is posted to the accounts in the general ledger.

Transaction 1:   Nov. 28, 1995   Stockholders invested $50,000 and formed Speedy Delivery Company.

GENERAL JOURNAL

Date	Account Titles and Explanation	Post. Ref.	Debit	Credit
1995 Nov. 28	Cash	100	5 0 0 0 0	
	Capital Stock	300		5 0 0 0 0
	Stockholders invested $50,000 cash in the business.			

GENERAL LEDGER

(Dr.)	**Cash**	Acct. No. 100	(Cr.)	(Dr.)	**Capital Stock**	Acct. No. 300	(Cr.)
1995 Nov. 28	50,000				1995 Nov. 28		50,000

No other transactions occurred in November. The company prepares financial statements at the end of each month. Illustration 2.4 shows the company's balance sheet at November 30, 1995.

The balance sheet reflects ledger account balances as of the close of business on November 30, 1995. These closing balances are the beginning balances on December 1, 1995. The ledger accounts show these closing balances as beginning balances (Beg. bal.).

Now assume that in December 1995, Speedy Delivery Company engages in the following transactions. The proper recording of each transaction is shown in the journal and then in the ledger accounts (in T-account form), and the effects of each transaction are described.

Illustration 2.4
BALANCE SHEET

SPEEDY DELIVERY COMPANY
Balance Sheet
November 30, 1995

Assets		Liabilities and Stockholders' Equity	
Cash	$50,000	Stockholders' equity:	
		Capital stock	$50,000
		Total liabilities and stock-	
Total assets	$50,000	holders' equity	$50,000

Transaction 2:   Dec. 1   Paid cash for four small delivery trucks, $40,000.

GENERAL JOURNAL

Date	Account Titles and Explanation	Post. Ref.	Debit	Credit
1995 Dec. 1	Trucks	150	40000	
	Cash	100		40000
	To record the purchase of four delivery trucks.			

GENERAL LEDGER

EFFECTS OF TRANSACTION

One asset, trucks, is increased (debited); and another asset, cash, is decreased (credited) by $40,000.

(Dr.)	**Trucks**	Acct. No. 150	(Cr.)
1995 **Dec. 1**	**40,000**		

(Dr.)	**Cash**	Acct. No. 100	(Cr.)
1995 Dec. 1 Beg. bal. 50,000		1995 **Dec. 1** 40,000	

Transaction 3:   Dec. 1   Paid $2,400 cash for insurance on the trucks to cover a one-year period from this date.

GENERAL JOURNAL

Date	Account Titles and Explanation	Post. Ref.	Debit	Credit
1995 Dec. 1	Prepaid Insurance	108	2400	
	Cash	100		2400
	Purchased truck insurance to cover a one-year period.			

GENERAL LEDGER

(Dr.)	**Prepaid Insurance**	Acct. No. 108	(Cr.)
1995 Dec. 1	2,400		

(Dr.)	**Cash**	Acct. No. 100	(Cr.)
1995 Dec. 1 Beg. bal. 50,000		1995 Dec. 1	40,000
		1	2,400

EFFECTS OF TRANSACTION

An asset, prepaid insurance, is increased (debited); and an asset, cash, is decreased (credited) by $2,400. The debit is to Prepaid Insurance rather than Insurance Expense because the policy covers more than the current accounting period of December (insurance policies are usually paid one year in advance). As you will see in Chapter 3, prepaid items are expensed as they are used. If this insurance policy was only written for December, the entire $2,400 debit would have been to Insurance Expense.

Transaction 4:   Dec. 1   Rented a building and paid $1,200 to cover a three-month period from this date.

GENERAL JOURNAL

Date		Account Titles and Explanation	Post. Ref.	Debit	Credit
1995 Dec.	1	Prepaid Rent	112	1 2 0 0	
		Cash	100		1 2 0 0
		Paid three months' rent on a building.			

GENERAL LEDGER

(Dr.)	**Prepaid Rent**	Acct. No. 112	(Cr.)
1995 Dec. 1	1,200		

(Dr.)	**Cash**	Acct. No. 100	(Cr.)
1995 Dec. 1 Beg. bal. 50,000		1995 Dec. 1	40,000
		1	2,400
		1	1,200

EFFECTS OF TRANSACTION

An asset, prepaid rent, is increased (debited); and another asset, cash, is decreased (credited) by $1,200. The debit is to Prepaid Rent rather than Rent Expense because the payment covers more than the current month. If the payment had just been for December, the debit would have been to Rent Expense.

Transaction 5:   Dec. 4   Purchased $1,400 of supplies on account to be used over the next several months.

GENERAL JOURNAL

Date		Account Titles and Explanation	Post. Ref.	Debit	Credit
1995 Dec.	4	Supplies on Hand	107	1 4 0 0	
		Accounts Payable	200		1 4 0 0
		To record the purchase of supplies for future use.			

GENERAL LEDGER

(Dr.) **Supplies on Hand** Acct. No. 107 *(Cr.)*	

1995
Dec. 4   1,400

(Dr.) **Accounts Payable** Acct. No. 200 *(Cr.)*	

1995
Dec. 4   1,400

EFFECTS OF TRANSACTION

An asset, supplies on hand, is increased (debited); and a liability, accounts payable, is increased (credited) by $1,400. The debit is to Supplies on Hand rather than Supplies Expense because the supplies are to be used over several accounting periods.

In each of the three preceding entries, an asset was debited rather than an expense. The reason for doing this was that the expenditure applies to (or benefits) more than just the current accounting period. Whenever a company will not fully use up an item such as insurance, rent, or supplies in the period when purchased, an asset should be debited. In practice, however, sometimes the expense is initially debited in these situations.

Companies sometimes buy items that they will fully use up within the current accounting period. For example, a company may buy supplies during the first part of the month that it intends to consume fully during that month. If the company will fully consume the supplies during the period of purchase, the best practice is to debit Supplies Expense at the time of purchase rather than Supplies on Hand. This same advice applies to insurance and rent. If a company purchases insurance that it will fully consume during the current period, the company should debit Insurance Expense at the time of purchase rather than Prepaid Insurance. Also, if a company pays rent that applies only to the current period, Rent Expense should be debited at the time of purchase rather than Prepaid Rent. As illustrated in Chapter 3, following this advice simplifies the procedures at the end of the accounting period.

Transaction 6:   Dec. 7   Received $4,500 from a customer in payment for future delivery services.

GENERAL JOURNAL

Date		Account Titles and Explanation	Post. Ref.	Debit	Credit
1995 Dec.	7	Cash	100	4 5 0 0	
		Unearned Delivery Fees	210		4 5 0 0
		To record the receipt of cash from a customer in			
		payment for future delivery services.			

GENERAL LEDGER

(Dr.)   **Cash**   Acct. No. 100   (Cr.)

1995			1995	
Dec.	1	Beg. bal. 50,000	Dec. 1	40,000
	7	4,500	1	2,400
			1	1,200

(Dr.)   **Unearned Delivery Fees**   Acct. No. 210   (Cr.)

	1995	
	Dec. 7	**4,500**

EFFECTS OF TRANSACTION

An asset, cash, is increased (debited); and a liability, unearned delivery revenue, is increased (credited) by $4,500. The credit is to Unearned Delivery Fees rather than Service Revenue because the $4,500 applies to more than just the current accounting period. Unearned Delivery Fees is a liability because, if the services are never performed, the $4,500 will have to be refunded. If the payment had been for services to be provided in December, the credit would have been to Service Revenue.

Transaction 7:   Dec. 15   Performed delivery services for a customer for cash, $5,000.

GENERAL JOURNAL

Date		Account Titles and Explanation	Post. Ref.	Debit	Credit
1995 Dec.	15	Cash	100	5 0 0 0	
		Service Revenue	400		5 0 0 0
		To record the receipt of cash for performing delivery			
		services for a customer.			

GENERAL LEDGER   **EFFECTS OF TRANSACTION**

		Acct. No.	
(Dr.)	**Cash**	100	*(Cr.)*

1995			1995		
Dec. 1	Beg. bal.	50,000	Dec. 1		40,000
7		4,500	1		2,400
15		**5,000**	1		1,200

An asset, cash, is increased (debited); and a revenue, service revenue, is increased (credited) by $5,000.

		Acct. No.	
(Dr.)	**Service Revenue**	400	*(Cr.)*

		1995	
		Dec. 15	**5,000**

Transaction 8:   Dec. 17   Paid the $1,400 account payable resulting from the transaction of December 4.

GENERAL JOURNAL

Date	Account Titles and Explanation	Post. Ref.	Debit	Credit
1995				
Dec. 17	Accounts Payable	200	1 4 0 0	
	Cash	100		1 4 0 0
	Paid the account payable arising from the purchase of			
	supplies on December 4.			

GENERAL LEDGER   **EFFECTS OF TRANSACTION**

		Acct. No.	
(Dr.)	**Accounts Payable**	200	*(Cr.)*

1995		1995	
Dec. 17	**1,400**	Dec. 4	1,400

A liability, accounts payable, is decreased (debited); and an asset, cash, is decreased (credited) by $1,400.

		Acct. No.	
(Dr.)	**Cash**	100	*(Cr.)*

1995			1995		
Dec. 1	Beg. bal.	50,000	Dec. 1		40,000
7		4,500	1		2,400
15		5,000	1		1,200
			17		**1,400**

Transaction 9:   Dec. 20   Billed a customer for delivery services performed, $5,700.

GENERAL JOURNAL

Date		Account Titles and Explanation	Post. Ref.	Debit	Credit
1995 Dec.	20	Accounts Receivable	103	5 7 0 0	
		Service Revenue	400		5 7 0 0
		To record the performance of delivery services on			
		account for which a customer was billed.			

GENERAL LEDGER

EFFECTS OF TRANSACTION

An asset, accounts receivable, is increased (debited); and a revenue, service revenue, is increased (credited) by $5,700.

	Acct. No.	
(Dr.) **Accounts Receivable**	103	*(Cr.)*

1995	
Dec. 20 **5,700**	

	Acct. No.	
(Dr.) **Service Revenue**	400	*(Cr.)*

	1995
	Dec. 15 5,000
	20 **5,700**

Transaction 10:   Dec. 24   Received a bill for advertising that appeared in a local newspaper in December, $50.

GENERAL JOURNAL

Date		Account Titles and Explanation	Post. Ref.	Debit	Credit
1995 Dec.	24	Advertising Expense	505	5 0	
		Accounts Payable	200		5 0
		Received a bill for advertising for the month of			
		December.			

GENERAL LEDGER

| (Dr.) | **Advertising Expense** | Acct. No. 505 | (Cr.) |

| 1995 | | |
| **Dec. 24** | **50** | |

| (Dr.) | **Accounts Payable** | Acct. No. 200 | (Cr.) |

1995		1995	
Dec. 17	1,400	Dec. 4	1,400
		24	50

EFFECTS OF TRANSACTION

An expense, advertising expense, is increased (debited); and a liability, accounts payable, is increased (credited) by $50. The reason for debiting an expense rather than an asset is because all the cost pertains to the current accounting period, the month of December. Otherwise, Prepaid Advertising (an asset) would have been debited.

Transaction 11:   Dec. 26   Received $500 on accounts receivable from a customer.

GENERAL JOURNAL

Date		Account Titles and Explanation	Post. Ref.	Debit	Credit
1995					
Dec.	26	Cash	100	5 0 0	
		Accounts Receivable	103		5 0 0
		Received $500 from a customer on accounts receivable.			

GENERAL LEDGER

| (Dr.) | | **Cash** | Acct. No. 100 | (Cr.) |

1995			1995	
Dec. 1	Beg. bal.	50,000	Dec. 1	40,000
7		4,500	1	2,400
15		5,000	1	1,200
26		**500**	17	1,400

| (Dr.) | **Accounts Receivable** | Acct. No. 103 | (Cr.) |

| 1995 | | 1995 | |
| Dec. 20 | 5,700 | **Dec. 26** | **500** |

EFFECTS OF TRANSACTION

One asset, cash, is increased (debited); and another asset, accounts receivable, is decreased (credited) by $500.

Transaction 12:   Dec. 28   Paid salaries of $3,600 to truck drivers for the first four weeks of December. (Payroll and other deductions are to be ignored since they have not yet been discussed.)

GENERAL JOURNAL

Date		Account Titles and Explanation	Post. Ref.	Debit	Credit
1995 Dec.	28	Salaries Expense	507	3 6 0 0	
		Cash	100		3 6 0 0
		Paid truck driver salaries for the first four weeks of			
		December.			

GENERAL LEDGER

(Dr.)	**Salaries Expense**	Acct. No. 507	(Cr.)
1995 Dec. 28	3,600		

EFFECTS OF TRANSACTION

An expense, salaries expense, is increased (debited); and an asset, cash, is decreased (credited) by $3,600.

(Dr.)		**Cash**	Acct. No. 100		(Cr.)
1995 Dec. 1	Beg. bal.	50,000	1995 Dec. 1	40,000	
7		4,500	1	2,400	
15		5,000	1	1,200	
26		500	17	1,400	
			28	**3,600**	

Transaction 13:   Dec. 29   Received and paid the utilities bill for December, $150.

GENERAL JOURNAL

Date		Account Titles and Explanation	Post. Ref.	Debit	Credit
1995 Dec.	29	Utilities Expense	511	1 5 0	
		Cash	100		1 5 0
		Paid the utilities bill for December.			

GENERAL LEDGER

EFFECTS OF TRANSACTION

An expense, utilities expense, is increased (debited); and an asset, cash, is decreased (credited) by $150.

(Dr.)	**Utilities Expense**	Acct. No. 511	*(Cr.)*

1995		
Dec. 29	**150**	

(Dr.)	**Cash**	Acct. No. 100	*(Cr.)*

1995			1995	
Dec. 1	Beg. bal.	50,000	Dec. 1	40,000
7		4,500	1	2,400
15		5,000	1	1,200
26		500	17	1,400
			28	3,600
			29	**150**

Transaction 14:   Dec. 30   Received a bill for gas and oil used in the trucks for December, $680.

GENERAL JOURNAL

Date	Account Titles and Explanation	Post. Ref.	Debit	Credit
1995 Dec. 30	Gas and Oil Expense	506	6 8 0	
	Accounts Payable	200		6 8 0
	Received a bill for gas and oil used in the trucks for			
	December.			

GENERAL LEDGER

EFFECTS OF TRANSACTION

An expense, gas and oil expense, is increased (debited); and a liability, accounts payable, is increased (credited) by $680.

(Dr.)	**Gas and Oil Expense**	Acct. No. 506	*(Cr.)*

1995		
Dec. 30	**680**	

(Dr.)	**Accounts Payable**	Acct. No. 200	*(Cr.)*

1995			1995	
Dec. 17		1,400	Dec. 4	1,400
			24	50
			30	**680**

Transaction 15:　Dec. 31　A dividend of $3,000 was paid to stockholders.

GENERAL JOURNAL

Date		Account Titles and Explanation	Post. Ref.	Debit	Credit
1995					
Dec.	31	Dividends	320	3 0 0 0	
		Cash	100		3 0 0 0
		Dividends were paid to stockholders.			

GENERAL LEDGER

(Dr.)	**Dividends**	Acct. No. 320	(Cr.)
1995 **Dec. 31**	**3,000**		

(Dr.)		**Cash**	Acct. No. 100	(Cr.)
1995			1995	
Dec. 1	Beg. bal.	50,000	Dec. 1	40,000
7		4,500	1	2,400
15		5,000	1	1,200
26		500	17	1,400
			28	3,600
			29	150
			31	**3,000**

EFFECTS OF TRANSACTION

The Dividends account is increased (debited); and an asset, cash, is decreased (credited) by $3,000.

Transaction 15 concludes the analysis of the Speedy Delivery Company transactions. The next section discusses and illustrates posting to three-column ledger accounts and cross-indexing.

THE USE OF THREE-COLUMN LEDGER ACCOUNTS

In practice, companies normally use three-column ledger accounts rather than T-accounts. The remainder of this chapter illustrates the use of three-column ledger accounts.

Posting to Three-Column Ledger Accounts

Objective 4
Post journal entries to the accounts in the ledger

A journal entry is like a set of instructions. The carrying out of these instructions is known as posting. As stated earlier, **posting** is recording in the ledger accounts the information contained in the journal. A journal entry directs the entry of a certain dollar amount as a debit in a specific ledger account and directs the entry of a certain dollar amount as a credit in a specific ledger account. Earlier, we posted the journal entries for the Speedy Delivery Company to T-accounts. In practice, however, these journal entries would be posted to three-column ledger accounts.

First, we use a new example, Jenks Company, to illustrate the posting process to three-column ledger accounts. (Later we will show you how to post the Speedy Delivery Company journal entries to three-column ledger accounts.)

In Illustration 2.5 (page 90), the first journal entry for the Jenks Company directs that $10,000 be posted in the ledger as a debit to the Cash account and as a credit to the Capital Stock account. The debit in the general ledger Cash account is posted by using the following procedure. The date, a short explanation, the journal designation ("G" for general journal) and the journal page number from which the debit is posted, and the $10,000 in the Debit column are entered in the Cash account. Then, the number of the account to which the debit is posted is entered in the Posting Reference column of the general journal. The credit is posted in a similar manner but as a credit to Account No. 300. The arrows in Illustration 2.5 show how these amounts were posted to the correct accounts.

Illustration 2.5 shows the three-column ledger account. In contrast to the two-sided T-account format shown so far, the three-column format has columns for debit, credit, and balance. The three-column form has the advantage that it shows the balance of the account after each item has been posted. In addition, in this chapter, we indicate whether each balance is a debit or a credit. In later chapters and in practice, the nature of the balance is usually not indicated since it is understood. Also, notice that we give an explanation for each item in the ledger accounts. Often accountants omit these explanations because each item can be traced back to the general journal for the explanation.

Posting is always from the journal to the ledger accounts. Postings can be made (1) at the time the transaction is journalized; (2) at the end of the day, week, or month; or (3) as each journal page is filled. The choice is a matter of personal taste. When posting the general journal, the date used in the ledger accounts is the date the transaction was recorded in the journal, not the date the journal entry was posted to the ledger accounts.

Cross-Indexing (Referencing)

Frequently, accountants must check and trace the origin of their transactions, so they provide for *cross-indexing*. **Cross-indexing** is the placing of (1) the account number of the ledger account in the general journal and (2) the general journal page number in the ledger account. As shown in Illustration 2.5, the account number of the ledger account to which the posting was made is placed in the Posting Reference column of the general journal. Note the arrow from Account No. 100 in the ledger to the 100 in the Posting Reference

A BROADER PERSPECTIVE

FEMALE GRADS DOMINATE NEW ACCOUNTING HIRES

New York—Six out of 10 new college accounting graduates hired last year were women, according to a new survey.

Their performance is particularly impressive in view of the fact that there were as many female accounting graduates as males last year.

The outlook for women in the profession this year, however, is not quite as bright. Projections indicate that the share of female graduates hired in 1991 will drop from 59 percent last year to 57 percent.

These and other statistics surfaced in the just-released 21st edition of "The Supply of Accounting Graduates and the Demand for Public Accounting Recruits," published by the American Institute of Certified Public Accountants.

The report is based on responses from 788 colleges and universities with accounting programs and 19,330 public accounting firms. Because the survey for the first time this year includes responses from sole practitioners and small firms in addition to all firms with more than 10 institute members, AICPA officials say comparisons with past surveys is difficult.

The AICPA has an explanation for the increase in proportion of new graduate recruits who are female in 1990 and 1991 relative to 1989 when the percentage was 48 percent. The gain, it says, can be largely attributed to the fact that

firms with under 10 AICPA members, who report hiring a greater proportion of females than other firms, now account for a larger share of recruits.

The comprehensive study turned up other significant data.

It shows, for instance, that more than 57,000 bachelor's and master's degrees in accounting were awarded in 1989–90, a number that is close to the 1988–89 total.

Graduate degrees, on the other hand, totaled 5,040, slightly less than the 5,230 awarded in 1988–89, despite a projected growth rate of 9 percent.

According to the study, CPA firms recruited fewer bachelor's graduates last year, while the number of master's recruits remained stable.

Of the graduates hired by public accounting firms last year, 69 percent were assigned to auditing; 12 percent to management advisory services; 18 percent to taxation; and one percent to other areas.

Seventeen percent of the accounting graduates were minorities, the study reports.

Thirty-four percent of the graduates with bachelor's degrees and 57 percent with master's degrees were hired by public accounting firms. On the other hand, 28 percent of the graduates with bachelor's degrees and 23 percent of those

column beside the first debit in the general journal. The number of the general journal page *from* which the entry was posted is placed in the Posting Reference column of the ledger account. Note the arrow from page 1 in the general journal to G1 in the Posting Reference column of the Cash account in the general ledger. The notation "G1" means general journal, page 1. The date of the transaction is also shown in the general ledger. Note the arrows from the date in the general journal to the dates in the general ledger.

Cross-indexing aids the tracing of any recorded transaction, either from general journal to general ledger or from general ledger to general journal. Normally, cross-reference numbers are not placed in the Posting Reference column of the general journal until the entry is posted. If this practice is

Proportion of Accounting
Graduates by Gender

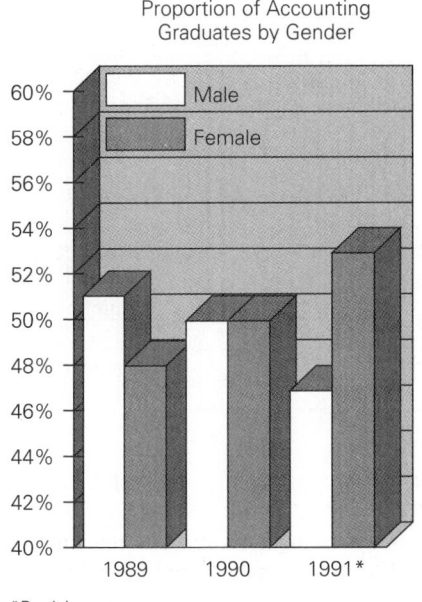

Proportion of New Graduate
Recruits by Gender

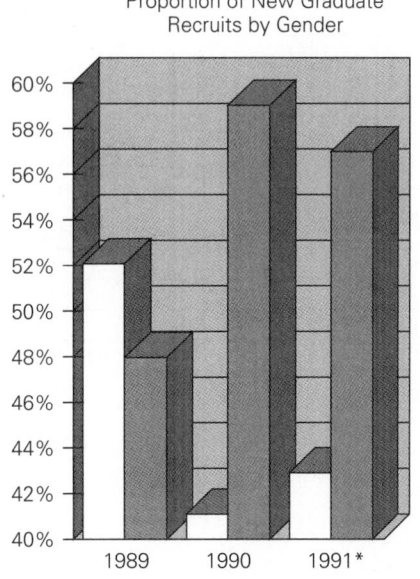

*Partial year.
Source: AICPA.

with master's were hired by employers in business and industry.

Commenting on the results of the study, Rick Elam, AICPA vice president-education, says "Stability in the number of accounting graduates entering the profession indicates that to-day's students are seeking a solid and rewarding profession in these uncertain economic times."

SOURCE: Reprinted by permission from *Accounting Today,* September 9, 1991, p. 3. © Copyright Lebber-Friedman Inc., 425 Park Avenue, New York, N.Y. 10022.

followed, the cross-reference numbers indicate that the entry has been posted.

An understanding of the posting and cross-indexing process can be obtained by tracing the entries from the general journal to the general ledger. The ledger accounts need not contain explanations of all the entries, since any needed explanations can be obtained from the general journal.

Compound Journal Entries

All the journal entries illustrated so far have involved one debit and one credit; these journal entries are called **simple journal entries.** Many business

Illustration 2.5
GENERAL JOURNAL AND GENERAL LEDGER; POSTING AND CROSS-INDEXING

JENKS COMPANY
GENERAL JOURNAL

Page 1

Date	Account Titles and Explanation	Post. Ref.	Debit	Credit
1995 Jan. 1	Cash	100	1 0 0 0 0	
	Capital Stock	300		1 0 0 0 0
	Stockholders invested $10,000 cash in the business.			
5	Cash	100	5 0 0 0	
	Notes Payable	201		5 0 0 0
	Borrowed $5,000 from the bank on a note.			

GENERAL LEDGER

Cash   *Account No. 100*

Date	Explanation	Post. Ref.	Debit	Credit	Balance
1995 Jan. 1	Stockholder investment	G1	1 0 0 0 0		1 0 0 0 0 Dr.
5	Bank loan	G1	5 0 0 0		1 5 0 0 0 Dr.

Notes Payable   *Account No. 201*

Date	Explanation	Post. Ref.	Debit	Credit	Balance
1995 Jan. 5	Borrowed cash	G1		5 0 0 0	5 0 0 0 Cr.

Capital Stock   *Account No. 300*

Date	Explanation	Post. Ref.	Debit	Credit	Balance
1995 Jan. 1	Cash from stockholders	G1		1 0 0 0 0	1 0 0 0 0 Cr.

transactions, however, affect more than two accounts. The journal entry for these transactions will involve more than one debit and/or credit. Such journal entries are called **compound journal entries.**

As an illustration of a compound journal entry, assume that on January 2, 1996, Speedy Delivery Company purchased $8,000 of machinery from Wilson Company. Speedy Delivery paid $2,000 cash with the balance due on March 3, 1996. The general journal entry for Speedy Delivery Company is:

	Debit	Credit
1996		
Jan. 2 Machinery	8,000	
Cash		2,000
Accounts Payable		6,000
Machinery purchased from Wilson Company.		

Note that two accounts, Cash and Accounts Payable, are credited in this one entry. However, the dollar totals of the debits and credits are equal.

Posting and Cross-Indexing—An Illustration

Illustration 2.6 shows how all the November and December transactions of Speedy Delivery Company presented on pages 76–86 would be journalized. As shown in Illustration 2.6, you skip a line between journal entries to show where one journal entry ends and another begins. This procedure is standard practice among accountants. Note that dollar signs are not used in journals or ledgers. When amounts are in even dollar amounts, the cents column may be left blank or zeros or a dash may be used. When lined accounting work papers are used, commas or a period are not needed to record an amount. When unlined paper is used, both commas and a period should be used.

Normally, journal entries would be posted to three-column ledger accounts. Each ledger account would appear on a separate page in the ledger. The "Solution to the Demonstration Problem" at the end of the chapter illustrates posting journal entries to three-column ledger accounts.

The Trial Balance

Objective 5
Prepare a trial balance to test the equality of debits and credits in the journalizing and posting process

Periodically, accountants use a *trial balance* to test the equality of their debits and credits. A **trial balance** is a listing of the ledger accounts and their debit or credit balances to determine that debits equal credits in the recording process. The accounts appear in the same order as in the general ledger and in the chart of accounts. Thus, they appear in the following order: assets, liabilities, stockholders' equity, dividends, revenues, and expenses. Within the assets category, the most liquid (closest to becoming cash) asset appears first and the least liquid appears last. Within the liabilities, those liabilities with the shortest "maturities" appear first. Illustration 2.7 shows the trial balance for Speedy Delivery Company. Note the listing of the ac-

Illustration 2.6
GENERAL JOURNAL (AFTER POSTING)

SPEEDY DELIVERY COMPANY
GENERAL JOURNAL

Page 1

Date		Account Titles and Explanation	Post. Ref.	Debit	Credit
1995					
Nov.	28	Cash	100*	5 0 0 0 0	
		Capital Stock	300		5 0 0 0 0
		Stockholders invested $50,000 cash in the business.			
Dec.	1	Trucks	150	4 0 0 0 0	
		Cash	100		4 0 0 0 0
		To record the purchase of four delivery trucks.			
	1	Prepaid Insurance	108	2 4 0 0	
		Cash	100		2 4 0 0
		Purchased truck insurance to cover a one-year period.			
	1	Prepaid Rent	112	1 2 0 0	
		Cash	100		1 2 0 0
		Paid three months' rent on a building.			
	4	Supplies on Hand	107	1 4 0 0	
		Accounts Payable	200		1 4 0 0
		To record the purchase of supplies for future use.			
	7	Cash	100	4 5 0 0	
		Unearned Delivery Fees	210		4 5 0 0
		To record the receipt of cash from a customer in			
		payment for future delivery services.			
	15	Cash	100	5 0 0 0	
		Service Revenue	400		5 0 0 0
		To record the receipt of cash for performing delivery			
		services for a customer.			
	17	Accounts Payable	200	1 4 0 0	
		Cash	100		1 4 0 0
		Paid the account payable arising from the purchase of			
		supplies on December 4.			

* These posting references would be inserted only after each amount has been posted.

Illustration 2.6
(*concluded*)

		GENERAL JOURNAL *(concluded)*				*Page 2*

Date		Account Titles and Explanation	Post. Ref.	Debit	Credit
1995 Dec.	20	Accounts Receivable	103	5700	
		Service Revenue	400		5700
		To record the performance of delivery services on			
		account for which a customer was billed.			
	24	Advertising Expense	505	50	
		Accounts Payable	200		50
		Received a bill for advertising for the month of			
		December.			
	26	Cash	100	500	
		Accounts Receivable	103		500
		Received $500 from a customer on accounts receivable.			
	28	Salaries Expense	507	3600	
		Cash	100		3600
		Paid truck driver salaries for the first four weeks of			
		December.			
	29	Utilities Expense	511	150	
		Cash	100		150
		Paid the utilities bill for December.			
	30	Gas and Oil Expense	506	680	
		Accounts Payable	200		680
		Received a bill for gas and oil used in the trucks for			
		December.			
	31	Dividends	320	3000	
		Cash	100		3000
		Dividends were paid to stockholders.			

ETHICS: A CLOSER LOOK

Jim Kranston was taking an accounting course at Western State University. He was also engaged in helping companies find an accounting system that would fit their information needs. He advised one of his clients to acquire a software computer package that could be used to correct the business transactions and would prepare the financial statements. The licensing agreement with the company that produced the software specified that the basic charge for one site is $4,000 and that $1,000 must be paid for each additional site at which the software is to be used.

Jim was pleased that his recommendation to acquire the software was followed. However, he was upset that the management of the company wanted him to install the software at eight other sites in the company and did not intend to pay the extra $8,000 due the software company. A member of management stated, "The software company will never know the difference and, besides, everyone else seems to be pirating software. If they do find out, we will pay the extra fee at that time. Our expenses are high enough without paying these unnecessary costs." Jim believed he might lose this client if he did not do as management instructed.

Required
a. What would you do if you were Jim?
b. What do you think management will do if Jim refuses to install the program at the other sites?

Illustration 2.7
TRIAL BALANCE

SPEEDY DELIVERY COMPANY
Trial Balance
December 31, 1995

Acct. No.	Account Title	Debits	Credits
100	Cash	$ 8,250	
103	Accounts Receivable.	5,200	
107	Supplies on Hand	1,400	
108	Prepaid Insurance	2,400	
112	Prepaid Rent	1,200	
150	Trucks	40,000	
200	Accounts Payable		$ 730
210	Unearned Delivery Fees		4,500
300	Capital Stock		50,000
320	Dividends	3,000	
400	Service Revenue.		10,700
505	Advertising Expense	50	
506	Gas and Oil Expense	680	
507	Salaries Expense	3,600	
511	Utilities Expense.	150	
		$65,930	$65,930

count numbers and account titles on the left, the column for debit balances, the column for credit balances, and the equality of the two totals.

When the trial balance does not balance, the first thing to do is to retotal the two columns. If this step does not locate the error, divide the difference in the totals by 2 and then by 9. If the difference is divisible by 2, you may have transferred a debit-balanced account to the trial balance as a credit, or a credit-balanced account as a debit. If the difference is divisible by 2, look for an amount in the trial balance that is equal to one half of the difference. Thus, if the difference is $800, look for an account with a balance of $400 and see if it is in the wrong column.

If the difference is divisible by 9, you may have made a transposition error in transferring a balance to the trial balance or a slide error. A transposition error occurs when you have reversed two numbers in an amount (e.g., writing 753 as 573 or 110 as 101). A slide error occurs when you have placed the decimal point incorrectly (e.g., $1,500 recorded as $15.00). Thus, when a difference is divisible by 9, compare the trial balance amounts with the general ledger account balances to see if you made a transposition or slide error in transferring the amounts.

If none of these steps locates the error, the error may be due to one of the following causes:

1. Failing to post part of a journal entry.
2. Posting a debit as a credit, or vice versa.
3. Incorrectly determining the balance of an account.
4. Recording the balance of an account incorrectly in the trial balance.
5. Omitting an account from the trial balance.
6. Making a transposition or slide error in the accounts or the journal.

Usually, you should work backward through the steps taken to prepare the trial balance. Assuming you have already retotaled the columns and traced the amounts appearing in the trial balance back to the general ledger account balances, use the following steps. Verify the balance of each general ledger account, verify postings to the general ledger, verify general journal entries, and then review the transactions and possibly the source documents.

The equality of the two totals in the trial balance does not necessarily mean that the accounting process has been error-free. Serious errors may have been made, such as failure to record a transaction, or posting a debit or credit to the wrong account. For instance, if a transaction involving payment of a $100 account payable is never recorded, the trial balance totals will still balance, but at an amount that is $100 too high. Both cash and accounts payable would be overstated by $100.

A trial balance can be prepared at any time—at the end of a day, a week, a month, a quarter, or a year. Typically, a trial balance is prepared before preparing the financial statements. Dollar signs may be used but are not required.

What you have learned in this chapter is basic to your study of accounting. The entire process of accounting is based on the double-entry concept. In Chapter 3, you will learn that adjustments are usually needed to bring the accounts to their proper balances before accurate financial statements can be prepared.

UNDERSTANDING THE LEARNING OBJECTIVES

1. Use the account as the basic classifying and storage unit for accounting information.
   - An account is a storage unit used to classify and summarize money measurements of business activities of a similar nature.
   - An account is set up whenever it is necessary to provide useful information about a particular business item to some party having a valid interest in the business.
2. Express the effects of business transactions in terms of debits and credits to different types of accounts.
   - A T-account resembles the letter T.
   - Debits are entries on the left-hand side of a T-account.
   - Credits are entries on the right-hand side of a T-account.
   - Asset, expense, and Dividends accounts are increased by debits.
   - Liability, stockholders' equity, and revenue accounts are increased by credits.
3. Record the effects of business transactions in a journal.
   - A journal contains a chronological record of the transactions of a business.
   - An example of a general journal is shown in Illustration 2.6.
   - Journalizing is the process of entering a transaction in a journal.
4. Post journal entries to the accounts in the ledger.
   - Posting is the process of transferring information recorded in the journal to the proper places in the ledger.
   - Cross-indexing is the placing of (1) the account number of the ledger account in the general journal and (2) the general journal page number in the ledger account.
   - An example of cross-indexing appears in Illustration 2.5.
5. Prepare a trial balance to test the equality of debits and credits in the journalizing and posting process.
   - A trial balance is a listing of the ledger accounts and their debit or credit balances.
   - If the trial balance does not balance, the accountant should work backward to discover the error.
   - A trial balance is shown in Illustration 2.7.

DEMONSTRATION PROBLEM

Rolling Hills Riding Stable, Incorporated, had the following balance sheet on June 30, 1995:

ROLLING HILLS RIDING STABLE, INCORPORATED
Balance Sheet
June 30, 1995
Assets

Cash	$ 7,500
Accounts receivable	5,400
Land	40,000
Total assets	$52,900

Liabilities and Stockholders' Equity

Liabilities:

Accounts payable		$ 800
Notes payable		40,000
Total liabilities.		$40,800

Stockholders' equity:

Capital stock	$10,000	
Retained earnings	2,100	
Total stockholders' equity		12,100
Total liabilities and stockholders' equity		$52,900

Transactions for July 1995 were as follows:

July 1   Additional shares of capital stock were issued for $25,000 cash.
　　　1   Paid for a prefabricated building constructed on the land at a cost of $24,000.
　　　8   Paid the accounts payable of $800.
　　 10   Collected the accounts receivable of $5,400.
　　 12   Horse feed to be used in July was purchased on credit for $1,100.
　　 15   Boarding fees for July were charged to customers in the amount of $4,500. (This amount is due on August 10.)
　　 24   Miscellaneous expenses of $800 for July were paid.
　　 31   Paid interest expense on the notes payable of $200.
　　 31   Salaries of $1,400 for the month were paid.
　　 31   Riding and lesson fees for July were billed to customers in the amount of $3,600. (They are due on August 10.)
　　 31   Paid a $1,000 dividend to the stockholders.

Required:

a. Prepare the journal entries to record the transactions for July 1995.

b. Post the journal entries to the ledger accounts after entering the beginning balances in those accounts. Insert cross-indexing references in the journal and ledger. Use the following chart of accounts:

100	Cash	320	Dividends
103	Accounts Receivable	402	Horse Boarding Fees Revenue
130	Land	404	Riding and Lesson Fees Revenue
140	Buildings	507	Salaries Expense
200	Accounts Payable	513	Feed Expense
201	Notes Payable	540	Interest Expense
300	Capital Stock	568	Miscellaneous Expense
310	Retained Earnings		

c. Prepare a trial balance.

Solution to demonstration problem

a.

ROLLING HILLS RIDING STABLE, INCORPORATED
GENERAL JOURNAL

Page 1

Date		Account Titles and Explanation	Post. Ref.	Debit	Credit
1995 July	1	Cash	100	2 5 0 0 0	
		Capital Stock	300		2 5 0 0 0
		Additional capital stock issued.			
	1	Buildings	140	2 4 0 0 0	
		Cash	100		2 4 0 0 0
		Paid for building.			
	8	Accounts Payable	200	8 0 0	
		Cash	100		8 0 0
		Paid accounts payable.			
	10	Cash	100	5 4 0 0	
		Accounts Receivable	103		5 4 0 0
		Collected accounts receivable.			
	12	Feed Expense	513	1 1 0 0	
		Accounts Payable	200		1 1 0 0
		Purchased feed on credit.			
	15	Accounts Receivable	103	4 5 0 0	
		Horse Boarding Fees Revenue	402		4 5 0 0
		Billed boarding fees for July.			
	24	Miscellaneous Expense	568	8 0 0	
		Cash	100		8 0 0
		Paid miscellaneous expense for July.			
	31	Interest Expense	540	2 0 0	
		Cash	100		2 0 0
		Paid interest.			
	31	Salaries Expense	507	1 4 0 0	
		Cash	100		1 4 0 0
		Paid salaries for July.			
	31	Accounts Receivable	103	3 6 0 0	
		Riding and Lesson Fees Revenue	404		3 6 0 0
		Billed riding and lesson fees for July.			
	31	Dividends	320	1 0 0 0	
		Cash	100		1 0 0 0
		Paid a dividend to stockholders.			

b.

ROLLING HILLS RIDING STABLE, INCORPORATED
GENERAL LEDGER

Cash   *Account No. 100*

Date		Explanation	Post. Ref.	Debit	Credit	Balance
1995						
June	30	Balance				7 5 0 0 Dr.
July	1	Stockholders' investment	G1	2 5 0 0 0		3 2 5 0 0 Dr.
	1	Buildings	G1		2 4 0 0 0	8 5 0 0 Dr.
	8	Accounts payable	G1		8 0 0	7 7 0 0 Dr.
	10	Accounts receivable	G1	5 4 0 0		1 3 1 0 0 Dr.
	24	Miscellaneous expense	G1		8 0 0	1 2 3 0 0 Dr.
	31	Interest expense	G1		2 0 0	1 2 1 0 0 Dr.
	31	Salaries expense	G1		1 4 0 0	1 0 7 0 0 Dr.
	31	Dividends	G1		1 0 0 0	9 7 0 0 Dr.

Accounts Receivable   *Account No. 103*

Date		Explanation	Post. Ref.	Debit	Credit	Balance
1995						
June	30	Balance				5 4 0 0 Dr.
July	10	Cash	G1		5 4 0 0	– 0 –
	15	Horse boarding fees	G1	4 5 0 0		4 5 0 0 Dr.
	31	Riding and lesson fees	G1	3 6 0 0		8 1 0 0 Dr.

Land   *Account No. 130*

Date		Explanation	Post. Ref.	Debit	Credit	Balance
1995						
June	30	Balance				4 0 0 0 0 Dr.

Buildings   *Account No. 140*

Date		Explanation	Post. Ref.	Debit	Credit	Balance
1995						
July	1	Cash	G1	2 4 0 0 0		2 4 0 0 0 Dr.

GENERAL LEDGER *(continued)*

Accounts Payable — Account No. 200

Date		Explanation	Post. Ref.	Debit	Credit	Balance
1995 June	30	Balance				800 Cr.
July	8	Cash	G1	800		-0-
	12	Feed expense	G1		1100	1100 Cr.

Notes Payable — Account No. 201

Date		Explanation	Post. Ref.	Debit	Credit	Balance
1995 June	30	Balance				40000 Cr.

Capital Stock — Account No. 300

Date		Explanation	Post. Ref.	Debit	Credit	Balance
1995 June	30	Balance				10000 Cr.
July	1	Cash	G1		25000	35000 Cr.

Retained Earnings — Account No. 310

Date		Explanation	Post. Ref.	Debit	Credit	Balance
1995 June	30	Balance				2100 Cr.

Dividends — Account No. 320

Date		Explanation	Post. Ref.	Debit	Credit	Balance
1995 July	31	Cash	G1	1000		1000 Dr.

GENERAL LEDGER *(continued)*

Horse Boarding Fees Revenue   *Account No. 402*

Date		Explanation	Post. Ref.	Debit	Credit	Balance
1995 July	15	Accounts receivable	G1		4 5 0 0	4 5 0 0 Cr.

Riding and Lesson Fees Revenue   *Account No. 404*

Date		Explanation	Post. Ref.	Debit	Credit	Balance
1995 July	31	Accounts receivable	G1		3 6 0 0	3 6 0 0 Cr.

Salaries Expense   *Account No. 507*

Date		Explanation	Post. Ref.	Debit	Credit	Balance
1995 July	31	Cash	G1	1 4 0 0		1 4 0 0 Dr.

Feed Expense   *Account No. 513*

Date		Explanation	Post. Ref.	Debit	Credit	Balance
1995 July	12	Accounts payable	G1	1 1 0 0		1 1 0 0 Dr.

Interest Expense   *Account No. 540*

Date		Explanation	Post. Ref.	Debit	Credit	Balance
1995 July	31	Cash	G1	2 0 0		2 0 0 Dr.

GENERAL LEDGER *(concluded)*

Miscellaneous Expense　　　　　　　　　　　　　*Account No. 568*

Date		Explanation	Post. Ref.	Debit	Credit	Balance
1995 July	24	Cash	G1	8 0 0		8 0 0 Dr.

c.

ROLLING HILLS RIDING STABLE, INCORPORATED
Trial Balance
July 31, 1995

Acct. No.	Account Title	Debits	Credits
100	Cash.	$ 9,700	
103	Accounts Receivable	8,100	
130	Land.	40,000	
140	Buildings	24,000	
200	Accounts Payable		$ 1,100
201	Notes Payable		40,000
300	Capital Stock.		35,000
310	Retained Earnings		2,100
320	Dividends	1,000	
402	Horse Boarding Fees Revenue		4,500
404	Riding and Lesson Fees Revenue		3,600
507	Salaries Expense	1,400	
513	Feed Expense	1,100	
540	Interest Expense	200	
568	Miscellaneous Expense	800	
		$86,300	$86,300

NEW TERMS

Account　A part of the accounting system used to classify and summarize the increases, decreases, and balances of each asset, liability, stockholders' equity item, dividends, revenue, and expense. The three-column account is normally used. It contains columns for debit, credit, and balance, *65*

Accrual basis of accounting　Recognizes revenues when sales are made or services are performed, regardless of when cash is received. Recognizes expenses as incurred, whether or not cash has been paid out. *74*

Chart of accounts　The complete listing of the account titles and account numbers of all of the accounts in the ledger; somewhat comparable to a table of contents. *73*

Compound journal entry　A journal entry with more than one debit and/or credit. *91*

Credit   The right side of any account; when used as a verb, to enter a dollar amount on the right side of an account; credits increase liability, stockholders' equity, and revenue accounts and decrease asset, expense, and Dividends accounts. *66*

Credit balance   The balance in an account when the sum of the credits to the account exceeds the sum of the debits to that account. *69*

Cross-indexing   The placing of (1) the account number of the ledger account in the general journal and (2) the general journal page number in the ledger account. *87*

Debit   The left side of any account; when used as a verb, to enter a dollar amount on the left side of an account; debits increase asset, expense, and Dividends accounts and decrease liability, stockholders' equity, and revenue accounts. *66*

Debit balance   The balance in an account when the sum of the debits to the account exceeds the sum of the credits to that account. *69*

Double-entry procedure   The accounting requirement that each transaction must be recorded by an entry that has equal debits and credits. *66*

Journal   A chronological (arranged in order of time) record of business transactions; the simplest form of journal is the two-column general journal. *71*

Journal entry   Shows all of the effects of a business transaction as expressed in terms of debit(s) and credit(s) and may include an explanation of the transaction. *72*

Journalizing   A step in the accounting recording process that consists of entering the effects of a transaction in a journal. *74*

Ledger   The complete collection of all of the accounts of a company; often referred to as the *general ledger. 73*

Nominal accounts   Income statement accounts (revenues and expenses) and the Dividends account. *73*

Note   An unconditional written promise to pay to another party the amount owed either when demanded or at a certain specified date. *67*

Permanent accounts   Balance sheet accounts; their balances are not transferred (or closed) to any other account at the end of the accounting period. *73*

Posting   Recording in the ledger accounts the information contained in the journal. *74, 86*

Real accounts   Balance sheet accounts (assets, liabilities, and stockholders' equity). *73*

Simple journal entry   An entry with one debit and one credit. *89*

T-account   An account resembling the letter T, which is used for illustrative purposes only. Debits are entered on the left side of the account, and credits are entered on the right side of the account. *65*

Temporary accounts   Nominal accounts; they temporarily contain the revenue, expense, and dividend information that is transferred (or closed) to a stockholders' equity account (Retained Earnings) at the end of the accounting period. *73*

Trial balance   A listing of the ledger accounts and their debit or credit balances to determine that debits equal credits in the recording process. *91*

SELF-TEST

True-False

Indicate whether each of the following statements is true or false.

1. A transaction must be journalized in the journal before it can be posted to the ledger accounts.

2. The left side of any account is the credit side.

3. Revenues, liabilities, and Capital Stock accounts are increased by debits.

4. The Dividends account is increased by debits.

5. If the trial balance has equal debit and credit totals, it cannot contain any errors.

Multiple-Choice

Select the best answer for each of the following questions.

1. When the stockholders invest cash in the business:
   a. Capital Stock is debited and Cash is credited.
   b. Cash is debited and Dividends is credited.
   c. Cash is debited and Capital Stock is credited.
   d. None of the above.

2. Assume that cash is paid for insurance to cover a three-year period. The recommended debit and credit are:
   a. Debit Insurance Expense, credit Cash.
   b. Debit Prepaid Insurance, credit Cash.
   c. Debit Cash, credit Insurance Expense.
   d. Debit Cash, credit Prepaid Insurance.

3. A company received cash from a customer in payment for future delivery services to be earned over a two-year period. The correct debit and credit are:
   a. Debit Cash, credit Unearned Delivery Fees.
   b. Debit Cash, credit Delivery Fee Revenue.
   c. Debit Accounts Receivable, credit Delivery Fee Revenue.
   d. None of the above.

4. A company performed delivery services for a customer for cash. The correct debit and credit are:
   a. Debit Cash, credit Unearned Delivery Fees.
   b. Debit Cash, credit Delivery Fee Revenue.
   c. Debit Accounts Receivable, credit Delivery Fee Revenue.
   d. None of the above.

5. A cash dividend of $1,000 was paid to stockholders. The correct journal entry is:

   a. Capital Stock 1,000
      Cash   1,000

   b. Cash 1,000
      Dividends.   1,000

   c. Dividends. 1,000
      Cash   1,000

   d. Cash 1,000
      Capital Stock . . .   1,000

Now turn to page 114 to check your answers.

QUESTIONS

1. Describe the steps in recording and posting the effects of a business transaction.
2. Give some examples of source documents.

3. Define an account. What are the two basic forms (styles) of accounts illustrated in the chapter?

4. What is meant by the term double-entry procedure, or duality?

5. Describe how you would determine the balance of a T-account.

6. Define debit and credit. Name the types of accounts that are:

    a. Increased by a debit.

    b. Decreased by a debit.

    c. Increased by a credit.

    d. Decreased by a credit.

    Do you think this system makes sense? Can you conceive of other possible methods for recording changes in accounts?

7. Why are expense and revenue accounts used when all revenues and expenses could be shown directly in the Retained Earnings account?

8. What is the purpose of the Dividends account and how is it increased?

9. Are the following possibilities conceivable in an entry involving only one debit and one credit? Why?

    a. Increase a liability and increase an expense.

    b. Increase an asset and decrease a liability.

    c. Increase a revenue and decrease an expense.

    d. Decrease an asset and increase another asset.

    e. Decrease an asset and increase a liability.

    f. Decrease a revenue and decrease an asset.

    g. Decrease a liability and increase a revenue.

10. Describe the nature and purposes of the general journal. What does "journalizing" mean? Give an example of a compound entry in the general journal.

11. Describe a ledger and a chart of accounts. How do these two compare with a book and its table of contents?

12. Describe the act of posting. What difficulties could arise if no cross-indexing existed between the general journal and the ledger accounts?

13. Which of the following cash payments would involve the immediate recording of an expense? Why?

    a. Paid vendors for office supplies previously purchased on account.

    b. Paid an automobile dealer for a new company auto.

    c. Paid the current month's rent.

    d. Paid salaries for the last half of the current month.

14. What types of accounts appear in the unadjusted trial balance? What are the purposes of this trial balance?

15. You have found that the total of the Debits column of the trial balance of Burns Company is $200,000, while the total of the Credits column is $180,000. What are some possible causes of this difference? If the difference between the columns is divisible by 9, what types of errors are possible?

16. Store equipment was purchased for $2,000. Instead of debiting the Store Equipment account, the debit was made to Delivery Equipment. Of what help will the trial balance be in locating this error? Why?

17. A student remembered that the side toward the window in the classroom was the debit side of an account. The student took an examination in a room where the windows were on the other side of the room and became confused and consistently reversed debits and credits. Would the student's trial balance have equal debit and credit totals? If there were no existing balances in any of the accounts to begin with, would the error prevent the student from preparing correct financial statements? Why?

18. *Real-world question*   Refer to "A Broader Perspective" on pages 88–89. Would you conclude that the opportunities for women are extremely limited in public accounting?

19. *Real-world question*   Refer to "A Broader Perspective" on pages 88–89. Was the proportion of masters degree recruits larger or smaller in 1990 than in 1989?

EXERCISES

Indicate rules of debit and credit (L.O. 1, 2)

2–1. Below is a diagram of the various types of accounts. Indicate where pluses (+) or minuses (−) should be inserted to indicate what effect debits and credits have on each account.

Asset Accounts		=	Liability Accounts		+	Stockholders' Equity Accounts	
Debit	Credit		Debit	Credit		Debit	Credit

Expense Accounts and Dividends Accounts		Revenue Accounts	
Debit	Credit	Debit	Credit

Prepare journal entries (L.O. 3)

2–2. Prepare the journal entry required for each of the following transactions:
   a. Cash was received for services performed for customers, $2,000.
   b. Services were performed for customers on account, $5,000.

Prepare journal entries (L.O. 3)

2–3. Prepare the journal entry required for each of the following transactions:
   a. Capital stock was issued for $200,000.
   b. Purchased machinery for cash, $30,000.

Prepare journal entries (L.O. 3)

2–4. Prepare the journal entry required for each of the following transactions:
   a. Capital stock was issued for $300,000 cash.
   b. A $50,000 loan was arranged with a bank. The bank increased the company's checking account by $50,000 after management of the company signed a written promise to return the $50,000 in 30 days.
   c. Cash was received for services performed for customers, $2,200.
   d. Services were performed for customers on account, $1,800.

Prepare journal
entries
(L.O. 3)

2–5. Prepare the journal entry (without dollar amounts) of a transaction that would involve the following combinations of types of accounts:

    a. An asset and a liability.

    b. An expense and an asset.

    c. A liability and an expense.

    d. Stockholders' equity and an asset.

    e. Two asset accounts.

    f. An asset and a revenue.

Record
transactions using
journal entries and
T-accounts
(L.O. 3, 4)

2–6. For each of the unrelated transactions below first give the journal entry to record the transaction. Then show how the journal entry would be posted to T-accounts. You need not include explanations or account numbers.

    a. Capital stock was issued for $150,000 cash.

    b. Salaries for a period were paid to employees, $20,000.

    c. Services were performed for customers on account, $30,000.

Explain sets of
debits and credits
(L.O. 1–4)

2–7. Explain each of the sets of debits and credits existing in the accounts below. There are 10 transactions to be explained. Each set is designated by the small letters to the left of the amount. For example, the first transaction is the issuance of capital stock for cash and is denoted by the letter *(a)*.

Cash

(a)	420,000	*(b)*	300,000
(d)	3,600	*(f)*	1,200
		(g)	7,200
		(i)	60,000
		(e)	4,000
Bal.	51,200		

Service Revenue

		(c)	3,600
		(j)	28,200
		Bal.	31,800

Accounts Receivable

(c)	3,600	*(d)*	3,600
(j)	28,200		
Bal.	28,200		

Rent Expense

(f)	1,200

Land

(b)	300,000
(i)	60,000
Bal.	360,000

Delivery Expense

(h)	2,400

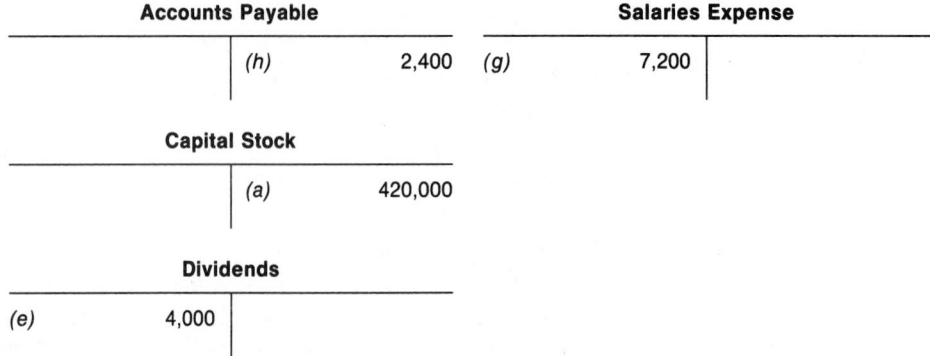

Accounts Payable		Salaries Expense	
	(h) 2,400	(g) 7,200	

Capital Stock	
	(a) 420,000

Dividends	
(e) 4,000	

2–8. Assume the ledger accounts given in Exercise 2–7 are those of Lopez Company as they appear at December 31, 1995. Prepare the trial balance as of that date.

2–9. Prepare journal entries to record each of the following transactions for Jakes Company. Use the letter of the transaction in place of the date. Include an explanation for each entry.

    a. Capital stock was issued for cash, $400,000.

    b. Purchased trucks by signing a note, $240,000.

    c. Earned (but did not yet receive) service revenue, $4,800.

    d. Collected the account receivable resulting from transaction *(c)*, $4,800.

    e. Paid the note payable for the trucks purchased, $240,000.

    f. Paid utilities for the month in the amount of $2,400.

    g. Paid salaries for the month in the amount of $7,200.

    h. Incurred delivery expenses in the amount of $1,920, but did not yet pay for them.

    i. Purchased more trucks for cash, $48,000.

    j. Performed delivery services on account, $24,000.

2–10. Using the data in Exercise 2–9, post the entries to T-accounts. Write the letter of the transaction in the account before the dollar amount. Determine a balance for each account.

2–11. Using your answer for Exercise 2–10, prepare a trial balance. Assume the date of the trial balance is March 31, 1995.

2–12. Sam Baker owns and manages a bowling center called Spare Lanes. He also maintains his own accounting records and was about to prepare financial statements for the year 1995. When he prepared the trial balance from the ledger accounts, the total of the debits column was $655,000, and the total of the credits column was $650,000. What are the possible reasons why the totals of the debits and credits are out of balance? How would you normally proceed to find an error if the two trial balance columns do not agree?

PROBLEMS

Prepare journal
entries
(L.O. 3)

2–1. Murphy Laundry Company, Inc., entered into the following transactions in August 1995:

Aug. 1 Received cash for capital stock issued to owners, $400,000.
       3 Paid rent for August on a building and laundry equipment rented, $7,000.
       6 Performed laundry services for $55,000 cash.
       8 Secured an order from a customer for laundry services of $42,000. The services are to be performed next month.
      13 Performed laundry services for $75,000 on account to various customers.
      15 Received and paid a bill for $900 for supplies used in operations.
      23 Cash collected from customers on account, $52,000.
      31 Paid $24,000 to employees for services performed in August.
      31 Received the electric and gas bill for August, $650, but did not pay it at this time.
      31 Paid cash dividend, $9,000.

Required:

Prepare journal entries for the above transactions in the general journal.

Record
transactions in
journal, post to
T-accounts, and
prepare trial
balance
(L.O. 3–5)

2–2. The transactions listed below are those of Sundown Company for April 1995:

Apr. 1 Cash of $240,000 was received for capital stock issued to the owners.
       3 Rent was paid for April, $1,600.
       6 Trucks were purchased for $28,000 cash.
       7 Office equipment was purchased on account from Wagner Company for $38,400.
      14 Salaries for first two weeks were paid, $5,600.
      15 $23,200 was received for services performed.
      18 An invoice was received from Roger's Gas Station for $200 for gas and oil used during April.
      23 A note was arranged with the bank for $40,000. The cash was received, and a note promising to return the $40,000 on May 30, 1995, was signed.
      29 Purchased trucks for $36,800 by signing a note.
      30 Salaries were paid, $7,200.

Required:

a. Prepare journal entries for the above transactions.
b. Post the journal entries to T-accounts. Enter the account number in the Posting Reference column of the journal as you post each amount. Use the following account numbers:

Acct. No.	Account Title
100	Cash
150	Trucks
172	Office Equipment
200	Accounts Payable
201	Notes Payable
300	Capital Stock
400	Service Revenue
506	Gas and Oil Expense
507	Salaries Expense
515	Rent Expense

c. Prepare a trial balance as of April 30, 1995.

Record transactions in journal, post to T-accounts, and prepare trial balance (L.O. 3–5)

2–3. The transactions below are those of Martino Company for the first week of April 1995.

Apr. 1   Martino Company was organized, and $160,000 of capital stock was issued for cash.

    1   The company borrowed $100,000 from its bank and issued its note payable to the bank.

    2   Paid $60,000 cash for land.

    2   Paid $190,000 cash for an office building located on the land purchased above.

    3   Purchased $24,000 of office equipment on account.

    4   Paid cash $1,600 for supplies to be consumed in April.

    5   Services performed on account were $1,000.

    6   Services performed for cash for the first week were $4,000.

    6   Paid salaries for the first week, $2,800.

Required:

a. Prepare journal entries for the above transactions.

b. Post the journal entries to T-accounts. Enter the account number in the Posting Reference column of the journal as you post each amount. Use the following account numbers:

Acct. No.	Account Title
100	Cash
103	Accounts Receivable
130	Land
140	Buildings
172	Office Equipment
200	Accounts Payable
201	Notes Payable
300	Capital Stock
400	Service Revenue
507	Salaries Expense
518	Supplies Expense

c. Prepare a trial balance as of April 6, 1995.

Prepare ledger
accounts,
journalize
transactions, post
to three-column
ledger accounts,
and prepare trial
balance
(L.O. 3–5)

2–4. Lassiter, Inc., was organized January 1, 1995. Its chart of accounts is as follows:

Acct. No.	Account Title
100	Cash
103	Accounts Receivable
150	Trucks
160	Office Furniture
172	Office Equipment
200	Accounts Payable
201	Notes Payable
300	Capital Stock
310	Retained Earnings
400	Service Revenue
506	Gas and Oil Expense
507	Salaries Expense
511	Utilities Expense
512	Insurance Expense
515	Rent Expense
530	Repairs Expense

Transactions for January are:

Jan. 1   The company received $240,000 cash and $120,000 of office furniture in exchange for $360,000 of capital stock.

2   Paid garage rent for January, $3,000.

4   Purchased office equipment on account, $6,600.

6   Purchased delivery trucks for $135,000; payment was made by giving cash of $75,000 and a 30-day note for the remainder.

12   Purchased insurance for January on the delivery trucks. The cost of the policy, $5,400, was paid in cash.

15   Received and paid January utilities bills, $480.

15   Paid salaries for first half of January, $1,800.

17   Cash received for delivery services to date amounted to $900.

20   Received bill for gasoline purchased and used in January, $90.

23   Purchased delivery trucks for cash, $54,000.

25   Cash sales of delivery services were $1,440.

27   Purchased an adding machine on account, $1,800.

31   Paid salaries for last half of January, $2,400.

31   Sales of delivery services on account amounted to $5,700.

31   Paid for repairs to a delivery truck, $560.

Required:

a. Prepare general ledger accounts for all the above accounts except Retained Earnings. The Retained Earnings account has a beginning balance of zero and maintains this balance throughout the period.

b. Journalize the transactions given for January 1995 in the general journal.

c. Post the journal entries to three-column ledger accounts.

d. Prepare a trial balance as of January 31, 1995.

Prepare journal
entries, post to
three-column
ledger accounts,
and prepare trial
balance
(L.O. 3–5)

2–5. The trial balance of Parkside Tennis Company at the end of the first 11 months of its fiscal year is given below.

PARKSIDE TENNIS COMPANY
Trial Balance
November 30, 1995

Acct. No.	Account Title	Debits	Credits
100	Cash	$162,360	
103	Accounts Receivable	163,500	
130	Land	120,000	
200	Accounts Payable		$ 37,500
201	Notes Payable		30,000
300	Capital Stock		120,000
310	Retained Earnings, January 1, 1995		107,400
413	Membership and Lesson Revenue		405,000
505	Advertising Expense	42,000	
507	Salaries Expense	132,000	
511	Utilities Expense	4,200	
515	Rent Expense	66,000	
518	Supplies Expense	4,500	
530	Repairs Expense	3,000	
531	Entertainment Expense	1,740	
540	Interest Expense	600	
		$699,900	$699,900

Transactions for December are:

Dec. 1 Paid building rent for December, $6,000.
  2 Paid vendors on account, $36,000.
  5 Purchased land for cash, $4,500.
  7 Sold memberships on account for December, $54,000.
  10 Paid the note payable of $30,000, plus interest of $300.
  13 Cash collections from customers on account, $72,000.
  19 Received a bill for repairs, $450.
  24 Paid the December utilities bill, $360.
  28 Received a bill for December advertising, $3,300.
  29 Paid the equipment repair bill received on the 19th, $450.
  30 Gave tennis lessons for cash, $9,000.
  30 Paid salaries, $12,000.
  30 Sales of memberships on account since December 7, $36,000 (for the month of December).
  30 Costs paid in entertaining customers in December, $510.
  30 Paid dividends of $3,000. (The Dividends account is No. 320.)

Required:

a. Open three-column general ledger accounts for each of the accounts in the trial balance. Place the word *Balance* in the explanation space and enter the date December 1, 1995, on this same line.

b. Prepare entries in the general journal for the transactions given above for December 1995.

c. Post the journal entries to three-column ledger accounts.

d. Prepare a trial balance as of December 31, 1995.

Prepare corrected
trial balance
(L.O. 5)

2–6. James Kelley prepared a trial balance for Baxter Company that did not balance. The trial balance he prepared was as follows:

BAXTER COMPANY
Trial Balance
December 31, 1995

Acct. No.	Account Title	Debits	Credits
100	Cash	$ 32,000	
103	Accounts Receivable	20,400	
170	Equipment	80,000	
200	Accounts Payable		$ 12,000
300	Capital Stock		60,000
310	Retained Earnings		20,000
320	Dividends	8,000	
400	Service Revenue		216,000
505	Advertising Expense	600	
507	Salaries Expense	88,000	
511	Utilities Expense	22,400	
515	Rent Expense	32,000	
		$283,400	$308,000

In trying to find out why the trial balance did not balance, James discovered the following errors:

1. Cash was understated (too low) by $4,000 because of an error in addition in determining the balance of that account in the ledger.
2. A credit of $2,400 to Accounts Receivable in the journal was not posted to the ledger account at all.
3. A debit of $8,000 for a semiannual dividend was posted as a credit to the Capital Stock account.
4. The balance of $6,000 in the Advertising Expense account was entered as $600 in the trial balance.
5. Miscellaneous Expense (Account No. 568), with a balance of $1,600, was omitted from the trial balance.

Required:

Prepare a correct trial balance as of December 31, 1995.

BUSINESS DECISION PROBLEM

Prepare journal
entries, post to
T-accounts, and
judge profitability
(L.O. 3, 4)

George Jeffers lost his job as a carpenter with a contractor when a recession hit the construction industry. George had been making $40,000 per year. He decided to form his own company, Jeffers Corporation, and do home repairs.

The following is a summary of the transactions of the business during the first three months of operations in 1994:

Jan. 15 Stockholders invested $40,000 in the business.

Feb. 25 Received payment of $8,800 for remodeling a basement into a recreation room. The homeowner purchased all of the building materials.

Mar.   5 Paid cash for an advertisement that appeared in the local newspaper, $220.

Apr. 10 Received $12,800 for converting a room over a garage into an office for a college professor. The professor purchased all of the materials for the job.

      11 Paid gas and oil expenses for automobile, $1,400.

      12 Miscellaneous business expenses were paid, $900.

      15 Paid dividends of $8,000.

Required:

a. Prepare journal entries for the above transactions.

b. Post the journal entries to T-accounts.

c. How profitable is this new venture? Should George stay in this business?

ANSWERS TO SELF-TEST

True-False

1. *True.* The journal is the book of original entry. Any amounts appearing in a ledger account must have been posted from the journal.

2. *False.* The left side of any account is the *debit* side.

3. *False.* These accounts are all increased by credits.

4. *True.* Since dividends reduce stockholders' equity, the Dividends account is increased by debits.

5. *False.* An entire journal entry may not have been posted, or a debit or credit might have been posted to the wrong account.

Multiple-Choice

1. *c.* An asset, Cash, is increased by a debit, and the Capital Stock account is increased by a credit.

2. *b.* Since the insurance covers more than the current accounting period, an asset is debited instead of an expense. The credit is to Cash.

3. *a.* The receipt of cash before services are performed creates a liability, Unearned Delivery Fees. To increase a liability, it is credited. Cash is debited to increase its balance.

4. *b.* Cash is increased by the debit, and Delivery Service Revenue is increased by the credit.

5. *c.* Dividends is increased by the debit, and Cash is decreased by the credit.

3

ADJUSTING THE ACCOUNTS AND COMPLETION OF THE ACCOUNTING CYCLE

LEARNING OBJECTIVES

After studying this chapter, you should be able to:

1. Describe the basic characteristics of the cash basis and the accrual basis of accounting.
2. Identify the reasons why adjusting entries must be made.
3. Identify the classes and types of adjusting entries.
4. Prepare adjusting entries.
5. Determine the effects of failing to prepare adjusting entries.
6. Prepare closing entries.
7. Prepare a classified balance sheet.
8. Prepare a work sheet for a service company (appendix).

Chapters 1 and 2 introduced the accounting process of analyzing, classifying, and summarizing business transactions into accounts. You learned how these transactions are entered into the journal and posted to the ledger accounts. You also know how the trial balance is used to test the equality of debits and credits in the journalizing and posting process. The purpose of the accounting process is to produce accurate financial statements. At this point in your study of accounting, you are concentrating on three financial statements—the income statement, the statement of retained earnings, and the balance sheet.

When you began to analyze business transactions in Chapter 1, you saw that the evidence of the transaction is usually a source document. A source document, you recall, is any written or printed evidence of a business transaction that describes the essential facts of that transaction. Examples of source documents are receipts for cash paid or received, checks written or received, bills sent to customers or bills received from suppliers, and so on. You should be familiar with some or all of these source documents by now.

The giving, receiving, or creating of a source document triggered the journal entries made in Chapter 2. Source documents are used to prepare journal entries during an accounting period.

The journal entries we will discuss in this chapter are *adjusting entries*. The arrival of the end of the accounting period triggers adjusting entries. The purpose of adjusting entries is to bring the accounts to their proper balances before the financial statements are prepared. In this chapter, you will first learn the difference between the cash basis and accrual basis of accounting. Then you will learn about the classes and types of adjusting entries and how to prepare them.

CASH VERSUS ACCRUAL BASIS ACCOUNTING

Objective 1
Describe the basic characteristics of the cash basis and the accrual basis of accounting

Some relatively small businesses and professionals such as physicians and lawyers may account for their revenues and expenses on a cash basis. The **cash basis of accounting** recognizes revenues when cash is received and recognizes expenses when cash is paid out. For example, under the cash basis, a company would treat services rendered to clients in 1994 for which the company collected cash in 1995 as 1995 revenues. Similarly, under the cash basis, a company would treat expenses incurred in 1994 for which the company disbursed cash in 1995 as 1995 expenses.

Since the cash basis of accounting does not match "efforts" and "accomplishments" in terms of expenses incurred and revenues earned, it is generally considered theoretically unacceptable. The cash basis is acceptable in practice only under those circumstances when it approximates the results that a company could obtain under the accrual basis of accounting. Companies using the cash basis do not have to prepare any adjusting entries unless they discover they have made a mistake in preparing an entry during the accounting period. Under certain circumstances, companies may use the cash basis for income tax purposes.

Throughout the text we use the accrual basis of accounting because most companies use the accrual basis. The **accrual basis of accounting** recognizes revenues when sales are made or services are performed, regardless of when cash is received. Expenses are recognized as incurred, whether or not cash has been paid out. For instance, assume a company performs services for a customer on account. Although the company has received no cash, the revenue is recorded at the time the company performs the service. Later, when the company receives the cash, no revenue is recorded because the company has already recorded the revenue. Under the accrual basis, adjusting entries are needed to bring the accounts up to date for unrecorded economic activity that has taken place.

Illustration 3.1 shows when revenues and expenses are recognized under the cash basis and under the accrual basis.

An example of economic activity that would require an adjusting entry is the purchase and gradual use of office supplies. When a company purchases

Illustration 3.1
CASH BASIS AND ACCRUAL BASIS OF ACCOUNTING COMPARED

	Cash Basis	*Accrual Basis*
Revenues are recognized	As cash is received	As earned (goods are delivered or services are performed)
Expenses are recognized	As cash is paid	As incurred to produce revenues

office supplies, the purchase is recorded in an asset account, Office Supplies on Hand. Even though the company uses the office supplies during the accounting period, their consumption is usually not recorded until the end of the period. The cost and nuisance of making an entry every time the company uses a small amount of office supplies outweighs the benefits of having accurate account balances during the period. Instead, an adjusting entry is made at the end of the period to bring the accounts to their proper balances before the financial statements are prepared.

THE NEED FOR ADJUSTING ENTRIES

Objective 2
Identify the reasons why adjusting entries must be made

The income statement of a business reports all revenues earned and all expenses incurred to generate those revenues during a given period. If the income statement does not report all revenues and expenses, it is incomplete, inaccurate, and possibly misleading. Similarly, a balance sheet that does not report all of an entity's assets, liabilities, and stockholders' equity at a specific point in time may be misleading. Each adjusting entry has a dual

Illustration 3.2
SUMMARY—FISCAL YEAR ENDINGS BY MONTH

	1990	*1989*	*1988*	*1987*
January	22	22	20	23
February.	15	15	13	13
March	14	16	15	14
April.	7	8	7	8
May	16	15	16	14
June.	62	57	54	42
July	16	16	14	14
August	17	16	15	15
September.	33	37	38	37
October	21	20	22	23
November	17	17	15	16
Subtotal	**240**	**239**	**229**	**219**
December	360	361	371	381
Total companies	**600**	**600**	**600**	**600**

SOURCE: American Institute of Certified Public Accountants, *Accounting Trends & Techniques* (New York: AICPA, 1991), p. 34.

A BROADER PERSPECTIVE

SKILLS FOR THE LONG HAUL

The decision has been made: You've opted to start your career by joining an international accounting firm. But you can't help wondering if you have the right skills both for short- and long-term success in public accounting. . . .

Most students understand that accounting knowledge, organizational ability and interpersonal skills are critical to success in public accounting. But it is important for the beginner to realize that different skills are emphasized at different points in a public accountant's career. . . .

Let's examine the duties and skills needed at each level—Staff Accountant (years 1–2), Senior Accountant (years 3–4), Manager/Senior Manager (years 5–11) and Partner (years 11+).

Staff Accountant—Enthusiastic Learner Let's travel with Tracy as she begins her career at the staff level. At the outset, she works directly under a senior accountant on each of her audits and is responsible for completing audits and administrative tasks assigned to her. Her duties include documenting workpapers, interacting with client accounting staff, clerical tasks and discussing questions that arise with her senior. Tracy will work on different audit engagements

during her first year and learn the firm's audit approach. She will be introduced to various industries and accounting systems.

The two most important traits to be demonstrated at the staff level are (1) a positive attitude and (2) the ability to learn quickly while adapting to unfamiliar situations.

* * * * *

Senior Accountant—Organizer and Teacher As a senior accountant, Tracy will be responsible for the day-to-day management of several audit engagements during the year. She will plan the audits, oversee the performance of interim audit testing and direct year-end field work. She will also perform much of the final wrap-up work, such as preparing checklists, writing the management letter and reviewing or drafting the financial statements. Throughout this process, Tracy will spend a substantial amount of time instructing and supervising staff accountants.

The two most critical skills needed at the senior level are (1) the ability to organize and control an audit and (2) the ability to teach staff accountants how to audit.

* * * * *

purpose: (1) to make the income statement report the proper revenue or expense and (2) to make the balance sheet report the proper asset or liability. Thus, every adjusting entry affects at least one income statement account and one balance sheet account.

Since those interested in the activities of a business need timely information, companies must prepare financial statements periodically. To prepare such statements, the accountant divides an entity's life into time periods. These time periods are usually equal in length and are called *accounting periods*. An **accounting period** may be one month, one quarter, or one year. An **accounting year,** or fiscal year, is an accounting period of one year. A **fiscal year** is any 12 consecutive months. The fiscal year may or may not coincide with the **calendar year,** which ends on December 31. Illustration 3.2

A BROADER PERSPECTIVE (*concluded*)

Manager/Senior Manager—General Manager and Salesperson Upon promotion to manager, Tracy will begin the transformation from auditor to executive. She will manage several audits at one time and become active in billing clients as well as negotiating audit fees. She will handle many important client meetings and closing conferences. Tracy will also become more involved in the firm's administrative tasks. . . . Finally, outside of her client service and administrative duties, Tracy will be evaluated to a large extent on her community involvement and ability to assist the partners in generating new business for the firm.

The two skills most emphasized at the manager level are (1) general management ability and (2) sales and communication skills.

* * * * *

Partner—Leader and Expert As a partner in the firm, Tracy will have many broad responsibilities. She will engage in high-level client service activities, business development, recruiting, strategic planning, office administration and counseling. Besides serving as the engagement partner on several audits, she will have ultimate responsibility for the quality of service provided to each of her clients. Although a certain industry or administrative function will become her specialty, she will often be called upon to perform a wide variety of audit and administrative duties when other partners have scheduling conflicts. She will be expected to serve as a positive example to those who work for her and will train others in her areas of expertise.

At the partnership level, what's looked for is leadership ability plus the ability to become an expert in a specific industry or administrative function.

* * * * *

In the Meantime Those planning on a public accounting career should do more than just learn accounting. To develop the needed skills, a broad education background in business and nonbusiness courses is required plus participation in extracurricular activities, that promote leadership and communication skills. It is never too early to start building the skills for long-term success.

SOURCE: Dana R. Hermanson and Heather M. Hermanson, *New Accountant*, January 1990, pp. 24–26, © 1990, New DuBois Corporation.

shows the fiscal year endings of a survey of 600 companies. More than half of the companies have a fiscal year that coincides with the calendar year. Companies in certain industries often have a fiscal year that differs from the calendar year. For instance, to avoid the Christmas holidays, many retail stores end their fiscal year on January 31. Other companies select a fiscal year ending at a time when inventories and business activity are lowest.

Periodic reporting and the matching principle necessitate the preparation of *adjusting entries*. **Adjusting entries** are journal entries made at the end of an accounting period or at any time financial statements are to be prepared to bring about a proper *matching* of revenues and expenses. The **matching principle** requires that expenses incurred in producing revenues be deducted from the revenues they generated during the accounting period.

This matching of expenses and revenues is necessary for the income statement to present an accurate picture of the profitability of a business. Adjusting entries reflect unrecorded economic activity that has taken place but has not yet been recorded. Why has the company not recorded this activity by the end of the period? The reason is either (1) it is more convenient and economical to wait until the end of the period to record the activity, or (2) no source document concerning that activity has yet come to the accountant's attention.

Adjusting entries bring the amounts in the general ledger accounts to their proper balances before the company prepares its financial statements. That is, **adjusting entries convert the amounts that are actually in the general ledger accounts to the amounts that should be in the general ledger accounts for proper financial reporting.** To make this conversion, the accounts are analyzed to determine which accounts need adjustment. For example, assume a company purchased a three-year insurance policy costing $600 at the beginning of the year and debited $600 to Prepaid Insurance. At year-end, the company should remove $200 of the cost from the asset and record it as an expense. Failure to do so misstates assets and net income on the financial statements.

Companies *continuously* receive benefits from many assets such as prepaid expenses (e.g., prepaid insurance and prepaid rent). Thus, the expense relating to these items could also be recognized *continuously* as time elapses. An entry could be made frequently, even daily, to record the expense incurred. Typically, however, the entry is not made until financial statements are to be prepared. Therefore, if monthly financial statements are prepared, monthly adjusting entries are required. By custom, and in some instances by law, businesses report to their stockholders at least annually. Accordingly, adjusting entries will be required at least once a year. Remember, however, that the entry transferring an amount from an asset account to an expense account should transfer only the cost of the portion of the asset that has expired.

CLASSES AND TYPES OF ADJUSTING ENTRIES

Objective 3
Identify the classes and types of adjusting entries

Adjusting entries can be grouped into two broad classes: deferred (meaning to postpone or delay) items and accrued (meaning to grow or accumulate) items. **Deferred items** consist of adjusting entries involving data previously recorded in accounts. These entries involve the transfer of data already recorded in asset and liability accounts to expense and revenue accounts, respectively. **Accrued items** consist of adjusting entries relating to activity on which no data have been previously recorded in the accounts. These entries involve the initial, or first, recording of assets and liabilities and the related revenues and expenses (Illustration 3.3).

Deferred items consist of two types of adjusting entries: asset/expense adjustments and liability/revenue adjustments. For example, prepaid insur-

Illustration 3.3
TWO CLASSES AND FOUR TYPES OF ADJUSTING ENTRIES

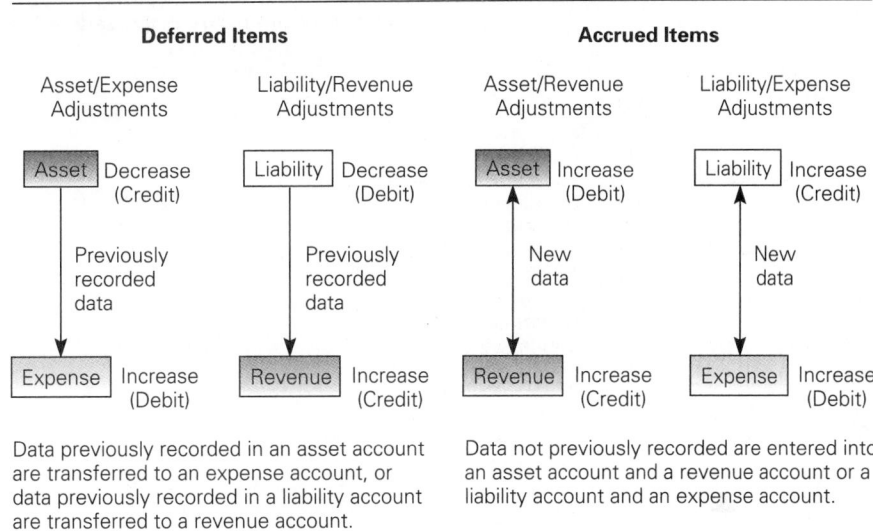

Deferred Items		Accrued Items	
Asset/Expense Adjustments	Liability/Revenue Adjustments	Asset/Revenue Adjustments	Liability/Expense Adjustments

Data previously recorded in an asset account are transferred to an expense account, or data previously recorded in a liability account are transferred to a revenue account.

Data not previously recorded are entered into an asset account and a revenue account or a liability account and an expense account.

ance and prepaid rent are shown as assets until they are used up; then they become expenses. Also, if a company receives cash for a service it has not yet rendered, the credit is to an unearned revenue (a liability account). However, as the company renders the service, the unearned revenue becomes earned revenue.

Accrued items also consist of two types of adjusting entries: asset/revenue adjustments and liability/expense adjustments. For example, assume a company performs a service for a customer but has not yet billed the customer. This transaction is recorded as an asset in the form of a receivable and as revenue because the company has earned a revenue. Also, assume a company owes its employees salaries that it has not yet paid. This transaction is recorded as a liability and an expense because the company has incurred an expense.

In this chapter, we use the Speedy Delivery Company example from Chapter 2 to illustrate each of the four types of adjusting entries: asset/expense, liability/revenue, asset/revenue, and liability/expense. Illustration 3.4 shows the trial balance of the Speedy Delivery Company at December 31, 1995. This trial balance is the same as the one shown in Chapter 2, Illustration 2.7. As you can see by looking at the trial balance, several accounts must be adjusted before accurate financial statements can be prepared. The adjustments for these accounts involve data that have already been recorded in the company's accounts.

Illustration 3.4
TRIAL BALANCE

SPEEDY DELIVERY COMPANY
Trial Balance
December 31, 1995

Acct. No.	Account Title	Debits	Credits
100	Cash	$ 8,250	
103	Accounts Receivable.	5,200	
107	Supplies on Hand	1,400	
108	Prepaid Insurance	2,400	
112	Prepaid Rent	1,200	
150	Trucks	40,000	
200	Accounts Payable		$ 730
210	Unearned Delivery Fees		4,500
300	Capital Stock		50,000
320	Dividends	3,000	
400	Service Revenue.		10,700
505	Advertising Expense	50	
506	Gas and Oil Expense.	680	
507	Salaries Expense	3,600	
511	Utilities Expense.	150	
		$65,930	$65,930

Type of Account	Acct. No.	Account Title	Description
Asset	121	Interest Receivable	The amount of interest earned but not yet received.
Contra assets*	104	Allowance for Uncollectible Accounts	The total amount of accounts receivable that is not expected to be collected. The balance of this account is deducted from that of Accounts Receivable on the balance sheet.
	151	Accumulated Depreciation— Trucks	The total depreciation cost taken on trucks. The balance of this account is deducted from that of Trucks on the balance sheet.
Liability	206	Salaries Payable	The amount of salaries earned by employees but not yet paid by the company.
Revenue	418	Interest Revenue	The amount of interest earned in the current period.
Expenses	512	Insurance Expense	The cost of insurance incurred in the current period.
	515	Rent Expense	The cost of rent incurred in the current period.
	518	Supplies Expense	The cost of supplies used in the current period.
	521	Depreciation Expense— Trucks	The portion of the cost of the trucks assigned to expense during the current period.
	534	Uncollectible Accounts Expense	The amount of expense resulting from accounts receivable that will not be collected.

* The balance of a contra asset is deducted from the balance of an asset account on the balance sheet. The reasons for using a contra asset account are explained later in the chapter.

In making adjustments for Speedy Delivery Company, we will need to add several additional accounts to the company's chart of accounts shown in Chapter 2 on page 75. These accounts are listed at the bottom of page 122.

Now you are ready to follow Speedy Delivery Company as it makes its adjustments for deferred items. If you find the process confusing, go back and study again the beginning of this chapter so you clearly understand the purpose of adjusting entries.

ADJUSTMENTS FOR DEFERRED ITEMS

*Objective 4
Prepare adjusting entries*

This section discusses the two types of adjustments for deferred items: asset/expense adjustments and liability/revenue adjustments. In the asset/expense group, you will learn how to prepare adjusting entries for prepaid expenses, depreciation expense, and uncollectible accounts expense. In the liability/revenue group, you will learn how to prepare adjusting entries for unearned revenues.

Asset/Expense Adjustments—Prepaid Expenses, Depreciation Expense, and Uncollectible Accounts Expense

Speedy Delivery Company must make several asset/expense adjustments for prepaid expenses. A **prepaid expense** is an asset awaiting assignment to expense, such as prepaid insurance, prepaid rent, and supplies on hand. As you will see, the nature of these three adjustments is the same.

Prepaid Insurance.   When a company pays an insurance policy premium in advance, the purchase creates the asset, *prepaid insurance*. This advance payment is an asset because the company will receive insurance coverage in the future. With the passage of time, however, the asset gradually expires. The portion that has expired becomes an expense. To illustrate this point, recall that in Chapter 2, Speedy Delivery Company purchased on account an insurance policy on its trucks for the period December 1, 1995, to November 30, 1996. The journal entry made on December 1, 1995, to record the purchase of the policy was:

```
1995
Dec. 1  Prepaid Insurance . . . . . . . . . . . . . . . . . .     2,400
            Accounts Payable . . . . . . . . . . . . . . . . .              2,400
        Purchased truck insurance to cover a one-year
        period.
```

The two accounts relating to insurance are Prepaid Insurance (an asset) and Insurance Expense (an expense). After posting the above entry, the Prepaid Insurance account has a $2,400 debit balance on December 1, 1995. The Insurance Expense account has a zero balance on December 1, 1995, because no time has elapsed to use any of the policy's benefits.

(Dr.)	**Prepaid Insurance**	(Cr.)	(Dr.)	**Insurance Expense**	(Cr.)
1995 Dec. 1 Bal.	2,400		1995 Dec. 1 Bal.	–0–	

By December 31, 1995, one month of the period covered by the policy has expired. Therefore, part of the **service potential** (or benefits that can be obtained from the asset) has expired. The asset will now provide less future services or benefits than when the company acquired it. We must recognize this reduction of the asset's ability to provide future services by treating the cost of the services received from the asset as an expense. For the Speedy Delivery Company example, the service received was one month of insurance coverage. Since the policy provides the same services for every month of its one-year life, we assign an equal amount ($200) of cost to each month. Thus, Speedy Delivery charges 1/12 of the annual premium to Insurance Expense on December 31, 1995. The adjusting journal entry is:

Adjustment 1— Insurance

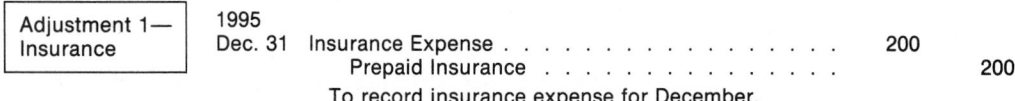

```
1995
Dec. 31  Insurance Expense . . . . . . . . . . . . . . . . .     200
             Prepaid Insurance  . . . . . . . . . . . . . . .            200
         To record insurance expense for December.
```

After posting the two journal entries above, the accounts in T-account format appear as follows:

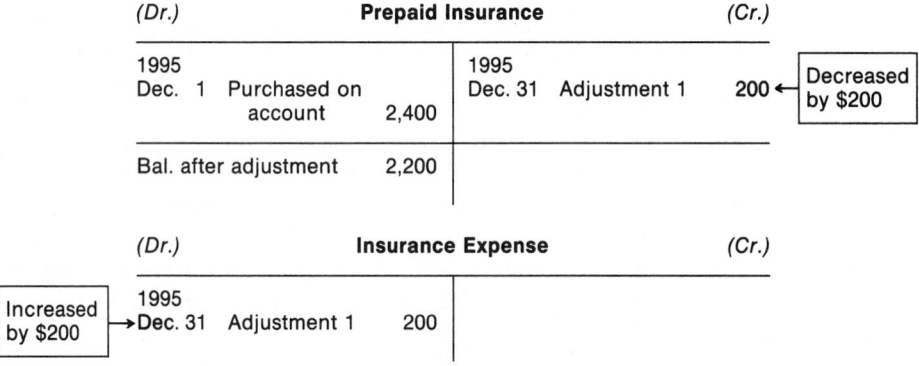

(Dr.)	**Prepaid Insurance**		(Cr.)	
1995 Dec. 1 Purchased on account	2,400	1995 Dec. 31 Adjustment 1	200 ←	Decreased by $200
Bal. after adjustment	2,200			

	(Dr.)	**Insurance Expense**	(Cr.)
Increased by $200 →	1995 Dec. 31 Adjustment 1	200	

In practice, accountants do not use T-accounts. Instead, they use three-column ledger accounts that have the advantage of showing a balance after each transaction. After posting the two entries above, the three-column ledger accounts appear as follows:

Prepaid Insurance   *Account No. 108*

Date		Explanation	Post. Ref.	Debit	Credit	Balance
1995						
Dec.	1	Purchased on account	G1*	2 4 0 0		2 4 0 0 Dr.
	31	Adjustment	G3*		2 0 0	2 2 0 0 Dr.

Insurance Expense   *Account No. 512*

Date		Explanation	Post. Ref.	Debit	Credit	Balance
1995						
Dec.	31	Adjustment	G3*	2 0 0		2 0 0 Dr.

* Assumed journal page number.

Before the above adjusting entry was made, the entire $2,400 insurance payment that the company paid on December 1, 1995, was a prepaid expense for 12 months of protection. As explained earlier, a prepaid expense is an asset awaiting assignment to expense. So on December 31, 1995, one month of protection had passed, and an adjusting entry transferred $200 of the $2,400 ($2,400/12 = $200) to insurance expense. On the income statement for the year ended December 31, 1995, Speedy Delivery reports one month of insurance expense, $200, as one of the expenses it incurred in generating that year's revenues. The remaining amount of the prepaid expense, $2,200, is reported as an asset on the balance sheet. The $2,200 prepaid expense represents the cost of 11 months of insurance protection that remains as a future benefit.

In initially recording the $2,400 insurance purchase, an alternative procedure could have been followed. Instead of debiting Prepaid Insurance, the Insurance Expense could have been debited as follows:

```
1995
Dec. 1  Insurance Expense. . . . . . . . . . . . . . . . .  2,400
            Cash . . . . . . . . . . . . . . . . . . . . . . .           2,400
        Purchased truck insurance to cover a one-year
        period.
```

If this had been done, the adjusting entry would have been a debit to Prepaid Insurance for $2,200, which would set up the asset in the books, and a credit to Insurance Expense for $2,200, reducing the period's expense. The result would be a $2,200 balance in the asset account and a $200 balance in the expense account, as shown in the T-accounts below. As you can see, the end result is the same either way, and either method is correct. The adjusting entry, however, will depend on which account the company originally debited for the prepayment. This is true of many of the other adjustments illustrated in this chapter.

(Dr.)	Insurance Expense		*(Cr.)*	
1995 Dec. 1	2,400	1995 Dec. 31 Adjustment	2,200 ←	Decreased by $2,200
Bal., 12/31/95	200			

	(Dr.)	Prepaid Insurance		*(Cr.)*
Increased by $2,200 →	1995 Dec. 31 Adjustment	2,200		

Prepaid Rent. Prepaid rent is another example of the gradual consumption of a previously recorded asset. Assume a company pays rent in advance to cover more than one accounting period. On the date it pays the rent, the company debits the prepayment to the Prepaid Rent account (an asset account). The company has not yet received benefits resulting from this expenditure. Thus, the expenditure creates an asset.

The measurement of rent expense is similar to insurance expense. Generally, the rental contract specifies the amount of rent per unit of time. If the prepayment covers a three-month rental, one third of this rental is charged to each month. The same amount is charged to each month even though some months have more days than other months.

For example, in Chapter 2, Speedy Delivery Company paid $1,200 rent in advance on December 1, 1995, to cover a three-month period beginning on that date. The journal entry made at that time was:

```
1995
Dec. 1  Prepaid Rent . . . . . . . . . . . . . . . . . . . . .   1,200
            Cash . . . . . . . . . . . . . . . . . . . . . .           1,200
        Paid three months' rent on a building.
```

The two accounts relating to rent are Prepaid Rent (an asset) and Rent Expense. After this entry is posted, the Prepaid Rent account has a $1,200 balance and the Rent Expense account has a zero balance because no part of the rent period has yet elapsed.

(Dr.)	Prepaid Rent	*(Cr.)*	*(Dr.)*	Rent Expense	*(Cr.)*
1995 Dec. 1 Bal. Cash paid	1,200		1995 Dec. 1 Bal.	–0–	

On December 31, 1995, an adjusting entry must be prepared. Since one third of the period covered by the prepaid rent has elapsed, one third of the $1,200 of prepaid rent is charged to expense. The required adjusting entry is:

Adjustment 2— Rent

1995
Dec. 31   Rent Expense   400
                   Prepaid Rent   400
             To record rent expense for December.

After posting this adjusting entry, the T-accounts appear as follows:

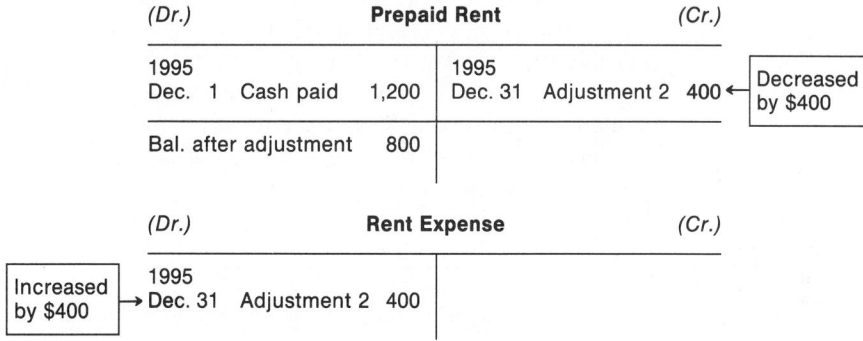

The $400 rent expense appears in the income statement for the year ended December 31, 1995. Speedy Delivery reports the remaining $800 of prepaid rent as an asset in the balance sheet on December 31, 1995. Thus, the adjusting entries have accomplished their purpose of maintaining the accuracy of the financial statements.

Supplies on Hand.   Almost every business uses supplies in its operations. Supplies may be classified simply as supplies (to include all types of supplies), or, more specifically, as office supplies (paper, stationery, floppy diskettes, pencils), selling supplies (gummed tape, string, paper bags or cartons, wrapping paper), or, possibly, cleaning supplies (soap, disinfectants). Frequently, companies buy supplies in bulk. These supplies are an asset until the company uses them. This asset may be called *supplies on hand* or *supplies inventory*. Even though these terms indicate a prepaid expense, the asset does not use "prepaid" in its title.

On December 4, 1995, Speedy Delivery Company purchased supplies for $1,400 and recorded the transaction as follows:

1995
Dec. 4   Supplies on Hand   1,400
                 Cash   1,400
             To record the purchase of supplies for future use.

Speedy Delivery's two accounts relating to supplies are Supplies on Hand (an asset) and Supplies Expense. After the above entry is posted, the Supplies on Hand account shows a debit balance of $1,400 and the Supplies Expense account has a zero balance as shown in the following T-accounts:

(Dr.)	Supplies on Hand	(Cr.)	(Dr.)	Supplies Expense	(Cr.)
1995 Dec. 4 Bal. Cash paid 1,400			1995 Dec. 4 Bal. –0–		

An actual physical inventory (a count of the supplies on hand) at the end of the month showed that only $900 of supplies were on hand at that time. Thus, the company must have used $500 of supplies in December. An adjusting journal entry is required to bring the two accounts pertaining to supplies to their proper balances. The adjusting entry recognizes the reduction in the asset (Supplies on Hand) and the recording of an expense (Supplies Expense) by transferring $500 from the asset to the expense. From the information given, the asset balance should be $900 and the expense balance, $500. So the following adjusting entry is made:

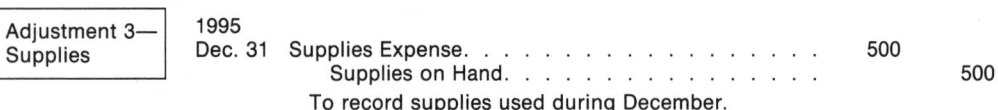

Adjustment 3— Supplies	1995 Dec. 31 Supplies Expense. 500
	Supplies on Hand. 500
	To record supplies used during December.

After posting this adjusting entry, the T-accounts appear as follows:

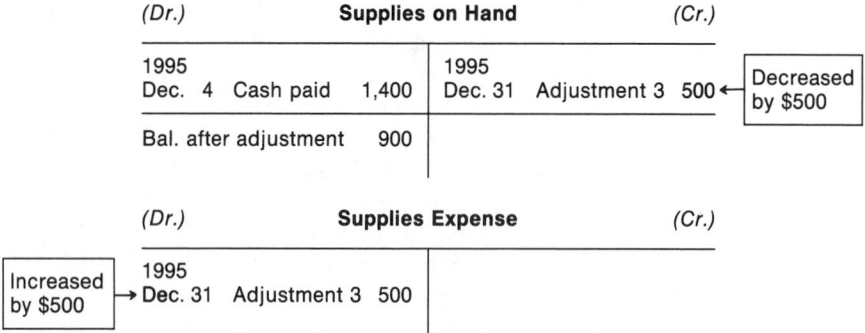

(Dr.)	Supplies on Hand	(Cr.)	
1995 Dec. 4 Cash paid 1,400	1995 Dec. 31 Adjustment 3 500		Decreased by $500
Bal. after adjustment 900			

Increased by $500	(Dr.)	Supplies Expense	(Cr.)
	1995 Dec. 31 Adjustment 3 500		

The entry to record the use of supplies could be made when the supplies are issued from the storeroom. However, such careful accounting for small items each time they are issued is usually too costly a procedure.

Adjusting entries for supplies on hand, like for any other prepaid expense, are made before financial statements are prepared. Supplies expense appears in the income statement. Supplies on hand is an asset in the balance sheet.

Sometimes companies buy assets relating to insurance, rent, and supplies knowing that they will fully use them up before the end of the current accounting period (usually one month or one year). If so, an expense account is usually debited at the time of purchase rather than debiting an asset account. This procedure avoids having to make an adjusting entry at the end of the accounting period. As mentioned earlier, sometimes an expense is debited even though the asset will benefit more than the current period. Then, at the end of the accounting period, the adjusting entry must transfer some of the cost from the expense to the asset. For instance, assume that on January 1, a company paid $1,200 rent to cover a three-year period and debited the $1,200 to Rent Expense. At the end of the year, $800 must be transferred from Rent Expense to Prepaid Rent.

Depreciation.   Just as prepaid insurance and prepaid rent indicate a gradual using up of a previously recorded asset, so does depreciation. However, the overall period of time involved in using up a depreciable asset (such as a building) is much longer and less definite than for prepaid expenses. Also, a prepaid expense generally involves a fairly small amount of money. Depreciable assets, however, usually involve larger sums of money.

A **depreciable asset** is a manufactured asset such as a building, machine, vehicle, or piece of equipment that provides service to a business. These assets in time lose their utility because of wear and tear from use or from obsolescence due to technological change. Since companies gradually use up these assets over time, depreciation expense is recorded on these assets. **Depreciation expense** is the amount of asset cost assigned as an expense to a particular time period. The process of recording depreciation expense is called **depreciation accounting.**

The three factors involved in computing depreciation expense are:

1. *Asset cost.*   The asset cost is the amount that a company paid to purchase the depreciable asset.
2. *Estimated salvage value.*   The estimated **salvage value (scrap value)** is the amount that the company can probably sell the asset for at the end of its estimated useful life.
3. *Estimated useful life.*   The estimated **useful life** of an asset is the estimated number of time periods that a company can make use of the asset. Useful life is an estimate, not an exact measurement, that a company must make in advance.

The equation for determining the amount of depreciation expense for each time period is:

$$\text{Depreciation expense for each time period} = \frac{\text{Asset cost} - \text{Estimated salvage value}}{\text{Estimated number of time periods in asset's useful life}}$$

Accountants use different methods for recording depreciation. The method illustrated here is the *straight-line method.* We discuss other depreciation methods in Chapter 7. Straight-line depreciation assigns the same amount of depreciation expense to each accounting period over the life of the asset. The **depreciation formula (straight-line)** to compute straight-line depreciation for a one-year period is:

$$\text{Annual depreciation} = \frac{\text{Asset cost} - \text{Estimated salvage value}}{\text{Estimated number of years of useful life}}$$

To illustrate the use of this formula, recall that on December 1, Speedy Delivery Company purchased four small trucks at a cost of $40,000. The journal entry made at that time was:

```
1995
Dec. 1  Trucks  . . . . . . . . . . . . . . . . . . . . . .  40,000
            Cash  . . . . . . . . . . . . . . . . . . . . .          40,000
            To record the purchase of four delivery trucks.
```

The estimated salvage value for each truck was $1,000, so Speedy Delivery estimated the total salvage value for all four trucks at $4,000. The company estimated the useful life of each truck to be four years. Using the straight-line depreciation formula, Speedy Delivery calculated the annual depreciation on the trucks as follows:

$$\text{Annual depreciation} = \frac{\$40,000 - \$4,000}{4 \text{ years}} = \$9,000$$

The amount of depreciation expense for one month would be $\frac{1}{12}$ of the annual amount. Thus, depreciation expense for December is $9,000 ÷ 12 = $750.

The difference between an asset's cost and its estimated salvage value is called an asset's **depreciable amount.** To satisfy the matching principle, the depreciable amount must be allocated as an expense to the various periods in the asset's useful life. This allocation is accomplished by debiting the amount of depreciation for a period to a depreciation expense account and crediting the amount to an accumulated depreciation account. Speedy Delivery's depreciation on its delivery trucks for December is $750. The company records the depreciation as follows:

Adjustment 4— Depreciation	

```
1995
Dec. 31  Depreciation Expense—Trucks  . . . . . . . . . . .     750
              Accumulated Depreciation—Trucks  . . . . . . .            750
              To record depreciation expense for December.
```

After posting the adjusting entry, the T-accounts appear as follows:

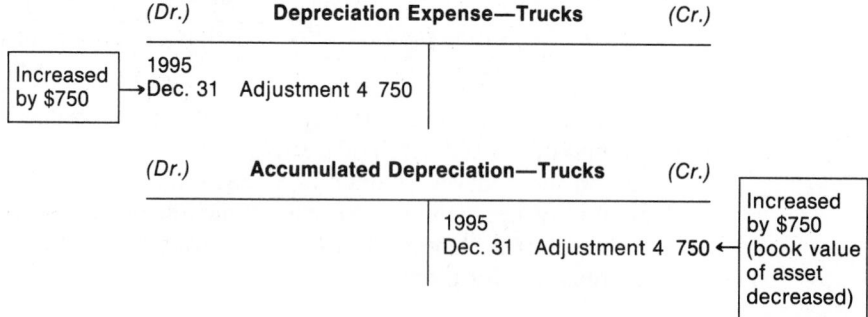

(Dr.)	**Depreciation Expense—Trucks**	(Cr.)

| Increased by $750 | 1995 Dec. 31 Adjustment 4 750 | |

(Dr.)	**Accumulated Depreciation—Trucks**	(Cr.)

| | | 1995 Dec. 31 Adjustment 4 750 | Increased by $750 (book value of asset decreased) |

Depreciation expense is reported in the income statement. Accumulated depreciation is reported in the balance sheet as a deduction from the related asset.

The **accumulated depreciation account** is a contra asset account that shows the total of all depreciation recorded on the asset up through the balance sheet date. A **contra asset account** is a deduction from the asset to which it relates in the balance sheet. The purpose of a contra asset account is to reduce the original cost of the asset down to its remaining undepreciated cost or book value. The *undepreciated cost of the asset* is the debit balance in the asset account (original cost) minus the credit balance in the accumulated depreciation contra account. Accountants also refer to an asset's cost less accumulated depreciation as the **book value** (or net book value) of the asset. Thus, book value is the cost not yet allocated to an expense. In the above example, the book value of the delivery equipment after the first month is:

Cost	$40,000
Less: Accumulated depreciation	750
Book value (or cost not yet allocated as an expense)	$39,250

The amount of the depreciation is credited to an accumulated depreciation account, which is a contra asset, rather than directly to the asset account. Contra accounts are used when it is desirable to show the statement reader the original amount of the account to which the contra account relates. For instance, for the asset Trucks, it is useful to know both the original cost of the asset and the total amount of depreciation that has been recorded on the asset. Therefore, the asset is used to show the original cost. The contra account, Accumulated Depreciation—Trucks, is used to show the total amount of recorded depreciation. By having both original cost and the accumulated depreciation amounts, a user can estimate the approximate percentage of the benefits embodied in the asset that the company has consumed. For instance, assume the accumulated depreciation amount is about three-fourths the cost of the asset. Then, the benefits would be approximately three-fourths consumed, and the company may have to replace the asset soon.

Thus, to provide more complete balance sheet information to users of financial statements, both the original acquisition cost and accumulated depreciation are shown. In the example described above for adjustment 4, the balance sheet at December 31, 1995, would show the asset and contra asset as follows:

Assets	
Trucks	$40,000
Less: Accumulated depreciation	750
	$39,250

As you may expect, the accumulated depreciation account balance increases each period by the amount of depreciation expense recorded until the remaining book value of the asset is equal to the estimated salvage value.

Uncollectible Accounts Receivable.   A seller doing business on a credit basis faces the virtual certainty that some customers' accounts will ultimately prove uncollectible. For example, assume that Speedy Delivery expects to collect only $4,500 out of $5,200 of accounts receivable outstanding at year-end. Normally, this would require the following entry:

Adjustment 5— Uncollectible Accounts	1995		
	Dec. 31	Uncollectible Accounts Expense.	700	
		Allowance for Uncollectible Accounts		700

After posting the adjusting entry, the T-accounts appear as follows:

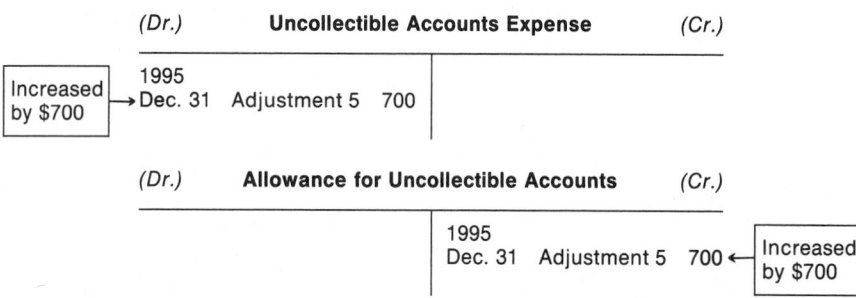

This entry serves two purposes: (1) uncollectible accounts are charged as an expense in the year the sale giving rise to them was made; that is, a proper matching results when, say, uncollectible accounts arising from credit sales made in 1995 are charged as an expense in 1995, (2) the accounts receivable at year-end are properly valued at their *net realizable value*— the amount of cash expected to be collected.

The **Uncollectible Accounts Expense** (also called **Bad Debts Expense**) account is an operating expense a business incurs as a result of customers not paying their bills when the company sells on credit. The **Allowance for Uncollectible Accounts** (also called *Allowance for Doubtful Accounts*) is a contra account (reduction account) to Accounts Receivable; it reduces Accounts Receivable to their net realizable value. The Accounts Receivable account is not reduced directly because it is not known at this time which customers' accounts will actually prove uncollectible. The $5,200 of accounts receivable and the related allowance for uncollectible accounts of $700 are reported as follows in the current assets section of the balance sheet:

Accounts receivable.	$5,200	
Less: Allowance for uncollectible accounts	700	4,500

Estimation Methods.   There are two basic methods of estimating the amount of uncollectible accounts to be charged to a given accounting period.

Percentage of Sales Method.   The *percentage of sales method* involves calculating the amount that has proven uncollectible from credit sales in previous years. The ratio of uncollectible accounts to credit sales is then used in estimating the amount for the uncollectible accounts adjusting entry. If cash sales are small or are a fairly constant percentage of total sales, the entry may be based on total net sales.

To illustrate, assume that the Boulder Company has found that 1% of its net sales is uncollectible. On the basis of this experience, each period the company may charge an amount equal to 1% of the net sales for the period to Uncollectible Accounts Expense and add a like amount to the Allowance for Uncollectible Accounts. If net sales for 1995 are $400,000, the entry will read:

```
Uncollectible Accounts Expense . . . . . . . . . . . . . .    4,000
     Allowance for Uncollectible Accounts. . . . . . . . . .             4,000
     To record uncollectible accounts expense.
```

Assuming that the gross (total) amount of accounts receivable is $100,000 and there was no previous balance in the allowance account, net accounts receivable would appear as follows on the balance sheet:

```
Accounts receivable. . . . . . . . . . . . . . . . .    $100,000
     Less: Allowance for uncollectible accounts. . . . .       4,000    $96,000
```

Sometimes the Allowance for Uncollectible Accounts account has a balance before adjustment. Under the percentage of sales method, any existing balance in the allowance account will *not* influence the size of the uncollectible accounts adjusting entry.

Some accountants believe this method is theoretically preferable because it bases the estimate of expense solely on the sales revenue of the same period and gives a more precise matching of expense and revenue than the alternative method.

Percentage of Accounts Receivable Method.   The *percentage of accounts receivable method* is designed to adjust the Allowance for Uncollectible Accounts balance to a certain percentage of accounts receivable. It may use one overall percentage or may use a different percentage for each age category of receivable. To illustrate the use of one overall percentage, assume that on the basis of past experience the Fox Company estimates that 5% of its outstanding receivables of $100,000 as of December 31, 1995, will ultimately prove to be uncollectible. The Allowance for Uncollectible Accounts already has a *debit* balance of $1,000. The journal entry to adjust the balance in the allowance account to its required $5,000 ($100,000 × 0.05) *credit* balance is as follows:

```
Uncollectible Accounts Expense . . . . . . . . . . . . . .    6,000
     Allowance for Uncollectible Accounts. . . . . . . . . .             6,000
     To adjust allowance for possible uncollectible accounts.
```

In T-account form, the effect of this entry can be shown as follows:

Uncollectible Accounts Expense		Allowance for Uncollectible Accounts	
Dec. 31 Adjustment 6,000		Beg. bal. 1,000	Dec. 31 Adjustment 6,000
			Bal. after adjustment 5,000

Thus, the percentage of accounts receivable method requires that you (1) determine the desired ending credit balance of Allowance for Uncollectible Accounts and (2) determine the amount that needs to be recorded in a journal entry to bring the account to this desired ending credit balance.

Aging Schedule.   Alternatively, an **aging schedule** may be used to apply a different percentage for each age category of receivable. An aging schedule for the Rogers Company is presented in Illustration 3.5, showing the age of each customer's account. As can be seen from Illustration 3.5, under this method the age of the accounts is the basis for estimating uncollectibility. For example, only 1% of the accounts not yet due (sales made less than 30 days prior to the end of the accounting period) is expected to be uncollectible. At the other extreme, 50% of all accounts over 90 days past due is expected to become worthless. The journal entry amount is still affected by the amount already in the allowance account prior to adjustment. For instance, Illustration 3.5 shows that $33,150 is needed in the allowance account. If the account already has a credit balance of $5,000 before adjustment, the adjusting entry would be made for $28,150.

Subsequent Write-offs.   Later, when an account is determined to be uncollectible, an entry is made debiting the Allowance for Uncollectible Accounts and crediting Accounts Receivable. Note that this entry has no effect on net income or on the valuation of the accounts receivable. The expense and the reduced valuation for the asset were recognized when the adjusting entry for estimated uncollectibles was made. The write-off entry merely gives recognition to an event that was anticipated when the allowance was established.

If, by chance, an error was made in writing off an individual customer's account (as shown by the collection of the account), an entry is made debiting Accounts Receivable and crediting the Allowance for Uncollectible Accounts for the full amount of the account previously written off. Then the cash collection is recorded as a debit to Cash and a credit to Accounts Receivable.

The allowance method is not acceptable for tax purposes. Instead, a company must wait until an account becomes uncollectible and then debit Uncollectible Accounts Expense and credit Accounts Receivable. This method is called *the direct write-off method.* The direct write-off method is not acceptable for accounting purposes unless the amounts involved are

Illustration 3.5
ACCOUNTS RECEIVABLE AGING SCHEDULE

			Number of Days Past Due			
Customer	Accounts Receivable Balance	Not Yet Due	1–30	31–60	61–90	Over 90
X	$ 8,000					$ 8,000
Y	16,000		$ 12,000	$ 4,000		
Z	4,000				$ 800	3,200
All others	800,000	$560,000	200,000	20,000	5,000	15,000
Totals	$828,000	$560,000	$212,000	$24,000	$5,800	$26,200
Estimated uncollectible percentage		1%	5%	10%	25%	50%
Estimated amount uncollectible	$ 33,150	$ 5,600	$ 10,600	$ 2,400	$1,450	$13,100

ROGERS COMPANY
Analysis of Accounts Receivable
December 31, 1995

immaterial. The direct write-off method (1) does not match (in the same accounting period) the uncollectible accounts expense against the sales revenue that resulted in the bad debts, and (2) fails to reduce accounts receivable down to their net realizable value on the balance sheet.

Liability/Revenue Adjustments—Unearned Revenues

A liability/revenue adjustment involving unearned revenues covers situations in which a customer has transferred assets, usually cash, to the selling company before the receipt of merchandise or services. When assets are received before being earned, a liability called **unearned revenue** is created. Such receipts are debited to the asset account, Cash, and credited to a liability account. The liability account credited may be called *Unearned Fees, Revenue Received in Advance, Advances by Customers,* or some similar title. The seller must either provide the services or return the customer's money. By performing the services, the company earns revenue and cancels the liability.

Companies receive advance payments for many items, such as delivery services, tickets, and magazine or newspaper subscriptions. While we only illustrate and discuss advanced receipt of delivery fees, the other items are treated similarly.

Unearned Delivery Fees. On December 7, Speedy Delivery Company received $4,500 from a customer in payment for future delivery services. The following journal entry was recorded:

```
1995
Dec. 7  Cash . . . . . . . . . . . . . . . . . . . . . . . . . .   4,500
            Unearned Delivery Fees . . . . . . . . . . . . .          4,500
        To record the receipt of cash from a customer in
        payment for future delivery services.
```

The two T-accounts relating to delivery fees are Unearned Delivery Fees (a liability) and Service Revenue. These accounts appear as follows on December 31, 1995 (before adjustment):

(Dr.)	**Unearned Delivery Fees**	(Cr.)
	1995 Dec. 7 Cash received in advance	4,500

(Dr.)	**Service Revenue**	(Cr.)
	1995 Bal. before adjustment	10,700*

*The $10,700 balance came from transactions discussed in Chapter 2.

The balance in the Unearned Delivery Fees liability account established when Speedy Delivery received the cash will be converted into revenue as the company performs the delivery services. Before Speedy Delivery prepares its financial statements, an adjusting entry must be made to transfer the amount of the services performed by the company from a liability account to a revenue account. If we assume that Speedy Delivery earned one third of the $4,500 in the Unearned Delivery Fees account by December 31, then the company will transfer $1,500 to the Service Revenue account as follows:

Adjustment 6—
Revenue
Earned

```
1995
Dec. 31  Unearned Delivery Fees . . . . . . . . . . . . . . .   1,500
             Service Revenue . . . . . . . . . . . . . . . . .          1,500
         To transfer a portion of delivery fees from the
         liability account to the revenue account.
```

After posting the adjusting entry, the T-accounts would appear as follows:

Decreased
by $1,500

(Dr.)	**Unearned Delivery Fees**	(Cr.)
1995 Dec. 31 Adjustment 6 1,500	1995 Dec. 7 Cash received in advance	4,500
	Bal. after adjustment	3,000

(Dr.)	**Service Revenue**	*(Cr.)*
	1995	
	Bal. before adjustment 10,700	
	Dec. 31 Adjustment 6 1,500	
	Bal. after adjustment 12,200	

Increased by $1,500

Speedy Delivery reports the service revenue in its income statement for 1995. The company reports the $3,000 balance in the Unearned Delivery Fees account as a liability in the balance sheet. In 1996, the company will likely earn the $3,000 and transfer it to a revenue account.

In initially recording the receipt of the $4,500 from a customer, an alternative procedure could have been followed. Instead of crediting Unearned Delivery Fees, the credit could have been to Service Revenue as follows:

```
1995
Dec. 7   Cash  . . . . . . . . . . . . . . . . . . . . . . . . . .   4,500
             Service Revenue.  . . . . . . . . . . . . . . . . .          4,500
         To record the receipt of cash from a customer in
         payment for future delivery services.
```

If this alternative had been chosen, the adjusting entry would have been a debit to Service Revenue for $3,000 and a credit to Unearned Delivery Fees for $3,000. This adjustment would establish the liability for the unearned portion of the delivery fees and would reduce the revenue by that same $3,000 amount. The end result is the same as the original procedure, as shown in the following T-accounts after adjustment:

Service Revenue

1995		1995	
Dec. 31 Adjustment 3,000		Bal. before adjustment 10,700	
		Dec. 7 Cash received 4,500	
		Bal. after adjustment 12,200	

Unearned Delivery Fees

	1995	
	Dec. 31 Adjustment 3,000	

Notice that the Service Revenue account has an ending balance of $12,200 and the Unearned Delivery Fees account has an ending balance of $3,000. These balances are the same as under the original procedure. The adjusting entry will depend on which account was originally credited for the receipt of $4,500 from the customer.

If Speedy Delivery does not perform the services, the company would have to refund the money to the delivery service customers. For instance, assume that for some reason, Speedy Delivery could not perform the remaining $3,000 of delivery services and would have to refund the money. Then, the company would make the following entry:

Unearned Delivery Fees	3,000	
Cash		3,000
To record the refund of unearned delivery fees.		

Thus, the company must either perform the services or refund the fees. This fact may serve to strengthen your understanding that unearned delivery fees and similar items are liabilities.

The adjusting entries for deferred items are made for data already recorded in a company's asset and liability accounts. Adjusting entries for accrued items, which we discuss in the next section, are made for business data not yet recorded in the accounting records. We will continue using Speedy Delivery Company for our example transactions.

ADJUSTMENTS FOR ACCRUED ITEMS

Accrued items require two types of adjusting entries: asset/revenue adjustments and liability/expense adjustments. The first group—asset/revenue adjustments—involves accrued assets; the second group—liability/expense adjustments—involves accrued liabilities.

Asset/Revenue Adjustments—Accrued Assets

Accrued assets are assets that exist at the end of an accounting period but have not yet been recorded. These assets represent rights to receive future payments that are not due at the balance sheet date. To present an accurate picture of the affairs of the business on the balance sheet, these rights must be recognized at the end of an accounting period by preparing an adjusting entry to correct the account balances. An example of this type of adjustment includes revenues earned but not recorded or billed. To indicate the dual nature of these adjustments, a related revenue is recorded in addition to the asset recorded. These adjustments may also be called **accrued revenues** because the revenues must also be recorded.

Interest Revenue.   Interest received periodically on savings accounts is literally earned moment by moment. Rarely is payment of the interest made on the last day of the accounting period. Thus, the accounting records normally will not show the amount of interest revenue earned, which affects the amount of total assets owned by the investor, unless the company makes an adjusting entry. The adjusting entry needed at the end of the accounting period debits a receivable account (an asset) and credits a revenue account to record the interest earned and the asset owned.

For example, assume Speedy Delivery Company has some money in a savings account. On December 31, 1995, the money on deposit has earned one month's interest, although the company has received no money for the interest. The interest earned in December is $600. An entry must be made to show the amount of interest earned by December 31, 1995, as well as the amount of the asset, interest receivable (the right to receive this interest). The entry to record the accrual of revenue is:

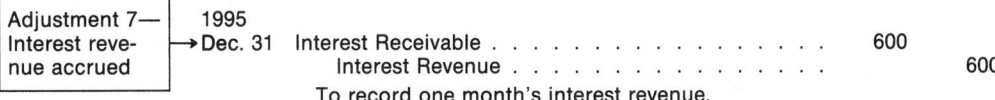

Adjustment 7— Interest revenue accrued	1995		
	Dec. 31	Interest Receivable	600	
		Interest Revenue		600
		To record one month's interest revenue.		

The T-accounts relating to interest would appear as follows:

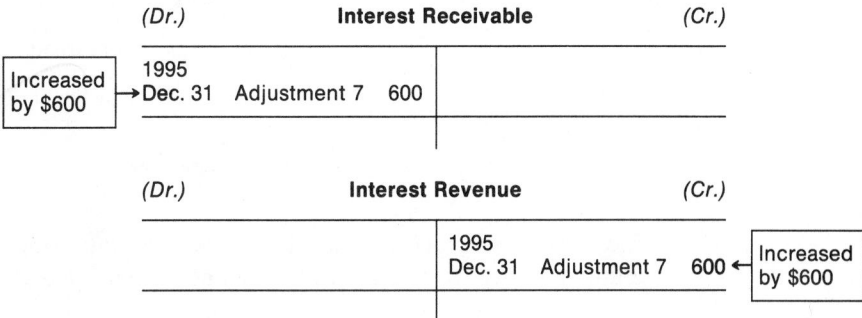

Speedy Delivery reports the $600 debit balance in Interest Receivable as an asset in the December 31, 1995, balance sheet. This asset accumulates gradually with the passage of time. The $600 credit balance in Interest Revenue is the interest earned during the month. You will recall that in **recording revenue under accrual basis accounting, it does not matter whether the company collects the actual cash during the year or not.** Regardless of whether the company receives the interest or not, the interest revenue earned is reported in the income statement for the year.

Unbilled Delivery Fees. A company may perform services for customers in one accounting period while it bills for the services in a different accounting period.

Speedy Delivery Company performed $1,000 of delivery services on account for a client in the last few days of December. Since it takes time to do the paper work, Speedy Delivery will bill the client for the services in January. The necessary adjusting journal entry at December 31, 1995, is:

Adjustment 8— Unbilled revenues	1995		
	Dec. 31	Accounts Receivable (or Delivery Fees Receivable) . .	1,000	
		Service Revenue		1,000
		To record unbilled delivery services performed in December.		

After posting the adjusting entry, the T-accounts will appear as follows:

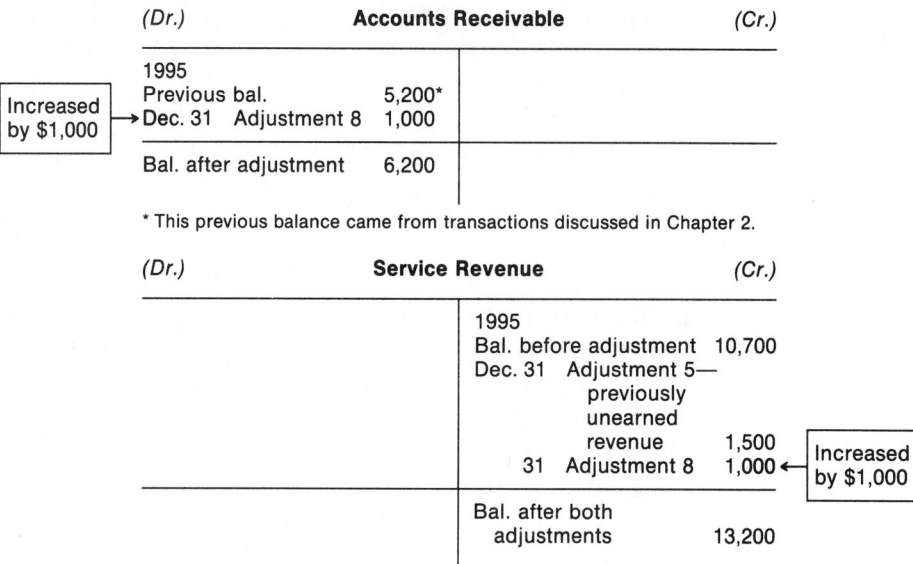

(Dr.)	Accounts Receivable		(Cr.)
1995			
Previous bal.		5,200*	
Dec. 31 Adjustment 8		1,000	
Bal. after adjustment		6,200	

Increased by $1,000

* This previous balance came from transactions discussed in Chapter 2.

(Dr.)	Service Revenue		(Cr.)
	1995		
	Bal. before adjustment		10,700
	Dec. 31 Adjustment 5—		
	previously		
	unearned		
	revenue		1,500
	31 Adjustment 8		1,000
	Bal. after both		
	adjustments		13,200

Increased by $1,000

The service revenue appears in the income statement, and the asset, accounts receivable, appears in the balance sheet.

Liability/Expense Adjustments—Accrued Liabilities

Accrued liabilities are liabilities that exist at the end of an accounting period but have not yet been recorded. They represent obligations to make payments not legally due at the balance sheet date, such as employee salaries. At the end of the accounting period, the company recognizes these obligations by preparing an adjusting entry including both a liability and an expense. For this reason, these obligations may also be called **accrued expenses.**

Salaries. The recording of the payment of employee salaries usually involves a debit to an expense account and a credit to Cash. Unless a company pays salaries on the last day of the accounting period for a pay period ending on that date, it must make an adjusting entry to record any salaries incurred but not yet paid.

Speedy Delivery Company paid $3,600 of salaries on Friday, December 28, 1995, to cover the first four weeks of December. The entry made at that time was:

```
1995
Dec. 28  Salaries Expense . . . . . . . . . . . . . . . . .   3,600
             Cash. . . . . . . . . . . . . . . . . . . . . .          3,600
         Paid truck driver salaries for the first four weeks of
         December.
```

Assuming that the last day of December 1995 falls on a Monday, the above expense account does not show salaries earned by employees for the last day of the month. Nor does the account show the employer's obligation to pay these salaries. The T-accounts pertaining to salaries appear as follows before adjustment:

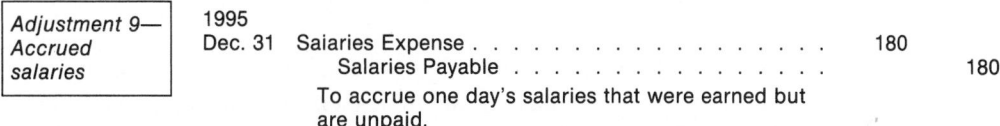

(Dr.)	Salaries Expense	(Cr.)	(Dr.)	Salaries Payable	(Cr.)
1995				1995	
Dec. 28	3,600			Dec. 28 Bal. –0–	

If salaries are \$3,600 for four weeks, they are \$900 per week. For a five-day workweek, daily salaries are \$180. Speedy Delivery needs the following adjusting entry on December 31 to accrue salaries for one day:

Adjustment 9—
Accrued
salaries

1995			
Dec. 31	Saiaries Expense	180	
	Salaries Payable		180
	To accrue one day's salaries that were earned but are unpaid.		

After adjustment, the two T-accounts involved appear as follows:

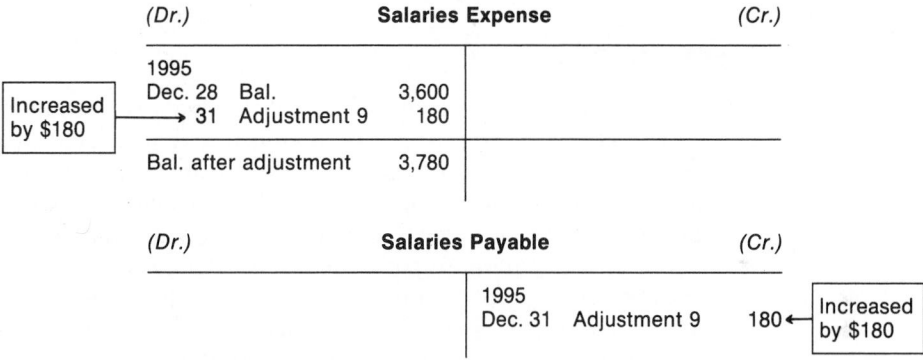

(Dr.)		Salaries Expense		(Cr.)
1995				
Increased by \$180	Dec. 28	Bal.	3,600		
→ 31	Adjustment 9	180		
Bal. after adjustment		3,780		

(Dr.)		Salaries Payable		(Cr.)
		1995		
		Dec. 31	Adjustment 9	180 ← *Increased by \$180*

The debit in the adjusting journal entry brings the month's salaries expense up to its correct \$3,780 amount for income statement purposes. The credit to Salaries Payable records the \$180 salary liability to employees. The balance sheet shows salaries payable as a liability.

Another example of a liability/expense adjustment is when a company incurs interest on a note payable. The debit would be to Interest Expense, and the credit would be to Interest Payable. Examples of this adjustment are given in Chapter 10.

EFFECTS OF FAILING TO PREPARE ADJUSTING ENTRIES

Objective 5
Determine the
effects of failing to
prepare adjusting
entries

Failure to prepare proper adjusting entries causes net income and the balance sheet to be in error. Illustration 3.6 shows the effect on net income and balance sheet items of failing to record each of the major types of adjusting entries.

Illustration 3.6
EFFECTS OF FAILURE TO RECOGNIZE ADJUSTMENTS

Failure to Recognize	Effect on Net Income	Effect on Balance Sheet Items
1. Consumption of the benefits of an asset (prepaid expense)	Overstates net income	Overstates assets Overstates retained earnings
2. Earning of previously un-earned revenues	Understates net income	Overstates liabilities Understates retained earnings
3. Accrual of assets	Understates net income	Understates assets Understates retained earnings
4. Accrual of liabilities	Overstates net income	Understates liabilities Overstates retained earnings

Using Speedy Delivery Company as an example, this chapter has discussed and illustrated many of the typical entries that companies must make at the end of an accounting period. You will study other examples of adjusting entries in later chapters.

CLOSING ENTRIES

Objective 6
Prepare closing entries

One step remains in our illustration of the financial accounting process—a step known as *closing the books*. As illustrated, after adjusting entries have been prepared and posted, the accounts contain basically two types of information: (1) information relating to the revenue and expense transactions for the period just ended (reported in the income statement) and (2) information on financial condition (reported in the balance sheet).

The first type of information is found in the expense and revenue accounts. As already indicated, these accounts are temporary subdivisions of the Retained Earnings account. They help the accountant fulfill a most important task—the determination of periodic net income. But after the financial statements for the period have been prepared, these temporary accounts have served their purpose. They must now be brought to a zero balance, or be "closed," to use accounting jargon. In this way, information pertaining to the next period can be gathered in them.

The balance in each expense and revenue account is transferred to an account called **Income Summary.** This is a *clearing* account used only at the end of the accounting period. It summarizes the expenses and revenues for the period, with the difference between these two being either net income or a net loss. Since revenue accounts have credit balances, they are debited and Income Summary credited. Conversely, expense accounts have debit balances, so they are credited and Income Summary debited. The Income Summary now contains either a debit (net loss) or a credit (net income) balance; it is then debited or credited to bring it to a zero balance. Retained Earnings is credited or debited to keep the entry in balance. With the making of this last entry, the books are closed. Note carefully that only expense and revenue accounts and the Income Summary account are closed. If dividends are recorded by debiting Retained Earnings and crediting Cash, no closing entry for that item is required. But, if dividends are recorded by debiting a separate Dividends account and crediting Cash, the Dividends account must be credited and Retained Earnings debited as part of the closing process.

The closing process, using T-accounts and assuming there is net income for the period, is as shown below.

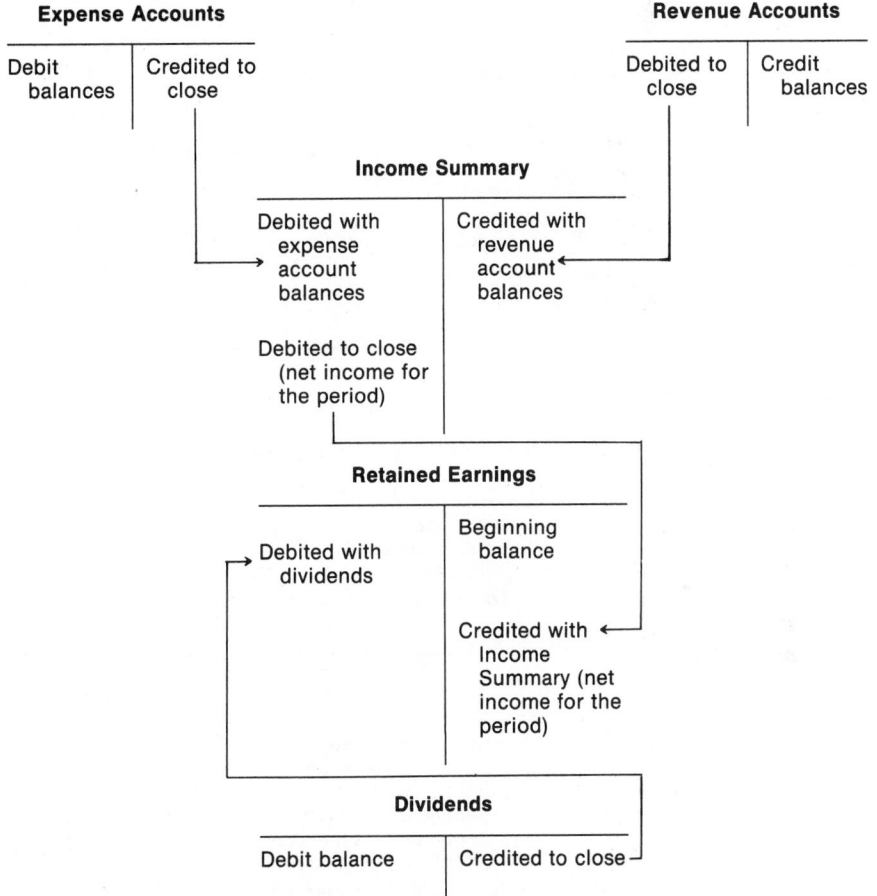

The **closing process** is (1) the act of transferring the balances in the revenue and expense accounts to a clearing account called Income Summary and then to Retained Earnings, and (2) the act of transferring the balance in the Dividends account (if it is used) to the Retained Earnings account. The closing process reduces revenue, expense, and Dividends account balances to zero so they will be ready to receive data for the next accounting period. Assume the income statement shown in Illustration 3.7 is for the Speedy Delivery Company. The accounts to be closed are all of the expense and revenue accounts shown in the income statement.

Illustration 3.7

SPEEDY DELIVERY COMPANY
Income Statement
For the Month Ended December 31, 1995

Revenues:

Service revenue		$13,200
Interest revenue		600
Total revenue.		$13,800

Expenses:

Advertising expense	$ 50	
Gas and oil expense	680	
Salaries expense	3,780	
Utilities expense	150	
Insurance expense	200	
Rent expense.	400	
Supplies expense.	500	
Depreciation expense—trucks.	750	
Uncollectible accounts expense	700	
Total expenses		7,210
Net income.		$ 6,590

In journal form, the closing entries would read:

```
1995
Dec. 31  Service Revenue . . . . . . . . . . . . . . . . . . .  13,200
         Interest Revenue . . . . . . . . . . . . . . . . . . .     600
              Income Summary. . . . . . . . . . . . . . . . .          13,800
         To close the revenue accounts.


     31  Income Summary. . . . . . . . . . . . . . . . . . . .   7,210
              Advertising Expense . . . . . . . . . . . . . . .             50
              Gas and Oil Expense . . . . . . . . . . . . . . .            680
              Salaries Expense . . . . . . . . . . . . . . . . .          3,780
              Utilities Expense . . . . . . . . . . . . . . . . .           150
              Insurance Expense . . . . . . . . . . . . . . . .            200
              Rent Expense . . . . . . . . . . . . . . . . . . .           400
              Supplies Expense. . . . . . . . . . . . . . . . .            500
              Depreciation Expense—Trucks . . . . . . . . . .            750
              Uncollectible Accounts Expense. . . . . . . . .            700
         To close the expense accounts.


     31  Income Summary. . . . . . . . . . . . . . . . . . . .   6,590
              Retained Earnings . . . . . . . . . . . . . . . .          6,590
         To close the Income Summary account.
```

When the entries are posted, each of the company's expense and revenue accounts will be reduced to a zero balance. Thus, they are ready to accumulate data on the operations for the year 1996. Note that Retained Earnings will have the same balance that it would have had if all expenses and revenues had been entered directly in it. But the use of expense and revenue accounts permits classification of these elements and makes them readily available for reporting in the income statement.

One more account must be closed. The Dividends account has a debit balance of $3,000. This account is closed directly to Retained Earnings as follows:

```
1995
Dec. 31   Retained Earnings . . . . . . . . . . . . . . . . .   3,000
              Dividends . . . . . . . . . . . . . . . . . . .           3,000
          To close the Dividends account.
```

The Use of a Work Sheet

The appendix to this chapter describes and illustrates how a work sheet could have been used in the above example. The use of such a work sheet is optional but often helpful.

The Financial Accounting Process Summarized

The steps involved in the operation of an accounting system are often referred to collectively as the accounting cycle. These steps include:

1. Journalizing transactions (and other events) in the journal.
2. Posting journal entries to ledger accounts.
3. Taking a trial balance of the accounts.
4. Journalizing the needed adjusting entries.
5. Posting the adjusting entries to the accounts.
6. Preparing the financial statements.
7. Journalizing the closing entries.
8. Posting the closing entries to the accounts.

THE CLASSIFIED BALANCE SHEET

Objective 7
Prepare a classi-
fied balance sheet

An **unclassified balance sheet** has only major categories labeled assets, liabilities, and stockholders' equity. A **classified balance sheet** subdivides at least some of the three major categories in order to provide useful information for interpretation and analysis by users of financial statements.

An example of a classified balance sheet is given in Illustration 3.8. It contains major categories of assets and liabilities. Accounts are then classified into these major categories. Notice that assets appear above liabilities and stockholders' equity in the illustration. This vertical format is as appropriate as the horizontal format for either a classified or unclassified balance sheet. The horizontal format has assets on the left side and liabilities and stockholders' equity on the right side.

Definitions of the items shown in Illustration 3.8 and listings of other classifications and items that could be included in a classified balance sheet follow the illustration.

Illustration 3.8
A CLASSIFIED BALANCE SHEET

WEST CORPORATION
Balance Sheet
June 30, 1995

Assets

Current assets:

Cash		$ 40,000
Accounts receivable.		55,000
Notes receivable		15,000
Prepaid insurance.		2,000
Total current assets			$112,000

Property, plant, and equipment:

Land		$114,000	
Building	$300,000		
Less: Accumulated depreciation	100,000	200,000	
Store equipment	$ 75,000		
Less: Accumulated depreciation	15,000	60,000	
Office equipment	$ 18,000		
Less: Accumulated depreciation	6,000	12,000	
Total property, plant, and equipment			386,000
Total assets.			$498,000

Liabilities and Stockholders' Equity

Current liabilities:

Accounts payable	$ 25,000
Notes payable.	6,000
Wages payable	800
Unearned subscriptions revenue	1,100
Total current liabilities.	$ 32,900

Long-term liabilities:

Notes payable, 10%, due in 2006	150,000
Total liabilities	$182,900

Stockholders' equity:

Capital stock	$250,000
Retained earnings.	65,100
Total stockholders' equity	315,100
Total liabilities and stockholders' equity	$498,000

Current Assets

Current assets are cash and other assets that will be converted to cash or used up during a relatively short period of time, usually a year or less. Current assets are normally listed in the order of liquidity (how readily they can be converted to cash).

The current assets commonly found in a service-type business are as follows:

Cash includes deposits in banks available for current operations at the balance sheet date, plus cash on hand consisting of currency, undeposited checks, drafts, and money orders. Normally, cash is the first current asset to appear in a balance sheet.

Marketable securities are *temporary investments* made to earn a return on idle cash. The purpose of such investments is to earn additional money on cash that is not required in the business at the present time but will probably be needed in a short time.

An **accounts receivable** is an amount owed to a concern by a customer (debtor). The account receivable arises when a service (or merchandise) is sold and cash is not received immediately. Normally, no written evidence of indebtedness is given by the customer except by affixing his or her signature to the sales invoice or delivery ticket.

A *note* is an unconditional written promise to pay a definite sum of money at a certain or determinable date, usually with interest at a specified rate. A note is a *note receivable* on the balance sheet of the enterprise to which the note is given and is a *note payable* on the balance sheet of the promisor. A note receivable arises (*a*) when a sale is made and a note is taken from the customer, (*b*) when a customer gives a note for an amount due on open account, or (*c*) when money is loaned and a note is received as evidence.

Interest receivable arises when interest has been earned but not collected at the balance sheet date because the amount is not due until later. Items similar to interest receivable that are also current assets are rent receivable and royalties receivable.

Prepaid expenses are items that have been paid for in advance of their usage. Such items will be used up during the next accounting period. If they were not paid for in advance, they would require the disbursement of cash in the following period.

Long-Term Investments

A **long-term investment** usually consists of securities of another company or enterprise held with the intention of (*a*) obtaining control of another company, (*b*) securing a permanent source of income for the investor, or (*c*) establishing friendly business relations. The long-term investment classification in the balance sheet (not shown in Illustration 3.8) does not include those securities purchased for short-term purposes with temporarily unneeded cash. For most businesses, long-term investments may take the form of capital stock of other corporations or bonds of other entities. Occasionally long-term investments include funds accumulated for specific purposes, buildings that are rented to others, and plant sites for future use.

Property, Plant, and Equipment

Property, plant, and equipment are types of assets acquired for use in a business rather than for resale. Property, plant, and equipment also are termed *plant assets* or *fixed assets*. They are called fixed assets because they are to be used for long-term purposes. Several of the more common types of property, plant, and equipment are described below:

Land is ground upon which the business buildings of the enterprise are located.

Buildings that appear in the property, plant, and equipment section of a balance sheet are structures used to carry on the business; buildings owned as investments are not included as plant assets.

Machinery is heavy equipment used in manufacturing a product or performing a service for a customer.

Store equipment, or **store fixtures,** includes items such as showcases, counters, tools, chairs, and cash registers.

Office equipment, or **office fixtures,** includes items such as file cabinets, calculators, typewriters, computers, desks, and chairs.

Delivery equipment, or trucks used in delivering goods to customers.

Accumulated depreciation is a contra asset account to depreciable assets such as buildings, machinery, and equipment. It shows total depreciation taken to date on the assets.

Intangible Assets

Intangible assets (not shown in Illustration 3.8) consist of the noncurrent, nonphysical assets of a business. Costs of intangible assets must be charged to expense over the period benefited. Among the intangible assets are special grants by governmental bodies, such as leaseholds, copyrights, patents, and goodwill.

Leaseholds are rights to use rented properties, usually for a number of years.

A **copyright** is granted by the federal government and gives the owner the exclusive privilege of publication for a period of time.

A **patent** is a right granted by the federal government to an inventor or the owner of an invention whereby he or she alone has the authority to manufacture a product or to use a process for a period of time.

Goodwill is an intangible value that is attached to a business because its management has the ability to earn larger net income per dollar of stockholders' equity than earned by competitors in the same industry. The ability to produce superior profits is a valuable resource of a business. Normally, goodwill will be recorded only when it is purchased, and then only at the price paid for it.

Current Liabilities

A **current liability** is a debt—usually due within one year—the payment of which normally will require the use of current assets. Examples of current liabilities follow:

Accounts payable are amounts owed to creditors for items purchased from them. In the balance sheet, accounts payable are shown in one amount, which is the sum of the individual accounts payable.

ETHICS   A CLOSER LOOK

The Carlton Delivery Service Company is owned by Shelly Birdsong. She had run the company for several years, but in 1994 she decided to hire Jack Stevens to manage the company and agreed to pay him a bonus of 10% of net income each year.

In late November 1995, Jack calculated the bonus he was going to receive for 1995. Net income was going to be about $40,000, giving him a bonus of $4,000.

Jack decided to make two changes that would have an impact on net income. First, he decided to use the current delivery trucks for six years instead of their original useful lives of three years. He believed that this change in policy would be cost effective for the company. He believed the quality of delivery service would not suffer significantly and the increased maintenance costs would be immaterial. This action would reduce depreciation expense for this year and each of the next three years by $40,000. (Depreciation on the old trucks would be $10,000 per year over their remaining lives as compared to $50,000 per year if new trucks were purchased at this time and depreciated over three years.)

Second, Jack decided to change the percentage that was used to record uncollectible accounts expense. The percentage used in the past was 5% of net sales. A large credit balance had developed in the Allowance for Uncollectible Accounts. This led Jack to believe that the percentage being used was too high. He decided to change the percentage to 3%. The result of this change would be to increase net income by $2,000.

As a result of these two changes, net income will be increased by $42,000 (from $40,000 to $82,000), and Jack's bonus will increase by $4,200 (from $4,000 to $8,200).

Required
a.   Did Jack behave unethically in making these changes?
b.   What would you do if you were Shelly Birdsong when you became aware of these decisions?

Notes payable are unconditional written promises to pay a certain sum of money at a definite future date. The notes may arise from borrowing money from a bank, the purchase of assets, or the giving of a note in settlement of an account payable. Notes payable to banks are known as *nontrade notes;* those arising from purchases are known as *trade notes.* Generally, only notes payable due in one year or less are included as current liabilities.

Taxes withheld from employees are items such as federal income taxes, state income taxes, and social security taxes withheld from employees' paychecks. These amounts will be paid to the proper governmental agencies.

Interest payable is interest that has accumulated on indebtedness, such as notes or bonds. This accrued interest has not been paid at the balance sheet date because the amount is not due until later.

Dividends payable are amounts declared payable to stockholders and represent a distribution of income. These declared dividends have not been paid at the balance sheet date and consequently are a liability of the corporation.

Salaries payable are amounts owed to employees for services rendered but for which payment has not been made at the balance sheet date. The wages have not been paid at the balance sheet date because they are not due until later.

Unearned revenues (revenues received in advance) result when payment is received for goods or services before it is earned, such as a subscription to a magazine. They represent a liability to return the asset received or to perform the agreed services or other contractual requirements, usually within the succeeding accounting period.

Long-Term Liabilities

Long-term liabilities are those not due for a relatively long period of time, usually more than one year. It is a good policy to show maturity dates in the balance sheet for all long-term liabilities.

Notes payable with maturity dates at least one year beyond the balance sheet date are long-term liabilities. **Bonds payable** are also long-term liabilities and are evidenced by formal printed certificates sometimes secured by liens (claims) on property, such as mortgages.

Stockholders' Equity

Stockholders' equity shows the owners' interest (equity) in the business. This interest is equal to the amount contributed plus the income left in the business.

Capital stock shows the capital paid into the company as the owners' investment.

Retained earnings show the cumulative income of the company less the amounts distributed to the owners in the form of dividends.

The chapter appendix describes a work sheet for a service company. The use of a work sheet is optional but helpful. Chapter 4 introduces accounting techniques for a merchandising company.

UNDERSTANDING THE LEARNING OBJECTIVES

1. Describe the basic characteristics of the cash basis and the accrual basis of accounting.
    *   The cash basis of accounting recognizes revenues when cash is received and recognizes expenses when cash is paid out.
    *   The accrual basis of accounting recognizes revenues when sales are made or services are performed, regardless of when cash is received; expenses are recognized as incurred, whether or not cash has been paid out.
    *   The accrual basis is more generally accepted than the cash basis because it provides a better matching of revenues and expenses.
2. Identify the reasons why adjusting entries must be made.
    *   Adjusting entries are needed to convert the amounts that are actually in the accounts to the amounts that should be in the accounts for proper periodic financial reporting.

- Adjusting entries reflect unrecorded economic activity that has taken place but has not yet been recorded.
3. Identify the classes and types of adjusting entries.
   - Deferred items consist of adjusting entries involving data previously recorded in accounts. Adjusting entries in this class normally involve moving data from asset and liability accounts to expense and revenue accounts. The two types of adjustments within this deferred items class are asset/expense adjustments and liability/revenue adjustments.
   - Accrued items consist of adjusting entries relating to activity on which no data have been previously recorded in the accounts. These entries involve the initial recording of assets and liabilities and the related revenues and expenses. The two types of adjustments within this accrued items class are asset/revenue adjustments and liability/expense adjustments.
4. Prepare adjusting entries.
   - Entries for deferred items and accrued items are illustrated in the chapter.
5. Determine the effects of failing to prepare adjusting entries.
   - Failure to prepare adjusting entries causes net income and the balance sheet to be in error.
6. Prepare closing entries.
   - Closing entries are necessary to reduce the balances of revenue, expense, and Dividends accounts to zero so they will be ready to receive data for the next accounting period.
   - Revenue account(s) are closed by debiting them and crediting the Income Summary account.
   - Expense account(s) are closed by crediting them and debiting the Income Summary account.
   - The balance in the Income Summary account represents the net income or net loss for the period.
   - To close the Income Summary account, the balance is transferred to the Retained Earnings account.
   - To close the Dividends account, the balance is transferred to the Retained Earnings account.
7. Prepare a classified balance sheet.
   - A classified balance sheet subdivides the major categories on the balance sheet into subcategories. For instance, a classified balance sheet subdivides assets into current assets; long-term investments; property, plant, and equipment; and intangible assets. It subdivides liabilities into current liabilities and long-term liabilities. Stockholders' equity at this point is no different in a classified balance sheet than in an unclassified balance sheet. Later chapters will show further subdivisions of the stockholders' equity section.
8. Prepare a work sheet for a service company (Appendix).
   - The work sheet is a columnar sheet of paper on which accountants

summarize information needed to make the adjusting and closing entries and to prepare the financial statements.

• Work sheets may vary in format. The work sheet illustrated in the chapter has 12 columns—two each for trial balance, adjustments, adjusted trial balance, income statement, statement of retained earnings, and balance sheet.

APPENDIX

THE WORK SHEET FOR A SERVICE COMPANY

*Objective 8
Prepare a work
sheet for a service
company*

In manually operated accounting systems containing large numbers of accounts, the accounting activities to be completed at the end of a financial reporting period may be organized and handled more efficiently through use of a work sheet. A **work sheet** is simply a sheet of paper containing a number of columns and lines for recording account titles, item descriptions, and dollar amounts. Since it is used internally only, it can take on a variety of forms. But to be of any real value, it will, at a minimum, contain columns for an unadjusted trial balance, adjusting entries, an income statement, and a balance sheet. A work sheet for Speedy Delivery Company is presented in Illustration 3.9 and discussed below.

The Trial Balance Columns

Instead of preparing a separate trial balance, the open accounts in the ledger are entered in the first pair of columns titled Trial Balance in the work sheet for the month ended December 31, 1995. The columns are summed, and the equality of the debits and credits in the ledger is shown by entering the totals ($65,930) immediately after the last item in the trial balance.

The Adjustments Columns

In the next pair of columns, all of the adjustments required to bring the accounts up to date prior to the preparation of financial statements are entered. The adjustments for Speedy Delivery Company are the ones presented in this chapter.

One advantage of a work sheet is that it assembles all of the accounts in one place, where they may easily be studied to determine the need for possible adjustment. As a result, entries are not likely to be overlooked.

After all of the adjusting entries are entered in the Adjustments columns, the two columns are totaled and their equality is noted as a partial check of the arithmetic accuracy of the work completed thus far.

The Adjusted Trial Balance Columns

After the adjustments have been entered, the adjusted balance of each account is determined and entered in the Adjusted Trial Balance columns.

Note carefully how the rules of debit and credit determine whether an entry increases or decreases the balance in the account. For example, Supplies on Hand has a debit balance of $1,400 which is decreased by a credit of $500 to a total of $900—the correct balance for financial reporting purposes.

The balances in the Adjusted Trial Balance columns are summed. The equality of the accounts with debit balances and those with credit balances is noted as a check upon the arithmetic accuracy of the work completed.

The Income Statement Columns

All of the accounts in the Adjusted Trial Balance columns that will appear in the Income Statement (the expense and revenue accounts) are now extended into the Income Statement columns—revenues as credits, expenses as debits. Each column is subtotaled, revealing revenues (credits) of $13,800 and expenses (debits) of $7,210. This means that the net income for the period amounted to $6,590. This amount is entered in the debit column to bring the two column totals into agreement. Note the similarity of the debit here to the debit in the Income Summary account to close or transfer net income to the Retained Earnings account. A net loss would, of course, be recorded in the opposite manner—that is, as a credit.

The Statement of Retained Earnings Columns

These columns contain the items that appear in the statement of retained earnings, namely: the $0 beginning balance of retained earnings as a credit, the $6,590 net income for the period as a credit, and the $3,000 of dividends as a debit. The columns are subtotaled, and the difference between the two subtotals, the ending balance of retained earnings, $3,590, is entered in the debit column in order to bring the two column totals into balance.

The Balance Sheet Columns

All of the asset, liability, and stockholders' equity accounts are extended into the Balance Sheet columns—assets as debits and the others as credits. Note that the ending $3,590 balance in Retained Earnings is carried into the credit column. Once again, to check the arithmetic accuracy of the work completed, the columns are totaled and their agreement is noted.

The Completed Work Sheet

Some accountants, in completing a work sheet, enter brief explanations keyed to the adjusting entries in the lower left-hand corner of the work

Illustration 3.9

SPEEDY DELIVERY COMPANY
Work Sheet
For the Month Ended December 31, 1995

Acct. No.	Account Titles	Trial Balance Debit	Trial Balance Credit	Adjustments Debit	Adjustments Credit	Adjusted Trial Balance Debit	Adjusted Trial Balance Credit	Income Statement Debit	Income Statement Credit	Statement of Retained Earnings Debit	Statement of Retained Earnings Credit	Balance Sheet Debit	Balance Sheet Credit
100	Cash	8,250				8,250						8,250	
103	Accounts Receivable	5,200		(8) 1,000		6,200						6,200	
107	Supplies on Hand	1,400			(3) 500	900						900	
108	Prepaid Insurance	2,400			(1) 200	2,200						2,200	
112	Prepaid Rent	1,200			(2) 400	800						800	
150	Trucks	40,000				40,000						40,000	
200	Accounts Payable		730				730						730
210	Unearned Delivery Fees		4,500	(6) 1,500			3,000						3,000
300	Capital Stock		50,000				50,000						50,000
310	Retained Earnings, 12/1/95		-0-				-0-				-0-		
320	Dividends	3,000				3,000				3,000			
400	Service Revenue		10,700		{(6) 1,500 / (8) 1,000}		13,200		13,200				
505	Advertising Expense	50				50		50					
506	Gas and Oil Expense	680				680		680					
507	Salaries Expense	3,600		(9) 180		3,780		3,780					
508	Utilities Expense	150				150		150					
		65,930	65,930										
512	Insurance Expense			(1) 200		200		200					
515	Rent Expense			(2) 400		400		400					
518	Supplies Expense			(3) 500		500		500					

No.	Account	Adjustments Dr	Adjustments Cr	Adjusted Trial Balance Dr	Adjusted Trial Balance Cr	Income Statement Dr	Income Statement Cr	Statement of Retained Earnings Dr	Statement of Retained Earnings Cr	Balance Sheet Dr	Balance Sheet Cr
521	Depreciation Expense—Trucks	(4) 750		750		750					
151	Accumulated Depreciation—Trucks		(4) 750		750						750
534	Uncollectible Accounts Expense	(5) 700		700		700					
104	Allowance for Uncollectible Accounts		(5) 700		700						700
121	Interest Receivable	(7) 600		600						600	
418	Interest Revenue		(7) 600		600		600				
206	Salaries Payable		(9) 180		180						180
		5,830	5,830	69,160	69,160	7,210	13,800	3,000	6,590	58,950	3,590
	Net Income					6,590			6,590		
						13,800	13,800	6,590	6,590		
	Retained Earnings, 12/31/95							3,590			3,590
										58,950	58,950

Adjustments explanations:
(1) To record insurance expense for December.
(2) To record rent expense for December.
(3) To record supplies expense during December.
(4) To record depreciation expense for December.
(5) To record uncollectible accounts expense for December.
(6) To transfer a portion of delivery fees from the liability account to the revenue account.
(7) To record one month's interest revenue.
(8) To record unbilled delivery services performed in December.
(9) To accrue one day's salaries that were earned but are unpaid.

> Adjustments explanations are optional.

> You may have to add accounts to enter the adjustments on the work sheet

> Column totals must be equal before proceeding.

> If the columns balance you are ready to prepare the financial statements.

Illustration 3.10

SPEEDY DELIVERY COMPANY
Statement of Retained Earnings
For the Month Ended December 31, 1995

Retained earnings, December 1, 1995	$ –0–
Net income for December	6,590
Total	$6,590
Less: Dividends	3,000
Retained earnings, December 31, 1995	$3,590

---

sheet. Such a practice is useful for complicated adjustments, but is not necessary for the relatively routine adjustments illustrated here.

When the work sheet has been completed, all of the information needed to prepare the financial statements is readily available. It need only be recast into a more formal format.

The income statement was shown in Illustration 3.7 (page 144). The statement of retained earnings and the balance sheet are shown in Illustrations 3.10 and 3.11, respectively.

Illustration 3.11

SPEEDY DELIVERY COMPANY
Balance Sheet
December 31, 1995
Assets

Cash		$ 8,250
Accounts receivable	$ 6,200	
Less: Allowance for uncollectible accounts	700	5,500
Supplies on hand		900
Prepaid insurance		2,200
Prepaid rent		800
Interest receivable		600
Trucks	40,000	
Less: Accumulated depreciation	750	39,250
Total assets		$57,500

Liabilities and Stockholders' Equity

Liabilities:		
Accounts payable		$ 730
Unearned delivery fees		3,000
Salaries payable		180
Total liabilities		$ 3,910
Stockholders' equity:		
Capital stock	$50,000	
Retained earnings	3,590	
Total stockholders' equity		53,590
Total liabilities and stockholders' equity		$57,500

Note, also, that it would be a relatively routine matter to journalize the adjusting and closing entries in the journal and then post them to the accounts. The adjusting entries can be readily prepared from information in the Adjustments columns and closing entries from the items in the Income Statement columns. But, since financial statements can be prepared from the work sheet, such entries are not likely to be entered formally in the journal and posted to the accounts at any time other than at the formal annual closing of the books. Thus, one of the real advantages of using a work sheet is that (monthly or quarterly) financial statements can be prepared without going through the work of journalizing and posting adjusting and closing entries. When adjusting and closing entries are prepared and posted, a post-closing trial balance is prepared to determine that the accounts are in balance.

The work sheet is a very convenient tool that assists in completing the accounting tasks at the end of the accounting period. While its use is optional, it is almost always used by accountants.

DEMONSTRATION PROBLEM 3–A

The trial balance of Korman Company for December 31, 1995, includes, among other items, the following account balances:

	Debits	Credits
Supplies on Hand	$ 6,000	
Prepaid Rent	25,200	
Buildings	200,000	
Accumulated Depreciation—Buildings . . .		$33,250
Salaries Expense	124,000	
Unearned Delivery Fees		4,000

Additional data

1. Some of the supplies represented by the $6,000 balance of the Supplies on Hand account have been consumed. An inventory count of the supplies actually on hand at December 31 totaled $2,400.
2. On May 1 of the current year, a rental payment of $25,200 was made for 12 months' rent; it was debited to Prepaid Rent.
3. The annual depreciation for the buildings is based on the cost shown in the Buildings account less an estimated salvage value of $10,000. The estimated useful lives of the buildings are 40 years each.
4. The salaries expense of $124,000 does not include $6,000 of unpaid salaries earned since the last payday.
5. The company has earned one fourth of the unearned delivery fees by December 31.
6. Delivery services of $600 were performed for a customer, but a bill has not yet been sent.

Required:

a. Prepare the adjusting journal entries for December 31, assuming adjusting entries are prepared only at year-end.

b. Based on the adjusted balance shown in the Accumulated Depreciation—Buildings account, how many years has Korman Company owned the building?

Solution to demonstration problem 3–A

a.

KORMAN COMPANY
GENERAL JOURNAL

Date		Account Titles and Explanation	Post. Ref.	Debit	Credit
1995 Dec.	31	Supplies Expense		3600	
		Supplies on Hand			3600
		To record supplies expense ($6,000 − $2,400).			
	31	Rent Expense		16800	
		Prepaid Rent			16800
		To record rent expense ($25,200 × 8/12).			
	31	Depreciation Expense—Buildings		4750	
		Accumulated Depreciation—Buildings			4750
		To record depreciation [($200,000 − $10,000) ÷ 40 years].			
	31	Salaries Expense		6000	
		Salaries Payable			6000
		To record accrued salaries.			
	31	Unearned Delivery Fees		1000	
		Service Revenue			1000
		To record delivery fees earned.			
	31	Accounts Receivable		600	
		Service Revenue			600
		To record delivery fees earned.			

b. Eight years; computed as:

$$\frac{\text{Total accumulated depreciation}}{\text{Annual depreciation expense}} = \frac{\$33,250 + \$4,750}{\$4,750} = 8$$

DEMONSTRATION PROBLEM 3–B

Post Company estimates its uncollectible accounts expense to be 1% of sales. Sales in 1995 were $1,125,000.

Required:

Prepare the journal entries for the following transactions:

a. The company prepared the adjusting entry for uncollectible accounts for 1995.
b. On January 15, 1996, the company decided that the account for John Nunn in the amount of $750 was uncollectible.
c. On February 12, 1996, John Nunn's check for $750 arrived.

Solution to demonstration problem 3–B

a. 1995
Dec. 31   Uncollectible Accounts Expense   11,250
　　　　　　Allowance for Uncollectible Accounts . . . .   　　　　11,250
　　　　　　To record estimated uncollectible accounts for
　　　　　　the year.

b. 1996
Jan. 15   Allowance for Uncollectible Accounts   750
　　　　　　Accounts Receivable—John Nunn . . . . . .   　　　　750
　　　　　　To write off the account of John Nunn as
　　　　　　uncollectible.

c. Feb. 12   Accounts Receivable—John Nunn   750
　　　　　　Allowance for Uncollectible Accounts . . . .   　　　　750
　　　　　　To correct the write-off of John Nunn's account
　　　　　　on January 15.

　　　　12   Cash   750
　　　　　　Accounts Receivable—John Nunn . . . . . .   　　　　750
　　　　　　To record the collection of John Nunn's
　　　　　　account receivable.

NEW TERMS

Accounting period   A time period normally of one month, one quarter, or one year into which an entity's life is arbitrarily divided for financial reporting purposes. *118*

Accounting year   An accounting period of one year. The accounting year may or may not coincide with the calendar year. *118*

Accounts payable   Amounts owed to creditors for items purchased from them. *148*

Accounts receivable   Amounts due from customers for services performed or merchandise sold on credit. *147*

Accrual basis of accounting   Recognizes revenues when sales are made or services are performed, regardless of when cash is received. Recognizes expenses as incurred, whether or not cash has been paid out. *116*

Accrued assets and liabilities   Assets and liabilities that exist at the end of an accounting period but have not yet been recorded; they represent rights to receive, or obligations to make, payments that are not legally due at the balance sheet date. Examples are accrued fees receivable and salaries payable. *138, 140*

Accrued items   See Accrued assets and liabilities. *120*

Accrued revenues and expenses   Other names for accrued assets and liabilities. *138, 140*

Accumulated depreciation account   A contra asset account that shows the total of all depreciation recorded on the asset up through the balance sheet date. *131, 148*

Adjusting entries   Journal entries made at the end of an accounting period to bring about a proper matching of revenues and expenses; reflect economic activity that has taken place but has not yet been recorded. Adjusting entries are made to bring the accounts to their proper balances before financial statements are prepared. *119*

Aging schedule   A means of classifying accounts receivable according to their age; used to determine the necessary balance in an Allowance for Uncollectible Accounts. A different uncollectibility percentage rate is used for each age category. *134*

Allowance for Uncollectible Accounts   A contra asset account to the Accounts Receivable account; it reduces accounts receivable to their net realizable value. Also called *Allowance for Doubtful Accounts* or *Allowance for Bad Debts*. *132*

Bad debts expense   See Uncollectible accounts expense.

Bonds payable   Long-term liabilities evidenced by formal printed certificates sometimes secured by liens (claims) on property. *150*

Book value   For depreciable assets, book value equals cost less accumulated depreciation. *131*

Buildings   Structures that are used to carry on the business. *148*

Calendar year   The normal year, which ends on December 31. *118*

Capital stock   Shows the capital paid into the company as the stockholders' investment. *150*

Cash   Includes deposits in banks available for current operations at the balance sheet date, plus cash on hand consisting of currency, undeposited checks, drafts, and money orders. *146*

Cash basis of accounting   Recognizes revenues when cash is received and recognizes expenses when cash is paid out. *116*

Classified balance sheet   Subdivides at least some of the major categories (assets, liabilities, and stockholders' equity) in order to provide useful information for interpretation and analysis by users of financial statements. *145*

Closing process   The act of transferring the balances in the revenue and expense accounts to a clearing account called Income Summary and then to the Retained Earnings account. The balance in the Dividends account is also transferred to the Retained Earnings account. *143*

Contra asset account   An account shown as a deduction from the asset to which it relates in the balance sheet; used to reduce the original cost of the asset down to its remaining undepreciated cost or book value. *131*

Copyright   Grants the owner the exclusive privilege of publication of written material. *148*

Current assets Cash and other assets that will be converted into cash or used up by the business during a relatively short period of time, usually a year or less. *146*

Current liabilities Debts, usually due within one year, the payment of which normally will require the use of current assets. *148*

Deferred items Adjusting entries involving data previously recorded in the accounts. Data are transferred from asset and liability accounts to expense and revenue accounts. Examples are prepaid expenses, depreciation, and unearned revenues. *120*

Delivery equipment Trucks used to deliver goods to customers. *148*

Depreciable amount The difference between an asset's cost and its estimated salvage value. *130*

Depreciable asset A manufactured asset such as a building, machine, vehicle, or equipment on which depreciation expense is recorded. *129*

Depreciation accounting The process of recording depreciation expense. *129*

Depreciation expense The amount of asset cost assigned as an expense to a particular time period. *129*

Depreciation formula (straight-line)   *129*

$$\frac{\text{Annual}}{\text{depreciation}} = \frac{\text{Asset cost} - \text{Estimated salvage value}}{\text{Estimated number of years of useful life}}$$

Dividends payable Amounts declared payable to stockholders and represent a distribution of income. *149*

Fiscal year An accounting year of any 12 consecutive months that may or may not coincide with the calendar year. For example, a company may have an accounting or fiscal year that runs from April 1 of one year to March 31 of the next. *118*

Goodwill An intangible value attaching to a business evidenced by the ability to earn larger net income per dollar of investment than that earned by competitors within the same industry. *148*

Income Summary account A clearing account used only at the end of an accounting period to summarize revenues and expenses for the period. *142*

Intangible assets Noncurrent, nonphysical assets of a business. *148*

Interest payable Arises when interest has been incurred but not yet paid at the balance sheet date because the amount is not due until later. *149*

Interest receivable Arises when interest has been earned but has not been collected at the balance sheet date. *147*

Land Ground on which the business buildings of the company are located. *148*

Leaseholds Rights to use leased properties. *148*

Long-term investment Usually securities of another company which the owner expects to hold over long periods of time, usually more than one year. *147*

Long-term liabilities Liabilities not due for a relatively long period of time, usually more than one year. *150*

Machinery   Heavy equipment used in manufacturing a product or performing a service for a customer. *148*

Marketable securities   Readily salable securities acquired with temporarily unneeded cash. *147*

Matching principle   An accounting principle requiring that expenses incurred in producing revenues be deducted from the revenues they generated during the accounting period. *119*

Note payable   An unconditional written promise to pay a definite sum of money at a certain or determinable date, usually with interest at a specified rate. *149*

Office equipment (office fixtures)   Items such as file cabinets, calculators, typewriters, computers, desks, and chairs. *148*

Patent   A right granted by the federal government to an inventor or the owner of an invention whereby he or she alone has the authority to manufacture a product or to use a process for a period of time. *148*

Prepaid expense   An asset awaiting assignment to expense. An example is prepaid insurance. Assets such as cash and accounts receivable are not prepaid expenses. *123, 147*

Property, plant, and equipment   They are acquired for use in a business rather than for resale; also called plant assets or fixed assets. *147*

Retained earnings   Show the cumulative income of the company less the amounts distributed to the owners in the form of dividends. *150*

Salaries payable   Amounts owed to employees for services rendered but for which payment has not been made at the balance sheet date. *149*

Salvage value (scrap value)   The amount that the company can probably sell the asset for at the end of its estimated useful life. *129*

Service potential   The benefits that can be obtained from assets. The future services that assets can render make assets "things of value" to a business. *124*

Stockholders' equity   Shows the owners' interest (equity) in the business. *150*

Store equipment (store fixtures)   Items such as showcases, counters, tools, chairs, and cash registers. *148*

Taxes withheld from employees   Income taxes and social security taxes withheld from employees. *149*

Unclassified balance sheet   Has only major categories labeled assets, liabilities, and stockholders' equity. *145*

Uncollectible accounts expense   An operating expense that a business incurs when it sells on credit; also called *doubtful accounts expense* or *bad debts expense. 132*

Unearned revenue   Assets received from customers before services are performed for them. Since the revenue has not been earned, it is a liability, often called *revenue received in advance* or *advances by customers. 135, 150*

Useful life   The estimated number of time periods that a company can make use of the asset. *129*

Work sheet   A columnar sheet of paper on which accountants have summarized information needed to make the adjusting and closing entries and to prepare the financial statements. *152*

SELF-TEST

True-False

Indicate whether each of the following statements is true or false.

1. Every adjusting entry affects at least one income statement account and one balance sheet account.
2. All calendar years are also fiscal years, but not all fiscal years are calendar years.
3. The accumulated depreciation account is an asset account that shows the amount of depreciation for the current year only.
4. The percentage-of-receivables method esti-

mates the uncollectible accounts from the credit sales of a given period.

5. Under the allowance method, income is recognized when an account receivable previously written off is collected.
6. The Unearned Delivery Fees account is a revenue account.
7. If all of the adjusting entries are not made, the financial statements will be incorrect.
8. After the closing process is complete, no balance can exist in any revenue, expense, Dividends, or Income Summary account.

Multiple-Choice

Select the best answer for each of the following questions.

1. An insurance policy premium of $1,200 was paid on September 1, 1995, to cover a one-year period from that date. An asset was debited on that date. Adjusting entries are prepared once a year, at year-end. The necessary adjusting entry at the company's year-end, December 31, 1995, is:

    a. Prepaid Insurance . . 400
        Insurance Expense .   400

    b. Insurance Expense . . 800
        Prepaid Insurance .   800

    c. Prepaid Insurance . . 800
        Insurance Expense .   800

    d. Insurance Expense . . 400
        Prepaid Insurance .   400

2. Refer to the previous problem. If an expense had been debited when the premium was paid on September 1, 1995, which of the choices in (1) would have been the correct adjusting entry on December 31, 1995?
3. The Supplies on Hand account has a balance of $1,500 at year-end. The actual amount of supplies on hand at the end of the period was $400. The necessary adjusting entry is:

    a. Supplies Expense. . . 1,100
        Supplies on Hand. .   1,100

    b. Supplies Expense. . .   400
        Supplies on Hand. .   400

    c. Supplies on Hand. . . 1,100
        Supplies Expense. .   1,100

    d. Supplies on Hand. . .   400
        Supplies Expense. .   400

4. A company purchased a truck for $20,000 on January 1, 1995. The truck has an estimated salvage value of $5,000 and is expected to last five years. Adjusting entries are prepared only at year-end. The necessary adjusting entry at December 31, 1995, the company's year-end, is:

    a. Depreciation Expense—Trucks . . . 4,000
        Accumulated Depreciation—Trucks   4,000

    b. Depreciation Expense—Trucks . . . 3,000
        Trucks   3,000

    c. Depreciation Expense—Trucks . . . 3,000
        Accumulated Depreciation—Trucks   3,000

d. Accumulated Depreci-
ation—Trucks . . . 3,000
Depreciation Ex-
pense—Trucks . 3,000

5. Which of the following statements is false?

a. Any existing balance in the Allowance for Uncollectible Accounts is ignored in calculating the uncollectible accounts expense under the percentage-of-sales method.

b. The percentage-of-receivables method may use either an overall rate or a different rate for each age category.

c. The Allowance for Uncollectible Accounts reduces accounts receivable to their net realizable value.

d. The allowance method must be used for tax purposes.

6. Clark Company uses the percentage-of-sales method in estimating uncollectible accounts. Clark expects 1% of net sales to be uncollectible for 1995. Total net sales for 1995 were $1,000,000, and the allowance account has a $3,000 debit balance. The uncollectible accounts expense for 1995 would be:

a. $13,000.
b. $10,000.
c. $7,000.
d. $9,970.
e. None of the above.

7. A company received cash of $24,000 on October 1, 1995, as subscriptions for a one-year period from that date. A liability account was credited when the cash was received. The magazine is to be published by the company and delivered to subscribers each month. The company prepares adjusting entries at the end of each month because it prepares financial statements each month. The adjusting entry the company would make at the end of each of the next 12 months would be:

a. Unearned Subscription
Fees 6,000
Subscription Fee
Revenue 6,000

b. Unearned Subscription
Fees 2,000
Subscription Fee
Revenue 2,000

c. Unearned Subscription
Fees 18,000
Subscription Fee
Revenue 18,000

d. Subscription Fee Revenue 2,000
Unearned Sub-
scription Fees . 2,000

8. When a company earns interest on a note receivable or on a bank account, the debit and credit are as follows:

	Debit	*Credit*
a.	Accounts Receivable	Interest Revenue
b.	Interest Receivable	Interest Revenue
c.	Interest Revenue	Accounts Receivable
d.	Interest Revenue	Interest Receivable

9. If $3,000 has been earned by a company's workers since the last payday in an accounting period, the necessary adjusting entry would be:

a. Debit an expense and credit a liability.
b. Debit an expense and credit an asset.
c. Debit a liability and credit an asset.
d. Debit a liability and credit an expense.

10. Which of the following statements is *false* regarding the closing process?

a. The Dividends account is closed to Income Summary.
b. The closing of expense accounts results in a debit to Income Summary.
c. The closing of revenues results in a credit to Income Summary.
d. The Income Summary account is closed to the Retained Earnings account.

11. Which of the following statements is *true* regarding the classified balance sheet?

a. Current assets include cash, accounts receivable, and equipment.

b. "Plant, property, and equipment" is one category of long-term assets.

c. Current liabilities include accounts payable, salaries payable, and notes receivable.

d. Stockholders' equity is subdivided into current and long-term categories.

Now turn to page 178 to check your answers.

QUESTIONS

1. Why are adjusting entries necessary? Why not treat every cash disbursement as an expense and every cash receipt as a revenue when the cash changes hands?

2. Give an example of each of the following:
   a. Equal growth of an expense and a liability.
   b. Earning of revenue that was previously recorded as unearned revenue.
   c. Equal growth of an asset and a revenue.
   d. Equal growth of an expense and decrease in an asset.

3. "Adjusting entries would not be necessary if the cash basis of accounting were followed (assuming no mistakes were made in recording cash transactions as they occurred). Under the cash basis, receipts that are of a revenue nature are considered revenue when received, and expenditures that are of an expense nature are considered expenses when paid. It is the use of the accrual basis of accounting, where an effort is made to match expenses incurred against the revenues they created, that makes adjusting entries necessary." Do you agree with this statement? Why?

4. Why don't accountants keep all the accounts at their proper balances continuously throughout the period so that adjusting entries would not have to be made before financial statements are prepared?

5. Identify the two major classes of adjusting entries and identify the types of adjusting entries that are included in each.

6. A fellow student makes the following statement: "It is easy to tell whether a company is using the cash or accrual basis of accounting. When an amount is paid for future rent or insurance services, a firm that is using the cash basis will debit an expense account while a firm that is using the accrual basis will debit an asset account." Is the student correct?

7. You notice that the Supplies on Hand account has a debit balance of $2,700 at the end of the accounting period. How would you determine the extent to which this account needs adjustment?

8. It may be said that some assets are converted into expenses as they expire and that some liabilities become revenues as they are earned. Give examples of asset and liability accounts for which the statement is true. Give examples of asset and liability accounts to which the statement does not apply.

9. What does the term *accrued liability* mean?

10. What is meant by the term *service potential?*

11. Give the depreciation formula for straight-line depreciation.

12. In view of the difficulty in estimating future events, would you recommend that accountants wait until collections are made from customers before recording sales revenue? Should they wait until known accounts prove to be uncollectible before charging an expense account?

13. What are the two major purposes to be accomplished in establishing an allowance for uncollectible accounts?

14. On the balance sheet what effect does the allowance for uncollectible accounts have on the accounts receivable balance?

15. What are the two basic methods for estimating uncollectible accounts for a period?

16. For a company using the allowance method of accounting for uncollectible accounts, which of the following directly affects its reported net income: (1) the establishment of the allowance, (2) the writing off of a specific account, or (3) the recovery of an account previously written off as uncollectible?

17. Explain why the direct write-off method of accounting for uncollectible accounts is generally unacceptable for accounting purposes.

18. When assets are received before they are earned, what type of account is credited? As the amounts are earned, what type of account is credited?

19. The accountant often speaks of expired costs. Do costs literally expire?

20. What does the word *accrued* mean? Is there a conceptual difference between interest payable and accrued interest payable?

21. It is more difficult to match expenses incurred with revenues earned than it would be to match expenses paid with revenues received. Do you think that the effort is worthwhile?

22. What are closing entries? In general, why must they be made?

23. How is a classified balance sheet different from an unclassified balance sheet?

24. (Based on the Appendix) Describe the purposes for which a work sheet is prepared.

The Coca-Cola Company

25. *Real-world question*   Refer to the balance sheet for December 31, 1991, of The Coca-Cola Company contained in its annual report in Appendix C at the end of the text. Approximately what percentage of the depreciable assets under property, plant, and equipment has been depreciated as of December 31, 1991?

MAYTAG CORPORATION

26. *Real-world question*   Refer to the financial statements of Maytag Corporation in Appendix C. What percentage of depreciable property, plant, and equipment has been depreciated as of December 31, 1991? (Construction in progress is not a depreciable asset.)

27. *Real-world question*   Referring to Appendix C at the end of the text, identify the classifications (or categories) of assets used by The Coca-Cola Company, Maytag Corporation, The Limited, Inc., and John H. Harland Company in their respective balance sheets.

28. *Real-world question*   Referring to Appendix C at the end of the text, identify the classifications (or categories) of liabilities used by The Coca-Cola Company, Maytag Corporation, The Limited, Inc., and John H. Harland Company in their respective balance sheets.

EXERCISES

Prepare and post adjusting entry for insurance under two methods (L.O. 4)

3–1. *a.* A one-year insurance policy was purchased on August 1 for $1,800 and the following entry was made at that time:

Prepaid Insurance 1,800
    Cash   1,800

What adjusting entry is necessary at December 31, the end of the accounting year?

b. Give the adjusting entry that would be necessary if the entry to record the purchase of the policy on August 1 had been:

Insurance Expense 1,800
    Cash   1,800

c. Show by the use of T-accounts that the end result is the same under either *(a)* or *(b)*.

Prepare adjusting entry for rent (L.O. 4)

3–2. Assume that rent of $18,000 was paid on September 1, 1995, to cover a one-year period from that date. Prepaid Rent was debited. If financial statements are prepared only on December 31 of each year, what adjusting entry is necessary on December 31, 1995, to bring the accounts involved to their proper balances?

Prepare adjusting entry for rent (L.O. 4)

3–3. If in Exercise 3–2, Rent Expense had been debited on September 1, 1995, what adjusting entry would have been necessary on December 31, 1995?

Determine date and entry for rent paid (L.O. 4)

3–4. At December 31, 1995, an adjusting entry was made as follows:

Rent Expense 12,000
    Prepaid Rent   12,000

You know that the gross amount of rent paid was $36,000, which was to cover a one-year period. Determine:

a. The opening date of the year to which the $36,000 of rent applies.

b. The entry that was made on the date the rent was paid.

Prepare entries for purchase of supplies and adjustment at year-end (L.O. 4)

3–5. Office supplies were purchased for cash on May 2, 1995, for $6,000. Show two ways in which this entry could be recorded. Then show the adjusting entry that would be necessary for each, assuming that $3,600 of the supplies remained at the end of the year.

Prepare adjusting entry for depreciation (L.O. 4)

3–6. Assume that a company acquired a building on January 1, 1995, at a cost of $3,600,000. The building has an estimated useful life of 40 years and an estimated salvage value of $400,000. What adjusting entry is needed on December 31, 1995, to record the depreciation for the entire year 1995?

Determine scrap value of building (L.O. 4)

3–7. A building is being depreciated by an amount of $108,000 per year. You know that it had an original cost of $1,200,000 and was expected to last 10 years. How must the $108,000 have been determined?

Prepare journal entries to record uncollectible accounts expense (L.O. 4)

3–8. The accounts of Drebbin Company as of December 31, 1995, show Accounts Receivable, $82,500; Allowance for Uncollectible Accounts, $525 (credit balance); Sales, $543,750; and Sales Returns and Allowances, $9,750. Prepare journal entries to adjust for possible uncollectible accounts under each of the following assumptions:

a. Uncollectible accounts are estimated at 1% of net sales.

b. The allowance is to be increased to 3% of accounts receivable.

Determine amount of uncollectible accounts adjusting entry (L.O. 4)

3–9. Torres Company had a balance of $120,000 in Accounts Receivable at December 31, 1995. A decision was made to adjust the balance in the Allowance for Uncollectible Accounts to 7% of the Accounts Receivable balance. Determine the required amount of the debit to Uncollectible Accounts Expense and credit to Allowance for Uncollectible Accounts if the existing balance in the allowance is (a) zero, (b) a $600 credit, and (c) a $600 debit.

Use aging schedule to estimate Allowance for Uncollectible Accounts (L.O. 4)

3–10. Compute the required balance of the Allowance for Uncollectible Accounts for the following receivables:

Accounts Receivable	Age (months)	Probability of Collection
$275,000	Less than 1	0.95
137,500	1–3	0.85
65,000	3–6	0.75
17,500	6–9	0.35
3,750	9–12	0.10

Record write-off and subsequent collection of account (L.O. 4)

3–11. On April 1, 1995, Bernstein Company, which uses the allowance method of accounting for uncollectible accounts, wrote off Jill Marks' $700 account. On December 14, 1995, the company received a check in that amount from Marks marked "in full payment of account." Prepare the necessary entries for all of the above.

Prepare entries for receipt of subscription fees and adjustment at year-end (L.O. 4)

3–12. On September 1, 1995, Stanton Company received a total of $120,000 as payment in advance for a number of one-year subscriptions to a monthly magazine. By the end of the year, one third of the magazines paid for in advance had been delivered. Give the entries to record the receipt of the subscriptions fees and to adjust the accounts at December 31 assuming annual financial statements are prepared at year-end.

Prepare adjusting entry for accrued legal services (L.O. 4)

3–13. Guilty and Innocent, a law firm, performed legal services in late December 1995 for clients. The $22,000 of services will be billed to the clients in January 1996. Give the adjusting entry that is necessary on December 31, 1995, if financial statements are prepared at the end of each month.

Prepare adjusting entry for accrued salaries (L.O. 4)

3–14. Taylor Company incurs sales salaries at the rate of $3,000 per day. The last payday in January is Friday, January 27. Salaries for Monday and Tuesday of the next week have not been recorded or paid as of January 31. Financial statements are prepared monthly. Give the necessary adjusting entry on January 31.

Determine effect on net income from failing to record adjusting entries (L.O. 5)

3–15. State the effect that each of the following would have on the amount of annual net income reported for 1995 and 1996.

a. No adjustment was made for accrued salaries of $3,000 as of December 31, 1995.

b. The collection of $1,600 for services yet unperformed as of December 31, 1995, was credited to a revenue account and not adjusted. The services are performed in 1996.

Prepare adjusting entry for accrued interest (L.O. 4)

3–16. A firm borrowed $50,000 on November 1. By December 31, $600 of interest had been incurred. Prepare the adjusting entry required on December 31.

Prepare closing entries (L.O. 6)

3–17. After adjustment, selected account balances of the Resteasy Campground are:

	Debits	Credits
Retained earnings.		$40,000
Campsite rental revenue.		60,000
Salaries expense	$21,000	
Depreciation expense	4,000	
Utilities expense.	13,000	
Dividends.	2,000	

In T-account format, give the entries required to close the books for the period. Enter the above balances in the accounts before doing so. Key the postings from the first closing entry with the number (1), the second with the number (2), and so on.

PROBLEMS

Prepare adjusting entries, post to ledger accounts, and state the correct figures for the financial statements (L.O. 4)

3–1. The following data pertain to the Lopez Company:

		Account Title	Trial Balance	Information for Adjustments
Item 1:	Equipment		$160,000	The equipment has an estimated useful life of five years and an estimated salvage value of $40,000.
	Accumulated Depreciation— Equipment		24,000	
Item 2:	Salaries Expense		3,000	Unpaid salaries incurred amount to $600.
Item 3:	Prepaid Insurance.		16,800	Of the prepaid insurance in the trial balance, only $6,800 is for additional protection after December 31.

Required:

For each of the items:

a. Prepare the adjusting journal entry, dating it December 31, 1995.

b. Set up ledger accounts showing debit, credit, and balance. Enter balances as given, if any, and post the adjusting entries made in part (a).

c. State the correct figures for the balance sheet. Show related accounts for each item as they should appear on that statement.

d. State the correct figures for the income statement.

Prepare adjusting entries (L.O. 4)

3–2. The trial balance of the Drake Company at December 31, 1995, includes, among other items, the following account balances:

	Debits	Credits
Prepaid insurance	$ 14,592	
Buildings	632,000	
Accumulated depreciation—buildings		$126,400
Salaries expense	110,000	
Prepaid rent	12,000	

Additional data

a. The debit balance in the Prepaid Insurance account is the advance premium for one year from September 1 of the current year.

b. The buildings are expected to last 25 years with no scrap value expected.

c. Salaries accrued and payable at December 31 amount to $5,200.

d. The debit balance in Prepaid Rent is for a one-year period that started March 1 of the current year.

Required:

Prepare the adjusting journal entries at December 31.

Prepare adjusting entries and post to ledger accounts (L.O. 4)

3–3. Among the account balances shown in the trial balance of the Lewis Company at December 31, 1995, of the current year are the following:

	Debits	Credits
Office supplies on hand	$ 6,960	
Prepaid insurance	9,600	
Buildings	168,000	
Accumulated depreciation—buildings		$39,000

Additional data

a. The inventory of supplies on hand at December 31 amounts to $1,200.

b. The balance in the Prepaid Insurance account is for a two-year policy taken out June 1 of the current year.

c. Depreciation for the buildings is based on the cost shown in the Buildings account, less salvage value estimated at $18,000. When acquired, the lives of the buildings were estimated at 50 years each.

Required:

a. Prepare the adjusting journal entries at December 31, 1995.

b. Open ledger accounts for each of the accounts involved, enter the balances as shown in the trial balance, post the adjusting entries, and calculate balances.

Write off uncollectible account, record expense under alternative methods of estimation (L.O. 4)

3–4. As of December 31, 1994, Lansing Company's accounts prior to adjustment show:

Accounts receivable.	$ 42,000
Allowance for uncollectible accounts (credit balance).	1,500
Sales.	450,000

Lansing Company follows a practice of estimating uncollectible accounts at 1% of sales.

On February 23, 1995, the account of Dan Hall in the amount of $600 was considered uncollectible and written off. On August 12, 1995, Hall remitted $375 and indicated that he intends to pay the balance due as soon as possible. By December 31, 1995, no further remittance had been received from Hall and no further remittance was expected.

Required:

a. Prepare journal entries to record all of the above transactions and adjusting entries.

b. Give the entry necessary as of December 31, 1994, if Lansing Company estimated its uncollectible accounts at 8% of outstanding receivables rather than at 1% of sales.

Calculate correct net income (L.O. 5)

3–5. The reported net income amounts for the Telly Company were: 1994, $180,000; and 1995, $220,000. *No* annual adjusting entries were made at either year-end for any of the transactions given below:

Transactions

a. A building was rented on April 1, 1994. Cash of $48,000 was paid on that date to cover a two-year period. Prepaid Rent was debited.

b. The balance in the Office Supplies on Hand account on December 31, 1994, was $8,000. An inventory of the supplies on December 31, 1994, revealed that only $5,000 was actually on hand at that date. No new supplies were purchased during 1995. At December 31, 1995, an inventory of the supplies revealed that $1,000 was on hand.

c. A building costing $1,000,000 and having an estimated useful life of 40 years and a salvage value of $200,000 was put into service on January 1, 1994.

d. Services were performed for a customer in December 1994. The $20,000 bill for these services was not sent until January 1995. The only transaction that was recorded was a debit to Cash and a credit to Service Revenue when payment was received in January.

Required:

Calculate the correct net income for 1994 and 1995. In your answer start with the reported net income amounts. Then show the effects of each correction (adjustment) using a plus or a minus to indicate whether reported income should be increased or decreased as a result of the correction. When the corrections are added to or deducted from the reported net income amounts, the result should be the correct net income amounts. The answer format should be as follows:

Explanation of Corrections	1994	1995
Reported net income.	$180,000	$220,000
To correct error in accounting for:		
a. Prepaid rent:		
Correct expense in 1994	−18,000	
Correct expense in 1995		−24,000

Prepare adjusting
entries
(L.O. 4)

3–6. The Bravo Company occupies rented quarters on the main street of the city. In order to get this location, it was necessary for the company to rent a store larger than needed, so a portion of the area is subleased (rented) to Fredrick's Restaurant. The partial trial balance of the Bravo Company as of December 31, 1994, is as follows:

BRAVO COMPANY
Partial Trial Balance
December 31, 1994

	Debits	Credits
Cash	$160,000	
Prepaid Insurance	11,400	
Store Equipment	176,000	
Accumulated Depreciation—Store Equipment		$ 19,200
Notes Payable		20,000
Service Revenue		600,000
Supplies Expense	10,800	
Rent Expense	14,400	
Store Salaries Expense	98,000	
Rent Revenue		8,800

Data to be considered:

a. Wages of the store clerks amount to $400 per day and were last paid through Wednesday, December 27. December 31 is a Sunday. The store is closed Sundays.

b. An analysis of the Store Equipment account disclosed:

Balance, January 1, 1994	$128,000
Addition, July 1, 1994	48,000
Balance, December 31, 1994, per trial balance	$176,000

The company estimates that all equipment will last 20 years from the date it was acquired and that the salvage value will be zero.

c. The store carries one combined insurance policy which is taken out once a year effective August 1. The premium on the policy now in force amounts to $7,200 per year.

d. Unused store supplies on hand at December 31, 1994, have a cost of $680.

e. December's rent from Fredrick's Restaurant has not yet been received, $800.

Required:

Present the period-end entries required by the statements of fact presented above. Show your calculations of the amounts as explanations of your entries.

Prepare journal entries under cash basis and accrual basis and determine difference in net income (L.O. 1)

3–7. On June 1, 1995, Jeff Zarley opened a swimming pool cleaning and maintenance service business, Zarley Company. He vaguely recalled the process of making journal entries and establishing ledger accounts from a high school bookkeeping course he had taken some years ago. At the end of June, he prepared an income statement for the month of June, but he had the feeling that he had not proceeded correctly. He contacted his brother, Jay, a recent college graduate majoring in accounting, for assistance.

Jay immediately noted that his brother had kept his records on a cash basis, so he set about to bring the books to a full accrual basis.

Transactions

June 1   Received cash of $9,000 from a motel chain in exchange for service agreements to clean and maintain their pools for the months of June, July, August, and September.

5   Paid rent for automotive and cleaning equipment to be used during the period June through September, $8,000. The payment covered the entire period.

8   Purchased a two-year liability insurance policy effective June 1 for $5,280 cash.

10   Received an advance of $2,500 from a Florida building contractor in exchange for an agreement to help service pools in his housing development during the months of October through May.

16   Paid wages for the first half of June, $4,800.

17   Paid $240 for advertising to be run in a local newspaper for two weeks in June and four weeks in July.

19   Paid the rent of $8,000 under a four-month lease on a building rented and occupied on June 1.

26   Purchased $4,000 of supplies for cash. (Only $600 of these supplies were used in June.)

29   Billed a customer for services rendered, $4,200.

30   Unpaid employee services received in the last half of June amounted to $5,000.

30   Received a bill for $400 for gas and oil used in June.

Required:

a. Prepare the entries for the transactions as Jeff must have recorded them under the cash basis of accounting.

b. Prepare the necessary adjusting entries as Jay must have prepared them to bring the books to a full accrual basis of accounting as of June 30.

Prepare T-accounts, income statement, balance sheet, and closing entries required (L.O. 6)

c. Calculate the change in the net income for June brought about by changing from the cash to the accrual basis of accounting.

3–8. The balances of all of the Berger Company accounts as of June 1, 1995, were as follows:

Cash	$33,600	Accounts payable	$16,000
Accounts receivable	34,400	Capital stock	48,000
		Retained earnings	4,000

The transactions (and certain other data) for the company for June were as follows:

1. Services rendered to a customer for cash, $32,000; on account, $64,000.
2. Paid rent for the six months ending November 30, $24,000. (Record entire amount as prepaid rent.)
3. Purchased equipment for cash, $38,400.
4. Supplies purchased on account, $6,400.
5. Received cash on account from a customer, $88,000.
6. Made payment on account to a supplier, $11,200.
7. Employee salaries incurred, $60,000; cash paid to employees, $52,000.
8. Paid utility bill of $1,600.
9. Paid dividend to stockholders, $2,400.
10. Equipment has an expected life of four years and no salvage value. It was acquired early in the month.
11. Adjust for prepaid rent that has expired.
12. Of the supplies purchased in (4), $5,600 were used by the end of the month.

Required:

a. Set up T-accounts and record the above data, including the beginning balances given above. (Ignore any possible federal income taxes.)

b. Prepare an income statement for the month of June.

c. Prepare a balance sheet as of June 30, 1995.

d. Enter in the T-accounts the closing entries that would be required if June 30, 1995, is the end of the accounting period. (Key these entries *a*, *b*, and *c* in the T-accounts.)

Prepare a corrected income statement (L.O. 4, 5)

3–9. Randy Duncan, president and sole stockholder of Duncan's Service, Inc., prepared the following income statement for the company's second month of operations, May 1995.

Service revenues		$10,000
Wages expense	$5,600	
Oil and gasoline expense	1,000	
Other expenses	1,400	8,000
Net income		$ 2,000

In preparing the above income statement, Randy merely looked at the checkbook and treated deposits of receipts from customers as revenue and checks drawn in payment for expenses as the expenses for the month. Further analysis shows that, of the $10,000 collected from customers in May, $1,200 was for services rendered in April. Services were rendered in May for which customers were billed $1,400, none of which was paid by the end of May. The $5,600 of wages paid included wages of $1,600 earned by employees in April. Wages earned in May but not paid by the end of May amounted to $600. A bill for $200 for gasoline and oil used in May remains unpaid at the end of May. The expenses shown above do not include depreciation on the equipment owned, which has a cost of $240,000, no salvage value, and an estimated life of 10 years.

Required:

Prepare a corrected income statement for May for Duncan's Service, Inc.

Prepare closing entries and a classified balance sheet (L.O. 6, 7)

3–10. You are given the following adjusted balances for the Clifford Company.

CLIFFORD COMPANY Adjusted Trial Balance December 31, 1995		
	Debits	*Credits*
Cash	$147,200	
Accounts Receivable	48,000	
Interest Receivable	400	
Notes Receivable	20,000	
Prepaid Insurance	2,400	
Supplies on Hand	1,800	
Land	32,000	
Buildings	190,000	
Accumulated Depreciation—Buildings		$ 40,000
Office Equipment	28,000	
Accumulated Depreciation—Office Equipment		8,000
Accounts Payable		43,000
Salaries Payable		8,500
Interest Payable		900
Notes Payable (due 1998)		64,000
Capital Stock		150,000
Retained Earnings		42,800
Dividends	40,000	
Commissions and Fees Revenue		378,520
Advertising Expense	14,000	
Commissions Expense	80,440	
Travel Expense	12,880	
Depreciation Expense—Buildings	8,500	
Salaries Expense	94,400	
Depreciation Expense—Office Equipment	2,800	
Supplies Expense	3,800	
Insurance Expense	3,600	
Building Repair Expense	1,900	
Utilities Expense	3,400	
Interest Expense	1,800	
Interest Revenue		1,600
	$737,320	$737,320

Required:

a. Prepare the closing journal entries.

b. Prepare a classified balance sheet.

Prepare work sheet and closing entries (L.O. 6, 8)

3–11. (Based on the Appendix) The trial balance and additional data given below are for the Stillwagon Company:

STILLWAGON COMPANY
Trial Balance
December 31, 1995

	Debits	Credits
Cash	$ 93,280	
Accounts Receivable	139,520	
Notes Receivable	170,000	
Supplies on Hand.	2,400	
Equipment	88,000	
Accumulated Depreciation—Equipment		$ 17,600
Accounts Payable.		82,000
Notes Payable		24,000
Capital Stock		300,000
Retained Earnings		21,640
Service Revenue		600,000
Interest Revenue		1,000
Interest Expense	600	
Sales Salaries Expense	141,600	
Advertising Expense	78,000	
Supplies Expense.	2,960	
General Office Expense	9,880	
Insurance Expense	4,800	
Office Salaries Expense	80,800	
Officers' Salaries Expense.	160,000	
Legal and Auditing Expenses	10,000	
Telephone Expense.	4,800	
Rent Expense.	57,600	
Dividends	2,000	
	$1,046,240	$1,046,240

Additional data as of December 31, 1995

a. Insurance unexpired, $1,000.

b. Supplies on hand, $1,400.

c. Prepaid rent expense (store only), $7,000.

d. The equipment has a 10-year estimated life with no salvage value.

e. Accrued sales salaries, $4,000.

f. Accrued office salaries, $3,000.

Required:

a. Prepare a 12-column work sheet for the year ended December 31, 1995. (See chapter appendix for an illustration.)

b. Prepare the December 31, 1995, closing entries, in general journal form.

BUSINESS DECISION PROBLEMS

*Explain why
adjusting entries
are made and
which accounts
need adjustment
(L.O. 2, 3)*

3–1. You have just been hired by the Sanders Company to help them prepare adjusting entries at the end of an accounting period. It becomes obvious to you that the management does not seem to have much of an understanding about the necessity for adjusting entries or which of the accounts might possibly need adjustment. The first step you take is to prepare the following unadjusted trial balance from the general ledger. It includes only those accounts from the ledger which had balances as of the end of the year.

	Debits	Credits
Cash	$100,000	
Accounts Receivable.	18,000	
Office Supplies on Hand	3,000	
Prepaid Insurance	2,700	
Office Equipment	120,000	
Accumulated Depreciation—Office Equipment		$ 45,000
Building	360,000	
Accumulated Depreciation—Building		105,000
Accounts Payable		9,000
Bank Loan Payable		15,000
Unearned Brokerage Commissions		30,000
Capital Stock		190,000
Retained Earnings.		69,300
Rental Commissions Revenue		270,000
Advertising Expense.	6,000	
Salaries Expense	112,500	
Utilities Expense.	7,500	
Miscellaneous Expense	3,600	
	$733,300	$733,300

Required:

a. Explain to management why adjusting entries in general are made.

b. Explain to management why some of the specific accounts appearing in the trial balance may need adjustment and what the nature of each adjustment might be (do not worry about specific dollar amounts).

*Prepare an
appraisal and an
approximate
income statement
(L.O. 1, 4)*

3–2. A friend of yours, Jack Biglow, is quite excited over the opportunity he has to purchase the land and several miscellaneous assets of Kraft Bowling Lanes Company for $375,000. Jack tells you that Mr. and Mrs. Kraft (the sole stockholders in the company) are moving due to Mr. Kraft's ill health. The annual rent on the building and equipment is $54,000.

   Mr. Kraft reports that the business earned a profit of $75,000 in 1995 (last year). Jack believes an annual profit of $75,000 on an investment of $375,000 is a really good deal. But, before completing the deal, he asks you to look it over. You agree and discover the following:

   1.   Mr. Kraft has computed his annual profit for 1995 as the sum of his cash dividends plus the increase in the Cash account: Dividends of $45,000 + Increase in Cash account of $30,000 = $75,000 profit.
   2.   As buyer of the business, Jack will take over responsibility for repayment

of a $300,000 loan (plus interest) on the land. The land was acquired at a cost of $624,000 seven years ago.

3. An analysis of the Cash account shows the following for 1995:

Rental revenues received		$420,000
Cash paid out in 1995 for—		
Salaries paid to employees in 1995	$240,000	
Utilities paid for 1995	18,000	
Advertising expenses paid	15,000	
Supplies purchased and used in 1995	24,000	
Interest paid on loan	18,000	
Loan principal paid	30,000	
Cash dividends	45,000	390,000
Increase in cash balance for the year		$ 30,000

4. You also find that the annual rent of $54,000, a December utility bill of $3,000, and an advertising bill of $4,500 have not been paid.

Required:

a. Prepare for Jack a written report giving your appraisal of Kraft Bowling Lanes Company as an investment. Comment on Mr. Kraft's method of computing the annual "profit" of the business.

b. Include in your report an approximate income statement for 1995.

ANSWERS TO SELF-TEST

True-False

1. *True.* Every adjusting entry involves either moving previously recorded data from an asset account to an expense account or from a liability account to a revenue account (or in the opposite direction) or simultaneously entering new data in an asset account and a revenue account or in a liability account and an expense account.

2. *True.* A fiscal year is *any* 12 consecutive months, so all calendar years are also fiscal years. A calendar year, however, must end on December 31, so it does not include fiscal years that end on any date other than December 31 (such as June 30).

3. *False.* The accumulated depreciation account is a *contra asset* that shows the total of all depreciation recorded on an asset up through the balance sheet date.

4. *False.* The percentage-of-receivables method estimates the uncollectible accounts based on outstanding receivables at year-end.

5. *False.* The original write-off entry is reversed, and then Cash is debited and Accounts Receivable is credited. Only under the direct write-off method is income recognized as a result of the subsequent recovery of accounts previously written off.

6. *False.* The Unearned Delivery Fees account is a liability. As the fees are earned, the amount in that account will be transferred to a revenue account.

7. *True.* If an adjusting entry is overlooked and not made, at least one income statement account and one balance sheet account will be incorrect.

8. *True.* All of these accounts are closed, or reduced to zero balances, as a result of the closing process.

Multiple-Choice

1. *d.* One third of the benefits have expired. Therefore, $400 must be moved from the asset to an expense.

2. *c.* Two thirds of the benefits have not expired. Therefore, $800 would have to be transferred from the expense to an asset.

3. *a.* $1,100 of the supplies have been used, so that amount must be moved from the asset to an expense.

4. *c.* The amount of annual depreciation is determined as ($20,000 − $5,000) divided by 5 = $3,000. The debit is to depreciation expense, and the credit is to the accumulated depreciation account, a contra asset.

5. *d.* The direct write-off method must be used for tax purposes.

6. *b.* $1,000,000 × .01 = $10,000. The current balance in the allowance account is ignored.

7. *b.* Each month $2,000 would be transferred from the liability account, Unearned Subscription Fees, to a revenue account.

8. *b.* An asset, Interest Receivable, is debited, and a revenue is credited.

9. *a.* The debit would be to Salaries Expense, and the credit would be to Salaries Payable.

10. *a.* The Dividends account is closed to the Retained Earnings account rather than to the Income Summary account.

11. *b.* "Plant, property, and equipment" is one of the long-term asset categories. Response (*a*) should not include equipment. Response (*c*) should not include notes receivable. Stockholders' equity is not subdivided into current and long-term categories.

4 MERCHANDISING TRANSACTIONS, INTRODUCTION TO INVENTORIES, AND CLASSIFIED INCOME STATEMENT

LEARNING OBJECTIVES

After studying this chapter, you should be able to:

1. Record journal entries for sales transactions involving merchandise.
2. Describe briefly cost of goods sold and the distinction between perpetual and periodic inventory procedures.
3. Record journal entries for purchase transactions involving merchandise.
4. Describe the freight terms and record transportation costs.
5. Determine cost of goods sold.
6. Prepare a classified income statement.
7. Prepare a work sheet and closing entries for a merchandising company.

In the first three chapters, you learned about the accounting process and how it begins with the recording of business transactions and results in the preparation of financial statements. As you studied the accounting process, you followed step by step the business transactions of a service company—Speedy Delivery Company. This company provided a delivery service to customers in return for a fee. Your study of accounting began with service companies as examples because they are the least complicated type of business. You are now ready to apply the accounting process to a more complex type of business—a merchandising company. The fundamental accounting concepts for service-type businesses also apply to merchandising businesses, but some additional accounts and techniques are needed to account for sales and purchases.

The normal flow of goods from manufacturer to final customer is as follows:

Merchandising Companies

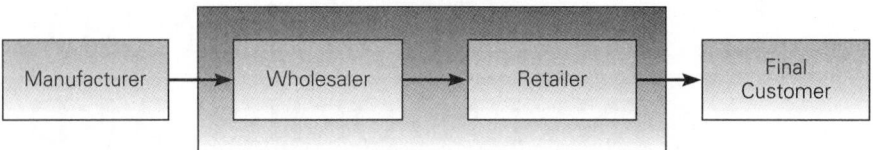

Manufacturers produce goods from raw materials and normally sell them to wholesalers. After performing certain functions, such as packaging or labeling, **wholesalers** normally sell the goods to retailers. **Retailers** sell the goods to final customers. The two middle boxes in the diagram above represent merchandising companies. These companies buy goods in finished form for resale.

In this chapter, you will see a comparison of the income statements of a service company and a merchandising company. Then, you will study how to record merchandise-related transactions. Finally, you will become familiar with the work sheet and the closing process for a merchandising company.

TWO INCOME STATEMENTS COMPARED—SERVICE COMPANY AND MERCHANDISING COMPANY

Illustration 4.1 compares the main divisions of an income statement of a service company with those of a merchandising company. To determine profitability or net income for a service company, total expenses incurred are deducted from revenues earned. A merchandising company is a more complex type of business and, therefore, has a more complex income statement.

As shown in Illustration 4.1, merchandising companies first must deduct from revenues the cost of the goods they sell to customers. Then, they

Illustration 4.1
CONDENSED INCOME STATEMENTS OF A SERVICE COMPANY AND A MERCHANDISING COMPANY COMPARED

SERVICE COMPANY Income Statement For the Year Ended December 31, 1995		MERCHANDISING COMPANY Income Statement For the Year Ended December 31, 1995	
Service revenues	$13,200	Sales revenues	$262,000
		Cost of goods sold	159,000
		Gross margin	$103,000
Expenses	6,510	Expenses	74,900
Net income	$ 6,690	Net income	$ 28,100

deduct other expenses. The income statement of a merchandising company has three main divisions: (1) sales revenues, (2) cost of goods sold, and (3) expenses. Sales revenues result from the sale of goods by the company; cost of goods sold (an expense) indicates how much the company paid for the goods that were sold; and expenses are the company's other expenses in running the business.

The next two sections of the chapter discuss the first two main divisions of the income statement of a merchandising company. The third division (expenses) is similar to expenses for a service company and has been illustrated in preceding chapters. As you study these chapter sections, keep in mind how the divisions of the merchandising income statement are related to each other and produce the final figure—net income or net loss—which indicates the profitability of the company.

SALES REVENUES

Objective 1
Record journal
entries for sales
transactions in-
volving merchan-
dise

The sale of goods occurs between two parties. The seller of the goods transfers them to the buyer in exchange for cash or a promise to pay later. This exchange is a relatively simple business transaction.

Sellers make sales to create revenues. As you recall, revenue is the inflow of assets resulting from the rendering of services or the sale of goods to customers. Illustration 4.1 showed a condensed income statement to emphasize its major divisions. Now the more complete income statement actually prepared by accountants is described. The merchandising company that we will use to illustrate the income statement is Hanlon Retail Food Store. This section first explains how to record sales revenues, including the effect of trade discounts. Next, you will learn how to record the two deductions from sales revenues—sales discounts and sales returns and allowances (Illustration 4.2). The amount that remains is **net sales.** The formula, then, for determining net sales is:

Net sales = Gross sales − (Sales discounts + Sales returns and allowances)

Illustration 4.2
PARTIAL INCOME STATEMENT OF MERCHANDISING COMPANY

HANLON RETAIL FOOD STORE
Partial Income Statement
For the Year Ended December 31, 1995

Operating revenues:		
Gross sales		$282,000
Less: Sales discounts.	$ 5,000	
Sales returns and allowances	15,000	20,000
Net sales.		$262,000

Recording Gross Sales

In a sales transaction, the seller transfers the legal ownership (title) of the goods to the buyer. Usually, the physical delivery of the goods occurs at the same time as the sale of the goods. A business document called an *invoice* (called a *sales invoice* by the seller and a *purchase invoice* by the buyer) is used as a basis for recording the sale.

An **invoice** is a document, prepared by the seller of merchandise and sent to the buyer, that contains the details of a sale, such as the number of units sold, unit price, total price billed, terms of sale, and manner of shipment. A retail company prepares the invoice at the point of sale. A wholesale company, which supplies goods to retailers, prepares the invoice after the shipping department notifies the accounting department that it shipped the goods to the retailer. Illustration 4.3 shows an invoice prepared by a wholesale company for goods sold to a retail company.

Using the invoice as the source document, a wholesale company records the revenue from the sale at the time of the sale for the following reasons:

1. The seller has passed *legal title* of the goods to the buyer, and the goods are now the responsibility and property of the buyer.
2. The seller has established the selling price of the goods.
3. The seller has completed its obligation.
4. The seller has exchanged the goods for another asset, such as cash or accounts receivable.
5. The seller can determine the costs incurred in selling the goods.

Each time a company makes a sale, the company earns revenue. This revenue increases a revenue account called *Sales*. Recall from Chapter 2 that revenues are increased by credits. Therefore, the Sales account is credited for the amount of the sale.

Illustration 4.3
INVOICE

BRYAN WHOLESALE CO.	Invoice No.: 1258
476 Mason Street	Date: Dec. 19, 1995
Detroit, Michigan 48823	

Customer's Order No.: 218
Sold to: Baier Company
Address: 2255 Hannon Street
Big Rapids, Michigan 48106   Date Shipped: Dec. 19, 1995
Terms: Net 30, FOB Destination   Shipped by: Nagel Trucking Co.

Description	Item Number	Quantity	Price per Unit	Total Amount
True-tone stereo radios	Model No. 5868-24393	200	$100	$20,000
		Total		$20,000

Usually sales are for cash or on account. When a sale is for cash, the credit to the Sales account is accompanied by a debit to Cash; when a sale is on account, the Sales account credit is accompanied by a debit to Accounts Receivable. For example, a $20,000 sale for cash is recorded as follows:

```
Cash . . . . . . . . . . . . . . . . . . . . . . . . . . . .   20,000
    Sales . . . . . . . . . . . . . . . . . . . . . . . . . .          20,000
    To record the sale of merchandise for cash.
```

A $20,000 sale on account is recorded as follows:

```
Accounts Receivable. . . . . . . . . . . . . . . . . . . .   20,000
    Sales . . . . . . . . . . . . . . . . . . . . . . . . . .          20,000
    To record the sale of merchandise on account.
```

A seller usually quotes the gross selling price, also called the *invoice price*, of goods to the buyer, but sometimes a seller quotes a list price of goods along with trade discounts that are available. In this latter situation, the buyer must calculate the gross selling price. The list price less all trade discounts is the **gross selling price.** Merchandising companies selling goods use the gross selling price as the amount of the credit to Sales.

Determining Gross Selling Price When Companies Offer Trade Discounts

A **trade discount** is a percentage deduction, or discount, from the specified list price or catalog price of merchandise. Trade discounts are used to:

1. Reduce the cost of catalog publication. A seller can use a catalog for a longer period of time when it prints list prices in the catalog and gives separate discount sheets to salespersons whenever prices change.
2. Grant quantity discounts.
3. Allow quotation of different prices to different types of customers, such as retailers and wholesalers.

The seller's invoice may show trade discounts. However, trade discounts are not recorded in the seller's accounting records because they are only used to calculate the gross selling price. Nor are trade discounts recorded on the books of the purchaser. To illustrate, assume an invoice contains the following data:

```
List price, 200 swimsuits at $24 . . . . . . .   $4,800
Less: Trade discount, 30%. . . . . . . . . . .    1,440
Gross selling price (invoice price) . . . . . .   $3,360
```

The seller records a sale of $3,360. The purchaser records a purchase of $3,360. **Thus, list prices and trade discounts are not entered on the books of either the seller or the purchaser.**

Sometimes the list price of a product is subject to several trade discounts; this series of discounts is called a **chain discount.** Chain discounts exist, for example, when a wholesaler receives two trade discounts because of certain services performed, such as packaging and distributing. When more than one discount is given, each discount is applied to the declining balance successively. If a product has a list price of $100 and is subject to trade discounts of 20% and 10%, the gross selling price (invoice price) would be $100 − 0.2($100) = $80; $80 − 0.1($80) = $72, computed as follows:

List price	$100
Less 20%	− 20
	$ 80
Less 10%	− 8
Gross selling price (invoice price)	$ 72

The same results can be obtained by multiplying the list price by the complements of the trade discounts allowed. The complement of 20% is 80% because 20% + 80% = 100%. The complement of 10% is 90% because 10% + 90% = 100%. Thus, the gross invoice price is $100 × 0.8 × 0.9 = $72.

Recording Deductions from Gross Sales

Two common deductions from gross sales are (1) sales discounts and (2) sales returns and allowances. These deductions are recorded in contra revenue accounts to the Sales account. Contra accounts have normal balances that are opposite the balance of the account they reduce. For example, since the Sales account normally has a credit balance, the Sales Discounts account and Sales Returns and Allowances account will have debit balances. The methods used to record these contra revenue accounts are explained in the paragraphs that follow.

Sales Discounts. Whenever a company sells goods on account, it clearly specifies terms of payment on the invoice. For example, the invoice in Illustration 4.3 states the terms of payment as "net 30."

"Net 30" is sometimes written as "n/30." This "n/30" term means that the buyer may not take a discount and must pay the entire amount of the invoice ($20,000) on or before 30 days after December 19, 1995 (invoice date)—on or before January 18, 1996. In Illustration 4.3, if the terms had read "n/10/EOM" (EOM means end of month), the buyer could not take a discount, and the invoice would be due on the 10th day of the month following the month of sale—or January 10, 1996. Credit terms vary from industry to industry.

In some industries, credit terms include a *cash discount* of 1% to 3% to induce early payment of an amount due. A **cash discount** is a deduction from the invoice price that can be taken only if the invoice is paid within a specified period of time. A cash discount differs from a trade discount in that a cash discount is a deduction from the gross sales price for the prompt payment of an invoice, while a trade discount is a deduction from the list price to determine the gross selling price (or invoice price). A cash discount is called a **sales discount** by the seller and a **purchase discount** by the buyer.

Companies often state cash discount terms as follows:

- 2/10, n/30—means a buyer may deduct a discount of 2% of the invoice price of the merchandise if the buyer pays within 10 days following the invoice date. If payment is not made within the discount period, the entire invoice price is due 30 days from the invoice date.
- 2/EOM, n/60—means a buyer may deduct a 2% discount from the invoice price if the buyer pays the invoice by the end of the month. If payment is not made within the discount period, the entire invoice price is due 60 days from the invoice date.
- 2/10/EOM, n/60—means a buyer may deduct a 2% discount from the invoice price if the buyer pays the invoice by the 10th day of the month following the month of sale. If payment is not made within the discount period, the entire invoice price is due 60 days from the invoice date.

Sellers cannot record the sales discount before they receive payment since they do not know before that time when the buyer will pay the invoice. A cash discount taken by the buyer reduces the amount of cash that the seller actually collects from the sale of the goods, so the seller must indicate this fact in the accounting records of the company. The following illustration shows how to record a sale and a subsequent sales discount.

Assume that on July 12, a business sold merchandise for $2,000 on account; terms are 2/10, n/30. On July 21 (nine days after invoice date), the business received a $1,960 check in payment of the account. The required journal entries for the seller are:

July 12	Accounts Receivable	2,000	
	Sales		2,000
	To record sale on account; terms 2/10, n/30.		
21	Cash	1,960	
	Sales Discounts	40	
	Accounts Receivable		2,000
	To record collection on account, less discount.		

The **Sales Discounts account** is a contra revenue account to the Sales account. In the income statement, this contra revenue account is deducted from gross sales. The Sales Discounts account is used (rather than directly reducing the Sales account) so the owners can examine the sales discounts figure to evaluate the company's sales discount policy. Note that the Sales Discounts account is not an expense incurred in generating revenue. Rather, the purpose of the account is to reduce recorded revenue to the amount actually realized from the sale.

Sales Returns and Allowances.   Merchandising companies usually allow a customer to return goods that are defective or unsatisfactory for a variety of reasons, such as wrong color, wrong size, wrong style, wrong amounts, or inferior quality. In fact, when the seller's policy is "satisfaction guaranteed," some companies allow customers to return goods simply because the customer does not like the merchandise. A **sales return** is merchandise returned by a buyer. Sellers and buyers regard a sales return as a cancellation of a sale. Alternatively, sometimes the customer keeps the unsatisfactory goods, and the seller gives the customer an allowance off the original price. A **sales allowance** is a deduction from the original invoiced sales price granted to a customer when the customer keeps the merchandise but is dissatisfied for any of a number of reasons, including inferior quality, damage, or deterioration in transit. In such cases, if a seller agrees to the sales return or sales allowance, the seller communicates with the buyer by sending a credit memorandum indicating that the seller is reducing (crediting) the account receivable with that buyer. A credit memorandum is a document that provides space for the name and address of the concerned parties and contains the preprinted words, "WE CREDIT YOUR ACCOUNT," followed by a space for the reason for the credit and the amount to be credited. A credit memorandum is used as the basis for recording a sales return or a sales allowance.

In theory, both sales returns and sales allowances could be recorded as debits to the Sales account because they cancel part of the recorded selling price. However, the amount of sales returns and sales allowances is useful information to stockholders and, therefore, should be shown separately. The amount of returns and allowances in relation to goods sold can be an indication of the quality of the goods (high-return percentage, low quality) or of pressure applied by salespersons (high-return percentage, high-pressure sales). Thus, sales returns and sales allowances are recorded in a separate *Sales Returns and Allowances account.* The **Sales Returns and Allowances account** is a contra revenue account (to Sales) used to record the selling price of merchandise returned by buyers or reductions in selling prices granted. (Some companies use separate accounts for sales returns and for sales allowances, but this text does not.)

Following are two examples illustrating the recording of sales returns in the Sales Returns and Allowances account:

1. Assume that a customer returns $300 of goods sold on account. If payment has not yet been received, the required entry is:

Sales Returns and Allowances	300	
Accounts Receivable		300
To record a sales return from a customer.		

2. Assume that the customer has already paid the account and the seller gives the customer a cash refund. Now, the credit is to Cash rather than Accounts Receivable. If the customer has taken a 2% discount when paying the account, the company would return to the customer the sales

price less the sales discount amount. For example, if a customer returns goods that sold for $300, on which a 2% discount was taken, the following entry would be made:

Sales Returns and Allowances	300	
Cash		294
Sales Discounts		6
To record a sales return from a customer who had taken a discount and was sent a cash refund.		

The debit to the Sales Returns and Allowances account is for the full selling price of the purchase. The credit of $6 reduces the balance of the Sales Discounts account.

Now we will illustrate the recording of a sales allowance in the Sales Returns and Allowances account. Assume that a company grants a $400 allowance to a customer for damage resulting from improperly packed merchandise. If the customer has not yet paid the account, the required entry would be:

Sales Returns and Allowances	400	
Accounts Receivable		400
To record sales allowance granted for damaged merchandise.		

If the customer has already paid the account, the credit is to Cash instead of Accounts Receivable. If the customer took a 2% discount when paying the account, the company would refund only the net amount ($392). Sales Discounts would be credited for $8. The entry would be:

Sales Returns and Allowances	400	
Cash		392
Sales Discounts		8
To record sales allowance when a customer has paid and taken a 2% discount.		

Reporting Net Sales in the Income Statement

Illustration 4.4 contains a partial income statement showing how a company would report sales, sales discounts, and sales returns and allowances. How-

Illustration 4.4
PARTIAL INCOME STATEMENT*

HANLON RETAIL FOOD STORE Partial Income Statement For the Year Ended December 31, 1995		
Operating revenues:		
Gross sales		$282,000
Less: Sales discounts	$ 5,000	
Sales returns and allowances	15,000	20,000
Net sales		$262,000

* This illustration is the same as Illustration 4.2, repeated here for your convenience.

ever, many times the income statement published in a company's annual report begins with "Net sales" because the details of this computation are not important to financial statement users outside the company.

COST OF GOODS SOLD

Objective 2
Describe briefly
cost of goods sold
and the distinction
between perpetual
and periodic
inventory proce-
dures

The second main division of an income statement for a merchandising business is cost of goods sold. **Cost of goods sold** is the cost to the seller of the goods sold to customers. For a merchandising company, the cost of goods sold can be relatively large. All merchandising companies have a quantity of goods on hand to sell to customers that is called *merchandise inventory*. **Merchandise inventory** (or **inventory**) is the quantity of goods on hand and available for sale at any given time. Cost of goods sold is determined by computing the cost of (1) the beginning inventory, (2) the net cost of goods purchased, and (3) the ending inventory.

Illustration 4.5 gives the cost of goods sold section of Hanlon Retail Food Store's income statement. The merchandise inventory on January 1, 1995, was $24,000. The net cost of purchases for the year was $166,000. Thus, Hanlon had $190,000 of merchandise available for sale during 1995. On December 31, 1995, the merchandise inventory was $31,000, meaning this amount was left unsold. Subtracting the unsold amount of inventory (the ending inventory), $31,000, from the amount Hanlon had available for sale during the year, $190,000, gives the cost of goods sold for the year of $159,000. Understanding this relationship, as shown on Hanlon Retail Food Store's partial income statement in Illustration 4.5, gives you the necessary background to determine the cost of goods sold as presented in this section. This illustration is repeated at the end of the following discussion.

Illustration 4.5
DETERMINATION OF COST OF GOODS SOLD FOR HANLON RETAIL FOOD STORE

Cost of goods sold:			
Merchandise inventory, January 1, 1995			$ 24,000
Purchases		$167,000	
Less: Purchase discounts.	$3,000		
Purchase returns and allowances	8,000	11,000	
Net purchases		$156,000	
Add: Transportation-in		10,000	
Net cost of purchases			166,000
Cost of goods available for sale.			$190,000
Less: Merchandise inventory, December 31, 1995 . .			31,000
Cost of goods sold			$159,000

Two Procedures for Accounting for Inventories

To determine the cost of goods sold, accountants must have accurate merchandise inventory figures. Accountants use two basic methods for determining the amount of merchandise inventory—perpetual inventory procedure and periodic inventory procedure. Perpetual inventory procedure is only mentioned briefly in this chapter. Periodic inventory procedure is used extensively in this chapter. In the next chapter, we emphasize perpetual inventory procedure and further compare it with periodic inventory procedure.

When discussing inventory, we need to clarify whether we are referring to the physical goods on hand or the Merchandise Inventory account, which is the financial representation of the physical goods on hand. The difference between perpetual and periodic inventory procedures is the frequency with which the Merchandise Inventory account is updated to reflect what is physically on hand. Under **perpetual inventory procedure,** the Merchandise Inventory account is continuously updated to reflect items on hand. For example, your supermarket uses a scanner to ring up your purchases. When your box of Rice Krispies crosses the scanner, the Merchandise Inventory account is adjusted to show that one less box of Rice Krispies is on hand. Hence, the name *perpetual inventory procedure.*

Under **periodic inventory procedure,** the Merchandise Inventory account is updated only periodically—after a physical count has been made. Hence, the name *periodic inventory procedure.* Usually, the physical count will only take place immediately before the preparation of financial statements.

Perpetual Inventory Procedure. Companies use *perpetual inventory procedure* in a variety of business settings. Historically, companies that sold merchandise with a high individual unit value, such as automobiles, furniture, and appliances, used perpetual inventory procedure. Today, computerized cash registers and accounting software programs can be designed to automatically keep track of inflows and outflows of each type of inventory item. This computerization makes it economical for many retail stores to use perpetual inventory procedure even for goods of low unit value, such as groceries.

Under perpetual inventory procedure, the Merchandise Inventory account provides close control over the actual goods on hand by showing the cost of the goods that are supposed to be on hand at any particular point in time. The Merchandise Inventory account is debited for each purchase and credited for each sale so that the current balance is shown in the account at all times. Also, the company usually maintains detailed unit records showing the quantities of each type of goods that should be on hand at any time. At the end of the accounting period, company personnel take a physical inventory by actually counting the number of units of inventory on hand. This physical count can be compared with the records showing the number of units that should be on hand. Chapter 5 describes perpetual inventory procedure in more detail.

Periodic Inventory Procedure.   Merchandising companies selling low unit value merchandise (such as nuts and bolts, nails, Christmas cards, or pencils) often find that if they have not computerized their inventory systems, the extra costs of record-keeping under perpetual inventory procedure more than outweigh the benefits. Close control of such items is not economically feasible. These merchandising companies often use periodic inventory procedure.

Under **periodic inventory procedure,** companies do not use the Merchandise Inventory account to record each purchase and sale of merchandise as under perpetual inventory procedure. Instead, a company makes adjustments to the Merchandise Inventory account only at the end of the accounting period to bring the account to its proper balance. Also, the company usually does not maintain other unit records that show the exact number of units that should be on hand. Thus, the use of periodic inventory procedure reduces record-keeping considerably, but it also reduces the control over inventory items.

As stated above, companies using periodic inventory procedure make no entries to the Merchandise Inventory account to record purchases or sales during the accounting period, nor do they usually maintain unit records. Thus, these companies have no up-to-date balance against which to check the physical inventory count at the end of the accounting period. Also, these companies make no attempt to determine the cost of goods sold at the time of each sale. Instead, the cost of all the goods sold during the accounting period is determined at the *end* of the period. The determination of cost of goods sold requires the knowledge of these three items:

1. Beginning inventory (cost of goods on hand at the beginning of the period).
2. Net cost of purchases during the period.
3. Ending inventory (cost of unsold goods on hand at the end of the period).

This information would be shown as follows:

Beginning inventory	$ 24,000
Add: Net cost of purchases during the period	140,000
Cost of goods available for sale during the period	$164,000
Deduct: Ending inventory	20,000
Cost of goods sold during the period	$144,000

From the above schedule you see that the company began the accounting period with $24,000 of merchandise and purchased an additional $140,000, making a total of $164,000 of goods that could have been sold during the period. Then, a physical inventory showed that $20,000 remained unsold at the end of the period, which implies that $144,000 was the cost of goods sold during the period. Of course, the $144,000 is not necessarily the precise amount of goods sold during the period because no actual record was made of the dollar amount of goods sold. Periodic inventory procedure basically assumes that everything not on hand at the end of the period has been sold. This method disregards problems such as theft or breakage because the Merchandise Inventory account contains no up-to-date balance at the end of the accounting period against which the physical count can be compared.

The main emphasis of this chapter will be on periodic inventory procedure. You are now ready for an in-depth discussion of the accounts and journal entries used under periodic inventory procedure.

Purchases of Merchandise

Under periodic inventory procedure, a merchandising company uses the **Purchases account** to record the cost of merchandise bought for resale during the current accounting period. The Purchases account is increased by debits and appears with the income statement accounts in the chart of accounts.

*Objective 3
Record journal
entries for pur-
chase transactions
involving mer-
chandise*

To illustrate entries affecting the Purchases account, assume that Hanlon Retail Food Store made two purchases of merchandise from Smith Wholesale Company. Hanlon purchased $30,000 of merchandise on credit (on account) on May 4 and on May 21 purchased $20,000 of merchandise for cash. The required journal entries for Hanlon are:

```
May  4  Purchases . . . . . . . . . . . . . . . . . . . . . .  30,000
                Accounts Payable . . . . . . . . . . . . . . .          30,000
           To record purchase of merchandise on account.

     21  Purchases . . . . . . . . . . . . . . . . . . . . . .  20,000
                Cash . . . . . . . . . . . . . . . . . . . . .          20,000
           To record purchase of merchandise for cash.
```

Deductions from Purchases

On the buyer's books, purchase discounts and purchase returns and allowances are deducted from purchases to arrive at net purchases. These items are recorded in contra accounts to the Purchases account.

Purchase Discounts.   Often companies purchase merchandise under credit terms that permit the buyer to deduct a stated cash discount if the buyer pays the invoice within a specified time period. Assume that credit terms for Hanlon's May 4 purchase are 2/10, n/30. If Hanlon pays for the merchandise by May 14, the store may take a 2% discount. Thus, Hanlon must pay only $29,400 to settle the $30,000 account payable. The entry to record the payment of the invoice on May 14 is:

```
May 14  Accounts Payable . . . . . . . . . . . . . . . . . .  30,000
                Cash . . . . . . . . . . . . . . . . . . . . .          29,400
                Purchase Discounts . . . . . . . . . . . . . .             600
           To record payment on account within discount
           period.
```

The purchase discount is recorded only when the invoice is paid within the discount period and the discount is taken. The **Purchase Discounts account** is a contra account to Purchases that reduces the recorded invoice price of the goods purchased to the price actually paid. Purchase discounts are reported in the income statement as a deduction from purchases.

Note that the May 4 purchase was recorded at the invoice price. This method is called the gross price method. An alternative is to record purchases net of the purchase discounts. This alternative is described below.

Companies base purchase discounts on the invoice price of goods. If an invoice shows purchase returns or allowances, they must be deducted from the invoice price before calculating purchase discounts. For example, in the preceding transaction, the invoice price of goods purchased was $30,000. If Hanlon returned $2,000 of the goods, the purchase discount is calculated on $28,000.

Net Price Method. Most well-managed companies take advantage of all the discounts made available to them by their suppliers. Effective internal control over cash disbursements makes certain that the company takes these discounts. A company should consider borrowing cash to pay invoices within the discount period.

For example, assume a company purchases goods for $10,000 under terms 2/10, n/30. The buyer is unable to pay at the end of 10 days but expects to be able to pay at the end of 30 days. To take the $200 discount offered, the buyer needs a $9,800 loan for 20 days, beginning on the last day of the 10-day discount period. The buyer would benefit if the interest cost of such a loan is less than $200.

Some companies prefer to use the net price method because (1) the accounting theory behind the method is superior, and (2) the method strengthens internal control.

Under the **net price method,** a purchase is recorded in Purchases and Accounts Payable net of the discount. Thus, the discount is *deducted* from the invoice price *before* entering the transaction in the accounts. To illustrate, assume a company makes a $1,500 purchase on May 14 under terms 2/10, n/30. The company pays the invoice on May 24 and takes the discount. The entries comparing the net price method and the gross price method are:

		Net Price Method		Gross Price Method	
May 14	Purchases	1,470		1,500	
	Accounts Payable.		1,470		1,500
	Purchased goods under terms 2/10, n/30.				
24	Accounts Payable.	1,470		1,500	
	Cash		1,470		1,470
	Purchase Discounts*				30
	Paid account within discount period.				

* This account would not appear in the net price entry.

Theoretically, the net price method is preferred over the gross price method because it records the goods at their actual cost. Thus, the cost principle of accounting is applied, and goods are recorded at the total amount of resources given up to acquire them. Also, the liability is shown in the Accounts Payable account at the amount for which it could be settled. In spite of these factors, many companies continue to use the gross price method.

Note that in the above net price example, the company did not show the discounts taken. However, if the company had not paid the invoice within 10 days, an entry would have been made to the **Discounts Lost account.** For example, assume that the invoice in the above example was paid on May 28 instead of May 24. Then, the entries for the payment comparing the net price and gross price methods are:

		Net Price Method		Gross Price Method	
May 28	Accounts Payable.	1,470		1,500	
	Discounts Lost*.	30			
	Cash.		1,500		1,500
	Paid account after discount had expired.				

* This account would not appear in the gross price entry.

Under the net price method, the only time discounts appear is when the company has lost them. When discounts of 2% or more are available, effective cash management calls for internal control procedures ensuring that the company pays all invoices within the discount period. The failure to take a discount highlights a deviation from company policy and directs management's attention to this fact. Calling management's attention to deviations is sometimes called *management by exception.* Losses resulting from inefficiency are contained in the Discounts Lost account, which is usually reported among nonoperating expenses near the bottom of the income statement. Some companies prefer the net price method because it strengthens internal control over cash disbursements.

Interest Rate Implied in Cash Discounts. To decide whether you should take advantage of discounts by using your cash or borrowing, you can make this simple analysis. Assume that you must pay $10,000 within 30 days or $9,800 within 10 days to settle a $10,000 invoice with terms of 2/10, n/30. By advancing payment 20 days from the final due date, you can secure a discount of $200. The interest expense incurred to borrow $9,800 at 12% per year for 20 days is $65.33. In this case, you would save $134.67 ($200 − $65.33) by borrowing the money and paying the invoice within the discount period.

In terms of an annual rate of interest, the 2% rate of discount for 20 days is equivalent to a 36% annual rate: (360 ÷ 20) × 2%. The formula is:

$$\text{Equivalent annual} \atop \text{rate of interest} = \frac{\text{The number of days in a year (assumed to be 360)}}{\text{The number of days from the end of the discount period until the final due date}} \times \text{The percentage} \atop \text{rate of discount}$$

All cash discount terms can be converted into their approximate annual interest rate equivalents by use of this formula. Thus, a company could afford to pay up to 36% [(360 ÷ 20) × 2%] on borrowed funds to take advantage of discount terms of 2/10, n/30. The company could pay 18% on terms of 1/10, n/30.

Purchase Returns and Allowances.   A purchase return occurs when a buyer returns merchandise to a seller. When a buyer receives an allowance (or reduction in the price of goods shipped), a purchase allowance results. In such cases, the buyer commonly uses a debit memorandum to notify the seller that the account payable with the seller is being reduced (Accounts Payable is debited). A debit memorandum is similar to a credit memorandum except for the preprinted words, "WE DEBIT YOUR ACCOUNT." The buyer may use a copy of a debit memorandum to record the returns or allowances or may wait for confirmation, usually in the form of a credit memorandum, from the seller.

Both returns and allowances serve to reduce the buyer's debt to the seller and to reduce the cost of the goods purchased. The buyer may want to know the amount of returns and allowances as the first step in controlling the costs incurred in returning unsatisfactory merchandise or negotiating purchase allowances. For this reason, purchase returns and allowances are recorded in a separate **Purchase Returns and Allowances account.** If Hanlon returned $350 of merchandise to Smith Wholesale before paying for the goods, the following journal entry would be made:

Accounts Payable	350	
Purchase Returns and Allowances		350
To record return of damaged merchandise to supplier.		

The entry would have been the same to record a $350 allowance. Only the explanation would change.

If Hanlon had already paid the account, the debit would be to Cash instead of Accounts Payable, since Hanlon would receive a refund of cash. If the company took a discount at the time it paid the account, then only the net amount would be refunded. For instance, if a 2% discount had been taken, Hanlon's journal entry for the return would be:

Cash	343	
Purchase Discounts	7	
Purchase Returns and Allowances		350
To record return of damaged merchandise to supplier and record receipt of cash.		

Purchase Returns and Allowances is a contra account to the Purchases account, and the income statement shows it as a deduction from purchases. Assuming that a company records purchases under the gross price method, when both purchase discounts and purchase returns and allowances are deducted from purchases, the result is **net purchases.**

Transportation Costs

Transportation costs are an important part of cost of goods sold. To understand how to account for transportation costs, you must know the meaning of the following terms:

Objective 4
Describe the freight terms and record transportation costs

- The term **FOB shipping point** means "free on board at shipping point"; that is, the buyer incurs all transportation costs after the merchandise has been loaded on a railroad car or truck at the point of shipment. Thus, the buyer is responsible for ultimately paying the freight charges.
- The term **FOB destination** means "free on board at destination"; that is, the seller ships the goods to their destination without charge to the buyer. Thus, the seller is ultimately responsible for paying the freight charges.
- **Passage of title** is a legal term used to indicate transfer of legal ownership of goods. Title to the goods normally passes from seller to buyer at the FOB point. Thus, when goods are shipped FOB shipping point, title usually passes to the buyer at the shipping point. When goods are shipped FOB destination, title usually passes at destination.
- When the *seller* must initially pay the freight at the time of shipment, companies use the term **freight prepaid.**
- When the *buyer* must initially pay the freight bill on the arrival of the goods, companies use the term **freight collect.**

To illustrate the use of these terms, assume that a company ships goods FOB shipping point, freight collect. Title passes at the shipping point. The buyer is responsible for paying the $100 freight costs and does so. No entry for freight charges is made on the seller's books. The entry on the *buyer's books* is:

```
Transportation-In (or Freight-In) . . . . . . . . . . . . . . .    100
    Cash . . . . . . . . . . . . . . . . . . . . . . . . . . . . .          100
    To record payment of freight bill on goods purchased.
```

The **Transportation-In account** is used to record inward freight costs incurred in the acquisition of merchandise. Transportation-In is an adjunct account in that it is added to net purchases to arrive at **net cost of purchases.** An **adjunct account** is closely related to another account (Purchases, in this instance), and its balance is added to the balance of the related account in the financial statements. Recall that a contra account is just the opposite of an adjunct account. A contra account, such as accumulated depreciation, is *deducted* from the related account in the financial statements.

If the seller ships the goods FOB destination, freight prepaid, the seller is responsible for and pays the freight bill. The seller does not bill a separate freight cost to the buyer, so the buyer shows no entry for freight on its books. The seller, however, has undoubtedly considered the freight cost in setting selling prices. The following entry is required on the *seller's books*:

```
Delivery Expense (or Transportation-Out Expense). . . . . . .    100
    Cash . . . . . . . . . . . . . . . . . . . . . . . . . . . .         100
    To record freight cost on goods sold.
```

When the terms are FOB destination, the seller records the freight costs as **delivery expense,** which is a selling expense shown on the income statement with other selling expenses.

FOB terms are especially important at the end of an accounting period. Goods that are in transit at the end of an accounting period belong to either the seller or the buyer, and one of these parties must include these goods in its ending inventory. Goods shipped FOB destination belong to the seller while in transit, and the seller should include these goods in its ending inventory. Goods shipped FOB shipping point belong to the buyer while in transit, and the buyer should record these goods as a purchase and include them in its ending inventory. For example, assume that a seller ships goods on December 30, 1994, and they arrive at their destination on January 5, 1995. If terms are FOB destination, the seller includes the goods in its December 31, 1994, inventory, and neither seller nor buyer records the exchange transaction until January 5, 1995. If terms are FOB shipping point, the buyer includes the goods in its December 31, 1994, inventory, and both parties record the exchange transaction as of December 30, 1994.

Sometimes the seller initially prepays the freight as a convenience to the buyer, even though the buyer is ultimately responsible for paying it. In such cases, the buyer merely reimburses the seller for the amount of freight paid. For example, assume that Wood Company sold merchandise to Loud Company with terms of FOB shipping point, freight prepaid. The freight charges were $100. The following entries are necessary on the books of the buyer and the seller:

```
Buyer—Loud Company                  Seller—Wood Company
Transportation-In . .    100        Accounts
    Accounts                            Receivable . . . .    100
        Payable . . .        100            Cash. . . . . .        100
```

Such entries are necessary because Wood initially paid the freight charges when the company was not required to ultimately do so. Therefore, Loud Company must reimburse Wood for the charges. If the buyer pays freight for the seller (e.g., FOB destination, freight collect), the buyer merely deducts the freight paid from the amount owed to the seller. The following entries are necessary on the books of the buyer and the seller:

```
Buyer—Loud Company                  Seller—Wood Company
Accounts Payable .    100           Delivery Expense . .    100
    Cash. . . . . .        100           Accounts
                                            Receivable . .        100
```

Purchase discounts may only be taken on the purchase price of goods. Therefore, if a buyer owes the seller for freight charges, the buyer cannot take a discount on the freight charges owed, even if the buyer makes payment within the discount period.

Illustration 4.6 summarizes the discussion of freight terms and the resulting journal entries to record the freight charges.

Merchandise Inventories

Merchandise inventory is the cost of goods on hand and available for sale at any given time. For the management of a company to determine the cost of goods sold in any accounting period, it needs inventory information. Management must know its cost of goods on hand at the start of the period (beginning inventory), the net cost of purchases made during the period, and the cost of goods on hand at the close of the period (ending inventory). Since

Illustration 4.6
SUMMARY OF SHIPPING TERMS

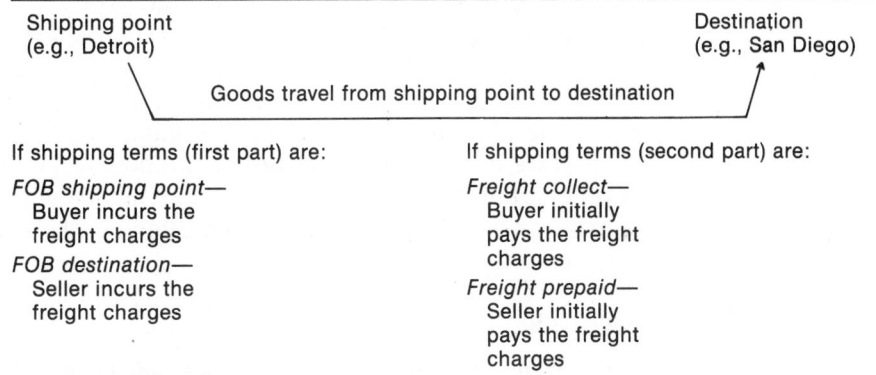

Shipping point
(e.g., Detroit)

Destination
(e.g., San Diego)

Goods travel from shipping point to destination

If shipping terms (first part) are:

FOB shipping point—
   Buyer incurs the
   freight charges
FOB destination—
   Seller incurs the
   freight charges

If shipping terms (second part) are:

Freight collect—
   Buyer initially
   pays the freight
   charges
Freight prepaid—
   Seller initially
   pays the freight
   charges

If the freight terms are combined as follows:

FOB shipping point, freight collect—Buyer both incurs and initially pays the freight charges. The proper party paid the freight. The buyer debits Transportation-In and credits Cash.

FOB destination, freight prepaid—Seller both incurs and initially pays the freight charges. The proper party paid the freight. The seller debits Delivery Expense and credits Cash.

FOB shipping point, freight prepaid—Buyer incurs the freight charges, and seller initially pays the freight charges. Buyer must reimburse seller for freight charges. The seller debits Accounts Receivable and credits Cash upon paying the freight. The buyer debits Transportation-In and credits Accounts Payable when informed of the freight charges.

FOB destination, freight collect—Seller incurs freight charges, and buyer initially pays freight charges. Buyer deducts freight charges from amount owed to seller. The buyer debits Accounts Payable and credits Cash when paying the freight. The seller debits Delivery Expense and credits Accounts Receivable when informed of the freight charges.

the ending inventory of the preceding period is the beginning inventory for the current period, management already knows the cost of the beginning inventory. Companies record purchases, purchase discounts, purchase returns and allowances, and transportation-in throughout the period. Therefore, management needs to determine only the cost of the ending inventory at the end of the period.

Taking a Physical Inventory. Under periodic inventory procedure, company personnel determine ending inventory cost by taking a *physical inventory*. Taking a **physical inventory** consists of counting physical units of each type of merchandise on hand. To calculate inventory cost, multiply the number of units of each kind of merchandise by its unit cost. Then combine the total costs of the various kinds of merchandise to provide the total ending inventory cost.

In taking a physical inventory, company personnel must be careful to ensure that they count all goods owned, regardless of where they are located, and include them in the inventory. Thus, companies should not record goods shipped to potential customers "on approval" as sold but should include these goods in their inventory. Similarly, companies should not record **consigned goods** (goods delivered to another party who will attempt to sell the goods for the owner at a commission) as sold goods. These goods remain the property of the owner (consignor) until sold by the consignee and must be included in the owner's inventory.

Merchandise in transit is merchandise in the hands of a freight company on the date of a physical inventory. As stated above, buyers must record merchandise in transit at the end of the accounting period as a purchase if the goods were shipped FOB shipping point and they have received title to the merchandise. In general, the goods belong to the party who must ultimately bear the transportation charges.

Determining Cost of Goods Sold

When accounting personnel know the beginning and ending inventories and the various items making up the net cost of purchases, they can determine the cost of goods sold.

Objective 5
Determine cost of goods sold

To illustrate, assume the following account balances for Hanlon Retail Food Store as of December 31, 1995:

Merchandise Inventory, January 1, 1995	$ 24,000 Dr.
Purchases	167,000 Dr.
Purchase Discounts.	3,000 Cr.
Purchase Returns and Allowances	8,000 Cr.
Transportation-In	10,000 Dr.

By taking a physical inventory, Hanlon determined the December 31, 1995, merchandise inventory to be $31,000. Hanlon then calculated its cost of goods sold as shown in Illustration 4.7. This computation appears in a section of the income statement directly below the calculation of net sales.

Illustration 4.7
DETERMINATION OF COST OF GOODS SOLD FOR HANLON RETAIL FOOD STORE*

Cost of goods sold:

Merchandise inventory, January 1, 1995			$ 24,000
Purchases		$167,000	
Less: Purchase discounts.	$3,000		
Purchase returns and allowances	8,000	11,000	
Net purchases		$156,000	
Add: Transportation-in		10,000	
Net cost of purchases			166,000
Cost of goods available for sale.			$190,000
Less: Merchandise inventory, December 31, 1995 . .			31,000
Cost of goods sold			$159,000

* This illustration is the same as Illustration 4.5, repeated here for your convenience.

In Illustration 4.7, Hanlon's beginning inventory ($24,000) plus net cost of purchases ($166,000) is equal to **cost of goods available for sale** ($190,000). Ending inventory cost ($31,000) is deducted from cost of goods available for sale to arrive at cost of goods sold ($159,000). The following diagram shows the relationship between these items:

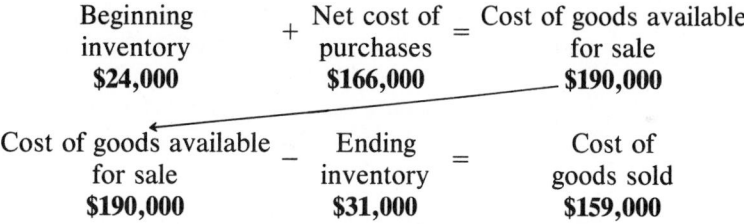

Another way of looking at this relationship is shown in the following diagram:

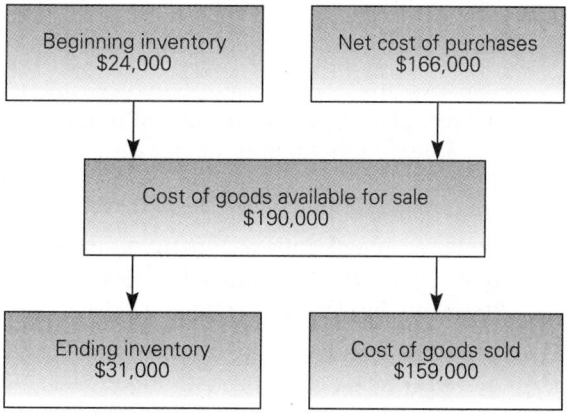

Beginning inventory and net cost of purchases combine to form cost of goods available for sale. The cost of goods available for sale is divided into ending inventory (which is the cost of goods not sold) and cost of goods sold.

To continue the calculation appearing in Illustration 4.7, net cost of purchases ($166,000) is equal to purchases ($167,000), *less* purchase discounts ($3,000) and purchase returns and allowances ($8,000), *plus* transportation-in ($10,000).

As shown in Illustration 4.7, ending inventory cost appears in the income statement as a deduction from cost of goods available for sale to compute cost of goods sold. Ending inventory cost (merchandise inventory) is also reported as a current asset in the end-of-period balance sheet.

Lack of Control under Periodic Inventory Procedure

Companies use periodic inventory procedure because of its simplicity and relatively low cost. However, as mentioned earlier, periodic inventory procedure provides for little control over inventory. Any items not included in the physical count of inventory at the end of the period are assumed to have been sold. Thus, even if the items have been stolen, they are assumed to have been sold, and their cost would be included in cost of goods sold.

To illustrate, assume that the cost of goods available for sale was $200,000 and ending inventory was $60,000. These figures suggest that the cost of goods sold was $140,000. Now assume that $2,000 of goods were actually shoplifted during the year. If such goods had not been stolen, the ending inventory would have been $62,000 and the cost of goods sold only $138,000. Thus, the $140,000 cost of goods sold calculated under periodic inventory procedure includes both the cost of the merchandise delivered to customers and the cost of merchandise stolen (if any).

CLASSIFIED INCOME STATEMENT

Objective 6
Prepare a classified income statement

In preceding chapters, we illustrated the unclassified (or single-step) income statement. An **unclassified income statement** has only two categories of items—revenues and expenses. In contrast, a **classified income statement** divides both revenues and expenses into operating and nonoperating items. The statement also separates operating expenses into selling and administrative expenses. A classified income statement, also called a multiple-step income statement, is introduced in this section.

Illustration 4.8 presents a classified income statement for Hanlon Retail Food Store. This statement uses the previously presented data on sales (Illustration 4.4) and cost of goods sold (Illustration 4.7), together with additional assumed data on operating expenses and other expenses and revenues. Note in Illustration 4.8 that a classified income statement has the following four major sections:

1. Operating revenues.
2. Cost of goods sold.

Illustration 4.8
CLASSIFIED INCOME STATEMENT FOR A MERCHANDISING COMPANY

HANLON RETAIL FOOD STORE
Income Statement
For the Year Ended December 31, 1995

Operating revenues:				
Gross sales				$282,000
Less: Sales discounts			$ 5,000	
Sales returns and allowances			15,000	20,000
Net sales				$262,000
Cost of goods sold:				
Merchandise inventory, January 1, 1995			$ 24,000	
Purchases		$167,000		
Less: Purchase discounts	$3,000			
Purchase returns and allowances	8,000	11,000		
Net purchases		$156,000		
Add: Transportation-in		10,000		
Net cost of purchases			166,000	
Cost of goods available for sale			$190,000	
Less: Merchandise inventory, December 31, 1995			31,000	
Cost of goods sold				159,000
Gross margin				$103,000
Operating expenses:				
Miscellaneous selling expenses:				
Sales salaries and commissions expense		$ 26,000		
Salespersons' travel expense		3,000		
Delivery expense		2,000		
Advertising expense		4,000		
Rent expense—store building		2,500		
Supplies expense		1,000		
Utilities expense		1,800		
Depreciation expense—store equipment		700		
Other selling expense		400	$ 41,400	
Miscellaneous administrative expenses:				
Salaries expense, executive		$ 29,000		
Rent expense—administrative building		1,600		
Insurance expense		1,500		
Supplies expense		800		
Depreciation expense—office equipment		1,100		
Other administrative expenses		300	34,300	
Total operating expenses				75,700
Income from operations				$ 27,300
Nonoperating revenues and expenses:				
Nonoperating revenues:				
Interest revenue				1,400
				$ 28,700
Nonoperating expenses:				
Interest expense				600
Net income				$ 28,100

3. Operating expenses.
4. Nonoperating revenues and expenses (other revenues and other expenses).

The classified income statement shows important relationships that help in analyzing how well the company is performing. For example, by deducting cost of goods sold from operating revenues, you can determine by what amount sales revenues exceed the cost of items being sold. If this margin, called gross margin, is lower than desired, a company may need to increase its selling prices or decrease its cost of goods sold. The classified income statement subdivides operating expenses into selling and administrative expenses. Thus, the statement users can see how much expense is being incurred in selling the product and how much in administering the business. Statement users can also make comparisons with other years' data for the same business and with other businesses. Nonoperating revenues and expenses appear at the bottom of the income statement because they are less significant in assessing the profitability of the business.

In the paragraphs that follow, we explain the major headings of the classified income statement shown in Illustration 4.8. The terms in some of these headings are already familiar to you.

1. **Operating revenues** are the revenues generated by the major activities of the business—usually the sale of products or services or both.

2. **Cost of goods sold** is the major expense in merchandising companies. Illustration 4.7 showed the cost of goods sold section of the classified income statement. This chapter has already discussed the items used in calculating cost of goods sold. The amount by which sales revenues exceed the cost of goods sold is usually shown in the top part of the income statement. The excess of net sales over cost of goods sold is the **gross margin or gross profit.** Gross margin may also be expressed as a percentage rate, computed by dividing gross margin by net sales. In Illustration 4.8, the gross margin rate is approximately 39.3% ($103,000/$262,000). The gross margin rate indicates that out of each sales dollar, approximately 39 cents is available to cover other expenses and produce income. Business owners watch the gross margin rate closely since a small percentage fluctuation can cause a large dollar change in net income. Also, a downward trend in the gross margin rate may indicate a problem, such as theft of merchandise.

3. **Operating expenses** for a merchandising company are those expenses, other than cost of goods sold, incurred in the normal business functions of a company. Usually, operating expenses are classified as either selling expenses or administrative expenses. **Selling expenses** are expenses a company incurs in selling and marketing efforts. Examples include salaries and commissions of salespersons, expenses for salespersons' travel, delivery, advertising, rent and utilities on a sales building, sales supplies used, and depreciation on delivery equipment used in sales. **Administrative expenses** are expenses a company incurs in the overall management of a busi-

ness. Examples include administrative salaries, rent and utilities on an administrative building, insurance expense, administrative supplies used, and depreciation on office equipment.

Certain operating expenses may be related partly to the selling function and partly to the administrative function. For example, a company might incur rent, taxes, and insurance on a building for both sales and administrative purposes. Expenses covering both the selling and administrative functions must be analyzed and prorated between the two functions on the income statement. For instance, if $1,000 of depreciation expense relates 60% to selling and 40% to administrative based on the square footage or number of employees, the income statement would show $600 as a selling expense and $400 as an administrative expense.

4. **Nonoperating revenues (other revenues)** are revenues not related to the sale of products or services regularly offered for sale by a business. An example of a nonoperating revenue is interest that a business earns on notes receivable. **Nonoperating expenses (other expenses)** are expenses not related to the acquisition and sale of the products or services regularly offered for sale. An example of a nonoperating expense is interest incurred on money borrowed by the company.

Important Relationships in the Income Statement

The more important relationships in the income statement of a merchandising firm can be summarized in equation form, as follows:

1. **Net sales** = Gross sales − (Sales discounts + Sales returns and allowances).
2. **Net purchases** = Purchases − (Purchase discounts + Purchase returns and allowances).
3. **Net cost of purchases** = Net purchases + Transportation-in.
4. **Cost of goods sold** = Beginning inventory + Net cost of purchases − Ending inventory.
5. **Gross margin** = Net sales − Cost of goods sold.
6. **Income from operations** = Gross margin − Operating (selling and administrative) expenses.
7. **Net income** = Income from operations + Nonoperating revenues − Nonoperating expenses.

Each relationship is important because of the way it relates to an overall measure of business profitability. For example, a company may produce a high gross margin on sales. However, because of large sales commissions and delivery expenses, the company may realize only a very small percentage of the gross margin as profit. The classifications in the income statement allow a user to focus on the whole picture as well as on how net income was derived (statement relationships).

Future illustrations may vary somewhat in form, but the basic organization of the classified income statement described above will be retained.

THE WORK SHEET FOR A MERCHANDISING COMPANY

Objective 7
Prepare a work sheet and closing entries for a merchandising company

Illustration 4.9 shows a work sheet for a merchandising company. To keep the illustration simple, a different retail company will be introduced. Lyons Company is a small sporting goods corporation. The illustration for Lyons Company focuses on the merchandise-related accounts. The fixed assets (land, building, and equipment) are not shown. Except for the merchandise-related accounts, the work sheet for a merchandising company is the same as for a service company. Recall from the appendix in Chapter 3 that use of a work sheet assists in the preparation of the adjusting and closing entries. The work sheet also contains all the information needed for the preparation of the financial statements.

To further simplify this illustration, assume Lyons needs no adjusting entries at month-end. The trial balance is taken from the ledger accounts at December 31, 1995. The $7,000 merchandise inventory in the trial balance is the beginning inventory. The sales and sales-related accounts and the purchases and purchases-related accounts summarize the merchandising activity for December 1995.

Completing the Work Sheet

Any revenue accounts (Sales) and contra purchases accounts (Purchase Discounts, Purchase Returns and Allowances) that appear in the Adjusted Trial Balance credit columns of the work sheet are carried to the Income Statement credit column. Beginning inventory, contra revenue accounts (Sales Discounts, Sales Returns and Allowances), Purchases, Transportation-In, and expense accounts (Selling Expenses, Administrative Expenses) shown in the Adjusted Trial Balance debit column are carried to the Income Statement debit column.

Note that the amount of ending merchandise inventory, $8,000, is entered in the Income Statement credit column because it is deducted from cost of goods available for sale (beginning inventory plus net cost of purchases) in determining cost of goods sold. The ending inventory is also entered in the Balance Sheet debit column to establish the proper balance in the Merchandise Inventory account. The reason both beginning and ending inventories are brought to the Income Statement columns is because both are used to calculate cost of goods sold in the income statement. Net income or net loss for the period will balance the Income Statement columns as it did in previous work sheets. Net income/loss is carried to the Statement of Retained Earnings credit/debit column. For Lyons Company, the net income is $5,843 for the month of December and is carried to the Statement of Retained Earnings credit column.

Illustration 4.9
WORK SHEET FOR A MERCHANDISING COMPANY

LYONS COMPANY
Work Sheet
For the Month Ended December 31, 1995

Acct. No.	Account Titles	Trial Balance Debit	Trial Balance Credit	Adjustments Debit	Adjustments Credit	Adjusted Trial Balance Debit	Adjusted Trial Balance Credit	Income Statement Debit	Income Statement Credit	Statement of Retained Earnings Debit	Statement of Retained Earnings Credit	Balance Sheet Debit	Balance Sheet Credit
100	Cash	19,663				19,663						19,663	
103	Accounts Receivable	1,880				1,880						1,880	
105	Merchandise Inventory	7,000				7,000		7,000	8,000			8,000	
200	Accounts Payable		700				700						700
300	Capital Stock		10,000				10,000						10,000
310	Retained Earnings, December 1		15,000				15,000				15,000		
320	Dividends	2,000				2,000				2,000			
410	Sales		14,600				14,600		14,600				
411	Sales Discounts	44				44		44					
412	Sales Returns and Allowances	20				20		20					
500	Purchases	6,000				6,000		6,000					
501	Purchase Discounts		82				82		82				
502	Purchase Returns and Allowances		100				100		100				
503	Transportation-In	75				75		75					
557	Miscellaneous Selling Expenses	2,650				2,650		2,650					
567	Miscellaneous Administrative Expenses	1,150				1,150		1,150					
		40,482	40,482			40,482	40,482	16,939	22,782				
	Net Income							5,843			5,843		
								22,782	22,782	2,000	20,843	29,543	10,700
	Retained Earnings, December 31									18,843			18,843
										20,843	20,843	29,543	29,543

The beginning balance in Retained Earnings is carried to the Statement of Retained Earnings credit column. The Dividends balance is carried to the Statement of Retained Earnings debit column. All other assets (Cash and Accounts Receivable) are carried to the Balance Sheet debit column. The liability (Accounts Payable), Capital Stock, and ending Retained Earnings balance are carried to the Balance Sheet credit column.

Financial Statements for a Merchandising Company

Once the work sheet has been completed, the financial statements are prepared. Next, any adjusting and closing entries are entered in the journal and posted to the ledger. This process clears the accounting records for the next accounting period. Finally, a post-closing trial balance is prepared.

Income Statement.   Illustration 4.10 shows the income statement Lyons prepared from its work sheet in Illustration 4.9. The focus in this income statement is on the determination of the cost of goods sold.

Statement of Retained Earnings.   The statement of retained earnings, as you recall, is a financial statement that summarizes the transactions affecting the Retained Earnings account balance. In Illustration 4.11, the state-

Illustration 4.10
INCOME STATEMENT FOR A MERCHANDISING COMPANY

LYONS COMPANY
Income Statement
For the Month Ended December 31, 1995

Operating revenues:			
Gross sales			$14,600
Less: Sales discounts		$ 44	
Sales returns and allowances		20	64
Net sales			$14,536
Cost of goods sold:			
Merchandise inventory, December 1, 1995		$ 7,000	
Purchases	$6,000		
Less: Purchase discounts . . . . $ 82			
Purchase returns and allowances 100	182		
Net purchases	$5,818		
Add: Transportation-in	75		
Net cost of purchases		5,893	
Cost of goods available for sale		$12,893	
Less: Merchandise inventory, December 31, 1995		8,000	
Cost of goods sold			4,893
Gross margin			$ 9,643
Operating expenses:			
Miscellaneous selling expenses		$ 2,650	
Miscellaneous administrative expenses		1,150	
Total operating expenses			3,800
Net income			$ 5,843

Illustration 4.11
STATEMENT OF RETAINED EARNINGS

<table>
<tr><td colspan="2" align="center">**LYONS COMPANY**
Statement of Retained Earnings
For the Month Ended December 31, 1995</td></tr>
<tr><td>Retained Earnings, December 1, 1995. . . . .</td><td>$15,000</td></tr>
<tr><td>Add: Net income for the month . . . .</td><td>5,843</td></tr>
<tr><td>Total . . . .</td><td>$20,843</td></tr>
<tr><td>Deduct: Dividends . . . .</td><td>2,000</td></tr>
<tr><td>Retained earnings, December 31, 1995 . . . .</td><td>$18,843</td></tr>
</table>

ment of retained earnings shows the increase in retained earnings resulting from net income and the decrease in retained earnings resulting from dividends.

Balance Sheet.   The balance sheet, Illustration 4.12, contains the assets, liabilities, and stockholders' equity items taken from the work sheet. Note the $8,000 ending inventory is shown as a current asset. The Retained Earnings account balance comes from the statement of retained earnings.

Closing Entries

Recall from Chapter 3 that the closing process normally takes place after the accountant has prepared the financial statements for the period. The closing

Illustration 4.12
BALANCE SHEET FOR A MERCHANDISING COMPANY

<table>
<tr><td colspan="3" align="center">**LYONS COMPANY**
Balance Sheet
December 31, 1995
Assets</td></tr>
<tr><td>Current assets:</td><td></td><td></td></tr>
<tr><td>Cash . . . .</td><td></td><td>$19,663</td></tr>
<tr><td>Accounts receivable . . . .</td><td></td><td>1,880</td></tr>
<tr><td>Merchandise inventory. . . . .</td><td></td><td>8,000</td></tr>
<tr><td>Total assets . . . .</td><td></td><td>$29,543</td></tr>
<tr><td colspan="3" align="center">**Liabilities and Stockholders' Equity**</td></tr>
<tr><td>Current liabilities:</td><td></td><td></td></tr>
<tr><td>Accounts payable . . . .</td><td></td><td>$ 700</td></tr>
<tr><td>Stockholders' equity:</td><td></td><td></td></tr>
<tr><td>Capital stock . . . .</td><td>$10,000</td><td></td></tr>
<tr><td>Retained earnings . . . .</td><td>18,843</td><td></td></tr>
<tr><td>Total stockholders' equity . . . .</td><td></td><td>28,843</td></tr>
<tr><td>Total liabilities and stockholders' equity. . . . .</td><td></td><td>$29,543</td></tr>
</table>

process closes revenue and expense accounts by transferring their balances to a clearing account called Income Summary and then to Retained Earnings. The closing process reduces the revenue and expense account balances to zero so that information for each accounting period may be accumulated separately from any previous period.

Closing entries may be prepared directly from the work sheet in Illustration 4.9. The closing entries for Lyons Company are given below.

The first journal entry *debits* all items appearing in the Income Statement credit column of the work sheet and *credits* Income Summary for the total of the column, $22,782.

	1995		
1st entry	Dec. 31	Merchandise Inventory (ending)	8,000	
		Sales.	14,600	
		Purchase Discounts.	82	
		Purchase Returns and Allowances.	100	
		Income Summary.		22,782
		To close accounts with a credit balance in the Income Statement columns and to establish ending merchandise inventory.		

The second entry *credits* all items appearing in the Income Statement debit column and *debits* Income Summary for the total of that column, $16,939.[1]

	Dec. 31	Income Summary.	16,939	
2nd entry		Merchandise Inventory (beginning)		7,000
		Sales Discounts		44
		Sales Returns and Allowances.		20
		Purchases		6,000
		Transportation-In		75
		Miscellaneous Selling Expenses		2,650
		Miscellaneous Administrative Expenses		1,150
		To close accounts with a debit balance in the Income Statement columns.		

In the third entry, the credit balance in the Income Summary account of $5,843 is closed to the Retained Earnings account.

	Dec. 31	Income Summary.	5,843	
3rd entry		Retained Earnings		5,843
		To close the Income Summary account to the Retained Earnings account.		

In the fourth entry, the Dividends account balance of $2,000 is closed to the Retained Earnings account.

---

[1] You may close debit balanced accounts (in the income statement) before credit balanced accounts. This practice does not affect the balance of the Income Summary account or the amount of net income.

Dec. 31	Retained Earnings	2,000	
	Dividends		2,000
	To close the Dividends account to the Retained Earnings account.		

4th entry

Note how the first three closing entries tie into the totals shown in the Income Statement columns of the work sheet in Illustration 4.9. In the first closing journal entry, the credit to the Income Summary account is equal to the subtotal of the Income Statement credit column. In the second entry, the debit to the Income Summary account is equal to the subtotal of the Income Statement debit column. The difference between the subtotals of the two Income Statement columns ($5,843) represents net income and is the amount of the third closing entry.

The effects of these closing entries are shown in the following T-accounts:

Merchandise Inventory

Bal. before closing	7,000	1995 Dec. 31 To close to Income Summary	7,000

1995
Dec. 31 To establish actual
               ending inventory
               balance
	8,000		

Sales

1995 Dec. 31 To close to Income Summary	14,600	Bal. before closing	14,600
		Bal. after closing	–0–

Sales Discounts

Bal. before closing	44	1995 Dec. 31 To close to Income Summary	44
Bal. after closing	–0–		

Sales Returns and Allowances

Bal. before closing	20	1995 Dec. 31 To close to Income Summary	20
Bal. after closing	–0–		

Purchases

Bal. before closing	6,000	1995 Dec. 31 To close to Income Summary	6,000
Bal. after closing	–0–		

Purchase Discounts

1995 Dec. 31 To close to Income Summary	82	Bal. before closing	82
		Bal. after closing	–0–

Purchase Returns and Allowances

1995 Dec. 31 To close to Income Summary	100	Bal. before closing	100
		Bal. after closing	–0–

Transportation-In

Bal. before closing	75	1995 Dec. 31 To close to Income Summary	75
Bal. after closing	–0–		

Miscellaneous Selling Expenses

Bal. before closing	2,650	1995 Dec. 31 To close to Income Summary	2,650
Bal. after closing	–0–		

Miscellaneous Administrative Expenses

		1995	
Bal. before closing	1,150	Dec. 31 To close to Income Summary	1,150
Bal. after closing	–0–		

Income Summary

1995		1995	
Dec. 31 From closing accounts appearing in Income Statement debit column of work sheet	16,939	Dec. 31 From closing accounts appearing in Income Statement credit column of work sheet	22,782
1995			
Dec. 31 To close to Retained Earnings account	5,843	Bal. (net income) before closing this account	5,843
		Bal. after closing	–0–

Retained Earnings

1995		1995	
Dec. 31 From closing Dividends account	2,000	Dec. 31 Beg. bal. From closing Income Summary account	15,000 5,843
		End. bal.	18,843

Dividends

		1995	
Bal. before closing	2,000	Dec. 31 To close to Retained Earnings account	2,000
Bal. after closing	–0–		

After the entries have been posted to the ledger, only the balance sheet accounts have balances. The revenue, expense, and Dividends accounts have zero balances. Lyons would now prepare a post-closing trial balance that would contain only balance sheet accounts (assets, liabilities, Capital Stock, and Retained Earnings). The chapter Appendix illustrates an alternative closing procedure.

You should now understand the distinction between accounting for a service company and a merchandising company. The next chapter discusses merchandise inventory carried by merchandising companies.

MARKET-VALUE RULES NOW ALL BUT CERTAIN

Williamsburg, Va.—New audit standards forcing the disclosures of balance sheet market values are a virtual certainty, declared one of the rule-writers involved in the decision.

The standard-setter, Clarence Sampson, a member of the Financial Accounting Standards Board, warned corporate accountants and money managers at a meeting of the Financial Executives Institute here that at best they could influence some of the details and timing of the controversial new rule. But he said time was running out.

"It would be much more effective if you would tell us how best to do it, rather than not to do it at all," said Sampson in public remarks that are among the frankest to date.

In response, John B. Sperry, a professor at Virginia Commonwealth University in Richmond, Va., and an outspoken figure in the profession, issued a call to arms.

"The public accounting profession has abrogated its responsibility to influence the FASB," Sperry declared as leader of a panel discussion following Sampson's appearance. "Put pressure on your auditing firm. The policy of the FASB is made in the national offices of the Big Six firms."

But Thomas Martin, an Ernst & Young partner, challenged Sperry's Big Six charge, telling the financial executives, "We're just as frustrated as you are."

Sampson's appearance at the meeting of the Financial Executives Institute came at a time of obvious strain with FASB. Just days before, a FASB board member, publicly branded anti-business, had failed to gain re-appointment to the board in what was widely interpreted to be a victory for the pro-business stance voiced by FEI members.

Sampson charged FASB's overseer, the Financial Accounting Foundation, had "no basis" for dropping former IBM Corp. executive C. Arthur Northrop, from the board.

But Sampson left an opening for FEI when he said major parts of the new standards would remain loose.

"We propose to leave it up to you as to what would be practicable," he said. "We also propose to avoid cramming some rules down your throats."

Anticipating objections from public accountants, however, Sampson added, "Subjectivity doesn't make auditors very happy. But it's not my job or yours to make things any easier for them. And it makes it more flexible for you."

As Sampson spoke, the period allowed for open comments was coming to an end. In all, FASB received 77 comment letters from the public. Three days of hearings are scheduled at the end of this month at FASB's offices in Norwalk, Conn.

"The board does believe that the market value of financial instruments in particular should be disclosed in some capacity," Sampson told the corporate financial officers.

But on other parts of the balance sheet, Sampson indicated, the board would be more lenient, perhaps allowing a whole new off-balance sheet statement of market values reminiscent of the currency-trading and the now long-forgotten inflation-adjustment supplements.

Although a number of experts who followed Sampson to the stage grudgingly agreed that market value accounting appeared inevitable, their opposition remained undiluted.

"No matter how you do it, market value would be extremely difficult and costly." declared Michael Walsch, a vice president at Signet Banking Corp. Martin's counter that audit costs would remain unchanged by the new rule were met with wry chuckles.

Walsch and Sperry agreed that the drive to market value could spur bankers into more risk-free lending, extending the nation's credit crunch.

SOURCE: Rick Telberg, *Accounting Today*, Reprinted by permission from *Accounting Today*, May 13, 1991, p. 3. Copyright Lebhar-Friedman, 425 Park Avenue, New York, NY 10022.

ETHICS   A CLOSER LOOK

Perry Publishing is the sole manufacturer and distributor of "quickie" books. "Quickie" books are paperback featurettes that Perry pieces together from various public sources on current "hot" topics, such as currently popular movie and music entertainers. Perry traditionally ships one initial pressing of several thousand books and rarely prints more than the initial quantity.

The books are then immediately shipped out and invoiced to grocery and discount store retailers, where the books have a typical shelf life of one to two months. However, the retailers do not pay for the books in advance and are usually shipped far more books than they will ever sell. But the retailers never send back the "quickie" books. Instead, within two to three months, the retailers pay for the copies they sell and return the book covers from those which they do not sell. Some books sell out completely while others flop miserably—selling "quickie" books can be a matter of luck.

Although Perry manufactures books year-round, it ships most of its books in late November and sells two-thirds of its books during the year-end Christmas season. Every year, when Perry prepares its year-end financial statements as of December 31, it treats all the "quickie" books it has shipped to retailers as sold. Any books returned from the Christmas season are reflected as returns during the following accounting period. Perry has adopted this accounting policy with regards to inventory because it feels it cannot realistically estimate how many returns it may experience.

Required
Comment on Perry's accounting policy for "quickie" book inventory. How might you improve this policy?

UNDERSTANDING THE LEARNING OBJECTIVES

1. Record journal entries for sales transactions involving merchandise.
    *   In a sales transaction, the seller transfers the legal ownership (title) of the goods to the buyer.
    *   An invoice is a document, prepared by the seller of merchandise and sent to the buyer, that contains the details of a sale, such as the number of units sold, unit price, total price, terms of sale, and manner of shipment.
    *   Usually sales are for cash or on account. When a sale is for cash, the debit is to Cash, and the credit is to Sales. When a sale is on account, the debit is to Accounts Receivable, and the credit is to Sales.
    *   When companies offer trade discounts, the gross selling price (gross invoice price) at which the sale is recorded is equal to the list price minus any trade discounts.
    *   Two common deductions from gross sales are (1) sales discounts and (2) sales returns and allowances. These deductions are recorded in contra revenue accounts to the Sales account. Both the Sales Discounts account and the Sales Returns and Allowances account nor-

mally have debit balances. Net sales = Sales − (Sales discounts + Sales returns and allowances).
- Sales discounts arise when the seller offers the buyer a cash discount of 1% to 3% to induce early payment of an amount due.
- Sales returns result from merchandise being returned by a buyer because the goods are considered unsatisfactory or have been damaged. A sales allowance is a deduction from the original invoiced sales price granted to a customer when the customer keeps the merchandise but is dissatisfied.

2. Describe briefly cost of goods sold and the distinction between perpetual and periodic inventory procedures.
   - Cost of goods sold = Beginning inventory + Net cost of purchases − Ending inventory. Net cost of purchases = Purchases − (Purchase discounts + Purchase returns and allowances) + Transportation-in.
   - Two methods of accounting for inventory are perpetual inventory procedure and periodic inventory procedure. Under perpetual inventory procedure, the inventory account is continuously updated during the accounting period. Under periodic inventory procedure, the inventory account is updated only periodically—after a physical count has been made.

3. Record journal entries for purchase transactions involving merchandise.
   - Purchases of merchandise are recorded by debiting Purchases and crediting Cash (for cash purchases) or crediting Accounts Payable (for purchases on account).
   - When the net price method is used, a purchase is recorded in Purchases and Accounts Payable *net* of the discount.
   - If a discount is missed, the Discounts Lost account is debited. This procedure focuses management's attention on discounts missed rather than on discounts taken.
   - Two common deductions from purchases are shown in (1) purchase discounts and (2) purchase returns and allowances. In the general ledger, both of these items normally carry credit balances. From the buyer's side of the transactions, cash discounts are purchase discounts, and merchandise returns and allowances are purchase returns and allowances.

4. Describe the freight terms and record transportation costs.
   - FOB shipping point means "free on board at shipping point"—the buyer incurs the freight.
   - FOB destination means "free on board at destination"—the seller incurs the freight.
   - Passage of title is a legal term used to indicate transfer of legal ownership of goods.
   - Freight prepaid is when the seller must initially pay the freight at the time of shipment.
   - Freight collect is when the buyer must initially pay the freight on the arrival of the goods.

5. Determine cost of goods sold.
   - Expansion and application of the relationship introduced in Learning Objective 2. Beginning inventory + Net cost of purchases = Cost of goods available for sale. Cost of goods available for sale − Ending inventory = Cost of goods sold.
6. Prepare a classified income statement.
   - A classified income statement has four major sections—operating revenues, cost of goods sold, operating expenses, and nonoperating revenues and expenses.
   - Operating revenues are the revenues generated by the major activities of the business—usually the sale of products or services or both.
   - Cost of goods sold is the major expense in merchandising companies.
   - Operating expenses for a merchandising company are those expenses other than cost of goods sold incurred in the normal business functions of a company. Usually, operating expenses are classified as either selling expenses or administrative expenses.
   - Nonoperating revenues and expenses are revenues and expenses not related to the sale of products or services regularly offered for sale by a business.
7. Prepare a work sheet and closing entries for a merchandising company.
   - Except for the merchandise-related accounts, the work sheet for a merchandising company is the same as for a service company.
   - Any revenue accounts and contra purchases accounts that appear in the Adjusted Trial Balance credit column of the work sheet are carried to the Income Statement credit column.
   - Beginning inventory, contra revenue accounts, Purchases, Transportation-In, and expense accounts shown in the Adjusted Trial Balance debit column are carried to the Income Statement debit column.
   - Ending merchandise inventory is entered in the Income Statement credit column and in the Balance Sheet debit column.
   - Closing entries may be prepared directly from the work sheet. The first journal entry debits all items appearing in the Income Statement credit column and credits Income Summary. The second entry credits all items appearing in the Income Statement debit column and debits Income Summary. The third entry debits Income Summary and credits the Retained Earnings account (assuming positive net income). The fourth entry debits the Retained Earnings account and credits the Dividends account.

APPENDIX

ALTERNATIVE CLOSING PROCEDURE

Many of the users of this text prefer the closing process illustrated in the chapter because it is easy to perform. If you are satisfied with that approach, you need not read this appendix. Some users, however, prefer an alternative procedure that they believe communicates more effectively the purposes behind the closing process. Since the end result of both methods is the same, both are correct. The procedure used depends on personal preference.

This appendix illustrates the alternative closing procedure. Under this alternative procedure, the beginning inventory balance and balances in all purchase-related accounts are transferred into the Cost of Goods Sold account in an *adjusting entry*. In a separate *adjusting entry*, the ending inventory is established by debiting Merchandise Inventory and crediting Cost of Goods Sold.

Using the same data from Illustration 4.9, the required adjusting entries for inventory and cost of goods sold under this alternative procedure are as shown below.

The first adjusting entry transfers into the Cost of Goods Sold account the net cost of all the goods available for sale during the year. At this point the Cost of Goods Sold account contains the cost of goods available for sale. The second adjusting entry then removes from the Cost of Goods Sold account the cost of goods unsold at year-end and establishes this amount as the ending inventory.

```
1995
Dec. 31  Cost of Goods Sold . . . . . . . . . . . . . . . .  12,893
            Purchase Discounts . . . . . . . . . . . . . .        82
            Purchase Returns and Allowances . . . . . . . .      100
                Merchandise Inventory (beginning) . . . . . . .          7,000
                Purchases . . . . . . . . . . . . . . . . . . .          6,000
                Transportation-In . . . . . . . . . . . . . . .             75
            To transfer the beginning inventory and the
            accounts comprising net purchases to the Cost of
            Goods Sold account.

      31  Merchandise Inventory (ending) . . . . . . . . . .   8,000
                Cost of Goods Sold . . . . . . . . . . . . . .          8,000
            To set up ending inventory and reduce Cost of
            Goods Sold by the cost of goods not sold.
```

The result of these two entries is that the Cost of Goods Sold account contains the amount of expense incurred during the year for merchandise delivered to customers. The Cost of Goods Sold account is closed as follows:

```
1995
Dec. 31  Income Summary. . . . . . . . . . . . . . . . . .  4,893
                Cost of Goods Sold. . . . . . . . . . . . . .          4,893
            To close Cost of Goods Sold to Income Summary.
```

This final entry would generally be included in the compound closing entry for all expenses closed at the end of the period rather than being journalized separately. A difference between the two alternatives is that the method in the chapter does not set up a ledger account for Cost of Goods Sold, while this method does.

Illustration 4.13 (pages 220–21) shows how a work sheet is prepared using this alternative procedure and focuses on the merchandise-related accounts.

Trial Balance Columns   The Trial Balance columns have the same data as shown in Illustration 4.9 in this chapter.

Adjusted Trial Balance Columns   Note that under this method the net balance in Cost of Goods Sold ($4,893) is shown in the Adjusted Trial Balance debit column. Also, the $8,000 ending inventory appears in this same column.

Income Statement Columns   The only purchase-related item that appears in the Income Statement columns is the cost of goods sold ($4,893).

Statement of Retained Earnings Columns   The Statement of Retained Earnings columns have the same data as shown in Illustration 4.9 in this chapter.

Balance Sheet Columns   The Balance Sheet columns have the same data as shown in Illustration 4.9 in this chapter.

Closing Entries   The closing entries under this alternative procedure are as follows:

1995					
Dec.	31	Sales		14,600	
		Income Summary			14,600
		To close accounts with a balance in the Income Statement credit column.			
	31	Income Summary		8,757	
		Sales Discounts			44
		Sales Returns and Allowances			20
		Miscellaneous Selling Expenses.			2,650
		Miscellaneous Administrative Expenses			1,150
		Cost of Goods Sold			4,893
		To close accounts with a balance in the Income Statement debit column.			
	31	Income Summary		5,843	
		Retained Earnings			5,843
		To close the Income Summary account to the Retained Earnings account.			
	31	Retained Earnings		2,000	
		Dividends			2,000
		To close the Dividends account to the Retained Earnings account.			

Illustration 4.13
WORK SHEET USING ALTERNATIVE PROCEDURE

LYONS COMPANY
Work Sheet
For the Month Ended December 31, 1995

Acct. No.	Account Titles	Trial Balance Debit	Trial Balance Credit	Adjustments Debit	Adjustments Credit	Adjusted Trial Balance Debit	Adjusted Trial Balance Credit	Income Statement Debit	Income Statement Credit	Statement of Retained Earnings Debit	Statement of Retained Earnings Credit	Balance Sheet Debit	Balance Sheet Credit
100	Cash	19,663				19,663						19,663	
103	Accounts Receivable	1,880				1,880						1,880	
105	Merchandise Inventory, Dec. 1	7,000			(1) 7,000								
200	Accounts Payable		700				700						700
300	Capital Stock		10,000				10,000						10,000
310	Retained Earnings, December 1		15,000				15,000				15,000		
320	Dividends	2,000				2,000				2,000			
410	Sales		14,600				14,600		14,600				
411	Sales Discounts	44				44		44					
412	Sales Returns and Allowances	20				20		20					

Acct. No.	Account	T.B. Dr.	T.B. Cr.	Adj. Dr.	Adj. Cr.	Adj. T.B. Dr.	Adj. T.B. Cr.	Inc. Stmt. Dr.	Inc. Stmt. Cr.	Ret. Earn. Dr.	Ret. Earn. Cr.	Bal. Sheet Dr.	Bal. Sheet Cr.
500	Purchases	6,000			(1) 6,000								
501	Purchase Discounts		82	(1) 82									
502	Purchase Returns and Allowances		100	(1) 100									
503	Transportation-In	75			(1) 75								
557	Miscellaneous Selling Expenses	2,650				2,650		2,650					
567	Miscellaneous Administrative Expenses	1,150				1,150		1,150					
		40,482	40,482										
504	Cost of Goods Sold			(1) 12,893	(2) 8,000	4,893		4,893					
105	Merchandise Inventory, Dec. 31*			(2) 8,000		8,000						8,000	
				21,075	21,075	40,300	40,300	8,757	14,600	2,000			10,700
	Net Income							5,843			5,843		
								14,600	14,600				
	Retained Earnings, December 31									18,843			18,843
										20,843	20,843	29,543	29,543

Adjustments:
(1) To transfer the beginning inventory and the accounts comprising net purchases to the Cost of Goods Sold account.
(2) To set up ending inventory and reduce Cost of Goods Sold by the cost of goods not sold.

* If desired, the $8,000 in the Adjustments debit column and in the Balance Sheet debit column may be placed on the same line as the $7,000 beginning inventory figure.

DEMONSTRATION PROBLEM 4–A

The following transactions occurred between Companies A and B during June 1995:

June 10   Company A purchased merchandise from Company B for $60,000; terms
          2/10/EOM, n/60, FOB destination.
     11   Company B paid freight of $900.
     14   Company A received an allowance of $3,000 from the gross invoice price
          because of damaged goods.
     23   Company A returned $6,000 of goods purchased because they were not the
          quality ordered.
     30   Company B received payment in full from Company A.

Required:

a. Journalize the transactions for Company A using the gross price method.
b. Journalize the transactions for Company B.

Solution to demonstration problem 4–A

a.

GENERAL JOURNAL

Date		Account Titles and Explanation	Post. Ref.	Debit	Credit
		Company A			
1995 June	10	Purchases		6 0 0 0 0	
		Accounts Payable			6 0 0 0 0
		Purchased merchandise from Company B; terms 2/10/EOM, n/60.			
	14	Accounts Payable		3 0 0 0	
		Purchase Returns and Allowances			3 0 0 0
		Received an allowance from Company B for damaged goods.			
	23	Accounts Payable		6 0 0 0	
		Purchase Returns and Allowances			6 0 0 0
		Returned merchandise to Company B because of improper quality.			
	30	Accounts Payable ($60,000 − $3,000 − $6,000)		5 1 0 0 0	
		Cash ($51,000 − $1,020)			4 9 9 8 0
		Purchase Discounts ($51,000 × 0.02)			1 0 2 0
		Paid amount due on June 10th purchase.			

b.

GENERAL JOURNAL

Date		Account Titles and Explanation	Post. Ref.	Debit	Credit
		Company B			
1995 June	10	Accounts Receivable		6 0 0 0 0	
		Sales			6 0 0 0 0
		Sold merchandise to Company A; terms 2/10/EOM, n/60.			
	11	Delivery Expense		9 0 0	
		Cash			9 0 0
		Paid freight on sale of merchandise shipped FOB destination.			
	14	Sales Returns and Allowances		3 0 0 0	
		Accounts Receivable			3 0 0 0
		Granted an allowance to Company A for damaged goods.			
	23	Sales Returns and Allowances		6 0 0 0	
		Accounts Receivable			6 0 0 0
		Merchandise returned from Company A due to improper quality.			
	30	Cash ($51,000 − $1,020)		4 9 9 8 0	
		Sales Discounts ($51,000 × 0.02)		1 0 2 0	
		Accounts Receivable ($60,000 − $3,000 − $6,000)			5 1 0 0 0
		Received the amount due from Company A.			

DEMONSTRATION PROBLEM 4–B

ANN'S MUSIC STORE
Trial Balance
July 31, 1995

Acct. No.	Account Title	Debits	Credits
100	Cash	$ 52,170	
103	Accounts Receivable.	6,900	
105	Merchandise Inventory, August 1, 1994	47,100	
108	Prepaid Insurance	1,080	
112	Prepaid Rent	7,200	
172	Office Equipment	18,000	
173	Accumulated Depreciation—Office Equipment		$ 6,750
200	Accounts Payable		12,000
300	Capital Stock		20,000
310	Retained Earnings, August 1, 1994		13,000
320	Dividends	30,000	
410	Sales		450,000
412	Sales Returns and Allowances	1,500	
500	Purchases	291,000	
502	Purchase Returns and Allowances		2,100
503	Transportation-In	7,800	
505	Advertising Expense	1,500	
507	Salaries Expense	34,800	
511	Utilities Expense	2,100	
518	Supplies Expense	2,700	
		$503,850	$503,850

Ann Parkman has prepared the above trial balance for Ann's Music Store, a small corporation. The following information will be used to prepare the work sheet.

1. A 12-month fire insurance policy was purchased for $1,080 on April 1, 1995, the date on which insurance coverage began.
2. On February 1, 1995, Ann paid $7,200 for the next 12 months' rent. The payment was recorded in the Prepaid Rent account.
3. Depreciation expense on the office equipment is $2,250.
4. Merchandise inventory at July 31, 1995, was $39,600.

Required:

a. Prepare a 12-column work sheet for Ann's Music Store for the fiscal year ended July 31, 1995. Use the chart of accounts on the inside covers of the text to assign additional account numbers as needed.
b. Prepare a classified income statement for the fiscal year ended July 31, 1995. The only selling expense is the advertising expense.
c. Prepare a statement of retained earnings for the fiscal year ended July 31, 1995.
d. Prepare a classified balance sheet for July 31, 1995.
e. Prepare closing entries.

Solution to demonstration problem 4–B

a.

ANN'S MUSIC STORE
Work Sheet
For the Year Ended July 31, 1995

Acct. No.	Account Titles	Trial Balance Debit	Trial Balance Credit	Adjustments Debit	Adjustments Credit	Adjusted Trial Balance Debit	Adjusted Trial Balance Credit	Income Statement Debit	Income Statement Credit	Statement of Retained Earnings Debit	Statement of Retained Earnings Credit	Balance Sheet Debit	Balance Sheet Credit
100	Cash	52,170				52,170						52,170	
103	Accounts Receivable	6,900				6,900						6,900	
105	Merchandise Inventory	47,100				47,100		47,100	39,600			39,600	
108	Prepaid Insurance	1,080			(1) 360	720						720	
112	Prepaid Rent	7,200			(2) 3,600	3,600						3,600	
172	Office Equipment	18,000				18,000						18,000	
173	Accumulated Depreciation—Office Equipment		6,750		(3) 2,250		9,000						9,000
200	Accounts Payable		12,000				12,000						12,000
300	Capital Stock		20,000				20,000						20,000
310	Retained Earnings, August 1, 1994		13,000				13,000				13,000		
320	Dividends	30,000				30,000				30,000			
410	Sales		450,000				450,000		450,000				
412	Sales Returns and Allowances	1,500				1,500		1,500					

No.	Account	Trial Balance Dr	Trial Balance Cr	Adjustments Dr	Adjustments Cr	Adjusted Trial Balance Dr	Adjusted Trial Balance Cr	Income Statement Dr	Income Statement Cr	Retained Earnings Dr	Retained Earnings Cr	Balance Sheet Dr	Balance Sheet Cr
500	Purchases	291,000				291,000		291,000					
502	Purchase Returns and Allowances		2,100				2,100		2,100				
503	Transportation-In	7,800				7,800		7,800					
505	Advertising Expense	1,500				1,500		1,500					
507	Salaries Expense	34,800				34,800		34,800					
511	Utilities Expense	2,100				2,100		2,100					
518	Supplies Expense	2,700				2,700		2,700					
		503,850	503,850										
512	Insurance Expense			(1) 360		360		360					
515	Rent Expense			(2) 3,600		3,600		3,600					
525	Depreciation Expense—Office Equipment			(3) 2,250		2,250		2,250					
				6,210	6,210	506,100	506,100	394,710	491,700				
	Net Income							96,990			96,990		
								491,700	491,700	30,000	109,990		41,000
	Retained Earnings, July 31, 1995									79,990			79,990
										109,990	109,990	120,990	120,990

Adjustments:
(1) Expiration of prepaid insurance ($1,080 × 4/12).
(2) Expiration of prepaid rent ($7,200 × 6/12).
(3) Depreciation expense on office equipment for the fiscal year ended July 31, 1995.

b.

ANN'S MUSIC STORE
Income Statement
For the Year Ended July 31, 1995

Operating revenues:

Gross sales			$450,000
Less: Sales returns and allowances			1,500
Net sales			$448,500

Cost of goods sold:

Merchandise inventory, August 1, 1994		$ 47,100	
Purchases	$291,000		
Less: Purchase returns and allowances	2,100		
Net purchases	$288,900		
Add: Transportation-in	7,800		
Net cost of purchases		296,700	
Cost of goods available for sale		$343,800	
Less: Merchandise inventory, July 31, 1995		39,600	
Cost of goods sold			304,200
Gross margin			$144,300

Operating expenses:

Selling expenses:

Advertising expense		$ 1,500	

Administrative expenses:

Salaries expense	$ 34,800		
Utilities expense	2,100		
Supplies expense	2,700		
Insurance expense	360		
Rent expense	3,600		
Depreciation expense—office equipment	2,250	45,810	
Total operating expenses			47,310
Net income			$ 96,990

---

c.

ANN'S MUSIC STORE
Statement of Retained Earnings
For the Year Ended July 31, 1995

Retained earnings, August 1, 1994	$ 13,000
Add: Net income for the year	96,990
Total	$109,990
Deduct: Dividends	30,000
Retained earnings, July 31, 1995	$ 79,990

---

d.

ANN'S MUSIC STORE
Balance Sheet
July 31, 1995
Assets

Current assets:

Cash	$52,170	
Accounts receivable	6,900	
Merchandise inventory	39,600	
Prepaid insurance	720	
Prepaid rent	3,600	
Total current assets		$102,990

Property, plant, and equipment:

Office equipment	$18,000	
Less: Accumulated depreciation	9,000	
Total property, plant, and equipment . . .		9,000
Total assets		$111,990

Liabilities and Stockholders' Equity

Liabilities:

Accounts payable		$ 12,000

Stockholders' equity:

Capital stock	$20,000	
Retained earnings	79,990	99,990
Total liabilities and stockholders' equity		$111,990

---

e. Closing entries:

1995
July 31 Merchandise Inventory   39,600
          Sales   450,000
          Purchase Returns and Allowances.   2,100
              Income Summary.   491,700
          To close accounts with credit balances in the Income
          Statement column and to set up the ending
          merchandise inventory.

      31 Income Summary.   394,710
              Merchandise Inventory   47,100
              Sales Returns and Allowances   1,500
              Purchases   291,000
              Transportation-In.   7,800
              Advertising Expense   1,500
              Salaries Expense.   34,800
              Utilities Expense   2,100
              Supplies Expense   2,700
              Insurance Expense   360
              Rent Expense   3,600
              Depreciation Expense—Office Equipment   2,250
          To close accounts with debit balances in the Income
          Statement column.

      31 Income Summary.   96,990
              Retained Earnings   96,990
          To close the Income Summary account to the
          Retained Earnings account.

      31 Retained Earnings   30,000
              Dividends   30,000
          To close Dividends account.

NEW TERMS

Adjunct account   Closely related to another account; its balance is added to the balance of the related account in the financial statements. *197*

Administrative expenses   Expenses a company incurs in the overall management of a business. *204*

Cash discount   A deduction from the invoice price that can be taken only if the invoice is paid within a specified period of time: to the seller, it is a sales discount; to the buyer, it is a purchase discount. *186*

Chain discount   Occurs when the list price of a product is subject to several of trade discounts. *186*

Classified income statement   Divides both revenues and expenses into operating and nonoperating items. The statement also separates operating expenses into selling and administrative expenses. Also called the multiple-step income statement. *202*

Consigned goods   Goods delivered to another party who will attempt to sell the goods for the owner at a commission. *200*

Cost of goods available for sale   Equal to beginning inventory plus net cost of purchases. *201*

Cost of goods sold   Shows the cost to the seller of the goods sold to customers; under periodic inventory procedure, cost of goods sold is computed as Beginning inventory + Net cost of purchases − Ending inventory. *190, 204, 205*

Delivery expense   A selling expense recorded by the seller for freight costs incurred when terms are FOB destination. *198*

Discounts Lost account   The account used to show the amount of discounts not taken when purchased merchandise is recorded using the net price method. *195*

FOB destination   Means "free on board at destination"; goods are shipped to their destination without charge to the buyer; the seller is responsible for paying the freight charges. *197*

FOB shipping point   Means "free on board at shipping point"; buyer incurs all transportation costs after the merchandise is loaded on a railroad car or truck at the point of shipment. *197*

Freight collect   Terms that require the buyer to pay the freight bill on arrival of the goods. *197*

Freight prepaid   Terms that indicate the seller has paid the freight bill at the time of shipment. *197*

Gross margin or gross profit   Net sales − Cost of goods sold; identifies the number of dollars available to cover expenses other than cost of goods sold; may be expressed as a percentage rate. *204, 205*

Gross selling price   The list price less all trade discounts. *185*

Income from operations   Gross margin − Operating (selling and administrative) expenses. *205*

Inventory   See Merchandise inventory.

Invoice   A document, prepared by the seller of merchandise and sent to the buyer, that contains the details of a sale, such as the number of units sold, unit price, total price billed, terms of sale, and manner of shipment; a purchase invoice from the buyer's point of view and a sales invoice from the seller's point of view. *184*

Manufacturers   Companies that produce goods from raw materials and normally sell them to wholesalers. *182*

Merchandise in transit   Merchandise in the hands of a freight company on the date of a physical inventory. *200*

Merchandise inventory   The quantity of goods on hand and available for sale at any given time. *190, 199*

Net cost of purchases   Net purchases + Transportation-in. *197, 205*

Net income   Income from operations + Nonoperating revenues − Nonoperating expenses. *205*

Net price method   An accounting procedure in which purchases and accounts payable are initially recorded at gross price less discount offered for prompt payment. Records discounts lost rather than discounts taken. *194*

Net purchases   Purchases − (Purchase discounts + Purchase returns and allowances). *197, 205*

Net sales   Gross sales − (Sales discounts + Sales returns and allowances). *183, 205*

Nonoperating expenses (other expenses)   Expenses incurred by a business that are not related to the acquisition and sale of the products or services regularly offered for sale. *205*

Nonoperating revenues (other revenues)   Revenues not related to the sale of products or services regularly offered for sale by a business. *205*

Operating expenses   Those expenses other than cost of goods sold incurred in the normal business functions of a company. *204*

Operating revenues   Those revenues generated by the major activities of a business. *204*

Passage of title   A legal term used to indicate transfer of legal ownership of goods. *197*

Periodic inventory procedure   A method of accounting for merchandise acquired for sale to customers wherein the cost of merchandise sold and the cost of merchandise on hand are determined only at the end of the accounting period by taking a physical inventory. *191, 192*

Perpetual inventory procedure   A method of accounting for merchandise acquired for sale to customers wherein the Merchandise Inventory account is continuously updated to reflect items on hand; this account is debited for each purchase and credited for each sale so that the current balance is shown in the account at all times. *191*

Physical inventory   Consists of counting physical units of each type of merchandise on hand. *200*

Purchase discount   See Cash discount.

Purchase Discounts account   A contra account to Purchases that reduces the recorded gross invoice cost of the purchase to the price actually paid. *194*

Purchase Returns and Allowances account   An account used under periodic inventory procedure to record the cost of merchandise returned to a seller and to record reductions in selling prices granted by a seller because merchandise was not satisfactory to a buyer; viewed as a reduction in the recorded cost of purchases. *196*

Purchases account   An account used under periodic inventory procedure to record the cost of goods or merchandise bought for resale during the current accounting period. *193*

Retailers   Companies that sell goods to final consumers. *182*

Sales allowance   A deduction from the original invoiced sales price granted to a customer when the customer keeps the merchandise but is dissatisfied for any of a number of reasons, including inferior quality or damage or deterioration in transit. *188*

Sales discount   See Cash discount.

Sales Discounts account   A contra revenue account to Sales; it is shown as a deduction from gross sales in the income statement. *187*

Sales return   From the seller's point of view, merchandise returned by a buyer for any of a variety of reasons; to the buyer, a purchase return. *188*

Sales Returns and Allowances account   A contra revenue account to Sales used to record the selling price of merchandise returned by buyers or reductions in selling prices granted. *188*

Selling expenses   Expenses a company incurs in selling and marketing efforts. *204*

Trade discount   A percentage deduction, or discount, from the specified list price or catalog price of merchandise to arrive at the gross invoice price; granted to particular categories of customers (e.g., retailers and wholesalers). Also see Chain discount. *185*

Transportation-In account   An account used under periodic inventory procedure to record inward freight costs incurred in the acquisition of merchandise; a part of cost of goods sold. *197*

Unclassified income statement   Shows only major categories for revenues and expenses. Also called the single-step income statement. *202*

Wholesalers   Companies that normally sell goods to retailers for resale. *182*

SELF-TEST

True-False

Indicate whether each of the following statements is true or false.

1. Sales discounts and sales returns and allowances are deducted from gross sales to determine net sales.

2. Under periodic inventory procedure, the cost of goods sold is reflected in the balance of the Purchases account.

3. Transportation costs on goods shipped FOB destination are added to net purchases to arrive at net cost of purchases.

4. An income statement that separates revenues and expenses into operating and nonoperating items is called a classified income statement.

5. The merchandise inventory amount in the Balance Sheet debit column of the work sheet is the ending inventory.

Multiple-Choice

Select the best answer for each of the following questions.

1. The entry on the books of the seller to record the return of merchandise sold on account for which no payment has been received is:
   a. Accounts Receivable (Dr.); Sales Returns and Allowances (Cr.).
   b. Sales (Dr.); Accounts Receivable (Cr.).
   c. Sales Returns and Allowances (Dr.); Accounts Receivable (Cr.).
   d. None of the above.

2. Cost of goods sold refers to:
   a. Cost of goods available for sale less ending inventory.
   b. Cost prices that are identified with the items that were sold during the period.
   c. Net cost of purchases plus beginning inventory.
   d. Net sales less gross margin.
   e. All of the above except (c)

3. An account payable of $400 is subject to a 2% discount if paid within the 10-day discount period. Part of the entry to record this payment under the gross price method would be:
   a. A credit to Accounts Payable of $392.
   b. A debit to Accounts Payable of $400.
   c. A credit to Accounts Payable of $400.

d. A credit to Cash of $400.

e. A debit to Purchase Discounts of $8.

4. In the income statement:

a. The amount shown as "Net sales" includes all cash sales plus only those charge sales for which cash has been received.

b. Expenses are subtracted from revenues to determine the balance of the Retained Earnings account.

c. Operating expenses are usually classified as either "Selling expenses" or "Administrative expenses."

d. Ending inventory is added to the net cost of purchases to determine goods available for sale.

e. "Net income from operations" and "Net income" are synonymous.

5. The closing entries for merchandise-related accounts include:

a. A credit to Merchandise Inventory for the cost of the beginning inventory.

b. A debit to Purchase Discounts.

c. A credit to Purchases.

d. A debit to Merchandise Inventory for the ending inventory.

e. All of the above.

Now turn to page 244 to check your answers.

QUESTIONS

1. Which account titles are likely to appear in the ledger of a merchandising company that do not appear in the ledger of a service enterprise?

2. What entry is made to record a sale of merchandise on account?

3. Describe trade discounts and chain discounts.

4. Sales discounts and sales returns and allowances are deducted from sales on the income statement to arrive at net sales. Why not deduct these directly from the Sales account by debiting Sales each time a sales discount, return, or allowance occurs?

5. What are the two basic procedures for accounting for inventory? How do these two procedures differ?

6. What useful purpose does the Purchases account serve?

7. Explain how use of the net price method of accounting for purchases can improve internal control.

8. How would purchase discounts lost be shown in the income statement?

9. What do the letters FOB stand for? When terms are *FOB destination,* who incurs the cost of freight?

10. What type of an expense is delivery expense? Where is this expense reported in the income statement?

11. Periodic inventory procedure is said to afford little control over inventory. Explain why.

12. How does the accountant arrive at the total dollar amount of the inventory after taking a physical inventory?

13. How is cost of goods sold determined under periodic inventory procedure?

14. If the cost of goods available for sale and the cost of the ending inventory are known, what other amount appearing on the income statement can be calculated?

15. What are the major sections in a classified income statement for a merchandising company, and in what order do these sections appear?

16. What is gross margin? Why might management be interested in the percentage of gross margin to net sales?

17. After closing entries are posted to the ledger, which types of accounts have balances? Why?

MAYTAG
CORPORATION

18. *Real-world question*   Based on the financial statements of Maytag Corporation contained in Appendix C, what were the 1991 selling, general, and administrative expenses?

THE LIMITED, INC.

19. *Real-world question*   Based on the financial statements of The Limited, Inc., contained in Appendix C, what were the 1991 cost of goods sold, occupancy, and buying costs?

HARLAND

20. *Real-world question*   Based on the financial statements of John H. Harland Company contained in Appendix C, what was the 1991 income from operations?

EXERCISES

Apply rules of debit and credit for merchandise-related accounts
(L.O. 1, 3)

4–1. In the following table, indicate how each account shown is increased and decreased (debit or credit), and indicate the normal balance (debit or credit).

Title of Account	Increased by (debit or credit)	Decreased by (debit or credit)	Normal Balance (debit or credit)
Merchandise Inventory			
Sales			
Sales Returns and Allowances			
Sales Discounts			
Accounts Receivable			
Purchases			
Purchase Returns and Allowances			
Purchase Discounts			
Accounts Payable			
Transportation-In			

Prepare entries for merchandise purchase/sale, return, and allowance on both buyer's and seller's books
(L.O. 1, 3)

4–2. *a.* Heard Company purchased $56,000 of merchandise from Manzano Company on account. Before paying its account, Heard Company returned damaged merchandise with an invoice price of $11,680. Assuming use of periodic inventory procedure and the gross price method, prepare entries on both companies' books to record the purchase/sale and the return.

b. Show how any of the required entries would change assuming that Manzano Company granted an allowance of $3,360 on the damaged goods instead of giving permission to return the merchandise.

Determine end of
discount period
and prepare entry
to record payment
(L.O. 1, 3)

4–3. What is the last payment date on which the cash discount can be taken on goods sold on March 5 for $102,400; terms 3/10/EOM, n/60? Assume that the bill is paid on this date and prepare the correct entry on both the buyer's and seller's books to record the payment. Use the gross price method.

Calculate effect of
trade and cash
discounts on
payment
(L.O. 1, 3)

4–4. You have purchased merchandise with a list price of $36,000. Because you are a wholesaler, you are granted trade discounts of 30%, 20%, and 10%. The cash discount terms are 2/EOM, n/60. How much will you remit if you pay the invoice by the end of the month of purchase? How much will you remit if you do not pay until the following month?

Calculate gross
invoice price and
final payment
(L.O. 1, 3)

4–5. Carroll Company sold merchandise with a list price of $30,000 on July 1, 1995. For each of the independent assumptions below, calculate (1) the gross selling price that would be used to record the sale and (2) the amount that the buyer would have to pay when paying the invoice.

Trade Discount Granted	Credit Terms	Date Paid
a. 30%, 20%	2/10, n/30	July 10
b. 40%, 10%	2/EOM, n/60	August 10
c. 30%, 10%, 5%	3/10/EOM, n/60	August 10
d. 40%	1/10, n/30	July 12

Determine cash
discount available
and amount of
cash paid
(L.O. 1, 3, 4)

4–6. Sinclair Company purchased goods at a gross selling price of $2,400 on August 1, 1995. Discount terms of 2/10, n/30 were available. For each of the following independent situations, determine (1) the cash discount available on the final payment and (2) the amount of cash paid if payment is made within the discount period.

Transportation Terms	Freight Paid (by)	Purchase Allowance Granted
a. FOB shipping point	$240 (buyer)	$480
b. FOB destination	120 (seller)	240
c. FOB shipping point	180 (seller)	720
d. FOB destination	192 (buyer)	120

Record purchases
using net price
method
(L.O. 3)

4–7. McGee Company uses the net price method for handling purchase discounts. Prepare the journal entries necessary to record the following 1995 transactions:

Oct. 6   Purchased $2,700 of merchandise from Lowry Company; terms 2/10, n/30.

   7   Purchased $9,000 of merchandise from Jennings Company; terms 2/10, n/30.

  17   Paid the invoice from Jennings Company for the October 7 purchase.

  31   Paid the invoice from Lowry Company for the October 6 purchase.

4–8. Gresham Company purchased goods for $42,000 on June 14 under the following terms: 3/10, n/30; FOB shipping point, freight collect. The bill for the freight amounted to $1,200.

    a. Assume the invoice was paid within the discount period, and prepare all entries required on Gresham Company's books using the gross price method.

    b. Assume that the invoice was paid on July 11. Prepare the entry to record the payment made on that date.

    c. Repeat *(a)* using the net price method.

    d. Repeat *(b)* using the net price method.

4–9. Kinsey Company uses periodic inventory procedure. Determine the cost of goods sold for the company assuming purchases during the period were $40,000, transportation-in was $300, purchase returns and allowances were $1,000, beginning inventory was $25,000, purchase discounts were $2,000, and ending inventory was $13,000.

4–10. In each case below, use the information provided to calculate the missing information:

	Case 1	Case 2	Case 3
Gross sales	$640,000	$?	$?
Sales discounts	?	25,600	19,200
Sales returns and allowances	19,200	44,800	32,000
Net sales	608,000	1,209,600	?
Merchandise inventory, January 1	256,000	?	384,000
Purchases.	384,000	768,000	?
Purchase discounts	7,680	13,440	12,800
Purchase returns and allowances.	24,320	31,360	32,000
Net purchases.	352,000	?	672,000
Transportation-in	25,600	38,400	32,000
Net cost of purchases	377,600	761,600	?
Cost of goods available for sale	?	1,081,600	1,088,000
Merchandise inventory, December 31 . . .	?	384,000	448,000
Cost of goods sold	320,000	?	640,000
Gross margin	?	512,000	320,000

4–11. In each of the following equations, supply the missing term(s):

    a. Net sales = Gross sales − (_____ _____ + Sales returns and allowances).

    b. Cost of goods sold = Beginning inventory + Net cost of purchases − _____ _____ .

    c. Gross margin = _____ _____ − Cost of goods sold.

    d. Income from operations = _____ _____ − Operating expenses.

    e. Net income = Income from operations + _____ _____ − _____ _____ .

Prepare partial
work sheet using
merchandise-related
accounts (L.O. 7)

4–12. Given the balances shown in the partial trial balance, indicate how the balances would be treated in the work sheet. The ending inventory is $96. (The amounts are unusually small for ease in rewriting the numbers.)

Account Titles	Trial Balance		Adjustments		Adjusted Trial Balance		Income Statement		Statement of Retained Earnings		Balance Sheet	
	Debit	Credit	Debit	Credit	Debit	Credit	Debit	Credit	Debit	Credit	Debit	Credit
Merchandise												
Inventory	120											
Sales		840										
Sales Discounts	18											
Sales Returns												
and Allowances	48											
Purchases	600											
Purchase												
Discounts		12										
Purchase Returns												
and Allowances		24										
Transportation-In	36											

Prepare and post
closing entries
using T-accounts
(L.O. 7)

4–13. Using the data in Exercise 4–12:
  a. Prepare closing entries for the accounts shown above. Do not close the Income Summary account.
  b. Show in T-account format how the accounts would appear after this portion of the closing process has been completed.

PROBLEMS

Journalize
merchandise
transactions for
two different
companies
(L.O. 1, 3, 4)

4–1. a. Fletcher Sporting Goods Company engaged in the following transactions in April 1995:

Apr. 1 Sold merchandise on account for $144,000; terms 2/10, n/30, FOB destination.
   5 $21,600 of the goods sold on account on April 1 were returned for full credit. Payment for these goods had not yet been received.
   8 A sales allowance of $2,880 was granted on the merchandise sold on April 1 because the merchandise was damaged in shipment.
   10 Payment was received for the net amount due from the sale of April 1.

b. Espinoza Stereo Company engaged in the following transactions in July 1995.

July 2 Purchased stereo merchandise on account at a cost of $21,600; terms 2/10, n/30, FOB destination.

15 Sold merchandise for $32,400; terms 2/10, n/30, FOB destination.

16 Paid freight costs on the merchandise sold, $1,080.

20 Espinoza Stereo Company was granted an allowance of $1,440 on the purchase of July 2 because of damaged merchandise.

31 Paid the amount due on the purchase of July 2.

Required:

Prepare journal entries to record the transactions.

Journalize merchandise transactions on both buyer's and seller's books (L.O. 1, 3, 4)

4-2. Knight Musical Instrument Company and Crisp Company engaged in the following transactions with each other during July 1995:

July 2 Knight Musical Instrument Company purchased merchandise on account with a list price of $48,000 from Crisp Company. The terms were 3/EOM, n/60, FOB shipping point, freight collect. Trade discounts of 15%, 10%, and 5% were granted by Crisp Company.

5 The buyer paid the freight bill on the purchase of July 2, $1,104.

6 The buyer returned damaged merchandise with an invoice price of $2,790 to the seller and received full credit.

On the last day of the discount period, the buyer paid the seller for the merchandise.

Required:

Prepare all the necessary journal entries for the buyer and the seller.

Journalize merchandise transactions on both buyer's and seller's books (L.O. 1, 3, 4)

4-3. Rogers Ski Shop and Carlson Company entered into the following transactions with each other during March 1995:

Mar. 1 Rogers Ski Shop purchased merchandise on account from Carlson Company, at a list price of $54,000. Trade discounts of 30%, 25%, and 5% were granted. Terms were 2/EOM, n/60, FOB shipping point.

4 The buyer paid the freight of $1,116.

25 The seller granted the buyer an allowance of $5,400 against the amount due because of damaged merchandise.

31 The buyer paid the amount due.

Required:

Journalize all the entries on the books of both the buyer and seller.

Prepare and post journal entries, and prepare trial balance and classified income statement (L.O. 1–6)

4-4. The data for June 1995 given below are for Acuff Company's first month of operations:

June 1 Acuff Company was organized, and the stockholders invested $504,000 cash, $168,000 of merchandise inventory, and a $144,000 plot of land.

4 Merchandise was purchased for cash, $216,000; FOB shipping point.

June 9   Cash of $5,040 was paid to a trucking company for delivery of the merchandise purchased June 4.

13   The company sold merchandise on account, $144,000; terms 2/10, n/30.

15   The company sold merchandise on account, $115,200; terms 2/10, n/30.

16   Of the merchandise sold June 13, $15,840 was returned for credit.

20   Salaries for services received were paid as follows: to office employees, $15,840; to salespersons, $41,760.

22   The company collected the amount due on the remaining $128,160 of accounts receivable arising from the sale of June 13.

24   The company purchased merchandise on account at a cost of $172,800; terms 2/10, n/30, FOB shipping point.

26   The company returned $28,800 of the merchandise purchased June 24 to the vendor for credit.

27   A trucking company was paid $3,600 for delivery to Acuff Company of the goods purchased June 24.

29   The company sold merchandise on account, $192,000; terms 2/10, n/30.

30   Sold merchandise for cash, $86,400.

30   Payment was received for the sale of June 15.

30   Paid store rent for June, $21,600.

30   Paid the amount due on the purchase of June 24.

Additional data

The inventory on hand at the close of business June 30 was $336,000 at cost.

Required:

a. Prepare journal entries for the transactions.

b. Post the journal entries to the proper ledger accounts. Use the account numbers shown in the chart of accounts on the inside covers of the text. Assume that all postings are from page 20 of the general journal.

c. Prepare a trial balance as of June 30, 1995.

d. Prepare a classified income statement for the month ended June 30, 1995. No adjusting entries are needed.

Prepare work sheet, classified income statement, statement of retained earnings, classified balance sheet, and closing entries
(L.O. 5–7)

4–5. The following data are for Holloway Lumber Company:

HOLLOWAY LUMBER COMPANY
Trial Balance
December 31, 1995

Acct. No.	Account Title	Debits	Credits
100	Cash.	$ 70,640	
103	Accounts Receivable	159,520	
105	Merchandise Inventory	285,200	
107	Supplies on Hand	5,360	
108	Prepaid Insurance	4,800	
112	Prepaid Rent.	57,600	
170	Equipment.	88,000	
171	Accumulated Depreciation—Equipment		$ 17,600
200	Accounts Payable		102,800
300	Capital Stock.		300,000
310	Retained Earnings		119,640
410	Sales		1,122,360
412	Sales Returns and Allowances	5,160	
418	Interest Revenue		1,000
500	Purchases	500,840	
502	Purchase Returns and Allowances.		4,040
503	Transportation-In	7,840	
505	Advertising Expense	78,000	
508	Sales Salaries Expense	138,400	
509	Office Salaries Expense.	80,800	
510	Officers' Salaries Expense	160,000	
511	Utilities Expense	4,800	
536	Legal and Accounting Expense	10,000	
540	Interest Expense	600	
567	Miscellaneous Administrative Expense.	9,880	
		$1,667,440	$1,667,440

Additional data

1. A total of $3,400 of the prepaid insurance has expired.
2. An inventory of supplies showed that $1,700 are still on hand.
3. Prepaid rent expired during the year is $50,600.
4. Depreciation expense on store equipment is $8,800.
5. Accrued sales salaries are $4,000.
6. Accrued office salaries are $3,000.
7. Merchandise inventory on hand is $350,000.

Required:

Prepare the following:

a. A work sheet for the year ended December 31, 1995. Refer to the chart of accounts on the inside covers of the text for any other account numbers you may need.

b. A classified income statement. The only selling expenses are sales salaries, advertising, supplies, and depreciation—equipment.

c. A statement of retained earnings.

d. A classified balance sheet.

e. The December 31, 1995, closing entries.

Prepare and post
journal entries,
prepare work
sheet, classified
income statement,
classified balance
sheet, and closing
entries
(L.O. 7)

4–6. Westdale Western Wear Company is a wholesaler of western wear clothing.
The company sells its merchandise to retailers. The company entered into the
following transactions in May 1995:

May 1   Westdale Western Wear Company was organized as a corporation.
The stockholders received $735,000 in capital stock by investing the
following assets in the business: $462,000 cash, $168,000 merchandise, and $105,000 land.

1   Paid rent on administrative offices for May, $25,200.

5   The company purchased merchandise from Lyle Company on account, $189,000; terms 2/10, n/30. Freight terms were FOB shipping
point.

8   Cash of $8,400 was paid to a trucking company for delivery of the
merchandise purchased May 5.

14   The company sold merchandise on account, $315,000; terms 2/10,
n/30.

15   Paid Lyle Company the amount due on the purchase of May 5.

16   Of the merchandise sold May 14, $13,860 was returned for credit.

19   Salaries for services received were paid for May as follows: office
employees, $16,800; salespersons, $33,600.

24   The company collected the amount due on $126,000 of the accounts
receivable arising from the sale of May 14.

25   The company purchased merchandise on account from Carlson
Company, $151,200; terms 2/10, n/30. Freight terms were FOB shipping point.

27   Of the merchandise purchased May 25, $25,200 was returned to the
vendor.

28   A trucking company was paid $2,100 for delivery to Westdale Western Wear Company of the goods purchased May 25.

29   The company sold merchandise on open account, $15,120; terms
2/10, n/30.

30   Cash sales were $74,088.

30   Cash of $100,800 was received from the sale of May 14.

31   Paid Carlson Company for the merchandise purchased on May 25,
taking into consideration the merchandise returned on May 27.

Additional data

The inventory on hand at the close of business on May 31 is $299,040.

Required:

From the data given for Westdale Western Wear Company:

a. Prepare journal entries for the transactions.

b. Post the journal entries to the proper ledger accounts. Use the account numbers
shown in the chart of accounts on the inside covers of the text. Assume that all
postings are from page 15 of the general journal.

c. Prepare a work sheet. (There were no adjusting journal entries.)

d. Prepare a classified income statement for the month ended May 31, 1995.

e. Prepare a classified balance sheet as of May 31, 1995.

f. Prepare and post the necessary closing entries.

BUSINESS DECISION PROBLEMS

Prepare income statement and balance sheet for merchandising company (L.O. 5, 6)

4–1. Rick Harris taught physical education classes at Mountain High School for 20 years. In 1994, Rick's uncle died and left Rick $400,000. Rick quit his teaching job in December 1994 and opened a hardware store in January 1995. On January 2, 1995, Rick deposited $240,000 in a checking account opened in the store's name, Harris's Hardware Store, for all the stock in the company. During the first week of January, Rick rented a building and paid the first year's rent of $19,200 in advance. Also during that week, he purchased the following assets for cash:

Delivery truck	$40,000
Store equipment.	20,000
Office equipment	12,000

During the remainder of the first six months of 1995, Rick received cash of $280,000 from customers and disbursed cash of $208,000 for merchandise purchases and $60,000 for operating expenses.

Rick never took an accounting course, but he was familiar with the term **net income**. He decided to compute his net income for the first six months of 1995 and prepared the following schedule:

Cash receipts.		$280,000
Cash disbursements:		
Delivery truck.	$ 40,000	
Store equipment	20,000	
Office equipment	12,000	
Prepaid rent	19,200	
Merchandise purchases	208,000	
Operating expenses.	60,000	359,200
Net loss		$ 79,200

Assume that the depreciation amounts for the six-month period are as follows:

Delivery truck	$4,000
Store equipment.	1,000
Office equipment	700

Also assume that you obtain the following information:

1. Harris owes $32,000 to creditors for merchandise purchases.
2. Customers owe Harris $40,000 on June 30, 1995, for goods purchased.
3. Merchandise costing $64,000 is on hand at the end of the six months.

Required:

a. Do you agree with Rick Harris's statement that his hardware store suffered a net loss of $79,200 for the six months ended June 30, 1995? If not, show how you would determine the net income (or net loss).

b. Is it possible to prepare a balance sheet on June 30, 1995, or does Mr. Harris have to wait until December 31, 1995, to prepare a balance sheet? If a balance sheet can be prepared on June 30, 1995, prepare one.

Classify income statement items (L.O. 6)

4–2. From the consolidated statements of income of The Coca-Cola Company in Appendix C, identify the 1991 net operating revenues; cost of goods sold; gross profit; selling, administrative, and general expenses; and operating income. Do the results of 1991 compare favorably with those of 1990?

ANSWERS TO SELF-TEST

True-False

1. *True.* To compute net sales, sales discounts and sales returns and allowances are deducted from gross sales.

2. *False.* The Purchases account balance shows the cost of merchandise acquired; cost of goods sold is determined by subtracting ending inventory from the total cost of goods available for sale.

3. *False.* FOB shipping point, not FOB destination, results in freight charges being added to purchases.

4. *True.* This type of income statement is a classified or multiple-step income statement.

5. *True.* The Balance Sheet columns of the work sheet show the ending balance of each real account.

Multiple-Choice

1. *c.* Sales returns and allowances are debited to the Sales Returns and Allowances account when incurred.

2. *e.* Net cost of purchases plus beginning inventory is cost of goods available for sale.

3. *b.* The entire entry for this transaction is:

Accounts Payable	400	
Purchase Discounts		8
Cash		392

4. *c.* A classified income statement consists of major sections, such as operating revenues, cost of goods sold, operating expenses, and nonoperating revenues and expenses and administrative expenses.

5. *e.* All of the entries mentioned in (a–d) are included in closing the merchandise-related accounts.

5 MEASURING AND REPORTING INVENTORIES

After studying this chapter, you should be able to:

1. Explain and calculate the effects of inventory errors on certain financial statement items.
2. Indicate which costs are properly included in inventory.
3. Calculate cost of ending inventory and cost of goods sold under the four major inventory costing methods using perpetual and periodic inventory procedures.
4. Explain the advantages and disadvantages of the four major inventory costing methods.
5. Record merchandise transactions under perpetual inventory procedure.
6. Apply net realizable value and the lower-of-cost-or-market method to inventory.
7. Estimate cost of ending inventory using the gross margin and retail inventory methods.

You may have been to a "pre-inventory sale" at your favorite retail store and witnessed the bargain prices designed to reduce the merchandise inventory on hand and to minimize the time and expense of "taking the inventory." A smaller inventory enhances the probability of taking an accurate inventory since the store has less merchandise to count. From Chapter 4 you know that companies use inventory amounts to determine the cost of goods sold, which is a major expense of a merchandising company that affects the company's net income. In this chapter, you will learn how important inventories are in preparing an accurate income statement, statement of retained earnings, and balance sheet.

This chapter discusses merchandise inventory carried by merchandising companies—retailers and wholesalers. Other types of inventory carried by manufacturers are discussed in a later chapter. **Merchandise inventory** is the quantity of goods held by a merchandising company for resale to customers.

The merchandise inventory figure used by accountants depends on the quantity of inventory items and the cost of the items. Merchandising companies determine the quantity of inventory items by a physical count. This chapter discusses four accepted methods of costing the items: (1) specific identification; (2) first-in, first-out (FIFO); (3) last-in, first-out (LIFO); and (4) weighted-average. Each method has advantages and disadvantages.

In studying this chapter, you should be impressed by the importance of having accurate inventory figures and the serious consequences of using inaccurate inventory figures. Then, you will understand why your favorite retail store is closing early to "take inventory" or why its employees are working late to "take inventory." You will connect this taking of inventory with the cost of goods sold figure on the store's income statement, the retained earnings amount shown on the statement of retained earnings, and the inventory figure and the retained earnings amount on the store's balance sheet.

INVENTORIES AND COST OF GOODS SOLD

Inventory is often the largest and most important asset owned by a merchandising business. The inventory of some companies, like car dealerships or jewelry stores, may cost several times more than any other asset the company owns. As an asset, the inventory figure has a direct impact on reporting the solvency of the company in the balance sheet. As a factor in determining cost of goods sold, the inventory figure has a direct impact on reported profitability of the company's operations as shown in the income statement. Thus, the importance of the inventory figure should not be underestimated.

Importance of Proper Inventory Valuation

*Objective 1
Explain and calculate the effects of inventory errors on certain financial statement items*

A merchandising company can prepare accurate income statements, statements of retained earnings, and balance sheets only if the company has correctly valued its inventory. On the income statement, inventory is used to determine the cost of goods sold. Since the cost of goods sold figure affects the company's net income, it also affects the balance of the Retained Earnings account shown on the statement of retained earnings. On the balance sheet, incorrect inventory amounts affect both the reported ending inventory and retained earnings. Inventories appear on the balance sheet under the heading "Current Assets," which reports current assets in a descending order of liquidity. Since inventories will be consumed or converted into cash within a year or one operating cycle, whichever is longer, the order of liquidity usually shows inventories following cash and receivables on the balance sheet.

You will recall that the cost of goods sold figure is determined by adding the beginning inventory to the net cost of purchases and deducting the ending inventory. In each accounting period, the appropriate expenses must be matched with the revenues of that period to determine the net income. Applied to inventory, matching involves determining (1) how much of the cost of goods available for sale during the period should be deducted from current revenues and (2) how much should be allocated to goods on hand and thus carried forward as an asset (merchandise inventory) in the balance sheet to be matched against future revenues. Cost of goods sold is determined by deducting the ending inventory from the cost of goods available for sale. As a result, a highly significant relationship exists: **net income for an accounting period depends directly on the valuation of ending inventory.** This relationship involves three items.

First, a merchandising company must be sure that it has properly valued its ending inventory. If the ending inventory is overstated, cost of goods sold will be understated, resulting in an overstatement of gross margin and net income. Also, overstatement of ending inventory will cause current assets, total assets, and retained earnings to be overstated. Thus, any change in the calculation of ending inventory will be reflected, dollar for dollar (ignoring any income tax effects), in net income, current assets, total assets, and retained earnings.

Second, when a company misstates its ending inventory in the current year, the company carries forward that misstatement into the next year. This misstatement occurs because **the ending inventory amount of the current year is the beginning inventory amount for the next year.**

Third, an error in one period's ending inventory automatically causes an error in the opposite direction in the next period. After two years, however, the error will "wash out," and assets and retained earnings will be properly stated.

Illustrations 5.1 and 5.2 prove that net income for an accounting period depends directly on the valuation of the inventory. Allen Company's income statements and the statements of retained earnings for years 1994 and 1995 show this relationship.

In Illustration 5.1, the correctly stated ending inventory for the year 1994 is $35,000. As a result, Allen has a gross margin of $135,000 and net income of $50,000. The statement of retained earnings shows a beginning retained earnings of $120,000 and an ending retained earnings of $170,000. When the ending inventory is overstated by $5,000, as shown on the right in Illustration 5.1, the gross margin is $140,000, and net income is $55,000. The statement of retained earnings then has an ending retained earnings of $175,000. The ending inventory overstatement of $5,000 causes a $5,000 overstatement of net income and a $5,000 overstatement of retained earnings. The balance sheet would show both an overstated inventory and an overstated retained earnings. Due to the error in ending inventory, both the stockholders and creditors may overestimate the profitability of the business.

Illustration 5.1
EFFECTS OF AN OVERSTATED ENDING INVENTORY

ALLEN COMPANY
For Year Ended December 31, 1994

	Ending Inventory Correctly Stated		Ending Inventory Overstated by $5,000	
Income Statement				
Sales.		$400,000		$400,000
Cost of goods available for sale	$300,000		$300,000	
Ending inventory	35,000		40,000	
Cost of goods sold		265,000		260,000
Gross margin.		$135,000		$140,000
Other expenses.		85,000		85,000
Net income.		$ 50,000		$ 55,000
Statement of Retained Earnings				
Beginning retained earnings.		$120,000		$120,000
Net income.		50,000		55,000
Ending retained earnings		$170,000		$175,000

Illustration 5.2
EFFECTS OF AN OVERSTATED BEGINNING INVENTORY

ALLEN COMPANY
For Year Ended December 31, 1995

	Beginning Inventory Correctly Stated		Beginning Inventory Overstated by $5,000	
Income Statement				
Sales.		$425,000		$425,000
Beginning inventory	$ 35,000		$ 40,000	
Purchases	290,000		290,000	
Cost of goods available for sale	$325,000		$330,000	
Ending inventory	45,000		45,000	
Cost of goods sold		280,000		285,000
Gross margin.		$145,000		$140,000
Other expenses.		53,500		53,500
Net income.		$ 91,500		$ 86,500
Statement of Retained Earnings				
Beginning retained earnings.		$170,000		$175,000
Net income.		91,500		86,500
Ending retained earnings		$261,500		$261,500

Illustration 5.2 is a continuation of Illustration 5.1 and gives Allen's operating results for the year ended December 31, 1995. Note that the ending inventory in Illustration 5.1 now becomes the beginning inventory in Illustration 5.2. However, Allen's inventory at December 31, 1995, is now an accurate inventory of $45,000. As a result, the gross margin in the income statement with the beginning inventory correctly stated is $145,000, and Allen has net income of $91,500 and an ending retained earnings of $261,500. In the income statement at the right, in which the beginning inventory is overstated by $5,000, the gross margin is $140,000 and net income is $86,500, with the ending retained earnings also at $261,500.

Thus, in contrast to an overstated ending inventory, which results in an overstatement of net income, an overstated beginning inventory results in an understatement of net income. If the beginning inventory is overstated, then cost of goods available for sale and cost of goods sold will also be overstated. Consequently, gross margin and net income will be understated. Note, however, that when net income in the second year is closed to retained earnings, the Retained Earnings account will be stated at its proper amount. The overstatement of net income in the first year is offset by the understatement of net income in the second year. For the two years combined, then, the net income is correct. At the end of the second year, the balance sheet contains the correct amounts for both inventory and retained earnings.

The effects of errors of inventory valuation are summarized as follows:

	Ending Inventory		Beginning Inventory	
	Understated	*Overstated*	*Understated*	*Overstated*
Cost of goods sold.	Overstated	Understated	Understated	Overstated
Net income	Understated	Overstated	Overstated	Understated

DETERMINING INVENTORY COST

Objective 2
Indicate which costs are properly included in inventory

To place the proper valuation on inventory, a business must answer the question: Which costs should be included in inventory cost? Then, when the business purchases identical goods at different costs, it must answer the question: Which cost should be assigned to the items sold? In this section, you will learn how accountants answer these questions.

The costs included in inventory depend on two variables: quantity and price. To arrive at a current inventory figure, companies must begin with an accurate physical count of inventory items. The quantity of inventory is multiplied by the unit cost to compute the cost of ending inventory. This section discusses first the taking of a physical inventory and then the methods of costing the physical inventory under both perpetual and periodic inventory procedures. The remainder of the chapter discusses departures from the cost basis of inventory measurement.

Taking a Physical Inventory

As briefly described in Chapter 4, to take a physical inventory, a company must count, weigh, measure, or estimate the physical quantities of the goods on hand. For example, a clothing store may count its suits; a hardware store may weigh such items as bolts, washers, and nails; a gasoline company may measure gasoline in storage tanks; and a lumberyard may estimate such items as quantities of lumber, coal, or other bulky materials. Throughout the taking of a physical inventory, the goal should be accuracy.

Taking a physical inventory may disrupt the normal operations of a business. Thus, the count should be administered as quickly and as efficiently as possible. The actual taking of the inventory is not considered an accounting function; however, accountants often plan and coordinate the count. Proper forms are required to record accurate counts and determine totals. Identification names or symbols must be chosen, and those persons who count, weigh, or measure the inventory items must know these symbols.

Taking a physical inventory often involves the use of inventory tags, such as the tag shown in Illustration 5.3. These tags are consecutively numbered for control purposes. A tag usually consists of a stub and a detachable duplicate section. The duplicate section facilitates checking in case of discrepancies. The format of the tags can vary. However, the tag usually provides space for (1) a detailed description and identification of inventory items by product, class, and model; (2) location of items; (3) quantity of items on hand; and (4) initials of the counters and checkers.

Illustration 5.3
INVENTORY TAG

Inventory Tag JMA Corp.
Inventory Tag No. _281_   Date _____
Description _____
_____
Location _____
Quantity Counted _____
Counted by _____
Checked by _____
Duplicate Inventory Tag
Inventory Tag No. _281_   Date _____
Description _____
_____
Location _____
Quantity Counted _____
Counted by _____
Checked by _____

The descriptive information and count may be entered on one copy of the tag by one team of counters. Another team of counters may record its count on the duplicate copy of the tag. Discrepancies between counts of the same items by different teams are reconciled by supervisors, and the correct counts are assembled on intermediate inventory sheets. When the inventory counts are completed and checked, the final sheets are sent to the accounting department for pricing and extensions (quantity × price). The tabulated result is the dollar amount of the physical inventory. Later in this chapter you will study the different methods accountants use to cost inventory.

Costs Included in Inventory Cost

Usually, inventory cost includes all the necessary outlays to obtain the goods, get the goods ready to sell, and have the goods in the desired location for sale to customers. Thus, inventory cost includes:

1. Seller's invoice price less any purchase discount.
2. Cost of the buyer's insurance to cover the goods while in transit.
3. Transportation charges when borne by the buyer.
4. Handling costs, such as the cost of pressing clothes wrinkled during shipment.

In theory, the cost of *each* unit of inventory should include its net invoice price plus its share of other costs incurred in shipment. The 1986 Tax Reform Act requires companies to make assignments of these costs to inventory for tax purposes. For accounting purposes, these cost assignments are recommended but not required.

Practical difficulties arise in allocating some of these costs to inventory items. Assume, for example, that the freight bill on a shipment of clothes does not state separately the cost of shipping one shirt. Also, assume that the company wants to include the freight cost as part of the inventory cost of the shirt. Then, the freight cost would have to be *allocated* in some manner to each unit because it cannot be measured directly. In practice, allocations of freight, insurance, and handling costs to the individual units of inventory purchased are often not worth the additional cost incurred to perform the allocations. Consequently, many companies have not assigned the costs of freight, insurance, and handling to inventory. Instead, they have expensed these costs as incurred. When companies omit these costs from both beginning and ending inventories, the omission minimizes the effect on net income of expensing these costs.

Even if a cost is derived for each unit in inventory, the inventory valuation problem is not solved. Two other aspects of the problem must be considered.

1. If goods were purchased at varying unit costs, how should cost of goods available for sale be allocated between the units sold and those that remain in inventory? For example, assume that Hi Fi Buys, Inc., pur-

chased two identical VCRs for resale. One was purchased for $450 and the other for $400. If one recorder was sold during the period, should Hi Fi Buys assign it a cost of $450, $400, or an average cost of $425?

2. Does the fact that current replacement costs are less than the costs of some units in inventory have any bearing on the amount at which inventory should be carried? Using the same example as above, if Hi Fi Buys can currently buy all VCRs at a price of $400, is it reasonable to carry some units in inventory at $450 rather than $400?

These questions are answered in the next section.

Inventory Valuation under Changing Prices

Inventories generally should be accounted for at historical cost, which is the cost at which the items were purchased. However, this rule does not indicate how to assign costs to ending inventory and to cost of goods sold when the goods have been purchased at different unit costs. For example, suppose that a retailer has three units of a given product on hand. One unit was bought for $20, another for $22, and a third for $24. If the retailer sells two of the units for $30 each, what is the cost of the two units sold?

Methods of Determining Inventory Cost

Objective 3
Calculate cost of ending inventory and cost of goods sold under the four major inventory costing methods using perpetual and periodic inventory procedures (applies to each method separately)

Four inventory costing methods have been developed to solve this type of problem. They are: (1) specific identification; (2) first-in, first-out (FIFO); (3) last-in, first-out (LIFO); and (4) weighted-average. These costing methods are explained below. Illustration 5.4 shows the frequency of use of these methods in a sample of 600 companies for the years 1987–90. Obviously, some companies use one method for certain inventory items and another method for other inventory items.

Before presenting the inventory costing methods, we present a brief introduction to perpetual inventory procedure and a comparison of periodic and perpetual inventory procedures.

Perpetual Inventory Procedure

In Chapter 4, the emphasis was on periodic inventory procedure. Under periodic inventory procedure, the Purchases account is debited when goods are acquired; other accounts, such as Purchase Discounts, Purchase Returns and Allowances, and Transportation-In, are used for purchase-related transactions. Cost of goods sold is determined only at the end of the period as the difference between cost of goods available for sale and ending inventory. No records are kept of the cost of items as they are sold, and no information is provided on possible inventory shortages. Any goods not in ending inventory are assumed to have been sold.

The recent development of inventory management software packages is causing more and more businesses to change from periodic to perpetual

Illustration 5.4
FREQUENCY OF USE OF INVENTORY METHODS

	Number of Companies			
	1990	*1989*	*1988*	*1987*
Methods:				
First-in, first-out (FIFO)	411	401	396	392
Last-in, first-out (LIFO)	366	366	379	393
Average cost.	195	200	213	216
Other	44	48	50	49
Total	1,016	1,015	1,038	1,050
Use of LIFO:				
All inventories	20	26	20	18
50% or more of inventories	186	191	207	221
Less than 50% of inventories	92	99	90	86
Not determinable.	68	50	62	68
Companies using LIFO	366	366	379	393

SOURCE: American Institute of Certified Public Accountants, *Accounting Trends & Techniques* (New York: AICPA, 1991), p. 144.

inventory procedure. Under perpetual inventory procedure, companies have no purchases and purchase-related accounts. Instead, all entries involving merchandise purchased for sale to customers are entered directly in the Merchandise Inventory account. Thus, **Merchandise Inventory is debited or credited in place of debiting or crediting Purchases, Purchase Discounts, Purchase Returns and Allowances, and Transportation-In. At the time of each sale, two entries are made. The first debits Accounts Receivable or Cash and credits Sales at the retail selling price. The second debits Cost of Goods Sold and credits Merchandise Inventory at cost.** Therefore, the Merchandise Inventory account at the end of the period will show the cost of the inventory that should be on hand. Comparison of this amount with the cost obtained by taking and pricing a physical inventory will reveal inventory shortages. Thus, perpetual inventory procedure is an important element in providing internal control over goods in inventory.

Perpetual Inventory Records. Even though companies can apply perpetual inventory procedure manually, the tracking of units and dollars in and out of inventory is much easier using a computer. With either manual or computer processing, a record will be maintained for each item in inventory. Illustration 5.5 gives an example of an inventory record for Entertainment World, a firm that sells many different brands of television sets. The inventory record in Illustration 5.5 shows the information on one particular brand and model of television set carried in inventory. Other information given on the record includes (1) the maximum and minimum number of units the company wishes to stock at any time, (2) when and how many units were acquired and at what cost, and (3) when and how many units were sold and

Illustration 5.5
PERPETUAL INVENTORY RECORD (FIFO METHOD)

	Item TV-96874			Maximum 26					
	Location			Minimum 6					

	Purchased			Sold			Balance		
1995 Date	Units	Unit Cost	Total Cost	Units	Unit Cost	Total Cost	Units	Unit Cost	Total
Beg. Inv.							8	$300	$2,400
July 5	10	$300	$3,000				18	300	5,400
7				12	$300	$3,600	6	300	1,800
12	10	315	3,150				6	300	1,800
							10	315	3,150
22				6	300	1,800			
				2	315	630	8	315	2,520
24	8	320	2,560				8	315	2,520
							8	320	2,560

what cost was assigned to cost of goods sold. The number of units on hand and their cost are readily available also. Entertainment World assumes that the first units acquired are the first units sold. This assumption is referred to as the first-in, first-out (FIFO) method of inventory costing and is discussed later.

Comparing Journal Entries under Periodic and Perpetual Inventory Procedures

As stated in the preceding section, several differences exist between accounting for inventories under periodic procedure and under perpetual procedure. These differences will be illustrated by using some of the data from Illustration 5.5 and making some additional assumptions. Later, some additional journal entries under perpetual inventory procedure will be illustrated.

The purchase on July 5 would be recorded as follows under each of the methods:

Periodic Procedure			**Perpetual Procedure**		
Purchases	3,000		Merchandise Inventory .	3,000	
Accounts Payable .		3,000	Accounts Payable .		3,000

Assuming the merchandise sold on July 7 was priced at $4,800, the sale would be recorded as follows:

Periodic Procedure			**Perpetual Procedure**		
Accounts Receivable . .	4,800		Accounts Receivable . .	4,800	
Sales		4,800	Sales		4,800
			Cost of Goods Sold .	3,600	
			Merchandise Inventory		3,600

Several other types of transactions that were not included in Illustration 5.5 could occur. A sample of these transactions follows:

1. Assume that two of the units purchased on July 5 were returned to the supplier because they were defective. The entries would be:

Periodic Procedure			**Perpetual Procedure**		
Accounts Payable	600		Accounts Payable . .	600	
Purchase Returns and			Merchandise		
Allowances		600	Inventory . . .		600

2. Assume instead that the supplier granted an allowance of $600 to the company because of the defective merchandise. The entries would be:

Periodic Procedure			**Perpetual Procedure**		
Accounts Payable	600		Accounts Payable . .	600	
Purchase Returns and			Merchandise		
Allowances		600	Inventory . . .		600

3. Assume that the company incurred and paid freight charges of $100 on the purchase of July 5. The entries would be:

Periodic Procedure			**Perpetual Procedure**		
Transportation-In . . .	100		Merchandise Inventory .	100	
Cash		100	Cash		100

Notice in the entries above that, under perpetual inventory procedure, the Merchandise Inventory account is used to record purchases, purchase returns and allowances, purchase discounts, and transportation-in. Also, when goods are sold, Cost of Goods Sold is debited (increased) and Merchandise Inventory is credited (reduced).

At the end of the accounting period, under perpetual procedure, the only merchandise-related expense account to be closed is Cost of Goods Sold. The Purchases, Purchase Returns and Allowances, Purchase Discounts, and Transportation-In accounts do not even exist.

An Extended Illustration of Four Inventory Methods under Perpetual and Periodic Inventory Procedures

The data for purchases, sales, and beginning inventory given in Illustration 5.6 will be used to illustrate each of the four inventory costing methods. Except for the specific identification method, each method is presented using, first, perpetual inventory procedure and, then, periodic inventory procedure. Total goods available for sale consist of 80 units with a total cost of $690. A physical inventory determined that 20 units are on hand at the end of the period. Sales revenue for the 60 units sold was $780. The questions to be answered are: What is the cost of the 20 units in inventory? What is the cost of the 60 units sold?

Illustration 5.6
BEGINNING INVENTORY, PURCHASES, AND SALES

Beginning Inventory and Purchases				*Sales*			
Date	*Units*	*Unit Cost*	*Total Cost*	*Date*	*Units*	*Price*	*Total*
Beginning inventory	10	$8.00	$ 80	March 10	10	$12.00	$120
March 2	10	8.50	85	July 14.	20	12.00	240
May 28	20	8.40	168	September 7	10	14.00	140
August 12	10	9.00	90	November 22.	20	14.00	280
October 12.	20	8.80	176				
December 21.	10	9.10	91				
	80		$690		60		$780

Ending inventory = 20 units, determined by taking a physical inventory.

Specific Identification   The **specific identification** method of inventory costing attaches the actual cost to an identifiable unit of product. This method is easily applied when large inventory items (such as autos) are purchased and sold. Under the specific identification method, each unit in inventory, unless it is unique, must be identified with a serial number plate or identification tag.

To illustrate, assume that the company in Illustration 5.6 can identify the 20 units on hand at year-end as 10 units from the August 12 purchase and 10 units from the December 21 purchase. The ending inventory is computed as shown in Illustration 5.7, where the **$181 ending inventory cost is subtracted**

Illustration 5.7
DETERMINING ENDING INVENTORY UNDER SPECIFIC IDENTIFICATION

	Units	*Unit Cost*	*Total Cost*
Ending inventory composed of purchases made on:			
August 12.	10	$9.00	$ 90
December 21	10	9.10	91
Ending inventory	20		$181
Cost of goods sold composed of:			
Beginning inventory	10	8.00	$ 80
Purchases made on:			
March 2.	10	8.50	85
May 28	20	8.40	168
October 12	20	8.80	176
			$509
Cost of goods available for sale			$690
Ending inventory			181
Cost of goods sold			$509

from the $690 cost of goods available for sale to obtain the $509 cost of goods sold. Note that you can also determine the cost of goods sold for the year by recording the cost of each unit sold. The $509 cost of goods sold is reported as an expense on the income statement, and the $181 ending inventory is a current asset on the balance sheet.

The specific identification costing method attaches cost to an identifiable unit of inventory. The method does not involve any assumptions about the flow of the costs as in the other inventory costing methods. The only difference is that perpetual inventory procedure records the cost of goods sold each time a sale occurs, and periodic inventory procedure determines cost of goods sold only after a physical inventory is taken at the end of the accounting period. Periodic and perpetual inventory procedures will produce the same results for the specific identification method.

<table>
<tr><td>

Objective 4
Explain the advantages and disadvantages of the four major inventory costing methods (applies to each method separately)

</td><td>

Advantages and Disadvantages of Specific Identification. Companies that use the specific identification method of inventory costing state their cost of goods sold and ending inventory at the actual cost of specific units sold and on hand. Some accountants argue that this method provides the most precise matching of costs and revenues and is, therefore, the most theoretically sound method. This statement is true for some one-of-a-kind items, such as autos or real estate. For these items, use of any other method would seem illogical.

</td></tr>
</table>

One disadvantage of the specific identification method is that it permits the manipulation of income. For example, assume that a company bought three identical units of a given product at different prices. One unit cost $2,000, the second cost $2,100, and the third cost $2,200. The company sold one unit for $2,800. The units are alike, so the customer does not care which of the identical units the company ships. However, the gross margin on the sale could be either $800, $700, or $600, depending on which unit the company ships.

FIFO (First-In, First-Out). Sometimes companies use a method that involves a cost flow assumption rather than using specific identification. For instance, the **FIFO (first-in, first-out)** method of inventory costing assumes that the costs of the first goods purchased are the first costs charged to cost of goods sold when the company actually sells the goods. Thus, the first goods purchased are assumed to be the first goods sold. In some companies, the first units "in" (bought) must be the first units "out" (sold) to avoid large losses from spoilage. Such items as fresh dairy products, fruits, and vegetables should be sold on a FIFO basis. In these cases, an assumed first-in, first-out flow corresponds with the actual physical flow of goods.

Since a company using FIFO assumes the older units to be the first units sold and the newer units to be still on hand, the ending inventory consists of the most recent purchases. Under perpetual inventory procedure, the ending balance in the Merchandise Inventory account will reflect these most recent purchases as a result of making the required entries during the period. Also, the cost of goods sold will already have been recorded in the Cost of Goods

Sold account. Under periodic inventory procedure, to determine the cost of the ending inventory at the end of the period under FIFO, you would begin by listing the cost of the most recent purchase. If the ending inventory contains more units than acquired in the most recent purchase, it will also include units from the next-to-the-latest purchase at the unit cost incurred, and so on. You would list these units from the latest purchases until the number of units agrees with the number of units in the ending inventory.

Illustration 5.8 shows how you would determine the cost of ending inventory under FIFO using perpetual inventory procedure. This illustration uses the same format as the perpetual inventory record shown earlier. The company keeps a record of the balance in the inventory account as it makes purchases and sells items from inventory. Notice in Illustration 5.8 that each time a sale occurs, the items sold are assumed to be the oldest items on hand. Thus, after each transaction, you can readily determine the balance in the Merchandise Inventory account from the perpetual inventory record. The balance after the December 21 purchase represents the 20 units from the most recent purchases. The total cost of ending inventory is $179, which the

Illustration 5.8
DETERMINING FIFO COST OF ENDING INVENTORY UNDER PERPETUAL INVENTORY PROCEDURE

Date	Purchased Units	Unit Cost	Total Cost	Sold Units	Unit Cost	Total Cost	Balance Units	Unit Cost	Total	
Beg. inv.							10	$8.00	$ 80	
Mar. 2	10	$8.50	$ 85				10	8.00	80	
							10	8.50	85	
Mar. 10				10	$8.00	$80 ←	10	8.50	85	Sales are assumed to be from the oldest units on hand.
May 28	20	8.40	168				10	8.50	85	
							20	8.40	168	
July 14				10	8.50	85 ←				
				10	8.40	84 ←	10	8.40	84	
Aug. 12	10	9.00	90				10	8.40	84	
							10	9.00	90	
Sept. 7				10	8.40	84 ←	10	9.00	90	
Oct. 12	20	8.80	176				10	9.00	90	Total of $179 would agree with balance already existing in Merchandise Inventory account.
							20	8.80	176	
Nov. 22				10	9.00	90 ←				
				10	8.80	88 ←	10	8.80	88	
Dec. 21	10	9.10	91				10	8.80	88 ⎫	
							10	9.10	91 ⎭	

Total cost of ending inventory = $179

company reports as a current asset on the balance sheet. During the accounting period, a total of $511 would have been debited to Cost of Goods Sold as sales occurred. Adding this $511 to the ending inventory of $179 accounts for all of the $690 cost of goods available for sale.

Illustration 5.9 shows how you can determine the cost of ending inventory under FIFO using periodic inventory procedure. The company assumes that 20 units in inventory consist of 10 units purchased December 21 and 10 units purchased October 12. As with the perpetual inventory procedure, the total cost of ending inventory is $179, and the cost of goods sold is $511. **Under FIFO, the use of perpetual and periodic inventory procedures will result in the same total costs for ending inventory and cost of goods sold.**

Illustration 5.10 shows the relationship between the cost of goods sold and the cost of ending inventory under FIFO using periodic inventory procedure. The cost of goods available for sale of 80 units for the period consists of the beginning inventory and all of the purchases during the period. Under FIFO, the ending inventory of 20 units is composed of the most recent purchases—10 units of December 21 purchase and 10 units of October 12 purchase—costing $179. Beginning inventory and other earlier purchases are assumed to have been sold during the period, representing the cost of goods sold of $511.

Advantages and Disadvantages of FIFO. The FIFO method has four major advantages: (1) it is easy to apply, (2) the assumed flow of costs corresponds with the normal physical flow of goods, (3) **no manipulation of**

Illustration 5.9
DETERMINING FIFO COST OF ENDING INVENTORY UNDER PERIODIC PROCEDURE

	Units	Unit Cost	Total Cost	
Ending inventory composed of purchases made on:				
December 21.	10	$9.10	$ 91	
October 12.	10	8.80	88	
Ending inventory.	20		$179 ←	
Cost of goods sold composed of:				
Beginning inventory	10	8.00	$ 80	
Purchases made on:				
March 2	10	8.50	85	
May 28	20	8.40	168	
August 12	10	9.00	90	
October 12.	10	8.80	88	Used to establish the ending balance in the Merchandise Inventory account.
			$511	
Cost of goods available for sale			$690	
Ending inventory			179	
Cost of goods sold			$511	

Illustration 5.10
FIFO FLOW OF COSTS

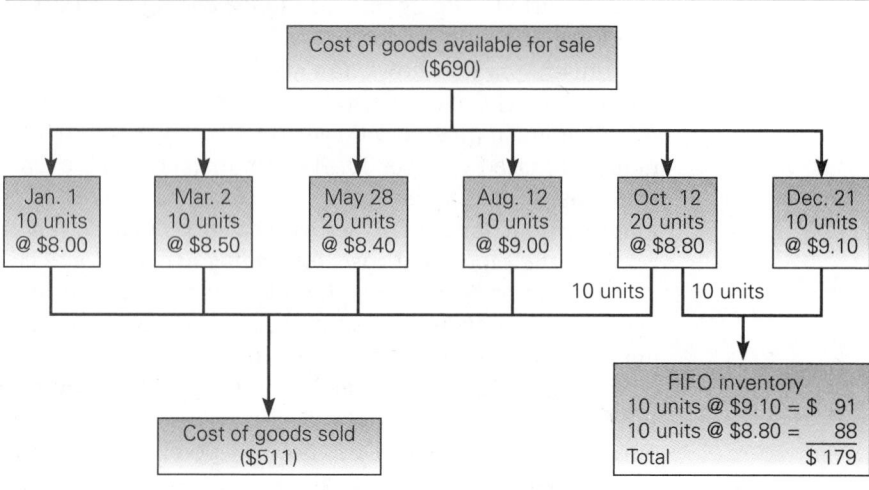

income is possible, and (4) the balance sheet amount for inventory is likely to approximate the current market value. All the advantages of FIFO occur because when a company sells goods, the first costs it removes from inventory are the oldest unit costs. A company cannot manipulate income by choosing which unit to ship because the cost of a unit sold is not determined by a serial number. Instead, the cost attached to the unit sold is always the oldest cost. Thus, under FIFO, purchases made at the end of the period have no effect on cost of goods sold or net income.

The disadvantages of FIFO include (1) the recognition of "paper" profits and (2) a heavier tax burden if used for tax purposes in periods of inflation. These disadvantages are discussed later as advantages of LIFO.

LIFO (Last-In, First-Out).   The **LIFO (last-in, first-out)** method of inventory costing assumes that the costs of the most recent purchases are the first costs charged to cost of goods sold when the company actually sells the goods. **The results can differ under perpetual and periodic inventory procedure.**

Illustration 5.11 shows the LIFO method using perpetual inventory procedure. Under perpetual inventory procedure, the inventory composition and balance are updated with each purchase and sale. Notice in Illustration 5.11 that each time a sale occurs, the items sold are assumed to be the most recent ones acquired. Despite the numerous purchases and sales during the year, the ending inventory still includes the 10 units from beginning inventory in our example. The remainder of the ending inventory consists of the last purchase because no sale occurred after the December 21 purchase. The

Illustration 5.11
DETERMINING LIFO COST OF ENDING INVENTORY UNDER PERPETUAL INVENTORY PROCEDURE

Date	Purchased			Sold			Balance			
	Units	Unit Cost	Total Cost	Units	Unit Cost	Total Cost	Units	Unit Cost	Total	
Beg. inv.							10	$8.00	$ 80	
Mar. 2	10	$8.50	$ 85				10	8.00	80	Sales are assumed to be from the most recent purchases.
							10	8.50	85	
Mar. 10				10	$8.50	$ 85	10	8.00	80	
May 28	20	8.40	168				10	8.00	80	
							20	8.40	168	
July 14				20	8.40	168	10	8.00	80	
Aug. 12	10	9.00	90				10	8.00	80	
							10	9.00	90	
Sept. 7				10	9.00	90	10	8.00	80	Balance of $171 would agree with balance already existing in the Merchandise Inventory account.
Oct. 12	20	8.80	176				10	8.00	80	
							20	8.80	176	
Nov. 22				20	8.80	176	10	8.00	80	
Dec. 21	10	9.10	91				10	8.00	80 }	
							10	9.10	91 }	

Total cost of ending inventory = $171

total cost of the 20 units in ending inventory is $171; the cost of goods sold is $519.

Illustration 5.12 shows the use of LIFO under periodic inventory procedure. Under periodic procedure, since the company charges the latest costs to cost of goods sold, the ending inventory consists of the oldest costs. Therefore, when determining the cost of inventory under periodic inventory procedure, the oldest units and their costs are listed first. Thus, the first units listed are those in beginning inventory, then the first purchase, and so on, until the number of units listed agrees with the number of units in ending inventory. Thus, ending inventory in Illustration 5.12 is composed of the 10 units from beginning inventory and the 10 units purchased on March 2. The total cost of these 20 units, $165, is the ending inventory cost; the cost of goods sold is $525.

Applying LIFO on a perpetual basis during the accounting period as shown in Illustration 5.11 results in different ending inventory and cost of goods sold figures than applying LIFO only at year-end using periodic inven-

Illustration 5.12
DETERMINING LIFO COST OF ENDING INVENTORY UNDER PERIODIC INVENTORY PROCEDURE

	Units	Unit Cost	Total Cost
Ending inventory composed of:			
Beginning inventory	10	$8.00	$ 80
March 2 purchase	10	8.50	85
Ending inventory	20		$165
Cost of goods sold composed of purchases made on:			
December 21	10	9.10	$ 91
October 12	20	8.80	176
August 12	10	9.00	90
May 28	20	8.40	168
			$525
Cost of goods available for sale			$690
Ending inventory			165
Cost of goods sold			$525

tory procedure. (Compare Illustrations 5.11 and 5.12 to verify that ending inventory and cost of goods sold are different under the two procedures.) For this reason, if LIFO is applied on a perpetual basis during the period, special adjustments are sometimes necessary at year-end to take full advantage of using LIFO for tax purposes. Complicated applications of LIFO perpetual inventory procedures that require such adjustments are beyond the scope of this text and are not illustrated here.

Illustrations 5.13 and 5.14 show the flow of inventory costs under LIFO using both the perpetual and periodic inventory procedures. Note that ending inventory and cost of goods sold are different under the two procedures.

Advantages and Disadvantages of LIFO. The advantages of the LIFO method are directly related to the fact that prices have risen almost constantly for decades. LIFO supporters claim that this upward trend in prices leads to inventory, or "paper," profits if the FIFO method is used. **Inventory, or "paper," profits** are equal to the current replacement cost to purchase a unit of inventory at the time of sale minus the unit's historical cost.

For example, assume a company has three units of a product on hand, each purchased at a different cost: $12, $15, and $20 (the most recent cost). The sales price of the unit normally will rise because the unit's replacement cost is rising. Assume that the company sells one unit for $30. FIFO gross margin would be $18 ($30 − $12), while LIFO would show a gross margin of $10 ($30 − $20). LIFO supporters would say that the extra $8 gross margin shown under FIFO represents inventory profit because that "profit" is merely the additional amount that the company must spend over cost of goods sold to purchase another unit of inventory ($8 + $12 = $20). Thus, the profit is not real; it exists only on paper. The company cannot distribute the

Illustration 5.13
LIFO FLOW OF COSTS UNDER PERPETUAL INVENTORY PROCEDURE

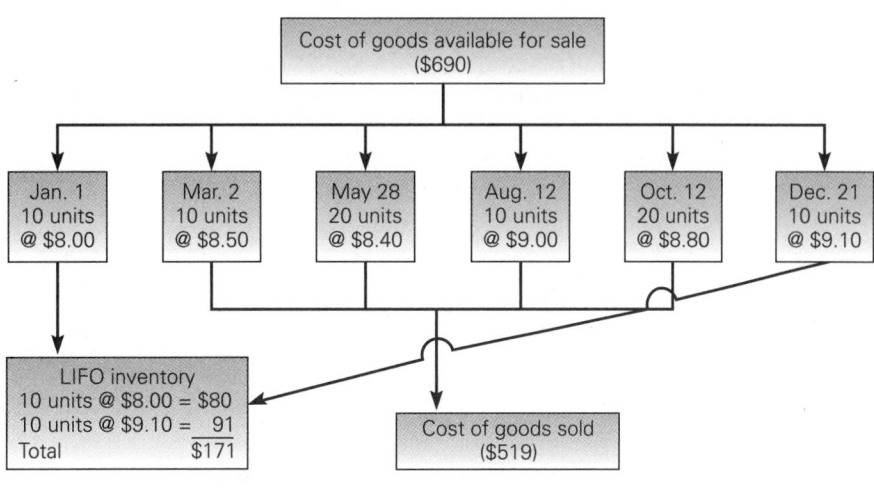

$8 to stockholders, but must retain it in the company if the company is to continue handling that particular product. LIFO shows the actual profits that the company can distribute to the stockholders while still replenishing inventory.

During periods of inflation, LIFO shows the largest cost of goods sold of any of the costing methods because the newest costs charged to cost of goods sold are also the highest costs. The larger the cost of goods sold, the

Illustration 5.14
LIFO FLOW OF COSTS UNDER PERIODIC INVENTORY PROCEDURE

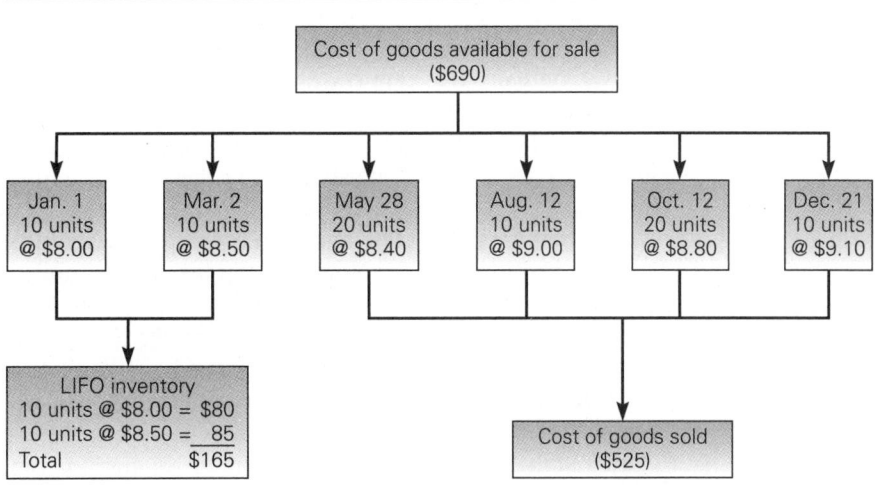

smaller the net income. If a company uses LIFO for income tax purposes, the resulting lower net income means lower income taxes. Companies may only use LIFO for tax purposes if they use it for financial statement purposes. Many companies use LIFO for financial statement purposes for this reason (Illustration 5.4, page 253).

To further illustrate the appeal of LIFO, assume that Company B has one unit of product Y on hand that cost $20. The company sold the unit for $30; other selling expenses totaled $7. Assume that the income tax rate is 50%. The company purchases an identical unit for $22 before the end of the accounting period. Using FIFO, Company B computes its net income as follows:

Net sales.	$30.00
Cost of goods sold	20.00
Gross margin.	$10.00
Expenses	7.00
Net operating margin	$ 3.00
Federal income taxes (50% rate).	1.50
Net income.	$ 1.50

According to the above schedule, the company is selling product Y at a price that is high enough to produce net income. However, consider the following:

Cash secured from sale.	$30.00
Expenses and taxes paid ($7.00 + $1.50).	8.50
Cash available for replacement of inventory	$21.50
Cost to replace inventory	22.00
Additional cash required to replace inventory . . .	$ 0.50

Thus, Company B is reporting net income of $1.50, but it cannot replace its inventory unless it obtains more cash.

Note how the results differ when Company B uses LIFO to measure inventory, as shown in the schedule at the top of the next page. In this case, inventory (or "paper") profits are $2, the difference between the original cost of the inventory ($20) and its replacement cost at the time the company sold the inventory ($22). Note that the tax savings under LIFO are equal to the tax rate times the inventory profits (0.5 × $2 = $1).

Those who favor LIFO argue that its use leads to a better matching of costs and revenues than the other methods. When a company uses LIFO, the income statement reports both sales revenue and cost of goods sold in current dollars. The resulting gross margin is a better indicator of management's ability to generate income than gross margin computed using FIFO, which may include substantial inventory profits.

Net sales.	$30.00
Cost of goods sold	22.00
Gross margin.	$ 8.00
Expenses	7.00
Net operating margin	$ 1.00
Federal income taxes (50% rate).	0.50
Net income.	$ 0.50
Cash secured from sale.	$30.00
Expenses and taxes paid ($7.00 + $0.50).	7.50
Cash available for replacement of inventory	$22.50
Cost to replace inventory	22.00
Cash available after replacement of inventory . . .	$ 0.50

Supporters of FIFO argue that LIFO (1) matches the cost of goods *not* sold against revenues, (2) grossly understates inventory, and (3) permits income manipulation.

The first criticism—that LIFO matches the cost of goods *not* sold against revenues—is an extension of the debate over whether the assumed flow of costs should agree with the physical flow of goods. LIFO supporters contend that it makes more sense to match current costs against current revenues than to worry about matching costs for the physical flow of goods.

The second criticism—that LIFO grossly understates inventory—is valid. A company may report LIFO inventory at a fraction of its current replacement cost, especially if the historical costs included are from several decades ago. LIFO supporters contend that the increased usefulness of the income statement more than offsets the negative effect of this undervaluation of inventory on the balance sheet.

The third criticism—that LIFO permits income manipulation—is also valid. Income manipulation is possible under LIFO. For example, assume that management wishes to reduce income. The company could purchase an abnormal amount of goods at current high prices near the end of the current period with the purpose of selling the goods in the next period. Under LIFO, these higher costs will be charged to cost of goods sold in the current period, resulting in a substantial decline in reported net income. To obtain higher income, management could delay making the normal amount of purchases until the next period and thus include some of the older, lower costs in cost of goods sold.

Weighted-Average. The **weighted-average method** of inventory costing is a means of costing ending inventory using a weighted-average unit cost. Companies most often use the weighted-average method to determine a unit cost for units that are basically the same, such as identical games in a toy store or identical electrical tools in a hardware store. Since the units are alike, they can be assigned the same unit cost.

Under perpetual inventory procedure, **a new weighted-average unit cost is computed after each purchase by dividing total cost of goods available for**

sale by total units available for sale. The unit cost is referred to as a moving weighted-average because it changes after each purchase. Illustration 5.15 shows how the moving weighted-average is computed using perpetual inventory procedure. The new weighted-average unit cost computed after each purchase is used as the unit cost for inventory items sold until a new purchase is made. The 20 units in ending inventory are valued at a unit cost of $8.929 for a total inventory cost of $178.58. Cost of goods sold under this procedure is $690 minus the $178.58, or $511.42.

Under periodic inventory procedure, a company determines the average cost at the end of the accounting period by dividing the total number of units purchased during the entire period plus those in beginning inventory into total cost of goods available for sale for the period. The ending inventory is carried at this per unit cost. Illustration 5.16 shows how a company uses the weighted-average method to determine inventory costs using periodic inventory procedure. Weighted-average cost per unit is computed by dividing the cost of units available for sale, $690, by the total number of units available

Illustration 5.15
DETERMINING ENDING INVENTORY UNDER WEIGHTED-AVERAGE METHOD USING PERPETUAL INVENTORY PROCEDURE

	Purchased			Sold			Balance			
Date	Units	Unit Cost	Total Cost	Units	Unit Cost	Total Cost	Units	Unit Cost	Total	
Beg. inv.							10	$8.00	$ 80.00	A new unit cost is calculated after each purchase.
Mar. 2	10	$8.50	$ 85				20	8.25[a]	165.00	
Mar. 10				10	$8.25	$ 82.50	10	8.25	82.50	
May 28	20	8.40	168				30	8.35[b]	250.50	The unit cost of sales is the most recently calculated unit cost.
July 14				20	8.35	167.00	10	8.35	83.50	
Aug. 12	10	9.00	90				20	8.675[c]	173.50	
Sept. 7				10	8.675	86.75	10	8.675	86.75	
Oct. 12	20	8.80	176				30	8.758[d]	262.75	
Nov. 22				20	8.758	175.17*	10	8.758	87.58	Balance of $178.58 would agree with balance already existing in the Merchandise Inventory account.
Dec. 21	10	9.10	91				20	$8.929[e]	$178.58	

[a] $165.00/20 = $8.25.
[b] $250.50/30 = $8.35.
[c] $173.50/20 = $8.675.
[d] $262.75/30 = $8.758.
[e] $178.58/20 = $8.929.
* Rounding difference

Illustration 5.16
DETERMINING ENDING INVENTORY UNDER WEIGHTED-AVERAGE METHOD USING PERIODIC INVENTORY PROCEDURE

	Units	Unit Cost	Total Cost
Beginning inventory	10	$8.00	$ 80.00
Purchases			
March 2	10	8.50	85.00
May 28	20	8.40	168.00
August 12	10	9.00	90.00
October 12	20	8.80	176.00
December 21	10	9.10	91.00
Total	80		$690.00

Weighted-average unit cost is $690 ÷ 80, or $8.625.
Ending inventory then is $8.625 × 20 . . . . 172.50

Cost of goods sold:
$8.625 × 60 . . . . $517.50

for sale, 80. Thus, the weighted-average cost per unit is $8.625, meaning that each unit sold or remaining in inventory is valued at $8.625.

Advantages and Disadvantages of Weighted-Average. When a company uses the weighted-average method and prices are rising, cost of goods sold is less than that obtained under LIFO, but more than that obtained under FIFO. Inventory is not as badly understated as under LIFO, but it is not as up to date as under FIFO. Weighted-average costing takes a "middle-of-the-road" approach. A company can manipulate income under the weighted-average costing method by buying or failing to buy goods near year-end. However, the effects of buying or not buying are reduced due to the averaging process.

Differences in Costing Methods Summarized

The four inventory costing methods—specific identification, FIFO, LIFO, and weighted-average—involve assumptions about how costs flow through a business. In some instances, assumed cost flows may correspond with the actual physical flow of goods. For example, fresh meats and dairy products must flow in a FIFO manner to avoid spoilage losses. In contrast, lumber or coal stacked in a pile will be used in a LIFO manner because the newest units purchased will be unloaded on top of the pile and sold first. Gasoline held in a tank is a good example of an inventory that has an average physical flow. As the tank is refilled, the new gasoline is mixed with the old. Thus, any amount used will consist of a blend of the old gas with the new.

Although physical flows are sometimes cited as support for an inventory method, accountants now recognize that an inventory method's assumed

Illustration 5.17
SUMMARY OF EFFECTS OF EMPLOYING DIFFERENT INVENTORY COSTING METHODS WITH SAME BASIC DATA—USE OF PERPETUAL INVENTORY PROCEDURE

	Specific Identification	FIFO	LIFO	Weighted-Average
Sales	$780.00	$780.00	$780.00	$780.00
Cost of goods sold:				
Beginning inventory.	$ 80.00	$ 80.00	$ 80.00	$ 80.00
Purchases	610.00	610.00	610.00	610.00
Cost of goods available for sale . . .	$690.00	$690.00	$690.00	$690.00
Ending inventory	181.00	179.00	171.00	178.58
Cost of goods sold	$509.00	$511.00	$519.00	$511.42
Gross margin	$271.00	$269.00	$261.00	$268.58

cost flows need not necessarily correspond with the actual physical flow of the goods. In fact, good reasons exist for simply ignoring physical flows and choosing an inventory method based on more significant criteria.

Illustrations 5.17 and 5.18 use the data from Illustration 5.6 to show the cost of goods sold, inventory cost, and gross margin for each of the four basic costing methods using perpetual and periodic inventory procedures, respectively.

The differences shown for the four methods occur because the company paid different prices for goods purchased. **No differences would occur if purchase prices were constant.** Since a company's purchase prices are seldom constant, the inventory costing method used by the company affects cost of goods sold, inventory cost, gross margin, and net income. Therefore,

Illustration 5.18
SUMMARY OF EFFECTS OF EMPLOYING DIFFERENT INVENTORY COSTING METHODS WITH SAME BASIC DATA—USE OF PERIODIC INVENTORY PROCEDURE

	Specific Identification	FIFO	LIFO	Weighted-Average
Sales	$780.00	$780.00	$780.00	$780.00
Cost of goods sold:				
Beginning inventory.	$ 80.00	$ 80.00	$ 80.00	$ 80.00
Purchases	610.00	610.00	610.00	610.00
Cost of goods available for sale . . .	$690.00	$690.00	$690.00	$690.00
Ending inventory	181.00	179.00	165.00	172.50
Cost of goods sold	$509.00	$511.00	$525.00	$517.50
Gross margin	$271.00	$269.00	$255.00	$262.50

companies must disclose on their financial statements which inventory costing method(s) was (were) used.

Which Is the "Correct" Method?   All four methods of inventory costing are acceptable; no single method is the only correct method. Different methods are attractive under different conditions.

If a company wants to match sales revenue with current cost of goods sold, it would use LIFO. If a company seeks to reduce its income taxes in a period of rising prices, it would also use LIFO. On the other hand, LIFO often charges against revenues the cost of goods not actually sold, and it may allow the company to manipulate net income by changing the time when the company makes additional purchases.

The FIFO and specific identification methods result in a more precise matching of historical cost with revenue. However, FIFO can give rise to "paper" profits, while specific identification can give rise to income manipulation. The weighted-average method also allows manipulation of income. Only under FIFO is the manipulation of net income not possible.

Changing Inventory Methods

Generally, companies may use the inventory method that best fits their individual circumstances. However, this freedom of choice does not include changing inventory methods every year or so, especially if the goal is to report higher income. Continuous switching of methods violates the *accounting principle of consistency,* which requires the repeated use of the same accounting methods in preparing financial statements. Consistency of methods in preparing financial statements enables financial statement users to compare statements from period to period and determine trends.

Companies may sometimes make a change in inventory method in spite of the principle of consistency. Improved financial reporting is the only justification for a change in inventory method. If a company changes its inventory method, the company must make a full disclosure of the change. Usually, the company makes a full disclosure in a footnote to the financial statements. The footnote consists of a complete description of the change, the reasons why the change was made, and, if possible, the effect of the change on net income.

For example, when J. M. Tull Industries, Inc., changed from lower of average cost or market to LIFO, the following footnote appeared in its annual report:

Note B. Change in accounting method for inventory. Effective with the year ending December 31, 1975, the company changed its method of determining inventory cost from the lower of average cost or market method to the last-in, first-out (LIFO) method for substantially all inventory. This change was made because management believes LIFO more clearly reflects income by providing a closer matching of current cost against current revenue.

Journal Entries under Perpetual Inventory Procedure

Now we illustrate in more detail the journal entries made when using perpetual inventory procedure. Data from Illustration 5.8 serve as the basis for some of the entries.

The Merchandise Inventory account is debited to record the increases in the asset due to purchase costs and transportation-in costs. Merchandise Inventory is credited to record the decreases in the asset brought about by purchase returns and allowances, purchase discounts, and cost of goods sold to customers. The balance in the account is the cost of the inventory that should be on hand at any date.

*Objective 5
Record merchandise transactions under perpetual inventory procedure.*

You would record the purchase of 10 units on March 2 in Illustration 5.8 as follows:

```
Mar. 2   Merchandise Inventory. . . . . . . . . . . . . . . . . . .  85
               Accounts Payable . . . . . . . . . . . . . . . . . . . .       85
               To record purchase of 10 units at $8.50 on account.
```

The 10 units purchased must also be recorded on the perpetual inventory record, as shown in Illustration 5.8.

The use of perpetual inventory procedure requires that two journal entries be made for each sale. One entry is at selling price—a debit to Accounts Receivable (or Cash) and a credit to Sales. The other entry is at cost—a debit to Cost of Goods Sold and a credit to Merchandise Inventory. Assuming that the 10 units sold on March 10 in Illustration 5.8 had a retail price of $13 each, you would record the following entries:

```
Mar. 10   Accounts Receivable . . . . . . . . . . . . . . . . . . . 130
                Sales  . . . . . . . . . . . . . . . . . . . . . . . .      130
                To record 10 units sold at $13 each on account.

      10   Cost of Goods Sold. . . . . . . . . . . . . . . . . . .   80
                Merchandise Inventory . . . . . . . . . . . . . . .       80
                To record cost of $8 on each of the 10 units sold.
```

When a company sells merchandise to customers, the company transfers the cost of the merchandise from an asset account (Merchandise Inventory) to an expense account (Cost of Goods Sold). The company makes this transfer because the sale reduces the asset, and the cost of the goods sold is one of the expenses of making the sale. Thus, the Cost of Goods Sold account accumulates the cost of all the merchandise that the company sells during a period.

A sales return also requires two entries—the first is the selling price, and the second is at cost.

Assume that a customer returned merchandise that cost $20 and was sold originally for $32. The entry to reduce the accounts receivable and to record the sales return of $32 is as follows:

```
Mar. 17  Sales Returns and Allowances . . . . . . . . . . . . . . .  32
             Accounts Receivable . . . . . . . . . . . . . . . . . .       32
         To record the reduction in amount owed by a customer
         upon return of goods.
```

The Merchandise Inventory account should be increased and the Cost of Goods Sold account should be decreased by $20 as follows:

```
Mar. 17  Merchandise Inventory . . . . . . . . . . . . . . . . .  20
             Cost of Goods Sold . . . . . . . . . . . . . . . . .       20
         To record replacement of goods returned to inventory.
```

Sales returns affect both revenues and cost of goods sold because the goods charged to cost of goods sold are actually returned to the seller. However, sales allowances granted to customers affect revenues only because the customers have returned no goods. Thus, if the company had granted a sales allowance of $32 on March 17, only the first entry would be required.

The balance of the Merchandise Inventory account is the cost of the inventory that should be on hand. This fact is one of the major reasons why some companies choose to use perpetual inventory procedure. The cost of inventory that should be on hand is readily available. Periodically, usually at year-end, a physical inventory is taken to determine the accuracy of the balance shown. Management may wish to investigate any major discrepancies between the balance shown in the account and the cost based on the physical count. Greater control over inventory is thereby achieved. If a shortage is discovered, an adjusting entry is required. The entry, assuming that a $15 shortage (at cost) is discovered, is:

```
Dec. 31  Loss from Inventory Shortage . . . . . . . . . . . . . . .  15
             Merchandise Inventory . . . . . . . . . . . . . . . .       15
         To record inventory shortage.
```

Assume that the Cost of Goods Sold account had a balance of $200,000 by year-end. At the end of the year, the Cost of Goods Sold account is closed to Income Summary. There are no other purchase-related accounts to be closed.

```
Dec. 31  Income Summary . . . . . . . . . . . . . . . . .  200,000
             Cost of Goods Sold . . . . . . . . . . . . . .          200,000
         To close Cost of Goods Sold account to Income
         Summary at the end of the year.
```

DEPARTURES FROM COST BASIS OF INVENTORY MEASUREMENT

As stated earlier, historical cost should generally be used to value inventories and cost of goods sold. However, in some circumstances, departures from historical cost are justified. One of these circumstances is when the utility or value of inventory items is less than the cost of those items. A decline in the selling price of the goods or in their replacement cost may indicate such a loss of utility. This section explains how accountants account for some of these departures from the cost basis of inventory measurement.

Net Realizable Value

Objective 6
Apply net realiz-
able value and
the lower-of-cost-
or-market method
to inventory

Companies should not carry goods in inventory at more than their net realizable value. **Net realizable value** is the estimated selling price of an item less the estimated costs that the company will incur in preparing the item for sale and selling it. Damaged, obsolete, or shopworn goods often have a net realizable value that is lower than their historical cost and must be written down to their net realizable value. The goods do not have to be damaged, obsolete, or shopworn for this situation to occur. Technological changes and increased competition have caused significant reductions in selling prices for such products as computers, VCRs, calculators, and microwave ovens.

To illustrate a necessary write-down in the cost of inventory, assume that an automobile dealer has a demonstrator on hand. The dealer acquired the auto at a cost of $8,000. The auto had an original selling price of $9,600. Since the dealer used the auto as a demonstrator and the new models are coming in, the auto now has an estimated selling price of only $8,100. However, the dealer can get the $8,100 only if the demonstrator receives some scheduled maintenance, including a tune-up and some paint damage repairs. This work and the sales commission will cost $300. The net realizable value of the demonstrator, then, is $7,800 (selling price of $8,100 less costs of $300). For inventory purposes, the required journal entry is:

Loss Due to Decline in Market Value of Inventory	200	
Merchandise Inventory		200
To write down inventory to net realizable value ($8,000 − $7,800).		

This entry treats the $200 inventory decline as a loss in the period in which the decline in utility occurred. Such an entry is necessary only when the net realizable value is less than cost. If net realizable value declines but still exceeds cost, the dealer would continue to carry the item at cost.

Lower-of-Cost-or-Market Method

The **lower-of-cost-or-market (LCM) method** is an inventory costing method that values inventory at the lower of its historical cost or its current market (replacement) cost. The term *cost* refers to historical cost of inventory as determined under the specific identification, FIFO, LIFO, or weighted-average inventory method. *Market* generally refers to a merchandise item's replacement cost in the quantity usually purchased. The basic assumption of the LCM method is that if the purchase price of an item has fallen, its selling price also has fallen or will fall. The LCM method has long been accepted in accounting.

Under LCM, inventory items are written down to market value when the market value is less than the cost of the items. For example, assume that the market value of the inventory is $39,600 and its cost is $40,000. Then, the company would record a $400 loss because the inventory has lost some of its revenue-generating ability. The company must recognize the loss in the period the loss occurred. On the other hand, if ending inventory has a market value of $45,000 and a cost of $40,000, the company would not recognize this increase in value. To do so would recognize revenue before the time of sale.

LCM Applied.   A company may apply LCM to each inventory item (such as Trivial Pursuit), each inventory class (such as games), or total inventory. Illustration 5.19 shows an application of the method to individual items and total inventory.

If LCM is applied on an item-by-item basis, ending inventory would be $5,000. The company would deduct the $5,000 ending inventory from cost of goods available for sale on the income statement and would report this inventory in the current assets section of the balance sheet. Under the class method, a company applies LCM to the total cost and total market for each class of items compared. One class might be games; another might be toys. Then, the company values each class at the lower of its cost or market amount. If LCM is applied on a total inventory basis, ending inventory would be $5,100, since total cost of $5,100 is lower than total market of $5,150.

The annual report of Du Pont contains an actual example of applying LCM. The report states that "substantially all inventories are valued at cost as determined by the last-in, first-out (LIFO) method; in the aggregate, such valuations are not in excess of market." The term *in the aggregate* means that Du Pont applied LCM to total inventory.

Illustration 5.19
APPLICATION OF LOWER-OF-COST-OR-MARKET METHOD

Item	Quantity	Unit Cost	Unit Market	Total Cost	Total Market	LCM on Item-by-Item Basis
1	100 units	$10	$9.00	$1,000	$ 900	$ 900
2	200 units	8	8.75	1,600	1,750	1,600
3	500 units	5	5.00	2,500	2,500	2,500
				$5,100	$5,150	$5,000

Estimating Inventory

Objective 7
Estimate cost of
ending inventory
using the gross
margin and retail
inventory methods

A company using periodic inventory procedure may wish to estimate its inventory for any of the following reasons:

1. To obtain an inventory cost for use in monthly or quarterly financial statements without taking a physical inventory. The effort of taking a physical inventory can be very expensive and disrupts normal business operations; once a year is often enough.
2. To compare with physical inventories to determine whether shortages exist.
3. To determine the amount recoverable from an insurance company when fire has destroyed inventory or the inventory has been stolen.

The paragraphs that follow discuss two recognized methods of estimating the cost of ending inventory—the gross margin method and the retail inventory method.

Gross Margin Method. The gross margin method is one method of estimating an inventory when a company uses periodic inventory procedure and has not taken a physical inventory. The steps in calculating ending inventory under the gross margin method are:

1. Estimate gross margin (based on net sales) using the same gross margin rate experienced in prior accounting periods.
2. Determine estimated cost of goods sold by deducting estimated gross margin from net sales.
3. Determine estimated ending inventory by deducting estimated cost of goods sold from cost of goods available for sale.

Thus, the **gross margin method** estimates ending inventory by deducting estimated cost of goods sold from cost of goods available for sale.

The gross margin method assumes that a fairly stable relationship exists between gross margin and net sales. In other words, gross margin has been a fairly constant percentage of net sales, and this relationship is assumed to

---

Illustration 5.20
INVENTORY ESTIMATION USING GROSS MARGIN METHOD

Merchandise inventory, January 1, 1995.		$ 40,000
Net cost of purchases		480,000
Cost of goods available for sale		$520,000
Less estimated cost of goods sold:		
Net sales	$700,000	
Gross margin (30% of $700,000)	210,000	
Estimated cost of goods sold		490,000
Estimated inventory, December 31, 1995		$ 30,000

A BROADER PERSPECTIVE

HAMPTON INDUSTRIES, INC. (DEC)

This item illustrates the type of disclosure regarding inventories that is presented in the footnotes to the financial statements. Notice that the company discloses the inventory costing methods used, as well as the bases for cost and market.

	1990	1989
Current assets:		
Cash	$ 1,438,627	$ 813,831
Accounts receivable, less allowance for doubtful accounts of $1,600,000 in 1990 and $375,000 in 1989.	23,671,421	22,984,286
Inventories (Note B).	37,879,268	44,875,037
Deferred income taxes	1,149,200	511,800
Other current assets.	1,150,766	1,535,702
Total current assets.	$65,289,282	$70,720,656

NOTES TO CONSOLIDATED FINANCIAL STATEMENTS

A (In Part): Summary of Significant Accounting Policies

Inventories

Inventories are carried at the lower of cost or market value. As described in Note B, the cost of substantially all inventory is determined by the last-in, first-out (LIFO) method.

B. Inventories

	1990	1989
Finished goods . . .	$27,821,339	$29,688,692
Work-in-process . . .	4,799,737	6,472,212
Piece goods.	4,398,234	7,933,969
Supplies and other. .	859,958	978,164
	$37,879,268	$44,875,037

Principally all inventories are valued at the lower of last-in, first-out (LIFO) cost or market. Information related to the first-in, first-out (FIFO) method may be useful in comparing operating results to those of companies not on LIFO. On a supplemental basis, if inventories had been valued at the lower of FIFO cost or market, inventories at December 29, 1990 and December 30, 1989 would be approximately $44,937,000 and $51,354,000, respectively. The LIFO valuation method had the effect of decreasing net earnings by $354,700 ($.09 per share) in 1990, $695,100 ($.18 per share) in 1989 and $357,400 ($.09 per share) in 1988.

SOURCE: American Institute of Public Accountants, *Accounting Trends & Techniques* (New York: AICPA, 1991), p. 147.

---

have continued into the current period. If this percentage relationship has changed, the gross margin method will not yield satisfactory results.

To illustrate the gross margin method of computing inventory, assume that Field Company has for several years maintained a rate of gross margin on net sales of 30%. The following data for 1995 are available: the January 1 inventory was $40,000; net cost of purchases of merchandise was $480,000; and net sales of merchandise were $700,000. As shown in Illustration 5.20, the inventory for December 31, 1995, can be estimated by deducting the estimated cost of goods sold from the actual cost of goods available for sale.

An alternative format for calculating estimated ending inventory is to use the standard income statement format and solve for the one unknown (ending inventory):

Net sales			$700,000
Less cost of goods sold:			
Merchandise inventory, January 1, 1995.	$ 40,000		
Net cost of purchases	480,000		
Cost of goods available for sale	$520,000		
Less estimated inventory, December 31, 1995 . . .	?		
Estimated cost of goods sold.			490,000 (70% of net sales)
Estimated gross margin			$210,000 (30% of net sales)

We know that:

$$\frac{\text{Cost of goods}}{\text{available for sale}} - \frac{\text{Ending}}{\text{inventory}} = \frac{\text{Cost of}}{\text{goods sold}}$$

Therefore (let X = Ending inventory):

$$\$520,000 - X = \$490,000$$
$$X = \$30,000$$

The gross margin method is not precise enough to be used for year-end financial statements. At year-end, a physical inventory must be taken and valued by the use of either the specific identification, FIFO, LIFO, or weighted-average inventory methods.

Retail Inventory Method.   Retail stores using periodic inventory procedure frequently use the retail inventory method (hence, the name *retail inventory*) to estimate ending inventory. Taking a physical inventory during an accounting period (such as monthly or quarterly) is too time consuming and significantly interferes with business operations. The **retail inventory method** estimates the cost of the ending inventory by applying a cost/retail price ratio to ending inventory stated at retail prices. The advantage of this method is that companies can estimate ending inventory (at cost) without taking a physical inventory. Thus, the use of this estimate permits the preparation of interim financial statements (monthly or quarterly) without taking a physical inventory.

The retail inventory method works as follows:

1. Accounting records must show the beginning inventory and the amount of goods purchased during the period at both cost and retail prices.
2. The cost/retail price ratio is found by dividing the cost of goods available for sale by the retail price of the goods available for sale.

3. Retail sales are then deducted from the retail price of the goods available for sale to determine ending inventory at retail.
4. The cost/retail price ratio or percentage is multiplied by the ending inventory at retail prices to reduce it to the ending inventory at cost.

Illustration 5.21 shows an example of the retail method. In the illustration, the cost ($22,000) and retail ($40,000) amounts for beginning inventory are available from the preceding period's computation. The amounts for purchases, purchase returns, purchase allowances, and transportation-in are obtained from the accounting records. The amounts for purchase allowances and transportation-in only appear in the cost column, as shown. The sales amount ($280,000) is obtained from the Sales account and is, of course, stated at retail (sales) prices. The difference between what was available for sale at retail prices and what was sold at retail prices (which, of course, is sales) equals what should be on hand (ending inventory of $60,000) expressed in retail prices. The retail price of the ending inventory needs to be converted into cost for use in the financial statements by multiplying it times the cost/retail price ratio. In the example, the cost/retail price ratio is 60%, which means that on the average, 60 cents of each sales dollar is cost of goods sold. Ending inventory at retail ($60,000) is multiplied by 60% to find inventory at cost ($36,000).

Once ending inventory has been estimated at cost ($36,000), the cost of ending inventory can be deducted from cost of goods available for sale ($204,000) to determine cost of goods sold ($168,000). Cost of goods sold can also be found by multiplying the cost/retail price ratio of 60% by sales of $280,000.

In 1996, the $36,000 and $60,000 amounts will appear on the schedule as beginning inventory at cost and retail, respectively. Other 1996 data regarding purchases, purchase returns, purchase allowances, and transportation-in

Illustration 5.21
INVENTORY ESTIMATION USING RETAIL INVENTORY METHOD

	Cost	Retail
Merchandise inventory, January 1, 1995	$ 22,000	$ 40,000
Purchases	182,000	303,000
Purchase returns	(2,000)	(3,000)
Purchase allowances	(3,000)	
Transportation-in	5,000	
Goods available for sale	$204,000	$340,000
Cost/retail price ratio: $204,000/$340,000 = 60%		
Sales		280,000
Ending inventory at retail prices		$ 60,000
Times cost/retail price ratio		×60%
Ending inventory at cost, December 31, 1995	$ 36,000	

ETHICS   A CLOSER LOOK

During the late 1980s, Jamey Mitchell opened and expanded his chain of computer stores and managed to make a moderate profit as more individuals and businesses purchased computers. His customer base was growing and seemed pleased with the service and support his company offered. Although he did not make a large profit by selling any one computer, he sold so many computers that he made his profit based on a large volume. In fact, over the years, Jamey's cash investments in his business increased as he expanded his inventory to keep pace with his company's sales growth.

As the 1990s approached, Jamey began to withdraw funds from the business for personal use. He believed that his company's sales growth justified the large inventory he maintained. Accordingly, Jamey obtained a $1,000,000 loan from a bank by using his entire inventory as collateral. If the value of his company's inventory ever fell below $1,000,000, Jamey would be required to repay the loan in full immediately.

In 1992, several computer "superstores" opened locations near Jamey's stores and began to compete with Jamey for computer sales. Computer manufacturers began to offer better and cheaper computers more frequently, but they did not give the retailers time to sell off their old and obsolete inventory. Jamey was having great difficulty selling these older computers when the "superstores" were selling the newer computers for less money than Jamey paid for his older computers. Both Jamey and his company became strapped for cash and did not have any other assets that could be readily converted to cash. At the end of the year, Jamey's accountant reviewed his inventory records and noticed that the company's $1,300,000 inventory included $700,000 in computers that were obsolete. The company had been offering the computers at a 50% discount off their cost and still was unable to sell them. Jamey had received a $250,000 offer from a liquidation broker for the $700,000 in obsolete computers, but Jamey was reluctant to sell them because he still hoped to sell them to his customers.

Jamey's accountant suggested that the carrying value of the obsolete computers should be reduced by $450,000 to their $250,000 net realizable value. Jamey preferred to maintain the computers at their original cost and simply accept a large loss on each obsolete computer he sold.

Required
a.   Is Jamey correct?
b.   Why does Jamey prefer to maintain the obsolete computers at their original cost?

will be included to determine goods available for sale at cost and at retail. From these amounts, a new cost/retail price ratio for 1996 will be computed.

At the end of each year, a physical inventory usually is taken at retail prices. Since the retail prices are marked on the individual items (while the cost is not), taking an inventory at retail prices is more convenient than taking an inventory at cost. The results of the physical inventory can then be compared to the calculation of inventory at retail under the retail inventory method to determine whether a shortage exists.

Both the gross margin and the retail inventory methods can be used to detect inventory shortages. To illustrate how shortages can be determined using the retail inventory method example given above, assume that a physical inventory taken on December 31, 1995, shows only $56,000 of retail-priced goods in the store. Comparing this amount to the $60,000 of goods that should be on hand (shown in Illustration 5.21) indicates a $4,000 inventory shortage at retail. The $4,000 will be converted to $2,400 of cost ($4,000 × 0.60) and reported as a "Loss from inventory shortage" in the income statement. Knowledge of such shortages may lead to management action to reduce or prevent them, such as increasing security or improving the training of employees.

You should now understand the importance of taking an accurate physical inventory and knowing how to assign a cost to this inventory. You also know how to estimate inventory under periodic procedure in the absence of a physical count.

In the next chapter, you will learn the general principles of internal control and how to control cash. Cash is one of a company's most important assets; however, it is also the company's most mobile asset. As you study the subject of controlling cash, you will realize that, to be successful, a company must attempt to hire and retain competent and trustworthy employees and must also establish an effective internal control structure.

UNDERSTANDING THE LEARNING OBJECTIVES

1. Explain and calculate the effects of inventory errors on certain financial statement items.
    - Net income for an accounting period depends directly on the valuation of ending inventory.
    - If ending inventory is overstated, cost of goods sold will be understated, resulting in an overstatement of gross margin, net income, and retained earnings.
    - When ending inventory is misstated in the current year, that misstatement is carried forward into the next year.
    - An error in the net income of one year caused by a misstated ending inventory automatically causes an error in net income in the opposite direction in the next period because of the misstated beginning inventory.
2. Indicate which costs are properly included in inventory.
    - Inventory cost includes all necessary outlays to obtain the goods, get the goods ready to sell, and have the goods in the desired location for sale to customers.
    - Inventory cost includes:
        a. Seller's gross selling price less purchase discount.
        b. Cost of insurance on the goods while in transit.
        c. Transportation charges when borne by the buyer.
        d. Handling costs, such as the cost of pressing clothes wrinkled during shipment.

3. Calculate cost of ending inventory and cost of goods sold under the four major inventory costing methods using perpetual and periodic inventory procedures.
    *   **Specific identification:** Attaches actual cost of each unit of product to units in ending inventory and cost of goods sold. Specific identification creates precise matching in determining net income.
    *   **FIFO (first-in, first-out):** Ending inventory consists of the most recent purchases. FIFO assumes that the costs of the first goods purchased are the first costs charged to cost of goods sold when the goods are actually sold. FIFO usually creates higher net income since the costs charged to cost of goods sold are lower.
    *   **LIFO (last-in, first-out):** Ending inventory consists of the oldest costs. LIFO assumes that the costs of the most recent purchases are the first costs charged to cost of goods sold. Net income is usually lower under LIFO since the costs charged to cost of goods sold are higher due to inflation. The ending inventory may differ between perpetual and periodic inventory procedures.
    *   **Weighted-average:** Ending inventory is priced using a weighted-average unit cost. Under perpetual procedure, a new weighted average is determined after each purchase. Under periodic procedure the average is determined at the end of the accounting period by dividing the total number of units purchased plus those in beginning inventory into total cost of goods available for sale. In determining cost of goods sold, this average unit cost is applied to each item. Under the weighted-average method, in a period of rising prices net income is usually higher than income under LIFO and lower than income under FIFO.
4. Explain the advantages and disadvantages of the four major inventory costing methods.
    *   **Specific identification:**
        Advantages: (1) States cost of goods sold and ending inventory at the actual cost of specific units sold and on hand, and (2) it provides the most precise matching of costs and revenues.
        Disadvantage: Income manipulation is possible.
    *   **FIFO:**
        Advantages: (1) FIFO is easy to apply, (2) the assumed flow of costs often corresponds with the normal physical flow of goods, (3) no manipulation of income is possible, and (4) the balance sheet amount for inventory is likely to approximate the current market value.
        Disadvantages: (1) Recognizes "paper" profits, and (2) tax burden is heavier if used for tax purposes.
    *   **LIFO:**
        Advantages: (1) LIFO reports both sales revenue and cost of goods sold in current dollars, and (2) lower income taxes result if used for tax purposes when prices are rising.

Disadvantages: (1) Matches the cost of goods *not* sold against revenues, (2) grossly understates inventory, and (3) permits income manipulation.

- **Weighted-average:**

  Advantages: Due to the averaging process, the effects of year-end buying or not buying are lessened.

  Disadvantages: Manipulation of income is possible.

5. Record merchandise transactions under perpetual inventory procedure.
   - Perpetual inventory procedure requires an entry to Merchandise Inventory whenever goods are purchased, returned, sold, or otherwise adjusted, so that inventory records reflect actual units on hand at all times. Thus, an entry is required to record cost of goods sold for each sale.

6. Apply net realizable value and the lower-of-cost-or-market method to inventory.
   - Companies should not carry goods in inventory at more than their net realizable value. Net realizable value is the estimated selling price of an item less the estimated costs that will be incurred in preparing the item for sale and selling it.
   - Inventory items are written down to market value when the market value is less than the cost of the items. If market value is greater than cost, the increase in value is not recognized. LCM may be applied to each inventory item, each inventory class, or total inventory.

7. Estimate cost of ending inventory using the gross margin and retail inventory methods.
   - The steps in calculating ending inventory under the gross margin methods are:
     a. Gross margin is estimated (based on net sales) using the same gross margin rate experienced in prior accounting periods.
     b. Estimated cost of goods sold is determined by deducting estimated gross margin from net sales.
     c. Estimated ending inventory is determined by deducting estimated cost of goods sold from cost of goods available for sale.
   - The retail inventory method estimates the cost of the ending inventory by applying a cost/retail price ratio to ending inventory stated at retail prices. The cost/retail price ratio is found by dividing the cost of goods available for sale by the retail price of the goods available for sale.

DEMONSTRATION PROBLEM 5–A

Following are data related to Castellanos Company's beginning inventory, purchases, and sales of a given item of product for the year 1995:

	Beginning Inventory and Purchases			Sales	
	Units	Unit Cost			Units
Beginning inventory. . . .	6,250 @	$1.50	February 3		5,250
March 15.	5,000 @	1.56	May 4		4,500
May 10	8,750 @	1.65	September 16.		8,000
August 12	6,250 @	1.74	October 9.		7,250
November 20	3,750 @	1.86			
	30,000				25,000

Required:

a. Compute the ending inventory under each of the following methods:
1. Specific identification (assume ending inventory consists of an equal number of units from the August 12 and November 20 purchases).
2. FIFO: *(a)* Assume use of perpetual inventory procedure.
   (b) Assume use of periodic inventory procedure.
3. LIFO: *(a)* Assume use of perpetual inventory procedure.
   (b) Assume use of periodic inventory procedure.
4. Weighted-average: *(a)* Assume use of perpetual inventory procedure.
   (b) Assume use of periodic inventory procedure.
   (Carry unit cost to four decimal places and round total cost to nearest dollar.)
b. Give the journal entries to record the individual purchases and sales (Cost of Goods Sold entry only) under the LIFO method and perpetual procedure.

Solution to demonstration problem 5–A

a. The ending inventory consists of:

	Units
Beginning inventory	6,250
Purchases	23,750
Goods available	30,000
Sales	25,000
Ending inventory	5,000

1. Ending inventory under specific identification:

Purchased	Units	Unit Cost	Total Cost
November 20	2,500	$1.86	$4,650
August 12.	2,500	1.74	4,350
			$9,000

2. Ending inventory under FIFO:
   (a) Perpetual:

Date	Purchased Units	Unit Cost	Total Cost	Sold Units	Unit Cost	Total Cost	Balance Units	Unit Cost	Total Cost
Beg. inv.							6,250	$1.50	$ 9,375
Feb. 3				5,250	$1.50	$ 7,875	1,000	1.50	1,500
Mar. 15	5,000	$1.56	$ 7,800				1,000	1.50	1,500
							5,000	1.56	7,800
May 4				1,000	1.50	1,500			
				3,500	1.56	5,460	1,500	1.56	2,340
May 10	8,750	1.65	14,438				1,500	1.56	2,340
							8,750	1.65	14,438
Aug. 12	6,250	1.74	10,875				1,500	1.56	2,340
							8,750	1.65	14,438
							6,250	1.74	10,875
Sept. 16				1,500	1.56	2,340			
				6,500	1.65	10,725	2,250	1.65	3,713
							6,250	1.74	10,875
Oct. 9				2,250	1.65	3,713			
				5,000	1.74	8,700	1,250	1.74	2,175
Nov. 20	3,750	1.86	6,975				1,250	1.74	2,175
							3,750	1.86	6,975

Ending inventory = (1,250 × $1.74) + (3,750 × $1.86) = $9,150

(b) Periodic:

Purchased	Units	Unit Cost	Total Cost
November 20	3,750	$1.86	$6,975
August 12.	1,250	1.74	2,175
	5,000		$9,150

* Note that the cost of ending inventory is the same as under perpetual.

3. Ending inventory under LIFO:
   (a) Perpetual:

Date	Purchased			Sold			Balance		
	Units	Unit Cost	Total Cost	Units	Unit Cost	Total Cost	Units	Unit Cost	Total Cost
Beg. inv.							6,250	$1.50	$ 9,375
Feb. 3				5,250	$1.50	$7,875	1,000	1.50	1,500
Mar. 15	5,000	$1.56	$ 7,800				1,000	1.50	1,500
							5,000	1.56	7,800
May 4				4,500	1.56	7,020	1,000	1.50	1,500
							500	1.56	780
May 10	8,750	1.65	14,438				1,000	1.50	1,500
							500	1.56	780
							8,750	1.65	14,438
Aug. 12	6,250	1.74	10,875				1,000	1.50	1,500
							500	1.56	780
							8,750	1.65	14,438
							6,250	1.74	10,875
Sept. 16				6,250	1.74	10,875			
				1,750	1.65	2,888	1,000	1.50	1,500
							500	1.56	780
							7,000	1.65	11,550
Oct. 9				7,000	1.65	11,550			
				250	1.56	390	1,000	1.50	1,500
							250	1.56	390
Nov. 20	3,750	1.86	6,975				1,000	1.50	1,500
							250	1.56	390
							3,750	1.86	6,975

Ending inventory = (1,000 × $1.50) + (250 × $1.56) + (3,750 × $1.86) = $8,865

(b) Periodic:

	Units	Unit Cost	Total Cost
Merchandise inventory, January 1	5,000	$1.50	$7,500

4. Ending inventory under weighted-average:
   (*a*) Perpetual:

	Purchased			Sold			Balance		
Date	Units	Unit Cost	Total Cost	Units	Unit Cost	Total Cost	Units	Unit Cost	Total Cost
Beg. inv.							6,250	$1.5000	$ 9,375
Feb. 3				5,250	$1.50	$ 7,875	1,000	1.5000	1,500
Mar. 15	5,000	$1.56	$ 7,800				6,000	1.5500[a]	9,300
May 4				4,500	1.55	6,975	1,500	1.5500	2,325
May 10	8,750	1.65	14,438				10,250	1.6354[b]	16,763
Aug. 12	6,250	1.74	10,875				16,500	1.6750[c]	27,638
Sept. 16				8,000	1.6750	13,400	8,500	1.6750	14,238
Oct. 9				7,250	1.6750	12,144	1,250	1.6750	2,094
Nov. 20	3,750	1.86	6,975				5,000	1.8138[d]	9,069

Ending inventory = (5,000 × $1.8138) = $9,069

[a] $\frac{\$9,300}{6,000} = \$1.550.$ [b] $\frac{\$16,762.50}{10,250} = \$1.6354.$ [c] $\frac{\$27,638}{16,500} = \$1.6750.$ [d] $\frac{\$9,069}{5,000} = \$1.8138.$

(*b*) Periodic:

Purchased	Units	Unit Cost	Total Cost
Merchandise inventory, January 1	6,250	$1.50	$ 9,375
March 15	5,000	1.56	7,800
May 10	8,750	1.65	14,438*
August 12.	6,250	1.74	10,875
November 20	3,750	1.86	6,975
	30,000		$49,463*

Weighted-average unit cost = $49,463 ÷ 30,000 = $1.6488
Ending inventory cost = $1.6488 × 5,000 = $8,244*

* Rounding difference.

b. Journal entries under LIFO perpetual:

Feb.	3	Cost of Goods Sold	7,875	
		Merchandise Inventory		7,875
		To record cost of $1.50 on 5,250 units sold.		
Mar.	15	Merchandise Inventory	7,800	
		Accounts Payable		7,800
		To record purchase of 5,000 units at $1.56 on account.		
May	4	Cost of Goods Sold	7,020	
		Merchandise Inventory		7,020
		To record cost of $1.56 on 4,500 units sold.		

May   10 Merchandise Inventory. 14,438
            Accounts Payable   14,438
         To record purchase of 8,750 units at $1.65 on
         account.

Aug. 12 Merchandise Inventory. 10,875
            Accounts Payable   10,875
         To record purchase of 6,250 units at $1.74 on
         account.

Sept. 16 Cost of Goods Sold 13,763
            Merchandise Inventory.   13,763
         To record cost of $1.74 and $1.65 on 6,250 units
         and 1,750 units sold, respectively.

Oct.   9 Cost of Goods Sold 11,940
            Merchandise Inventory.   11,940
         To record costs of $1.65 and $1.56 on 7,000 units
         and 250 units sold, respectively.

Nov. 20 Merchandise Inventory. 6,975
            Accounts Payable   6,975
         To record purchase of 3,750 units at $1.86 on
         account.

DEMONSTRATION PROBLEM 5–B

a. Natalie Company reported annual net income as follows:

1992	$13,600
1993	14,200
1994	12,000

Analysis of the inventories shows that certain clerical errors were made with the following results:

	Incorrect Inventory Amount	Correct Inventory Amount
December 31, 1992	$2,400	$2,840
December 31, 1993	2,800	2,340

Required:

What is the corrected net income for 1992, 1993, and 1994?

b. The records of Lewis Corporation show the following account balances on the day a fire destroyed the company's inventory:

Merchandise inventory, January 1	$ 20,000
Net cost of purchases (to date)	100,000
Sales (to date)	$150,000
Average rate of gross margin for the past five years	30% of net sales

Required:

Compute an estimated value of the ending inventory using the gross margin method.

c. The records of Dexter Company show the following account balances at year-end:

	Cost	Retail
Merchandise inventory, January 1	$ 8,800	$12,500
Purchases	34,000	50,000
Transportation-in	950	
Sales		$50,500

Required:

Compute the estimated ending inventory at cost using the retail inventory method.

Solution to demonstration problem 5–B

a.

	1992	1993	1994	Total
Net income as reported	$13,600	$14,200	$12,000	$39,800
Adjustments:				
(1)	440			
(2)		(440)		
		(460)		
(3)			460	
Adjusted net income	$14,040	$13,300	$12,460	$39,800

(1) Ending inventory understated ($2,840 − $2,400 = $440).
(2) Beginning inventory understated ($2,840 − $2,400 = $440).
    Ending inventory overstated ($2,800 − $2,340 = $460).
(3) Beginning inventory overstated ($2,800 − $2,340 = $460).

b. Computation of inventory:

Merchandise inventory, January 1		$ 20,000
Net cost of purchases		100,000
Cost of goods available for sale		$120,000
Less estimated cost of goods sold:		
Net sales	$150,000	
Gross margin ($150,000 × 0.30)	45,000	
Estimated cost of goods sold		105,000
Inventory at cost, estimated by gross		
margin method.		$ 15,000

c.

	Cost	Retail
Merchandise inventory, January 1	$ 8,800	$12,500
Purchases	34,000	50,000
Transportation-in.	950	—
Goods available for sale	$43,750	$62,500
Cost/retail price ratio:		
$43,750/$62,500 = 70%		
Sales		$50,500
Ending inventory at retail price		$12,000
Times cost/retail price ratio		×70%
Ending inventory at cost, December 31	$ 8,400	

NEW TERMS

FIFO (first-in, first-out) A method of costing inventory that assumes the costs of the first goods purchased are the first costs charged to cost of goods sold when the company actually sells the goods. *257*

Gross margin method A procedure for estimating inventory cost in which estimated cost of goods sold (determined using an estimated gross margin) is deducted from the cost of goods available for sale to determine estimated ending inventory. The estimated gross margin is calculated using gross margin rates (in relation to net sales) of prior periods. *274*

Inventory, or "paper," profits Equal to the current replacement cost to purchase a unit of inventory at time of sale minus the unit's historical cost. *262*

LIFO (last-in, first-out) A method of costing inventory that assumes the costs of the most recent purchases are the first costs charged to cost of goods sold when the company actually sells the goods. *260*

Lower-of-cost-or-market (LCM) method An inventory costing method that values inventory at the lower of its historical cost or its current market (replacement) cost. *272*

Merchandise inventory   The quantity of goods held by a merchandising company for resale to customers. *246*

Net realizable value   Estimated selling price of an item less the estimated costs that will be incurred in preparing the item for sale and selling it. *272*

Retail inventory method   A procedure for estimating the cost of the ending inventory by applying a cost/retail price ratio to ending inventory stated at retail prices. *276*

Specific identification   An inventory costing method that attaches the actual cost to an identifiable unit of product. *256*

Weighted-average method   A method of costing ending inventory using a weighted-average unit cost. Under perpetual inventory procedure, a new weighted average is calculated after each purchase. Under periodic procedure, the weighted average is determined by dividing the total number of units purchased plus those in beginning inventory into total cost of goods available for sale. Units in the ending inventory are carried at this per unit cost. *265*

SELF-TEST

True-False

Indicate whether each of the following statements is true or false.

1. Overstated ending inventory results in an overstatement of cost of goods sold and an understatement of gross margin and net income.

2. In a period of rising prices, FIFO results in the lowest cost of goods sold.

3. Under LCM, inventory is written down to market value when the market value is less than the cost, and inventory is written up to market value when the market value is greater than the cost.

Multiple-Choice

Select the best answer for each of the following questions.

On July 1, 1995, Elmer Company began the accounting period with inventory of 3,000 units at $7.50 each. During the period, the company purchased an additional 5,000 units at $9.00 each and sold 4,600 units. Assume the use of periodic inventory procedure for Questions 1–6.

1. Cost of ending inventory using FIFO is:
   a. $26,100.
   b. $30,600.
   c. $30,000.

4. Under the gross margin method, an estimate must first be made of gross margin to determine estimated cost of goods sold and estimated ending inventory.

5. To use the retail inventory method, both cost and retail prices must be known for the goods available for sale.

6. Under perpetual procedure, cost of goods sold is determined as a result of the closing entries made at the end of the period.

   d. $36,900.
   e. None of the above.

2. Cost of goods sold using FIFO is:
   a. $41,400.
   b. $37,500.
   c. $36,900.
   d. $30,600.
   e. None of the above.

3. Cost of ending inventory using LIFO is:
   a. $26,100.
   b. $28,687.50.
   c. $39,000.

d. $30,600.
e. None of the above.

4. Cost of goods sold using LIFO is:
   a. $38,812.50.
   b. $28,500.
   c. $36,900.
   d. $41,400.
   e. None of the above.

5. Cost of ending inventory using weighted-average is:
   a. $28,687.50.
   b. $39,400.
   c. $30,600.
   d. $27,412.50.
   e. None of the above.

6. Cost of goods sold using weighted-average is:

   a. $36,800.
   b. $40,087.50.
   c. $38,812.50.
   d. $28,500.
   e. None of the above.

7. During a period of rising prices, which inventory method might be expected to give the highest net income?
   a. Weighted-average.
   b. FIFO.
   c. LIFO.
   d. Specific identification.
   e. Cannot determine.

Now turn to page 302 to check your answers.

QUESTIONS

1. Why is proper inventory valuation so important?

2. Why does an understated ending inventory understate net income for the period by the same amount?

3. Why does an error in ending inventory affect two accounting periods?

4. What is the meaning of "to take a physical inventory"?

5. What is the accountant's responsibility regarding the taking of a physical inventory?

6. Which cost elements are included in inventory? What practical problems arise by including the costs of such elements?

7. Which accounts that are used under periodic inventory procedure are not used under perpetual inventory procedure?

8. What entries are necessary under perpetual procedure when goods are sold?

9. Why is there closer control over inventory under perpetual procedure than under periodic procedure?

10. Why is perpetual inventory procedure being used increasingly in business?

11. What is the cost flow assumption? What is meant by the physical flow of goods? Does a relationship between cost flows and the physical flow of goods exist, or should such a relationship exist?

12. Indicate how a company can manipulate its net income if it uses LIFO. Is the same opportunity available under FIFO? Why or why not?

13. What are the main advantages of using FIFO and LIFO?

14. Which inventory method is the "correct" one? Can a company change inventory methods?

15. Why are ending inventory and cost of goods sold the same under FIFO perpetual and FIFO periodic?

16. Would you agree with the following statement? Reducing the amount of taxes payable currently is a valid objective of business management and, since LIFO results in such a reduction, all businesses use LIFO.

17. What is net realizable value, and how is it used?

18. Why is it considered acceptable accounting practice to recognize a loss by writing down an item in inventory to market, but unacceptable to recognize a gain by writing up an inventory item?

19. Under what conditions will the gross margin method of computing an estimated inventory yield approximately correct amounts?

20. What are the main reasons for estimating ending inventory?

21. Should a company rely exclusively on the gross margin method to determine the ending inventory and cost of goods sold for the end-of-year financial statements?

22. How can the retail method be used to estimate inventory?

MAYTAG
CORPORATION

23. *Real-world question*   Based on the financial statements of Maytag Corporation contained in Appendix C, what was the 1991 beginning inventory?

THE LIMITED, INC.

24. *Real-world question*   Based on the financial statements of The Limited, Inc., contained in Appendix C, what was the 1991 ending inventory?

HARLAND

25. *Real-world question*   Based on the financial statements of John H. Harland Company contained in Appendix C, what was the 1991 beginning inventory?

EXERCISES

Determine effects
of inventory errors
(L.O. 1)

5-1. Angie Company reported annual net income as follows:

1993	$60,560
1994	60,960
1995	51,248

Analysis of its inventories shows that the following incorrect inventory amounts were used (the correct amounts are also shown):

	Incorrect Inventory Amount	Correct Inventory Amount
December 31, 1993	$ 9,600	$11,200
December 31, 1994	10,800	9,200

Compute the annual net income for each of the three years assuming the correct inventories had been used.

Compute the impact on net income under specific identification (L.O. 3, 4)

5–2. Becky Motor Company manufactures trucks and identifies each truck with a unique serial plate. On December 31, a customer ordered five trucks from the company. The company currently has twenty trucks in its inventory. Ten of these trucks cost $5,000 each, and the other 10 cost $6,250 each. If Becky wished to minimize its net income, which trucks would it ship? By how much is it possible to reduce net income by selecting units from one group versus the other group?

Compute ending inventory using FIFO perpetual inventory procedure (L.O.3)

5–3. Winters Company inventory records show:

	Units	Unit Cost	Total Cost
Beginning inventory	3,000	$ 9.50	$28,500
Purchases:			
February 14	900	9.75	8,775
March 18.	2,400	10.00	24,000
July 21.	1,800	10.08	18,144
September 27	1,800	10.15	18,270
November 27	600	10.25	6,150
Sales:			
April 15	2,800		
August 20	2,000		
October 3	1,500		

The December 31 inventory was 4,200 units. Winters Company uses perpetual inventory procedure. Present a schedule showing the measurement of the ending inventory using the FIFO method.

Compute ending inventory under LIFO perpetual inventory procedure (L.O. 3)

5–4. Using the data in Exercise 5–3 for Winters Company, present a schedule showing the measurement of the ending inventory using the LIFO method.

Compute ending inventory using weighted-average perpetual inventory procedure (L.O. 3)

5–5. Dana Company had a beginning inventory of 80 units at $3 (total = $240) and the following inventory transactions during 1994:

1. January 8, sold 20 units.
2. January 11, purchased 40 units at $3.75.
3. January 15, purchased 40 units at $4.00.
4. January 22, sold 40 units.

Using the information above, price the ending inventory at its weighted-average cost, assuming perpetual inventory procedure.

Compute cost of ending inventory using FIFO, LIFO, and weighted-average under periodic inventory procedure (L.O. 3)

5–6. Listed below are the purchases of product A made by Parello Company in its first year of operations:

	Units	Unit Cost
January 2	1,400 @	$1.85
March 31	1,200 @	1.75
July 5.	2,400 @	1.90
November 1.	1,800 @	2.00

The ending inventory of the year consisted of 2,400 units. Periodic inventory procedure is used.

a. Compute the cost of the ending inventory using each of the following methods: (1) FIFO, (2) LIFO, and (3) weighted-average.

b. Which method would yield the highest amount of gross margin? Explain why it does.

Prepare journal entries for inventory under FIFO perpetual inventory procedure (L.O. 3, 5)

5–7. The following are selected transactions and other data of the Shellnut Company:

1. Purchased 20 units @ $90 per unit on account on September 18, 1995.

2. Sold 6 units on account for $144 per unit on September 20, 1995.

3. At year-end, a physical inventory was taken, and a shortage of $660 was discovered.

Prepare journal entries for the above transactions using FIFO perpetual inventory procedure. Assume the beginning inventory consists of 20 units @ $84 per unit.

Prepare journal entries under FIFO perpetual inventory procedure (L.O. 3, 5)

5–8. Following are selected transactions of Bunby Company:

1. Purchased 100 units of merchandise at $60 each; terms 2/10, n/30.

2. Paid the invoice in transaction (1) within the discount period.

3. Sold 80 units at $96 each for cash.

4. Purchased 100 units at $90; terms 2/10, n/30.

5. Paid the invoice in transaction (4) within the discount period.

6. Sold 60 units at $138 each for cash.

Prepare journal entries for the six numbered items above. Assume goods acquired are recorded at net invoice prices, accounted for under perpetual inventory procedure, and the FIFO inventory method is used.

Prepare journal entries affecting inventory using LIFO perpetual inventory procedure (L.O. 3, 5)

5–9. Joyner Company had the following transactions during February:

1. Purchased 270 units at $32.50.

2. Sold 216 units at $45.

3. Purchased 340 units at $37.50.

4. Sold 245 units at $47.50.

5. Sold 135 units at $50.

The beginning inventory consisted of 135 units purchased at a cost of $27.50.

Prepare the journal entries relating to inventory for the five transactions above, assuming inventory is accounted for using perpetual procedure and the LIFO inventory method. Do not record the entry for sales.

Prepare journal
entries affecting
inventory using
weighted-average
periodic inventory
procedure
(L.O. 3)

5–10. Following are inventory data for 1994 for Morrow Company:

1. January 1 inventory on hand, 400 units @ $7.20.
2. January sales were 80 units.
3. February sales totaled 120 units.
4. March 1, purchased 200 units @ $7.56.
5. Sales for March through August were 160 units.
6. September 1, purchased 40 units @ $8.28.
7. September through December sales were 180 units.

Prepare only the journal entries affecting inventory assuming use of periodic inventory procedure. A physical inventory on December 31, 1994, showed 100 units on hand. Determine the cost of the ending inventory using the weighted-average method.

Compute
inventory profit
under FIFO
(L.O. 3, 4)

5–11. A company purchased 1,000 units of a product at $6 and 2,000 units at $6.60. All of these units were sold at $19 each at a time when the current cost to replace the units sold was $6.90. Compute the amount of gross margin under FIFO that LIFO supporters would call inventory, or "paper," profits.

Compare effect on
net income under
FIFO and LIFO
(L.O. 3, 4)

5–12. Garner Company's inventory of a certain product was 12,000 units with a cost of $40 each on January 1, 1994. During 1994, numerous units of this product were purchased and sold. Also during 1994, the purchase price of this product fell steadily until at year-end it was $30. The inventory at year-end was 18,000 units. State which of the two methods of inventory measurement, LIFO or FIFO, would have resulted in higher reported net income, and explain briefly.

Compute value of
ending inventory
using LCM applied
on an item-by-item
basis
(L.O. 6)

5–13. Your assistant has compiled the following data to assist you in determining the decline in inventory from cost to the LCM method applied on an item-by-item basis:

Item	Quantity (units)	Unit Cost	Unit Market	Total Cost	Total Market
A	300	$14.40	$13.80	$4,320	$4,140
B	300	7.20	8.40	2,160	2,520
C	900	5.40	5.40	4,860	4,860
D	500	3.00	3.30	1,500	1,650

Determine the dollar amount of the ending inventory using the LCM method, determined on an item-by-item basis, and the amount of the decline from cost to lower of cost or market.

Compute value of
total inventory
using LCM
(L.O. 6)

5–14. Use the data in Exercise 5–13 above to compute the cost of the ending inventory using the LCM method applied to the total inventory.

Compute carrying
cost of inventory
items
(L.O. 6)

5–15. Roberta Motor Company owns an automobile that it has used as a demonstrator for eight months. The auto has a list or sticker price of $18,750 and cost Roberta $16,250. At the end of the fiscal year, the auto is on hand and has an expected selling price of $17,500. Costs expected to be incurred to sell the auto include tune-up and maintenance costs of $500, advertising of $125, and a commission of 5% of selling price to the employee selling the auto. Compute the amount at which the auto should be carried in inventory.

Determine the
proper value of
damaged
inventory
(L.O. 6)

5–16. Buford Stereo Shop has a stereo system it uses as a floor model. The stereo cost $900 and had an original selling price of $1,200. After six months, the stereo is damaged and is to be replaced by a newer model. The stereo has an estimated selling price of $720, but when the company performs $120 in repairs, it can be sold for $960. Prepare the journal entry, if any, that must be made on Buford's books to record the decline in market value.

Estimate ending
inventory using
gross margin
method
(L.O. 7)

5–17. Garcia Company takes a physical inventory at the end of each calendar-year accounting period to establish the ending inventory amount for financial statement purposes. Its financial statements for the past few years indicate an average gross margin on net sales of 25%. On July 18, a fire destroyed the entire store building and its contents. The records were in a fireproof vault and are intact. Through July 17, these records show:

Merchandise inventory, January 1	$ 336,000
Merchandise purchases	4,704,000
Purchase returns	67,200
Transportation-in	252,000
Sales	7,168,000
Sales returns	336,000

The company was fully covered by insurance and asks you to determine the amount of its claim for loss of merchandise.

Estimate ending
inventory using
gross margin
method
(L.O. 7)

5–18. McKenzie Company takes a physical inventory at the end of each calendar-year accounting period. Its financial statements for the past few years indicate an average gross margin on net sales of 30%.

On June 12, a fire destroyed the entire store building and the inventory. The records were in a fireproof vault and are intact. Through June 11, these records show:

Merchandise inventory, January 1	$ 30,000
Merchandise purchases	750,000
Purchase returns	9,000
Transportation-in	51,000
Net sales	930,000

The company was fully covered by insurance and asks you to determine the amount of its claim for loss of merchandise.

Estimate ending
inventory using
retail inventory
method
(L.O. 7)

5–19. Lilly Company, Inc., records show the following account balances for the year ending December 31, 1994:

	Cost	Retail
Beginning inventory	$20,500	$28,750
Purchases	12,500	18,750
Transportation-in.	250	
Sales		26,250

Using the above data, compute the estimated cost of the ending inventory using the retail inventory method.

PROBLEMS

Determine effects
of inventory errors
(L.O. 1)

5–1. Poole Company reported net income of $179,025 for 1994, $185,700 for 1995, and $162,900 for 1996, using the incorrect inventory amounts shown for December 31, 1994, and 1995. The correct inventory amounts for those dates are also given. The correct December 31, 1996, inventory amount was used in calculating 1996 net income.

	Incorrect	Correct
December 31, 1994	$36,300	$42,600
December 31, 1995	42,000	35,100

Required:

Prepare a schedule that shows: *(a)* the reported net income for each year, *(b)* the amount of correction needed for each year, and *(c)* the correct net income for each year.

Determine effects
of inventory errors
(L.O. 1)

5–2. An examination of the financial records of Blackmon Company on December 31, 1994, disclosed the following with regard to merchandise inventory for 1994 and prior years:

1. December 31, 1990, inventory was correct.
2. December 31, 1991, inventory was overstated $50,000.
3. December 31, 1992, inventory was overstated $25,000.
4. December 31, 1993, inventory was understated $55,000.
5. December 31, 1994, inventory was correct.

The reported net income for each year was:

1991	$ 96,000
1992	136,000
1993	167,500
1994	211,500

Required:

a. Prepare a schedule of corrected net income for each of the four years—1991–94.

b. What error(s) would have been included in each December 31 balance sheet? Assume each year's error is independent of the other years' errors.

c. Comment on the implications of your corrected net income as contrasted with reported net income.

Maximize and minimize gross margin and net income using specific identification (L.O. 3, 4)

5–3. Dixon Company sells home computers and uses the specific identification method to account for its inventory. On November 30, 1994, the company had 23 Orange III model home computers on hand that were acquired on the following dates and at these stated costs:

	Units	Unit Cost
July 3.	5	@ $2,560
September 10.	10	@ 2,400
November 29	8	@ 2,800

Dixon sold 18 Orange III computers at $3,680 each in December. There were no purchases of this model in December.

Required:

a. Compute the gross margin on December sales of Orange III computers assuming the company shipped those units that would maximize reported gross margin.

b. Repeat part *(a)* assuming the company shipped those units that would minimize reported gross margin for December.

c. In view of your answers to parts *(a)* and *(b)*, what would be your reaction to an assertion that the specific identification method should not be considered an acceptable method for costing inventory?

Prepare journal entries for purchases and sales using FIFO perpetual inventory procedure (L.O. 3, 5)

5–4. The inventory records of Pike Company show the following:

Mar. 1 Beginning inventory consists of 10 units costing $10 per unit.
    3 Sold 5 units at $23.50 per unit.
   10 Purchased 16 units at $12 per unit.
   12 Sold 8 units at $24 per unit.
   20 Sold 7 units at $24 per unit.
   25 Purchased 16 units at $12.50 per unit.
   31 Sold 8 units at $24 per unit.

Assume all purchases and sales are made on credit.

Required:

Using FIFO perpetual inventory procedure, prepare the appropriate journal entries for March.

Compute ending
inventory under
FIFO, LIFO, and
weighted-average
using perpetual
and periodic
inventory
procedures
(L.O. 3)

5–5. The purchases and sales of a certain product for Key Company for April 1994 are shown below. There was no inventory on April 1.

Purchases			Sales	
	Units	Unit Cost		Units
April 3	3,200 @	$8.25	April 6	1,500
April 10	1,600 @	8.50	April 12	1,400
April 22	2,000 @	8.75	April 25	2,300
April 28	1,800 @	9.00		

Required:

a. Compute the ending inventory as of April 30, 1994, using perpetual inventory procedure, under each of the following methods: (1) FIFO, (2) LIFO, and (3) weighted-average (carry unit cost to four decimal places and round total cost to nearest dollar).

b. Repeat (a) using periodic inventory procedure.

Prepare journal
entries for
purchases and
sales using LIFO
perpetual and
periodic inventory
procedures
(L.O. 5)

5–6. Refer to the data in Problem 5–5.

Required:

a. Using LIFO perpetual inventory procedure, prepare the journal entries for the purchases and sales (Cost of Goods Sold entry only).

b. Repeat (a) using LIFO periodic inventory procedure, including closing entries.

Compute ending
inventory and cost
of goods sold
under FIFO and
LIFO using
perpetual and
periodic inventory
procedures
(L.O. 3)

5–7. Listed below are the purchases and sales of a certain product made by Doris Company during 1994. The company had 25,000 units of this product on hand at January 1, 1994, with a cost of $2.50 per unit.

Purchases			Sales		
	Units	Unit Cost		Units	Unit Cost
February 20	5,000 @	$2.60	February 2	7,500 @	$3.50
April 18	12,500 @	2.65	April 23	10,000 @	3.65
August 28	12,500 @	2.80	September 3	10,000 @	3.83
December 22	10,000 @	3.00	December 24	18,750 @	4.00

Required:

a. Assuming use of perpetual inventory procedure, compute the cost of ending inventory and the cost of goods sold under the following methods: (1) FIFO and (2) LIFO.

b. Repeat (a) assuming use of periodic inventory procedure.

Compute ending
inventory and cost
of goods sold
under FIFO, LIFO,
and weighted-
average using
perpetual and
periodic inventory
procedures
(L.O. 3)

5–8. Following are data relating to the beginning inventory, purchases, and sales of a given item of product of Rutherford Company for the year 1995:

	Units	Unit Cost
Merchandise inventory, January 1.	1,400 @	$1.26
Purchases:		
February 2	1,000 @	1.20
April 5	2,000 @	.90
June 15.	1,200 @	.75
September 30.	1,400 @	.72
November 28	1,800 @	1.05
Sales:		
March 10	900	
May 15	1,800	
July 6.	800	
August 23.	600	
December 22	2,500	

Required:

a. Assuming use of perpetual inventory procedure, compute the ending inventory and cost of goods sold under each of the following methods: (1) FIFO, (2) LIFO, and (3) weighted-average (carry unit cost to four decimal places and round total cost to nearest dollar).

b. Repeat (a) assuming use of periodic inventory procedure.

Compute gross
margin using
LIFO and FIFO
illustrating effects
of end-of-year
purchases
(L.O. 3, 4)

5–9. Mitchell Company accounts for a certain product that it handles using LIFO periodic inventory procedure. Data relative to this product for the year ended December 31, 1994, are:

Merchandise inventory, January 1, 6,000 units @ $7.20.

Purchases			Sales		
	Units	Unit Cost		Units	Unit Cost
January 5. . . .	12,000 @	$ 9.00	January 10 . . .	8,000 @	$14.40
March 31	36,000 @	10.80	April 2	30,000 @	16.20
August 12 . . .	24,000 @	13.50	August 22 . . .	32,000 @	18.00
December 26 . .	12,000 @	14.40	December 24 . .	6,000 @	19.80

Required:

a. Compute the gross margin earned on sales of this product for 1994.

b. Repeat part (a) assuming that the December 26 purchase was made in January of 1995.

c. Recompute the gross margin assuming that 20,000 rather than 12,000 units were purchased on December 26 at the same cost per unit.

d. Solve parts (a), (b), and (c) using the FIFO method.

Compute ending
inventory using
LCM
(L.O. 6)

5–10. The accountant for Gomez Company prepared the following schedule of the company's inventory at December 31, 1994, and used the LCM method applied to total inventory in determining cost of goods sold.

Item	Quantity	Unit Cost	Unit Market
Q	8,400	$1.80	$1.80
R	4,800	1.50	1.44
S	10,800	1.20	1.14
T	9,600	1.05	1.08

Required:

a. State whether this approach is an acceptable method of inventory measurement and show the calculations used to determine the amounts.
b. Compute the amount of the ending inventory using the LCM method on an item-by-item basis.
c. State the effect on net income in 1994 if the method in *(b)* was used rather than the method referred to in *(a)*.

Estimate inventory
using gross
margin method
(L.O. 6)

5–11. As part of a loan agreement with a local bank, Florence Company must present quarterly and cumulative income statements for the year 1994. The company uses periodic inventory procedure and marks its merchandise to sell at a price that will yield a gross margin of 30%. Selected data for the first six months of 1994 are as follows:

	First Quarter	Second Quarter
Sales	$62,000	$64,000
Purchases	40,000	46,000
Purchase returns and allowances	2,400	2,800
Purchase discounts	800	880
Sales returns and allowances	2,000	1,200
Transportation-in.	2,000	2,080
Miscellaneous selling expenses	6,400	6,000
Miscellaneous administrative expenses	2,400	2,000

The cost of the physical inventory taken December 31, 1993, was $7,600.

Required:

a. Indicate how income statements can be prepared without taking a physical inventory at the end of each of the first two quarters of 1994.
b. Prepare income statements for the first quarter, the second quarter, and the first six months of 1994.

Estimate ending
inventory using
retail inventory
method
(L.O. 7)

5–12. Lewis Company records show the following information for 1995.

	Cost	Retail
Sales	—	$175,200
Purchases	$135,000	210,000
Transportation-in	13,140	—
Merchandise inventory,		
January 1	6,000	8,700
Purchase returns	7,560	9,300

Required:

Compute the estimated year-end inventory balance at cost using the retail method of estimating inventory.

BUSINESS DECISION PROBLEMS

Determine tax
effects of FIFO,
LIFO, and
weighted-average
(L.O. 3, 4)

5–1. Kline Company, which began operations on January 2, 1994, sells a single product, product X. Purchases for the year were:

	Units	Unit Price
January 2	2,000 @	$4.00
February 15	3,200 @	4.00
April 8	4,000 @	4.15
June 6	1,600 @	4.25
August 19	3,200 @	4.30
October 5	2,400 @	4.50
November 22	1,600 @	4.80

Periodic inventory procedure is used. On December 31, a physical inventory shows 3,200 units on hand.

Mr. Kline is trying to decide which of the following inventory costing methods he should adopt for tax purposes: FIFO, LIFO, or weighted-average. Since Mr. Kline is short of cash, he wants to minimize the amount of the company's income taxes payable.

Required:

What will be the cost of goods sold and the cost of the ending inventory under each of these three inventory costing methods? Which of the three inventory costing methods will minimize the company's income taxes payable?

Determine
insurance
settlement using
gross margin
method
(L.O. 7)

5–2. Amy Dalton owns and operates a sporting goods store. On February 2, 1994, the store suffered extensive fire damage, and all of the inventory was destroyed. Ms. Dalton uses periodic inventory procedure and has the following information in her accounting records, which were undamaged:

Merchandise inventory,	
January 1	$20,000
Purchases:	
January 8	8,000
January 20	12,000
January 30	16,000
Net Sales:	
During January	60,000
February 1 and 2	4,000

Ms. Dalton also knows that her gross margin rate on net sales has been 40% for the past three years. Ms. Dalton's insurance company has offered to pay $14,000 to settle her inventory loss unless she can show that she suffered a greater loss.

Required:

Should Ms. Dalton settle for $14,000? If not, how can she show that she suffered a greater loss? What is the estimated loss?

ANSWERS TO SELF-TEST

True-False

1. *False.* Overstated ending inventory results in an understatement of cost of goods sold and an overstatement of gross margin and net income.

2. *True.* The cost of goods sold consists of the earliest purchases at the lowest costs in a period of rising prices.

3. *False.* Under LCM, inventory is adjusted to market value only when the market (replacement) value is less than the cost.

4. *True.* The first step in the gross margin method is to estimate gross margin using the gross margin rate experienced in the past.

5. *True.* The cost/retail ratio is computed by dividing the cost of goods available for sale by the retail price of the goods available for sale.

6. *False.* Under perpetual procedure, the Cost of Goods Sold account is updated as sales occur.

Multiple-Choice

1. *b.* The cost of ending inventory using FIFO consists of the most recent purchase:

   Cost of ending inventory $= 3,400 \times \$9$
   $= \$30,600$

2. *c.* The cost of goods sold using FIFO is:

   $$\text{Cost of goods available for sale} = (3,000 \times \$7.50) + (5,000 \times \$9)$$
   $$= \$67,500$$

   $$\text{Cost of goods sold} = \$67,500 - \$30,600$$
   $$= \$36,900$$

3. *a.* The cost of ending inventory using LIFO is:

   $(3,000 \times \$7.50) + (400 \times \$9) = \$26,100$

4. *d.* The cost of goods sold using LIFO is:

   $\$67,500 - \$26,100 = \$41,400$

5. *a.* The cost of ending inventory using weighted-average cost is computed:

   Unit cost $= \$67,500 \div 8,000 = \$8.4375$
   Cost of ending inventory $= 3,400 \times \$8.4375$
   $= \$28,687.50$

6. *c.* The cost of goods sold using weighted-average cost is:

   $\$67,500 - \$28,687.50 = \$38,812.50$

7. *b.* During a period of rising prices, FIFO results in the lowest cost of goods sold, thus the highest net income.

III

FINANCIAL ACCOUNTING: ASSETS, LIABILITIES, AND STOCKHOLDERS' EQUITY

CONTROL OF CASH

LEARNING OBJECTIVES

After studying this chapter, you should be able to:

1. Describe the necessity for and features of internal control.
2. Define cash and list the objectives sought by management in handling a company's cash.
3. Identify procedures for controlling cash receipts and disbursements.
4. Prepare a bank reconciliation and make necessary journal entries based on that schedule.
5. Explain why a petty cash fund is used, describe its operations, and make the necessary journal entries.
6. Describe the operation of the voucher system and make entries in its special journals—the voucher register and the check register.

So far in this text you have studied examples of small corporations. When a corporation is small, the president can make all the important decisions and usually maintain a close watch over the affairs of the business. Often the president personally signs the checks. However, as the business grows and the need arises for additional employees, including other officers and managers, the president begins to lose absolute control and must trust employees to take over some of the affairs of the business. At this point, the president realizes that precautions must be taken to protect the company's interests. As a result, the president establishes an internal control structure.

The **internal control structure** of a company is defined as "the policies and procedures established to provide reasonable assurance that specific entity objectives will be achieved."[1] The three elements of an internal con-

---

[1] AICPA, *Statement on Auditing Standards No. 55,* "Consideration of the Internal Control Structure in a Financial Statement Audit" (New York, 1988), p. 4.

trol structure are the control environment, the accounting system, and the control procedures.

The **control environment** reflects the overall attitude, awareness, and actions of the board of directors, management, and owners. The **accounting system** consists of the methods and records established to identify, assemble, analyze, classify, record, and report an entity's transactions to provide complete, accurate, and timely financial information. The **control procedures** of a company are those policies and procedures, in addition to the control environment and the accounting system, that management has established to provide reasonable assurance that the company will achieve its specific objectives. These control procedures may involve procedures pertaining to proper authorization, segregation of duties, design and use of adequate documents and records, adequate safeguards over access to assets, and independent checks on performance.

You may think that the sole purpose of internal control is to prevent theft and fraud. However, internal control serves many purposes. Company policies must be implemented, especially those policies that require compliance with federal law. Personnel must perform their assigned duties to promote efficiency of operations. Correct accounting records must be maintained so that accurate and reliable information is presented in the accounting reports.

This chapter discusses the internal control structure that a company establishes to protect its assets and promote the accuracy of its accounting records. You will learn how internal control is established through control of cash receipts and cash disbursements, proper use of the bank checking account, preparation of the bank reconciliation, protection of petty cash funds, and usage of the voucher system. The internal control structure is enhanced by hiring competent and trustworthy employees, a fact you will appreciate if you ever become a business owner.

INTERNAL CONTROL

Objective 1
Describe the
necessity for and
features of inter-
nal control

An effective *internal control structure* of a company includes its plan of organization and all the procedures and actions taken by the company to:

1. Protect its assets against theft and waste.
2. Ensure compliance with company policies and federal law.
3. Evaluate the performance of all personnel in the company so as to promote efficiency of operations.
4. Ensure accurate and reliable operating data and accounting reports.

As you study the basic procedures and actions of an effective internal control structure, you will realize that even small, one-owner businesses can benefit from using some internal control measures. Preventing theft and waste is only a part of internal control.

In general terms, the purpose of internal control is to ensure the efficient operations of a business, thus enabling the business to effectively reach its goals. Since additional control procedures are necessary in a computer environment, a discussion of these controls concludes this section on internal control.

Protection of Assets

Assets can be protected by (1) segregation of employee duties, (2) assignment of specific duties to each employee, (3) rotation of employee job assignments, and (4) use of mechanical devices.

Segregation of Employee Duties.   To accomplish **segregation of duties,** the employee responsible for safeguarding an asset must be someone other than the employee who maintains the accounting records for that asset. Also, responsibility for related transactions should be divided among employees so that one employee's work serves as a check on the work of other employees.

When a company segregates the duties of employees, then collusion between at least two employees is necessary to steal assets and cover up the theft in the accounting records. For example, an employee could not steal cash from a company and have the theft go undetected unless someone changes the cash records to cover the shortage. To change the records, the employee stealing the cash must also maintain the cash records or be in collusion with the employee who maintains the cash records.

Assignment of Specific Duties to Each Employee.   When the responsibility for a particular work function is assigned to one employee, that employee is accountable for specific tasks. Then, if a problem occurs, the employee responsible can be quickly identified.

When a company gives each of its employees specific duties, it can easily trace lost documents or determine how a particular transaction is recorded. Also, the employee responsible for a given task is the person best able to provide information about that task. In addition, being responsible for specific duties gives people a sense of pride and importance that usually makes them want to perform to the best of their ability.

Rotation of Employee Job Assignments.   Some companies rotate job assignments where feasible. This policy discourages employees from engaging in long-term schemes to steal from the company. Employees realize that if they steal from the company, the next employee assigned to that position may discover the theft.

Frequently, companies have the policy that all employees must take an annual vacation. This policy also discourages theft because many dishonest schemes collapse when the employee does not attend to the scheme on a daily basis.

Use of Mechanical Devices.   Companies can use mechanical devices to help protect their assets. Devices such as check protectors (machines that perforate the check amount into the check), cash registers, and time clocks make it impossible for employees to alter certain company documents and records.

Compliance with Company Policies and Federal Law

Internal control policies are effective only when the employees of a company follow those policies. To ensure that employees carry out its internal control policies, a company must hire competent and trustworthy employees. Thus, the execution of effective internal control begins with the time and effort a company expends in hiring employees. Once the company hires the employees, it must train those employees and clearly communicate to them company policies, such as obtaining proper authorization before making a cash disbursement. Frequently, written job descriptions are effective in establishing the responsibilities and duties of employees. The initial training of employees should be such that they know what their duties are and how to perform them.

In publicly held corporations, the company's internal control structure must satisfy the requirements of federal law. In December 1977, Congress enacted the Foreign Corrupt Practices Act (FCPA). This law requires publicly held corporations to devise and maintain an effective system of internal control and to keep accurate accounting records. The passage of this law came about partly because of the cover-ups in company accounting records of bribes and kickbacks made to foreign governments or government officials. The FCPA made this specific type of bribery illegal.

Evaluation of Personnel Performance

To evaluate how well company employees are doing their jobs, many companies use an internal auditing staff. **Internal auditing** consists of investigating and evaluating employees' compliance with the company's policies and procedures. Companies employ **internal auditors** to perform these audits. These individuals are trained in company policies and internal auditing duties. For instance, internal auditors might periodically test the effectiveness of controls and procedures involving cash receipts and cash disbursements.

Internal auditors should encourage operating efficiency throughout the company and be constantly alert for breakdowns in the company's internal control structure. In addition, internal auditors make recommendations for the improvement of the company's internal control structure when necessary. All companies and nonprofit organizations can benefit from internal auditing. However, internal auditing is especially necessary in large organizations because the stockholders and top management cannot be personally involved with all aspects of the business.

Accuracy of Accounting Records

Companies should maintain complete and accurate accounting records. The best method to ensure that such accounting records are kept is to hire and train competent and honest individuals. Periodically, supervisors should evaluate an employee's performance to make sure the employee is following company policies. Inaccurate or inadequate accounting records serve as an invitation to theft by dishonest employees because the theft can be more easily concealed.

Most accounting transactions are supported by one or more business documents. These source documents are an integral part of the internal control structure. For optimal control, source documents should be serially numbered. (Transaction documentation and related aspects of internal control will be presented throughout the text.)

Since source documents serve as documentation of business transactions, from time to time the validity of these documents should be checked. For example, to review a merchandise transaction, the documents used to record the transaction should be checked against the proper accounting records. When the accounting department records a merchandise transaction, it should receive copies of the following four documents:

1. A **purchase requisition** (Illustration 6.1) is a written request from an employee inside the company to the purchasing department to purchase certain items.
2. A **purchase order** (Illustration 6.2) is a document sent from the purchasing department to a supplier requesting that merchandise or other items be shipped to the purchaser.
3. An **invoice** (Illustration 6.3) is the statement sent by the supplier to the purchaser requesting payment for the merchandise shipped.
4. A **receiving report** is a document prepared by the receiving department showing the descriptions and quantities of all items received from a supplier in a particular shipment. A copy of the purchase order can serve as a receiving report if the quantity ordered is omitted. Then, the receiving department personnel will not know what quantity to expect and probably will count the quantity received more accurately.

These four documents together serve as authorization to pay for merchandise and should be checked against the accounting records. Without these documents, a company might fail to pay a legitimate invoice, pay fictitious invoices, or pay an invoice more than once. Companies can accomplish proper internal control only by periodically checking the source documents of business transactions with the accounting records of those transactions. Illustration 6.4 shows the flow of documents and goods in a merchandise transaction.

Illustration 6.1
PURCHASE REQUISITION

Purchase Requisition   No. ___2416___

BRYAN WHOLESALE COMPANY

From: _Automotive Supplies Department_   **Date:** _November 20, 1995_

To: _Purchasing Department_   **Suggested supplier:** _Wilkes Radio Company_

Please purchase the following items:

Description	Item Number	Quantity	Estimated Price
True-tone stereo radios	Model No. 5868-24393	200	$50 per unit

Reason for request:

Customer order
Baier Company

To be filled in by purchasing department:

Date ordered _11/21/95_

Purchase order number _N-145_

Approved _R.S.T._

Illustration 6.2
PURCHASE ORDER

Purchase Order   No. ___N-145___

BRYAN WHOLESALE COMPANY
476 Mason Street
Detroit, Michigan 48823

To: _Wilkes Radio Company_
2515 West Peachtree Street
Atlanta, Georgia 30303

Ship to: _Above address_

Date: _November 21, 1995_

Ship by: _December 20, 1995_

FOB terms requested: _Destination_

Discount terms requested: _2/10, n/30_

Please send the following items:

Description	Item Number	Quantity	Price per Unit	Total Amount
True-tone stereo radios	5868-24393	200	$50	$10,000

Ordered by: _Jane Knight_   Please include order number on all invoices and shipments.

Illustration 6.3
INVOICE

	Invoice	Invoice No.: _1574_
	WILKES RADIO COMPANY **2515 West Peachtree Street** **Atlanta, Georgia 30303**	Date: _Dec. 15, 1995_

Customer's Order No.: _N-145_

Sold to: _Bryan Wholesale Co._

Address: _476 Mason Street_

Detroit, Michigan 48823   **Date shipped:** _Dec. 15, 1995_

Terms: _2/10, n/30, FOB destination_   **Shipped by:** _Nagel Trucking Co._

Description	Item Number	Quantity	Price per Unit	Total Amount
True-tone stereo radios	Model No. 5868-24393	200	$50	$10,000
	Total			$10,000

Unfortunately, even if a company implements all of the above features in its internal control structure, theft may still occur. If employees are dishonest, they can usually figure out a way to steal from a company, thus circumventing even the most effective internal control structure. Therefore, companies should carry adequate casualty insurance on assets. This insurance will reimburse the company for loss of a nonmonetary asset such as specialized equipment. Companies should also have **fidelity bonds** on employees handling cash and other negotiable instruments. These bonds will ensure that a company is reimbursed for losses due to theft of cash and other monetary assets. With both casualty insurance on assets and fidelity bonds on employees, a company can recover at least a portion of any loss that occurs.

Internal Control in a Computer Environment

The use of computers to maintain financial records necessitates the use of the same internal control principles of separation of duties and control over access that are used in a manual accounting system. The exact control steps taken depend on whether a company is using mainframe computers and minicomputers or microcomputers.

Mainframe computers and minicomputers are used in the accounting environments of large corporations. Because of the size and complexity of

Illustration 6.4
FLOW OF DOCUMENTS AND GOODS IN A
MERCHANDISING TRANSACTION

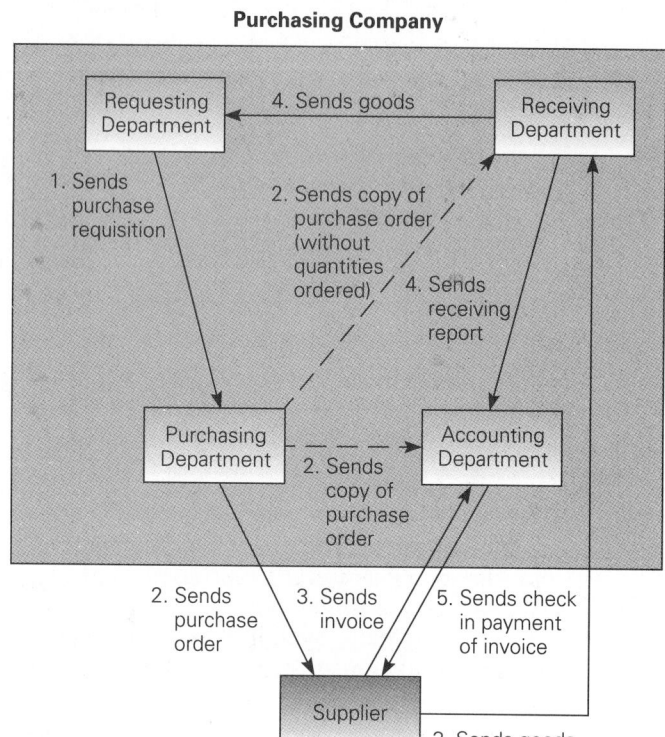

Steps

1. Requesting department sends purchase requisition to purchasing department.
2. Purchasing department sends purchase order to supplier, with copies going to the receiving department (without quantities ordered) and the accounting department.
3. Supplier sends goods to receiving department, where goods received are checked against purchase order, and sends invoice to accounting department.
4. Receiving department sends goods to requesting department and sends receiving report to accounting department.
5. Accounting department checks receiving report against purchase order and invoice and sends check in payment of invoice to the supplier.

these computers, specially trained persons are needed to keep these computer systems operating. Systems specialists operate the computer system itself, while programmers develop the programs that direct the computer to perform specific tasks. In a mainframe or minicomputer environment, internal control should include the following:

1. Computer access should be controlled by placing the computer in an easily secured room, and only persons authorized to operate the computer should be allowed to enter the room.
2. Systems specialists who operate the computer should not have access to programming, and programmers should not have access to the computer. This policy prevents a person from making unauthorized changes to programs.
3. Some programs, such as ones used to print monthly accounts receivable statements to send to credit customers, should be run only during an authorized time period. If programs and data are stored on magnetic tape, the tapes should be stored under lock and key and under the control of a "librarian." The librarian should be independent of the computer systems and programming functions.

Many smaller companies use microcomputers instead of a mainframe or a minicomputer. The use of microcomputers causes the control environment to change somewhat. Small companies generally do not employ systems specialists and programmers. Instead, these companies usually use "off the shelf programs" such as accounting, spreadsheet, database management, and word processing packages. The data created by use of these programs are valuable (e.g., the company's accounting records) and often sensitive. Thus, controls are also important in a microcomputer environment.

In a microcomputer environment, the following controls can be useful:

1. Each microcomputer should be kept under lock and key, and only persons authorized to use that computer should have a key.
2. Each computer user should have tight control over his or her diskettes on which programs and data are stored. Just as one person maintains custody over a certain set of records in a manual system, in a computer system one person maintains custody over diskettes containing a certain type of information (such as the accounts receivable subsidiary ledger). These diskettes should be locked up at night, and backup copies should be made and retained in a different secured location.
3. Passwords should be required (and kept secret) to gain entry into data files maintained on the hard disk.
4. In situations where a local area network (LAN) is present that links the microcomputers into one system, only certain computers and persons in the network should have access to some data files (the accounting records, for example).

The use of computers in accounting does not lessen the need for internal control. In fact, access to a computer by an unauthorized person could result in significant theft in a shorter span of time than in a manual system.

Controlling Cash

In the preceding section, you learned about some of the general principles of internal control. This section focuses specifically on the control of cash. Since cash is the most liquid of all assets, a business cannot survive and prosper if it does not have adequate control over its cash.

In accounting, **cash** includes coins; currency; undeposited negotiable instruments such as checks, bank drafts, and money orders; amounts in checking and savings accounts; and demand certificates of deposit. A **certificate of deposit (CD)** is an interest-bearing deposit in a bank that can be withdrawn at will (demand CD) or at a fixed maturity date (time CD). Cash only includes demand CDs that may be withdrawn at any time without prior notice or penalty. Cash does not include postage stamps, IOUs, time CDs, or notes receivable.

In the general ledger, usually two cash accounts are maintained—Cash (bank checking and savings account balances) and Petty Cash. The balances of these two accounts are combined into one amount and reported as "Cash" on the company's balance sheet.

Since many business transactions involve cash, it is a vital factor in the operation of a business. Of all the company's assets, cash is the most easily mishandled either through theft or carelessness. To control and manage its cash, a company should:

1. Account for all cash transactions accurately so that correct information will be available regarding cash flows and balances.
2. Make certain that enough cash is available to pay bills as they come due.
3. Avoid holding too much idle cash because excess cash could be invested to generate income, such as interest.
4. Prevent loss of cash due to theft or fraud.

The need to control cash is clearly evident. Although you might think first about how to protect cash from the greedy hands of a dishonest employee, as you can see from the list above, the control of cash has many aspects. Without the proper timing of cash flows and the protection of idle cash, a business cannot survive. This section discusses cash receipts and cash disbursements. Later in the chapter, you will learn about the importance of preparing a bank reconciliation for each bank checking account and controlling the petty cash fund. The voucher system is also described.

Controlling Cash Receipts

When a merchandising company sells its merchandise, it may receive cash immediately or several days or weeks later. The cash received immediately *dures for control-ling cash receipts and disbursements*

over the counter is usually recorded and placed in a cash register. The presence of the customer as the sale is *rung up* usually ensures that the cashier enters the correct amount of the sale in the cash register. At the end of each day, the cash in each cash register should be reconciled with the cash register tape or computer printout for that register. When payment is received later, it is almost always in the form of checks. A record of the checks received should be prepared as soon as they are received. Some merchandising companies receive all their cash receipts on a delayed basis in the form of payments on accounts receivable (see the cash receipts cycle for merchandise transactions in Illustration 6.5).

Although businesses vary their specific procedures for controlling cash receipts, they usually observe the following principles:

1. A record of all cash receipts should be prepared as soon as cash is received. Most thefts of cash occur before a record is made of the receipt. Once a record is made, it is easier to trace a theft.
2. All cash receipts should be deposited as soon as feasible, preferably on the day they are received or on the next business day. Undeposited cash is more susceptible to misappropriation.
3. The employee who handles cash receipts should not also be the employee who records the receipts in the accounting records. This control feature follows the general principle of *segregation of duties* given earlier in the chapter, as does item 4 below.
4. If possible, the employee who receives the cash should not also be the employee who disburses the cash. This control measure is possible in all but the smallest companies.

Illustration 6.5
CASH RECEIPTS CYCLE FOR MERCHANDISE TRANSACTIONS

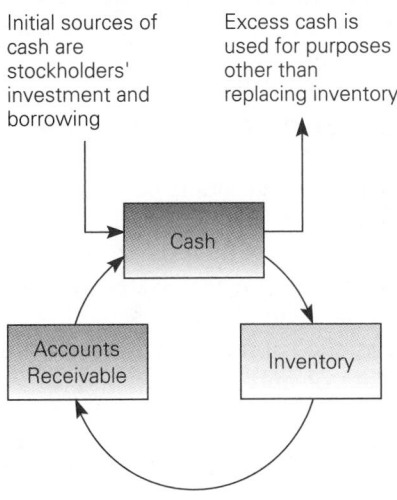

Initial sources of cash are stockholders' investment and borrowing

Excess cash is used for purposes other than replacing inventory

Cash initially comes into the business from stockholders' investment (capital stock) and borrowing. Cash is then invested in inventory and other assets. When inventory is sold, cash may be received immediately, or receipt may be delayed and involve accounts receivable. The inventory generally is sold at more than cost so the company can make a profit. Each time the cycle is completed, the amount of cash grows and may be used for purposes other than replacing inventory.

Controlling Cash Disbursements

Controls are also needed over cash disbursements. Since a company spends most of its cash by check, many of the internal controls for cash disbursements deal with checks and authorizations for cash payments. The basic principle of segregation of duties is also applied in controlling cash disbursements. Following are some basic control procedures for cash disbursements:

1. All disbursements should be made by check or from petty cash. Proper approval for all disbursements should be obtained, and a permanent record of each disbursement should be created. In many retail stores, refunds for returned merchandise are made from the cash register. If this practice is followed, refund tickets should be prepared and approved by a supervisor before cash is refunded.
2. All checks should be serially numbered, and access to checks should be limited to employees authorized to write checks.
3. Preferably, two signatures should be required on each check so that one person alone cannot withdraw funds from the bank account.
4. If possible, the employee who authorizes payment of a bill should not be allowed to sign checks. Otherwise, the checks could be written to "friends" in payment of fictitious invoices.
5. Approved documents should be required to support all checks issued.
6. The employee authorizing cash disbursements should make certain that payment is for a legitimate purpose and is made out for the exact amount and to the proper party.
7. When liabilities are paid, the supporting documents should be stamped "paid," and the date and number of the check issued should be indicated. These procedures lessen the chance of paying the same debt more than once.
8. Those employees who sign checks should not have access to canceled checks and should not prepare the bank reconciliation. This policy makes it more difficult for an employee to conceal a theft.
9. The bank reconciliation should be prepared each month, preferably by an employee who has no other cash duties, so that errors and shortages will be quickly discovered.
10. All checks incorrectly prepared should be voided. These checks should be physically marked "void" and retained to prevent their unauthorized use.
11. Large companies may need a voucher system (described later) for close control of cash disbursements.
12. Use of the net price method of recording purchases (described in Chapter 4) helps avoid loss of purchase discounts by calling attention to discounts missed.

Illustration 6.6 shows an overview of some of the internal control considerations relating to cash.

Illustration 6.6
SOME INTERNAL CONTROL CONSIDERATIONS REGARDING CASH

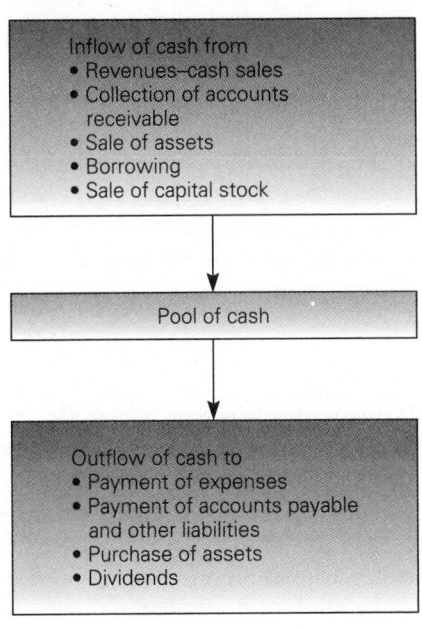

Internal control considerations

1. Are all cash receipts being properly recorded and actually going into the company's pool of cash, or are individuals siphoning off some of these receipts for their own use?
2. Is the pool of cash protected from theft? Is the cash on hand managed so as to produce income for the company and yet be available when needed to make legitimate disbursements?
3. Is there close control over cash disbursements to ensure that only legitimate disbursements are made in the proper amounts and on a timely basis?

Most companies use checking accounts to handle their cash transactions. The company deposits its cash receipts in a bank checking account and writes checks to pay its bills. The bank sends the company a statement each month. The company checks this statement against its records to determine if it must make any corrections or adjustments in either the company's balance or the bank's balance. You will learn how to do this later in the chapter when the bank reconciliation is discussed. In the next section, you will learn about the bank checking account. If you have a personal checking account, some of this information will be familiar to you.

THE BANK CHECKING ACCOUNT

Banks seek to earn income by providing a variety of services to individuals, businesses, and other entities such as churches or libraries. One of these services is the checking account. A **checking account** is a money balance maintained in the bank that is subject to withdrawal by the depositor, or owner of the money, on demand. To provide depositors with an accurate record of depositor funds received and disbursed, a bank uses the business documents discussed in this section.[2]

The Signature Card

A bank requires a new depositor to complete a **signature card,** which provides the signatures of persons authorized to sign checks drawn on an account. The bank retains the card and uses it to identify signatures on checks paid by the bank. The bank does not compare every check with this signature card. Usually, it makes a comparison only when the depositor disputes the validity of a check paid by the bank or when a check for an unusually large sum is presented for payment.

Deposit Ticket

When depositors make a bank deposit, they prepare a deposit ticket or slip. A **deposit ticket** is a form that shows the date and the items that make up the deposit (Illustration 6.7). The ticket is often preprinted to show the depositor's name, address, and account number. Items comprising the deposit—cash and a list of checks—are entered on the ticket when the deposit is made. After making the deposit, the depositor is given a receipt showing the date of the deposit and the amount deposited.

Illustration 6.7
DEPOSIT TICKET

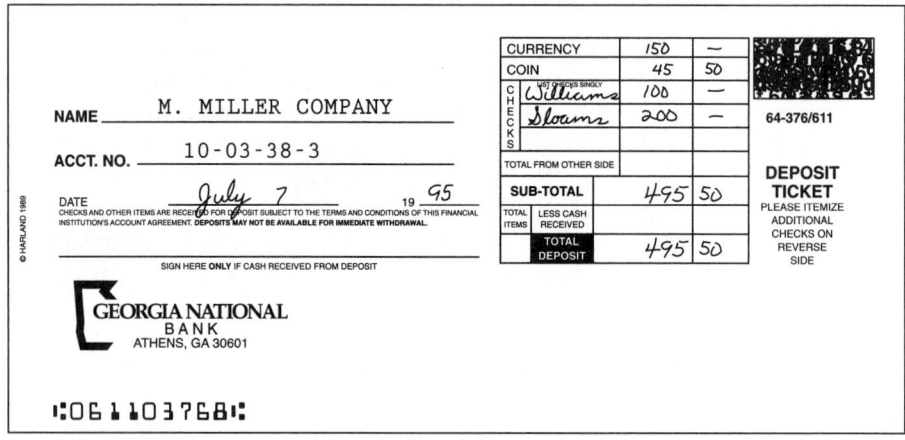

---

[2] Due to relaxed federal regulations, institutions other than banks—such as savings and loan associations and credit unions—now offer checking account services. All of these institutions function somewhat similarly; but, for simplicity's sake, only banks will be discussed here.

Check

A **check** is a written order on a bank to pay a specific sum of money to the party designated as the payee by the party issuing the check. Thus, every check transaction involves three parties: the *bank,* the **payee** (party to whom the check is made payable), and the **drawer** (depositor). Most depositors use serially numbered checks that are preprinted with information about the depositor, such as name, address, and telephone number. Often a business check will have an attached remittance advice. A **remittance advice** informs the payee why the drawer (or maker) of the check is making this payment. Before the check is cashed or deposited, the payee detaches the remittance advice from the check (Illustration 6.8).

Bank Statement

A **bank statement** is a statement issued (usually monthly) by a bank describing the activities in a depositor's checking account during the period. Illustration 6.9 shows a bank statement that includes the following data:

Illustration 6.8
CHECK WITH ATTACHED REMITTANCE ADVICE

M. MILLER COMPANY
1216 Dawson Rd.
Albany, Ga. 30605

GEORGIA NATIONAL BANK
ATHENS, GA 30601

NO 2897

64-376
611

EXPENSE CHECK

July 8, 19 95

PAY Five hundred sixty and no/100------------------ DOLLARS $ 560.00

TO THE ORDER OF K.F. Frazer Co.

M. Miller

⑈002897⑈ ⑆061103768⑆ 01⑈00⑈024⑈

M. W. V. HARLAND NO. 805

DETACH AND RETAIN THIS STATEMENT
THE ATTACHED CHECK IS IN PAYMENT OF ITEMS DESCRIBED BELOW. IF NOT CORRECT PLEASE NOTIFY US PROMPTLY. NO RECEIPT DESIRED.
GEORGIA NATIONAL BANK

DATE	DESCRIPTION	AMOUNT
7/8/95	P.O. No. R2130--Payment of your invoice #4501	$560.00

1. Deposits made to the checking account during the period.
2. Checks paid out of the depositor's checking account by the bank during the period. These checks have *cleared* the bank and are *canceled*.
3. Other deductions from the checking account for items such as service charges, NSF (nonsufficient funds) checks, safe-deposit box rent, and check printing fees. Banks assess **service charges** on the depositor to cover the cost of handling the checking account, such as check clearing charges. An **NSF check** is a customer's check returned from the customer's bank to the depositor's bank because the funds in the customer's checking account balance were insufficient to cover the check. The depositor's bank deducts the amount of the returned check from the depositor's checking account. Since the customer still owes the depositor money, the depositor will restore the amount of the NSF check to the account receivable for that customer in the company's books.
4. Other additions to the checking account for items such as proceeds of a note collected by the bank for the depositor and interest earned on the account.

In addition to the data shown in the bank statement in Illustration 6.9, bank statements also can show nonroutine deposits made to the depositor's checking account. Such deposits are not made directly by the depositor but by a third party. For example, the bank may have received a wire transfer of funds for the depositor.

A **wire transfer of funds** is an interbank transfer of funds by telephone. Companies that operate in many widely scattered locations and therefore have checking accounts with several different local banks often use an interbank transfer of funds. These companies may set up special procedures to avoid accumulating too much idle cash in local bank accounts. One such procedure involves the use of special-instruction bank accounts. For example, **transfer bank accounts** may be set up so local banks automatically transfer to a central bank (by wire or bank draft) all amounts on deposit in excess of a stated amount. In this way, funds not needed for local operations are sent quickly to company headquarters, where the company can use the funds or invest them.

Frequently, the bank returns canceled checks and original deposit tickets with the bank statement. Since it is expensive to sort, handle, and mail these items, some banks no longer return them to the depositor. These banks usually store the documents on microfilm, with photocopies available if needed. Most depositors need only a detailed bank statement, as shown in Illustration 6.9, and not the original documents to show what transactions occurred during a given period.

When banks debit or credit a depositor's checking account, they prepare debit and credit memoranda (memos). These memos may also be returned with the bank statement. A **debit memo** is a form used by a bank to explain a deduction from the depositor's account; a **credit memo** explains an addition

Illustration 6.9
BANK STATEMENT

THE
GEORGIA
NATIONAL
B A N K

DIRECT INQUIRIES TO THE ABOVE ADDRESS OR CALL (404) 548-5511

P. O. BOX 1684
ATHENS, GEORGIA 30603

CHECKING STATEMENT

R. L. LEE COMPANY
1021 ROY LANE
ATHENS, GA 30603

01 45 65 2

ACCOUNT NUMBER 01-45-65-2	STATEMENT DATE 5/31/95	21 ENCLOSURES

BEGINNING BALANCE $2,248.00	ADDITIONS $12,358.00	SUBTRACTIONS $11,354.00	ENDING BALANCE $3,252.00

SUBTRACT 22 ITEMS

CHECKS	AMOUNT	DATE PAID	CHECKS	AMOUNT	DATE PAID	CHECKS	AMOUNT	DATE PAID
9515*	351.00	5/3	9531	1,250.00	5/8	9537	111.00	5/22
9519*	154.00	5/3	9532	800.00	5/15	9538	2,071.00	5/23
9527	208.00	5/7	9533	925.00	5/15	9539	413.00	5/25
9528	467.00	5/7	9534	417.00	5/18	9540	1,093.00	5/25
9529	125.00	5/7	9535	230.00	5/17	9541	1,005.00	5/25
9530	411.00	5/8	9536	169.00	5/21	9542	818.00	5/29
						9543	211.00	5/29

NSF CHECK   102.00 5/30
SERVICE CHARGE   8.00 5/31
SAFE DEPOSIT BOX RENT   15.00 5/31
*PRECEDING CHECK(S) NOT PAID DURING THIS PERIOD

ADD 23 ITEMS

AMOUNT	DATE	AMOUNT	DATE	AMOUNT	DATE
624.00	5/1	514.00	5/10	333.00	5/22
776.00	5/2	401.00	5/11	407.00	5/23
526.00	5/3	702.00	5/14	371.00	5/24
474.00	5/4	303.00	5/15	331.00	5/25
631.00	5/7	471.00	5/16	507.00	5/28
608.00	5/8	653.00	5/17	601.00	5/29
1,225.00**	5/8	414.00	5/18	400.00	5/30
667.00	5/9	419.00	5/21		

**NOTE COLLECTED FROM A CUSTOMER

ENDING BALANCE FOR EACH DAY YOUR ACCOUNT HAD ACTIVITY

BALANCE	DATE	BALANCE	DATE	BALANCE	DATE
2,248.00	4/30	5,327.00	5/10	6,371.00	5/22
2,872.00	5/1	5,728.00	5/11	4,707.00	5/23
3,648.00	5/2	6,430.00	5/14	5,078.00	5/24
3,669.00	5/3	5,008.00	5/15	2,898.00	5/25
4,143.00	5/4	5,479.00	5/16	3,405.00	5/28
3,974.00	5/7	5,902.00	5/17	2,977.00	5/29
4,146.00	5/8	5,899.00	5/18	3,275.00	5/30
4,813.00	5/9	6,149.00	5/21	3,252.00	5/31

Illustration 6.10
DEBIT MEMORANDUM (TOP) AND CREDIT MEMORANDUM (BOTTOM)

GENERAL LEDGER	R. L. Lee Company	Acct. No. 01 45 65 2	
DEBIT ACCT. TITLE	1021 Roy Lane Athens, GA 30603	DATE May 31, 1995	
	DESCRIPTION	AMOUNT	
Safe Deposit Box Rental			
CONTRA ENTRY			
DRAWN BY _CWT_ CENTER [ ] APPROVED BY _MRC_ TOTAL		15	00

BANKERS SYSTEMS, INC., ST. CLOUD, MN 56301

⑆037600800⑆

GENERAL LEDGER	R. L. Lee Company	Acct. No. 01 45 65 2	
CREDIT ACCT. TITLE	1021 Roy Lane Athens, GA 30603	DATE 5/8/95	
	DESCRIPTION	AMOUNT	
Collection of note for the Lee Company from X Company			
CONTRA ENTRY			
DRAWN BY _CWT_ CENTER [ ] APPROVED BY _MRC_ TOTAL		1,225	00

BANKERS SYSTEMS, INC., ST. CLOUD, MN 56301

⑆037600208⑆

to the depositor's account. The terms *debit memo* and *credit memo* may seem reversed, but remember that the depositor's checking account is a liability—an account payable—of the bank. So, when the bank seeks to reduce a depositor's balance, a debit memo is prepared. To increase the balance, a credit memo is prepared. Illustration 6.10 shows examples of debit and credit memos. Some banks no longer mail these documents to the depositor and rely instead on explanations in the bank statement.

Information that the depositor did not know before receiving the bank statement (items 3 and 4 on page 322) requires new journal entries on the company's books. After the entries have been made to record the new information, the balance in the Cash account is the actual cash available to the company. When the depositor has already received notice of NSF checks and other bank charges or credits, the needed journal entries may have been made earlier. In this chapter, we assume no entries have been made for these items unless stated otherwise.

When a company receives its bank statement, it must reconcile the balance shown by the bank with the cash balance shown in the company's books. If you have a personal checking account, you also should reconcile your bank statement with your checkbook. You can use the reconciliation form on the back of the bank statement to list your checks that have not yet been paid by the bank and your deposits not yet shown on the bank statement. Some small businesses may also use this form. However, they may instead prepare a separate bank reconciliation, which you will learn how to prepare in the next section.

BANK RECONCILIATION

Objective 4
Prepare a bank reconciliation and make necessary journal entries based on that schedule

A **bank reconciliation,** often called a *bank reconciliation statement* or *schedule*, is a schedule the company (depositor) prepares to *reconcile,* or explain, the difference between the cash balance shown on the bank statement and the cash balance on the company's books. The bank reconciliation is prepared to determine the company's actual cash balance. Illustration 6.11 shows an example of a bank reconciliation.

The bank reconciliation is divided into two main sections. One section, at the top in Illustration 6.11, begins with the balance shown on the bank

Illustration 6.11
BANK RECONCILIATION

	R. L. LEE COMPANY		
	Bank Reconciliation		
	May 31, 1995		
①	Balance per bank statement, May 31, 1995.		$3,252
②	Add: Deposit in transit		452
			$3,704
③	Less: Outstanding checks:		
	No. 9544.	$322	
	No. 9545.	168	
	No. 9546.	223	713
	Adjusted balance, May 31, 1995.		$2,991
①	Balance per ledger, May 31, 1995		$1,891
④	Add: Note collected (including interest of $25)		1,225
			$3,116
⑤	Less: NSF check (R. Johnson)	$102	
⑥	Safe-deposit box rent.	15	
⑥	Service charges	8	125
	Adjusted balance, May 31, 1995.		$2,991

statement. The second section, at the bottom in Illustration 6.11, begins with the company's balance as shown on the company's books. Adjustments are made to both the *bank* and *book* balances; after these adjustments, both adjusted balances should be the same.

The steps in preparing a bank reconciliation are as follows:

a. *Deposits.*   Compare the deposits listed on the bank statement with the deposits on the company's books. This comparison can be made by placing check marks in the bank statement and in the company's books by the deposits that agree. Then determine the deposits in transit. A **deposit in transit** is typically a day's cash receipts recorded in the depositor's books in one period but recorded as a deposit by the bank in the succeeding period. The most common deposit in transit is the deposit of the cash receipts of the last business day of the month. Normally, deposits in transit occur only near the end of the period covered by the bank statement. For example, a deposit made in a bank's night depository on May 31 would be recorded by the company on May 31 and by the bank on June 1. Thus, the deposit will not appear on a bank statement for the month ended May 31. The deposits in transit listed in last month's bank reconciliation should also be checked against the bank statement. Any deposit made during the month that is missing from the bank statement (unless it involves a deposit made at the end of the period) should be investigated immediately.

b. *Paid checks.*   If canceled checks are returned with the bank statement, first compare them to the bank statement to be sure the amounts on the statement agree with the checks. Then, sort the checks in numerical order. Next, determine which checks are outstanding. **Outstanding checks** are checks issued by a depositor that have not yet been paid by the bank on which they are drawn. The party receiving the check may not deposit it immediately. Once deposited, checks may take several days to clear the banking system. The outstanding checks are determined by a process of elimination. The check numbers that have cleared the bank are compared with a list of the check numbers issued by the company. Check marks are used in the company's record of checks issued to identify those checks returned by the bank. Checks issued that have not yet been returned by the bank are the outstanding checks. If the bank does not return checks but provides only a listing of the cleared checks on the bank statement, the outstanding checks are determined by comparing this list with the company's record of checks issued.

Sometimes checks written long ago will still be outstanding. Checks outstanding as of the beginning of the month will appear on the prior month's bank reconciliation. Most of these will have cleared during the current month; those that have not cleared should be listed as still outstanding on the current month's reconciliation.

c. *Bank debit and credit memos.* Verify all debit and credit memos on the bank statement. Debit memos reflect deductions for such items as service charges, NSF checks, safe-deposit box rent, and notes paid by the bank for the depositor. Credit memos reflect additions for such items as wire transfers of funds from another bank in which the company sends funds to the home office bank and notes collected for the depositor by the bank. Check the bank debit and credit memos with the depositor's books to see if they have already been recorded. Journal entries should be made for any such items not already recorded in the company's books.

d. *Errors*. List any errors found. A common error is that the depositor records a check in the accounting records at an amount that differs from the actual amount on the check. For example, a $47 check may be recorded at $74. The check will clear the bank at the amount written on the check ($47), but the depositor frequently does not catch the error until the bank statement or canceled checks are reviewed.

Deposits in transit, outstanding checks, and bank service charges usually account for the difference between the company's Cash account balance and the bank balance. (These same items can cause a difference between your personal checkbook balance and the bank balance shown on your bank statement.) Remember that **all items shown on the bank reconciliation as adjustments of the book (ledger) balance will require journal entries to adjust the Cash account** (items 4, 5, and 6 in Illustration 6.11 and in the following example); **items appearing on the bank balance side do not require entries by the depositor** (items 2 and 3). Any bank errors, of course, should be called to the bank's attention.

To illustrate the preparation of the bank reconciliation shown in Illustration 6.11, assume the following (these items are keyed by number into that illustration):

1. On May 31, 1995, R. L. Lee Company showed a balance in its Cash account of $1,891. On June 2, Lee received its bank statement for the month ended May 31, which showed an ending balance of $3,252.

2. A matching of debits to the Cash account on the books with deposits on the bank statement showed that the $452 receipts of May 31 were included in Cash but not included as a deposit on the bank statement. This deposit was in the bank's night deposit chute on May 31.

3. A comparison of checks issued with checks that had cleared the bank showed three checks outstanding:

No. 9544	$322
No. 9545	168
No. 9546	223
Total.	$713

4. Included with the bank statement was a credit memo for $1,225 (principal of $1,200 + interest of $25) for collection of a note owed to Lee by Shipley Company.

5. Included with the bank statement was a $102 debit memo for an NSF check written by R. Johnson and deposited by Lee.
6. Charges made to Lee Company's account include $15 for safe-deposit box rent and $8 for service charges.

After reconciling the book and bank balances as shown in Illustration 6.11, Lee Company finds that its actual cash balance is $2,991. The following entries are needed to record information from the bank reconciliation:

---

④ Cash   1,225
       Notes Receivable—Shipley Company   1,200
       Interest Revenue   25
   To record note collected from Shipley Company.

⑤ Accounts Receivable—R. Johnson*   102
       Cash   102
   To charge NSF check back to customer, R. Johnson.

⑥ Bank Service Charge Expense (or Miscellaneous Expense)   23
       Cash   23
   To record bank service charges.

* This debit would be posted to the Accounts Receivable control account in the general ledger and to R. Johnson's account in an accounts receivable subsidiary ledger. An accounts receivable subsidiary ledger contains an account for each customer who has purchased goods or services on account. Appendix B at the end of the text contains a full description of control accounts and subsidiary ledgers.

The income statement for the period ending May 31, 1995, would include the $23 bank service charge as an expense. The May 31 balance sheet would show $2,991 cash, the actual cash balance.

The three entries above could be combined into one compound entry as follows:

Cash   1,100
Bank Service Charge Expense   23
Accounts Receivable—R. Johnson   102
   Notes Receivable   1,200
   Interest Revenue   25
To correct the accounts for needed changes identified in the bank reconciliaton.

The deposit in transit and the outstanding checks have already been recorded in the depositor's books and will be handled routinely when they reach the bank. Since these items appear on the bank balance side of the reconciliation, they require no entry in the company's books. These items will be processed by the bank in the subsequent period.

When a company maintains more than one checking account, it must reconcile each account separately with the balance on the bank statement for

A BROADER PERSPECTIVE

ORGANIZATIONS STEP UP GLOBALIZATION EFFORTS

The globalization of the accounting profession is running on the fast track as international organizations expand horizons and seek to harmonize worldwide accounting standards.

Jeffreys Henry International, Independent Accountants International, HLB International, and HI International have not only been recruiting new members but have set up training programs to help their affiliated firms here and abroad adapt to the changing face of global accounting.

Jeffreys Henry International has been one of the more agressive of the international organizations. The Toronto-based association has just completed a three-year global master business plan, which has seen it grow from a strong European base into a worldwide network of 56 firms reporting combined fee billing close to $170 million, says Philip Zimmerman, chairman of the accounting association.

The North American region now has 20 members, up from nine three years ago, while a newly-formed Asia Pacific region now has nine members.

Zimmerman acknowledges that Jeffreys Henry is seeking members in several countries. In Europe, he points out, a Danish firm has applied and other prospective members are being considered.

Recent regional meetings in Dusseldorf, Chicago, and Singapore focused on such issues as implications of the proposed free trade agreement between Mexico, the United States and Canada and the standardization of international reporting and audit requirements, which seems inevitable in the wake of the European integration and the formation of the North American trading bloc.

The European region is taking steps to conduct an audit school later this year, says Zimmerman, also a partner with the New York firm of Paneth, Haber & Zimmerman.

Meanwhile, the ranks of such organizations as HI International in New York, are continuing to swell.

Crowe Chisek & Co., the large South Bend, Indiana-based accounting firm, is the newest member in the HI fold, which includes more than 70 affiliated firms worldwide.

According to Ronald S. Cohen, Crowe Chisek managing partner, international network affiliation is extremely important today because of the increasing globalization of the marketplace, and the changing laws resulting from the establishment of the European Community '92.

On another front, the Miami-based Independent Accountants International is spearheading a comprehensive accounting and bookkeeping instructional program to assist its member firm in Budapest, Hungary, Interexpert Hungaria.

With new businesses entering Hungary, and with the limited knowledge of administration of private businesses in Hungary, IA International executive director Art Goessel says his organization decided to help improve accounting and bookkeeping knowledge by sponsoring an accounting and bookkeeping training program for Interexpert.

At the same time, HLB International, another worldwide organization of professional accounting firms based in London, has extended its reach with new member firms in Hungary and Korea. They are Tudorg Informics & Organization in Budapest and Sam-Kyeong Accounting Firm in Seoul.

HLB now has member firms in 56 countries and correspondents in 16 more. Annual billings are in excess of $350 million.

SOURCE: *Accounting Today,* Reprinted by permission from *Accounting Today,* August 26, 1991, p. 10. Copyright Lebhor-Friedman, Inc., 425 Park Avenue, New York, NY 10022.

that account. The depositor should also check carefully to see that the bank did not make an error in keeping the transactions of the two accounts separate.

Certified and Cashier's Checks

To make sure a check will not *bounce* and become an NSF check, a payee may demand a certified or cashier's check from the maker. Both certified checks and cashier's checks are liabilities of the issuing bank rather than the depositor. As a result, these checks usually are accepted without question.

- A **certified check** is a check written, or drawn, by a *depositor* and taken to the depositor's bank for certification. The bank will stamp *certified* across the face of the check and insert the name of the bank and the date; the certification will be signed by a bank official. The bank will certify a check only when the depositor's balance is large enough to cover the check. The bank deducts the amount of the check from the depositor's account at the time it certifies the check.
- A **cashier's check** is a check drawn by a *bank* made out to either the depositor or a third party after deducting the amount of the check from the depositor's account or receiving cash from the depositor.

  In this section, you learned that all cash receipts should be deposited in the bank and all cash disbursements should be made by check. However, the next section explains the convenience of having small amounts of cash (petty cash) available for minor expenditures.

PETTY CASH FUNDS

Objective 5
Explain why a petty cash fund is used, describe its operations, and make the necessary journal entries

At times, every business finds it convenient to have small amounts of cash available for immediate payment of items such as delivery charges, postage stamps, taxi fares, supper money for employees working overtime, and other small items. To permit these disbursements to be made in cash and still maintain adequate control over cash, companies frequently establish a **petty cash fund** of a round figure such as $100 or $500.

  Usually one individual, called the *petty cash custodian* or *cashier,* is responsible for the operation of the fund, which includes control of the petty cash fund and documenting the disbursements made from the fund. By assigning the responsibility for the fund to one individual, the company has internal control over the cash in the fund. In this section, you will learn how to both establish and operate a petty cash fund.

Establishing the Fund

The petty cash fund is established by writing a check for, say, $100. The amount of a petty cash fund should be large enough to make disbursements for a reasonable period, such as a month.

For example, assume a $100 petty cash fund is to be established. A check in that amount is drawn, payable to the petty cash custodian. The following entry is required:

Petty Cash	100	
Cash		100
To establish a petty cash fund.		

The check is cashed, and the money is turned over to the petty cash custodian, who normally places the money in a small box that can be locked. The fund is now ready to be disbursed as needed.

Operating the Fund

One of the conveniences of the petty cash fund is that payments from the fund require no journal entries at the time of payment. Thus, using a petty cash fund avoids the need for making many entries for small amounts. Only when the fund is reimbursed, or when the end of the accounting period arrives, will an entry be made in the journal.

When cash is disbursed from the fund, the petty cash custodian prepares a petty cash voucher, which should be signed by the person receiving the funds. A **petty cash voucher** (Illustration 6.12) is a document or form that shows the amount of and reason for a petty cash disbursement. A voucher should be prepared for each disbursement from the fund. If an invoice for the expenditure is provided, the invoice should be stapled to the petty cash voucher. The employee responsible for petty cash is at all times accountable for having cash and petty cash vouchers equal to the total amount of the fund.

Illustration 6.12
PETTY CASH VOUCHER

PETTY CASH VOUCHER NO. ___359___

To ___Local Cartage, Inc.___   Date ___June 29,___ ___1995___

EXPLANATION	ACCT. NO.	AMOUNT	
Freight on parts	27	12	57

APPROVED   RECEIVED
BY ___A.E.S.___   PAYMENT ___Ken Black___

Replenishing the Fund

The petty cash fund should be replenished at the end of the accounting period, or sooner if it becomes low. The reason for replenishing the fund at the end of the accounting period is that no record of the fund expenditure is in the accounts until the check is written and a journal entry is made. (The fund is sometimes referred to as an *imprest* fund since it is replenished when it becomes low.) The petty cash vouchers are presented to the employee having authority to order that the fund be reimbursed. The vouchers are examined by that employee; and if all is in order, a check is drawn to restore the fund to its original amount.

To determine which accounts to debit, the petty cash vouchers are summarized according to the reasons for expenditure. The petty cash vouchers are then stamped or defaced to prevent reuse. The journal entry to record replenishing the fund would debit the various accounts indicated by the summary and credit Cash.

For example, assume the $100 petty cash fund currently has a money balance of $7.40. A summary of the vouchers shows payments of $22.75 for transportation-in, $50.80 for stamps, and $19.05 for an advance to an employee; these payments total $92.60. After the vouchers have been examined and approved, a check is drawn for $92.60 which, when cashed, restores the cash in the fund to its $100 balance. The journal entry to record replenishment is:

Transportation-In.	22.75	
Postage Expense.	50.80	
Receivable from Employees (or Advances to Employees)	19.05	
Cash		92.60
To replenish petty cash fund.		

Note that the entry to record replenishing the fund does not credit the Petty Cash account. Entries are made to the Petty Cash account only when the fund is established, when the end of the accounting period arrives and the fund is not replenished, or when the size of the fund is changed.

At the end of an accounting period, any petty cash disbursements for which the fund has *not* yet been replenished must be recorded. Since the fund has not been replenished, **the credit would be to Petty Cash rather than Cash.** Failure to make an entry at the end of an accounting period would cause errors in both the income statement and balance sheet. The easiest way to record these disbursements is to replenish the fund. Replenishing the fund at the end of an accounting period is handled exactly as at any other time.

If, after a period of time, the petty cash custodian finds that the petty cash fund is larger than needed, the excess petty cash should be deposited in the company's checking account. **The required entry to record a decrease in**

the size of the fund debits Cash and credits Petty Cash for the amount returned and deposited. On the other hand, a petty cash fund may be too small, requiring replenishment every few days. **The entry to record an increase in the size of the fund debits Petty Cash and credits Cash for the amount of the increase.**

To illustrate, the entry to *decrease* the size of the petty cash fund by $50 would be:

Cash	50	
Petty Cash.		50
To decrease the size of the petty cash fund by $50.		

The entry to *increase* the size of the petty cash fund by $600 would be:

Petty Cash	600	
Cash		600
To increase the size of the petty cash fund by $600.		

Cash Short and Over

Errors can be made in making change from the petty cash fund. These errors cause the amount of cash in the fund to be more or less than the amount of the fund less the total vouchers. When the fund is restored to its original amount, the credit to Cash is for the difference between the established amount and the actual cash in the fund. Debits are made for all vouchered items. Any discrepancy should be debited or credited to an account called *Cash Short and Over*. The Cash Short and Over account is an expense or a revenue, depending on whether it has a debit or credit balance.

To illustrate, assume in the preceding example that the balance in the fund was only $6.10 instead of $7.40. To restore the fund to $100, a check for $93.90 is needed. Since the petty cash vouchers total only $92.60, the fund is short $1.30. In this case, the entry for replenishment is:

Transportation-In.	22.75	
Postage Expense.	50.80	
Receivable from Employees.	19.05	
Cash Short and Over.	1.30	
Cash		93.90
To replenish petty cash fund.		

Entries in the Cash Short and Over account may be entered from other change-making activities. For example, assume that a clerk accidentally shortchanges a customer $1 and that total cash sales for the day are $740.50. At the end of the day, actual cash will be $1 over the sum of the sales tickets or the total of the cash register tape. The journal entry to record the day's cash sales is:

Cash 741.50		
Sales	740.50	
Cash Short and Over.	1.00	
To record cash sales for the day.		

THE VOUCHER SYSTEM

*Objective 6
Describe the
operation of the
voucher system
and make entries
in its special
journals—the
voucher register
and the check
register*

Companies often suffer substantial losses from the embezzlement of cash. Frequently, the embezzlement results from the paying of fictitious invoices. Thus, every business must make sure that its cash payments are proper and timely. In small companies, such a problem often does not exist because the owner usually has personal knowledge of all transactions and personally signs all checks. However, in larger companies, the owners and high-level officers may have no direct part in the payment process. These companies can effectively control cash disbursements by using the voucher system.

The use of a voucher system can be expensive. Only those companies with the size and need for a voucher system should consider installing one.

The **voucher system** is a set of procedures, special journals, and authorization forms designed to provide control over cash payments. The special journals used in the voucher system are the voucher register and the check register. These journals are defined later in this section. (Other special journals, such as the sales journal and cash receipts journal, would still be used. These journals are illustrated and discussed in Appendix B at the end of the text.)

When a company uses the voucher system, each transaction that involves a cash payment is entered on a voucher (Illustration 6.13) and recorded in the voucher register before payment. A **voucher** is a form with spaces provided for data about a liability that must be paid. The data include items such as creditor's name and address, description of the goods or services received, invoice number, terms of payment, due date, and amount due, and often show the ledger accounts and amounts to be debited. The voucher also has spaces for signatures of those approving the payment.

An invoice or other business document is the basis for making a journal entry in the voucher register. The voucher usually forms a *jacket* for the invoice, purchase order, and receiving report. Each voucher should undergo careful examination and receive either approval or disapproval for payment. By the time a voucher is approved for payment, several employees have confirmed that the claim being paid is proper and accurate, thus reducing the chances of embezzlement.

Illustration 6.13
VOUCHER

ATWELL SUPPLY COMPANY
Atwell Plaza
Atwell, Texas 78712

VOUCHER

VOUCHER NO. ___141___
OUR P.O. NO. ___2514___
VENDOR'S INVOICE ___416___
PAID BY CHECK NO. ___587___
DATE PAID ___7/18/95___

Payable To: Gregory Corporation
48 Cadillac Square
Detroit, Michigan 48226

DATE		ACCT. NO.	DESCRIPTION	QUANTITY	UNIT PRICE	TOTAL
July	14	126	X-16 Transistors	100	$2.00	$200.00
			TOTAL			$200.00
			DISCOUNT	2%		4.00
			NET PAYABLE			$196.00

TERMS 2/10, n/30

EXPLANATIONS: *Due date is August 13, 1995.*

AUDITED AS TO CORRECTNESS A.T.	APPROVED FOR PAYMENT L.S.W.	ENTERED IN VOUCHER REGISTER R.E.L.	DATE ENTERED 7/14/95

Procedures for Preparing a Voucher

The preparation of a voucher begins with the receipt of an invoice from a supplier or with approved evidence that a liability has been incurred and cash should be disbursed. Then, the procedures are as follows:

1. Basic data are entered on the voucher from the invoice.
2. The invoice, voucher, and receiving report are sent to the employees

responsible for verifying the correctness of the description of the goods as to quantity and quality, dollar amounts, and other details. Each employee initials the voucher when satisfied as to its correctness.

3. When the voucher and accompanying documents are returned to the accounting department, a notation is made on the voucher as to the proper accounts to be debited and credited.

4. After a final review by an authorized employee, the proper entry is made in the voucher register, and the voucher is filed in the unpaid voucher file.

The name *voucher system* comes from the fact that **every check issued is authorized by a voucher.** A voucher really can be any written form that serves as a receipt or evidence of authority to act. However, as applied to the voucher system, a voucher is a form that confirms a liability and, as such, serves as the basis for an accounting entry.

In some businesses, the discount and payment terms run from the invoice date. Then, a voucher should be prepared for each invoice (Illustration 6.13). The voucher should be filed according to the date on which the discount period terminates or payment is due. However, when the discount and payment terms are computed from the end of the month, the voucher may be modified, reducing the number of vouchers prepared and the entries made in the voucher register. Then, all invoices received from a particular creditor are accumulated and listed on one voucher at the end of the month. One check is written on the due date to pay for all invoices listed on the voucher. These vouchers are filed according to their individual due dates.

Special Journals Used

When a voucher system is used, the voucher register replaces the purchases journal, and the check register replaces the cash disbursements journal. (The purchases journal and cash disbursements journal are illustrated and discussed in Appendix B at the end of the text.) Illustration 6.14 shows a voucher register, and Illustration 6.15 shows a check register for Jackson Company, assuming the journals have been posted.

Voucher Register. A **voucher register** is a multicolumn special journal containing a record of all vouchers prepared, listed chronologically by date and voucher number. A brief explanation of each transaction may also be included. Since each entry in the voucher register includes a credit to an account called the *Vouchers Payable account,* a column titled *Vouchers Payable Cr.* is included in the voucher register (Illustration 6.14). In addition to this credit column, the voucher register has debit columns for the accounts most frequently debited when a liability is incurred, as well as a column to enter the other accounts debited (Other Accounts Dr. column).

At the end of each month, the Vouchers Payable Cr. column total is posted to the general ledger control account, Vouchers Payable. In Illustration 6.14, a voucher is prepared for each invoice. Note that the vouchers in this illustration are recorded net of purchase discounts allowed. If a discount is missed, another voucher is prepared for the discount lost (Illustration 6.14, line 13). (As described below, the voucher system can also be used when purchases are recorded at the gross amount.) The total of each of the specifically titled columns is posted to the designated account. The debits in the Other Accounts Dr. column are posted individually to the accounts named, usually on a daily basis. The account numbers appearing below each of these columns indicate that the column total has been posted to that account. The total of the Other Accounts Dr. column is not posted because each of the amounts it includes affects a different account. Therefore, an (X) appears beneath the total of the Other Accounts Dr. column, and a ($\sqrt{}$) appears to the right of each amount in the column. This indicates that the amount has been posted to the account shown.

Check Register. A **check register** is a special journal showing all checks issued, chronologically listed by date and by check number. One line is allotted to each check. No check may be issued unless authorized by an approved voucher.

The check register in Illustration 6.15 shows the entry and procedure when a check is issued in payment of a voucher. Note that Check No. 1352 is marked *void*. This notation usually means that a mistake was made in writing the check, and another check had to be prepared.

The net price method was used in Illustration 6.15, so the check register has only one money column. The column total is posted in the general ledger as a debit to Vouchers Payable and a credit to Cash. If the gross price method is used, invoices are entered gross (before discount deductions) in the voucher register, and a Purchase Discounts Cr. column should be included in the check register. Separate columns would be needed for the debit to Vouchers Payable and the credit to Cash, since the dollar amounts posted to these two accounts would differ by the amount of the discount taken (see Demonstration Problem 6-C for an example).

In a voucher system, the voucher register and the check register are the two primary journals from which postings are made to the Vouchers Payable control account in the general ledger. These two journals replace the traditional purchases and cash disbursements journals. However, a sales journal, cash receipts journal, and general journal would still be used.

Procedures for Paying a Voucher

When a voucher is due for payment, it is removed from the unpaid voucher file in the accounting department. A check is prepared for the amount payable. The check, voucher, and supporting documents are then typically sent to the person authorized to sign checks, usually the treasurer (the top financial officer in the company). The treasurer examines the documents. If they

Illustration 6.14
VOUCHER REGISTER

JACKSON COMPANY
VOUCHER REGISTER

Line No.	Voucher Date 1995		Voucher No.	Payee	Explanation	Terms	Date Paid*		Check No.*	Vouchers Payable Cr. 205
1	May	2	223	Hanley Company	Ring binders	2/10, n/30	May	12	1350	980.00
2		4	224	Moore Transport	Transportation, binders	Cash		5	1347	13.00
3		6	225	White Stationery Company	Office supplies	2/10, n/30		12	1351	102.00
4		8	226	Specialty Advertisers	Advertising	Cash		8	1348	1,200.00
5		10	227	Blanch Company	Office equipment and supplies	Cash		10	1349	1,010.00
6										
7		14	228	Swanson Company	Filler paper	2/10, n/30		26	1356	3,920.00
8		16	229	Rizzo Company	Office desk	n/30		25	1355	640.00
9		18	230	Warren Company	Spiral binders	2/10, n/30		28	1357	4,900.00
10		20	231	First National Bank	Mortgage payment			20	1353	154.00
11		22	232	Falconer Company	Books	n/30				10,000.00
12		24	233	Petty cash	Reimbursement			24	1354	132.00
13		26	234	Swanson Company	Discount lost (No. 228)			26	1356	80.00
14		28	235	Celoron Company	Drawing sets	2/20, n/30				9,800.00
15		31	236	Payroll account	Salaries and wages			31	1358	24,000.00
16										56,931.00
										(205)

* Added later when paid.

are in order, the treasurer initials the voucher to show that final approval has been given and signs the check. The check is mailed to the creditor, usually with a remittance advice attached. The voucher is then returned to the accounting department.

On receipt of the paid voucher, the accounting department makes an entry in the check register showing the date paid, check number, voucher number, and amount paid. The check number and date paid are also inserted

Page No.: *15*
Month: *May 1995*

Discounts Lost Dr. 543	Purchases Dr. 500	Transportation-In Dr. 503	Salaries Expense Dr. 507	Supplies Expense Dr. 518	Advertising Expense Dr. 505	Other Accounts Dr.			
						Account Name	Acct. No.	Amount Dr.	✓
	980.00								
		13.00							
				102.00					
					1,200.00				
						Office Equipment	172	1,000.00	✓
						Supplies on Hand	107	10.00	✓
	3,920.00								
						Office Equipment	172	640.00	✓
	4,860.00	40.00							
						Mortgage Note Payable	218	44.00	✓
						Interest Expense	540	110.00	✓
	10,000.00								
		31.88		60.12	40.00				
80.00									
	9,800.00								
			24,000.00						
80.00	29,560.00	84.88	24,000.00	162.12	1,240.00			1,804.00	
(543)	(500)	(503)	(507)	(518)	(505)			(x)	

in the voucher register and on the voucher itself. The voucher then is filed in the paid voucher file.

Files Maintained in a Voucher System

Two files are maintained in a voucher system—unpaid voucher file and paid voucher file.

Illustration 6.15
CHECK REGISTER

			JACKSON COMPANY		Page No.: *24*	
			CHECK REGISTER		Month: *May 1995*	

Line No.	Date 1995		Payee	Voucher No.	Check No.	Vouchers Payable Dr. 205, Cash Cr. 100
1	May	5	Moore Transport	224	1347	13.00
2		8	Specialty Advertisers	226	1348	1,200.00
3		10	Blanch Company	227	1349	1,010.00
4		12	Hanley Company	223	1350	980.00
5		12	White Stationery Company	225	1351	102.00
6		20	VOID		1352	
7		20	First National Bank	231	1353	154.00
8		24	Petty cash	233	1354	132.00
9		25	Rizzo Company	229	1355	640.00
10		26	Swanson Company	228} 234}	1356	4,000.00
11		28	Warren Company	230	1357	4,900.00
12		31	Payroll account	236	1358	24,000.00
						37,131.00
						(205)(100)

The **unpaid voucher file** contains all vouchers that have been prepared and approved as proper liabilities but have not yet been paid. These vouchers are filed according to their due dates. The unpaid voucher file takes the place of the accounts payable subsidiary ledger. The total of the vouchers in the unpaid voucher file should equal the total of the *open* items (those items not paid) in the voucher register and also should equal the balance in the Vouchers Payable control account in the general ledger.

The **paid voucher file** contains all vouchers that have been paid. These vouchers are often filed by voucher number in numerical order, but they can be filed by vendor name. Vouchers become a permanent and convenient reference for anyone who wants to check the details of past cash disbursements.

Illustration 6.16
VOUCHERS PAYABLE ACCOUNT

GENERAL LEDGER

Vouchers Payable   *Account No. 205*

Date		Explanation	Post. Ref.	Debit	Credit	Balance
1995 May	1	Beginning balance				– 0 –
	31	From voucher register			5 6 9 3 1	5 6 9 3 1
	31	From check register		3 7 1 3 1		1 9 8 0 0

Unpaid Vouchers at the End of the Period

At the end of the accounting period, the total of unpaid vouchers is shown in three places. First, the individual unpaid vouchers are shown in the voucher register, consisting of the vouchers for which no data appear in the Date Paid and Check No. columns (Illustration 6.14, lines 11 and 14). Second, the total is shown as the ending balance in the Vouchers Payable account, shown in Illustration 6.16 for Jackson Company. Third, the total is shown in a schedule prepared at the end of the period—the schedule of unpaid vouchers. Illustration 6.17 shows the schedule of unpaid vouchers for Jackson Company. In a balance sheet prepared at the end of an accounting period, the total of unpaid vouchers would normally be labeled as "Accounts payable" rather than "Vouchers payable."

Now that you have learned how to control a company's most liquid asset, cash, you are ready to study about plant assets in the next chapter. These long-term assets include land and depreciable assets such as buildings, machinery, and equipment.

Illustration 6.17
SCHEDULE OF UNPAID VOUCHERS

JACKSON COMPANY
Schedule of Unpaid Vouchers
May 31, 1995

Voucher No.	Name	Amount
232	Falconer Company	$10,000
235	Celoron Company	9,800
		$19,800

ETHICS A CLOSER LOOK

Cliff Hagen owns Hagen's Haven, a diner and yogurt shoppe in a small strip mall. At one point, the restaurant was a small place with a few customers whom Cliff could easily serve by himself. However, after 10 years, the business grew to such a point that Cliff hired several waitresses and busboys to handle the additional customer traffic. Cliff also began to take several afternoons and weekends off.

During Cliff's absences, the restaurant would sometimes need groceries or other supplies, so money was taken out of the register and replaced with receipts for the supplies purchased. Cliff found the register reconciliations and accounting more difficult when he had to contend with these little receipts, so he established a $300 petty cash fund. Cliff told his employees that whenever they needed money, they should take the money from the petty cash fund and that he would inspect, reconcile, and replenish the fund every Friday.

One waitress whom Cliff trusted felt the minimum wages she received were not enough, so she took advantage of the petty cash fund. She saved her personal grocery receipts and then simply placed them in the petty cash box whenever she took money from the box. Over several months, she managed to steal several hundred dollars before Cliff detected the phony receipts.

Required
a. Were the waitress' actions justified?
b. What steps might Cliff have taken to either prevent the opportunity for theft or quickly detect the fraud?

UNDERSTANDING THE LEARNING OBJECTIVES

1. Describe the necessity for and features of internal control.
    • The internal control structure of a company includes its plan of organization and all the procedures and actions taken by the company to protect its assets against theft and waste, ensure compliance with company policies and federal law, evaluate the performance of all personnel in the company so as to promote efficiency of operations, and ensure accurate and reliable operating data and accounting records.
    • The purpose of internal control is to ensure the efficient operations of a business.
2. Define cash and list the objectives sought by management in handling a company's cash.
    • Cash includes coins; currency; undeposited negotiable instruments such as checks, bank drafts, and money orders; amounts in checking and savings accounts; and demand certificates of deposit.
    • To protect their cash, companies should account for all cash transactions accurately, make certain enough cash is available to pay bills as they come due, avoid holding too much idle cash, and prevent loss of cash due to theft or fraud.

3. Identify procedures for controlling cash receipts and disbursements.
    *   Procedures for controlling cash receipts include such basic principles as recording all cash receipts as soon as cash is received; depositing all cash receipts as soon as feasible, preferably on the day they are received or on the next business day; and preventing the employee who handles cash receipts from also recording the receipts in the accounting records or from disbursing cash.
    *   Procedures for controlling cash disbursements include, among others, making all disbursements by check or from petty cash, using checks that are serially numbered, requiring two signatures on each check, and having a different person authorize payment of a bill than the persons allowed to sign checks.
4. Prepare a bank reconciliation and make necessary journal entries based on that schedule.
    *   A bank reconciliation is prepared to *reconcile,* or explain, the difference between the cash balance shown on the bank statement and the cash balance shown on the company's books.
    *   A bank reconciliation is shown in Illustration 6.11.
    *   Journal entries are needed for all items that appear in the bank reconciliation as adjustments to the balance per ledger to arrive at the adjusted cash balance.
5. Explain why a petty cash fund is used, describe its operation, and make the necessary journal entries.
    *   Companies establish a petty cash fund to permit minor disbursements to be made in cash and still maintain adequate control over cash.
    *   When the cash in the petty cash fund becomes low, the fund should be replenished. A journal entry is necessary to record the replenishment.
6. Describe the operation of the voucher system and make entries in its special journals—the voucher register and the check register.
    *   The voucher system is a set of procedures, special journals, and authorization forms designed to provide control over cash payments.
    *   A voucher is a form with spaces provided for data about a liability that must be paid and for signatures of persons who must approve the expenditure.
    *   A voucher register is a multicolumn special journal containing a record of all vouchers prepared, listed chronologically by date and voucher number.
    *   A check register is a special journal showing all checks issued, listed chronologically by date and check number.

DEMONSTRATION PROBLEM 6–A

You are the manager of a restaurant that has an ice cream parlor as a separate unit. Your accountant comes in once a year to prepare financial statements and the tax return. In the current year, you have a feeling that even though business seems good, net income is going to be lower. You ask the accountant to prepare condensed statements on a monthly basis. All sales are priced to yield an estimated gross margin of 40%. You, your accountant, and several of the accountant's assistants take physical inventories at the end of each of the four months indicated below. The resulting sales, cost of goods sold, and gross margins are:

	March		April		May		June	
	Restau-rant	Ice Cream Parlor	Restau-rant	Ice Cream Parlor	Restau-rant	Ice Cream Parlor	Restau-rant	Ice Cream Parlor
Sales	$54,450	$79,500	$58,575	$64,125	$57,150	$58,500	$61,875	$53,250
Cost of goods sold . . .	34,913	47,250	35,700	46,500	34,463	46,125	38,250	46,688
Gross margin	$19,537	$32,250	$22,875	$17,625	$22,687	$12,375	$23,625	$ 6,562

Required:

What would you suspect after analyzing these reports? What sales control procedures would you recommend to correct the situation? All of the points covered in this problem were not specifically covered in the chapter, although the principles were. Use logic, common sense, and knowledge gained elsewhere in coming up with some of the control procedures.

Solution to demonstration problem 6–A

The gross margin percentages are as follows:

	March	April	May	June
Restaurant	35.88%	39.05%	39.70%	38.18%
Ice cream parlor	40.57	27.49	21.15	12.32

Either cash or inventory is being stolen or given away in the ice cream parlor. Employees or outsiders may be pocketing cash. Or the employees may be giving extra-large ice cream cones to friends, or eating the ice cream themselves. Several things could be done to improve the sales control procedures:

1. The manager could hire an investigator to come in and watch the employees in action. If cash is being pocketed, the employees could be fired.
2. The prices of ice cream cones could be changed to odd amounts so that employees would not be as able to make change without going to the cash register. Also, the "No Sale" lever could be removed from the cash register.
3. The customers could be encouraged to ask for their cash register receipts by having a monthly drawing (for some prize) by cash register receipt number.
4. The cash register should be placed in a prominent position so that each customer could see the amount recorded for each sale. The customer is not going to be willing to pay 65 cents when the employee rings up 50 cents.
5. The cash register tapes should be inaccessible to the employees. The manager (and possibly assistant manager) should have the only keys to the cash registers.

6. Mention to the employees that you have an effective control structure. The employees do not have to know what the structure is.
7. Pay the employees a competitive wage.
8. Require that all sales be rung up immediately after the sale.
9. The manager or assistant manager should reconcile the cash register tapes at the end of each day.

DEMONSTRATION PROBLEM 6–B

The following data pertain to Baker Company:

1. Balance per bank statement, dated March 31, 1995, is $6,675.
2. Balance of the Cash account on the company's books as of March 31, 1995, is $6,688.50.
3. The $1,950 deposit of March 31 was not shown on the bank statement.
4. Of the checks recorded as cash disbursements in March, some checks, totaling $1,575, have not yet cleared the bank.
5. Service and collection charges for the month were $15.
6. The bank erroneously charged the Baker Company account for the $300 check of another company. The check was included with the canceled checks returned with the bank statement.
7. The bank credited the company's account with the $1,500 proceeds of a noninterest-bearing note that it collected for the company.
8. A customer's $112.50 check marked NSF was returned with the bank statement.
9. As directed, the bank paid and charged to the company's account a $761.25 noninterest-bearing note of Baker Company. This payment has not been recorded by the company.
10. The bank credited the company for $30 of interest earned on the company's checking account.
11. An examination of the cash receipts and the deposit tickets revealed that the bookkeeper erroneously recorded a customer's check of $222.75 as $202.50.

Required:

a. Prepare a bank reconciliation as of March 31, 1995.
b. Prepare the necessary journal entry or entries to adjust the Cash account.

Solution to demonstration problem 6-B

a.
BAKER COMPANY
Bank Reconciliation
March 31, 1995

Balance per bank statement, March 31, 1995		$6,675.00
Add: Deposit in transit	$1,950.00	
Check charged in error	300.00	2,250.00
		$8,925.00
Less: Outstanding checks.		1,575.00
Adjusted balance, March 31, 1995		$7,350.00
Balance per ledger, March 31, 1995		$6,688.50
Add: Note collected.	$1,500.00	
Interest earned on checking account	30.00	
Error in recording customer's check	20.25	1,550.25
		$8,238.75
Less: Service and collection charges	$ 15.00	
NSF check	112.50	
Baker Company note charged against account	761.25	888.75
Adjusted balance, March 31, 1995		$7,350.00

b.

1995
Mar. 31 Cash	661.50	
Bank Service Charge Expense	15.00	
Accounts Receivable.	112.50	
Notes Payable.	761.25	
Notes Receivable		1,500.00
Interest Revenue.		30.00
Accounts Receivable.		20.25
To record adjustments to Cash account.		

Alternatively:

1995
Mar. 31 Cash	1,550.25	
Notes Receivable		1,500.00
Interest Revenue.		30.00
Accounts Receivable.		20.25
To record additions to Cash account.		
Bank Service Charge Expense	15.00	
Accounts Receivable.	112.50	
Notes Payable	761.25	
Cash		888.75
To record deductions from Cash account.		

DEMONSTRATION PROBLEM 6-C

Classic Company uses a voucher system to control cash disbursements. Purchases are recorded at gross selling prices. As of April 30, 1995, two vouchers are unpaid:

Voucher No. 404 payable to Garland Company for $2,550 and Voucher No. 405 payable to Sharper Company for $150.

Classic Company engaged in the following transactions affecting vouchers payable:

May 1 Prepared Voucher No. 406 payable to Kramer Company for merchandise purchased; price on invoice dated April 30 is $1,200. Terms are 2/10, n/30, FOB destination.

2 Issued Check No. 385 in payment of Voucher No. 405; no discount was offered on this purchase.

4 Received a credit memo for $300 for merchandise returned to Garland Company. Purchase was originally recorded in Voucher No. 404. (Record in general journal with notation of return on Voucher No. 404.)

5 Prepared Voucher No. 407 payable to Carson Brothers for merchandise with an invoice price of $2,850 on invoice dated May 3; terms are 2/10, n/30, FOB shipping point, freight prepaid. Supplier paid $150 freight bill and added $150 to the invoice for a total billing of $3,000.

6 Prepared Voucher No. 408 payable to CSS, Inc., for cost incurred to deliver merchandise sold, $360; terms n/10.

8 Issued Check No. 386 to pay Voucher No. 404, less return and less a 2% discount.

9 Issued Check No. 387 to pay Voucher No. 406.

12 Prepared Voucher No. 409 payable to Paul Insurance Company for $900, the three-year premium on an insurance policy. Issued Check No. 388 to pay Voucher No. 409.

13 Issued Check No. 389 to pay Voucher No. 407.

15 Prepared Voucher No. 410 payable to Cash for $6,000 in salaries for the first half of May. Issued Check No. 390 in payment of Voucher No. 410. Cashed the check and paid employees in cash.

16 Issued Check No. 391 to pay Voucher No. 408.

23 Prepared Voucher No. 411 payable to Busch Company for merchandise with an invoice price of $900 on invoice dated May 22; terms are 2/10, n/30, FOB shipping point, freight collect.

24 Prepared Voucher No. 412 payable to Harper Transit, Inc., for $150 freight on merchandise purchased on May 23.

26 Prepared Voucher No. 413 payable to Converse Telephone Company for $375 for monthly telephone service.

28 Prepared Voucher No. 414 payable to Baker Delivery, Inc., for costs incurred to deliver merchandise sold, $240; terms n/30.

31 Prepared Voucher No. 415 payable to Cash for salaries for the last half of May, $6,600. Issued Check No. 392 in payment of Voucher No. 415. Cashed the check and paid employees in cash.

Required:

a. Record the transactions above using a voucher register (page 12), check register (page 5), and a general journal (page 17). You need not include account numbers.

b. Prepare a Vouchers Payable account (Account No. 205) and post the portions of the entries that affect this account.

c. Prepare a schedule (list) of unpaid vouchers to prove the accuracy of the balance in the Vouchers Payable account.

Solution to demonstration problem 6–C

a. The voucher register is on the following page.

CLASSIC COMPANY
Check Register   *Page 5*

Date 1995		Payee	Voucher No.	Check No.	Vouchers Payable Dr.	Purchase Discounts Cr.	Cash Cr.
May	2	Sharper Company	405	385	150		150
	8	Garland Company	404	386	2,250	45	2,205
	9	Kramer Company	406	387	1,200	24	1,176
	12	Paul Insurance Company	409	388	900		900
	13	Carson Brothers	407	389	3,000	57	2,943
	15	Cash	410	390	6,000		6,000
	16	CSS, Inc.	408	391	360		360
	31	Cash	415	392	6,600		6,600
					20,460	126	20,334

CLASSIC COMPANY
GENERAL JOURNAL   *Page*

Date		Account Titles and Explanation	Post. Ref.	Debit	Credit
1995 May	4	Vouchers Payable		300	
		Purchase Returns and Allowances			300
		To record receipt of credit memo for merchandise returned;			
		Voucher No. 404.			

CLASSIC COMPANY
VOUCHER REGISTER

Voucher Date 1995	Voucher No.	Payee	Terms	Date Paid	Check No.	Vouchers Payable Cr.	Purchases Dr.	Transportation-In Dr.	Delivery Expense Dr.	Salaries Expense Dr.	Other Accounts Dr. Account Name	Post. Ref.	Amount Dr.
May 1	406	Kramer Company	2/10, n/30	May 9	387	1,200	1,200						
5	407	Carson Brothers	2/10, n/30	13	389	3,000	2,850	150					
6	408	CSS, Inc.	n/10	16	391	360			360				
12	409	Paul Insurance Company		12	388	900					Prepaid Insurance		900
15	410	Cash		15	390	6,000				6,000			
23	411	Busch Company	2/10, n/30			900	900						
24	412	Harper Transit, Inc.				150		150					
26	413	Converse Telephone Company				375					Utilities Expense		375
28	414	Baker Delivery, Inc.	n/30			240			240				
31	415	Cash		31	392	6,600				6,600			
						19,725	4,950	300	600	12,600			1,275

b.

CLASSIC COMPANY
GENERAL LEDGER

Vouchers Payable *Account No. 205*

Date		Explanation	Post. Ref.	Debit	Credit	Balance
1995 Apr.	30	Beginning balance				2 7 0 0 Cr.
May	4	Credit memo; Voucher No. 404	G17	3 0 0		2 4 0 0 Cr.
	31		VR12		1 9 7 2 5	2 2 1 2 5 Cr.
	31		CR5	2 0 4 6 0		1 6 6 5 Cr.

c.

CLASSIC COMPANY
Schedule of Unpaid Vouchers
May 31, 1995

Voucher No.	Name	Amount
411	Busch Company	$ 900
412	Harper Transit, Inc.	150
413	Converse Telephone Company . .	375
414	Baker Delivery, Inc.	240
		$1,665

NEW TERMS

Accounting system Methods and records established to identify, assemble, analyze, classify, record, and report an entity's transactions to provide complete, accurate, and timely financial information. *308*

Bank reconciliation A schedule the company (depositor) prepares to *reconcile,* or explain, the difference between the cash balance shown on the bank statement and the cash balance on the company's books; often called a *bank reconciliation statement* or *schedule. 325*

Bank statement A statement issued (usually monthly) by a bank describing the activities in a depositor's checking account during the period. *321*

Cash Includes coins; currency; certain undeposited negotiable instruments such as checks, bank drafts, and money orders; amounts in checking and savings accounts; and demand certificates of deposit. *316*

Cashier's check A check drawn by a bank made out to either the depositor or a third party after deducting the amount of the check from the depositor's account or receiving cash from the depositor. *330*

Certificate of deposit (CD) An interest-bearing deposit in a bank that can be withdrawn at will (demand CD) or at a fixed maturity date (time CD). *316*

Certified check A check written, or drawn, by a depositor and taken to the depositor's bank for certification. The check is deducted from the depositor's balance immediately and becomes a liability of the bank. Thus, the check will usually be accepted without question. *330*

Check   A written order on a bank to pay a specific sum of money to the party designated as the payee by the party issuing the check. *321*

Checking account   A money balance maintained in the bank that is subject to withdrawal by the depositor, or owner of the money, on demand. *319*

Check register   A special journal showing all checks issued, chronologically listed by date and by check number. *337*

Control environment   Reflects the overall attitude, awareness, and actions of the board of directors, management, and owners. *308*

Control procedures   Policies and procedures, in addition to the control environment and the accounting system that management has established to provide reasonable assurance that the company will achieve its specific objectives. *308*

Credit memo   A form used by a bank to explain an addition to the depositor's account. *322*

Debit memo   A form used by a bank to explain a deduction from the depositor's account. *322*

Deposit in transit   Typically, a day's cash receipts recorded in the depositor's books in one period but recorded as a deposit by the bank in the succeeding period. *326*

Deposit ticket   A form that shows the date and the items that make up the deposit. *320*

Drawer   The party (depositor) writing a check. *321*

Fidelity bonds   Ensure that a company is reimbursed for losses due to theft of cash and other monetary assets. *313*

Internal auditing   Consists of investigating and evaluating employees' compliance with the company's policies and procedures. Internal auditing is performed by company personnel. *310*

Internal auditors   Auditors employed by the company to perform internal audits. These auditors are trained in company policies and in internal auditing duties such as testing effectiveness of controls and procedures involving cash receipts and cash disbursements. *310*

Internal control structure   Policies and procedures established to provide reasonable assurance that specific entity objectives will be achieved. *307*

Invoice   Statement sent by the supplier to the purchaser requesting payment for the merchandise shipped. *311*

NSF check   A customer's check returned from the customer's bank to the depositor's bank because the funds in the customer's checking account balance were insufficient to cover the check. *322*

Outstanding checks   Checks issued by a depositor that have not yet been paid by the bank on which they are drawn. *326*

Paid voucher file   A permanent file used in a voucher system where paid vouchers are filed in numerical sequence. *340*

Payee   The party to whom a check is made payable. *321*

Petty cash fund   A nominal sum of money established as a separate fund from which minor cash disbursements for valid business purposes are made. The cash in the fund plus the vouchers covering disbursements must always equal the balance at which the fund was established and at which it is carried in the Petty Cash account. *330*

Petty cash voucher   A document or form that shows the amount of, and reason for, a petty cash disbursement. *331*

Purchase order   A document sent from the purchasing department to a supplier requesting that merchandise or other items be shipped to the purchaser. *311*

Purchase requisition   A written request from an employee inside the company to the purchasing department to purchase certain items. *311*

Receiving report   A document prepared by the receiving department showing the descriptions and quantities of all items received from a supplier in a particular shipment. *311*

Remittance advice   Informs the payee why the drawer (or maker) of the check is making this payment. *321*

Segregation of duties   Having the employee responsible for safeguarding an asset be someone other than the employee who maintains the accounting records for that asset. *309*

Service charges   Charges assessed by the bank on the depositor to cover the cost of handling the checking account. *322*

Signature card   Provides the signatures of persons authorized to sign checks drawn on an account. *320*

Transfer bank accounts   A bank account set up so that local banks automatically transfer to a central bank (by wire or written bank draft) all amounts on deposit in excess of a stated amount. *322*

Unpaid voucher file   Contains all vouchers that have been prepared and approved as proper liabilities but have not yet been paid. Serves as an accounts payable subsidiary ledger under a voucher system; unpaid vouchers are filed according to their due dates. *340*

Voucher   A form with spaces provided for data about a liability that must be paid. The data include items such as creditor's name and address, description of the goods or services received, invoice number, terms of payment, due date, and amount due, and often show the ledger accounts and amounts to be debited. The voucher also has spaces for signatures of those approving the liability for payment. *334*

Voucher register   A multicolumn special journal used in a voucher system; the voucher register contains a record of all vouchers prepared, listed in order by date and voucher number. A brief explanation of each transaction also may be included. In addition to a credit column for Vouchers Payable, a voucher register normally has various debit columns for accounts such as Purchases, Salaries, and Transportation-In. *336*

Voucher system   A set of procedures, special journals, and authorization forms designed to provide control over cash payments. *334*

Wire transfer of funds   Interbank transfer of funds by telephone. *322*

SELF-TEST

True-False

Indicate whether each of the following statements is true or false.

1. Cash includes coin, currency, postdated checks, money orders, and money on deposit with banks.

2. To effectively manage its cash, a company should make certain that enough cash is available to pay bills as they come due.

3. The cash balance shown on the bank statement is usually equal to the cash balance in the depositor's books.

4. A deposit in transit will require an entry in the depositor's books after the bank reconciliation is prepared.

5. For control purposes, a company should issue checks for every payment, regardless of its amount.

6. In a voucher system, the voucher register and the check register replace the traditional purchases and cash disbursement journals.

Multiple-Choice

Select the best answer for each of the following questions.

1. The objectives of the internal control structure of a company include all of the following except:
   a. Compliance with company policies and federal law.
   b. Protection of its assets.
   c. Increase in accuracy and reliability of accounting data.
   d. Ensurance of a certain level of profit.
   e. Evaluation of personnel performance to promote efficiency of operations.

Use the following information to answer Question 2.

Balance per bank statement	$5,853.60
Balance per ledger.	5,608.80
Deposits in transit	813.60
Outstanding checks	1,283.40
NSF check	183.60
Service charges	41.40

2. The adjusted cash balance is:
   a. $5,383.80.
   b. $5,158.80.
   c. $4,914.00.
   d. $5,189.00.
   e. $5,628.60.

3. In a bank reconciliation, deposits in transit should be:
   a. Deducted from the balance per books.
   b. Deducted from the balance per bank statement.
   c. Added to the balance per ledger.
   d. Added to the balance per bank statement.
   e. Disregarded in the bank reconciliation.

4. After the bank reconciliation is prepared, the entry to record bank service charges would have a credit to:
   a. Bank Service Charge Expense.
   b. Cash.
   c. Petty Cash.
   d. Cash Short and Over.
   e. None of the above.

5. The entry to replenish the petty cash fund for disbursements made for stamps includes:
   a. A credit to Petty Cash.
   b. A credit to Postage Expense.
   c. A debit to Accounts Payable.
   d. A credit to Cash.
   e. None of the above.

6. A voucher system:
   a. Eliminates the need for cash disbursement records.
   b. Is an internal control system for cash receipts.

c. Is designed to provide control over cash payments.

d. Is a desirable addition to the accounting system of any concern.

e. Is not related to internal control.

Now turn to page 364 to check your answers.

QUESTIONS

1. What purposes does an internal control structure accomplish?

2. Identify some features which, if present, would strengthen an internal control structure.

3. Name some control documents that are used in merchandise transactions.

4. What are the four objectives sought in effective cash management?

5. Cite some essential internal control features regarding cash receipts.

6. The bookkeeper of a given company was stealing remittances received from customers in payment of their accounts. To cover the theft, the bookkeeper made out false credit memoranda indicating returns and allowances made by or granted to the customers. What feature of a system of internal control, if operative, would have prevented this scheme?

7. Cite some essential internal control features regarding cash disbursements.

8. "The difference between a company's Cash ledger account balance and the balance in the bank statement is usually a matter of timing." Do you agree or disagree? Why?

9. Why might a company's management wish to determine the cash position daily?

10. Explain how the use of transfer bank accounts can bring about effective cash management.

11. Indicate the method of operation of a petty cash fund and the advantages obtained through its use. Indicate how control is maintained over petty cash transactions.

12. What is the advantage of recording purchases at the net invoice price?

13. Describe how the use of a voucher system provides close control over cash disbursements.

The Coca-Cola Company

14. *Real-world question* From the consolidated balance sheet of The Coca-Cola Company in Appendix C, identify the total 1991 cash and cash equivalents and marketable securities. Explain the definition of cash equivalents and marketable securities in accordance with the footnotes.

MAYTAG
CORPORATION

15. *Real-world question* Based on the financial statements of Maytag Corporation contained in Appendix C, what was the 1991 ending cash and cash equivalents balance?

THE LIMITED, INC

16. *Real-world question*   Based on the financial statements of The Limited, Inc., in Appendix C, what was the February 2, 1991, cash and cash equivalents balance? When does this company's fiscal year end?

HARLAND

17. *Real-world question*   Based on the financial statements of John H. Harland Company contained in Appendix C, what was the 1991 ending short-term investments balance?

EXERCISES

Answer true-false questions about internal control (L.O. 1)

6–1. State whether each of the following statements about internal control is true or false:

a. Those persons responsible for safeguarding an asset should maintain the accounting records for that asset.

b. Complete, accurate, and up-to-date accounting records should be maintained.

c. Whenever possible, responsibilities should be assigned and duties subdivided in such a way that only one person is responsible for a given function.

d. Employees should be assigned to one job and should remain in that job so that skill levels will be as high as possible.

e. The use of check protectors, cash registers, and time clocks is recommended.

f. An internal auditing function should not be implemented because it leads the employees to believe that management does not trust them.

g. One of the best protections against theft is to hire honest, competent employees.

h. A foolproof internal control structure can be devised if management puts forth the effort.

Answer multiple-choice question about internal control (L.O. 1)

6–2. Concerning internal control, which one of the following statements is correct? Explain.

a. Broadly speaking, internal control is only necessary in large organizations.

b. The purposes of internal control are to check the accuracy of accounting data, safeguard assets against theft, promote efficiency of operations, and ensure that management's policies are being followed.

c. Once an internal control structure has been established, it should be effective as long as the formal organization remains unchanged.

d. An example of internal control is having one individual count the day's cash receipts and compare the total with the total of the cash register tapes.

Determine available cash balance from bank statement and Cash account data (L.O. 4)

6–3. The Penny Company's Cash account balance was $390,825 at the end of August. The bank statement showed a balance of $386,100 for the same date. Checks outstanding totaled $132,000, and deposits in transit totaled $151,500.

If these are the only pertinent data available to you, what was the correct amount of cash against which the Penny Company could have written checks as of the end of August?

Prepare bank reconciliation statement and specify cash available (L.O. 4)

6–4. From the following data, prepare a bank reconciliation statement and determine the correct available cash balance for the Brooks Company as of October 31, 1995:

Balance per bank statement, October 31, 1995	$27,948
Ledger account balance	22,056
Note collected by bank not yet entered in ledger	6,000
Bank charges not yet entered by Brooks Company	36
Deposit in transit	3,360
Outstanding checks:	
No. 527	768
No. 528	576
No. 529	1,440
No. 531	504

Prepare bank reconciliation statement and necessary journal entries (L.O. 4)

6–5. From the following information for the Knight Company:

a. Prepare a bank reconciliation statement as of September 30, 1995.

b. Give the necessary journal entries to correct the Cash account.

Balance per bank statement, September 30, 1995	$97,800
Ledger account balance as of September 30, 1995	87,900
Note collected by bank	6,000
Bank charges	60
Deposits in transit	5,544
NSF check deposited and returned	504
Check of Howard Company deducted in error	300
Outstanding checks	10,308

Determine checks outstanding (L. O. 4)

6–6. As of March 1 of the current year, the Jones Company had outstanding checks of $84,000. During March the company issued an additional $360,000 of checks. As of March 31 the bank statement showed that $336,000 of checks had cleared the bank during the month. What is the amount of outstanding checks as of March 31?

Determine deposits in transit (L.O. 4)

6–7. The Crowley Company's bank statement as of August 31, 1995, shows total deposits into the company's account of $139,020 and a total of 14 deposits. On July 31 deposits of $7,800 and $6,750 were in transit. The total cash receipts for August amounted to $141,360, and the company's records show 13 deposits made in August. What is the amount of deposits in transit at August 31?

Record reimbursement of petty cash fund (L.O. 5)

6–8. On August 31, 1995, the Fleming Company's petty cash fund contained:

Coin and currency	$249.00
IOU from employee	30.00
Vouchers covering expenditures for:	
Postage	120.00
Taxi fares	51.00
Entertainment of a customer	138.00

The Petty Cash account shows a balance of $600. If financial statements are prepared for each calendar month, what journal entry is required on August 31? The petty cash fund was not replenished at this time.

Record reimbursement of petty cash fund (L.O. 5)

6–9. Use the data in Exercise 8 above. If the fund were replenished on August 31, 1995, what journal entry would be required? Which of the accounts debited would not appear in the income statement?

List the procedures to follow for processing an invoice (L.O. 6)

6–10. You are the chief accountant of the Meyer Company. An invoice has just been received from the Day Company in the amount of $12,000, with terms of 2/10, n/30. List the procedures you would follow in processing this invoice up through the point of filing it in the unpaid vouchers file.

Determine vouchers payable balance; compute current month's vouchers paid (L.O. 6)

6–11. Refer to Illustration 6.14.

a. Assume that all vouchers written before May 1, 1995, have been paid. By only looking at the voucher register, what is the balance in the Vouchers Payable account on May 31, 1995?

b. All checks written in May were in payment of May vouchers. By only looking at the voucher register, determine the total dollar amount of vouchers paid in May.

Prepare general journal entries to record selected transactions and indicate whether recorded in voucher or check register (L.O. 6)

6–12. Jenks Company uses a voucher system. Recently, the company had the following transactions:

a. Prepared Voucher No. 801 for purchase of merchandise from Wilke Company, $3,000.

b. Issued Check No. 723 to pay Voucher No. 801.

c. Prepared Voucher No. 802 to set up a petty cash fund, $900.

d. Issued Check No. 724 to pay Voucher No. 802.

e. Prepared Voucher No. 804 for $120 freight on merchandise in Voucher No. 801.

f. Prepared Voucher No. 805 to replenish petty cash when it contained cash of $168 and receipts for postage, $396; supplies, $204; and miscellaneous expenses, $120.

g. Issued Check No. 725 to pay Voucher No. 805.

Prepare entries in general journal form to record the above transactions. Identify the journal or book of original entry in which each transaction would normally appear.

Describe what amounts and information would appear in a voucher system to record payment for purchase under net price procedure when discount is lost (L.O. 6)

6–13. Assume that Bailey Company uses a voucher register and a check register exactly like Illustration 6.14 and Illustration 6.15. On May 1, Bailey Company purchased merchandise from Powers Company, $6,000; terms 2/10, n/30. Bailey prepared Voucher No. 567 for $5,880. On May 29, Bailey paid for the merchandise purchased from Powers Company and missed the discount (Check No. 489).

State what information should be entered in the voucher register and the check register to record the payment of May 29. Assume that the last voucher used was 598.

PROBLEMS

Prepare bank
reconciliation
statement with
necessary journal
entries
(L.O. 4)

6–1. The bank statement for the Cacey Company's general checking account with the First National Bank for the month ended August 31, 1995, showed an ending balance of $31,854, service charges of $60, an NSF check returned of $1,260, and the collection of a $6,000 note plus interest of $60. Further investigation revealed that a wire transfer of $10,800 from the bank account maintained by a branch office of the company had not been recorded by the company as having been deposited in the First National Bank account. In addition, a comparison of deposits with receipts showed a deposit in transit of $12,600. Checks outstanding amounted to $9,036 while the cash ledger balance was $19,878.

Required:

a. Prepare a bank reconciliation statement for the Cacey Company account for the month ended August 31, 1995.

b. Prepare all necessary journal entries.

Prepare bank
reconciliation
statement with
necessary journal
entries
(L.O. 4)

6–2. The bank statement for Evans Company's account with the First National Bank for the month ended April 30, 1995, showed a balance of $65,316. On this date the company's Cash account balance was $57,162. Returned with the bank statement were (1) a debit memo for service charges of $60, (2) a debit memo for a customer's NSF check of $600, and (3) a credit memo for a $13,200 wire transfer of funds on April 14 from the State Bank, the local bank used by the company's branch office. Further investigation revealed that outstanding checks amounted to $7,800, the cash receipts of April 30 of $9,726 did not appear as a deposit on the bank statement, and the canceled checks included a check for $2,460 (drawn by the president of the company to cover travel expenses on a recent trip) which the company has yet to record.

Required:

a. Prepare a bank reconciliation statement for the month ended April 30, 1995.

b. Prepare any necessary journal entries.

Prepare bank
reconciliation
statement with
necessary journal
entries
(L.O. 4)

6–3. The following data pertain to the Gilbert Company:

(1) Balance per the bank statement dated June 30, 1995, is $183,420.

(2) Balance of the Cash in Bank account on the company books as of June 30, 1995, is $53,910.

(3) Outstanding checks as of June 30, 1995, are $90,000.

(4) Bank deposit of June 30 for $14,130 was not included in the deposits per the bank statement.

(5) The bank had collected a $135,000, 6%, 30-day note and the interest of $675, which it credited to the Gilbert Company account. The bank charged the company a collection fee of $90 on the above note.

(6) The bank erroneously charged the Gilbert Company account for a $63,000 check of the Hilbert Company. The check was found among the canceled checks returned with the bank statement.

(7) Bank service charges for June, exclusive of the collection fee, amounted to $450.

(8) Among the canceled checks was one for $3,105 given in payment of an account. The bookkeeper had recorded the check at $4,320 in the company records.

(9) A check of Mr. Wall, a customer, for $18,900, deposited on June 20, was returned by the bank marked NSF. No entry has been made to reflect the returned check on the company records.

(10) A check for $7,560 of Ms. Maceda, a customer, which had been deposited in the bank, was erroneously recorded by the bookkeeper as $8,370.

Required:

Prepare a bank reconciliation statement as of June 30, 1995. Also prepare any necessary adjusting journal entries.

Prepare bank reconciliation statement with necessary journal entries (L.O. 4)

6-4. The following data pertain to the Ortega Company. The reconciliation statement as of June 30, 1995, showed a deposit in transit of $8,100 and three checks outstanding:

No. 553.	$3,600
No. 570.	6,600
No. 571.	4,800

During July the following checks were written and entered in the Cash account.

No. 572	$4,500	No. 578	$ 6,900
No. 573	4,950	No. 579	8,460
No. 574	8,460	No. 580	1,080
No. 575	3,810	No. 581	14,562
No. 576	7,598	No. 582	14,400
No. 577	5,070	No. 583	5,544

As of July 31, all of the checks written, except No. 578, had been mailed to the payees. Check No. 578 was kept in the vault pending receipt of a statement from the payee. Four deposits were made at the bank as follows:

July 7.	$45,000
14.	57,600
14.	34,200
28.	41,400

The bank statement, which was received on August 2, correctly included all deposits and showed a balance as of July 31 of $151,560. The following checks were returned: Nos. 570, 571, 572, 573, 574, 575, 576, 577, 580, and 581. With the paid checks there were three debit memoranda for:

(1) Fee of $24 for the collection on July 30 of a $6,600 noninterest-bearing note payable to the Flores Company for which a credit memorandum was enclosed.

(2) Monthly service charge of $30.

(3) Payment of a $4,500 noninterest-bearing note of the Ortega Company.

The bank statement included a credit for $18,000 dated July 29. The bank telephoned the company on the morning of August 3 to explain that this credit was in error because it represented a transaction between the bank and the Orville Company.

The balance in the Cash account on the books of the Ortega Company as of July 31 is $92,610.

Required:

Prepare a bank reconciliation statement for the Ortega Company as of July 31, 1995. Also prepare any necessary adjusting entries.

Prepare bank reconciliation statement with necessary journal entries (L.O. 4)

6–5. The following information is taken from the books and records of the Carter Company:

Balance per bank statement, July 31, 1995	$137,334
Balance per ledger, July 31, 1995	139,452
Collections received on the last day of July and debited to Cash in Bank on books but not entered by bank until August	31,872
Debit memo for customer's check returned unpaid (uncollectible check is on hand, but no entry for the return has been made on the books).	3,000
Debit memo for bank service charge for July	90
Check issued but not paid by bank	30,204
Credit memo for proceeds of a note receivable which was left at the bank for collection but has not been recorded on the books as collected ($48 of this is interest revenue)	4,800
Check for an account payable entered on books as $2,880 but issued and paid by the bank in the correct amount of $5,040.	

Required:

Prepare a bank reconciliation statement and the necessary journal entries to adjust the accounts.

Prepare bank reconciliation statement with necessary journal entries; comment on control of cash receipts (L.O. 2,4)

6–6. The following data for March 1995 are summarized from the accounts of Pierce Company. The accountant also acts as cashier.

Cash Receipts		Cash Disbursements	
Mar. 2	$ 9,900	Check No. 911	$ 7,956
4	28,800	No. 912	11,034
5	11,700	No. 913	13,122
11	25,200	No. 914	7,992
13	31,500	No. 915	14,526
14	37,800	No. 916	21,600
19	9,000	No. 917	34,200
20	7,200	No. 918	24,300
27	540	No. 919	6,750
29	3,330 70	No. 920	6,300
	164970		

At March 1 the checks outstanding were:

No. 209	$ 810
No. 792	14,400
No. 796	5,022
No. 910	11,358

There were no deposits in transit. The balance of the Cash in Bank account per books was $138,150 at March 31. The bank statement for the month of March is as follows:

| | BANK STATEMENT | | |
Date	Checks	Deposits	Balance
Mar. 1			153,000
3		9,900	162,900
4	7,956		
4	11,034		143,910
6		40,500	184,410
9	14,526		
9	7,992		161,892
16		94,500	256,392
19	21,600		
19	24,300		210,492
24		16,200	226,692
25	5,022		
25	11,358		210,312
26	34,200		
26	9,000 NSF		167,112
27	9,000 DM		158,112
29		3,420	161,532
31	36 DM		161,496

The debit memoranda (DM) are for the payment of a company note and for the monthly service charge.

Required:

a. Prepare a bank reconciliation statement as of March 31, 1995.

b. Journalize the entry or entries necessary to correct the books.

c. Comment on the company's control of cash receipts.

Prepare necessary journal entries involving petty cash fund (L.O. 5)

6–7. Following are selected transactions of the Baker Company during 1995:

Mar. 1   Established a petty cash fund of $3,000 which will be under the control of the assistant office manager.

Apr. 3   Fund is replenished on this date. Prior to replenishment, the fund consisted of the following:

Coin and currency	$1,707.48
Payroll check issued by Baker Company to part-time office worker, Jill Jones, properly endorsed by Jones (cashed by the assistant office manager) . .	170.88
Petty cash vouchers indicating disbursements for:	
Postage stamps	420.00
Supper money for office employees working overtime	144.00
Office supplies	130.80
Window washing service	240.00
Flowers for wedding of employee	60.00
Flowers for hospitalized employee	60.00
Employee IOU	60.00

The employee's IOU is to be deducted from his paycheck.

Required:

Present journal entries for the above transactions.

Prepare necessary
journal entries
involving petty
cash fund
(L.O. 5)

6–8. The following data pertain to the petty cash fund of the Lighthouse Company:

Nov. 2   A $3,600 check is drawn and cashed, and the cash is placed in the care of the assistant office manager to be used as a petty cash fund.

Dec. 17   The fund is replenished. An analysis of the fund shows:

Coins and currency	$ 884.43
Petty cash vouchers for:	
Delivery expenses	1,040.85
Freight-in	1,566.72
Postage stamps purchased	90.00

31   The end of the accounting period falls on this date. The fund was not replenished. Its contents on this date consist of:

Coins and currency	$3,012.30
Petty cash vouchers for:	
Delivery expenses	189.90
Postage stamps	217.80
Employee's IOU	180.00

Required:

Present journal entries to record the above transactions.

Prepare entries in
voucher and
check registers,
using net price
method for
purchase
discounts
(L.O. 6)

6–9. Woodson Company was organized January 1 of the current year, 1995. The company uses a voucher register and a check register with the same column headings as in Illustrations 6.14 and 6.15, except that only four voucher register debit columns are used—Purchases, Transportation-In, Discounts Lost, and Other Accounts. Vouchers are prepared for the net amount of the invoice. For discounts lost, a new voucher is prepared for the amount of the discount.

Transactions:

Jan. 2   Received merchandise from Lind Company with terms of 2/10, n/30. The invoice received was in the amount of $15,600.

   3   Paid transportation charges to Moyer Trucking Company on purchase of January 2, $261.

   6   Paid Wilson Display Company $9,900 for billboard advertising for a three-month period beginning February 1, 1995.

  15   Paid Lind Company for the purchase of January 2.

  17   Received merchandise from Bradly Company with terms of 2/10, n/30. The invoice received was for $12,600.

  18   Received merchandise from Casp Company with terms of 2/10, n/30. The invoice received was for $53,250. Paid net amount today to establish a good credit rating.

  23   Received invoice for $5,400 from Office Equipment, Inc., for office equipment recently received. Terms are 2/10, n/30.

  31   The Bradly Company voucher of January 17 was misfiled and had not been paid as of the end of the month. A voucher was prepared for the discount missed.

Required:

Enter the above approved transactions for January in these registers and total the registers. Start with Voucher No. 1 and Check No. 1. You need not include account numbers.

BUSINESS DECISION PROBLEM

Decribe method
used to steal cash;
determine amount
stolen; prepare
correct bank
reconciliation
statement;
describe internal
control
procedures that
would have
prevented such
theft
(L.O. 1,3,4)

The outstanding checks of the Zing Company at November 30, 1995, were:

No. 237	$1,125.00
No. 271	1,225.13
No. 3686	763.88
No. 3687	904.50
No. 3688	1,577.25

During the month, checks numbered 3689–3728 were issued, and all of these checks cleared the bank except Nos. 3727 and 3728 for $1,083.38 and $816.75, respectively. Check Nos. 3686, 3687, and 3688 also cleared the bank.

The bank statement on December 31 showed a balance of $26,937. Service charges amounted to $22.50, and two checks were returned by the bank, one marked NSF in the amount of $128.25 and the other marked "No account" in the amount of $2,250.

Wilson recently retired as the office manager-cashier-bookkeeper for the company and was replaced by Garcia. Garcia noted the absence of an internal control structure but was momentarily deterred from embezzling for lack of a scheme of concealment. Finally, Garcia hit upon several schemes. The $2,250 check marked "No account" by the bank was the product of one scheme. Garcia took cash receipts and replaced them with a check drawn upon a nonexistent account to make it appear that a customer had given the company a worthless check.

The other scheme was more subtle. Garcia pocketed cash receipts to bring them down to an amount sufficient to prepare the following reconciliation statement:

Balance, Cash account, December 31, 1995		$30,630.15
Deduct:		
Worthless check	$2,250.00	
NSF check	128.25	
Service charges	22.50	2,400.75
Adjusted balance, December 31, 1995		$28,229.40
Balance per bank statement, December 31, 1995		$26,937.00
Add: Deposit in transit		3,192.53
		$30,129.53
Deduct: Outstanding checks:		
No. 3727	$1,083.38	
No. 3728	816.75	1,900.13
Adjusted balance, December 31, 1995		$28,229.40

Required:

a. State the nature of the second scheme used by Garcia. How much in total does it appear Garcia has stolen by use of the two schemes together?

b. Prepare a correct bank reconciliation statement as of December 31, 1995.

c. Suggest procedures which would have defeated the attempts of Garcia to steal funds and conceal these actions.

ANSWERS TO SELF-TEST

True-False

1. *False.* Postdated checks are not included as cash.

2. *True.* A company should make sure that enough cash is available to pay bills as they come due.

3. *False.* The cash balance on a bank statement is not usually the same as the cash balance in the depositor's books because of such items as deposits in transit, outstanding checks, bank service charges, etc.

4. *False.* A deposit in transit is one of the items that has been correctly recorded as a debit to the Cash account of the depositor and will be recorded as a deposit by the bank after the bank employees open the night deposit chute.

5. *False.* For convenience, a company may use a petty cash fund for small amounts of cash payments such as delivery charges, postage stamps, etc.

6. *True.* When a voucher register and check register are used, there is no need for a purchases journal or cash disbursements journal. However, a sales journal, cash receipts journal, and general journal would still be used.

Multiple-Choice

1. *d.* An effective internal control structure does not necessarily guarantee a certain level of profits.

2. *a.*

Balance per bank statement	$5,853.60
Add: Deposits in transit	813.60
Less: Outstanding checks	(1,283.40)
Adjusted balance	$5,383.80
Balance per ledger	$5,608.80
Less: NSF check	(183.60)
Service charges	(41.40)
Adjusted balance	$5,383.80

3. *d.* Deposits in transit have been recorded in the company's accounting records but have not yet been recorded in the bank's records.

4. *b.* The entry to record bank service charges on the books is:

Bank Service Charge Expense. . 41.40
    Cash 41.40

5. *d.* The entry to replenish the petty cash fund has a credit to Cash, not Petty Cash.

Postage Expense. xxx
    Cash   xxx

6. *c.* A voucher system is an internal control structure for cash disbursements. Some small companies do not need such a voucher system because the owner usually has enough knowledge of all transactions and personally signs all checks.

PROPERTY, PLANT, AND EQUIPMENT

LEARNING OBJECTIVES

After studying this chapter, you should be able to:

1. List the characteristics of plant assets and identify the costs of acquiring plant assets.
2. List the four major factors affecting depreciation expense.
3. Describe the various methods of calculating depreciation expense.
4. Distinguish between capital and revenue expenditures for plant assets.
5. Describe the subsidiary records used to control plant assets.

In Chapter 3, you were introduced to the classified balance sheet. The asset section of a classified balance sheet is divided into (1) current assets, (2) property, plant, and equipment, and (3) other categories such as "intangible assets" and "long-term investments." Current assets were discussed in previous chapters. This chapter begins a discussion of property, plant, and equipment, which are often called **plant and equipment** or simply **plant assets.**

Plant assets are long-lived assets because their useful lives are expected to last for more than one year. Long-lived assets consist of tangible assets and intangible assets. **Tangible assets** have physical characteristics that we can see and touch. These tangible assets include (1) plant assets such as buildings, machinery, vehicles, and furniture, which are discussed in this chapter; and (2) natural resources such as gas and oil, which are discussed in Chapter 8. *Intangible assets* (also discussed in Chapter 8) have no physical characteristics that we can see and touch but represent exclusive privileges and rights to their owners.

You should be aware that a difference exists between the physical life of an asset and its economic life. For example, on TV you may have seen a demolition crew setting off explosives in a huge building and wondered why a decision was made to destroy what looked like a perfectly good building.

The reason the building was destroyed was because the building had "lived" its economic life. The land on which the building stood could be put to better use, possibly by constructing a new building.

NATURE OF PLANT ASSETS

Objective 1
List the character-
istics of plant
assets and identify
the costs of ac-
quiring plant
assets

To be classified as a *plant asset,* an asset must (1) be tangible, that is, capable of being seen and touched; (2) have a useful service life of more than one year; and (3) be used in business operations rather than held for resale. Common plant assets are buildings, machines, tools, and office equipment. On the balance sheet, you will find these assets included under the heading "Property, plant, and equipment."

Plant assets include all long-lived tangible assets that are used to generate the principal revenues of the business. Inventory is a tangible asset but not a plant asset because inventory is usually not long-lived and it is held for sale rather than for use. What represents a plant asset to one company may be inventory to another. For example, a business such as a retail appliance store may classify a delivery truck as a plant asset because the truck is used to deliver merchandise, but a business such as a truck dealership would classify the same delivery truck as inventory because the truck is held for sale. Also, land held for speculation or not yet put into service is a long-term investment rather than a plant asset because the land is not being used by the business. However, standby equipment that is used only in peak or emergency periods is classified as a plant asset because the equipment is used in the operations of the business.

Accountants view plant assets as a collection of *service potentials* that are consumed over a long period of time. For example, over several years, a delivery truck may provide 100,000 miles of delivery services to an appliance business. A new building may provide 40 years of shelter, while a machine may perform a particular operation on 400,000 parts. In each instance, purchase of the plant asset actually represents the advance payment or prepayment for expected services. Plant asset costs are a *form of prepaid expense*. As was the case with short-term prepayments, the accountant must allocate the cost of these services to the accounting periods benefited.

Accounting for plant assets presents the following four challenges:

1. Record the acquisition cost of the asset.
2. Record the allocation of the asset's original cost to periods of its useful life through depreciation.
3. Record subsequent expenditures on the asset.
4. Account for the disposal of the asset.

These four accounting challenges are shown in Illustration 7.1. Note how the asset's life begins with its procurement and the recording of its acquisition cost, which is usually in the form of a dollar purchase; then, as the asset provides services through time, accountants must record the asset's depreci-

Illustration 7.1
FOUR CHALLENGES IN RECORDING LIFE HISTORY OF A DEPRECIABLE ASSET

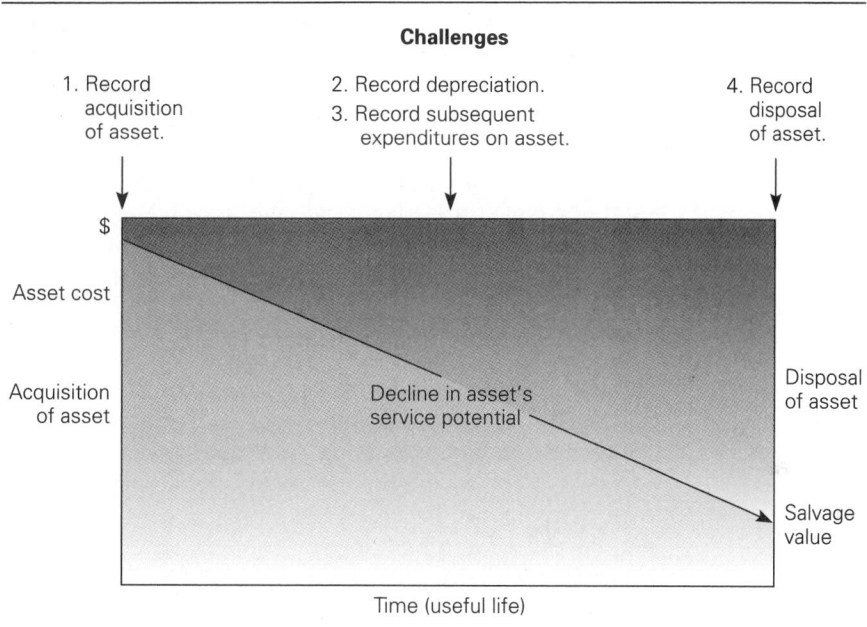

ation and any subsequent expenditures related to the asset; and, finally, accountants must record the disposal of the asset. The first three challenges are discussed in this chapter; the disposal of an asset is discussed in Chapter 8. The last section in this chapter explains how accountants use subsidiary ledgers to control assets.

Remember that in recording the life history of an asset, accountants seek to match expenses related to the asset with the revenues generated by the asset. Since the measurement of periodic expense associated with plant assets affects net income, accounting for property, plant, and equipment is important to financial statement users.

INITIAL RECORDING OF PLANT ASSETS

When a company acquires a plant asset, accountants record the asset at the cost of acquisition (historical cost) because this cost is objective, verifiable, and the best measure of an asset's fair market value at the time of purchase. Even if the market value of the asset changes over time, the **acquisition cost** continues to be the amount reported in the asset account in subsequent accounting periods.

The acquisition cost of a plant asset is the amount of cash/or cash equivalents given up to acquire that asset and place it in operating condition at its proper location. Thus, cost includes all normal, reasonable, and necessary expenditures to obtain the asset and get it ready for use. Acquisition cost also includes the repair and reconditioning costs for used or damaged assets. Unnecessary costs (such as traffic tickets or fines) that must be paid as a result of hauling machinery to a new plant are not part of the acquisition cost of the asset.

In this section, you will learn which costs are capitalized (debited to an asset account) for (1) land and land improvements, (2) buildings, (3) group purchases of assets, (4) machinery and other equipment, (5) self-constructed assets, (6) noncash acquisitions, and (7) gifts of plant assets.

Land and Land Improvements

The cost of land includes its purchase price and other costs such as option cost, if any; real estate commissions; title search and title transfer fees; title insurance premiums; existing mortgage note assumed; unpaid taxes (back taxes) assumed by purchaser; cost of surveying, clearing, and grading; and local assessments for sidewalks, streets, sewers, and water mains. **When land purchased as a building site contains an unusable building that must be removed, the entire purchase price should be debited to Land, including the cost of removing the building less any cash received from the sale of salvaged items, such as crops or fruit on the land, that occurs while the land is being readied for use.**

To illustrate, assume that Spivey Company purchased an old farm on the outskirts of San Diego, California, as a factory site. The company paid $225,000 for the property. In addition, the company agreed to pay unpaid property taxes from previous periods (called *back taxes*) of $12,000. Attorneys' fees and other legal costs relating to the purchase of the farm totaled $1,800. The farm buildings were demolished at a cost of $18,000. Some of the structural pieces of the buildings were salvaged and sold for $3,000. The purpose of the demolition was to construct a new building at the site. Since new construction was to take place, the city assessed Spivey Company $9,000 for water mains, sewers, and street paving. The cost of the land is computed as follows:

	Land
Cost of factory site.	$225,000
Back taxes	12,000
Attorneys' fees and other legal costs	1,800
Demolition.	18,000
Sale of salvaged parts	(3,000)
City assessment	9,000
	$262,800

All costs relating to the farm purchase and razing of the old buildings are assignable to the Land account because the old buildings purchased with the land were not usable. The real goal was to purchase the land, but the land was not available without the buildings.

Land is considered to have an unlimited life and is therefore not depreciable. However, **land improvements,** including driveways, temporary landscaping, parking lots, fences, lighting systems, and sprinkler systems, are attachments to the land that have limited lives and therefore are depreciable. Depreciable land improvements should be recorded in a separate account called Land Improvements. The cost of permanent landscaping, including leveling and grading, should be recorded in the Land account.

Buildings

When an existing building is purchased, its cost includes purchase price, repair and remodeling costs, unpaid taxes assumed by the purchaser, legal costs, and real estate commissions paid.

The cost of constructing new buildings is often more difficult to determine. Usually this cost includes architect's fees; building permits; payments to contractors; *cost of digging the foundation;* labor and materials to build the building; salaries of officers supervising the construction; and insurance, taxes, and *interest during the construction period.* **Any miscellaneous amounts earned from the building during construction reduce the cost of the building.** For example, if a small completed portion of the building is rented out during construction of the remainder of the building, the rental proceeds are credited to the Buildings account rather than to a revenue account.

Group Purchases of Assets

Sometimes land and other assets are purchased for a lump sum. When land and buildings are purchased together and both are to be used, the total cost should be divided so that separate ledger accounts may be established for land and for buildings. This division of cost is necessary to establish the proper balances in the appropriate accounts, which is especially important later because reported income will be affected by the depreciation recorded on the buildings.

Returning to our example of Spivey Company, suppose one of the existing buildings was going to be remodeled for use by the company. Then, Spivey would have to determine what portion of the purchase price of the farm, back taxes, and legal fees ($225,000 + $12,000 + $1,800 = $238,800) it could assign to the buildings and what portion it could assign to the land. (The net cost of demolition would not be incurred, and the city assessment would be incurred at a later time.) Spivey would assign the $238,800 to the land and the buildings on the basis of their appraised values. For example, assume that the land itself was appraised at $162,000 and the buildings were appraised at $108,000. The cost assignable to each of these plant assets would be determined as follows:

Asset	Appraised Value	Percent of Total Value
Land	$162,000	60% (162/270)
Buildings . . .	108,000	40 (108/270)
	$270,000	100% (270/270)

	Percent of Total Value	×	Purchase Price	=	Cost Assigned
Land	60%	×	$238,800*	=	$143,280
Buildings	40	×	238,800	=	95,520
					$238,800

* The purchase price is the sum of the cash price, back taxes, and legal fees.

The journal entry to record the purchase of the land and buildings would be:

Land	143,280	
Buildings	95,520	
Cash		238,800
To record purchase of land and buildings.		

When the city eventually assesses the charges for the water mains, sewers, and street paving, these costs will still be debited to the Land account as they were in the previous example.

Machinery and Other Equipment

When machinery or other equipment (such as delivery or office equipment) is purchased, its cost includes the seller's *net* invoice price (whether the discount is taken or not), transportation charges, insurance in transit, cost of installation, costs of accessories, testing and break-in costs, and other costs needed to put the machine or equipment in operating condition in its intended location for use. **The cost of machinery does not include costs of removing and disposing of a replaced, old machine that has been used in operations.** Such costs are part of the gain or loss on disposal of the old machine, as discussed in Chapter 8.

To illustrate, assume that Clark Company purchased new equipment to replace old equipment that it has used in operations for five years. The company paid a net purchase price of $150,000, brokerage fees of $5,000, legal fees of $2,000, and freight and insurance in transit of $3,000. In addition to these expenses, the company paid $1,500 to remove old equipment and

$2,000 to install new equipment. The cost of new equipment is computed as follows:

Net purchase price	$150,000
Brokerage fees	5,000
Legal fees	2,000
Freight and insurance in transit	3,000
Installation costs	2,000
Total cost.	$162,000

Self-Constructed Assets

If a company builds a plant asset for its own use, the cost would include cost of materials and labor directly traceable to construction of the asset. Also included in the cost of the asset are indirect costs, such as interest costs related to the asset, and amounts paid for utilities (such as heat, light, and power) and for supplies used during construction. To determine how much of these indirect costs should be capitalized, the company compares utility and supply costs during the construction period with utility and supply costs paid in a period when no construction occurred. The increase is recorded as part of the asset's cost. For example, assume a company normally incurred a $600 utility bill for June. This year a machine was constructed during June, and the utility bill was $975. The $375 increase would be recorded as part of the machine's cost.

To illustrate further, assume that Tanner Company needed a new die-casting machine and received a quote from Smith Company for $23,000, plus $1,000 freight costs. Tanner decided to build the machine rather than buy it. The company incurred the following costs to build the machine: materials, $4,000; labor, $13,000; and indirect services of heat, power, and supplies, $3,000. The machine should be recorded at its cost of $20,000 ($4,000 + $13,000 + $3,000) rather than $24,000, the price that would have been paid if the machine had been purchased. The $20,000 is the cost of the resources given up to construct the machine. Also, recording the machine at $24,000 would require Tanner to recognize a gain on construction of the assets. Accountants generally do not subscribe to the idea that a business can earn revenue (or realize a gain), and therefore net income, by dealing with itself.

The general guidelines discussed and illustrated above can be applied to other plant assets, such as furniture and fixtures. The accounting methods are the same.

Noncash Acquisitions

When a plant asset is purchased for cash, its acquisition cost is simply the agreed cash price. However, when plant assets are acquired in exchange for other noncash assets (shares of stock, a customer's note, or tract of land) or as gifts, a cash price is more difficult to establish. Three possible asset valuation bases are discussed in this section.

Fair Market Value. **Fair market value** is the price that would be received for an item being sold in the normal course of business (not at a forced liquidation sale). Accountants seek to record noncash exchange transactions at fair market value.

The general rule on noncash exchanges is that **the noncash asset received is valued at its fair market value or the fair market value of what was given up, whichever is more clearly evident.** The reason for not using the book value of the old asset to value the new asset is that the asset being given up is often carried in the accounting records at historical cost or book value. Neither amount may adequately represent the actual fair market value of either the old or the new asset. Therefore, if the fair market value of one of the assets is clearly evident, this amount is more representative of the value that should be recorded for the new asset in the accounting records at the time of the exchange.

Appraised Value. Exchanges of items, neither of which has a clearly determinable fair market value, may be recorded at their appraised values as determined by a professional appraiser. **Appraised value** is an expert's opinion as to what an item's fair market price would be if the item were sold. Appraisals are often used to value works of art, rare books, and antiques.

Book Value. The **book value** of an asset is its recorded cost less accumulated depreciation. An old asset's book value is usually not a valid indication of the new asset's fair market value. The book value of an asset given up is an acceptable basis for measuring the value of the new asset received only if a better basis is not available.

Gifts of Plant Assets

Occasionally, a company will receive an asset without giving up anything for it. For example, to attract industry to an area and provide jobs for local residents, a city may give a tract of land to a company on which to build a factory. Although such a gift costs the recipient company nothing, the asset (land) is usually recorded at its fair market value. Gifts of plant assets are recorded at fair market value because accounting seeks to provide information on all assets owned by the company. Omitting some assets may make information provided misleading. Assets received as gifts are credited to Paid-In Capital—Donations, which appears in the stockholders' equity section of the balance sheet.

DEPRECIATION OF PLANT ASSETS

Depreciation is recorded on all plant assets except land. Since the amount of depreciation may be relatively large, depreciation expense is often a significant factor in determining net income. For this reason, most financial statement users are interested in the amount of, and the methods used to compute, a company's depreciation expense.

Depreciation is the amount of plant asset cost allocated to each accounting period benefiting from the plant asset's use and is a *process of allocation, not valuation*. Since eventually all assets except land wear out or become so inadequate or outmoded that they are sold or discarded, depreciation must be recorded on every plant asset except land. Depreciation is recorded even when the market value of a plant asset temporarily rises above its original cost because eventually the asset will no longer be useful to its current owner.

Major causes of depreciation are (1) physical deterioration, (2) inadequacy for future needs, and (3) obsolescence. **Physical deterioration** results from the use of the asset—wear and tear—and the action of the elements. For example, an automobile may have to be replaced after a time because its body rusted out. The **inadequacy** of a plant asset is its inability to produce enough products or provide enough services to meet current demands. For example, an airline cannot provide air service for 125 passengers on a flight serviced by a plane with a seating capacity of 90. The **obsolescence** of an asset is its decline in usefulness brought about by inventions and technological progress. For example, the development of the xerographic process of reproducing printed matter rendered almost all previous methods of duplication obsolete.

The use of a plant asset in business operations transforms a plant asset cost into an operating expense. Depreciation, then, is an operating expense resulting from the use of a depreciable plant asset.

Because depreciation expense does not require a current cash outlay, it is often called a *noncash expense*. Cash was given up in the period when the asset was acquired, not during the periods when depreciation expense is recorded.

Factors Affecting Depreciation

Objective 2
List the four major factors affecting depreciation expense

To compute depreciation expense, accountants consider four major factors:

1. Cost of the asset.
2. Estimated salvage value of the asset. **Salvage value** (or **scrap value**) is the amount of money the company expects to recover, less disposal costs, on the date a plant asset is scrapped, sold, or traded in.
3. Estimated useful life of the asset. **Useful life** refers to the length of time the company owning the asset intends to use it; useful life is not necessarily the same time period as either economic life or physical life. The economic life of a car may be 7 years and its physical life may be 10 years, but if a company has a policy of trading cars every 3 years, the useful life for depreciation purposes is 3 years. Useful life may be ex-

pressed in years, months, working hours, or units of production. Obsolescence may also affect useful life. For example, a machine may be capable of producing units for 20 years, but it is expected to be obsolete in 6 years. Thus, its estimated useful life is 6 years—not 20.

4. Depreciation method to be used in depreciating the asset. The four common depreciation methods are discussed in the next section.

Illustration 7.2 shows the relationship among these factors. Assume Ace Company purchased an office building for a cost of $100,000. The building has an estimated salvage value of $15,000 and a useful life of 20 years. The depreciable cost of the building is $85,000 (cost less estimated salvage value), and this depreciable base is allocated over the useful life of the building using a proper depreciation method under the circumstances.

Now you know the nature of plant assets and how to initially record them. Next, you are ready to study the various plant asset depreciation methods accountants use. You may have read about some of these depreciation methods in the business section of your daily newspaper.

Depreciation Methods[1]

Objective 3
Describe the
various methods
of calculating
depreciation ex-
pense

Today, many different methods are available for calculating depreciation on assets. This section discusses and illustrates the most common methods—straight-line, units-of-production, and two accelerated depreciation methods (sum-of-the-years'-digits and double-declining-balance).

As is true for inventory methods, a company is normally free to adopt the method(s) of depreciation it believes most appropriate for its business operations. The theoretical guideline is to use a depreciation method that

Illustration 7.2
FACTORS AFFECTING DEPRECIATION

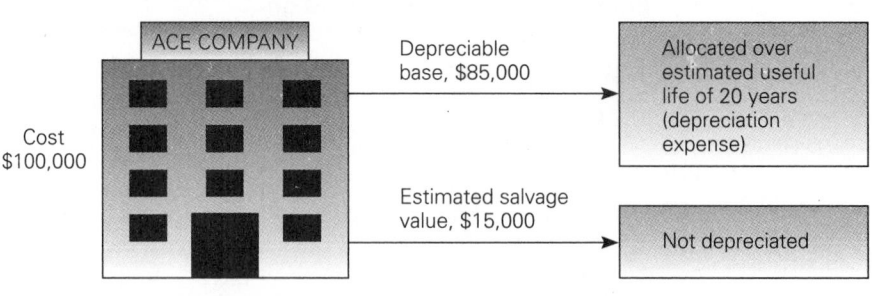

---

[1] Because depreciation expense is an estimate, calculations may be rounded to the nearest dollar.

Illustration 7.3
DEPRECIATION METHODS USED

	Number of Companies			
	1990	1989	1988	1987
Straight-line	560	562	563	559
Declining-balance.	38	40	44	44
Sum-of-the-years'-digits	11	16	11	12
Accelerated method—not specified	69	69	70	76
Units-of-production	50	50	53	51
Other	8	8	9	12

SOURCE: American Institute of Certified Public Accountants, *Accounting Trends & Techniques* (New York: AICPA, 1991), p. 325.

reflects most closely the underlying economic circumstances. Thus, companies should adopt the depreciation method that allocates plant asset cost to accounting periods according to the benefits received from the use of the asset. Illustration 7.3 shows the frequency of use of these methods for a sample of 600 companies. You can see that most companies use the straight-line method for financial reporting purposes. Also, some companies use one method for certain assets and another method for other assets.

In practice, the measurement of benefits from the use of a plant asset is impractical and often not possible. As a result, a depreciation method must meet only one standard—the depreciation method *must* allocate plant asset cost to accounting periods in a systematic and rational manner. The four methods discussed in this section meet this requirement.

Regardless of the method or methods chosen, the company must disclose its depreciation method(s) in the footnotes to its financial statements. This information is included in the first footnote, which contains a summary of significant accounting policies.

The disclosure is generally straightforward: Sears, Roebuck and Co.'s Annual Report states simply that "depreciation is provided principally by the straight-line method." Companies may use different depreciation methods for different assets. General Electric uses an accelerated method for most of its property, plant, and equipment; however, some assets are depreciated on a straight-line basis, while the company's mining properties are depreciated under the units-of-production method.

The illustrations of the four depreciation methods given below are based on the following data: On January 1, 1995, a machine was purchased for $54,000 with an estimated useful life of 10 years, or 50,000 units of output, and an estimated salvage value of $4,000.

Straight-Line Method.   The **straight-line depreciation** method has been the most widely used depreciation method in the United States for many years because it is easily applied. (You have already applied this method in Chapter 3.) To apply the straight-line method, an equal amount of plant asset cost is charged to each accounting period. The formula for calculating depreciation under the straight-line method is:

$$\frac{\text{Depreciation}}{\text{per period}} = \frac{\text{Asset cost} - \text{Estimated salvage value}}{\text{Number of accounting periods}}{\text{in estimated useful life}}$$

Using our example of a machine purchased for $54,000, the depreciation is:

$$\frac{\$54,000 - \$4,000}{10 \text{ years}} = \$5,000 \text{ per year}$$

Illustration 7.4 presents a schedule of annual depreciation entries, cumulative balances in the accumulated depreciation account, and the book (or carrying) values of the $54,000 machine.

Use of the straight-line method is appropriate for assets where (1) time rather than obsolescence is the major factor limiting the asset's life and (2) relatively constant amounts of periodic services are received from the asset. Assets that possess these features include items such as pipelines, fencing, and storage tanks.

Units-of-Production (Output) Method.   The **units-of-production depreciation** method assigns an equal amount of depreciation to each unit of product manufactured or service rendered by an asset. Since this method of depreciation is based on physical output, it is applied in situations where usage rather than obsolescence is the main factor leading to the demise of the asset. Under this method, first the depreciation charge per unit of output is

Illustration 7.4
STRAIGHT-LINE DEPRECIATION SCHEDULE

End of Year	Depreciation Expense Dr.; Accumulated Depreciation Cr.	Total Accumulated Depreciation	Book Value
			$54,000
1	$ 5,000	$ 5,000	49,000
2	5,000	10,000	44,000
3	5,000	15,000	39,000
4	5,000	20,000	34,000
5	5,000	25,000	29,000
6	5,000	30,000	24,000
7	5,000	35,000	19,000
8	5,000	40,000	14,000
9	5,000	45,000	9,000
10	5,000	50,000	4,000*
	$50,000		

* Estimated salvage value.

computed; then this figure is multiplied by the number of units of goods or services produced during the accounting period to find the period's depreciation expense. The formula is:

$$\frac{\text{Depreciation}}{\text{per unit}} = \frac{\text{Asset cost} - \text{Estimated salvage value}}{\substack{\text{Estimated total units of production}\\ \text{(or service) during useful life of asset}}}$$

$$\frac{\text{Depreciation}}{\text{per period}} = \frac{\text{Depreciation}}{\text{per unit}} \times \frac{\text{Number of units of goods}}{\text{or services produced}}$$

The depreciation charge for the $54,000 machine is determined as follows:

$$\frac{\$54,000 - \$4,000}{50,000 \text{ units}} = \$1 \text{ per unit}$$

If the machine produced 1,000 units in 1995 and 2,500 units in 1996, depreciation expense for those years would be $1,000 and $2,500, respectively.

Accelerated Depreciation Methods. **Accelerated depreciation methods** record higher amounts of depreciation during the early years of an asset's life and lower amounts in the asset's later years. A business might choose an accelerated depreciation method for the following reasons:

1. The value of the benefits received from the asset decline with age (for example, office buildings).
2. The asset is a high-technology asset subject to rapid obsolescence (for example, computers).
3. Repairs increase substantially in the asset's later years, and under this method the depreciation and repairs together remain fairly constant over the asset's life (for example, automobiles).

The two most common accelerated methods of depreciation are the *sum-of-the-years'-digits (SOYD)* method and the *double-declining-balance (DDB)* method.

Sum-of-the-Years'-Digits Method. The **sum-of-the-years'-digits (SOYD)** method is so called because the consecutive digits for each year of an asset's estimated life are added together and used as the denominator of a fraction. The numerator is the number of years of useful life remaining at the *beginning* of the accounting period. To compute that period's depreciation expense, this fraction is then multiplied by the acquisition cost of the asset less the estimated salvage value. The formula is:

$$\frac{\text{Depreciation}}{\text{per period}} = \frac{\substack{\text{Number of years of useful}\\ \text{life remaining at beginning}\\ \text{of accounting period}}}{\text{SOYD}} \times \left(\frac{\text{Asset}}{\text{cost}} - \frac{\text{Estimated}}{\text{salvage value}}\right)$$

The years are totaled to find SOYD. For an asset with a 10-year useful life, SOYD = 10 + 9 + 8 + 7 + 6 + 5 + 4 + 3 + 2 + 1 = 55. Alternatively, rather than adding the digits for all years together, the following formula can be used to find the SOYD for any given number of periods:

$$SOYD = \frac{n(n + 1)}{2}$$

where n is the number of periods in the asset's useful life. Thus, SOYD for an asset with a 10-year useful life is:

$$SOYD = \frac{10(10 + 1)}{2} = 55$$

The SOYD method is applied to the data given earlier for the $54,000 machine as follows. First, determine that at the beginning of year 1 (1995), the machine has 10 years of useful life remaining. Then, using the formula above, compute the first year's depreciation as $10/55$ times $50,000 (the $54,000 cost less the $4,000 salvage value). The depreciation for the first year is $9,091, as shown in Illustration 7.5. Note that the fraction gets smaller every year, resulting in a declining depreciation charge for each successive year.

Double-Declining-Balance Method.   The **double-declining-balance (DDB)** method of computing periodic depreciation charges is applied by first calculating the straight-line depreciation rate. The straight-line rate is calculated by dividing 100% by the number of years of useful life of the asset. Then multiply this rate by 2. The resulting double-declining rate is applied to the

Illustration 7.5
SUM-OF-THE-YEARS'-DIGITS DEPRECIATION SCHEDULE

End of Year		Depreciation Expense Dr.; Accumulated Depreciation Cr.	Total Accumulated Depreciation	Book Value
				$54,000
1.	$50,000* × $10/55$	$ 9,091	$ 9,091	44,909
2.	$50,000 × $9/55$	8,182	17,273	36,727
3.	$50,000 × $8/55$	7,273	24,546	29,454
4.	$50,000 × $7/55$	6,364	30,910	23,090
5.	$50,000 × $6/55$	5,455	36,365	17,635
6.	$50,000 × $5/55$	4,455	40,910	13,090
7.	$50,000 × $4/55$	3,636	44,546	9,454
8.	$50,000 × $3/55$	2,727	47,273	6,727
9.	$50,000 × $2/55$	1,818	49,091	4,909
10.	$50,000 × $1/55$	909	50,000	4,000
		$50,000		

* $54,000 cost − $4,000 salvage value.

declining book value of the asset. **Salvage value is ignored in making the calculations.** However, at the point where book value is equal to the salvage value, no more depreciation is taken. The formula for DDB depreciation is:

$$\frac{\text{Depreciation}}{\text{per period}} = \left(2 \times \frac{\text{Straight-line}}{\text{rate}}\right) \times \left(\frac{\text{Asset}}{\text{cost}} - \frac{\text{Accumulated}}{\text{depreciation}}\right)$$

The calculations for the $54,000 machine using the DDB method are shown in Illustration 7.6. The straight-line rate is 10% (100%/10 years), which, when doubled, yields a DDB rate of 20%. (Expressed as fractions, the straight-line rate is $\frac{1}{10}$, and the DDB rate is $\frac{2}{10}$.) Since at the beginning of year 1 no accumulated depreciation has been recorded, the calculation is based on cost. In each of the following years, the calculation is based on book value at the beginning of the year.

In the 10th year, depreciation could be increased to $3,247 if the asset is to be retired and its salvage value is still $4,000. This higher depreciation amount for the last year ($3,247) would reduce the book value of $7,247 down to the salvage value of $4,000. If an asset is continued in service, depreciation should only be recorded until the asset's book value equals its estimated salvage value.

Illustration 7.7 summarizes the four depreciation methods.

Illustration 7.8 compares the three depreciation methods discussed above—straight-line, sum-of-the-years'-digits, and double-declining-balance—using the same example of a machine purchased on January 1, 1995, for $54,000. The machine has an estimated useful life of 10 years and an estimated salvage value of $4,000.

Illustration 7.6
DOUBLE-DECLINING-BALANCE (DDB) DEPRECIATION SCHEDULE

End of Year	Depreciation Expense Dr.; Accumulated Depreciation Cr.	Total Accumulated Depreciation	Book Value
			$54,000
1. (20% of $54,000)	$10,800	$10,800	43,200
2. (20% of $43,200)	8,640	19,440	34,560
3. (20% of $34,560)	6,912	26,352	27,648
4. (20% of $27,648)	5,530	31,882	22,118
5. (20% of $22,118)	4,424	36,306	17,694
6. (20% of $17,694)	3,539	39,845	14,155
7. (20% of $14,155)	2,831	42,676	11,324
8. (20% of $11,324)	2,265	44,941	9,059
9. (20% of $9,059)	1,812	46,753	7,247
10. (20% of $7,247)	1,449*	48,202	5,798

* This amount could be $3,247 so as to reduce the book value to the estimated salvage value of $4,000. Accumulated depreciation would then be $50,000.

Illustration 7.7
SUMMARY OF DEPRECIATION METHODS

Method	Base	Calculation
Straight-line	Asset cost − Estimated salvage value	Base ÷ Number of accounting periods in estimated useful life
Units-of-production	Asset cost − Estimated salvage value	(Base ÷ Estimated total units of production) × Units produced this period
Sum-of-the-years'-digits	Asset cost − Estimated salvage value	Base × (Number of years of useful life remaining at beginning of accounting period ÷ SOYD)
Double-declining-balance	Asset cost − Accumulated depreciation	Base × (2 × Straight-line rate)

Partial-Year Depreciation

So far we have assumed that the assets were put into service at the beginning of an accounting period and have ignored the fact that assets are often put into service *during* an accounting period. When assets are acquired sometime during an accounting period, the first recording of depreciation is usually for a partial year. The depreciation for the partial year is normally calculated to the nearest full month the asset was in service. For example, an asset purchased on or before the 15th day of the month is treated as if it were purchased on the 1st day of the month; an asset purchased after the 15th of the month is treated as if it were acquired on the 1st day of the following month.

In this section, you will learn how to calculate partial-year depreciation for each of the four depreciation methods—straight-line, units-of-production, sum-of-the-years'-digits, and double-declining-balance. The example used is a machine purchased for $7,600 on September 1, 1995, with an estimated salvage value of $400 and an estimated useful life of five years.

Straight-Line Method. Partial-year depreciation calculations for the straight-line depreciation method are relatively easy. First, find the 12-month charge by the normal computation explained earlier. Then, multiply this annual amount by the fraction of the year for which the asset was in use. For example, for the $7,600 machine purchased September 1, 1995 (estimated salvage value, $400; and estimated useful life, five years), the annual straight-line depreciation is [($7,600 − $400)/5 years] = $1,440. The machine will be used four months prior to the end of the accounting year, December 31, or one third of a year. The 1995 depreciation is ($1,440/3) = $480.

Units-of-Production Method. The units-of-production method requires no unusual computations to record depreciation for a partial year. The partial-year depreciation is still computed by multiplying the depreciation charge per unit by the number of units produced. The charge for a

Illustration 7.8
COMPARISON OF STRAIGHT-LINE, SUM-OF-THE-YEARS'-DIGITS, AND
DOUBLE-DECLINING-BALANCE DEPRECIATION METHODS

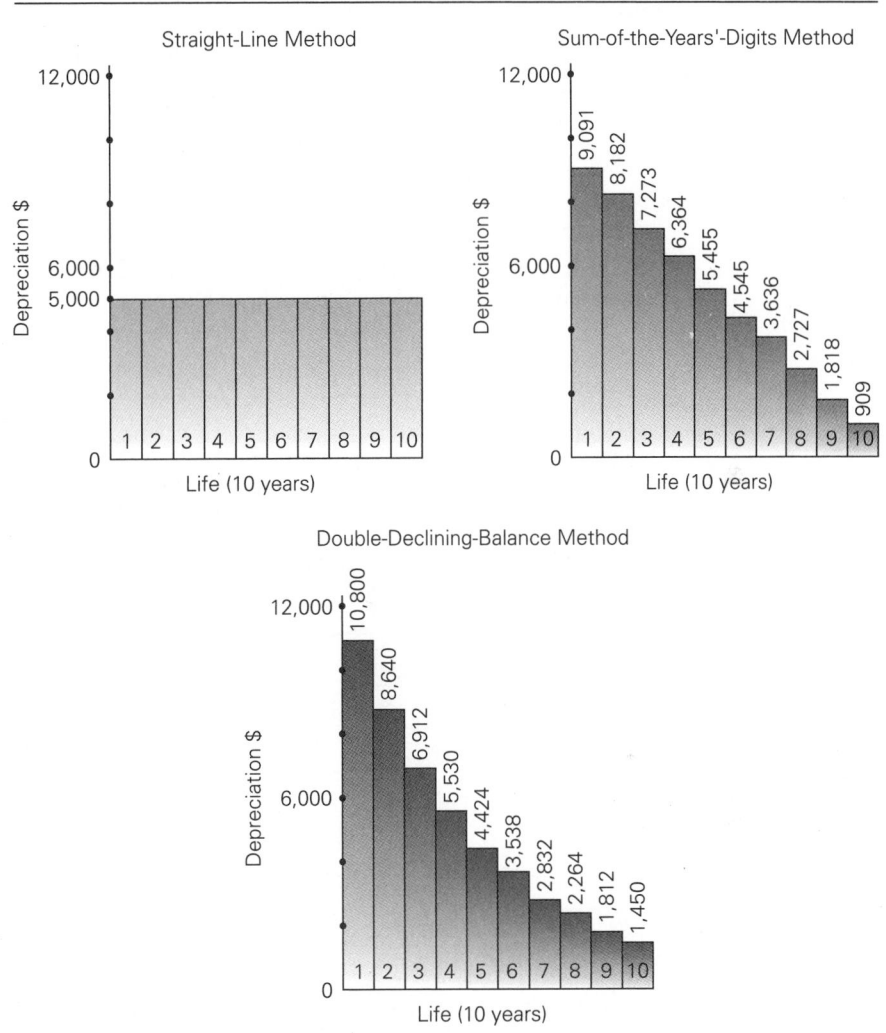

partial year will probably be less than for a full year because fewer units of goods or services are produced.

Sum-of-the-Years'-Digits Method.   Under the SOYD method, the computation of partial-year depreciation is more complex. Problems occur because the 12 months for which depreciation is computed using the SOYD fraction do not correspond with the 12 months for which the financial statements are being prepared. For example, the depreciation recorded in 1995 on the $7,600 asset is for the last four months of 1995, which is the first one third of the first year of the asset's life. The depreciation for the four months of 1995 is computed as ($7,600 − $400) × 5/15 × 1/3; thus, depreciation is $800. In 1996, the depreciation recorded is $2,240, computed as follows:

For the first two thirds of the year:	($7,200 × 5/15 × 2/3) =	$1,600
For the last one third of the year:	($7,200 × 4/15 × 1/3) =	640
Total depreciation expense for 1996		$2,240

With the SOYD method, annual depreciation charges will have to be computed in this same way throughout the asset's life as follows:

Year	Depreciation for Each Year of Life of Asset (September 1–August 31)	Depreciation for Each Calendar Year (January 1–December 31)	
		1995:	
		Sept. 1–Dec. 31($2,400 × 1/3) =	$ 800
1	$7,200 × 5/15 = $2,400	1996:	
		Jan. 1–Aug. 31 ($2,400 × 2/3) = $1,600	
		Sept. 1–Dec. 31($1,920 × 1/3) = 640	
			2,240
2	$7,200 × 4/15 = 1,920	1997:	
		Jan. 1–Aug. 31 ($1,920 × 2/3) = $1,280	
		Sept. 1–Dec. 31($1,440 × 1/3) = 480	
			1,760
3	$7,200 × 3/15 = 1,440	1998:	
		Jan. 1–Aug. 31 ($1,440 × 2/3) = $ 960	
		Sept. 1–Dec. 31 ($960 × 1/3) = 320	
			1,280
4	$7,200 × 2/15 = 960	1999:	
		Jan. 1–Aug. 31 ($960 × 2/3) = $ 640	
		Sept. 1–Dec. 31 ($480 × 1/3) = 160	
			800
5	$7,200 × 1/15 = 480	2000:	
		Jan. 1–Aug. 31 ($480 × 2/3) =	320
	Total depreciation= $7,200	Total depreciation =	$7,200

Double-Declining-Balance Method. Under the double-declining-balance method, it is relatively easy to determine depreciation for a partial year and then for subsequent full years. For the partial year, simply multiply the fixed rate times the cost of the asset times the fraction of the partial year. For example, DDB depreciation on the $7,600 asset for 1995 is ($7,600 × 0.4 × 1/3) = $1,013. For subsequent years, the depreciation is computed using the regular procedure of multiplying the book value at the beginning of the period by the fixed rate. In this case, the 1996 depreciation would be $[(\$7,600 - \$1,013) \times 0.4] = \$2,635$.

Changes in Estimates

After an asset is depreciated down to its estimated salvage value, no more depreciation is recorded on the asset even if it continues to be used. However, when the estimated useful life of an asset or its salvage value is found to be incorrect *before* the asset is depreciated down to its estimated salvage value, revised depreciation charges are computed. These revised charges do not correct *past* depreciation taken; **they merely compensate for past incorrect charges through changed expense amounts in current and future periods.** The new depreciation charge per period is computed by dividing the book value less the newly estimated salvage value by the estimated periods of useful life remaining.

For example, assume that a machine cost $30,000, has an estimated salvage value of $3,000, and originally had an estimated useful life of eight years. At the end of the fourth year of the machine's life, the balance in its accumulated depreciation account (assuming use of the straight-line method) was $(\$30,000 - \$3,000) \times \frac{4}{8} = \$13,500$. Now assume that at the beginning of the fifth year it is estimated that the asset will last six more years. The newly estimated salvage value is $2,700. The revised depreciation per period is determined as follows:

Original cost	$30,000
Less: Accumulated depreciation at the end of 4th year . . .	13,500
Book value at the beginning of 5th year	$16,500
Revised salvage value.	2,700
Remaining depreciable base.	$13,800
Revised depreciation per period: $13,800/6	$ 2,300

Had the units-of-production method been in use, a revision of the life estimate would be in the form of units. Thus, to determine depreciation expense, a new per unit depreciation charge must be computed by dividing book value less salvage value by the estimated remaining units of production. This per unit charge is then multiplied by the periodic production to determine depreciation expense.

Continuing the above machine example and using the double-declining-balance method, the book value at the beginning of year 5 would be $9,492.19 (cost of $30,000 less accumulated depreciation of $20,507.81). Depreciation expense for year 5 would be calculated as twice the new straight-line rate times book value. The straight-line rate is $100\%/6 = 16.67\%$. So twice the straight-line rate is 33.33%, or $\frac{1}{3}$. Thus, $\frac{1}{3} \times \$9,492.19 = \$3,164.06$. Under the sum-of-the-years'-digits method, a new fraction must be calculated. The sum-of-the-years'-digits is now $6 + 5 + 4 + 3 + 2 + 1 =$

21. The fraction for year 5 is ⁶⁄₂₁. Depreciation under the sum-of-the-years'-digits method would be computed as follows:

Book value at the beginning of 5th year	$10,500.00
Revised salvage value.	2,700.00
Remaining depreciable base.	$ 7,800.00
Depreciation expense for year 5: $7,800 × ⁶⁄₂₁	$ 2,228.57

Depreciation for Tax Purposes

Tax depreciation is substantially different than depreciation used for accounting purposes. In accounting, depreciation methods are designed to match the expense of a capital investment against the revenue the investment produces. The depreciable period or useful life used for tax purposes is based on law and not on the actual useful life of the asset; thus, no attempt is made to match revenues and expenses.

Before 1981, several depreciation methods were available for tax purposes, including methods described in this chapter. The Economic Recovery Tax Act of 1981 introduced a new depreciation system known as the *Accelerated Cost Recovery System (ACRS)*. However, the Tax Reform Act of 1986 substantially modified the ACRS rules. For purposes of discussion, we shall refer to these rules as **modified ACRS.**

The assets are grouped into one of eight different classes (see the table at the top of the next page). Each class has an assigned life over which costs of the assets (not reduced by salvage) are depreciated.

Assets in the 3-, 5-, 7-, and 10-year classes may be depreciated by using either the 200% declining-balance method, earlier referred to as the double-declining-balance method, or the straight-line method. Assets in the 15- and 20-year classes may be depreciated by using either the 150% declining-balance method or the straight-line method. Assets in the 27.5- and 31.5-year classes must be depreciated by using straight-line depreciation. The Internal Revenue Service provides tables that may be used in applying these methods. The declining-balance methods result in faster write-offs in the first few years of an investment's life. Cash saved from reduced taxes in the early years of life of the assets can be invested in new productive assets or can be applied to the replacement of the old assets when they become obsolete or worn out.

Tax depreciation methods are not generally acceptable for financial reporting purposes because they have little relation to the actual useful life of the asset, and these methods do not necessarily match revenues and expenses. Thus, tax depreciation methods only apply to the preparation of income tax returns.

Class of Investment	Kinds of Assets
3 years	Investment in some short-lived assets.
5 years	Automobiles, light-duty trucks, and machinery and equipment used in research and development.
7 years	All other machinery and equipment, such as dies, drills or presses, furniture, and fixtures.
10 years	Some longer-lived equipment.
15 years	Sewage treatment plants and telephone distribution plants.
20 years	Sewer pipes and very long-lived equipment.
27.5 years	Residential rental property.
31.5 years	Nonresidential real estate.

Depreciation and Financial Reporting

APB Opinion No. 12 requires that the methods of depreciation used and the amount of depreciation expense for the period be separately disclosed in the body of the income statement or in the notes to the financial statements. Major classes of plant assets and their related accumulated depreciation amounts are to be reported as shown in Illustration 7.9 (using assumed data).

The presentation of cost less accumulated depreciation in the balance sheet gives the statement user a better understanding of the percentages of a company's plant assets that have been used up than if the balance sheet presented only the book value (remaining undepreciated cost) of the assets. For example, reporting buildings of $75,000 less $45,000 of accumulated depreciation, resulting in a net amount of $30,000, is quite different from merely reporting $30,000 of buildings. In the first case, the statement user

Illustration 7.9
PARTIAL BALANCE SHEET

REED COMPANY
Partial Balance Sheet
June 30, 1995

Property, plant, and equipment:		
Land		$30,000
Buildings	$75,000	
Less: Accumulated depreciation	45,000	30,000
Equipment.	$ 9,000	
Less: Accumulated depreciation	1,500	7,500
Total property, plant, and equipment		$67,500

A BROADER PERSPECTIVE

MET-PRO CORPORATION (JAN.)

	1991	1990
Total current assets	$18,910,499	$18,521,209
Property, plant and equipment, at cost, net—Note 5	9,220,082	7,943,024
Costs in excess of net assets of businesses acquired	1,687,093	1,716,961
Deferred income taxes	54,300	—
Other assets	1,071,453	512,945
	$30,943,427	$28,694,139

NOTES TO FINANCIAL STATEMENTS

1 (In Part): Summary of Significant Accounting Policies

Property, plant and equipment:
    Property, plant and equipment is recorded at cost. Depreciation is computed principally by use of the straight-line method based upon the estimated useful lives of the various classes of assets. Expenditures for maintenance and repairs are charged to expense as incurred. Renewals and betterments are capitalized (see Note 5).

5. Property, Plant and Equipment
    Property, plant and equipment was comprised of the following [see the table below]:

    Depreciation and amortization of property, plant and equipment charged to operations amounted to $939,167, $936,755 and $929,909, for the years ended in 1991, 1990 and 1989, respectively

    During the year ended January 31, 1991, the Company entered into a $2.3 million contract for the design and construction of a facility to replace an existing facility in Hatfield, Pennsylvania. Subsequent to January 31, 1991, the Company received a $2.5 million loan commitment from a bank for the construction of this facility. As of January 31, 1991, no borrowings had been made under this commitment.

    Also during the year ended January 31, 1991, the Company acquired a larger plant facility in Owosso, Michigan, to replace an existing facility there. The move into the new facility was completed prior to January 31, 1991. The former facility, with a net book value of approximately $763,000, has been reclassified into other assets.

SOURCE: American Institute of Certified Public Accountants, *Accounting Trends & Techniques* (New York: AICPA, 1991), p. 160.

	Estimated Useful Life (Years)	January 31, 1991	January 31, 1990
Land	—	$ 1,350,739	$ 802,833
Building and improvements	10–40	7,288,651	6,286,289
Machinery and equipment	5–10	5,985,218	5,694,102
Furniture and fixtures	5–20	1,866,869	1,794,572
Automotive equipment	3 and 4	579,340	458,830
Leasehold improvements	Term of lease	248,860	238,576
Construction in progress		36,191	—
		$17,355,868	$15,275,202
Less accumulated depreciation		8,135,786	7,332,178
		$ 9,220,082	$ 7,943,024

can see that the assets are about 60% used up. In the latter case, the statement user has no way of knowing whether the assets are new or old.

A Misconception.   Some financial statement users mistakenly believe that the amount of accumulated depreciation represents funds available for replacing old plant assets with new assets. **However, the accumulated depreciation account balance does not represent cash; accumulated depreciation shows simply how much of an asset's cost has been charged to expense.** The plant asset and its contra account, accumulated depreciation, are used so that data on the total original acquisition cost and accumulated depreciation are readily available to meet reporting requirements.

Costs or Market Values in the Balance Sheet.   Plant assets are reported in the balance sheet at *original* cost less accumulated depreciation. One of the justifications for reporting the remaining undepreciated costs of the asset rather than market values is the going-concern concept. As you recall from Chapter 1, the going-concern concept assumes that the company will remain in business indefinitely, which implies the company will use its plant assets rather than sell them. Market values generally are not considered relevant for use in the primary financial statements, although they may be reported in supplemental statements.

Furthermore, an asset cannot be written up to a market value above its cost merely because its value has increased. Neither can an asset be written down below its cost if future revenues from using the asset are expected to exceed its cost.

RECORD SUBSEQUENT EXPENDITURES (CAPITAL AND REVENUE) ON ASSETS

*Objective 4
Distinguish between capital and revenue expenditures for plant assets*

Companies often make expenditures on plant assets after they have been in use for some time. These expenditures are debited to (1) an asset account, (2) an accumulated depreciation account, or (3) an expense account.

Expenditures debited to an asset account or to an accumulated depreciation account are called **capital expenditures.** Capital expenditures increase the book value of plant assets. **Revenue expenditures,** on the other hand, do not qualify as capital expenditures because they help to generate the current period's revenues rather than future periods' revenues. As a result, revenue expenditures are expensed immediately and are reported in the income statement as expenses.

Expenditures Capitalized in Asset Accounts

Betterments or improvements to existing plant assets are capital expenditures because they increase the *quality* of services obtained from the asset. Because betterments or improvements add to the service-rendering ability of assets, they are charged to the asset accounts. For example, installing an air conditioner in an automobile that did not previously have one is a betterment. Such an expenditure is debited to the asset account, Automobiles.

Expenditures Capitalized as Charges to Accumulated Depreciation

Occasionally, expenditures made on plant assets extend the *quantity* of services *beyond the original estimate* but do not improve the quality of the services. Since these expenditures will benefit an increased number of future periods, they are capitalized rather than expensed. However, since there is no visible, tangible addition to, or improvement in, the quality of services, the expenditures are charged to the accumulated depreciation account. Such expenditures are viewed as canceling a part of the existing accumulated depreciation and are often called **extraordinary repairs.**

To illustrate, assume that after operating a press for four years, a company spent $5,000 to recondition the press. The effect of the reconditioning is to increase the machine's life to 14 years instead of the original estimate of 10 years. The journal entry to record the extraordinary repair is:

Accumulated Depreciation—Machinery	5,000	
Cash (or Accounts Payable)		5,000
To record the cost of reconditioning a press.		

When the press was acquired, it cost $40,000. The press had an estimated useful life of 10 years and no salvage value. At the end of the fourth year, the balance in its accumulated depreciation account under the straight-line method is [($40,000 ÷ 10) × 4] = $16,000. After the $5,000 spent to recondition the press is debited to the accumulated depreciation account, the balances in the asset account and its related accumulated depreciation account are as shown in the second money column:

	Before Extraordinary Repair	After Extraordinary Repair
Press	$40,000	$40,000
Accumulated depreciation	16,000	11,000
Book value (end of four years)	$24,000	$29,000

The effect of the expenditure, then, is to increase the carrying amount (book value) of the asset by reducing its contra account, accumulated depreciation. Under the straight-line method, the new book value of the press, $29,000, is divided equally among the 10 remaining years in amounts of $2,900 per year (assuming that salvage value is still zero).

As a practical matter, expenditures for major repairs not extending the asset's life are also sometimes charged to accumulated depreciation to avoid distortion of net income that might result if these expenditures were expensed in the year incurred. Then, a revised depreciation expense must be calculated, and the cost of major repairs is spread over a number of years. This treatment is not theoretically correct.

To illustrate, assume the same facts as in the above example except that the $5,000 expenditure did not extend the life of the asset. However, because of the size of this expenditure, it is still charged to accumulated depreciation. Now the $29,000 remaining book value would be spread over the remaining six years of the life of the press. Under the straight-line method, annual depreciation would then be ($29,000 ÷ 6) = $4,833.

Expenditures Charged to Expense

Recurring and/or minor expenditures that neither add to the asset's quality of service-rendering ability nor extend its quantity of services beyond the asset's original estimated useful life are treated as expenses. Thus, regular maintenance (lubricating a machine) and ordinary repairs (replacing a broken fan belt on an automobile) are expensed immediately as revenue expenditures. For example, if the company mentioned previously spends $190 to repair the press after using it for some time, this amount should be debited to Maintenance Expense or Repairs Expense.

In many companies, any expenditure below an arbitrary minimum, such as $100, is charged to expense regardless of its impact on the asset's useful life. This practice is followed to avoid calculating and preparing adjusting entries for depreciation for such a nominal cost.

Low-Cost Items.   Most businesses purchase **low-cost items** that provide years of service at a relatively low unit cost, such as paperweights, hammers, wrenches, and drills. Because of the small dollar amounts involved, it is impractical to use the ordinary depreciation methods for such assets, and it is often costly to maintain records of individual items. Also, the effect of the costs of such items on the financial statements is not significant. Accordingly, it is more efficient to record the items as expenses when they are purchased. This practice of accounting for such low unit cost items as expenses is an example of the modifying convention of materiality that we will discuss in Chapter 11.

Illustration 7.10 shows a graphical summary of these expenditures on plant assets after acquisition.

Errors in Classification

In practice, it is often difficult to distinguish between an expenditure that should be debited to the asset account and an expenditure that should be debited to the accumulated depreciation account. For example, some expenditures seem to affect both the quality and quantity of services. Even if the wrong account is debited for the expenditure, the book value of the plant asset at that point will be the same amount it would have been if the correct

Illustration 7.10
EXPENDITURES ON PLANT ASSETS AFTER ACQUISITION

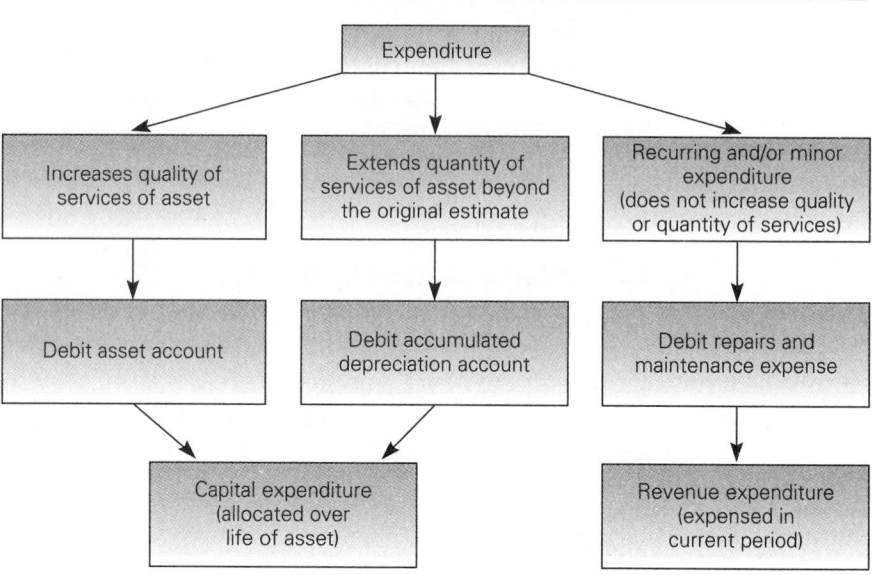

account had been debited. However, both the asset and accumulated depreciation accounts will be misstated.

As an example of the effect of misstated asset and accumulated depreciation accounts, assume Watson Company had an asset that had originally cost $15,000 and had been depreciated to a book value of $6,000 at the beginning of 1995. At that time, the equipment was estimated to have a remaining useful life of two years. The company spent $4,000 in early January 1995 to install a new motor in the equipment. This motor was expected to extend the useful life of the asset four years beyond the original estimate. Since the expenditure served to extend the life, it should be capitalized by a debit to the accumulated depreciation account. The calculations for depreciation expense if the entry were made correctly and if the expenditure had been improperly charged (debited) to the asset account are shown in Illustration 7.11.

If an expenditure that should be expensed is capitalized, the effects are more significant. Assume now that $6,000 in repairs expense is incurred for a plant asset that originally cost $40,000 and had a useful life of four years and no estimated salvage value. This asset had been depreciated using the straight-line method for one year and had a book value of $30,000 ($40,000 cost − $10,000 first-year depreciation) at the beginning of 1995. The $6,000 that should have been charged to repairs expense in 1995 was capitalized instead. The charge for depreciation should have remained at $10,000 for

Illustration 7.11
EXPENDITURE EXTENDING PLANT ASSET LIFE

	December 31, 1994	After Expenditure Entry	
		Correct	Incorrect
Cost.	$15,000	$15,000	$19,000†
Accumulated depreciation	9,000	5,000*	9,000
Book value	$ 6,000	$10,000	$10,000
Remaining life.	2 years	6 years	6 years
Depreciation expense per year	$ 3,000	$ 1,667	$ 1,667

* ($9,000 − $4,000)

† ($15,000 + $4,000)

each of the next three years. With the incorrect entry, however, depreciation increases.

Regardless of whether the repair was debited to the asset account or the accumulated depreciation account, the depreciation expense amount will be changed to $12,000 for each of the next three years [($30,000 book value + $6,000 repairs expense) ÷ 3 more years of useful life]. As a result, net

Illustration 7.12
EFFECT OF REVENUE EXPENDITURE TREATED AS CAPITAL EXPENDITURE

	For 1995 under Correctly Expensing	For 1995 under Incorrectly Capitalizing
1995 depreciation expense	$10,000	$12,000
1995 repair expense	6,000	–0–
1995 net income overstated by $4,000, which affects retained earnings	$16,000	$12,000
Asset cost	$40,000	$46,000
Accumulated depreciation	20,000	22,000
Book value.	$20,000	$24,000

	For 1996 under Correctly Expensing	For 1996 under Incorrectly Capitalizing
1996 depreciation expense	$10,000	$12,000
1996 repair expense	–0–	–0–
1996 net income understated by $2,000, which affects retained earnings	$10,000	$12,000
Asset cost	$40,000	$46,000
Accumulated depreciation	30,000	34,000
Book value.	$10,000	$12,000

income for the year 1995 will be overstated $4,000 due to the effects of these two errors: (1) repairs expense is understated by $6,000, causing income to be overstated by $6,000; and (2) depreciation expense is overstated by $2,000, causing income to be understated by $2,000. In 1996, depreciation will again be overstated by $2,000, causing 1996 income to be understated by $2,000.

You should realize that the $6,000 recording error affects more than just the expense accounts and net income. Plant asset and Retained Earnings accounts on the balance sheet will also reflect the impact of this error. Illustration 7.12 shows the effect of incorrectly capitalizing the $6,000 to the asset account rather than correctly expensing it.

SUBSIDIARY RECORDS USED TO CONTROL PLANT ASSETS

*Objective 5
Describe the
subsidiary records
used to control
plant assets*

Most companies maintain formal records (ranging from handwritten documents to computer tapes) to ensure control over their plant assets. These records include an asset account and a related accumulated depreciation account in the general ledger for *each* major class of depreciable plant assets, such as buildings, factory machinery, office equipment, delivery equipment, and store equipment.

Since the general ledger account frequently cannot contain detailed information about each item in a major class of depreciable plant assets, many companies use plant asset subsidiary ledgers. For example, the general ledger account for office equipment may contain entries for such items as microcomputers, FAX machines, copying machines, calculators, dictating equipment, and filing cabinets, but it cannot contain detailed information about these items. Plant asset subsidiary ledgers and detailed records provide more information and make it possible for the company to maintain better control over plant and equipment.

When subsidiary ledgers are kept for each major class of plant and equipment, there may be a subsidiary ledger for factory machinery, office equipment, and other classes of depreciable plant assets. Then there may be an additional subsidiary ledger for each type of asset within each category. For example, the subsidiary office equipment ledger may contain accounts for microcomputers, typewriters, copying machines, calculators, and so on. (The subsidiary ledger concept is discussed and illustrated in Appendix B at the end of the text.) Also, a detailed record will normally exist for each item represented in a subsidiary ledger account. For example, if there is a subsidiary ledger account for microcomputers, there may be a separate detailed record for each microcomputer represented in the microcomputer subsidiary ledger account. Each detailed record should include information such as the following: a description of the asset, identification or serial number, location of the asset, date of acquisition, cost, estimated salvage value, estimated useful life, annual depreciation, accumulated depreciation, insurance cover-

ETHICS   A CLOSER LOOK

Since the 1970s, Mesa Management Company has developed and managed shopping center sites on behalf of the real estate investors who purchased interests in the properties. Mesa's management fee is 25% of the net income that each property generates for its investors. As the economy grew, more investors were interested in the great returns provided by shopping centers because the cash generated by the ongoing operations of the properties more than offset the cost of financing the shopping centers. At some future point, the properties would be sold at a profit after their values had appreciated considerably.

Not coincidentally, Mesa's revenues grew as it continued to handle more shopping center sites. Mesa always managed to sell its properties within three to five years after initial development without making any additional revenue or capital expenditures. However, during the late 1980s, the real estate market for shopping center developments slowed down considerably, and Mesa was forced to keep many properties far longer than it had intended. Mesa also had difficulty obtaining tenants for many of its strip malls.

Even as some of the properties became at least five years old, Mesa had not performed common ongoing expenditures such as spot-painting, repainting the parking lot spaces, and replacing worn carpeting. Mesa has budgeted $10 million to improve the appearance and quality of the shopping center sites and increase the likelihood that the sites could be sold. Mesa plans to treat this investment as a capital expenditure to be debited to the plant asset accounts.

Required
a. Comment on Mesa's accounting policy with regards to this investment.
b. Why would Mesa prefer this policy?

Illustration 7.13
DETAILED RECORD OF A SPECIFIC PLANT ASSET

Item IBM PS/2, 50Z			Insurance coverage:	
Id. No. Z-43806			United Ins. Co.	
Location Rm. 403, Adm. bldg.			Pol. No. 0052-61481-24	
Date acquired Jan. 1, 1992			Amt. $3,000	
Cost $3,000			Repairs:	
Estimated salvage value	$200		6/13/93	$140
Estimated useful life	4 yrs.			
Depreciation per year	$700			
Accumulated depreciation:			Disposal date _____	
12/31/92	$ 700			
12/31/93	1,400		Gain or loss _____	
12/31/94	_____			
12/31/95	_____			

age, repairs, and gain or loss on final disposal of the asset. Illustration 7.13 shows how the detailed record for one particular microcomputer might appear as of December 31, 1993.

To enhance control over plant and equipment, the identification or serial number for each asset should be stenciled on or otherwise attached to the asset. Periodically, a physical inventory should be taken to determine whether all items shown in the accounting records actually exist, whether they are located where they should be, and whether they are still being used. A company that does not use detailed records and identification numbers or take physical inventories may find it difficult to determine whether assets have been discarded or stolen.

The general ledger control account balance for each major class of plant and equipment should equal the total of the amounts shown in the subsidiary ledger accounts for that class of plant assets. Also, the totals shown in the detailed records for a specific subsidiary ledger account (such as microcomputers) should equal the balance of that account. Each time a plant asset is acquired, exchanged, or disposed of, an entry should be posted to both a general ledger control account and the appropriate subsidiary ledger account. The detailed record for the item(s) affected also should be updated.

In this chapter, you learned how to account for the acquisition of plant assets and depreciation. The next chapter discusses how to record the disposal of plant assets and how to account for natural resources and intangible assets.

UNDERSTANDING THE LEARNING OBJECTIVES

1. List the characteristics of plant assets and identify the costs of acquiring plant assets.
    *   To be classified as a plant asset, an asset must (1) be tangible, (2) have a useful service life of more than one year, and (3) be used in business operations rather than held for resale.
    *   In accounting for plant assets, accountants must:
        1. Record the acquisition cost of the asset.
        2. Record the allocation of the asset's original cost to periods of its useful life through depreciation.
        3. Record subsequent expenditures on the asset.
        4. Account for the disposal of the asset.
2. List the four major factors affecting depreciation expense.
    *   Accountants consider four major factors in computing depreciation: (1) cost of the asset, (2) estimated salvage value of the asset, (3) estimated useful life of the asset, and (4) depreciation method to use in depreciating the asset.
3. Describe the various methods of calculating depreciation expense.

- **Straight-line method:**
  Assigns an equal amount of depreciation to each period. The formula for calculating straight-line depreciation is:

$$\frac{\text{Depreciation}}{\text{per period}} = \frac{\text{Asset cost} - \text{Estimated salvage value}}{\substack{\text{Number of accounting periods} \\ \text{in estimated useful life}}}$$

- **Units-of-production method:**
  Assigns an equal amount of depreciation to each unit of product manufactured by an asset. The units-of-production depreciation formulas are:

$$\frac{\text{Depreciation}}{\text{per unit}} = \frac{\text{Asset cost} - \text{Estimated salvage value}}{\substack{\text{Estimated total units of production (or service)} \\ \text{during useful life of asset}}}$$

$$\frac{\text{Depreciation}}{\text{per period}} = \frac{\text{Depreciation}}{\text{per unit}} \times \frac{\text{Number of units of goods}}{\text{or services produced}}$$

- **Sum-of-the-years'-digits (SOYD) method:**
  SOYD is an accelerated depreciation method. The SOYD depreciation formulas are:

$$\frac{\text{Depreciation}}{\text{per period}} = \frac{\substack{\text{Number of years} \\ \text{of useful life} \\ \text{remaining at beginning} \\ \text{of accounting period}}}{\text{SOYD}} \times \left(\frac{\text{Asset}}{\text{cost}} - \frac{\text{Estimated}}{\text{salvage value}} \right)$$

$$\text{Sum-of-the-years'-digits (SOYD)} = \frac{n(n+1)}{2}$$

- **Double-declining-balance method:**
  DDB is an accelerated depreciation method. Salvage value is ignored in making annual calculations. The formula for DDB depreciation is:

$$\frac{\text{Depreciation}}{\text{per period}} = (2 \times \text{Straight-line rate}) \times \left(\frac{\text{Asset}}{\text{cost}} - \frac{\text{Accumulated}}{\text{depreciation}} \right)$$

4. Distinguish between capital and revenue expenditures for plant assets.
   - Capital expenditures are debited to an asset account or an accumulated depreciation account and increase the book value of plant assets. Expenditures that increase the quality of services or extend the quantity of services beyond the original estimate are considered to be capital expenditures.
   - Revenue expenditures are expensed immediately and reported in the income statement as expenses. Recurring and/or minor expenditures

that neither add to the asset's quality of service-rendering abilities nor extend its quantity of services beyond the asset's original estimated useful life are treated as expenses.

5. Describe the subsidiary records used to control plant assets.
   - Plant asset subsidiary ledgers contain detailed information about each item in a major class of depreciable plant assets that cannot be maintained in the general ledger account.
   - Control over plant and equipment is enhanced by plant asset subsidiary ledgers and other detailed records. Information in a detailed record may include a description of the asset, identification or serial number, location of the asset, date of acquisition, cost, estimated salvage value, estimated useful life, annual depreciation, accumulated depreciation, insurance coverage, repairs, and gain or loss on final disposal of the asset. A periodic physical inventory should be taken to determine whether items in accounting records actually exist.

DEMONSTRATION PROBLEM 7–A

Chancy Company purchased a 2-square-mile farm under the following terms: cash paid, $972,000; mortgage note assumed, $480,000; and accrued interest on mortgage note assumed, $12,000. The company paid $110,400 for brokerage and legal services to acquire the property and secure clear title. Chancy planned to subdivide the property into residential lots and to construct homes on these lots. Clearing and leveling costs of $43,200 were paid. Crops on the land were sold for $28,800. A house on the land, to be moved by the buyer of the house, was sold for $10,080. The other buildings were torn down at a cost of $19,200, and salvaged material was sold for $20,160.

Approximately 6 acres of the land were deeded to the township for roads, and another 10 acres were deeded to the local school district as the site for a future school. After the subdivision was completed, this land would have an approximate value of $15,360 per acre. The company secured a total of 1,200 salable lots from the remaining land.

Required:

Present a schedule showing in detail the composition of the cost of the 1,200 salable lots.

Solution to demonstration problem 7–A

CHANCY COMPANY
Schedule of Cost of 1,200 Residential Lots

Costs incurred:

Cash paid	$972,000	
Mortgage note assumed.	480,000	
Interest accrued on mortgage note assumed	12,000	
Broker and legal services	110,400	
Clearing and leveling costs	43,200	
Tearing down costs	19,200	$1,636,800
Less proceeds from sale of:		
Crops	$ 28,800	
House	10,080	
Salvaged materials	20,160	59,040
Net cost of land to be subdivided into 1,200 lots		$1,577,760

DEMONSTRATION PROBLEM 7–B

Samantha Company acquired and put into use a machine on January 1, 1995, at a total cost of $90,000. The machine was estimated to have a useful life of 10 years and a salvage value of $10,000. It was also estimated that the machine would produce one million units of product during its life. The machine produced 90,000 units in 1995 and 125,000 units in 1996.

Required:

Compute the amounts of depreciation to be recorded in 1995 and 1996 under each of the following:

a. Straight-line method.
b. Units-of-production method.
c. Sum-of-the-years'-digits method.
d. Double-declining-balance method.
e. Assume 30,000 units were produced in the first quarter of 1997. Compute depreciation for this quarter under each of the four methods.

Solution to demonstration problem 7–B

a. Straight-line method:

1995: ($90,000 − $10,000)/10 = $8,000

1996: ($90,000 − $10,000)/10 = $8,000

b. Units-of-production method:

1995: [($90,000 − $10,000)/1,000,000] × 90,000 = $ 7,200

1996: [($90,000 − $10,000)/1,000,000] × 125,000 = $10,000

c. Sum-of-the-years'-digits method:

1995: ($90,000 − $10,000) × $^{10}/_{55}$ = $\underline{\underline{\$14,545.45}}$

1996: ($90,000 − $10,000) × $^{9}/_{55}$ = $\underline{\underline{\$13,090.91}}$

d. Double-declining-balance method:

1995: $90,000 × 20% = $\underline{\underline{\$18,000}}$

1996: ($90,000 − $18,000) × 20% = $\underline{\underline{\$14,400}}$

e. Straight-line: ($90,000 − $10,000)/10 × ¼ = $\underline{\underline{\$2,000}}$

Units-of-production: (30,000 × $0.08) = $\underline{\underline{\$2,400}}$

Sum-of-the-years'-digits: ($90,000 − $10,000) × $^{8}/_{55}$ × ¼ = $\underline{\underline{\$2,909.09}}$

Double-declining-balance:

($90,000 − $18,000 − $14,400) × 0.2 × ¼ = $\underline{\underline{\$2,880}}$

NEW TERMS

Accelerated depreciation methods   Record higher amounts of depreciation during the early years of an asset's life and lower amounts in later years. *377*

Acquisition cost   Amount of cash and/or cash equivalents given up to acquire a plant asset and place it in operating condition at its proper location. *367*

Appraised value   An expert's opinion as to what an item's market price would be if the item were sold. *372*

Betterments (improvements)   Capital expenditures that are properly charged to asset accounts because they add to the service-rendering ability of the assets; they increase the quality of services that can be obtained from an asset. *387*

Book value   An asset's recorded cost less its accumulated depreciation. *372*

Capital expenditures   Expenditures that are debited to an asset account or to an accumulated depreciation account. *387*

Depreciation   The amount of plant asset cost allocated to each accounting period benefiting from the plant asset's use. (*373*) The **straight-line-depreciation** method charges an equal amount of plant asset cost to each period. (*375*) The **units-of-production depreciation** method assigns an equal amount of depreciation for each unit of product manufactured or service rendered by an asset. (*376*) The **sum-of-the-years'-digits (SOYD)** (*377*) and the **double-declining-balance (DDB)** (*378*) methods assign decreasing amounts of depreciation to successive periods of time.

Double-declining-balance depreciation   (DDB)   See Depreciation.

Extraordinary repairs   Expenditures that are viewed as canceling a part of the existing accumulated depreciation because they increase the quantity of services expected from an asset. *388*

Fair market value   The price that would be received for an item being sold in the normal course of business (not at a forced liquidation sale). *372*

Inadequacy   The inability of a plant asset to produce enough products or provide enough services to meet current demands. *373*

Land improvements   Attachments to land, such as driveways, landscaping, parking lots, fences, lighting systems, and sprinkler systems, that have limited lives and therefore are depreciable. *369*

Low-cost items   Items that provide years of services at a relatively low unit cost, such as hammers, paperweights, and drills. *389*

Modified ACRS   A tax method of depreciation that assigns assets into particular groups that have specified lives for depreciation purposes. The 1986 Tax Reform Act modified the Accelerated Cost Recovery System. *384*

Obsolescence   Decline in usefulness of an asset brought about by inventions and technological progress. *373*

Physical deterioration   Results from use of the asset—wear and tear—and the action of the elements. *373*

Plant and equipment   A shorter title for property, plant, and equipment; also called *plant assets*. Included are land and manufactured or constructed assets such as buildings, machinery, vehicles, and furniture. *365*

Revenue expenditures   Expenditures (on a plant asset) that are immediately expensed. *387*

Salvage value   The amount of money the company expects to recover, less disposal costs, on the date a plant asset is scrapped, sold, or traded in. Also called *scrap or residual value*. *373*

Straight-line-depreciation   See Depreciation.

Sum-of-the-years'-digits depreciation (SOYD)   See Depreciation.

Tangible assets   Assets that we can see and touch such as land, building, and equipment. *365*

Units-of-production depreciation   See Depreciation.

Useful life   Refers to the length of time the company owning the asset intends to use it. *373*

SELF-TEST

True-False

Indicate whether each of the following statements is true or false.

1. The cost of land includes its purchase price and other related costs, including the cost of removing an old unusable building that is on the land.

2. Depreciation is the process of valuation of an asset to arrive at its market value.

3. The purpose of depreciation accounting is to provide the cash required to replace plant assets.

4. Expenditures made on plant assets that increase the quality of services are debited to the Accumulated Depreciation account.

5. Plant asset subsidiary ledgers are used to increase control over plant assets.

Multiple-Choice

Select the best answer for each of the following questions.

1. On January 1, 1995, Jackson Company purchased equipment for $400,000, and installation and testing costs totaled $40,000. The equipment has a useful life of 10 years and an estimated salvage value of $40,000. If Jackson uses the straight-line depreciation method, the depreciation expense for 1995 is:
   a. $36,000.
   b. $40,000.
   c. $44,000.
   d. $20,000.
   e. $88,000.

2. In Question 1, if the equipment were purchased on July 1, 1995, and Jackson used the double-declining-balance method, the depreciation expense for 1995 would be:
   a. $88,000.
   b. $72,000.
   c. $36,000.
   d. $44,000.
   e. $40,000.

3. In Question 1, if Jackson acquired the asset on January 1, 1995, and uses the sum-of-the-years'-digits method, the depreciation expense for 1995 is:
   a. $72,727.
   b. $80,000.
   c. $65,454.
   d. $7,272.
   e. $8,000.

4. Hammons Company purchased a computer on January 2, 1995, for $10,000. The computer had an estimated salvage value of $3,000 and a useful life of five years. At the beginning of 1997, the estimated salvage value changed to $1,000, and the computer is expected to have a remaining useful life of two years. Using the straight-line method, the depreciation expense for 1997 is:
   a. $1,400.
   b. $1,750.
   c. $2,250.
   d. $1,800.
   e. $3,100.

5. The result of recording a capital expenditure as a revenue expenditure is an:
   a. Overstatement of current year's expense.
   b. Understatement of current year's expense.
   c. Understatement of subsequent year's net income.
   d. Overstatement of current year's net income.
   e. None of the above.

Now turn to page 408 to check your answers.

QUESTIONS

1. What is the main distinction between inventory and plant assets?

2. Which of the following items are properly classifiable as plant assets on the balance sheet?
   a. Future advertising paid to inform the public about new energy-saving programs at a manufacturing plant.
   b. A truck acquired by a manufacturing company to be used to deliver the company's products to wholesalers.
   c. An automobile acquired by an insurance company to be used by one of its salespersons.
   d. Calculators acquired by an office supply company to be resold to customers.
   e. The cost of constructing and paving a driveway that has a useful life of 10 years.

3. In any exchange of noncash assets, the accountant's task is that of finding the most appropriate valuation to assign to the assets received. What is the general rule for determining the most appropriate valuation in such a situation?

4. Why should periodic depreciation be recorded on all plant assets except land?

5. Harper Company is offered $400,000 for a tract of land carried in its accounts at $160,000. Should it accept the offer? Why or why not?

6. Define the terms *inadequacy* and *obsolescence* as used in accounting for plant assets.

7. What four factors must be known to compute depreciation on a plant asset?

8. What is the sum-of-the-years'-digits for a machine that has an estimated useful life of nine years?

9. The Lawson Company has just acquired new factory machines and is trying to determine which depreciation method to use. List the relative merits of using each of the following methods:
   a. Straight-line.
   b. Units-of-production.
   c. Accelerated.

10. What does the balance in the accumulated depreciation account represent? Can this balance be used to replace the related plant asset at the end of its useful life?

11. Distinguish between capital expenditures and revenue expenditures.

12. For each of the following, state whether the expenditure made should be charged to an expense, an asset, or an accumulated depreciation account:
   a. Cost of installing air-conditioning equipment in a car that previously did not have air conditioning.
   b. Painting of an owned factory building every other year.
   c. Cost of replacing the roof on a 10-year-old building that was purchased new and has an estimated total life of 40 years. The replacement did not extend the life beyond the original estimate.
   d. Cost of repairing an electric motor.

13. *Real-world question*   In the financial statements of Met-Pro Corporation, in "A Broader Perspective" (page 386), determine the total accumulated depreciation and the total historical cost of all property, plant, and equipment.

The Coca-Cola Company

14. *Real-world question*   From the consolidated balance sheet of The Coca-Cola Company in Appendix C, identify the December 31, 1991, amount of gross property, plant, and equipment and the amount of net property, plant, and equipment. What percentage of the depreciable assets have been depreciated?

MAYTAG CORPORATION

15. *Real-world question*   Based on the financial statements of Maytag Corporation contained in Appendix C, what was the December 31, 1991, balance in the Land account?

THE LIMITED, INC.

16. *Real-world question*   Based on the financial statements of The Limited, Inc., contained in Appendix C, what was the February 1, 1992, net property and equipment balance?

HARLAND

17. *Real-world question*   Based on the financial statements of John H. Harland Company contained in Appendix C, what was the December 31, 1991, ending balance of accumulated depreciation and amortization?

EXERCISES

Determine cost of land
(L.O. 1)

7–1. Clark Company recently bought a plot of land for $490,000 for construction of a new warehouse. Legal fees connected with the transaction were $4,800. Back taxes on the property amounted to $12,000, for which Clark Company assumed the liability. Demolition costs incurred to raze (destroy) the old warehouse on the property were $17,800. What is the cost of the land?

Determine cost of land and building when acquired together
(L.O. 1)

7–2. Payne Company acquired real property consisting of a tract of land and two buildings for $960,000 cash. The company intended to raze (destroy) the old factory building and to remodel and use the old office building. To allocate the cost of the property acquired, the company had the property appraised. The appraised values were: land, $360,000; factory building, $360,000; and office building, $480,000. The factory building was demolished at a net cost of $48,000. The office building was remodeled at a cost of $96,000. The cost of a new identical office building was estimated to be $540,000. Present a schedule or schedules showing the determination of the amounts at which the assets acquired should be carried in the Payne Company accounts. Show calculations.

Determine cost of equipment
(L.O. 1)

7–3. Daniels Company purchased an earthmover for $44,000, less a 2% cash discount. One of the company's employees drove the equipment to the company's storage lot. The company was fined $700 because the employee had failed to obtain a permit to drive the equipment on city streets. Break-in and testing costs totaled $6,000. What is the cost of the equipment?

Record cost of office furniture, repairs, and depreciation
(L.O. 1,3,4)

7–4. The Reed Company purchased some office furniture on March 1, 1994, for $13,000 cash. Cash of $200 was paid for freight and cartage costs. The furniture is being depreciated over a four-year life under the straight-line method, assuming $720 of salvage value. The company employs a calendar-year accounting period and records depreciation for the full month in which an asset is installed. On July 1, 1995, $90 was spent to refinish the furniture. Prepare journal entries for the Reed Company to record all of the above data, including the annual depreciation adjustments, through 1995.

Compute difference in income taxes payable between DDB and straight-line
(L.O. 3)

7–5. Kestler Company purchased a new machine on January 2, 1994, at a cash cost of $360,000. The machine is estimated to have a life of five years with no salvage value at the end of that time. If federal income taxes are levied at a rate of 50% of net income, how much would the income taxes payable for the years 1994 and 1995 be reduced if the company could choose the double-declining-balance method of computing depreciation rather than the straight-line method?

Compute SOYD
depreciation for
two years
(L.O. 3)

7–6. Coleman Company acquired equipment costing $120,000 on April 1, 1994. The equipment has an estimated salvage value of $8,000 and an estimated useful life of seven years. The machine is being depreciated using the sum-of-the-years'-digits method. Compute the depreciation for the years ended December 31, 1994, and 1995.

Compute annual
depreciation for
two years under
each of four
different methods
(L.O. 3)

7–7. On January 2, 1994, a new machine was acquired for $300,000. The machine has an estimated salvage value of $12,000 and an estimated useful life of 10 years. The machine is expected to produce a total of 500,000 units of product throughout its useful life. Compute depreciation for 1994 and 1995 using each of the following methods:

    a. Straight-line.

    b. Units-of-production (assume 30,000 and 50,000 units were produced in 1994 and 1995, respectively).

    c. Double-declining-balance.

    d. Sum-of-the-years'-digits.

Compute straight-
line depreciation
given reduced
estimated life
(L.O. 3)

7–8. The Higgins Company acquired a delivery truck on January 2, 1994, for $84,000. The truck has an estimated salvage value of $4,500 and an estimated useful life of eight years. The truck is being depreciated on a straight-line basis. At the beginning of 1997, it is estimated that the truck has a remaining useful life of seven years. What are the depreciation charges for 1994 and for 1997?

Determine
whether
expenditures are
capital or revenue
expenditures
(L.O. 4)

7–9. Classify each of the following as either a capital expenditure or an expense:

    a. Painting of office building at a cost of $3,400. The building is painted every year.

    b. Addition of a new wing on the building at a cost of $670,000.

    c. Expansion of a paved parking lot at a cost of $180,000.

    d. Replacement of a stairway with an escalator at a cost of $48,000.

    e. Lubricating a machine at a cost of $600.

    f. Replacing a broken fan belt at a cost of $370.

PROBLEMS

Determine
building account
balance, and
prepare journal
entry to record it
(L.O. 1)

7–1. Lamar Company purchased land and a building having appraised values of $720,000 and $1,200,000, respectively. The terms of the sale were that Lamar would pay $978,000 in cash and assume responsibility for a $600,000 mortgage note, $30,000 of accrued interest, and $72,000 of unpaid property taxes. Lamar intends to use the building as an office building.

Required:

Prepare a journal entry to record the purchase.

Determine cost of
land
(L.O. 1)

7–2. The Malone Company purchased a two-square-mile farm from its owner under the following terms: cash paid, $773,000; mortgage note assumed, $386,000; and accrued interest on mortgage note assumed, $9,800. The company paid $84,000 for brokerage and legal services to acquire the property and secure clear title. It planned to subdivide the property into residential lots and to construct homes on these lots. Clearing and leveling costs of $34,000 were paid. Crops on the land were sold for $26,000. A house on the land, to be moved by the buyer, was sold for $22,400. The other buildings were razed at a cost of $30,000, and salvaged material was sold for $12,600. Approximately six acres of land were deeded to the township for roads, and another 10 acres were deeded to the local school district as the site for a future school. After the subdivision was completed, this land would have an approximate value of $11,600 per acre. The company secured a total of 1,200 salable lots from the remaining land.

Required:

Present a schedule showing in detail the composition of the cost of the 1,200 salable lots.

Determine correct valuations of assets
(L.O. 1)

7–3. Hilliard Company planned to erect a new factory building and a new office building in Atlanta, Georgia. Preliminary studies showed two possible sites as available and desirable. Further studies showed the second site to be preferable. A report on this property showed an appraised value of $1,200,000 for land and orchard and $800,000 for a building.

After considerable negotiation, the company and the owner reached the following agreement. Hilliard Company was to pay $1,040,000 in cash, assume a $600,000 mortgage note on the property, assume the accrued interest on the mortgage note of $12,800, and assume unpaid property taxes of $48,000. Hilliard Company paid $132,000 cash for brokerage and legal services in acquiring the property.

Shortly after acquiring the property, Hilliard Company sold the fruit on the trees for $17,600, remodeled the building into an office building at a cost of $256,000, and removed the trees from the land at a cost of $60,000. Construction of the factory building is to begin in a week.

Required:

Prepare a schedule showing the proper valuation of the assets acquired by the Hilliard Company.

Determine correct cost of equipment and place in T-account form
(L.O. 1)

7–4. When you were hired as manager of the Sunshine Company on January 1, 1995, the company bookkeeper gave you the following information regarding one of its equipment accounts (in T-account form):

Equipment—Machine C

1994			1994		
Jan. 1	Disposition cost of Machine B	6,000	Jan. 1	Cash from sale of Machine B	5,000
1	Material used in building Machine C	220,000	Dec. 31	Depreciation on Machine C for year ended 12/31/94 (10% of $426,600)	42,660
1	Labor used in building Machine C	160,000			
1	Cost of installing Machine C	27,600			
1	Net income from building Machine C rather than purchasing it . .	24,000			

Required:

Construct the theoretically correct equipment account for Machine C.

Determine
building account
balance and
prepare correcting
entries
(L.O. 1)

7–5. The Meeler Company has the following entries in its Building account:

1994
May 5 Cost of land and building purchased $1,600,000
     5 Broker fees incident to purchase   72,000
1995
Jan. 3 Contract price of new wing added to south end of building   440,000
     15 Cost of new machinery, estimated life ten years   1,600,000
June 10 Real estate taxes for six months ending 6/30/95   36,000
Aug. 10 Cost of parking lot for employees in back of building . . .   49,600
Sept. 6 Replacement of broken windows   1,600
Oct. 10 Repairs due to regular usage.   18,400
1994
Dec. 31 Transfer to Land account, as per allocation of purchase
         cost authorized in minutes of board of directors.   240,000
1995
Jan. 5 Proceeds from lease of second floor for six months ended
         12/31/94.   40,000

The original property was acquired on May 5, 1994. The Meeler Company immediately engaged a contractor to construct a new wing on the south end of the building. While the new wing was being constructed, the company leased the second floor as temporary warehouse space to the Jane Company. During this period (July 1 through December 31, 1994) the company installed new machinery costing $1,600,000 on the first floor of the building. Regular operations began on January 2, 1995.

Required:

a. Compute the correct balance for the Building account as of December 31, 1995. The building is expected to last 40 years. The company employs a calendar-year accounting period.

b. Prepare the necessary journal entries to correct the records of the Meeler Company at December 31, 1995. No depreciation entries are required.

Compute
depreciation for
various assets
using straight-line
and
units-of-production
depreciation
methods
(L.O. 3)

7–6. The Douglas Company's fiscal year ends May 31. The company has its own fleet of delivery vehicles, which include the following:

Description	Date Acquired	Cost	Expected Life	Expected Salvage Value
Sedan No. 3	June 1, 1993	$ 64,000	4 years	$ 9,600
Truck No. 2	June 1, 1989	96,000	100,000 miles	8,000
Truck No. 5	Jan. 1, 1995	224,000	150,000 miles	22,400
Trailer No. 8	Apr. 1, 1992	128,000	400,000 miles	–0–

Speedometer readings at May 31, show the following:

	1994	1995	Total Mileage for Year Ended May 31, 1995
Sedan No. 3.	15,000 miles	28,000 miles	13,000 miles
Truck No. 2.	120,000	150,000	30,000
Truck No. 5.	0	20,000	20,000
Trailer No. 8.	50,000	75,000	25,000

Required:

Set up a schedule showing in full detail the amount of depreciation to be recorded for the year ended May 31, 1995, on each of the above assets. Use the straight-line method for Sedan No. 3 and the units-of-production (number of miles driven) method for the other vehicles.

Compute depreciation for first year under each of four different methods (L.O. 1,3)

7–7. Cooper Company acquired a machine on July 1, 1994, at a cash cost of $288,000 and immediately spent $12,000 to install it. The machine was estimated to have a useful life of eight years and a salvage value of $18,000 at the end of this time. It was further estimated that the machine would produce 500,000 units of product during its life. In the first year, the machine produced 100,000 units.

Required

Prepare journal entries to record depreciation for the fiscal year ended June 30, 1995, if the company used:

a. The straight-line method.
b. The units-of-production method.
c. The double-declining-balance method.
d. The sum-of-the-years'-digits method.

Compute depreciation for first year under each of four different methods (L.O. 1,3)

7–8. Griffin Company acquired equipment on January 2, 1995, at a cash cost of $1,300,000. Transportation charges amounted to $16,000, and installation and testing costs totaled $40,000. The equipment was damaged while being installed, and the cost of repairing the damage was $8,000.

The equipment was estimated to have a useful life of nine years and a salvage value of $24,000 at the end of its life. It was further estimated that the equipment would be used in the production of 660,000 units of product during its life. During 1995, 220,000 units of product were produced.

Required:

Prepare journal entries to record depreciation for the year ended December 31, 1995, if the company used:

a. The straight-line-method.
b. The units-of-production method.
c. The double-declining-balance method.
d. The sum-of-the-years'-digits method.

Compute first year depreciation using three methods; assume life expectancy change (L.O. 1,3)

7–9. Nichols Company purchased a machine on January 2, 1993, at an invoice price of $250,400. Transportation charges amounted to $2,800, and $6,000 was spent to install the machine. The costs of removing an old machine to make room for the new one amounted to $2,400; $800 was received for the scrap material from the old machine.

Required:

a. State the amount of depreciation that would be recorded on the machine for the first year on the straight-line basis, the double-declining-balance basis, and the sum-of-the-years'-digits basis, assuming an estimated life of eight years and no salvage value.

b. Give the journal entry needed at December 31, 1995, to record depreciation, assuming a revised total life expectancy of 12 years for the machine. Assume that depreciation has been recorded through December 31, 1994, on a straight-line basis.

Determine cost of machine; prepare entry for depreciation under DDB and assume change in estimated life (L.O. 1,3)

7–10. The Nelson Corporation acquired a new computer on July 1, 1994. The computer had an invoice price of $288,000, but the company received a 3% cash discount by paying the bill at the date of acquisition. While transporting the computer to its new location, a Nelson employee was fined $800 for speeding. Nelson paid the fine. Installation and testing costs totaled $28,416. The computer is estimated to have a $11,200 salvage value and a seven-year useful life.

Required:

a. Prepare the journal entry to record the acquisition of the computer.
b. Prepare the journal entry to record depreciation for 1994 under the double-declining-balance method.
c. Assume that at the beginning of 1997 it is estimated that the computer will last another six years. Prepare the journal entry to record depreciation for 1997. Assume that depreciation has been recorded through 1996 on a straight-line basis and that the expected salvage value remains at $11,200.

Compute straight-line depreciation after major part is replaced (L.O. 3,4)

7–11. A machine belonging to the Dilliard Company that cost $120,000 has an estimated life of 20 years. After 10 years, an extremely important machine part, representing about 40% of the original cost, is worn out and replaced. The replacement cost is $36,000, and the useful life of the new part is the same as the remaining useful life of the machine.

Required:

a. Prepare journal entries to record the removal of the old part from the asset and accumulated depreciation accounts and the addition of the new part to the asset account. Assume that depreciation has already been brought up to date.
b. Compute the annual depreciation charge after replacement, using the straight-line method.

Compute straight-line depreciation (L.O. 1,3)

7–12. Johnson Company purchased a machine at a cash cost of $360,000. An electric motor was purchased for cash and attached to the machine at a total cost of $192,000. The machine was installed in a production center on the first floor at a cost of $72,000 on July 1, 1994. Its estimated life was 15 years, with no salvage value expected. On July 1, 1999, the machine (and motor unit) was moved from its first-floor location to the second floor and the entire unit was installed at a cost of $116,000. The estimated life of the unit in its second-floor location is 10 years, with no salvage value expected.

Required:

Compute the depreciation charge for the year ending June 30, 2000, using the straight-line method.

BUSINESS DECISION PROBLEM

Compute three years' depreciation using two methods; compute tax savings; and advise on which company to purchase (L.O. 3)

Bower Company and Gant Company are quite similar except for the following: Bower Company uses double-declining-balance depreciation, whereas Gant Company uses straight-line depreciation. On January 2, 1995, both companies acquired the following plant assets with the related costs, salvage values, and useful lives:

Plant Asset	Cost	Salvage Value	Useful Life
Building	$500,000	Negligible	40 years
Land	200,000	—	—
Machinery	400,000	Negligible	16 years

The companies reported the following net income for the years 1995, 1996, and 1997.

	Net Income	
Year	Bower Company	Gant Company
1995	$ 95,000	$ 98,750
1996	100,000	102,500
1997	110,000	111,250

David Rogers is interested in buying one of the companies. He notices that Gant Company's income exceeds Bower Company's income each year. But Bower Company has more working capital (current assets minus current liabilities) than Gant Company. Rogers has engaged you to advise him on buying one of the companies.

Required:

a. Compute the amount of depreciation recorded by each of the companies in 1995, 1996, and 1997.

b. Compute the amount of tax savings Bower Company would obtain by using double-declining-balance depreciation instead of straight-line depreciation. (Assume a 40% tax rate and that this method can be used for tax purposes.) Also, round calculations to the nearest dollar.

c. Which company would you advise Mr. Rogers to buy? Why?

ANSWERS TO SELF-TEST

True-False

1. *True*. The cost of land includes all normal, reasonable, and necessary expenditures to obtain the land and get it ready for use.

2. *False*. Depreciation is a process of allocation, not valuation, and the book value of an asset is usually quite different than its market value.

3. *False*. Depreciation accounting does not provide funds required to replace plant assets. Instead, accumulated depreciation

simply shows how much of an asset's cost has been charged to expense.

4. *False*. Expenditures that improve the quality of services are debited to the asset account.

5. *True*. Plant asset subsidiary ledgers provide detailed information that the general ledger account cannot provide and thus give better control over plant assets.

Multiple-Choice

1. *b.* The depreciation expense for 1995 using the straight-line method is computed as follows:

$$(\$440,000 - \$40,000)/10 = \$40,000$$

2. *d.*

$$\text{Double-declining-balance rate} = 2\times(100\%/10)$$
$$= 20\%$$

$$\text{Depreciation expense for 1994} = (20\% \times \$440,000) \times \tfrac{6}{12}$$
$$= \$44,000$$

3. *a.*

$$\text{SOYD} = \frac{10(10 + 1)}{2} = 55$$

$$\text{Depreciation expense} = \frac{10}{55} \times (\$440,000 - \$40,000)$$
$$= \$72,727$$

4. *e.* At the beginning of 1997, the balance of accumulated depreciation is $2,800 (annual depreciation of $1,400 × 2) and book value is $7,200 ($10,000 − $2,800). The revised annual depreciation expense is $3,100 [($7,200 − $1,000)/2].

5. *a.* The error in recording a capital expenditure as a revenue expenditure results in an overstatement of current year's expense, as well as an understatement of current year's net income.

8

PLANT ASSET DISPOSALS, NATURAL RESOURCES, AND INTANGIBLE ASSETS

LEARNING OBJECTIVES

After studying this chapter, you should be able to:

1. Calculate and prepare entries for the sale, retirement, and destruction of plant assets.
2. Describe and record exchanges of dissimilar and similar plant assets.
3. Discuss the differences between accounting principles and tax rules in the treatment of gains and losses from the exchange of plant assets.
4. Determine the periodic depletion cost of a natural resource and calculate depreciation of plant assets located on extractive industry property.
5. Prepare entries for the acquisition and amortization of intangible assets.

The study of long-term assets, which includes plant assets, natural resources, and intangible assets, began in Chapter 7. Discussion in that chapter focused on determining plant asset cost, computing depreciation, and distinguishing between capital and revenue expenditures. This chapter begins by discussing the disposal of plant assets. The next topic is accounting for natural resources such as ores, minerals, oil and gas, and timber. The final topic is accounting for intangible assets such as patents, copyrights, franchises, trademarks and trade names, leases, and goodwill.

Although several long-term assets are discussed in this chapter, you will see that accounting for all long-term assets is basically the same. When a company purchases a long-term asset, the asset is recorded at cost. As the company receives benefits from the asset and the future service potential is reduced, the cost is transferred from an asset account to an expense account. Finally, the asset is sold, retired, or traded in on a new asset. Since the lives of long-term assets can extend for many years, the methods accountants use in reporting such assets can have a dramatic effect on the financial statements of many accounting periods.

DISPOSAL OF PLANT ASSETS

All plant assets except land eventually wear out or become inadequate or obsolete and must be sold, retired, or traded for new assets. **When a plant asset is disposed of, both the asset's cost and accumulated depreciation must be removed from the accounts.** Overall, then, all asset disposals have the following in common:

1. The asset's depreciation must be brought up to date.
2. To record the disposal, you must:
   - *a.* Write off the asset's cost.
   - *b.* Write off the accumulated depreciation.
   - *c.* Record any consideration (usually cash) received or paid or to be received or paid.
   - *d.* Record the gain or loss, if any.

As you study this section, remember these common procedures used by accountants to record the disposal of plant assets. In the paragraphs that follow, we discuss accounting for the (1) sale of plant assets, (2) retirement of plant assets without sale, (3) destruction of plant assets, (4) exchange of plant assets, and (5) cost of dismantling and removing plant assets.

Sale of Plant Assets

Objective 1
Calculate and prepare entries for the sale, retirement, and destruction of plant assets

Companies frequently dispose of plant assets by selling them. By comparing an asset's book value (cost less accumulated depreciation) with its selling price (or net amount realized if there are selling expenses), the company may show either a gain or loss. If the sales price is greater than the asset's book value, the company will show a gain. If the sales price is less than the asset's book value, the company will show a loss. Of course, if the sales price is equal to the asset's book value, no gain or loss occurs.

To illustrate accounting for the sale of a plant asset, assume that equipment costing $45,000, with accumulated depreciation of $14,000, is sold for $35,000. A gain of $4,000 is realized as computed below:

Equipment cost	$45,000
Accumulated depreciation	14,000
Book value	$31,000
Sales price	35,000
Gain realized	$ 4,000

The journal entry to record the sale is:

Cash	35,000	
Accumulated Depreciation—Equipment	14,000	
Equipment		45,000
Gain on Disposal of Plant Assets		4,000
To record sale of equipment at a price greater than book value.		

If on the other hand, the equipment is sold for $28,000, a loss of $3,000 ($31,000 book value − $28,000 sales price) is realized. The journal entry to record the sale is:

Cash	28,000	
Accumulated Depreciation—Equipment	14,000	
Loss from Disposal of Plant Assets	3,000	
Equipment		45,000
To record sale of equipment at a price less than book value.		

If the equipment is sold for $31,000, no gain or loss occurs. The journal entry to record the sale is:

Cash	31,000	
Accumulated Depreciation—Equipment	14,000	
Equipment		45,000
To record sale of equipment at a price equal to book value.		

Accounting for Depreciation to Date of Disposal.   When a plant asset is sold or otherwise disposed of, it is important to record the depreciation up to the date of sale or disposal. For example, if an asset is sold on April 1 and depreciation was last recorded on December 31, depreciation for three months (January 1–April 1) should be recorded. If depreciation is not recorded for the three months, operating expenses for that period will be understated, and the gain on the sale of the asset will be understated or the loss overstated.

To illustrate, assume that on August 1, 1996, Ray Company sold a machine for $1,500. When the machine was purchased on January 2, 1988, it cost $12,000 and was being depreciated at the straight-line rate of 10% per year. As of December 31, 1995, after closing entries were made, the machine's accumulated depreciation account had a balance of $9,600. Before a gain or loss can be determined and before an entry can be made to record the sale, the following entry must be made to record depreciation for the seven months ended July 31, 1996:

July 31	Depreciation Expense—Machinery	700	
	Accumulated Depreciation—Machinery		700
	To record depreciation for seven months ($12,000 × 0.10 × 7/12).		

The $200 loss on the sale is computed as shown below:

Machine cost.	$12,000
Accumulated depreciation ($9,600 + $700).	10,300
Book value.	$ 1,700
Sales price.	1,500
Loss realized.	$ 200

The journal entry to record the sale is:

Cash	1,500	
Accumulated Depreciation—Machinery	10,300	
Loss from Disposal of Plant Assets	200	
Machinery.		12,000
To record sale of machinery at a price less than book value.		

Retirement of Plant Assets without Sale

When a plant asset is retired from service, the asset's cost and accumulated depreciation must be removed from the plant asset accounts. For example, Hayes Company would make the following journal entry when it retired a fully depreciated machine that cost $15,000 and had no salvage value:

Accumulated Depreciation—Machinery	15,000	
Machinery		15,000
To record the retirement of a fully depreciated machine.		

Occasionally, a company continues to use a plant asset after it has been fully depreciated. In such a case, **the asset's cost and accumulated depreciation should not be removed from the accounts until the asset is sold, traded, or retired from service**. Of course, no more depreciation may be recorded on a fully depreciated asset because total depreciation expense taken on an asset may not exceed its cost.

Sometimes a plant asset is retired from service or discarded before it is fully depreciated. If the asset is to be sold as scrap (even if not immediately), its cost and accumulated depreciation should be removed from the asset and accumulated depreciation accounts. In addition, its estimated salvage value should be recorded in a Salvaged Materials account, and a gain or loss on disposal should be recognized. To illustrate, assume that a machine with a $10,000 original cost and $7,500 of accumulated depreciation is retired. If the machine's estimated salvage value is $500, the following entry is required:

Salvaged Materials	500	
Accumulated Depreciation—Machinery	7,500	
Loss from Disposal of Plant Assets	2,000	
Machinery		10,000
To record retirement of machinery, which will be sold for scrap at a later time.		

Destruction of Plant Assets

Plant assets are sometimes wrecked in accidents or destroyed by fire, flood, storm, or other causes. Losses are normally incurred in such situations. For example, assume that an *uninsured* building costing $40,000 with accumulated depreciation of $12,000 was completely destroyed by a fire. The journal entry is:

Fire Loss	28,000	
Accumulated Depreciation—Buildings.	12,000	
Buildings		40,000
To record fire loss.		

If the building was *insured*, only the amount of the fire loss exceeding the amount to be recovered from the insurance company would be debited to the Fire Loss account. To illustrate, assume that in the example above, the building was partially insured and that $22,000 is recoverable from the insurance company. The journal entry is:

Receivable from Insurance Company	22,000	
Fire Loss	6,000	
Accumulated Depreciation—Buildings.	12,000	
Buildings		40,000
To record fire loss and amount recoverable from insurance company.		

Exchanges of Plant Assets (Nonmonetary Assets)

Nonmonetary assets are those items whose price may change over time, such as inventories, property, plant, and equipment. In accounting for the exchange of nonmonetary assets, ordinarily the recorded amount should be based on the fair market value of the asset given up or the fair value of the asset received, whichever is more clearly evident. If a gain or loss results from the exchange, the loss is always recognized; the gain may or may not be recognized, depending on whether the asset exchanged is similar or dissimilar to the asset received.

Similar assets are those of the same general type, that perform the same function, or that are employed in the same line of business. Examples of the exchange of similar assets include exchanging a building for another building, a delivery truck for another delivery truck, and equipment for other equipment. Conversely, examples of the exchange of dissimilar assets include exchanging a building for land, and equipment for inventory.

In general, losses on nonmonetary assets are recognized, regardless of whether the assets are similar or dissimilar in nature. Gains are recognized if the assets are dissimilar in nature because the earnings process related to those assets is considered to be completed. With one exception, gains are deferred on the exchange of similar nonmonetary assets. The exception occurs when monetary consideration is received in addition to the similar asset. In this case, a partial gain may be recognized when cash is received along with an asset. Because the specific details of monetary consideration are reserved for an intermediate accounting text, assume in the examples given that cash has been paid, not received. Both gains and losses on the disposal of nonmonetary assets are computed by comparing the book value of the asset given up with the fair market value of the asset given up.

The proper accounting for exchanges of dissimilar and similar plant assets is illustrated below.

Objective 2
Describe and
record exchanges
of dissimilar and
similar plant as-
sets

Exchanges of Dissimilar Plant Assets.   Sometimes a machine is traded for a dissimilar plant asset such as a truck. Exchanges of dissimilar plant assets are accounted for by recording the new asset at the fair market value of the asset received or the asset(s) given up, whichever is more clearly evident.[1] The cash price of the new asset may be stated; if so, the cash price should be used to record the new asset. If the cash price is not stated, the fair market value of the old asset plus any cash paid is assumed to be the cash price and is used to record the new asset. Thus, the asset received would normally be recorded at either (1) the stated cash price of the new asset or (2) a known fair market value of the asset given up plus any cash paid.

The book value of the old asset is removed from the accounts by debiting accumulated depreciation and crediting the old asset. The Cash account is credited for any amount paid. If the amount at which the new asset is recorded exceeds the book value of the old asset plus any cash paid, a gain is recorded to balance the journal entry. If the situation is vice versa, a loss is recorded to balance the journal entry.

To illustrate such an exchange, assume that an old factory machine is exchanged for a new delivery truck. The machine cost $45,000 and had an up-to-date accumulated depreciation balance of $38,000. The truck had a $55,000 cash price and was acquired by trading in the machine with a fair value of $3,000 and paying $52,000 cash. The journal entry to record the exchange is:

Trucks.	55,000	
Accumulated Depreciation—Machinery	38,000	
Loss from Disposal of Plant Assets	4,000	
Machinery.		45,000
Cash		52,000
To record loss on exchange of dissimilar plant assets.		

The $4,000 loss on the exchange can also be computed as the book value of the old asset less the fair market value of the old asset. The calculation is as follows:

---

[1] APB, *APB Opinion No. 29,* "Accounting for Nonmonetary Transactions" (New York: AICPA, May 1973), par. 16.

Machine cost.	$45,000
Accumulated depreciation	38,000
Book value.	$ 7,000
Fair market value of old asset	
(trade-in allowance)	3,000
Loss realized.	$ 4,000

To illustrate the recognition of a gain from an exchange of dissimilar plant assets, assume that the fair market value of the above machine was $9,000 instead of $3,000, and that $46,000 was paid in cash. The gain would be $2,000 ($9,000 fair market value less $7,000 book value). The journal entry to record the exchange would be:

Trucks.	55,000	
Accumulated Depreciation—Machinery	38,000	
Machinery		45,000
Cash		46,000
Gain on Disposal of Plant Assets		2,000
To record gain on exchange of dissimilar plant assets.		

The gain of $2,000 on the exchange can also be computed as the fair market value of the old asset less the book value of the old asset. The calculation is as follows:

Machine cost.	$45,000
Accumulated depreciation	38,000
Book value.	$ 7,000
Fair market value of old asset	
(trade-in allowance)	9,000
Gain realized.	$ 2,000

Remember, both gains and losses are always recognized on exchanges of dissimilar plant assets. As shown below, gains on exchanges of similar plant assets should not be recognized.

Exchanges of Similar Plant Assets.   Plant assets such as automobiles, trucks, and office equipment are often exchanged by trading the old asset for a similar new one. When such an exchange occurs, the company usually receives a trade-in allowance for the old asset,[2] and the balance is paid in cash. The cash price of the new asset is often stated. If not, the cash price is assumed to be the fair market value of the old asset plus the cash paid.

---

[2] Trade-in allowance is sometimes expressed as the difference between *list* price and cash paid, but we choose to define it as the difference between *cash* price and cash paid because this latter definition seems to agree with current practice for exchange transactions.

When similar assets are exchanged, the general rule that new assets are recorded at the fair market value of what is given up or received is modified slightly. **The new asset is recorded at (1) the cash price of the asset received or (2) the book value of the old asset plus the cash paid, whichever is lower.** When this rule is applied to exchanges of similar assets, **losses are recognized, but gains are not.**

To illustrate the accounting for exchanges of similar plant assets, assume that $50,000 cash and delivery truck No. 1—which cost $45,000, had $38,000 of accumulated depreciation, and had a $5,000 fair market value—were exchanged for delivery truck No. 2. The new truck has a cash price (fair market value) of $55,000. A loss of $2,000 is realized on the exchange.

Cost of delivery truck No. 1	$45,000
Accumulated depreciation	38,000
Book value	$ 7,000
Fair market value of old asset	
(trade-in allowance)	5,000
Loss on exchange of plant assets	$ 2,000

The journal entry to record the exchange is:

Trucks (cost of No. 2).	55,000	
Accumulated Depreciation—Trucks	38,000	
Loss from Disposal of Plant Assets	2,000	
Trucks (cost of No. 1).		45,000
Cash		50,000
To record loss on exchange of similar plant assets.		

Note that exchanges of similar plant assets are recorded just like exchanges of dissimilar plant assets when a *loss* **occurs from the exchange.**

Accounting for any gain resulting from exchanges of similar plant assets is handled differently than a gain resulting from exchanges of dissimilar plant assets. To illustrate, assume that in the preceding example, delivery truck No. 1 (now with a fair market value of $9,000) and $46,000 cash were given in exchange for delivery truck No. 2. A gain of $2,000 is indicated on the exchange:

Cost of delivery truck No. 1	$45,000
Accumulated depreciation	38,000
Book value.	$ 7,000
Fair market value of old asset	
(trade-in allowance)	9,000
Gain indicated	$ 2,000

The journal entry to record the exchange is:

Trucks (cost of No. 2) ($7,000 + $46,000)	53,000	
Accumulated Depreciation—Trucks	38,000	
Trucks (cost of No. 1).		45,000
Cash		46,000

To record exchange of similar plant assets.

When similar assets are exchanged, a gain is not recognized. The new asset is recorded at book value of the old asset ($7,000) plus cash paid ($46,000). The gain is deducted from the cost of the new asset ($55,000). Thus, the cost basis of the new delivery truck is equal to $55,000 less the $2,000 gain, or $53,000. This $53,000 cost basis is used in recording depreciation on the truck and determining any gain or loss on its disposal.

Book value of old truck (No. 1)	$ 7,000
Cash paid	46,000
Cost of new truck (No. 2)	$53,000
Fair market value of new truck (No. 2)	$55,000 (equal)
Less: Gain indicated	2,000
Cost of new truck (No. 2)	$53,000

The justification used by the Accounting Principles Board for not recognizing gains on exchanges of similar plant assets is that "revenue should not be recognized merely because one productive asset is substituted for a similar productive asset but rather should be considered to flow from the production and sale of the goods or services to which the substituted productive asset is committed."[3] In effect, the gain on an exchange of similar plant assets is realized in future accounting periods in the form of increased net income resulting from smaller depreciation charges on the newly acquired asset. In the preceding example, annual depreciation expense is less if it is based on the truck's $53,000 cost basis than if it is based on the truck's $55,000 cash price. Thus, future net income per year will be larger.

Objective 3
Discuss the differences between accounting principles and tax rules in the treatment of gains and losses from the exchange of plant assets

Tax Rules and Plant Asset Exchanges.   The Internal Revenue Code does not allow recognition of *gains or losses* for income tax purposes when similar productive assets are exchanged. For income tax purposes, the cost basis of the new asset is the book value of the old asset plus any additional cash (called **boot**) paid.

Accounting principles and income tax laws agree on the treatment of gains, but they disagree on the treatment of losses. Thus, in the previous example involving a $2,000 loss on the exchange of delivery trucks, the loss should not be recognized for income tax purposes. In this case, the loss is

---

[3] *APB Opinion No. 29,* par. 16.

treated as an adjustment of the cost of the new asset. The transaction would be recorded as follows for income tax purposes:

Trucks (cost of No. 2) ($7,000 + $50,000)	57,000	
Accumulated Depreciation—Trucks	38,000	
Trucks (cost of No. 1).		45,000
Cash		50,000
To record exchange of similar plant assets using tax method.		

The new asset is recorded at the $7,000 book value of the old asset plus the cash payment of $50,000. The unrecognized loss of $2,000 is added to the cost basis of the new asset. This $57,000 cost basis is used in recording depreciation on the truck and determining any gain or loss on its disposal. The cost basis of the new asset is computed as follows:

Book value of old truck (No. 1)	$ 7,000
Cash paid	50,000
Cost of new truck (No. 2)	$57,000
Fair market value of new truck (No. 2)	$55,000 (equal)
Add: Unrecognized loss	2,000
Cost of new truck (No. 2)	$57,000

Illustration 8.1 summarizes the rules for recording exchanges of plant assets for accounting and income tax purposes. Studying this illustration may help you remember how to record exchange transactions.

Illustration 8.1
SUMMARY OF RULES FOR RECORDING EXCHANGES OF PLANT ASSETS

	Dissimilar Assets	Similar Assets		
	For Both Accounting and Tax Purposes	For Accounting Purposes		For Tax Purposes
Recognize Gains?	Yes	No		No
Recognize Losses?	Yes	Yes		No
Record New Asset at:	Cash price of new asset **or** fair market value of old asset plus cash paid	**If loss:** Cash price of new asset **or** fair market value of old asset plus cash paid	**If gain:** Book value of old asset plus cash paid	Book value of old asset plus cash paid

Because of differences between accounting principles and income tax laws, two sets of depreciation records must be kept if a *material* (relatively large) *loss* occurs on an exchange of similar plant assets. One set of depreciation records is based on the accounting valuation of the new asset (cash price of new asset or fair market value of old asset plus cash paid) and is used to determine net income for financial reporting purposes; the second set is based on the tax valuation of the new asset (book value of old asset plus cash paid).

If the loss is immaterial, some companies follow the tax method in their books to account for a loss from an exchange of similar plant assets to avoid keeping two sets of accounting records. For example, assume a company that earns approximately $1,000,000 per year suffers a $25 loss on an exchange of plant assets. In relation to $1,000,000, $25 is immaterial, and the company need only keep one set of accounting records regarding the exchange and not show the loss.

Removal Costs

Removal costs are incurred to dismantle and remove a company's old plant asset. These costs are deducted from salvage proceeds to determine the asset's net salvage value. Removal costs are associated with the old asset, not the new asset acquired as a replacement.

The next section discusses natural resources. Again you will note the underlying accounting principle of matching expenses of an accounting period with the revenues earned in that *same* accounting period.

NATURAL RESOURCES

Resources supplied by nature, such as ore deposits, mineral deposits, oil reserves, gas deposits, and timber stands, are known as **natural resources** or **wasting assets.** Natural resources represent inventories of raw materials that can be consumed (exhausted) through extraction or removal from their natural setting (e.g., removing oil from the ground).

On the balance sheet, natural resources are classified as a separate group among noncurrent assets under headings such as "Timber stands" and "Oil reserves." Natural resources are typically recorded at their cost of acquisition plus exploration and development costs; they are reported on the balance sheet at total cost less accumulated depletion. (Accumulated depletion is similar to the accumulated depreciation used for plant assets.) When analyzing the financial condition of companies owning natural resources, caution must be exercised because the historical costs reported for the natural resources may only be a small fraction of their current value.

Depletion

Depletion is the exhaustion of a natural resource that results from the physical removal of a part of the resource. In each accounting period, the depletion recognized is an estimate of the cost of the natural resource that was removed from its natural setting during the period. **Depletion is recorded by debiting a Depletion account and crediting an Accumulated Depletion account, which is a contra account to the natural resource asset account.**

By crediting the Accumulated Depletion account instead of the asset account, the original cost of the entire natural resource continues to be reported on the financial statements, and statement users can see the percentage of the resource that has been removed. This depletion cost is combined with other extraction, mining, or removal costs to determine the total cost of the resource available. This total cost is assigned to either the cost of natural resources sold or the inventory of the natural resource still on hand. Thus, it is possible that all, some, or none of the depletion and removal costs recognized in an accounting period will be expensed in that period, depending on the portion sold. If all of the resource is sold, all of the depletion and removal costs are expensed. The cost of any portion not yet sold will be part of the cost of inventory.

Objective 4
Determine the periodic depletion cost of a natural resource and calculate depreciation of plant assets located on extractive industry property

Computing Periodic Depletion Cost. Depletion charges usually are computed by the units-of-production method. Total cost is divided by the estimated number of units—tons, barrels, or board feet—**that can be economically extracted** from the property. This calculation provides a per unit depletion cost. For example, assume that in 1995 a company paid $650,000 for a tract of land containing ore deposits. The company spent $100,000 in exploration costs. The results indicated that approximately 900,000 tons of ore can be economically removed from the land, after which the land will be worth $50,000. Costs of $200,000 were incurred to develop the site, including the cost of running power lines and building roads. Total cost subject to depletion is the net cost assignable to the natural resource plus the exploration and development costs. When the property is purchased, a journal entry is made to assign the purchase price to the two assets purchased—the natural resource and the land. The entry would be:

Land	50,000	
Ore Deposits	600,000	
Cash		650,000
To record purchase of land and mine.		

After the purchase, all other costs mentioned above are debited to the natural resource account. The entry would be:

Ore Deposits ($100,000 + $200,000)	300,000	
Cash		300,000
To record costs of exploration and development.		

The formula for finding depletion cost per unit is:

$$\frac{\text{Depletion cost}}{\text{per unit}} = \frac{\text{Cost of site} - \text{Residual value of land} + \text{Costs to develop site}}{\text{Number of units that can be economically extracted}}$$

In some instances, companies buy only the right to extract the natural resource from someone else's land. **When the land is not purchased, its residual value is irrelevant and should be ignored.** If there is an obligation to restore the land to a usable condition, these estimated restoration costs should be added to the costs to develop the site.

In the above example where the land was purchased, the total costs of the mineral deposits is equal to the cost of the site ($650,000) minus the residual value of land ($50,000) plus costs to develop the site ($300,000), or a total of $900,000. The unit (per ton) depletion charge is $1, or $900,000/900,000 tons.

The formula to compute the depletion cost of a period is:

$$\begin{array}{c} \text{Depletion cost} \\ \text{of a period} \end{array} = \begin{array}{c} \text{Depletion cost} \\ \text{per unit} \end{array} \times \begin{array}{c} \text{Number of units extracted} \\ \text{during period} \end{array}$$

In this example, if 100,000 tons are mined in 1995, the entry to record the depletion cost of $100,000 ($1 × 100,000) for the period is:

Depletion   100,000
    Accumulated Depletion—Ore Deposits*   100,000
    To record depletion for 1995.

* Instead of crediting the accumulated depletion account, the Ore Deposits account could have been credited directly. But for reasons indicated earlier, the credit is usually to an accumulated depletion account.

The Depletion account contains the "in the ground" cost of the ore or natural resource mined. This cost is combined with other extractive costs to determine the total cost of the ore mined. To illustrate, assume that in addition to the $100,000 depletion cost, mining labor costs totaled $320,000, and other mining costs, such as depreciation, property taxes, power, and supplies, totaled $60,000. If 80,000 tons were sold and 20,000 remained on hand at the end of the period, the total cost of $480,000 would be allocated as follows:

Depletion cost.	$100,000
Mining labor costs.	320,000
Other mining costs.	60,000
Total cost of 100,000 tons mined ($4.80 per ton).	$480,000
Less: Ore inventory (20,000 tons at $4.80)	96,000
Cost of ore sold (80,000 tons at $4.80)	$384,000

Note that the average cost per ton to mine 100,000 tons was $4.80 ($480,000/100,000). The income statement would show cost of ore sold of $384,000. Depletion would not be reported separately as an expense because depletion is included in cost of ore sold. The balance sheet would show inventory of ore on hand (a current asset) at $96,000 ($4.80 × 20,000). The balance sheet would also report the cost less accumulated depletion of the natural resource as follows:

| Ore deposits . . . . | $900,000 | |
| Less: Accumulated depletion . . . . . . | 100,000 | $800,000 |

Another method of calculating depletion cost is the percentage of revenue method. This method, used only for income tax purposes and not for financial statements, is not discussed in this text.

Depreciation of Plant Assets Located on Extractive Industry Property. Depreciable plant assets erected on extractive industry property are depreciated in the same manner as other depreciable assets. **If such assets will be abandoned when the natural resource is exhausted, they should be depreciated over the shorter of the (a) physical life of the asset or (b) life of the natural resource.** In some cases, periodic depreciation charges are computed using the units-of-production method. Using this method matches the life of the plant asset with the life of the natural resource. This method is recommended where the *physical* life of the plant asset equals or exceeds the life of the natural resource but its *useful* life is limited to the life of the natural resource.

Assume mining property is acquired and a building on the site is purchased for exclusive use in the mining operations. Also assume that the units-of-production method is used for computing building depreciation. Relevant facts are:

Building cost	$310,000
Estimated physical life of building.	20 years
Estimated salvage value of building (after mine exhausted).	$ 10,000
Capacity of mine.	1,000,000 tons
Expected life of mine.	10 years

Since the life of the mine (10 years or 1,000,000 tons) is shorter than the life of the building (20 years), the building should be depreciated over the life of the mine. In this case, the depreciation charge should be based on tons of ore rather than years because the mine's "life" could be longer or shorter than 10 years, depending on how rapidly the ore is removed from the mine.

Suppose that during the first year of operations, 150,000 tons of ore are extracted. Building depreciation for the first year is $45,000, computed as follows:

$$\text{Depreciation per unit} = \frac{\text{Asset cost} - \text{Estimated salvage value}}{\begin{array}{c}\text{Total tons of ore in mine that}\\ \text{can be economically extracted}\end{array}}$$

$$= \frac{\$310,000 - \$10,000}{1,000,000 \text{ tons}} = \$0.30 \text{ per ton}$$

$$\text{Depreciation for year} = \text{Depreciation per unit} \times \text{Units extracted}$$

$$= \$0.30 \text{ per ton} \times 150,000 \text{ tons} = \$45,000$$

A BROADER PERSPECTIVE

MURPHY OIL CORPORATION (DEC.)

Costs and Expenses (thousands of dollars):	1990	1989	1988
Crude oil, products, and related operating expenses	$1,370,131	$1,028,457	$ 886,965
Drilling and other operating expenses	138,856	144,685	155,273
Exploration expenses, including undeveloped lease amortization	63,421	48,594	59,805
Selling and general expenses.	90,557	85,203	78,825
Depreciation, depletion, amortization, and abandonments	213,540	210,110	212,764
Interest expense.	36,553	45,368	36,856
Interest capitalized.	(3,743)	(3,828)	(2,157)
Total costs and expenses	$1,909,315	$1,558,589	$1,428,331

NOTES TO CONSOLIDATED FINANCIAL STATEMENTS

Note A (In Part): Significant Accounting Policies

Depreciation and Depletion—Depreciation and depletion of producing oil and gas properties are provided under the units-of-production method on a property-by-property basis. Developed reserves are used to compute unit rates for unamortized tangible and intangible development costs, and proved reserves are used for unamortized leasehold costs. Estimated costs (net of salvage value) of dismantling oil and gas production facilities are computed and included in depreciation and depletion using the units-of-production method. Depreciation of refining and marketing facilities is calculated using the composite straight-line method. Depletion of timber is based on board feet cut. Depreciation of each drilling barge and related equipment is determined by dividing the cost less accumulated depreciation and salvage value by the estimated remaining useful life of the barge. Diving equipment, office buildings, pipelines, and other properties are depreciated by individual unit based on the straight-line method.

SOURCE: Based on American Institute of Certified Public Accountants, *Accounting Trends & Techniques* (New York: AICPA, 1991), pp. 326–27.

Depreciation on the building would be included on the income statement as part of the cost of ore that was sold and would be carried as part of inventory cost for those tons of ore that were not sold during the period. Accumulated depreciation on the building would be reported on the balance sheet with the related asset account.

Plant assets and natural resources are tangible assets used by a company to produce revenues. A company may also acquire intangible assets to assist in producing revenues.

INTANGIBLE ASSETS

Intangible assets have no physical characteristics but are of value because of the advantages or exclusive privileges and rights they provide to a business. Intangible assets generally arise from two sources: (1) exclusive privileges granted by governmental authority or by legal contract, such as patents, copyrights, franchises, trademarks and trade names, and leases; and (2) superior entrepreneurial capacity or management know-how and customer loyalty, which is called *goodwill*.

All intangible assets are nonphysical, but not all nonphysical assets are classified as intangibles. For example, accounts receivable and prepaid expenses are nonphysical, but they are classified as current assets rather than intangible assets. Intangible assets are generally both nonphysical and noncurrent; they are reported in a separate long-term section of the balance sheet entitled "Intangible assets."

Acquisition of Intangible Assets

Objective 5
Prepare entries for the acquisition and amortization of intangible assets

Like most other assets, intangible assets are recorded initially at cost. However, computing an intangible asset's acquisition cost differs from computing a plant asset's acquisition cost. **Only outright purchase costs are included in the acquisition cost of an intangible asset;** the acquisition cost does *not* include cost of internal development or self-creation of the asset. If an intangible asset is internally generated in its entirety, none of its costs will be capitalized. Therefore, some companies have extremely valuable assets that may not even be recorded in their asset accounts. The reasons for this practice can be understood by studying the history of accounting for research and development costs.

Research and development (R&D) costs are costs incurred in a planned search for new knowledge and in translating such knowledge into new products or processes. Prior to 1975, research and development costs were often capitalized as intangible assets when future benefits were expected from their incurrence. Since it was often difficult to determine the costs applicable to future benefits, many companies expensed all such costs as they were incurred. Other companies capitalized those costs that related to proven products and expensed the rest as incurred.

As a result of these varied accounting practices, the Financial Accounting Standards Board in *Statement No. 2* in 1974 ruled that all research and development costs, other than those directly reimbursable by government agencies and others, must be expensed when incurred. Immediate expensing is justified on the grounds that (1) the amount of costs applicable to the future cannot be measured with any high degree of precision; (2) doubt exists as to whether any future benefits will be received; and (3) even if benefits are expected, they cannot be measured. Thus, research and development costs no longer appear as intangible assets on the balance sheet. The same line of reasoning is applied to other costs associated with internally generated intangible assets, such as the internal costs of developing a patent.

Amortization of Intangible Assets

Amortization is the systematic write-off of the cost of an intangible asset to expense. A portion of an intangible asset's cost is allocated to each accounting period in the economic (useful) life of the asset. All intangible assets are subject to amortization, which is similar to plant asset depreciation. Generally, amortization is recorded by debiting Amortization Expense and crediting the intangible asset account. An accumulated amortization account could be used to record amortization. However, usually the information gained from such accounting would not be significant because intangibles do not normally account for as significant an amount of total asset dollars as do plant assets.

Intangibles should be amortized over the shorter of (1) their economic life, (2) their legal life, or (3) 40 years. The 40-year limitation was established by the Accounting Principles Board. *APB Opinion No. 17* requires an intangible asset acquired after October 31, 1970, to be amortized over a period not to exceed 40 years. Straight-line amortization must be used unless another method of amortization (such as units-of-production) can be shown to be superior. Straight-line amortization is calculated in the same way as straight-line depreciation for plant assets.

Patents

A **patent** is a right granted by the federal government giving the owner the exclusive right to manufacture, sell, lease, or otherwise benefit from an invention for a limited period of time. The value of a patent lies in its ability to produce revenue. Patents have a legal life of 17 years. Protection for the patent owner begins at the time of patent application and lasts for 17 years from the date the patent is granted.

The purchase of a patent should be recorded in the Patents account at cost. The Patents account should also be debited for the cost of the *first* successful defense of the patent in lawsuits (assuming an outside law firm was hired rather than using internal legal staff). Also, the cost of any competing patents that were purchased to ensure revenue-generating capability of the purchased patent should be debited to the Patents account.

The cost of a purchased patent should be amortized over the shorter of 17 years (or remaining legal life) or its estimated useful life. If a patent cost $40,000 and has a useful life of 10 years, the journal entries to record the patent and periodic amortization are:

Patents	40,000	
Cash		40,000
To record purchase of patent.		
Patent Amortization Expense	4,000	
Patents		4,000
To record patent amortization.		

If the patent becomes worthless before it is fully amortized, the unamortized balance in the Patents account should be charged to expense.

As noted on page 426 in the discussion on research and development costs, all R&D costs incurred in the internal development of a product, process, or idea that is later patented must be expensed, rather than capitalized. In the above example, the cost of the purchased patent was amortized over its useful life of 10 years. If the patent had been the result of an internally generated product or process, its cost of $40,000 would have been expensed as incurred, in accordance with *Statement No. 2* of the Financial Accounting Standards Board.

Copyrights

A **copyright** is an exclusive right granted by the federal government giving the owner protection against the illegal reproduction by others of the owner's written works, designs, and literary productions. The copyright period is for the life of the author (creator) plus 50 years. Since most publications have a limited life, the cost of the copyright may appropriately be charged to expense on a straight-line basis over the life of the first edition published or based on projections of the number of copies to be sold per year.

Franchises

A **franchise** is a contract between two parties granting the franchisee (the purchaser of the franchise) certain rights and privileges ranging from name identification to complete monopoly of service. In many instances, both parties are private businesses. For example, an individual who wishes to open a hamburger restaurant may purchase a McDonald's franchise; the two parties involved are the individual business owner and McDonald's Corporation. This franchise would allow the business owner to use the McDonald's golden arch, and would provide the owner with advertising and many other benefits. The legal life of a franchise may be limited by contract.

The parties involved in a franchise arrangement are not always private businesses. A franchise may also be granted to a private company by a government agency. A city may give a franchise to a utility company, giving the utility company the exclusive right to provide service to a particular area.

In addition to providing benefits, a franchise usually places certain restrictions on the franchisee. These restrictions are generally related to rates or prices charged; they may also be in regard to product quality or to the particular supplier from whom supplies and inventory items must be purchased.

If periodic payments to the grantor of the franchise are required, they should be debited to a Franchise Expense account. If a lump-sum payment is made to obtain the franchise, the cost should be recorded in an asset account entitled Franchise and amortized over the shorter of the legal life (if limited by contract), the economic life of the franchise, or 40 years.

Trademarks; Trade Names

A **trademark** is a symbol, design, or logo that is used in conjunction with a particular product or company. A **trade name** is a brand name under which a product is sold or a company does business. Often trademarks and trade names are extremely valuable to a company, but if they have been internally developed, they will have no recorded asset cost. However, if such items are purchased by a business from an external source, they are recorded at cost and amortized over their economic life or 40 years, whichever is shorter.

Leases

A **lease** is a contract to rent property. The owner of the property is the grantor of the lease and is called the *lessor*. The person or company obtaining rights to possess and use the property is called the *lessee*. The rights granted under the lease are called a **leasehold.** The accounting for a lease depends on whether it is a capital lease or an operating lease.

Capital Leases.   A **capital lease** transfers to the lessee virtually all rewards and risks that accompany ownership of property. A lease is a capital lease if, among other provisions, it (1) transfers ownership of the leased property to the lessee at the end of the lease term or (2) contains a bargain purchase option that permits the lessee to buy the property at a price significantly below fair market value at the end of the lease term.

A capital lease is a means of financing property acquisitions and has the same economic impact as a purchase made on an installment plan. Thus, the lessee in a capital lease must record the leased property as an asset and the lease obligation as a liability. Because a capital lease is an asset, the leased property is depreciated over its useful life to the lessee. A part of each lease payment is recorded as interest expense, with the balance viewed as a payment on the lease liability.

The proper accounting for capital leases for both lessees and lessors has been an extremely difficult problem. Further discussion of capital leases is left for an intermediate accounting text.

Operating Leases.   If a lease does not qualify as a capital lease, it is an **operating lease.** A one-year lease on an apartment and a week's rental of an automobile are examples of operating leases. Such leases make no attempt to transfer any of the rewards and risks of ownership to the lessee. As a result, there may be no recordable transaction when a lease is signed.

In some situations, the lease may call for an immediate cash payment that must be recorded. Assume, for example, that a business signed a lease that required the immediate payment of the annual rent of $15,000 for each of the first and fifth years of a five-year lease. The lessee would record the payment as follows:

Prepaid Rent.	15,000	
Leasehold	15,000	
Cash		30,000

To record first and fifth years' rent on a five-year lease.

Since the Leasehold account is actually a long-term prepaid rent account for the fifth year's annual rent, it is classified as an intangible asset until the beginning of the fifth year. Then the Leasehold account is reclassified as a current asset and may be transferred into a Prepaid Rent account. Accounting for the balance in the Leasehold account depends on the terms of the lease. In the above example, the $15,000 in the Leasehold account will be charged to expense over the fifth year only. The balance in Prepaid Rent will be charged to expense in the first year. Thus, assuming the lease year and fiscal year coincide, the entry for the first year is:

Rent Expense	15,000	
Prepaid Rent.		15,000

To record rent expense.

The entry in the fifth year is:

Rent Expense	15,000	
Leasehold		15,000

To record rent expense.

The accounting for the second, third, and fourth years will be the same as for the first year. The rent will be recorded in Prepaid Rent when paid in advance for the year and then expensed. As stated above, the amount in the Leasehold account may be transferred to Prepaid Rent at the beginning of the fifth year by debiting Prepaid Rent and crediting Leasehold. If this entry was made, the credit in the above entry would have been to Prepaid Rent.

In some cases, when a lease is signed, a lump-sum payment is paid that does not cover a specific year's rent. This payment is debited to the Leasehold account and amortized over the life of the lease. The straight-line method is required unless another method can be shown to be superior. Assume the $15,000 rent for the fifth year in the above example was, instead, a lump-sum payment on the lease in addition to the annual rent payments. An annual adjusting entry to amortize the $15,000 over five years is required. The entry would read:

Rent Expense	3,000	
Leasehold		3,000

To amortize leasehold.

In this example, the annual rental expense is $18,000: $15,000 annual cash rent plus $3,000 amortization of leasehold ($15,000/5).

Periodic rent may be based on current-year sales or usage rather than being a constant amount. For example, if a lease called for rent equal to 5% of current-year sales and sales were $400,000 in 1995, the rent for 1995 would be $20,000. The rent would either be paid or adjusted to the correct amount at the end of the year.

Leasehold Improvements

A **leasehold improvement** is any physical alteration made by the lessee to the leased property in which benefits are expected beyond the current accounting period. Leasehold improvements made by a lessee usually become the property of the lessor after the lease has expired. However, since leasehold improvements are an asset of the lessee during the lease period, they should be debited to a Leasehold Improvements account. Leasehold improvements are then amortized to expense over the period of time benefited by the improvements. The amortization period for leasehold improvements should be the shorter of the life of the improvements or the life of the lease. If the lease can (and probably will) be renewed at the option of the lessee, the option period should be included in the life of the lease.

As an illustration, assume that on January 2, 1995, Wolf Company leases a building for 20 years under a nonrenewable lease at an annual rental of $20,000, payable on each December 31. Wolf immediately incurs a cost of $80,000 for improvements to the building, such as interior walls for office separation, ceiling fans, and recessed lighting. The improvements have an estimated life of 30 years. The $80,000 should be amortized over the 20-year lease period, since that period is shorter than the life of the improvements, and Wolf will not be able to use the improvements beyond the life of the lease. If only annual financial statements are prepared, the following journal entry will properly record the rental expense for the year ended December 31, 1995:

Rent Expense (or Leasehold Improvement Expense) . . .	4,000	
Leasehold Improvements		4,000
To record amortization of leasehold improvement.		
Rent Expense	20,000	
Cash		20,000
To record annual rent.		

Thus, the total cost to rent the building each year equals the $20,000 cash rent plus the amortization of the leasehold improvements.

Although leaseholds are intangible assets, leaseholds and leasehold improvements are sometimes shown in the property, plant, and equipment section of the balance sheet.

Goodwill

In accounting, **goodwill** is an intangible value attached to a company resulting mainly from the company's management skill or know-how and a favorable reputation with customers. A company's value may be greater than the total of the fair market value of its tangible and identifiable intangible assets. This greater value means that the company is able to generate an above-average income on each dollar invested in the business. Thus, proof of the existence of goodwill for a company can be found only in its ability to generate superior earnings or income.

A Goodwill account will appear in the accounting records only if goodwill has been purchased. Goodwill cannot be purchased by itself; an entire business or a part of a business must be purchased to obtain the accompanying intangible asset, goodwill.

To illustrate, assume that Lenox Company purchased all of Martin Company's assets for $700,000. Lenox also agreed to assume responsibility for a $350,000 mortgage note payable owed by Martin. Goodwill is determined as the difference between the amount paid for the business including the debt assumed ($700,000 + $350,000 = $1,050,000) and the *fair market value* of the assets purchased. Notice that fair market value of the assets rather than book value is used to determine the amount of goodwill. The following shows the computation for the amount of goodwill purchased by Lenox:

Cash paid		$ 700,000
Mortgage note payable assumed.		350,000
Total price paid.		$1,050,000
Less fair market values of individually identifiable assets:		
Accounts receivable.	$ 95,000	
Merchandise inventory	100,000	
Land	240,000	
Buildings.	275,000	
Equipment	200,000	
Patents.	65,000	975,000
Goodwill		$ 75,000

The $75,000 is the amount of goodwill to be recorded as an intangible asset on the books of Lenox Company; **all of the other assets will be recorded at their fair market values,** and the liability will be recorded at the amount due. Specific reasons for the existence of goodwill in a company might include good reputation, customer loyalty, superior product design, unrecorded intangible assets (because they were developed internally), and superior human resources. Since these positive factors are not individually quantifiable, they are all grouped together and referred to as *goodwill*. The journal entry to record the above purchase is:

Accounts Receivable	95,000
Merchandise Inventory	100,000
Land	240,000
Buildings	275,000
Equipment.	200,000
Patents	65,000
Goodwill.	75,000
Cash	700,000
Mortgage Note Payable.	350,000
To record the purchase of Martin Company's assets and assumption of mortgage note payable.	

Goodwill, like all other intangibles, must be amortized. No legal life exists for goodwill, and the useful life of goodwill usually cannot be reasonably estimated. If, for example, the new owner made substantial changes in the method of doing business, goodwill that existed at the purchase date could rapidly disappear. Therefore, current accounting practice requires the amortization of goodwill over a period not to exceed 40 years. This requirement is necessary because the value of purchased goodwill will eventually disappear. Other goodwill may be generated in its place, but the organization cannot record its internally created goodwill any more than it can record other internally generated intangible assets.

The entry to amortize the $75,000 goodwill over a 40-year period is:

Goodwill Amortization Expense	1,875	
Goodwill.		1,875
To amortize goodwill ($75,000/40 years).		

Reporting Amortization

Illustration 8.2 shows the frequencies of intangible assets being amortized by a sample of 600 companies for the years 1987–90.

Amortization expense for most intangible assets discussed in this chapter appears among the operating expenses on the income statement. The account titles used are all of this type: "Amortization of Goodwill (or Pat-

Illustration 8.2
INTANGIBLE ASSETS HELD BY SAMPLE OF 600 COMPANIES

	Number of Companies			
	1990	*1989*	*1988*	*1987*
Assets being amortized:				
Goodwill recognized in a business combination	379	367	340	338
Patents, patent rights.	62	62	67	59
Trademarks, brand names, copyrights	46	38	41	34
Licenses, franchises, memberships	16	19	22	26
Other—described.	57	52	47	20

SOURCE: American Institute of Certified Public Accountants, *Accounting Trends & Techniques* (New York: AICPA, 1991), p. 174.

Illustration 8.3
RULES FOR AMORTIZATION OF INTANGIBLE ASSETS

Intangible Asset	Useful Life	Amortized over Shorter of	
		Legal Life	Maximum Life (years)
Patents	?	17 years	40
Copyrights	?	Life of author plus 50 years	40
Franchises	?	No limit (unless limited by contract)	40
Trademarks; trade names	?	No limit	40
Leasehold improvements	?	Life of lease	40
Goodwill	?	No limit	40

ents, Copyrights, Franchises, Leaseholds) Expense.'' Periodic amortization of leaseholds and leasehold improvements is often reported as rent expense. The amortization of goodwill is an expense in determining accounting income but is not a deductible expense in determining taxable income.

Illustration 8.3 summarizes the amortization rules for intangible assets.

Balance Sheet Presentation

Illustration 8.4 shows a partial balance sheet for Reed Company. Unlike plant assets or natural resources, intangible assets are usually presented at a net amount in the balance sheet.

Illustration 8.4
PARTIAL BALANCE SHEET

REED COMPANY
Partial Balance Sheet
June 30, 1995

Property, plant, and equipment:		
Land.		$ 30,000
Buildings	$ 75,000	
Less: Accumulated depreciation.	45,000	30,000
Equipment.	$ 9,000	
Less: Accumulated depreciation.	1,500	7,500
Total property, plant, and equipment		$ 67,500
Natural resources:		
Mineral deposits	$300,000	
Less: Accumulated depletion	100,000	$200,000
Total natural resources		$200,000
Intangible assets:		
Patents		$ 10,000
Goodwill.		20,000
Total intangible assets		$ 30,000

ETHICS   A CLOSER LOOK

Ed Bentley owns two businesses: Bentley Transportation Company (BTC) and Bentley Leasing. BTC is a local shuttle service with no major assets, while Bentley Leasing purchases and leases shuttle vans to BTC for use in its operations and handles the routine maintenance on the vans. BTC leases only from Bentley Leasing, and Bentley Leasing provides no other company with leased assets. Bentley Leasing purchases accident and liability insurance on the vans.

The operating lease for a newly purchased shuttle van runs for one year. At the end of the first year, a separate lease is prepared for an additional two or three years. When the leases are due for renewal at the end of the first year, Ed typically inflates the rental amount in the new leases to help Bentley Leasing cover the cost of maintenance.

Bentley Leasing typically keeps shuttle vans for three or four years. Bentley Leasing then trades in the older vans for newer ones and pays any difference in cash. When the initial operating lease for a newly purchased van is prepared, Ed includes a nonrefundable deposit which covers the cash paid when the older van was traded in.

Required
a. Why do you think Ed created Bentley Leasing to lease vans to BTC? Is this arrangement legal? Is this arrangement ethical?
b. Discuss how Ed handles the leasing of shuttle vans. Do you believe that the leases are operating leases?

This chapter concludes your study of accounting for long-term assets. In Chapter 9, you will learn about the stockholders' equity section of the balance sheet and the transactions that cause changes in the items in that section.

UNDERSTANDING THE LEARNING OBJECTIVES

1. Calculate and prepare entries for the sale, retirement, and destruction of plant assets.
    *   By comparing an asset's book value (cost less accumulated depreciation) with its sales price, the company may show either a gain or a loss. If sales price is greater than book value, the company will show a gain. If sales price is less than book value, the company will show a loss. If sales price equals book value, no gain or loss results.
    *   When a plant asset is retired from service, the asset's cost and accumulated depreciation must be removed from the plant asset accounts.
    *   Plant assets are sometimes wrecked in accidents or destroyed by fire, flood, storm, and other causes. If the asset was not insured, the loss is equal to the book value of the asset. If the asset was insured, only the amount of the loss exceeding the amount to be recovered from the insurance company would be debited to a loss account.

2. Describe and record exchanges of dissimilar and similar plant assets.
   - In exchanges of dissimilar assets, the asset received is recorded at either (1) the stated cash price of the new asset or, if the cash price is not stated, (2) the known fair market value of the asset given up plus any cash paid.
   - In exchanges of similar assets, the new asset is recorded at (1) the cash price of the asset received or (2) the book value of the old asset plus the cash paid, whichever is lower.
3. Discuss the differences between accounting principles and tax rules in the treatment of gains and losses from the exchange of plant assets.
   - When dissimilar assets are exchanged, gains and losses are recognized for both accounting and tax purposes.
   - When similar assets are exchanged, losses are recognized for accounting purposes, but gains are not. For income tax purposes, neither gains nor losses are recognized; the new asset is recorded at the book value of the old asset plus any cash paid.
4. Determine the periodic depletion cost of a natural resource and calculate depreciation of plant assets located on extractive industry property.
   - Depletion charges usually are computed by the units-of-production method. Total cost is divided by the estimated number of units that are economically extractable from the property. This calculation provides a per unit depletion cost that is multiplied by the units extracted each year to obtain the depletion cost for that year.
   - Depreciable assets located on extractive industry property should be depreciated over the shorter of the (a) physical life of the asset or (b) life of the natural resource. The periodic depreciation charges usually are computed using the units-of-production method. Using this method matches the life of the plant asset with the life of the natural resource.
5. Prepare entries for the acquisition and amortization of intangible assets.
   - Only outright purchase costs are included in the acquisition cost of an intangible asset. If an intangible asset is internally generated, its cost is immediately expensed.
   - Intangibles should be amortized over the shorter of (1) their economic life, (2) their legal life, or (3) 40 years. Straight-line amortization must be used unless another method can be shown to be superior.

DEMONSTRATION PROBLEM 8–A

On January 2, 1992, Donald Company purchased a machine for $72,000 cash. The machine has an estimated useful life of six years and an estimated salvage value of $3,600. The straight-line method of depreciation is being used.

Required:

a. Compute the book value of the machine as of July 1, 1995.

b. Assume the machine was disposed of on July 1, 1995. Prepare the journal entries to record the disposal of the machine under each of the following unrelated assumptions:

1. The machine was sold for $24,000 cash.
2. The machine was sold for $36,000 cash.
3. The machine and $48,000 cash were exchanged for a new machine that had a cash price of $78,000. Use the accounting method rather than the income tax method.
4. The machine was completely destroyed by fire. Cash of $21,600 is expected to be recovered from the insurance company.

Solution to demonstration problem 8–A

a.

DONALD COMPANY
Schedule to Compute Book Value
July 1, 1995

Cost	$72,000
Less accumulated depreciation:	
$\dfrac{\$72,000 - \$3,600}{6 \text{ years}} = \$11,400 \text{ per year}$	
$11,400 × 3½ years = $39,900	39,900
Book value	$32,100

b. 1.

Cash	24,000	
Accumulated Depreciation—Machinery	39,900	
Loss from Disposal of Plant Assets	8,100	
Machinery		72,000
To record sale of machinery at a loss.		

2.

Cash	36,000	
Accumulated Depreciation—Machinery	39,900	
Machinery		72,000
Gain on Disposal of Plant Assets		3,900
To record sale of machinery at a gain.		

3.

Machinery (new)	78,000	
Accumulated Depreciation—Machinery	39,900	
Loss from Disposal of Plant Assets	2,100	
Machinery (old)		72,000
Cash		48,000
To record exchange of machines.		

4.

Receivable from Insurance Company	21,600	
Accumulated Depreciation—Machinery	39,900	
Fire Loss	10,500	
Machinery		72,000
To record loss of machinery.		

DEMONSTRATION PROBLEM 8–B

Clinton Company acquired on January 1, 1995, a tract of property containing timber at a cost of $16,000,000. After the timber is removed, the land will be worth about $6,400,000 and will be sold to another party. Costs of developing the site were $1,600,000. A building was erected at a cost of $320,000. The building had an estimated physical life of 20 years and will have an estimated salvage value of $160,000 when the timber is gone. It was expected that 50,000,000 board feet of timber can be economically cut. During the first year, 16,000,000 board feet were cut. The units-of-production basis is used to depreciate the building.

Required:

Prepare the entries to record:

a. The acquisition of the property.

b. The development costs.

c. Depletion cost for the first year.

d. Depreciation on the building for the first year.

Solution to demonstration problem 8–B

a. Land. 6,400,000
       Timber Stands 9,600,000
           Cash.   16,000,000
       To record purchase of land and timber.

b. Timber Stands 1,600,000
           Cash.   1,600,000
       To record costs of development of the site.

c. Depletion 3,584,000
           Accumulated Depreciation—Timber Stands   3,584,000
       To record depletion for 1995:
           ($9,600,000 + $1,600,000)/50,000,000 = $0.224 per
           board foot. $0.224 × 16,000,000 = $3,584,000.

d. Depreciation Expense—Buildings   51,200
           Accumulated Depreciation—Buildings.   51,200
       To record depreciation expense:
           $$\frac{\$320,000 - \$160,000}{50,000,000 \text{ board feet}} = \$0.0032 \text{ per board foot.}$$
           $0.0032 × 16,000,000 = $51,200

DEMONSTRATION PROBLEM 8–C

On January 2, 1995, Bedford Company purchased a 10-year sublease on a warehouse for $60,000. Bedford will also pay annual rent of $12,000. Bedford immediately incurred costs of $40,000 for improvements to the warehouse, such as lighting fixtures, replacement of a ceiling, heating system, and loading dock. The improvements have an estimated life of 12 years and no residual value.

Required:

Prepare the entries to record:

a. The payment for the sublease on a warehouse.

b. The rent payment for the first year.

c. The payment for the improvements.

d. Amortization of the leasehold for the first year.

e. Amortization of the leasehold improvements for the first year.

Solution to demonstration problem 8–C

a. Leasehold 60,000
      Cash   60,000
      To record purchase of sublease on warehouse.

b. Rent Expense 12,000
      Cash   12,000
      To record annual rent payment.

c. Leasehold Improvements 40,000
      Cash   40,000
      To record payment for leasehold improvements.

d. Rent Expense 6,000
      Leasehold   6,000
      To record leasehold amortization for 1995:

$$\text{Annual amortization} = \frac{\$60{,}000}{10 \text{ years}}$$
$$= \$6{,}000$$

e. Rent Expense 4,000
      Leasehold Improvements   4,000
      To amortize leasehold improvements:

$$\text{Annual amortization} = \frac{\$40{,}000}{10 \text{ years}}$$
$$= \$4{,}000$$

NEW TERMS

Amortization The term used to describe the systematic write-off of the cost of an intangible asset to expense. *427*

Boot The additional cash outlay made when one asset is exchanged for a similar one. *419*

Capital lease A lease that transfers to the lessee virtually all of the rewards and risks that accompany ownership of property. *429*

Copyright An exclusive right granted by the federal government giving the author (creator) protection against the illegal reproduction by others of the author's written works, designs, and literary productions. *428*

Depletion   The exhaustion of a natural resource; an estimate of the cost of the resource that was removed from its natural setting during the period. *421*

Franchise   A contract between two parties granting the franchisee (the purchaser of the franchise) certain rights and privileges ranging from name identification to complete monopoly of service. *428*

Goodwill   An intangible value attached to a company resulting mainly from the company's management skill or know-how and a favorable reputation with customers. Evidenced by the ability to generate an above-average rate of income on each dollar invested in the business. *431*

Intangible assets   Items that have no physical characteristics but are of value because of the advantages or exclusive privileges and rights they provide to a business. *426*

Lease   A contract to rent property. Grantor of the lease is the *lessor;* the party obtaining the rights to possess and use property is the *lessee. 429*

Leasehold   The rights granted under a lease. *429*

Leasehold improvement   Any physical alteration made by the lessee to the leased property in which benefits are expected beyond the current accounting period. *431*

Natural resources   Ore deposits, mineral deposits, oil reserves, gas deposits, and timber stands supplied by nature. *421*

Operating lease   A lease that does not qualify as a capital lease. *429*

Patent   A right granted by the federal government giving the owner the exclusive right to manufacture, sell, lease, or otherwise benefit from an invention for a limited period of time. *427*

Research and development (R&D) costs   Costs incurred in a planned search for new knowledge and in translating such knowledge into a new product or process. *426*

Trademark   A symbol, design, or logo that is used in conjunction with a particular product or company. *429*

Trade name   A brand name under which a product is sold or a company does business. *429*

Wasting assets   See Natural resources.

SELF-TEST

True-False

Indicate whether each of the following statements is true or false.

1. When a plant asset is still being used after it has been fully depreciated, depreciation can be taken in excess of its cost.

2. Neither generally accepted accounting principles (GAAP) nor income tax rules permit the recording of gains on exchanges of similar assets.

3. In an exchange of dissimilar assets, the new asset is recorded at the fair market value of the asset received or the fair market value of the asset given up plus cash paid, whichever is more clearly evident.

4. In calculating depletion, the residual value of acquired land containing an ore deposit is included in total costs subject to depletion.

5. All recorded intangible assets are subject to amortization.

Multiple-Choice

Select the best answer for each of the following questions.

1. When a fully depreciated asset is still in use:
   a. Prior years' depreciation should be adjusted.
   b. The cost should be adjusted to market value.
   c. Part of the depreciation should be reversed.
   d. The cost and accumulated depreciation should remain in the ledger and no more depreciation should be taken.
   e. It should be written off the books.

2. A truck costing $60,000 and having an estimated salvage value of $6,000 and an original life of five years is exchanged for a new truck. The cash price of the new truck is $76,000, and a trade-in allowance of $30,000 is received. The old truck has been depreciated for three years using the straight-line method. The new truck would be recorded at:
   a. $73,600.
   b. $76,000.
   c. $46,000.
   d. $57,600.
   e. None of the above.

3. In Question 2, the gain or loss on the exchange under income tax rules will be:

   a. Gain of $2,400.
   b. Loss of $6,000.
   c. Gain of $30,000.
   d. Gain of $18,400.
   e. None of the above.

4. Land containing a mine having an estimated 1,000,000 tons of economically extractable ore is purchased for $500,000. After the ore deposit is removed, the land will be worth $100,000. If 100,000 tons of ore are mined and sold during the first year, the depletion cost charged to expense for the year is:
   a. $400,000.
   b. $50,000.
   c. $40,000.
   d. $500,000.
   e. None of the above.

5. Steve Company purchased a patent for $48,000. The patent is expected to have value for 10 years even though its legal life is 17 years. The amortization for the first year is:
   a. $48,000.
   b. $4,800.
   c. $2,824.
   d. $4,320.
   e. None of the above.

Now turn to page 448 to check your answers.

QUESTIONS

1. When depreciable plant assets are sold for cash, how is the gain or loss measured?

2. A plant asset that cost $30,000 and has a related accumulated depreciation account balance of $30,000 is still being used in business operations. Would it be appropriate to continue recording depreciation on this asset? Explain. When should the asset's cost and accumulated depreciation be removed from the accounting records?

3. Factory equipment and $20,000 cash are exchanged for a delivery truck. How should the cost basis (cash price) of the delivery truck be measured?

4. A plant asset is disposed of by exchanging it for a new asset of a similar type. How should the cost basis of the new asset be measured under generally accepted accounting principles?

5. A plant asset is exchanged for an asset of a similar type. What is the cost basis of the new asset for tax purposes?

6. *a.* Distinguish between depreciation, depletion, and amortization. Name two assets that are subject to depreciation, to depletion, to amortization.

   b. Distinguish between tangible and intangible assets, and classify the above-named assets accordingly.

7. A building with an estimated physical life of 40 years was constructed at the site of a coal mine. The coal mine is expected to be completely exhausted within 20 years. Over what length of time should the building be depreciated, assuming that it will be abandoned after all the coal has been extracted? Why?

8. You note that a certain store seems to have a steady stream of regular customers, a favorable location, courteous employees, high-quality merchandise, and a reputation for fairness in dealing with customers, employees, and suppliers. Does it follow automatically that this business has goodwill?

9. What is the difference between a leasehold (under an operating lease contract) and a leasehold improvement? Is there any difference in the accounting procedures applicable to each?

10. What reasons justify the immediate expensing of most research and development costs?

11. Over what length of time should intangible assets be amortized?

12. Santos Company leased a tract of land for 40 years at an agreed annual rental fee of $24,000. The effective date of the lease was July 1, 1994. During the last six months of 1994, Santos constructed a building on the land at a cost of $600,000. The building was placed in operation on January 2, 1995, at which time it was estimated to have a physical life of 50 years. Over what period of time should the building be depreciated? Why?

13. Describe the typical accounting for a patent.

The Coca-Cola Company

14. *Real-world question* From the consolidated balance sheet of The Coca-Cola Company in Appendix C, identify the December 31, 1991, balance for intangible assets. What percentage increase does this amount represent over the 1990 ending balance, and what percentage did the intangible assets balance represent of the 1990 and 1991 total assets?

MAYTAG CORPORATION

15. *Real-world question* Based on the financial statements of Maytag Corporation contained in Appendix C, what was the 1991 allowance for amortization of intangibles?

EXERCISES

Record sale of vehicle (L.O. 1)

8–1. A tow truck originally costing $30,000 was sold for $5,000 cash. Accumulated depreciation on the truck amounted to $27,000. Prepare the journal entry to record the sale of the truck.

<table>
<tr><td>

Record
destruction of
machinery by
fire—uninsured
and insured asset
(L.O. 1)
</td><td>

8–2. A machine costing $16,000, on which $12,000 of depreciation has been accumulated, is completely destroyed by fire. What journal entry should be made to record the machine's destruction and the resulting fire loss under each of the following unrelated assumptions:

a. The machine is *not* insured.

b. The machine *is* insured, and it is estimated that $3,000 will be recovered from the insurance company.
</td></tr>

<tr><td>

Update
depreciation and
record exchange
of equipment
(L.O. 2)
</td><td>

8–3. Brooks Company owns plant equipment acquired on December 31, 1992, at a cost of $130,000. At the time of purchase, the equipment was estimated to have a useful life of six years and a $4,000 salvage value. Depreciation of $42,000 has been recorded through December 31, 1994, on a straight-line basis. Because of technological changes, on August 31, 1995, the equipment is traded in for similar new equipment with a fair market value of $120,000. Cash of $50,000 is paid in addition to the old equipment. Prepare the journal entry to record the trade-in under generally accepted accounting principles.
</td></tr>

<tr><td>

Record variety of
cases involving
sale, retirement, or
exchange of
equipment
(L.O. 1–3)
</td><td>

8–4. Equipment costing $44,000 which had been depreciated $30,000 was disposed of on January 2, 1994. What journal entries are required to record the equipment's disposition under each of the following unrelated assumptions?

a. The equipment was sold for $18,000 cash.

b. The equipment was sold for $11,600 cash.

c. The equipment was retired from service and hauled to the junk yard. No material was salvaged.

d. The equipment was exchanged for similar equipment having a cash price of $60,000. A trade-in allowance of $20,000 was received, and the balance was paid in cash.

e. The equipment was exchanged for similar equipment having a cash price of $60,000. A trade-in allowance of $10,000 was received, and the balance was paid in cash. (Record this transaction twice: first, for tax purposes, and second, for financial reporting purposes.)
</td></tr>

<tr><td>

Record exchanges
of dissimilar plant
assets
(L.O. 2)
</td><td>

8–5. Honor Company gave cash of $10,000 and traded a vehicle costing $29,000 with accumulated depreciation of $19,400 for an office computer. The computer had a cash price of $22,000. Prepare the journal entry to record the exchange. Assume that depreciation expense is up-to-date.
</td></tr>

<tr><td>

Determine
depletion cost and
expense
(L.O. 4)
</td><td>

8–6. Carl Company paid $2 million for the right to extract all of the mineral-bearing ore, estimated at 5 million tons, from a certain tract of land. During the first year, the company extracted 500,000 tons of the ore and sold 400,000 tons. What part of the $2 million should be charged to expense during the first year?
</td></tr>

<tr><td>

Compute periodic
depletion cost per
unit
(L.O. 4)
</td><td>

8–7. Clark Mining Company purchased a tract of land containing ore for $350,000. After spending $50,000 in exploration costs, the company determined that 600,000 tons of ore existed on the tract, but only 500,000 tons could be economically removed. No other costs were incurred. When the company finishes with the tract, it estimates the land will be worth $100,000. Determine the depletion cost per unit.
</td></tr>
</table>

Calculate
depreciation
expense using the
units-of-production
method for plant
assets on
extractive industry
property
(L.O. 4)

8–8. Janson Drilling Company acquired mining property and purchased a building at the site for exclusive use in mining operations. Given the information below, determine the building depreciation expense using the units-of-production method.

Building cost	$460,000
Estimated salvage value	$ 40,000
Capacity of mine	2,000,000 tons
Expected life of mine	15 years
Units extracted during year	250,000 tons

Determine patent
cost and periodic
amortization
(L.O. 5)

8–9. The Wyatt Company purchased a patent on January 1, 1978, at a total cost of $272,000. In January 1989 the company hired an outside law firm and successfully defended a suit alleging infringement of another's patent rights. The legal fees amounted to $60,000. What will be the amount of patent cost amortized in 1994? (The useful life of the patent is the same as its legal life—17 years.)

Record leasehold;
record rent
accrued and
leasehold
amortization
(L.O. 5)

8–10. Agnus Company leased a building under an operating lease for a 20-year period beginning January 1, 1994. The company paid $160,000 in cash and agreed to make annual payments equal to 1 percent of the first $1,000,000 of sales and one half of 1% of all sales over $1,000,000. Sales for 1994 amounted to $3,000,000. Payment of the annual amount will be made on January 12, 1995. Prepare journal entries to record the cash payment of January 1, 1994, and the proper expense to be recognized for the use of the leased building in 1994.

Record franchise;
accrued franchise
fees, and record
amortization
(L.O. 5)

8–11. Bob Molly paid Sally's Sandwiches $60,000 for the right to operate a fast-food restaurant using the Sally's Sandwiches name. The franchise agreement stated that Bob was to pay an operating fee of 1% of net sales for advertising and other services rendered by Sally's Sandwiches. Bob plans on operating the restaurant for about 15 years; operations began January 1, 1995. Net sales for the year were $800,000, with operating expenses of $140,000. Give the entries needed to record the payment of $60,000 and to record expenses for 1995 relating to the franchise.

Determine amount
of goodwill
(L.O. 5)

8–12. On April 1, 1995, Akron Metal Company purchased all of the assets of Dayton Brick Company for $900,000 and agreed to accept responsibility for a $140,000 mortgage note payable. The book value of the assets was $600,000; the fair market value was $1,020,000. Determine the amount of goodwill purchased by Akron Metal Company.

PROBLEMS

Update
depreciation and
record sale of
computer
(L.O. 1)

8–1. Janet Company purchased a personal computer on April 1, 1991, for $25,000. At the time of purchase, the computer had an expected life of six years and estimated salvage value of $1,600. The computer is being depreciated annually on a straight-line basis; accumulated depreciation through 1994 was $14,625. The computer was sold on June 1, 1995, for $8,000 cash.

Required:

Prepare journal entries to record the above data for 1995. Assume Janet has a calendar-year accounting period.

Update
depreciation and
record exchange
of autos under the
tax method and
generally accepted
accounting
principles
(L.O. 2, 3)

8–2. Walter Company purchased a new 1995 automobile on October 1, 1995. The cash price of the new car was $29,000. Walter paid $16,000 cash and received a trade-in allowance of $13,000 for a 1993 model. The 1993 model had been acquired on October 1, 1993, at a cost of $24,400. Depreciation of $6,062 had been recorded through December 31, 1994, on a straight-line basis, with four years of useful life expected. Salvage value was estimated to be $5,000. At the time of the trade-in, the 1993 automobile had a fair market value of $13,000.

Required:

Prepare journal entries to record the exchange of automobiles using (a) the tax method and (b) the theoretically correct accounting method.

Update
depreciation and
record six cases
of asset disposal
(L.O. 1, 2)

8–3. On January 2, 1991, Salty Company purchased a delivery truck for $84,000 cash. The truck has an estimated useful life of six years and an estimated salvage value of $40,000. The double-declining-balance method of depreciation is being used.

Required:

a. Prepare a schedule that shows how the truck's book value on January 1, 1994, would be computed.

b. Assume that the truck is to be disposed of on July 1, 1994. What journal entry is required to record depreciation for the six months ended June 30, 1994?

c. Prepare the journal entries to record the disposition of the truck on July 1, 1994, under each of the following unrelated assumptions:

(1) The truck is sold for $12,000 cash.

(2) The truck is sold for $28,000 cash.

(3) The truck is retired from service, and it is expected that $6,000 will be received from the sale of salvaged materials.

(4) The truck and $80,000 cash are exchanged for office equipment having a cash price of $112,000.

(5) The truck and $88,000 cash are exchanged for a new delivery truck which has a cash price of $120,000.

(6) The truck is completely destroyed in an accident. Cash of $11,200 is expected to be recovered from the insurance company.

Record exchange
of plant asset for a
dissimilar asset
under generally
accepted
accounting
principles
(L.O. 2)

8–4. On January 4, 1995, Morgan Company traded a delivery truck for an assortment of office equipment. The truck originally cost $25,000 and had accumulated depeciation of $15,000. The fair market value of the truck was $12,000. The cash value of the equipment was not known. In addition to the truck, Morgan paid $4,000 cash.

Required:

Prepare the journal entry to record the exchange of plant assets. Assume depreciation expense on the truck is up-to-date.

Determine
depletion for
period and
depreciation on
mining equipment;
compute average
cost per ton of ore
mined
(L.O. 4)

8–5. Shelby Company acquired a mine for $18 million. The mine contained an estimated 9 million tons of ore. It was also estimated that the land would have a value of $1,600,000 when the mine was exhausted and that only 8 million tons of ore could be economically extracted. A building was erected on the property at a cost of $2,400,000. The building has an estimated useful life of 35 years and no scrap value. Specialized mining equipment was installed at a cost of $3,300,000. This equipment has an estimated useful life of seven years and an estimated $84,000 salvage value. The company began operating on July 1, 1994. During the fiscal year ended June 30, 1995, 800,000 tons of ore were extracted. The company decided to use the units-of-production method to record depreciation on the building and the sum-of-the-years'-digits method to record depreciation on the equipment.

Required:

Prepare journal entries to record the depletion and depreciation charges for the fiscal year ended June 30, 1995. Show calculations.

Compute cost and
amortization of
patent
(L.O. 5)

8–6. The Kyle Company purchased a patent for $240,000 on January 2, 1994. The patent was estimated to have a useful life of 10 years. The $240,000 cost was properly charged to an asset account and amortized in 1994. On July 1, 1995, the company hired an outside law firm and incurred legal and court costs of $72,000 in a successful defense of the patent in an infringement suit.

Required:

Compute the patent amortization cost for 1995.

Record leasehold
amortization;
record
depreciation and
trade-in
(L.O. 2, 5)

8–7. On July 1, 1995, the Dover Company had the following balances in its plant asset and accumulated depreciation accounts:

	Asset	Accumulated Depreciation
Land	$ 400,000	
Leasehold.	300,000	
Buildings	3,752,000	$517,000
Equipment	1,632,000	520,000
Trucks	284,000	85,300

Additional information

(1) The leasehold covers a plot of ground leased on July 1, 1990, for a period of 25 years.
(2) The office building is on the leased land and was completed on July 1, 1991, at a cost of $1,152,000. Its physical life is set at 40 years. The factory building is on the owned land and was completed on July 1, 1990, at a cost of $2,600,000. Its life is also set at 40 years. Neither building has any expected salvage value.
(3) Equipment is depreciated at 6% per year of its cost.
(4) The company owns three trucks—A, B, and C. Truck A, purchased on July 1, 1993, at a cost of $64,000, has a life of three years and a scrap value

of $4,000. Truck B, purchased on January 2, 1994, at a cost of $100,000, has a life of four years and a scrap value of $8,000. Truck C, purchased on January 2, 1995, at a cost of $120,000, has a life of five years and a scrap value of $12,000.

The following events occurred in the fiscal year ended June 30, 1996:

1995
July 1 Rent for July 1, 1995–June 30, 1996, on leased land is paid, $38,000.
Oct. 1 Truck A was traded in on Truck D. Cash price of the new truck is $128,000. Cash of $108,000 is paid. Truck D has a life of four years and a scrap value of $7,000.
1996
Feb. 2 Truck B is sold for $56,000 cash.
June 1 Truck C (uninsured) is completely demolished in an accident.

Required:

Prepare journal entries to record the above transactions and the necessary June 30, 1996, adjusting entries. Use the straight-line depreciation method.

Record
amortization
expense for a
variety of
intangible assets
(L.O. 5)

8–8. Following are selected transactions and other data relating to the Maple Company for the year ended December 31, 1994.

  a. The company rented the second floor of a building for five years on January 2, 1994, and paid the annual rent of $20,000 for the first and fifth years in advance.

  b. In 1993 the company incurred legal fees of $60,000 (paid to an outside law firm) in applying for a patent and paid a fee of $20,000 to a former employee who conceived of a device that substantially reduced the cost of manufacturing one of the company's products. The patent on the device has a market value of $600,000 and is expected to be useful for 10 years.

  c. In 1993 the company entered into a 10-year operating lease on several floors of a building, paying $40,000 in cash immediately and agreeing to pay $20,000 at the end of each of the 10 years of life in the lease. It then incurred costs of $80,000 to install partitions, shelving, and fixtures. These items would normally last 25 years.

  d. The company spent $24,000 promoting a trademark in a manner that it believed enhanced its value considerably. The trademark has an indefinite life.

  e. The company incurred costs amounting to $200,000 in 1993 and $260,000 in 1994 for research and development of new products that are expected to enhance the company's revenues for at least five years.

Required:

For each of the situations described above, prepare only the journal entries to record the expense applicable to 1994.

Calculate goodwill
and prepare
journal entry
(L.O. 5)

8–9. On April 30, 1994, Mayflower Company purchased all of the assets of John Company for $1,700,000, and assumed $110,000 of various liabilities owed by John Company. The fair market values of the assets purchased are as follows:

Accounts receivable.	$150,000
Inventories.	230,000
Land	500,000
Building	160,000
Equipment	540,000
Trademarks	160,000

Required:

a. Compute the amount of goodwill purchased by Mayflower Company.

b. Give the entry to record the purchase of John Company's assets and assumption of liabilities.

BUSINESS DECISION PROBLEMS

Record exchange of similar assets; adjust accounts for errors in accounting for depreciable assets (L.O. 2, 3)

8–1. Billingsley Company acquired machine A for $120,000 on January 2, 1992. Machine A had an estimated useful life of four years and no salvage value. The machine was depreciated on the straight-line basis. On January 2, 1994, machine A was exchanged for machine B. Machine B had a cash price of $144,000. In addition to machine A, cash of $120,000 was given up in the exchange. The company recorded the exchange in accordance with income tax regulations instead of in accordance with generally accepted accounting principles. Machine B has an estimated useful life of five years and no salvage value. The machine is being depreciated using the straight-line method.

Required:

a. What journal entry did the Billingsley Company make when it recorded the exchange of machines? (Show computations.)

b. What journal entry should the Billingsley Company have made to record the exchange of machines in accordance with generally accepted accounting principles?

c. Assume the error is discovered on December 31, 1995, before adjusting journal entries have been made. What journal entries should be made to correct the accounting records? (Adjustments of prior years' net income because of errors should be debited or credited to Retained Earnings.) What adjusting journal entry should be made to record depreciation for 1995? (Ignore income taxes.)

d. What effect did the error have on reported net income for 1994? (Ignore income taxes.)

e. How should machine B be reported on the December 31, 1995, balance sheet?

Determine depreciable life. (L.O. 4)

8–2. The financial statements of Murphy Oil Corporation in "A Broader Perspective," note (A), explain the Company's method of depreciation and depletion.

Required:

Discuss the length of time over which the drilling barges and diving equipment should be depreciated.

ANSWERS TO SELF-TEST

True-False

1. *False.* No more depreciation can be taken on a fully depreciated plant asset.
2. *True.* Gains cannot be recognized on exchanges of similar assets. Losses are recognized for accounting purposes, but not for tax purposes.
3. *True.* The new asset is recorded at the fair market value of the asset received or given up, whichever is more clearly evident.
4. *False.* The residual value of land should be deducted from total costs subject to depletion.
5. *True.* All recorded intangible assets should be amortized over their economic life, their legal life, or 40 years, whichever is shorter.

Multiple-Choice

1. *d.* The cost and accumulated depreciation should not be removed from the asset's account until the disposal of the asset.

2. *a.* On the date of exchange, the book value of the old truck is $27,600 ($60,000 minus accumulated depreciation of $32,400). The trade-in allowance of $30,000 indicates a gain on exchange of $2,400. In an exchange of similar assets, a gain is not recognized, but reduces the cost of a new asset. Therefore, the cost of the new truck is $73,600 ($76,000 minus $2,400), and no gain is recognized.

3. *e.* A gain resulting from an exchange of similar assets is not recognized under income tax rules.

4. *c.* The depletion charge for the first year is:

$$\text{Depletion charge per ton} = (\$500,000 - \$100,000)/1,000,000$$

$$= \$0.40$$

$$\text{Depletion charge for the year} = \$0.40 \times 100,000$$

$$= \$40,000$$

Since all of the ore that was extracted was sold, all of the $40,000 is expensed as cost of ore sold.

5. *b.* The patent is amortized over 10 years:

$$\text{Annual amortization expense} = \$48,000/10$$

$$= \$4,800$$

9

STOCKHOLDERS' EQUITY

LEARNING OBJECTIVES

After studying this chapter, you should be able to:

1. State the advantages and disadvantages of the corporate form of business.
2. List the various kinds of stock and describe the differences between them.
3. Present in proper form the stockholders' equity section of a balance sheet.
4. Account for the issuances of stock for cash.
5. Determine book values of both preferred and common stock.
6. Identify the different sources of paid-in capital and describe how they would be presented on a balance sheet.
7. Account for a cash dividend, a stock dividend, a stock split, and a retained earnings appropriation.
8. Account for the acquisition and reissuance of treasury stock.
9. Describe the proper accounting treatment of discontinued operations, extraordinary items, and changes in accounting principles.
10. Define prior period adjustments and show their proper presentation in the financial statements.
11. Compute earnings per share.

THE CORPORATION

A **corporation** is an entity recognized by law as possessing an existence separate and distinct from its owners; that is, it is a separate legal entity. Endowed with many of the rights and obligations possessed by a person, a corporation can, for example, enter into contracts in its own name; buy, sell, or hold property; borrow money; hire and fire employees; and sue and be sued.

Corporations have proved to be remarkably well-suited vehicles for obtaining the huge amounts of capital necessary for large-scale business operations. Corporations acquire their capital by issuing **shares of stock,** which are the units into which the ownership of a corporation is divided. Investors buy shares of stock in a corporation for two basic reasons. First, investors expect the value of their shares to increase over time so that the stock may be sold in the future at a profit. Also, while investors hold stock, they expect the corporation to pay them dividends (usually in cash) in return for using their money. The latter part of this chapter discusses the various kinds of dividends and their accounting treatment.

Advantages of the Corporate Form of Business

*Objective 1
State the advantages and disadvantages of the corporate form of business*

Corporations have many advantages compared to single proprietorships and partnerships. Some of the major advantages of a corporation over a single proprietorship are the same advantages a partnership has over a single proprietorship. Although corporations usually have more owners than partnerships, both have a broader base for investment, risk, responsibilities, and talent than do single proprietorships. Since corporations are more comparable to partnerships than to single proprietorships, the discussion of advantages that follows contrasts the partnership with the corporation.

1. *Easy transfer of ownership.*   In a partnership, a partner cannot transfer ownership in the business to another person if the other partners do not want the new person involved in the partnership. In a publicly held (owned by many stockholders) corporation, shares of stock are traded on a stock exchange between unknown parties; one owner usually cannot dictate to whom shares can or cannot be sold by another owner.
2. *Limited liability.*   Each partner in a partnership is personally responsible for all the debts of the business. In a corporation, the stockholders are not personally responsible for the corporation's debts; the maximum amount a stockholder can lose is the amount of his or her investment. However, when a small, closely held corporation (owned by only a few stockholders) borrows money, banks and lending institutions often require an officer of the small corporation to sign the loan agreement. Then, the officer will have to repay the loan if the corporation does not.
3. *Continuous existence of the entity.*   In a partnership, many circumstances, such as the death of a partner, can cause the termination of the business entity. These same circumstances have no effect on a corporation because it is a legal entity, separate and distinct from its owners.
4. *Easy capital generation.*   The easy transfer of ownership and the limited liability of stockholders are attractive features to potential investors. Thus, it is relatively easy for a corporation to raise capital by issuing shares of stock to many investors. Corporations with thousands of stockholders are not uncommon.
5. *Professional management.*   Generally, the partners in a partnership are

also the managers of that business, but they may or may not have the necessary expertise to manage a business. In a publicly held corporation, most of the owners (stockholders) do not participate in the day-to-day operations and management of the entity. Usually, professionals are hired to run the business on a daily basis.

6. *Separation of owners and entity.*   Since the corporation is considered a separate legal entity, the owners do not have the power to bind the corporation to business contracts. This feature eliminates the potential problem of mutual agency that exists between partners in a partnership. In a corporation, one stockholder cannot jeopardize other stockholders through poor decision making.

Disadvantages of the Corporate Form of Business

The corporate form of business has its disadvantages. These disadvantages include the following:

1. *Double taxation.*   Because a corporation is a separate legal entity, its net income is subject to double taxation. The corporation pays a tax on its income, and stockholders pay a tax on corporate income received as dividends.

2. *Government regulation.*   Because corporations are created by law, they are subject to greater regulation and control than are single proprietorships and partnerships.

3. *Entrenched, inefficient management.*   A corporation may be burdened with an inefficient management that remains in control because it can use corporate funds to solicit the needed stockholder votes to back its positions. Stockholders scattered across the country, who individually own only small portions of a corporation's stock, usually find it difficult to organize themselves and oppose existing management.

4. *Limited ability to raise creditor capital.*   The limited liability of stockholders makes a corporation an attractive means for accumulating stockholder capital. At the same time, this limited liability feature limits the amount of creditor capital a corporation can amass because *creditors cannot look to the personal assets of stockholders for satisfaction of the debts of a corporation if the corporation cannot pay.* Thus, beyond a certain point, creditors will not lend some corporations money without the personal guarantee of a stockholder or officer of the corporation to repay the loan if the corporation does not.

CAPITAL STOCK AUTHORIZED AND OUTSTANDING

Objective 2
List the various kinds of stock and describe the differences between them

The corporate charter states the number of shares and the par value, if any, per share of each class of stock that the corporation is permitted to issue. **Capital stock authorized** is the number of shares of stock that a corporation is entitled to issue as designated in its charter. **Par value** is an arbitrary amount printed on each stock certificate that may be assigned to each share of a given class of stock, usually at the time of incorporation.

A corporation might not issue all of its authorized stock immediately; some stock might be held for future issuance when additional funds are needed. If all authorized stock has been issued and more funds are needed, the consent of the state of incorporation will be required to increase the number of authorized shares.

The authorization to issue stock is not a transaction that results in a journal entry with a debit and credit. Instead, the authorization is noted in the capital stock account in the ledger (and often in the general journal) as a reminder of the number of shares authorized. **Capital stock issued** is the number of shares of stock that have been sold and issued to stockholders.

Capital stock outstanding is the number of authorized shares of stock that have been issued and that are currently held by stockholders. The total ownership of a corporation rests with the holders of the capital stock outstanding. If, for example, a corporation is authorized to issue 10,000 shares of capital stock but has issued only 8,000 shares, the holders of the 8,000 shares own 100% of the corporation.

Each outstanding share of stock of a given class is identical to any other outstanding share of that class with respect to the rights and privileges possessed. Shares authorized but not yet issued are referred to as **unissued shares** (the above example has 2,000 unissued shares). No rights or privileges attach to these shares until they are issued; they are not, for example, entitled to dividends, nor can they be voted at stockholders' meetings.

The number of shares issued and the number of shares outstanding may be different. Issued stock includes shares that have been issued at some point in time, while outstanding shares are those shares that are currently held by stockholders. All outstanding stock is issued stock, but the reverse is not necessarily true. The difference is due to shares, called *treasury stock,* that have been returned to the corporation by stockholders. Treasury stock is discussed later in the chapter.

CLASSES OF CAPITAL STOCK

A corporation may issue two classes of capital stock—common and preferred. These classes are discussed in the following sections.

Common Stock

If a corporation issues only one class of stock, this stock is known as *common stock*. The rights of the stockholder are enjoyed equally by all the holders of shares. **Common stock** is usually referred to as the *residual equity* in the corporation. This term means that all other claims against the corporation rank ahead of the claims of the common stockholder.

Illustration 9.1
CAPITAL STRUCTURES

	1990	*1989*	*1988*	*1987*
Common stock with:				
No preferred stock	447	438	440	430
One class of preferred stock.	118	117	117	128
Two classes of preferred stock.	28	36	38	36
Three or more classes of preferred stock . . .	7	9	5	6
Total companies	600	600	600	600
Companies included above with two or more classes of common stock	56	58	60	52

SOURCE: American Institute of Certified Public Accountants, *Accounting Trends & Techniques* (New York: AICPA, 1991), p. 233.

Preferred Stock

Preferred stock is capital stock that carries certain features or rights not carried by common stock. Different classes of preferred stock may exist, each with slightly different characteristics.

Companies issue preferred stock for the following reasons: (1) to avoid the use of bonds that have fixed interest charges that must be paid regardless of the amount of net income; (2) to avoid issuing so many additional shares of common stock that earnings per share will be less in the current year than in prior years; and (3) to avoid diluting the common stockholders' control of the corporation, since preferred stockholders generally have no voting rights.

Unlike common stock, which has no set maximum or minimum dividend, the dividend return on preferred stock is usually stated at an amount per share or as a percentage of par value. Therefore, the amount of the dividend per share is usually fixed.

Illustration 9.1 shows the various classes and combinations of capital stock outstanding for a sample of 600 companies.

TYPES OF PREFERRED STOCK

When a corporation issues both preferred and common stock, the preferred stock may be:

1. Preferred as to dividends. If it is, it may be:
   a. Noncumulative or cumulative.
   b. Participating or nonparticipating.
2. Preferred as to assets in the event of liquidation.
3. Convertible or nonconvertible.
4. Callable.

Stock Preferred as to Dividends

A **dividend** is a distribution of assets (usually cash) that represents a withdrawal of earnings by the owners. Dividends are similar in nature to withdrawals by single proprietors and partners.

Stock preferred as to dividends means that the preferred stockholders are entitled to receive a specified dividend per share before any dividend on common stock is paid. A **dividend on preferred stock** is the amount paid to preferred stockholders as a return for the use of their money. For no-par preferred stock, the dividend is stated as a specific dollar amount per share per year, such as $4.40. For par value preferred stock, the dividend is usually stated as a percentage of the par value, such as 8% of par value, although the dividend can also be stated as a specific dollar amount per share. Most preferred stock has a par value.

Dividends on preferred stock usually are paid quarterly. A dividend—in full or in part—can be paid on preferred stock only if it is declared by the board of directors. In some states, preferred stock dividends can be declared only if the corporation has retained earnings (income that has been retained in the business) at least equal in dollar amount to the dividend declared.

Noncumulative Preferred Stock. **Noncumulative preferred stock** is preferred stock on which the right to receive a dividend expires if the dividend is not declared. When noncumulative preferred stock is outstanding, a dividend omitted or not paid in any one year need not be paid in any future year. Because omitted dividends are usually lost forever, noncumulative preferred stocks are not attractive to investors and rarely are issued.

Cumulative Preferred Stock. **Cumulative preferred stock** is preferred stock for which the right to receive a basic dividend, usually each quarter, accumulates if the dividend is not paid. Unpaid cumulative preferred dividends must be paid before any dividends can be paid on the common stock. For example, assume a company has cumulative, $10 par value, 10% preferred stock outstanding of $100,000, common stock outstanding of $100,000, and retained earnings of $30,000. No dividends have been paid for two years. The preferred stockholders are entitled to dividends of $20,000 ($10,000 per year times two years) before any dividends can be paid to the common stockholders.

Dividends in arrears are cumulative unpaid dividends, including the quarterly dividends not declared for the current year. Dividends in arrears are never shown as a liability of the corporation since they are not a legal liability until declared by the board of directors. However, since the amount of dividends in arrears may influence the decisions of users of a corporation's financial statements, such dividends should be, and usually are, disclosed in a footnote. An appropriate footnote might read: "Dividends in the amount of $20,000, representing two years' dividends on the company's 10%, cumulative preferred stock, were in arrears as of December 31, 1995."

Participating Preferred Stock.   **Participating preferred stock** allows the preferred stockholders to receive dividends above the stated preference dividend rate under certain conditions that are specified in the preferred stock contract. The participation feature can work in two ways. For example, assume that the preferred stock contract states that when the total dividend distributed to stockholders in a given year exceeds $8 per share to preferred stockholders and $8 per share to common stockholders, the remaining amount will be distributed in an equal amount per share to all stockholders. (The participation also may be based on the relative total par values of the outstanding shares instead of the number of shares outstanding.) If there are 2,000 shares of preferred stock and 4,000 shares of common stock outstanding and the participation is stated as an equal amount per share, a distribution of $108,000 would be shared as follows:

		Preferred	Common
1. Preferred stockholders are paid their dividends (2,000 shares × $8)		$16,000	
2. Common stockholders are paid an amount equal to the preferred dividend per share (4,000 shares × $8)			$32,000
3. The remainder of the dividend is divided so as to pay the same amount per share:			

	Shares	Ratio		
Preferred	2,000	(2⁄6 × $60,000)	20,000	
Common	4,000	(4⁄6 × $60,000)		40,000
Total	6,000			
Total dividend			$36,000	$72,000

The preferred stockholders receive the first $16,000 of the current year's dividends. The common stockholders receive the next $32,000 of dividends. Any dividends over $48,000 per year are paid in an equal amount per share. In years when dividends are not sufficient to pay at least $48,000 of dividends, the distribution would be as follows:

Amount of Dividends to Be Paid	Split between	
	Preferred	Common
$16,000	$16,000	$–0–
24,000	16,000	8,000
32,000	16,000	16,000
40,000	16,000	24,000

Nonparticipating Preferred Stock.   Participating preferred stock was popular in the early 1900s but has seldom been issued since that time. Most preferred stock is nonparticipating. **Nonparticipating preferred stock** is preferred stock that is entitled to its cumulative stated dividend only, regardless of the size of the dividend paid on common stock.

Stock Preferred as to Assets

Most preferred stocks are preferred as to assets in the event of dissolution and liquidation of the corporation. **Stock preferred as to assets** is preferred stock that receives special treatment in case of liquidation. Preferred stockholders are entitled to receive the par value (or a larger stipulated liquidation value) per share before any assets may be distributed to common stockholders. If the corporation has cumulative preferred dividends in arrears at liquidation, they usually are payable even if there are not enough accumulated earnings to cover the dividends. Also, the cumulative dividend for the current year is payable. Stock may be preferred as to assets, dividends, or both.

Convertible Preferred Stock

Convertible preferred stock is preferred stock that is convertible into common stock of the issuing corporation. Many preferred stocks do not carry this special feature; they are nonconvertible. Holders of convertible preferred stock may exchange it, at their option, for a certain number of shares of common stock of the same corporation.

Investors find convertible preferred stock attractive because of the greater probability that the dividends on the preferred stock will be paid (as compared to dividends on common shares) and because the conversion privilege may be the source of substantial price appreciation. To illustrate this latter feature, assume that Olsen Company issued 1,000 shares of 6%, $100 par value convertible preferred stock at $100 per share. The stock is convertible at any time into four shares of Olsen $10 par value common stock, which has a current market value of $20 per share. In the next several years, the company reported much higher net income and increased the dividend on the common stock from $1 to $2 per share. Assume that the common stock then sells at $40 per share. The preferred stockholders can (1) convert each share of preferred stock into four shares of common stock and increase the annual dividend they receive from $6 to $8; (2) sell their preferred stock at a substantial gain, since it will sell in the market at approximately $160 per share, the market value of the four shares of common stock into which it is convertible; or (3) continue to hold their preferred shares in the expectation of realizing an even larger gain at a later date.

If all 1,000 shares of $100 par value Olsen Company preferred stock are converted into 4,000 shares of $10 par value common stock, the entry is:

```
Preferred Stock. . . . . . . . . . . . . . . . . . . . . . .  100,000
    Common Stock . . . . . . . . . . . . . . . . . . . . .            40,000
    Paid-In Capital in Excess of Par Value—Common . . . .            60,000
    To record the conversion of preferred stock into common
    stock.
```

Callable Preferred Stock

Most preferred stocks are callable at the option of the issuing corporation. **Callable preferred stock** means that the corporation can inform nonconvertible preferred stockholders that they must surrender their stock to the company and convertible preferred stockholders that they must either surrender their stock or convert it to common shares.

Preferred shares are usually callable at par value plus a small premium of 3% or 4% of the par value of the stock. This **call premium** is the difference between the amount at which a corporation calls its preferred stock for redemption and the par value of the stock.

An issuing corporation may force conversion of *convertible* preferred stock by calling in the preferred stock for redemption. If these stockholders do not want to surrender their stock, they will have to convert it to common shares. When preferred stockholders surrender their stock, the corporation pays these stockholders par value plus the call premium, any dividends in arrears from past years, and a prorated portion of the current period's dividend. If the market value of common shares is higher than the amount the stockholders would receive in redemption, obviously they should convert their preferred shares to common shares. For instance, assume that a stockholder owns 1,000 shares of convertible preferred stock. Each share is callable at $104 per share, convertible to two common shares (currently selling at $62 per share), and entitled to $10 of unpaid dividends. If the issuing corporation calls in its preferred stock, the stockholder would receive either (1) $114,000, or [($104 + $10) × 1,000], if the shares are surrendered or (2) common shares worth $124,000, or ($62 × 2,000), if the shares are converted. Obviously, the stockholder should convert these preferred shares to common shares.

You may wonder why a corporation would call in its preferred stock. Corporations call in preferred stock for many reasons: (1) the outstanding preferred stock may require, for example, a 12% annual dividend at a time when the company can secure capital to retire the stock by issuing a new 8% preferred stock; (2) the issuing company may have been sufficiently profitable to enable it to retire the preferred stock out of earnings; or (3) the company may wish to force conversion of its convertible preferred stock because the cash dividend on the equivalent common shares will be less than the dividend on the preferred shares.

BALANCE SHEET PRESENTATION OF STOCK

*Objective 3
Present in proper form the stockholders' equity section of a balance sheet*

At this point, it may be helpful to see how capital stock is reported in the balance sheet. The stockholders' equity section of a corporation's balance sheet contains two main elements: paid-in capital and retained earnings. **Paid-in capital** is the part of stockholders' equity that normally results from cash or other assets invested by owners. Paid-in capital may result from services performed for the corporation in exchange for capital stock and from certain other transactions to be discussed later in this chapter. As stated earlier, **retained earnings** is the part of stockholders' equity resulting from accumulated net income, reduced by dividends and net losses. The Retained Earnings account is increased *periodically* by net income earned

A BROADER PERSPECTIVE

COCA-COLA ENTERPRISES INC. (DEC.)
PARTIAL BALANCE SHEET ($000)

	1990	1989
Shareholders' equity		
(In thousands except share data):		
Preferred stock, $1 par value		
Authorized—100,000,000 shares;		
Issued and outstanding—2,500 shares, at aggregate liquidation		
preference.	$ 250,000	$ 250,000
Common stock, $1 par value		
Authorized—500,000,000 shares;		
Issued—140,471,081 shares and 140,363,166 shares, respectively . . .	140,471	140,363
Paid-in capital	1,262,755	1,262,288
Reinvested earnings	382,243	311,198
Common stock in treasury, at cost		
25,636,358 shares and 17,317,010 shares, respectively	(408,990)	(283,712)
	$1,626,479	$1,680,137

NOTES TO CONSOLIDATED FINANCIAL STATEMENTS

Preferred Stock

In May 1988, the Company issued 2,500 shares of variable dividend rate nonvoting preferred stock at a purchase price of $100,000 per share. The holders are entitled to cumulative dividends at a rate determined by an auction approximately every forty-nine days. The weighted average dividend rate of the preferred stock was 6.5% and 7.3% during 1990 and 1989, respectively.

The preferred stock is subject to redemption at the Company's option, at any time, at $101,000 per share (plus accrued dividends) through May 4, 1991 and at $100,000 per share (plus accrued dividends) thereafter.

Holders of the preferred stock are permitted to elect two additional directors to the Company's Board of Directors if the Company is in arrears for the equivalent of six quarterly dividend payments. The Company is current on all preferred dividend payments.

SOURCE: American Institute of Certified Public Accountants, *Trends & Techniques* (New York: AICPA, 1991), p. 239.

and decreased by net losses. In addition, Retained Earnings is *decreased* by *dividends* declared to stockholders. Since Retained Earnings is a capital account and represents accumulated net income retained in the company, it normally has a *credit* balance. Retained earnings is discussed in more detail later in this chapter.

The following illustration shows the proper financial reporting for preferred and common stock. Assume that a corporation is authorized to issue 10,000 shares of $100 par value, 6%, cumulative, convertible preferred stock, all of which have been issued and are outstanding; and 200,000 shares of $10 par value common stock, of which 80,000 shares have been issued and are outstanding. The stockholders' equity section of the balance sheet (assuming $450,000 of retained earnings) is:

Stockholders' equity:		
Paid-in capital:		
Preferred stock—$100 par value, 6%, cumulative,		
convertible (5 common for 1 preferred); authorized,		
issued, and outstanding, 10,000 shares	$1,000,000	
Common stock—$10 par value; authorized, 200,000		
shares; issued and outstanding, 80,000 shares	800,000	
Total paid-in capital		$1,800,000
Retained earnings		450,000
Total stockholders' equity.		$2,250,000

Notice that the balance sheet lists preferred stock before common stock (because the preferred stock is preferred as to dividends, assets, or both). The conversion rate may be disclosed in a parenthetical note within the description of preferred stock or in a footnote.

STOCK ISSUANCES FOR CASH

Issuance of Par Value Stock for Cash

*Objective 4
Account for the
issuances of stock
for cash*

Each share of capital stock (common or preferred) is either with par value or without par value, depending on the terms of the corporation's charter. As stated earlier, **par value** is an arbitrary amount assigned to each share of a given class of stock and printed on the stock certificate. The par value, if any, is stated in the charter and printed on the stock certificates issued. Par value may be any amount—1 cent, 10 cents, $16\frac{2}{3}$ cents, $1, $5, or $100. Low par values of $10 or less are common in our economy.

Par value gives no clue as to the stock's market value. Shares with a par value of $5 have sold in the market for well over $600, and many $100 par value preferred stocks have sold for considerably less than par. Par value is not even a reliable indicator of the price at which shares can be issued. Even in new corporations, shares are often issued at prices well in excess of par value and may even be issued for less than par value if state laws permit (however, the stock may carry a contingent liability for the amount of the discount). Par value does give the accountant a constant amount at which to record capital stock issuances in the capital stock accounts. Also, the total par value of all issued shares is generally the legal capital of the corporation. The concept of legal capital exists to help protect creditors from losses. **Legal capital** (or **stated capital**) is an amount prescribed by law below which a corporation may not reduce stockholders' equity through declaration of dividends or other payments to stockholders. Maintaining legal capital does not guarantee that a company will be able to pay its debts, but it does serve to keep a company from compensating stockholders to the detriment of creditors.

To illustrate the issuance of stock for cash, assume that 10,000 authorized shares of $20 par value common stock are issued at $22 per share. The following entry is made:

Cash	220,000	
Common Stock		200,000
Paid-In Capital in Excess of Par Value—Common . . .		20,000
To record the issuance of 10,000 shares of stock for cash.		

Notice that the credit to the Common Stock account is the par value ($20) times the number of shares issued. The excess over par value ($20,000) is credited to Paid-In Capital in Excess of Par Value and is part of the paid-in capital contributed by the stockholders. Thus, **paid-in capital in excess of par (or stated) value** represents capital contributed to a corporation in addition to that assigned to the shares issued and recorded in capital stock accounts.

The paid-in capital section of the balance sheet appears as follows:

Paid-in capital:	
Common stock—par value, $20; 10,000 shares authorized, issued, and outstanding	$200,000
Paid-in capital in excess of par value—common.	20,000
Total paid-in capital	$220,000

Issuance of No-Par Stock with a Stated Value for Cash

No-par stock is stock without a par value. When no-par stock with a stated value is issued, the shares are carried in the capital stock account at the stated value. **Stated value** is an arbitrary amount assigned by the board of directors to each share of a given class of no-par stock. Any amounts received in excess of the stated value per share represent a part of the capital of the corporation and should be credited to Paid-In Capital in Excess of Stated Value. The legal capital of a corporation issuing no-par shares with a stated value is generally equal to the total stated value of the shares issued.

To illustrate, assume that the DeWitt Corporation, which is authorized to issue 10,000 shares of capital stock without par value, assigns a stated value of $20 per share to its stock. The 10,000 authorized shares are issued for cash at $22 per share. The entry to record this transaction is:

Cash	220,000	
Common Stock		200,000
Paid-In Capital in Excess of Stated Value—Common . .		20,000
To record issuance of 10,000 shares for cash.		

The paid-in capital section of the balance sheet appears as follows:

Paid-in capital:	
Common stock—without par value; stated value, $20;	
10,000 shares authorized, issued, and outstanding	$200,000
Paid-in capital in excess of stated value—common.	20,000
Total paid-in capital	$220,000

The $20,000 received over and above the stated value of $200,000 is carried permanently as paid-in capital because it is a part of the capital originally contributed by the stockholders. However, the legal capital of the DeWitt Corporation is $200,000.

Issuance of No-Par Stock without a Stated Value for Cash

If a corporation issues no-par stock without a stated value, the entire amount received is credited to the capital stock account. For instance, consider the above illustration of DeWitt Corporation involving the issuance of no-par stock. If no stated value had been assigned, the entry would have been as follows:

Cash	220,000	
Common Stock		220,000
To record the issuance of 10,000 shares for cash.		

Since shares may be issued at different times and at differing amounts, the credits to the capital stock account will not be at a uniform amount per share, in contrast to when par value shares or shares with a stated value are issued.

To continue our example, the paid-in capital section of the company's balance sheet would be as follows:

Paid-in capital:	
Common stock—without par or stated value; 10,000 shares	
authorized, issued, and outstanding	$220,000
Total paid-in capital.	$220,000

The actual capital contributed by stockholders is $220,000. In some states, the entire amount received for shares without par or stated value is the amount of legal capital. The legal capital in this example would then be equal to $220,000.

Stockholders' equity:			
Paid-in capital:			
Preferred stock—$100 par value, 6%			
cumulative; 1,000 shares authorized, issued,			
and outstanding	$100,000		
Common stock—without par			
value, stated value $5; 100,000 shares			
authorized, 80,000 shares issued			
and outstanding	400,000	$500,000	
Paid-in capital in excess of par (or			
stated) value:			
From preferred stock issuances	$ 5,000		
From common stock issuances	20,000	25,000	
Total paid-in capital			$525,000
Retained earnings.			200,000
Total stockholders' equity			$725,000

BOOK VALUE

*Objective 5
Determine book
values of both
preferred and
common stock*

The total book value of a corporation's outstanding shares is equal to the recorded net asset value of the corporation—that is, assets minus liabilities. Quite simply, **the amount of net assets is equal to stockholders' equity.** When *only* common stock is outstanding, **book value per share** is computed by dividing total stockholders' equity by the total number of common shares outstanding. In calculating book value, an assumption is made that (1) the corporation could be liquidated without incurring any further expenses, (2) the assets could be sold at their recorded amounts, and (3) the liabilities could be satisfied at their recorded amounts.

Assume the stockholders' equity of a corporation is as follows:

Stockholders' equity:		
Paid-in capital:		
Common stock—without par value, stated value $10;		
authorized, 20,000 shares; issued and outstanding,		
15,000 shares	$150,000	
Paid-in capital in excess of stated value.	10,000	
Total paid-in capital		$160,000
Retained earnings		50,000
Total stockholders' equity		$210,000

The book value per share of the stock is determined as follows:

Total stockholders' equity	$210,000
Total shares outstanding	÷15,000
Book value per share	$ 14

When two or more classes of capital stock are outstanding, the computation of book value per share is more complex. The book value for each share of stock depends on the rights of the preferred stockholders. Preferred stockholders typically are entitled to a specified liquidation value per share, plus cumulative dividends in arrears, if any, since most preferred stocks are preferred as to assets and are cumulative. In each case, the specific provisions in the preferred stock contract will govern.

To illustrate, the Celoron Corporation's stockholders' equity is as follows:

Stockholders' equity:
  Paid-in capital:
    Preferred stock—$100 par value, 6% cumulative;
      5,000 shares authorized, issued, and
      outstanding . . . . $ 500,000
    Common stock—$10 par value, 200,000 shares
      authorized, issued, and outstanding   2,000,000
    Paid-in capital in excess of par value—preferred   200,000
                                                                 ──────────
        Total paid-in capital $2,700,000
  Retained earnings   400,000
                                                                            ──────────
        Total stockholders' equity. $3,100,000

The preferred stock is 6%, cumulative, and nonparticipating. It is preferred as to dividends and as to assets in liquidation to the extent of the liquidation value of $100 per share, plus any cumulative dividends on the preferred stock. Dividends for four years are unpaid. Book values of the two classes of stock are calculated as follows:

		Total	*Per Share*
Total stockholders' equity		$3,100,000	
Book value of preferred stock (5,000 shares):			
Liquidation value (5,000 shares × $100) . . .	$500,000		
Dividends (4 years at $30,000)	120,000	620,000	$124.00*
Book value of common stock (200,000 shares).		$2,480,000	12.40†

* $620,000 ÷ 5,000 shares.
† $2,480,000 ÷ 200,000 shares.

Notice that the paid-in capital in excess of par value—preferred did not get assigned to the preferred stock in determining the book values. Only the liquidation value and cumulative dividends on the preferred stock are assigned to the preferred stock.

Assume now that the features attached to the preferred stock in the above example are the same except that the preferred stockholders have the right to receive $103 per share in liquidation. The book values of the two classes of stock would be:

	Total	Per Share
Total stockholders' equity	$3,100,000	
Book value of preferred stock (5,000 shares):		
Liquidation value (5,000 shares × $103) $515,000		
Dividends (4 years at $30,000) 120,000	635,000	$127.00*
Book value of common stock (200,000 shares) . .	$2,465,000	12.33†

* $635,000 ÷ 5,000 shares.
† $2,465,000 ÷ 200,000 shares.

Book value rarely equals market value of a stock because many of the assets have changed in value due to inflation. Thus, the shares of many corporations are traded regularly at market prices that are different from their book values.

PAID-IN (OR CONTRIBUTED) CAPITAL

*Objective 6
Identify the different sources of paid-in capital and describe how they would be presented on a balance sheet*

As you have learned in the early part of this chapter, *paid-in capital,* or *contributed capital,* refers to all of the contributed capital of a corporation, including that capital carried in the capital stock accounts. In the general ledger, no account titled ''Paid-In Capital'' is maintained. Instead, a separate account is established for each source of paid-in capital.

Illustration 9.2 summarizes several sources of stockholders' equity and gives examples of general ledger account titles used to record increases and decreases in capital from each of these sources. Earlier in this chapter was a discussion on some of these general ledger accounts. The remainder of this chapter will discuss other general ledger accounts used to record sources of stockholders' equity.

The stockholders' equity section of a balance sheet should show the different sources of the corporation's paid-in capital since these sources are important information. For example, these additional sources may be from stock dividends, treasury stock transactions, or donations.

Paid-In Capital—Stock Dividends

When a corporation declares a stock dividend, the corporation distributes additional shares of stock (instead of cash) to its present stockholders. In a later section, this chapter discusses and illustrates how the issuance of a stock dividend results in a credit to a Paid-In Capital—Stock Dividends account.

Paid-In Capital—Treasury Stock Transactions

Another source of capital is treasury stock transactions. **Treasury stock** is the corporation's own stock, either preferred or common, that has been issued and then reacquired by the issuing corporation; it is legally available

Illustration 9.2
SOURCES OF STOCKHOLDERS' EQUITY

Sources of Stockholders' Equity	*Illustrative General Ledger Account Titles*
I. Capital paid in (or contributed).	
A. For, or assigned to, shares:	
1. Issued to the extent of par or stated value or the amount received for shares without par or stated value.	Common Stock 5% Preferred Stock
2. Subscribed but not issued to the extent of par or stated value or the amount subscribed for shares without par or stated value.	Common (Preferred) Stock Subscribed
3. To be distributed as a stock dividend.	Stock Dividend Distributable—Common (Preferred)
4. In addition to par or stated value:	
a. In excess of par.	Paid-In Capital in Excess of Par Value—Common (Preferred)
b. In excess of stated value.	Paid-In Capital in Excess of Stated Value—Common (Preferred)
c. Resulting from declaration of stock dividends.	Paid-In Capital—Stock Dividends
d. Resulting from reissue of treasury stock at a price above its acquisition price.	Paid-In Capital—Common (Preferred) Treasury Stock Transactions
B. Other than for shares, whether from stockholders or from others.	Paid-In Capital—Donations
II. Capital accumulated by retention of earnings (retained earnings).	
A. Appropriated retained earnings.	Appropriation per Loan Agreement
B. Free and unappropriated retained earnings.	Retained Earnings (Unappropriated)

for reissuance. If a corporation reacquires shares of its own outstanding capital stock at one price and later reissues them at a higher price, corporate capital is increased by the difference between the two prices. If the reissue price is *less* than acquisition cost, corporate capital is decreased. Treasury stock transactions are discussed at length later in this chapter.

Paid-In Capital—Donations

Occasionally, a corporation receives gifts of assets, such as a gift of a $500,000 building. These donated gifts increase stockholders' equity and are called *donated capital*. The entry to record the gift of a $500,000 building is a debit to Buildings and a credit to Paid-In Capital—Donations. This entry should be made in the amount of the $500,000 fair market value of the gift when received.

RETAINED EARNINGS

The *retained earnings* portion of stockholders' equity results from accumulated earnings, reduced by net losses and dividends. Like paid-in capital, retained earnings is a source of assets received by a corporation. Paid-in capital is the actual investment by the stockholders; retained earnings is the investment by the stockholders through earnings not yet withdrawn.

The balance in the corporation's Retained Earnings account is the corporation's net income, less net losses, from the date the corporation began to the present, less the sum of dividends paid during this period. Net income increases Retained Earnings, while net losses and dividends decrease Retained Earnings in any given year. Thus, the balance in Retained Earnings represents the corporation's accumulated net income not distributed to stockholders.

When the Retained Earnings account has a debit balance, a **deficit** exists. A deficit is shown as retained earnings with a negative amount in the stockholders' equity section of the balance sheet. The title of the general ledger account need not be changed even though it contains a debit balance. The most common credits and debits made to Retained Earnings are for income (or losses) and dividends. Occasionally, other entries are made to the Retained Earnings account. We will discuss some of these entries later in the chapter.

PAID-IN CAPITAL AND RETAINED EARNINGS ON THE BALANCE SHEET

The following stockholders' equity section of a balance sheet presents the various sources of capital in proper form:

Stockholders' equity:		
Paid-in capital:		
Preferred stock—6%, $100 par value; authorized,		
issued, and outstanding, 4,000 shares	$ 400,000	
Common stock—no par value, $5 stated value;		
authorized, issued, and outstanding, 400,000		
shares	2,000,000	$2,400,000
Paid-in capital—		
From preferred stock issuances*	$ 40,000	
From donations	10,000	50,000
Total paid-in capital		$2,450,000
Retained earnings		500,000
Total stockholders' equity		$2,950,000

* This label is not the exact account title but is representative of the descriptions used on balance sheets. The exact account title could be used, but shorter descriptions are often shown.

In highly condensed, published balance sheets, the details regarding the sources of the paid-in capital in excess of par or stated value are often omitted and replaced by a single item, such as:

Paid-in capital in excess of par (or stated) value $50,000

DIVIDENDS

Dividends are distributions of earnings by a corporation to its stockholders. Usually dividends are paid in cash, but additional shares of the corporation's own capital stock may also be distributed as dividends. Occasionally, dividends are paid in merchandise or other assets. Since dividends are the means whereby the owners of a corporation share in the earnings of the corporation, they are charged against retained earnings.

Before dividends can be paid, they must be declared by the board of directors and recorded in the corporation's minutes book. Three dividend dates are significant:

1. **Date of declaration.** This date indicates when the board of directors takes action in the form of a motion and declares that dividends should be paid. The board action creates the liability for dividends payable (or stock dividends distributable for stock dividends).
2. **Date of record.** The board of directors establishes this date; the date of record determines the stockholders who will receive the dividends. The corporation's records (the stockholders ledger) determine the corporation's stockholders as of the date of record.
3. **Date of payment.** This date indicates when the corporation will pay the dividend to the stockholders.

To illustrate how these three dates relate to an actual situation, assume the board of directors of the Allen Corporation declared a cash dividend on May 5, 1995 (date of declaration). The cash dividend declared is $1.25 per share to stockholders of record on July 1, 1995 (date of record), payable on July 10 (date of payment). Since financial transactions occur on both the date of declaration (a liability is incurred) and on the date of payment (cash is paid), journal entries will be required on both of these dates. No journal entry is required on the date of record.

Cash Dividends

Cash dividends are cash distributions of net income by a corporation to its stockholders. To illustrate the entries for cash dividends, consider the following example. On January 21, 1995, a corporation's board of directors declared a 2% quarterly cash dividend on $100,000 of outstanding preferred stock. This dividend is one fourth of the annual dividend on 1,000 shares of $100 par value, 8% preferred stock. The dividend will be paid on March 1, 1995, to stockholders of record on February 5, 1995. The entries at the declaration and payment dates are as follows (**no entry is made on the date of record**):

```
1995
Jan.  21  Retained Earnings. . . . . . . . . . . . . .   2,000
              Dividends Payable. . . . . . . . . . . .            2,000
          Dividend declared: 2% on $100,000 of
          outstanding preferred stock, payable March 1,
          1995, to stockholders of record on February
          5, 1995.

Mar.   1  Dividends Payable. . . . . . . . . . . . . .   2,000
              Cash . . . . . . . . . . . . . . . . . .            2,000
          Paid the dividend declared on January 21,
          1995.
```

Often a cash dividend is stated as so many dollars per share. For instance, the quarterly dividend could have been stated as $2 per share. When a cash dividend is declared, some companies debit a Dividends account instead of Retained Earnings. (Both methods are acceptable.) The Dividends account is then closed to Retained Earnings at the end of the fiscal year.

Once a cash dividend is declared and notice of the dividend is given to stockholders, it generally cannot be rescinded unless all stockholders agree to such action.[1] Thus, the credit balance in the Dividends Payable account appears as a current liability on the balance sheet.

Stock Dividends

Stock dividends are payable in additional shares of the declaring corporation's capital stock. When stock dividends are declared, additional shares of the same class of stock as that held by the stockholders are issued to those stockholders.

Corporations usually account for stock dividends by transferring a sum from retained earnings to permanent paid-in capital. The amount transferred for stock dividends depends on the size of the stock dividend. Most states permit corporations to debit Retained Earnings or any paid-in capital accounts other than those representing legal capital for stock dividends. In most circumstances, however, Retained Earnings will be debited for the declaration of a stock dividend.

Stock dividends have no effect on the total amount of stockholders' equity or on net assets. They merely decrease retained earnings and increase

---

[1] Stockholders might agree to rescind (cancel) a dividend that has already been declared if the company is in difficult financial circumstances and needs to retain the cash to pay bills or acquire assets that are needed to continue operations.

paid-in capital by an equal amount. Immediately after the distribution of a stock dividend, each share of similar stock has a lower book value per share. This decrease occurs because more shares are outstanding with no increase in total stockholders' equity.

Stock dividends do not affect the individual stockholder's percentage of ownership in the corporation. For example, if a stockholder owns 1,000 shares in a corporation having 100,000 shares of stock outstanding, that stockholder owns 1% of the outstanding shares. After a 10% stock dividend, the stockholder will still own 1% of the outstanding shares—1,100 of the 110,000 outstanding shares.

A corporation might declare a stock dividend for several reasons:

1. Retained earnings may have become large relative to total stockholders' equity, or the corporation may simply desire a larger permanent capitalization.
2. The market price of the stock may have risen above a desirable trading range. A stock dividend will generally reduce the per share market value of the company's stock.
3. The board of directors of the corporation may wish to have more stockholders (who might then buy its products) and expects to eventually increase their number by increasing the number of shares outstanding. Some of the stockholders receiving the stock dividend are likely to sell the shares to other persons.
4. Stock dividends may be used to silence stockholders' demands for cash dividends from a corporation that does not have sufficient cash to pay cash dividends.

A stock dividend is categorized as a small stock dividend or a large stock dividend according to the percentage of shares issued as a stock dividend, and different accounting treatments are used for each.

Recording Small Stock Dividends. A stock dividend of less than 20 to 25% of the outstanding shares is considered a *small stock dividend* and is assumed to have little effect on the market value (quoted market price) of the shares. Thus, the dividend is accounted for at the current market value of the outstanding shares.

Assume a corporation is authorized to issue 20,000 shares of $100 par value common stock, of which 8,000 shares are outstanding. Its board of directors declares a 10% stock dividend (800 shares). The quoted market price of the stock is $125 per share immediately before the stock dividend is announced. Since the distribution is less than 20 to 25% of the outstanding shares, the dividend is accounted for at market value. The entry for the declaration of the stock dividend on August 10, 1995, is:

```
Aug.  10  Retained Earnings (or Stock Dividends) (800
              shares × $125) . . . . . . . . . . . . . .  100,000
                 Stock Dividend Distributable—Common
                    (800 shares × $100) . . . . . . . . . .        80,000
                 Paid-In Capital—Stock Dividends
                    (800 shares × $25). . . . . . . . . . .        20,000
              To record the declaration of a 10% stock
              dividend; shares to be distributed on
              September 20, 1995, to stockholders of record
              on August 31, 1995.
```

The entry to record the issuance of the shares is:

```
Sept.  20  Stock Dividend Distributable—Common  . . . .   80,000
               Common Stock . . . . . . . . . . . . . .          80,000
           To record the distribution of 800 shares of
           common stock as authorized in stock
           dividend declared on August 10, 1995.
```

The **Stock Dividend Distributable—Common account** is a stockholders' equity (paid-in capital) account credited for the par or stated value of the shares distributable when recording the declaration of a stock dividend. Since a stock dividend distributable is not to be paid with assets, it is not a liability. If a balance sheet is prepared between the date the 10% dividend is declared and the date the shares are issued, the proper statement presentation of the effects of the stock dividend is:

```
Stockholders' equity:
  Paid-in capital:
    Common stock—$100 par value; authorized, 20,000
       shares; issued and outstanding, 8,000 shares . . . .  $800,000
    Stock dividend distributable on September 20, 1995, 800
       shares at par value. . . . . . . . . . . . . . .          80,000
    Total par value of shares issued and to be issued . . . .  $880,000
    Paid-in capital from stock dividends. . . . . . . . . .       20,000
       Total paid-in capital . . . . . . . . . . . . . . .              $  900,000
  Retained earnings . . . . . . . . . . . . . . . . . .                    150,000
       Total stockholders' equity . . . . . . . . . . .                 $1,050,000
```

Suppose, on the other hand, that the common stock in the above example is no-par stock and has a stated value of $50 per share. In this case, the entry to record the declaration of the stock dividend (when the market value is $125) is:

```
Retained Earnings (800 shares × $125) . . . . . . . . . .  100,000
    Stock Dividend Distributable—Common
       (800 shares × $50). . . . . . . . . . . . . . .            40,000
    Paid-In Capital—Stock Dividends (800 shares × $75)  . .       60,000
    To record the declaration of a stock dividend.
```

The entry to record the issuance of the stock dividend is:

Stock Dividend Distributable—Common	40,000	
Common Stock		40,000
To record the issuance of the stock dividend.		

Recording Large Stock Dividends. A stock dividend of more than 20 to 25% of the outstanding shares is considered a *large stock dividend*. Since one purpose of a large stock dividend is to reduce the market value of the stock so the shares can be traded more easily, the old market value of the stock should not be used in the entry. Such dividends are accounted for at their *par* or *stated* value rather than at their current market value. Stocks without par or stated value are accounted for at the amounts established by the laws of the state of incorporation or by the board of directors.

To illustrate the treatment of a stock dividend of more than 20 to 25%, assume X Corporation has been authorized to issue 10,000 shares of $10 par value common stock, of which 5,000 shares are outstanding. X Corporation declared a 30% stock dividend (1,500 shares) on September 20, 1995, to be issued on October 15, 1995. The required entries are:

Sept. 20 Retained Earnings (or Stock Dividends) (1,500 shares × $10).	15,000	
Stock Dividend Distributable—Common		15,000
To declare a 30% stock dividend.		
Oct. 15 Stock Dividend Distributable—Common	15,000	
Common Stock		15,000
To issue the 30% stock dividend.		

Note that in contrast to the small stock dividend that was accounted for at current market value, the 30% stock dividend is accounted for at par value (1,500 shares × $10 = $15,000). Because of the differences in accounting for large and small stock dividends, the relative size of the stock dividend must be determined before making any journal entries.

Illustration 9.3 shows the effect of a small and large stock dividend on the stockholders' equity.

Stock Splits

A **stock split** is a distribution of 100% or more of additional shares of the issuing corporation's stock accompanied by a corresponding reduction in the par value per share. The corporation receives no assets in this transaction. The purpose of a stock split is to cause a large reduction in the market price per share of the outstanding stock. A two-for-one split doubles the number of shares outstanding, a three-for-one split triples the number of shares, and so on. The par value per share is reduced at the same time so that the total dollar amount credited to common stock remains the same. For instance, in a two-for-one split, the par value per share is halved, and the fair market

Illustration 9.3
STOCK DIVIDENDS

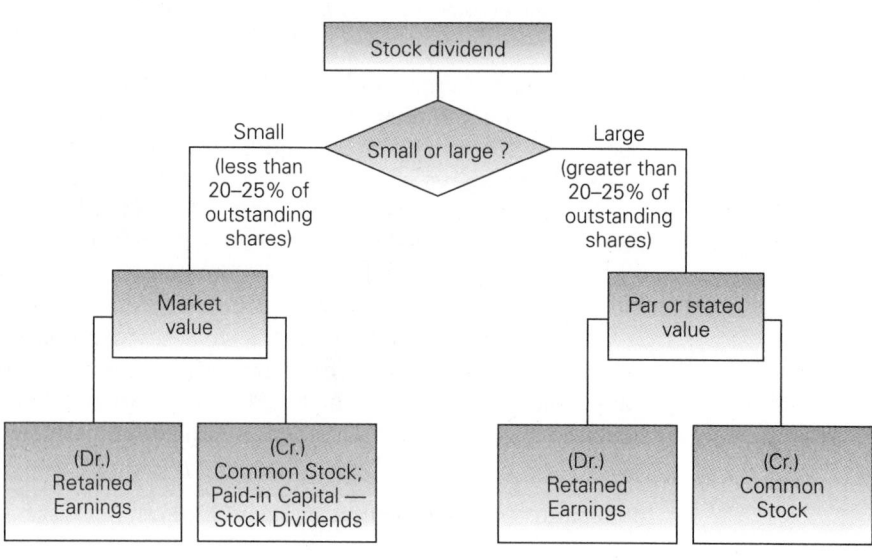

value would likely be halved also.[2] If the corporation issues 100% more stock without a reduction in the par value per share, the transaction is considered a 100% stock dividend rather than a two-for-one stock split.

The entry to record a stock split depends on the particular circumstances. Usually, only the number of shares outstanding and the par or stated value need to be changed in the records. (The number of shares authorized may also change.) Thus, a two-for-one stock split in which the par value of the shares is decreased from $20 to $10 would be recorded as:

```
Common Stock—$20 par value. . . . . . . . . . . . . .  100,000
     Common Stock—$10 par value. . . . . . . . . . . .            100,000
   To record a two-for-one stock split; 5,000 shares of $20
   par value common stock were replaced by 10,000 shares
   of $10 par value common stock.
```

Illustration 9.4 summarizes the effects of stock dividends and stock splits. Stock dividends and stock splits have no effect on the total amount of stockholders' equity. In addition, stock splits have no effect on the total amount of paid-in capital or retained earnings. They merely increase the number of shares outstanding and decrease the par value per share. Stock

---

[2] If a corporation *reduces* the par value of its stock without issuing more shares, say, from $100 to $60 per share, then $40 per share must be removed from the appropriate capital stock account and credited to Paid-In Capital—Recapitalization. Further discussion of this process, called *recapitalization,* is beyond the scope of this text.

Illustration 9.4
SUMMARY OF EFFECTS OF STOCK DIVIDENDS AND STOCK SPLITS

	Total Stockholders' Equity	Common Stock	Paid-In Capital— Common	Retained Earnings	Number of Shares Outstanding	Par Value per Share
Stock dividends:						
Small.	No effect	Increases	Increases*	Decreases	Increases	No effect
Large	No effect	Increases	No effect	Decreases	Increases	No effect
Stock splits.	No effect	No effect	No effect	No effect	Increases	Decreases

* Assuming current market price is greater than par value.

dividends increase paid-in capital and decrease retained earnings by equal amounts.

RETAINED EARNINGS APPROPRIATIONS

Appropriations of retained earnings may be made for pending litigation, for debt retirement, for contingencies in general, and for other purposes. Such appropriations do not reduce total retained earnings. Their purpose is merely to disclose to balance sheet readers that a portion of retained earnings is not available for cash dividends. Thus, the recording of these appropriations simply guarantees that the corporation will limit its outflow of cash dividends while repaying a loan, expanding a plant, or taking on some other costly endeavor. Recording retained earnings appropriations does not involve the setting aside of cash for the indicated purpose. The establishment of a separate fund would require a specific directive from the board of directors. Thus, the only entry required to record the appropriation of $25,000 of retained earnings to fulfill the provisions in a loan agreement is:

```
Retained Earnings . . . . . . . . . . . . . . . . . . . . . . . . 25,000
    Appropriation per Loan Agreement . . . . . . . . . . . .          25,000
    To record restriction on retained earnings.
```

When the retained earnings appropriation has served its purpose of restricting dividends and the loan has been repaid, the board of directors may decide to return the appropriation intact to Retained Earnings. The entry to do this is:

```
Appropriation per Loan Agreement . . . . . . . . . . . . . 25,000
    Retained Earnings . . . . . . . . . . . . . . . . . . . . . .          25,000
    To return balance in Appropriation per Loan Agreement
    account to Retained Earnings.
```

Retained Earnings Appropriations on the Balance Sheet

On the balance sheet, retained earnings appropriations should be shown in the stockholders' equity section as follows:

Stockholders' equity:

Paid-in capital:

Preferred stock—8%, $50 par value; 500 shares authorized,
issued, and outstanding. $25,000

Common stock—$5 par value; 10,000 shares authorized,
issued, and outstanding. 50,000

Total paid-in capital . . . . $ 75,000

Retained earnings:

Appropriated:

Per loan agreement. $25,000

Unappropriated. 20,000

Total retained earnings 45,000

Total stockholders' equity. $120,000

Note that a retained earnings appropriation does not reduce stockholders' equity but merely earmarks (restricts) a portion of that equity for a specific reason.

Changes in the composition of retained earnings reveal important information about a corporation to financial statement users. As shown in earlier chapters, a separate formal statement is issued to disclose such changes. This statement is called the *statement of retained earnings*.

STATEMENT OF RETAINED EARNINGS

A **statement of retained earnings** is a formal statement showing the items causing changes in unappropriated and appropriated retained earnings during a stated period of time. Changes in unappropriated retained earnings usually consist of the addition of net income (or deduction of net loss) and the deduction of dividends and appropriations. Changes in appropriated retained earnings consist of increases or decreases in appropriations.

Illustration 9.5 shows a statement of retained earnings. Ward Corporation's only new appropriation during 1995 was an additional $35,000 for plant expansion. This new $35,000 is added to the $25,000 beginning balance in that account and subtracted from unappropriated retained earnings. An alternative to the statement of retained earnings is the statement of stockholders' equity.

STATEMENT OF STOCKHOLDERS' EQUITY

Most corporations include four financial statements in their annual reports: a balance sheet, an income statement, a statement of stockholders' equity (in place of a statement of retained earnings), and a statement of cash flows (to be discussed in Chapter 21). A **statement of stockholders' equity** is a summary of the transactions affecting the accounts in the stockholders' equity

Illustration 9.5
STATEMENT OF RETAINED EARNINGS

WARD CORPORATION
Statement of Retained Earnings
For Year Ended December 31, 1995

Unappropriated retained earnings:		
January 1, 1995, balance		$180,000
Add: Net income		80,000
		$260,000
Less: Dividends	$15,000	
Appropriation for plant expansion.	35,000	50,000
Unappropriated retained earnings, December 31, 1995		$210,000
Appropriated retained earnings:		
Appropriation for plant expansion, January 1, 1995, balance . .	$25,000	
Add: Increase in 1995	35,000	$ 60,000
Appropriation for contract obligation, January 1, 1995, balance .		20,000
Appropriated retained earnings, December 31, 1995		$ 80,000
Total retained earnings, December 31, 1995		$290,000

Illustration 9.6
STATEMENT OF STOCKHOLDERS' EQUITY

LARKIN CORPORATION
Statement of Stockholders' Equity
For the Year Ended December 31, 1995

	$50 Par Value, 6% Preferred Stock	$20 Par Value Common Stock	Paid-In Capital in Excess of Par Value	Retained Earnings	Treasury Stock	Total
Balance, January 1, 1995.	$250,000	$300,000	$200,000	$500,000	$(42,000)	$1,208,000
Issuance of 10,000 shares of						
common stock		200,000	100,000			300,000
5% stock dividend on common						
stock, 1,250 shares		25,000	27,500	(52,500)		–0–
Purchase of 1,200 shares of						
treasury stock					(48,000)	(48,000)
Net income				185,000		185,000
Cash dividends:						
Preferred stock				(15,000)		(15,000)
Common stock				(25,000)		(25,000)
Balance, December 31, 1995 . . .	$250,000	$525,000	$327,500	$592,500	$(90,000)	$1,605,000

section of the balance sheet during a stated period of time. These transactions include activities affecting both paid-in capital and retained earnings accounts. Thus, the statement of stockholders' equity includes the information contained in a statement of retained earnings plus some additional information. The columns in the statement of stockholders' equity reflect the major account titles within the stockholders' equity section: the types of stock issued and outstanding, paid-in capital in excess of par (or stated) value, retained earnings, and treasury stock. Each row indicates the effects of major transactions affecting one or more stockholders' equity accounts.

Illustration 9.6 shows a statement of stockholders' equity. The first row indicates the beginning balances of each account in the stockholders' equity section. This summary shows that Larkin Corporation issued 10,000 shares of common stock, declared a 5% stock dividend on common stock, repurchased 1,200 shares of treasury stock, earned net income of $185,000, and paid cash dividends on both its preferred and common stock. After the transactions' effects are indicated within each row, each column's components are added or subtracted to determine the ending balance in each stockholders' equity account.

TREASURY STOCK

*Objective 8
Account for the
acquisition and
reissuance of
treasury stock*

Treasury stock is the corporation's own capital stock that has been issued and then reacquired by the corporation; it has not been canceled and is legally available for later reissuance. Also, treasury stock is *not* classified as *unissued stock* because unissued stock is stock that has never been issued.

As you may recall, if a corporation has additional *authorized* but *unissued* shares of stock that are to be issued after the date of original issue, the preemptive right requires that additional authorized and unissued shares must, in most states, be offered first to existing stockholders on a pro rata basis. However, treasury stock may be reissued without violating the preemptive right provisions of state laws; that is, treasury stock does not have to be offered to current stockholders on a pro rata basis.

A corporation may reacquire its own capital stock as treasury stock to (1) cancel and retire the stock, (2) reissue the stock later at a higher price, (3) reduce the number of shares outstanding and thereby increase earnings per share, or (4) use the stock for issuance to employees. If the intent of reacquisition is cancellation and retirement, the treasury shares exist only until they are retired and canceled by a formal reduction of corporate capital.

For dividend or voting purposes, most state corporate laws consider treasury stock as issued but not outstanding, since the shares are no longer in the possession of stockholders. Also, treasury shares are not considered outstanding in calculating earnings per share. However, treasury shares usually are considered outstanding for purposes of determining legal capital, which would include outstanding shares plus treasury shares.

In states that consider treasury stock as part of legal capital, the cost of treasury stock may not exceed the amount of retained earnings at the date the shares are reacquired. This regulation protects creditors by preventing the corporation from using funds to purchase its own stock instead of paying its debts when the corporation is in financial difficulty. Thus, if a corporation is subject to such a law (as is assumed in this text), the retained earnings available for dividends are limited to the amount in excess of the cost of the treasury shares on hand.

Acquisition and Reissuance of Treasury Stock

When treasury stock is acquired, the stock is recorded at cost as a debit in a stockholders' equity account called *Treasury Stock*.[3] Reissuances are credited to the Treasury Stock account at the cost of acquisition. Any excess of the reissue price over cost is credited to **Paid-In Capital—Treasury Stock Transactions** because it represents additional paid-in capital.

To illustrate, assume that on February 18, 1995, the Hillside Corporation reacquired 100 shares of its outstanding common stock for $55 each. (The company's stockholders' equity consisted solely of common stock and retained earnings.) On April 18, 1995, the company reissued 30 shares for $58 each. The entries to record these events are:

```
1995
Feb. 18   Treasury Stock—Common (100 shares × $55) . . . . .   5,500
               Cash. . . . . . . . . . . . . . . . . . . . . . .          5,500
          Acquired 100 shares of treasury stock at $55.

Apr. 18   Cash (30 shares × $58) . . . . . . . . . . . . . . . .   1,740
               Treasury Stock—Common (30 shares × $55) . . . .          1,650
               Paid-In Capital—Common Treasury Stock
                  Transactions . . . . . . . . . . . . . . . . .             90
          Reissued 30 shares of treasury stock at $58; cost is
          $55 per share.
```

When the reissue price of subsequent shares is *less* than the acquisition price, the difference between cost and reissue price is debited to Paid-In Capital—Common Treasury Stock Transactions. This account, however, is not permitted to develop a debit balance. By definition, no paid-in capital account can have a debit balance. If Hillside reissued an additional 20 shares at $52 per share on June 12, 1995, the entry would be:

```
June 12   Cash (20 shares × $52) . . . . . . . . . . . . . . . .   1,040
          Paid-In Capital—Common Treasury Stock Transactions.      60
               Treasury Stock—Common (20 shares × $55) . . . .          1,100
          Reissued 20 shares of treasury stock at $52; cost is
          $55 per share.
```

---

[3] Another acceptable method of accounting for treasury stock transactions is called the par value method. Further discussion of the par value method is left to intermediate accounting texts.

At this point, the credit balance in the Paid-In Capital—Common Treasury Stock Transactions account would be $30. If the remaining 50 shares are reissued on July 16, 1995, for $53 per share, the entry would be:

```
July 16   Cash (50 shares × $53) . . . . . . . . . . . . . . .    2,650
              Paid-In Capital—Common Treasury Stock Transactions .      30
              Retained Earnings. . . . . . . . . . . . . . . . .        70
                  Treasury Stock—Common (50 shares × $55) . . . .              2,750
              Reissued 50 shares of treasury stock at $53; cost is
              $55 per share.
```

Note that the Paid-In Capital—Common Treasury Stock Transactions account credit balance has been exhausted. If more than $30 is debited to that account, it would develop a debit balance. Thus, the remaining $70 of the excess of cost over reissue price is regarded as a special distribution to the stockholders involved and is debited to the Retained Earnings account.

When stockholders *donate* stock to a corporation, the treatment is slightly different. Since donated treasury shares have no cost, only a memo entry is made when they are received.[4] The only formal entry required is to debit Cash and credit the Paid-In Capital—Donations account when the stock is reissued. For example, if donated treasury stock is sold for $5,000, the entry would be:

```
Cash . . . . . . . . . . . . . . . . . . . . . . . . . . . .    5,000
    Paid-In Capital—Donations . . . . . . . . . . . . . . . .          5,000
    To record the sale of donated treasury stock.
```

Treasury Stock on the Balance Sheet

When treasury stock is held on a balance sheet date, it is customarily shown on that statement at cost, as a deduction from the sum of total paid-in capital and retained earnings, as follows.

Stockholders' equity:		
Paid-in capital:		
Common stock—$10 par value; authorized and issued,		
20,000 shares, of which 2,000 shares are in the treasury . .	$200,000	
Retained earnings (including $22,000 restricted by acquisition		
of treasury stock)	80,000	
Total paid-in capital and retained earnings		$280,000
Less: Treasury stock at cost, 2,000 shares		22,000
Total stockholders' equity		$258,000

---

[4] The method illustrated here is called the *memo* method. Other acceptable methods of accounting for donated stock are the *cost* method and *par value* method. These latter two methods are discussed in intermediate accounting texts.

Illustration 9.7
STOCKHOLDERS' EQUITY SECTION OF THE BALANCE SHEET

HYPOTHETICAL CORPORATION
Partial Balance Sheet
December 31, 1995

Stockholders' equity:

Paid-in capital:

Preferred stock—8%, $100 par value; 2,000 shares authorized, issued, and outstanding			$ 200,000
Common stock—$10 par value; authorized, 100,000 shares, issued, 80,000 shares of which 1,000 are held in the treasury		$800,000	
Stock dividend distributable on common stock on January 15, 1996, 7,900 shares		79,000	879,000

Paid in capital—

From common stock issuances		$ 40,000	
From stock dividends		60,000	
From treasury stock transactions		30,000	
From donations.		50,000	180,000
Total paid-in capital.			$1,259,000

Retained earnings:

Appropriated:

Per loan agreement.		$250,000	
Unappropriated (restricted to the extent of $20,000, the cost of treasury shares held).		150,000	
Total retained earnings			400,000
Total paid-in capital and retained earnings			$1,659,000
Less: Treasury stock, common, 1,000 shares at cost			20,000
Total stockholders' equity			$1,639,000

Stockholders' Equity on the Balance Sheet

Much of what has been discussed so far in this chapter can be summarized through presentation of the stockholders' equity section of the balance sheet of a hypothetical corporation (Illustration 9.7). This partial balance sheet shows (1) the amount of capital assigned to shares outstanding; (2) the capital contributed for outstanding shares in addition to that assigned to the shares; (3) other forms of paid-in capital; and (4) retained earnings, appropriated and unappropriated.

NET INCOME INCLUSIONS AND EXCLUSIONS

Objective 9
Describe the proper accounting treatment of discontinued operations, extraordinary items, and changes in accounting principles

Accounting has long faced the problem of what to include in the net income reported for a period. Should net income include only the revenues and expenses related to normal operations? Or should it include the results of discontinued operations and unusual, nonrecurring gains and losses? And further, should the determination of net income for 1995, for example, include an item that can be clearly associated with a prior year, such as additional federal income taxes for 1994? Or should such items, including corrections of errors, be carried directly to retained earnings? How are the effects of making a change in accounting principle (like a change in depreciation methods) to be reported?

APB Opinion No. 9 (December 1966) sought to provide answers to some of these questions. The *Opinion* directed that unusual and nonrecurring items that have an earnings or loss effect should be classified as extraordinary items (reported in the income statement) or as prior period adjustments (reported in the statement of retained earnings). Extraordinary items were to be reported separately after net income from regular continuing activities.

Illustrations 9.8 (p. 483) and 9.10 (p. 486) show the reporting of discontinued operations, extraordinary items, changes in accounting principle, and prior period adjustments. For Illustrations 9.8 and 9.10, assume that the Anson Company has 1,000,000 shares of common stock outstanding and the company's earnings are taxed at 40%. Also, assume the following:

1. Anson sold its Cosmetics Division on August 1, 1995, at a loss of $500,000. The net operating loss of that division through July 31, 1995, was $2,000,000.
2. Anson had a taxable gain in 1995 of $40,000 from voluntary early retirement of debt (extraordinary item).
3. Anson changed depreciation methods in 1995 (change in accounting principle), and the cumulative effect of the changes was a $6,000 decrease in prior years' depreciation expense.
4. In 1995, it was discovered that the $200,000 cost of land acquired in 1994 had been expensed for both financial accounting and tax purposes. A prior period adjustment was made in 1995.

Now the effects of these assumptions will be explained in greater detail.

Discontinued Operations

A **discontinued operation** occurs when a segment (usually an unprofitable department or division) of a business is sold to another company or has been abandoned. When a company discontinues a segment, it shows the information relating to the segment in a special section of the income statement immediately after income from continuing operations and before extraordinary items. Two items of information are reported:

1. The income or loss (net of tax effect) from the segment's operations for the portion of the current year before it was discontinued.
2. The gain or loss (net of tax effect) on disposal of the segment.

To illustrate, Anson's sale of its Cosmetics Division on August 1 led to a before-tax loss of $500,000. The after-tax loss was $500,000 × 60% = $300,000. The operating loss before taxes through July 31 was $2,000,000. The after-tax operating loss for that period was $2,000,000 × 60% = $1,200,000. This information is included on the income statement, as shown in Illustration 9.8.

Illustration 9.8
NET INCOME INCLUSIONS AND EXCLUSIONS

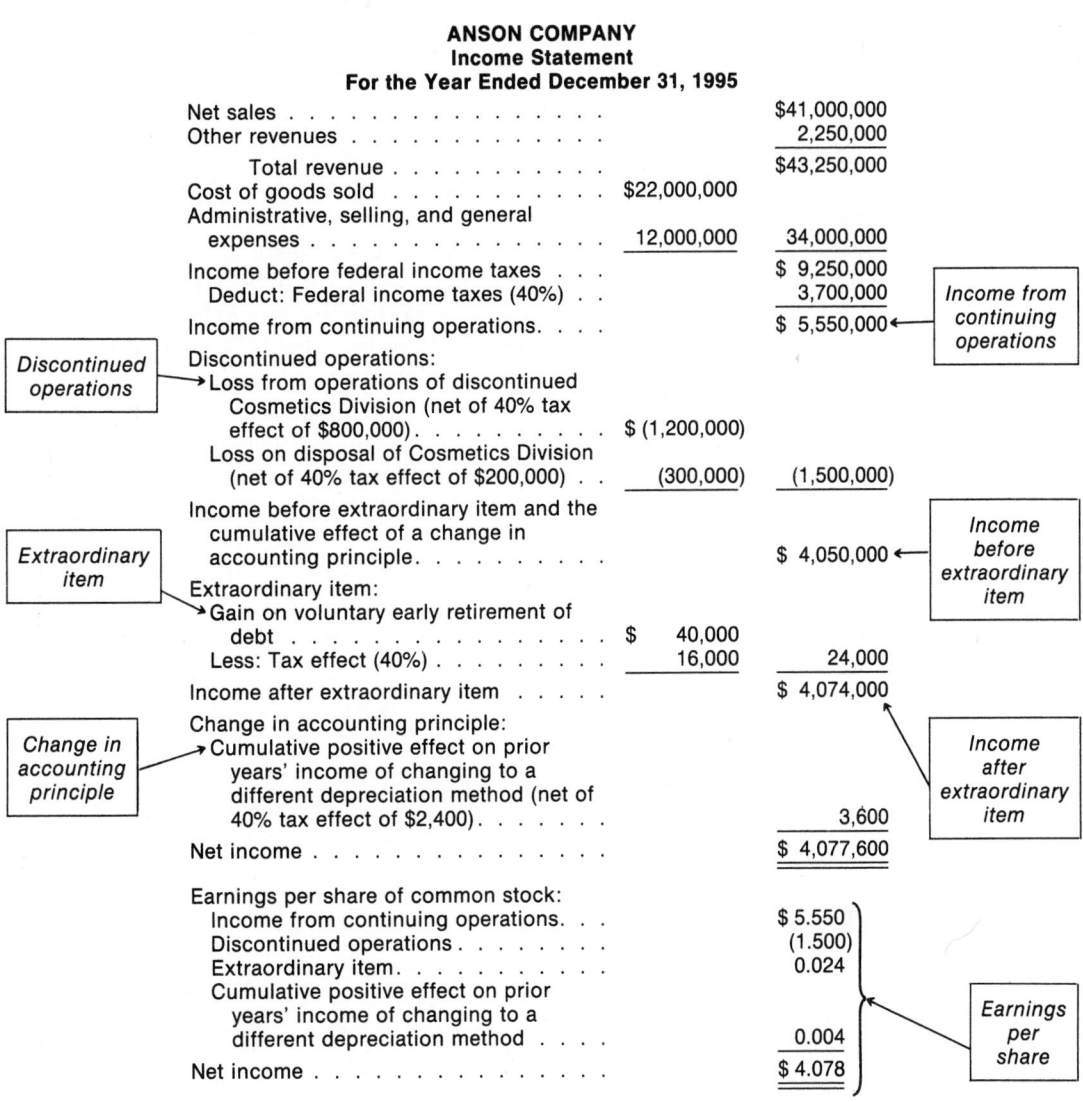

ANSON COMPANY
Income Statement
For the Year Ended December 31, 1995

Net sales		$41,000,000
Other revenues		2,250,000
Total revenue		$43,250,000
Cost of goods sold	$22,000,000	
Administrative, selling, and general expenses	12,000,000	34,000,000
Income before federal income taxes . . .		$ 9,250,000
Deduct: Federal income taxes (40%) . .		3,700,000
Income from continuing operations. . . .		$ 5,550,000

Income from continuing operations

Discontinued operations

Discontinued operations:		
Loss from operations of discontinued Cosmetics Division (net of 40% tax effect of $800,000).	$ (1,200,000)	
Loss on disposal of Cosmetics Division (net of 40% tax effect of $200,000) . .	(300,000)	(1,500,000)

Extraordinary item

Income before extraordinary item and the cumulative effect of a change in accounting principle.		$ 4,050,000

Income before extraordinary item

Extraordinary item:		
Gain on voluntary early retirement of debt	$ 40,000	
Less: Tax effect (40%)	16,000	24,000
Income after extraordinary item		$ 4,074,000

Change in accounting principle

Change in accounting principle:		
Cumulative positive effect on prior years' income of changing to a different depreciation method (net of 40% tax effect of $2,400).		3,600
Net income		$ 4,077,600

Income after extraordinary item

Earnings per share of common stock:	
Income from continuing operations. . .	$ 5.550
Discontinued operations	(1.500)
Extraordinary item.	0.024
Cumulative positive effect on prior years' income of changing to a different depreciation method	0.004
Net income	$ 4.078

Earnings per share

Extraordinary Items

Prior to 1973, companies tended to report a gain or loss as an extraordinary item if it was *either* unusual in nature *or* occurred infrequently. As a result, companies were inconsistent in the financial reporting of certain gains and losses. This inconsistency led to the issuance of *APB Opinion No. 30* (September 1973). *Opinion No. 30* redefined **extraordinary items** as those that are unusual in nature *and* that occur infrequently. Note that both conditions must be met—unusual nature and infrequent occurrence. Whether an item is unusual and infrequent is to be determined in light of the environment in which the company operates. Examples of extraordinary items include gains or losses that are the direct result of a major casualty (a flood), a confiscation of property by a foreign government, or a prohibition under a newly enacted law. *FASB Statement No. 4* further directs that gains and losses from the voluntary early *extinguishment* (retirement) of debt are extraordinary items.

Extraordinary items are to be included in the determination of periodic net income, but disclosed separately (net of their tax effects, if any) in the income statement. As shown in the income statement presented in Illustration 9.8, income before extraordinary items must be reported, and then income after extraordinary items is reported. **Income before extraordinary items** is income from continuing operations less applicable income taxes plus or minus the gain or loss from discontinued operations.

Gains or losses related to ordinary business activities are not extraordinary items regardless of their size. For example, material write-downs of uncollectible receivables, obsolete inventories, and intangible assets are not extraordinary items. However, such items may be separately disclosed as part of income from continuing operations.

Illustration 9.9 shows that in a sample of 600 companies for the years 1987–90, both the number of companies reporting extraordinary items and the total number of extraordinary items decreased significantly in 1988 and 1989.

Changes in Accounting Principle

A company's reported net income and financial position can be altered materially by *changes in accounting principle*. **Changes in accounting principle** are changes in accounting methods pertaining to such items as inventory and

Illustration 9.9
EXTRAORDINARY ITEMS

	1990	1989	1988	1987
Nature:				
Debt extinguishments	36	16	26	53
Operating loss carryforwards	24	26	35	80
Litigation settlements.	2	3	6	2
Other	5	9	6	9
Total Extraordinary Items	67	54	73	144
Number of companies:				
Presenting extraordinary items	63	49	67	127
Not presenting extraordinary items	537	551	533	473
Total companies	600	600	600	600

SOURCE: Based on American Institute of Certified Public Accountants, *Accounting Trends & Techniques* (New York: AICPA, 1991), p. 357.

depreciation. Examples of changes in accounting principle are a change in inventory valuation method from FIFO to LIFO or a change in depreciation method from accelerated to straight-line.

According to *APB Opinion No. 20,* a company should consistently apply the same accounting methods from one period to another. However, a company may make a change if the newly adopted method is preferable and if the change is adequately disclosed in the financial statements. In the period in which a company makes a change in principle, it must disclose on the financial statements the nature of the change, its justification, and its effect on net income. Also, the company must show on the income statement for the year of the change (Illustration 9.8) the cumulative effect of the change on prior years' income (net of tax).

As an example of a change in accounting principle, assume that Anson purchased a machine on January 2, 1993, for $30,000. The machine has a useful life of five years with no salvage value expected. Anson decided to depreciate the machine for financial reporting purposes using the sum-of-the-years'-digits method. At the beginning of 1995, the company decided to change to the straight-line method of depreciation. The cumulative effect of the change in accounting principle is computed as follows:

Under sum-of-the-years'-digits depreciation:		
Depreciation for 1993: $30,000 × 5/15.	$10,000	
Depreciation for 1994: $30,000 × 4/15.	8,000	
Balance in accumulated depreciation at beginning of 1995	$18,000	Difference $6,000
Under straight-line depreciation (if it had been used):		
Depreciation for 1993: $30,000/5.	$ 6,000	
Depreciation for 1994: $30,000/5.	6,000	
Balance that would have been in accumulated depreciation at beginning of 1995	$12,000	

The accumulated depreciation account balance would have been $6,000 less under the straight-line method. Also, depreciation expense over the two years would have been $6,000 less. Assume that federal income tax would have been $2,400 more ($6,000 × 0.4). The net effect of the change is $6,000 − $2,400 = $3,600. Therefore, Anson corrects the appropriate account balances by reducing (debiting) the accumulated depreciation account balance by $6,000, crediting an account entitled Cumulative Effect of Change in Accounting Principle for $3,600 (which will be closed to Retained Earnings during the normal closing process), and crediting Federal Income Taxes Payable for $2,400. The journal entry would be:

Accumulated Depreciation—Machinery	6,000	
Cumulative Effect of Change in Accounting Principle		3,600
Federal Income Taxes Payable		2,400

To record the effect of changing from sum-of-the-years'-digits depreciation to straight-line depreciation on machinery.

The cumulative effect of changing to the straight-line depreciation method is reported in Illustration 9.8 at the after-tax amount of $3,600.

Prior Period Adjustments

Objective 10
Define prior period adjustments and show their proper presentation in the financial statements

According to *FASB Statement No. 16,* **prior period adjustments** consist almost entirely of corrections of errors in previously published financial statements. Corrections of abnormal, nonrecurring errors that may have been caused by the improper use of an accounting principle or by mathematical mistakes are considered to be prior period adjustments. Normal, recurring corrections and adjustments, which follow inevitably from the use of estimates in accounting practice, are not treated as prior period adjustments. Also, mistakes corrected in the same year they occur are not prior period adjustments. To illustrate a prior period adjustment, suppose that Anson purchased land in 1994 at a total cost of $200,000 and recorded this amount in an expense account instead of in the Land account. Discovery of the error on May 1, 1995, after publication of the 1994 financial statements, would require a prior period adjustment. The adjustment would be recorded directly in the Retained Earnings account. Assuming the error had resulted in an $80,000 underpayment of taxes in 1994, the entry to correct the error would be:

```
May 1  Land . . . . . . . . . . . . . . . . . . . . . . . . . . .  200,000
           Federal Income Taxes Payable . . . . . . . . .            80,000
           Retained Earnings (or Prior Period Adjustment—
             Land) . . . . . . . . . . . . . . . . . . . . . .      120,000
       To correct an accounting error expensing land.
```

Prior period adjustments are not reported on the income statements but are shown in the current-year financial statements as adjustments to the opening balance of retained earnings on the statement of retained earnings (Illustration 9.10).

Illustration 9.10
STATEMENT OF RETAINED EARNINGS

ANSON COMPANY
Statement of Retained Earnings
For the Year Ended December 31, 1995

Retained earnings, January 1, 1995.	$5,000,000
Prior period adjustment:	
Prior period adjustment → Correction of error expensing land (net of tax effect of $80,000)	120,000
Retained earnings, January 1, 1995, as adjusted	$5,120,000
Add: Net income	4,077,600
	$9,197,600
Less: Dividends.	500,000
Retained earnings, December 31, 1995	$8,697,600

ETHICS   A CLOSER LOOK

Ace Corporation is a 20-year-old, publicly traded company that generates $50,000,000 in annual sales of commercial food preparation equipment. Most of Ace's growth in sales has come from selling the same basic product line to newly opened restaurants. Consequently, Ace has managed to modestly increase its profits over the previous year's performance and consequently declare a higher dividend for its shareholders during most years.

In the past five years, however, the restaurant industry in which most Ace customers compete has suffered from a major shakeup. Several major established restaurant chains and more than a few new startups failed, which flooded the restaurant equipment market with used equipment that sells for half the cost of new equipment. Ace's equipment sales this year have declined while it waits for this temporary glut to disappear, and the company may post a slight loss (the company's first) as a result.

Most of Ace's stockholders are investors who expect the company's profits, share value, and dividends to increase. Although they are sympathetic to tough economic times, the stockholders will sell off their shares and refuse to buy additional shares in the future if the company's fortunes decline. To keep its stockholders content, Ace plans to make an accounting change in its depreciation policy on its auto fleet from double-declining-balance to straight-line. The company would show a slight profit this year and hopefully give its management time to boost the company's sales and profitability during the next year.

a. Are the company's plans to change its depreciation policy for its auto fleet appropriate?
b. Are the stockholders' expectations realistic?

Accounting for Tax Effects

Most discontinued operations, extraordinary items, changes in accounting principle, and prior period adjustments affect the amount of income taxes a corporation must pay. A question arises as to how to report the income tax effect of these items. *FASB Statement No. 96*[5] requires that all of these items be reported *net of their tax effects,* as shown in Illustrations 9.8 and 9.10. **Net-of-tax effect** means that items are shown at the dollar amounts remaining after deducting the income tax effects. Thus, the total effect of a discontinued operation, an extraordinary item, a change in accounting principle, or a prior period adjustment is shown in one place in the appropriate financial statement. The reference to "Income from continuing operations" on the income statement represents the results of transactions (including income taxes) that are normal for the business and may be expected to recur. Note that the tax effect of an item may be shown separately, as it is for the gain on voluntary early retirement of debt in Illustration 9.8, or may be

---

[5] FASB, *Statement of Financial Accounting Standards No. 96,* "Accounting for Income Taxes" (Stamford, Conn., 1987). Copyright © by the Financial Accounting Standards Board, High Ridge Park, Stamford, Connecticut 06905, U.S.A.

mentioned parenthetically with only the net amount shown (see loss from discontinued operations and change in accounting principle in Illustration 9.8 and correction of error in Illustration 9.10).

EARNINGS PER SHARE

Objective 11
Compute earnings
per share

A major item of interest to investors and potential investors is how much a company earned during the current year, both in total and for each share of stock outstanding. The earnings per share amount is calculated only for the common shares of ownership. **Earnings per share (EPS)** is computed as net income available to common stockholders in a period divided by the average number of common shares outstanding during that period. **Income available to common stockholders** is net income less any dividends on preferred stock. The regular preferred dividend on cumulative preferred stock (but *not* a dividend in arrears) is deducted, whether or not declared, but only declared dividends are deducted on noncumulative preferred stock.

To illustrate, assume that Hoffman Company had 5,000 shares of common stock outstanding with net income of $24,000 during 1995. EPS would be computed as follows:

$$\text{EPS} = \frac{\text{Net income available to common stockholders}}{\text{Average number of common shares outstanding}}$$

$$= \frac{\$24,000}{5,000 \text{ shares}}$$

$$= \$4.80 \text{ per share}$$

EPS is usually calculated and presented for each major category on the face of the income statement. In other words, an EPS calculation is made for income from continuing operations, discontinued operations, extraordinary items, changes in accounting principle, and net income. Note in Illustration 9.8 that the EPS amounts are reported at the bottom of the income statement.

Summary of Illustrative Financial Statements

Note especially the following facts in Illustrations 9.8 and 9.10:

1. Income from continuing operations of $5,550,000 is more representative of the continuing earning power of the company than is the net income figure of $4,077,600.
2. The special items shown below income from continuing operations are reported at their actual impact on the company—that is, net of their tax effect.

3. EPS is reported both before ($5.550) and after ($4.078) the discontinued operations, extraordinary item, and the cumulative effect of a change in accounting principle.
4. The correction of the $200,000 error adds only $120,000 to retained earnings. This result occurs because the mistake was included in the 1994 tax return and taxes were therefore underpaid by $80,000. In the 1995 return, the $80,000 of taxes would have to be paid.

This chapter completes the study of stockholders' equity. In Chapter 10, you will learn about bonds—another source of capital for companies and a vehicle for investment by investors.

UNDERSTANDING THE LEARNING OBJECTIVES

1. State the advantages and disadvantages of the corporate form of business.
    - Advantages:
      (1) Easy transfer of ownership.
      (2) Limited liability.
      (3) Continuous existence of the entity.
      (4) Easy capital generation.
      (5) Professional management.
      (6) Separation of owners and entity.
    - Disadvantages:
      (1) Double taxation.
      (2) Government regulation.
      (3) Entrenched, inefficient management.
      (4) Limited ability to raise creditor capital.
2. List the various kinds of stock and describe the differences between them.
    - Capital stock authorized—the number of shares of stock that a corporation is entitled to issue as designated in its charter.
    - Capital stock issued—the number of shares of stock that have been sold and issued to stockholders.
    - Capital stock outstanding—the number of authorized shares of stock that have been issued and that are still currently held by stockholders.
    - Two classes of capital stock:
      (1) Common stock—represents the residual equity.
      (2) Preferred stock—may be preferred as to dividends and/or assets. Also may be participating, cumulative, and/or callable.
3. Present in proper form the stockholders' equity section of a balance sheet.
    - If the company has paid-in capital in excess of par value:

Stockholders' equity:
Paid-in capital:

Preferred stock—$100 par value, 6% cumulative; 1,000 shares authorized, issued, and outstanding	$100,000		
Common stock—without par value, stated value $5; 100,000 shares authorized, 80,000 shares issued and outstanding	400,000	$500,000	
Paid-in capital in excess of par (or stated) value:			
From preferred stock issuances	$ 5,000		
From common stock issuances	20,000	25,000	
Total paid-in capital			$525,000
Retained earnings.			200,000
Total stockholders' equity			$725,000

4. Account for the issuances of stock for cash.
  • The following examples illustrate the issuance for cash of (1) stock with a par value, (2) no-par value stock with a stated value, and (3) no-par value stock without a stated value.
  • Issuance of par value stock for cash—10,000 shares of $20 par value common stock issued for $22 per share.

Cash	220,000	
Common Stock		200,000
Paid-In Capital in Excess of Par		
Value—Common		20,000

  • Issuance of no-par, stated value stock for cash—10,000 shares (no-par value) with $20 per share stated value issued for $22 per share.

Cash	220,000	
Common Stock		200,000
Paid-In Capital in Excess of Stated		
Value—Common		20,000

  • Issuance of no-par stock without a stated value for cash—10,000 shares (no-par value) issued at $22 per share.

Cash	220,000	
Common Stock		220,000

5. Determine book values of both preferred and common stock.
  • *Example:* A corporation has 200,000 shares of common stock and 5,000 shares of preferred stock outstanding. Preferred stock is 6% cumulative, and nonparticipating. It is preferred as to dividends and as to assets in liquidation to the extent of the liquidation value of $100 per share, plus any cumulative dividends on the preferred stock. Dividends for three years are unpaid. Total stockholders' equity is $4,100,000. Calculations are as follows:

	Total	Per Share
Total stockholders' equity.	$4,100,000	
Book value of preferred stock (5,000 shares):		
Liquidation value (5,000 × $100). $500,000		
Dividends (3 years at $30,000) 90,000	590,000	$118.00
Book value of common stock (200,000 shares).	$3,510,000	$ 17.55

6. Identify the different sources of paid-in capital and describe how they would be presented on a balance sheet.

   - Paid-in capital is presented in the stockholders' equity section of the balance sheet. Each source of paid-in capital is listed separately.
   - Sources of paid-in capital are:
     (1) Common stock.
     (2) Preferred stock.
     (3) In excess of par value or stated value (common and preferred).
     (4) Stock dividends.
     (5) Treasury stock transactions.
     (6) Donations.

7. Account for a cash dividend, a stock dividend, a stock split, and a retained earnings appropriation.
   - Cash dividend of 3% on $100,000 of outstanding common stock declared on July 1 and paid on September 15.

```
July     1   Retained Earnings. . . . . . . . . . . . . .    3,000
                 Dividends Payable . . . . . . . . . . . . ..            3,000

Sept. 15   Dividends Payable . . . . . . . . . . . . . .    3,000
                 Cash . . . . . . . . . . . . . . . . . . .            3,000
```

   - Ten percent stock dividend on 10,000 shares of common stock outstanding; par value, $100; market value at declaration, $125 per share.

```
Jan. 1   Retained Earnings (1,000 shares × $125) . .   125,000
              Stock Dividend Distributable—Common
                 (1,000 shares × $100) . . . . . . . .             100,000
              Paid-In Capital—Stock Dividends
                 (1,000 shares × $25)  . . . . . . . .              25,000

Feb. 1   Stock Dividend Distributable—Common  . .   100,000
              Common Stock . . . . . . . . . . . . .              100,000
```

   - Thirty percent stock dividend on 10,000 shares of common stock outstanding: declared on January 1 and payable on February 1; par value, $100.

```
Jan. 1   Retained Earnings (3,000 shares × $100) . .   300,000
            Stock Dividend Distributable—Common                    300,000

Feb. 1   Stock Dividend Distributable—Common  . .   300,000
            Common Stock . . . . . . . . . . .                     300,000
```

- Stock split: 1,000 shares of $50 par value common stock replaced by 2,000 shares of $25 par value common stock.

```
Common Stock—$50 par value  . . . . . . . . .   50,000
   Common Stock—$25 par value  . . . . . . .              50,000
```

- Retained earnings appropriation: $75,000 appropriated for plant expansion.

```
Retained Earnings . . . . . . . . . . . . . .   75,000
   Retained Earnings Appropriated for Plant
      Expansion . . . . . . . . . . . . . . .             75,000
```

8. Account for the acquisition and reissuance of treasury stock.
   - Treasury stock transactions: 100 shares of common stock were reacquired at $100 each and reissued for $105 each.

```
Treasury Stock—Common (100 shares × $100) . . .   10,000
   Cash . . . . . . . . . . . . . . . . . . . .             10,000

Cash (100 shares × $105) . . . . . . . . . . . .   10,500
   Treasury Stock—Common (100 shares × $100) .             10,000
   Paid-In Capital—Common Treasury Stock
      Transactions (100 shares × $5) . . . . . .              500
```

9. Describe the proper accounting treatment of discontinued operations, extraordinary items, and changes in accounting principles.
   - The income or loss (net of tax effect) from the segment's operations for the portion of the current year before it was discontinued is reported on the income statement after "Income from continuing operations."
   - The gain or loss (net of tax effect) on disposal of the segment is also reported in that same section of the income statement.
   - Extraordinary items are those items that are both unusual in nature and infrequent in occurrence. Extraordinary items are shown on the income statement (net of tax effects) after "Income from continuing operations."
   - In the period in which a change in principle is made, the nature of the change, its justification, and its effect on net income must be disclosed in the financial statements. Also, the cumulative effect of the change on prior years' income (net of tax) must be shown on the income statement for the year of change after "Income from continuing operations."

10. Define prior period adjustments and show their proper presentation in the financial statements.
   - Prior period adjustments consist of errors in previously published financial statements. Prior period adjustments are shown as a correc-

tion to the beginning retained earnings balance on the statement of retained earnings.

11. Compute earnings per share.
    - Earnings per share is computed as net income available to common stockholders in a period divided by the average number of common stock shares outstanding during that period.
    - EPS is usually calculated and presented for each major category on the face of the income statement.

DEMONSTRATION PROBLEM 9–A

Tulip Company has paid all required preferred dividends through December 31, 1989. Its outstanding stock consists of 10,000 shares of $250 par value common stock and 4,000 shares of 6%, $250 par value preferred stock. During five successive years, the company's dividend declarations were as follows:

1990	$170,000
1991	105,000
1992	15,000
1993	30,000
1994	135,000

Required:

Compute the amount of dividends that would have been paid to each class of stock in each of the last five years assuming the preferred stock is:

a. Cumulative and nonparticipating.

b. Noncumulative and nonparticipating.

Solution to demonstration problem 9–A

TULIP COMPANY

		Assumptions	
Year	Dividends to	(a)	(b)
1990	Preferred.	$ 60,000*	$ 60,000
	Common.	110,000	110,000
1991	Preferred.	60,000	60,000
	Common.	45,000	45,000
1992	Preferred.	15,000	15,000
	Common.	–0–	–0–
1993	Preferred.	30,000	30,000
	Common.	–0–	–0–
1994	Preferred.	135,000†	60,000‡
	Common.	–0–	75,000

* 4,000 shares × $250 × 0.06 = $60,000.

† $60,000 + $45,000 preferred dividend missed in 1992 + $30,000 preferred dividend missed in 1993.

‡ Only the basic $60,000 dividend is paid because the stock is noncumulative.

DEMONSTRATION PROBLEM 9–B

Following are selected transactions of Teeth Company:

1. The company reacquired 200 shares of its own $200 par value common stock, previously issued at $210 per share, for $41,200.
2. Fifty of the treasury shares were reissued at $220 per share, cash.
3. Seventy of the treasury shares were reissued at $190 per share, cash.
4. Stockholders of the corporation donated 100 shares of their common stock to the company.
5. The 100 shares of treasury stock received by donation were reissued for $18,000.

Required:

Prepare the necessary journal entries to record the above transactions.

Solution to demonstration problem 9–B

1. Treasury Stock.   41,200
       Cash   41,200
       Acquired 200 shares at $41,200 ($206 per share).

2. Cash (50 shares × $220)   11,000
       Treasury Stock—Common (50 shares × $206)   10,300
       Paid-In Capital—Common Treasury Stock
          Transactions.   700
       Reissued 50 shares at $220 per share; cost is $10,300.

3. Cash (70 shares × $190)   13,300
   Paid-In Capital—Common Treasury Stock Transactions
       (50 shares × $14)   700
   Retained Earnings   420
       Treasury Stock—Common (70 shares × $206)   14,420
       Reissued 70 shares at $190 per share; cost is $14,420.

4. Stockholders donated 100 shares of common stock to the company. (Only memo entry is made.)

5. Cash   18,000
       Paid-In Capital—Donations (100 shares × $180) . . .   18,000
       Reissued donated shares at $180 per share.

DEMONSTRATION PROBLEM 9–C

Selected account balances of Tennis Corporation at December 31, 1995, are:

Common Stock (no par value; 100,000 shares authorized, issued, and outstanding; stated value of $40 per share)	$4,000,000
Retained Earnings	1,140,000
Dividends Payable (in cash, declared December 15 on preferred stock). . .	32,000
Preferred Stock (8%, par value $400; 1,000 shares authorized, issued, and outstanding)	400,000
Paid-In Capital from Donation of Plant Site	200,000
Paid-In Capital in Excess of Par Value—Preferred.	16,000

Required:

Present in good form the stockholders' equity section of the balance sheet.

Solution to demonstration problem 9–C

TENNIS CORPORATION
Partial Balance Sheet
December 31, 1995

Stockholders' equity:

Paid-in capital:

Preferred stock—8%, par value $400; 1,000 shares authorized, issued, and outstanding.	$ 400,000	
Common stock—no par value, stated value of $40 per share; 100,000 shares authorized, issued, and outstanding	4,000,000	
Paid-in capital from donation of plant site	200,000	
Paid-in capital in excess of par value—preferred.	16,000	
Total paid-in capital		$4,616,000
Retained earnings		1,140,000
Total stockholders' equity		$5,756,000

NEW TERMS

Book value per share   Stockholders' equity per share; the amount per share each stockholder would receive if the corporation were liquidated without incurring any further expenses and if assets were sold and liabilities liquidated at their recorded amounts. *464*

Callable preferred stock   If the stock is nonconvertible, it must be surrendered to the company when the holder is requested to do so. If the stock is convertible, it may be either surrendered or converted into common shares when called. *458*

Call premium (on preferred stock)   The difference between the amount at which a corporation calls its preferred stock for redemption and the par value of the stock. *459*

Capital stock authorized   The number of shares of stock that a corporation is entitled to issue as designated in its charter. *453*

Capital stock issued   The number of shares of stock that have been sold and issued to stockholders. *454*

Capital stock outstanding   The number of shares of authorized stock that have been issued and that are currently held by stockholders. *454*

Cash dividends   Cash distributions of net income by a corporation to its stockholders. *469*

Changes in accounting principle   Changes in accounting methods pertaining to such items as inventory and depreciation. *484*

Common stock   Shares of stock representing the residual equity in the corporation. If only one class of stock is issued, it is known as *common stock*. All other claims rank ahead of common stockholders' claims. *454*

Convertible preferred stock   Preferred stock that is convertible into common stock of the issuing corporation. *458*

Corporation   An entity recognized by law as possessing an existence separate and distinct from its owners; that is, it is a separate legal entity. A corporation is granted many of the rights, and placed under many of the obligations, of a natural person. In any given state, all corporations organized under the laws of that state are **domestic corporations;** all others are **foreign corporations.** *451*

Cumulative preferred stock   Preferred stock for which the right to receive a basic dividend accumulates if dividends are not paid; unpaid cumulative preferred dividends must be paid before any common stock dividends can be paid. *456*

Date of declaration (of dividends)   The date the board of directors takes action in the form of a motion that dividends be paid. *469*

Date of payment (of dividends)   The date of actual payment of a dividend, or issuance of additional shares in the case of a stock dividend. *469*

Date of record (of dividends)   The date of record established by the board that determines the stockholders who will receive dividends. *469*

Deficit   A debit balance in the Retained Earnings account. *468*

Discontinued operation   A department or division of a business that is sold to another company or has been abandoned. *482*

Dividend   A distribution of assets (usually cash) that represents a withdrawal of earnings by the owners. Dividends are similar in nature to withdrawals by sole proprietors and partners. *456, 469*

Dividend on preferred stock   The amount paid to preferred stockholders as a return for the use of their money; usually a fixed or stated amount expressed in dollars per share or as a percentage of par value per share. *456*

Dividends in arrears   Cumulative unpaid dividends, including quarterly dividends not declared for the current year. *456*

Earnings per share (EPS)   Earnings to the common stockholders on a per share basis, computed as net income available to common stockholders divided by the average number of common shares outstanding. *488*

Extraordinary items   Items that are both unusual in nature and infrequent in occurrence; reported in the income statement net of their tax effects, if any. *483*

Income available to common stockholders   Net income less any dividends on preferred stock. *488*

Income before extraordinary items   Income from operations less applicable income taxes, if any, plus or minus any gain or loss from discontinued operations. *484*

Legal capital (stated capital)   An amount prescribed by law (often par value or stated value of shares issued) below which a corporation may not reduce stockholders' equity through the declaration of dividends or other payments to stockholders. *461*

Net-of-tax effect   Used for discontinued operations, extraordinary items, changes in accounting principle, and prior period adjustments, whereby items are shown at the dollar amounts remaining after deducting the effects of such items on income taxes, if any, payable currently. *487*

Noncumulative preferred stock   Preferred stock on which the right to receive a dividend expires if the dividend is not declared. *456*

Nonparticipating preferred stock   Preferred stock that is entitled to its cumulative stated dividend only, regardless of the size of the common stock dividend. *457*

No-par stock   Capital stock without par value, to which a stated value may or may not be assigned. *462*

Paid-in capital   Amount of stockholders' equity that normally results from the cash or other assets invested by owners; it may also result from services provided for shares of stock and certain other transactions. *459*

Paid-in capital in excess of par (or stated) value—common or preferred   Capital contributed to a corporation in addition to that assigned to the shares issued and recorded in capital stock accounts. *462*

Paid-In Capital—Treasury Stock Transactions   The account credited when treasury stock is reissued for more than its cost; this account is debited to the extent of its credit balance when such shares are reissued at less than cost. *479*

Participating preferred stock   Preferred stock that is entitled to receive dividends above the stated preference rate under certain conditions specified in the preferred stock contract. *457*

Par value   An arbitrary amount printed on each stock certificate that may be assigned to each share of a given class of stock, usually at the time of incorporation. *453, 461*

Preferred stock   Capital stock that carries certain features or rights not carried by common stock. Preferred stock may be preferred as to dividends, preferred as to assets, or preferred as to both dividends and assets. Preferred stock may be callable and/or convertible and may be cumulative or noncumulative and participating or nonparticipating. *455*

Prior period adjustments   Consist almost entirely of corrections of errors in previously published financial statements. Prior period adjustments are reported in the statement of retained earnings net of their tax effects, if any. *486*

Retained earnings   That part of stockholders' equity resulting from earnings; the account to which the results of corporate activity, including prior period adjustments, are carried and to which dividends and certain items resulting from capital transactions are charged. *459*

Shares of stock   Units of ownership in a corporation. *452*

Stated value   An arbitrary amount assigned by the board of directors to each share of a given class of no-par stock. *462*

Statement of retained earnings   A formal statement showing the items causing changes in unappropriated and appropriated retained earnings during a stated period of time. *476*

Statement of stockholders' equity   A summary of the transactions affecting the accounts in the stockholders' equity section of the balance sheet during a stated period of time. *476*

Stock Dividend Distributable—Common account   The stockholders' equity (paid-in capital) account credited for the par or stated value of the shares distributable when recording the declaration of a stock dividend. *472*

Stock dividends   Dividends that are payable in additional shares of the declaring corporation's capital stock. *470*

Stock preferred as to assets   Means that in liquidation, the preferred stockholders are entitled to receive the par value (or a larger stipulated liquidation value) per share before any assets may be distributed to common stockholders. *458*

Stock preferred as to dividends   Means that the preferred stockholders are entitled to receive a specified dividend per share before any dividend on common stock is paid. *456*

Stock split   A distribution of 100% or more of additional shares of the issuing corporation's stock accompanied by a corresponding reduction in the par value per share. The purpose of a stock split is to cause a large reduction in the market price per share of the outstanding stock. *473*

Treasury stock   Shares of capital stock issued and reacquired by the issuing corporation; they have not been formally canceled and are available for reissuance. *466, 478*

Unissued shares   Capital stock authorized but not yet issued. *454*

SELF-TEST

True-False

Indicate whether each of the following statements is true or false.

1. A person may favor the corporate form of organization for a risky business enterprise primarily because a corporation's shares can be easily transferred.

2. The par value of a share of capital stock is no indication of the market value or book value of the share of stock.

3. The Retained Earnings account describes one source of paid-in capital of a corporation.

4. Since treasury stock has been issued once, it may be reissued without violating the pre-emptive right of the stockholders.

5. The payment of a cash dividend decreases a corporation's current liabilities.

6. The declaration of a stock dividend increases a corporation's current liabilities.

7. Damage suffered from destruction by an earthquake of a plant in Georgia would probably be an extraordinary item.

Multiple-Choice

Select the best answer for each of the following questions.

1. Which of the following is not an advantage of the corporate form of organization?
    a. Separate legal entity.
    b. Limited liability of stockholders.
    c. Double taxation.
    d. Easy transfer of ownership.

2. An arbitrary amount assigned to each share of a given class of stock and printed on the stock certificate is:
    a. Market value.
    b. Par value.

    c. Redemption value.
    d. Liquidation value.

3. Which of the following stocks could have dividends in arrears?
    a. Common stock.
    b. Noncumulative preferred stock.
    c. Participating preferred stock.
    d. Cumulative preferred stock.

4. Eugene Corporation issued 5,000 shares of $40 par value common stock at $70 per share. The amount that would be credited to Common Stock is:
    a. $200,000.

b. $150,000.

c. $550,000.

d. $350,000.

e. None of the above.

5. You are given the following information: Capital Stock, $40,000 ($40 par), Paid-In Capital in Excess of Par Value—Common, $100,000, and Retained Earnings, $200,000. Assuming only one class of stock, the book value per share is:

a. $340.

b. $140.

c. $40.

d. $200.

e. None of the above.

6. White Company issued 20,000 shares of $20 par value common stock at $24 per share. White reacquired 2,000 shares of its own stock at a cost of $30 per share. The entry to record the reacquisition is:

a. Premium on
      Treasury Stock . 20,000
    Treasury Stock . . 40,000
        Cash   60,000

b. Premium on
      Treasury Stock . 12,000
    Treasury Stock . . 48,000
        Cash   60,000

c. Treasury Stock . . 60,000
        Cash   60,000

d. Treasury Stock . . 40,000
    Paid-In Capital—
    Treasury Stock
    Transactions. . . 20,000
        Cash   60,000

7. If the company reissues 1,000 shares of the treasury stock for $36 per share in (6), the entry is:

a. Cash 36,000
    Treasury Stock .   30,000
    Paid-In Capital—
    Treasury Stock
    Transactions. .   6,000

b. Cash 36,000
    Treasury Stock .   36,000

c. Cash 36,000
    Treasury Stock .   30,000
    Retained
    Earnings . . .   6,000

d. Cash 36,000
    Treasury Stock .   20,000
    Retained
    Earnings . . .   16,000

8. Treasury stock should be shown on the balance sheet as a:

a. Reduction of the corporation's stockholders' equity.

b. Current asset.

c. Current liability.

d. Investment asset.

9. An individual stockholder is entitled to receive any dividends declared on stock owned, provided the stock is held on the:

a. Date of declaration.

b. Date of record.

c. Date of payment.

d. Last day of a fiscal year.

10. ABC Corporation declared the regular quarterly dividend of $1.00 per share. ABC had issued 21,000 shares and subsequently reacquired 1,000 shares as treasury stock. What would be the total amount of the dividend?

a. $24,000.

b. $28,000.

c. $20,000.

d. $4,000.

11. Which of the following items is not reported as a separate line item below income from continuing operations, net of tax effects, in the income statement?

a. Extraordinary items.

b. Prior period adjustments.

c. Discontinued operations.

d. Changes in accounting principle.

Now turn to page 511 to check your answers.

QUESTIONS

1. Cite the major advantages of the corporate form of business organization and indicate why each is considered an advantage.

2. What is meant by the statement that corporate income is subject to double taxation? Cite several other disadvantages of the corporate form of organization.

3. What are the basic rights associated with a share of capital stock if there is only one class of stock outstanding?

4. What are the differences between par value stock and stock with no-par value?

5. Corporate capital stock is seldom issued for less than par value. Give two reasons why this statement is true.

6. What are the meanings of the terms *stock preferred as to dividends* and *stock preferred as to assets?*

7. What do the terms *(a) cumulative* and *noncumulative* and *(b) participating* and *nonparticipating* mean in regard to preferred stock?

8. What are dividends in arrears, and how should they be disclosed in the financial statements?

9. A corporation has 1,000 shares of 8%, $100 par value, cumulative, preferred stock outstanding. Dividends on this stock have not been declared for three years. Is the corporation legally liable to its preferred stockholders for these dividends? How should this fact be shown in the balance sheet, if at all?

10. Explain why a corporation might issue a preferred stock that is both convertible into common stock and callable.

11. Explain the nature of the account entitled, Paid-In Capital in Excess of Par Value. Under what circumstances is this account credited?

12. Wright Corporation issued 5,000 shares of $50 par value common stock at $60 per share. What is the legal capital of Wright Corporation, and why is the amount of legal capital important?

13. What assumptions are made in determining book value?

14. Assuming there is no preferred stock outstanding, how can the book value per share of common stock be determined? Of what significance is the book value per share? What is the relationship of book value per share to market value per share?

15. Name several sources of paid-in capital. Would it suffice to maintain one account called Paid-In Capital for all sources of paid-in capital? Why or why not?

16. What are the main parts of the stockholders' equity in a corporation? Explain the difference between them.

17. Does accounting for treasury stock resemble accounting for an asset? Is treasury stock an asset? If not, where is it properly shown on a balance sheet?

18. What are some possible reasons for a corporation to reacquire its own capital stock as treasury stock?

19. What is the effect of each of the following on the total stockholders' equity of a corporation: *(a)* declaration of a cash dividend, *(b)* payment of a cash dividend

already declared, *(c)* declaration of a stock dividend, and *(d)* issuance of a stock dividend already declared?

20. The following dates are associated with a cash dividend of $25,000: July 15, July 31, and August 15. Identify each of the three dates and describe the journal entry required on each, if any.

21. How should a declared but unpaid cash dividend be shown on the balance sheet? A declared but unissued stock dividend?

22. What are the possible reasons for a corporation to declare a stock dividend?

23. Why is a dividend consisting of the distribution of additional shares of the common stock of the declaring corporation not considered income to the recipient stockholders?

24. Describe a discontinued operation.

25. What are extraordinary items? Where and how are they reported?

26. Give an example of a change in accounting principle. How is each change reported?

27. What are prior period adjustments? Where and how are they reported?

28. Why are stockholders and potential investors interested in the amount of a corporation's earnings per share? What does the earnings per share amount reveal that total income does not?

MAYTAG
CORPORATION

29. *Real-world question*   Based on the financial statements of Maytag Corporation contained in Appendix C, what was the number of shares of common stock authorized?

THE LIMITED, INC.

30. *Real-world question*   Based on the financial statements of The Limited, Inc., contained in Appendix C, what was the amount of the February 1, 1992, ending paid-in capital (not including common stock)?

HARLAND

31. *Real-world question*   Based on the financial statements of John H. Harland Company contained in Appendix C, how many shares of common stock had been issued as of December 31, 1991?

The Coca-Cola Company

32. *Real-world question*   From the consolidated statements of shareholders' equity of The Coca-Cola Company in Appendix C, identify the 1991 total amount for each of the following items:

a. Sales to employees exercising stock options.

b. Purchase of common stock for treasury.

c. Total cash dividends.

d. Balance—December 31, 1991 for each item listed.

MAYTAG
CORPORATION

33. *Real-world question*   Based on the financial statements of Maytag Corporation contained in Appendix C, what was the number of shares of common stock in the treasury as of December 31, 1991?

THE LIMITED, INC.

34. *Real-world question*   Based on the financial statements of The Limited, Inc., contained in Appendix C, what was the cost of treasury stock on hand as of February 1, 1992?

HARLAND

35. *Real-world question*   Based on the financial statements of John H. Harland Company contained in Appendix C, what was the number of shares in the treasury as of December 31, 1991?

EXERCISES

Determine dividends for common and preferred stock (L.O. 3)

9–1. Sammy Corporation has outstanding 1,000 shares of noncumulative, nonparticipating preferred stock and 2,000 shares of common stock. The preferred stock is entitled to an annual dividend of $80 per share before dividends are declared on common stock. What are the total dividends received by each class of stock if Sammy Corporation distributes $224,000 in dividends in 1995?

Determine dividends for common and preferred stock (L.O. 3)

9–2. Smith Corporation has 2,000 shares outstanding of cumulative, nonparticipating preferred stock and 6,000 shares of common stock. The preferred stock is entitled to an annual dividend of $18 per share before dividends are declared on common stock. No preferred dividends were paid for last year and the current year. What are the total dividends received by each class of stock if Smith Corporation distributes $108,000 in dividends?

Determine dividends for common and preferred stock for five-year period (L.O. 3)

9–3. The preferred stock contract of Capital Corporation specifies that the preferred shares will participate on an equal amount per share basis with the common shares after $8 has been distributed per share of preferred stock and common stock. There are 1,000 shares of noncumulative preferred stock outstanding and 9,000 shares of common stock outstanding. Determine the dividends that will be paid to each class for the following years:

Year	Total Dividend to Be Distributed
1994	$ 8,000
1995	40,000
1996	80,000
1997	100,000
1998	120,000

Journalize stock issuance (L.O. 5)

9–4. Howard Company issued 10,000 shares of common stock for $840,000 cash. The common stock has a par value of $80 per share. Give the journal entry for the stock issuance.

Prepare entries for stock issuance (L.O. 5)

9–5. Stanford Company issued 30,000 shares of $80 par value common stock for $2,720,000. What is the journal entry for this transaction? What would the journal entry be if the common stock has no-par or stated value?

Compute the book value and average price of common stock (L.O. 6)

9–6. The stockholders' equity section of Hollis Company's balance sheet is as follows:

Stockholders' equity:		
Paid-in capital:		
Common stock—without par value, $10 stated value; authorized 100,000 shares; issued and outstanding, 70,000 shares.	$700,000	
Paid-in capital in excess of stated value	272,000	
Total paid-in capital		$ 972,000
Retained earnings.		108,000
Total stockholders' equity		$1,080,000

Compute the average price at which the 70,000 issued shares of common stock were sold. Compute the book value per share of common stock.

Prepare journal entries for reacquisition and reissuance of treasury stock (L.O. 3)

9–7. Watkins Company had outstanding 50,000 shares of $30 stated value common stock, all issued at $36 per share, and had retained earnings of $1,200,000. The company reacquired 2,000 shares of its stock for cash at book value from the widow of a deceased stockholder.

a. Give the entry to record the reacquisition of the stock.

b. Give the entry to record the subsequent reissuance of this stock at $75 per share.

c. Give the entry required if the stock is instead reissued at $45 per share and there were no prior treasury stock transactions.

Prepare journal entry(ies) for reissuance of donated stock (L.O. 3)

9–8. Snow Company received 200 shares of its $100 stated value common stock on December 1, 1995, as a donation from a stockholder. On December 15, 1995, it reissued the stock for $31,200 cash. Give the journal entry or entries necessary for these transactions.

Prepare journal entries for cash dividend (L.O. 2)

9–9. Brown Company has issued all of its authorized 5,000 shares of $200 par value common stock. On February 1, 1995, the board of directors declared a dividend of $6 per share payable on March 15, 1995, to stockholders of record on March 1, 1995. Give the necessary journal entries.

Prepare journal entries for cash dividend when treasury stock is held (L.O. 2)

9–10. The stockholders' equity section of Orange Company's balance sheet on December 31, 1995, shows 100,000 shares of authorized and issued $80 stated value common stock, of which 9,000 shares are held in the treasury. On this date, the board of directors declared a cash dividend of $8 per share payable on January 21, 1996, to stockholders of record on January 10. Give dated journal entries for the above.

Prepare journal entry for small stock dividend and discuss large stock dividend (L.O. 2)

9–11. Adams Company has outstanding 75,000 shares of common stock without par or stated value, which were issued at an average price of $72 per share, and retained earnings of $2,880,000. The current market price of the common stock is $108 per share. Total authorized stock consists of 500,000 shares.

a. Give the required entry to record the declaration of a 10% stock dividend.

b. If, alternatively, the company declared a 30% stock dividend, what additional information would you need before making a journal entry to record the dividend?

Prepare journal
entries for stock
split and small
stock dividend
(L.O. 2)

9–12. Greene Corporation's stockholders' equity consisted of 60,000 authorized shares of $40 par value common stock, of which 30,000 shares had been issued at par, and retained earnings of $1,500,000. The company then split its stock, two for one, by changing the par value of the old shares and issuing new $20 par shares.

a. Give the required journal entry to record the stock split.

b. Suppose instead that the company declared and later issued a 10% stock dividend. Give the required journal entries, assuming that the market value on the date of declaration was $50 per share.

Calculate EPS;
present
information in
income statement
format
(L.O. 6)

9–13. The following information relates to Kullison Corporation for the year ended December 31, 1995:

Common stock outstanding	75,000 shares
Income from continuing operations.	$3,808,000
Loss on discontinued operations (net of tax)	600,000
Extraordinary gain (net of tax)	360,000

Calculate EPS for the year ended December 31, 1995. Present the information in the same format as would be used in the corporation's income statement.

Calculate EPS;
comment on
resulting amounts
(L.O. 6)

9–14. Sundance Company had an average number of shares of common stock outstanding of 200,000 in 1995 and 215,000 in 1996. Net income for these two years was as follows:

1995	$1,840,000
1996	1,920,000

a. Calculate EPS for the years ended December 31, 1995, and 1996.

b. What might the resulting figures tell a stockholder or a potential investor?

PROBLEMS

Determine
dividends for
common stock
and cumulative
and
noncumulative
preferred stock
(L.O. 3)

9–1. The outstanding capital stock of Preston Corporation consisted of 3,000 shares of 10% preferred stock, $400 par value, and 30,000 shares of no-par common stock with a stated value of $400. The preferred was issued at $659.20, the common at $768 per share. On January 1, 1990, the retained earnings of the company were $400,000. During the succeeding five years, net income was as follows:

1990	$1,228,000
1991	816,000
1992	76,800
1993	256,000
1994	1,060,000

No dividends were in arrears as of January 1, 1990, and during the five years 1990–94, the board of directors declared dividends in each year equal to net income of the year.

Required:

Prepare a schedule showing the dividends declared each year on each class of stock assuming the preferred stock is:

a. Cumulative and nonparticipating.

b. Noncumulative and nonparticipating.

Prepare partial balance sheet involving par value stock
(L.O. 4)

9–2. Certain post-closing account balances for Dixie, Inc., as of December 31, 1995, were as follows:

DIXIE, INC.
Partial List of Post-Closing Account Balances
December 31, 1995

Paid-In Capital in Excess of Par Value—Preferred	$ 60,000
Preferred Stock (8%, $400 par value, 3,000 shares authorized, issued, and outstanding)	1,200,000
Paid-In Capital in Excess of Par Value—Common	144,000
Common Stock ($200 par value, 30,000 shares authorized; 8,000 shares issued and outstanding)	1,600,000
Retained Earnings	1,508,000

Required:

From the above list of account balances, prepare the stockholders' equity section of the December 31, 1995, balance sheet in proper form.

Prepare stockholders' equity section; determine book values of stock; and determine dividends for each class of stock
(L.O. 3, 6)

9–3. On January 2, 1993, the date Logue Company received its charter, it issued all of its authorized 3,000 shares of no-par cumulative preferred stock at $104 and all of its 12,000 authorized shares of no-par common stock at $40 per share. The preferred stock has a stated value of $50 per share, is entitled to a basic dividend of $6 per share, is callable at $106 beginning in 1995, and is entitled to $100 per share plus cumulative dividends in the event of liquidation. The common stock has a stated value of $10 per share.

On December 31, 1994, the end of the second year of operations, retained earnings were $90,000. No dividends have been declared or paid on either class of stock.

Required:

a. Prepare the stockholders' equity section of Logue Company's December 31, 1994, balance sheet.

b. Compute the book value of each class of stock assuming the preferred stock is nonparticipating.

c. If $42,000 of dividends were declared as of December 31, 1994, compute the amount paid to each class of stock assuming the preferred stock is nonparticipating.

Compute total
market value for
common stock;
compute book
value of common
and preferred
stock
(L.O. 6)

9–4. The common stock of Diaz Corporation is selling on a stock exchange for $75 per share. The stockholders' equity of the corporation at December 31, 1995, consists of:

Stockholders' equity:		
Paid-in capital:		
Preferred stock—9% cumulative and nonparticipating, $100 par value, 3,000 shares authorized, issued, and outstanding	$ 300,000	
Common stock—$60 par value, 30,000 shares authorized, issued, and outstanding	1,800,000	
Total paid-in capital.		$2,100,000
Retained earnings		295,500
Total stockholders' equity		$2,395,500

Assume that in liquidation the preferred stock is entitled to par value plus cumulative unpaid dividends.

Required:

a. What is the total market value of all of the corporation's common stock?

b. If all dividends have been paid on the preferred stock as of December 31, 1995, what are the book values of the preferred stock and the common stock?

c. If two years' dividends were due on the preferred stock as of December 31, 1995, what are the book values of the preferred stock and common stock?

Compute book
values of a
stockholder's
preferred and
common stock
(L.O. 6)

9–5. Gray Corporation has an agreement with each of its 15 preferred and 30 common stockholders that in the event of the death of a stockholder, it will purchase at book value from the stockholder's estate or heirs the shares of Gray Corporation stock held by the deceased at the time of death. The book value is to be computed in accordance with generally accepted accounting principles.

Following is the stockholders' equity section of the Gray Corporation's December 31, 1995, balance sheet.

Stockholders' equity:		
Paid-in capital:		
$24 no-par preferred stock—$80 stated value; 3,000 shares authorized, issued, and outstanding	$ 240,000	
Common stock—$100 par value, 60,000 shares authorized, issued, and outstanding	6,000,000	
Paid-in capital in excess of stated value—preferred.	1,344,000	
Paid-in capital in excess of par value—common	48,000	
Total paid-in capital		$ 7,632,000
Retained earnings		2,880,000
Total stockholders' equity		$10,512,000

The preferred stock is cumulative and entitled to $480 per share plus cumulative dividends in liquidation. No dividends have been paid for 1½ years.

A stockholder who owned 100 shares of preferred stock and 1,000 shares of common stock died on December 31, 1995. You have been employed by the stockholder's executor to compute the book value of each class of stock and to determine the price to be paid for the stock held by her late husband.

Required:

Prepare a schedule showing the computation of the amount to be paid for the deceased stockholder's preferred and common stock.

Present stockholders' equity section of balance sheet (L.O. 1)

9–6. Following are selected data and accounts of Burger, Inc., as of May 31, 1995:

Paid-In Capital in Excess of Par Value—Preferred	$ 8,400
Retained Earnings, Unappropriated	144,000
Allowance for Uncollectible Accounts	48,000
Common Stock (without par value, stated value $60; 20,000 shares authorized, issued, and outstanding)	1,200,000
Appropriation for Retirement of Bonds	180,000
Dividends Payable (cash)	7,200
Paid-In Capital in Excess of Stated Value—Common	48,000
Notes Payable (17%, due April 1, 2001)	720,000
Preferred Stock (7%, par value $120; 2,000 shares authorized, issued, and outstanding)	240,000
Paid-In Capital—Donations	36,000

Required:

Present the stockholders' equity section of the company's balance sheet as of May 31, 1995.

Prepare journal entries for cash dividend and small stock dividend (L.O. 2)

9–7. The only stockholders' equity items of Goldwell Company at June 30, 1995, are:

Stockholders' equity:		
Paid-in capital:		
Common stock—$400 par value, 5,000 shares authorized, 3,000 shares issued and outstanding	$1,200,000	
Paid-in capital in excess of par value	480,000	
Total paid-in capital		$1,680,000
Retained earnings		480,000
Total stockholders' equity		$2,160,000

On August 4, 1995, a 4% cash dividend was declared, payable on September 3. On November 16, a 10% stock dividend was declared. The shares were issued on December 1. The market value of the common stock was $720 per share on November 16 and $708 per share on December 1.

Required:

Prepare journal entries for the above dividend transactions.

Prepare
stockholders'
equity section of
balance sheet
(L.O. 3)

9–8. The bookkeeper of C. L. Davis Company has prepared the following incorrect statement of stockholders' equity for the year ended December 31, 1995:

Stockholders' equity:		
Paid-in capital:		
Preferred stock—6%, cumulative		
(8,000 shares)	$ 418,000	
Common stock—50,000 shares	1,190,000	
Total paid-in capital		$1,608,000
Retained earnings		682,000
Total stockholders' equity.		$2,290,000

The authorized stock consists of 12,000 shares of preferred stock with a $50 par value and 75,000 shares of common stock, $20 par value. The preferred stock was issued on two occasions: (1) 5,000 shares at par, and (2) 3,000 shares at $56 per share. The 50,000 shares of common stock were issued at $26 per share. Five thousand shares of treasury common stock were reacquired for $110,000; the bookkeeper deducted the cost of the treasury stock from the Common Stock account.

Required:

Prepare the correct stockholders' equity section of the balance sheet at December 31, 1995.

Prepare statement
of retained
earnings
(L.O. 2)

9–9. Following are selected data of Datex Corporation at December 31, 1995:

Net income for the year	$384,000
Dividends declared on preferred stock	54,000
Retained earnings appropriated for future plant expansion	
during the year	180,000
Dividends declared on common stock	48,000
Retained earnings, January 1, unappropriated.	540,000
Directors ordered that the balance in the "Appropriation per loan	
agreement," related to a loan repaid on March 31, 1995, be returned	
to unappropriated retained earnings	360,000

Required:

Prepare a statement of retained earnings for the year ended December 31, 1995.

Prepare journal
entries for
treasury stock
transactions and
for cash dividend;
present
stockholders'
equity section of
balance sheet
(L.O. 2, 3)

9–10. The stockholders' equity of Grape Company on December 31, 1993, consisted of 1,000 authorized, issued, and outstanding shares of $36, no-par, cumulative preferred stock, stated value $120 per share, which were originally issued at $596 per share; 100,000 shares authorized, issued, and outstanding of no-par, $80, stated value common stock, which were originally issued at $80; and retained earnings of $560,000. Following are selected transactions and other data relating to 1994. No previous treasury stock transactions had occurred.

1. The company reacquired 2,000 shares of its common stock at $168.
2. One thousand of the treasury shares were reissued at $144.

3. Stockholders donated 1,000 shares of common stock to the company. These shares were immediately reissued at $128 to provide working capital.
4. The first quarter's dividend of $9.00 per share was declared and paid on the preferred stock. No other dividends were declared or paid during 1994.

The company suffered a net loss of $112,000 for the year 1994.

Required:

a. Prepare journal entries for the numbered transactions above.
b. Prepare the stockholders' equity section of the December 31, 1994, balance sheet.

Present income statement and statement of retained earnings (L.O. 2, 4, 5)

9–11. Selected data for Diana Company for 1994 are given below:

Common stock—$10 par value.	$1,000,000
Sales, net.	870,000
Selling and administrative expenses	160,000
Cash dividends declared and paid	60,000
Cost of goods sold	400,000
Depreciation expense	60,000
Interest revenue.	10,000
Loss on write-down of obsolete inventory.	20,000
Retained earnings (as of 12/31/93)	1,000,000
Operating loss on Candy Division up to point of sale in 1994.	20,000
Loss on disposal of Candy Division.	100,000
Earthquake loss.	48,000
Cumulative negative effect on prior years' income of changing from straight-line to an accelerated method of computing depreciation.	32,000

Assume the applicable federal income tax rate is 40%. All of the items of expense, revenue, and loss are included in the computation of taxable income. The earthquake loss resulted from the first earthquake experienced at the company's location. In addition, the company discovered that in 1993 it had erroneously charged to expense the $80,000 cost of a tract of land purchased that year and had made the same error on its tax return for 1993.

Required:

a. Prepare an income statement for the year ended December 31, 1994.
b. Prepare a statement of retained earnings for the year ended December 31, 1994.

BUSINESS DECISION PROBLEMS

Compute dividends on preferred stock and common stock and determine their relationship to

9–1. Northern Company and Southern Company are two companies that have extremely stable net income amounts of $12,000,000 and $8,000,000, respectively. Both companies distribute all their net income as dividends each year. Northern Company has 100,000 shares of $200 par value, 6% preferred stock, and 500,000 shares of $20 par value common stock outstanding. Southern Company has 50,000 shares of $100 par value, 8% preferred stock, and 400,000

stock prices
(L.O. 3)

shares of $20 par value common stock outstanding. Both preferred stocks are cumulative and nonparticipating.

Required:

a. Compute the annual dividend per share of preferred stock and per share of common stock for each company.

b. Based solely on the above information, which common stock would you predict to have the higher market price per share? Why?

Determine book values and their relationship to investment decisions
(L.O. 6)

9–2. Joe Brown recently inherited $384,000 cash that he wishes to invest in one of the following securities: common stock of the Bowden Corporation or common stock of the Maxwell Corporation. Both corporations manufacture the same types of products and have been in existence for five years. The stockholders' equity sections of the two corporations' latest balance sheets are shown below:

BOWDEN CORPORATION

Stockholders' equity:

Paid-in capital:

Common stock—$100 par value, 30,000 shares authorized, issued, and outstanding	$3,000,000
Retained earnings	2,760,000
Total stockholders' equity	$5,760,000

MAXWELL CORPORATION

Stockholders' equity:

Paid-in capital:

Preferred stock—8%, $400 par value, cumulative and nonparticipating, 4,000 shares authorized, issued, and outstanding	$1,600,000	
Common stock—$100 par value, 40,000 shares authorized, issued, and outstanding	4,000,000	
Total paid-in capital		$5,600,000
Retained earnings		448,000
Total stockholders' equity		$6,048,000

The Bowden Corporation has paid a cash dividend of $4.80 per share each year since its creation; its common stock is currently selling for $472 per share. The Maxwell Corporation's common stock is currently selling for $384 per share. The current year's dividend and three prior years' dividends on the preferred stock are in arrears. The preferred stock has a liquidation value of $480 per share.

Required:

a. What is the book value per share of the Bowden Corporation common stock and the Maxwell Corporation common stock? Is book value the major determinant of market value of the stock?

b. Based solely on the above information, which investment would you recommend? Why?

Determine amount
of dividends
received and
effects on stock
prices
(L.O. 2)

9–3. The stockholders' equity section of the Allen Corporation's balance sheet for June 30, 1995, is shown below:

Stockholders' equity:

Paid-in capital:		
Common stock—$20 par value; authorized 200,000 shares; issued and outstanding 80,000 shares.	$1,600,000	
Paid-in capital in excess of par value	960,000	
Total paid-in capital		$2,560,000
Retained earnings		1,520,000
Total stockholders' equity		$4,080,000

On July 1, 1995, the corporation's directors declared a 10% stock dividend distributable on August 2 to stockholders of record on July 16. On November 1, 1995, the directors voted a $2.40 per share annual cash dividend payable on December 2 to stockholders of record on November 16. For four years prior to 1995, the corporation had paid an annual cash dividend of $2.52.

Bill Hale purchased 8,000 shares of Allen Corporation's common stock five years ago. The market value of his stock was $48 per share on July 1, 1995, and $43.64 per share on July 16, 1995.

Required:

a. What amount of cash dividends will Hale receive in 1995? How does this amount differ from the amount of cash dividends Hale received in the previous four years?

b. For what logical reason did the price of the stock drop from $48 to $43.64 on July 16, 1995?

c. Is Hale better off as a result of the stock dividend and the $2.40 cash dividend than he would have been if he had just received the $2.52 cash dividend? Why?

ANSWERS TO SELF-TEST

True-False

1. *False.* This is not the primary reason a person may prefer the corporate form of business organization in a situation involving considerable risk. The primary reason is that stockholders can lose only the amount of capital they have invested in a corporation.

2. *True.* Par value is simply the amount per share that is credited to the Capital Stock account for each share issued and is no indication of the market value or the book value of the stock.

3. *False.* The paid-in capital of a corporation only includes capital contributed by stockholders or others. The Retained Earnings account balance reflects the excess of the company's aggregate net income since its formation over all dividends distributed and aggregate net losses.

4. *True.* Treasury stock may be reissued without violating the preemptive right.

5. *True.* The payment of a cash dividend decreases the current liability, dividends pay-

able, set up by the declaration of the cash dividend.

6. *False.* The declaration of a stock dividend does not increase current liabilities because

the stock dividend is not to be paid with assets.

7. *True.* Such losses are likely to be unusual in nature and nonrecurring.

Multiple-Choice

1. *c.* This feature of corporations is one of the disadvantages of the corporate form of organization.

2. *b.* Par value is an arbitrary amount assigned to each share of a given class of stock and is printed on the stock certificate.

3. *d.* Dividends in arrears are cumulative unpaid dividends. Only cumulative preferred stock could have dividends in arrears.

4. *a.* The amount credited to the Common Stock account is computed as follows:

$$5,000 \text{ shares} \times \$40 = \$200,000$$

5. *a.* The book value of common stock is computed as follows:

Total book value of stockholders' equity ($40,000 + $100,000 + $200,000)	$340,000
Total shares	÷1,000
Book value per share	$ 340

6. *c.* When treasury stock is reacquired, the stock is recorded at cost in a debit-balance

stockholders' equity account, Treasury Stock.

7. *a.* The excess of the reissue price over the cost of treasury stock is recorded in the Paid-In Capital—Treasury Stock Transactions account.

8. *a.* Treasury stock is customarily shown as a deduction from total stockholders' equity.

9. *b.* The date of record determines who is to receive the dividends.

10. *c.* The total amount of dividends is computed as follows:

Total outstanding shares at declaration: (21,000 − 1,000) shares. . . .	20,000
Dividend per share	× $1.00
Total dividend amount	$20,000

11. *b.* Prior period adjustments are shown as adjustments to the opening balance of retained earnings on the statement of retained earnings.

10 DEBT FINANCING AND BOND INVESTMENTS

LEARNING OBJECTIVES

After studying this chapter, you should be able to:

1. Account for notes receivable and payable, including calculation of interest.
2. Record the discounting of a customer's note at a bank.
3. Describe the features of bonds and tell how bonds differ from shares of stock.
4. List the advantages and disadvantages of financing with long-term debt and prepare examples showing how financial leverage is employed.
5. Prepare journal entries for bonds issued at face value.
6. Explain how interest rates affect bond prices and what causes a bond to sell at a premium or a discount.
7. Apply the concept of present value to compute the price of a bond.
8. Prepare journal entries for bonds issued at a discount or a premium.
9. Prepare journal entries for bond redemptions and bond conversions.
10. Prepare journal entries for bond investments.
11. Explain future value and present value concepts and make required calculations (appendix).

In previous chapters, you learned that corporations obtain cash for recurring business operations from stock issuances, profitable operations, and short-term borrowing (current liabilities). However, when situations arise that require large amounts of cash, such as the purchase of a building, corporations also raise cash from long-term borrowing, that is, by issuing bonds. The issuing of bonds results in a Bonds Payable account. After discussing short-term financing, the next part of this chapter discusses the issuing of bonds and accounting for bonds payable from the issuer's point of view.

The final part of this chapter looks at bond transactions from the investors' point of view. Since corporations are legal entities, they, like individuals, can invest in stocks and bonds issued by other corporations that are regularly traded on national exchanges. These types of investments can offer a rate of return substantially greater than a savings account.

SHORT-TERM FINANCING

Why would a business need short-term financing; that is, why would it need to use the bank's or some other creditor's money for short periods of time? A business usually expects the cash inflow from the sale of goods or services to exceed the cash outflow for the purchase of goods for resale or for the purchase of supplies, labor services, utilities, and so on. Also, some expenses, such as depreciation expense, do not involve an outflow of cash in the current period. But at certain times in the life of a business the inflow of cash may not be greater than the outflow of cash from operations. This can be caused by: (1) the delay in the receipt of cash due to giving customers credit terms on amounts due (though the business at least partly offsets this by the use of credit on its own purchases in order to delay the payment of cash); (2) the seasonal buildup of inventory, such as that which occurs in department stores just before the Christmas holidays; or (3) an expansion in operations caused by an expected future increase in sales. Some of the ways in which a business can obtain short-term financing are discussed below.

Short-Term Commercial Bank Loans

When a business needs additional financing it may go to a commercial bank to borrow on a short-term basis. When the loan is granted, the bank normally asks the borrower to sign a promissory note. A **promissory note** is an unconditional promise in writing made and signed by the borrower (the **maker**) obligating the borrower to pay the lender (the **payee**) or someone else who legally acquired the note a certain sum of money on demand or at a definite time. Normally, only the maker and the payee are parties to the instrument, but sometimes others who legally acquire the note or guarantee payment also become parties.

Nature of Interest.   Most notes bear an explicit (or stated) charge for interest. **Interest** is the fee charged for the use of money through time. It is an expense to the maker of the note and a revenue to the payee of the note. In commercial transactions interest is commonly figured on the basis of 360 days per year. The elapsed time in a fraction of a year between two stated days is computed by counting the exact number of days—omitting the day the money is borrowed but counting the day it is paid back. A note falling due on a Sunday or a holiday is due on the following business day.

Assume that we desire to calculate the interest on a $1,000 note with an interest rate of 6% and a life of 60 days. It can be done thus:

$$\text{Principal} \times \text{Rate of interest} \times \text{Time} = \text{Interest}$$

$$\$1{,}000 \times \frac{6}{100} \times \frac{60}{360} = \$10$$

Giving Your Own Note to the Bank.   In some instances in which a borrower presents his or her own noninterest-bearing note to a bank with a request for a loan, the bank computes the amount of interest on the face value of the note, deducts the amount computed from the face value, and gives the balance, the proceeds, to the borrower. This transaction is called **discounting a note payable.** The amount deducted is often called the **bank discount** or the **discount on notes payable,** and the process of computing the amount is referred to as discounting. To illustrate this process, assume that a bank discounts a customer's $20,000, 90-day, noninterest-bearing note at 12%. The calculation of interest is:

$$\$20{,}000 \times \frac{12}{100} \times \frac{90}{360} = \$600$$

The $600 interest is deducted from the $20,000, and the borrower receives $19,400. Assuming the above transaction occurred on December 1, 1995, it would be recorded by the borrower as follows:

Cash		Notes Payable—Discount		Notes Payable	
12/1 19,400		12/1 600			12/1 20,000

Note that the borrower does not receive $20,000, but $19,400. Since the borrower will pay $600 for the use of this sum for a period of 90 days, the rate of interest is actually higher than 12%. (If $600 is the interest on $20,000 at 12% for 90 days, then $600 is more than 12% on $19,400 for 90 days.) Note also that the bank must discount this note in order to introduce interest into the transaction. If the bank advanced $20,000 on this noninterest-bearing note, it would not earn any interest from this loan because at maturity it will receive only $20,000.

The Notes Payable—Discount account used above is a contra account to Notes Payable. Assuming that December 31, 1995, is the end of the borrower's accounting period, it would be necessary to record interest expense for the month of December as follows (the debit and credit are dated 12/31, and the debit balance of $600 shown in Notes Payable—Discount is the balance in the account *before* making the latest entry):

Interest Expense		Notes Payable—Discount	
12/31 200		Bal. 600	12/31 200

In the current liability section of the December 31, 1995, balance sheet, the note and the discount would appear as follows:

Notes payable. $20,000
Less: Discount 400 $19,600

When the note is paid at maturity the accounts would be affected as follows (maturity date is March 1, 1996):

Cash				Notes Payable—Discount			
Bal.	xxx	3/1	20,000	Bal. after 12/31 adjustment 400		3/1	400

Notes Payable				Interest Expense			
3/1	20,000	Bal.	20,000	3/1	400		

In journal entry form this transaction would appear as follows:

```
1996
Mar. 1  Notes Payable . . . . . . . . . . . . . . . . . . . .  20,000
        Interest Expense. . . . . . . . . . . . . . . . . . .     400
           Cash . . . . . . . . . . . . . . . . . . . . . .            20,000
           Notes Payable—Discount . . . . . . . . . . .                   400
        To record payment of the note.
```

The above changes reduce the Notes Payable—Discount and Notes Payable accounts to zero balances. Notice that the difference in the cash paid out ($20,000) and that originally received ($19,400) is equal to the total interest expense ($600). The interest relates to a 90-day period, 30 days of which fall in the year ending December 31, 1995, and 60 days of which fall in the following year. Thus, the amount charged to interest expense should be $200 in 1995 and $400 in 1996.

An alternative approach the borrower may use in discounting a note payable at the bank is to compute interest on the amount requested, add this to the amount requested, and draw a note for the total of the two. Thus, the borrower would sign a 90-day, noninterest-bearing note for $20,600 and would receive $20,000. At the date of borrowing the entry would be:

Cash		Notes Payable—Discount		Notes Payable	
(a)	20,000	(a)	600	(a)	20,600

The borrower could use a second alternative loan arrangement by giving a $20,000, 90-day, 12% interest-bearing note and actually receiving $20,000 in cash. At the date of borrowing the required entry is:

Cash		Notes Payable	
(a)	20,000	(a)	20,000

At maturity the borrower pays both the face amount of the note and interest at the rate stated in the note on that face amount (a total of $20,600). The $600 paid over and above the $20,000 face of the note represents interest expense to the borrower.

Notes Arising from Business Transactions

A company may have notes receivable and/or notes payable arising from transactions with customers or suppliers. When a company is the maker of a note with a supplier as the payee, the company has *received* short-term financing from that supplier. When a company is the payee of a note and a customer is the maker, the company has *supplied* short-term financing to that customer. A note may result from the conversion of an overdue open account or directly from merchandise transactions. To illustrate, assume that on October 6, 1995, Fox Company, the payee, receives from Kent Company, the maker, a 60-day, $18,000 note. The interest rate is 12%, and the note results from the previous sale (on October 4) of merchandise by Fox Company to Kent Company. Kent Company uses periodic inventory procedure. The interest will be earned over the life of the note and will not be paid until maturity, December 5, 1995. The entries for both the payee and the maker are:

FOX COMPANY, PAYEE

To record sale:

Accounts Receivable		Sales	
10/4 18,000			10/4 18,000

To record receipt of note:

Notes Receivable		Accounts Receivable	
10/6 18,000		Bal. 18,000	10/6 18,000

To record receipt of principal and interest:

Cash		Notes Receivable	
12/5 18,360		Bal. 18,000	12/5 18,000

Interest Revenue	
	12/5 360

KENT COMPANY, MAKER

To record purchase:

	Purchases				Accounts Payable	
10/4	18,000				10/4	18,000

To record giving of note:

	Accounts Payable					Notes Payable	
10/6	18,000	Bal.	18,000			10/6	18,000

To record payment of principal and interest:

	Notes Payable					Cash		
12/5	18,000	Bal.	18,000	Bal.	xxx	12/5	18,360	

	Interest Expense	
12/5	360	

A note becomes a **dishonored note** if the maker fails to pay it at maturity. The payee of the note may debit either Accounts Receivable or Dishonored Notes Receivable and credit Notes Receivable for the face of the note. If interest is due, it should be debited to the same account to which the dishonored note is debited and credited to Interest Revenue. The maker should merely debit the amount of interest incurred to Interest Expense and credit Interest Payable. When a note cannot be paid at maturity, the maker sometimes either pays the interest on the original note or includes it in the face of a new note given to take the place of the old note.

Discounting Notes Receivable

*Objective 2
Record the discounting of a customer's note at a bank*

When a company issues its own note payable to a bank, it is directly liable to the bank at the maturity date of the loan. Such notes payable are shown in the balance sheet as liabilities.

Instead of borrowing directly, a company may use another method of obtaining short-term financing from a bank—**discounting a note receivable.** A note receivable held by the company may be endorsed and then sold to a bank. The bank discounts the note and gives the company cash in exchange for it. The company that sells the note receivable is contingently, instead of directly, liable to the lending bank; that is, the company must pay the bank the amount due at the **maturity date** only if the maker of the note fails to pay the obligation. Illustration 10.1 shows the process of discounting a note receivable.

Illustration 10.1
ACTIONS BETWEEN MAKER, PAYEE, AND BANK

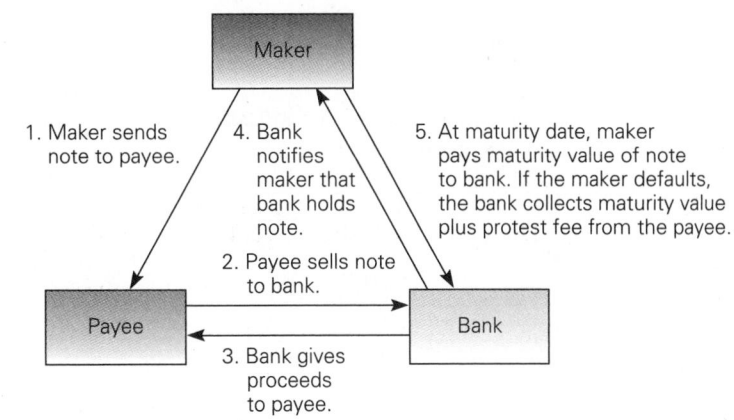

The cash proceeds from notes receivable discounted are computed as follows:

1. Determine the **maturity value** of the note (face value plus interest). This is the amount the bank will collect at maturity. For a noninterest-bearing note, the face of the note equals the maturity value. For an interest-bearing note, the face of the note plus interest for the life of the note equals the maturity value.
2. Determine the **discount period;** that is, count the exact number of days from the date of sale of the note to the date of maturity. Exclude the date of sale but include the date of maturity in the count. An efficient way of calculating the discount period is to determine the number of days the company held the note and deduct that period from the life of the note. The discount period, of course, can never be longer than the life of the note.
3. Using the **discount rate** charged by the bank, compute the **bank discount** on the maturity value (principal plus interest) for the discount period.
4. Deduct the bank discount from the maturity value to find the **cash proceeds.**

The contingent liability for the notes receivable discounted is usually shown in a note to the financial statements. If the original maker does not pay the bank at the maturity date, the company that sold the note to the bank will be held liable.

Example.   Assume that on May 4, 1995, Carlson Company received a $10,000 note from Thomas (the maker). The note bears interest at 12% and matures in 60 days from May 4. On May 14, 1995, Carlson Company (the endorser) sold the note to the Michigan National Bank, which discounted the note at 14%. The discount and the cash proceeds are determined as follows:

Face value of note.	$10,000.00
Add: Interest at 12% for 60 days	200.00
Maturity value	$10,200.00
Less: Bank discount on $10,200 at 14% for 50 days	198.33
Cash proceeds.	$10,001.67

The entry for Carlson would be:

Cash		Interest Revenue	
5/14 10,001.67			5/14 1.67

Notes Receivable	
5/4 10,000.00	5/14 10,000.00

If the book value of the note had exceeded the proceeds, the difference would have been debited to an Interest Expense account.

Balance Sheet Presentation of Notes Receivable Discounted. In the above illustration a balance sheet prepared for Carlson Company as of December 31, 1995, should show a contingent liability in the amount of $10,000 for notes receivable discounted. Assume that the total of all notes receivable that have not been discounted is $60,000. An acceptable method of presenting this information in the balance sheet is:

Assets	
Current assets:	
Cash	$xx,xxx
Accounts receivable.	xx,xxx
Notes receivable (Note 1)	60,000

Note 1: At December 31, 1995, the company is contingently liable for a customer's $10,000 note receivable that it has endorsed and discounted at the local bank. This note is not included in the $60,000 of notes shown.

Although the contingent liability is actually for the note plus the accrued interest to maturity ($10,200), for convenience it is customarily shown only for the face value of the note ($10,000).

Discounted Notes Receivable Paid by Maker. When a note receivable has been sold, it is usually the duty of the endorsee (the holder) to present the note to the maker for payment at maturity. Sometimes the note designates the place of payment. If the maker pays the endorsee (the bank in the above illustrations) at maturity, the endorser is thereby relieved of the contingent liability. If the note is not paid at maturity, the endorsee can collect from the endorser, who, in turn, can try to collect from the maker.

Assume that Thomas (above) pays his $10,000 note plus interest of $200 to the Michigan National Bank on July 3, 1995—the note's maturity date. Carlson Company, which sold the note to the bank, has been relieved of the possibility of being held liable for the note.

However, if Thomas dishonors the note at maturity instead of paying it, the Michigan National Bank will collect the principal ($10,000), interest ($200), and any protest fee (assume it is $5) from Carlson Company. Carlson Company will show the following changes in its accounts:

Accounts Receivable		Cash		
10,205		Bal.	xxx	10,205

Carlson Company will then try to collect $10,205 from Thomas. If this cannot be done, the $10,205 should be removed from the Accounts Receivable account and written off as an uncollectible account.

LONGER-TERM FINANCING

Although it is conceivable that once a company begins operations it can finance the acquisition of additional long-term or plant assets out of operating cash flows, this is often not possible. It is quite common for companies to use long-term sources of financing to acquire such assets. Chapter 9 discussed the use of capital stock to acquire long-term funds. This chapter discusses some of the more common forms of long-term debt financing.

Notes Payable

Notes payable may be either short or long term, but they are usually short term. Since these notes have been discussed earlier, we will not deal with them again in this section except to say that when payables (or receivables) have maturities exceeding approximately one year they are to be recorded at their present cash value.[1] The procedure is similar to that used in calculating the proceeds of a discounted bank loan. To illustrate, assume that we are the maker of a $1,000 face value note bearing no explicit rate of interest, and the note is due one year from its date. (Even though this does not exceed "approximately one year" and technically would not have to be recorded at its present value, we will assume that the company chooses to do so). Assume also that the rate of interest to be used in reducing this note to its present value is 16%. To solve for the present value, we have to ask the

---

[1] "Interest on Receivables and Payables," *APB Opinion No. 21* (New York: AICPA, 1971).

question, "What amount, if invested at 16%, would grow to $1,000 one year from now?" If we let x equal that amount, our formula would be:

$$x + 0.16x = \$1,000$$

$$1.16x = \$1,000$$

$$x = \frac{\$1,000}{1.16}$$

$$x = \$862.07$$

Assuming that the note payable resulted from the purchase of a machine, it would be recorded as follows:

Machinery		Notes Payable—Discount		Notes Payable	
(a) 862.07		(a) 137.93			(a) 1,000

At the due date, $1,000 would be paid to the payee and $137.93 would be (or would have been) recorded as interest expense. The accounting for the interest in this type of transaction is quite similar to that used when a company discounts its own note at the bank.

BONDS PAYABLE   20+ yr.

*Objective 3
Describe the
features of bonds
and tell how
bonds differ from
shares of stock*

A **bond** is a long-term debt, or liability, owed by its issuer. Physical evidence of the debt lies in a negotiable bond certificate. In contrast to long-term notes, which usually mature in 10 years or less, bond maturities often run for 20 years or more.

Generally, a bond issue consists of a large number of $1,000 bonds rather than one large bond. For example, a company seeking to borrow $100,000 would issue one hundred (100) $1,000 bonds rather than one (1) $100,000 bond. This practice enables investors with limited cash to purchase some of the bonds.

Bonds derive their value primarily from two promises made by the borrower to the lender or bondholder. The borrower promises to pay (1) the **face value** or *principal amount* of the bond on a specific maturity date in the future and (2) *periodic interest* at a specified rate on face value at stated dates, usually semiannually, until the maturity date.

Large companies often have numerous long-term notes and bond issues outstanding at any one time. The various issues generally have different stated interest rates and will mature at different points in the future. Companies present this information in the footnotes to their financial statements. Illustration 10.2 shows a portion of the long-term borrowings footnote from Du Pont's 1990 Annual Report. All the items labeled "debentures" are bond issues outstanding.

1. face
    value
1. Po. Int.

Comparison with Stock

A bond differs from a share of stock in several ways:

1. A bond is a debt or liability of the issuer, while a share of stock is a unit of ownership.
2. A bond has a maturity date when it must be paid. A share of stock does not mature; stock remains outstanding indefinitely unless the company decides to retire it.
3. Most bonds require stated periodic interest payments by the company. In contrast, dividends to stockholders are payable only when declared; even preferred dividends need not be paid in a particular period if the board of directors so decides.

4. Bond interest is deductible by the issuer in computing both net income and taxable income, while dividends are not deductible in either computation.

Selling (Issuing) Bonds

A company seeking to borrow millions of dollars generally will not be able to borrow from a single lender. By selling (issuing) bonds to the public, the company is able to secure the necessary funds.

Usually companies sell their bond issues through an investment company or banker called an **underwriter.** The underwriter performs many tasks for the bond issuer, such as advertising, selling, and delivering the bonds to the purchasers. Often the underwriter guarantees the issuer a fixed price for the bonds, expecting to earn a profit by selling the bonds for more than the fixed price.

When a company sells bonds to the public, many purchasers buy the bonds. Rather than deal with each purchaser individually, the issuing company appoints a *trustee* to represent the bondholders. The **trustee** usually is a bank or trust company. The main duty of the trustee is to see that the borrower fulfills the provisions of the *bond indenture*. A **bond indenture** is the contract or loan agreement under which the bonds are issued. The indenture deals with matters such as the interest rate, maturity date and maturity amount, possible restrictions on dividends, repayment plans, and other provisions relating to the debt. If the issuing company does not adhere to the bond indenture provisions, the issuer is said to be in default. The trustee is expected to take action to force the issuer to comply with the indenture.

Characteristics of Bonds

As stated earlier, a bond is a long-term liability that derives its value from two promises made to the purchasers: (1) the issuing company will repay the principal at a specified later time, and (2) the issuing company will make periodic interest payments (usually every six months) until that time. Bonds

Illustration 10.2
DU PONT'S LONG-TERM BORROWINGS (in $ thousands)

December 31	1990	1989
U.S. dollar:		
Industrial development bonds due 2001–2022	$ 197	$ 223
Zero coupon convertible notes due 2010 ($2,127.5 face value,		
7.75% yield to maturity)[1]	485	—
Medium-term notes due 1991–2015[2]	720	446
10.13% notes due 1992	251	252
7.50% notes due 1993	250	250
9.00% notes due 1994	254	255
Floating rate notes due 1994[3].	150	—
11.25% notes due 1995	—	150
8.45% notes due 1996	300	300
8.65% notes due 1997	300	—
8.70% notes due 1998	117	133
8.00% notes due 1998	42	46
9.13% debentures due 1999	94	102
7.50% debentures due 1999	50	54
9.15% notes due 2000[4]	309	—
8.88% debentures due 2001	150	160
6.00% debentures due 2001 ($660 face value, 13.95% yield to		
maturity).	369	358
8.25% notes due 2002	55	60
8.45% debentures due 2004	198	198
8.50% debentures due 2006	182	182
9.38% debentures due 2009	180	190
8.50% debentures due 2016	285	300
9.00% European Currency Unit (ECU) notes due 1992[5].	109	109
12.375% Italian Lira notes due 1994[6]	101	—
Other loans (various currencies) due 1991–2013[7]	573	467
Unamortized discount[8].	(138)	(155)
	$5,583	$4,080

[1] In 1990, the company issued zero coupon convertible subordinated notes at an issue price of $465. The notes are convertible at the option of the holder at any time prior to maturity into the company's common stock at a conversion rate of 4.613 shares per thousand dollars of principal amount at maturity. On conversion, the company may elect to pay the holder an amount in cash equal in value to the number of converted shares of common stock; however, the holder will not receive any cash payment representing accrued original issue discount. The notes are redeemable at any time, in whole or in part, at the option of the company at a price equal to the issue price plus accrued original issue discount; provided that the notes may not be redeemed prior to June 14, 1992, unless certain market conditions exist. The notes will be purchased by the company at the option of the holder on June 14, 1995, June 14, 2000, and June 14, 2005 at a price equal to the issue price plus accrued original issue discount.

[2] Average interest rates at December 31, 1990 and 1989 were 8.17 percent and 8.27 percent. At December 31, 1990, the company had outstanding four interest rate swap agreements maturing at various dates between January 10, 1992 and November 5, 1993 that effectively converted $95 of long-term fixed rate borrowings to floating rate obligations with an effective interest rate less than that generally available for the company's commercial paper.

[3] The interest rate on these notes is 75 basis points above the Bond Equivalent Yield of the 91-day Treasury Bill Rate and is adjusted weekly. Concurrent with the issuance of these notes, the company entered into an interest rate swap agreement that effectively converted these notes to an 8.87 percent fixed rate obligation.

[4] Concurrent with the issuance of these notes, the company entered into an interest rate swap agreement that effectively converted these notes to an 8.67 percent fixed rate obligation over the term of the notes. Under the terms of this swap agreement the counterparty has the option at the end of the third year to convert the swap to a floating rate essentially equivalent to the rate the company pays on its commercial paper.

Illustration 10.2
(concluded)

---

(5) In 1989, the company issued notes denominated as 100 million European Currency Units (ECUs) with a 9 percent interest rate. Concurrent with the issuance of these notes, the company entered into a currency swap agreement that effectively established U.S. dollar-denominated principal ($109) and interest (8.73 percent) obligations over the term of the ECU notes.

(6) In 1990, the company issued notes denominated as 125 billion Italian Lire with a 12.375 percent interest rate. Concurrent with the issuance of these notes, the company entered into two combined interest rate and currency swaps that effectively established U.S. dollar-denominated principal ($101) and interest obligations over the term of the notes. U.S. dollar interest payable under the swap agreements is at a floating rate of interest less than that generally available for the company's commercial paper.

(7) Includes a 1990 bank loan in the amount of 4 billion Belgian Financial Francs ($129 at the year-end exchange rate). Under the terms of the loan, interest is payable quarterly and the interest rate is adjustable every six months based on an arithmetic mean of certain public issues quoted by the Cote Officielle de la Bourse de Luxembourg. No principal repayments are scheduled during the first three years; after that period, repayments must be made (minimum 500 million Francs per year) each year until the loan is retired. The company is entitled, at its option, to prepay all or part of the loan at the end of each six month interest settlement period. The company has entered into forward exchange contracts that effectively convert interest payments for the current interest settlement period to U.S. dollar-denominated amounts.

Also includes notes denominated as 160 million Australian dollars with a 16.5 percent interest rate issued in 1989 by the company's majority-owned Canadian subsidiary which were effectively converted to a 149 million Canadian dollar obligation with an implicit 12.43 percent annual cost through a series of currency swap agreements and forward exchange contracts.

(8) Unamortized discount results principally from revaluation of debt acquired from Conoco in 1981, based on an imputed rate of 15.63 percent. The face amount of such debt included above at December 31, 1990 and 1989 was $684 and $772.

---

may differ in other respects; they may be secured or unsecured bonds, registered or unregistered (bearer) bonds, and term or serial bonds. We discuss these differences and others below.

Certain bond features are matters of legal necessity, such as how a company pays interest and transfers ownership. Such features usually do not affect the issue price of the bonds. Other features, such as convertibility into common stock, are called *sweeteners* because they are designed to make the bonds more attractive to potential purchasers. These sweeteners may increase the issue price of a bond.

Secured Bonds.   A **secured bond** is a bond for which a company has pledged specific property to ensure its payment. Mortgage bonds are the most common type of secured bonds. A **mortgage** is a legal claim (lien) on specific property that gives the bondholder the right to possess the pledged property if the company fails to make required payments.

Unsecured Bonds.   An **unsecured bond** is called a **debenture bond,** or simply a **debenture.** A debenture is an unsecured bond backed only by the general creditworthiness of the issuer, not by a lien on any specific property. A financially sound company will be able to issue debentures more easily than a company experiencing financial difficulty.

Registered Bonds.   A **registered bond** is a bond with the owner's name on the bond certificate and in the register of bond owners kept by the bond issuer or its agent, the registrar. Bonds may be registered as to principal (or face value of the bond) or as to both principal and interest. Most bonds in our economy are registered as to principal only. If a bond is registered as to both principal and interest, the bond interest is paid by check. Ownership of registered bonds is transferred by endorsing the bond and registering it in the new owner's name. Registered bonds are easily replaced if lost or stolen.

Unregistered (Bearer) Bonds. An **unregistered (bearer) bond** is assumed to be the property of its holder or bearer, since the owner's name does not appear on the bond certificate or in a separate record. Ownership is transferred by physical delivery of the bond.

Coupon Bonds. A **coupon bond** is a bond not registered as to interest. Coupon bonds carry detachable coupons for the interest they pay. At the end of each interest period, the coupon for the period is clipped and presented to a stated party, usually a bank, for collection.

Term Bonds and Serial Bonds. A **term bond** is a bond that matures on the same date as all other bonds in a given bond issue. **Serial bonds** are bonds in a given bond issue with maturities spread over several dates. For instance, one fourth of the bonds may mature on December 31, 1996, another one fourth on December 31, 1997, and so on.

Callable Bonds. A **callable bond** contains a provision that gives the issuer the right to call (buy back) the bond before its maturity date. The provision is similar to the call provision in some preferred stocks. A company might exercise this call right if outstanding bonds bear interest at a much higher rate than the company would have to pay if it issued new but similar bonds. The exercise of the call provision normally requires the company to pay the bondholder a call premium of about $30 to $70 per $1,000 bond. A **call premium** is the price paid in excess of face value that the issuer of bonds must pay to redeem (call) bonds before their maturity date.

Convertible Bonds. A **convertible bond** is a bond that may be exchanged for shares of stock of the issuing corporation at the bondholder's option. A convertible bond has a stipulated conversion rate of some number of shares for each $1,000 bond. Any type of bond may be convertible, but this feature usually is added to rather risky debenture bonds to make them more attractive to investors.

Bonds with Stock Warrants. A **stock warrant** allows the bondholder to purchase shares of common stock at a fixed price for a stated period of time. Warrants issued with long-term debt may be nondetachable or detachable. A bond with *nondetachable warrants* is virtually the same as a convertible bond; the holder must surrender the bond to acquire the common stock. *Detachable warrants* allow bondholders to keep their bonds and still purchase shares of stock through exercise of the warrants.

Junk Bonds. **Junk bonds** are high-interest rate, high-risk bonds that were issued in the 1980s to finance corporate restructurings. These restructurings took the form of management buyouts (called leveraged buyouts or LBOs), hostile takeovers of companies by outside parties, or friendly takeovers of companies by outside parties. As of the early 1990s, junk bonds were out of favor because many of the issuers had defaulted on their interest payments and some of the issuers had declared bankruptcy or sought relief from the bondholders by negotiating new debt terms.

Advantages of Issuing Debt

*Objective 4
List the advantages and disadvantages of financing with long-term debt and prepare examples showing how financial leverage is employed*

Several advantages come from raising cash by issuing bonds rather than stock. First, the current stockholders do not have to dilute or surrender their control of the company when funds are obtained by borrowing rather than issuing more shares of stock. Second, it may also be less expensive to issue debt rather than additional stock because the interest payments made to bondholders are tax deductible while dividends are not. Finally, probably the most important reason to issue bonds is that the use of debt may increase the earnings of stockholders through favorable financial leverage.

Favorable Financial Leverage.   A company has **favorable financial leverage** when it uses borrowed funds to increase earnings per share (EPS) of common stock. Increased EPS usually results from earning a higher rate of return than the rate of interest paid for the borrowed money. For example, suppose a company borrowed money at 10% and earned a 15% rate of return. The 5% difference increases earnings.

Illustration 10.3 (on page 531) provides a more comprehensive example of favorable financial leverage. The two companies in the illustration are identical in every respect except in the way they are financed. Company A issued only capital stock, while Company B issued equal amounts of 10% bonds and capital stock. Both companies have $20,000,000 of assets, and both earned $4,000,000 of income from operations. If we divide income from operations by assets ($4,000,000 ÷ $20,000,000), we see that both companies earned 20% on assets employed. Yet B's stockholders fared far better than A's. The ratio of net income to stockholders' equity is 18% for B, while it is only 12% for A.

Assume that both companies issued their stock at the beginning of 1995 at $10 per share. B's $1.80 EPS are 50% greater than A's $1.20 EPS. This EPS difference probably would cause B's shares to sell at a substantially higher market price than A's shares. B's larger EPS would also allow a larger dividend on B's shares.

Company B in Illustration 10.3 is employing financial leverage, or is said to be **trading on the equity.** The company is using its stockholders' equity as a basis for securing funds on which it pays a fixed return. Company B expects to earn more from the use of such funds than their fixed after-tax cost. As a result, Company B increases its rate of return on stockholders' equity and EPS.[1]

---

[1] Issuing bonds is only one method of using leverage. Other methods of using financial leverage include issuing preferred stock or long-term notes.

A BROADER PERSPECTIVE

COMPANIES LOCKING IN CHEAPER DEBT

NEW YORK—The record pace at which companies are refinancing their long-term debt is some of the best news the economy has gotten this year.

Like millions of homeowners refinancing their mortgages, corporations are racing to issue debt at today's low interest rates to pay off debt issued at higher rates in the 1980s and earlier. So far this year, companies have issued $28.2 billion of bonds. If that pace keeps up, this will be a record year for corporate bond sales.

The billions of dollars companies will save on interest payments this year mean:

- Higher net income, which should boost stock prices. That could lead some companies to raise dividend payments to shareholders.
- Higher federal tax payments, which should make at least a small dent in the budget deficit. Interest payments are tax-deductible. As they decrease, a company's taxable income increases.
- More money to spend developing new products or investing for expansion—buying heavy equipment or expanding plants, for example.
- Less pressure to lay off workers to cut costs. If companies use the extra cash to expand, some eventually may hire more workers as a result of the interest savings.

* * * * *

Interest rates have been declining since early 1990, so the idea of replacing old debt is nothing new to U.S. corporations. But when the Federal Reserve Board cut the discount rate a full percentage point to 3.5% on Dec. 20, it set off a corporate stampede to the debt markets. This week, 10-year notes from companies that have good credit ratings were yielding about 7.75%, down from about 9.6% three years ago. Commercial paper—securities that companies sell to borrow for periods of a few days to 38 weeks—now offers interest rates of a little more than 4%, vs. 9% three years ago.

Companies have slowed down bond sales the past few days. But they're likely to speed up again soon, analysts say. "If corporate treasurers begin to sense rates have bottomed, you will have quite a logjam in the not-too-distant future," says John Lonski, analyst at Moody's Investor Services. "It will be just like the rush you see with homeowners trying to refinance" after mortgage rates begin to edge up.

* * * * *

Many large, financially strong companies do benefit. But not all companies are welcome at the refinancing party. Small companies that have less than $30 million in annual revenue don't have access to public debt markets that large companies do, says David Gladstone of venture capital firm Allied Capital. "They aren't participating in all this wonderful refinancing that's going on," he says. "Small companies have been shut out of the credit markets."

Small companies have trouble because they don't borrow enough at one time to interest institutional investors who buy corporate notes, bonds and mortgages, Gladstone says. Most banks that do business with small companies have tightened lending standards and won't refinance loans. So, small companies "are continuing to muddle through with the debt they piled on in past periods," he says.

And companies that borrowed heavily using junk bonds in the 1980s are not big players in the rush to refinance. A handful of companies that loaded up on junk debt are beginning to tap into the bond market, Kiernan says. Mostly, though, those companies are benefiting from another financing outlet: They're tapping into the record-level stock market, selling stock and using the proceeds to pay debt.

* * * * *

SOURCE: Susan Antilla, *USA TODAY*, January 29, 1992, pp. 1B, 2B. Reprinted with permission.

A BROADER PERSPECTIVE (*concluded*)

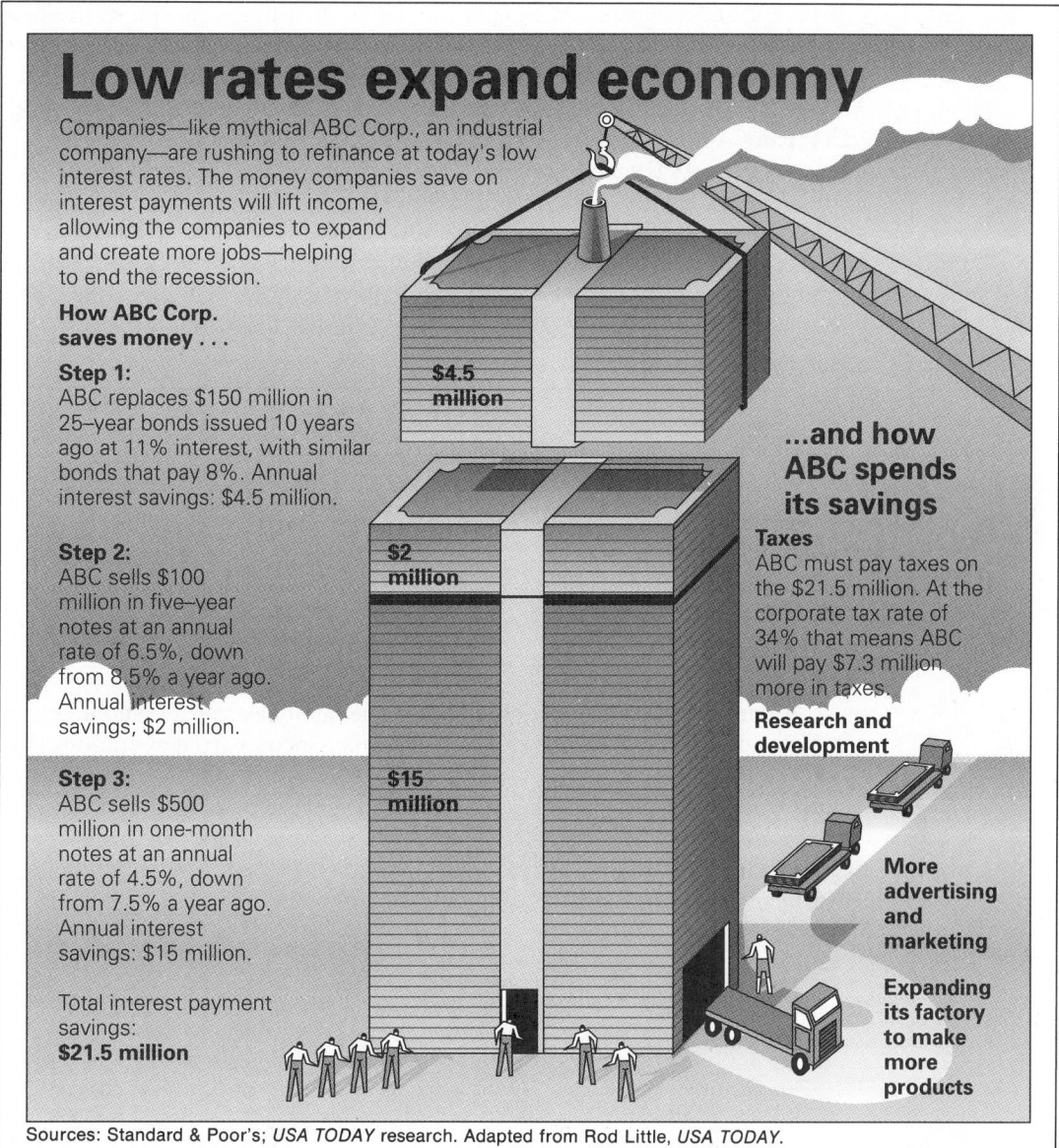

Low rates expand economy

Companies—like mythical ABC Corp., an industrial company—are rushing to refinance at today's low interest rates. The money companies save on interest payments will lift income, allowing the companies to expand and create more jobs—helping to end the recession.

How ABC Corp. saves money . . .

Step 1:
ABC replaces $150 million in 25–year bonds issued 10 years ago at 11% interest, with similar bonds that pay 8%. Annual interest savings: $4.5 million.

Step 2:
ABC sells $100 million in five–year notes at an annual rate of 6.5%, down from 8.5% a year ago. Annual interest savings; $2 million.

Step 3:
ABC sells $500 million in one-month notes at an annual rate of 4.5%, down from 7.5% a year ago. Annual interest savings: $15 million.

Total interest payment savings:
$21.5 million

$4.5 million

$2 million

$15 million

...and how ABC spends its savings

Taxes
ABC must pay taxes on the $21.5 million. At the corporate tax rate of 34% that means ABC will pay $7.3 million more in taxes.

Research and development

More advertising and marketing

Expanding its factory to make more products

Sources: Standard & Poor's; *USA TODAY* research. Adapted from Rod Little, *USA TODAY.*

Disadvantages of Issuing Debt

Several disadvantages accompany the use of debt financing. First, the borrower has a fixed interest payment that must be met each period to avoid default. Second, use of debt also reduces a company's ability to withstand a major loss. For example, assume that instead of having net income, both Company A and Company B in Illustration 10.3 sustain a net loss in 1995 of $11,000,000. At the end of 1995, Company A will still have $9,000,000 of stockholders' equity and can continue operations with a chance of recovery, as shown below. Company B, on the other hand, would have negative stockholders' equity of $1,000,000, and the bondholders could force the company to liquidate if B could not make interest payments as they came due. The result of sustaining the loss by the two companies is as follows:

COMPANIES A AND B
Partial Balance Sheets
December 31, 1995

	Company A	Company B
Stockholders' equity:		
Paid-in capital:		
Common stock.	$ 20,000,000	$ 10,000,000
Retained earnings	(11,000,000)	(11,000,000)
Total stockholders' equity	$ 9,000,000	$ (1,000,000)

A third disadvantage of debt financing is that it also causes a company to experience unfavorable financial leverage when income from operations falls below a certain level. **Unfavorable financial leverage** results when the cost of borrowed funds exceeds the revenue they generate; it is the reverse of *favorable financial leverage*. In the above example, if income from operations fell to $1,000,000, the rates of return on stockholders' equity would be 3% for A and zero for B, as shown in the following schedule.

COMPANIES A AND B
Income Statements
For the Year Ended December 31, 1995

	Company A	Company B
Income from operations	$1,000,000	$1,000,000
Interest expense.		1,000,000
Income before federal income taxes	$1,000,000	$ –0–
Deduct: Federal income taxes (40%)	400,000	–0–
Net income	$ 600,000	$ –0–
Rate of return on stockholders' equity:		
Company A ($600,000/$20,000,000)	3%	
Company B ($0/$10,000,000)		0%

Illustration 10.3
FAVORABLE FINANCIAL LEVERAGE

COMPANIES A AND B CONDENSED STATEMENTS
Balance Sheets
December 31, 1995

	Company A	Company B
Total assets	$20,000,000	$20,000,000
Bonds payable, 10%		$10,000,000
Stockholders' equity (capital stock).	$20,000,000	10,000,000
Total equities	$20,000,000	$20,000,000

Income Statements
For the Year Ended December 31, 1995

	Company A	Company B
Income from operations	$ 4,000,000	$ 4,000,000
Interest expense.		1,000,000
Income before federal income taxes	$ 4,000,000	$ 3,000,000
Deduct: Federal income taxes (40%)	1,600,000	1,200,000
Net income	$ 2,400,000	$ 1,800,000
Number of common shares outstanding	2,000,000	1,000,000
Earnings per share (EPS) (Net income ÷ Number of common shares outstanding)	$1.20	$1.80
Rate of return on assets employed (Income from operations ÷ Total assets; both companies $4,000,000/$20,000,000)	20%	20%
Rate of return on stockholders' equity (Net income ÷ Stockholders' equity):		
Company A ($2,400,000/$20,000,000)	12%	
Company B ($1,800,000/$10,000,000)		18%

The fourth disadvantage of issuing debt is that loan agreements often require the maintenance of a certain amount of working capital (Current assets − Current liabilities) and place limitations on dividends and additional borrowings.

Accounting for Bonds Issued at Face Value

Objective 5
Prepare journal entries for bonds issued at face value

When a company issues bonds, it incurs a long-term liability on which periodic interest payments must be made, usually twice a year. If interest dates fall on other than balance sheet dates, the company will need to accrue interest in the proper periods. The following examples illustrate the accounting for bonds issued at face value on an interest date and issued at face value between interest dates.

Bonds Issued at Face Value on an Interest Date. Valley Company's accounting year ends on December 31. On December 31, 1995, Valley issued 10-year, 12% bonds with a $100,000 face value, for $100,000. The bonds are dated December 31, 1995, call for semiannual interest payments on June 30 and December 31, and mature on December 31, 2005. Valley made the required interest and principal payments when due. The entries for the 10 years are summarized below.

On December 31, 1995, the date of issuance, the entry is:

```
1995
Dec. 31  Cash . . . . . . . . . . . . . . . . . . . . . . . .  100,000
             Bonds Payable. . . . . . . . . . . . . . . .              100,000
         To record bonds issued at face value.
```

On each June 30 and December 31 for 10 years, beginning June 30, 1996 (ending June 30, 2005), the entry would be:

```
Each
year
June 30
and
Dec. 31  Bond Interest Expense ($100,000 × 0.12 × ½) . . .    6,000
             Cash . . . . . . . . . . . . . . . . . . . . . .              6,000
         To record periodic interest payment.
```

On December 31, 2005, the maturity date, the entry would be:

```
2005
Dec. 31  Bond Interest Expense . . . . . . . . . . . . . .      6,000
         Bonds Payable. . . . . . . . . . . . . . . . . .    100,000
             Cash . . . . . . . . . . . . . . . . . . . . . .            106,000
         To record final interest and bond redemption
         payment.
```

Note that no adjusting entries are needed because the interest payment date falls on the last day of the accounting period. The income statement for each of the 10 years 1996–2005 would show Bond Interest Expense of $12,000 ($6,000 × 2); the balance sheet at the end of each of the years 1995–2003 would report bonds payable of $100,000 in long-term liabilities. At the end of 2004, the bonds would be reclassified as a current liability because they will be paid within the next year.

The real world is more complicated. For example, assume the Valley bonds were dated October 31, 1995, issued on that same date, and pay interest each April 30 and October 31. In this case, an adjusting entry is needed on December 31 to accrue interest for two months, November and December. That entry would be:

```
1995
Dec. 31  Bond Interest Expense ($100,000 × 0.12 × 2/12) . .    2,000
             Bond Interest Payable . . . . . . . . . . . .              2,000
         To accrue two months' interest expense.
```

The April 30, 1996, entry would be:

```
1996
Apr. 30  Bond Interest Expense ($100,000 × 0.12 × 4/12) . .    4,000
         Bond Interest Payable . . . . . . . . . . . . .        2,000
            Cash . . . . . . . . . . . . . . . . . . . .                  6,000
            To record semiannual interest payment.
```

The October 31, 1996, entry would be:

```
1996
Oct. 31  Bond Interest Expense . . . . . . . . . . . . .        6,000
            Cash . . . . . . . . . . . . . . . . . . . .                  6,000
            To record semiannual interest payment.
```

Each year similar entries would be made for the semiannual payments and the year-end accrued interest. The $2,000 Bond Interest Payable would be reported as a current liability on the December 31 balance sheet for each year.

Bonds Issued at Face Value between Interest Dates. Bonds are not always issued on the date they start to bear interest. Regardless of when the bonds are physically issued, interest starts to accrue from the *most recent* interest date. The bonds are reported to be selling at a stated price "plus accrued interest." The issuer of the bonds must pay holders of the bonds a full six months' interest at each interest date. Thus, investors purchasing bonds after the bonds begin to accrue interest must pay the seller for the unearned interest accrued since the preceding interest date. The bondholders will be reimbursed for this accrued interest when they receive their first six months' interest check.

Using the facts for the Valley bonds dated December 31, 1995, suppose Valley issued its bonds on May 31, 1996, instead of on December 31, 1995. The entry required is:

```
1996
May 31  Cash . . . . . . . . . . . . . . . . . . . . . . .    105,000
           Bonds Payable. . . . . . . . . . . . . . . . .              100,000
           Bond Interest Payable ($100,000 × 0.12 × 5/12) .              5,000
           To record bonds issued at face value plus
           accrued interest.
```

This entry records the $5,000 received for the accrued interest as a debit to Cash and a credit to Bond Interest Payable.

The entry required on June 30, 1996, when the full six months' interest is paid, is:

```
1996
June 30  Bond Interest Expense ($100,000 × 0.12 × 1/12) . .    1,000
         Bond Interest Payable . . . . . . . . . . . . .        5,000
            Cash . . . . . . . . . . . . . . . . . . . .                  6,000
            To record bond interest payment.
```

This entry records $1,000 interest expense on the $100,000 of bonds that were outstanding for one month. The $5,000 is the amount previously collected from the bondholders on May 31 as accrued interest and is now being returned to them.

Bond Prices and Interest Rates

Objective 6
Explain how interest rates affect bond prices and what causes a bond to sell at a premium or discount

The price of a bond issue often differs from its face value. The amount a bond sells for above face value is called a **premium.** The amount a bond sells for below face value is called a **discount.** A difference between face value and issue price exists whenever the market rate of interest for similar bonds differs from the contract rate of interest on the bonds. The **market interest rate** (also called the **effective rate** or **yield**) is the minimum rate of interest that investors will accept on bonds of a particular risk category. The higher the risk category, the higher the minimum rate of interest that investors will accept. The **contract rate of interest** (also called the **stated, coupon,** or **nominal rate**) is stated in the bond indenture, printed on the face of each bond, and is used to determine the amount of cash that will be paid each interest period. The market rate fluctuates from day to day, responding to factors such as the interest rate the Federal Reserve Board charges banks to borrow from it, government actions to finance the national debt, and the supply of, and demand for, money.

Market and contract rates of interest are likely to differ. The contract rate must be set before the bonds are actually sold to allow time for such activities as printing the bonds. Assume, for instance, that the contract rate for a bond issue is set at 12%. If the market rate is equal to the contract rate, the bonds will sell at their face value. However, by the time the bonds are sold, the market rate could be higher or lower than the contract rate. As shown in Illustration 10.4, if the market rate is lower than the contract rate, the bonds will sell for more than their face value. Thus, if the market rate is 10% and the contract rate is 12%, the bonds will sell at a premium. Investors will be attracted to bonds offering a contract rate higher than the market rate and will bid up their price. If the market rate is higher than the contract rate, the bonds will sell for less than their face value. Thus, if the market rate is 14% and the contract rate is 12%, the bonds will sell at a discount. Investors will not be interested in bonds bearing a contract rate less than the market rate unless the price is reduced. The effect of selling bonds at a premium or a discount is to allow the purchasers of the bonds to earn the market rate of interest on their investment.

Computing Bond Prices

Objective 7
Apply the concept of present value to compute the price of a bond

Computing long-term bond prices involves finding *present values* using compound interest. The appendix to this chapter explains the concepts of future value and present value. If you do not understand these concepts, you should read the appendix before continuing with this section.

Illustration 10.4
BOND PREMIUMS AND DISCOUNTS

	Market Rate	Contract Rate
Bonds sell at a *premium* if Market rate < Contract rate	10%	12%
Bonds sell at a *face value* if Market rate = Contract rate	12%	12%
Bonds sell at a *discount* if Market rate > Contract rate	14%	12%

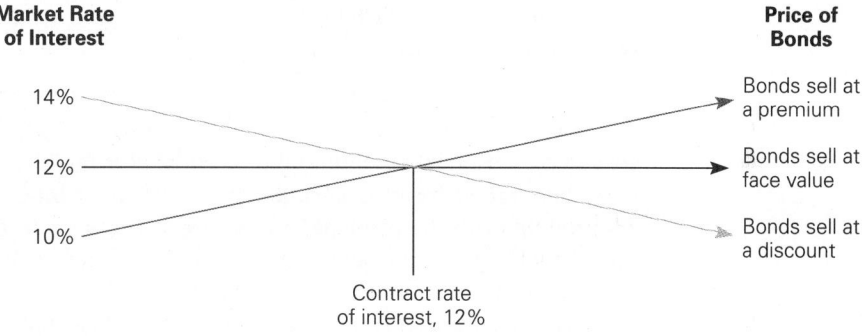

Buyers and sellers negotiate a price that will yield the going rate of interest for bonds of a particular risk class. The price investors will pay for a given bond issue is equal to the present value of the bonds. Present value is computed by discounting the promised cash flows from the bonds—principal and interest—using the market, or effective, rate. Market rate is used because the bonds must yield at least this rate or investors will be attracted to alternative investments. The life of the bonds is stated in terms of interest (compounding) periods. The interest rate used is the effective rate *per interest period*, which is found by dividing the annual rate by the number of times interest is paid per year. For example, if the annual rate is 12%, the semiannual rate would be 6%.

Bond prices usually are quoted as percentages of face value—100 means 100% of face value, 97 means 97% of face value, and 103 means 103% of face value. For example, 100, $1,000 face value bonds issued at 103 have a price of $103,000. Regardless of the issue price, at maturity the issuer of the bonds must pay back the investor(s) the face value of the bonds.

Bonds Issued at Face Value. The following example illustrates the specific steps involved in computing the price of bonds. Assume Carr Company issues 12% bonds with a $100,000 face value to yield 12%. The bonds are dated and issued on June 30, 1995, call for semiannual interest payments on June 30 and December 31, and mature on June 30, 1998.[2] The bonds will sell at face value because they offer 12% and investors seek 12%. Potential purchasers have no reason to offer a premium or demand a discount. One way to prove the bonds would be sold at face value is by showing that their present value is $100,000:

	Cash Flow	×	Present Value Factor	=	Present Value
Principal of $100,000 due in six interest periods multiplied by present value factor for 6% from Table E.3, Appendix E (end of text).	$100,000	×	0.70496	=	$ 70,496
Interest of $6,000 due at end of each of six interest periods multiplied by present value factor for 6% from Table E.4, Appendix E (end of text)	6,000	×	4.91732	=	29,504
Total price (present value)					$100,000

This schedule shows that if investors seek an effective rate of 6% per six-month period, they should pay $100,000 for these bonds. **Notice that the same number of interest periods and semiannual interest rates are used in discounting both the principal and interest payments to their present values.** The entry to record the sale of these bonds on June 30, 1995, debits Cash and credits Bonds Payable for $100,000.

Bonds Issued at a Discount.   Assume the $100,000, 12% Carr bonds are sold to yield a current market rate of 14% annual interest, or 7% per semiannual period. The present value (selling price) of the bonds is computed as follows:

	Cash Flow	×	Present Value Factor	=	Present Value
Principal of $100,000 due in six interest periods multiplied by present value factor for 7% from Table E.3, Appendix E (end of text)	$100,000	×	0.66634	=	$66,634
Interest of $6,000 due at end of each of six interest periods multiplied by present value factor for 7% from Table E.4, Appendix E (end of text)	6,000	×	4.76654	=	28,599
Total price (present value)					$95,233

Note that in computing the present value of the bonds, the actual $6,000 cash interest payment that will be made each period is still used. **The amount of cash the company pays as interest does not depend on the market interest rate.** However, the market rate per semiannual period—7%—does change, and this new rate is used to find interest factors in the tables.

---

[2] Bonds do not normally mature in such a short time; we use a three-year life for illustrative purposes only.

*Objective 8
Prepare journal
entries for bonds
issued at a dis-
count or a pre-
mium*

The journal entry to record issuance of the bonds is:

```
1995
June 30   Cash . . . . . . . . . . . . . . . . . . . . . . .   95,233
             Discount on Bonds Payable  . . . . . . . . . .    4,767
                Bonds Payable. . . . . . . . . . . . . .             100,000
          To record bonds issued at a discount.
```

In recording the bond issue, Bonds Payable is credited for the face value of
the debt. The difference between face value and price received is debited to
Discount on Bonds Payable, a contra account to Bonds Payable. Carr reports the bonds payable and discount on bonds payable in the balance sheet
as follows:

Long-term liabilities:
    Bonds payable, 12%, due June 30, 1998 . . . . $100,000
        Less: Discount on bonds payable 4,767 $95,233

The $95,233 is called the carrying value, or net liability, of the bonds.
Carrying value is the face value of the bonds minus any unamortized discount or plus any unamortized premium. The next section discusses unamortized premium on bonds payable.

Bonds Issued at a Premium.   Assume that Carr issued the $100,000 face
value of 12% bonds to yield a current market rate of 10%. The bonds would
sell at a premium calculated as follows:

	Cash Flow	Present Value × Factor =	Present Value
Principal of $100,000 due in six interest periods multiplied by present value factor for 5% from Table E.3, Appendix E (end of text)	$100,000 ×	0.74622 =	$ 74,622
Interest of $6,000 due at end of each of six interest periods multiplied by present value factor for 5% from Table E.4, Appendix E (end of text)	6,000 ×	5.07569 =	30,454
Total price (present value).			$105,076

The journal entry to record the issuance of the bonds is:

```
1995
June 30   Cash . . . . . . . . . . . . . . . . . . . . . . .   105,076
             Bonds Payable. . . . . . . . . . . . . . .              100,000
             Premium on Bonds Payable . . . . . . . . .                5,076
          To record bonds issued at a premium.
```

The carrying value of these bonds at issuance is $105,076, consisting of face
value of $100,000 and premium of $5,076. The premium is an adjunct account shown on the balance sheet as an addition to bonds payable as follows:

Long-term liabilities:		
Bonds payable, 12%, due June 30, 1998	$100,000	
Add: Premium on bonds payable.	5,076	$105,076

Discount/Premium Amortization

When a company issues bonds at a premium or discount, bond interest expense recorded each period differs from bond interest payments. A discount *increases* and a premium *decreases* the amount of interest expense. For example, if Carr issues bonds with a face value of $100,000 for $95,233, the total interest cost of borrowing would be $40,767: $36,000 (which is six payments of $6,000) plus the discount of $4,767. If the bonds had been issued at $105,076, the total interest cost of borrowing would be $30,924: $36,000 less the premium of $5,076. The $4,767 discount or $5,076 premium must be allocated or charged to the six periods that benefit from the use of borrowed money. Two methods are available for amortizing a discount or premium on bonds—the straight-line method and the effective interest rate method.

The straight-line method records interest expense at a *constant amount*; the effective interest rate method records interest expense at a *constant rate*. *APB Opinion No. 21* states that the straight-line method may be used **only when it does not differ materially from the effective interest rate method.** In many cases, the differences will not be material.

The Straight-Line Method. The **straight-line method of amortization** is a procedure that allocates an equal amount of discount or premium to each month the bonds are outstanding. The amount is calculated by dividing the discount or premium by the total number of months from the *date of issuance* to the maturity date. For example, if Carr sells its $100,000 face value bonds for $95,233, the $4,767 discount would be charged to interest expense at a rate of $132.42 per month (equal to $4,767/36). Total discount amortization for six months would be $794.52, computed as follows: $132.42 × 6. Interest expense for each six-month period then would be $6,794.52, calculated as follows: $6,000 + ($132.42 × 6). The entry to record the expense on December 31, 1995, would be:

```
1995
Dec. 31  Bond Interest Expense . . . . . . . . . . . . .  6,794.52
              Cash. . . . . . . . . . . . . . . . . . . .              6,000.00
              Discount on Bonds Payable ($132.42 × 6) . .                794.52
            To record interest payment and discount
            amortization.
```

By the maturity date, all of the discount will have been amortized.

To illustrate the straight-line method applied to a premium, recall earlier that Carr sold its $100,000 face value bonds for $105,076. Carr would amortize the $5,076 premium on these bonds at a rate of $141 ($5,076/36) per month. The entry for the first period's semiannual interest expense on bonds sold at a premium is:

```
1995
Dec.  31  Bond Interest Expense . . . . . . . . . . . . . . .  5,154
          Premium on Bonds Payable ($141 × 6). . . . . . . .    846
              Cash. . . . . . . . . . . . . . . . . . . .            6,000
              To record interest payment and premium
              amortization.
```

By the maturity date, all of the premium will have been amortized.

The Effective Interest Rate Method.   *APB Opinion No. 21* recommends an amortization procedure called the **effective interest rate method,** or simply the **interest method.** Under the interest method, **interest expense for any interest period is equal to the effective (market) rate of interest on the date of issuance times the carrying value of the bonds at the beginning of that interest period.** Using the Carr example of 12% bonds with a face value of $100,000 sold to yield 14%, the carrying value at the beginning of the first interest period is the selling price of $95,233. The interest expense for the first semiannual period would be recorded as follows:

```
1995
Dec.  31  Bond Interest Expense ($95,233 × 0.14 × ½) . . . . .  6,666
              Cash ($100,000 × 0.12 × ½) . . . . . . . . . . .          6,000
              Discount on Bonds Payable . . . . . . . . . .              666
              To record discount amortization and interest
              payment.
```

Note that interest expense is the carrying value times the *effective interest rate*. The cash payment is the face value times the *contract rate*. The discount amortized for the period is the difference between the two amounts.

After the above entry, the carrying value of the bonds is $95,899, or $95,233 + $666. The balance in the Discount on Bonds Payable account was reduced by $666 to $4,101, or $4,767 − $666. Assuming the accounting year ends on December 31, the entry to record the payment of interest for the second semiannual period on June 30, 1996, is:

```
1996
June  30  Bond Interest Expense ($95,899 × 0.14 × ½) . . . . .  6,713
              Cash ($100,000 × 0.12 × ½) . . . . . . . . . . .          6,000
              Discount on Bonds Payable . . . . . . . . . .              713
              To record discount amortization and interest
              payment.
```

The effective interest rate method is also applied to premium amortization. If the Carr bonds had been issued at $105,076 to yield 10%, the premium would be $5,076. Interest expense would be calculated in the same manner as for bonds sold at a discount. However, the entry would differ somewhat, showing a debit to the premium account. The entry for the first interest period is:

```
1995
Dec. 31  Bond Interest Expense ($105,076 × 0.10 × ½) . . . . .  5,254
           Premium on Bonds Payable . . . . . . . . . . . .     746
              Cash ($100,000 × 0.12 × ½) . . . . . . . . . .           6,000
           To record interest payment and premium
           amortization.
```

After the first entry, the carrying value of the bonds is $104,330, or $105,076 − $746. The premium account now carries a balance of $4,330, or $5,076 − $746. The entry for the second interest period is:

```
1996
June 30  Bond Interest Expense ($104,330 × 0.10 × ½) . . . .  5,216*
           Premium on Bonds Payable . . . . . . . . . . . .     784
              Cash ($100,000 × 0.12 × ½) . . . . . . . . . .           6,000
           To record interest payment and premium
           amortization.

           * Rounded down.
```

Discount and Premium Amortization Schedules. A discount amortization schedule (Illustration 10.5) and a premium amortization schedule (Illustration 10.6) can be used to aid in preparing entries for interest expense. Usually, companies prepare such schedules when they first issue bonds, often using computer programs designed for this purpose. The companies then refer to the schedules whenever they make journal entries to record interest. Note that in each period the amount of interest expense changes; interest expense gets larger when a discount is involved and smaller when a premium is involved. This fluctuation occurs because the carrying value to which a constant interest rate is applied changes each interest payment date. With a discount, carrying value increases; with a premium, it decreases. However, the actual cash paid as interest is always a constant amount determined by multiplying the bond's face value by the contract rate.

Illustration 10.5
DISCOUNT AMORTIZATION SCHEDULE FOR BONDS PAYABLE

(A) Interest Payment Date	(B) Interest Expense Debit ($E \times 0.14 \times ½$)	(C) Cash Credit ($100,000 × 0.12 × ½)	(D) Discount on Bonds Payable Credit ($B − C$)	(E) Carrying Value of Bonds Payable (previous balance in $E + D$)
Issue price				$ 95,233
12/31/95	$ 6,666	$ 6,000	$ 666	95,899
6/30/96	6,713	6,000	713	96,612
12/31/96	6,763	6,000	763	97,375
6/30/97	6,816	6,000	816	98,191
12/31/97	6,873	6,000	873	99,064
6/30/98	6,936*	6,000	936	100,000
	$40,767	$36,000	$4,767	

* Includes rounding difference.

Illustration 10.6
PREMIUM AMORTIZATION SCHEDULE FOR BONDS PAYABLE

(A) Interest Payment Date	(B) Interest Expense Debit $(E \times 0.10 \times 1/2)$	(C) Cash Credit ($100,000 \times$ $0.12 \times 1/2)$	(D) Premium on Bonds Payable Debit $(C - B)$	(E) Carrying Value of Bonds Payable (previous balance in E − D)
Issue price				$105,076
12/31/95	$ 5,254	$ 6,000	$ 746	104,330
6/30/96	5,216*	6,000	784	103,546
12/31/96	5,177	6,000	823	102,723
6/30/97	5,136	6,000	864	101,859
12/31/97	5,093	6,000	907	100,952
6/30/98	5,048	6,000	952	100,000
	$30,924	$36,000	$5,076	

* Rounded down.

Recall from the earlier discussion that the issue price was $95,233 for the discount situation and $105,076 for the premium situation. Note that total interest expense of $40,767 for the discount situation in Illustration 10.5 is equal to $36,000 (which is six $6,000 payments) *plus* the $4,767 discount. This amount agrees with the earlier computation of total interest expense. In Illustration 10.6 total interest expense in the premium situation is $30,924, or $36,000 (which is six $6,000 payments) *less* the $5,076 premium. In both illustrations, at the maturity date the carrying value of the bonds is equal to the face value because the discount or premium has been fully amortized.

Adjusting Entry for Partial Period. Illustrations 10.5 and 10.6 can be used to obtain amounts needed if Carr must accrue interest for a partial period. Instead of a calendar-year accounting period, assume the fiscal year of the bond issuer ends on August 31. Using the information provided in the premium amortization schedule (Illustration 10.6), the adjusting entry needed on August 31, 1995, is:

```
1995
Aug. 31   Bond Interest Expense ($5,254 × 2/6) . . . . . . . . .   1,751
              Premium on Bonds Payable ($746 × 2/6). . . . . . . .    249
              Bond Interest Payable ($6,000 × 2/6). . . . . . . .            2,000
          To record two months' accrued interest.
```

This entry records interest for two months, July and August, of the six-month interest period ending on December 31, 1995. The first line of Illustration 10.5 shows the interest expense and premium amortization for the six months. The above entry thus records two sixths (or one third) of the amounts for this six-month period. The remaining four months' interest is recorded when the first payment is made on December 31, 1995. That entry reads:

```
1995
Dec. 31  Bond Interest Payable . . . . . . . . . . . . . . .  2,000
         Bond Interest Expense ($5,254 × 4/6) . . . . . . . . .  3,503
         Premium on Bonds Payable ($746 × 4/6) . . . . . . . .   497
              Cash . . . . . . . . . . . . . . . . . . . . .          6,000
              To record four months' interest expense and
              semiannual interest payment.
```

Similar entries for August 31 and December 31 will be made in the remaining years in the life of the bonds. The amounts will differ, however, because the interest method of accounting for bond interest is being used. The entry for each June 30 would be as indicated in Illustration 10.6.

Redeeming Bonds Payable

Objective 9
Prepare journal entries for bond redemptions and bond conversions

Bonds may be (1) paid at maturity, (2) called, or (3) purchased in the market and retired. Each action is referred to as redemption of bonds or the extinguishment of debt. If a company pays its bonds at maturity, it would have already amortized any related discount or premium. The only entry required at maturity would debit Bonds Payable and credit Cash for the face amount of the bonds as follows:

```
1998
June 30  Bonds Payable . . . . . . . . . . . . . . . . .  100,000
             Cash . . . . . . . . . . . . . . . . . . . . .          100,000
             To pay bonds on maturity date.
```

An issuer may redeem some or all of its outstanding bonds before maturity by calling them. Or bonds may be purchased in the market and retired. In either case, the accounting is the same. Assume that on January 1, 1997, Carr calls bonds totaling $10,000 of the $100,000 face value bonds in Illustration 10.6 at 103, or $10,300. Accrued interest, if any, will be added to the price. In this example, however, assume that the interest due on this date has been paid. A look at the last column on the line dated 12/31/96 in Illustration 10.6 reveals that the carrying value of the bonds is $102,723, which consists of Bonds Payable of $100,000 and Premium on Bonds Payable of $2,723. Since 10% of the bond issue is being redeemed, 10% must be removed from each of these two accounts. A loss is incurred for the excess of the price paid for the bonds, $10,300, over their carrying value, $10,272. The required entry is:

```
1997
Jan. 1  Bonds Payable . . . . . . . . . . . . . . . . . .  10,000
        Premium on Bonds Payable ($2,723 ÷ 10) . . . . . .    272
        Loss on Bond Redemption ($10,272 − $10,300) . . .     28
             Cash . . . . . . . . . . . . . . . . . . . . .          10,300
             To record bonds redeemed.
```

According to *FASB Statement No. 4,* gains and losses from *voluntary early* retirement of bonds are extraordinary items, if material. Such gains and losses are reported in the income statement, net of their tax effects, as described in Chapter 9.

Serial Bonds

To avoid the burden of redeeming an entire bond issue at one time, **serial bonds** may be issued that mature over several dates. Assume that on June 30, 1990, Jasper Company issued $100,000 face value, 12% serial bonds at 100. Interest is payable each year on June 30 and December 31. A total of $20,000 of the bonds mature each year starting on June 30, 1995. Jasper has a calendar-year accounting period. Entries required for 1995 for interest expense and maturing debt are:

```
1995
June 30   Bond Interest Expense ($100,000 × 0.12 × ½). . . .   6,000
              Cash . . . . . . . . . . . . . . . . . . . .            6,000
          To record interest payment.

      30   Serial Bonds Payable . . . . . . . . . . . . . .  20,000
              Cash . . . . . . . . . . . . . . . . . . . .           20,000
          To record retirement of serial debt.

Dec. 31   Bond Interest Expense ($80,000 × 0.12 × ½) . . . .   4,800
              Cash . . . . . . . . . . . . . . . . . . . .            4,800
          To record payment of semiannual interest
          expense.
```

Note that interest expense for the last six months of 1995 is calculated only on the remaining outstanding debt ($100,000 original issue less the $20,000 that matured on June 30, 1995). Each year after the amount of bonds maturing that year is retired, interest expense decreases proportionately. The $20,000 amount maturing the next year is reported as a current liability on each year-end balance sheet. The remaining debt is a long-term liability.

Bond Redemption or Sinking Funds

Bond investors are naturally concerned about the safety of their investments. They fear the company may default on paying the entire principal at the maturity date. This concern has led to the inclusion of provisions in some bond indentures that require companies to make periodic payments to a **bond redemption fund,** often called a **sinking fund.** These payments are used by the fund trustee (usually a bank) to redeem a stated amount of bonds annually and pay the accrued bond interest. The trustee determines which bonds are to be called and uses the cash deposited in the fund only to redeem these bonds and pay their accrued interest.

To illustrate, assume Hand Company has 12% coupon bonds outstanding that pay interest on March 31 and September 30 and were issued at face value. The bond indenture requires that Hand pay a trustee the sum of $53,000 each September 30. The trustee is to use the funds to call $50,000 of

Hand's bonds (assuming no call premium) and to pay $3,000 accrued interest on bonds called. The entry for the payment to the trustee is:

```
Sept. 30  Sinking Fund . . . . . . . . . . . . . . . . . . .   53,000
              Cash . . . . . . . . . . . . . . . . . . . .              53,000
              To record payment to trustee of required deposit.
```

The trustee calls $50,000 of bonds, pays for the bonds and accrued interest, and notifies Hand. The trustee also bills Hand for its fee and expenses incurred of $325. Assuming no interest has been recorded on these bonds for the period ended September 30, the entries are:

```
Sept. 30  Bonds Payable . . . . . . . . . . . . . . . . .   50,000
          Bond Interest Expense. . . . . . . . . . . . . .    3,000
              Sinking Fund . . . . . . . . . . . . . . . .              53,000
              To record bond redemption and interest paid by
              trustee.

       30  Sinking Fund Expense. . . . . . . . . . . . . .      325
              Cash . . . . . . . . . . . . . . . . . . . .                 325
              To record trustee fee and expenses.
```

If a balance exists in the Sinking Fund account at year-end, it is included in a category labeled "Investments" or "Other Assets" on the balance sheet. The $50,000 of bonds that must be retired during the coming year usually is described as "Current maturity of long-term debt" and reported as a current liability on the balance sheet.

The existence of a sinking fund does not necessarily mean that the company has created a retained earnings appropriation entitled "Appropriation for Bonded Indebtedness." A sinking fund usually is contractual (required by the bond indenture), and an appropriation of retained earnings is simply an announcement by the board of directors that dividend payments will be limited over the term of the bonds. The former requires cash to be paid in to a trustee, and the latter is a restriction of retained earnings available for dividends to owners. Also, even if the indenture does not require a sinking fund, the corporation may decide to (1) pay into a sinking fund and not appropriate retained earnings, (2) appropriate retained earnings and not pay into a sinking fund, (3) do neither, or (4) do both.

Convertible Bonds

A company may add to the attractiveness of its bonds by giving the bond-holders the option to *convert* the bonds to shares of the issuer's common stock. The conversions of *convertible bonds* are accounted for by treating the carrying value of bonds surrendered as the capital contributed for shares issued.

Suppose a company has $10,000 face value of bonds outstanding. Each $1,000 bond is convertible into 50 shares of the issuer's $10 par value common stock. On May 1, when the carrying value of the bonds was $9,800, all of the bonds were presented for conversion. The entry required is:

May 1 Bonds Payable 10,000
              Discount on Bonds Payable   200
              Common Stock ($10,000 ÷ $1,000 = 10 bonds;
                  10 bonds × 50 shares × $10 par).   5,000
              Paid-In Capital in Excess of Par Value—Common .   4,800
          To record bonds converted to common stock.

The entry eliminates the $9,800 book value of the bonds from the accounts by debiting Bonds Payable for $10,000 and crediting Discount on Bonds Payable for $200. Common Stock is credited for the par value of the 500 shares issued (500 shares × $10 par). The excess amount ($4,800) is credited to Paid-In Capital in Excess of Par Value—Common.

BOND INVESTMENTS

*Objective 10
Prepare journal
entries for bond
investments*

Companies may purchase bonds as either short- or long-term investments. Usually, companies make short-term investments in bonds to earn income on what might otherwise be idle cash. These investments may yield a higher return than other available alternatives. Long-term investments in bonds are usually made for reasons other than a return on idle cash. Sometimes companies invest on a long-term basis in other companies to guarantee needed raw materials; or, a company could become a dealer or distributor of another company's products. In any event, the most common reason for long-term investments is to establish a long-term relationship between two companies.

When short-term bond investments are marketable (readily salable), accountants consider them as a temporary use of cash available for operations and report them as current assets. Long-term investments are reported in the investments section of the balance sheet below current assets, whether they are marketable or not.

To aid in assessing the risk of various bond investments, the evaluations of bond rating services may be used. The two leading bond rating services are Moody's Investors Service and Standard & Poor's Corporation. The ratings used by these services are:

	Moody's	Standard & Poor's
Highest quality to upper medium	Aaa	AAA
	Aa	AA
	A	A
Medium to speculative	Baa	BBB
	Ba	BB
	B	B
Poor to lowest quality	Caa	CCC
	Ca	CC
	C	C
In default, value is questionable		DDD
		DD
		D

Junk bonds are normally rated at Ba (Moody's) and BB (Standard & Poor's) or below. As a company's prospects change over time, the ratings of its outstanding bonds will normally change because of the higher or lower probability that the company can pay the interest and principal on the bonds when due. A severe recession may cause many companies' bond ratings to decline.

Bond prices are quoted in certain newspapers. For instance, Citicorp's bonds were recently quoted as follows in *The Wall Street Journal:*

Issue (Rating: Moody's/S&P)	Coupon	Maturity	Price	Change	Yield	Change
Citicorp (Baa/A)	9.000	04/15/99	80.799	0.010	12.800	unch

The information indicates that the bonds are rated Baa by Moody's and A by Standard & Poor's. Thus, the two rating services differ slightly as to the risk of the bonds. The bonds carry a coupon rate of 9%. The bonds mature on April 15, 1999. The current price is $80.799 per hundred, or $807.99 for a $1,000 bond. The price the preceding day was $80.789, since the change was 0.010, or 80.799 compared to 80.789. The current price yields a return to investors of 12.8%, which is unchanged from the preceding day because the change in price was so small. As the market rate of interest changes from day to day, the market price of the bonds varies inversely. Thus, if the market rate of interest declines, the market price of bonds increases, and vice versa.

Short-Term Bond Investments

Short-term bond investments are recorded in a single account at cost, which includes the price paid for the bonds and often includes a broker's commission. These investments are listed among the current assets on the balance sheet. As explained earlier, if investors purchase bonds between interest dates, they pay the accrued interest and collect the amount paid later when they receive the semiannual interest. **Premiums and discounts on short-term bond investments are not amortized because the length of time the bonds will be held is not known.**

To illustrate, assume that on May 31, 1995, Bay Company purchased as a short-term investment $10,000 face value, 12% bonds of Ace Company at 102, plus $100 of accrued interest from April 30. A $70 broker's commission was also paid. The entry required is:

```
1995
May  31  Temporary Investments (or Marketable Securities)
             ($10,200 + $70) . . . . . . . . . . . . . . . . . .   10,270
         Bond Interest Receivable ($10,000 × 0.12 × 1/12). . .       100
             Cash . . . . . . . . . . . . . . . . . . . . . . .              10,370
         To record bonds purchased.
```

On September 30, 1995, Bay sold the Ace bonds at 103.5, plus accrued interest of $500. A $70 broker's commission was charged on the sale. Before computing the gain or loss on the sale, the broker's commission is deducted from selling price to compute net proceeds to the seller ($10,350 − $70 = $10,280). The gain or loss is the difference between net proceeds and cost. In this example, the gain is $10, or $10,280 − $10,270. Note that accrued interest does not affect the amount of gain or loss because it is paid for by the purchaser. The entry to record the sale is:

```
1995
Sept. 30   Cash ($10,350 + $500 − $70) . . . . . . . . . .   10,780
              Temporary Investments . . . . . . . . . .            10,270
              Bond Interest Receivable (from above entry) .           100
              Bond Interest Revenue ($10,000 × 0.12 × 4/12)          400
              Gain on Sale of Temporary Investments  . . .            10
           To record sale of temporary investments.
```

The purchaser will receive the semiannual interest check from Ace to cover the $500 of accrued interest paid to Bay. Bay records only $400 of the $500 of interest received as interest revenue, since it held the bonds for only four months.

Long-Term Bond Investments

Long-term investments in bonds also are recorded in a single account at cost, which includes any premium or discount. These investments are listed in an "Investments" category among the assets on the balance sheet. A premium or discount on long-term bond investments is amortized, although it is not recorded in a separate account by the investing company as it is by the issuing company.

Bonds Purchased at a Discount.   Assume that on June 30, 1995, Mann Company purchased as a long-term investment $100,000 face value of Carr Company's 12% bonds for $95,233 (including broker's commission), a price that yields 14%. These bonds are the same Carr Company bonds that were described in Illustration 10.5. The entry to record the purchase is:

```
1995
June 30   Bond Investments . . . . . . . . . . . . . . . .   95,233
              Cash . . . . . . . . . . . . . . . . . . . .            95,233
           To record bonds purchased at a discount.
```

Note that the debit to the Bond Investments account included the broker's commission paid to acquire the bonds.

Since Mann intends to hold the bonds to maturity, the discount is amortized over the remaining life of the bonds. Although either the straight-line method or the interest method could be used to amortize the discount, we are using the interest method. Under this method, interest revenue on bonds purchased by Mann is computed in the same manner as the issuer's interest expense—the bond price is multiplied by the effective interest rate per period. To compute Mann's discount amortization, we can use a similar procedure to that used for Carr—compute the difference between interest revenue (expense) and cash received (paid). The first period's interest revenue is

$6,666, or $95,233 × 0.14 × ½. The cash received is $6,000, or $100,000 × 0.12 × ½. The discount amortized is $666, or $6,666 − $6,000. If Mann has a calendar-year accounting period, the required adjusting entry is:

```
1995
Dec. 31  Cash . . . . . . . . . . . . . . . . . . . . . . . .   6,000
             Bond Investments . . . . . . . . . . . . . . . . .     666
                 Bond Interest Revenue . . . . . . . . . . . . .            6,666
             To record accrued bond interest revenue.
```

Note that in the entry, the amount added to the Bond Investments account is equal to the discount amortized on the issuer's books. The discount is amortized even though it is not set up in a separate account on the investor's books. The original discount is $4,767, and this amount must be included in bond interest revenue on Mann's books during the life of the bonds. Illustration 10.7 shows how the $4,767 is added to periodic interest revenue and to Bond Investments. The debits gradually increase the Bond Investments account balance to the face value of $100,000 by the maturity date.

Mann's December 31, 1995, balance sheet would show Bond Investments of $95,899. If Mann's fiscal year ended on November 30, the adjusting entry on that date would be the same as the December 31 entry, except all amounts would be five sixths of the December 31 amounts and Bond Interest Receivable instead of Cash would be debited.

If the straight-line method were used, discount amortization would be $794.50 per period, or $4,767/6. Bond interest revenue would be $6,794.50, or $6,000 + $794.50.

Bonds Purchased at a Premium.   To illustrate accounting for bonds purchased at a premium, assume that on June 30, 1995, Ladd Company paid $105,076 for $100,000 face value of 12% bonds, a price that yields 10%. Ladd

Illustration 10.7
DISCOUNT AMORTIZATION SCHEDULE FOR BOND INVESTMENTS

(A) Interest Payment Date	(B) Cash Debit ($100,000 × 0.12 × ½)	(C) Bond Interest Revenue Credit (E × 0.14 × ½)	(D) Bond Investments Debit (C − B)	(E) Carrying Value of Bond Investments (previous balance in E + D)
Purchase price				$ 95,233
12/31/95	$ 6,000	$ 6,666	$ 666	95,899
6/30/96	6,000	6,713	713	96,612
12/31/96	6,000	6,763	763	97,375
6/30/97	6,000	6,816	816	98,191
12/31/97	6,000	6,873	873	99,064
6/30/98	6,000	6,936*	936	100,000
	$36,000	$40,767	$4,767	

* Includes rounding difference.

has a calendar-year accounting period. These bonds are the Carr Company bonds shown in Illustration 10.6. The entry to record the purchase would be:

```
1995
June 30  Bond Investments . . . . . . . . . . . . . . .  105,076
              Cash . . . . . . . . . . . . . . . . .           105,076
         To record bonds purchased at a premium.
```

Here again, interest revenue for the first interest period can be computed by multiplying the purchase price by the effective rate: $105,076 \times 0.10 \times \frac{1}{2} = \$5,254$. The entry to record the $5,254 is:

```
1995
Dec. 31  Cash . . . . . . . . . . . . . . . . . . . . . . .  6,000
              Bond Investments . . . . . . . . . . . . . .         746
              Bond Interest Revenue . . . . . . . . . . . .       5,254
         To record bond interest revenue received.
```

The premium is amortized by crediting the Bond Investments account. If bonds are held to maturity, the balance in the Bond Investments account would be gradually decreased to the maturity value of $100,000, as shown in Illustration 10.8. Bond interest revenue for the second six months can be read from Illustration 10.7, or it can be computed: $(\$105,076 - \$746) \times 0.10 \times \frac{1}{2} = \$5,216$.

If we used the straight-line method, the periodic amortization of the premium would be $846, or $5,076 ÷ 6. Interest revenue would be a constant semiannual $5,154, or $6,000 − $846.

Sale of Bond Investments

When a company sells its bond investments, usually a gain or loss must be recorded. The difference between the price received and the carrying value

Illustration 10.8
PREMIUM AMORTIZATION SCHEDULE FOR BOND INVESTMENTS

(A) Interest Payment Date	(B) Cash Debit ($100,000 × 0.12 × ½)	(C) Bond Interest Revenue Credit (E × 0.10 × ½)	(D) Bond Investments Credit (B − C)	(E) Carrying Value of Bond Investments (previous balance in E − D)
Purchase price.				$105,076
12/31/95	$ 6,000	$ 5,254	$ 746	104,330
6/30/96	6,000	5,216*	784	103,546
12/31/96	6,000	5,177	823	102,723
6/30/97	6,000	5,136	864	101,859
12/31/97	6,000	5,093	907	100,952
6/30/98	6,000	5,048	952	100,000
	$36,000	$30,924	$5,076	

* Rounded down.

ETHICS   A CLOSER LOOK

Jack and Jim Esterly inherited 600,000 shares (40%) of the common stock of the Esterly Clothing Company from their father, who had founded the company 43 years earlier. Jack now serves as president of the company, and Jim serves as vice president and treasurer. The company produces a line of fine clothing that is sold nationwide and earns an average of $8,000,000 per year. Located in New Haven, Connecticut, the company has provided steady employment for approximately 20% of the city's population. The city has benefited from the revenues the company attracted to the area and from the generous gifts provided by the father.

The remainder of the common stock is widely held and is traded in the over-the-counter market. No other stockholder holds more than 4% of the stock. The stock has recently traded at $40 per share. The company has $20,000,000 of 10% bonds outstanding, which mature in 15 years.

The brothers do not enjoy the work. They also are frustrated by the fact that they do not own a controlling interest (more than 50%) of the company and cannot always impose their will. The other members of the board of directors sometimes vote against actions the brothers want to take. If they had a controlling interest, they could make important decisions without obtaining the agreement of the other members of the board of directors.

With the assistance of a New York City brokerage house, the brothers decided to pursue a plan that could increase their wealth. The company would offer to buy back a certain number of shares of common stock at $50 per share. These shares would then be canceled, and the brothers would have controlling interest. Some of the other board members went along with this plan because they wanted to sell their own shares at a profit.

The stock buy-back would be financed by issuing 10-year, 18%, high-interest bonds (called *junk bonds*). The brokerage house has located some financial institutions that would be willing to buy the bonds. The interest payments on the junk bonds would be $3,000,000 per year. The brothers thought the company could make these payments if the country soon pulled out of the recession. If need be, wages could be reduced under the threat of closing the plant or the company's pension plan could be terminated.

If the junk bonds could be paid at maturity, the brothers would own a controlling interest in what could be an extremely valuable company. If the interest payments cannot be met or if the junk bonds are defaulted at maturity, the company could eventually be forced to liquidate. The risks are high, but so are the potential rewards.

If another party entered the picture at this point and bid an even higher amount for the stock, the brothers could sell their shares and exit the company. The brothers hoped that another buyer might bid as much as $60 per share so they could sell their shares and pursue other interests. The changes a new buyer might make are unpredictable at this point.

Required
a.   What motivates the brothers to pursue this new strategy?
b.   Are the brothers the only ones assuming the risks?
c.   How will workers, the city, the holders of the original bond issue, and the other present stockholders be affected if the junk bonds are issued and are then defaulted?
d.   How might these parties (stakeholders) be affected if a new buyer outbids the management?
e.   What ethical considerations are involved?

of the bonds on the date they are sold determines whether the bonds are sold at a gain or a loss. Suppose that on June 30, 1997, Ladd Company sold all of its bonds, which had a carrying value of $101,859 (Illustration 10.8), for $102,500 less a $500 broker's commission. The required entry is:

```
1997
June 30  Cash . . . . . . . . . . . . . . . . . . . . . .   102,000
             Bond Investments . . . . . . . . . . . . .               101,859
             Gain on Sale of Bond Investments . . . . . .                  141
             To record sale of bond investments.
```

Since the bond sale occurred on an interest payment date, the payment of interest had already been recorded, and no accrued interest existed. Ladd's gain (or loss, if one had occurred) on the sale is reported on the income statement as a nonoperating item, not as an extraordinary item.

Valuation of Bond Investments

Short-term bond investments are reported at cost (or sometimes at lower-of-cost-or-market). Long-term bond investments are reported at amortized cost. Amortized cost is equal to acquisition cost plus discount amortized or less premium amortized. An exception exists when a substantial, permanent decline in market value occurs. Long-term bond investments are then written down by debiting an account called Loss on Market Decline of Bond Investments and crediting Bond Investments.

Once long-term bond investments have been written down, traditional accounting conservatism dictates that they may not be written up, not even to their original cost, if market price recovers. The written down amount serves as the basis for computing gain or loss when the bonds are sold.

Chapter 11 discusses accounting theory and international accounting. Both of these topics are vital to acquiring a strong background in accounting.

UNDERSTANDING THE LEARNING OBJECTIVES

1. Account for notes receivable and payable, including calculation of interest.
    *   A promissory note is an unconditional written promise by a borrower (maker) to pay the lender (payee) or someone else who legally acquired the note a certain sum of money on demand or at a definite time.
    *   Interest is the fee charged for the use of money through time. Interest = Principal × Rate of interest × Time.
    *   Companies sometimes need short-term financing. Short-term financing may be secured by issuing interest-bearing notes or by issuing noninterest-bearing notes.
    *   An interest-bearing note specifies the interest rate that will be charged on the principal borrowed.

- A noninterest-bearing note does not have a stated interest rate applied to the face value of the note.

2. Record the discounting of notes receivable.
   - The cash proceeds are computed by determining the maturity value of the note, the discount period, and the amount of the discount charged by the bank. The bank discount is deducted from the maturity value to find the cash proceeds.

3. Describe the features of bonds and tell how bonds differ from shares of stock.
   - A bond is a liability (with a maturity date) that bears interest that is deductible in computing both net income and taxable income.
   - A stock is a unit of ownership on which a dividend is paid only if declared, and dividends are not deductible in determining net income or taxable income.
   - Bonds may be secured or unsecured, registered or unregistered, callable, and/or convertible.

4. List the advantages and disadvantages of financing with long-term debt and prepare examples showing how financial leverage is employed.
   - Advantages include stockholders retaining control of the company, tax deductibility of interest, and possible creation of favorable financial leverage.
   - Disadvantages include having to make a fixed interest payment each period, reduction in a company's ability to withstand a major loss, possible limitations on dividends and future borrowings, and possible reduction in earnings per share caused by unfavorable financial leverage.

5. Prepare journal entries for bonds issued at face value.
   - If bonds are issued at face value on an interest date, no accrued interest is recorded.
   - If bonds are issued between interest dates, accrued interest must be recorded.

6. Explain how interest rates affect bond prices and what causes a bond to sell at a premium or discount.
   - If the market rate is lower than the contract rate, the bonds will sell for more than their face value, and a premium will be recorded.
   - If the market rate is higher than the contract rate, the bonds will sell for less than their face value, and a discount will be recorded.

7. Apply the concept of present value to compute the price of a bond.
   - The present value of the principal plus the present value of the interest payments is equal to the price of the bond.
   - The contract rate of interest is used to determine the amount of future cash interest payments.
   - The effective rate of interest is used to discount the future payment of principal and of interest back to the present value.

8. Prepare journal entries for bonds issued at a discount or premium.
   - When bonds are issued, Cash is debited, and Bonds Payable is credited. If the bonds were issued at a discount, Discount on Bonds Payable is also debited. If the bonds were issued at a premium, Premium on Bonds Payable is also credited. If the bonds are issued between interest dates, Bond Interest Payable is also credited.
   - Any premium or discount must be amortized over the period the bonds are outstanding.
   - Under the effective interest rate method, interest expense for any period is equal to the effective (market) rate of interest at date of issuance times the carrying value of the bond at the beginning of that interest period.
   - Under the straight-line method of amortization, an equal amount of discount or premium is allocated to each month the bonds are outstanding.

9. Prepare journal entries for bond redemptions and bond conversions.
   - When bonds are redeemed before they mature, a loss or gain (an extraordinary item, if material) on bond redemption may occur.
   - A bond sinking fund might be required in the bond indenture.
   - Bonds may be convertible into shares of stock. The carrying value of the bonds is considered to be the capital contributed for shares of stock issued.

10. Prepare journal entries for bond investments.
    - When bonds are purchased as a long-term investment, Bond Investments is debited, and Cash is credited.
    - Premiums and discounts on short-term bond investments are not amortized because the length of time the bonds will be held is not known.
    - Premiums or discounts on bond investments are not recorded in a separate account. Instead, they affect the amount recorded in the Bond Investments account.
    - Premiums and discounts on long-term bond investments are amortized in a manner similar to that used for bonds payable.

11. Explain future value and present value concepts and make the required calculations (appendix).
    - The future value of an investment is the amount to which a sum of money invested today will grow in a stated time period at a specified interest rate.
    - Present value is the current worth of a future cash receipt and is the reciprocal of future value. To discount future receipts is to bring them back to their present values.

APPENDIX

FUTURE VALUE AND PRESENT VALUE

Objective 11
Explain future
value and present
value concepts
and make required
calculations

The concepts of interest, future value, and present value are widely applied in business decision making. Therefore, accountants need to understand these concepts to properly record certain business transactions.

The Time Value of Money

The concept of the time value of money stems from the logical preference for a dollar today rather than a dollar at any future date. Most individuals would prefer having a dollar today rather than at some future date because (1) the risk exists that the future dollar will never be received; and (2) if the dollar is on hand now, it can be invested, resulting in an increase in total dollars possessed at that future date.

Most business decisions involve a comparison of cash flows in and out of the company. To be useful in decision making, such comparisons must be in terms of dollars of the same point in time. That is, the dollars held now must be accumulated or rolled forward, or future dollars must be discounted or brought back to the present before comparisons are valid. Such comparisons involve future value and present value concepts.

Future Value

The **future value or worth** of any investment is the amount to which a sum of money invested today will grow in a stated time period at a specified interest rate. The interest involved may be simple interest or compound interest. **Simple interest** is interest on principal only. For example, $1,000 invested today for two years at 12% simple interest will grow to $1,240 since interest is $120 per year. The principal of $1,000, plus 2 × $120, is equal to $1,240. **Compound interest** is interest on principal *and* on interest of prior periods. For example, $1,000 invested for two years at 12% compounded annually will grow to $1,254.40 as shown below.

Principal or present value	$1,000.00
Interest, year 1 = $1,000 × 0.12 =	120.00
Value at end of year 1	$1,120.00
Interest, year 2 = $1,120 × 0.12 =	134.40
Value at end of year 2 (future value)	$1,254.40

Illustration 10.9 graphically portrays these computations of future worth and shows how $1,000 grows to $1,254.40 with a 12% interest rate compounded annually. The effect of compounding is $14.40—the interest in the second year that was based on the interest computed for the first year, or $120 × 0.12 = $14.40.

Illustration 10.9
COMPOUND INTEREST AND FUTURE VALUE

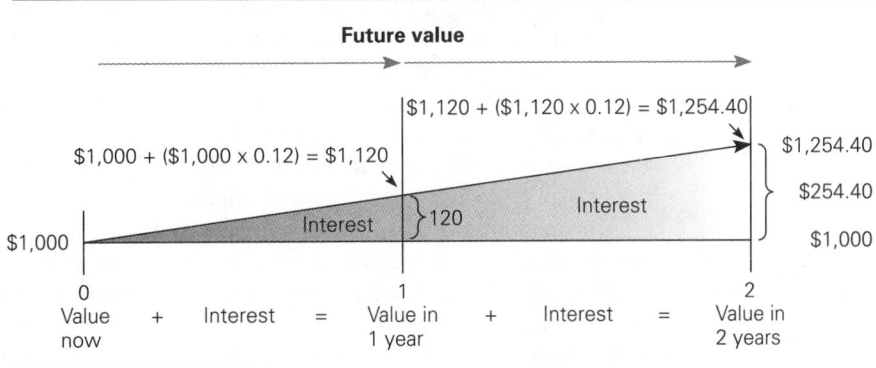

The task of computing the future worth to which any invested amount will grow at a given rate for a stated period is aided by the use of interest tables. An example is Table E.1 in Appendix E at the end of this text. To use the Appendix E tables, first determine the number of compounding periods involved. A compounding period may be any length of time, such as a day, a month, a quarter, a half-year, or a year, but normally not more than a year. The number of compounding periods is equal to the number of years in the life of the investment times the number of compoundings per year. Five years compounded annually is five periods, five years compounded quarterly is 20 periods, and so on.

Next, determine the interest rate per compounding period. Interest rates are usually quoted in annual terms; in fact, federal law requires statement of the interest rate in annual terms in some situations. Divide the annual rate by the number of compounding periods per year to get the proper rate per period. Only with an annual compounding will the annual rate be the rate per period. All other cases involve a lower rate. For example, if the annual rate is 12% and interest is compounded monthly, the rate per period (one month) will be 1%.

To use the tables, find the number of periods involved in the Period column. Move across the table to the right, stopping in the column headed by the Interest Rate per Period, which yields a number called a *factor*. **The factor shows the amount to which an investment of $1 will grow for the periods and the rate involved.** To compute future worth of the investment, multiply the number of dollars in the given situation by this factor. For example, suppose your parents tell you that they will invest $8,000 at 12% for four years and give you the amount to which this investment grows if you graduate from college in four years. How much will you receive at the end of four years if the interest rate is 12% compounded annually? How much will you receive if the interest rate is 12% compounded quarterly?

To calculate these amounts, look at Appendix E, Table E.1. In the intersection of the 4 period row and the 12% column, you find the factor 1.57352. Multiplying this factor by $8,000 yields $12,588.16, the answer to the first question. To answer the second question, look at the intersection of the 16 period row and the 3% column. The factor is 1.60471, and the value of your investment is $12,837.68. The more frequent compounding would add $12,837.68 − $12,588.16 = $249.52 to the value of your investment. The reason for this difference in amounts is that 12% compounded quarterly is a higher rate than 12% compounded annually.

Future Value of an Annuity.   An **annuity** is a series of equal cash flows (often called *rents*) spaced equally in time. The semiannual interest payments received on a bond investment are a common example of an annuity. Assume that $100 will be received at the end of each of the next three semiannual periods. The interest rate is 6% per semiannual period. It is possible, using Table E.1, to find the future value of each of the $100 receipts as follows:

```
Future value (after three periods) of $100 re-
  ceived at the end of the—
  First period:     1.12360 × $100 = $112.36
  Second period: 1.06000 ×   100 =  106.00
  Third period:   1.00000 ×   100 =  100.00
Total future value  . . . . . . .  $318.36
```

Such a procedure would become quite tedious if the annuity consisted of many receipts. Fortunately, tables are available to calculate the total future value directly. See Appendix E, Table E.2. For the annuity described above, one single factor can be identified by looking at the 3 period row and 6% column. The factor is 3.18360, and when multiplied by $100, yields $318.36, which is the same answer as above. Illustration 10.10 graphically presents the future value of an annuity.

Illustration 10.10
FUTURE VALUE OF AN ANNUITY

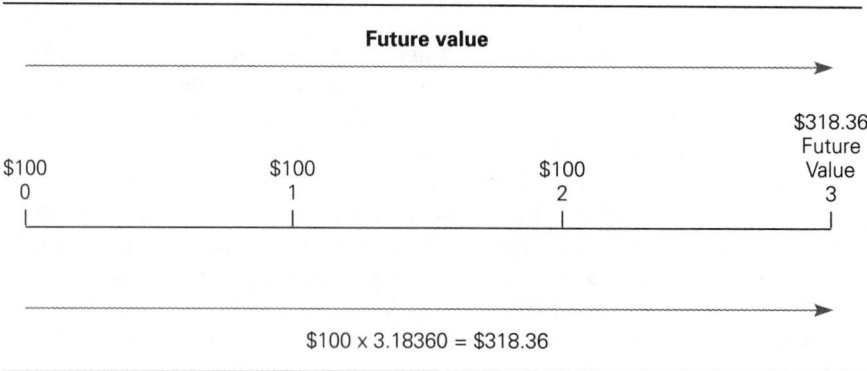

$100 × 3.18360 = $318.36

Present Value

Present value is the current worth of a future cash receipt and is the reciprocal of future value. In future value, a sum of money is possessed now, and its future value must be calculated. In present value, rights to future cash receipts are possessed now, and their current worth is to be calculated. Future cash receipts are discounted to find their present values. **To discount future receipts is to bring them back to their present values.**

Assume that you have the right to receive $1,000 in one year. If the appropriate interest rate is 12% compounded annually, what is the present value of this $1,000 future cash receipt? You know that the present value is less than $1,000 because $1,000 due in one year is not worth $1,000 today. You also know that the $1,000 due in one year is equal to some amount, P, plus interest on P at 12% for one year. Thus, $P + 0.12P = \$1,000$, or $1.12P = \$1,000$. Dividing $1,000 by 1.12, you get $892.86; this amount is the present value of your future $1,000. If the $1,000 was due in two years, you would find its present value by dividing $892.86 by 1.12, which equals $797.20. Portrayed graphically, present value looks similar to future value, except for the direction of the arrows (Illustration 10.11).

Table E.3 (Appendix E) contains present value factors for combinations of a number of periods and interest rates. Table E.3 is used in the same manner as Table E.1. For example, the present value of $1,000 due in four years at 16% compounded annually is $552.29, computed as $1,000 × 0.55229. The 0.55229 is the present value factor found in the intersection of the 4 period row and the 16% column.

As another example, suppose that you wish to have $4,000 in three years to pay for a vacation in Europe. If your investment will increase at a 20% rate compounded quarterly, how much should you invest now? To find the amount, you would use the present value factor found in Appendix E, Table E.3, 12 period row, 5% column. This factor is 0.55684, which means that an investment of about 55½ cents today would grow to $1 in 12 periods at 5%

Illustration 10.11
COMPOUND INTEREST AND PRESENT VALUE

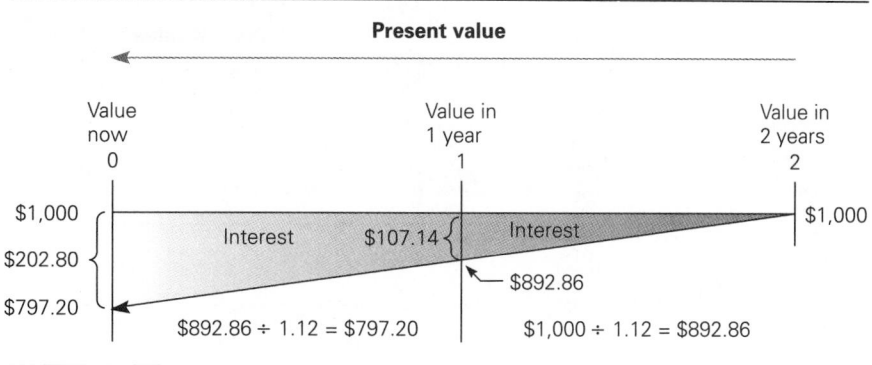

Present value

per period. To have $4,000 at the end of three years, you must invest $4,000 times this factor (0.55684), or $2,227.36.

Present Value of an Annuity.   The semiannual interest payments on a bond are a common example of an annuity. An illustration will be used to show how to calculate the present value of an annuity. Assume that $100 will be received at the end of each of the next three semiannual periods. The interest rate is 6% per semiannual period. By using Table E.3 (Appendix E), you can find the present value of each of the three $100 payments as follows:

Present value of $100 due in:	
1 period: 0.94340 × $100 =	$ 94.34
2 periods: 0.89000 × 100 =	89.00
3 periods: 0.83962 × 100 =	83.96
Total present value	$267.30

Such a procedure could become quite tedious if the annuity consisted of a large number of payments. Fortunately, tables are also available showing the present values of an annuity of $1 per period for varying interest rates and periods. See Appendix E, Table E.4. For the annuity described above, a single factor can be obtained from the table to represent the present value of an annuity of $1 per period for three (semiannual) periods at 6% per (semiannual) period. This factor is 2.67301; it is equal to the sum of the present value factors for $1 due in one period, $1 in two periods, and $1 in three periods found in Appendix E, Table E.3. When this factor is multiplied by $100, the number of dollars in each payment, it yields the present value of the annuity, $267.30. Illustration 10.12 graphically presents the present value of this annuity and shows that we find the present value of the three $100 cash flows by multiplying the $100 by a present value of an annuity factor, 2.67301.

Suppose you won a prize in a lottery that awarded you your choice of receiving $10,000 at the end of each of the next five years or $35,000 cash

Illustration 10.12
PRESENT VALUE OF AN ANNUITY

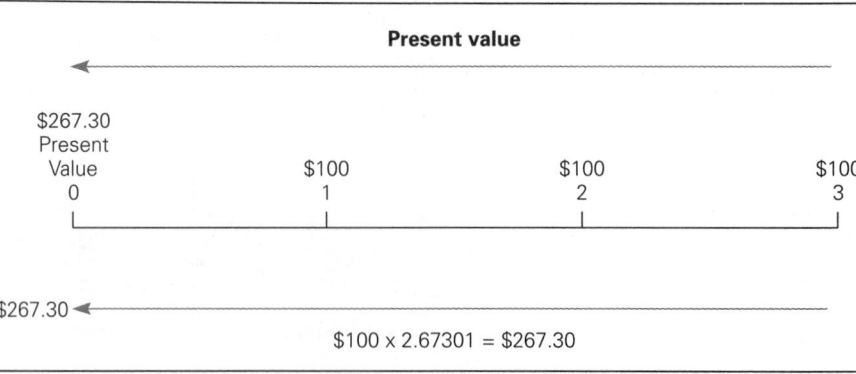

today. You believe you can earn interest on invested cash at 15% per year. Which option should you choose? To answer the question, you should compute the present value of an annuity of $10,000 per period for five years at 15%. The present value is $33,521.60, or $10,000 × 3.35216. You should accept the immediate payment of $35,000 since it has the larger present value.

The future and present value concepts presented in this appendix will be useful as you study capital budgeting in Chapter 20 and will be applicable in many of your other courses.

DEMONSTRATION PROBLEM 10–A

a. Prepare the entries on the books of Cromwell Company assuming the company borrowed $10,000 at 7% from First National Bank and signed a 60-day noninterest-bearing note payable on December 1, 1994, accrued interest on December 31, 1994, and paid the debt on the maturity date.

b. Prepare the entries on the books of Cromwell Company assuming it purchased equipment from Jones Company for $5,000 and signed a 30-day, 9% interest-bearing note payable on February 24, 1995. The note was paid on its maturity date.

Solution to demonstration problem 10–A

a. 1994
Dec. 1   Cash 9,883.33
              Bank Discount 116.67
                   Notes Payable 10,000.00

       31   Interest Expense 58.33
               Bank Discount 58.33
               ($10,000 × 0.07 × 30/360) = $58.33

       1995
Jan. 30   Notes Payable 10,000.00
              Interest Expense 58.33
                   Bank Discount 58.33
                   Cash 10,000.00

b. 1995
Feb. 24   Purchases 5,000.00
                   Notes Payable 5,000.00

Mar. 26   Notes Payable 5,000.00
              Interest Expense 37.50
                   Cash 5,037.50
              ($5,000 × 0.09 × 30/360) = $37.50

DEMONSTRATION PROBLEM 10–B

A $22,500, 90-day, 12% note dated June 15, 1995, was received by Lyle Company from Stone Company in payment of its account.

Required:

Prepare the journal entries in the records of Lyle Company for each of the following:

a. Lyle Company received the note on June 15, 1995.

b. Lyle Company discounted the note on July 15, 1995, at 10% at Citizens National Bank.

c. Stone Company paid the note at maturity.

d. Assume that Stone Company did not pay the note at maturity. Citizens National Bank charged the note to Lyle Company and charged a protest fee of $30.

e. On September 15, Lyle Company decided that the note was uncollectible.

Solution to demonstration problem 10–B

a. 1995
June 15 Notes Receivable 22,500.00
                Accounts Receivable—Stone Company . .   22,500.00
        To record receipt of a note from Stone
        Company.

b. July 15 Cash 22,788.75
                Notes Receivable 22,500.00
                Interest Revenue 288.75
        To record the discounting of the Stone
        Company note.
        Computation of cash proceeds:
          Maturity value
            [$22,500 + ($22,500
                × 0.12 × $90/360$)] $23,175.00
          Discount = $23,175
                × 10% × $60/360$ 386.25
                                                    $22,788.75

c.   No entry.

d. Sept. 13 Accounts Receivable—Stone Company 23,205.00
                Cash 23,205.00
        To record the charge made against Lyle
        Company account for the Stone Company
        note of $22,500, interest of $675, and protest
        fee of $30.

e.   15 Allowance for Uncollectible Accounts* 23,205.00
                Accounts Receivable—Stone Company . .   23,205.00
        To write off the Stone Company note as
        uncollectible.

        * This debit assumes that notes receivable were taken into consideration when an allowance
        was established. If not, the debit should be to Loss from Dishonored Notes Receivable.

DEMONSTRATION PROBLEM 10–C

Jackson Company issued $100,000 face value of 15%, 20-year bonds on April 30, 1995. The bonds are dated April 30, 1995, call for semiannual interest payments on April 30 and October 31, and are issued to yield 16% (8% per period).

Required:

a. Compute the amount received for the bonds.

b. Prepare an amortization schedule. Enter data in the schedule for only the first two interest periods. Use the interest method.

c. Prepare journal entries to record issuance of the bonds, the first six months' interest expense on the bonds, the adjustment needed on December 31, 1995 (assuming Jackson's accounting year ends on that date), and the second six months' interest expense on April 30, 1996.

Solution to demonstration problem 10–C

a. Price received:

Present value of principal: $100,000 × 0.04603
    (see Appendix E, Table E.3, 40 period row, 8% column) . . . . $ 4,603
Present value of interest: $7,500 × 11.92461
    (see Appendix E, Table E.4, 40 period row, 8% column) 89,435

        Total $94,038

b.

(A) Interest Payment Date	(B) Bond Interest Expense Debit (E × 0.16 × ½)	(C) Cash Credit ($100,000 × 0.15 × ½)	(D) Discount on Bonds Payable Credit (B − C)	(E) Carrying Value of Bonds Payable (previous balance in E + D)
Issue price				$94,038
10/31/95	$7,523	$7,500	$23	94,061
4/30/95	7,525	7,500	25	94,086

c.

JACKSON COMPANY
GENERAL JOURNAL

1995

Apr. 30 Cash 94,038
        Discount on Bonds Payable 5,962
            Bonds Payable 100,000

        Issued $100,000 face value of 20-year, 15% bonds
        to yield 16%.

Oct. 31 Bond Interest Expense. 7,523
            Discount on Bonds Payable 23
            Cash 7,500

        Paid semiannual bond interest expense.

Dec. 31 Bond Interest Expense ($7,525 × ⅓) 2,508
            Discount on Bonds Payable 8
            Bond Interest Payable ($7,500 × ⅓) 2,500

        To record accrual of two months' interest
        expense.

1996

Apr. 30 Bond Interest Payable 2,500
        Bond Interest Expense ($7,525 × ⅔) 5,017
            Discount on Bonds Payable 17
            Cash 7,500

        Paid semiannual bond interest expense.

DEMONSTRATION PROBLEM 10–D

On May 31, 1995, Martin Company purchased $10,000 face value of 8%, 10-year bonds issued by Shane Company. The bonds mature on May 31, 2005, call for semiannual interest payments on May 31 and November 30, and were issued for cash of $8,754, a price that yields an effective rate of 10%. The bonds are considered a long-term investment by Martin Company, which has a December 31 accounting year-end.

Required:

Prepare journal entries to record the investment in the Shane bonds, to record the interest collected on November 30, 1995, and to adjust the accounts on December 31, 1995. Use the effective interest rate method.

Solution to demonstration problem 10–D

MARTIN COMPANY
GENERAL JOURNAL

1995			
May 31	Bond Investments.	8,754	
	Cash.		8,754
	To record purchase of $10,000 face value of bonds.		
Nov. 30	Cash ($10,000 × 0.08 × ½)	400	
	Bond Investments.	38	
	Bond Interest Revenue ($8,754 × 0.10 × ½)		438
	To record semiannual interest revenue.		
Dec. 31	Bond Interest Receivable ($10,000 × 0.08 × 1/12)	67	
	Bond Investments.	6	
	Bond Interest Revenue [($8,754 + $38) × 0.10 × 1/12]		73
	To accrue one month's interest revenue.		

NEW TERMS

Annuity A series of equal cash flows equally spaced in time. *556*

Bank discount The difference between the maturity value of a note and the actual amount—the note's proceeds—given to the borrower. *515, 519*

Bearer bond See Unregistered bond.

Bond A long-term debt, or liability, owed by its issuer. A **bond certificate** is a negotiable instrument and is the formal, physical evidence of the debt owed. *522*

Bond indenture The contract or loan agreement under which bonds are issued. *523*

Bond redemption (or sinking) fund A fund used to bring about gradual redemption of a bond issue. *543*

Callable bond A bond that gives the issuer the right to call (buy back) the bond before its maturity date. *526*

Call premium The price paid in excess of face value that the issuer of bonds must pay to redeem (call) bonds before their maturity date. *526*

Carrying value (of bonds)   The face value of bonds minus any unamortized discount or plus any unamortized premium. Sometimes referred to as **net liability** on the bonds when used for bonds payable. *537*

Cash proceeds   The maturity amount of a note less the bank discount. *519*

Compound interest   Interest calculated on the principal and on interest of prior periods. *554*

Contract rate of interest   The interest rate printed on the bond certificates and specified on the bond indenture; also called the **stated, coupon,** or **nominal rate.** *534*

Convertible bond   A bond that may be exchanged for shares of stock of the issuing corporation at the bondholders' option. *526*

Coupon bond   A bond not registered as to interest; it carries detachable coupons that are to be clipped and presented for payment of interest due. *526*

Debenture bond   An unsecured bond backed only by the general creditworthiness of its issuer. *525*

Discounting a note payable   The act of borrowing on a noninterest-bearing note drawn for a maturity amount, from which a bank discount is deducted, and the proceeds are given to the borrower. *515*

Discounting a note receivable   The act of selling a note receivable with recourse to a bank. *Discounting* means that the bank deducts the interest from the maturity value of the note immediately and gives the seller of the note only the proceeds. *With recourse* means that if the maker does not pay the bank at maturity, the bank can collect the maturity value from the company that discounted the note at the bank. *518*

Discount (on bonds)   Amount a bond sells for below its face value. *534*

Discount on Notes Payable   A contra account used to reduce Notes Payable from face value to the net amount of the debt. *515*

Discount period   The exact number of days from the date of sale (or discounting) of a note to the date of maturity *519*

Discount rate   The rate of interest the bank charges on a discounted note. *519*

Dishonored note   A note that the maker failed to pay at maturity. *518*

Effective interest rate method (interest method)   A procedure for calculating periodic interest expense (or revenue) in which the first period's interest is computed by multiplying the carrying value of bonds payable (bond investments) by the market rate at the issue date. The difference between computed interest expense (revenue) and the interest paid (received), based on the contract rate times face value, is the discount or premium amortized for the period. Computations for subsequent periods are based on carrying value at the beginning of the period. *539*

Face value   Principal amount of a bond. *522*

Favorable financial leverage   An increase in EPS and rate of return on stockholders' equity resulting from earning a higher rate of return on borrowed funds than the fixed cost of such funds. **Unfavorable financial leverage** results when the cost of borrowed funds exceeds the income they generate, resulting in decreased income to stockholders. *527*

Future value or worth   The amount to which a sum of money invested today will grow in a stated time period at a specified interest rate. *554*

Interest   The fee charged for use of money over a period of time (I = P × R × T). *514*

Interest method   See Effective interest rate method.

Junk bonds   High-interest rate, high-risk bonds that were issued in the 1980s to finance corporate restructurings. *526*

Maker (of a note)   The party who prepares a note and is responsible for paying the note at maturity. *514*

Market interest rate   The minimum rate of interest investors will accept on bonds of a particular risk category. Also called **effective rate** or **yield.** *534*

Maturity date   The date on which a note becomes due and must be paid. *518*

Maturity value   The amount that the maker must pay on the note on its maturity date. *519*

Mortgage   A legal claim (lien) on specific property that gives the bondholder the right to possess the pledged property if the company fails to make required payments. A bond secured by a mortgage is called a **mortgage bond.** *525*

Payee (of a note)   The party who receives a note and will be paid cash at maturity. *514*

Premium (on bonds)   Amount a bond sells for above its face value. *534*

Present value   The current worth of a future cash receipt(s); computed by discounting future receipts at a stipulated interest rate. *557*

Promissory note   An unconditional written promise by a borrower (maker) to pay a definite sum of money to the lender (payee) on demand or at a specific date. *514*

Registered bond   A bond with the owner's name on the bond certificate and in the register of bond owners kept by the bond issuer or its agent, the registrar. *525*

Secured bond   A bond for which a company has pledged specific property to ensure its payment. *525*

Serial bonds   Bonds in a given bond issue with maturities spread over several dates. *526, 543*

Simple interest   Interest on principal only. *554*

Sinking fund   See Bond redemption fund.

Stock warrant   A right that allows the bondholder to purchase shares of common stock at a fixed price for a stated period of time. Warrants issued with long-term debt may be **detachable** or **nondetachable.** *526*

Straight-line method of amortization   A procedure that, when applied to bond discount or premium, allocates an equal amount of discount or premium to each period in the life of a bond. *538*

Term bond   A bond that matures on the same date as all other bonds in a given bond issue. *526*

Trading on the equity   A company using its stockholders' equity as a basis for securing funds on which it pays a fixed return. *527*

Trustee   Usually a bank or trust company appointed to represent the bondholders in a bond issue and to enforce the provisions of the bond indenture against the issuer. *523*

Underwriter   An investment company that performs many tasks for the bond issuer in issuing bonds; may also guarantee the issuer a fixed price for the bonds. *523*

Unfavorable financial leverage   Results when the cost of borrowed funds exceeds the revenue they generate; it is the reverse of **favorable financial leverage.** *530*

Unregistered (bearer) bond   Ownership transfers by physical delivery. *526*

Unsecured bond   A **debenture bond,** or simply a **debenture.** *525*

SELF-TEST

True-False

Indicate whether each of the following statements is true or false.

1. When a noninterest-bearing note is issued to a bank, the difference between the cash proceeds and the maturity amount is debited to the Discount on Notes Payable.

2. An unsecured bond is also called a debenture bond.

3. Callable bonds may be called at the option of the holder of the bonds.

4. Favorable financial leverage results when borrowed funds are used to increase earnings per share of common stock.

5. If the market rate of interest exceeds the contract rate, the bonds will be issued at a discount.

6. The straight-line method of amortization is the recommended method.

Multiple-Choice

Select the best answer for each of the following questions.

1. To calculate interest on a promissory note, all of the following elements must be known except:
    a. The face value of the note.
    b. The stated interest rate.
    c. The life of the note.
    d. The name of the payee.
    e. None of the above.

2. When a note receivable is discounted with recourse at a bank, which of the following would be false?
    a. The net proceeds to the seller are equal to the maturity amount less bank discount.
    b. The party discounting the note should disclose a contingent liability of the note.
    c. Interest expense or interest revenue may be recorded depending on the difference between the proceeds and face value of the note.
    d. The seller must pay the maturity value to the bank if the note is dishonored.
    e. The proceeds could be more or less than the maturity value.

3. Allen Company issued its own $5,000, 60-day, noninterest-bearing note to a bank. If the note is discounted at 9%, the proceeds to Allen are:
    a. $5,000.
    b. $5,075.
    c. $4,550.
    d. $4,925.
    e. None of the above.

4. Harner Company issued $100,000 of 12% bonds on March 1, 1995. The bonds are dated January 1, 1995, and were issued at 96 plus accrued interest. The entry to record the issuance would be:

a. Cash   98,000
    Discount on Bonds
        Payable.   4,000
            Bonds Payable .   100,000
            Bond Interest
                Payable. . . .   2,000

b. Cash   102,000
            Bonds Payable .   100,000
            Bond Interest
                Payable. . . .   2,000

c. Cash   96,000
    Discount on Bonds
        Payable.   4,000
            Bonds Payable .   100,000

d. None of the above.

5. If the bonds in (4) had been issued at 104, the
    entry to record the issuance would have
    been:

a. Cash   104,000
        Bonds Payable .   100,000
        Premium on
            Bonds Pay-
                able   4,000

b. Cash   102,000
        Bonds Payable .   100,000
        Bond Interest
            Payable. . . .   2,000

c. Cash   106,000
        Bonds Payable .   100,000
        Premium on
            Bonds Pay-
                able   4,000
        Bond Interest
            Expense . . .   2,000

d. None of the above.

6. On January 1, 1995, the Alvarez Company
    issued $400,000 face value of 8%, 10-year
    bonds for cash of $328,298, a price to yield
    11%. The bonds pay interest semiannually

and mature on January 1, 2005. Using the
effective interest rate method, the bond interest expense for the first six months of 1995
would be:

a. $36,113.
b. $18,056.
c. $32,000.
d. $16,000.

7. If the straight-line amortization method had
    been used in (6), the interest expense for the
    first six months would have been:

a. $39,170.
b. $32,000.
c. $18,000.
d. $19,585.

8. Assume that the Hanford Insurance Company
    bought 20% of the Alvarez bonds in (6). As-
    suming the discount is amortized at each
    interest date using the effective interest rate
    method, the journal entry to record the re-
    ceipt of the first six months of interest would
    be:

a. Cash   3,200
    Bonds Investments . . .   411
        Bond Interest
            Revenue   3,611

b. Cash   3,200
        Bond Interest
            Revenue   3,200

c. Cash   3,611
        Bond Interest
            Revenue   3,611

d. Cash   4,022
        Bond Investments . .   411
        Bond Interest
            Revenue   3,611

Now turn to page 575 to check your answers.

QUESTIONS

1. Why might a business have need for short-term financing even when cash in-
    flows are expected to exceed cash outflows?

2. How is interest calculated on a note?

3. How is interest introduced into a situation where a note is noninterest-bearing?

4. What does it mean for a note to be dishonored?

5. Describe the process of discounting a note receivable. What happens if the maker fails to pay the bank at maturity?

6. How are the cash proceeds determined when a note receivable is discounted?

7. What effect does the maturity date have on the carrying value of notes payable?

8. What are the advantages of obtaining long-term funds by the issuance of bonds rather than additional shares of capital stock? What are the disadvantages?

9. What is a bond indenture? What parties are usually associated with it? Explain why.

10. Explain what is meant by the terms *coupon, callable, convertible,* and *debenture.*

11. What is meant by the term *trading on the equity?*

12. When bonds are issued between interest dates, why should the issuing corporation receive cash equal to the amount of accrued interest (accrued since the preceding interest date) in addition to the issue price of the bonds?

13. Why might it be more accurate to describe a sinking fund as a bond redemption fund?

14. Indicate how each of the following items should be classified in a balance sheet on December 31, 1995.
    a. Cash balance in a sinking fund.
    b. Accrued interest on bonds payable.
    c. Debenture bonds payable due in 2005.
    d. Premium on bonds payable.
    e. First-mortgage bonds payable, due July 1, 1996.
    f. Discount on bonds payable.
    g. First National Bank—Interest account.
    h. Convertible bonds payable due in 1998.

15. Why is the effective interest rate method of computing periodic interest expense considered theoretically preferable to the straight-line method?

16. Why would an investor whose intent is to hold bonds to maturity pay more for the bonds than their face value?

17. Describe the amortization of a premium or discount on a short-term bond investment.

18. Describe the amortization of a premium or discount on a long-term bond investment.

19. Under what circumstances should bond investments be written down below their carrying value?

20. *Real-world question*   Refer to "A Broader Perspective" on page 528. Why are so many of the companies mentioned refinancing?

21. *Real-world question*   A recent annual report of Fuqua Industries contained the following paragraph in the notes to the financial statements:

The 9⅞% Senior Subordinated Debentures are redeemable at the option of Fuqua at 103.635% of the principal amount plus accrued interest if redeemed prior to March 15, 1990, and at decreasing prices thereafter. Mandatory sinking fund payments of $3,000,000 (which Fuqua may increase to $6,000,000 annually) began in 1982 and are intended to retire, at par plus accrued interest, 75% of the issue prior to maturity.

Answer the following questions about this quote:

a. What does the term *debentures* mean?

b. How much is the call premium initially? Does this premium decrease over time?

c. Under what circumstances might Fuqua want to increase the sinking fund payments?

EXERCISES

Use T-accounts to record short-term borrowing transactions (L.O. 1)

10–1. John Stewart went to the bank and asked to borrow $24,000 at 10½% for a 60-day period. Using T-accounts, show how to record each of the following transactions:

a. He signed a note for $24,000. Interest was deducted from the face amount in determining the proceeds.

b. He received $24,000 and signed a note for the interest plus the amount borrowed.

c. He received $24,000 and signed an interest-bearing note for that amount. The interest is to be paid at the maturity date.

Prepare journal entries for repayment of loan (L.O. 1)

10–2. Using T-accounts, give the entries at the maturity date for each of the alternatives given in 1, assuming that the loan is repaid. Also assume that repayment is made before the end of the accounting period.

Prepare entries for note (L.O. 1)

10–3. Crimins gives his 90-day, $45,000, 12% note to Lopez in exchange for merchandise. Using T-accounts, give the entries each will make on the maturity date, assuming that payment is made.

Prepare entries for default (L.O. 1)

10–4. Referring to Exercise 10–3 above and using T-accounts, give the entries for each at the maturity date assuming that Crimins defaults.

Prepare entries at date of discounting of note (L.O. 2)

10–5. Lewis Company gave a 120-day, $60,000, 12% note to River Company on July 6, 1995. River Company sold the note to the bank on August 20, 1995. The rate of discount was 12%. Determine the entries each company would make on the date of discounting.

Prepare entries at maturity date (L.O. 2)

10–6. In Exercise 10–5, if Lewis Company fails to make payment on the maturity date, what entry or entries are required on the books of each company?

Prepare entries for bond issuance on date of bonds (L.O. 3, 6)

10–7. Brinkley Corporation issued $400,000 of 12% bonds on the date of the bonds, January 1, 1995. Prepare the entry for their issuance if they were sold at:

a. Face value.

b. A discount of $16,000.

c. A premium of $16,000.

Prepare entries for bond issuance between interest dates (L.O. 3, 6)

10–8. Prindle Corporation issued $100,000 of 12% bonds on March 1, 1995, which was two months after the January 1, 1995, date of the bonds. The accrued interest was $2,000. Prepare the entry for their issuance if they were sold at:

a. Face value.

b. A discount of $4,000.

c. A premium of $4,000.

Record issuance of bonds, adjusting entry, and payment of interest (L.O. 3)

10–9. On September 30, 1995, Romero Company issued $960,000 face value of 18%, 10-year bonds dated August 31, 1995, at 100, plus accrued interest. Interest is paid semiannually on February 28 and August 31. Romero's accounting year ends on December 31. Prepare journal entries to record the issuance of these bonds, the accrual of interest at year-end, and the payment of the first interest coupon.

Record bond investments, adjusting entry, and collection of interest (L.O. 8)

10–10. Stanley Company, with an accounting year ending on December 31, bought $40,000 face value of the bonds in Exercise 10–9 on September 30 as a long-term investment. Prepare entries to record the purchase, the necessary year-end adjusting entry, and the receipt of the first six months' interest.

Compute bond interest expense; show how bond price is determined (L.O. 4–6)

10–11. On December 31, 1995, Springer Company issued $400,000 face value of 8%, 10-year bonds for cash of $328,298, a price to yield 11%. The bonds pay interest semiannually and mature December 31, 2004.

a. State which is higher, the market rate of interest or the contract rate.

b. Compute the bond interest expense for the first six months of 1996 using the interest method.

c. Show how the $328,298 price must have been determined.

Record bond investment and first period's interest (L.O. 8)

10–12. Ruiz Company purchased bonds with a face value of $80,000 issued by Springer Company (Exercise 10–11) as a long-term investment on December 31, 1995. Prepare the journal entry to record the investment. Also, prepare the entry to record the receipt of interest on the bonds to the nearest dollar for the first six months of 1996 using the interest method.

Calculate interest using straight-line amortization (L.O. 6, 8)

10–13. Compute the annual interest expense on the bonds in Exercise 10–11 and the interest revenue on the bonds in Exercise 10–12, assuming the bond discount is amortized using the straight-line method.

Prepare entry to record interest payment (L.O. 6)

10–14. After recording the payment of the interest coupon due on June 30, 1995, the accounts of the Woody Company showed Bonds Payable of $800,000 and Premium on Bonds Payable of $28,192. Interest is payable semiannually on June 30 and December 31. The five-year, 12% bonds have a face value of $800,000 and were originally issued to yield 10%. Prepare the entry to record the payment of interest on December 31, 1995. Use the interest method.

Record call of bonds and payment of interest (L.O. 7)

10–15. On June 30, 1995 (a semiannual interest payment date), Simpson Company redeemed all of its $400,000 face value of 10% bonds outstanding by calling them at 106. The bonds were originally issued on June 30, 1991, at 100. Prepare the entry to record the payment of the interest and the redemption of the bonds on June 30, 1995. If the bonds had been issued at a premium or discount, how would the unamortized portion of the premium or discount be treated at redemption?

Record conversion
of bonds
(L.O. 7)

10–16. After interest was paid on September 30, 1995, $128,000 face value of Charleston Company's $1,280,000 face value of outstanding bonds were converted into 8,000 shares of the company's $10 par value common stock. Prepare the entry to record the conversion assuming the bonds were issued at 100.

Record accrued
interest and the
purchase and
retirement of
bonds
(L.O. 7)

10–17. On August 31, 1995, Tacoma Company, as part of the provisions of its bond indenture, acquired $120,000 of its outstanding bonds on the open market at 96 plus accrued interest. These bonds were originally issued at face value and carry a 12% interest rate, payable semiannually. The bonds are dated November 30, 1984, and pay semiannual interest on May 31 and November 30. Prepare the entries required to record the accrual of the interest to the acquisition date on the bonds acquired and the acquisition of the bonds.

Record interest
received for
six-month period
given adjusting
entry previously
made
(L.O. 8)

10–18. On December 31, 1995, the end of its accounting year, Kling Company prepared an adjusting entry to record $13,334 of accrued interest revenue earned on 12% bonds with a $300,000 face value that were purchased on August 31, 1995, to yield 14%. The bonds are dated August 31, 1995, and call for semiannual interest payments on August 31 and February 28. Prepare the entry on February 28, 1996, to record the interest revenue, the discount amortization, and the collection of interest.

Record sinking
fund transactions
(L.O. 7)

10–19. Brewer Company is required to make a deposit of $144,000 plus semiannual interest expense of $4,320 on October 31, 1995, to the trustee of its sinking funds so that the trustee can redeem $144,000 of Brewer Company's bonds on that date. The bonds were issued at 100. Prepare the entries required on October 31 to record the sinking fund deposit, the bond retirement, payment of interest (due on that date), and payment of trustee expenses, assuming the latter amount is $450.

Prepare journal
entries related to
temporary
investment in
bonds
(L.O. 8)

10–20. On June 30, 1995, Cane Company purchased as a temporary investment $80,000 face value of Ace Company's 12% bonds at 101. In addition to the purchase price, Cane paid $1,600 of accrued interest from April 30 and a $560 broker's commission.

On September 30, 1995, Cane sold the Ace bonds at 102.5, plus accrued interest of $4,000, and less a $560 broker commission. Prepare journal entries on Cane Company's books to record the purchase and sale of the Ace Company bonds.

Determine present
value of lump sum
(based on
Appendix)
(L.O. 9)

10–21. What is the present value of a lump-sum payment of $66,000 due in five years if the market rate of interest is 10% per year (compounded annually) and the present value of $1 due in five periods at 10% is 0.62092?

Determine present
value of an
annuity (based on
Appendix)
(L.O. 9)

10–22. What is the present value of a series of semiannual payments (an annuity) of $24,000 due at the end of each six months for the next five years if the market rate of interest is 10% per year and the present value of an annuity of $1 for 10 periods at 5% is 7.72173?

Determine present
value of an
annuity (based on
Appendix)
(L.O. 9)

10–23. Sam Latona bought a ticket in the New York State lottery for $1, hoping to strike it rich. To his amazement, he won $4,000,000. Payment was to be received in equal amounts at the end of each of the next 20 years. Sam heard from relatives and "friends" he had not heard from in years. They all wanted to renew their relationship with this "new millionaire." Federal and state income taxes were going to be about 40% (31% for federal and 9% for state) on each year's income from the lottery check. The discount rate to use in all present value calculations is 12%.

a. How much will Sam actually receive after taxes each year?

b. Is Sam a millionaire in terms of the present value of his cash inflow after taxes?

c. What is the present value of the net amount the state has to pay out? Remember that the state gets part of the money back in the form of taxes.

Determine future value of an annuity (based on Appendix) (L.O. 9)

10–24. After Sam Latona won $4,000,000 in the New York State lottery, he decided to purchase $10,000 of lottery tickets at the end of each year for the next 20 years. He was hoping to hit the lottery again, but he never did. If the state can earn 12% on ticket revenue received, how much will the annuity of $10,000 from Sam grow to by the end of 20 years?

PROBLEMS

Using T-accounts prepare journal entries to record discounting of company's own note (L.O. 1)

10–1. On November 1, 1995, the Conyers Company presented its own $100,000 120-day, noninterest-bearing note to the B&D National Bank, which discounted it at 12%.

Required:

Using T-accounts, give the entries required on Conyer's books as of November 1, December 31 (the company's closing date), and the maturity date.

Prepare entries to record a number of note transactions, discounting of a note (customer's and own), adjusting entries for interest, and payment of notes (L.O. 1, 2)

10–2. Following are selected transactions of the Dogwood Company:

1995

Oct. 31   Presented its own 30-day, $30,000, noninterest-bearing note to the First State Bank, which discounted it at 11%.

Nov. 8   Received a $20,000, 30-day, 12% note from the Lively Company in settlement of an account receivable. The note is dated November 8.

15   Purchased merchandise by issuing its own 60-day note for $12,000. The note is dated November 15 and bears interest at 12%.

20   Sold the Lively Company note to the First State Bank, which discounted the note at 13%.

30   The First State Bank notified the Dogwood Company that it had charged the note of October 31 against the company's checking account.

Required:

Assume that all notes falling due after November 30 were paid in full on their due dates by their respective makers. Give the journal entries required on Dogwood's books for each of the above transactions and each of the necessary adjustments assuming a fiscal year accounting period ending on November 30. Also give the journal entries required on Dogwood's books for payment of the notes due after November 30.

Compute two
prices for bond
issue and first
period's interest
(L.O. 5, 6)

10–3. Sanchez Company is seeking to issue $400,000 face value of 10%, 15-year bonds. The bonds are dated June 30, 1995, call for semiannual interest payments, and mature on June 30, 2010. The interest method is used to amortize any premium or discount.

Required:

a. Compute the price investors should offer if they seek a yield of 8% on these bonds. Also, compute the first six months' interest assuming the bonds are issued at this price.

b. Repeat part *(a)* assuming investors seek a yield of 12%.

Record bond
interest expense
payment and
accrual for partial
period
(L.O. 6)

10–4. On March 31, 1995, Rayburn Corporation issued $320,000 face value of 10%, 10-year bonds. The bonds call for semiannual interest payments on March 31 and September 30 and mature on March 31, 2005. Rayburn received cash of $283,294, a price that yields 12%.

Required:

Assume that Rayburn's accounting year ends on December 31. Prepare entries to record the bond interest expense on September 30, 1995, the adjustment needed on December 31, 1995, and the bond interest expense on March 31, 1996, using the interest method.

Record issuance
of bonds and
payment of
interest; record
purchase and
accrual of interest
on investor's
books
(L.O. 3, 8)

10–5. On December 1, 1995, Ling Corporation issued $900,000 of 16%, 10-year bonds dated September 30, 1995, at 100. Interest on the bonds is payable semiannually on March 31 and September 30 on presentation of the appropriate coupon. All of the bonds are of $1,000 denomination. The company's accounting period ends on December 31.

All of the first interest period's coupons on the bonds are presented to the company's bank and paid on March 31, 1996. All of the second interest period's coupons on the bonds are received and paid on September 30, 1996.

Required:

a. Prepare all necessary journal entries for the above transactions through September 30, 1996, including the adjusting entry needed at December 31, 1995.

b. Chand Company purchased $300,000 of Ling Corporation's bonds on December 1, 1995, as a long-term investment. Chand Company prepares financial statements on December 31. Prepare all journal entries for Chand Company relating to the bonds through December 31, 1995.

Compute issue
price of bonds;
prepare
amortization
schedule; prepare
journal entries
(L.O. 5, 6)

10–6. Zip Company issued $640,000 face value of 15%, 20-year bonds on September 30, 1995. The bonds are dated September 30, 1995, call for semiannual interest payments on March 31 and September 30, and are issued to yield 16% (8% per period).

Required:

a. Compute the amount received for the bonds.

b. Prepare an amortization schedule similar to that shown in Illustration 10.5. Enter data in the schedule for the first two interest periods only. Use the interest method.

c. Prepare journal entries to record the issuance of the bonds, the adjustment needed on December 31, 1995, and payment of the first six months' interest expense on the bonds, assuming Zip Company has a calendar-year accounting period.

Record bond investment, full and partial period's interest, and sale of bonds (L.O. 8)

10–7. Lindy Company purchased, as a long-term investment, $64,000 face value of the Zip Company bonds (Problem 10–6) when they were issued on September 30, 1995.

Required:

a. Prepare entries to record the purchase of the bonds, the receipt of the first six months' interest, and the adjustment needed on June 30, 1996, assuming the company's fiscal year ends on that date. Use the interest method.
b. Assume that the Lindy Company sold all of these bonds on September 30, 2005, for cash of $63,680 after detaching the interest coupon due on this date. The bonds have a carrying value, properly adjusted to that date, of $60,886. Prepare the journal entry to record the sale.

Compute price of bonds; prepare amortization schedule; journalize bond issuance, payment of first period's interest, and accrual of partial period's interest (L.O. 5, 6)

10–8. Aleo Company issued $400,000 face value of 18%, 20-year bonds on March 31, 1995. The bonds are dated March 31, 1995, call for semiannual interest payments on March 31 and September 30, and are issued to yield 16% (8% per period).

Required:

a. Compute the amount received for the bonds.
b. Prepare an amortization schedule similar to that shown in Illustration 10.6. Enter data in the schedule for the first two interest periods only. Use the interest method.
c. Prepare entries to record the issuance of the bonds, the first six months' interest on the bonds, and the adjustment needed on December 31, 1995, assuming Aleo's fiscal year ends on that date.

Record bond investment, collection of full period's interest, accrual of partial period's interest, and call of bonds (L.O. 7, 8)

10–9. Pavin Corporation, with a December 31 accounting year-end, purchased as a long-term investment $120,000 face value of the Aleo Company's bonds (Problem 10–8) when they were issued on March 31, 1995.

Required:

a. Prepare journal entries to record the purchase of the bonds, the receipt of the first six months' interest, and the adjustment needed on December 31, 1995. Use the interest method.
b. Assume that on September 30, 2005, Aleo called all of the bonds at 105. The properly adjusted carrying value of the bonds on this date was $131,836. Pavin received a check for $126,000. The collection of the semiannual interest due on this date had already been recorded. Prepare the entry to record the receipt of the check from Aleo Company for the redemption of the bonds.
c. If the investment had been a short-term investment, would the premium be amortized?

Record serial
bond transactions
and show financial
reporting
(L.O. 7)

10–10. Faxton Company issued $560,000 face value of 16% serial bonds on June 30, 1995, at face value. The bonds are dated June 30, pay interest semiannually on June 30 and December 31, and mature at the rate of $112,000 per year. The first group of bonds matures on June 30, 2000. The company's accounting period ends on December 31.

Required:

a. Prepare journal entries to record the interest payment of June 30, 2000; the maturing of $112,000 of bonds on June 30, 2000; and the entry to record the interest payment on December 31, 2000.

b. Show how the bonds will be presented in the company's balance sheet for December 31, 2000.

BUSINESS DECISION PROBLEMS

Analyze two
financing
proposals; decide
whether
investment should
be made
(L.O. 2)

10–1. The management of a company is trying to decide whether to invest $8,000,000 on plant expansion and $4,000,000 to finance a related increase in inventories and accounts receivable. The $12,000,000 expansion is expected to increase business volume substantially. Profit forecasts indicate that income from operations will rise from $6,400,000 to $8,800,000. The income tax rate is 40%. Net income last year was $3,660,000. Interest expense on debt now outstanding is $280,000 per year. There are 200,000 shares of common stock currently outstanding.

The $12,000,000 needed can be obtained in two alternative ways:

1. Finance entirely by issuing additional shares of common stock at an expected issue price of $150 per share.

2. Finance two thirds with bonds, one third with additional stock. The bonds would have a 20-year life, bear interest at 10%, and would sell at face value. The issue price of the stock would be $160 per share.

Required:

Should the investment be made? If so, which financing plan would you recommend? (Hint: Calculate EPS for last year and for future years under each of the alternatives.)

Choose which of
two bond issues
to purchase
(L.O. 5)

10–2. You are an investor in stocks and bonds of various companies. An account executive of a brokerage firm has brought the following bonds to your attention:

1. Company A bonds—remaining life, 12 years; interest rate 6%, payable semiannually. Price: $13,000 per $20,000 bond.

2. Company B bonds—remaining life, 13 years; interest rate 15%, payable semiannually. Price: $23,000 per $20,000 bond.

From a study of available alternatives, you reach the conclusion that either of these bonds would be a suitable investment if the yield were 12% (6% per period).

Required:

In which of the above bonds should you invest, if either? Explain.

Decide whether to
convert or
surrender bonds
(real-world
problem)
(L.O. 7)

10-3. A recent annual report of Emhart Corporation contained the following paragraph in its notes to the financial statements:

The 6¾% convertible subordinated debentures may be converted into shares of common stock at a price of $26.50 per share at any time prior to maturity. They are redeemable at prices decreasing from 105 percent of face amount currently to 100 percent in July 1993. At December 31, 1988, a total of 1,886,794 common shares were reserved for the conversion of the debentures.

Required:

Answer the following questions about this quote:

a. If you held one $1,000 bond, how many shares of stock would you receive if you converted the bond into shares of stock? (Hint: You can use the principal amount of the bond to buy shares of stock at the stated price.)

b. Assume you held one $1,000 bond and the bond was called by the company at a price of 105% of the face amount. If the current market price per share of the stock was $29, would you convert the bond into shares of stock or would you surrender the bond?

ANSWERS TO SELF-TEST

True-False

1. *True*. The maturity amount and the face amount of the note are the same for a noninterest-bearing note. The discount reduces the net liability to the amount of cash received.

2. *True*. These unsecured bonds are also called debenture bonds and are backed only by the general creditworthiness of the issuer.

3. *False*. Callable bonds may be called at the option of the issuer.

4. *True*. This statement is the definition of favorable financial leverage. However, unfavorable financial leverage can result when favorable financial leverage was planned. Unfavorable financial leverage will result if earnings before interest and taxes are much

lower than anticipated. Then earnings per share for the common stockholders would be lower than they would have been without the borrowing.

5. *True*. Purchasers will not be willing to pay the face amount if the market rate of interest exceeds the contract rate. By paying less than the face value, purchasers can earn the market rate of interest on the bonds.

6. *False*. The effective interest rate method is the recommended method. The straight-line method may only be used when the results are not materially different from the effective interest rate method.

Multiple-Choice

1. *d*. The name of the payee is not needed to compute interest expense on a promissory note.

2. *e*. The proceeds are always less than the maturity value.

3. *d*. The proceeds from a bank are computed as follows:

$$\text{Discount amount} = \$5,000 \times 0.09 \times {}^{60}\!/_{360}$$
$$= \$75$$
$$\text{Proceeds} = \$5,000 - \$75 = \$4,925$$

4. *a*. The discount of $4,000 must be recorded. Also, the accrued interest must be recognized ($100,000 \times 12\% \times {}^{2}\!/_{12} = \$2,000$).

5. *c.* The premium is $4,000, and the accrued interest is $2,000. Both must be recognized.

6. *b.* The interest is ($328,298 × 0.11 × ½) = $18,056.

7. *d.* The interest would have been ($400,000 × 0.04) + ($71,702/20) = $19,585.

8. *a.* The debit to Cash is ($80,000 × 0.04) = $3,200. The credit to Bond Interest Expense is ($65,660 × 0.055) = $3,611. The debit to Bond Investments is ($3,611 − $3,200) = $411.

11 ACCOUNTING THEORY AND INTERNATIONAL ACCOUNTING

LEARNING OBJECTIVES

After studying this chapter, you should be able to:

1. Identify and discuss the underlying assumptions or concepts of accounting.
2. Identify and discuss the major principles of accounting.
3. Identify and discuss the modifying conventions (or constraints) of accounting.
4. Describe the Conceptual Framework Project of the Financial Accounting Standards Board.
5. Discuss the differences in international accounting among nations (appendix).

In the preceding chapters, you learned how accountants use the accounting process (or cycle) to account for the activities of a business. Chapter 1 made a brief mention of the body of theory underlying accounting procedures. Other chapters have also mentioned theoretical concepts. In this chapter, we discuss accounting theory in greater depth. Now that you have learned some accounting procedures, you are better able to relate these theoretical concepts to accounting practice. **Accounting theory** is "a set of basic concepts and assumptions and related principles that explain and guide the accountant's actions in identifying, measuring, and communicating economic information."[1]

To some people, the word *theory* has the connotation of being abstract and "out of reach." In accounting, understanding the theory behind the accounting process helps one make decisions in diverse accounting situations. Accounting theory provides a logical framework for accounting practice.

---

[1] American Accounting Association, *A Statement of Basic Accounting Theory* (Sarasota, Fla., 1966), pp. 1–2.

The first part of the chapter describes underlying accounting assumptions or concepts, the measurement process used in accounting, major accounting principles, and modifying conventions or constraints. This body of accounting theory has developed over the years and is contained in authoritative accounting literature and textbooks. The second part of the chapter describes the results of a major effort by the Financial Accounting Standards Board to construct a conceptual framework for accounting. This conceptual framework builds on the accounting theory that has developed over time and serves as a basis for formulating accounting standards in the future. By presenting the traditional body of theory first and the conceptual framework second, we give you a sense of the historical development of accounting theory. While there is some overlap between the two parts of the chapter, we reemphasize the fact that the conceptual framework builds on traditional theory rather than replacing it.

The chapter appendix discusses international accounting. As businesses expand their operations across international borders, accountants must become aware of the accounting challenges this expansion presents.

TRADITIONAL ACCOUNTING THEORY

Traditional accounting theory consists of underlying assumptions, rules of measurement, accounting principles, and modifying conventions (or constraints). The following sections describe each of these important aspects of accounting theory that have a great influence on accounting practice.

UNDERLYING ASSUMPTIONS OR CONCEPTS

Objective 1
Identify and discuss the underlying assumptions or concepts of accounting

The major underlying assumptions or concepts of accounting are (1) business entity, (2) going concern (continuity), (3) money measurement, (4) stable dollar, and (5) periodicity (time periods). This section discusses the effects of these assumptions on the accounting process.

Business Entity

Data gathered in an accounting system are assumed to relate to a specific business unit or entity. The **business entity concept** assumes that each business has an existence separate from its owners, creditors, employees, customers, other interested parties, and other businesses. For each business (such as a horse stable or a fitness center), the business, not the business owner, is the accounting entity. Financial statements must be identified as belonging to a particular business entity. The content of the financial statements must be limited to reporting the activities, resources, and obligations of that entity.

A business entity may be made up of several different *legal* entities. For instance, a large business (such as General Motors Corporation) may consist of several separate corporations, each of which is a separate legal entity. For reporting purposes, however, the corporations may be considered as one business entity because they have a common ownership.

Going Concern (Continuity)

Accountants record business transactions for an entity assuming the entity is a "going concern." The **going-concern (continuity) assumption** states that an entity will continue to operate indefinitely unless strong evidence exists that the entity will terminate. The termination of an entity occurs when a company ceases business operations and sells its assets. The process of termination is called **liquidation.** If liquidation appears likely, the going-concern assumption is no longer valid.

The going-concern assumption is often cited to justify the use of historical costs rather than market values in measuring assets. Market values are thought to be of little or no significance to an entity intending to use its assets rather than sell them. On the other hand, if an entity is to be liquidated, liquidation values should be used to report assets.

The going-concern assumption permits the accountant to record certain items as assets. For example, printed advertising matter may be on hand to promote a special sale next month. This advertising material may have little, if any, value to anyone but its owner. However, since the owner expects to continue operating long enough to benefit from the advertising, the accountant classifies the expenditure as an asset, prepaid advertising, and not an expense.

Money Measurement

The economic activity of a business is normally recorded and reported in money terms. **Money measurement** is the use of a monetary unit of measurement, such as the dollar, instead of physical or other units of measurement. The use of a particular monetary unit provides accountants with a common unit of measurement to report economic activity. Without a monetary unit, it would be impossible to add such items as buildings, equipment, and inventory on a balance sheet.

Financial statements identify their unit of measure (the dollar in the United States) so the statement user can make valid comparisons of amounts. For example, it would be difficult to compare relative asset amounts or profitability of a company reporting in U.S. dollars with a company reporting in Japanese yen.

Stable Dollar

In the United States, accountants make another assumption regarding money measurement—the stable dollar assumption. Under the **stable dollar assumption,** the dollar is accepted as a *reasonably stable* unit of measurement. Thus, accountants make no adjustments in the primary financial statements for the changing value of the dollar.

A difficulty with following the stable dollar assumption occurs in depreciation accounting. Assume, for example, that a company acquired a building in 1964 and computed the 30-year straight-line depreciation on the building without adjusting for any changes in the value of the dollar. Thus, the depreciation deducted in 1994 is the same as the depreciation deducted in 1964. The company makes no adjustments for the difference between the values of the 1964 dollar and the 1994 dollar. Both dollars are treated as *equal monetary units* of measurement even though substantial price inflation has occurred over the 30-year period. Accountants and business executives have expressed concern over this inflation problem, especially since 1970.

Periodicity (Time Periods)

According to the **periodicity (time periods) assumption,** an entity's life can be divided into time periods (such as months or years) for purposes of reporting its economic activities. After accountants divide an entity's life into time periods, they attempt to prepare accurate reports on the entity's activities for these periods. Although these time-period reports provide useful and timely financial information for investors and creditors, they may be inaccurate for some of these time periods because accountants use estimates, such as depreciation expense and other adjusting entries.

Accounting reports cover relatively short periods of time. The time periods are usually of equal length so that statement users can make valid comparisons of a company's performance from period to period. The length of the accounting period must be stated in the financial statements. For instance, so far in this text, the income statements were for either a one-month or a one-year period. Companies that publish their financial statements, such as publicly held corporations, generally prepare monthly statements for internal management and publish financial statements quarterly and annually for statement users outside the company.

Accrual Basis and Periodicity. In Chapter 3, you learned that financial statements more accurately reflect the financial status and operations of a company when prepared under the accrual basis of accounting rather than the cash basis. Under the cash basis of accounting, revenues are recorded when cash is received, and expenses are recorded when cash is paid. Under the accrual basis, however, revenues are recorded when services are rendered or products are sold, and expenses are recorded when incurred.

The periodicity assumption makes necessary the adjusting entries prepared under the accrual basis. Without the periodicity assumption, a business would have only one time period running from the inception of the business to its termination. Then, the concepts of cash basis and accrual basis accounting would be irrelevant because all revenues and all expenses would be recorded in that one time period and would not have to be assigned to artificially short time periods of one year or less.

Approximation and Judgment because of Periodicity. To provide periodic financial information, accountants must often make estimates of such things as expected uncollectible accounts and useful lives of depreciable assets. Uncertainty about future events prevents precise measurement and makes estimates necessary in accounting. However, the estimates are often reasonably accurate.

OTHER BASIC CONCEPTS

Other basic accounting concepts that affect the accounting for entities are (1) general-purpose financial statements, (2) substance over form, (3) consistency, (4) double-entry, and (5) articulation. A discussion of these basic accounting concepts follows.

General-Purpose Financial Statements

As you know, financial statements present the results of the financial accounting process. Accountants prepare these general-purpose financial statements at regular intervals to meet many of the information needs of external parties and top-level internal managers. In contrast, accountants can gather special-purpose financial information for a specific decision, usually on a one-time basis. For example, management may need specific information to decide whether or not to purchase a new computer. Since special-purpose financial information must be specific, this information is best obtained from the detailed accounting records rather than from the financial statements.

Substance over Form

In some business transactions, the economic substance of the transaction may conflict with its legal form. For example, a contract that is legally a lease may, in fact, be equivalent to a purchase. A company may have a three-year contract to lease (rent) an automobile at a stated monthly rental fee. At the end of the lease period, the company will receive title to the auto after paying a nominal sum (say, $1). The economic substance of this transaction is a purchase rather than a lease of the auto. Thus, under the substance-over-form concept, the auto is shown as an asset on the balance sheet and is depreciated instead of showing rent expense on the income statement. Accountants should record the *economic substance* of a transaction rather than be guided by the *legal form* of the transaction.

Consistency

When discussing inventories in Chapter 5, we introduced the consistency concept. **Consistency** generally requires that a company use the same accounting principles and reporting practices through time. This concept prohibits indiscriminate switching of principles or methods, such as changing inventory methods every year. However, consistency does not prohibit a change in accounting principles if the information needs of financial statement users are better served by the change. When a company makes a change in principles, it must make the following disclosures in the financial statements: (1) nature of the change; (2) reasons for the change; (3) effect of the change on current net income, if significant; and (4) cumulative effect of the change on past income.

Double-Entry

Chapter 2 introduced the basic accounting concept of the double-entry method of recording transactions. Under the double-entry approach, every transaction has a two-sided effect on *each* party engaging in the transaction. Thus, to record a transaction, each party debits at least one account and credits at least one account. The total debits equal the total credits in each journal entry.

Articulation

In the early chapters, you also learned that financial statements are fundamentally related and *articulate* (interact) with each other. For example, the amount of net income is carried from the income statement to the statement of retained earnings. The ending balance on the statement of retained earnings is carried to the balance sheet to bring total assets and total equities into balance.

Illustration 11.1 is a summary of the underlying assumptions or concepts. The next section discusses the measurement process used in accounting.

Illustration 11.1
THE UNDERLYING ASSUMPTIONS OR CONCEPTS

Assumption or Concept	Description	Importance
Business entity	Each business has an existence separate from its owners, creditors, employees, customers, other interested parties, and other businesses.	Defines scope of the business. Identifies which transactions should be recorded on the company's books. Examples in Chapter 1 were horse stable and physical fitness center.
Going concern (continuity)	An entity will continue to operate indefinitely unless strong evidence exists that the entity will terminate.	Allows a company to continue carrying plant assets at their historical costs in spite of a change in their market values.
Money measurement	The use of a monetary unit of measurement, such as the dollar, instead of physical or other units of measurement.	Provides accountants with a common unit of measure to report economic activity. This concept permits us to add and subtract items on the financial statements.
Stable dollar	The dollar is accepted as a reasonably stable unit of measure.	Permits us to make no adjustments in the financial statements for the chang-

**Illustration 11.1
(concluded)**

Assumption or Concept	Description	Importance
		ing value of the dollar. This assumption works fairly well in the United States because of our relatively low rate of inflation.
Periodicity (time periods)	An entity's life can be subdivided into time periods (such as months or years) for purposes of reporting its economic activities.	Permits us to prepare financial statements that cover periods shorter than the entire life of a business. Thus, we have an idea as to how well a business is performing before it terminates its operations. The need for adjusting entries arises because of this concept and the use of accrual accounting.
General-purpose financial statements	Only one set of financial statements is prepared to serve the needs of all types of users.	Allows companies to prepare only one set of financial statements instead of a separate set for each potential user of those statements. The financial statements should be free of bias so they do not favor the interests of any one type of user.
Substance over form	Accountants should record economic substance of a transaction rather than its legal form.	Encourages the accountant to record the true nature of a transaction rather than its apparent nature. This approach is the accounting equivalent of "tell it like it is." If an apparent lease transaction has all the characteristics of a purchase, it should be recorded as a purchase.
Consistency	Generally requires that a company use the same accounting principles and reporting practices every accounting period.	Prevents a company from changing accounting methods whenever it likes to present a "better picture" or to manipulate income. The inventory and depreciation chapters both mentioned the importance of this concept.
Double-entry	Every transaction has a two-sided effect on each company or party engaging in the transaction.	Uses a system of checks and balances to help identify whether or not errors have been made in recording transactions. When the debits do not equal the credits, this inequality immediately signals us to stop and find the error.
Articulation	Financial statements are fundamentally related and articulate (interact) with each other.	Changes in account balances that occur during an accounting period are reflected in financial statements that are related to one another. For instance, earning revenue increases net income on the income statement, retained earnings on the statement of retained earnings, and assets and retained earnings on the balance sheet. The statement of retained earnings ties the income statement and the balance sheet together.

MEASUREMENT IN ACCOUNTING

In the Introduction to this text, accounting was defined as "the process of identifying, measuring, and communicating economic information to permit informed judgments and decisions by the users of the information."[2] In this section, we focus on the *measurement* process of accounting.

Accountants measure a business entity's assets, liabilities, and stockholders' equity and any changes that occur in them. The effects of these changes are assigned to particular time periods (periodicity) to find the net income or net loss of the accounting entity.

Measuring Assets and Liabilities

Accounting measures the various assets of a business in different ways. Cash is measured at its specified amount. Claims to cash, such as notes and accounts receivable, are measured at their expected cash inflows, taking into consideration possible uncollectibles. Inventories, prepaid expenses, plant assets, and intangibles are measured at their historical costs (actual amounts paid). Some items, such as inventory, are later carried at the lower-of-cost-or-market value. Plant assets and intangibles are later carried at original cost less accumulated depreciation or amortization. Liabilities are measured in terms of the cash that will be paid or the value of services that will be performed to satisfy the liabilities.

Measuring Changes in Assets and Liabilities

From the previous chapters, you have learned that accountants can easily measure some changes in assets and liabilities, such as the exchange of one asset for another of equal value, acquisition of an asset on credit, and payment of a liability. Other changes in assets and liabilities, such as those recorded in adjusting entries, are more difficult to measure because they often involve estimates and/or calculations. The accountant must determine when a change has taken place and the amount of the change. These decisions involve matching revenues and expenses and are guided by the principles discussed below.

THE MAJOR PRINCIPLES

*Objective 2
Identify and discuss the major principles of accounting*

As stated in the Introduction to this text, generally accepted accounting principles (GAAP) set forth standards or methods for presenting financial accounting information. A standardized presentation format enables users to compare the financial information of different companies more easily. Generally accepted accounting principles have been either developed through accounting practice or established by authoritative organizations. Major au-

---

[2] Ibid., p. 1.

thoritative organizations that have contributed to the development of the principles are the American Institute of Certified Public Accountants (AICPA), the Financial Accounting Standards Board (FASB), the Securities and Exchange Commission (SEC), the American Accounting Association (AAA), the Financial Executives Institute (FEI), and the Institute of Management Accountants (IMA).

In this section, you will study the following principles:

1. Exchange-price (or cost) principle.
2. Matching principle.
3. Revenue recognition principle.
4. Expense recognition principle.
5. Gain and loss recognition principle.
6. Full disclosure principle.

Exchange-Price (or Cost) Principle

When a transfer of resources takes place between two parties, such as buying merchandise on account, the accountant must follow the exchange-price (or cost) principle when presenting that information. The **exchange-price (or cost) principle** requires transfers of resources to be recorded at prices agreed on by the parties to the exchange at the time of exchange. This principle sets forth (1) what goes into the accounting system—transaction data; (2) when it is recorded—at the time of exchange; and (3) the amounts—exchange prices—at which assets, liabilities, stockholders' equity, revenues, and expenses are recorded.

As applied to most assets, this principle is often called the **cost principle,** meaning that purchased or self-constructed assets are initially recorded at historical cost. **Historical cost** is the amount paid, or the fair value of the liability incurred or other resources surrendered, to acquire an asset and place it in a condition and position for its intended use. For instance, when the cost of a plant asset (such as a machine) was recorded in Chapter 7, its cost included the net purchase price plus any costs of reconditioning, testing, transporting, and placing the asset in the location for its intended use. The term *exchange-price principle* is preferred to *cost principle* because it seems inappropriate to refer to liabilities, stockholders' equity, and such assets as cash and accounts receivable as being measured in terms of cost.

Matching Principle

Using the **matching principle,** net income of a period is determined by associating or relating revenues earned in a period with expenses incurred to generate those revenues. The logic underlying this principle is that whenever economic resources are used, someone will want to know what was accomplished and at what cost. Every evaluation of economic activity will involve matching benefit with sacrifice. The application of the matching principle is discussed and illustrated next.

Revenue Recognition Principle

Revenue is not difficult to define or measure; it is the inflow of assets from the sale of goods and services to customers, measured by the amount of cash expected to be received from customers. However, the crucial question for the accountant is *when* to record a revenue. Under the **revenue recognition principle,** revenues should be *earned* and *realized* before they are recognized (recorded).

    Earning of Revenue.   All economic activities undertaken by a company to create revenues are part of the earning process. The actual receipt of cash from a customer may have been preceded by many activities, including (1) placing advertisements, (2) calling on the customer several times, (3) submitting samples, (4) acquiring or manufacturing goods, and (5) selling and delivering goods. Costs are incurred by the company for these activities. Although revenue was actually being earned by these activities, in most instances accountants do not recognize revenue until the time of sale because of the requirement that revenue be *substantially* earned before it is recognized (recorded). This requirement is called the **earning principle.**

    Realization of Revenue.   Under the **realization principle,** the accountant does not recognize (record) revenue until the seller acquires the right to receive payment from the buyer. The seller acquires the right to receive payment from the buyer at the time of sale for merchandise transactions or when services have been performed in service transactions. Legally, a sale of merchandise occurs when title to the goods passes to the buyer. The time at which title passes normally depends on the shipping terms—FOB shipping point or FOB destination (as discussed in Chapter 4). As a practical matter, accountants generally record revenue when goods are delivered.

    The advantages of recognizing revenue at the time of sale are that (1) the actual transaction—delivery of goods—is an observable event; (2) revenue is easily measured; (3) risk of loss due to price decline or destruction of the goods has passed to the buyer; (4) revenue has been earned, or substantially so; and (5) because the revenue has been earned, expenses and net income can be determined. As discussed below, the disadvantage of recognizing revenue at the time of sale is that the revenue might not be recorded in the period during which most of the activity creating it occurred.

    Exceptions to the Realization Principle.   The following examples illustrate instances when practical considerations may cause accountants to vary the point of revenue recognition from the time of sale. These examples illustrate the effect that the business environment has on the development of accounting principles and standards.

    Cash Collection as Point of Revenue Recognition.   Some small companies record revenues and expenses at the time of cash collection and payment, which may not occur at the time of sale. This procedure is known as the *cash basis* of accounting. The cash basis is acceptable primarily in service enterprises that do not have substantial credit transactions or inventories, as is the case with doctors or dentists.

Installment Basis of Revenue Recognition.   When a company is going to collect the selling price of goods sold in installments (such as monthly or annually) and considerable doubt exists as to collectibility, the company may use the installment basis of accounting. Companies make these sales in spite of the doubtful collectibility of the account because their margin of profit is high and the goods can be repossessed if the payments are not received. Under the **installment basis,** the percentage of total gross margin (selling price of a good minus its cost) recognized in a period is equal to the percentage of total cash from a sale that is received in that period. Thus, the gross margin recognized in a period is equal to the amount of cash received times the gross margin percentage (gross margin divided by selling price). The formula to recognize gross profit on cash collections made on installment sales of a certain year is:

$$\frac{\text{Cash}}{\text{collections}} \times \frac{\text{Gross margin}}{\text{percentage}} = \frac{\text{Gross margin}}{\text{recognized}}$$

To be more precise, we expand the descriptions in the formula as follows:

$$\begin{matrix}\text{Cash collections} \\ \text{this year resulting} \\ \text{from installment} \\ \text{sales made in a} \\ \text{certain year}\end{matrix} \times \begin{matrix}\text{Gross margin} \\ \text{percentage} \\ \text{for the year} \\ \text{of sale}\end{matrix} = \begin{matrix}\text{Gross margin} \\ \text{recognized this year} \\ \text{on cash collections} \\ \text{this year from} \\ \text{installment sales made} \\ \text{in a certain year}\end{matrix}$$

To illustrate, assume a company sold a stereo set. The facts of the sale are:

Date of Sale	Selling Price	Cost	Gross Margin (Selling price − Cost)	Gross Margin Percentage (Gross margin ÷ Selling price)
October 1, 1995	$500	$300	($500 − $300) = $200	($200 ÷ $500) = 40%

The buyer makes 10 equal monthly installment payments of $50 each to pay for the set (10 × $50 = $500). If the company receives three monthly payments in 1995, the total amount of cash received in 1995 is $150 (3 × $50). The gross margin to recognize in **1995** is:

$$\begin{matrix}\text{1995 cash} \\ \text{collections from} \\ \text{1995 installment} \\ \text{sales}\end{matrix} \times \begin{matrix}\text{Gross margin} \\ \text{percentage} \\ \text{on 1995} \\ \text{installment} \\ \text{sales}\end{matrix} = \begin{matrix}\text{1995 gross margin} \\ \text{recognized on 1995} \\ \text{cash collections} \\ \text{from 1995 installment} \\ \text{sales}\end{matrix}$$

$$\mathbf{\$150} \quad \times \quad \mathbf{40\%} \quad = \quad \mathbf{\$60}$$

The company collects the other installments when due so it receives a total of $350 in 1996 from 1995 installment sales. The gross margin to recognize in **1996** on these cash collections is shown on the next page.

1996 cash collections from 1995 installment sales	$\times$	Gross margin percentage on 1995 installment sales	$=$	1996 gross margin recognized on 1996 cash collections from 1995 installment sales
$350	$\times$	**40%**	$=$	**$140**

In summary, the total receipts and gross margin recognized in the two years are as follows:

Year	Total Amount of Cash Received	Gross Margin Recognized
1995	$150 (30%)	$ 60 (30%)
1996	350 (70%)	140 (70%)
Total	$500 100%	$200 100%

The installment basis of revenue recognition may be used for tax purposes only in very limited circumstances. **Since the installment basis delays revenue recognition beyond the time of sale, it is acceptable for accounting purposes only when considerable doubt exists as to collectibility of the installments.**

Revenue Recognition on Long-Term Construction Projects.   Revenue from a long-term construction project can be recognized under two different methods: (1) the completed-contract method or (2) the percentage-of-completion method. The **completed-contract method** does not recognize any revenue until the period in which the project is completed. At that point, all revenue is recognized even though the contract may have required three years to complete. Thus, the **completed-contract method recognizes revenues at the time of sale,** as is true for most sales transactions. Costs incurred on the project are carried forward in an inventory account (Construction in Process) and are charged to expense in the period in which the revenue is recognized.

Some accountants argue that waiting so long to recognize any revenue is unreasonable. Revenue-producing activities have been performed during each year of construction, and revenue should be recognized in each year of construction even if estimates are needed. The **percentage-of-completion method** is a method of recognizing revenue based on the estimated stage of completion of a long-term project. The stage of completion is measured by comparing actual costs incurred in a period with the total estimated costs to be incurred on the project.

To illustrate, assume that a company has a contract to build a dam for $44 million. The estimated construction cost is $40 million. Estimated gross margin is calculated as follows:

Sales Price of Dam	Estimated Costs to Construct Dam	Estimated Gross Margin (Sales price − Estimated costs)
$44 million	$40 million	($44 million − $40 million) = $4 million

The $4 million gross margin is recognized in the financial statements by recording the "assigned" amount of revenue for the year and then deducting actual costs incurred that year.

The formula to recognize revenue is:

$$\left(\begin{array}{l}\text{Actual construction} \\ \text{costs incurred} \\ \text{during the period}\end{array} \div \begin{array}{l}\text{Total estimated} \\ \text{construction costs} \\ \text{for the} \\ \text{entire project}\end{array}\right) \times \begin{array}{l}\text{Total} \\ \text{sales} \\ \text{price}\end{array} = \begin{array}{l}\text{Revenue} \\ \text{recognized} \\ \text{(assigned)} \\ \text{for period}\end{array}$$

Suppose that by the end of the first year (1995), the company had incurred *actual* construction costs of $30 million. The $30 million of construction costs is 75% of the total estimated construction costs ($30 million ÷ $40 million = 75%). Under the percentage-of-completion method, the 75% figure would be used to *assign* revenue to the first year. In 1996, another $6 million of construction costs is incurred. In 1997, the final $4 million of construction costs is incurred. The amount of revenue to assign to each year is determined as follows:

Year	Ratio of Actual Construction Costs to Total Estimated Construction Costs	×	Agreed Price of Dam	=	Amount of Revenue to Recognize (Assign)
1995	($30 million ÷ $40 million) = 75%				
	75%	×	$44 million	=	$33 million
1996	($ 6 million ÷ $40 million) = 15%				
	15%	×	$44 million	=	$6.6 million
1997	($ 4 million ÷ $40 million) = 10%				
	10%	×	$44 million	=	$4.4 million

The amount of gross margin to recognize in each year is as follows:

Year	Assigned Revenues	− Actual Construction Costs	= Recognized Gross Margin
1995	$33.0 million	− $30.0 million	= $3.0 million
1996	6.6	− 6.0	= 0.6
1997	4.4	− 4.0	= 0.4
Total	$44.0 million	− $40.0 million	= $4.0 million

Period costs, such as general and administrative expenses, would be deducted from gross margin to determine net income. For instance, assuming general and administrative expenses were $100,000 in 1996, net income would be ($600,000 − $100,000) = $500,000.

Illustration 11.2 shows the frequencies of references to the methods of accounting for long-term contracts in the financial statements of a sample of 600 companies for the years 1987–90. The percentage-of-completion method seems to be the most widely used.

Revenue Recognition at Completion of Production. Recognizing revenue at the time of completion of production or extraction is called the **production basis.** The production basis is considered an acceptable procedure when accounting for many farm products (wheat, corn, and soybeans) and for certain precious metals (gold). Accountants justify recognizing revenue before the sale of these products because (1) the products are homogeneous in nature, (2) they can usually be sold at their market prices, and (3) unit production costs for these products are often difficult to determine.

Recognizing revenue on completion of production or extraction is accomplished by debiting inventory (an asset) and crediting a revenue account for the expected selling price of the goods. All costs incurred in the period can then be treated as expenses. For example, assume that 1,000 ounces of gold are mined at a time when gold sells for $400 per ounce. The entry to record the extraction of 1,000 ounces of gold would be:

Inventory of Gold 400,000
    Revenue from Extraction of Gold   400,000
    To record extraction of 1,000 ounces of gold. Selling price
    is $400 per ounce.

If the gold is later sold at $400 per ounce, Cash is debited and Inventory of Gold is credited for $400,000 as follows:

Cash 400,000
    Inventory of Gold   400,000
    To record sale of 1,000 ounces of gold at $400 per ounce.

If expenses in producing the gold amounted to $300,000, net income on the gold mined would be $100,000.

Illustration 11.2
METHODS OF ACCOUNTING FOR LONG-TERM CONTRACTS

	Number of Companies			
	1990	1989	1988	1987
Percentage-of-completion.	91	92	86	89
Units-of-delivery	34	33	37	35
Completed contract	9	6	8	6
Not determinable.	4	2	3	2

SOURCE: American Institute of Certified Public Accountants, *Accounting Trends & Techniques* (New York: AICPA, 1991, p. 347).

Expense Recognition Principle

Expense recognition is closely related to, and sometimes discussed as part of, the revenue recognition principle. The **expense recognition principle** states that expenses should be recognized (recorded) as they are incurred to produce revenues. An *expense* is the outflow or using up of assets in the generation of revenue. An expense is incurred *voluntarily* to produce revenue. For instance, the cost of a television set delivered by a dealer to a customer in exchange for cash is an asset "consumed" to produce revenue. Similarly, the cost of such services as labor are voluntarily incurred to produce revenue.

The Measurement of Expense.   Most assets used in operating a business are measured in terms of their historical costs. Therefore, expenses, such as depreciation, resulting from the consumption of those assets in producing revenues are measured in terms of the historical costs of those assets. Other expenses, such as wages, are paid for currently and are measured in terms of their current costs.

The Timing of Expense Recognition.   The matching principle implies that a relationship exists between expenses and revenues. For certain expenses, such as cost of goods sold, this relationship is easily seen. However, when a direct relationship cannot be seen, the costs of assets with limited lives may be charged to expense in the periods benefited on a systematic and rational allocation basis. Depreciation of plant assets is an example.

Product costs are costs incurred in the acquisition or manufacture of goods. Included as product costs for purchased goods are invoice, freight, and insurance-in-transit costs. For manufacturing companies, product costs include all costs of materials, labor, and factory operations necessary to produce the goods. Product costs are assumed to attach to the goods purchased or produced and are carried in inventory accounts as long as the goods are on hand. Product costs are charged to expense when the goods are sold. The result is a precise matching of cost of goods sold expense to its related revenue.

Period costs are costs that cannot be traced to specific products and are expensed in the period in which incurred. Selling and administrative costs are examples of period costs.

Gain and Loss Recognition Principle

The **gain and loss recognition principle** states that gains may be recorded only when realized, but losses should be recorded when they first become evident. Thus, losses are recognized at an earlier point than are gains. This principle is related to the conservatism concept.

Gains typically result from the sale of long-term assets for more than their book value, as was illustrated in Chapter 8. Gains should not be recognized until they are realized through sale or exchange. Recognizing potential gains before they are actually realized is forbidden in accounting.

Losses consume assets, as do expenses. However, unlike expenses, they do not produce revenues. Losses are usually *involuntary,* such as the loss suffered from destruction by fire on an uninsured building. A loss on the sale of a building may be "voluntary" if management decided to sell the building even though it meant incurring a loss. Losses should be recorded when they first become evident, as in Chapter 5 when we applied the lower-of-cost-or-market method and recorded the loss from market decline of inventory before we actually sold the inventory.

Illustration 11.3
THE MAJOR PRINCIPLES

Principle	Description	Importance
Exchange-price (or cost) principle	Requires transfers of resources to be recorded at prices agreed on by the parties to the exchange at the time of the exchange.	Tells the accountant to record a transfer of resources at an objectively determinable amount at the time of the exchange. Also, self-constructed assets are recorded at their actual cost rather than at some estimate of what they would have cost if they had been purchased. Chapter 7 relies heavily on this principle in recording the acquisition of plant assets.
Matching principle	Net income of a period is determined by associating or relating revenues earned in a period with expenses incurred to generate those revenues.	Identifies how to calculate net income under the accrual concept of income. Chapter 3 first illustrated the matching principle, but all chapters reinforce the importance of this fundamental principle.
Revenue recognition principle	Revenues should be earned and realized before they are recognized (recorded).	Informs accountant that revenues generally should be recognized when services are performed or goods are sold. Exceptions are made for installment sales, long-term construction projects, certain farm products, and precious metals.
Expense recognition principle	Expenses should be recognized (recorded) as they are incurred to produce revenues.	Indicates that expenses are to be recorded as soon as they are incurred rather than waiting until some future time.
Gain and loss recognition principle	Gains may only be recorded when realized, but losses should be recorded when they first become evident.	Tells the accountant to be conservative when recognizing gains and losses. Gains can only be recognized when they have been realized through sale (or exchange). Losses should be recognized as soon as they become evident. Thus, potential losses can be recorded, but only gains that have actually been realized can be recorded.
Full disclosure principle	Information important enough to influence the decisions of an informed user of the financial statements should be disclosed.	Requires the accountant to disclose everything that is important. A good rule to follow is—if in doubt, disclose. Another good rule is—if you are not consistent, disclose all the facts and the effect on income.

Full Disclosure Principle

The **full disclosure principle** states that information important enough to influence the decisions of an informed user of the financial statements should be disclosed. Depending on its nature, this information should be disclosed either in the financial statements, in notes to the financial statements, or in supplemental statements. For instance, Appendix C at the end of this text illustrates how The Coca Cola Company discloses information in notes to its financial statements. In judging whether or not to disclose information, it is better to err on the side of too much disclosure rather than too little. Many lawsuits against CPAs and their clients have resulted from inadequate or misleading disclosure of the underlying facts.

Illustration 11.3 summarizes the major principles and describes the importance of each one.

MODIFYING CONVENTIONS (OR CONSTRAINTS)

*Objective 3
Identify and discuss the modifying conventions (or constraints) of accounting*

In certain instances, accounting principles are not strictly applied because of modifying conventions (or constraints). **Modifying conventions** are customs emerging from accounting practice that alter the results that would be obtained from a strict application of accounting principles. Three such modifying conventions are cost-benefit, materiality, and conservatism.

Cost-Benefit. The **cost-benefit consideration** involves deciding whether the benefits of including optional information in financial statements exceed the costs of providing the information. Users tend to think information is cost free since they incur none of the costs of providing the information. Preparers realize that providing information is costly. The benefits of using information should exceed the costs of providing it. The measurement of benefits is nebulous and inexact, which makes application of this modifying convention difficult in practice.

Materiality. **Materiality** is a modifying convention that allows the accountant to deal with immaterial (unimportant) items in an expedient but theoretically incorrect manner. The fundamental question the accountant must ask in judging the materiality of an item is whether a knowledgeable user's decisions would be different if the information were presented in the theoretically correct manner. If not, the item is immaterial and may be reported in a theoretically incorrect but expedient manner. For instance, since small dollar amount items (such as the cost of calculators) often do not make a difference in a statement user's decision to invest in the company, they are considered *immaterial* (unimportant) and may be expensed when purchased. However, because large dollar amount items (such as the cost of mainframe computers) usually do make a difference in such a decision, they are considered *material* (important) and should be recorded as assets and depreciated. The accountant should record all material items in a theoretically correct manner. **Immaterial items may be recorded in a theoretically**

incorrect manner simply because it is more convenient and less expensive to do so. For example, the purchase of a wastebasket may be debited to an expense account rather than an asset account even though the wastebasket has an expected useful life of 30 years. It simply is not worth the cost of recording depreciation expense on such a small item over its life.

Materiality has been defined by the FASB as "the magnitude of an omission or misstatement of accounting information that, in the light of surrounding circumstances, makes it probable that the judgement of a reasonable person relying on the information would have been changed or influenced by the omission or misstatement."[3] The term *magnitude* in this definition suggests that the materiality of an item may be assessed by looking at its *relative* size. A $10,000 error in an expense in a company with earnings of $30,000 is material. The same error in a company earning $30,000,000 may not be material.

Illustration 11.4
MODIFYING CONVENTIONS

Modifying Convention	Description	Importance
Cost-benefit	Optional information should only be included in financial statements if the benefits of providing it exceed its costs.	Lets the accountant know that information that is not required should not be made available if the costs exceed its benefits. An example may be companies going to the expense of providing information on the effects of inflation when the inflation rate is low and/or users do not seem to benefit significantly from the information.
Materiality	Only items that would affect a knowledgeable user's decision are considered to be material (important) and must be reported in a theoretically correct way.	Allows accountant to treat immaterial (relatively small dollar amount) information in a theoretically incorrect but expedient manner. For instance, a wastebasket can be expensed rather than capitalized and depreciated even though it may last for 30 years.
Conservatism	Transactions should be recorded in such a manner that net assets and net income are not overstated.	Warns the accountant that net assets and net income are not to be overstated. "Anticipate (and record) all possible losses and do not anticipate (or record) any possible gains" is common advice under this constraint. Also, conservative application of the matching principle involves making sure that adjustments for expenses for such items as uncollectible accounts, warranties, and depreciation are adequate.

---

[3] FASB, *Statement of Financial Accounting Concepts No. 2,* "Qualitative Characteristics of Accounting Information" (Stamford, Conn., 1980), p. xv. Copyright © by the Financial Accounting Standards Board, High Ridge Park, Stamford, Connecticut 06905, U.S.A. Quoted (or excerpted) with permission. Copies of the complete documents are available from the FASB.

Materiality involves more than the relative size of dollar amounts. Often the nature of the item may make it material. For example, it may be quite significant to know that a company is paying bribes or making illegal political contributions, even if the dollar amounts of such items are relatively small.

Conservatism.   **Conservatism** means being cautious or prudent and making sure that net assets and net income are not overstated. Such overstatements can mislead potential investors and creditors regarding making an investment in the company or a loan to the company. You saw conservatism applied when (1) the lower-of-cost-or-market rule was used for inventory in Chapter 5 and (2) when a gain could not be recognized on a trade-in of similar assets in Chapter 8. Accountants must realize a fine line exists between conservative and incorrect accounting.

Illustration 11.4 is a summary of the modifying conventions and the importance of each one.

The remainder of this chapter discusses the Conceptual Framework Project of the Financial Accounting Standards Board. The Conceptual Framework Project is designed to resolve some disagreements as to the proper theoretical foundation for accounting. Only the portions of the project relevant to this text are presented.

THE FINANCIAL ACCOUNTING STANDARDS BOARD'S CONCEPTUAL FRAMEWORK PROJECT

Objective 4
Describe the
Conceptual
Framework Pro-
ject of the Finan-
cial Accounting
Standards Board

The exact nature of the basic concepts and related principles composing accounting theory has been debated for years. The debate continues today even though numerous references can be found to "generally accepted accounting principles" (GAAP). To date, all attempts to present a concise statement of GAAP have received only limited acceptance.

Due to this limited success, many accountants suggest that the starting point in reaching a concise statement of GAAP is to seek agreement on the objectives of financial accounting and reporting. The belief is that if a person (1) carefully studies the environment, (2) knows what objectives are sought, (3) can identify certain qualitative traits of accounting information, and (4) can define the basic elements of financial statements, that person can discover the principles and standards that will lead to the attainment of the stated objectives. The FASB has taken the first three steps in "Objectives of Financial Reporting by Business Enterprises" and in "Qualitative Characteristics of Accounting Information."[4] The fourth step is represented by two

---

[4] FASB, *Statement of Financial Accounting Concepts No. 1,* "Objectives of Financial Reporting by Business Enterprises" (Stamford, Conn., 1978); and *Statement of Financial Accounting Concepts No. 2,* "Qualitative Characteristics of Accounting Information" (Stamford, Conn., 1980). Copyright © by the Financial Accounting Standards Board, High Ridge Park, Stamford, Connecticut 06905, U.S.A. Quoted (or excerpted) with permission. Copies of the complete documents are available from the FASB.

concepts statements entitled "Elements of Financial Statements of Business Enterprises" and "Elements of Financial Statements."[5]

OBJECTIVES OF FINANCIAL REPORTING

Financial reporting objectives are the broad overriding goals sought by accountants engaging in financial reporting. According to the FASB, the first objective of financial reporting is to:

> provide information that is useful to present and potential investors and creditors and other users in making rational investment, credit, and similar decisions. The information should be comprehensible to those who have a reasonable understanding of business and economic activities and are willing to study the information with reasonable diligence.[6]

The term *other users* is interpreted broadly and includes employees, security analysts, brokers, and lawyers. Financial reporting should provide information to all who are willing to learn to use it properly.

The second objective of financial reporting is to:

> provide information to help present and potential investors and creditors and other users in assessing the amounts, timing, and uncertainty of prospective cash receipts from dividends [owner withdrawals] or interest and the proceeds from the sale, redemption, or maturity of securities or loans. Since investors' and creditors' cash flows are related to enterprise cash flows, financial reporting should provide information to help investors, creditors, and others assess the amounts, timing, and uncertainty of prospective net cash inflows to the related enterprise.[7]

This objective ties the cash flows of investors (owners) and creditors to the cash flows of the enterprise, a tie-in that appears entirely logical. Enterprise cash inflows are the source of cash for dividends, interest, and redemption of maturing debt.

Third, financial reporting should:

> provide information about the economic resources of an enterprise, the claims to those resources (obligations of the enterprise to transfer resources to other entities and owners' equity), and the effects of transactions, events, and circumstances that change its resources and claims to those resources.[8]

---

[5] FASB, *Statement of Financial Accounting Concepts No. 3,* "Elements of Financial Statements of Business Enterprises" (Stamford, Conn., 1980); and *Statement of Financial Accounting Concepts No. 6,* "Elements of Financial Statements" (Stamford, Conn., 1985). Copyright © by the Financial Accounting Standards Board, High Ridge Park, Stamford, Connecticut 06905, U.S.A. Quoted (or excerpted) with permission. Copies of the complete documents are available from the FASB.

[6] FASB, *Statement of Financial Accounting Concepts No. 1,* p. viii.

[7] Ibid.

[8] Ibid.

A number of conclusions can be drawn from these three objectives and from a study of the environment in which financial reporting is carried out. For example, financial reporting should:

1. Provide information about an enterprise's past performance because such information is used as a basis for prediction of future enterprise performance.
2. Focus on earnings and its components, despite the emphasis in the objectives on cash flows. (Earnings computed under the accrual basis generally provide a better indicator of ability to generate favorable cash flows than do statements prepared under the cash basis.)

On the other hand, financial reporting does not seek to:

1. Measure the value of an enterprise but rather provides information that may be useful in determining its value.
2. Evaluate management's performance, predict earnings, assess risk, or estimate earning power but rather provides information to persons who wish to make these evaluations.

These conclusions are some of those reached in *Statement of Financial Accounting Concepts No. 1.* As the Board stated, these statements "are intended to establish the objectives and concepts that the Financial Accounting Standards Board will use in developing standards of financial accounting and reporting."[9] How successful the Board will be in the approach adopted remains to be seen.

QUALITATIVE CHARACTERISTICS

Qualitative characteristics are those characteristics that accounting information should possess to be useful in decision making. This criterion is difficult to apply. The usefulness of accounting information in a given instance depends not only on information characteristics but also on the capabilities of the decision makers and their professional advisers, if any. Accountants cannot specify who the decision makers are, their characteristics, the decisions to be made, or the methods chosen to make the decisions; therefore, attention is directed to characteristics of accounting information. The FASB's graphic summarization of the problems faced is presented in Illustration 11.5.[10]

Relevance

For information to have **relevance,** it must be pertinent to or affect a decision. The information must "make a difference" to someone who does not

---

[9] Ibid., p. i.
[10] FASB, *Statement of Financial Accounting Concepts No. 2,* p. 15.

Illustration 11.5
A HIERARCHY OF ACCOUNTING QUALITIES

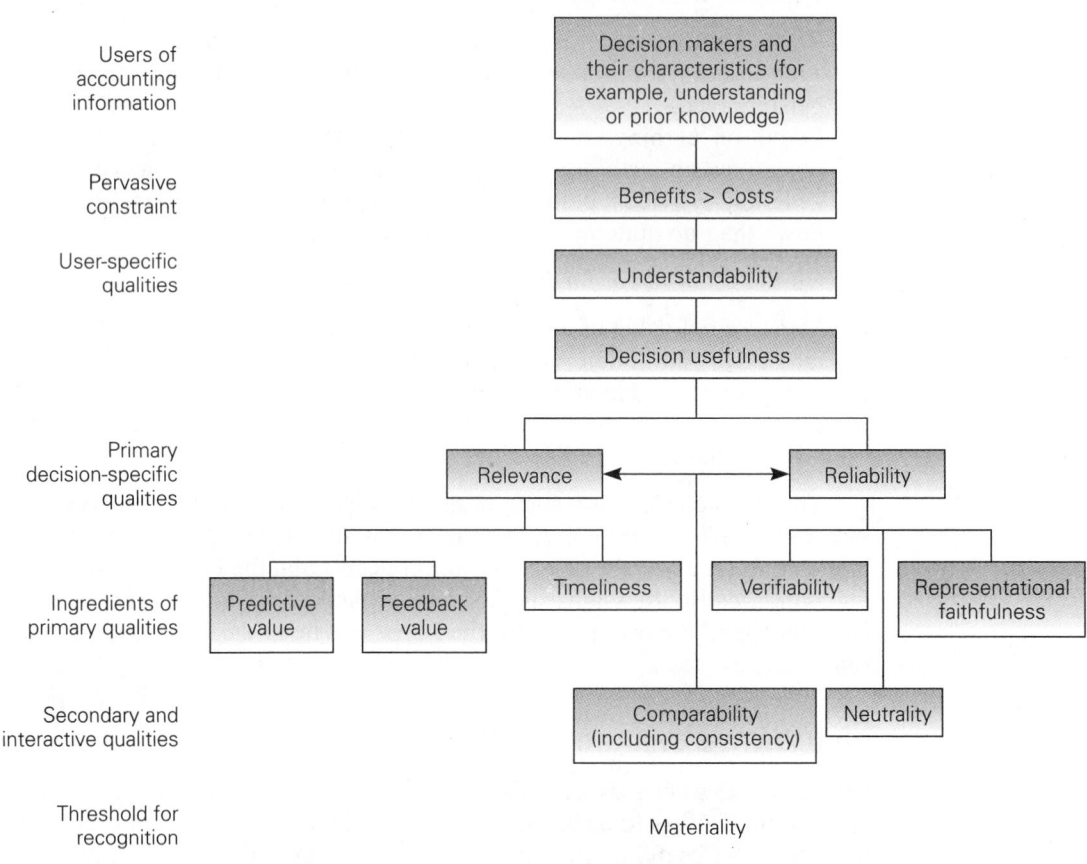

already have the information. Relevant information is capable of making a difference in a decision either by affecting user predictions of outcomes of past, present, or future events or by confirming or correcting expectations. Note that information need not be a prediction to be useful in developing, confirming, or altering expectations. Expectations are commonly based on the present or past. For example, any attempt to predict future earnings of a company would quite likely start with a review of present and past earnings. Also, information that merely confirms prior expectations may be less useful, but this information is still relevant because it reduces uncertainty.

Certain types of accounting information have been criticized because of an alleged lack of relevance. For example, some would argue that a cost of $1 million paid for a tract of land 40 years ago and reported in the current balance sheet at that amount is irrelevant (except for possible tax implications) to users for decision making today. Such criticism has encouraged research into the types of information relevant to users. Suggestions have been made that a different valuation basis, such as current cost, be used in reporting such assets.

Predictive Value and Feedback Value. Since actions taken now can affect only future events, information is obviously relevant when it possesses **predictive value,** or improves users' abilities to predict outcomes of events. Information that reveals the relative success of users in predicting outcomes possesses **feedback value.** Feedback reports on past activities and can make a difference in decision making by (1) reducing uncertainty in a situation, (2) refuting or confirming prior expectations, and (3) providing a basis for further predictions. For example, a report on the first quarter's earnings of a company reduces the uncertainty surrounding the amount of such earnings, confirms or refutes the predicted amount of such earnings, and provides a possible basis on which to predict earnings for the full year. You should remember that although accounting information may possess predictive value, it does not consist of predictions. Making predictions is a function performed by the decision maker, not the accountant.

Timeliness. **Timeliness** requires that accounting information be provided at a time when it may be considered in reaching a decision. Utility of information decreases with age—to know what the net income for 1994 was in early 1995 is much more useful than to receive this information a year later. If information is to be of any value in decision making, it must be available *before* the decision is made. If not, the information is of little value. In determining what constitutes timely information, consideration must be given to the other qualitative characteristics and to the cost of gathering information. For example, a timely estimated amount for uncollectible accounts may be more valuable than a later, verified actual amount. Timeliness alone cannot make information relevant, but information that was potentially relevant might be rendered irrelevant by a lack of timeliness.

Reliability

In addition to being relevant, information must be reliable to be useful. Information has **reliability** when it faithfully depicts for users what it purports to represent. Thus, accounting information is reliable if users can depend on it to reflect the underlying economic activities of the organization. The reliability of information depends on its representational faithfulness, verifiability, and neutrality. The information must also be complete and free of bias.

Representational Faithfulness. Insight into this quality may be gained by considering a map. A map possesses representational faithfulness when it shows roads and bridges (among other things) where roads and bridges actually exist. A correspondence exists between what is shown on the map and what is present physically. Similarly, **representational faithfulness** exists when accounting statements on economic activity correspond to the actual underlying activity. Where there is no correspondence, the cause may be (1) bias or (2) lack of completeness.

1. **Effects of bias.**   Accounting measurements are biased if they are consistently too high or too low. **Bias** in accounting measurements may exist due to the choice of measurement method or to bias introduced either deliberately or through lack of skill by the measurer.

2. **Completeness.**   To be free from bias, information must be sufficiently complete to ensure that it validly represents underlying events and conditions. **Completeness** means that all significant information must be disclosed in a way that aids understanding and does not mislead. Relevance of information also may be reduced if information that would make a difference to a user is omitted. Currently, full disclosure generally requires presentation of a balance sheet, an income statement, a statement of cash flows, and necessary notes to the financial statements and supporting schedules. A statement of changes in stockholders' equity (which includes information contained in a statement of retained earnings), is also required in annual reports of corporations. Such statements must be complete, with items properly classified and segregated (such as reporting sales revenue separately from other revenues). Required disclosures may be made in (1) the body of the financial statements, (2) the notes to such statements, (3) special communications, and/or (4) the president's letter or other management reports in the annual report.

Another aspect of completeness is that full disclosure must be made of all changes in accounting principles and their effects.[11] Disclosure should also be made of unusual activities (loans to officers), changes in expectations (losses on inventory), depreciation expense for the period, long-term obligations entered into that are not recorded by the accountant (a 20-year lease on a building), new arrangements with certain groups (pension and profit-sharing plans for employees), and significant events that occur after the date of the statements (loss of a major customer). Accounting policies (major principles and their manner of application) followed in preparing the financial statements should also be disclosed.[12] Because of its emphasis on disclosure, this aspect of reliability is often called the *full disclosure principle*.

Verifiability.   Financial information has **verifiability** when it can be substantially duplicated by independent measurers using the same measurement methods. Verifiability is directed toward eliminating measurer bias, rather than measurement method bias. The requirement that financial information is derived from objective evidence is based on demonstrated needs of users for reliable, unbiased financial information. Unbiased information is espe-

---

[11] APB, *APB Opinion No. 20,* "Accounting Changes" (New York: AICPA, July 1971).

[12] APB, *APB Opinion No. 22,* "Disclosure of Accounting Policies" (New York: AICPA, April 1972).

cially needed when parties with opposing interests (credit seekers and credit grantors) rely on the same information. Reliability of information is enhanced if the information is verifiable.

Financial information will never be free of subjective opinion and judgment; it will always possess varying degrees of verifiability. Some measurements can be supported by canceled checks and invoices. Other measurements, such as periodic depreciation charges, can never be verified because of their very nature. Thus, financial information in many instances is verifiable only in that it represents a consensus as to what would be reported if the same procedures had been followed by other accountants.

Neutrality. **Neutrality** in accounting information means that the information should be free of measurement method bias. The primary concern should be relevance and reliability of the information that result from application of the principle, not the effect that the principle may have on a particular interest. Nonneutral accounting information is designed to favor one set of interested parties over others. For example, a particular form of measurement might favor stockholders over creditors, or vice versa. "To be neutral, accounting information must report economic activity as faithfully as possible, without coloring the image it communicates for the purpose of influencing behavior in *some particular direction*."[13] Accounting standards should not be developed and used like certain tax regulations that deliberately seek to foster or restrain certain types of activity. Verifiability seeks to eliminate measurer bias; neutrality seeks to eliminate measurement method bias.

Comparability (and Consistency)

When **comparability** in financial information exists, reported differences and similarities in information are real and are not the result of differing accounting treatments. Comparable information will reveal relative strengths and weaknesses in a single company through time and between two or more companies at the same point in time.

Consistency requires that a company use the same accounting principles and reporting practices through time. Consistency leads to comparability of financial information for a single company through time. Comparability between companies is more difficult to achieve because the same activities may be accounted for in different ways. For example, Company B may use one method of depreciation, while Company C accounts for an identical asset in similar circumstances using another method. A high degree of intercompany comparability in accounting information will not exist unless accountants are required to account for the same activities in the same manner across companies and through time.

---

[13] FASB, *Statement of Financial Accounting Concepts No. 2*, par. 100.

Pervasive Constraints

As Illustration 11.5 shows, two pervasive constraints must be considered in providing useful information. First, the benefits secured from the information must be greater than the costs of providing that information. Second, only material items need be disclosed and accounted for strictly in accordance with generally accepted accounting principles (GAAP). Both cost-benefit and materiality were discussed earlier in the chapter.

THE BASIC ELEMENTS OF FINANCIAL STATEMENTS

Thus far we have discussed objectives of financial reporting and qualitative characteristics of accounting information. A third important task in developing a conceptual framework for any discipline is that of identifying and defining its basic elements. The FASB identified and defined the basic elements of financial statements in *Concepts Statement No. 3*. Later, some of the definitions were revised in *Concepts Statement No. 6*. Most of the terms were defined earlier in this text in a less technical way to convey a general understanding of the terms. The more technical definitions are listed below. (These items are not repeated in this chapter's "New Terms.")

Assets are probable future economic benefits obtained or controlled by a particular entity as a result of past transactions or events.

Liabilities are probable future sacrifices of economic benefits arising from present obligations of a particular entity to transfer assets or provide services to other entities in the future as a result of past transactions or events.

Equity or net assets is the residual interest in the assets of an entity that remains after deducting its liabilities. In a business enterprise, the equity is the ownership interest. In a not-for-profit organization, which has no ownership interest in the same sense as a business enterprise, net assets is divided into three classes based on the presence or absence of donor-imposed restrictions—permanently restricted, temporarily restricted, and unrestricted net assets.

Comprehensive income is the change in equity of a business enterprise during a period from transactions and other events and circumstances from nonowner sources. It includes all changes in equity during a period except those resulting from investments by owners and distributions to owners.

Revenues are inflows or other enhancements of assets of any entity or settlements of its liabilities (or a combination of both) from delivering or producing goods, rendering services, or other activities that constitute the entity's ongoing major or central operations.

Expenses are outflows or other using up of assets or incurrences of liabilities (or a combination of both) from delivering or producing goods, rendering services, or carrying out other activities that constitute the entity's ongoing major or central operations.

Gains are increases in equity (net assets) from peripheral or incidental transactions of an entity and from all other transactions and other events and circumstances affecting the entity except those that result from revenues or investments by owners.

Losses are decreases in equity (net assets) from peripheral or incidental transactions of an entity and from all other transactions and other events and circumstances affecting the entity except those that result from expenses or distributions to owners.

Investments by owners are increases in equity of a particular business enterprise resulting from transfers to it from other entities of something valuable to obtain or increase ownership interests (or equity) in it. Assets are most commonly received as investments by owners, but that which is received may also include services or satisfaction or conversion of liabilities of the enterprise.

Distributions to owners are decreases in equity of a particular business enterprise resulting from transferring assets, rendering services, or incurring liabilities by the enterprise to owners. Distributions to owners decrease ownership interest (or equity) in an enterprise.[14]

Note that the requirement that assets and liabilities be based on past transactions normally rules out the recording of contracts that are mutual promises to do something, such as entering into an employment contract with an officer. For a similar reason, the accountant refuses to record an asset and a liability when a contract is signed whereby the entity agrees to purchase a certain number of units of a product over a future period of time.

RECOGNITION AND MEASUREMENT IN FINANCIAL STATEMENTS

In December 1984, the FASB issued *Statement of Financial Accounting Concepts No. 5,* "Recognition and Measurement in Financial Statements of Business Enterprises,"[15] describing recognition criteria and providing guidance as to the timing and nature of information to be included in financial statements. The recognition criteria established in the *Statement* are fairly consistent with those used in current practice. The *Statement* indicates, however, that when information that is more useful than currently reported information is available at a reasonable cost, it should be included in financial statements.

A slightly modified income statement format is recommended. The income statement may become a statement of earnings and comprehensive

---

[14] FASB, *Statement of Financial Accounting Concepts No. 6.*

[15] FASB, *Statement of Financial Accounting Concepts No. 5,* "Recognition and Measurement in Financial Statements of Business Enterprises" (Stamford, Conn., 1984). Copyright © by the Financial Accounting Standards Board, High Ridge Park, Stamford, Connecticut 06905, U.S.A. Copies of the complete document are available from the FASB. (In case you are wondering why we do not mention *Statement of Financial Accounting Concepts No. 4,* it pertains to accounting for not-for-profit organizations and is, therefore, not relevant to this text.)

ETHICS   A CLOSER LOOK

Sam Jenkins is a partner in the XYZ CPA firm. One of his assignments is serving on the audit of Massey's, Inc., a large retail chain. The company underwent a "leveraged buyout" several years ago when the company's management bought a controlling interest in the company. The buyout was financed through the use of high-interest bonds (called *junk bonds*).

The economy is currently in a recession, and economists cannot agree on when the recession is likely to end. The company's sales have reached an all-time low. It seems that people are not spending money at up-scale stores such as Massey's. Instead, they are buying at the discount stores.

As part of the audit, the partner on the job has to decide whether or not the client is a "going concern." In other words, is the client apt to continue in business next year, or will the client probably have to go out of business? The company cannot meet its interest payments next year unless the current recession ends soon.

Sam believes the most likely scenario is that the company will have to declare bankruptcy next year and seek protection from its creditors. Even under "Chapter 11 bankruptcy," the company must eventually be able to reorganize as a profitable entity or be forced into liquidation by its creditors.

Sam knows that if the auditor's opinion includes a statement that the company may not be a going concern, this very action could cause the creditors to demand immediate payment of the amounts due to them and could lead to liquidation of the company. Yet, if he does not include such a statement in the auditor's report, he and his firm might be successfully sued by persons relying on the auditor's report—if it is proven that the evidence available at the time of the audit casts substantial doubt about the company's ability to continue in existence. The client has pleaded with Sam not to include the statement in the auditor's report so the company will have a chance of "working out" of its bad situation. Sam is worried about what to do and is beginning to lose sleep over his dilemma.

Required
a. Restate Sam's dilemma.
b. What is an underlying ethical consideration in this situation?
c. Who could be hurt if Sam does not include the statement?
d. Who could be hurt if Sam does include the statement?
e. What should Sam do?

income. "Earnings" would generally be computed in the same way as income after extraordinary items (covered in Chapter 9) is presently calculated. Then, cumulative account adjustments (such as changes in accounting principle) and other nonowner changes in equity would be added or deducted in arriving at "comprehensive income." The lower part of the statement would appear as shown at the top of the next page.

The *Statement* also indicates that a balance sheet does not show the value of a business, but when used in combination with other information and other financial statements, the balance sheet is helpful in estimating the value of a business. The importance of cash flow information (covered in Chapter 13) is also mentioned.

Earnings	xx
+ or − Cumulative account adjustments (e.g., cumulative effect of changes in accounting principle) .	xx
+ or − Other nonowner changes in equity (e.g., gains or losses on market changes in noncurrent marketable equity securities)	xx
Comprehensive income	xx

The chapter appendix discusses international accounting. As we move toward a global economy, this topic becomes vitally important. The next chapter begins the coverage of managerial accounting. Although managerial accounting pertains to service and merchandising companies as well, Chapter 12 introduces a third type of company—manufacturing companies.

UNDERSTANDING THE LEARNING OBJECTIVES

1. Identify and discuss the underlying assumptions or concepts of accounting.
    *   The major underlying assumptions or concepts of accounting are (1) business entity, (2) going concern (continuity), (3) money measurement, (4) stable dollar, and (5) periodicity.
    *   Other basic accounting concepts that affect the accounting for entities are (1) general-purpose financial statements, (2) substance over form, (3) consistency, (4) double entry, and (5) articulation.
2. Identify and discuss the major principles of accounting.
    *   The major principles include exchange-price (or cost), matching, revenue recognition, expense recognition, gain and loss recognition, and full disclosure. Major exceptions to the realization principle include cash collection as point of revenue recognition, installment basis of revenue recognition, the percentage-of-completion method of recognizing revenue on long-term construction projects, and revenue recognition at completion of production.
3. Identify and discuss the modifying conventions (or constraints) of accounting.
    *   Modifying conventions include cost-benefit, materiality, and conservatism.
4. Describe the Conceptual Framework Project of the Financial Accounting Standards Board.
    *   The FASB has defined the objectives of financial reporting, qualitative characteristics of accounting information, and elements of financial statements.
    *   Financial reporting objectives are the broad overriding goals sought by accountants engaging in financial reporting.
    *   Qualitative characteristics are those characteristics that accounting

information should possess to be useful in decision making. The two primary qualitative characteristics are relevance and reliability. Another qualitative characteristic is comparability.

- Pervasive constraints include cost-benefit analysis and materiality.
- The basic elements of financial statements have been identified and defined by the FASB.
- The FASB has also described revenue recognition criteria and provided guidance as to the timing and nature of information to be included in financial statements.

5. Discuss the differences in international accounting among nations (Appendix).

- Accounting principles differ among nations because they were developed independently.
- There have been attempts at harmonizing accounting principles throughout the world.
- Various differences in accounting principles that exist between nations are described.

APPENDIX

INTERNATIONAL ACCOUNTING*

Why Accounting Principles and Practices Differ among Nations

*Objective 5
Discuss the differences in international accounting among nations*

In today's world, we do not find it surprising to discover a British bank in Atlanta, Coca-Cola in Paris, and French airplanes in Zaire. German automobile parts are assembled in Spain and sold in the United States. Japan buys oil from Saudi Arabia and sells cameras in Italy. Russian livestock eat American grain, and the British sip tea from Sri Lanka and China. Business has become truly international, but accounting, often described as the language of business, does not cross borders so easily. Accounting principles and reporting practices differ from country to country, and international decision making is made more difficult by the lack of a common communication system. However, since business is practiced at an international level, accounting must find a way to provide its services at that level.

The problem is that accounting reflects the national economic and social environment in which it is practiced, and this environment is not the same in Bangkok as in Boston. Some economies, for example, are mainly agricultural. Others are based on manufacturing, trade, or service industries. Still others export natural resources, such as oil or gold, while a few derive most of their income from tourism. Accounting for inventories and natural re-

---

* The authors wish to express their appreciation to William P. Hauworth II, Partner, Arthur Andersen & Co., Chicago, Illinois, for updating this appendix.

sources, cost accounting techniques, and methods of foreign currency translation have a different orientation, emphasis, and degree of refinement in these different economies.

Other accounting differences stem from the various legal or political systems of nations. In centrally controlled economies (of which there are a declining number), for instance, the state owns all or most of the property. It makes little sense to prescribe full disclosure of accounting procedures to protect investors when little or no private ownership of property exists. In these nations with centrally controlled economies, an accounting profession is virtually nonexistent. Some of these countries standardize their accounting methods and incorporate them into law. One of the great challenges for Western nations over the next few decades is to assist the nations of Eastern Europe and the former Soviet Union to build an accounting profession within those nations to serve the companies that will evolve under their new market-oriented economies. Creation of an accounting profession will enhance the ability of these nations to do business with the West.

In most market-oriented economies, the development of accounting principles and reporting practices is left mainly to the private sector. Where uniformity exists, it occurs more by general agreement or consensus of interested parties than by governmental decree. In countries where business firms are predominately family owned, disclosure practices usually are less complete than in countries where large, publicly held corporations dominate. The requirement in many countries that the financial statements must conform to the tax return contributes to diversity in accounting practices among countries.

The degree of development of the accounting profession and the general level of education of a country also influence accounting practices and procedures. Nations that lack a well-organized accounting profession may adopt, almost in total, the accounting methods of other countries. Commonwealth countries, for example, tend to follow British accounting standards; the former French colonies of Africa use French systems; Bermuda follows Canadian pronouncements; and the influence of the United States is widespread. At the same time, levels of expertise vary. In countries that have little knowledge or understanding of statistics, nothing is gained by advocating statistical accounting and auditing techniques. Accounting systems designed for electronic data processing are not helpful in countries where few or no businesses use computers.

Even in advanced countries, genuine differences of opinion exist regarding accounting theory and appropriate accounting methods. American standards, for example, require the periodic amortization of goodwill to expense, but British and Dutch standards do not. The lack of agreement on the objectives of financial statements and the lack of any effort in most countries to articulate objectives also contribute to diversity. Accounting methods also differ within nations. Most countries, including the United States, permit several depreciation methods and two or more inventory costing methods.

Attempted Harmonization of Accounting Practices

The question arises as to whether financial statements that reflect the economic and social environment of, say, France can also be useful to a potential American investor. Can some of the differences between French and American accounting be eliminated or at least explained so that French and American investors will understand each other's reports and find them useful when they make decisions?

Several organizations are working to achieve greater understanding and harmonization of different accounting practices. These organizations include the Organization for Economic Cooperation and Development (OECD), the European Community (EC), the International Accounting Standards Committee (IASC), and the International Federation of Accountants (IFAC). These organizations study the information needs and accounting and reporting practices of different nations and some of them issue pronouncements recommending specific practices and procedures for adoption by all members.

The IASC is making a significant contribution to the development of international accounting standards. It was founded in London in 1973 by the professional accountancy bodies of 10 countries: Australia, Canada, France, Germany, Ireland, Japan, Mexico, the Netherlands, the United Kingdom and the United States. The IASC selects a topic for study from lists of problems submitted by the profession all over the world. After research and discussion by special committees, the IASC issues an exposure draft of a proposed standard for consideration by the profession and the business and financial communities. After about six months' further study of the topic in light of the comments received, the IASC issues the final international accounting standard. To date, 26 standards have been issued on topics as varied as *Disclosure of Accounting Policies* (IAS 1), *Depreciation Accounting* (IAS 4), *Statement of Changes in Financial Position* (IAS 7), and *Revenue Recognition* (IAS 18). Setting international standards is not easy. If the standards are too detailed or rigid, the flexibility needed to reflect different national environments will be lost. On the other hand, if pronouncements are vague and allow too many alternative methods, there is little point in setting international standards.

One major problem is obtaining compliance with these standards. There is no organization, nor is there likely to be an organization, to ensure compliance with international standards. Adoption is left to national standard-setting bodies or legislatures, which may or may not adopt a recommended international standard. Generally, members commit themselves to support the objectives of the international body. The members promise to use their best endeavors to see that international standards are formally adopted by local professional accountancy bodies, by government departments or other authorities that control the securities markets, and by the industrial, business, and financial communities of their respective countries.

The American Institute of Certified Public Accountants (AICPA), for example, issued a revised statement in 1975 reaffirming its support for the implementation of international standards adopted by the IASC. The AICPA's position is that international accounting standards must be specifically adopted by the Financial Accounting Standards Board (FASB), which is not a member of the IASC, to achieve acceptance in the United States. However, if no significant difference exists between an international standard and U.S. practice, compliance with U.S. generally accepted accounting principles (GAAP) constitutes compliance with the international standard. Where a significant difference exists, the AICPA publishes the IASC standard together with comments on how it differs from GAAP in the United States and undertakes to urge the FASB to give early consideration to harmonizing the differences.[16] Significant support for IASC standards has also resulted from a resolution adopted by the World Federation of Stock Exchanges in 1975. The resolution binds members to require conformance with IASC standards in securities listing agreements.[17]

Although these developments are important for the international harmonization of accounting, the success of international pronouncements ultimately depends on the willingness of the members to support them. In some cases, national legislation is required and may be slow or difficult to pass. The EC, for example, issues "Directives" that must be accepted as compulsory objectives by the 12 member states (Belgium, Denmark, France, Germany, Greece, Ireland, Italy, Luxembourg, the Netherlands, Portugal, Spain, and the United Kingdom) but are translated into national legislation at the discretion of each member state. The EC's important *Fourth Directive* was adopted in 1978 to regulate the preparation, content, presentation, audit, and publication of the accounts and reports of companies. It applies to all limited-liability companies (corporations) registered in the EC, except banks and insurance companies. Under the directive, member states were to introduce legislation by July 1980 so that accounts in all EC countries would conform to the directive as of the fiscal year beginning January 1, 1982.

The general movement toward international harmonization of accounting standards is increasing in other areas of society. The accounting profession, national standard-setting bodies, universities, academic societies, and multinational corporations have all shown an increased interest in international accounting problems in recent years. The AICPA has an International Practice Division as a formal part of its organization. The American Accounting Association officially established an International Accounting section in 1976 and has approximately one dozen international accounting organizations as Associate Members. The University of Lancaster (England) and the University of Illinois have international accounting research centers that

---

[16] American Institute of Certified Public Accountants, *CPA Letter,* August 1975.

[17] *CA Magazine,* January 1975, p. 52.

A BROADER PERSPECTIVE

E&Y ON TOP OF THE GLOBAL ACCOUNTING MARKET

Princeton, N.J.—Ernst & Young ranks first in the world in the number of audit clients, according to a new study by an independent researcher.

The study, conducted by the Center for International Financial Analysis & Research Inc., listed E&Y as the leader in both the number of companies audited (3,321) and also in the value of the companies audited ($10.2 billion). The study analyzed 1990 information from more than 22,000 publicly held companies. [See the International Accounting Scoreboard on the next page.]

Coming in second in both categories was Klynveld Peat Marwick Goerdeler (KPMG) with Deloitte Ross Tohmatsu (DRT) third in number of audit clients and Coopers & Lybrand (C&L) third in total value audited. Value audited includes a total of assets for financial companies and sales for all other client firms.

The study emphasizes the continued dominance of the Big Six, which audited 67 percent of all companies. The Big Six audited companies [with] 86 percent of all sales or assets among the companies studied, emphasizing that Big Six hegemony among larger clients.

The Big Six market share changed little over the 1989 study, said Vinod B. Bavishi, CIFAR executive director.

* * * * *

CIFAR also used the 1990 study to measure the impact of the 1989 mergers which created E&Y from Ernst & Whinney and Arthur Young, and DRT from Deloitte Haskins & Sells and Touche Ross International.

The E&Y merger pushed that firm to the top position in the United States in terms of clients while it also increased the number of worldwide partners by 8 percent.

* * * * *

"The world is becoming smaller," said Bavishi. He said that market forces are driving the harmonization of international accounting standards and that money managers will demand comparisons be made even if accountants cannot agree to standards.

Those areas included treatment of depreciation, which CIFAR found to be extremely diverse, particularly in the manufacturing industries. It also found inconsistency in the treatment of consolidation of subsidiaries along with distorted performance from the use of discretionary or general reserves, allowed in countries such as Japan and Germany.

SOURCE: *Accounting Today,* January 6, 1992, p. 6. Reprinted with permission.

support research studies and conduct international conferences and seminars. Georgia State University received a Touche Ross & Co. grant to internationalize its accounting curriculum. Many universities currently offer courses in international business and accounting.

All this activity helps increase the flow of information and our understanding of the accounting and reporting practices in other parts of the world. Greater understanding improves the likelihood that unnecessary differences will be eliminated and enhances the general acceptance of international standards.

The difficulty of achieving harmonization was illustrated in a recent

INTERNATIONAL ACCOUNTING SCOREBOARD

	Number of Companies	% of Total Companies	Total Sales and/or Assets (U.S.$ Billions)	% of Total Sales/Assets	Number of Offices	Total Partners	% of Total Partners	Average Partners per Office
Ernst & Young International	3,231	14.62	$10,228	22.29	777	5,700	13.41	7.34
KPMG Klynveld Peat Marwick Goerdeler	3,163	14.32	8,466	18.45	864	6,530	15.36	7.56
Deloitte Ross Tohmatsu International	2,726	12.34	6,935	15.12	722	4,823	11.36	6.68
Coopers & Lybrand	2,380	10.77	6,639	14.47	737	5,152	12.12	6.99
Price Waterhouse	1,691	7.65	4,584	9.99	496	3,113	7.32	6.27
Arthur Andersen	1,627	7.36	2,815	6.14	289	2,478	5.83	8.57
BDO Binder	351	1.59	636	1.39	377	1,556	3.66	4.13
Horwath International	348	1.58	154	0.34	212	824	1.94	3.89
Grant Thornton International	312	1.41	210	0.46	323	1,248	2.94	3.86
Dunwoody Robson McGladrey & Pullen	149	0.67	67	0.15	270	1,052	2.47	3.90
Moores Rowland International	118	0.53	107	0.23	314	1,228	2.89	3.91
Clark Kenneth Leventhal	106	0.48	108	0.24	102	466	1.10	4.57
Pannell Kerr Forster	104	0.47	177	0.39	247	766	1.80	3.10
Summit International Associates Inc.	104	0.47	45	0.10	176	861	2.03	4.89
Nexia International	102	0.46	147	0.32	285	992	2.33	3.48
Hodgson Landau Brands International	51	0.23	23	0.05	215	703	1.65	3.27
BKR International	36	0.16	254	0.55	103	452	1.06	4.39
DFK International	35	0.16	31	0.07	199	518	1.22	2.60
Moore Stephens	31	0.14	15	0.03	186	565	1.33	3.04
TGI	25	0.11	9	0.02	187	639	1.50	3.42
Independent Accountants International	22	0.10	32	0.07	167	536	1.26	3.21
Midsnell International	17	0.08	91	0.20	161	432	1.02	2.68
The International Group of Accounting Firms	15	0.07	4	0.01	119	481	1.13	4.04
Jeffreys Henry International	12	0.05	0	*	94	350	0.82	3.72
AFAi/Alliott Pierson International	9	0.04	1	*	156	487	1.15	3.12
GMN International	9	0.04	0	*	70	208	0.49	2.97
ACPA International	5	0.02	1	*	69	221	0.52	3.20
No Auditor	663	3.00	76	0.17				
Non-Affiliated Firms	4,654	21.06	4,026	8.78				

* Very small percentage.

SOURCE: Center for International Financial Analysis & Research Inc.

effort to gain international agreement on the treatment of goodwill.[18] The International Accounting Standards Committee issued an exposure draft, known as E32, that included a provision that goodwill be recorded as an asset and amortized against earnings over a period of five years. If a company wanted to use a longer period, it would have to justify its position and explain it in the financial statements.

Currently, the United Kingdom and the Netherlands write off goodwill immediately against "reserves" (a part of stockholders' equity) and bypass the income statement. This method gives them an advantage when making acquisitions because future earnings are not reduced by the amortization of goodwill. Some countries record goodwill as an asset but have amortization periods that exceed five years. For instance, in the United States goodwill can be written off over a period not to exceed 40 years. Other countries, such as Holland, permit either approach.

Companies in the United Kingdom generally oppose the change because it would reduce reported earnings and would remove their advantage in making acquisitions. However, they might be willing to support a change if the write-off period were longer, say, 20 years. The Dutch seem to be opposed to any change in their current accounting for goodwill. The French generally agreed with the proposal but would like a longer write-off period. Arthur Wyatt, the U.S. delegate to the IASC, felt that executives of U.S. companies might oppose a five-year write-off period because it would reduce income and affect their compensation plans that are often tied to income. If harmonization is to be achieved regarding accounting for goodwill, compromise will be necessary.

The remainder of this appendix gives examples of the accounting methods used in different countries and of the concepts that underlie them to illustrate the difficulty of achieving international harmonization.

Foreign Currency Translation

Foreign currency translation is probably the most common problem in an international business environment. Foreign currency translation has two main components: accounting for transactions in a foreign currency and translating the financial statements of foreign enterprises into a different, common currency. This topic is presented here to give you an idea of the complexity of the harmonization effort.

Accounting for Transactions in a Foreign Currency.   Suppose an American automobile dealership imports vehicles from Japan and promises to pay for them in yen 90 days after receiving them. If no change in the dollar-yen exchange rate occurs between the date the goods are received and the date the invoice is paid, no problem exists. Both the purchase and the payment

---

[18] This discussion is based on an article by Anne O'Carroll, "IASC's Goodwill Proposal Draws Much Negative Criticism," *Corporate Accounting International*, no. 1 (November 1989), pp 8–9.

will be recorded at the same dollar value. But if the yen appreciates against the dollar during the 90-day period, the importer must pay more dollars for the yen needed on the settlement date.[19] Which exchange rate should the importer use to record the purchase of the vehicles—the rate in effect on the purchase date or on the payment date?

One approach to the problem is to regard the purchase of the automobiles and settlement of the invoice as two separate transactions and record them at two different exchange rates. The difference between the amount recorded in Accounts Payable on the purchase date and the amount of cash paid on the settlement date is considered an exchange gain or loss. This approach, known as the **time-of-transaction method,** was the prescribed or predominant practice in 61 of 64 countries surveyed in 1979,[20] including the United States.[21] The time-of-transaction method is also the method recommended in the IASC's Statement No. 21, *Accounting for the Effects of Changes in Foreign Exchange Rates,* issued in July 1983.

Another approach, known as the **time-of-settlement method**, regards the transaction and its settlement as a single event. If this method is used, the amount recorded on the purchase date is regarded as an estimate of the settlement amount. Any fluctuations in the exchange rate between the purchase date and the settlement date are accounted for as part of the transaction and are not treated as a separate gain or loss. Consequently, the effect on earnings is not recognized until the purchased items are sold.

Although the time-of-transaction method is widely used, the treatment of resulting exchange gains and losses is not uniform. If the gains or losses are realized (that is, if settlement is made within the same accounting period as the purchase), most countries recognize the gains and losses in the income statement for that period. If the **exchange gains or losses** are unrealized—that is, if they result from translating accounts payable (or accounts receivable for the vendor) at the balance sheet date—the treatment varies. Recording unrealized losses was the prescribed or predominant practice in 54 countries in 1979. Only 40 countries, however, similarly recognized exchange gains in income, the remaining nations preferring to defer them until settlement. In the United States, under the provisions of FASB *Statement No. 52,* both realized and unrealized transaction gains and losses are recognized in the earnings of the period in which the exchange rate changes.

---

[19] This example ignores the possibility that the importer might obtain a forward exchange contract, a discussion of which is beyond the scope of this text.

[20] Price Waterhouse International *International Survey.* Data on the different methods used and on the number of countries using each method described in these examples are derived substantially from this publication.

[21] FASB, *Statement of Financial Accounting Standards No. 8,* "Accounting for the Translation of Foreign Currency Transactions and Foreign Currency Financial Statements" (Stamford, Conn., 1975). The "time-of-transaction" method is also prescribed by FASB *Statement No. 52,* "Foreign Currency Translation" (Stamford, Conn., 1981), which supersedes FASB *Statement No. 8.*

Translating Financial Statements.   Financial statements of foreign subsidiaries are translated into a single common unit of measurement, such as the dollar, for purposes of consolidation. Considerable argument has arisen in recent years regarding the correct way to make this translation; that is, which exchange rate should be used to translate items in the balance sheet and income statement, and what treatment is appropriate for any resulting exchange gains and losses? Items translated at the historical rate cannot result in exchange gains or losses. However, items translated at the exchange rate in effect on the balance sheet date (the **current rate**) can result in exchange gains and losses if the current rate differs from the rate in effect when those items were recorded (the **historical rate**). If the current rate is used, a related question arises: Should the resulting exchange gains or losses be recognized immediately in income or deferred in some way?

The methods used to translate financial statements fall basically into two groups: translation of all items at the current rate and translation of some items at the current rate and others at the historical rates. The two groups are based on different concepts of both consolidation and international business.

The Current-Rate Approach.   The **current-rate or closing-rate approach** translates all assets and liabilities at the current rate, the exchange rate in effect on the balance sheet date. The main advantage of this method is its simplicity; it treats all items uniformly. The approach is based on the view that a foreign subsidiary is a separate unit from the domestic parent company. The subsidiary's assets are viewed as being acquired largely out of local borrowing. Multinational groups, therefore, consist of entities that operate independently but contribute to a central fund of resources. Consequently, in consolidation it is believed that stockholders of the parent company are interested primarily in the parent company's net investment in the foreign subsidiary.

The Current/Historical-Rates Approach.   The **current/historical-rates approach** regards the parent company and its foreign subsidiaries as a single business undertaking. Assets owned by a foreign subsidiary are viewed as indistinguishable from assets owned by the parent company. Foreign assets should, therefore, be reflected in consolidated statements in the same way that similar assets of the parent company are reported, that is, at historical cost in the parent company's currency.

Three translation methods are commonly used under this approach. The **current-noncurrent method** translates current assets and current liabilities at the current rate—the rate in effect on the balance sheet date—while noncurrent items are translated at their respective historical rates. The *historical rate* is the rate in effect when an asset or liability is originally recorded. Under the **monetary-nonmonetary method,** the current rate is used for monetary assets and liabilities—that is, for those that have a fixed, nominal value in terms of the foreign currency—while historical rates are applied to nonmonetary items. The **temporal method** is a variation of the monetary-nonmonetary method. Cash, receivables and payables, and other assets and liabilities carried at current prices (e.g., marketable securities carried at current market value) are translated at the current rate of exchange. All other assets and liabilities are translated at historical rates.

Disagreement over the appropriate translation method seems likely to continue because of the different concepts of parent-subsidiary relations on which they are founded. In 1979, only six countries prescribed a single method. The temporal method was required in Austria, Canada, Bermuda, Jamaica, and the United States (under FASB *Statement No. 8*), while Uruguay required the current-rate method. Since that time the United States and Canada have changed to the current-rate method (FASB *Statement No. 52*). Apart from these 6 nations, 24 countries, including most of Europe, Japan, and Australia, predominantly followed the current-rate approach, while in 25 countries, including Germany, South Africa, and most of Central and South America, some variation of the current/historical-rates approach was common practice.

The treatment of exchange gains and losses produced by translating items at the current rate varies and is not strictly related to the translation method used. In 1979, the predominant practice in 42 nations, including much of Europe, Latin America, Japan, and the United States, was to recognize all gains and losses immediately in income. Eighteen of these countries used the current-rate translation method, and 23 followed one of the current/historical-rates methods. Alternative treatments of translation gains and losses included recording them directly in stockholders' equity (Australia), recognizing some of them immediately in income and deferring others (United Kingdom), and recognizing some in income and deferring and amortizing others over the remaining life of the items concerned (Canada and Bermuda).

Since the issuance of FASB *Statement No. 52,* the immediate recognition of translation gains and losses in income is not permitted in the United States. Instead, they are reported separately and accumulated in a separate component of stockholders' equity until the parent company's investment in the foreign subsidiary is sold or liquidated, at which time they are reported as part of the gain or loss on sale or liquidation of the investment.

Inventories

Variations in accounting for inventories relate principally to the basis for determining cost and whether cost, once determined, should be increased or decreased to reflect the market value of the inventories.

Determination of Cost.   Although other methods are occasionally used in some countries, this text discusses three principal bases for determining inventory cost: first-in, first-out (FIFO); last-in, first-out (LIFO); and average cost.

The most frequently used methods in 1979 were FIFO and average cost.

Each of these methods was predominant in 31 countries, although no country required the use of one method to the exclusion of the other. FIFO was more common in Europe, although Austria, France, Greece, and Portugal used an average method. FIFO also predominated in Australia, Canada, South Africa, and the United States. The average method was generally followed in Latin America, Japan, and much of Africa. LIFO was the principal method in only one country—Italy—although it was a common minority method in Japan, the United States, most of Latin America, and several European countries. LIFO was considered an unacceptable method in Australia, Brazil, France, Ireland, Malawi, Norway, Peru, and the United Kingdom. IASC's Statement No. 2, *Valuation and Presentation of Inventories in the Context of the Historical Cost System,* supports the preference of the majority of countries and recommends the use of FIFO or average cost.

Market Value of Inventories. Only seven countries in 1979 did not require or predominantly follow the principle that inventories should be carried at the lower-of-cost-or-market value. Five of these countries, including Japan, used cost, even when cost exceeded market value. In the other two countries—Portugal and Switzerland—most enterprises wrote down inventories to amounts below both cost and market value, a practice permitted by law.

The main difference in the countries that did use the lower-of-cost-or-market approach was in the interpretation of "market value." Forty-eight countries equated market value with net realizable value, meaning estimated selling price in the ordinary course of business less costs of completion and necessary selling expenses. This view was essentially required in 22 countries, including Australia, France, Ireland, South Africa, and the United Kingdom. *IASC Statement No. 2* also requires this interpretation. Austria, Greece, Italy, and Venezuela interpreted market value as replacement cost—the current cost of replacing the inventories in their present condition and location.

The United States defines market value as replacement cost, with the stipulation that it cannot exceed net realizable value or fall below net realizable value reduced by the normal profit margin. In 1979, Chile, the Dominican Republic, Mexico, Panama, and the Philippines also used this interpretation of market value.

Accounting for the Effects of Changing Prices

The final example of international differences illustrates an opportunity for international harmonization that is almost unique. Accounting for the effects of changing prices is a relatively recent development, so it may be possible to achieve a general international approach to the problem before national practices become too varied and too entrenched.

Two approaches to accounting for the effects of changing prices on business enterprises are usually advocated: general price-level (constant-dollar) accounting and current-cost accounting. The FASB, in *Statement No. 33,* required both methods.[22] However, *Statement No. 82* eliminated the requirements to use the first of these methods.[23] The first approach attempts to reflect the effects of changes in general purchasing power on historical-cost financial statements, while the second is concerned with the impact of specific price changes. FASB *Statement No. 89* made reporting the effects of inflation completely optional.[24]

A number of countries are concerned about the loss of relevance of historical-cost financial reporting in inflationary environments, and several have adopted one of the two standard approaches—constant dollar or current cost. Some countries, usually those with the longest history of severe inflation, have issued standards that are mandatory for all enterprises, or at least for large or publicly held entities. In other countries, the accounting profession recommends, but does not prescribe, a form of inflation-adjusted statements, usually as supplementary information. Few countries, however, are prepared to abandon the present system based on historical cost and nominal units of currency for their primary financial statements, at least until decision makers have had sufficient experience with inflation accounting to give an opinion on its utility. Exceptions to this view are Argentina, Brazil, and Chile, which now require incorporation of general price-level accounting in the primary financial statements of all enterprises.

The United Kingdom's standard, until it was withdrawn, prescribed the provision of current-cost information either in the primary financial statements or as supplementary statements or additional information. New Zealand requires a supplementary income statement and balance sheet on a current-cost basis. Australia and South Africa recommend, but do not yet require, similar supplementary current-cost statements. Germany recommends the incorporation of current-cost information in notes to the historical-cost financial statements; while in the Netherlands, some companies prepare the primary statements on a current-cost basis, and some provide only supplementary information.

The fact that the accountancy bodies of various nations are adopting neither a uniform approach nor a uniform application of any approach, even with something as relatively new as accounting for changing prices, highlights the difficulty of achieving international harmonization of accounting standards. Adoption of different approaches to accounting for changing prices by different countries will make the preparation of consolidated financial statements by multinational corporations especially difficult, while at the

---

[22] FASB, *Statement of Financial Accounting Standards No. 33,* "Financial Reporting and Changing Prices" (Stamford, Conn., 1979).

[23] FASB, *Statement of Financial Accounting Standards No. 82,* "Financial Reporting and Changing Prices: Elimination of Certain Disclosures" (Stamford, Conn., 1984).

[24] FASB, *Statement of Financial Accounting Standards No. 89,* "Financial Reporting and Changing Prices" (Stamford, Conn., 1987).

same time comparability of the financial reports of companies in different nations will be further reduced. However, even if all countries adopted a similar approach, a major barrier to comparability would still remain: the price indexes used in each country to compute adjustments for price changes are not comparable in composition, accuracy, frequency of publication, or timeliness.

Many accountants are reluctant to see current-cost-adjusted statements replace historical-cost financial statements because they believe historical cost is the most objective basis of valuation. However, business entities may be more likely to favor inflation accounting, once they become accustomed to it, because of its tax implications—assuming the tax law will permit the method. Since inflation accounting generally leads to lower profit figures than those computed on the historical-cost basis, companies have a strong incentive to adopt inflation accounting in those countries where computation of the tax liability is based on reported net income. Governments, on the other hand, could then decide to prohibit the use of inflation accounting for tax purposes when a decline in tax revenues becomes apparent.

The current trend in the use of approaches to accounting for changing prices appears to be toward current-cost accounting and away from general price-level accounting. It has been suggested that, of the two approaches, governments prefer current-cost accounting, and this preference may influence the decisions of the accounting profession in some countries. As one British writer has pointed out:

> No government wants to have the effects of its currency debasement measured by anyone—certainly not by every business enterprise in the country. Much better to point the finger at all those individual prices moving around because of the machinations of big business, big labour and big aliens.[25]

Whether current-cost accounting will become common practice or whether some combination of current-cost and general price-level accounting will gain favor should depend on the usefulness to decision makers of the information provided by each approach. One thing is clear: As inflation again becomes a problem, more countries will adopt some form of inflation accounting. The opportunity to achieve a higher level of international harmonization while national standards are still at the development stage should not be missed.

We have attempted in these few pages to provide a broad and general picture of the variety of accounting principles and reporting practices that exist across the world. Articulation among countries is a challenging problem—and one that will receive increasing attention in the years to come.

Selected Bibliography

The following sources will provide you with additional information about international accounting.

---

[25] P. H. Lyons, "Farewell to Historical Costs?" *CA Magazine,* February 1976, p. 23.

Arthur Andersen & Co. (London). *European Review,* nos. 1–5 (January 1981–May 1982).

Choi, Frederick D. S., and Gerhard G. Mueller. *An Introduction to Multinational Accounting.* Englewood Cliffs, N.J.: Prentice-Hall, 1984.

Choi, Frederick D. S., and Richard M. Levich. "Behavioral Effects of International Accounting Diversity." *Accounting Horizons*, vol. 5, no. 2 (June 1991), pp. 1–13.

Gandy, Lisa A. "German and Japanese Annual Reports Lack Sufficient Information." *Corporate Accounting International,* no. 1 (November 1989), pp. 14–15.

Gray, Sidney J., and Clare B. Roberts. "East-West Accounting Issues: A New Agenda." *Accounting Horizons*, vol. 5, no. 1 (March 1991), pp. 42–50.

Hauworth, William P., II. "A Comparison of Various International Proposals on Inflation Accounting: A Practitioner's View." Monograph, 1980.

Hobson, D. "International Harmonization." *Public Finance and Accountancy* (May 1983), pp. 34–36.

Horner, Lawrence D. "Efficient Markets and Universal Standards." *Chief Executive* (Winter 1985), p. 38.

International Financial Reporting Standards: Problems and Prospects. ICRA Occasional Paper No. 13. Lancaster, England: International Centre for Research in Accounting, University of Lancaster, 1977.

London, David Aron. "Soviets Begin to Westernize Accounting Standards with East-West Joint Ventures." *Corporate Accounting International,* no. 1 (November 1989), pp. 6–7.

O'Carroll, Anne. "IASC's Goodwill Proposal Draws Much Negative Criticism." *Corporate Accounting International,* no. 1 (November 1989), pp. 8–9.

Price Waterhouse International. *International Survey of Accounting Principles and Reporting Practices,* 1979.

Purvis, S. E. C., Helen Gernon, and Michael A. Diamond. "The IASC and Its Comparability Project: Prerequisits for Success." *Accounting Horizons*, vol. 5, no. 2 (June 1991), pp. 25–44.

Smith, Bradford E. "Red Revolution Jostles World Rule Makers." *Accounting Today* (January 22, 1990), p. 12.

Stamp, Edward. *The Future of Accounting and Auditing Standards. ICRA Occasional Paper No. 18.* Lancaster, England: International Centre for Research in Accounting, University of Lancaster, 1979.

Stamp, Edward, and Maurice Moonitz. "International Auditing Standards—Parts I and II." *The CPA Journal* LII, nos. 6 and 7 (June–July 1982).

DEMONSTRATION PROBLEM

For each of the transactions or circumstances described below and the entries made, state which, if any, of the assumptions, concepts, principles, or modifying conventions of accounting have been violated. For each violation, give the entry to correct the improper accounting assuming the books have not been closed.

During the year, Dorsey Company did the following:

1. Had its buildings appraised. They were found to have a market value of $410,000, although their book value was only $380,000. The accountant debited

the Buildings and Accumulated Depreciation—Buildings accounts for $15,000 each and credited Paid-in Capital from Appreciation. No separate mention was made of this action in the financial statements.

2. Purchased a number of new electric pencil sharpeners for its offices at a total cost of $60. These pencil sharpeners were recorded as assets and are being depreciated over five years.

3. Produced a number of agricultural products at a cost of $26,000. These costs were charged to expense when the products were harvested. The products were set up in inventory at their market value of $35,000, and the Farm Revenues Earned account was credited for $35,000.

Solution to demonstration problem

1. The realization principle and the modifying convention of conservatism may have been violated. Such write-ups simply are not looked on with favor in accounting. To correct the situation, the entry made needs to be reversed:

Paid-in Capital from Appreciation.	30,000	
Buildings		15,000
Accumulated Depreciation—Buildings		15,000

2. Theoretically, no violations occurred, but the cost of compiling insignificant information could be considered a violation of acceptable accounting practice. As a practical matter, the $60 could have been expensed on materiality grounds.

3. No violations occurred. The procedures followed are considered acceptable for farm products that are interchangeable and readily marketable. No correcting entry is needed, provided due allowance has been made for the costs to be incurred in delivering the products to the market.

NEW TERMS

Accounting theory "A set of basic concepts and assumptions and related principles that explain and guide the accountant's actions in identifying, measuring, and communicating economic information." *577*

Bias Measurements that are consistently too high or too low. The bias may be (1) caused by choice of measurement method, (2) introduced deliberately, or (3) the result of lack of skill by the measurer. *600*

Business entity concept The specific unit for which accounting information is gathered. Business entities have a separate existence from owners, creditors, employees, customers, other interested parties, and other businesses. *578*

Comparability A qualitative characteristic of accounting information; when information is comparable, it reveals differences and similarities that are real and are not the result of differing accounting treatments. *601*

Completed-contract method A method of recognizing revenue on long-term projects under which no revenue is recognized until the period in which the project is completed; similar to recognizing revenue upon the completion of a sale. *588*

Completeness A qualitative characteristic of accounting information; requires disclosure of all significant information in a way that aids understanding and does not mislead; sometimes called the **full disclosure principle.** *600*

Conservatism Being cautious or prudent and making sure that net assets and net income are not overstated. *595*

Consistency Requires a company to use the same accounting principles and reporting practices through time. *581, 600*

Cost-benefit consideration Determining whether the benefits of including information in financial statements exceed the costs of providing the information. *593*

Cost principle See Exchange-price principle.

Current/historical-rates approach Regards the parent company and its foreign subsidiaries as a single business undertaking. All assets are shown at historical cost in the parent company's currency. *614*

Current-noncurrent method Translates current assets and current liabilities at the current rate. *614*

Current rate Exchange rate in effect on the balance sheet date. *614*

Current-rate or closing-rate approach The current-rate or closing-rate method translates all assets and liabilities at current rate, the exchange rate in effect on the balance sheet date. *614*

Earning principle The requirement that revenue be substantially earned before it is recognized (recorded). *586*

Exchange gains or losses (time-of-transaction method) The difference between the amount recorded in Accounts Payable on the purchase date and amount of cash paid on the settlement date. *613*

Exchange-price (or cost) principle Transfers of resources are recorded at prices agreed on by the parties to the exchange at the time of the exchange. *585*

Expense recognition principle Expenses should be recognized as they are incurred to produce revenues. *591*

Feedback value A qualitative characteristic that information has when it reveals the relative success of users in predicting outcomes. *599*

Financial reporting objectives The broad overriding goals sought by accountants engaging in financial reporting. *596*

Full disclosure principle Information important enough to influence the decisions of an informed user of the financial statements should be disclosed. *593*

Gain and loss recognition principle Gains may be recorded only when realized, but losses should be recorded when they first become evident. *591*

Gains Typically result from the sale of long-term assets for more than their book value. *591*

Going concern (continuity) assumption The assumption that an entity will continue to operate indefinitely unless strong evidence exists that the entity will terminate. *579*

Historical cost The amount paid, or the fair value of a liability incurred or other resources surrendered, to acquire an asset and place it in a condition and position for its intended use. *585*

Historical rate   The exchange rate in effect when an asset or liability is originally recorded. *614*

Installment basis   A revenue recognition procedure in which the percentage of total gross margin recognized in a period on an installment sale is equal to the percentage of total cash from the sale that is received in that period. *587*

Liquidation   Terminating a business by ceasing business operations and selling off its assets. *579*

Losses   Asset expirations that are usually involuntary and do not create revenues. *592*

Matching principle   The principle that net income of a period is determined by associating or relating revenues earned in a period with expenses incurred to generate those revenues. *585*

Materiality   A modifying convention that allows the accountant to deal with immaterial (unimportant) items in an expedient but theoretically incorrect manner; also a qualitative characteristic specifying that financial accounting report only information significant enough to influence decisions or evaluations. *593*

Modifying conventions   Customs emerging from accounting practice that alter the results that would be obtained from a strict application of accounting principles; conservatism is an example. *593*

Monetary-nonmonetary method   The current exchange rate is used in translating monetary assets and liabilities, while the historical rate is applied to nonmonetary items. *614*

Money measurement   Use of a monetary unit of measurement, such as the dollar, instead of physical or other units of measurement—feet, inches, grams, and so on. *579*

Neutrality   A qualitative characteristic that requires accounting information to be free of measurement method bias. *601*

Percentage-of-completion method   A method of recognizing revenue based on the estimated stage of completion of a long-term project. The stage of completion is measured by comparing actual costs incurred in a period with total estimated costs to be incurred in all periods. *588*

Period costs   Costs that cannot be traced to specific products and are expensed in the period in which incurred. *591*

Periodicity (time periods) assumption   An assumption of the accountant that an entity's life can be divided into time periods for purposes of reporting its economic activities. *580*

Predictive value   A qualitative characteristic that information has when it improves users' abilities to predict outcomes of events. *599*

Product costs   Costs incurred in the acquisition or manufacture of goods. Product costs are accounted for as if they were attached to the goods, with the result that they are charged to expense when the goods are sold. *591*

Production basis   A method of revenue recognition used in limited circumstances that recognizes revenue at the time of completion of production or extraction. *590*

Qualitative characteristics   Characteristics that accounting information should possess to be useful in decision making. *597*

Realization principle   A principle that directs that revenue is recognized only after the seller acquires the right to receive payment from the buyer. *586*

Relevance   A qualitative characteristic requiring that information be pertinent to or affect a decision. *597*

Reliability   A qualitative characteristic requiring that information faithfully depict for users what it purports to represent. *599*

Representational faithfulness   A qualitative characteristic requiring that accounting statements on economic activity correspond to the actual underlying activity. *599*

Revenue recognition principle   The principle that revenues should be earned and realized before they are recognized (recorded). *586*

Stable dollar assumption   An assumption that the dollar is a reasonably stable unit of measurement. *579*

Temporal method   Cash, receivables and payables, and other assets and liabilities carried at current prices are translated at the current rate of exchange. All other assets and liabilities are translated at historical rates. *614*

Timeliness   A qualitative characteristic requiring that accounting information be provided at a time when it may be considered before making a decision. *599*

Time-of-settlement method   Regards the transaction in a foreign currency and its settlement as a single event and records it at the settlement date exchange rate. *613*

Time-of-transaction method   Regards the transaction in a foreign currency and the settlement of the invoice as two separate transactions and records them at two different exchange rates. *613*

Verifiability   A qualitative characteristic of accounting information; information is verifiable when it can be substantially duplicated by independent measurers using the same measurement methods. *600*

SELF-TEST

True-False

Indicate whether each of the following statements is true or false.

1. The business entity concept assumes that each business has an existence separate from all parties except its owners.

2. When the substance of a transaction differs from its legal form, the accountant should record the economic substance.

3. The matching principle is fundamental to the accrual basis of accounting.

4. Exceptions to the realization principle include the installment basis of revenue recognition

for sales revenue and the completed-contract method for long-term construction projects.

5. Immaterial items do not have to be recorded at all.

6. The Conceptual Framework Project resulted in identifying two primary qualitative characteristics that accounting information should possess—relevance and reliability.

7. *(Based on Appendix)*   Pronouncements issued by the International Accounting Standards Committee (IASC) must be followed by member nations.

Multiple-Choice

Select the best answer for each of the following questions.

1. The underlying assumptions of accounting include all the following except:
   a. Business entity.
   b. Going concern.
   c. Matching.
   d. Money measurement and periodicity.

2. The concept that requires that all companies use the same accounting practices and reporting practices through time is:
   a. Substance over form.
   b. Consistency.
   c. Articulation.
   d. None of the above.

3. Which of the following statements is false regarding the revenue recognition principle?
   a. Revenue must be substantially earned before it is recognized.
   b. The accountant usually recognizes revenue before the seller acquires the right to receive payment from the buyer.
   c. Some small companies use the cash basis of accounting.
   d. Under the installment basis, the gross margin recognized in a period is equal to the amount of cash received from installment sales times the gross margin percentage for the year of sale.

4. Assume the following facts regarding the construction of a bridge:

Construction costs this period. . .	$ 3,000,000
Total estimated construction costs.	10,000,000
Total sales price	15,000,000

The revenue that should be recognized this period under the percentage-of-completion method is:
   a. $3,000,000.
   b. $4,500,000.
   c. $5,000,000.
   d. $6,500,000.

5. Modifying conventions include all of the following except:
   a. Periodicity.
   b. Cost-benefit.
   c. Materiality.
   d. Conservatism.

6. Which of the following is not part of the Conceptual Framework Project?
   a. Objectives of financial reporting.
   b. Quantitative characteristics.
   c. Qualitative characteristics.
   d. Basic elements of financial statements.

7. *(Based on Appendix)* Which of the following statements is true regarding the environment of international accounting?
   a. More and more nations are switching to a market-oriented economy.
   b. The accounting practices around the world are almost completely harmonized.
   c. The other nations of the world are willing to accept accounting methods used in the United States as the best methods to use in their own country.
   d. The topic of international accounting is becoming less and less relevant over time.

Now turn to page 632 to check your answers.

QUESTIONS

1. Name the assumptions underlying generally accepted accounting principles. Comment on the validity of the stable unit of measurement assumption during periods of high inflation.

2. Why does the accountant use the business entity concept?

3. When is the going-concern assumption not to be used?

4. What is meant by the term *accrual basis of accounting?* What is its alternative?

5. What does it mean to say that accountants record substance rather than form?

6. If a company changes an accounting principle because the change better meets the information needs of users, what disclosures must be made?

7. What is the exchange-price (or cost) principle? What is the significance of adhering to this principle?

8. What two requirements generally must be met before revenue will be recognized in a period?

9. Under what circumstances, if any, is the receipt of cash an acceptable time to recognize revenue?

10. What two methods may be used in recognizing revenues on long-term construction contracts?

11. Define expense. What principles guide the recognition of expense?

12. How does an expense differ from a loss?

13. What is the full disclosure principle?

14. What role does cost-benefit play in financial reporting?

15. What is meant by the accounting term *conservatism?* How does it affect the amounts reported in the financial statements?

16. Does materiality relate only to the relative size of dollar amounts?

17. Identify the three major parts of the Conceptual Framework Project that are included in the text.

18. What are the two primary qualitative characteristics?

19. *(Based on Appendix)* Why do differences exist in accounting standards and practices from nation to nation?

20. *(Based on Appendix)* How successful have efforts at harmonization been to date?

21. (*Based on Appendix*) Why do former Soviet Bloc nations have to develop internationally acceptable accounting and reporting standards? What is the present status of the accounting profession in these nations?

22. *Real-world question* A recent annual report of the American Ship Building Company stated:

Revenues, costs, and profits applicable to construction and conversion contracts are included in the consolidated statements of operations using the . . . percentage-of-completion accounting method. . . . The completed contract method was used for income tax reporting in the years this method was allowed.

Why might the management of a company want to use two different methods for accounting and tax purposes?

23. *Real-world question* A recent annual report of the Chevron Corporation stated:

Environmental expenditures that relate to current or future revenues are expensed or capitalized as appropriate. Expenditures that relate to an existing condition caused by past operations, and do not contribute to current or future revenue generation, are expensed.

What principle of accounting is being followed by this policy?

EXERCISES

Match theory terms with definitions (L.O. 1–3)

11–1. Match the items in Column A with the proper descriptions in Column B.

Column A	Column B
1. Going concern (continuity).	a. An assumption relied on in the preparation of the primary financial statements that would be unreasonable when the inflation rate is high.
2. Consistency.	
3. Disclosure.	
4. Periodicity.	
5. Conservatism.	b. Concerned with relative dollar amounts.
6. Stable dollar.	c. The usual basis for the recording of assets.
7. Matching.	
8. Materiality.	d. Required if the accounting treatment differs from that previously used for a particular item.
9. Exchange-price.	
10. Business entity.	
	e. An assumption that would be unreasonable to use in reporting on a firm that had become insolvent.
	f. None of these.
	g. Requires a company to use the same accounting procedures and practices through time.
	h. An assumption that the life of an entity can be subdivided into time periods for reporting purposes.
	i. Discourages undue optimism in measuring and reporting net assets and net income.
	j. Requires separation of personal activities from business activities in the recording and reporting processes.

Compute income under accrual basis and installment method (L.O. 2)

11–2. Morrison Company sells its products on an installment sales basis. Data for 1995 and 1996 are shown below.

	1995	1996
Installment sales	$200,000	$240,000
Cost of goods sold on installment sales . . .	140,000	180,000
Other expenses.	30,000	40,000
Cash collected from 1995 sales	120,000	60,000
Cash collected from 1996 sales		160,000

a. Compute the net income for 1996 assuming use of the accrual (sales) basis of revenue recognition.

b. Compute the net income for 1996 assuming use of the installment method of recognizing gross margin.

Recognize
revenue under
percentage-of-
completion
method
(L.O. 2)

11–3. A company has a contract to build a ship at a price of $500 million and an estimated cost of $400 million. In 1995, costs of $100 million were incurred. Under the percentage-of-completion method, how much revenue would be recognized in 1995?

Compute effect on
financial
statements of
incorrectly
expensing an
asset
(L.O. 2)

11–4. A company follows a practice of expensing the premium on its fire insurance policy when the policy is paid. In 1995, the company charged to expense the $12,000 premium paid on a three-year policy covering the period July 1, 1995, to June 30, 1998. In 1992, a premium of $9,000 was charged to expense on the same policy for the period July 1, 1992, to June 30, 1995.

a. State the principle of accounting that was violated by this practice.

b. Compute the effects of this violation on the financial statements for the calendar year 1995.

c. State the basis on which the company's practice might be justified.

Compute gross
margin under
GAAP and then
comment on
recognizing
revenue as
production is
completed
(L.O. 2)

11–5. Silver Moon Company produces a product at a cost of $120 per unit that it sells for $180. The company has been successful and is able to sell all of the units that it can produce. During 1995, the company manufactured 50,000 units, but because of a transportation strike, it was able to sell and deliver only 40,000 units.

a. Compute the gross margin for 1995 following the realization principle. The cost of the units sold should be entitled "cost of goods sold" and treated as an expense.

b. Describe any circumstances under which the realization principle is ignored and revenue is recognized as production is completed.

Match accounting
qualities with
proper
descriptions
(L.O. 4)

11–6. Match the descriptions in the second column with the proper terms in the first column. Some descriptions will be used more than once.

Terms	Descriptions
1. Relevance.	*a.* Users of accounting information.
2. Feedback value.	*b.* A pervasive constraint.
3. Decision makers.	*c.* A user-specific quality.
4. Representational faithfulness.	*d.* A primary decision-specific quality.
5. Reliability.	*e.* An ingredient of a primary quality.
6. Comparability.	*f.* A secondary and interactive quality.
7. Benefits>costs.	*g.* A threshold for recognition.
8. Predictive value.	
9. Timeliness.	
10. Decision usefulness.	
11. Verifiability.	
12. Understandability.	
13. Neutrality.	
14. Materiality.	

PROBLEMS

Compute income
assuming
revenues are
recognized at time
of sale and then
assuming
installment
method is used
(L.O. 2)

11–1. Kramer Video, Inc., sells video recorders under terms calling for a small down payment and monthly payments spread over three years. Following are data for the first three years of the company's operations:

	1995	1996	1997
Gross margin rate	30%	40%	50%
Cash collected in 1997:			
From 1995 sales			$216,000
From 1996 sales			288,000
From 1997 sales			468,000

Total sales in 1997 were $1,440,000, while general and selling expenses amounted to $432,000 in 1997.

Required:

a. Compute net income for 1997 assuming that revenues are recognized at the time of sale.

b. Compute net income for 1997 using the installment method of accounting for sales and gross margin.

Compute income
under completed-
contract and
percentage-of-
completion
methods
(L.O. 2)

11–2. The following data relate to the Lopez Construction Company's long-term construction projects for the year 1995:

	Completed Projects	Incomplete Projects
Contract price	$18,000,000	$96,000,000
Costs incurred prior to 1995	3,700,000	16,000,000
Costs incurred in 1995	11,100,000	32,000,000
Estimated costs to be incurred in future years	–0–	32,000,000

General and administrative expenses incurred in 1995 amounted to $2,000,000, none of which is to be considered a construction cost.

Required:

a. Compute net income for 1995 under the completed-contract method.

b. Compute net income for 1995 using the percentage-of-completion method.

Match principles, assumptions, or concepts with certain accounting procedures followed (L.O. 1–3)

11–3. For each of the numbered items listed below, state the letter or letters of the principle(s), assumption(s), or concept(s) used to justify the accounting procedure followed. The accounting procedures are all correct.

A—Business entity.
B—Conservatism.
C—Earning principle of revenue recognition.
D—Going concern (continuity).
E—Exchange-price principle.
F—Matching principle.
G—Period cost (or principle of immediate recognition of expense).
H—Realization principle.
I—Stable dollar assumption.

1. The estimated liability for federal income taxes was increased by $12,000 over the amount reported on the tax return to cover possible differences found by the Internal Revenue Service in determining the amount of income taxes payable.
2. A truck purchased in January was reported at 80% of its cost even though its market value at year-end was only 70% of its cost.
3. The collection of $20,000 of cash for services to be performed next year was reported as a current liability.
4. The president's salary was treated as an expense of the year even though he spent most of his time planning the next two years' activities.
5. No entry was made to record the company's receipt of an offer of $230,000 for land carried in its accounts at $150,000.
6. A stock of printed stationery, checks, and invoices with a cost of $5,600 was treated as a current asset at year-end even though it had no value to others.
7. A tract of land acquired for $100,000 was recorded at that price even though it was appraised at $122,000, and the company would have been willing to pay that amount.
8. The company paid and charged to expense the $6,000 paid to Louis Brown for rental of a truck owned by him. Louis Brown is the sole stockholder in the company.
9. $16,800 of interest collected on $140,000 of 12% bonds was recorded as interest revenue even though the general level of prices increased 16% during the year.

Answer matching
question
regarding the
Conceptual
Framework
Project
(L.O. 4)

11–4. Match the descriptions in Column B with the proper terms in Column A.

Column A	Column B
1. Financial reporting objectives.	a. Information is free of measurement method bias.
2. Qualitative characteristics.	b. The benefits exceed the costs.
3. Relevance.	c. Relatively large items must be accounted for in a theoretically correct way.
4. Predictive value.	d. The information can be substantially duplicated by independent measurers using the same measurement methods.
5. Feedback value.	
6. Timeliness.	e. When information improves users' ability to predict outcomes of events.
7. Reliability.	f. Broad overriding goals sought by accountants engaging in financial reporting.
8. Representational faithfulness.	g. When information is pertinent or bears on a decision.
9. Verifiability.	
10. Neutrality.	h. The characteristics that accounting information should possess to be useful in decision making.
11. Comparability.	i. Information that reveals the relative success of users in predicting outcomes.
12. Consistency.	j. When accounting statements on economic activity correspond to the actual underlying activity.
13. Cost-benefit.	k. When information is provided at a time so that it may be considered in decision making.
14. Materiality.	l. When information faithfully depicts for users what it purports to represent.
	m. Requires a company to use the same accounting principles and reporting practices through time.
	n. When reported differences and similarities in information are real and not the result of differing accounting treatments.

Answer
multiple-choice
questions
regarding
international
accounting (based
on Appendix)
(L.O. 5)

11–5. Select the best answer to each of the following questions:

1. Methods that are used to account for transactions between companies in different nations when goods are received on one date and the invoice is paid on another date include:
   a. Time-of-transaction method.
   b. Time-of-settlement method.
   c. Current-rate method.
   d. *(a)* and *(b)* are correct.

2. Which of the following statements is **false** regarding translating financial statements of foreign subsidiaries?
   a. Under the *current-rate approach,* all assets and liabilities are translated at the exchange rate in effect on the balance sheet date.
   b. Under the *current-noncurrent method,* current assets and current liabilities are translated at the current rate, and noncurrent items are translated at their historical rates.
   c. Under the *monetary-nonmonetary method,* nonmonetary assets and liabilities are translated at their historical rate.
   d. The nations of the world now have settled on the current-rate method.

3. Variations between nations in accounting for inventories include all *except* which of the following?
   a. The basis for determining cost.
   b. Whether "cost" should be increased or decreased to reflect changes in market value.
   c. Whether inventories should be written down to an amount below both cost and market.
   d. Whether standard costs should be used.

4. In accounting for the effects of inflation, the approach that seems to be favored by most nations that have adopted an approach is:
   a. Current cost.
   b. Constant dollar (general price-level) adjusted statements.
   c. A combination of *(a)* and *(b)* in one set of financial statements.
   d. Both *(a)* and *(b)* as two sets of financial statements.

BUSINESS DECISION PROBLEM

Evaluate correctness of accounting practices and give reasons for conclusions (L.O. 1–3)

Jerry Newman recently received his accounting degree from State University and went to work for a Big-Six CPA firm. After he had been with the firm for about six months, he was sent to the Western Clothing Company to work on the audit. He was not very confident of his knowledge at this early point in his career. He noticed, however, that some of the company's transactions and events were recorded in a way that might be in violation of accounting theory and generally accepted accounting principles.

Required:

Study each of the following facts and see if you believe that the auditors should challenge the financial accounting practices used or the intentions of management. Give the reasoning behind your conclusions. (Some of the situations covered relate to other chapters you have studied in this text.)

1. The company recorded purchases of merchandise at the net price rather than the gross selling price.

2. Goods shipped to the company from a supplier, FOB destination, were debited to Purchases. The goods were not included in ending inventory because the goods had not yet arrived.

3. The company held the books open at the end of 1995 so they could record some early 1996 sales as 1995 revenue. The justification for this practice was that 1995 was not a good year in terms of profits.

4. The company counted some items twice in taking the physical inventory at the end of the year. The person taking the inventory said he had forgotten to include some items in last year's physical inventory, and counting some items twice would make up for the items missed last year so that net income this year would be "about correct."

5. The company switched from FIFO to LIFO in accounting for inventories. The preceding year it had switched from the weighted-average method to FIFO. The reason given for the most recent change was that federal income taxes

would be lower. No indication of this switch was to appear in the financial statements.

6. Since things were pretty hectic at year-end, the accountant made no effort to reconcile the bank account. His reason was that the bank probably had not made any errors. The bank balance was lower than the book balance, so the accountant debited Miscellaneous Expense and credited Cash for the difference.

7. When a customer failed to pay the amount due, the accountant debited Uncollectible Accounts Expense and credited Accounts Receivable. The amount of accounts written off in this manner was huge. When the company later collects an account that has already been written off, Cash is debited and Miscellaneous Revenue is credited.

8. The company's buildings were appraised for insurance purposes. The appraised values were $10,000,000 higher than the book value. The accountant debited Buildings and credited Paid-in Capital from Appreciation for the difference.

9. A machine was completely depreciated and was still being used. The accountant left the asset and its related accumulated depreciation on the books, stopped recording depreciation on the machine, and did not go back and correct earlier years' net income and reduce accumulated depreciation.

10. One of the senior members of management stated that the company planned to replace all of the furniture next year. He said that the cash in the Accumulated Depreciation account would be used to pay for the furniture.

11. The accountant stated that even though research and development costs incurred to develop a new product would benefit future periods, these costs must be expensed as incurred. This year $200,000 of these costs were charged to expense.

12. An old truck was traded for a new truck. Since the trade-in value of the old truck was higher than its book value, a gain was recorded on the transaction.

13. The company paid for a franchise giving it the exclusive right to operate in a given geographical area for 60 years. The accountant is amortizing the asset over 60 years.

14. The company leases a building and has a nonrenewable lease that expires in 15 years. The company made some improvements to the building. Since the improvements will last 30 years, they are being written off over 30 years.

ANSWERS TO SELF-TEST

True-False

1. *False*. The business entity concept assumes that each business has an existence separate from its owners, creditors, employees, customers, other interested parties, and other businesses.

2. *True*. Accountants should be guided by the economic substance of a transaction rather than its legal form.

3. *True*. The accrual basis of accounting seeks to match effort and accomplishment by matching expenses against the revenues they created.

4. *False*. Exceptions include the installment basis for sales and the percentage-of-completion method for long-term construction projects.

5. *False.* Immaterial items do have to be recorded, but they can be recorded in an incorrect way (e.g., expensing a wastebasket that will last many years).

6. *True.* Relevance and reliability are the two primary characteristics.

7. *False.* The IASC can only recommend specific practices and procedures for adoption by member nations.

Multiple-Choice

1. *c.* The matching concept is one of the major principles of accounting rather than an assumption.

2. *d.* If you answered *(b)*, you should note that the consistency concept requires that a given company (not all companies) use the same accounting principles and reporting practices through time.

3. *b.* Usually, the accountant does not recognize revenue until the seller acquires the right to receive payment from the buyer.

4. *b.* $\$3,000,000/\$10,000,000 \times \$15,000,000 = \$4,500,000$.

5. *a.* Periodicity is an underlying assumption rather than a modifying convention.

6. *b.* The category, quantitative characteristics, is not part of the Conceptual Framework Project.

7. *a.* The move from communism toward democracy is causing former Soviet Bloc nations to pursue a market-oriented economy.

IV

MANAGERIAL ACCOUNTING: CONCEPTS AND SYSTEMS

CHAPTER 12

MANAGERIAL ACCOUNTING CONCEPTS

CHAPTER 13

JOB ORDER COST SYSTEMS

CHAPTER 14

PROCESS COST SYSTEMS

12 MANAGERIAL ACCOUNTING CONCEPTS

LEARNING OBJECTIVES

After studying this chapter, you should be able to:

1. Describe the uses of managerial accounting information.
2. Describe the three basic components of manufacturing costs incurred in the production of a product.
3. Compare product costs to period costs and fixed costs to variable costs, and explain why proper classification of these costs is essential.
4. Determine the cost of inventories under periodic inventory procedure.
5. Compare financial reporting by a merchandiser to that of a manufacturer, and prepare a statement of cost of goods manufactured, an income statement, and a balance sheet for a manufacturer.
6. Diagram the pattern of cost flows for a manufacturing company using perpetual inventory procedure, and prepare journal entries.
7. Describe the just-in-time (JIT) production system and prepare journal entries.
8. Prepare a work sheet for a manufacturing company using periodic inventory procedure (appendix).

The remaining chapters in this text focus on managerial accounting. This chapter provides an overview of managerial accounting, shows differences between the accounting practices of merchandisers and manufacturers, and classifies and defines cost terms. Further, the chapter discusses periodic inventory procedure, activity-based costing, financial reporting by manufacturing companies, and perpetual inventory procedure. The chapter also presents recent developments including the just-in-time (JIT) production system and managerial accounting in high-tech companies. The appendix contains an example of a work sheet for a manufacturing company using periodic inventory procedure.

OVERVIEW OF MANAGERIAL ACCOUNTING

*Objective 1
Describe the uses
of managerial
accounting infor-
mation*

Managerial accounting information is intended for internal use. Managers need information to make good decisions. These management decisions include:

1. *Financing decisions*—deciding what funds the company needs to run the business, and whether the company should secure these funds from owners or creditors.
2. *Resource allocation decisions*—deciding how the company should invest the funds, such as whether to purchase automated teller machines in a bank or laser surgical devices in hospitals.
3. *Production decisions*—deciding which products the company should produce and how to improve product quality and also reduce production costs.
4. *Marketing decisions*—deciding on selling prices and marketing budgets and determining which products and markets are profitable.

The kind of information used by managers may range from broad, long-range planning data to detailed explanations of why actual costs varied from cost estimates in a particular period.

Managerial accounting information should:

1. Relate to the part of the company that the manager oversees. For example, a production manager will want information on costs of production but not on advertising.
2. Involve planning for the future. For instance, a company may prepare a budget that shows financial plans for the coming year.
3. Meet two tests: the accounting information must be useful (relevant) and must not cost more to gather and process than it is worth.

Differences between Financial and Managerial Accounting

Most managerial decisions require more detailed data than provided by external financial reports. For instance, the external financial statements of General Electric show single amounts on the balance sheet for inventory and on the income statement for the cost of goods sold. For managerial purposes, however, detailed data about the cost of each of several hundred products would typically be useful.

The fundamental differences between managerial and financial accounting are listed at the top of the next page.

One of the challenges currently facing accountants is designing systems with sufficient flexibility to provide data for multiple purposes. Another challenge facing managers is understanding accounting well enough to know which information to request and what may be expected from accountants.

	Financial Accounting	*Managerial Accounting*

Users

External users of information—usually stockholders, financial analysts, and creditors.

Internal users of information—usually managers.

Compliance with
Generally Accepted Accounting Principles

Must comply with generally accepted accounting principles.

Need not comply with generally accepted accounting principles. Internal cost-benefit evaluation determines how much information is enough.

Future versus Past

Uses historical data.

May use estimates of the future for budgeting and decision making.

Detail Presented

Summary data are presented.

More detailed data are required about product costs, revenues, and profits.

Ethical Issues in Managerial Accounting

Managerial accountants face many choices involving ethics. For example, managers are responsible for achieving accounting targets such as net income for a company's division. Failure to achieve these targets can have serious negative consequences for these managers. If a division or company is having trouble achieving financial performance targets, managers may be tempted to manipulate the accounting numbers, even to commit fraud.

In its Standards of Ethical Conduct for Management Accountants, the Institute of Management Accountants (IMA) states that management accountants have an obligation to maintain the highest levels of ethical conduct by maintaining professional competency, refraining from disclosing confidential information, and maintaining integrity and objectivity in their work.[1] The standards recommend that when ethical conflicts occur, accountants should first follow the company's established policies that deal with such conflicts. If these policies do not resolve the conflict, accountants should consider discussing the matter with superiors. If necessary, accountants should go as high as the audit committee of the board of directors. In extreme cases, the accountants may have no alternative but to resign.

This section explained the differences between *financial* and *managerial* accounting. In the next section, you will see that differences between *mer-*

---

[1] See *Standards of Ethical Conduct for Management Accountants* (Montvale, N.J.: National Association of Accountants, June 1, 1983.) The Institute of Management Accountants was formerly called the National Association of Accountants.

chandising and *manufacturing* operations require accountants to use different procedures.

MERCHANDISER AND MANUFACTURER ACCOUNTING DIFFERENCES

Previous chapters in this text dealt with service and merchandising organizations. The remaining chapters discuss issues involving manufacturing companies as well as service and merchandising companies. We begin by discussing the unique accounting features of manufacturing companies.

If you owned a bicycle store, you would purchase bicycles and accessories and sell them to customers. To determine your profitability, you would subtract the cost of bicycles and accessories purchased from your gross sales as cost of goods sold. If, instead, you owned the manufacturing company that made the bicycles, your cost of goods sold would be based on the cost of manufacturing those bicycles.

Unlike many service companies, merchandising and manufacturing companies often carry inventories. However, tracing manufacturing costs through several inventory accounts into cost of goods sold is more complex than accounting for a merchandiser's inventory and cost of goods sold. This chapter explains and illustrates the accounting procedures for manufacturing costs. Terms such as raw materials, work in process, finished goods, direct labor, indirect labor, and manufacturing overhead are part of manufacturing accounting. The basic accounting process we have discussed throughout the text also applies to manufacturing companies.

Illustration 12.1
COMPARISON OF INVENTORY COST FLOWS

Merchandising company

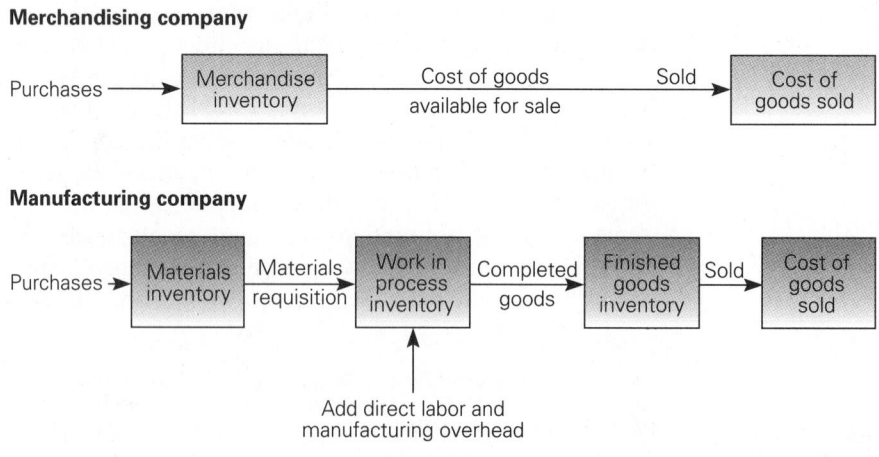

Manufacturing company

Illustration 12.2
COST OF GOODS SOLD COMPARISON

Merchandiser		*Manufacturer*	
Cost of goods sold:		Cost of goods sold:	
Merchandise inventory, January 1 . . .	$ 25,000	Finished goods inventory, January 1 . .	$ 40,000
Net cost of purchases	165,000	Cost of goods manufactured (from statement of cost of goods manufactured)	250,000
Cost of goods available for sale	$190,000	Cost of goods available for sale	$290,000
Merchandise inventory, December 31 .	30,000	Finished goods inventory, December 31	50,000
Cost of goods sold	$160,000	Cost of goods sold	$240,000

Managerial accounting provides data for three major objectives: (1) determining the cost of products, (2) planning and controlling the cost, and (3) supporting management decisions. In Part IV of this text, we focus on the accounting processes to measure the cost of products in manufacturing companies.

Perhaps the most important accounting difference between merchandisers and manufacturers is the difference in their activities. A merchandiser purchases goods that are already in their finished state and ready to be sold. On the other hand, a manufacturer purchases raw materials and uses production equipment and employee labor to transform the raw materials into finished products. Thus, a merchandiser has only one type of inventory—merchandise available for sale. A manufacturer has three types—unprocessed **materials,** partially complete **work in process,** and ready-for-sale **finished goods.** Manufacturers, then, must use three different types of inventory accounts (instead of one) to show the cost of inventory in various stages of production. Illustration 12.1 shows how the inventory cost flows differ between merchandising and manufacturing companies.

Illustration 12.2 compares the cost of goods sold section of a merchandiser's income statement to the cost of goods sold section of a manufacturer's income statement. Two major differences occur in the cost of goods sold sections. First, a merchandiser refers to goods ready to be sold as *merchandise inventory*; a manufacturer refers to these goods as *finished goods inventory*. Second, a merchandiser's cost of purchases is equivalent to the manufacturer's cost of goods manufactured.

The next section concentrates on manufacturing costs; it classifies and defines the various costs incurred by manufacturers.

COST CLASSIFICATIONS

A **cost** is a financial measure of the resources used or given up to achieve a stated purpose. In manufacturing companies, costs can be classified as (1) manufacturing or nonmanufacturing costs, (2) product costs or period costs, and (3) fixed costs or variable costs. This section discusses each of these cost classifications.

Manufacturing Costs

Objective 2
Describe the three
basic components
of manufacturing
costs incurred in
the production of
a product

The total cost of manufacturing a product is referred to as **manufacturing cost, factory cost, inventoriable cost,** or **product cost.** Manufacturing cost includes three cost elements: (1) direct material costs, (2) direct labor costs, and (3) manufacturing overhead costs. Inventory and cost of goods sold costs are made up of manufacturing costs.

Direct Materials. **Direct materials** are materials (1) included in the finished product, (2) used only in the manufacture of the product, and (3) clearly and easily traceable to the product. For example, iron ore is a direct material to a steel company because the iron ore is clearly traceable to the finished product, steel. In turn, steel becomes a direct material to an automobile manufacturer.

The cost of direct materials includes the invoice price plus delivery charges of the actual quantity used. Some companies also include storage and handling costs. Direct materials inventory may be accounted for using any of the inventory costing methods discussed in Chapter 5, including specific identification, FIFO, LIFO, or average cost.

Some materials (such as glue and thread used in making furniture) may become part of the finished product, but tracing those materials to the product would require great cost and effort. For this reason, we refer to these materials as *indirect materials* or supplies and include them in manufacturing overhead. **Indirect materials** are materials that are used in the manufacture of a product that for practical reasons cannot or will not be traced directly to the manufactured products.

Direct Labor. **Direct labor** costs include labor costs of all employees actually working on materials to convert them to finished goods. As with direct material costs, direct labor costs of a product include only those labor costs that are clearly traceable to, or readily identifiable with, the finished product. You can identify direct labor costs by showing that these costs vary in direct proportion to the number of units the company produces. Thus, the labor of machinists, assemblers, cutters, and painters is direct labor.

Usually, we measure direct labor cost by multiplying the number of direct labor-hours by the hourly wage rate. Many employees, however, receive fringe benefits—employer's share of payroll taxes, pension costs, health insurance, paid vacations, and so on. Occasionally, fringe benefit costs are accounted for as direct labor. Normally, however, they are included in manufacturing overhead because they can be traced to one particular product only at great cost and effort.

Some labor costs (e.g., wages of materials handlers, custodial workers, and supervisors) tend to vary directly with the number of product units produced. However, these costs are not accounted for as direct labor because it is too expensive to trace these costs to product units. These labor costs are called *indirect labor* and are accounted for as manufacturing overhead, discussed below. **Indirect labor** consists of labor costs that for practical reasons cannot or will not be traced to the manufactured products.

Manufacturing Overhead. Accountants use many alternative names for manufacturing overhead, including factory indirect costs, factory burden, and manufacturing expense. **Manufacturing overhead** is a catchall classification, since it includes all manufacturing costs except those costs accounted for as direct materials and direct labor. Manufacturing overhead costs are manufacturing costs that the company must incur but cannot or will not trace directly to specific units. As noted earlier, manufacturing overhead may include certain materials and labor costs that could theoretically be accounted for as direct materials or direct labor.

Manufacturing overhead contains a number of other costs that relate to the manufacturing process, such as depreciation and maintenance on machines, supervisors' salaries, and factory utility costs. Illustration 12.3 summarizes most manufacturing overhead costs and gives some examples of indirect materials and indirect labor.

Note from Illustration 12.3 that overtime wage premiums on direct labor are commonly included in manufacturing overhead rather than in direct labor cost. The logic behind this practice is that normally employees work overtime because of an overall production backlog and not the need to manufacture a given product line. For example, in a company that manufactures three products, employees may work overtime on any one of the three products, depending on the **arbitrary scheduling by the production manager.** In such situations, the overtime is due to the combined time requirements of all three products. For this reason, the overtime should not be directly charged to any one product unless that product is clearly the sole cause of the overtime.

Manufacturing Cost Terminology. For decision-making purposes, accountants often classify costs according to their relation to the finished

Illustration 12.3
MANUFACTURING OVERHEAD COSTS—EXAMPLES

Indirect materials:
  Lubricants
  Adhesives
  Cleaners, etc.
Indirect labor:
  Cost accountant
  Engineers
  Janitors
  Materials storeroom personnel
  Timekeepers
  Toolroom personnel, etc.
Depreciation on factory buildings and
  equipment
	Insurance and taxes on factory property
	  and inventories
	Overtime wage premiums on direct labor
	Payroll taxes and fringe benefits for
	  manufacturing employees
	Repairs and maintenance on factory
	  buildings and equipment
	Utilities for factory buildings
	Write-off of hand tools

product or the manufacturing process. Special terms such as *prime cost* and *conversion cost* are used to identify these classifications. The sum of direct materials costs and direct labor costs incurred to manufacture a product is called **prime cost** because these costs are the primary costs of production. The sum of direct labor costs and manufacturing overhead costs is called **conversion cost** because these costs are incurred in the conversion of the direct materials into finished goods. Illustration 12.4 shows the relationship between prime cost and conversion cost.

Nonmanufacturing Costs

Nonmanufacturing costs differ from manufacturing costs in that they relate to selling and administrative functions rather than to manufacturing. Nonmanufacturing costs are not included in inventory. Instead, these costs are charged to expense in the period they are incurred. Accountants generally classify nonmanufacturing costs as selling costs or administrative costs.

Selling costs are costs that a manufacturing company incurs to obtain customer orders and get the finished product in the customer's possession. Examples of selling costs are advertising, market research, sales salaries and commissions, and storage and delivery of finished goods. Remember that retailers, wholesalers, manufacturers, and service organizations all have selling costs. Selling costs incurred in 1995 appear as expenses on that year's income statement. They are not part of cost of goods sold.

Administrative costs are nonmanufacturing costs that include the costs of top administrative functions and various staff departments such as accounting, data processing, and personnel. Examples of administrative costs are executive salaries, clerical salaries, office expenses, office rent, donations, research and development costs, and legal costs. As with selling costs, all organizations have administrative costs. Administrative costs incurred in 1995 appear as expenses on that year's income statement. They are not part of cost of goods sold.

Product and Period Costs

Objective 3
Compare product costs to period costs and fixed costs to variable costs, and explain why proper classification of these costs is essential

Cost classifications are important for decision making and financial reporting. Companies installing or redesigning computer systems should get as much feedback from managers as possible to classify costs correctly. Classifying costs into product costs and period costs is important for income determination purposes.

Product costs are costs a company assigns to units of a product produced. For manufacturing companies, these costs are direct materials, direct labor, and manufacturing overhead.

Period costs relate more closely to periods of time rather than to the production of specific products. For this reason, period costs are expensed (deducted from revenues) in the period in which they are incurred.

To illustrate, assume a company pays its sales manager a fixed salary. In

Illustration 12.4
COST RELATIONSHIPS

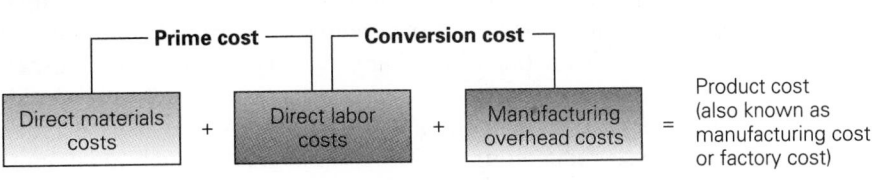

addition to the manager's regular activities, the manager may be working on projects that will benefit the company in future accounting periods. However, the company expenses the sales manager's salary in the period in which it is incurred because the expense cannot be traced to the production of a product. **For external financial reporting, accountants treat all selling and nonfactory administrative costs as period costs.** For managerial purposes, managers can include these costs in the total cost of a product. For example, to determine whether a particular type of water ski is profitable, management can add selling and administrative costs to product costs to compute the total cost of the ski.

Illustration 12.5 shows how a manufacturing company reports product costs and period costs in its financial statements. **Note that the company**

Illustration 12.5
STATEMENT ANALYSIS OF PERIOD AND PRODUCT COSTS

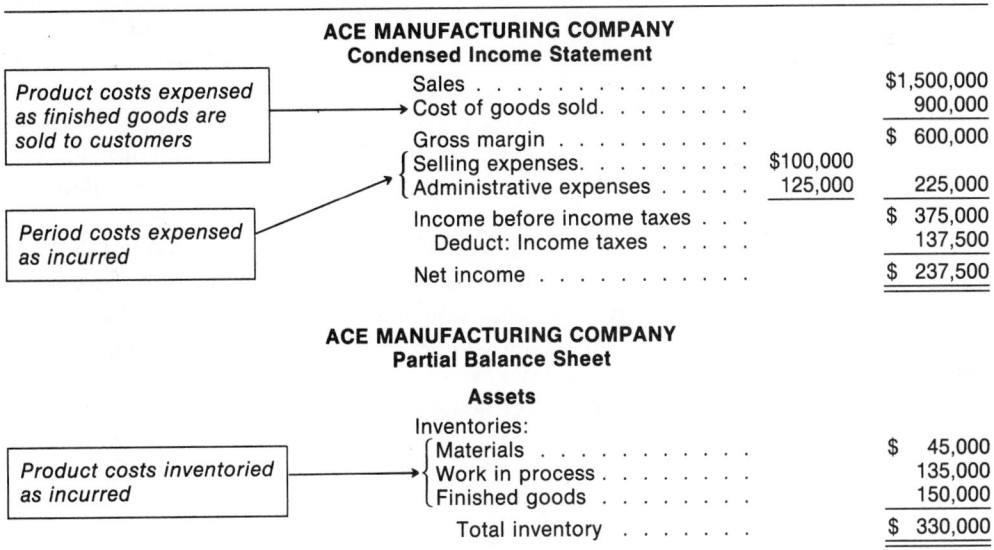

| | ACE MANUFACTURING COMPANY | | |
	Condensed Income Statement		
Product costs expensed as finished goods are sold to customers	Sales		$1,500,000
	Cost of goods sold.		900,000
	Gross margin		$ 600,000
Period costs expensed as incurred	Selling expenses.	$100,000	
	Administrative expenses	125,000	225,000
	Income before income taxes . . .		$ 375,000
	Deduct: Income taxes		137,500
	Net income		$ 237,500

| | ACE MANUFACTURING COMPANY | |
	Partial Balance Sheet	
	Assets	
	Inventories:	
Product costs inventoried as incurred	Materials	$ 45,000
	Work in process	135,000
	Finished goods	150,000
	Total inventory	$ 330,000

expenses product costs in the period the goods are sold and not when the company incurs the costs. If a company incurs product costs toward the end of period 1 and sells the goods in period 2, the company expenses those product costs against revenues of period 2. As shown in Illustration 12.5, Ace Manufacturing Company sold $900,000 of finished products to customers and expensed this amount as cost of goods sold. Ace expensed its period costs—selling and administrative expenses ($225,000)—as incurred. Ace deducted the $225,000 from gross margin to compute its income before income taxes.

The three ending inventories of a manufacturing company are (1) materials, (2) work in process, and (3) finished goods. Illustration 12.5 shows these three items as assets under "Inventories" in the partial balance sheet of Ace Manufacturing Company. Ace expenses the product costs in these inventories in the period the goods are sold to customers. When Ace sells items from the finished goods inventory, it reports these costs as an expense (cost of goods sold) on the income statement for the period of sale.

Fixed and Variable Costs

So far we have classified costs by their relationships to the manufacturing process and to accounting periods. We can also classify costs by how they respond to changes in the volume of manufacturing activity. Costs that are not affected in total amount during an accounting period by the volume of production activity are called *fixed costs*. Costs that vary in total amount directly with changes in the volume of production activity are called *variable costs*.

Fixed costs remain constant in total amount over a range of manufacturing activity levels. For example, an annual automobile license may cost you $200 whether you drive the auto 1,000 or 100,000 miles during the year. The same may be true for your annual auto insurance premium. Property taxes, depreciation, rent, and executives' salaries are also examples of fixed costs. Fixed costs are basically time related, such as a president's one-year salary. Variable costs, discussed below, increase in total as the volume of activity increases.

Fixed costs present a special problem in determining the unit cost of a product. Although total fixed costs do not change with the volume of production activity, cost per unit may vary widely when output varies. For example, assume that a company rents a factory building for $100,000 per year. The rental cost per ton of output is $1 if the company produces 100,000 tons, $0.50 if it produces 200,000 tons, and only $0.10 if it produces 1 million tons. You can see from this example that the fixed cost per unit decreases as the number of units produced increases. Also, the fixed cost per unit will increase as the number of units produced decreases.

Variable costs are costs that vary directly in total amount with changes in the volume of production activity or output. Direct materials are a good example of a variable cost. For example, every washing machine produced by a manufacturer has one motor. If the motors cost $50 each, the motor cost for one machine is $50; for two machines, $100; for three machines, $150; and so on. Assume the profit plans call for the production of 10,000 washing machines. Then, the planned cost of the motors is $500,000. Similarly, the labor cost to install the motors would be a variable cost.

In conclusion, since fixed costs are basically time related, total fixed cost remains constant with volume changes. However, fixed cost per unit varies inversely with the change in activity. In contrast, variable costs remain constant on a per unit basis. However, total variable costs change in direct relation to the change in activity.

Now that you understand how accountants classify manufacturing costs, you are ready to learn how they assign various costs to manufacturing inventories.

PERIODIC INVENTORY PROCEDURE

Objective 4
Determine the
cost of inventories
under periodic
inventory proce-
dure

A manufacturer may use either periodic or perpetual inventory procedure to assign a cost to its inventory. Recall from Chapter 5 that under periodic inventory procedure, accounts are brought to their proper balances only at the end of the accounting period by taking a physical inventory. Under perpetual inventory procedure, the inventory accounts are maintained at their proper balances throughout the period. This section discusses periodic inventory procedure applied in a manufacturing company. Perpetual inventory procedure is discussed in a later section in the chapter.

Accounts Used for Materials and Other Inventories

Under periodic inventory procedure, a manufacturer uses the Materials Purchases, Materials Purchase Discounts, Materials Purchase Returns and Allowances, Transportation-In, and Materials Inventory accounts in the same manner as does a retailer. During the period, the manufacturer debits purchases to the Materials Purchases account and debits transportation charges incurred on the purchases to Transportation-In. The manufacturer credits discounts to Materials Purchase Discounts and credits returns and allowances to Materials Purchase Returns and Allowances. Each of these accounts is closed through Manufacturing Summary to Income Summary at the end of the accounting period. The Materials Inventory account contains the beginning inventory amount until year-end. At year-end, the ending inventory is entered in the Materials Inventory account during the closing process.

As with Materials Inventory, when a manufacturer uses periodic inventory procedure, Work in Process Inventory and Finished Goods Inventory accounts will contain the beginning inventory amount until year-end. At year-end, the manufacturer takes a physical inventory and enters the amount of ending inventory in the accounts.

The following T-accounts show the entries of a manufacturer using periodic inventory procedure:

Materials Purchases

Purchases of materials entered here	Closed through Manufacturing Summary to Income Summary at end of period

Materials Inventory

Beginning balance	xx	Beginning balance is closed through Manufacturing Summary to Income Summary at end of period
Ending balance	xx	
Ending balance is entered at end of period based on a physical inventory		

Materials Purchase Discounts

Closed through Manufacturing Summary to Income Summary at end of period	Cash discounts taken on purchases entered here

Work in Process Inventory

Beginning balance	xx	Beginning balance is closed through Manufacturing Summary to Income Summary at end of period
Ending balance	xx	
Ending balance is entered at end of period based on a physical inventory		

Materials Purchase Returns and Allowances

Closed through Manufacturing Summary to Income Summary at end of period	Cost of materials returned to suppliers and amount of any allowances granted on purchases entered here

Finished Goods Inventory

Beginning balance	xx	Beginning balance is closed to Income Summary at end of period
Ending balance	xx	
Ending balance is entered at end of period based on a physical inventory		

Transportation-In

Freight charges incurred on purchases entered here	Closed through Manufacturing Summary to Income Summary at end of period

Measuring per Unit Inventory Costs

Before determining the total cost of work in process and finished goods inventory, the accountant must calculate the per unit costs of direct materials, direct labor, and manufacturing overhead. Then, the unit costs will be multiplied times the relevant quantities to determine total inventory costs.

Direct Materials Cost. Accountants establish the materials cost in each unit of work in process and finished goods by referring to a materials specification list. This list gives the types and quantities of materials used in manufacturing each product. To obtain the direct materials cost per unit, the relevant quantities are multiplied by the purchase invoice unit price.

Direct Labor Cost.   Manufacturers typically base the direct labor cost in each unit of a product on management observations. These observations determine the *normal* time it takes workers to complete a unit of product. By multiplying this time by the hourly wage rate, management estimates the direct labor cost per unit.

Manufacturing Overhead Cost.   Manufacturing overhead costs are not clearly traceable to units of product. Accountants use a *manufacturing overhead rate* to allocate these costs to a product. The **manufacturing overhead rate** expresses manufacturing overhead costs in relation to some measure of manufacturing activity. Accountants frequently express manufacturing overhead rates as either (1) a percentage of some other cost like direct labor or materials or (2) a certain dollar amount per an activity base like machine-hours or direct labor-hours.

Manufacturing overhead costs may have many different causes or sources. In labor intensive workplaces, direct labor is usually a major portion of product costs, and indirect labor costs, overtime pay, and fringe benefit costs might comprise a major portion of manufacturing overhead costs. In an automated workplace, direct labor cost is often a minor cost factor, and the existence of factory machinery and the computers to operate them may be the cause of much of the manufacturing overhead.

In the past, manufacturing was more labor intensive, so many companies used direct labor as the activity base to apply manufacturing overhead. As companies become more automated, they generally move to the use of machine-hours as an activity base for allocating manufacturing overhead. Even in the service sector, we find many companies using computer machine-hours as an activity base to apply overhead in calculating the cost of services performed for a client.

In the following example for estimating total inventory costs under periodic inventory procedure, we will assume that the company applies manufacturing overhead based on machine-hours.

Estimating Total Inventory Costs

As stated above, when a manufacturer is using periodic inventory procedure, inventory quantities are determined at year-end by taking a physical count of the materials, work in process, and finished goods on hand. Once the *quantity* of these inventories has been established, their *cost* must be estimated. Materials inventory cost is then calculated by multiplying the unit purchase price by the quantity of each type of item.

Estimating the cost of work in process inventory and finished goods inventory is more complicated. For the average unit in work in process inventory and then for each unit in finished goods inventory, a manufacturer must estimate the—

1. Direct materials cost contained in each unit.
2. Direct labor cost incurred for each unit.
3. Manufacturing overhead applicable to each unit.

The amounts of materials *may* differ, while the amounts of labor and overhead *will* differ, for units in work in process inventory and units in finished goods inventory. Materials may be added at the beginning of the process, uniformly throughout the process, or near the end of the process. Direct labor and manufacturing overhead are incurred throughout the manufacturing process. The sum of the three cost elements represents the product cost per unit contained in each of the inventories. The relevant product costs per unit are then multiplied by the number of units in work in process inventory and the number of units in finished goods inventory to obtain the total costs of these inventories.

The following example illustrates the method for computing the cost of ending work in process and finished goods inventories. Assume the data below pertain to the Fleetwing Parachute Company.

Direct materials used (30,000 units)	$180,000
Direct labor (52,000 hours)	520,000
Manufacturing overhead (26,000 machine-hours)	416,000
Ending inventories (determined by physical count):	
Work in process	8,000 units
Finished goods	2,000 units
Units sold during the period	20,000 units

Fleetwing manufactures only one product—parachutes. Each unit of product in work in process inventory and finished goods inventory contains one unit of direct materials. The direct materials cost per unit is $180,000 ÷ 30,000 units = $6.

Management estimates that each completed unit of product contains two hours of direct labor. Each unit still in production contains an average of one hour of direct labor. The direct labor cost per hour is $520,000 ÷ 52,000 hours = $10. Thus, the direct labor cost per unit is $20 for finished goods and $10 for work in process.

Manufacturing overhead costs are applied using machine-hours as the activity base. Management estimates that each completed unit contains one machine-hour and each unit still in production contains one-half machine-hour. The manufacturing overhead rate per hour is $16, computed as follows:

$$\text{Manufacturing overhead rate} = \frac{\text{Total manufacturing overhead cost}}{\text{Total machine-hours}}$$

$$= \frac{\$416,000}{26,000 \text{ machine-hours}}$$

$$= \$16 \text{ per machine-hour}$$

Thus, the manufacturing overhead cost per unit is $16 for finished goods and $8 for work in process.

Illustration 12.6
COMPUTE WORK IN PROCESS AND FINISHED GOODS

	Estimated Cost per Unit					Estimated Total Inventory Cost		
Inventory	Direct Materials	+ Direct Labor	+ Manufacturing Overhead*	= Unit Cost	Unit Cost	× Units in Inventory	= Total Ending Inventory Cost
Work in process	$6	+ $10	+ $ 8	= $24	$24	× 8,000	= $192,000
Finished goods	6	+ 20	+ 16	= 42	42	× 2,000	= 84,000

* Manufacturing overhead rate $= \dfrac{\text{Total manufacturing overhead cost}}{\text{Total machine-hours}}$

$= \dfrac{\$416,000}{26,000 \text{ machine-hours}} = \$16$ per machine-hour

Work in process used one-half machine-hour per unit in process = 0.50 hour × $16 = $8. Finished goods used one machine-hour per unit finished = 1 hour × $16 = $16.

Illustration 12.6 shows how the costs of the ending inventories of work in process and finished goods can now be determined.

The chapter appendix illustrates the use of a work sheet by a manufacturing company using periodic inventory procedure. The closing process is also described and illustrated.

The Fleetwing example applied overhead to products using a simple approach—namely, applying overhead based on machine-hours worked. In practice, many companies use such a simplistic approach. Other companies have begun implementing a more complex approach to provide more information about the causes of costs. This approach is known as *activity-based costing* (also called *transactions-based costing*).

ACTIVITY-BASED COSTING

Activity-based costing is a method of assigning costs to goods and services that assumes all costs are caused by the activities used to produce those goods and services. This method provides more insight into the causes of costs than conventional costing methods. Conventional costing methods divide the total costs by the number of units to compute a unit cost. In contrast, activity-based costing starts with the detailed activities required to produce a product or service and computes a product's cost using the following three steps:

1. Identify the activities or transactions that cause costs to be incurred. These activities are called *cost drivers*. **Cost drivers** are causes of costs incurred. Machine-hours could be a cost driver. So could the number of times a new drawing is needed because a product has been redesigned.
2. Assign a cost to each cost driver.
3. Sum the costs of the cost drivers that make up the product.

Illustration 12.7
ACTIVITY-BASED COSTING FOR A CIRCUIT BOARD—HEWLETT-PACKARD

Overhead Costs

Activities (cost drivers)	Cost per Cost Driver		Number of Cost Drivers per Circuit Board		Cost per Circuit Board
Different parts purchased (affects cost of purchasing)	$0.10 per part	×	94 parts	=	$ 9.40
Manual insertions of components	$0.35 per insertion	×	13 insertions	=	4.55
Hours of testing	$70.00 per hour	×	0.20 hours per circuit board	=	14.00
	Other items have been omitted to simplify this exhibit. They totaled $19.52 per circuit board.			=	19.52
Total overhead (includes labor)					$ 47.47
Total direct materials					75.17
Total cost to make one circuit board					$122.64

SOURCE: D. Berlant, R. Browning, and G. Foster, "How Hewlett-Packard Gets Numbers It Can Trust," *Harvard Business Review*, January–February 1990, pp. 178–83.

For example, Hewlett-Packard recently installed activity-based costing in its Roseville, California, Networks Division.[2] To compute a cost for personal computer circuit boards, the accountants identified such cost drivers as the number of parts in the product, number of times components were inserted in the circuit boards, hours of testing, and several others. The accountants assigned a cost to each cost driver as shown in Illustration 12.7. Then, they summed these costs and added the total to direct materials costs to compute the product's unit manufacturing cost. (Like many high-tech companies, Hewlett-Packard puts direct labor into overhead because direct labor costs are too small to be separately accounted for.) Activity-based costing has enabled Hewlett-Packard managers to identify which cost drivers have a major impact on product costs. From this information, managers have redesigned certain products to reduce costs.

The financial statements prepared by a manufacturing company differ from those prepared by service and merchandising companies. The next section describes and illustrates the financial statements of manufacturing companies.

FINANCIAL REPORTING BY MANUFACTURING COMPANIES

One of the major differences between merchandisers and manufacturers is in their types of inventories. Inventories are reported on the balance sheet and

---

[2] D. Berlant, R. Browning, and G. Foster, "How Hewlett-Packard Gets Numbers It Can Trust," *Harvard Business Review*, January–February 1990, pp. 178–83.

also affect income (through cost of goods sold) on the income statement. Thus, the balance sheet and income statement of a merchandiser differ from the balance sheet and income statement of a manufacturer. In addition, manufacturers prepare a statement of cost of goods manufactured.

The Statement of Cost of Goods Manufactured

Objective 5
Compare financial reporting by a merchandiser to that of a manufacturer, and prepare a statement of cost of goods manufactured, an income statement, and a balance sheet for a manufacturer

The **statement of cost of goods manufactured** supports the cost of goods manufactured figure on the income statement. The two most important figures on this statement are (1) the cost to manufacture and (2) the cost of goods manufactured. Be careful not to confuse the terms *cost to manufacture* and *cost of goods manufactured* with each other or with cost of goods sold. Illustration 12.8 shows the relationship of cost to manufacture, cost of goods manufactured, and cost of goods sold. **Cost to manufacture** includes the costs of all *resources* put into production during the period. **Cost of goods manufactured** consists of the total costs of all *goods completed* during the period and includes "cost to manufacture" plus the beginning work in process inventory minus the ending work in process inventory. Cost of goods sold includes the cost of goods manufactured plus the beginning finished goods inventory minus the ending finished goods inventory.

Illustration 12.9 shows the 1995 statement of cost of goods manufactured for Flanigan Manufacturing Company. Note how the statement gives the costs incurred for materials, direct labor, and manufacturing overhead. The total of these three costs is the cost to manufacture during the period. When we add beginning work in process inventory to the cost to manufacture and deduct ending work in process inventory, we obtain cost of goods manufac-

Illustration 12.8
RELATIONSHIP OF COST TO MANUFACTURE, COST OF GOODS MANUFACTURED, AND COST OF GOODS SOLD

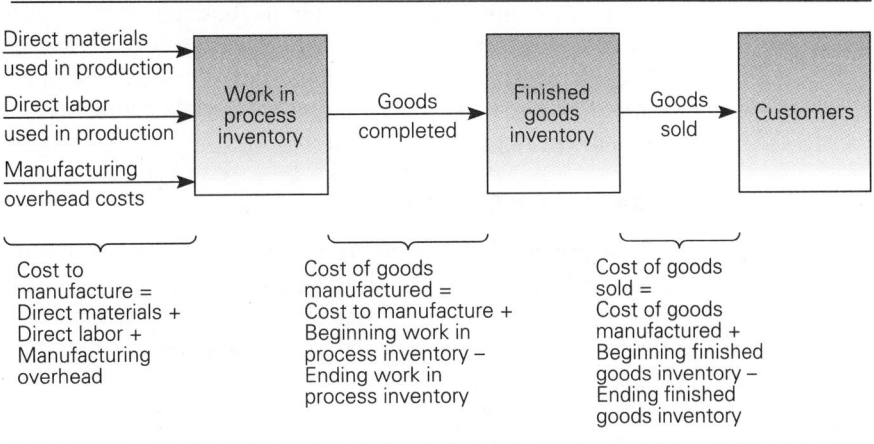

Illustration 12.9
STATEMENT OF COST OF GOODS MANUFACTURED

FLANIGAN MANUFACTURING COMPANY
Statement of Cost of Goods Manufactured
For the Year Ended December 31, 1995

Materials:

Materials inventory, January 1	$ 40,000	
Materials purchases (net)	480,000	
Transportation-in	6,000	
Materials available for use	$526,000	
Less: Materials inventory, December 31	38,000	
Materials used		$ 488,000
Direct labor		380,000

Manufacturing overhead:

Indirect labor	$ 65,000	
Supervisors' salaries expense	130,000	
Maintenance and repairs expense	17,000	
Factory utilities expense	5,000	
Factory property taxes expense	15,000	
Depreciation expense—factory building	20,000	
Depreciation expense—factory equipment	46,000	
Insurance expense—factory	6,000	
Total manufacturing overhead		304,000
Cost to manufacture		$1,172,000
Add: Work in process inventory, January 1		84,000
		$1,256,000
Less: Work in process inventory, December 31		80,000
Cost of goods manufactured		$1,176,000

---

tured (completed). Cost of goods sold does not appear on the cost of goods manufactured statement but is shown on the income statement.

In Illustration 12.9, all materials (both direct and indirect) are included in the Materials Inventory account. Therefore, materials used consist of both direct materials and indirect materials. These amounts could have been separated, and the amount of indirect materials could have been included under manufacturing overhead as a line item.

The Income Statement

Since a manufacturer incurs more types of costs than a merchandiser who buys goods ready for sale, the income statement preparation for a manufacturer is usually more complex than for a merchandiser. To make the manufacturer's income statement more understandable to financial statement readers, only the cost of goods manufactured is shown. Manufacturers prepare a statement of cost of goods manufactured to support the amount of cost of goods manufactured shown in their income statements.

Illustration 12.10
INCOME STATEMENT OF A MANUFACTURER

FLANIGAN MANUFACTURING COMPANY
Income Statement
For the Year Ended December 31, 1995

Operating revenues:		
Sales		$1,800,000
Cost of goods sold:		
Finished goods inventory, January 1	$ 56,000	
Cost of goods manufactured (see statement of cost		
of goods manufactured in Illustration 12.9)	1,176,000	
Cost of goods available for sale	$1,232,000	
Less: Finished goods inventory, December 31	60,000	
Cost of goods sold		1,172,000
Gross margin		$ 628,000
Operating expenses:		
Selling expenses	$ 200,000	
Administrative expenses	185,000	
Other operating expenses	1,500	
Total operating expenses		386,500
Income from operations		$ 241,500
Nonoperating revenues and expenses:		
Interest expense		20,000
Income before income taxes		$ 221,500
Deduct: Income taxes		107,000
Net income		$ 114,500

Illustration 12.10 shows the income statement for Flanigan Manufacturing Company. Notice the relationship of the statement of cost of goods manufactured in Illustration 12.9 to the income statement in Illustration 12.10. The cost of goods manufactured appears in the cost of goods sold section as an addition to the beginning inventory of finished goods to derive the cost of goods available for sale. Cost of goods manufactured is presented in the same place that purchases would be presented on a merchandiser's income statement. When companies release financial statements to the public, they usually include the previous years' income statements alongside the current year's statement for comparison.

The Balance Sheet

The balance sheet for a merchandiser reports a single inventory amount. However, the balance sheet for a manufacturer typically shows materials, work in process, and finished goods inventories separately. A manufacturer's balance sheet may also show greater detail in the property, plant, and equipment section because of the significant investment in plant assets.

Periodic inventory procedure is designed to determine the *total* cost of goods manufactured and the *total* cost of goods sold at the *end* of the accounting period so that financial statements can be prepared. The next section will illustrate perpetual inventory procedure, which is used by many manufacturing companies.

PERPETUAL INVENTORY PROCEDURE—THE GENERAL COST ACCUMULATION MODEL

Objective 6
Diagram the pattern of cost flows for a manufacturing company using perpetual inventory procedure, and prepare journal entries

A primary accounting objective in manufacturing companies is to measure the cost of manufacturing a product line on a *per unit* basis *during* the period. This measurement enables managers to make timely cost control and product pricing decisions. Under perpetual inventory procedure, unit product costs are determined during the period rather than estimated at the end of the period. The costs of direct materials, direct labor, and manufacturing overhead are transferred during the period to Work in Process Inventory and then to Finished Goods Inventory accounts as goods are processed. Thus, unit costs can be determined during the period instead of waiting until the end of the period.

Product and Cost Flows

Next, we will describe the basic pattern of cost accumulation under perpetual inventory procedure in a manufacturing environment. Illustration 12.11 shows how the flow of costs under perpetual inventory procedure matches the physical flow of products through the production process.

The production process begins when materials are received from suppliers and placed in the materials storeroom. When needed for production, the materials are moved from the materials storeroom to the production departments. During production, the materials are processed by laborers and ma-

Illustration 12.11
PRODUCT AND COST FLOWS

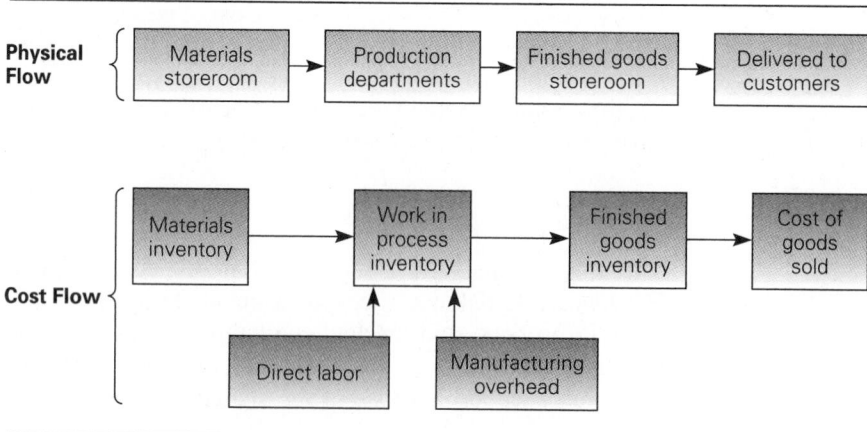

chines and become partially manufactured products. At any time during production, these partially manufactured products are collectively known as **work in process.** Eventually the products are completed, at which time they are known as **finished goods.** The completed products are then moved to the finished goods storeroom for later sale and delivery to customers.

The accounting flow of costs using perpetual inventory procedure follows the physical flow of the manufacturing process, except when using the just-in-time (JIT) production system discussed later. The accounting records show the flow of direct material costs from Materials Inventory into Work in Process Inventory. Here, the costs of direct labor and other factory services are added. When the products are completed and transferred to the finished goods storeroom, their costs are removed from Work in Process Inventory and assigned to Finished Goods Inventory. As the goods are sold, the related costs are transferred from Finished Goods Inventory to Cost of Goods Sold.

Illustration 12.12 shows the manufacturing cost flows along with the selling, administrative, interest, and tax expenses of a company. These three expense categories plus the cost of goods sold are the total expenses of the company and are deducted from sales to arrive at net income.

Manufacturing Cost Flows Using Perpetual Inventory Procedure Illustrated

Illustration 12.13 shows the July cost and revenue flowchart of a manufacturing company. Note how the T-accounts trace the flow of materials, labor, and manufacturing overhead costs through the production process to finished goods inventory. The illustration also shows the sale of finished goods inventory to customers and the closing of the revenue and expense accounts for the month. The paragraphs that follow explain the procedures used in Illustration 12.13 step by step, including the journal entries necessary to record the transactions. July's beginning inventories are materials, $10,000; work in process, $20,000; and finished goods, $40,000.

Flow of Direct and Indirect Materials Cost. During July, the company purchased $40,000 of materials and supplies on account, including transportation-in. The company also issued $28,000 of direct materials and $2,000 of indirect materials (supplies) from the storeroom to production. The required entries (keyed numerically to the entries in the T-accounts in Illustration 12.13) are:

(1)   Materials Inventory   40,000
        Accounts Payable.   40,000
        To record purchases of materials and supplies on
        account.

(2)   Work in Process Inventory.   28,000
        Manufacturing Overhead   2,000
           Materials Inventory   30,000
        To record direct and indirect materials issued to
        production.

Illustration 12.12
A MANUFACTURING COMPANY'S TOTAL OPERATIONS

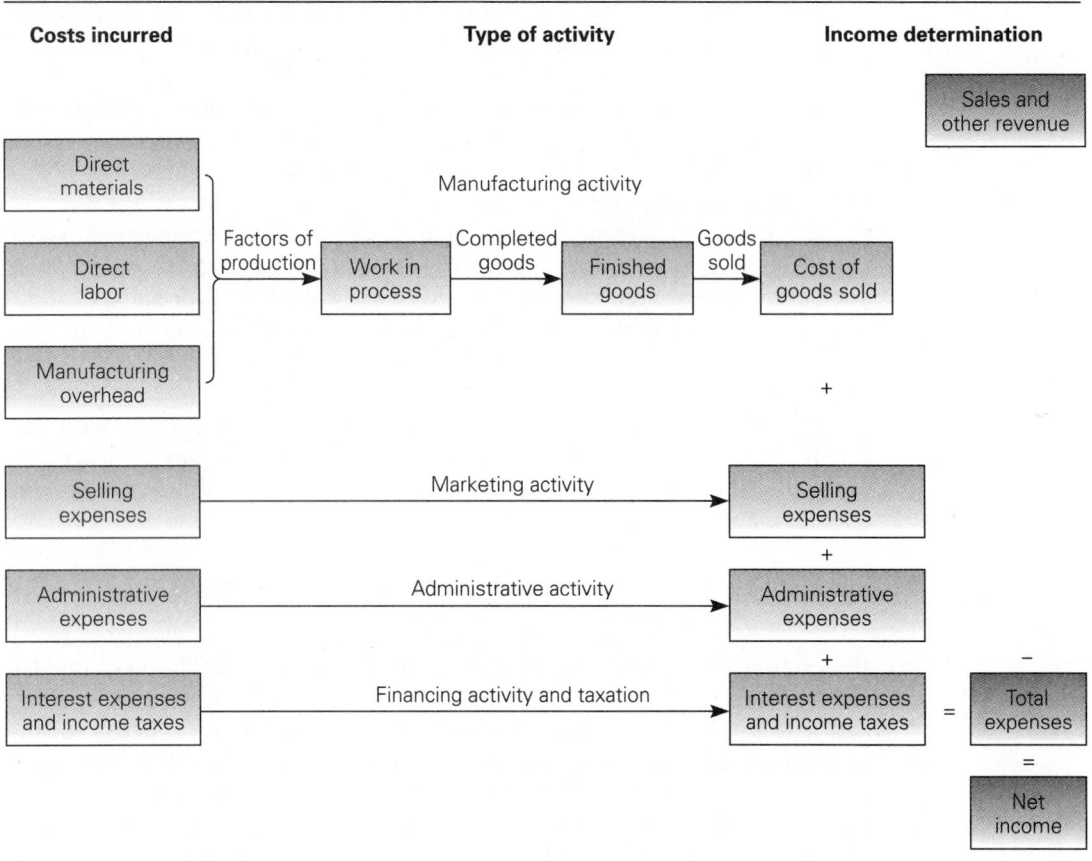

Note that the $40,000 purchases of direct and indirect materials (supplies) are debited to Materials Inventory. However, when the materials are issued to production, direct materials and indirect materials are separated. Direct materials are debited to Work in Process Inventory. Indirect materials are debited to Manufacturing Overhead because they are not easily traceable to specific products.

Flow of Labor Costs.   Under perpetual inventory procedure, two separate accounting activities—*payroll accounting* and *labor cost accounting*—are used to account for labor costs. *Payroll accounting* determines the total wages earned, the various deductions, and the net pay of each employee. *Labor cost accounting* determines the accounts that are to be charged with the various labor costs. The two accounting activities are tied together by an account that is common to both activities—the *Payroll Summary* account.

The Payroll Summary account is a temporarily established clearing account that is debited when the payroll department prepares payrolls and credited when the factory accounting department distributes labor costs. The Payroll Summary account has a zero balance at the end of any accounting period. The account has a balance during the period because of the time lag between payroll preparation and distribution of payroll costs as direct and indirect labor.

In Illustration 12.13, the factory payroll for July amounted to $75,000—$60,000 direct labor and $15,000 indirect labor. Payroll withholding from employees' paychecks amounted to $3,500 for social security taxes (FICA), $8,000 for income taxes, and $500 for union dues. The entries required are:

(3)	Payroll Summary	75,000	
	FICA Taxes Payable.		3,500
	Employees' Income Taxes Payable.		8,000
	Employees' Union Dues Payable.		500
	Payroll Payable.		63,000
	To record factory payroll and various withholdings.		
(4)	Work in Process Inventory.	60,000	
	Manufacturing Overhead	15,000	
	Payroll Summary		75,000
	To distribute labor costs for July.		

The Payroll Payable shown in entry (3) will be paid in cash to the employees. The amounts withheld will be paid at a later date in the employees' name to the federal government (social security taxes and federal income taxes) and the labor union (union dues). Entry (4) adds to Work in Process Inventory all labor costs traceable to the products being manufactured (direct labor). Nontraceable labor costs (indirect labor) are transferred to Manufacturing Overhead.

Flow of Overhead Costs. During July, the indirect costs of operating the factory were: repairs paid in cash, $1,000; property taxes, $1,500; expiration of prepaid equipment rent, $2,500; expiration of prepaid insurance, $2,000; payroll taxes accrued, $3,500; utilities accrued, $4,000; and factory building depreciation, $5,500. The following entry (5) shows the recording of these indirect costs.

(5)	Manufacturing Overhead	20,000	
	Cash		1,000
	Property Taxes Payable		1,500
	Prepaid Rent		2,500
	Prepaid Insurance		2,000
	Payroll Taxes Payable		3,500
	Accounts Payable		4,000
	Accumulated Depreciation—Factory Building		5,500
	To record factory indirect costs for July.		

Illustration 12.13
COST AND REVENUE FLOWCHART (PERPETUAL INVENTORY)

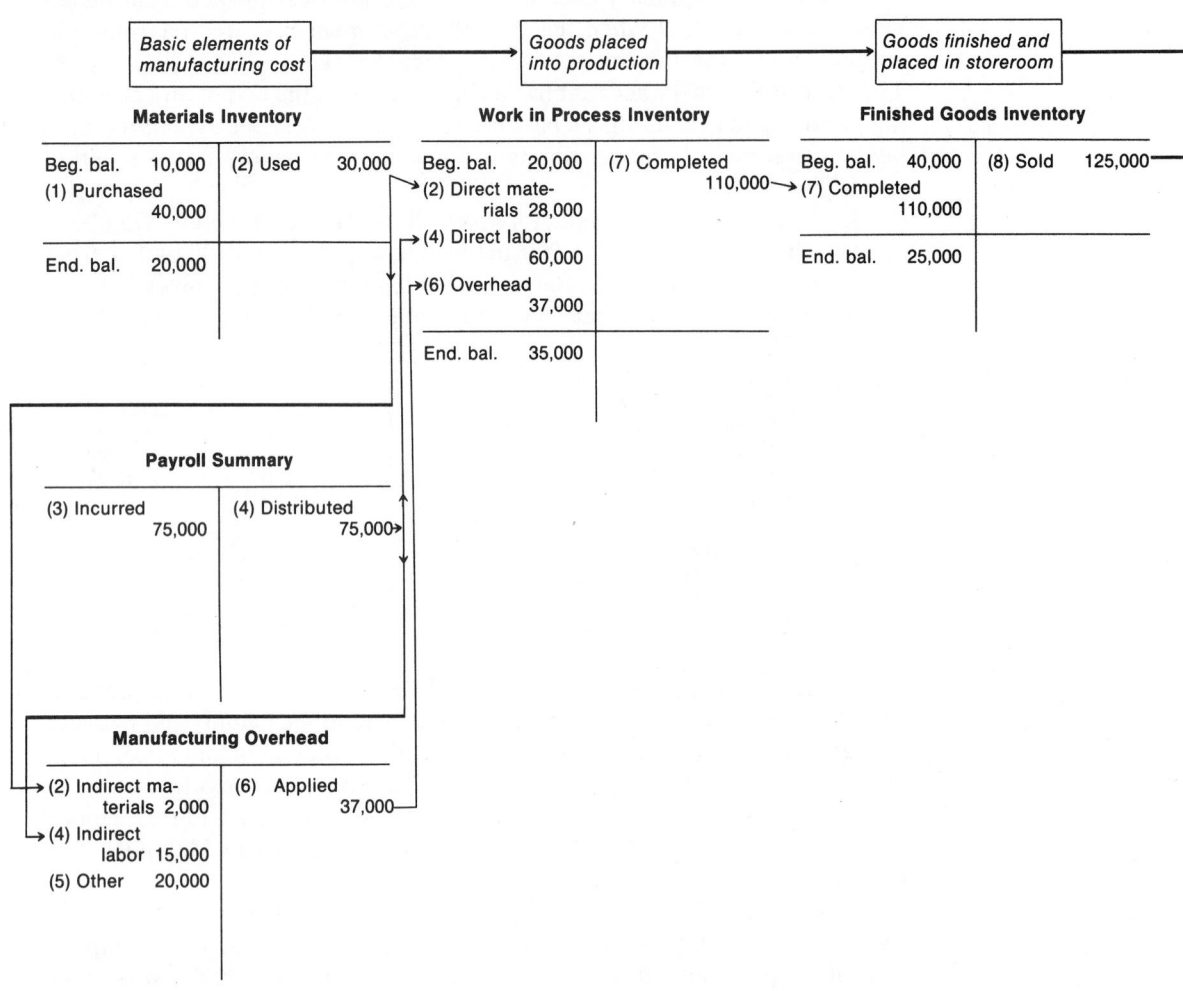

Manufacturing overhead costs are as much a part of production costs as are the costs of direct materials and direct labor. Manufacturing overhead costs must, therefore, be added to the Work in Process Inventory account. Entries (2), (4), and (5) included manufacturing overhead costs that totaled $37,000 (or $2,000 + $15,000 + $20,000). Entry (6) assigns this $37,000 of manufacturing overhead costs to Work in Process Inventory.

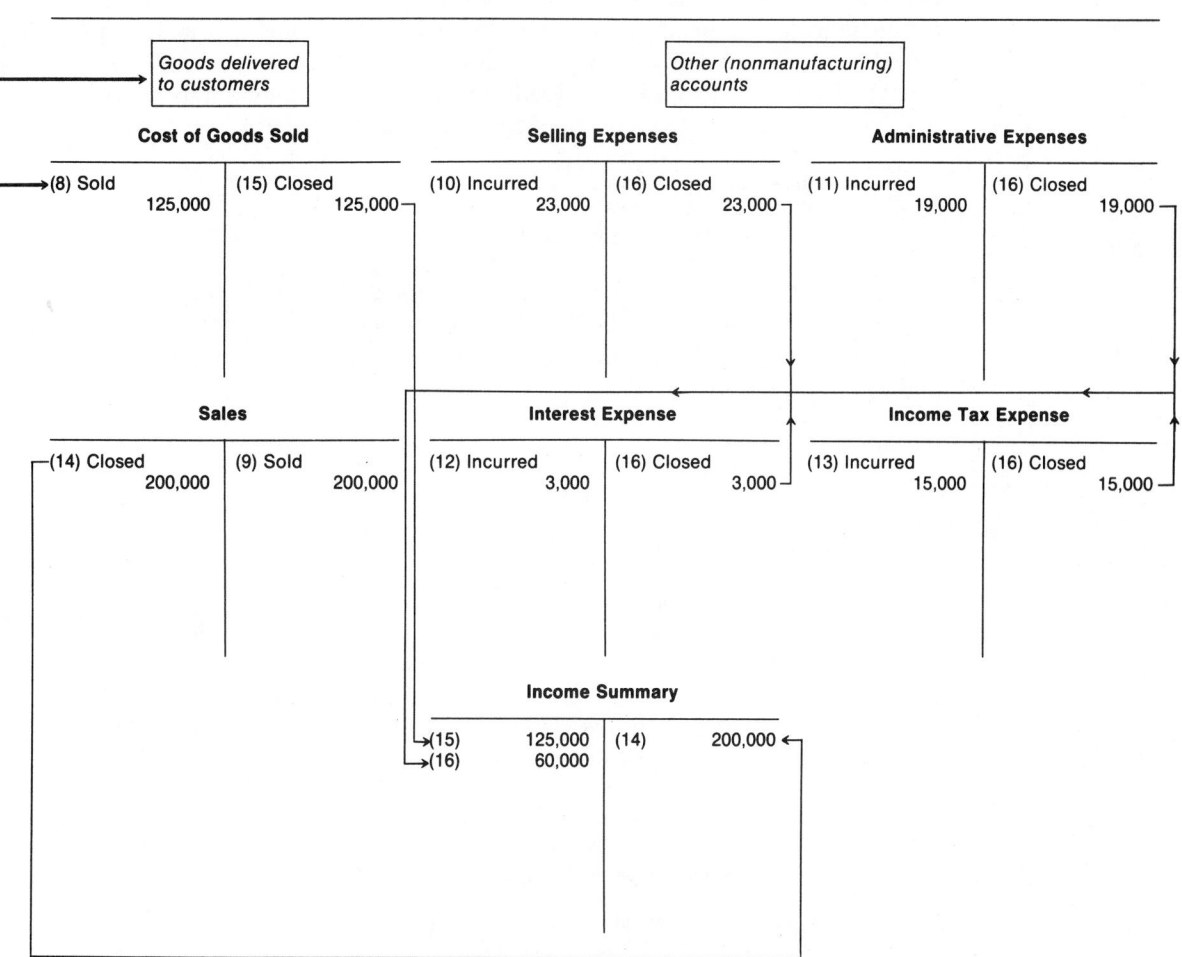

Note: The purpose of this illustration is to show the flow of inventory costs through a manufacturing company using perpetual inventory procedure. The numbers in parentheses represent the journal entry numbers from the discussion portion of the example. Only the portions of the journal entry that relate to inventory costing, expenses, or revenues are included in the above T-accounts. Debits or credits to noninventory balance sheet accounts that are not relevant to the discussion of inventory cost flows are not illustrated here.

(6)	Work in Process Inventory.	37,000	
	Manufacturing Overhead		37,000
	To assign overhead to work in process.		

Manufacturing overhead costs are generally assigned to production using a predetermined overhead rate. For purposes of this illustration, however, it is assumed that *all* overhead costs incurred during July are assigned to production.

Flow of Finished Goods.   Illustration 12.13 shows that for product cost purposes, Work in Process Inventory is charged with materials, labor, and manufacturing overhead costs. When the goods are completed and transferred out of production, an entry is made to transfer their cost from Work in Process Inventory to Finished Goods Inventory. Assuming goods costing $110,000 were completed and transferred, the entry needed is:

```
(7)  Finished Goods Inventory. . . . . . . . . . . . .  110,000
         Work in Process Inventory  . . . . . . . . . .           110,000
     To record transfer of completed goods.
```

Now assume the manufacturer in Illustration 12.13 sold goods costing $125,000 on account for $200,000. The following entries are required to transfer the cost of the inventory out of finished goods to cost of goods sold and to record the sale:

```
(8)  Cost of Goods Sold. . . . . . . . . . . . . . .  125,000
         Finished Goods Inventory. . . . . . . . . . .           125,000
     To record cost of goods sold.

(9)  Accounts Receivable . . . . . . . . . . . . . .  200,000
         Sales  . . . . . . . . . . . . . . . . . . . .           200,000
     To record sales on account.
```

We are now ready to complete the explanation of the entries in Illustration 12.13. Assume the company incurred the following expenses in July: selling, $23,000; administrative, $19,000; interest, $3,000; and income tax, $15,000. The required entries are:

```
(10)  Selling Expenses . . . . . . . . . . . . . . . . .  23,000
          Various asset and liability accounts . . . . . . . .          23,000
      To record selling expenses incurred in July.

(11)  Administrative Expenses  . . . . . . . . . . . . . .  19,000
          Various asset and liability accounts . . . . . . . .          19,000
      To record administrative expenses incurred in July.

(12)  Interest Expense . . . . . . . . . . . . . . . . .  3,000
          Interest Payable  . . . . . . . . . . . . . . . .          3,000
      To record interest expense incurred in July.

(13)  Income Tax Expense . . . . . . . . . . . . . . .  15,000
          Income Taxes Payable . . . . . . . . . . . . .          15,000
      To record estimated income taxes for July.
```

As indicated in entries (10) and (11) above, the manufacturer would keep subsidiary records or accounts for the various types of selling and administrative expenses incurred. The credits in these entries would be to accounts such as Cash, Accounts Payable, Salaries Payable, Accumulated Depreciation, and Prepaid Expenses.

Usually, the accounts are closed only at the end of the accounting year. However, entries (14), (15), and (16) record the closing of the revenue and expense accounts for July.

(14) Sales	200,000	
Income Summary.		200,000
To close Sales account.		

(15) Income Summary.	125,000	
Cost of Goods Sold.		125,000
To close Cost of Goods Sold account.		

(16) Income Summary.	60,000	
Selling Expenses		23,000
Administrative Expenses		19,000
Interest Expense		3,000
Income Tax Expense		15,000
To close other expense accounts.		

Entries (15) and (16) could be combined into one entry. Although it is not shown in Illustration 12.13, the closing process would be completed by transferring net income to the Retained Earnings account.

Income Summary.	15,000	
Retained Earnings		15,000
To close Income Summary account.		

So far in this chapter, we have discussed manufacturing companies that have inventories. Recent innovations in manufacturing methods have the potential to revolutionize both the production process and accounting procedures. The next section in this chapter discusses one of these innovations— the *just-in-time (JIT) production system.*

JUST-IN-TIME PRODUCTION SYSTEM

*Objective 7
Describe the just-in-time (JIT) production system and prepare journal entries*

Under the **just-in-time (JIT) production system,** materials are purchased just in time for production, parts of final products are produced just when needed for the next step in the production process, and finished goods are provided just in time for sale. The principal feature of the JIT system is that production does not begin on an item until an order is received. When the order is received, raw materials are ordered and the production cycle begins. As soon as the order is filled, production ends.

In theory, a JIT system eliminates the need for inventories because no production takes place until management knows that the item will be sold. In practice, companies using this system will normally have a backlog of orders so they can keep their production operations going. The benefits of the JIT system would be lost if a company had to shut down its operations for lengthy periods of time while waiting for a new order.

Effect of Just-in-Time on Accounting

Since JIT production responds to the receipt of an order for goods, a JIT accounting system will normally debit all costs directly to Cost of Goods Sold and bypass the usual inventory accounts. When inventories exist and must be reported in the financial statements, the inventory amounts are "backed out" of the Cost of Goods Sold account.

For example, Arizona Sunscreen uses the JIT system. Direct materials costs are $3.00 per bottle, and other manufacturing costs are $1.50 per bottle. The company received an order for 10,000 bottles of Sunscreen. Materials costs of $30,000 were incurred as were other manufacturing costs of $15,000. Assume that $6,000 of these other costs are wages, and the remaining $9,000 are manufacturing overhead costs on account. The journal entries to record these events are:

Cost of Goods Sold	30,000	
Accounts Payable		30,000
To record the use of materials.		
Cost of Goods Sold	15,000	
Wages Payable.		6,000
Accounts Payable		9,000
To record other manufacturing costs.		

All of the manufacturing costs are charged directly to Cost of Goods Sold.

Assume the manufacturer has 1,000 bottles left in Finished Goods Inventory when financial reports are prepared. These bottles are complete units that have not been shipped. The 1,000 units in Finished Goods Inventory are backed out of Cost of Goods Sold based on a unit cost of $4.50 ($3.00 for materials and $1.50 for other manufacturing costs) for a total of $4,500 (1,000 units × $4.50). The journal entry to transfer the cost of Finished Goods Inventory is:

Finished Goods Inventory	4,500	
Cost of Goods Sold.		4,500
To record inventories.		

Illustration 12.14 shows the T-accounts for Cost of Goods Sold and Finished Goods Inventory. This method of backing inventory amounts out of Cost of Goods Sold is often called *backflush accounting*.

JIT production simplifies accounting procedures. If the costs of sunscreen bottles were charged to production using traditional costing methods, the materials costs would be debited to a Materials Inventory account. As the materials were used, their costs would be transferred to Work in Process Inventory. The other manufacturing costs also would be charged to Work in Process Inventory. As goods were completed, costs would be transferred out of Work in Process Inventory into Finished Goods Inventory and, finally, into Cost of Goods Sold.

Illustration 12.14
JUST-IN-TIME COST FLOWS

Cost of Goods Sold			
Materials	30,000		
Other manufacturing	15,000	Finished goods	4,500

Finished Goods Inventory		
Finished goods	4,500	

Accounting systems are simplified under JIT. A substantial amount of time can be saved given the large volume of accounting entries required in complex operations. A Hewlett-Packard plant saved an estimated 100,000 journal entries per month when it switched to JIT, for example.[3]

Advantages of Just-in-Time

By reducing inventories, a JIT system offers potentially substantial cost savings. This system releases investment dollars that can be used elsewhere, frees space that the inventory previously occupied, and simplifies the accounting system. Companies have found that to implement JIT, they must also concentrate on eliminating manufacturing defects. No excess units are carried to fill customer orders in case defective units are manufactured. Thus, JIT is tied to quality improvements.

What Is Needed for Just-in-Time to Work

Use of a JIT system means that goods will not be produced to stockpile in inventory. Thus, to make JIT work, a company must begin with a backlog of orders from customers. If the company does not have a backlog, its production would stop after the company fills an order and remain idle until a new order is received. Such a stoppage could create chaos in the factory. In addition, the company must have reliable suppliers who can readily supply materials so that production can begin upon receipt of an order. A delay in waiting for materials could interrupt the production process and create customer dissatisfaction.

When companies reduce their inventory levels, they generally make smaller batches of a product. For example, Levi Strauss Company would

---

[3] R. Hunt, L. Garrett, and C. M. Merz, "Direct Labor Cost Not Always Relevant at H-P," *Management Accounting,* February 1985, pp. 58–62.

A BROADER PERSPECTIVE

THE NEW THEORY OF PRODUCTION

According to noted management author Peter Drucker, managerial accounting is one of the four basic concepts on which the "factory of 1999" will be built and managed. In addition to managerial accounting, these concepts are statistical quality control, a modular approach to organizing the production process, and a systems approach that combines the physical process of making things with the economics of running a business.

Drucker says, "Bean counters do not enjoy a good press these days. They are blamed for all the ills that afflict U.S. manufacturing. But the bean counters will have the last laugh. In the factory of 1999, manufacturing accounting will play as big a role as it ever did and probably an even bigger one" [p. 96]. In this new business enterprise, managerial accountants will integrate production, economics, and business strategy.

In the 1920s, new managerial accounting methods supported decentralized management and enabled companies such as General Motors and General Electric to develop into worldwide industry leaders. Managerial accounting techniques developed in the 1920s are out of date today, according to Drucker, because the manufacturing environment has moved from labor-intensive processes to machine-intensive processes. Yet traditional costing methods assign overhead costs to products as a proportion of the direct labor in those products.

When direct labor is less than five percent of the cost of making a product, as it is in high-tech companies, it is unrealistic to assign overhead costs to products as a proportion of the direct labor in the product. Instead, accountants should find ways to assign overhead to products based on the company's activities that cause the overhead.

Author's note: To deal with the problems noted by Drucker, many companies are experimenting with a method called *activity-based costing,* which is discussed in this chapter and later chapters in this book.

SOURCE: Based on the article by Peter F. Drucker, "The Emerging Theory of Manufacturing," *Harvard Business Review,* May–June 1990, pp. 94–102.

make just enough pairs of a particular style and size jeans to fill customer orders, then switch to another style or size. Companies making smaller batches of products need machines that will enable them to change from one product to another quickly and efficiently.

In recent years, computer-operated *flexible manufacturing systems* have been developed to change production quickly from one type of product to another. With computer-operated flexible manufacturing systems, companies can quickly fill customer orders and substantially reduce inventory levels.

MANAGERIAL ACCOUNTING IN HIGH-TECH COMPANIES

Many companies have recently installed computer-assisted methods of manufacturing, merchandising, or providing services. These new technologies

Lisa and Glenn were drinking coffee together during their break. ''I have a problem that I'd like your advice about,'' said Glenn. ''I prepare all the staff's expense reports. Most of the time their accommodations and business meals far exceed the limits allowed by the company. On several occasions, I know that some of them have taken their families and friends along on the trip and charged the bills to clients' accounts.''

''How do they get away with it?'' asked Lisa.

''They tell me to add some of their colleagues' names to the list of people who went on the trip so that the costs are within the company limits,'' said Glenn.

''Have you talked to your supervisor about this?'' asked Lisa.

''My supervisor said that as long as the clients foot the bill, there was no problem with padding the clients' expenses.''

''I just don't feel good about this situation,'' continued Glenn. ''Morally and ethically I think it is wrong for me to knowingly go along with these practices; besides, I would be very angry if I were a client and found out I had been overcharged.''

''Can you talk to your supervisor's boss?'' Lisa suggested.

''If my supervisor found out, I'd be in big trouble,'' said Glenn. ''Besides, maybe all the higher-ups condone this practice. Maybe everyone pads expense accounts. Maybe I have to go along with this practice to keep my job.''

Required
What should Glenn do?

have had a major impact on managerial accounting. For example, where robots and computer-assisted manufacturing methods have replaced people, labor costs have shrunk from between 20% and 40% of product costs to less than 5%. Accounting in traditional settings required much more work to keep track of labor costs than in the new settings.

In highly automated environments, overhead costs have become a larger part of total product cost. Accountants have had to become more sophisticated in finding the causes of these overhead costs.

Overhead is now assumed to be caused by machine-hours, complexity of the production process, amount of product testing required, and many other activities. Activity-based costing, discussed earlier in this chapter, is an example of the type of effort accountants will be required to make in the future to find the causes of overhead costs.

UNDERSTANDING THE LEARNING OBJECTIVES

1. Describe the uses of managerial accounting information.
   • Managerial accounting is intended for internal use to provide more detailed information to managers. Managers use the information to

make good management decisions, which include financial, resource allocation, production, and marketing decisions.

- The information managers receive and use should (1) relate to the part of the company that the manager oversees, (2) involve planning for the future, and (3) be relevant and cost effective.

- The main differences between managerial and financial accounting is that managerial accounting is more detailed and intended for internal use, while financial accounting is broader in scope and intended for external use.

2. Describe the three basic components of manufacturing costs incurred in the production of a product.

- **Direct materials costs** are (1) included in the finished product, (2) used only in the manufacture of the product, and (3) clearly and easily traceable to the product. These costs include the invoice price of the actual quantity used plus delivery charges.

- **Direct labor costs** (1) include labor costs of all employees actually working on materials to convert them into finished goods; (2) include only those labor costs that are clearly traceable to, or readily identifiable with, the finished product; and (3) are usually measured by multiplying the number of direct labor-hours by the hourly wage rate.

- **Manufacturing overhead costs** (1) include all manufacturing costs except those accounted for as direct materials and direct labor; (2) are manufacturing costs that the company must incur but cannot or will not trace directly to specific units; and (3) include a number of costs that relate to the manufacturing process, such as depreciation and maintenance on machines, supervisors' salaries, and factory utility costs.

- **Prime costs** are direct materials and direct labor.

- **Conversion costs** are costs of converting materials to finished goods and are made up of direct labor and manufacturing overhead.

3. Compare product costs to period costs and fixed costs to variable costs, and explain why proper classification of these costs is essential.

- **Product costs** are costs a manufacturing company incurs in the manufacture of products and assigns to units of a product. These costs include costs of direct materials, direct labor, and manufacturing overhead.

- **Period costs** are costs that relate to periods of time rather than the production of products. These costs cannot be traced directly to the manufacture of a specific product. All selling and nonfactory administrative costs are treated as period costs.

- **Fixed costs** remain constant in total amount over a range of manufacturing activity levels.

- **Variable costs,** such as direct materials, vary or change in total as volume changes. Fixed costs do not change as volume changes.

- Proper classification between product costs and period costs is essential because product costs are not expensed when incurred but are expensed in the period the goods are sold, while period costs are expensed in the period in which they are incurred. This distinction is important for income determination purposes. The distinction between fixed costs and variable costs is important for decision making, as discussed later in the book.

4. Determine the cost of inventories under periodic inventory procedure.
    *   Under periodic inventory procedure, accounts are brought to their proper balances only at the end of the accounting period by taking a physical inventory.
    *   Purchases are debited to Materials Purchases; transportation charges incurred on purchases are debited to Transportation-In; cash discounts on purchases are credited to Materials Purchase Discounts; and returns of purchased materials and allowances granted on purchases are credited to Materials Purchase Returns and Allowances. Each of these accounts is closed through Manufacturing Summary to Income Summary at the end of the accounting period.
    *   The Materials Inventory account contains the beginning inventory amount until year-end, when the ending inventory is entered in the account during the closing process.
    *   Inventory quantities are determined at year-end by taking a physical count of the materials, work in process, and finished goods on hand.
        (1) Materials inventory cost is calculated by multiplying the unit purchase price by the quantity of each type of item.
        (2) Estimating the cost of work in process or finished goods inventory is more complicated. A manufacturer must estimate the *(a)* direct materials cost contained in each unit, *(b)* direct labor cost incurred for each unit, and *(c)* manufacturing overhead applicable to each unit.

5. Compare financial reporting by a merchandiser to that of a manufacturer, and prepare a statement of cost of goods manufactured, an income statement, and a balance sheet for a manufacturer.
    *   One of the major differences between merchandisers and manufacturers is in their types of inventories. Inventories are reported on the balance sheet and also affect income (through cost of goods sold) on the income statement. Thus, the balance sheet and income statement of a merchandiser will differ from the balance sheet and income statement of a manufacturer.
    *   The statement of cost of goods manufactured supports the cost of goods manufactured figure on the income statement and has two important calculations of—
        (1) Cost to manufacture, which includes the costs of all resources put into production during the period.
        (2) Cost of goods manufactured, which consists of the cost of all goods completed during the period.

- The manufacturer's income statement shows the cost of goods manufactured, which is added to the beginning inventory of finished goods to derive the cost of goods available for sale.
- The manufacturer's balance sheet (1) shows materials, work in process, and finished goods inventories separately; and (2) may also show greater detail in the property, plant, and equipment section because of the significant investment in plant assets.

6. Diagram the pattern of cost flows for a manufacturing company using perpetual inventory procedure, and prepare journal entries.
   - Under perpetual inventory procedure, unit product costs are determined during the period, rather than estimated at the end of the period, by transferring the cost of direct materials, direct labor, and manufacturing overhead to Work in Process Inventory and then to Finished Goods Inventory accounts as goods are processed.
   - The accounting flow of costs under perpetual inventory procedure follows the physical flow of the manufacturing process. The accounting records show the flow of direct materials costs from Materials Inventory into Work in Process Inventory. Here, the costs of direct labor and manufacturing overhead are added. When the products are completed and transferred to the finished goods storeroom, their costs are removed from Work in Process Inventory and assigned to Finished Goods Inventory. As the goods are sold, the related costs are transferred from Finished Goods Inventory to Cost of Goods Sold.
   - Cost of goods sold + Selling expenses + Administrative expenses + Interest expense and income tax expense = Total expenses; total expenses are deducted from sales and other revenue to arrive at net income.

7. Describe the just-in-time (JIT) production system and prepare journal entries.
   - The just-in-time (JIT) production system manages purchasing and production so that materials are purchased just in time for production, parts of final products are produced just when needed for the next step in the production process, and finished goods are provided just in time for sale. The principal feature of the JIT system is that production does not begin on an item until an order is received, and production ends when the order is filled. In theory, JIT substantially reduces or eliminates the need for inventories.
   - JIT accounting procedures normally debit all costs directly to cost of goods sold and bypass the usual inventory accounts. When inventories are reported in the financial statements, the inventory amounts are "backed out" of the Cost of Goods Sold account.
   - JIT can save record-keeping costs, free resources previously tied up in inventory, reduce inventory storage and related costs, and help managers identify production problems previously buried in inventory.

- To use a JIT system effectively, a company needs to have a backlog of orders from customers and reliable suppliers with materials readily available so that the company can keep the production line moving.

8. Prepare a work sheet for a manufacturing company using periodic inventory procedure (appendix).

- Manufacturing companies using periodic inventory procedure follow procedures similar to merchandisers using periodic inventory procedure.

- The work sheet for a manufacturer includes Manufacturing Statement columns that show the total of all manufacturing costs incurred during the period.

APPENDIX

THE WORK SHEET FOR A MANUFACTURING COMPANY USING PERIODIC INVENTORY PROCEDURE

Objective 8
Prepare a work sheet for a manufacturing company using periodic inventory procedure

Manufacturers prepare a statement of cost of goods manufactured to support the cost of goods sold figure on the income statement. A work sheet, also called a *spreadsheet,* can be used to aid in preparing the statement of cost of goods manufactured (as well as adjusting and closing entries). These work sheets are generally prepared on a computer using spreadsheet software. The work sheet for a manufacturing company has a pair of columns for the **statement of cost of goods manufactured** (manufacturing statement), as shown in Illustration 12.15. This example focuses on the production-related accounts. (We could also have had a pair of columns for the Statement of Retained Earnings. If so, the beginning Retained Earnings of $103,500 and the net income of $114,500 would have been totaled [$218,000] before being transferred to the credit Balance Sheet column.)

The Flanigan Manufacturing Company trial balance is taken from its ledger accounts at year-end. Administrative and selling expenses have been summarized to emphasize the company's production activities. Beginning-of-year inventory account balances for Materials Inventory, Work in Process Inventory, and Finished Goods Inventory are $40,000, $84,000, and $56,000, respectively. Year-end inventory account balances are $38,000, $80,000, and $60,000, respectively.

Adjustments Columns

The required adjustments for Flanigan Manufacturing Company appear in the *Adjustments* columns on the work sheet. The following information was used to prepare the adjustments:

1. The uncollectible accounts expense was estimated to be $1,500 for the year.

Illustration 12.15
MANUFACTURING WORK SHEET

FLANIGAN MANUFACTURING COMPANY
Work Sheet for the Year Ended December 31, 1995

Account Titles	Trial Balance Debit	Trial Balance Credit	Adjustments Debit	Adjustments Credit	Manufacturing Statement Debit	Manufacturing Statement Credit	Income Statement Debit	Income Statement Credit	Balance Sheet Debit	Balance Sheet Credit
Cash	62,000								62,000	
Accounts Receivable	160,000								160,000	
Allowance for Uncollectible Accounts		500		(1) 1,500						2,000
Prepaid Insurance	7,500			(4) 6,500					1,000	
Inventories:										
Materials	40,000				40,000	38,000			38,000	
Work in Process	84,000				84,000	80,000			80,000	
Finished Goods	56,000						56,000	60,000	60,000	
Factory Building	400,000								400,000	
Accumulated Depreciation—Factory Building		40,000		(2) 20,000						60,000
Factory Equipment	460,000								460,000	
Accumulated Depreciation—Factory Equipment		92,000		(3) 46,000						138,000
Land	32,000								32,000	
Accounts Payable		60,000								60,000
Mortgage Payable, 10%		200,000								200,000
Common Stock—$5 Par Value		600,000								600,000
Retained Earnings		103,500								103,500
Sales		1,800,000						1,800,000		
Materials Purchases (net)	480,000				480,000					
Transportation-In	6,000				6,000					

Account	Trial Balance Dr	Trial Balance Cr	Adjustments Dr	Adjustments Cr	Manufacturing Dr	Manufacturing Cr	Income Statement Dr	Income Statement Cr	Balance Sheet Dr	Balance Sheet Cr
Direct Labor	371,000		(5) 9,000		380,000					
Indirect Labor	62,500		(5) 2,500		65,000					
Supervisors' Salaries Expense	127,000		(5) 3,000		130,000					
Maintenance and Repairs Expense	17,000				17,000					
Factory Utilities Expense	5,000				5,000					
Selling Expenses	199,500		(5) 500				200,000			
Administrative Expenses	184,500		(4) 500				185,000			
Interest Expense	20,000						20,000			
Factory Property Taxes Expense	15,000				15,000					
Income Tax Expense	107,000						107,000			
	2,896,000	2,896,000								
Uncollectible Accounts Expense			(1) 1,500				1,500			
Depreciation Expense— Factory Building			(2) 20,000		20,000					
Depreciation Expense— Factory Equipment			(3) 46,000		46,000					
Insurance Expense—Factory			(4) 6,000		6,000					
Payroll Payable				(5) 15,000						15,000
			89,000	89,000		118,000				
Manufacturing Summary (cost of goods manufactured)						1,176,000	1,176,000			
					1,294,000	1,294,000	1,745,500	1,860,000	1,293,000	1,178,500
Net income							114,500			114,500
							1,860,000	1,860,000	1,293,000	1,293,000

(1) To record uncollectible accounts expense for the year.
(2) To record depreciation expense on factory building.
(3) To record depreciation expense on factory equipment.
(4) To record and distribute cost of expired insurance.
(5) To record and distribute cost of accrued payroll.

2. Depreciation on the factory building was $20,000.
3. Depreciation on the factory equipment was $46,000.
4. Insurance expiring during the year was $6,500. Of this amount, $6,000 applied to the factory building and equipment, and $500 applied to administrative offices (administrative expense).
5. Factory payroll accrued since the last payday was distributed as follows: direct labor, $9,000; supervisors' salaries, $3,000; indirect labor, $2,500; and finished goods storeroom personnel (selling expense), $500. Nonfactory employees were paid on December 31.

Based on the above information, the following adjusting entries must be recorded on the work sheet of Flanigan Manufacturing Company (Illustration 12.15):

(1)	Uncollectible Accounts Expense	1,500	
	Allowance for Uncollectible Accounts		1,500
	To record uncollectible accounts expense for the year.		
(2)	Depreciation Expense—Factory Building	20,000	
	Accumulated Depreciation—Factory Building		20,000
	To record depreciation on factory building.		
(3)	Depreciation Expense—Factory Equipment	46,000	
	Accumulated Depreciation—Factory Equipment		46,000
	To record depreciation on factory equipment.		
(4)	Insurance Expense—Factory	6,000	
	Insurance Expense—Administrative	500	
	Prepaid Insurance		6,500
	To record and distribute cost of expired insurance.		
(5)	Direct Labor	9,000	
	Supervisors' Salaries Expense	3,000	
	Indirect Labor	2,500	
	Selling Expenses	500	
	Payroll Payable		15,000
	To record and distribute cost of accrued payroll.		

Manufacturing Statement Columns

The *Manufacturing Statement* columns show the total of all manufacturing costs *incurred* during the period. The total is referred to as cost to manufacture for the period. The first element of total manufacturing cost is materials used in production. The beginning materials inventory plus materials purchases and related transportation costs represent the total cost of materials available for production. Therefore, Materials Inventory, Materials Purchases (net), and Transportation-In are included in the Manufacturing Statement debit column of the work sheet. Materials remaining in inventory at the end of the period were not used, so the ending balance in Materials Inventory is included in the Manufacturing Statement credit column to remove that amount from the cost of materials issued to production.

Direct labor incurred in production and all manufacturing overhead costs incurred during the period are included in the Manufacturing Statement debit column because these items increase the cost of goods produced during the period.

Cost to manufacture, the total of all manufacturing costs for the period, represents the costs added to production. **Cost of goods manufactured** represents the total cost of all goods completed during the period and removed from production.

To determine the cost of goods manufactured, add the beginning work in process inventory to manufacturing costs for the period and subtract the ending work in process inventory. Thus, the beginning balance of Work in Process Inventory is included in the Manufacturing Statement debit column, and the ending balance of Work in Process Inventory is included in the credit column. Note that **the excess of total debits over total credits represents the cost of goods manufactured and is the total cost of all goods completed during the period.**

The Closing Entries

Closing entries for a manufacturing company using periodic inventory procedure are slightly different from closing entries prepared for a merchandiser. This difference is due to the use of a Manufacturing Summary account, which records the cost of goods produced during the period. As shown below, all of the items in the Manufacturing Statement columns are closed to the Manufacturing Summary account first (this balance is the cost of goods manufactured and is placed in the Income Statement debit column); then all items in the Income Statement columns are closed to Income Summary. Finally, the Income Summary account is closed to Retained Earnings.

Closing the Accounts in the Manufacturing Statement Columns

The first closing entry closes all of the accounts appearing in the Manufacturing Statement debit column (Illustration 12.15) by crediting those accounts. The debit is to Manufacturing Summary for the subtotal of the Manufacturing Statement debit column, $1,294,000.

1995				
Dec.	31	Manufacturing Summary	1,294,000	
		Materials Inventory (beginning)		40,000
		Work in Process Inventory (beginning) .		84,000
		Materials Purchases (net).		480,000
		Transportation-In.		6,000
		Direct Labor		380,000
		Indirect Labor		65,000
		Supervisors' Salaries Expense		130,000

```
1995
Dec.  31      Maintenance and Repairs Expense  . . .            17,000
              Factory Utilities Expense . . . . . . . . .         5,000
              Factory Property Taxes Expense  . . . .           15,000
              Depreciation Expense—Factory Building            20,000
              Depreciation Expense—Factory
                   Equipment. . . . . . . . . . . . . .          46,000
              Insurance Expense—Factory . . . . . .              6,000
           To close all accounts in the Manufacturing
           Statement debit column to Manufacturing
           Summary.
```

The second closing entry sets up the inventories that appear in the Manufacturing Statement credit column by debiting those accounts. The credit is to Manufacturing Summary for the subtotal of the Manufacturing Statement credit column, $118,000.

```
1995
Dec.  31   Materials Inventory (ending) . . . . . . . .        38,000
           Work in Process Inventory (ending). . . . .         80,000
               Manufacturing Summary. . . . . . . .                     118,000
            To set up the ending inventories of
            materials and work in process.
```

At this point in the closing process, the Manufacturing Summary account has a debit balance of $1,176,000. This amount represents the cost of goods manufactured during the period.

Closing the Accounts in the Income Statement Columns

The third closing entry closes all of the accounts in the Income Statement debit column by crediting those accounts. The debit is to the Income Summary account for the subtotal of the Income Statement debit column, $1,745,500.

```
1995
Dec.  31   Income Summary . . . . . . . . . . . . .        1,745,500
               Finished Goods Inventory (beginning) . .                  56,000
               Selling Expenses. . . . . . . . . . . .                  200,000
               Administrative Expenses . . . . . . . .                  185,000
               Interest Expense . . . . . . . . . . . .                  20,000
               Income Tax Expense . . . . . . . . . .                   107,000
               Uncollectible Accounts Expense  . . . .                    1,500
               Manufacturing Summary . . . . . . . .                  1,176,000
            To close all accounts in the Income
            Statement debit column to Income
            Summary.
```

The fourth closing entry establishes the ending Finished Goods Inventory balance and closes the Sales account by debiting those accounts. The credit is to the Income Summary account for the subtotal of the Income Statement credit column, $1,860,000.

```
1995
Dec.  31  Finished Goods Inventory (ending) . . . . .      60,000
          Sales . . . . . . . . . . . . . . . . .  1,800,000
              Income Summary . . . . . . . . . .                    1,860,000
          To set up the ending Finished Goods
          Inventory and close Sales to the Income
          Summary account.
```

At this point in the closing process, the Income Summary account has a credit balance of $114,500, which is the amount of net income on the work sheet. The fifth (and last) closing entry closes the Income Summary account by debiting Income Summary and crediting Retained Earnings:

```
1995
Dec.  31  Income Summary . . . . . . . . . . . . .     114,500
              Retained Earnings . . . . . . . . . . .                 114,500
          To close the Income Summary account to
          Retained Earnings.
```

DEMONSTRATION PROBLEM

Project Sound, Inc., makes VCRs. The following events occurred during October.

The beginning inventories on October 1 were: materials, $10,000; work in process, $30,000; and finished goods, $30,000. During October, the company purchased $90,000 of materials and supplies on account and issued $66,000 of direct materials and $4,000 of indirect materials (supplies) from the storeroom to production.

The factory payroll for October was $160,000—direct labor of $130,000 and indirect labor of $30,000. Indirect costs of operating the factory during the period included repairs of $2,000 paid in cash, property taxes of $3,000 on account, expiration of prepaid equipment rent of $5,000, expiration of prepaid insurance of $4,000, employer's payroll taxes accrued of $7,000, utilities of $8,000 paid in cash, and factory building depreciation of $11,000.

Goods costing $250,000 were completed and transferred from Work in Process Inventory to Finished Goods Inventory. Goods costing $270,000 were sold on account for $400,000.

Selling expenses of $80,000, administrative expenses of $60,000, interest expense of $5,000, and corporate income tax expense of $30,000 were incurred.

Required:

a. Prepare journal entries to show the flow of costs through accounts. Include closing entries.
b. Prepare a cost and revenue flowchart like the one in Illustration 12.13. Use perpetual inventory procedure.

Solution to demonstration problem

a. Journal entries:

1. Materials Inventory.	90,000	
Accounts Payable		90,000
To record purchases of materials and supplies on account.		
2. Work in Process Inventory	66,000	
Manufacturing Overhead	4,000	
Materials Inventory.		70,000
To record direct and indirect materials issued to production.		
3. Payroll Summary.	160,000	
Payroll Withholding Accounts		30,000
Payroll Payable		130,000
To record factory payroll and payroll withholding accounts.		
4. Work in Process Inventory	130,000	
Manufacturing Overhead	30,000	
Payroll Summary.		160,000
To distribute labor costs for October.		
5. Manufacturing Overhead	40,000	
Cash		10,000
Property Taxes Payable		3,000
Prepaid Equipment Rent		5,000
Prepaid Insurance		4,000
Payroll Taxes Payable		7,000
Accumulated Depreciation—Factory Building . . .		11,000
To record factory indirect costs for October.		
6. Work in Process Inventory	74,000	
Manufacturing Overhead		74,000
To assign overhead to work in process.		
7. Finished Goods Inventory	250,000	
Work in Process Inventory		250,000
To record transfer of completed goods.		
8. Cost of Goods Sold	270,000	
Finished Goods Inventory		270,000
To record cost of goods sold.		
9. Accounts Receivable	400,000	
Sales		400,000
To record sales on account.		
10. Selling Expenses	80,000	
Various Asset and Liability Accounts		80,000
To record selling expenses incurred in October.		
11. Administrative Expenses	60,000	
Various Asset and Liability Accounts		60,000
To record Administrative expenses incurred in October.		

12.	Interest Expense	5,000	
	Interest Payable		5,000
	To record interest expense incurred in October.		

13.	Income Tax Expense	30,000	
	Income Taxes Payable		30,000
	To record estimated income taxes for October.		

14.	Sales	400,000	
	Income Summary		400,000
	To close Sales account.		

15.	Income Summary	270,000	
	Cost of Goods Sold		270,000
	To close Cost of Goods Sold account.		

16.	Income Summary	175,000	
	Selling Expenses		80,000
	Administrative Expenses		60,000
	Interest Expense		5,000
	Income Tax Expense		30,000
	To close other expense accounts.		

b. Flow of costs and revenues:*

Materials Inventory

Beg. bal. 10,000	(2) Used
(1) Purchased 90,000	70,000
End bal. 30,000	

Work in Process Inventory

Beg. bal. 30,000	(7) Completed
(2) Direct materials 66,000	250,000
(4) Direct labor 130,000	
(6) Overhead 74,000	
End bal. 50,000	

Finished Goods Inventory

Beg. bal. 30,000	(8) Sold
(7) Completed 250,000	270,000
End bal. 10,000	

Payroll Summary

| (3) Incurred 160,000 | (4) Distributed 160,000 |

Manufacturing Overhead

(2) Indirect materials 4,000	(6) Applied 74,000
(4) Indirect labor 30,000	
(5) Other 40,000	

* This illustration includes *only* the entries relevant for cost flows.

Cost of Goods Sold	

(8) Sold
     270,000
	(15) Closed
	        270,000

Selling Expenses	

(10) Incurred
       80,000
	(16) Closed
	        80,000

Administrative Expenses	

(11) Incurred
       60,000
	(16) Closed
	        60,000

Sales	

(14) Closed
       400,000
	(9) Sold
	       400,000

Interest Expense	

(12) Incurred
        5,000
	(16) Closed
	        5,000

Income Tax Expense	

(13) Incurred
       30,000
	(16) Closed
	        30,000

Income Summary	
(15) 270,000 (16) 175,000	(14) 400,000

NEW TERMS

Activity-based costing   A method of assigning costs to goods and services that assumes all costs are caused by the activities used to produce those goods and services. *651*

Administrative costs   Nonmanufacturing costs that include the costs of top administrative functions and various staff departments such as accounting, data processing, and personnel. *644*

Conversion cost   The sum of direct labor and manufacturing overhead costs. *644*

Cost   A financial measure of the resources used or given up to achieve a stated purpose. *641*

Cost driver   Activity or transaction that causes costs to be incurred. Machine-hours can be a cost driver, for example. *651*

Cost of goods manufactured   Consists of the total costs of all goods completed during the period; total manufacturing cost plus beginning work in process inventory minus ending work in process inventory. *653, 675*

Cost to manufacture   Includes the costs of all resources put into production during the period. *653*

Direct labor   Labor costs of all employees actually working on materials to convert them to finished goods. *642*

Direct materials   Materials that are (1) included in the finished product, (2) used only in the manufacture of the product, and (3) clearly and easily traceable to the product. *642*

Factory cost   See Manufacturing cost.

Finished goods   Completed manufactured products ready to be sold; also, Finished Goods Inventory is the title of an inventory account maintained for such products. *641, 657*

Fixed costs   Costs that remain constant in total amount over a range of manufacturing activity levels. *646*

Indirect labor   The services of factory employees that for practical reasons cannot or will not be traced to the manufactured products. *643*

Indirect materials   Materials used in the manufacture of a product that for practical reasons cannot or will not be traced directly to the manufactured products. *642*

Inventoriable cost   See Manufacturing cost.

Just-in-time (JIT) production system   JIT production manages purchasing and production so that materials are purchased just in time for production, parts of products are produced just when needed for the next step in the production process, and finished goods are provided just in time for sale. *663*

Managerial accounting   Information is intended for internal use. The purpose is to generate detailed information managers can use to make management decisions. *638*

Manufacturing cost   The cost incurred to produce or create a product; it includes direct materials, direct labor, and manufacturing overhead costs. *642*

Manufacturing overhead   All manufacturing costs except for those costs accounted for as direct materials and direct labor. *643*

Manufacturing overhead rate   Expresses manufacturing overhead costs in relation to some measure of manufacturing activity. *649*

Materials   Unprocessed items that will be used in the manufacturing process. *641*

Period costs   Costs related more closely to periods of time than to the production of products. Period costs cannot be traced directly to the manufacture of a specific product; they are expensed in the period in which they are incurred. *644*

Prime cost   The sum of the direct materials costs and direct labor costs incurred to manufacture a product. *644*

Product costs   Costs a company assigns to units produced. For manufacturing companies, these costs are direct materials, direct labor, and manufacturing overhead. See also Manufacturing cost. *642, 644*

Selling costs   Costs incurred to obtain customer orders and get the finished product in the customer's possession. *644*

Statement of cost of goods manufactured   An accounting report showing the cost to manufacture and the cost of goods manufactured. *653, 671*

Variable costs   Costs that vary directly in total amount with changes in the volume of production activity or output. *646*

Work in process   Partially completed products; also, Work in Process Inventory is the title of an inventory account maintained for such products. *641, 657*

SELF-TEST

True-False

Indicate whether each of the following statements is true or false.

1. The sum of direct labor costs and manufacturing overhead costs is called *prime cost*.

2. Managerial accounting is for internal use and generally gives more detailed information than financial accounting.

3. A manufacturer produces personal computers requiring a screen for each one. The screens are considered direct materials and are variable costs.

4. JIT production is made in response to the receipt of an order for goods, and the accountant will normally debit all costs directly to Cost of Goods Sold and bypass the usual inventory accounts.

Multiple-Choice

Select the best answer for each of the following questions.

1. Under which cost category are indirect labor costs included?
   a. Administrative expense.
   b. Manufacturing overhead.
   c. Direct labor.
   d. None of the above.

2. Under which cost category are employees' benefits normally included?
   a. Direct labor.
   b. Manufacturing overhead.
   c. Direct materials.
   d. None of the above.

3. All selling and nonfactory administrative costs are treated as:
   a. Period costs.
   b. Selling costs.
   c. Manufacturing overhead costs.
   d. Administrative costs.

4. One of the steps that activity-based costing uses to determine a product's cost is to identify cost drivers, which are activities or transactions that cause costs to be incurred. Which of the following could be considered a cost driver?
   a. Direct labor-hours.
   b. The number of different parts of a product.
   c. Machine-hours.
   d. All of the above.

5. Using the following data, determine the manufacturing overhead rate per hour using machine-hours to apply manufacturing overhead to Work in Process Inventory.

Direct materials used to make 10,000 shirts	$100,000
Direct labor (50,000 hours)	250,000
Manufacturing overhead (12,500 machine-hours)	200,000

   a. $28.
   b. $36.
   c. $44.
   d. $16.

6. On the statement of cost of goods manufactured, what are the two most important figures?
   a. Cost to manufacture and cost of goods manufactured.
   b. Manufacturing overhead and direct labor.
   c. Work in process and cost of goods manufactured.
   d. Cost to manufacture and cost of goods sold.

7. Which of the following entries would be made to record factory payroll and various payroll withholding accounts?
   a. Credit Payroll Summary account; debit Payroll Withholding accounts and Payroll Payable account.
   b. Debit Payroll Summary account; credit Payroll Withholding accounts and Payroll Payable account.
   c. Debit Payroll Payable account; credit FICA Taxes Payable and Employees' Federal Income Taxes Payable accounts.
   d. Credit Manufacturing Overhead account; debit Payroll Summary account.

Now turn to page 694 to check your answers.

QUESTIONS

1. For what types of decisions do managers use managerial accounting information?

2. What are the major differences between managerial and financial accounting?

3. Identify the three elements of cost incurred in manufacturing a product, and indicate the distinguishing characteristics of each.

4. Why might a company claim that the total cost of employing a person is $10.30 per hour even though the employee's wage rate is $6.50 per hour? How should this difference be classified and why?

5. What is the typical accounting for the overtime wage premium paid to a direct laborer? Why?

6. Identify the two broad classifications of costs incurred by manufacturing companies and which types of items are included in each. Discuss the importance of classifying costs correctly.

7. Why are certain costs referred to as period costs? What are the major types of period costs incurred by a manufacturer?

8. Explain the differences between fixed costs and variable costs.

9. What are the main differences between activity-based costing and conventional costing methods?

10. Activity-based costing methods use three steps in computing the cost of a product or service. What are these steps?

11. Explain how the income statement of a manufacturing company differs from the income statement of a merchandising company.

12. What is the general content of a statement of cost of goods manufactured? What is its relationship to the income statement?

13. Under perpetual inventory procedure, what is the relationship between cost flows in the accounts and the flow of physical products through a factory?

14. Elimination of inventories through a JIT system is believed to result in a number of different types of cost savings. Itemize the types of savings that result from a JIT system.

15. What is the difference between accounting for costs under a JIT system and under a traditional costing system?

16. What operating conditions are necessary for a company to make use of a JIT system?

17. *Real-world question*   Refer to this chapter's "A Broader Perspective" on page 666. Why are traditional managerial accounting techniques out of date, according to Drucker?

The Coca-Cola Company

18. *Real-world question*   Refer to Appendix C at the end of this text. For The Coca-Cola Company, how much were its beginning and ending raw materials and

supplies, work-in-process, and finished goods inventories for 1991? (Hint: Recall that the 1990 ending inventory is the 1991 beginning inventory.)

The Coca-Cola Company

19. *Real-world question*   Refer to Appendix C at the end of this text. Why are The Coca-Cola Company's work in process inventories so low compared to its materials and finished goods inventories?

EXERCISES

Classify costs
(L.O. 2)

12–1. Given below are some costs incurred by a maker of video tapes. Classify these costs as direct materials, direct labor, manufacturing overhead, selling, or administrative.

 a. President's salary.
 b. Cost of labels.
 c. Cost of the plant's janitorial supplies.
 d. Wages of assembly-line workers.
 e. Cost of promotional displays.
 f. Plant supervisor's salary.
 g. Cost accountant's salary.
 h. Advertising.
 i. Cost of plastic used for cases.
 j. Cost of market research survey.

Identify prime
costs and
conversion costs
(L.O. 2)

12–2. Which of the costs listed in Exercise 12–1 would be considered prime costs? Which costs would be considered conversion costs?

Classify items as
product or period
costs
(L.O. 3)

12–3. Classify the costs listed in Exercise 12–1 as either product costs or period costs. Which of these costs would most likely vary directly with the number of video tapes produced?

Compute
manufacturing
overhead rate
(L.O. 4)

12–4. Compute the manufacturing overhead rate for the Boston Company based on machine-hours, given the following information:

Machine-hours	20,000
Manufacturing overhead costs.	$360,000

Calculate
estimated ending
inventory costs
(L.O. 4)

12–5. The following data pertain to the Rockies Company for its intermediate downhill ski called Superglas, for the year ended December 31, 1995 (each unit is one pair of skis):

Estimated direct materials cost per unit included in work in process inventory for Superglas.	$60
Estimated direct materials cost per unit included in finished goods inventory for Superglas.	$60
Estimated direct labor cost per unit included in work in process inventory for Superglas.	$30
Estimated direct labor cost per unit included in finished goods inventory for Superglas.	$50
Manufacturing overhead rate—60% of direct labor cost	
Units of Superglas included in ending work in process inventory . .	400 units
Units of Superglas included in ending finished goods inventory. . .	200 units

Rockies Company uses periodic inventory procedure. Compute the ending work in process inventory and ending finished goods inventory for Superglas.

Compute cost of goods manufactured (L.O. 5)

12–6. The following data pertain to Italis, Inc., a frozen pizza maker, for the year ended December 31, 1995:

Materials inventory, January 1, 1995	$110,000
Materials inventory, December 31, 1995.	130,000
Materials purchases (net)	340,000
Direct labor	455,000
Work in process inventory, January 1, 1995	65,000
Work in process inventory, December 31, 1995	97,500
Manufacturing overhead	260,000
Finished goods inventory, January 1, 1995	160,000
Finished goods inventory, December 31, 1995.	280,000

Compute the cost of goods manufactured and the cost of goods sold.

Prepare journal entries for labor costs (L.O. 5)

12–7. Assume Toni was paid $980 for 46 hours as a worker at Hewlett-Packard. This sum consisted of 40 hours regular time at $20 per hour and 6 hours overtime at time and a half.

a. Prepare the entry to distribute the labor costs to the accounts.

b. Prepare the entry to distribute the labor costs to the accounts assuming Toni is an accountant in administration at corporate headquarters.

c. Prepare the entry assuming Toni is a factory supervisor.

Prepare cost and revenue flowchart using perpetual procedure (L.O. 6)

12–8. Tia Company, a manufacturer of calculators, uses perpetual procedure for its inventories. The following data are for June:

1. Materials purchased on account, $175,000.
2. Direct materials issued, $225,000.
3. Repairs and maintenance on factory buildings, $30,000.
4. Factory depreciation, taxes, and utilities, $187,500.
5. Factory payroll for June, $140,000, including $13,000 of indirect labor. (Assume no withholdings.)
6. Manufacturing overhead is assigned in full to production.
7. Cost of goods completed and transferred, $618,750.
8. Cost of goods sold, $637,500.
9. Sales for June on account, $1,125,000.

The June 1 inventory balances were:

Materials.	$ 70,000
Work in process	150,000
Finished goods.	50,000

Prepare a cost and revenue flowchart similar to the one in Illustration 12.13, incorporating the above data.

Prepare journal entries under perpetual inventory procedure (L.O. 6)

12–9. Prepare journal entries to record the transactions in Exercise 12–8.

Prepare entries for JIT inventory accounting (L.O. 7)

12–10. Seattle Peripherals, Inc., manufactures hard discs for personal computer systems. The company uses a JIT system. An order for 600 hard discs was received. To fill this order, materials costing $8,000 were ordered. Manufacturing costs of $25,000 were incurred, of which $6,000 was for wages. All items are purchased on account.

After the production was finished, but before some of the goods were sold, the company needed to compute an inventory value for financial statement purposes. Finished goods inventory was $1,340.

Prepare journal entries for these transactions.

Prepare entries for JIT inventory accounting (L.O. 7)

12–11. Quantro Biotech, Inc., manufactures surgical tools. An order was received for 500 items. Materials costing $11,500 were ordered on account. Additional manufacturing costs were $45,000, of which $24,000 was accounts payable and the balance was wages payable. At the end of the accounting period, $2,700 of goods were still in finished goods inventory.

Prepare the journal entries to show the flow of costs under a JIT system.

PROBLEMS

Classify costs (L.O. 2)

12–1. Just as the cost results for Spikes, Inc., for November arrived on your desk, your boss called to ask what the manufacturing costs were for the month. Here are the data you just received:

Administrative costs	$ 95,000
Indirect materials.	20,000
Direct materials	195,000
Indirect labor	15,000
Direct labor	120,000
Selling costs.	50,000
Manufacturing overhead not already listed above	180,000

Required:

a. How much are the manufacturing costs for November? How much are the non-manufacturing costs?

b. How much are the prime costs for November? How much are the conversion costs?

Classify costs as period, product, fixed, and variable (L.O. 3)

12–2. Your company is installing a new computerized accounting system. The information systems team wants your advice about classifying the following costs:

a. Direct materials (recycled paper).

b. Sales commissions paid as a percent of sales.

c. General manager's salary.

d. Depreciation on administrative office equipment.

e. Indirect materials.

f. Sales manager's salary, which does not change as sales volume changes.

Required:

a. Which of these costs are product costs? Which are period costs?

b. Which of these costs are likely to be variable costs? Which are likely to be fixed costs?

Calculate manufacturing overhead rate and cost of ending inventories under periodic inventory procedure (L.O. 4)

12–3. El Naturel, Inc., makes two types of body lotions: Naturel and Nature's-Best. (Nature's-Best was developed from plants and contains no harsh chemicals.) The company uses periodic inventory procedure. El Naturel incurred the following manufacturing costs for the first quarter of 1995:

Direct materials used	$1,000,000
Direct labor	1,850,000
Manufacturing overhead	1,302,000

Manufacturing overhead is applied on the basis of machine-hours. During the first quarter, 186,000 machine-hours were expended. The work in process and finished goods inventories were $194,400 and $804,000, respectively, on January 1, 1995. The production department provided the following information relating to the cost of the work in process and finished goods inventories on March 31, 1995.

	Units in Inventory*	Estimated Cost per Unit — Direct Materials	Estimated Cost per Unit — Direct Labor	Machine-Hours per Unit for Applying Manufacturing Overhead
Work in process:				
Naturel	1,000	$13.00	$30.00	6
Nature's-Best	2,000	19.00	15.00	2
Finished goods:				
Naturel	4,000	28.00	45.00	9
Nature's-Best	5,220	26.00	36.00	5

* Each unit is one case of containers.

Required:

a. Compute the manufacturing overhead rate based on machine-hours.

b. Using the rate computed in *(a),* determine the cost of work in process and finished goods inventories as of March 31, 1995.

Prepare statement of cost of goods manufactured (L.O. 5)

12–4. The following account balances for 1995 are from a work sheet prepared by Jeremy Manufacturing Company at December 31, 1995:

Beginning inventories:	
Materials (beginning balance, January 1, 1995)	$ 12,250
Work in Process (beginning balance, January 1, 1995)	19,250
Materials Purchases (net)	120,000
Transportation-In	17,500
Direct Labor	87,500
Indirect Labor	35,000
Supervisors' Salaries Expense	20,000
Factory Utilities Expense	14,000
Factory Supplies Expense	10,500
Depreciation Expense—Factory Building	28,000
Depreciation Expense—Equipment	15,000
Other Manufacturing Overhead	52,500
Ending inventories:	
Materials	21,000
Work in Process	5,250

Required:

a. Using this information, prepare a statement of cost of goods manufactured for Jeremy Manufacturing Company for the year ended December 31, 1995.

b. Write a short report (approximately 50 words) to the plant manager summarizing the results of plant operations for the year. The plant manager is not an accountant and does not understand accounting concepts.

Prepare statement of cost of goods manufactured and income statement (L.O. 5)

12–5. The following account information is based on events at Casida Company for the year ended December 31, 1995:

Sales	$ 900,000
Materials Purchases	135,000
Transportation-In	1,500
Inventories:	
Materials—Beginning of year	18,000
End of year	15,000
Work in Process—Beginning of year	39,000
End of year	32,400
Finished Goods—Beginning of year	54,000
End of year	45,000
Direct Labor	158,000
Indirect Materials	4,800
Overtime Wages	9,600
Employer's Payroll Taxes—Factory	51,000
Factory Utilities Expense	6,000
Maintenance and Repairs Expense—Factory	1,800

Selling Expenses.	$100,000
Administrative Expenses	200,000
Factory Property Taxes Expense	1,320
Corporate Income Tax Expense.	20,000
Insurance Expense—Factory	1,800
Depreciation Expense—Factory Building	9,000
Depreciation Expense—Factory Equipment	12,000

Required:

a. Prepare a statement of cost of goods manufactured for Casida Company for the year ended December 31, 1995.

b. Prepare an income statement for Casida Company for the year ended December 31, 1995.

c. Management has established target ratios for gross margin and net income. The gross margin/sales target is 0.4 (40% of sales) and the net income/sales target is 0.15 (15% of sales). Did Casida achieve its goals?

Prepare statement of cost of goods manufactured and income statement (L.O. 5)

12–6. The following account balances were taken from the completed work sheet of Paisley Manufacturing Company at December 31, 1995:

Direct Labor	$190,000
Indirect Labor	26,250
Factory Supervision Expense	46,200
Selling and Administrative Salaries Expense	100,000
Factory Supplies Expense	6,300
Inventories, January 1, 1995:	
Materials.	8,400
Work in Process	21,000
Finished Goods	18,900
Inventories, December 31, 1995:	
Materials.	12,600
Work in Process	26,250
Finished Goods	23,100
Materials Purchases	120,000
Transportation-In.	6,300
Insurance Expense (70% applicable to factory).	10,500
Repairs and Maintenance Expense	1,575
Utilities Expense (70% applicable to factory)	3,150
Payroll Taxes (factory)	31,500
Depreciation Expense (80% applicable to factory)	42,000
Delivery Expense.	16,800
Sales	700,000
Other Selling and Administrative Expenses	21,000

Required:

a. Prepare a statement of cost of goods manufactured for the year ended December 31, 1995.

b. Prepare an income statement for the year ended December 31, 1995 (ignore income taxes).

Prepare cost and revenue flowchart for perpetual inventory procedure (L.O. 6)

12–7. Nabil Company uses perpetual inventory procedure. The following data are for June:

1. Materials purchased on account, $70,640.
2. Direct materials issued, $94,080. (No indirect materials were issued.)
3. Repairs and maintenance on factory buildings, $11,000.
4. Factory depreciation, taxes, and utilities, $69,888.
5. Factory payroll for June, $60,480, including $5,376 of indirect labor.
6. Actual manufacturing overhead is assigned to production.
7. Cost of goods completed and transferred, $262,080.
8. Cost of goods sold, $268,800.
9. Sales for June on account, $504,000.

The June 1 inventory balances were:

Materials.	$27,880
Work in process	68,200
Finished goods.	21,160

Required:

Using T-accounts, prepare a cost and revenue flowchart similar to the one shown in Illustration 12.13.

Prepare journal entries and ending inventory balances for perpetual inventory procedure (L.O. 6)

12–8. Tyler Company uses perpetual inventory procedure. Assume the inventories at August 1, 1995, were as follows:

Materials inventory.	$19,480
Work in process inventory	27,880
Finished goods inventory.	38,800

Transactions:

1. During August, $67,200 of raw materials were purchased on account and $55,600 were issued to production, none of which were indirect materials.
2. The factory payrolls (gross for August) were $79,800. Direct labor was $58,800, and indirect labor was $21,000. Payroll withholdings included FICA taxes, $5,040; income taxes, $15,120; and union dues, $1,260.
3. The indirect costs of production included machinery repairs, $1,260; equipment rental, $2,520; utilities, $8,400; payroll taxes, $5,040; amortization of prepaid insurance, $3,360; and factory building depreciation, $2,688. The first three expenditures were for cash.
4. Overhead was assigned in full to production.
5. Goods costing $117,600 were completed and transferred to finished goods inventory.
6. Goods costing $126,000 were sold on account for $180,000.

Required:

a. Give the journal entries for the preceding transactions.

b. Using T-accounts, compute the balance in each of the three inventory accounts at August 31, 1995.

Prepare journal
entries, income
statement, and
closing entries
under perpetual
inventory
procedure
(L.O. 6)

12–9. Ramone Manufacturing Company, which uses perpetual inventory procedure, had the following transactions for May 1995:

1. Materials and supplies purchased on account, $49,400.
2. Materials issued to production, $58,800; and indirect materials issued, $4,200.
3. Repairs and maintenance on factory equipment, $3,150.
4. Recorded factory depreciation, $21,000; property taxes, $8,400; and utilities, $14,280.
5. Administrative salaries paid, $26,200.
6. Depreciation on administration building, $10,500.
7. Factory payroll (gross), $37,800; withholding of FICA taxes, $2,310; and income taxes, $6,720.
8. Factory payroll distribution: direct labor, $34,440; and indirect labor, $3,360.
9. Paid advertising expense, $1,050; and delivery expense, $735.
10. Sales salaries and commissions paid, $10,450.
11. Actual manufacturing overhead cost was assigned to production.
12. Cost of goods completed and transferred, $163,800.
13. Sales on account, $325,000; and cost of goods sold, $178,000.
14. Other selling expenses, $588; other administrative expenses, $1,050; and interest expense, $84, were paid in cash.
15. Income taxes were accrued at 40% of pretax income.

Required:

a. Prepare journal entries to record the May transactions.

b. Prepare an income statement for Ramone Manufacturing Company for May 1995.

c. Prepare closing entries at May 31, 1995.

Compare JIT
accounting to a
traditional system
(L.O. 7)

12–10. Miami Precision Instruments produces ultrasound monitors. The company has a large backlog of orders and had no beginning inventories because all units in production last year were sold by the end of the year. At the start of this year, an order was received for 4,000 monitors.

The company purchased and used $200,000 of materials in production for this order. Direct labor costs of $650,000 and overhead costs of $1,040,000 were incurred. All costs were incurred on account. Ten percent of these costs were still in finished goods inventory at the end of the period.

Required:

a. Use T-accounts to show the flow of costs under a traditional costing system.

b. Use T-accounts to show the flow of costs using a JIT system.

Prepare work
sheet, all financial
statements, and
closing entries
(based on the
appendix)
(L.O. 8)

12–11. Jones Products, Inc., uses periodic inventory procedure and prepared the following trial balance and supplementary information as of December 31, 1995, the end of its first year of operations:

	Debits	Credits
Cash	$ 66,605	
Accounts Receivable	220,500	
Prepaid Factory Insurance	14,238	
Factory Supplies on Hand	22,374	
Office Supplies on Hand	9,645	
Factory Machinery	540,000	
Factory Equipment	100,200	
Office Equipment	36,700	
Accounts Payable		$ 52,545
Mortgage Notes Payable		120,000
Common Stock		700,000
Sales		966,705
Sales Returns and Allowances	4,500	
Sales Discounts	9,255	
Materials Purchases	183,450	
Direct Labor	252,740	
Factory Supervision Expense	48,750	
Indirect Labor	25,500	
Heat, Light, and Power Expense—Factory	50,346	
Machine Maintenance Expense	13,800	
Factory Rent Expense	30,000	
Factory Property Taxes Expense	4,800	
General Factory Expense	17,280	
Sales Office Salaries Expense	61,360	
Advertising Expense	12,600	
Sales Office Rent Expense	7,200	
Officers' Salaries Expense	60,391	
Office Salaries Expense	33,051	
Miscellaneous Office Expense	7,965	
Administrative Office Rent Expense	3,300	
Interest Expense	2,700	
	$1,839,250	$1,839,250

Supplementary information:

Inventories, December 31, 1995:	
Materials	$26,700
Work in process.	9,600
Finished goods	34,800

Information needed for adjustments:	
1. Estimated uncollectible accounts expense for the year:	
1% of net sales.	
2. Factory insurance expired.	$ 3,438
3. Factory supplies used.	19,599
4. Office supplies used	8,265

Depreciation rates per year:	
5. Factory machinery	10%
6. Factory equipment	15%
7. Office equipment	7%
8. Accrued factory payroll at December 31, 1995:	
Direct labor	$10,650
Factory supervision.	1,425
	$12,075

9. Accrued salaries at December 31, 1995:	
Sales office salaries.	$ 3,000
Officers' salaries	1,710
	$ 4,710

10. Accrued rent of office (administrative)	$ 300
11. Accrued interest on mortgage note	900

Required:

Using the information given, prepare the following for the year ended December 31, 1995:

a. Work sheet. (Do not use columns for the statement of retained earnings, and round all amounts to the nearest dollar.)
b. Statement of cost of goods manufactured.
c. Income statement (ignore income taxes).
d. Balance sheet.
e. Entries to set up the ending inventories and to close the accounts.

BUSINESS DECISION PROBLEM

Classify costs by behavior and type of production cost (L.O. 3)

12–1. Anderson Consultants provides information services and accounting advice to companies that are upgrading their computerized accounting systems. Several of the consultants decided to meet for lunch to discuss how to classify various costs incurred by their clients. These costs may be fixed or variable with respect to some measure of volume or output and may be classified as direct materials (DM), direct labor (DL), or manufacturing overhead (MO).

1. Energy costs to run machines in manufacturing.
2. Paint used in toy manufacturing.
3. Insurance on factory building and equipment.
4. A production department supervisor's salary.
5. Rent on factory machinery.
6. Iron ore in a steel mill.
7. Oil, gasoline, and grease for forklift trucks.
8. Services of painters in a building construction company.
9. Cutting tools used in machining operations.
10. Cost of food in a factory employees' cafeteria.
11. Payroll taxes and fringe benefits related to direct labor.
12. The plant electricians' salaries.
13. Sand used in glass manufacturing.
14. Copy editor's salary for a book publisher.

Required:

a. List the numbers 1 through 14 down the left side of a sheet of paper. After each number write the letters V (for variable) and F (for fixed) and either DM (for direct materials), DL (for direct labor), or MO (for manufacturing overhead) to show how you would classify the numbered cost items given above.

b. Which of your own answers given for *(a)* could you challenge? Discuss.

ANSWERS TO SELF-TEST

True-False

1. *False.* The sum of direct materials costs and direct labor costs is called prime cost.
2. *True.* Managerial accounting is for internal use by managers and gives more detailed information than financial accounting.
3. *True.* Direct materials can be traced directly to the product. Variable costs remain constant on a per unit basis but change in total in direct relation to the change in the level of activity.
4. *True.* The JIT production system does operate as described. When inventories exist and must be reported in the financial statements, the inventory amounts are "backed out" of the Cost of Goods Sold account.

Multiple-Choice

1. *b.* Indirect labor costs are part of manufacturing overhead.
2. *b.* Employees' benefits are normally part of manufacturing overhead.
3. *a.* Selling and nonfactory administrative costs are period costs.
4. *d.* Direct labor-hours, the number of different parts, and machine-hours could all be cost drivers.
5. *d.* $\dfrac{\$200,000}{12,500} = \dfrac{\text{Total manufacturing overhead cost}}{\text{Total machine-hours}} = \$16$
6. *a.* "Cost to manufacture" includes the costs of all resources put into production during the period. "Cost of goods manufac-

tured" consists of the cost of all goods completed during the period and includes "cost to manufacture," plus the beginning work in process inventory minus the ending work in process inventory.

7. *b.* Example:

Payroll Summary	75,000	
FICA Taxes Payable . . .		3,500
Employees' Income Taxes Payable.		8,000
Employees' Union Dues Payable.		500
Payroll Payable		63,000

To record factory payroll and various withholdings.

JOB ORDER COST SYSTEMS

LEARNING OBJECTIVES

After studying this chapter, you should be able to:

1. Compare and contrast different production methods and accounting systems.
2. Define job order costing and describe where job order cost systems are typically used.
3. Describe the documents used to accumulate product costs in a job order cost system.
4. Describe job order cost flows, beginning with the initial materials requisition and ending with the sale of the final product.
5. Show how a predetermined overhead rate is computed and how it is used to assign overhead to production.
6. Transfer any overapplied or underapplied overhead to Cost of Goods Sold.
7. Demonstrate job order cost flows with a comprehensive example.
8. Demonstrate job order cost flows in a service organization.

This chapter is the first of two chapters that present contrasting cost systems. Chapter 13 discusses the job order cost system, and Chapter 14 covers the process cost system. We assume companies use perpetual inventory procedure for both systems.

The goal of both cost systems is to **determine before year-end the unit costs of the products being manufactured.** These unit costs provide important data for management. Throughout the accounting period, unit costs are used to compute (1) cost of goods sold, (2) cost of work in process and finished goods ending inventories, (3) payments to be received under contracts based on "full" costs,[1] and (4) selling prices.

---

[1] A "full" cost contract basically guarantees the manufacturer total recovery of the costs incurred in producing the product (including overhead) and, usually, a specified profit margin.

The chapter begins with a discussion of cost accounting systems for different types of production. Then, the chapter covers accumulating costs and basic records used in a job order cost system. Accounting procedures, the use of predetermined overhead rates, and under- and overapplied overhead are discussed. In the final portion of the chapter, an example is given of the job order cost method. Also, activity-based costing and job costing in service organizations are discussed.

COST ACCOUNTING SYSTEMS FOR DIFFERENT TYPES OF PRODUCTION

Objective 1
Compare and contrast different production methods and accounting systems

Illustration 13.1 shows that different companies use different cost accounting systems, depending on the type of product. First, companies producing individual, dissimilar products known as "jobs" use job order costing. Second, some companies, such as furniture manufacturers, produce batches. They produce all of the components of a single product (e.g., coffee tables) in one batch. They would then produce the components of another product (e.g., dining room sets) in a new batch. (Some university food service companies prepare meals this way.) Companies such as these use job costing methods to accumulate the cost of each batch.

The next two production methods shown in Illustration 13.1 use process costing methods described in Chapter 14, so we give just a brief overview here. Repetitive manufacturing lends itself to the use of automated equipment that minimizes the amount of manual material handling. Automobile assembly plants, food processing plants, and computer terminal assembly plants are examples of repetitive manufacturing.

Finally, continuous flow processing is the opposite of job shops. These companies mass-produce a single, homogeneous product in a continuing process. Process systems are used in manufacturing chemicals, grinding flour, and refining oil.

Illustration 13.1
PRODUCTION ACTIVITIES

Type of Production	Cost Accounting System	Type of Product	Length of Production Run
Job shop Consulting firm, custom home builder	Job order costing	Customized	Short, possibly only one product per run
Batch production Furniture manufacturer	Mostly job order costing	Several different products	Relatively short
Repetitive manufacturing Computer terminals, automobiles	Mostly process costing	Standardized with some options	Relatively long
Continuous flow processing Oil refinery, chemicals	Process costing	Standardized	Long production run

ACCUMULATING COSTS USING A JOB ORDER COST SYSTEM

Objective 2
Define job order
costing and de-
scribe where job
order cost systems
are typically used

A **job order cost system (job costing)** is a manufacturing cost system that accumulates costs incurred to produce a product according to the individual jobs. Manufacturers generally use a job order cost system when they can separately identify products or when they produce goods to meet a customer's particular needs.

Who uses job order costing? Examples include homebuilders who specifically design houses for each customer and accumulate the costs separately for each job, and caterers who accumulate the costs of each banquet separately. Consulting, law, and public accounting firms use job order costing to measure the costs of serving each client. Motion pictures, printing, and other industries where many dissimilar products are produced use job order costing. Hospitals use job order costing to determine the cost of a patient's care.

Under job order costing, an up-to-date record of the costs incurred on each job is kept to provide management with timely cost data. Reports to management can be revised as often as desired, even daily, on such matters as materials used, labor costs incurred, manufacturing overhead assigned, goods completed, total production costs incurred, and budgeted and actual cost comparisons.

As the *key document* in the job cost system, the job order cost record maintains up-to-date information for each job. The **job order cost record,** which is typically a computer record, summarizes the costs of direct materials, direct labor, and manufacturing overhead incurred for a job.

Illustration 13.2
COST FLOWS IN A JOB ORDER COST SYSTEM

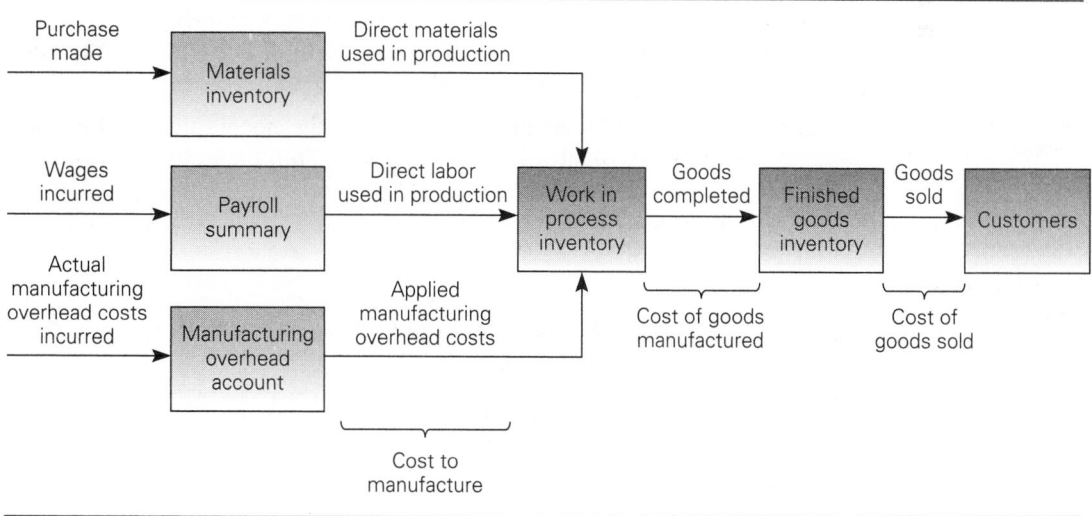

Illustration 13.2 presents an overview of cost flows in a job order cost system. You will note that the pattern of cost flows is the same as that discussed in Chapter 12. This chapter describes the methods in more detail than Chapter 12, but the "big picture" is the same.

BASIC RECORDS USED IN A JOB ORDER COST SYSTEM

*Objective 3
Describe the documents used to accumulate product costs in a job order cost system*

Job order cost systems are almost always computerized. Illustration 13.3 shows the following basic records or source documents used to record costs in a job order cost system:

1. A **stores (or materials) record** is kept for each type of direct and indirect material maintained in inventory. The stores record shows the quantities (and costs) of each type of material received, issued to a job, and left on hand for which the storekeeper is responsible. When a job is started, the production department enters orders for direct materials from the store-room on a **materials requisition.** This form shows the types and quantities of the materials ordered.
2. The **work (labor time) ticket** shows who worked on each job for how many hours and at what wage rate.
3. The **manufacturing overhead cost record** summarizes the various factory indirect costs incurred. One sheet is maintained for each production center.
4. The **job order cost record** summarizes all costs—direct materials, direct labor, and applied overhead—of producing a given job or batch of products. One record is maintained for each job. When goods are completed and transferred, the job order cost records are transferred to a completed jobs file. The number of units and their unit costs are recorded in files supporting the Finished Goods Inventory account.
5. A **finished goods record** is a running record of the number of units and costs of products completed, sold, and on hand.

*Objective 4
Describe job order cost flows, beginning with the initial materials requisition and ending with the sale of the final product*

The flow of manufacturing costs through the accounting system of a company is shown in Illustration 13.4. To gain a full understanding of a job order cost system, this illustration should be studied carefully and related to the documents shown in Illustration 13.3.

ACCOUNTING PROCEDURES FOR MATERIALS, LABOR, AND MANUFACTURING OVERHEAD

This section explains the specific procedures followed in accounting for materials, labor, and manufacturing overhead costs in a job order cost system.

Illustration 13.3
BASIC RECORDS IN A JOB ORDER COST SYSTEM

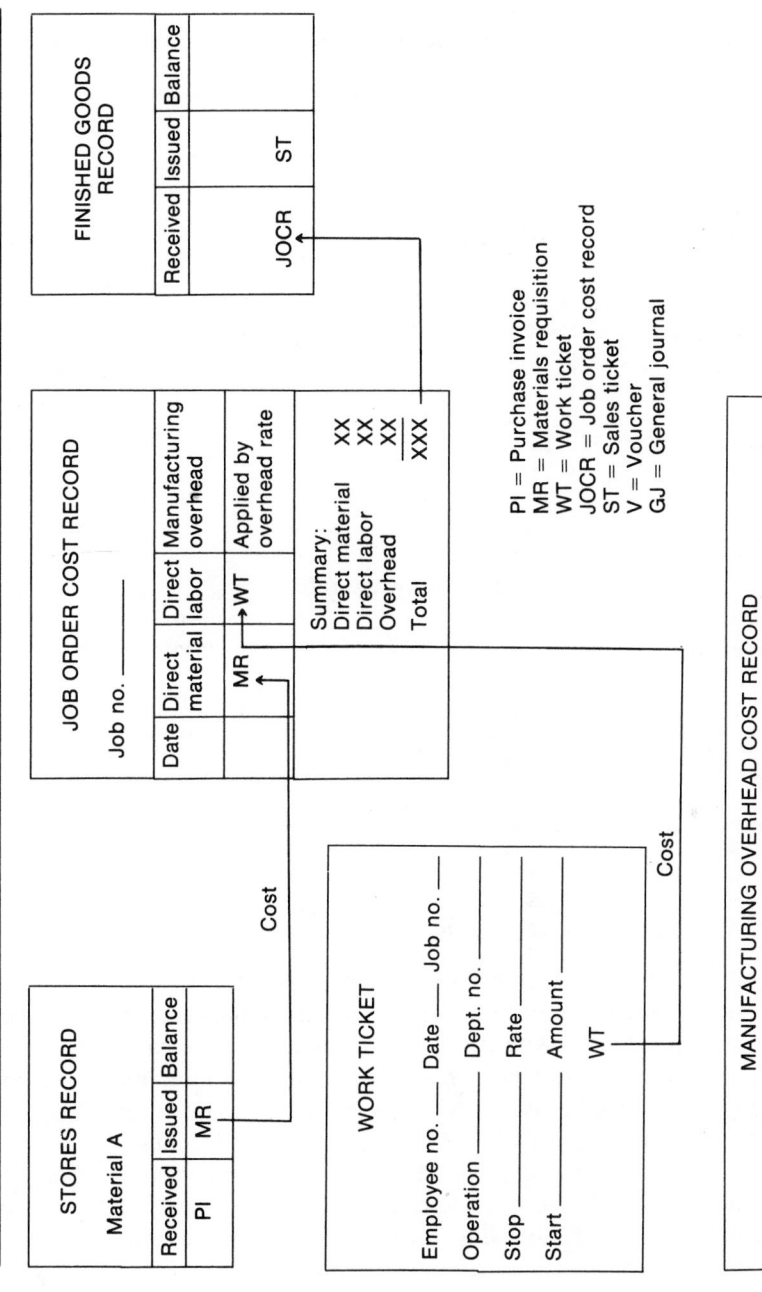

Illustration 13.4
COST FLOWS IN A JOB ORDER COST SYSTEM

Materials Inventory		Work in Process Inventory†		Finished Goods Inventory	
Beginning balance	Direct materials used	Beginning balance	Goods completed	Beginning balance	Goods sold
Purchases	Indirect materials used	Direct materials		Goods completed	
		Direct labor			
		Manufacturing overhead			

Payroll Summary		Cost of Goods Sold	
Factory labor	Direct labor	Goods sold	Closed to Income Summary
	Indirect labor		

Manufacturing Overhead	
Actual overhead incurred*	Applied to production

* Includes indirect materials, indirect labor, and other overhead.

† A separate Work in Process Inventory account may be used for each job, as illustrated later in the chapter.

Accounting for Materials

As companies receive materials from vendors, they place these materials in the materials storeroom. A **stores (or materials) record** is a perpetual inventory record showing the quantities and costs of each type of material received, issued to a job, and left on hand. Accountants keep a computer file for each type of direct and indirect material in inventory. These files are the subsidiary ledger for the Materials Inventory account.

When a production center needs materials in production, a supervisor fills out a *materials requisition* or types the request into the computer. A **materials requisition** (Illustration 13.5) is a written order directing the store's clerk to issue certain materials to a production center. The requisition shows the types, quantities, and costs of the materials ordered from the storeroom and identifies the job to which the cost of those materials is to be assigned.

Some jobs involve products that are frequently manufactured. In this case, companies typically use a *bill of materials* to requisition materials. The

A BROADER PERSPECTIVE

A HOLLYWOOD MYSTERY: JOB COSTING FOR MOVIES

Producers of movies and television shows have been criticized for their procedures in costing movies and television shows. In the entertainment industry, costs are inventoried by job; that is, by movie or television show.

Many shows are unsuccessful—"flops." Some studios have been criticized for assigning the costs of flops to successful shows to reduce the profits of the successful shows. The studios reduce the profits of the successful shows because they have profit-sharing agreements with actors, actresses, and other people associated with the successful show. By reducing the profits of the successful shows they reduce the amounts paid to these people.

From the studios' point of view, however, "flops" have to be paid for out of the revenues generated by successful shows, so they feel justified in thinking about shows in batches of products, some of which are profitable and some unprofitable.

Orion Pictures, maker of academy award winner "Dances with Wolves," was recently criticized for failing to write off the cost of unsuccessful shows. Instead, the company carried the cost of "flops" in inventory, thereby overstating assets and overstating profits. "While Orion recorded profits every year but 1986, it was also showing rising assets—a growing proportion of which were actually failed films that hadn't been written down." [Mayer, p. 8] By early 1991, the bubble had burst, and in view of its large negative cash flows, Orion faced a plummeting stock price, debt restructuring, and possible bankruptcy.

SOURCES: Authors' research and articles by Jane Mayer, "Hollywood Mystery: Woes at Orion Stayed Invisible for Years," *The Wall Street Journal,* October 16, 1991, pp. A1, A8; and Leslie Brenner "Pix Fix Bad Add?, *Harper's Magazine,* January 1991, p. 61.

---

bill of materials is a control document showing the type and quantity of each item of material going into a completed unit.

Each materials requisition and bill of materials is accumulated by job number. At the end of the day, the amount of direct materials issued for each job is entered into the job order cost record for that particular job. When a company classifies the materials issued as indirect materials, it accumulates these requisitions separately and charges the total amount to manufacturing overhead at the end of the day. Illustration 13.3 shows how the information from the materials requisition is used in the stores record, the job order cost record, and the manufacturing overhead cost record.

Accounting for Labor

A job order cost system requires that labor costs be accumulated and recorded for each job. As each employee works on a particular job assignment, that employee fills out a **work (labor time) ticket.** The work ticket is a form that companies use to record labor costs. The information on the work ticket includes employee number, job number, number of hours worked, and any other important information. At the end of the day, work tickets for each job

Illustration 13.5
MATERIALS REQUISITION

MATERIALS REQUISITION

Storekeeper: Issue Following to Bearer

Req. No.   R4
Date   6/4/95
Dept No.   1

Charge   Job No. 201   Dept.   Assembly

Item	Quantity	Stock No.	Cost	Amount
DG	8,000	16	$3.00	$24,000

Entered on
Job Order Cost Sheet

Signed:
KMS

Inventory Store Manager   *JPS*
Production Manager   *LFS*

---

are accumulated. The total direct labor costs for each job are then entered on the job order cost record. Illustration 13.3 shows a work ticket.

Companies also use work tickets to accumulate and record indirect labor costs. Employees who are assigned work not directly related to any job (such as general maintenance work) also record their time on a work ticket. Work not directly related to any job is indirect labor, which is accounted for as part of manufacturing overhead. At the end of the day, the indirect labor work tickets are accumulated. The total indirect labor cost is then recorded on the manufacturing overhead cost record.

Work tickets serve two purposes. First, they permit the daily accumulation and recording of direct and indirect labor costs for each job. Second, they provide control over the labor cost of each employee. Employees must fill out work tickets for each task they perform, so all the hours of each employee should be accounted for on one or more work tickets.

Accounting for Manufacturing Overhead

To exert some control over manufacturing overhead costs incurred, each production center or department must summarize its manufacturing overhead costs. A **manufacturing overhead cost record** summarizes the various manufacturing overhead costs incurred. The file of manufacturing overhead cost records serves as the subsidiary ledger for the Manufacturing Overhead account. An example of a manufacturing overhead cost record was shown in Illustration 13.3.

Predetermined Overhead Rates.   Most manufacturing and service operations compute unit costs at the time the production center completes the job. Accountants have already entered the direct materials and direct labor costs from the materials requisitions and work tickets to the job order cost record. Now they must assign to each job its share of the manufacturing overhead costs.

In Chapter 12, the manufacturing overhead rate was computed using actual overhead costs for the period. The formula to calculate an **actual overhead rate** is:

$$\text{Actual overhead rate} = \frac{\text{Total actual manufacturing overhead cost}}{\text{Total actual (manufacturing) activity}}$$

Recall that we measured manufacturing activity using machine-hours, direct labor-hours, or some other cost driver.

Although an actual rate is simple to compute, manufacturing companies do not commonly use it because often the information is available too late for decision making. Also, the results are misleading because overhead rates may fluctuate significantly from month to month. When these fluctuations occur, similar jobs completed in different months will have overhead costs and total costs that differ.

Most manufacturing companies prefer to use a *predetermined* overhead rate rather than waiting to accumulate all overhead costs during a period and developing an actual manufacturing overhead rate. To calculate a **predetermined overhead rate,** a company divides the *estimated* total manufacturing overhead costs for a period by an *expected* total level of activity.

$$\frac{\text{Predetermined}}{\text{overhead rate}} = \frac{\text{Estimated total manufacturing overhead costs}}{\text{Expected total activity}}$$

This activity could be total expected machine-hours, total expected direct labor-hours, total expected direct labor cost, or some other measure of activity for the period. Companies set predetermined overhead rates at the *beginning* of the year in which they will use them.

Overhead Cost Drivers.   A **cost driver** is a measure of activity, such as machine-hours or computer time, that causes manufacturing overhead costs. An appropriate cost driver should be used to calculate manufacturing overhead rates and to apply manufacturing overhead to work in process inventory.

Direct labor has traditionally been used as a cost driver. Over the years, however, direct labor has become less of a factor in the cost of some products in certain industries. One reason for this change is the automation of various activities in the production process. Companies are now using computers and robots for many tasks formerly performed by humans. This increased automation means that where direct labor is decreasing in importance, manufacturing overhead may be increasing due to the depreciation of automated equipment (computers, robots, etc.).

For largely automated operations, direct labor probably has little to do with the incurrence of manufacturing overhead. Thus, direct labor may not be an appropriate base for computing overhead rates. Instead, companies should use a base that acts as a cost driver in the incurrence of manufacturing overhead cost.

However, direct labor is not decreasing in importance in all industries. In some industries, direct labor is still a significant factor. Thus, every organization should determine if either direct labor cost or hours is still an appropriate base in calculating overhead rates. If not, a switch to machine-hours, computer time, or some other base may be desirable.

Reasons for Using Predetermined Rates. A manufacturing company uses a predetermined overhead rate for the following reasons:

1. A company usually does not incur overhead costs uniformly throughout the year. For example, heating costs are larger during winter. However, allocating less cost to a unit produced in the summer than to one produced in the winter serves no useful purpose. With a predetermined rate, companies can apply overhead based on machine-hours, direct labor cost, direct labor-hours, or some other measure of activity rather than actual overhead incurred in a particular month.
2. Some overhead costs, like factory building depreciation, are fixed costs. Thus, if the volume of goods produced varies from month to month, the company must use a predetermined rate to avoid sharp fluctuations in average unit cost.
3. Predetermined rates enable managers to know the total (approximate) production unit costs sooner. Using a predetermined rate, companies can assign overhead costs to production when they assign direct materials and direct labor costs. Without a predetermined rate, companies do not know unit costs until the end of the month or even later when bills arrive. For example, the electric bill for July will probably not arrive until August. If the company uses actual overhead, it cannot determine its July unit costs until August.

Objective 5
Show how a predetermined overhead rate is computed and how it is used to assign overhead to production

Computing Predetermined Overhead Rates. Companies compute predetermined overhead rates in the same basic manner as actual rates. However, these companies use *predicted* levels of activity and cost rather than *actual* levels. As part of the budgeting process, managers identify the expected level of manufacturing activity for the next year. These managers express this activity level as a specified base, such as machine-hours, direct labor-hours, direct labor costs, or some other cost driver. Next, managers estimate the year's overhead costs based on the expected level of activity.

This process of determining the expected level of activity and the estimated overhead costs and then calculating the predetermined overhead rate may be performed for the company as a whole (if the company desires a single, companywide overhead rate), or it may be performed separately for each production center (department) within the company. The following example illustrates the calculation of a predetermined overhead rate for a single production center. Assume that the expected level of activity in a certain production center is 60,000 machine-hours. Also assume that the estimated overhead costs at that level of activity are $540,000.

The predetermined overhead rate would be:

$$\frac{\text{Predetermined}}{\text{overhead rate}} = \frac{\text{Estimated total manufacturing overhead costs}}{\text{Expected total activity (such as machine-hours)}}$$

$$= \frac{\$540,000}{60,000 \text{ hours}} = \$9 \text{ per machine-hour}$$

The Work in Process Inventory account must contain amounts for direct materials, direct labor, and manufacturing overhead. The company will use the predetermined overhead rate to apply overhead to the Work in Process Inventory account. The account already contains actual amounts for direct materials and direct labor that were posted from the materials requisitions and the work tickets. In the above example, the company applies overhead to Work in Process Inventory at $9 for each **actual** machine-hour worked on a job. If the production center used 2,000 machine-hours, the journal entry to apply overhead is:

```
Work in Process Inventory . . . . . . . . . . . . . . . . .   18,000
      Manufacturing Overhead . . . . . . . . . . . . . . .              18,000
      To apply overhead to Work in Process Inventory using a
      predetermined overhead rate of $9 per machine-hour.
```

Note that the credit in the above entry is to the Manufacturing Overhead account. Actual manufacturing overhead is accumulated in the Manufacturing Overhead account on the debit side. When overhead is applied to Work in Process Inventory, the Manufacturing Overhead account is credited. The amounts used for estimated overhead costs and expected level of activity could be *exactly* the same as the actual amounts incurred for overhead and machine-hours. Then the Manufacturing Overhead account would have a zero balance at the end of the period.

Underapplied or Overapplied Overhead.   In practice, the amounts used in computing the predetermined overhead rate usually will not exactly equal the actual overhead costs or the machine-hours incurred. Therefore, the Manufacturing Overhead account normally has a debit or credit balance at the end of the period. **Underapplied (underabsorbed) overhead** (a debit balance) is the amount by which actual overhead costs incurred in a period exceed the overhead applied to production in that period. **Overapplied**

(overabsorbed) overhead (a credit balance) is the amount by which the overhead applied to production exceeds the actual overhead costs incurred in that same period. Remember that we apply overhead to Work in Process Inventory (production) by using the *predetermined* overhead rate times the *actual* level of activity (such as machine-hours) incurred during the period.

To illustrate the use of a predetermined overhead rate during a period, consider the following facts:

Estimated manufacturing overhead per year	$48,000
Expected level of activity for year	80,000 machine-hours
Predetermined overhead rate ($48,000 ÷ 80,000 hours). . .	$0.60 per machine-hour
Actual overhead costs incurred during year	$45,000
Actual machine-hours	70,000

The following journal entries are necessary to record the above information:

Manufacturing Overhead.	45,000	
Various accounts		45,000
To record actual manufacturing overhead costs incurred during period (machinery repairs, indirect material, etc.).		
Work in Process Inventory	42,000	
Manufacturing Overhead.		42,000
To apply manufacturing overhead to Work in Process Inventory at predetermined rate of $0.60 per machine-hour for 70,000 machine-hours used.		

In reality, accountants do not make these entries at a single point in time for the total amount. They record actual manufacturing overhead (the first entry above) continuously during the period as indirect materials are issued to production, as work tickets are accumulated for indirect labor, and as other circumstances require entries (machinery repair, utility bills, etc.). The second entry above records applied manufacturing overhead.

Based on these two entries, the Manufacturing Overhead account will appear as follows:

Manufacturing Overhead

Actual costs	45,000	Applied to production	42,000
Balance	3,000		

The $3,000 debit balance is the amount of *underapplied* overhead during the period.

Reasons for Underapplied or Overapplied Manufacturing Overhead. Two different factors are responsible for underapplied or overapplied overhead for the period. The first factor involves the difference between indirect manufacturing costs actually incurred and the amount management estimated for the period. The second factor involves the difference between the expected level of manufacturing activity used to set the predetermined overhead rate and the actual level of activity on which overhead is applied.

A difference between actual and estimated overhead costs can arise because unanticipated events cause overhead costs to be more or less than the budgeted amount. These unanticipated events could be high heating bills caused by a severe winter, excess repairs to factory machinery, or increases in prices of supplies. Events that cause actual overhead costs to exceed expected costs tend to result in underapplied overhead. Unanticipated cost savings, on the other hand, tend to cause overapplied overhead.

Unanticipated events can also cause the expected and actual levels of activity to differ. For example, a company could find itself without essential raw materials and have to cut back production. Alternatively, a company could produce a product that becomes a ''fad'' and have to increase production to meet demand.

Recall that every manufacturing company has some overhead costs that are fixed costs and do not change with the level of manufacturing activity. As a result, *total actual* overhead costs do not vary in direct proportion to the actual level of activity. However, *applied* overhead costs do vary in direct proportion to the actual level of activity. This result occurs because companies apply overhead to Work in Process Inventory at a constant amount per actual unit of activity (such as machine-hours). Therefore, if actual operations are at a higher level of activity than that used to set the predetermined overhead rate, the company will apply more overhead to Work in Process Inventory than originally anticipated. This higher level of activity will tend to cause overapplied overhead. Operating at a lower level than originally expected will tend to cause underapplied overhead.

Objective 6
Transfer any over-
applied or under-
applied overhead
to Cost of Goods
Sold

Disposition of Underapplied or Overapplied Manufacturing Overhead.   A company can carry forward an underapplied or overapplied manufacturing overhead balance in monthly or quarterly (interim) financial statements if it is possible that the remainder of the year's operations will reduce or offset the balance. If a significant balance in overhead remains at year-end, a company can allocate (or dispose of) it to Work in Process Inventory, Finished Goods, and Cost of Goods Sold. This allocation can be made by recomputing the cost of production for the year using actual overhead rates and adjusting the three account balances to their appropriate actual amounts. As an alternative, a company can charge off underapplied overhead as a loss of the period, particularly if the loss resulted from idle production capacity or unusual circumstances.

In practice, however, companies *usually transfer underapplied or overapplied overhead to Cost of Goods Sold*. This transfer results in little distortion of net income or assets if the amount transferred is small or if the company sells most of the goods produced during the year. Thus, if the $3,000 underapplied overhead in the previous example is a year-end balance, the company could dispose of it with the following journal entry:

```
Cost of Goods Sold . . . . . . . . . . . . . . . . . .    3,000
    Manufacturing Overhead. . . . . . . . . . . . . . .              3,000
  To dispose of underapplied overhead.
```

Average Cost per Unit.   Throughout the production process, companies record manufacturing costs on a job order cost record. When a job is finished, all costs are totaled. Then, the company computes the **average cost per unit** of the job with the following formula:

$$\frac{\text{Average cost}}{\text{per unit}} = \frac{\text{Total manufacturing cost of job}}{\substack{\text{Total number of finished units} \\ \text{(good units) in job}}}$$

This information is used for decision making and cost control, and to value the inventory on the balance sheet.

JOB ORDER COSTING—AN EXAMPLE

Some companies that use a job order cost system maintain only one Work in Process Inventory account for all jobs and rely on the job order cost record for details about a particular job. Other companies maintain a Work in Process Inventory control account in the general ledger and have a Work in Process Inventory account for each job in a subsidiary ledger. Still other companies maintain a separate Work in Process Inventory account in the general ledger for each job. In the illustrations that follow and in some of this chapter's exercises and problems, we will use a separate Work in Process Inventory account for each job.

*Objective 7
Demonstrate job
order cost flows
with a comprehen-
sive example*

To illustrate a job order costing system, the following example of Custom Manufacturing shows transactions for July and their journal entries.

On July 1, Custom Manufacturing had beginning inventories as follows:

```
Materials inventory. . . . . . . . . . . . . . . . . . . . . .    $20,000
Work in process inventory (Job No. 106: direct materials,
    $4,200; direct labor, $5,000; and overhead, $4,000). . . .     13,200
Finished goods inventory (Job No. 105) . . . . . . . . . .          5,500
```

Job No. 105 was completed, but had not been shipped to the customer as of June 30. Job No. 106 was in process at the beginning of July and was completed in July. Job No. 107 was started in July but not completed.

The transactions and the journal entries to record these transactions are given below. Illustration 13.6 shows the supporting records, and Illustration 13.7 shows the flow of costs through accounts.

1.   Purchased $25,000 of materials on account.

```
Materials Inventory . . . . . . . . . . . . . . . . . . . .    25,000
    Accounts Payable. . . . . . . . . . . . . . . . . . . .              25,000
  To record purchase of direct materials.
```

Illustration 13.6
SUPPORTING INVENTORY RECORDS AND JOB ORDER COST RECORDS

STORES RECORD

Material

Date	Received	Issued	Balance
July 1 bal.			$20,000
During July	$25,000		45,000
		$ 9,000	36,000
		14,000	22,000
		1,000	21,000

JOB ORDER COST RECORD   Job No. 106

Date	Direct Materials	Direct Labor	Manufacturing Overhead
July 1 bal.	$ 4,200	$5,000	$4,000
During July	9,000	4,000	3,200
	$13,200	$9,000	$7,200

Job completed. Total cost, $29,400.

JOB ORDER COST RECORD   Job No. 107

Date	Direct Materials	Direct Labor	Manufacturing Overhead
During July	$14,000	$16,000	$12,800

Job incomplete on July 31. Total cost, $42,800.

FINISHED GOODS RECORD

Job No. 105

Date	Received	Issued	Balance
July 1 bal.			$5,500
During July		$5,500	—0—

FINISHED GOODS RECORD

Job No. 106

Date	Received	Issued	Balance
During July	$29,400		$29,400

Illustration 13.7
JOB ORDER COST FLOWS—CUSTOM MANUFACTURING

Work in Process Inventory—Job No. 106			
Beginning inventory:			
Materials	4,200		
Labor	5,000		
Overhead	4,000		
Total	13,200		
Current period:		Completed	29,400
Materials	9,000		
Labor	4,000		
Overhead	3,200		
Total	16,200		
Ending inventory	–0–		

Finished Goods Inventory			
July 1 balance	5,500	Sold	5,500
Completed	29,400		
July 31 balance	29,400		

Work in Process Inventory—Job No. 107	
Beginning inventory –0–	
Current period:	
Materials	14,000
Labor	16,000
Overhead	12,800
Total	42,800
Ending inventory:	
Materials	14,000
Labor	16,000
Overhead	12,800
Total	42,800

Manufacturing Overhead			
Materials used	1,000	Applied to production	16,000
Labor cost incurred	5,000		
Indirect manufacturing costs incurred	15,000		
Underapplied balance	5,000		

2. Issued direct materials: $9,000 to Job No. 106, and $14,000 to Job No. 107. Indirect materials issued to all jobs, $1,000. Each job has a separate Work in Process Inventory account corresponding to each job's job order cost record.

Work in Process Inventory—Job No. 106	9,000	
Work in Process Inventory—Job No. 107	14,000	
Manufacturing Overhead	1,000	
Materials Inventory		24,000

To record direct and indirect materials issued.

3. Factory payroll for the month, $25,000; FICA and income taxes withheld, $4,000.

Payroll Summary	25,000	
Various liability accounts for taxes withheld		4,000
Wages Payable		21,000

To record factory payroll for July.

4. Factory payroll paid, $21,000.

Wages Payable	21,000	
Cash		21,000

To record cash paid to factory employees in July.

5. Payroll costs assigned: direct labor, $20,000 (Job No. 106, $4,000; Job No. 107, $16,000); and indirect labor, $5,000.

Work in Process Inventory—Job No. 106	4,000	
Work in Process Inventory—Job No. 107	16,000	
Manufacturing Overhead	5,000	
Payroll Summary		25,000

To distribute factory labor costs incurred.

6. Other indirect manufacturing costs incurred:

Payroll taxes accrued	$ 3,000
Repairs (on account)	1,000
Property taxes accrued	4,000
Heat, light, and power (on account)	2,000
Depreciation	5,000
	$15,000

Manufacturing Overhead	15,000	
Accounts Payable		3,000
Payroll Taxes Payable		3,000
Property Taxes Payable		4,000
Accumulated Depreciation		5,000

To record overhead costs incurred.

7. Manufacturing overhead applied to production. Assume a predetermined rate of $8 per machine-hour, with 400 machine-hours on Job No. 106 and 1,600 machine-hours on Job No. 107.

Job No. 106 ($8 × 400)	$ 3,200
Job No. 107 ($8 × 1,600)	12,800
	$16,000

Work in Process Inventory—Job No. 106	3,200	
Work in Process Inventory—Job No. 107	12,800	
Manufacturing Overhead		16,000
To record application of overhead to production.		

8. Job No. 106 was completed. It cost $29,400 for the total work done on the job, including costs in beginning Work in Process Inventory on July 1.

Finished Goods Inventory	29,400	
Work in Process Inventory—Job No. 106		29,400
To record completed production for July.		

9. Job No. 105 was sold on account in July for $9,000.

Accounts Receivable	9,000	
Sales.		9,000
To record sales on account for July.		

Cost of Goods Sold	5,500	
Finished Goods Inventory		5,500
To record cost of goods sold in July.		

After the above entries have been posted, the Work in Process Inventory and Finished Goods Inventory accounts appear (in T-account form) in Illustration 13.7.

10. At the end of the month, the Manufacturing Overhead account will show underapplied overhead of $5,000 as shown in Illustration 13.7.

The journal entry to dispose of underapplied overhead to Cost of Goods Sold will read:

Cost of Goods Sold	5,000	
Manufacturing Overhead		5,000
To dispose of underapplied overhead.		

On July 31, the Work in Process Inventory account has a balance of $42,800, which agrees with the total costs charged thus far to Job No. 107, as shown in Illustration 13.7. The balance consists of direct materials, $14,000; direct labor, $16,000; and manufacturing overhead, $12,800. Finished Goods Inventory has a balance on July 31 of $29,400, supported by the finished goods inventory record for Job No. 106 in Illustration 13.6.

Companies often make entries like those above from cost summaries at the end of the month. However, if management wants to be informed more frequently as to costs incurred, accountants can record the details of the various costs more often, even daily.

ACTIVITY-BASED COSTING

This chapter assumes that a company used a single predetermined overhead rate. Some companies, however, use multiple predetermined rates. This practice is called *activity-based costing,* which was introduced in Chapter 12.

Companies use activity-based costing because they engage in multiple activities that cause overhead costs. These companies have a different activity base for each activity because some jobs or departments are more labor intensive, machine intensive, and so on, than others. As a product moves through production, overhead is applied in each department according to the department's predetermined rate for that activity. The total of all these overhead applications represents the total overhead cost of the job.

JOB COSTING IN SERVICE ORGANIZATIONS

*Objective 8
Demonstrate job
order cost flows in
a service organiza-
tion*

Service organizations, such as engineering firms, consulting firms, law firms, and public accounting firms, also use job order costing. The costing procedure is basically the same in both service and manufacturing organizations, except that many service firms use no direct materials.

To illustrate job order costing in a service organization, we describe cost flows in a consulting firm. You will note many parallels to the manufacturing example previously described.

The firm started in July with the following inventory balances:

Work in process inventory (Job No. 116: direct labor, $10,000; and overhead, $12,000)	$22,000
Finished goods inventory (Job No. 115)	15,000

Job No. 115 was billed to the customer during July. Job No. 116, which was in process at the beginning of July, was completed in July. Job No. 117 was started but not completed by the end of July.

The transactions and the journal entries to record these transactions are given below.

1. Payroll for the month, $25,000; FICA and income taxes withheld, $4,000.

Payroll Summary	25,000	
Various liability accounts for taxes withheld		4,000
Wages Payable		21,000
To record workers' payroll for July.		

2. Payroll paid, $21,000.

Wages Payable	21,000	
Cash		21,000
To record cash paid to employees in July.		

3. Payroll costs assigned: direct labor, $20,000 (Job No. 116, $4,000 and Job No. 117, $16,000); and indirect labor, such as secretarial support, $5,000.

Work in Process Inventory—Job No. 116	4,000	
Work in Process Inventory—Job. No. 117	16,000	
Overhead	5,000	
Payroll Summary		25,000
To distribute labor costs incurred.		

4. Other overhead costs incurred:

Payroll taxes accrued	$ 3,000
Travel, meals, and lodging for consultants (cash)	6,000
Supplies (on account)	2,000
Copy services (on account)	1,500
Mailing and express services (cash)	1,500
Depreciation on computers and office equipment	5,000
Other (on account)	4,000
	$23,000

Overhead	23,000	
Accounts Payable		7,500
Payroll Taxes Payable		3,000
Cash		7,500
Accumulated Depreciation		5,000
To record overhead costs incurred.		

5. Overhead applied to production: Assume a predetermined rate of $30 per consultant labor-hour, with 200 labor-hours on Job No. 116 and 700 labor-hours on Job No. 117.

Job No. 116 ($30 × 200)	$ 6,000
Job No. 117 ($30 × 700)	21,000
	$27,000

Work in Process Inventory—Job No. 116	6,000	
Work in Process Inventory—Job No. 117	21,000	
Overhead		27,000
To record application of overhead to production.		

6. Job No. 116 completed.

Finished Goods Inventory	32,000	
Work in Process Inventory—Job No. 116		32,000
To record completed production for July that has not yet been billed to the customer.		

ETHICS   A CLOSER LOOK

Jennifer Jones, an accountant for a consulting firm, has just received the monthly cost reports for three jobs she supervises: one for Microsoot, Inc., one for Antel, and one for OBM. After reading the figures for Microsoot, she immediately called her boss.

"We're going to be way over budget on the Microsoot account," she informed her boss. "The job is only 75% complete, but we've spent all the money we budgeted for the entire job."

"What! Why didn't you tell me sooner?" asked Jennifer's boss angrily.

"I just received the report," Jennifer explained. "This problem didn't show up until this month. Last month we were on target with the budget."

"You had better watch these job costs more carefully in the future." advised Jennifer's boss. "Meanwhile, charge the rest of the costs needed to complete Microsoot's job to your other two accounts, Antel and OBM. Those accounts are so big they won't notice the extra costs. Besides, we get reimbursed for costs on the OBM job, so we won't lose any money on this problem you have with the Microsoot account." Jennifer's boss then hung up the phone.

Required:
a.   What should Jennifer do?
b.   Does it matter that Jennifer's company is reimbursed for costs on the OBM account?

---

7.   Sales on account for the month: Job No. 115, cost $15,000; revenue, $25,000.

Accounts Receivable	25,000	
Sales.		25,000
To record sales on account for July.		
Cost of Goods Sold.	15,000	
Finished Goods Inventory		15,000
To record cost of goods sold in July.		

In this case, we assume the company invoiced the customer for the jobs when completed. Some service companies invoice as the job is being done. If so, the entries are the same as above, but the cost flows are for parts of jobs instead of completed jobs.

After the above entries have been posted, the Work in Process Inventory and Finished Goods Inventory accounts appear (in T-account form) in Illustration 13.8.

On July 31, the Work in Process Inventory account has a balance of $37,000, which agrees with the total costs charged thus far to Job No. 117, as shown in Illustration 13.8. The balance consists of direct labor, $16,000; and overhead, $21,000. Finished Goods Inventory has a balance on July 31 of $32,000 for Job No. 116, which is completed, but the customer has not yet been invoiced for it.

Illustration 13.8
FLOW OF COSTS IN A SERVICE ORGANIZATION

Work in Process Inventory—Job No. 116			
Beginning balance:			
Direct labor	10,000		
Overhead			
applied	12,000		
Total	22,000		
Current period:		Completed	32,000
Direct labor	4,000		
Overhead			
applied	6,000		
Total	10,000		
Ending inventory	–0–		

Finished Goods Inventory			
July 1 balance	15,000	Sold	15,000
Completed	32,000		
July 31 balance	32,000		

Work in Process Inventory—Job No. 117		
Beginning balance –0–		
Current period:		
Direct labor	16,000	
Overhead		
applied	21,000	
Total	37,000	
Ending balance:		
Direct labor	16,000	
Overhead		
applied	21,000	
Total	37,000	

Overhead			
Indirect labor	5,000	Applied to	
Other overhead		production	27,000
costs	23,000		
Underapplied			
balance	1,000		

8. The journal entry to dispose of underapplied overhead to Cost of Goods Sold is:

```
Cost of Goods Sold . . . . . . . . . . . . . . . . . . . 1,000
     Overhead . . . . . . . . . . . . . . . . . . . . .        1,000
   To dispose of underapplied overhead.
```

As shown in this example, the flow of costs in service organizations such as law firms, accounting firms, and consulting firms is similar to the flow of costs in manufacturing companies.

As mentioned at the beginning of this chapter, two cost accumulation systems exist. Job order costing, one of these systems, was the focus of this chapter. We discuss process costing, the other major costing system, in Chapter 14.

UNDERSTANDING THE LEARNING OBJECTIVES

1. Compare and contrast different production methods and accounting systems.
   - Job shops use job order costing.
   - Batch production uses methods like job order costing, where a batch of products is like a job.
   - Repetitive manufacturing uses methods similar to process costing.
   - Continuous flow processing uses process costing.
2. Define job order costing and describe where job order cost systems are typically used.
   - A job order cost system is a manufacturing cost system that accumulates costs incurred to produce a product according to individual jobs.
   - Like process costing, job order costing has the goal of determining before year-end the unit costs of the products being manufactured.
   - A job order cost system is generally used when manufacturers can separately identify products or when they produce goods to meet a customer's particular needs.
   - Job order costing is commonly used in construction, motion pictures, printing, and other industries producing many heterogeneous (dissimilar) products.
3. Describe the documents used to accumulate product costs in a job order cost system.
   - *Stores (or materials) record.* A stores (or materials) record is kept for each type of direct and indirect material maintained in inventory. This record shows the quantities (and costs) of each type of material received, issued, and on hand for which the storekeeper is responsible.
   - *Work (labor time) ticket.* The work ticket shows who worked on each job for how many hours and at what wage rate. Employees must account for all of their daily hours on one or more work tickets.

- *Manufacturing overhead cost record.*   The manufacturing overhead cost record summarizes the various factory indirect costs incurred. One record is maintained for each production center.
- *Job order cost record.*   The job order cost record summarizes all costs—direct materials, direct labor, and applied manufacturing overhead—of producing a given job or batch of products. One record is maintained for each job.
- *Finished goods record.*   A finished goods record is a running record of the number of units and costs of products completed, sold, and on hand. A record is maintained for each type of job.

4. Describe job order cost flows, beginning with the initial materials requisition and ending with the sale of the final product.
- *Materials.*   Purchases of materials are debited to Materials Inventory. As the direct materials are used, Materials Inventory is credited, and Work in Process Inventory is debited. Indirect materials used are credited to Materials Inventory and debited to Manufacturing Overhead as part of the actual overhead incurred.
- *Labor.*   Direct labor is debited to Work in Process Inventory as the labor is applied in the production of goods and is credited to Payroll Summary. Indirect labor is also credited to Payroll Summary but is debited to Manufacturing Overhead as part of the actual overhead incurred.
- *Manufacturing overhead.*   Manufacturing overhead is estimated by the use of predetermined overhead rates and is debited to Work in Process Inventory and credited to Manufacturing Overhead as the overhead applied to production.
- *Goods completed.*   Completed goods are credited to Work in Process Inventory and debited to Finished Goods Inventory.

5. Show how a predetermined overhead rate is computed and how it is used to assign overhead to production.
- The formula for the predetermined rate is:

$$\text{Predetermined overhead rate} = \frac{\text{Estimated total manufacturing overhead costs}}{\text{Expected level of activity (such as machine-hours)}}$$

- Management is responsible for identifying the expected level of manufacturing activity for the next year and the estimated overhead costs for the next year.
- The entry to record predetermined overhead is to debit Work in Process Inventory and credit Manufacturing Overhead.
- *Underapplied or overapplied overhead:* The actual overhead (the debit to Manufacturing Overhead) is compared to the applied overhead (the credit to Manufacturing Overhead). The amount by which the actual overhead incurred exceeds the applied overhead is called

underapplied overhead. The amount by which applied overhead exceeds actual overhead is called *overapplied overhead.*

6. Transfer any overapplied or underapplied overhead to Cost of Goods Sold.
   - Any overapplied manufacturing overhead is disposed of by crediting Cost of Goods Sold and debiting Manufacturing Overhead. Any underapplied manufacturing overhead is disposed of by debiting Cost of Goods Sold and crediting Manufacturing Overhead.
7. Demonstrate job order cost flows with a comprehensive example.
   - Costs of jobs are assigned to a Work in Process Inventory account for each job that corresponds to the job order cost record for that job.
   - When complete, jobs are assigned to Finished Goods Inventory corresponding to the finished goods record.
8. Demonstrate job order cost flows in a service organization.
   - The flow of costs in service organizations that produce jobs, such as law firms, public accounting firms, and consulting firms, is similar to the flow of costs in manufacturing companies.
   - In contrast to manufacturers, many service firms have little or no materials costs.

DEMONSTRATION PROBLEM 13-A

Mobile Construction Company uses perpetual inventory procedure and a job order cost system to account for the mobile homes it builds. Each home is a separate job. As of January 1, 1995, its records showed:

Inventories:	
Materials and supplies.	$ 48,000
Work in process (Job Nos. 212 and 213)	103,200
Finished goods (Job No. 211)	120,000

The work in process inventory consisted of two jobs:

Job No.	Direct Materials	Direct Labor	Construction Overhead*	Total
212	$18,000	$24,000	$12,000	$ 54,000
213	20,400	19,200	9,600	49,200
	$38,400	$43,200	$21,600	$103,200

* Construction overhead is treated just like manufacturing overhead in the text examples.

Cost and sales data for 1995 are summarized below:

1. Materials purchased on account, $200,000.
2. Construction payrolls accrued, $408,000; FICA taxes withheld, $20,400; and income taxes withheld, $36,000.

3. Construction overhead costs incurred, other than indirect materials and indirect labor: depreciation, $12,000; heat, light, power, and miscellaneous, $12,000.
4. Direct materials requisitioned: Job No. 212, $31,000; Job No. 213, $58,000; Job No. 214, $96,000; and indirect materials requisitioned, $5,000.
5. Payrolls distributed: direct labor—Job No. 212, $48,000; Job No. 213, $96,000; Job No. 214, $144,000; construction supervision, $48,000; and other indirect labor, $72,000.
6. Overhead is assigned to work in process at 50% of direct labor cost.
7. Job Nos. 212 and 213 were completed.
8. Job Nos. 211 and 212 were sold for $540,000.

Required:

Prepare general journal entries to record the data above, as well as all closing entries for which you have sufficient information.

Solution to demonstration problem 13–A

MOBILE CONSTRUCTION COMPANY
General Journal

(1)	Materials Inventory.	200,000	
	Accounts Payable		200,000
	To record materials purchased on account.		
(2)	Payroll Summary.	408,000	
	FICA Taxes Payable		20,400
	Employees' Income Taxes Payable		36,000
	Wages Payable.		351,600
	To record accrued factory payrolls.		
(3)	Construction Overhead.	24,000	
	Accumulated Depreciation		12,000
	Various accounts (Accounts Payable, Accrued Liabilities Payable, Cash, etc.)		12,000
	To record various construction overhead costs incurred.		
(4)	Work in Process Inventory—Job No. 212.	31,000	
	Work in Process Inventory—Job No. 213.	58,000	
	Work in Process Inventory—Job No. 214.	96,000	
	Construction Overhead.	5,000	
	Materials Inventory.		190,000
	To record requisitions of materials.		

(5)	Work in Process Inventory—Job No. 212.	48,000	
	Work in Process Inventory—Job No. 213.	96,000	
	Work in Process Inventory—Job No. 214.	144,000	
	Construction Overhead.	120,000	
	Payroll Summary.		408,000

To distribute labor costs:

Direct labor to Work in Process Inventory and
  Construction Overhead:

Construction supervisor	$ 48,000
Other indirect labor	72,000
	$120,000

(6)	Work in Process Inventory—Job No. 212.	24,000	
	Work in Process Inventory—Job No. 213.	48,000	
	Work in Process Inventory—Job No. 214.	72,000	
	Construction Overhead.		144,000

Overhead assigned: Job No. 212, $24,000 (= 50% ×
$48,000); Job No. 213, $48,000 (= 50% × $96,000);
and Job No. 214, $72,000 (= 50% × $144,000).

(7)	Finished Goods Inventory.	408,200	
	Work in Process Inventory—Job No. 212.		157,000
	Work in Process Inventory—Job No. 213.		251,200

Completed and transferred Jobs 212 and 213. The following amounts were
computed by adding beginning Work in Process balances to the current month's
debits to Work in Process for direct materials, direct labor, and construction
overhead:

Job No. 212 . . . . $157,000 (= $54,000 + $31,000 + $48,000 + $24,000)
Job No. 213 . . . . 251,200 (= $49,200 + $58,000 + $96,000 + $48,000)
                          $408,200

(8)	Accounts Receivable.	540,000	
	Sales		540,000

To record sales on account.

	Cost of Goods Sold	277,000	
	Finished Goods Inventory.		277,000

To record cost of goods sold ($277,000 = $120,000
+ $157,000).

(9)	Cost of Goods Sold	5,000	
	Construction Overhead.		5,000

To close underapplied construction overhead
(actual = $149,000, applied = $144,000).

(10)	Sales	540,000	
	Income Summary		540,000

To close Sales account.

	Income Summary	282,000	
	Cost of Goods Sold		282,000

To close Cost of Goods Sold account ($282,000 =
$277,000 + $5,000).

DEMONSTRATION PROBLEM 13–B

Different companies may use different bases in computing their predetermined overhead rates. From the following estimated data, compute the predetermined rate to be used by each company.

	Company		
	A	B	C
Machine-hours.	103,000	212,000	125,000
Direct labor-hours	52,000	48,000	39,000
Direct labor cost.	$650,000	$735,000	$420,000
Manufacturing overhead	$845,000	$864,000	$750,000

Basis for determining predetermined overhead rate:

Company	Basis
A	Machine-hours
B	Direct labor cost
C	Direct labor-hours

Solution to demonstration problem 13–B

Company A:

$$\frac{\text{Predetermined}}{\text{overhead rate}} = \frac{\$845,000}{103,000} = \$8.20 \text{ per machine-hour}$$

Company B:

$$\frac{\text{Predetermined}}{\text{overhead rate}} = \frac{\$864,000}{\$735,000} = 118\% \text{ of direct labor cost}$$

Company C:

$$\frac{\text{Predetermined}}{\text{overhead rate}} = \frac{\$750,000}{39,000} = \$19.23 \text{ per direct labor-hour}$$

NEW TERMS

Actual overhead rate Total actual manufacturing overhead divided by total actual manufacturing activity. *705*

Average cost per unit Total manufacturing cost of a job divided by the total number of finished units (good units) in the job. *710*

Bill of materials A control document that shows the type and quantity of each item of material going into a completed unit. *703*

Cost driver A measure of activity, such as machine-hours or computer time, that is a causal factor in the incurrence of manufacturing overhead costs in an organization. *705*

Finished goods record   A running record of the number of units and costs of products completed, sold, and on hand. *700*

Job order cost record   A form used to summarize the costs of direct materials, direct labor, and manufacturing overhead incurred for a job. *699, 700*

Job order cost system (job costing)   A manufacturing cost system that accumulates costs incurred to produce a product according to individual jobs, such as a building, a consulting job, or a batch of 100 computer desks. *699*

Manufacturing overhead cost record   A record that summarizes the various manufacturing overhead costs incurred. *700, 704*

Materials requisition   A written order directing the store's clerk to issue certain materials to a production center; it shows the types, quantities, and costs of materials ordered. *700, 702*

Overapplied (overabsorbed) overhead   The amount by which the overhead applied to production exceeds the actual overhead costs incurred in that same period. *707*

Predetermined overhead rate   Calculated by dividing estimated total manufacturing overhead costs for a period by the expected total level of activity, such as total expected machine-hours or total expected direct labor-hours for the period. *705*

Stores (or materials) record   A perpetual inventory record that shows the quantities (and costs) of each type of material received, issued to a job, and left on hand for which the storekeeper is responsible. *700, 702*

Underapplied (underabsorbed) overhead   The amount by which actual overhead costs incurred in a period exceed the overhead applied to production in that period. *707*

Work (labor time) ticket   A form used to record labor costs. The information on the work ticket includes employee number, job number, number of hours worked, and any other important information; may be prepared for both direct and indirect labor. *700, 703*

SELF-TEST

True-False

Indicate whether each of the following statements is true or false.

1. A winery is an example of a company that would use a job order cost system.

2. Indirect labor costs appear on a work (labor time) ticket.

3. A predetermined overhead rate is calculated by dividing estimated total overhead costs by expected level of activity.

4. To compute the average cost per unit in a job, the following formula is used:

$$\text{Average cost per unit} = \frac{\text{Total manufacturing cost of job}}{\text{Total number of finished units (good units) in job}}$$

5. Overhead cannot be entered in the Work in Process Inventory account when using a predetermined overhead rate. Only when the actual overhead costs are determined is the overhead entered.

Multiple-Choice

Select the best answer for each of the following questions.

1. The goal of a job order cost system is to determine before year-end the unit cost of products (jobs) being manufactured. These product costs are used to compute which of the following:
   a. Predetermined overhead rate.
   b. Payments to be received under contracts based on costs.
   c. Selling price per unit.
   d. (a) and (b).

2. A job order cost system is not used:
   a. When a company produces many dissimilar products.
   b. By manufacturers and service companies.
   c. When goods are produced to meet a customer's particular needs.
   d. By an automobile manufacturer.

3. What is the key document in a job order cost system?
   a. Work ticket.
   b. Manufacturing overhead cost record.
   c. Finished goods record.
   d. Job order cost record.

4. You are given the following data:

Estimated manufacturing overhead per year. .	$24,000
Expected level of activity per year. . .	40,000 machine-hours
Predetermined overhead rate. . . .	$0.60 per machine-hour
Actual overhead costs incurred during year	$22,500
Actual machine-hours .	35,000

Which of the following are the correct journal entries for the above data when a predetermined overhead rate is used?

   a. Manufacturing
      Overhead   22,500
          Various accounts .   22,500

      Work in Process
      Inventory   21,000
          Manufacturing
          Overhead   21,000

   b. Manufacturing
      Overhead   22,500
          Various accounts .   22,500

      Work in Process
      Inventory   24,000
          Manufacturing
          Overhead   24,000

   c. Manufacturing
      Overhead   24,000
          Various accounts .   24,000

      Work in Process
      Inventory   22,500
          Manufacturing
          Overhead   22,500

   d. Various accounts . . .   22,500
          Manufacturing
          Overhead   22,500

      Manufacturing
      Overhead   21,000
          Work in Process
          Inventory   21,000

5. The expected level of activity in a certain production center is 30,000 machine-hours. Estimated overhead costs are: indirect materials and indirect labor = $500,000; other overhead = $100,000.

   Which of the following is the predetermined overhead rate per machine-hour?
   a. $13.
   b. $12.
   c. $15.
   d. $20.

6. Which of the following describe(s) the advantages of using a predetermined overhead rate:
   a. Overhead costs are applied evenly throughout the year rather than fluctuating from month to month.
   b. Actual levels rather than predicted levels of activity and cost are used to determine the rate.
   c. Total unit costs of production are known sooner than when using actual overhead rates.
   d. (a) and (c) above.

Now turn to page 734 to check your answers.

QUESTIONS

1. What are the two major types of cost accumulation systems under perpetual inventory procedure? What is the common goal of these systems?

2. Describe a job order cost system and give an example of a situation in which it can be used.

3. Briefly describe the basic records (source documents) used in a job order cost system.

4. Describe the information documented on the job order cost record and explain how it is used.

5. Explain the limitations of direct labor as a cost driver.

6. What are three major reasons for using predetermined manufacturing overhead rates?

7. What is the formula for computing a predetermined overhead rate? If the expected level of activity in a production center is 50,000 machine-hours and the estimated overhead costs are $750,000, what is the predetermined overhead rate? Show the calculation.

8. Explain why total actual overhead costs *do not* vary in direct proportion to the actual level of activity, and explain why applied overhead *does* vary in direct proportion to the level of activity.

9. What are underapplied and overapplied overhead? What type of balance does each have in the Manufacturing Overhead account?

10. Explain why the Manufacturing Overhead account could have an underapplied or overapplied balance remaining at the end of the period.

11. What are the three alternative methods of disposing of overapplied or underapplied manufacturing overhead? Which alternative is normally used as a practical matter?

12. Direct materials were issued to the following jobs: material A was issued to Job No. 101, $2,000, Job No. 102, $1,000, and Job No. 103, $5,000; material B was issued to Job No. 101, $5,000, Job No. 102, $2,000, and Job No. 103, $3,000. Indirect materials were issued to all jobs, $3,000.
   Record the direct and indirect materials in journal entry form.

13. *Real-world question*   Refer to "A Broader Perspective" on page 703. What did movie producers do with costs to reduce the profits of successful shows?

14. *Real-world question*   Besides the law firms, consulting firms, and public accounting firms listed in the text, name three service organizations that perform services that could be accounted for as jobs.

EXERCISES

Identify basic
source documents
(L.O. 3)

13–1. Indicate the source document that would most likely contain the following information:
   1. The receipt of materials to a job.
   2. The amount of direct labor cost incurred on a particular job.
   3. The amount of payroll taxes incurred for the previous month.

4. The power (electricity) used for the previous month.

5. The manufacturing overhead applied to a particular job.

Compute job costs; prepare journal entries related to production activities (L.O. 4)

13–2. In June, Honey Company worked only on Job No. 714, completing it on June 30. There were no prior costs accumulated on Job No. 714. During the month, the company purchased and used $5,500 of direct materials, used 1,920 machine-hours, and incurred $9,600 of direct labor costs. Assuming manufacturing overhead is applied at the rate of $5 per machine-hour, what is the total cost of Job No. 714? Prepare journal entries to assign the materials, labor, and manufacturing overhead costs to production and to record the transfer of Job No. 714 to finished goods inventory.

Compute cost of a job and give journal entry to record its completion (L.O. 4)

13–3. Job No. 301 has, at the end of the second week in March, an accumulated total cost of $19,000. In the third week, $5,000 of direct materials were used on the job, 300 hours of direct labor were charged to the job at $22.50 per hour, and manufacturing overhead was applied on the basis of $11.50 per machine-hour for fixed overhead and $9 per machine-hour for variable overhead. Job No. 301 was the only job completed in the third week. Job No. 301 used 160 machine-hours. Compute the cost of Job No. 301, and give the journal entry required to record its completion.

Compute overhead rates (L.O. 5)

13–4. Different companies may use different bases in computing their predetermined overhead rates. From the following estimated data, compute the predetermined rate to be used by each company.

	Company		
	Albert	Charles	Edward
Machine-hours	200,000	420,000	250,000
Direct labor-hours	100,000	96,000	78,000
Direct labor cost.	$1,600,000	$1,470,000	$820,000
Manufacturing overhead	$ 800,000	$ 864,000	$750,000

Basis for determining predetermined overhead rate:

Company	Basis
Albert	Machine-hours
Charles	Direct labor cost
Edward	Direct labor-hours

Prepare journal entry to dispose of overhead (L.O. 6)

13–5. Refer to the data in Exercise 13–4. Assume the actual hours and cost data were:

	Albert	Charles	Edward
Actual:			
Manufacturing overhead	$ 900,000	$ 800,000	$750,000
Direct labor cost.	$1,700,000	$1,400,000	$800,000
Direct labor-hours	90,000	92,000	76,000
Machine-hours	210,000	400,000	260,000

a. Compute overapplied or underapplied overhead.

b. Prepare journal entries to transfer overapplied or underapplied overhead to Cost of Goods Sold.

Compute job cost per unit; prepare journal entries to record transfer and sale (L.O. 7)

13–6. *a.* As of October 1, Job No. 410 had already accumulated $19,000 in total costs. During October, Job No. 410 required $25,200 of direct materials and $50,400 of direct labor. Manufacturing overhead is applied to production at the rate of 75% of direct labor costs. Actual manufacturing overhead was $46,000, all on account. Give the journal entries necessary to record the transfer of Job No. 410 to finished goods inventory and its sale at 150% of manufacturing cost. Then dispose of the balance in Manufacturing Overhead in the usual manner.

b. Alternatively, assume that overhead is applied at $6 per machine-hour, with Job No. 410 using 6,700 machine-hours. Give the journal entries necessary to record the transfer of Job No. 410 to finished goods inventory and its sale at 150% of cost. Then dispose of the balance in Manufacturing Overhead in the usual manner.

Demonstrate job order cost flows in a comprehensive example (L.O. 7)

13–7. Brooke House Manufacturing Company uses a job order cost system to account for its jobs, which are do-it-yourself dollhouse kits. As of January 1, 1995, its records showed:

Inventories:	
Materials and supplies	$60,000
Work in process (Job Nos. 22 and 23)	92,000
Finished goods (Job No. 21)	80,000

The work in process inventory consisted of two jobs:

Job No.	Direct Materials	Direct Labor	Manufacturing Overhead	Total
22	$18,000	$20,000	$11,000	$49,000
23	20,000	14,000	9,000	43,000
	$38,000	$34,000	$20,000	$92,000

Cost and sales data for 1995 are summarized below:

1. Materials purchased on account, $300,000.

2. Manufacturing payrolls accrued, $210,000; FICA taxes withheld, $20,000; and income taxes withheld, $36,000.

3. Manufacturing overhead costs incurred, other than indirect materials and indirect labor: depreciation, $50,000; heat, light, power, miscellaneous, $30,000 (all on account).

4. Direct materials requisitioned: Job No. 22, $30,000; Job No. 23, $60,000; Job No. 24, $90,000; and indirect materials requisitioned, $5,000.

5. Payrolls distributed: direct labor—Job No. 22, $50,000; Job No. 23, $100,000; Job No. 24, $40,000; indirect labor, $20,000.

6. Overhead is assigned to work in process at $50 per machine-hour. Job No.

22 used 500 machine-hours, Job No. 23 used 1,000 machine-hours, and Job No. 24 used 300 machine-hours in January.

7. Job Nos. 22 and 23 were completed.

8. Jobs 21 and 22 were sold for $650,000, total.

Required:

Prepare general journal entries to record the above and dispose of underapplied or overapplied manufacturing overhead. A separate Work in Process Inventory account is used for each job.

Demonstrate job cost flows in a service organization (L.O. 8)

13–8. New Venture Consultants uses a job order cost system. The following data pertain to the month of December:

1. No jobs were in beginning Work in Process Inventory or Finished Goods Inventory.

2. Three jobs were started: Nos. 222, 223, and 224. Job No. 222 was completed, and the customer was billed for $6,000 (on account). Job No. 223 was completed and remains in Finished Goods Inventory awaiting billing to the client at the end of the month. Job No. 224 was still in process at month-end.

3. Direct labor costs incurred for:
   Job No. 222 . . . . 100 hours @ $21/hour
   Job No. 223 . . . . 150 hours @ $18/hour
   Job No. 224 . . . . 60 hours @ $17/hour

4. Assume overhead is applied at the rate of $11 per direct labor-hour.

5. Actual overhead was $3,500.

Required:

Prepare journal entries to record the above data and dispose of underapplied or overapplied manufacturing overhead. A separate Work in Process Inventory account is used for each job.

PROBLEMS

Compute predetermined overhead rate and job costs (L.O. 4, 5)

13–1. a. Carlson Company has established the following estimates for 1995:

	Assembly	Packaging
Manufacturing overhead	$ 500,000	$ 800,000
Direct labor cost.	$1,080,000	$1,320,000
Direct labor-hours	75,000	110,000
Machine-hours	37,500	100,000

Carlson Company uses predetermined rates to apply manufacturing overhead. These rates are based on machine-hours in assembly and on direct labor cost in packaging.

b. During June, the job cost sheet for Job No. 410 showed the following:

	Assembly	Packaging
Direct materials used	$14,400	$14,400
Direct labor cost	$10,800	$ 4,500
Direct labor-hours	750	375
Machine-hours	375	250

Required:

a. Compute the predetermined manufacturing overhead rate for each department.

b. Using the predetermined overhead rate for each department computed in *(a)*, compute the total manufacturing overhead cost for Job No. 410.

Compute predetermined overhead rate and overhead cost of one job (L.O. 5)

13–2. Kent Company uses a job order cost system, applying manufacturing overhead at predetermined rates based on direct labor-hours in Department Y and machine-hours in Department Z. Budgeted estimates for 1995 are:

	Department Y	Department Z
Manufacturing overhead	$108,000	$144,000
Direct labor cost	$ 90,000	$ 99,000
Direct labor-hours	18,000	24,000
Machine-hours	12,000	36,000

Detailed cost records show the following for Job No. 105, which was completed in 1995:

	Department Y	Department Z
Direct materials cost	$6,000	$250
Direct labor cost	$5,000	$300
Direct labor-hours	100	60
Machine-hours	30	40

Required:

a. Compute the predetermined overhead rates for 1995 for Departments Y and Z.

b. Compute the amount of manufacturing overhead applied to Job No. 105 in each department.

c. Compute the cost of Job No. 105.

Compute predetermined overhead rate and under- or overapplied overhead (L.O. 5, 6)

13–3. Langley Truck Lines transports office equipment for various office equipment manufacturers. Langley applied overhead to jobs using a predetermined overhead rate based on truck miles. Budgeted data for 1995 are:

Budgeted truck miles	10 million
Budgeted overhead for hauling operations (equivalent to manufacturing overhead)	$12 million

Required:

a. Compute the predetermined overhead rate.

b. Assume that in 1995, actual manufacturing overhead for hauling operations amounted to $16 million, and 17 million truck miles were driven. Compute the amount of underapplied or overapplied manufacturing overhead for 1995.

c. Prepare the journal entry to transfer underapplied or overapplied overhead to Cost of Goods Sold.

Comprehensive example (L.O. 7)

13–4. Sprawling Landscaping Company uses a job order cost system. As of January 1, its records showed the following inventory account balances:

Materials (shrubs, trees, etc.)	$27,000
Work in Process	51,600
Finished Goods.	60,000

The Work in Process Inventory consisted of two jobs:

Job No.	Direct Materials	Direct Labor	Manufacturing Overhead	Total
212 (10 Downing St.)	$ 9,000	$12,000	$ 4,800	$25,800
213 (1010 Wilshire Blvd.)	10,200	9,600	6,000	25,800
	$19,200	$21,600	$10,800	$51,600

Summarized below are production and sales data for the company for January:

1. Materials purchased, $97,000.
2. Landscaping payroll costs incurred, $200,000.
3. Overhead costs incurred (other than indirect labor and indirect materials): depreciation, $6,000; and miscellaneous, $6,000 (all on account).
4. Materials requisitioned: direct materials for Job No. 212, $15,000, for Job No. 213, $28,800, and for Job No. 214, $48,800; supplies (indirect materials) requisitioned, $2,400.
5. Landscaping payroll distributed: direct labor to Job No. 212, $20,000, to Job No. 213, $48,000, and to Job No. 214, $72,000; indirect labor, $60,000.
6. Overhead is assigned to work in process at $6 per labor-hour, with 8,000 labor-hours to Job No. 212 and 2,000 labor-hours each to Job Nos. 213 and 214.
7. Job Nos. 212 and 213 were completed and transferred to Finished Goods Inventory.
8. Sales revenues for January were $100,000; cost of goods sold, $80,000, all for jobs completed before January 1.

Required:

a. Prepare journal entries to record the above transactions. The company uses only one Work in Process Inventory account.

b. Prepare all closing entries for which you have information.

c. Set up T-accounts for Materials Inventory, Payroll Summary, Manufacturing Overhead, Work in Process Inventory, Finished Goods Inventory, and Cost of Goods Sold. Show the flow of costs through those accounts.

d. Show that the total cost charged to incomplete jobs agrees with the balance in the Work in Process Inventory account.

Comprehensive example in a service organization (L.O. 8)

13-5. The Good Life Catering uses a job order cost system with a separate Work in Process Inventory account for each job. Its activities in November 1995, its first month of operations, are summarized below:

	Job		
	Second Rate University	*Leisure Life Home*	*Lincoln Grade School*
Direct materials cost (food)	$54,000	$36,000	$81,000
Direct labor cost	$45,000	$40,500	$54,000
Labor-hours	2,900	3,500	3,800

Overhead is applied at a rate of $17.50 per labor-hour. All jobs were completed in November. The Lincoln Grade School job was not billed and remains in Finished Goods Inventory on November 30.

Required:

a. Compute the amount of overhead charged to each job.

b. Compute the total cost of each job.

c. Prepare journal entries to record the costs and to record the transfer of completed jobs to Finished Goods Inventory and to Cost of Goods Sold.

BUSINESS DECISION PROBLEM

Determine how overhead should be applied; give advantages of predetermined rate; justify use of applied overhead (L.O. 5)

Green Manufacturing Company produces one product, grass seed. The demand for the grass seed is highly seasonal, and because of this fact, Green adjusts its production schedule so that it is in line with demand (the seeds are susceptible to spoilage). The president of Green, Lisa Bass, has received complaints from the sales department that it is having difficulty in setting a stable price for the grass seed. The sales department is under orders from Mrs. Bass to set prices on the basis of "cost plus 30% of cost." The sales department complains that the cost figures it receives from the production manager vary widely from quarter to quarter, and that variation in turn causes the selling price to fluctuate.

In an attempt to settle the dispute, Mrs. Bass calls the production manager, Robert Reed, into her office for a conference. Mr. Reed reports that he has no choice but to change the cost every quarter, as to do otherwise would mean that a loss would result during periods of low demand. He tells Mrs. Bass that he has the numbers to back up this statement and reminds Mrs. Bass that "figures don't lie." As proof, he offers the following information:

	First Quarter	Second Quarter	Third Quarter	Fourth Quarter
Direct materials.	$108,900	$ 43,560	$ 21,780	$ 87,120
Direct labor	135,000	54,000	27,000	108,000
Variable manufacturing overhead	26,100	10,440	5,220	20,880
Fixed manufacturing overhead	180,000	180,000	180,000	180,000
Total.	$450,000	$288,000	$234,000	$396,000
Number of pounds to be produced . . .	90,000	36,000	18,000	72,000
Cost per pound.	$5.00	$8.00	$13.00	$5.50

Mrs. Bass realizes that the root of the problem is manufacturing overhead. Manufacturing overhead costs cannot be reduced enough to make a difference during the periods of low demand. She asks Mr. Reed to find a better way to allocate the manufacturing overhead costs to each pound of grass seed produced in order to arrive at a more uniform cost figure per pound.

Required:

a. How would you recommend to Mr. Reed that manufacturing overhead costs be assigned to production? How would this approach differ from his present method?
b. What benefits would be gained by using your recommended solution?
c. To justify your recommendation made in (a) above, recalculate the per pound cost of the grass seed using your recommendation. (Round calculation of fixed overhead to the nearest $100.)

ANSWERS TO SELF-TEST

True-False

1. *False.*   A job order cost system is used primarily by industries where many dissimilar products are produced. A winery produces a product, wine, for which each unit is essentially the same as each other unit.

2. *True.*   Besides using work tickets for direct labor costs, companies also use work tickets to accumulate and record indirect labor costs. At the end of the day, the work tickets are accumulated, and the total indirect labor cost is recorded on the manufacturing overhead cost record.

3. *True.*   Estimated total overhead cost is divided by expected level of activity.

4. *True.*   This formula is valid for calculating the average cost per unit.

5. *False.*   Using a predetermined overhead rate, overhead can be applied during the period to the Work in Process Inventory account as work on a job progresses.

Multiple-Choice

1. *b.*   Unit costs are not used to compute the predetermined overhead rate. Although costs are one factor used in setting selling prices, they are usually not used to *compute* selling prices. They are used to compute cost of goods sold and payments to be received under contracts based on costs.

2. *d.*   Job order costing is not used by an automobile manufacturer.

3. *d.* The job order cost record is the key document in a job order cost system.
4. *a.* The first set of entries is correct (35,000 hours × $0.60 = $21,000).
5. *d.* Total manufacturing overhead = $600,000 (= $500,000 + $100,000)

$$\frac{\$600,000}{30,000 \text{ hours}} = \begin{array}{c} \$20 \text{ per hour predetermined} \\ \text{overhead rate} \end{array}$$

6. *d.* Both *(a)* and *(c)* are advantages of using a predetermined rate.

PROCESS COST SYSTEMS

LEARNING OBJECTIVES

After studying this chapter, you should be able to:

1. Describe the types of operations for which a process cost system is used.
2. Distinguish between process and job order cost systems.
3. Discuss the concept of equivalent units in a process cost system.
4. Compute equivalent units of production and unit costs under the average cost procedure.
5. Prepare a production cost report for a process cost system and discuss its relationship to the Work in Process Inventory account.
6. Compute equivalent units of production and unit costs under the first-in, first-out (FIFO) system (Appendix 14–A).
7. Discuss how common costs are allocated to joint products (Appendix 14–B).

This chapter continues the discussion of the two major types of cost accumulation systems under perpetual inventory procedure. (Recall that Illustration 13.1 in Chapter 13 summarizes alternative production methods and cost systems.) In Chapter 13, we explained and illustrated job order costing. We also stated that the **job order cost system (job costing)** is a manufacturing cost system that accumulates costs incurred to produce a product according to individual jobs. Manufacturers generally use job order costing when they can separately identify their products or when they produce goods to meet a customer's particular needs.

The subject of this chapter is process costing. The chapter begins with a discussion of the nature of a process cost system. In this discussion, we review the similarities and differences between job order costing and process costing. This review is followed by an extended illustration of process costing, which includes a discussion of equivalent units of production and the production cost report. In the chapter appendixes, we discuss and illustrate FIFO process costing and the allocation of joint product costs.

NATURE OF A PROCESS COST SYSTEM

*Objective 1
Describe the types of operations for which a process cost system is used*

Many businesses manufacture large quantities of a single product or similar products on a continuous basis over long periods (e.g., Pepsi-Cola making soft drinks, Georgia-Pacific making lumber, or Kellogg making breakfast cereals). For these kinds of products, manufacturers do not have separate job orders. Instead, production is an ongoing process.

A **process cost system (process costing)** is a manufacturing cost system that accumulates costs incurred to produce a product according to the processes or departments a product goes through on its way to completion. Companies making paint, gasoline, steel, rubber, plastic, and similar products use process costing. In these types of operations, accountants must accumulate costs for *each process* that a product undergoes. The processes or departments, known as **processing centers,** serve as cost centers. After accumulating costs for the entire period (usually a month), accountants divide the costs by the number of units produced (tons, pounds, gallons, or feet). This calculation gives the average unit cost.

*Objective 2
Distinguish between process and job order cost systems*

The two cost accumulation systems—job order costing and process costing—are similar in some ways. They also differ, however, in other ways. Similarities between job order costing and process costing are:

1. Both job order and process cost systems have the same *goal*: to determine the unit cost of products.
2. Both job order and process cost systems have the same *cost flows*. Accountants first record production in separate accounts for materials inventory, labor, and overhead. Then, they transfer the costs to one or more Work in Process Inventory account(s).
3. Both job order and process cost systems make use of *predetermined overhead rates* (defined in Chapter 13) to apply manufacturing overhead.
4. Both job order and process cost systems have the same *source documents* to record direct and indirect materials (materials requisitions) and direct and indirect labor (work tickets).
5. Both job order and process cost systems record actual *overhead as it is incurred*.
6. Both job order and process cost systems measure *over- or underapplied overhead at the end of a specified time period*.

Job order costing and process costing also have their differences. The differences between these two systems are:

1. *Types of products produced.* Companies that use job order costing work on many different jobs with different production requirements

Illustration 14.1
COST FLOWS IN A PROCESS COST SYSTEM

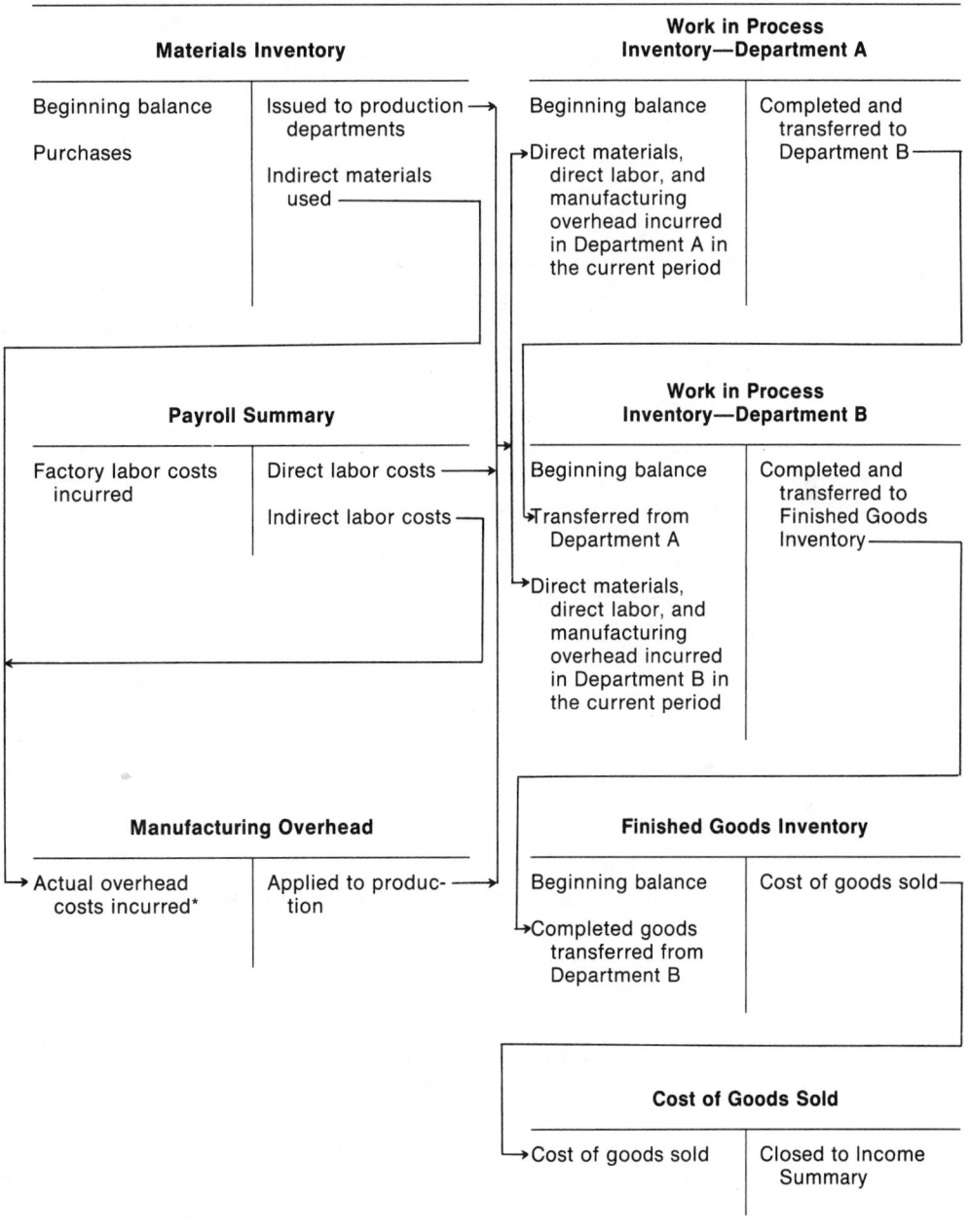

* Includes indirect materials, indirect labor, and other manufacturing-related overhead.

Illustration 14.2
POSSIBLE PRODUCTION FLOW COMBINATIONS

A. One product is processed sequentially, yielding one final product.

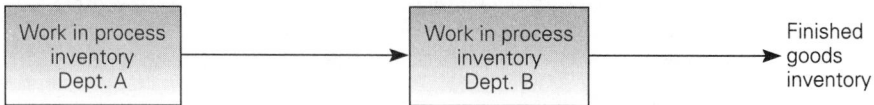

B. Two products are combined and then processed further to yield one final product.

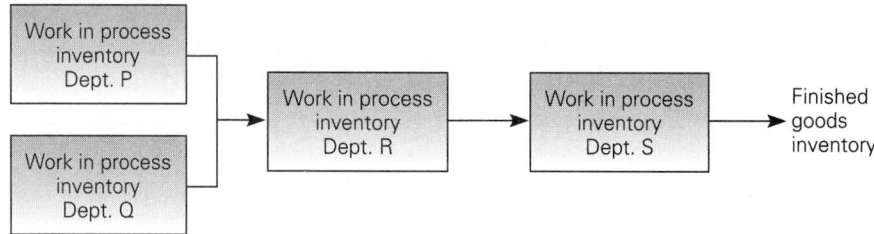

C. One product is further processed in two different ways, yielding two different final products.

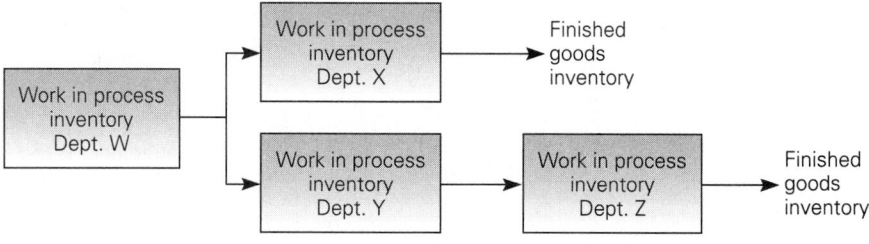

during each period. Companies that use process costing produce a single product, either on a continuous basis or for long periods. All the products that the company produces under process costing are the same.

2. *Cost accumulation procedures employed.* Job order costing accumulates costs by individual jobs. Process costing accumulates costs by process or department.

3. *Key documents used.* The job order cost record is the key document in job order costing. The departmental production cost report is the key document in process costing.

4. *Work in Process Inventory accounts.* Job order cost systems have one Work in Process Inventory account per job (or could have one for all jobs). Process cost systems have a Work in Process Inventory account for each department or process.

Illustration 14.1 shows the cost flows of a process cost system that processes the products in a specified sequential order. That is, the production and processing of products begin in Department A. From Department A, products go to Department B. Department B inputs direct materials and further processes the products. Then, Department B transfers the products to Finished Goods Inventory. For illustration purposes, we will assume that all the process cost systems in this chapter are sequential. You should be aware, however, that many production flow combinations exist. Illustration 14.2 presents three possible production flow combinations.

PROCESS COSTING ILLUSTRATED

Assume that Ajax Company sells a chemical product used for cleaning that the company processes in two departments. Department A crushes, powders, and blends the basic materials. Department B packages the product and transfers it to finished goods. Illustration 14.3 shows this manufacturing process.

The June production and cost data for Ajax Company are:

	Department A	Department B
Beginning inventory	–0–	–0–
Units started, completed, and transferred	11,000	9,000
Units on hand at June 30, partially completed	–0–	2,000
Direct materials	$16,500	$1,100
Direct labor	$ 5,500	$5,880
Actual manufacturing overhead	$ 4,500	$5,600
Applied manufacturing overhead	$ 4,400	$5,880

Ajax's accountant applies manufacturing overhead in Department A on the basis of a predetermined rate of 80% of direct labor cost. The accountant applies manufacturing overhead in Department B at a predetermined rate of 100% of direct labor cost.

From these data, we can construct and summarize the Work in Process Inventory—Department A account as follows:

Work in Process Inventory—Department A

Direct materials	16,500	Transferred to	
Direct labor	5,500	Department B—	
Applied overhead (80%		11,000 units @ $2.40	26,400
of direct labor cost)	4,400		
Total	26,400		

Department A completed all the units it started in June and transferred them to Department B. All the costs assigned to these units were also transferred to Department B. Ajax's accountant computed the unit costs in Department A by dividing the $26,400 total costs by the 11,000 units completed and transferred. The result is $2.40, the average unit cost of the 11,000 units.

Illustration 14.3
PRODUCT FLOWS IN A PROCESS COST SYSTEM
(Ajax Company example)

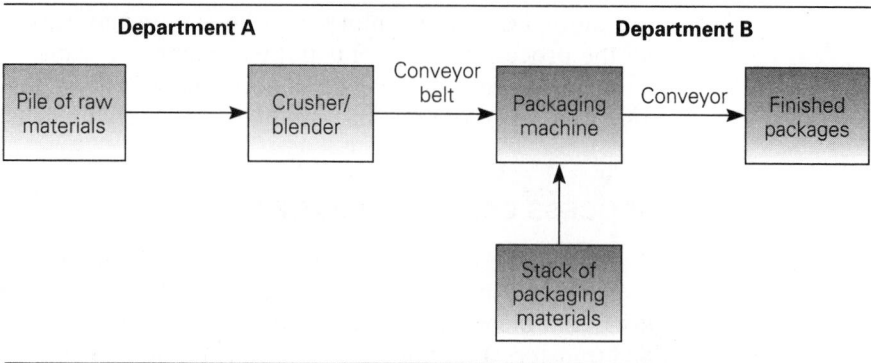

Computations are often more complex. A complication exists whenever partially completed inventories are present, as is true for Department B. Before Department B transfers the cost of completed units, its Work in Process Inventory account for June is:

Work in Process Inventory—Department B

Transferred in from	
Department A	26,400
Direct materials	1,100
Direct labor	5,880
Overhead (100% of	
direct labor cost)	5,880
Total	39,260

Recall that direct materials, direct labor, and manufacturing overhead are product costs. That is, the costs *attach* to the product. Thus, the "Transferred in from Department A" in the above T-account represents the direct materials, direct labor, and overhead costs assigned to products in Department A. These costs have *followed* the physical units to Department B.

Now, Ajax's accountant must divide the $39,260 total costs charged to Department B in June between the units transferred out and those remaining on hand in the department. The accountant cannot divide $39,260 by 11,000 to get an average unit cost because the 11,000 units are not alike. Department B has 9,000 finished units and has 2,000 units that are only partially finished. To solve this problem, the accountant uses the concept of equivalent units, which we discuss next.

Equivalent Units of Production

Objective 3
Discuss the concept of equivalent units in a process cost system

Essentially, the concept of **equivalent units** involves expressing a given number of partially completed units as a smaller number of fully completed units. For example, if we bring 1,000 units to a 40% state of completion, these units are equivalent to 400 units that are 100% complete. Accountants base this concept on the fact that a company must incur approximately the same amount of costs to bring 1,000 units to a 40% level of completion as it would incur to complete 400 units.

Illustration 14.4 presents pictorially the concept of equivalent units. As you examine the diagram, think of the amount of water in the glasses as costs that the company has already incurred.

Objective 4
Compute equivalent units of production and unit costs under the average cost procedure

The first step in computing Department B's equivalent units for Ajax Company is to determine the stage of completion of the 2,000 unfinished units. These units are 100% complete as to **transferred-in costs** because if they were not, Department A would not have transferred the units to Department B. In Department B, however, the units may be in different stages of completion regarding the materials, labor, and manufacturing overhead costs. Assume that Department B adds all materials at the beginning of the production process. Then, both ending inventory and units transferred out would be 100% complete as to materials. Therefore, equivalent production for materials would be 11,000 units.

Accountants usually assume that units are at the same stage of completion for both labor and manufacturing overhead. This assumption is made because often manufacturing overhead is applied to work in process on a direct labor basis. (Recall that direct labor and manufacturing overhead

Illustration 14.4
THE CONCEPT OF EQUIVALENT UNITS

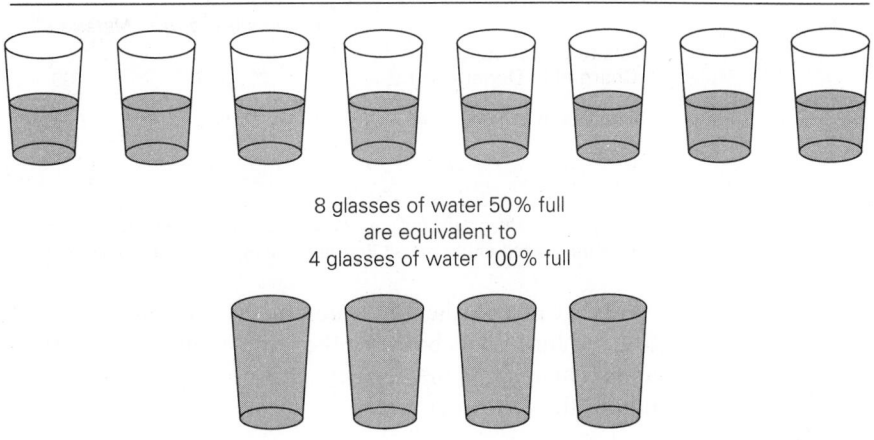

8 glasses of water 50% full
are equivalent to
4 glasses of water 100% full

together are known as *conversion cost*.) Let us assume that, on the average, the 2,000 units in ending inventory are 40% complete as to conversion. Department B transferred out 9,000 units fully completed and brought 2,000 units to a 40% completion state. Thus, the equivalent (fully completed) units for labor and manufacturing overhead would be 9,800, or 9,000 + (2,000 × 40%). Department B now has an equivalent of 800 fully completed units (2,000 × 40%) in ending inventory.

The formula for equivalent units of production for each cost element (transferred in, materials, and conversion) is:

$$\begin{array}{c} \text{Equivalent units} \\ \text{of production} \end{array} = \begin{array}{c} \text{Units} \\ \text{completed} \end{array} + \left(\begin{array}{c} \text{Units in} \\ \text{ending inventory} \end{array} \times \begin{array}{c} \text{Percentage} \\ \text{complete} \end{array} \right)$$

When we know the equivalent units of production, we can compute unit costs for transferred-in, materials, and conversion elements. The formulas for the unit cost for each cost element are:

$$\text{Unit cost for transferred in} = \frac{\text{Total transferred-in costs}}{\text{Equivalent units—transferred in}}$$

$$\text{Unit cost for materials} = \frac{\text{Total materials costs}}{\text{Equivalent units—materials}}$$

$$\text{Unit cost for conversion} = \frac{\text{Total conversion costs}}{\text{Equivalent units—conversion}}$$

Now we can compute unit costs for each cost element in Department B as follows:

	Transferred In	Materials	Conversion	Total
Costs to be accounted for:				
Charged to Department B	$26,400	$ 1,100	$11,760*	$39,260
Equivalent units	11,000	11,000	9,800†	
Unit costs	$2.40	$0.10	$1.20	$3.70

* Conversion costs consist of Direct labor + Overhead ($11,760 = $5,880 + $5,880).
† Units transferred out (9,000) + Equivalent units in ending inventory (800).

We can use the $3.70 computed unit cost to divide Department B's $39,260 June costs between the units completed and transferred out and the units remaining in the department's ending inventory. We make this calculation in the following table:

PROCESS COSTING AND JUST-IN-TIME PRODUCTION

Borg-Warner recently implemented just-in-time production at its automotive division in Ithaca, New York. Although not completely eliminated, inventory was cut in half. Before introducing just-in-time, the layout of the factory allowed "piles" of inventory to accumulate between workstations. Managers referred to the accounting system as "pile accounting" because accountants had to keep track of the materials and conversion cost of inventory in each pile.

After introducing just-in-time production (JIT), the company stopped producing partially finished products into piles. Using JIT, a new batch of products was not started in the process until the previous batch was transferred to the next stage of the production process. Now, "production moves between machines like water flowing through a pipeline—it flows freely until an object blocks the flow. Then the input

valve must be shut off until the line is cleared. Similarly, on the factory floor there is nowhere for parts to go when the flow of product is stopped. Therefore, the entire line or process must be shut down." [p. 32]

The JIT method requires total quality control. Before JIT, units were measured as completed regardless of their quality. Now, defective output is rejected and charged back to the department that produced it. "The system can be compared to an automotive repair shop. The customer pays only when the car has been repaired properly and released. The auto shop receives no credit or payment for cars that are 'almost repaired.'" [p. 33]

SOURCE: Article by Al Phillips and Dan E. Collins, "How Borg-Warner Made the Transition from Pile Accounting to JIT," *Management Accounting*, October 1990, pp. 32–35.

	Transferred In (@ $2.40)	Materials (@ $0.10)	Conversion (@ $1.20)	Total
Costs accounted for:				
Units completed and transferred out (9,000 units)	$21,600	$ 900	$10,800	$33,300
Units remaining in ending inventory (2,000 units)	4,800	200	960*	5,960
Costs accounted for	$26,400	$1,100	$11,760	$39,260

* Equivalent units = 800 units (800 × $1.20 = $960).

The $33,300 total costs transferred out of Department B consist of $21,600 transferred in from Department A (9,000 × $2.40), $900 of materials costs (9,000 × $0.10), and $10,800 of conversion costs (9,000 × $1.20), or a total cost of $3.70 per unit times 9,000 units. The 2,000 units of ending inventory in Department B are fully complete as to materials and 40% complete as to conversion. We calculate the ending inventory cost as follows:

Costs from Department A (2,000 × $2.40)		$4,800
Costs added by Department B:		
Materials (2,000 × $0.10).	$200	
Conversion (800 equivalent units × $1.20).	960	1,160
Total cost of ending inventory		$5,960

Ajax carries units transferred out of Department B in Finished Goods Inventory at a cost of $3.70 each until they are sold. Then, Ajax charges the costs to Cost of Goods Sold.

Journal Entry Analysis

We have discussed how to determine the cost of each cost element placed in production, transferred to finished goods inventory, and charged to Cost of Goods Sold. Now let's look at the June journal entries for these activities.

(1) Work in Process Inventory—Department A 16,500
Work in Process Inventory—Department B 1,100
    Materials Inventory 17,600
    To record materials placed in production in June.

(2) Payroll Summary 11,380
    Various withholding accounts and wages payable. . . 11,380
    To record factory payroll for June.

(3) Work in Process Inventory—Department A 5,500
Work in Process Inventory—Department B 5,880
    Payroll Summary 11,380
    To assign factory labor costs (assuming that all such costs are chargeable directly to production departments).

(4) Manufacturing Overhead. 10,100
    Various accounts—Cash, Accounts Payable, accruals, and accumulated depreciation 10,100
    To record actual overhead costs incurred in June.

(5) Work in Process Inventory—Department A 4,400
Work in Process Inventory—Department B 5,880
    Manufacturing Overhead. 10,280
    To apply overhead to production using predetermined rates based on direct labor cost: Department A, 80%; and Department B, 100%.

(6) Work in Process Inventory—Department B 26,400
    Work in Process Inventory—Department A 26,400
    To record transfer of goods from Department A to Department B.

(7) Finished Goods Inventory 33,300
    Work in Process Inventory—Department B 33,300
    To record transfer of completed goods from Department B to finished goods.

If Ajax sold 6,000 completed units in June at $10 per unit on account, it would make the following entries:

(8)	Accounts Receivable	60,000	
	Sales		60,000
	To record sales on account.		

(9)	Cost of Goods Sold	22,200	
	Finished Goods Inventory		22,200
	To record cost of goods sold in June, 6,000 units @ $3.70.		

If Manufacturing Overhead is closed at the end of the month, the entry to dispose of the overapplied overhead to Cost of Goods Sold is:

Manufacturing Overhead	180	
Cost of Goods Sold		180
To dispose of overapplied overhead of $180 (or $10,280 applied − $10,100 actual) to Cost of Goods Sold.		

Production Cost Report

Objective 5
Prepare a production cost report for a process cost system and discuss its relationship to the Work in Process Inventory account

The key document in a process costing system is *the production cost report*. A **production cost report** shows both the flow of units and the flow of costs through the Work in Process Inventory account of a processing center. It also shows how accountants divide these costs between the cost of units completed and transferred out and the cost of units still in the processing center's ending work in process inventory. This report makes the equivalent unit and unit cost computations easier.

To illustrate the preparation of a production cost report with partially completed beginning and ending work in process inventories, assume the following June 1995 data for Department 3 of Storey Company:

Units		
Units in beginning inventory, complete as to materials, 60% complete as to conversion costs		6,000
Units transferred in from Department 2		18,000
Units completed and transferred out		16,000
Units in ending inventory, complete as to materials, 50% complete as to conversion costs		8,000
Costs		
Cost of beginning inventory:		
Costs transferred in from preceding department in May	$12,000	
Materials added in May in Department 3	6,000	
Conversion costs (equal amounts of labor and overhead)	3,000	$21,000
Costs transferred in from preceding department in June		37,200
Costs added in Department 3 in June:		
Materials	$18,480	
Conversion (equal amounts of labor and overhead)	18,000	36,480
Total costs of beginning inventory and units placed in production in Department 3 in June		$94,680

The preparation of the production cost report includes the following four steps:

1. Trace the physical flow of the units through the production department.
2. Convert actual units to equivalent units.
3. Compute unit costs for each cost element.
4. Distribute the total cost between the units completed and transferred out of the department and the units remaining in the ending inventory.

Using the June data, Storey developed the production cost report for Department 3 shown in Illustration 14.5.

Illustration 14.5
PRODUCTION COST REPORT

STOREY COMPANY
Production Cost Report—Department 3
For the Month of June 1995

	Actual Units	Equivalent Units		
		Transferred In	Materials	Conversion
UNITS:				
Units in beginning inventory	6,000			
Units transferred in from Department 2 . . .	18,000			
Units to be accounted for	24,000			
Units completed and transferred out	16,000	16,000	16,000	16,000
Units in ending inventory*	8,000	8,000	8,000	4,000
Units accounted for	24,000	24,000	24,000	20,000

	Transferred In	Materials	Conversion	Total
COSTS:				
Costs to be accounted for:				
Costs in beginning inventory	$12,000	$ 6,000	$ 3,000	$21,000
Costs transferred in from Department 2 in June	37,200			37,200
Costs added in Department 3		18,480	18,000	36,480
Costs to be accounted for	$49,200	$24,480	$21,000	$94,680
Equivalent units (as above)	24,000	24,000	20,000	
Unit cost (per equivalent unit)†	$2.05	$1.02	$1.05	$4.12
Costs accounted for:				
Costs completed and transferred out (16,000 units)	$32,800	$16,320	$16,800	$65,920
Costs remaining in ending inventory (8,000 units)*	16,400	8,160	4,200	28,760
Costs accounted for	$49,200	$24,480	$21,000	$94,680

* Inventory is complete as to materials added, 50% complete as to conversion.

† Unit cost equals "costs to be accounted for" divided by equivalent units.

The first step in the preparation of a production cost report is to trace the physical flow of actual units in and out of Department 3. The section entitled "UNITS" in Illustration 14.5 shows that Department 3 had 6,000 units in the June beginning inventory. Department 3 also had 18,000 units transferred in from the previous department. Thus, a total of 24,000 units must be accounted for in Department 3. Of these 24,000 units, Department 3 completed and transferred out 16,000 units (either to the next processing department or to finished goods). At the end of the month, Department 3 had 8,000 partially completed units. These 8,000 units are the June ending inventory. Now we are ready for the second step in the preparation of the production cost report—convert actual units to equivalent units.

Storey Company's cost of production report uses the **average cost procedure. Under the average cost procedure, the number of equivalent units for each cost element equals the number of units transferred out plus the number of equivalent units of that cost element in the ending inventory.** (The average cost procedure does not consider the number of units in the beginning inventory and the degree of completion of the beginning inventory.) Alternatively, Storey could use FIFO. We use the average cost procedure in this chapter because it is simpler and is used extensively in practice. Chapter Appendix 14–A describes process costing using FIFO.

In the Storey example, the units in the ending inventory are fully complete as to costs transferred in and as to materials. Therefore, the number of equivalent units for each of these cost elements is 24,000, or 16,000 units completed and transferred out + [8,000 units in the ending inventory × 100% complete for transferred-in cost and for materials]. The equivalent units for conversion costs are 20,000, or 16,000 units completed and transferred out + [8,000 units in ending inventory × 50% complete for conversion].

Once a company has computed its equivalent units, the company must calculate its unit costs (the third step in preparing the production cost report). Each cost element of production—costs transferred in, materials, and conversion—has accumulated costs. Notice in Illustration 14.5 that for each cost element, we total the costs of beginning inventory and the costs of the current month. We refer to the total costs charged to a department as *costs to be accounted for*. These costs have either been transferred out or will appear in the ending inventory of Department 3.

To determine the cost per equivalent unit for each cost element, divide the total cost for each cost element by the equivalent units of production related to that cost element. (Since we totaled all costs for each cost element before the division, we can average the computed unit costs across the current and prior periods.) Illustration 14.5 shows the average per unit costs for June as transferred-in costs, $2.05; materials, $1.02; and conversion, $1.05. Management monitors these costs closely for cost control purposes, watching for extreme fluctuations from one month to the next.

The last step in preparing the production cost report is to allocate costs between the units completed and transferred out and the units remaining in ending inventory. The units that were transferred out were fully complete as to all elements of production. Therefore, we can multiply the 16,000 units by $4.12, the total cost per unit. The result, $65,920, is the amount Storey assigns to the next department as *cost transferred in* or to finished goods as the cost of completed current period production. We now compute the cost of ending work in process inventory as follows:

8,000 equivalent units transferred in @ $2.05	$16,400
8,000 equivalent units of materials costs @ $1.02	8,160
4,000 equivalent units of conversion costs @ $1.05	4,200
Total cost of ending inventory	$28,760

The sum of the ending inventory cost and the cost of the units transferred out must equal the total costs to be accounted for. This built-in check determines whether the company has properly followed the procedures of cost allocation. As shown in the production cost report, Department 3 adds the $65,920 cost transferred out to the $28,760 ending inventory cost. The total equals the $94,680 for which Department 3 must account.

Some companies do not use the production cost report, instead replacing it with three schedules. The first schedule is the schedule of equivalent production. This schedule shows the computation of equivalent units of production for the period for transferred-in, materials, and conversion costs. The second schedule is the unit cost analysis schedule. This schedule shows all the costs charged to the Work in Process Inventory account of each production process department. Then, it shows the cost per equivalent unit for transferred-in, materials, and conversion costs. The third schedule is the cost summary schedule. This schedule makes use of the results of the preceding two schedules to distribute the total costs accumulated during the period among all the units of output.

FIFO Method

We have described process costing using an average costing method. Companies that use a process cost system may use the *first-in, first-out (FIFO) method* instead of the average cost procedure. The FIFO method is more complex. Chapter Appendix 14–A illustrates this method.

PROCESS COSTING IN SERVICE ORGANIZATIONS

Service organizations that provide similar services to a variety of customers are potential users of process costing. For example, a clinic dispensing flu shots and a photo shop that processes your pictures could use process costing. In manufacturing, the difficult task is to match costs in a period with the units produced that period, which is why companies compute equivalent units of production.

ETHICS   A CLOSER LOOK

Tony Perkins works in the inventory control group at a company that produces footballs. A good friend of Tony's manages the production department in the same company. At the end of a recent month, Tony reviewed the production department's production cost report and found the department had no beginning work in process inventory, had started 39,000 footballs, and had produced only 35,000. "That leaves 4,000 footballs in ending inventory," Tony thought. "That's a lot of footballs they didn't finish."

Later, Tony visited his friend, Samuel, who managed the production department. "Why all the ending inventory?" Tony asked.

"One of my best workers has been having a lot of family problems and hasn't been as efficient. He set one of the machines incorrectly so that we have to redo 3,500 footballs. The other 500 are complete now and have been transferred out. Our entire operation has been slowed by the machine problem."

"Samuel, you know company policy is to send all defective products to the recycling company as it is more cost effective than to fix defects," said Tony.

"We can't do that!" exclaimed Samuel. "We'd all be in trouble if plant management found out. The worker who messed up would probably be fired and that is the last thing he needs with all his other problems. This is our little problem, and we'll take care of it."

Required
a. What should Tony do?
b. Would your answer to (a) change if Tony learned that the production department had fixed the footballs and sent them on to the next department?

Service companies generally complete the service by the end of the period and have no work in process at the end of the period. Nurses do not leave for home halfway through a flu shot, and the photo shop usually processes your pictures within a few hours. Consequently, there is no need to compute equivalent units, which simplifies process costing when used in service organizations.

You may encounter some service companies that have partially completed work at the end of the period. Certain types of dry cleaning and photo processing may still be "in process" at the end of a period. You can apply the methods described for manufacturing in this chapter to those service companies. For "materials," you could substitute any significant supplies, and for "conversion costs," you could substitute service labor and overhead.

EFFECT OF JUST-IN-TIME PRODUCTION SYSTEMS

Managers using just-in-time (JIT) production systems seek to drive inventory levels to zero or near zero levels. Managers frequently target work in process inventory to apply JIT.

Managers who apply JIT and drive work in process inventories to zero eliminate the task of computing equivalent units and allocating costs to ending inventory. This savings in accounting costs is one of the benefits of JIT.

Now that you have studied both job order costing (Chapter 13) and process costing (this chapter), you can appreciate why companies must accurately account for product unit costs. Without accurate cost accounting information, a manufacturing company cannot determine the cost of its products for managerial decision making or prepare accurate financial statements.

UNDERSTANDING THE LEARNING OBJECTIVES

1. Describe the types of operations for which a process cost system is used.
    - Process cost systems are used for businesses that manufacture large quantities of a single product or similar products on a continuous basis over long periods.
    - Paint, paper, chemicals, photo processing, gasoline, rubber, and plastics are examples of products that should be accounted for under a process cost system.
2. Distinguish between process and job order cost systems.
    - *Types of products produced under each system.*   Companies that use job order costing work on many different jobs with different production requirements during each period. Companies that use process costing produce a single homogeneous product, either on a continuous basis or for long periods.
    - *Cost accumulation procedures used under each system.*   Job order costing accumulates costs by individual jobs. Process costing accumulates costs by process or department.
    - *Key document used under each system.*   The job order cost record is the key document in job order costing. The department production cost report is the key document in process costing.
    - *Work in Process Inventory accounts.*   Job order cost systems have one Work in Process Inventory account per job or one for all jobs. Process cost systems have one Work in Process Inventory account for each department or process.
3. Discuss the concept of equivalent units in a process cost system.
    - Whenever partially completed inventories are present, the number of equivalent units of production must be computed. Essentially, the concept of equivalent units involves expressing a given number of partially completed units as a smaller number of fully completed units.
    - As a simple example of equivalent units, two apples that are half eaten are equivalent to one whole apple eaten. In manufacturing, we

estimate the degree of completion for a group of products with respect to transferred-in costs, materials costs, and conversion costs (direct labor and overhead). Accountants base the concept of equivalent units on the fact that a company must incur approximately the same amount of costs to partially complete a large number of units as to totally complete a smaller number of units.

4. Compute equivalent units of production and unit costs under the average cost procedure.
   - Accountants compute equivalent units of production for transferred-in units, materials, and conversion. For each of these categories, the number of units transferred out is added to the equivalent units remaining in ending work in process in the department.
   - Unit costs for the three categories—transferred-in units, materials, and conversion—are determined by dividing the equivalent units into the costs in beginning inventory plus the costs transferred in or added in the department during this period.

5. Prepare a production cost report for a process cost system and discuss its relationship to the Work in Process Inventory account.
   - A production cost report shows both the flow of units and the flow of costs through a processing center. The report is divided into two parts. The first part traces the physical flow of the units through the production department and converts actual units to equivalent units. The second part shows the costs to be accounted for, computes unit costs based on equivalent units as determined in the first part, and shows how the costs were accounted for by adding the costs completed and transferred out to the costs remaining in ending inventory. The costs to be accounted for and the costs accounted for must balance.
   - The production cost report describes cost and unit flows through the Work in Process Inventory account of a processing center. Each processing department normally has its own Work in Process Inventory account and related production cost report. The separate items that make up work in process inventory, that is, direct labor, direct materials, applied overhead, and cost of units transferred in and out, can be traced from the production cost report to the Work in Process Inventory account (and vice versa) during a given period.

6. Compute equivalent units of production and unit costs under the first-in, first-out (FIFO) system (Appendix 14–A).
   - Equivalent units of production are computed by taking the equivalent units of work done to complete the beginning inventory, plus units started and completed during the current period, plus equivalent units of work done on the ending inventory. As is true under the average cost method, the equivalent units usually differ between materials and conversion.
   - Unit costs for the three categories—transferred-in units, materials,

and conversion—are determined by dividing costs to be accounted for during the period by units produced during the period.

7. Discuss how common costs are allocated to joint products (Appendix 14–B).
   - The physical measures method allocates joint product costs based on physical measures, such as units, pounds, or liters.
   - The relative sales value method is the most commonly used method to allocate joint product costs. This method is based on the relative sales value of the products at the split-off point.

APPENDIX 14–A

THE FIFO PROCESS COST METHOD

Objective 6
Compute equivalent units of production and unit costs under the first-in, first-out (FIFO) system

In this chapter, the discussion assumed the use of the average cost method for determining unit cost under process costing. Another acceptable method for determining unit cost under process costing is the **first-in, first-out (FIFO)** cost method.

The following table shows how the method of equivalent units computation differs between the average cost method and the FIFO cost method.

Average Cost Method	*FIFO Cost Method*

Equivalent units of production
= Units completed this period
+ Equivalent units of work done on the
  ending inventory
	Equivalent units of production
	= Equivalent units of work done to
	  complete the beginning inventory
	+ Units started and completed this period
	+ Equivalent units of work done on the
	  ending inventory

To illustrate the computation of equivalent units under the FIFO method, assume the following facts:

Beginning inventory, 3,000 units, 40% complete; all completed and transferred out
Units started this period, 10,000 units
Ending inventory, 5,000 units, 20% complete

The equivalent production for the period would be:

Equivalent units of work done to complete the beginning inventory equals 3,000 units times 60%, because they were already 40% complete at the beginning of the period (3,000 × 0.60)	1,800
Units started and completed this period (10,000 − 5,000 in ending inventory)	5,000
Equivalent units of work done to partially complete the ending inventory (5,000 × 0.20)	1,000
Equivalent units of production	7,800

As is true under the average cost method, the equivalent units usually differ between materials and conversion.

This appendix presents a detailed illustration of the FIFO process costing system.

FIFO Process Costing—An Illustration

To illustrate more completely the operation of the FIFO process cost method, we will use an example of June 1995 production costs for a company with two departments—Department A and Department B. Both departments add materials only at the beginning of processing. Department A has no May 31 inventory. The May 31 inventory in Department B consists of 2,000 units that are fully complete as to materials and 50% complete as to conversion. This inventory has accumulated costs of $6,180.

The following transactions and additional data summarize manufacturing operations in both departments for June 1995:

(1) Raw materials purchased on account, $25,000.
(2) Direct materials issued: Department A (14,000 units at $1.50), $21,000; and Department B (10,000 units at $0.13), $1,300. Indirect materials issued: Department A, $400; and Department B, $200.
(3) Factory payroll for the month, $15,000; FICA taxes withheld, $750; and income taxes withheld, $1,250.
(4) Payroll distributed: direct labor, Department A, $6,600, Department B, $5,400; and indirect labor, building occupancy department, $3,000.
(5) Other manufacturing overhead incurred:

Repairs (on account)	$1,500
Depreciation	3,000
Payroll taxes	1,000
Property taxes	1,200
Insurance	600
Utilities (on account)	800
	$8,100

(6) Manufacturing overhead is applied at a rate of 80% of direct labor cost in Department A and at a rate of 100% of direct labor cost in Department B.
(7) Production reports show the following for June:

	Department A	Department B
Beginning inventory	–0–	2,000
Units started	14,000	10,000
Units completed and transferred	10,000	9,000
Units in inventory, June 30	4,000	3,000
Estimated percentage of completion	50%	33⅓%

(8)   Sales for the month on account, 15,000 units at $6 per unit.

(9)   The company computed cost of goods sold at $55,866 on a FIFO basis.

The general journal entries and their explanations follow.

(1)   Materials Inventory   25,000
         Accounts Payable   25,000
      To record materials purchased on account.

(2)   Work in Process—Department A   21,000
      Work in Process—Department B   1,300
      Manufacturing Overhead   600
         Materials Inventory   22,900
      To record direct and indirect materials requisitioned.

(3)   Payroll Summary   15,000
         FICA Taxes Withheld   750
         Income Taxes Withheld   1,250
         Payroll Payable   13,000
      To record factory payroll for the month.

(4)   Work in Process—Department A   6,600
      Work in Process—Department B   5,400
      Manufacturing Overhead   3,000
         Payroll Summary   15,000
      To assign labor costs to departments.

(5)   Manufacturing Overhead   8,100
         Accounts Payable   2,300
         Accumulated Depreciation—Plant and Equipment . .   3,000
         Payroll Taxes Payable   1,000
         Property Taxes Payable   1,200
         Prepaid Insurance   600
      To record various overhead costs incurred.

(6)   Work in Process—Department A   5,280
      Work in Process—Department B   5,400
         Manufacturing Overhead   10,680
      To record assignment of overhead to production.

(7)   Work in Process—Department B   24,900
         Work in Process—Department A   24,900
      To record transfer of completed production from
      Department A to Department B. (For details of
      computation, see production cost report of Department
      A in Illustration 14.6.)

      Finished Goods   34,120
         Work in Process—Department B   34,120
      To record transfer of completed production from
      Department B to storeroom. (For details of
      computation, see production cost report for
      Department B in Illustration 14.7.)

(8)   Accounts Receivable   90,000
         Sales   90,000
      To record sales for the month.

(9) Cost of Goods Sold 55,866
        Finished Goods 55,866
    To record cost of goods sold.

(10) Cost of Goods Sold 1,020
        Manufacturing Overhead 1,020
    To dispose of underapplied overhead of $1,020
    (= [$600 + $3,000 + $8,100] − $10,680 applied), if
    overhead is closed at the end of the month.

The Production Cost Report. As noted in the above journal entries for June's manufacturing operations, the *production cost report* provided the dollar amounts of certain entries. The chapter illustration of the production cost report shows the units and costs charged to a department, the disposition of these units and costs, and typical supporting details and computations.

Production Cost Report—Department A. To illustrate flexibility in format, Illustration 14.6 shows the production cost report for Department A in a different format than the one in the chapter. Note that first Department A placed 14,000 units in production. Then, Department A completed and transferred out 10,000 units. Department A retained the remaining 4,000 partially completed units in the department. The footnote in the illustration shows the computation of equivalent units.

The costs section of the report shows that the only costs to be accounted for were those added in the department in June. These costs include materials, $21,000, and conversion, $11,880, totaling $32,880. Department A had no beginning inventory and no transfers in. Note how Department A determines its unit costs for each of the two elements of manufacturing costs ($1.50 for materials and $0.99 for conversion). Also, the total current unit cost is $2.49. The report then shows the disposition of the costs—the cost of the units transferred to Department B and the amount remaining in Department A as the cost of the ending inventory (based on current unit cost). The units transferred to Department B have the same unit cost as the unit cost in Department A for the month. The current unit cost and the cost of the transferred units is not always the same, as we will show for Department B in Illustration 14.7.

Production Cost Report—Department B. The report for Department B (Illustration 14.7) is similar to that for Department A. Note how the illustration highlights the current unit cost of the operations performed in the department. Note also that the costs Department B must account for include the costs in the beginning inventory and the cost of the units transferred in from Department A. Department B determines the cost of the ending inventory through use of the current month's unit cost ($1.33). All of Department B's other costs are included in the costs of the 9,000 units transferred to Finished Goods.

In the production cost report in Illustration 14.7, we determine the cost of units transferred out by subtracting the cost of the ending inventory from

Illustration 14.6
PRODUCTION COST REPORT—DEPARTMENT A

DEPARTMENT A
Production Cost Report
For the Month Ended June 30, 1995

UNITS:

Units in beginning inventory	–0–
Units started during period	14,000
Units to be accounted for.	14,000
Units completed and transferred out.	10,000
Units in ending inventory	4,000
Units accounted for	14,000

	Equivalent Units	Total Cost	Current Unit Cost
COSTS:			
Costs to be accounted for:			
Costs added during the month:			
Direct materials	14,000*	$21,000	$1.50
Conversion.	12,000*	11,880	0.99
Costs added in month and costs to be accounted for. .		$32,880	$2.49
Costs accounted for:			
Cost of ending inventory:			
Direct materials (4,000 × 100% × $1.50)		$ 6,000	
Conversion (4,000 × 50% × $0.99).		1,980	
Total cost of ending inventory.		$ 7,980	
Cost of 10,000 units transferred out		24,900	$2.49
Costs accounted for		$32,880	

* Supporting computations and data:

	Materials	Conversion
Computations of equivalent units:		
Equivalent units to complete beginning inventory.	–0–	–0–
Units started and completed.	10,000	10,000
Equivalent units in partially completed ending inventory	4,000	2,000
Equivalent units of production for month.	14,000	12,000

Ending inventory is 100% complete for materials and 50% complete as to processing or conversion costs.

Illustration 14.7
PRODUCTION COST REPORT—DEPARTMENT B

DEPARTMENT B
Production Cost Report
For the Month Ended June 30, 1995

UNITS:

Units in beginning inventory	2,000
Units started during period	10,000
Units to be accounted for.	12,000
Units completed and transferred out.	9,000
Units in ending inventory	3,000
Units accounted for	12,000

	Equivalent Units	Total Cost	Current Unit Cost
COSTS:			
Costs to be accounted for:			
Costs added during the month:			
Direct materials	10,000*	$ 1,300	$0.13
Conversion.	9,000*	10,800	1.20
Costs added during the month		$12,100	$1.33
Costs in beginning inventory		6,180	
Costs transferred in from Department A		24,900	
Total costs to be accounted for		$43,180	
Costs accounted for:			
Cost of ending inventory:			
Transferred in from Department A (3,000 units at $2.49)		$ 7,470	
Direct materials (3,000 × 100% × $0.13)		390	
Conversion (3,000 × ⅓ × $1.20).		1,200	
Total cost of ending inventory.		$ 9,060	
Cost of 9,000 units transferred out.		34,120	$3.791
Costs accounted for		$43,180	

* Supporting computations and data:

	Materials	Conversion
Computations of equivalent units:		
Equivalent units to complete beginning inventory.	–0–	1,000
Units started and completed.	7,000	7,000
Equivalent units in partially completed ending inventory	3,000	1,000
Equivalent units of production for the month.	10,000	9,000

Beginning and ending inventories are complete as to materials. Beginning inventory is 50% complete and ending inventory 33⅓% complete as to processing.

the total costs to be accounted for ($43,180 − $9,060 = $34,120). We can compute the $3.791 average unit cost by dividing $34,120 by the 9,000 units transferred. The footnote in the illustration shows the computation of the equivalent units.

APPENDIX 14–B

ALLOCATION OF JOINT PRODUCT COSTS

Objective 7
Discuss how
common costs are
allocated to joint
products

A company incurs **joint product costs (common costs)** when it produces two or more products through the same production process or from a common raw material. The company produces these products simultaneously. The products are not identifiable as different individual products until a particular point in the manufacturing process known as the *split-off point.*

The **split-off point** is a certain stage of production at which the separate products become identifiable from a common processing unit. We refer to any costs beyond the split-off point as *separable costs* because they can be directly traced to individual products. Examples of industries that process joint products are petroleum, lumber, flour milling, meat packing, chemicals, and tobacco. Illustration 14.8 shows the joint production process.

Since we cannot identify joint product costs with individual products, we must use cost allocation. The accounting problem we face is how to allocate the joint costs that a company incurred *before* the products became separately identified. Commonly used methods to allocate joint costs are the *physical measures method* and the *relative sales value method.*

Physical Measures Method

The **physical measures method** allocates joint product costs on the basis of physical measures such as units, pounds, or liters.

To illustrate, assume that Roy Company produces two grades of oil,

Illustration 14.8
JOINT PRODUCTION PROCESS

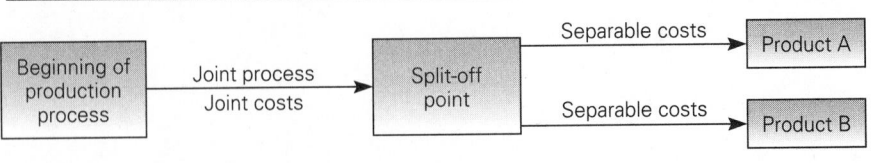

product A and product B, through a joint process. The cost and production data of Roy Company for July are:

	Product A	Product B	Total
Units produced.	15,000 liters	25,000 liters	40,000 liters
Unit selling price at split-off.	$15	$6	
Revenue at split-off.	$225,000	$150,000	
Joint product costs:			
Direct materials			$125,000
Direct labor			105,000
Manufacturing overhead			70,000
			$300,000

The physical measures method uses a ratio of the physical volume of each product to total volume as a basis for allocation of joint costs. We allocate the cost to each product as follows:

	Total Liters	Ratio	Joint Costs	Allocated Joint Costs
Product A	15,000	$\dfrac{15,000}{40,000}$ × $300,000	=	$112,500
Product B	25,000	$\dfrac{25,000}{40,000}$ × $300,000	=	187,500
	40,000			$300,000

If Roy sells both products without further processing, the gross margin for product A will be $112,500, or $225,000 less $112,500 allocated joint costs. Product B will show a loss of $37,500, or $150,000 less $187,500 allocated joint costs. Even though the physical measures method is easy to use, it often has no relationship to the revenue-generating power of each product. In this instance, product B suffers a loss of $37,500 because the company allocated a high portion of joint costs based on product B's high volume even though its selling price is less than that of product A.

Relative Sales Value Method

The **relative sales value method** is the most commonly used basis to allocate joint product costs at the split-off point. Accountants base the relative sales value method on the assumption that the market value of each product is the most reasonable basis for allocating joint costs.

Using the relative sales value method, Roy Company would allocate the joint costs as follows:

	Sales Value at Split-off	Ratio	Joint Costs	Allocated Joint Costs
Product A:				
($15 × 15,000)	$225,000	$\dfrac{\$225,000}{\$375,000}$ × $300,000 =		$180,000
Product B:				
($6 × 25,000)	150,000	$\dfrac{\$150,000}{\$375,000}$ × $300,000 =		120,000
	$375,000			$300,000

The allocation ratios of 60% and 40%, respectively, for product A and product B result in allocated joint costs of $180,000 to product A and $120,000 to product B.

To compare the physical measures method and the relative sales value method, assume Roy Company has no inventory at the end of July. A partial July income statement would appear as follows:

	Product A		Product B	
	Physical Measures Method	Relative Sales Value Method	Physical Measures Method	Relative Sales Value Method
Sales.	$225,000	$225,000	$150,000	$150,000
Cost of goods sold	112,500	180,000	187,500	120,000
Gross margin	$112,500	$ 45,000	$ (37,500)	$ 30,000
Gross margin percentage	50%	20%	—*	20%

* Percentage cannot be calculated for a negative amount.

As you can see, under the relative sales value method both products have the same gross margin percentage of 20%. The major advantage of the relative sales value method is that it allocates joint costs according to the relative revenue-generating ability of the individual products.

DEMONSTRATION PROBLEM

Cairn Company uses a process cost system to accumulate the costs it incurs to produce plastic dishes from recycled plastic. The May 1 inventory of the finishing department consisted of 36,000 units, fully complete as to materials and 80% complete as to conversion. The beginning inventory cost of $270,995 consisted of $200,400 of costs transferred in from the molding department, $30,000 of finishing department materials costs, and $40,555 of finishing department conversion costs. The costs incurred in the finishing department for May are shown in the next table.

The finishing department received 120,000 units from the molding department in May. During May, 127,200 units were completed by the finishing department and

Costs from molding department (excluding costs in beginning inventory)	$720,000
Costs added in finishing department in May (excluding costs in beginning inventory):	
Materials . . . . $ 63,600	
Conversion 131,376	194,976
	$914,976

transferred out. As of May 31, 28,800 units, complete as to materials and 60% complete as to conversion, were left in inventory of the finishing department.

Required:

a. Prepare a production cost report for the finishing department for May.
b. Compute the finishing department's average unit cost for conversion in April.

Solution to demonstration problem

a.

CAIRN COMPANY
Finishing Department
Production Cost Report
For the Month Ending May 31

	Actual Units	*Equivalent Units*		
		Transferred In	Materials	Conversion
UNITS:				
Units in May 1 inventory.	36,000			
Units transferred in	120,000			
Units to be accounted for	156,000			
Units completed and transferred out . . .	127,200	127,200	127,200	127,200
Units in May 31 inventory*.	28,800	28,800	28,800	17,280†
Units accounted for.	156,000	156,000	156,000	144,480

* Inventory is complete as to materials, 60% complete as to conversion.
† (28,800 × 60% = 17,280).

	Transferred In	Materials	Conversion	Total
COSTS:				
Costs to be accounted for:				
Costs in May 1 inventory	$200,400	$ 30,000	$ 40,555	$ 270,955
Costs transferred in.	720,000			720,000
Costs added in department		63,600	131,376	194,976
Costs to be accounted for.	$920,400	$ 93,600	$171,931	$1,185,931
Equivalent units (as above)	156,000	156,000	144,480	
Unit costs	$5.90	$0.60	$1.19	$7.69
Cost accounted for:				
Units completed and transferred out (127,200 units)	$750,480	$ 76,320	$151,368	$ 978,168
Units remaining in May 31 inventory (28,800 units, 60% complete as to conversion).	169,920	17,280	20,563	207,763
Costs accounted for	$920,400	$ 93,600	$171,931	$1,185,931

b. The unit cost of conversion in the finishing department in April was $1.41, calculated as ($40,555 ÷ [0.8 × 36,000]).

NEW TERMS*

Average cost procedure   A method of computing equivalent units where the number of equivalent units for each cost element equals the number of units transferred out plus the number of equivalent units of that cost element in the ending inventory. *749*

Equivalent units   A method of expressing a given number of partially completed units as a smaller number of fully completed units; for example, bringing 1,000 units to a 75% level of completion is the equivalent of bringing 750 units to a 100% level of completion. *743*

First-in, first-out (FIFO) method   A method of determining unit cost. This method computes equivalent units by adding equivalent units of work needed to complete the units in beginning inventory, work done on units started and completed during the period, and work done on partially completed units in ending inventory. *754*

Job order cost system (job costing)   A manufacturing cost system that accumulates costs incurred to produce a product according to individual jobs. *737*

Joint product costs (common costs)   Costs incurred when a company produces two or more products through the same production process or from a common raw material. *760*

Physical measures method   A method of allocating joint product costs on the basis of physical measures such as units, pounds, or liters. *760*

Process cost system (process costing)   A manufacturing cost system that accumulates costs incurred to produce a product according to the processes or departments a product goes through on its way to completion. *738*

Processing center   An individual process or department in a process cost system that serves as a cost center where accountants accumulate costs for the entire period in question. *738*

Production cost report   A report that shows both the flow of units and the flow of costs through the Work in Process Inventory account of a processing center. It also shows how accountants divide these costs between the cost of units completed and transferred out and the cost of units still in the processing center's ending inventory. *747*

Relative sales value method   A method of allocating joint product costs on the basis of the relative sales value of the products at the split-off point. *761*

Split-off point   A certain stage of production at which the separate products become identifiable from a common processing unit. *760*

Transferred-in costs   Costs associated with physical units that were accumulated in previous processing centers. *743*

---

* Some terms listed in Chapter 13 are repeated here for your convenience.

SELF-TEST

True-False

Indicate whether each of the following statements is true or false.

1. Processing centers in a company using a process cost system serve as cost centers where costs are accumulated over long periods (usually a year).

2. Process cost systems have one Work in Process Inventory account per job.

3. To determine equivalent units, one needs to know the stage of completion of ending inventory.

4. After the equivalent units of production are known, unit costs for transferred-in, materials, and conversion costs can be calculated.

5. *(Based on Appendix 14–B)*   A common basis for allocating joint product costs at the split-off point is the physical measures method.

Multiple-Choice

Select the best answer for each of the following questions.

1. Which of the following statements *does not* apply to process cost systems?
   a. Uses predetermined overhead rate.
   b. The job order cost record is the key document used.
   c. Costs of production are first recorded in separate accounts for materials inventory, labor, and overhead, then transferred to Work in Process Inventory.
   d. Measures overapplied and underapplied overhead.

2. Which of the following formulas is the correct formula for equivalent units of production using the average cost method? Equivalent units of production equal:

   a.
$$\text{Units completed and transferred out} - \left(\begin{array}{c} \text{Units in} \\ \text{ending} \\ \text{inventory} \end{array} \times \begin{array}{c} \text{Percentage} \\ \text{complete} \end{array} \right)$$

   b.
$$\text{Units completed and transferred out} + \left(\begin{array}{c} \text{Units in} \\ \text{ending} \\ \text{inventory} \end{array} \times \begin{array}{c} \text{Percentage} \\ \text{complete} \end{array} \right)$$

   c.
$$\text{Units completed and transferred out} - \left(\begin{array}{c} \text{Units in} \\ \text{beginning} \\ \text{inventory} \end{array} \times \begin{array}{c} \text{Percentage} \\ \text{complete} \end{array} \right)$$

   d. None of the above.

3. Using the following data, compute the ending inventory cost.

   2,000 units are in ending inventory in Department B. The unit cost of goods transferred in from Department A is $1.20. The 2,000 units are fully complete as to materials and 20% complete as to conversion. The unit cost for materials = $0.05, and conversion unit cost = $0.60.

   a. $1,370.
   b. $2,060.
   c. $1,850.
   d. $2,740.

4. Preparation of a production cost report includes which of the following?
   a. Tracing physical flow of units through a production department.
   b. Computing unit costs for each cost element.
   c. Converting actual units to equivalent units.
   d. Distributing the total cost between the units completed and transferred and the units remaining in the ending inventory.
   e. All of the above.

5. *(Based on Appendix 14–A)*   Compute the equivalent units of production under the FIFO method using the data below.

   Beginning inventory, 1,500 units—40% complete
   Units started this period, 5,000 units

Ending inventory, 1,500 units—20% complete

a.	4,700.	c.	4,400.
b.	4,900.	d.	4,600.

Now turn to page 773 to check your answers.

QUESTIONS

1. Define process costing and describe the types of operations accounted for under this cost system.

2. How does a process cost system differ from a job order cost system? What factors should be taken into consideration in determining which type of system should be employed?

3. What is meant by the term *equivalent units?* Of what use is the computation of the numbers of equivalent units of production?

4. Distinguish between the number of units completed and transferred during a period and the equivalent units for the same period.

5. Under what circumstances would the number of equivalent units of materials differ from the equivalent units of labor and overhead in the same department in the same period? Under what circumstances would they be the same?

6. When transferring goods from one department to another, which accounts will be debited and credited?

7. Units are usually assumed to be at the same stage of completion for both labor and overhead. What is the reason for this assumption?

8. What is the basic information conveyed by a production cost report?

9. What are the four steps in preparing a production cost report?

10. What is meant by average cost procedure? What other two cost flow assumptions could be used?

11. Less effort is required to operate a job cost system than a process cost system. Do you agree or disagree? Explain.

12. *(Based on Appendix 14–A)*   Show the differences between computing equivalent units of production using the average cost method and FIFO cost method.

13. *(Based on Appendix 14–B)*   Describe the relative sales value method and show how it is used.

14. *Real-world question*   Refer to "A Broader Perspective" on page 745. What changes at Borg-Warner affected the company's cost system? How was the cost system affected?

The Coca-Cola Company

15. *Real-world question*   Refer to Appendix C at the end of this text. Do you think The Coca-Cola Company uses a process cost system or a job order cost system? Why?

The Coca-Cola Company

16. *Real-world question*   Refer to Appendix C at the end of this text. Suppose

Coca-Cola made an error in estimating the stage of completion of its ending work in process inventory in 1991. Suppose the costs in beginning inventory and the costs transferred in were correct. However, the company overstated the stage of completion for both materials and conversion costs in ending Work in Process Inventory causing ending Work in Process Inventory to be 10% too high. The beginning and ending Finished Goods Inventory amounts are correct. What effect would this error have on Coca-Cola's 1991 financial statements?

17. *Real-world question*   Name five companies that probably use process costing.

EXERCISES

Compute equivalent units (L.O. 4)

14–1. The 6,000 units in the April ending inventory were 80% complete as to materials and 40% complete as to conversion. Determine the number of equivalent units for materials and conversion in the ending inventory.

Compute equivalent units (L.O. 4)

14–2. Using the average cost method, compute the equivalent units in each case given below:

a. Units started in production during the month, 17,000; units completed and transferred, 13,200; and units in process at end of month (100% complete as to materials; 60% complete as to conversion), 3,800.

b. Units in process at beginning of month (100% complete as to materials; 30% complete as to processing), 4,000; units started during month, 13,000; and units in process at end of month (100% complete as to materials; 40% complete as to conversion), 5,000.

Compute equivalent units (L.O. 4)

14–3. In Department F, materials are added at the beginning of the process. Assume that 800 units were in beginning inventory, 10,900 units were started during the month, and 7,100 units were completed and transferred to finished goods inventory. The ending inventory in Department F in June was 20% complete as to conversion costs. Under the average cost method, what are the equivalent units of production for materials and conversion?

Compute equivalent units (L.O. 4)

14–4. In Department Z, materials are added uniformly throughout processing. The beginning inventory was considered 40% complete, as was the ending inventory. Assume that 3,000 units were in the beginning inventory, 9,000 units were in the ending inventory, and 50,000 units were completed and transferred. If the average unit costs are to be computed, what is the equivalent production for the period?

Compute costs of the units completed and transferred (L.O. 4)

14–5. If in Exercise 14–4 the total costs charged to the department amounted to $619,200, including the $18,090 cost of the beginning inventory, what is the cost of the units completed and transferred?

Calculate cost per equivalent unit; determine costs of units transferred (L.O. 4)

14–6. The following data relate to Department X, in which all materials are added at the start of processing and in which the weight of the finished product is equal to the weight of the direct materials used:

Inventory, November 1:	
Materials cost (1,200 pounds)	$ 3,516
Conversion cost (20% complete).	458

Costs incurred this period:

Direct materials used (8,000 pounds at $2.01)	16,080
Direct labor (900 hours at $6.60).	5,940
Overhead (at $6 per machine-hour; 1,485 machine-hours incurred) .	8,910

Inventory, November 30:
Materials cost (1,800 pounds, 100% complete)
Conversion cost (1,800 pounds, ⅔ complete)

Using the above data, compute:

a. The number of pounds transferred out of the department in November.

b. The unit cost per equivalent unit for materials and conversion (use the average cost method).

c. The cost of the product transferred out.

Compute equivalent units and conversion cost element in ending inventory (L.O. 4)

14–7. Wesley Company manufactures golf bags. On March 31, Department Q had an ending inventory of 53,200 units, 60% complete as to conversion. What is the equivalent number of units for conversion in the ending inventory? If the conversion cost per equivalent unit is $2.15, how much is the conversion cost element in the ending inventory?

PROBLEMS

Calculate equivalent units, costs per equivalent units, cost of goods completed, and cost of ending inventory (L.O. 4)

14–1. The following data pertain to a production center of Garbco Company, a maker of garbage bins:

Work in process inventory, August 1, 4,200 units (a unit equals one bin):	
Direct materials	$ 6,932
Direct labor	2,526
Manufacturing overhead (at $6 per machine-hour; 639 machine-hours were incurred)	3,834
	$13,292

Units started in August.	11,600

Costs incurred in August:

Direct materials	$17,400
Direct labor	24,000
Manufacturing overhead applied (6,000 machine-hours were incurred)	?

The ending inventory consisted of 6,000 units (100% complete as to materials, 70% complete as to conversion).

Required:

Compute the following:

a. Number of units completed and transferred to finished goods inventory.

b. The equivalent units of production for materials and conversion using the average cost method.

c. Cost per equivalent unit. Round to the nearest cent.

d. Cost of units completed and transferred.

e. Cost of ending inventory.

Prepare
production cost
report
(L.O. 5)

14–2. The following information relates to The Swing Company for its line of children's swing sets for the month ended June 30, 1995:

Units in beginning inventory (a unit equals one swing set)	4,400
Costs of units in beginning inventory:	
Materials	$ 40,500
Conversion	$ 18,990
Units placed in production	108,000
Costs incurred during current period:	
Materials	$239,376
Conversion	$215,310
Units remaining in ending inventory	
(100% complete as to materials, 60% complete as to conversion) .	6,000

Required:

Prepare a production cost report for the month ended June 30, 1995, using the average cost method.

Prepare
production cost
report
(L.O. 5)

14–3. Quick Food Company uses a process cost system to account for the costs incurred in making its single product, a nutritional snack called Quick Snack. This product is processed first in Department A and then in Department B. Materials are added in both departments. Production for May 1995 was as follows:

	Department A	Department B
Units started or transferred in.	200,000	157,500
Units completed and transferred out	157,500	133,000
Stage of completion of May 31 inventory:		
Materials	100%	80%
Conversion	50%	40%
Direct materials costs	$126,000	$ 21,364
Conversion costs	$368,225	$249,900

No beginning inventory existed in either department.

Required:

a. Prepare a production cost report for Department A in May.

b. Prepare a production cost report for Department B in May.

Prepare
production cost
report
(L.O. 5)

14–4. Gifford Company manufactures frozen dinners and determines product costs using a process cost system. Following are cost and production data for the mixing department for March 1995:

	Units	Materials Costs	Conversion Costs
Inventory, March 1	56,000	$ 6,810	$ 9,120
Placed in production in March . . .	133,000	15,870	21,309
Inventory, March 31	63,000	?	?

The March 31 inventory was 100% complete as to materials and 30% complete as to conversion.

Required:

Prepare a production cost report for the month ended March 31 using the average cost method.

Prepare production cost report using FIFO (based on Appendix 14–A) (L.O. 6)

14–5. Refer to the facts given in Problem 14–4.

Required:

a. Prepare a production cost report for the month ended March 31, using FIFO. The March 1 inventory was 100% complete as to materials and 25% complete as to conversion. Round unit costs to the nearest cent.

b. Why are ending inventory amounts different than those for Problem 14–4?

Allocate common costs to joint products (based on Appendix 14–B) (L.O. 7)

14–6. Glacier Mining Company produces two products from ore—copper and zinc. The following events took place in June:

	Copper	Zinc	Total
Units produced	40,000	60,000	100,000
Unit selling price at split-off . . .	$2.00	$1.00	
Joint costs			$110,000

Required:

a. Allocate the joint costs to the two products using the physical measures method.

b. Allocate the joint costs to the two products using the relative sales value method.

c. Explain the difference in unit costs using the two methods.

d. Which method do you think better allocates joint costs? Why?

BUSINESS DECISION PROBLEM

Determine how production costs should be allocated (L.O. 6)

Vilnova Manufacturing Company manufactures thousands of armchairs every year. While the company has developed a per unit cost for its armchairs, it has not been able to accurately break down its costs in each of its three departments: cutting, assembling, and packaging. Rita Reno, the production manager, has been concerned with cost overruns during July in the assembling department.

On July 1, the assembling department had 6,000 units in its work in process inventory. These units were 100% complete as to materials and 40% complete as to conversion. The department had incurred $12,300 in materials costs and $95,232 in conversion costs in processing these 6,000 units.

The department handled 30,000 units during the month, including the 6,000 units in beginning inventory on July 1. At the end of the month, the department's work in process included 3,600 units that were 100% complete as to materials and 30%

complete as to conversion. The month's costs were allocated based on the number of units processed during the month as follows:

	Materials	Conversion
Costs	$58,800	$273,000
Units handled during month . . .	30,000	30,000
Cost per unit	$1.96	$9.10

The $11.06 per unit cost was systematically allocated and resulted in the following costs:

	Beginning Work in Process	Work Started and Completed	Ending Work in Process
Costs transferred in	$105,600		
Costs incurred during the month:			
Units	6,000	20,400	3,600
Cost per unit	$11.06	$11.06	$11.06
Allocated costs	$ 66,360	$225,624	$39,816
Total costs	$171,960	$225,624	$39,816
Total per unit cost	$28.66		

Ms. Reno realized that this per unit cost allocation is incorrect because the beginning work in process has too high a per unit cost. She asks you to develop a better method of allocating these costs for the month ended July 31, 1995.

Required:

a. How would you recommend to Ms. Reno that July's costs be assigned to the units produced? How would this approach differ from her present method?

b. To justify your recommendation, recalculate July's costs using your recommendation. Present your analysis in a production cost report.

COMPREHENSIVE REVIEW PROBLEM

Covers material discussed in Chapters 12 through 14. Topics include product costing, cost flows, job costing, and underapplied/overapplied overhead

P.R. Company assembles speech output computer devices. These devices allow people with speech disabilities to communicate. The speech output computer devices go through several departments where subassemblies are unpacked and checked, the circuit boards are attached, the products are tested and repaired if defective, and the computers are packed carefully for shipping. Each order is treated as a job, and the entire job is shipped at once. The company keeps track of costs by job and calculates the equivalent stage of completion for each job based on labor-hours.

The company has grown rapidly, but has yet to show a profit. You have been called in as a consultant. Management believes some jobs are profitable and others are not, but it is not clear which jobs are profitable. You find the accounting system is almost nonexistent, but you piece together the following information for April:

1. Production:
    a. Completed Job No. 101.

      b.   Started and completed Job No. 102.

      c.   Started Job No. 103.

2. Inventory values:

      a.   Work in process inventory:

March 31: Job No. 101—Direct materials	$40,000
—Direct labor: 480 hours @ $18 . . .	8,640
—Overhead	14,400
April 30: Job No. 103 —Direct materials	40,000
—Direct labor: 520 hours @ $18 . . .	9,360
—Overhead	15,600

      b.   Job No. 101 was exactly one-half completed in labor-hours at the beginning of April, and Job No. 103 was exactly one-half completed in labor-hours at the end of April. However, all of the direct materials necessary to complete the entire job were charged to each job as soon as the job was started.

      c.   No direct materials inventories or finished goods inventories existed at either March 31 or April 30.

3. Manufacturing overhead is applied at $30 per direct labor-hour. Actual overhead for April was $49,000.

4. Cost of goods sold (before adjustment for over- or underapplied overhead):

Job No. 101:		Job No. 102:	
Materials	$40,000	Materials	?
Labor	?	Labor	?
Overhead	?	Overhead	?
Total	?	Total	?

5. Overhead was applied to jobs using a predetermined rate per labor-hour. The same rate had been used since the company began operations. Over- or underapplied overhead is debited or credited to Cost of Goods Sold at the end of each month.

6. All direct materials were purchased on account. Direct materials purchased and used in April amounted to $100,000.

7. Direct labor costs charged to jobs in April were $27,720. All labor costs were the same rate per hour for all laborers in April.

Required:

a. Show the transactions in journal entry and T-account form. A separate Work in Process Inventory account should be used for each job.

b. Compute the cost of each job, whether sold or in inventory.

ANSWERS TO SELF-TEST

True-False

1. *False.* Processing centers are cost centers where costs are accumulated for short periods, such as a month.

2. *False.* Process cost systems have a Work in Process Inventory account for each department or process.

3. *True.* The stage of completion of ending inventory is needed to compute equivalent units.

4. *True.* Unit costs can be calculated after the equivalent units for each cost element are known.

5. *True.* The physical measures method is a common basis for allocating joint product costs at split-off.

Multiple-Choice

1. *b.* The department production cost report is the key document.

2. *b.* Units completed and transferred out

$$+ \left(\begin{array}{c} \text{Units in} \\ \text{ending inventory} \end{array} \times \begin{array}{c} \text{Percentage} \\ \text{complete} \end{array} \right)$$

$$= \begin{array}{c} \text{Equivalent units} \\ \text{of production} \end{array}$$

3. *d.*

Costs from Dept. A		
(2,000 × $1.20).		$2,400
Costs added by Dept. B:		
Materials (2,000 × $0.05) .	$100	
Conversion (400 × $0.60).	240	340
Total cost of ending		
inventory		$2,740

4. *e.* The production cost report includes all of these data.

5. *a.* The equivalent production for the period would be:

Equivalent units of work done to complete the beginning inventory (1,500 × 0.60)	900
Units started and completed this period in ending inventory (5,000 − 1,500)	3,500
Equivalent units of work done to partially complete the ending inventory (1,500 × 0.20)	300
Equivalent units of production	4,700

V

MANAGERIAL ACCOUNTING: DECISION MAKING, PLANNING, AND CONTROL

15

COST-VOLUME-PROFIT ANALYSIS

LEARNING OBJECTIVES

After studying this chapter, you should be able to:

1. Explain and describe different cost behavior patterns.
2. Calculate the break-even point for a company.
3. Explain the effects of changing costs or selling price on the break-even point; calculate the margin of safety.
4. List the assumptions underlying cost-volume-profit analysis.
5. Demonstrate various applications of cost-volume-profit analysis.

In making decisions, management must frequently distinguish between short-run decision making and long-run decision making. The term **short run** describes a time frame during which a company's management cannot change the effects of certain past decisions. The short-run time frame is often considered to be one year or less. In the short run, many costs, such as depreciation expense, are assumed to be fixed and unchangeable. Since all costs are subject to change in the long run, short-run decision making uses different criteria than long-run decision making.

In this chapter, you will be introduced to some of the analytical tools that can be used to make short-run decisions. The chapter begins with a discussion of cost behavior patterns because the classification of costs as fixed or variable is the first step in using the analytical tools. You will find this chapter discusses fixed and variable costs in greater depth than Chapter 12. Our goal in this chapter is to explain how to apply cost concepts to profit planning using cost-volume-profit analysis.

COST BEHAVIOR PATTERNS

Objective 1
Explain and de-
scribe different
cost behavior
patterns

Illustration 15.1 shows four basic cost behavior patterns: fixed, variable, mixed (semivariable), and step. As discussed in earlier chapters, **fixed costs** remain constant over some relevant range of output and are often described as time-related costs. Depreciation, insurance, property taxes, and adminis- trative salaries are examples of fixed costs.

In contrast, **variable costs** vary directly with changes in volume of pro- duction or sales. Direct materials, direct labor, and sales commissions are examples of variable costs. Mixed costs and step costs have both fixed and variable characteristics. These costs must be analyzed to separate the fixed and variable portions contained in each.

A **mixed cost** contains a fixed portion of cost that will be incurred even when the facility is idle and a variable portion that will increase directly with volume. Electricity is an example of a mixed cost. A company must incur a certain amount of cost to have any electrical service. As the company in- creases its volume of activity, it runs more machines and runs them longer. Also, the company may extend its hours of operation. Illustration 15.2 shows how to separate the fixed and variable portions of a mixed cost such as electricity.

A **step cost** remains constant at a certain fixed amount over a short range of output (or sales). Then, at certain points, the step costs increase to higher amounts. Visually, step costs appear like stair steps. A step cost with many small steps is called a **step variable cost;** a step cost with only a few large steps is called a **step fixed cost.** Both step variable costs and step fixed costs have fixed and variable portions.

An example of a step variable cost is the cost of water. The utility company charges a flat fee for providing water (fixed component) and an additional amount that depends on the quantity of water used (variable com- ponent). The variable charge for electricity is often given on an hour-by-hour basis. The charge for water, however, may be stated in increments such as $10 for the first 1,000 gallons or less, $5 additional for use of 1,001 to 5,000

Illustration 15.1
FOUR COST PATTERNS

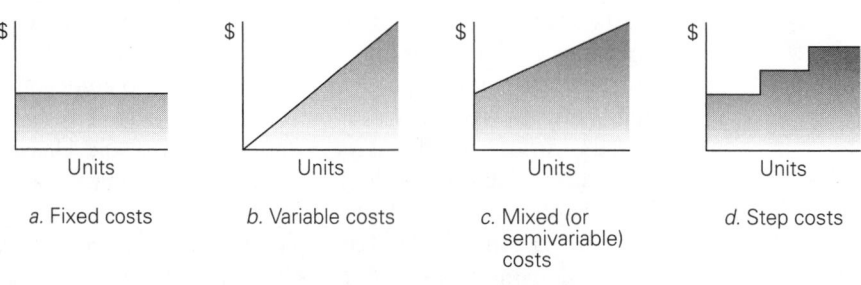

a. Fixed costs	b. Variable costs	c. Mixed (or semivariable) costs	d. Step costs

Illustration 15.2
SEPARATION OF MIXED COSTS

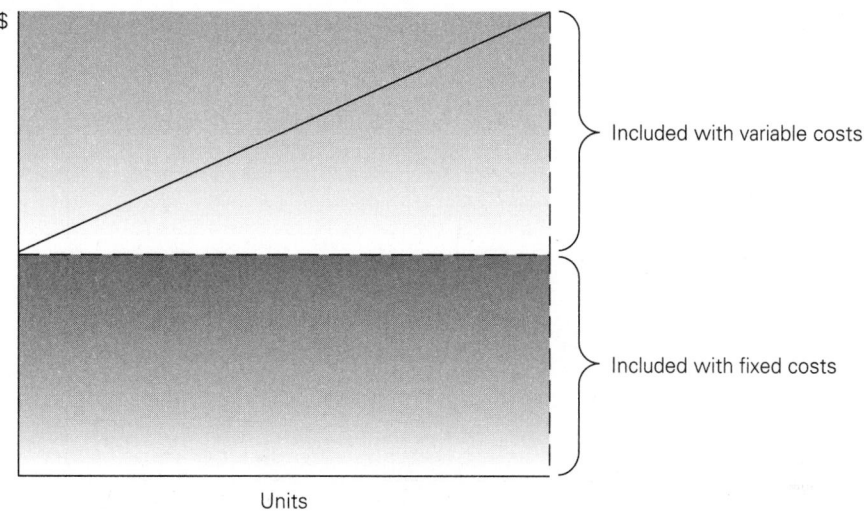

For decision making, management must separate mixed costs and step

gallons, $8 additional for use of 5,001 to 10,000 gallons, and so on. Illustration 15.3 shows the separation of a step variable cost into its fixed and variable portions.

Supervisors' salaries are an example of a step fixed cost when companies hire additional supervisors as production increases. At any level of production from 1 unit to 40,000 units, one supervisor is necessary at a salary of $20,000 per year. If the company produces at a level of 40,001 units but below 100,000 units, the company must hire a second supervisor at an additional cost of $20,000. Illustration 15.4 shows a step fixed cost for supervisors' salaries based on production.

For decision making, management must separate mixed costs and step costs into their fixed and variable components. Mixed costs and step variable costs can be easily broken down into these two components. The fixed portion of these costs is included with other fixed costs, while the variable portion is shown as directly increasing with increases in volume. As stated above, Illustration 15.2 shows the separation of a mixed cost into fixed and variable portions; Illustration 15.3 shows the separation of a step variable cost. A step fixed cost, however, is fixed over a relatively wide range of activity. Thus, for decision-making purposes, management treats a step fixed cost as entirely fixed. Management estimates the level of operations and then treats the step fixed cost expected at that level as a fixed cost for decision making.

Although we have described four different types of cost patterns (fixed,

**Illustration 15.3
SEPARATION OF A STEP VARIABLE COST**

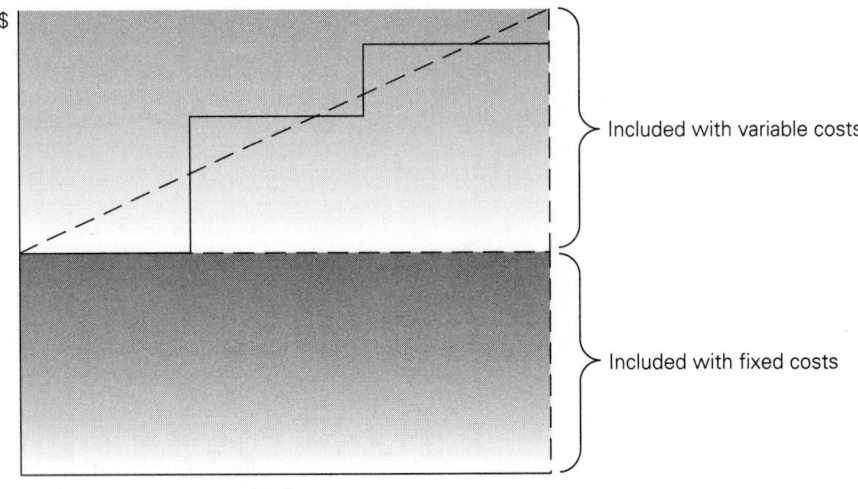

Even though step variable costs do not vary directly with changes in volume, they can be treated for planning purposes as though they are directly variable costs. The slanted dashed line represents the smoothing of the step variable cost into a directly variable cost.

**Illustration 15.4
A STEP FIXED COST**

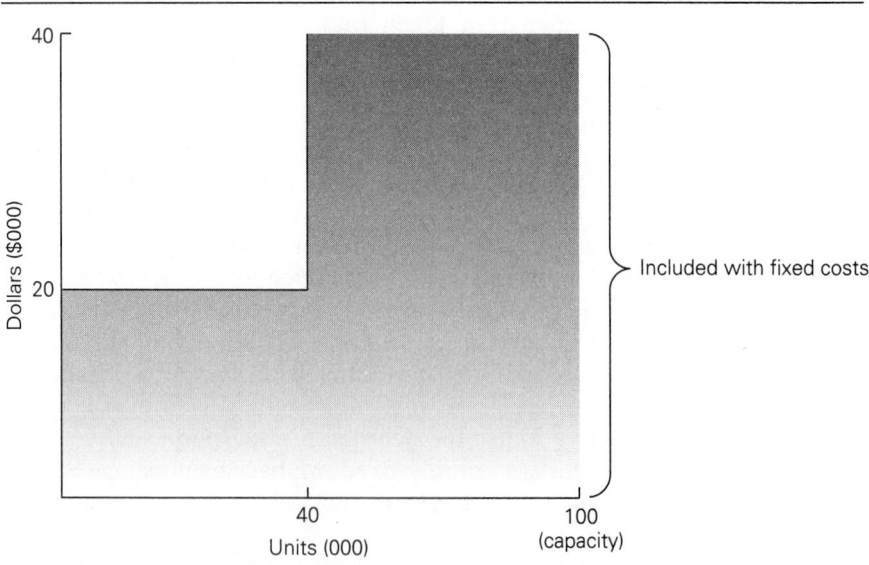

variable, mixed, and step), the fixed and variable categories may be used to include all cost patterns.

Before proceeding to the next discussion on analyzing costs, you should be aware that some variable costs do not vary in a strictly linear relationship with volume. Rather, they vary in a curvilinear pattern—a 10% increase in volume may yield an 8% change in costs at lower output levels and an 11% change in costs at higher output levels. Illustration 15.5 diagrams a curvilinear relationship. In the remainder of this chapter, however, we assume that variable costs vary in a linear relationship with volume to simplify the analysis.

Methods for Analyzing Costs

Several methods are available for breaking down a mixed cost or a step variable cost into its fixed and variable cost components. Two of these procedures are the *scatter diagram* and the *high-low method*.

The Scatter Diagram. A **scatter diagram** shows plots of actual costs incurred for various levels of output or sales. The dots on the scatter diagram in Illustration 15.6 represent total actual maintenance costs for a company's fleet of delivery trucks at various levels of past activity. Costs associated with activities from different time periods must be adjusted for inflation to make them comparable. A line is drawn through what appears visually to be the center of the pattern formed by the dots. In Illustration 15.6, the fixed element of the mixed cost is $23,000, since that figure is the amount of cost at

**Illustration 15.5
CURVILINEAR COST PATTERN**

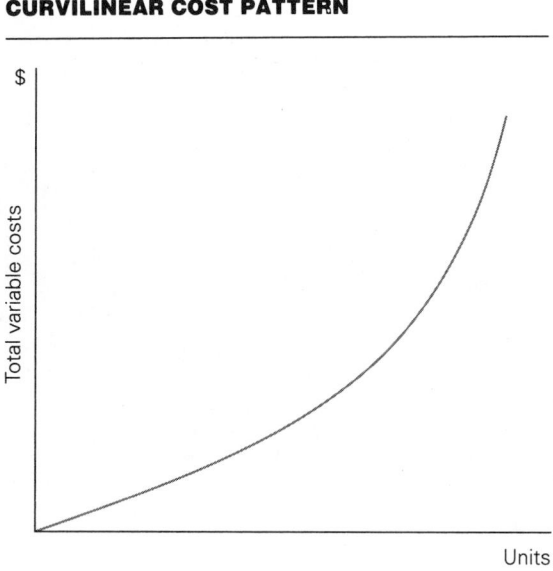

zero volume of output. The line rises from $23,000 to $63,000 over the range of 100,000 miles. We can now compute the variable cost portion as follows:

$$\frac{\$63,000 - \$23,000}{100,000 \text{ miles}} = \$0.40 \text{ per mile}$$

The data in Illustration 15.6 suggest that the company's truck maintenance costs can be estimated at $23,000 plus 40 cents for every mile driven.

Many companies use a more sophisticated technique, called the **least-squares method,** to derive the line that best fits the data, known as a *regression line*. This line divides mixed costs into their fixed and variable portions. The least-squares method is covered in statistics and cost accounting texts.

The High-Low Method.   The **high-low method** is also used to identify the behavior of mixed costs. This method uses only the highest and lowest points (levels of operation) on a scatter diagram to fit a line to the data.

To illustrate, the lowest point in Illustration 15.6 is $38,000 of expense at 30,000 miles driven, and the highest point is $60,000 at 80,000 miles. The amount of variable cost per mile is found as follows:

$$\frac{\text{Change in cost}}{\text{Change in units}} = \frac{\$60,000 - \$38,000}{80,000 - 30,000 \text{ miles}} = \frac{\$22,000}{50,000 \text{ miles}} = \$0.44 \text{ per mile}$$

Illustration 15.6
SCATTER DIAGRAM

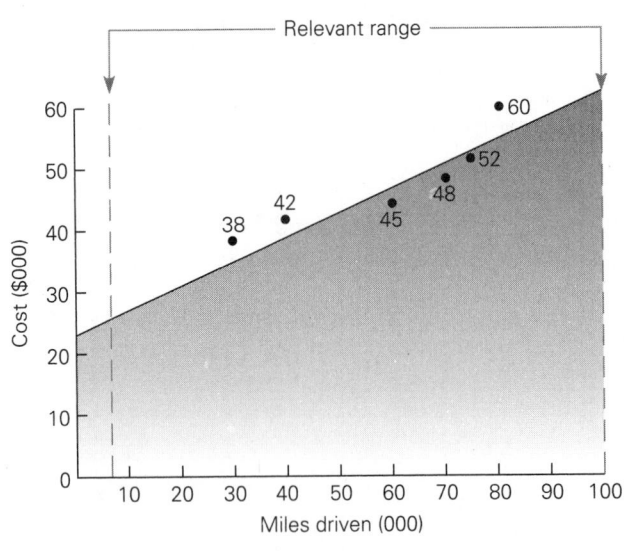

The fixed portion is then found as follows:

Total cost at 80,000 miles of output.	$60,000
Less: Variable cost at that level of output (80,000 × $0.44)	35,200
Fixed cost at all levels of output within the relevant range	$24,800

The high-low method is less precise than the scatter diagram since it uses only two data points in the computation. Either or both points may not be representative of the data as a whole.

Now that you understand cost patterns and how to analyze costs, we will apply these concepts to specific tools that managers use in short-term decision making. The first of these tools is *cost-volume-profit (CVP) analysis*.

COST-VOLUME-PROFIT (CVP) ANALYSIS

Objective 2
Calculate the break-even point for a company

Companies use **cost-volume-profit (CVP) analysis** (sometimes called **break-even analysis**) to determine what effects changes in their selling prices, costs, and/or volume will have on income in the short run. The starting point of this analysis is the company's break-even point. A company is said to *break even* for a given period if sales revenue and costs charged to that period are equal. Thus, the **break-even point** is that level of operations at which a company realizes no net income or loss.

A careful and accurate cost-volume-profit (CVP) analysis requires knowledge of costs and their behavior (i.e., fixed or variable) as volume changes. The types and quantities of cost data accumulated depend on the costs of obtaining the data compared to the benefits of having more refined information. Within this constraint, break-even points should be computed for each area of decision making within the company. Some important classifications of cost data for break-even analysis are by product, territory, salesperson, or class of customer.

This section first explains how to calculate the break-even point. Next, we illustrate a break-even chart and describe actions that a company can take to change the break-even point. Then, we show you how to calculate a company's margin of safety. Also, we describe the assumptions used in CVP analysis. Finally, we illustrate CVP analysis for both single and multiproduct companies.

Calculation of the Break-Even Point

A company may express a break-even point in dollars of sales revenue or number of units produced or sold. No matter how a company expresses its break-even point, it is still the point of zero income or loss.

To illustrate the calculation of a break-even point, assume Video Productions produces video tapes that sell for $20 per unit. Fixed costs per period total $40,000, while variable cost per unit is $12. The **variable cost ratio** is 60% ($12/$20). That is, for each dollar of sales, the company incurs $0.60 of variable cost. The sales revenue needed to break even is that point at which the company covers all costs but generates no income. Therefore, the break-even point can be expressed as:

$$\text{Sales} = \text{Fixed costs} + \text{Variable costs}$$

or

$$S = FC + VC$$

Substituting the Video Productions' fixed costs and variable cost ratio into the formula gives the following:

$$
\begin{aligned}
S &= \$40{,}000 + 0.60S \\
S - 0.60S &= \$40{,}000 \\
0.40S &= \$40{,}000 \\
S &= \$40{,}000 \div 0.40 \\
S &= \$100{,}000
\end{aligned}
$$

Sales revenue at the break-even point is $100,000. To compute the break-even point in units, simply divide the $100,000 of sales by the $20 selling price per unit. This calculation gives a break-even point of 5,000 units.

If desired, the break-even point can be expressed in terms of capacity. Newspaper reports often refer to the break-even point of the automobile industry, or of a company in that industry, as being a stated percentage of capacity, for example, 55%. If in the example presented above, the output capacity of the plant was 25,000 units, then the break-even point would be 20% of plant capacity, calculated as 5,000/25,000.

Alternatively, we could first calculate the break-even point in units. This calculation involves a concept known as *contribution margin*. The **contribution margin** is the amount by which revenue exceeds variable costs of producing that revenue; it can be calculated on a per unit or total sales volume basis. On a per unit basis, the contribution margin for Video Productions is $8, which equals the selling price of $20 less the variable cost per unit of $12. The contribution margin indicates the amount of money remaining after the company covers its variable costs. This remainder *contributes* to the coverage of fixed costs and to the generation of net income. We can compute the break-even point (BEP) in units by dividing total fixed costs by the contribution margin per unit.

$$BEP_{units} = \frac{\text{Fixed costs}}{\text{Contribution margin per unit}}$$

$$BEP_{units} = \frac{\$40{,}000}{\$8 \text{ per unit}}$$

$$= 5{,}000 \text{ units}$$

Earlier, we stated that the break-even point in sales dollars could be found by using the formula $S = FC + VC$. Another method that companies use to find the break-even point in sales dollars is to divide the total fixed costs by the *contribution margin ratio*. The **contribution margin ratio** expresses the contribution margin per unit as a percentage of selling price per unit. Video Productions' contribution margin ratio is:

$$\frac{\text{Contribution margin per unit}}{\text{Selling price per unit}} = \frac{\$20 - \$12}{\$20} = \frac{\$8}{\$20} = 0.40$$

Using this ratio, we can calculate Video Productions' break-even point in sales dollars as:

$$\text{BEP}_{\text{dollars}} = \frac{\text{Fixed costs}}{\text{Contribution margin ratio}}$$

$$\text{BEP}_{\text{dollars}} = \frac{\$40,000}{0.40}$$

$$= \$100,000$$

Cost-Volume-Profit Chart

A **cost-volume-profit (CVP) chart** is a graph that shows the relationships between sales revenues, costs, volume, and profit and also shows the break-even point. Illustration 15.7 presents the CVP chart for Video Productions. Each CVP chart or calculation is valid only for a specified *relevant range* of volume.

The **relevant range** is the range of production or sales volume over which the basic cost behavior assumptions will hold true. For volumes outside these ranges, costs will behave differently and will alter the assumed relationships. For example, if Video Productions produced more than 10,000 units, it might need to increase plant capacity (thus incurring additional fixed costs) or to use extra shifts (thus incurring overtime charges and other inefficiencies). In either case, the cost relationships first assumed would no longer be valid.

Illustration 15.7 shows cost data for Video Productions in a relevant range of output from 500 to 10,000 units. It shows that the break-even volume of sales is $100,000 (5,000 units at $20 per unit). At this level of sales, fixed costs plus variable costs equal sales revenue, as shown below.

Revenues.	$100,000
Less: Variable costs.	60,000
Contribution margin.	$ 40,000
Less: Fixed costs	40,000
Net income	$ –0–

Illustration 15.7
THE COST-VOLUME-PROFIT CHART

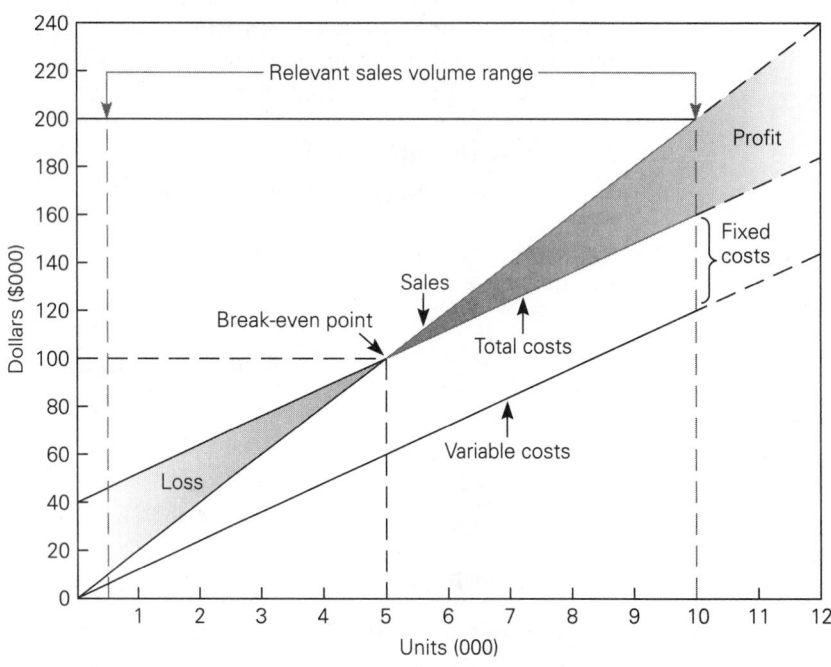

Illustration 15.8 shows how the CVP chart can be relabeled to indicate the contribution margin. It also shows that total contribution margin equals fixed costs at the break-even point.

The CVP charts in Illustrations 15.7 and 15.8 show that in a period of complete idleness, Video Productions will produce a loss of $40,000 (the amount of fixed costs). However, when Video Productions has an output of 10,000 units, the company will have net income of $40,000. Other points on the graphs show that sales of 7,500 units will result in $150,000 of revenue. At that point, Video Productions' total costs amount to $130,000, leaving net income of $20,000. The charts also show that you can find net income at any level of output by multiplying the contribution margin per unit by the number of units sold and subtracting total fixed costs from the result.

Changing the Break-Even Point

Objective 3
Explain the effects of changing costs or selling price on the break-even point; calculate the margin of safety

A company can raise or lower its break-even point by changing its selling price, variable cost per unit, or total fixed costs. By lowering its break-even point, a company can earn income at a lower volume of operations. If the company increases its selling price or lowers its variable cost per unit, it will lower its break-even point because its contribution margin per unit will be

Illustration 15.8
COST-VOLUME-PROFIT CHART SHOWING THAT FIXED COSTS EQUAL
CONTRIBUTION MARGIN AT BREAK-EVEN POINT

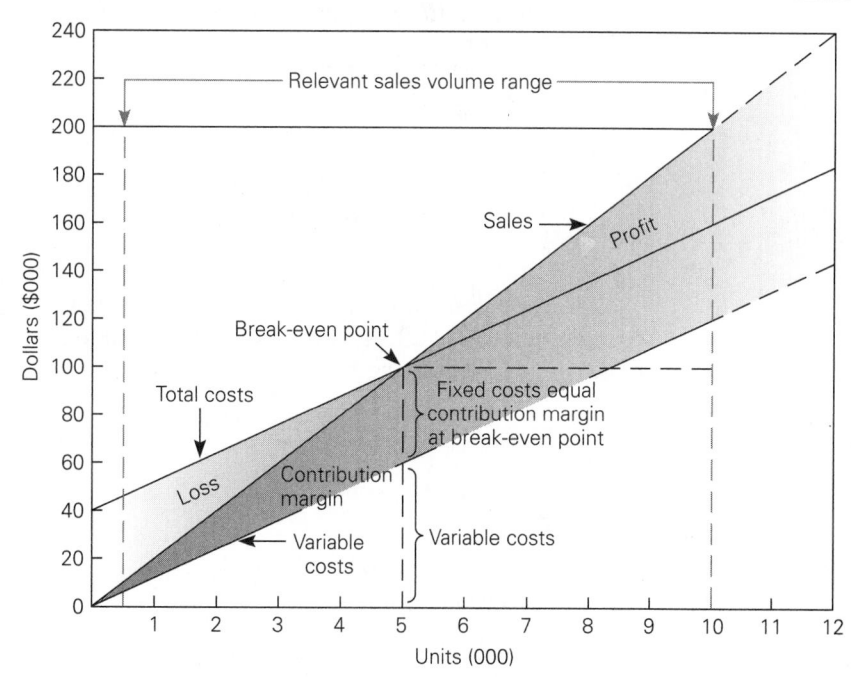

larger. A larger contribution margin means that the company can use more of the selling price of each unit to cover fixed costs. Similarly, if a company decreases its total fixed costs, it must sell fewer units to cover the smaller amount of fixed costs.

These actions in reverse will create a higher break-even point. That is, lowering the selling price, increasing the variable cost per unit, or increasing total fixed costs will raise the break-even point.

To illustrate the effect of changing the (1) selling price, (2) variable cost per unit, or (3) total fixed costs to lower the break-even point, consider the following situation for Smogchek, a company that performs tests on automobiles to see if they pass the state's automobile emissions standards. Smogchek charges $60 for each test. Variable cost per test is $15, or 25% of selling price, and fixed costs are $27,000 per month. The break-even point is $36,000 of sales revenue, computed as follows:

$$S = FC + VC$$
$$S = \$27,000 + 0.25S$$
$$0.75S = \$27,000$$
$$S = \$36,000$$

As shown below, companies have some flexibility in the means of adjusting their break-even points. Of course, companies attempt to operate at a level of operations *above* the break-even point to make a profit.

Increasing Selling Price.   If Smogchek can increase its selling price to $75 while keeping variable costs and fixed costs the same, the variable cost rate becomes 20%, or $15/$75. The break-even point will then decrease to $33,750 of sales:

$$S = FC + VC$$
$$S = \$27{,}000 + 0.20S$$
$$0.80S = \$27{,}000$$
$$S = \$33{,}750$$

Reduce Variable Cost per Unit.   If Smogchek can reduce the variable cost per unit to $13.20 and thus reduce the variable cost rate to 22% of selling price, or $13.20/$60, the break-even point can be lowered:

$$S = FC + VC$$
$$S = \$27{,}000 + 0.22S$$
$$0.78S = \$27{,}000$$
$$S = \$34{,}615$$

Reduce Total Fixed Costs.   If Smogchek can reduce its total fixed costs by $3,000 to $24,000, the break-even point is again reduced:

$$S = FC + VC$$
$$S = \$24{,}000 + 0.25S$$
$$0.75S = \$24{,}000$$
$$S = \$32{,}000$$

Margin of Safety

If a company's current sales are above its break-even point, then the company has a *margin of safety* equal to current sales less break-even sales. The **margin of safety** is the amount by which sales can decrease before the company incurs a loss. For example, assume that a company currently has sales of $250,000 and its break-even sales are $200,000. The margin of safety is $50,000, computed as follows:

$$\text{Margin of safety} = \text{Current sales} - \text{Break-even sales}$$
$$= \$250{,}000 - \$200{,}000$$
$$= \$50{,}000$$

Sometimes companies express the margin of safety as a percentage, called the *margin of safety rate*. The **margin of safety rate** is equal to (Current sales − Break-even sales)/Current sales. Using data from the company just discussed, the margin of safety rate would be computed as follows:

$$\text{Margin of safety rate} = \frac{\text{Current sales} - \text{Break-even sales}}{\text{Current sales}}$$

$$= \frac{\$250,000 - \$200,000}{\$250,000}$$

$$= 20\%$$

This calculation shows that sales volume could drop by 20% before the company would incur a loss.

ASSUMPTIONS MADE IN COST-VOLUME-PROFIT ANALYSIS

Objective 4
List the assumptions underlying cost-volume-profit analysis

The assumptions underlying CVP analysis are:

1. Selling price, variable cost per unit, and total fixed costs remain constant throughout a relevant range of output. This assumption means that a company can sell more units or fewer units at the same price and that the company has no change in technical efficiency as volume changes.
2. The number of units produced equals the number of units sold.
3. In multiproduct situations, the product mix is known in advance. (We discuss multiproduct situations later in this chapter.)
4. Costs can be accurately classified into their fixed and variable portions.

These assumptions can be criticized as being unrealistic in many situations, but they simplify the analysis a great deal.

Cost-Volume-Profit Analysis Illustrated

CVP analysis has many applications. This section illustrates several applications using airline data.

Objective 5
Demonstrate the various applications of cost-volume-profit analysis

Calculating the Break-Even Point.   The management of a major airline wishes to know how many seats must be sold on Flight 529 to break even. To solve this problem, management must first identify and separate costs into fixed and variable categories.

The fixed costs of Flight 529 are the same regardless of the number of seats filled. Fixed costs include items such as the fuel required to fly the plane and crew (with no passengers) to its destination; depreciation on the plane used on the flight; and salaries of required crew members, gate attendants, and maintenance and refueling personnel.

The variable costs will vary directly with the number of passengers. Variable costs include meals and beverages provided to passengers, baggage handling costs, and the cost of the additional fuel required to fly the plane with passengers to its destination. Each variable cost should be expressed on a per person basis.

Assume that after company analysts have analyzed the various costs and separated them into fixed or variable categories, they find the fixed costs for Flight 529 are $12,000 and variable costs are $25 per passenger. Tickets are sold for $125. Thus, the variable cost ratio is 20% ($25/$125). The contribution margin ratio is 80% [($125 − $25)/$125].

We can express the break-even point in sales revenue (dollars) or in number of passengers. The sales revenue needed to break even is:

$$\text{Sales} = \text{Fixed costs} + \text{Variable costs}$$
$$S = FC + VC$$
$$S = \$12{,}000 + 0.20S$$
$$0.80S = \$12{,}000$$
$$S = \$15{,}000$$

The break-even point in dollars can also be found as follows:

$$BEP_{\text{dollars}} = \frac{\text{Fixed costs}}{\text{Contribution margin ratio}}$$

$$= \frac{\$12{,}000}{0.80}$$

$$= \$15{,}000$$

We can find the break-even point in number of passengers (units) by dividing fixed costs by the contribution margin per unit:

$$BEP_{\text{units}} = \frac{\text{Fixed costs}}{\text{Contribution margin per unit (or passenger)}}$$

$$= \frac{\$12{,}000}{\$125 - \$25}$$

$$= 120 \text{ passengers}$$

Calculating Sales Volume Needed for Desired Net Income.   With a simple adjustment in the break-even formulas, CVP analysis can also show the sales volume needed to generate some desired level of net income (ignoring taxes). To make this adjustment, management adds the desired income amount to the total costs that must be covered. From this calculation, management can determine the sales volume in dollars or units needed to provide the desired net income. For example, if the airline wishes to earn $8,000 of income on Flight 529, the company can calculate the amount of necessary sales revenue by the following formula:

$$\text{Sales} = \text{Fixed costs} + \text{Variable costs} + \text{Desired net income}$$

or

$$S = FC + VC + NI$$
$$S = \$12{,}000 + 0.20S + \$8{,}000$$
$$0.80S = \$20{,}000$$
$$S = \$25{,}000$$

Now suppose the airline's management wants to know how many passenger tickets the airline must sell to earn $8,000. Remembering that the contribution margin per ticket is $100, the number of tickets to be sold is computed as follows:

$$\text{Number of units} = \frac{\text{Fixed costs} + \text{Desired net income}}{\text{Contribution margin per unit}}$$

$$= \frac{\$12,000 + \$8,000}{\$100}$$

$$= \frac{\$20,000}{\$100}$$

$$= 200 \text{ tickets}$$

Calculating the Effect on Net Income of Changing Price.   The airline management can also use the break-even formula to determine the effect of changing the price used in the formula. To illustrate, assume that Flight 529 normally carries 150 passengers (sales of $18,750 and net income of $3,000) and the airline decided to increase ticket prices by 5%. If variable and fixed costs remain constant and passenger load does not change, net income will rise from $3,000 to $3,937.50 as shown below.

$$S = FC + VC + NI$$
$$\$18,750(1.05) = \$12,000 + 0.20(\$18,750) + NI$$
$$\$19,687.50 = \$12,000 + \$3,750 + NI$$
$$\$19,687.50 = \$15,750 + NI$$
$$NI = \$3,937.50$$

In the Flight 529 case, we assume that variable costs would remain constant at 20% of original sales because a change in selling price does not affect the variable costs associated with providing flight service. Thus, income would rise by the entire amount of the price increase ($19,687.50 − $18,750 = $937.50) because all variable costs and fixed costs are already covered by the original selling price.

Calculating Sales Needed to Maintain Net Income When Costs Change.   The break-even formula also has another application. Management can use the formula to calculate the sales needed to maintain a certain income level when costs change. For example, if the price of fuel rises, both fixed costs and variable costs will increase for the airline. Assume that total fixed costs increase by $4,030 from $12,000 to $16,030 and variable costs increase by $6.25 to $31.25 per passenger. The ticket price remains at $125. Variable costs are now 25% ($31.25/$125) of sales price. To maintain the current net income of $3,000 (on $18,750 of sales), the airline will need to increase sales revenue to $25,373 as shown below.

$$S = FC + VC + NI$$
$$S = \$16,030 + 0.25S + \$3,000$$
$$0.75S = \$19,030$$
$$S = \$25,373 \text{ (or 203 tickets at \$125 each)}$$

Other Uses of CVP Analysis.   Management can also use its knowledge of CVP relationships to determine whether to increase sales promotion costs

ANALYZING COST BEHAVIOR IN HOSPITALS

Healthcare costs, rising faster than inflation, now account for more than 10% of total gross national product. Concerns about these rising costs have prompted hospital administrators to improve cost accounting practices so they can understand how to cut costs without reducing the quality of healthcare services provided. These cost systems typically break down costs into fixed and variable components by service. "For example, if it costs $100 to do 10 laboratory tests, do 11 tests cost $110? It's possible the extra test may cost only $3 because all of the fixed cost was already covered by the first 10 tests." [p. 25.]

Knowing the cost function is $70 fixed costs plus $3 variable cost per laboratory test is more informative than knowing the cost is $100 for 10 tests. Armed with the breakdown of costs into fixed and variable components, the laboratory administrators know they could afford to charge less than $10 per test if the volume increases. On the other hand, they know that if volume decreases below 10 tests, charging $10 per test will not be sufficient to cover costs.

SOURCE: Judith Nemes, "Tight Margins Lead Hospital to Cost Accounting Systems," *Modern Healthcare,* December 17, 1990, pp. 23–30.

in an effort to increase sales volume or to accept an order at a lower-than-usual price. In general, the careful study of break-even charts helps management plan future courses of action. Indeed, one could say that to be successful, management must become "break-even minded."

Calculating Break-Even for a Multiproduct Company

When computing the break-even point for a multiproduct company, only dollars of sales are used. For CVP purposes, a multiproduct company must assume a constant product mix. **Product mix** refers to the proportion of the company's total sales attributable to each type of product sold. To illustrate the computation of the break-even point for Wonderfood, a multiproduct company that makes three types of cereal, assume the following historical data:

| | \multicolumn{8}{c}{Product} | | | | | | | |
| | 1 | | 2 | | 3 | | Total | |
	Amount	Per-cent	Amount	Per-cent	Amount	Per-cent	Amount	Per-cent
Sales	$60,000	100	$30,000	100	$10,000	100	$100,000	100
Less: Variable costs	40,000	67	16,000	53	4,000	40	60,000	60
Contribution margin	$20,000	33	$14,000	47	$ 6,000	60	$ 40,000	40

The relationships shown in the total column are used to compute the break-even point. Variable costs are 60% ($60,000/$100,000) of total sales. If the product mix is assumed to remain constant and fixed costs for the company are $50,000, break-even sales are $125,000, computed as follows:

$$S = FC + VC$$
$$S = \$50,000 + 0.60S$$
$$0.40S = \$50,000$$
$$S = \$125,000$$

The $125,000 sales can be specified by product by multiplying total sales dollars by the percent of product mix of each of the three products. The product mix for products 1, 2, and 3 is 60:30:10, respectively, that is, out of $100,000 total sales, there would be $60,000 sales of product 1, $30,000 sales of product 2, and $10,000 sales of product 3. Therefore, the company will have to sell $75,000 of product 1 (0.6 × $125,000), $37,500 of product 2 (0.3 × $125,000), and $12,500 of product 3 (0.1 × $125,000) to break even.

If there is any expected change in the mix of products sold, the break-even point will also change. The break-even point changes because each product has a different contribution margin. Also, if historical patterns of selling prices or variable costs are not expected to hold true in the future, projected sales and variable expenses should be used to determine expected percentages of variable expenses to total sales.

To illustrate the effects of such changes, assume that the product mix for products 1, 2, and 3 is expected to change to 20:30:50 in the upcoming period, as shown in the following chart. Also assume that total sales are expected to remain at $100,000 and that the variable costs for product 3 are expected to fall to 33% of the selling price. To compute the new break-even point, we again use the relationship shown in the total column.

	Product							
	1		2		3		Total	
	Amount	Per-cent	Amount	Per-cent	Amount	Per-cent	Amount	Per-cent
Sales.	$20,000	100	$30,000	100	$50,000	100	$100,000	100
Less: Variable costs.	13,333	67	16,000	53	16,667	33	46,000	46
Contribution margin	$ 6,667	33	$14,000	47	$33,333	67	$ 54,000	54

As shown in the total column, variable costs are expected to fall to 46% of total sales in the upcoming period. The new break-even point will be $92,593 computed as follows:

$$S = FC + VC$$
$$S = \$50,000 + 0.46S$$
$$0.54S = \$50,000$$
$$S = \$92,593$$

Notice that the new break-even point is lower than the old one. Sales shifted from the lowest contribution margin product (product 1) to the highest contribution margin product (product 3), thereby increasing the contribution margin dollars available to cover fixed costs. Therefore, the company will have to sell $18,519 of product 1 (0.2 × $92,593), $27,778 of product 2 (0.3 × $92,593), and $46,296 of product 3 (0.5 × $92,593) to break even.

EFFECT OF AUTOMATION ON COST-VOLUME-PROFIT ANALYSIS

Increased automation does not affect the fundamental CVP model or the types of analysis we have discussed. However, increased automation does affect the relative size of fixed and variable costs. As companies become more automated, they substitute machinery for labor. Companies that make this substitution often increase fixed costs and decrease variable costs. For example, when banks installed automated teller machines, their labor costs decreased but their fixed costs, including machine depreciation, increased.

Illustration 15.9
EFFECTS OF AUTOMATION

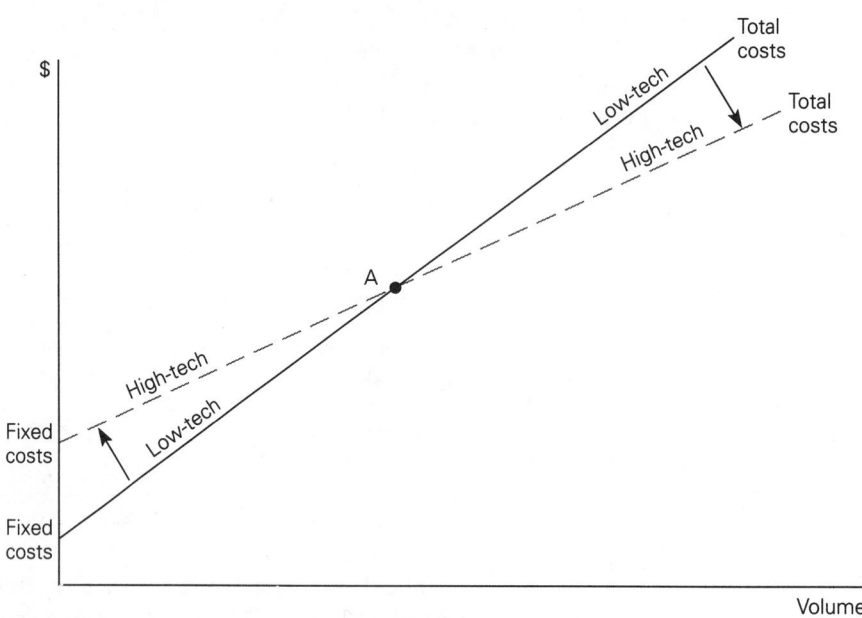

When a company substitutes fixed costs for variable costs, the total cost line shifts up as shown in Illustration 15.9. Becoming more automated increases total costs at low levels of volume, but it decreases total costs at high levels of volume. What does increased automation do to the company's break-even point? The answer depends on where the sales revenue line crosses the total cost line. If the sales revenue line crosses the total cost line at a low volume (to the left of point A in Illustration 15.9), then increasing automation increases the company's break-even point. However, if this intersection occurs at a high volume (to the right of point A), then increasing automation lowers total costs, and the company's break-even point will be lowered.

USING COMPUTER SPREADSHEETS FOR COST-VOLUME-PROFIT ANALYSIS

Computer spreadsheet packages are well suited for CVP analysis because they enable managers to answer "what-if" questions. The cost and revenue items in CVP analysis are estimates, not actual results. Since these estimates are used in planning and decision making, plans or decisions might have to change if the estimates change.

Consider the following example: Management of Prince Cruises wants to know what the income before income taxes would be for a proposed product, a Caribbean cruise. The analyst prepared the following formulas for the spreadsheet:

- Revenue equals ticket price times number of passengers (amounts to be inserted for ticket price and number of passengers).
- Variable costs equal (amount to be inserted) percent of revenue.
- Fixed costs equal $200,000.
- Income equals revenue minus variable costs minus fixed costs.

Management then inserted fixed costs and various values for ticket price, number of passengers, and percent of variable cost to revenue, all per cruise. Illustration 15.10 shows the results. Based on these results, management

Illustration 15.10
SPREADSHEET ANALYSIS OF CVP RELATIONSHIPS

Fixed Cost	Ticket Price	Number of Passengers	Percent Variable Cost to Revenue	Income
$200,000	$3,000	100	30	$10,000
200,000	3,000	80	30	−32,000
200,000	3,000	100	25	25,000
200,000	3,000	80	25	−20,000
200,000	4,000	70	30	−4,000
200,000	4,000	50	30	−60,000
200,000	4,000	70	25	10,000
200,000	4,000	50	25	−50,000

ETHICS   A CLOSER LOOK

Bailey Romich works in product development for a company that sells computer speech output devices to disabled people. These devices enable people who are unable to speak to communicate with a computer synthesized voice. Bailey has been obtaining data necessary to develop a CVP analysis for a new speech output device, one that can speak in different languages.

Bailey's boss asked him to prepare a spreadsheet analysis for the new device that contained several alternative assumptions about the product's selling price, sales volume, fixed cost, and variable cost to produce. Bailey did a careful analysis and presented his findings to the company's New Product Review Committee. Bailey's boss and the committee were very impressed with Bailey's presentation. Based on Bailey's projection of a low break-even point, the committee recommended that the new product be produced.

Three months later, Bailey retrieved his file on the foreign language speech output device analysis to answer a question from one of the committee members. As he reviewed his work, he had a sinking feeling in his stomach. He had forgotten to include the variable costs of advertising the product in his analysis. The New Product Review Committee and Bailey's boss had assumed that Bailey had included variable advertising costs in the variable costs that he had presented, but Bailey could see that he had omitted them. He projected variable advertising costs to be about 10% of the product's selling price.

Required
a.   Assume the product has not yet been produced. What should Bailey do?
b.   Would your answer to *(a)* change if the product had already been produced?

sees what combination of ticket price, number of passengers, and variable cost ratio is required for the cruise to be profitable.

We show only a few of the possible combinations in Illustration 15.10 to save space. Spreadsheets provide the advantage of a large number of possible combinations with minimal data entry.

Differential analysis is another analytical tool of short-term decision making that relies heavily on cost concepts. The next chapter illustrates the use of this tool in making important business decisions.

UNDERSTANDING THE LEARNING OBJECTIVES

1.   Explain and describe different cost behavior patterns.
   •   *Fixed costs.* These costs remain constant over some relevant range of output and are often described as time-related costs. Depreciation and insurance are examples.
   •   *Variable costs.* These costs vary directly with changes in the volume of production or sales. Direct labor and direct materials are examples.
   •   *Mixed costs.* These costs contain a fixed portion of cost that will be incurred even when the facility is completely idle and a variable

portion that will increase directly with production volume. Electricity is an example of a mixed cost.

- *Step costs*. These costs remain constant at a certain fixed amount over a short range of output (or sales) but then increase to higher amounts at certain points. The cost of water and supervisors' salaries are examples.

2. Calculate the break-even point for a company.
    - Cost-volume-profit analysis (sometimes called *break-even analysis*) is used to determine what effects any changes in a company's selling prices, costs, and/or volume will have on income in the short run.
    - The break-even point is that level of operations at which a company realizes no income or loss.
    - The break-even point can be expressed as:

Sales = Fixed costs + Variable costs

3. Explain the effects of changing costs or selling price on the break-even point; calculate the margin of safety.
    - A break-even point can be lowered or raised by changing selling price, variable cost per unit, or fixed costs. Lowering the break-even point means that the company can earn income at a lower volume of operations. If the selling price is increased or the variable cost per unit is decreased, the break-even point will be lower because the contribution margin per unit is larger. A larger contribution margin means that more of the selling price of each unit can be used to cover fixed costs. Similarly, if fixed costs are decreased, fewer units must be sold to cover the smaller amount of fixed costs.
    - The margin of safety can be expressed as follows:

Margin of safety = Current sales − Break-even sales

4. List the assumptions underlying cost-volume-profit analysis.
    - Selling price, variable cost per unit, and total fixed costs remain constant through the relevant range.
    - The number of units produced equals the number of units sold.
    - In multiproduct situations, the product mix is known in advance.
    - Costs can be accurately classified into their fixed and variable portions.

5. Demonstrate various applications of cost-volume-profit analysis.
    - One application is the calculation of the break-even point in a multiproduct company. The break-even point is computed in sales dollars as follows:

Sales = Fixed costs + Variable costs

    - Another application is the calculation of the sales volume needed for a desired net income. This calculation can be expressed by the following formula:

$$\text{Sales} = \text{Fixed costs} + \text{Variable costs} + \text{Desired net income}$$

- The calculation of the effect on net income of changing the price is another application. The break-even formula is used for this calculation.
- In addition, an application is the calculation of the sales needed to maintain net income when costs change. The break-even formula is also used for this calculation.

DEMONSTRATION PROBLEM

Hammer Sound System, Inc., a producer of car speakers, has fixed costs of $500,000 per year and variable costs of $7.50 per unit. Its product sells for $12.50 per unit. Full capacity is 200,000 units. Variable costs are 60% of sales ($7.50/$12.50).

Required:

a. Compute the break-even point in (1) sales dollars, (2) units, and (3) percentage of capacity.

b. Compute the number of units the company must sell if it wishes to have net income of $300,000.

Solution to demonstration problem

a.   (1)   Sales (S) = Fixed costs (FC) + Variable costs (VC)

$$S = \$500,000 + 0.60S$$
$$0.40S = \$500,000$$
$$S = \underline{\underline{\$1,250,000}}$$

(2)   Break-even point in units = $1,250,000 ÷ $12.50 = 100,000 units

or $\dfrac{\$500,000}{\$12.50 - \$7.50}$ = $\underline{\underline{100,000 \text{ units}}}$

(3)   Break-even point as percentage of capacity = 100,000 ÷ 200,000 = 50.0%.

b.   Number of units = $\dfrac{\text{Fixed cost} + \text{Desired net income}}{\text{Contribution margin}}$

$$= \frac{\$500,000 + \$300,000}{\$12.50 - \$7.50}$$

$$= \frac{\$800,000}{\$5}$$

$$= \underline{\underline{160,000 \text{ units}}}$$

NEW TERMS*

Break-even analysis   See Cost-volume-profit (CVP) analysis. *783*

Break-even point   That level of operations at which revenues for a period are equal to the costs assigned to that period so no net income or loss results. *783*

Contribution margin   The total contribution margin is the amount by which revenue exceeds the variable costs of producing that revenue. The contribution margin per unit is selling price minus variable cost per unit. *784*

Contribution margin ratio   Contribution margin per unit divided by selling price per unit. *785*

Cost-volume-profit (CVP) analysis   An analysis of the effect that any changes in a company's selling prices, costs, and/or volume will have on income (profits) in the short run. Also called break-even analysis. *783*

Cost-volume-profit (CVP) chart   A graph that shows the relationships between sales revenues, costs, volume, and profit and also shows the break-even point. *785*

Fixed costs   Costs that remain constant (in total) over some relevant range of output. *778*

High-low method   A method used in dividing mixed costs into their fixed and variable portions. The high point and low point of actual costs are used to draw a line representing a total mixed cost. *782*

Least-squares method   A method used for dividing mixed costs into their fixed and variable portions; this method uses statistical techniques to estimate the regression line representing a total mixed cost. *782*

Margin of safety   Amount by which sales can decrease before the company incurs a loss. *788*

Margin of safety rate   Margin of safety expressed as a percentage; is equal to (Current sales − Break-even sales) ÷ Current sales. *788*

Mixed cost   Contains a fixed portion of cost that will be incurred even when the plant is completely idle and a variable portion that will increase directly with production volume. *778*

Product mix   The proportion of the company's total sales attributable to each type of product sold. Product mix may be defined either in terms of sales dollars or in terms of the number of units sold. *792*

Relevant range   The range of production or sales volume over which the basic cost behavior assumptions will hold true. *785*

Scatter diagram   A diagram that shows plots of actual costs incurred for various levels of output or sales. The diagram is used in dividing mixed costs into their fixed and variable portions. *781*

Short run   The time during which a company's management cannot change the effects of certain past decisions; often determined to be one year or less; in the short run, many costs are assumed to be fixed and unchangeable. *777*

---

* Some terms listed in earlier chapters are repeated here for your convenience.

Step cost   A cost that remains constant at a certain fixed amount over a short range of output (or sales) but then increases to higher amounts at certain points. *778*

Step fixed cost   A step cost with only a few large steps. *778*

Step variable cost   A step cost with many small steps. *778*

Variable cost ratio   Variable costs expressed as a percentage of sales; used to find the break-even point. *784*

Variable costs   Costs that vary (in total) directly with changes in volume of production or sales. *778*

SELF-TEST

True-False

Indicate whether each of the following statements is true or false.

1. The high-low method is less precise than the scatter diagram for identifying the behavior of mixed costs.

2. A break-even point can be expressed in dollars of sales revenue or units.

3. Total contribution margin indicates the amount of income remaining after variable costs and fixed costs are covered.

4. The margin of safety is equal to current sales minus break-even sales.

5. When computing the break-even point for a multiproduct company, units produced are used as a measure of volume in making the calculations.

Multiple-Choice

Select the best answer for each of the following questions.

1. Under which of the following cost behavior patterns would production supervisors' salaries be categorized?
   a. Variable cost.
   b. Fixed cost.
   c. Mixed cost.
   d. Step cost.

2. Which of the following statements describe(s) the underlying assumptions of cost-volume-profit analysis?
   a. The number of units produced equals the number of units sold.
   b. Selling price, variable cost per unit, and total fixed costs remain constant throughout the relevant range.
   c. In multiproduct situations, the product mix is known in advance.
   d. Costs can be accurately classified into their fixed and variable portions.
   e. All of the above.

3. Calculate the amount of sales revenue needed to break even from the following data:

Selling price per unit.	$ 5
Fixed costs	15,000
Variable cost/per unit	3

   a. $40,000.
   b. $37,500.
   c. $50,000.
   d. $35,000.

4. Calculate the contribution margin from the following per unit data:

Selling price.	$30
Fixed costs	6
Variable costs	8

   a. $24.
   b. $20.
   c. $22.
   d. $18.

5. Calculate the break-even point in units using the following data:

Selling price per unit	$ 40
Fixed costs.	48,000
Variable cost per unit	8

   a. 1,500 units.
   b. 1,800 units.
   c. 1,275 units.
   d. 2,000 units.

6. Which of the following are characteristics of step costs?
   a. Has a fixed component.
   b. Has a portion that can change in steps as production levels change.
   c. Can remain constant over some relevant range of output.
   d. All of the above.

Now turn to page 808 to check your answers.

QUESTIONS

1. Name and describe the four cost behavior patterns.

2. What are the various ways in which the cost line for a mixed cost can be determined? Describe each method.

3. What is meant by the term *break-even point?* What factors must be taken into consideration in determining it?

4. What are the different ways in which the break-even point can be expressed?

5. How is the relevant range related to break-even analysis?

6. Why is break-even analysis considered appropriate only for short-run decisions?

7. What is the formula for calculating the break-even point in sales revenue?

8. What formula is used to solve for the break-even point in units? How can this formula be altered to calculate the number of units that must be sold to achieve a desired level of income?

9. Why might a business wish to lower its break-even point? How would it go about lowering the break-even point? What effect would you expect the mechanization and automation of production processes to have upon the break-even point?

10. How is the break-even point calculated for a multiproduct company?

11. What does the label *units* on the horizontal axis of the break-even chart mean?

MAYTAG
CORPORATION

12. *Real-world question*   Refer to the income statement for Maytag Corporation in Appendix C at the end of this text. For this question, refer to the amounts for 1991. Consider only revenue; cost of sales; and selling, general, and administrative expenses. Ignore taxes, interest, and other items on the income statement. Assume that for 1991, 90% of Maytag's selling, general, and administrative expenses were fixed, and 30% of cost of goods sold was fixed. At what level of revenues would Maytag break even in 1991?

MAYTAG
CORPORATION

13. *Real-world question*   Refer to Question 12. What assumptions did you make to derive Maytag's break-even point?

14. *Real-world question* Assume your college is considering hiring a lecturer to teach a special class in communication skills. Identify at least two different types of costs that college administrators might consider in deciding whether to hire the lecturer and add the class.

15. *Real-world question* Two enterprising students are considering renting space and opening a class video tape service. They would hire camera operators to video tape large introductory classes. The students taking the classes would be charged a fee to rent the tape or to view it on one of the video tape service's television sets. Identify as many costs of this business as you can and indicate which would be variable and which would be fixed.

EXERCISES

Analyze mixed cost using high-low method (L.O. 1)

15–1. Use the high-low method to determine the fixed and variable components of a mixed cost, given the following observations:

Volume (units)	Cost
3,400	$3,000
9,600	5,800

Match cost behavior types with diagrams (L.O. 1)

15–2. Name and match the type of cost behavior with the appropriate diagram below.

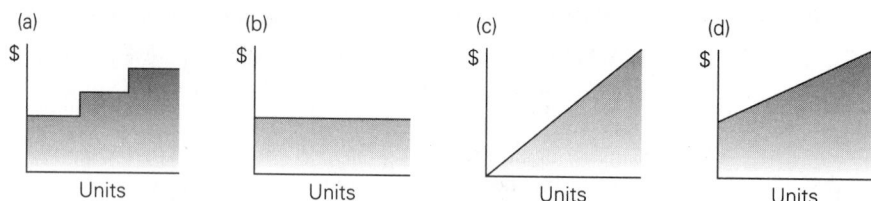

Compute break-even point in sales dollars (L.O. 2)

15–3. Compute the break-even point in sales dollars if fixed costs are $154,000 and variable costs are 50% of sales.

Compute break-even point in units (L.O. 2)

15–4. Moscow Company sells rubber boots for $16, with fixed costs of $140,000 and variable cost of $8.00 per unit. Find the break-even point in units.

Compute break-even point in sales dollars (L.O. 2)

15–5. Velencia Company sells each unit it produces for $5. Calculate the break-even point in dollars given the following cost observations:

Volume (units)	Cost
8,000	$ 60,000
58,000	180,000

Compute break-even point in sales dollars and units under varying assumptions; comment on results
(L.O. 4)

15–6. Kentucky Company currently sells each unit it produces for $8.00. Variable cost is $2.00 per unit, and fixed costs are $66,000. Compute the break-even point in both dollars and units under each of the following independent assumptions. Comment on why the break-even points are different.

a. The costs and selling price are as given above.

b. Fixed costs are increased to $69,300.

c. Selling price is increased by 2%.

d. Variable cost is increased to $3.24 per unit.

Decide whether to increase advertising; compute margin of safety
(L.O. 3, 5)

15–7. A company sells a product for $50 each, with variable cost of $25 per unit. Fixed costs are $2,000,000. The company currently sells 200,000 units per year. Should this company undertake an advertising campaign that will result in a $200,000 increase in fixed costs, a $5 per unit decrease in variable cost, and a 10% increase in sales? What would the margin of safety be before and after the campaign?

Compute break-even point in units and sales volume to achieve a specified level of income
(L.O. 5)

15–8. If a company has fixed costs of $312,000 and variable cost of $17.20 per unit, how many units would have to be sold at $25.20 each to break even? How many units would have to be sold to earn $240,000? If 60,000 units are 100% of capacity, what percentage of capacity do the two levels of output represent?

Compute multiproduct break-even point and margin of safety
(L.O. 3, 5)

15–9. Rico Company sells three products. Last year's sales were $160,000 for product L, $230,000 for product M, and $126,000 for product N. Variable costs were L, $90,000; M, $154,000; and N, $79,200. Fixed costs were $86,400. Determine the break-even point in dollars and the margin of safety.

Compute multiproduct break-even point
(L.O. 5)

15–10. If the company in Exercise 15–9 changes its product mix (in sales dollars) to 2:2:1, with total dollar sales being the same as last year, what will be the new break-even point? Comment on why it has changed.

PROBLEMS

Analyze mixed cost using high-low method and scatter diagram
(L.O. 1)

15–1. Your boss assigns you the task of estimating total public relations costs to the company. This cost is a mixed cost. You are supplied with the following data (adjusted to current dollars) from past years:

Year	Hours	Costs
1985	400	$6,000
1986	500	6,480
1987	450	6,600
1988	550	6,960
1989	500	6,960
1990	650	7,440
1991	700	8,040
1992	900	8,640
1993	1,000	9,600

Required:

a. Using the high-low method, determine the total amount of fixed costs and the amount of variable cost per hour. Draw the cost line.

b. Prepare a scatter diagram, plot the actual costs, and visually fit a linear cost line to the points. Estimate the amount of total fixed costs and the amount of variable cost per hour.

Identify points on a break-even chart (L.O. 2)

15–2. Use the graph below for this problem.

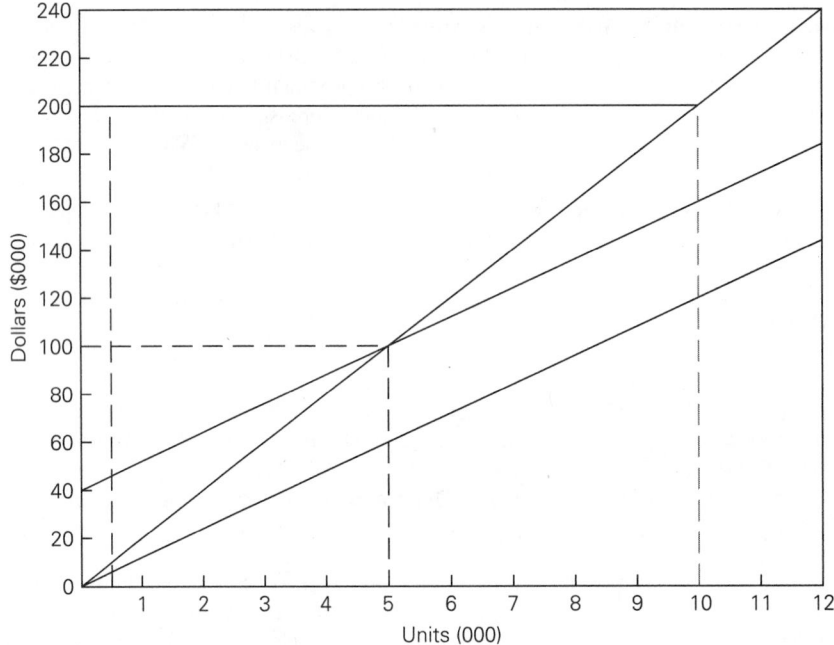

Required:

a. Label the relevant range, total costs, variable costs, fixed costs, break-even point, and profit and loss areas.

b. At 6,000 units, what are the variable costs, fixed costs, sales, and contribution margin amounts in dollars?

c. Does a profit or loss result? How much?

Determine break-even point under varying assumptions (L.O. 2)

15–3. The management of Skidadle Company wants to know the break-even point for its new line of high competition skis under each of the following independent assumptions. Selling price in each case is $50 per unit unless otherwise stated. (One "unit" is one pair of skis.)

  a. Fixed costs are $600,000, and variable cost is $30 per unit.

  b. Fixed costs are $600,000, and variable cost is $20 per unit.

  c. Fixed costs are $300,000, and variable cost is $20 per unit.

  d. Fixed costs are $300,000; selling price is $37.50; variable cost is $26.25 per unit.

Required:

Using the above assumptions, compute the break-even point in both sales dollars and units.

Compute the level of sales needed to achieve specified level of income (L.O. 4)

15–4. Refer to Problem 15–3.

Required:

Using the data in Problem 15–3 *(a)* through *(d)*, determine the level of sales required to achieve a net income of $240,000.

Determine break-even point under varying assumptions (L.O. 4)

15–5. a. Assume that fixed costs of R Corporation are $150,000 per year, variable cost is $4.80 per unit, and selling price is $12 per unit. Determine the break-even point in sales dollars.

b. S Company breaks even when sales amount to $4,900,000. In 1995, its sales were $7,200,000, and its variable costs amounted to $2,160,000. Determine the amount of its fixed costs.

c. The sales of T Corporation in 1995 amounted to $20,000,000, its variable costs were $5,000,000, and its fixed costs were $10,000,000. At what level of sales would the T Corporation break even?

d. What would have been the net income of the T Corporation in *(c)* above if sales volume had been 10% higher but selling prices had remained unchanged?

e. What would have been the net income of the T Corporation in *(c)* above if variable costs had been 10% lower?

f. What would have been the net income of the T Corporation in *(c)* above if fixed costs had been 10% lower?

g. Determine the break-even point in sales dollars for the T Corporation on the basis of the data given in *(e)* above and then in *(f)* above.

Required:

Using the above assumptions, answer each of the above questions.

Compute break-even point and sales needed to achieve a specific level of income (L.O. 5)

15–6. If Animalcare Laboratories has fixed costs of $360,000, variable cost of $7.20 per lab test, and a selling price of $16.80 per lab test, how many tests must be performed to break even? How many tests will it have to perform to earn $60,000 before taxes? (Assume each test is "sold.")

Required

Compute the break-even point in number of tests and the number of tests needed to be performed to earn $60,000.

Prepare cost-volume-profit chart; compute break-even point; prepare income statement for two companies (L.O. 5)

15–7. The operating results for two companies are presented below.

	Company A	Company B
Sales (20,000 units).	$1,000,000	$1,000,000
Variable costs	240,000	500,000
Contribution margin	760,000	500,000
Fixed costs	500,000	200,000
Income before income taxes	260,000	300,000

Required:

a. Prepare a cost-volume-profit chart for Company A, indicating the break-even point, the contribution margin, and the areas of income and losses.

b. Compute the break-even point of both companies in sales dollars and units.

c. Assume that without changes in selling price, the sales of each company decline by 20%. Prepare condensed income statements, similar to the statements above, for both companies.

Compute
break-even point;
compute expected
net income; make
leasing decision
(L.O. 5)

15–8. Citadel Company, a leading manufacturer of CDs, incurred $250,000 of fixed costs while selling 20,000 CDs at $60 each. Variable cost was $20 per CD.

A new machine used in the production of CDs has recently become available and is more efficient than the machine currently being used. The new machine would reduce Citadel's variable costs by 20% and can be leased on an annual basis for $9,600 per year.

Required:

a. Compute the break-even point in units assuming use of the old machine.

b. Compute the break-even point in units assuming use of the new machine.

c. Assuming that total sales remain at $1,200,000 and that the new machine is leased, compute expected net income.

d. Should the new machine be leased? Why?

Decide whether to
undertake a sales
promotion
campaign and
whether to hire an
efficiency expert
(L.O. 5)

15–9. a. Lehr Company reports sales of $360,000, variable costs of $180,000, and fixed costs of $54,000. If the company spends $36,000 on a sales promotion campaign, management estimates that sales can be increased by $135,000.

b. The following data pertain to the McNeil Corporation:

Sales	$720,000
Variable costs	432,000
Fixed costs.	140,000

The president is considering hiring an efficiency expert at $36,000 this year who can reduce variable costs by 25%. Assume that sales will remain at the same level.

Required:

a. For *(a)*, determine whether the sales promotion campaign should be undertaken. Provide calculations.

b. For *(b)*, determine whether the efficiency expert should be hired. Provide calculations.

Compute
multiproduct
break-even point
assuming change
in product mix
(L.O. 5)

15–10. Jeep City, Inc., sells three types of Jeeps. It has fixed costs of $500,000 per month. The sales and variable costs of these products for April follow:

	Product		
	Jeep 1	Jeep 2	Jeep 3
Sales	$500,000	$750,000	$1,250,000
Variable costs	300,000	400,000	600,000

Required:

a. Compute the break-even point in sales dollars.
b. Assume the sales mix in May is expected to be in the ratio 5 : 3 : 2 with total sales and fixed costs being the same as in April. What would be the break-even point in sales dollars in May?

BUSINESS DECISION PROBLEMS

Compute
break-even point
and projected net
income for two
investment
alternatives;
determine best
alternative
(L.O. 5)

15–1. Vitrovia Company is operating at almost 100% of capacity. The company expects the demand for its product to increase by 25% next year (1995). To satisfy the demand for its product, the company is considering two alternatives. The first alternative will increase fixed costs by 15% but will not have an effect on variable costs. The second alternative will not affect fixed costs but will cause variable costs to increase to 60% of the selling price of the company's product.

Vitrovia Company's condensed income statement for 1994 is shown below:

Sales		$3,600,000
Costs:		
Variable	$1,620,000	
Fixed	760,000	2,380,000
Income before taxes . . .		$1,220,000

Required:

a. Determine the break-even point in sales dollars for 1995 under each of the alternatives.
b. Determine projected income before income taxes for 1995 under each of the alternatives.
c. Which alternative would you recommend? Why?

Compute
break-even point;
determine point at
which factory
should shut down
rather than
produce
(L.O. 5)

15–2. When the plant of Sheen Company is completely idle, fixed costs amount to $720,000. When the plant operates at levels of 50% of capacity and below, its fixed costs are $840,000; at levels above 50% of capacity, its fixed costs are $1,120,000. The company's variable costs at full capacity (100,000 units) amount to $1,500,000.

Required:

a. Assuming that the company's product sells for $60 per unit, what is the company's break-even point in sales dollars?

b. Using only the data given, at what level of sales would closing the factory be more economical than operating it? In other words, at what level will operating losses approximate the losses incurred if the factory is closed down completely?

c. Assume that Sheen Company is operating at half of its capacity. It decides to reduce the selling price from $60 per unit to $36 per unit to increase sales. At what percentage of capacity must the company operate to break even at the reduced sales price?

ANSWERS TO SELF-TEST

True-False

1. *True*. The high-low method is less precise than the scatter diagram since it uses only two data points in the computation.

2. *True*. Break-even point can also be expressed in terms of capacity.

3. *False*. Total contribution margin is the amount by which revenue exceeds variable costs of producing that revenue.

4. *True*. Margin of safety = Current sales − Break-even sales.

5. *False*. Dollars of sales are used as the measure of volume when a company has many different products.

Multiple-Choice

1. *d*. The cost of production supervisors' salaries is a step cost.

2. *e*. All of these are underlying assumptions of CVP analysis.

3. *b*. Sales = Fixed costs + Variable costs

   or

   $$S = FC + VC$$
   $$S = \$15,000 + 0.60S$$
   $$S - 0.60S = \$15,000$$
   $$0.40S = \$15,000$$
   $$S = \$15,000 \div 0.40$$
   $$S = \$37,500$$

4. *c*. $\dfrac{\text{Contribution}}{\text{margin per unit}} = \dfrac{\text{Selling}}{\text{price}} - \dfrac{\text{Variable cost}}{\text{per unit}}$

   $$\$30 - \$8 = \$22$$

5. *a.* $\text{BEP}_{units} = \dfrac{\text{Fixed costs}}{\text{Contribution margin per unit}}$

   $$\text{BEP}_{units} = \dfrac{\$48,000}{\$32 \text{ per unit}}$$
   $$= 1,500 \text{ units}$$

6. *d*. Step costs have all of these characteristics.

16

SHORT-TERM DECISION MAKING: DIFFERENTIAL ANALYSIS

After reading this chapter, you should be able to:

1. Explain differential analysis and describe its components.
2. Demonstrate applications of differential analysis.
3. Compare and contrast absorption costing and direct costing.
4. Describe the differences in net income under absorption costing and direct costing.
5. Explain distribution cost analysis and how it is used.

We begin this chapter by discussing differential analysis, which is used to select the best solution to a particular short-run problem. The second major topic in the chapter, absorption costing versus direct costing, focuses on whether to treat fixed manufacturing costs as product costs or period costs. The chapter concludes by discussing distribution costs, which are costs of selling and delivering products and services to customers. Managers often ignore these costs in business decisions because they are not part of inventory costs.

DIFFERENTIAL ANALYSIS

*Objective 1
Explain differential analysis and describe its components*

Differential analysis involves analyzing the different costs and benefits that would arise from alternative solutions to a particular situation. **Relevant revenues or costs** in a given situation are future revenues or costs that differ depending on which alternative course of action is selected. **Differential revenue** is the difference in revenues between two alternatives. **Differential cost or expense** is the difference between relevant costs for two alternatives.[1]

---

[1] Some authors equate relevant cost and differential cost. This text uses the term *relevant* to identify which costs should be considered in a situation and the term *differential* to identify the amount by which these costs differ.

Future costs that do not differ between alternatives are irrelevant and may be ignored since they will affect both alternatives similarly. Past costs, also known as **sunk costs,** are also not relevant in decision making because the costs have already been incurred and, therefore, cannot be changed no matter which alternative is selected.

For certain decisions, revenues do not differ between alternatives. Under those circumstances, management should select the alternative with the least cost. In other situations, costs do not differ between alternatives. Accordingly, management should select the alternative that results in the greatest revenue. However, many times both future costs and revenues differ between alternatives. In these situations, management should select the alternative that results in the greatest positive difference between future revenues and expenses (costs).

To illustrate relevant, differential, and sunk costs, assume that Joanna Bennett invested $400 in a tiller so she could till gardens to earn $1,500 during the summer. Joanna is now offered the opportunity to work at a horse stable feeding horses and cleaning stalls for $1,200 for the summer. The costs that Joanna would incur in tilling are $100 for transportation and $150 for supplies. The costs she would incur at the horse stable are $100 for transportation and $50 for supplies. If Joanna works at the stable, she would still have the tiller, and she could loan it to her parents and friends at no charge.

The tiller cost of $400 is not *relevant* to the decision because it is a *sunk* cost. The transportation cost of $100 is also not relevant because it is the same for both alternatives. The relevant costs and revenues are shown below.

	Performing Tilling Service	Working at Horse Stable	Differential
Revenues	$1,500	$1,200	$300
Costs	150	50	100
Net benefit in favor of tilling service. .			$200

Based on this differential analysis, Joanna Bennett should perform her tilling service rather than work at the stable. Of course, the analysis considers only cash flows, and nonmonetary considerations (such as her love for horses) could sway the decision.

In many situations, total variable costs differ between alternatives, while total fixed costs do not. However, we cannot assume that variable costs are always differential costs and fixed costs are never differential costs. For example, the differential cost between operating at a production level of 40,000 units versus a production level of 60,000 units might include increases in both variable and fixed costs. This increase in fixed costs could be the result of a step fixed cost, such as that related to the number of supervisors necessary for a particular production level.

Before studying the applications of differential analysis, you must realize that (1) two types of fixed costs exist, and (2) opportunity costs are also relevant in choosing between alternatives. For this reason, this section discusses committed fixed costs, discretionary fixed costs, and opportunity costs before concentrating on the applications of differential analysis.

Nature of Fixed Costs

Up to this point in the discussion, we have treated fixed costs as if they were all alike. Now we identify two types of fixed costs—committed fixed costs and discretionary fixed costs.

Committed Fixed Costs.   **Committed fixed costs** relate to the basic facilities and organizational structure that a company must have to continue operations. These costs cannot be changed in the short run without seriously disrupting operations. Examples of committed fixed costs are depreciation on buildings and equipment and salaries of key executives. In the short run, these costs are not subject to the discretion or control of management. These costs result from past decisions that *committed* the company for a period of several years. For instance, once a company constructs a building to house production operations, it is committed to the use of the building for many years. Thus, the depreciation on that building is not as subject to management's control as are some other types of fixed costs.

Discretionary Fixed Costs.   In contrast to committed fixed costs, **discretionary fixed costs** are subject to management control from year to year. Each year, management decides how much to spend on advertising, research and development, and employee training and development programs. Since management makes these decisions each year, these costs are under management's *discretion*. Management is not locked in or committed to a certain level of expense for more than one budget period. The next period management may change the level of expense or eliminate the expense completely.

Management's philosophy can affect to some extent which fixed costs are committed and which are discretionary. For instance, during the recession of the early 1990s, some companies terminated persons in the upper levels of management, while other companies kept their "management team" intact. Thus, in some companies the salaries of top-level managers were discretionary costs, while in other companies these salaries were committed costs.

The discussion of committed fixed costs and discretionary fixed costs is relevant to CVP analysis. If almost all of a company's fixed costs are committed fixed costs, then the company will have more difficulty reducing its break-even point for the next budget period than if most of the company's fixed costs are discretionary in nature. A company with a large proportion of discretionary fixed costs may be able to reduce fixed costs dramatically in a recessionary period. By making such a reduction, the company may be able to "run lean" and show some income even when economic conditions are difficult. Thus, the company may enhance its chances of long-run survival.

Opportunity Costs

Another cost concept relevant to decision making is opportunity cost. An **opportunity cost** is the potential benefit that is foregone from *not* following the next best alternative course of action. For example, assume that the two best uses of a plot of land are as a mobile home park (annual income of $100,000) and as a golf driving range (annual income of $60,000). The opportunity cost of using the land as a mobile home park is $60,000, while the opportunity cost of using the land as a driving range is $100,000.

Companies do not record opportunity costs in the accounting records because they are the costs of *not* following a certain alternative. Thus, opportunity costs are not transactions that occurred; instead, they are transactions that did not occur. However, opportunity cost is a relevant cost in many decision problems because it represents a real sacrifice that occurs because one alternative is chosen instead of another.

APPLICATIONS OF DIFFERENTIAL ANALYSIS

*Objective 2
Demonstrate applications of differential analysis*

To illustrate the application of differential analysis to specific decision problems, we will now consider five types of decisions: (1) setting prices of products; (2) accepting or rejecting special orders; (3) eliminating products, segments, or customers; (4) processing or selling joint products; and (5) deciding to make products or buy them. These five types of decisions are not the only applications of differential analysis, but they represent typical short-term business decisions to which differential analysis can properly be applied.

Setting Prices of Products

When applying differential analysis to pricing decisions, each possible price for a given product represents an alternative course of action. The sales revenues for each alternative and the costs that differ between alternatives are the relevant amounts in these decisions. Total fixed costs often remain the same between pricing alternatives and, if so, may be ignored. In selecting a price for a product, the goal is to select the price at which total future revenues will exceed total future costs by the greatest amount.

A high price is not necessarily the price that will maximize income. The product may have many substitutes. If a company sets a high price, the number of units sold may decline substantially as customers switch to lower-priced competitive products. Thus, in the maximization of income, the expected volume of sales at each price is as important as the contribution margin per unit of product sold. In making any pricing decision, management should seek the combination of price and volume that will produce the largest *total* profit. This combination is often difficult to identify in an actual situation because management may have to estimate the number of units that can be sold at each price.

For example, assume that a company selling fried chicken in the New York market estimates product demand for its large bucket of chicken for a particular period as:

Choice	Demand
1	15,000 units at $6 per unit
2	12,000 units at $7 per unit
3	10,000 units at $8 per unit
4	7,000 units at $9 per unit

The fixed costs are not affected by the different volume alternatives. Variable costs are $5 per unit. What price should be set for the product? Based on the calculations shown below, the company should select a price of $8 per unit (choice 3) because this price will result in the greatest total contribution margin and profit.

Choice	Contribution Margin per Unit*	×	Number of Units	=	Total Contribution Margin
1	$1		15,000		$15,000
2	2		12,000		24,000
3	3		10,000		30,000
4	4		7,000		28,000

* Sales price − Variable cost.

Accepting or Rejecting Special Orders: Providing Discounts

Sometimes management is faced with the opportunity to sell its product in two or more markets at two or more different prices. Movie theaters, for example, sell tickets at discount prices to particular groups of people, such as children, students, or senior citizens. Differential analysis can be used to determine whether companies should sell their products at prices below regular levels.

The desirability of keeping physical facilities and personnel working at capacity is obvious. Efficient business management requires keeping the cost of idleness at a minimum. When operations are at a level less than full capacity, management should seek additional business. Management may decide to accept such additional business at prices lower than average unit costs if the differential revenues from the additional business exceed the differential costs.

To illustrate, assume Rios Company produces and sells a single product with a variable cost of $8 per unit. Annual capacity is 10,000 units, and annual fixed costs total $48,000. The selling price is $20 per unit, and production and sales are budgeted at 5,000 units. Thus, budgeted income before income taxes is $12,000, computed as follows:

Sales (5,000 units at $20)		$100,000
Costs:		
Fixed.	$48,000	
Variable (5,000 units at $8).	40,000	88,000
Income before income taxes		$ 12,000

Assume the company receives an order for 3,000 units from a foreign distributor at a price of $10 per unit. This $10 price is half of the regular selling price per unit and is also less than the average cost per unit of $17.60 ($88,000 ÷ 5,000 units). However, the $10 price offered exceeds the variable cost per unit by $2. If the company accepts the order, income before taxes will be $18,000, computed as follows:

Sales (5,000 units at $20; 3,000 units at $10) . . .		$130,000
Costs:		
Fixed.	$48,000	
Variable (8,000 units at $8).	64,000	112,000
Income before income taxes		$ 18,000

If Rios Company continues to operate at 50% capacity (producing 5,000 units), it would produce income before taxes of only $12,000. By accepting the order, the new units would have a contribution margin of $2 per unit. Thus, income before taxes will increase by $6,000. Since the regular market is unlikely to be affected by the export of the product at a sharply reduced price, the company should accept the order assuming it does not violate international trade agreements.

Differential analysis would provide the following calculations:

	(1) Accept Order	(2) Reject Order	Differential
Revenues	$130,000	$100,000	$30,000
Costs	64,000	40,000	24,000
Net benefit in favor of accepting order			$ 6,000

In summary, variable costs set a floor for the selling price in cost analyses. Even if the price exceeds variable costs only slightly, the additional business may make a contribution to income. However, "contribution pricing'' of marginal business often brings only short-term increases in income. Companies should appraise such pricing in light of the long-range effects on company and industry price structures. In the long run, companies must cover full costs.

Adding or Dropping Products, Segments, or Customers

Periodically, management has to decide whether to add or drop certain products, segments, or customers. If you have seen a store or a plant open or close in your area, then you have seen the results of these decisions. Differential analysis is useful in this type of decision making. A company's income statement does not automatically associate costs with certain products, segments, or customers. Companies must reclassify costs as those costs that the proposed action would change and those costs that it would not change.

If companies add or drop products, variable costs will usually increase or decrease. The fixed costs may change, but will not in many cases. The decisions to add or drop a product are based only on the differential items; that is, the costs and revenues that would change.

To illustrate, assume that the Campus Bookstore is considering eliminating its arts supply department. If the bookstore drops the arts supply department, it will lose revenues of $100,000 annually. The bookstore's management assigns costs of $110,000, $80,000 variable and $30,000 fixed, to the arts supply department. Therefore, the arts supply department has an apparent annual loss of $10,000 ($100,000 revenue minus $110,000 costs). However, careful cost analysis reveals that if the arts supply department were dropped, the reduction in costs would be only $80,000. The $30,000 fixed costs would continue to be incurred and would need to be covered by other activities. The differential analysis is:

	(1) Retain Arts Supply Department	(2) Drop Arts Supply Department	Differential
Revenues . . . . —	$100,000	$ –0–	$100,000
Costs	110,000	30,000	80,000
Net benefit of retaining arts supply department			$ 20,000

This illustration shows that the arts supply department has been contributing $20,000 ($100,000 revenues minus $80,000 variable costs) annually to cover the fixed costs of the business. Consequently, its elimination could be a costly mistake unless a more profitable use exists for the released facilities.

If the company has a profitable alternative use for the released facilities, the potential income from that alternative represents an opportunity cost of retaining the product, segment, or customer. Assume, for example, that the bookstore could use the facilities currently occupied by the arts supply department to open a new computer department to display and sell personal computers, printers, and software. This new department would contribute $30,000 to the bookstore's income.

In this case, the relevant costs in the decision to retain the arts supply department are $110,000 ($80,000 of variable manufacturing costs and $30,000 of opportunity cost), while the relevant revenues are still $100,000. Therefore, the bookstore has a net disadvantage of keeping the arts supply department because it loses $10,000 compared to assigning the space to a computer department.

Processing or Selling Joint Products

Sometimes several products result from a common raw material or production process; these products are called **joint products.** For instance, when companies refine crude oil, they produce a wide variety of fuels, solvents, lubricants, and residual petrochemicals. These companies can process these products further or sell them in their current condition.

Management can use differential analysis to decide whether to process a joint product further or to sell it in its present condition. **Joint costs** are those costs incurred up to the point where the joint products split off from each other. These costs are sunk costs in deciding whether to process a joint product further before selling it or to sell the product in its condition at split off.

The following example will illustrate the issue of whether to process or sell joint products. Assume that Atlantic Paper produces two paper products, A and B, from a common manufacturing process. Each of the products could be sold in its present form or could be processed further and sold at a higher price. Data for both products are given below.

Product	Selling Price per Unit at Split-Off Point	Cost per Unit of Further Processing	Selling Price per Unit after Further Processing
A	$10	$6	$21
B	12	7	18

The differential revenues and costs of further processing the two products are as follows:

Product	Differential Revenue of Further Processing	Differential Cost of Further Processing	Net Advantage (Disadvantage) of Further Processing
A	$11	$6	$ 5
B	6	7	(1)

USING ACTIVITY-BASED COSTING TO MAKE MARKETING DECISIONS

Marketing cost analysis provides relevant data for managerial decisions to add or drop territories and products. Applying principles of activity-based costing to marketing activities helps marketing managers make decisions about product line or territory profitability.

For example, suppose the Nike shoe company considers opening a territory in Russia. The first step is to determine what activities would be required to market shoes in Russia. These activities would include selling, warehousing, order filling, providing credit and collecting on accounts receivable, and shipping, in addition to advertising and promotion. The second step is to identify measures of the activities. Some examples of activity measures are shown in the table.

The next step is to estimate the cost of each activity. Finally, management would estimate the number of activities required to open the sales territory in Russia which, multiplied by the

Activity	Measures
Selling.	Number of sales calls
	Number of orders obtained
	Volume of sales
Warehousing.	Number of items stored
	Volume of items stored
Credit and collection . . .	Number of customer orders
	Dollar amount of customer orders on account

cost per activity, would provide an estimate of the cost of marketing in the new territory.

SOURCE: Article by Ronald Lewis, "Activity-Based Costing for Marketing," *Management Accounting,* November 1991, pp. 33–38.

Based on this analysis, Atlantic Paper should process product A further since it will increase income by $5 per unit sold. The company should not process product B further because that would decrease income by $1 per unit sold.

Companies use this same form of differential analysis to decide whether they should discard or process further their by-products. **By-products** are additional products resulting from production of a main product; sometimes companies consider by-products to be waste materials. For example, the bark from trees that are cut into lumber is a by-product of lumber production. Although a by-product, this bark can be converted into fuel or landscaping material. If the differential revenue of further processing exceeds the differential cost, then further processing should be done. As companies increase their concerns about the effects of waste on the environment, they find that more and more waste products can be converted into by-products.

Deciding to Make or Buy

Managers can also apply differential analysis to make-or-buy decisions. A **make-or-buy decision** occurs when management must decide whether to make or purchase a part or material used in making another product. Management must compare the price it would pay for the part if it were purchased with the *additional costs* that would be incurred to manufacture the part. If most of the manufacturing costs are fixed and would exist in any case, the part should probably be made rather than bought.

To illustrate the application of differential analysis to make-or-buy decisions, assume that General Motors manufactures a part costing $6 for use in its automobile engines. Cost components are materials, $3.00; labor, $1.50; fixed overhead costs, $1.05; and variable overhead costs, $0.45. The part could be purchased for $5.25. Since fixed overhead would presumably continue even if the part were purchased, manufacture of the part should be continued. The added costs of manufacturing amount to only $4.95 ($3.00 + $1.50 + $0.45). This amount is 30 cents per unit less than the purchase price of the part, as shown in the following analysis:

	(1) Make	(2) Buy	Differential
Costs	$4.95	$5.25	$0.30
Net advantage of making			$0.30

In make-or-buy decisions, management should also consider the opportunity cost of not utilizing the space for some other purpose. In the above example, if the opportunity cost of not using this space in its best alternative use is more than 30 cents per unit times the number of units produced, then the part should be purchased.

In some manufacturing situations, a portion of fixed costs can be avoided by buying from an outside source. For example, suppose eliminating a part would reduce production such that a supervisor's salary could be saved. In such a situation, these fixed costs should be treated the same as variable costs in the analysis, since they would then be relevant costs.

Sometimes the cost to manufacture is about the same as the cost of purchasing the part or material. In this case, management should place considerable weight on other factors, such as the competency of existing personnel to manufacture the product and the quality of outside suppliers.

The proper treatment of fixed manufacturing overhead costs is subject to some debate. The next section on absorption costing versus direct costing discusses the treatment of these costs first as product costs and then as period costs.

ABSORPTION VERSUS DIRECT COSTING

*Objective 3
Compare and
contrast absorp-
tion costing and
direct costing*

As the final consideration in short-term decision making, we introduce a new form of income statement and product costing. Currently, the most commonly accepted theory and method of product costing is called *absorption or full costing.* Under **absorption (or full) costing,** all product costs, including fixed manufacturing overhead, are accounted for as product costs and are allocated to the units of product produced during a period. In Chapters 12–14, the discussion of product costing was based on absorption costing.

Another method, **direct (or variable) costing,** includes only variable manufacturing costs as product costs. All fixed manufacturing overhead costs are charged to expense in the period in which they are incurred. The difference between the income statements under the two methods is that absorption costing focuses on gross margin, while direct costing focuses on contribution margin.

The differences between absorption costing and direct costing can be seen by comparing the income statements that would result from applying each technique to the same data. Assume Bradley Company had the following data relating to manufacturing and sales activities for May 1995.

BRADLEY COMPANY
May 1995

Beginning inventory (units). . .	–0–	Variable costs (per unit):	
Production (units)	10,000	Direct materials	$2.00
Sales (units).	9,000	Direct labor	1.00
Fixed costs:		Manufacturing overhead	0.30
Manufacturing overhead . . .	$ 6,000	Total	$3.30
Selling expenses	15,000		
Administrative expenses . . .	12,000	Variable selling expenses (per unit)	$0.20
		Selling price (per unit)	8.00

Absorption Costing

Under absorption costing, fixed manufacturing overhead costs would be applied to the units of production at the rate of $0.60 per unit, calculated as $6,000/10,000 units. Therefore, the cost per unit of inventory is $3.90, the total of the direct materials, direct labor, and variable and fixed manufacturing overhead. All selling and administrative expenses are period costs. Illustration 16.1 contains the income statement for Bradley Company prepared under absorption costing.

Generally, variable and fixed manufacturing costs do not appear as separate line items on the income statement; they are presented this way simply to illustrate that the fixed manufacturing costs are included in ending inventory. Ending inventory is priced at "full cost" of $3.90 per unit, or $39,000/10,000. Also, no distinction is usually made between fixed and variable

Illustration 16.1
INCOME STATEMENT UNDER ABSORPTION COSTING

BRADLEY COMPANY
Income Statement
For the Period Ending May 31, 1995

Sales (9,000 units at $8)		$72,000
Cost of goods sold:		
Variable costs of production (10,000 units at $3.30)	$33,000	
Fixed manufacturing overhead costs	6,000	
Total costs of producing 10,000 units.	$39,000	
Less: Ending inventory (1,000 units at $3.90)	3,900	35,100
Gross margin on sales.		$36,900
Operating expenses:		
Selling expenses ($15,000 fixed plus 9,000 at $0.20 each)	$16,800	
Administrative expenses	12,000	28,800
Income before income taxes		$ 8,100

selling expenses. These expenses are totaled and shown under operating expenses of the period.

Absorption costing is required for external financial statement presentation and also for tax purposes. However, as shown throughout this chapter, a full cost approach is not necessarily the best approach for internal management decision making. Management often needs information on contribution margin rather than gross margin to calculate break-even points and make decisions regarding special-order pricing. Direct costing presents this information in a more obvious and prominent form.

Direct Costing

Under direct costing, companies treat only *variable* costs of production (direct materials, direct labor, and variable manufacturing overhead) as product costs. Recall from Chapter 12 that product costs attach to the product and only become an expense (cost of goods sold) when products are sold. All *fixed* manufacturing overhead costs are considered period costs and are charged to expense in the period incurred. The logic behind this expensing of fixed manufacturing overhead is that the company would incur such costs whether a plant was in production or idle. Therefore, these fixed costs do not specifically relate to the manufacture of products.

Illustration 16.2 presents Bradley's direct costing income statement for May 1995. This statement uses the **contribution margin format.** In contrast to traditional income statements, like the one in Illustration 16.1, the contribution margin format subtracts variable costs from revenues to show the contribution margin and then subtracts fixed costs from the contribution margin to show income.

Illustration 16.2
CONTRIBUTION MARGIN INCOME STATEMENT UNDER DIRECT COSTING

BRADLEY COMPANY
Income Statement
For the Period Ending May 31, 1995

Sales (9,000 units at $8)		$72,000
Variable costs:		
Variable production costs incurred (10,000 units at $3.30)	$33,000	
Less: Ending inventory (1,000 units at $3.30)	3,300	29,700
Manufacturing margin		$42,300
Variable selling expenses (9,000 units at $0.20)		1,800
Contribution margin		$40,500
Fixed costs:		
Manufacturing overhead	$ 6,000	
Selling expenses	15,000	
Administrative expenses	12,000	33,000
Income before income taxes		$ 7,500

Notice that Bradley's direct costing income statement carries the goods in inventory at $3.30 per unit rather than at the $3.90 full cost. The statement shows all variable costs at the top of the statement as deductions from sales to disclose contribution margin for the month. All fixed costs are classified as period costs no matter what the source of the cost (manufacturing, selling, or administrative).

Comparing the Two Methods

Comparing the two income statements in Illustrations 16.1 and 16.2, a $600 difference exists in income before income taxes for the month; and a $600 difference exists in ending inventory valuation, as shown in Illustration 16.3. These differences are due to the treatment of fixed manufacturing overhead costs. Under absorption costing, each unit in ending inventory carries $0.60 of fixed overhead cost as part of product cost. At the end of the month, Bradley has 1,000 units in inventory. Therefore, ending inventory under absorption costing includes $600 of fixed manufacturing overhead costs ($0.60 × 1,000 units) and is valued at $600 more than under direct costing.

Under direct costing, companies charge off, or expense, *all* the fixed manufacturing overhead costs during the period rather than deferring these costs and carrying them forward to the next period as part of inventory cost. Therefore, $6,000 of fixed manufacturing overhead costs appear on the direct costing income statement as an expense, rather than $5,400 ($6,000 fixed manufacturing overhead costs minus $600 fixed manufacturing overhead included in inventory) under absorption costing. Consequently, income before income taxes under direct costing is $600 less than under absorption costing because more expense is charged off during the period.

Illustration 16.3
COMPARISON OF RESULTS UNDER ABSORPTION AND
DIRECT COSTING

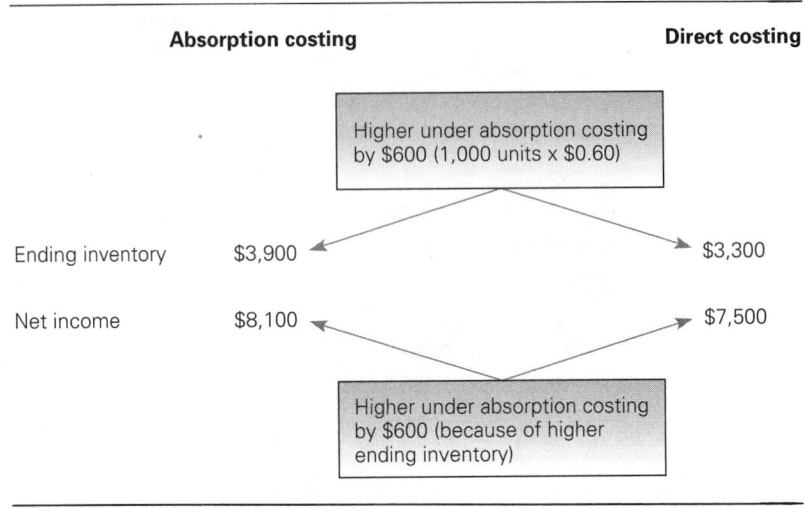

Absorption costing   Direct costing

Higher under absorption costing
by $600 (1,000 units x $0.60)

Ending inventory $3,900 $3,300

Net income $8,100 $7,500

Higher under absorption costing
by $600 (because of higher
ending inventory)

Objective 4
Describe the
differences in net
income under
absorption costing
and direct costing

As a final point of emphasis, recognize that the difference between the absorption costing and direct costing methods is *solely* in the treatment of fixed manufacturing overhead costs and income statement presentation. *Both* methods treat selling and administrative expenses as period costs. Regarding selling and administrative expenses, the only difference is their placement on the income statement and the segregation of variable and fixed selling and administrative expenses. Variable selling and administrative expenses are *not* part of product cost under either method. Illustration 16.4 contrasts this difference.

The comparison of absorption costing and direct costing is slightly more complicated when both beginning and ending inventories are involved. Assuming fixed costs per unit remain the same from period to period, the analysis is made as described above if ending inventory is greater than beginning inventory (even if beginning inventory is not zero). However, if the amount of inventory decreases, the effect on net income is reversed.

We can estimate the effects of inventory another way. First, find the difference in income before taxes by determining whether the amount of fixed manufacturing overhead costs included in inventory cost under absorption costing increased or decreased from the beginning to the end of the period. If fixed manufacturing overhead costs included in inventory increased during the period, then income before income taxes under direct costing will be less than under absorption costing. If the amount of fixed manufacturing overhead costs included in inventory decreased during the period, income before income taxes under direct costing will be greater than

Illustration 16.4
COMPARISON OF ABSORPTION AND DIRECT COSTING

	Absorption Costing		Direct Costing	
Expense	Product Cost	Period Cost	Product Cost	Period Cost
Direct costs:				
Direct materials	x		x	
Direct labor	x		x	
Indirect costs:				
Variable manufacturing overhead.	x		x	
Fixed manufacturing overhead	x			x
Other expenses:				
Selling		x		x
Administrative.		x		x

under absorption costing. (The Demonstration Problem at the end of this chapter illustrates how to determine net income when both beginning and ending inventories are involved.)

As a general rule, the difference in income before income taxes under absorption costing and direct costing can be related to the *change* in inventories. Assuming a relatively constant level of production, if inventories increase during the year, then production exceeded sales, and reported income before income taxes will be less under direct costing than under absorption costing. Conversely, if inventories decreased, then sales exceeded production, and income before income taxes will be larger under direct costing than under absorption costing.

Currently accepted practice requires that *all* costs of producing a product be attached to that product and treated as expense only when the product is sold. Direct costing is not currently acceptable for income measurement or inventory valuation in external financial statements that must comply with generally accepted accounting principles or for tax purposes in the United States. Managers may use it for internal company reports, however. The type of information accumulated under direct costing, especially the classification of costs as fixed and variable, is very useful to management in understanding relationships between costs, volume, and profits. Since direct costing is such a valuable management tool, its use is likely to increase.

DISTRIBUTION COST ANALYSIS

Objective 5
Explain distribution cost analysis and how it is used

The analytical tools discussed in this chapter are designed to give consideration to both manufacturing and nonmanufacturing costs. Some of the most important nonmanufacturing costs are costs of selling and delivering products and services to customers. In fact, distribution costs are the major costs incurred in many businesses.

One method of cost analysis that is gaining popularity is distribution cost analysis. **Distribution costs** are expenses such as advertising, shipping, sales salaries, sales commissions, and handling costs incurred in selling and delivering products and services to customers. **Distribution cost analysis** is the process of assembling the various items of distribution cost into meaningful groupings such as by segment, territory, salesperson, or customers and then analyzing the results. This analysis permits managers to evaluate performance and to consider alternative ways to sell and deliver their goods and services.

To illustrate, assume that Tidwell Stores groups its distribution costs by geographical segments. The costs are further subdivided by product groups and salespersons. In analyzing the results, Tidwell found that distribution costs for selling product A in Segment 1 were $0.10 per dollar of sales salaries and $0.18 per dollar of sales salaries in Segment 2. Further analysis discovered (among other things) that the salespersons in Segment 1 used the company's new 800 WATS line number to stay in touch with small customers, while salespersons in Segment 2 still tried to make frequent personal visits to all customers.

In many situations such as that described, management discovers that one segment uses more efficient and effective sales techniques (conference calls) and less costly transportation means (railroad rather than air) than the other segments. Identifying better marketing and transportation techniques and spreading their use to other segments can improve the entire company's net income. Where problems persist that are due to human factors, companies may need to replace or retrain certain personnel.

The specific uses of distribution cost analysis are to:

1. Identify the types and amounts of expense incurred in each separate marketing activity.
2. Evaluate marketing methods, policies, and procedures.
3. Determine the marketing costs and profitability of a company's various segments, territories, salespersons, products, or consumers.
4. Determine the relationship between cost and order size as a basis for minimizing losses on small orders and as a basis for quantity discount schedules that conform to the Robinson-Patman Act. (This act prohibits price differences to customers unless justified by differences in distribution costs.)

The basic steps in distribution cost analysis are to (1) determine the cost of performing each distribution activity or function of the business; (2) arrange the costs into meaningful groupings (segments, territories, salespersons, products, or customers); (3) analyze the results; and (4) take corrective action based on the analysis.

Distribution costs are as important as manufacturing costs and all other costs in determining net income. Yet, they are sometimes minimized in

ETHICS   A CLOSER LOOK

Andre Lebaque started a company several years ago that makes leather and suede coats. He sells these coats to boutique stores for $180 per coat. His variable cost per unit is $60, and fixed costs are $1,000,000 per year. All variable costs are manufacturing costs. He has been selling about 10,000 coats a year, thus enjoying good profits.

A small local company recently told Andre it would be interested in buying his company. The selling price was negotiable, but would be based heavily on the current year's net income. Andre's fiscal year ends in three months.

Andre asked his financial adviser for advice about ways to make the company profitable. His adviser made several suggestions, including one "to increase production and ending inventories so some of this year's fixed costs would be expensed in later years." When Andre asked for an explanation, the adviser stated that under absorption costing, fixed manufacturing costs are product costs. They are not expensed on the income statement until the goods are sold.

"For example," explained Andre's adviser, "about 70% of your fixed costs are manufacturing costs. These costs go into inventory when the product is manufactured and are expensed when it is sold. If the product has been manufactured but not sold, the fixed manufacturing cost remains in ending inventory. For example, if in one year you produced 20,000 coats and sold 10,000, I estimate you could increase your income before income taxes by $350,000. The buyers won't understand what you are doing because they aren't familiar with accounting practices."

Required
a. Is the analyst correct?
b. What should Andre do?

making decisions. Manufacturing, merchandising, and service companies need to give considerable attention to controlling distribution costs.

The focus of this chapter has been short-term decision making. Part of decision making involves planning through the use of budgets. Chapter 17 discusses budgeting—an important tool of company management.

UNDERSTANDING THE LEARNING OBJECTIVES

1. Explain differential analysis and describe its components.
   - Differential analysis involves analyzing the different costs and benefits that would arise from alternative solutions to a particular situation.
   - The different components are:
     1. *Relevant revenues or costs.* These revenues/costs are future revenues or costs that differ depending on which alternative course of action is selected.
     2. *Differential revenue.* This revenue is the difference in revenue between two alternatives.

    3. *Differential cost or expense.* This cost/expense is the difference between relevant costs for two alternatives.

    4. *Sunk costs.* These costs are past costs and are not relevant in decision making.

2. Demonstrate applications of differential analysis.
- Five types of decisions are involved in differential analysis:
    1. *Setting prices of products.* In selecting a price for a product, the goal is to select the price at which total future revenues will exceed total future costs by the greatest amount or, in other words, the price that will result in the greatest total profit.
    2. *Accepting or rejecting special orders.* Variable costs set a floor for the selling price in cost analysis. Such pricing should be appraised in light of the long-range effects on company and industry price structures. In the long run, companies must cover full costs.
    3. *Adding or dropping products, segments, or customers.* Costs must be reclassified as those costs that would be changed by adding or dropping a product, a segment, or a class of customers and those costs that would not. The decisions to add or drop a product, a segment, or a class of customers are based only on the differential items; that is, the costs and revenues that would change.
    4. *Processing or selling joint products.* Joint costs are those costs incurred up to the point where the joint products split off from each other. These costs are sunk costs in deciding whether to process a joint product further before selling it or to sell it in its condition at split off. If the differential revenue of further processing exceeds the differential cost, then further processing should be done.
    5. *Deciding to make or buy.* A make-or-buy decision concerns whether to manufacture or purchase a part or material used in the manufacture of another product. The price that would be paid for the part if it was purchased is compared with the additional costs that would be incurred if the part was manufactured.

3. Compare and contrast absorption costing and direct costing.
- Similarities between absorption costing and direct costing:
    1. Both methods of costing treat selling and administrative expenses as period costs.
    2. Both methods treat variable manufacturing costs as product costs.
- Differences between absorption and direct costing:
    1. Under absorption costing, all manufacturing costs are treated as product costs, including fixed manufacturing overhead.
    2. Under direct costing, all the fixed manufacturing overhead costs are charged off during the period rather than being deferred and carried forward to the next period as part of inventory cost.

4. Describe the differences in net income under absorption costing and direct costing.
   - The difference in income before income taxes under the two methods can be related solely to the *change* in inventories. Assuming a relatively constant level of production, if inventories increased during the year, then production exceeded sales, and reported income before income taxes will be less under direct costing than under absorption costing. Conversely, if inventories decreased, then sales exceeded production, and income before income taxes will be higher under direct costing than under absorption costing.
5. Explain distribution cost analysis and how it is used.
   - Distribution cost analysis is a process of assembling the various items of distribution cost (e.g., advertising, shipping, sales salaries, and so on) into meaningful groupings such as by segment, territory, salesperson, or customer. The results are then analyzed and corrective action is taken if necessary.
   - The specific uses of distribution cost analysis are to:
     1. Identify the types and amounts of expense incurred in each separate marketing activity.
     2. Evaluate marketing methods, policies, and procedures.
     3. Determine the marketing cost and profitability of a company's various segments, territories, salespersons, products, or consumers.
     4. Determine the relationship between cost and order size as a basis for minimizing losses on small orders and as a basis for quantity discount schedules that conform to the Robinson-Patman Act. (This act prohibits price differences to customers unless justified by differences in distribution costs.)

DEMONSTRATION PROBLEM

The Philadelphia Division of Pride Company produces a single product that it sells for $12 each. Production costs include $2.40 per unit variable costs and $198,000 per year of fixed manufacturing overhead costs. Normal activity for fixed manufacturing overhead cost absorption is 55,000 units per year. Thus, fixed manufacturing overhead costs are applied at $3.60 per unit. Selling and administrative expenses are $15,000 plus $0.60 per unit sold.

On December 31, 1994, the division's finished goods inventory consisted of 10,000 units with a total cost of $60,000 ($24,000, variable: $36,000, fixed). Sales and production data for 1995 are:

Sales in units.	50,000
Dollars of sales.	$600,000
Production in units	55,000
Variable production costs	$132,000

Required:

a. Prepare an income statement for the division for 1995 under absorption costing.

b. Prepare an income statement for the division for 1995 under direct costing.

Solution to demonstration problem

a. Income statement under absorption costing:

PRIDE COMPANY (Philadelphia Division)
Income Statement
For the Year Ended December 31, 1995

Sales (50,000 units at $12)			$600,000
Cost of goods sold:			
Beginning finished goods inventory (absorption cost $6 per unit)		$ 60,000	
Variable production costs ($2.40 per unit) . . .	$132,000		
Fixed manufacturing overhead costs absorbed ($3.60 per unit).	198,000		
Cost of goods manufactured		330,000	
Ending finished goods inventory (absorption cost $6 per unit)		(90,000)	
Cost of goods sold			300,000
Gross margin on sales			$300,000
Selling and administrative expenses.			45,000
Income before income taxes			$255,000

b. Income statement under direct costing:

PRIDE COMPANY (Philadelphia Division)
Income Statement
For the Year Ended December 31, 1995

Sales (50,000 units at $12)		$600,000
Cost of goods sold:		
Beginning finished goods inventory (absorption cost $2.40 per unit).	$ 24,000	
Direct cost of goods manufactured ($2.40 per unit)	132,000	
Ending finished goods inventory (absorption cost $2.40 per unit).	(36,000)	
Cost of goods sold.		120,000
Manufacturing margin		$480,000
Variable selling and administrative expenses		30,000
Contribution margin		$450,000
Period costs:		
Fixed manufacturing overhead	$198,000	
Fixed selling and administrative expenses.	15,000	213,000
Income before income taxes		$237,000

NEW TERMS

Absorption (or full) costing   A concept of costing under which all production costs, including fixed manufacturing overhead, are accounted for as product costs and allocated to the units produced during a period. *819*

By-products   The additional products (which sometimes have a small market value compared to the main product) that result from the production of the main product or products. *817*

Committed fixed costs   Costs relating to the basic facilities and organizational structure that a company must have to continue operations. *811*

Contribution margin format   Subtracts variable costs from revenues to show the contribution margin and then subtracts fixed costs from the contribution margin to show income. *820*

Differential analysis   An analysis of the different costs and benefits that would arise from alternative solutions to a particular problem. *809*

Differential cost or expense   The difference between the amounts of relevant costs for two alternatives. *809*

Differential revenue   The difference between the amounts of relevant revenues for two alternatives. *809*

Direct (or variable) costing   A concept of costing under which only variable manufacturing costs are accounted for as product costs and charged to the units produced during a period. All fixed manufacturing overhead is charged to expense in the period in which it is incurred. *819*

Discretionary fixed costs   Fixed costs that are subject to management control from year to year. An example is advertising expense. *811*

Distribution cost analysis   The process of assembling the various items of distribution cost into meaningful groupings such as by segment, territory, salesperson, or customers and then analyzing the results. *824*

Distribution costs   The expenses incurred in selling and delivering products and services to customers. *824*

Joint costs   Those costs incurred up to the point where joint products split off from each other. *816*

Joint products   Two or more products resulting from a common raw material or manufacturing process. *816*

Make-or-buy decision   Concerns whether to manufacture or purchase a part or material used in the manufacture of another product. *818*

Opportunity cost   The potential benefit that is foregone from not following the next best alternative course of action. *812*

Relevant revenues or costs   Revenues or costs that will differ in the future depending on which alternative course of action is selected. *809*

Sunk costs   Past costs about which nothing can be done. They are not relevant in decision making because the costs have already been incurred. *810*

SELF-TEST

True-False

Indicate whether each of the following statements is true or false.

1. Opportunity costs are costs of transactions that have occurred.

2. Public relations expense would be considered a discretionary fixed cost.

3. Contribution margin is often more valuable to management than gross margin when making decisions on special order pricing.

4. Under direct costing, all of the fixed manufacturing overhead costs are charged off during the period rather than being deferred as part of inventory costs into the next period.

5. Variable selling and administrative expenses are not part of product costs under either absorption or direct costing methods.

Multiple-Choice

Select the best answer for each of the following questions.

1. Differential analysis is best described by which of the following statements?
    a. Determines the difference in revenues between two alternatives.
    b. Estimates future revenues and costs that differ depending on the course of action selected.
    c. Determines the difference between relevant costs for two alternatives.
    d. Analyzes opportunity costs.

2. In selecting a price for a product using differential analysis, which of the following decisions should be made?
    a. The expected volume of sales at each price should be estimated.
    b. The price that will result in the greatest total profit should be selected.
    c. Total future revenues should exceed total future costs by the greatest amount for the alternative selected.
    d. All of the above.

3. If no beginning inventory existed, the company had fixed manufacturing overhead costs, and production units exceeded sales units, then:
    a. Income before income taxes under direct costing would be lower than under absorption costing.
    b. Income before income taxes under direct

costing would be higher than under absorption costing.
    c. Income before income taxes under absorption costing would be the same as direct costing.
    d. None of the above.

4. Direct costing is currently considered acceptable for:
    a. Income measurement for external reporting under generally accepted accounting principles.
    b. Inventory valuation for external reporting under generally accepted accounting principles.
    c. Tax purposes.
    d. Internal company reports.

5. Which of the following choices best explains the basic steps in distribution cost analysis?
    a. Determining the fixed and variable aspects of distribution costs and arranging the costs into meaningful groups.
    b. Identifying types of expenses incurred with distribution costs and arranging costs into segments.
    c. Assessing and determining costs of performing each distribution activity, arranging costs into meaningful groups, analyzing the results, and taking action.
    d. None of the above.

Now turn to page 839 to check your answers.

QUESTIONS

1. Identify some types of decisions that can be made using differential analysis.

2. What is a committed fixed cost? Give some examples.

3. What is a discretionary fixed cost? Give some examples.

4. Give an example of a fixed cost that might be considered committed for one company and discretionary for another.

5. What is the disadvantage of a company having all committed fixed costs? Explain.

6. What is an opportunity cost? Give an example.

7. What essential feature distinguishes direct costing from absorption costing?

8. Under what specific circumstances would you expect net income to be larger under direct costing than under absorption costing? What is the specific reason for this difference?

9. Explain the concept of distribution cost analysis.

10. Describe the basic steps when using distribution cost analysis and why it is important to managers.

11. *Real-world question*   When the Los Angeles Kings acquired hockey star Wayne Gretzky, they paid $15 million to the Edmonton Oilers and gave the Oilers a young star plus three draft choices. What costs and revenues do you think would be differential for the Los Angeles Kings in acquiring Gretzky?

12. *Real-world question*   Give an example in which your campus bookstore replaced one of its departments with another that it currently does not have. (For example, it stopped selling magazines and started selling cameras.) Which revenues and costs would be differential?

13. *Real-world question*   Assume McDonald's, of McDonald's fast-food restaurants, currently buys its french fries from agricultural growers and food processors such as Ore-Ida Foods. In doing so, McDonald's has decided to buy the materials for its french fries instead of "make" them. (Assume that "making" french fries includes growing the potatoes.) What factors went into McDonald's decision to "buy" instead of "make" french fries?

The Coca-Cola Company

14. *Real-world question*   Refer to The Coca-Cola Company's financial statements in Appendix C at the end of this text. Does Coca-Cola use direct costing or absorption costing?

The Coca-Cola Company

15. *Real-world question*   Refer to Note 18, "Lines of Business," in Coca-Cola's financial statements in Appendix C at the end of this text. Suppose Coca-Cola dropped its Foods business segment that earned $103.7 million in operating income in 1991. Would Coca-Cola's total operating income have dropped by $103.7 million if it had dropped the Foods segment? Do you think it would have dropped by more or by less than $103.7 million?

EXERCISES

<table>
<tr><td>

Identify relevant
and differential
revenues and
costs
(L.O. 1)

</td><td>

16-1. Assume you had invested $144 in cosmetics to set up a business selling cosmetics for the summer. During the first week, you are presented with two opportunities. You can sell cosmetics at a friend's store for $760 or you can help cater a wedding for $600. The additional costs you will incur are $120 and $48, respectively. These costs include $15.00 under each alternative for a white apron. Prepare a schedule showing the net benefit or advantage of selecting one alternative over the other.

</td></tr>
<tr><td>

Decide which offer
to accept
(L.O. 2)

</td><td>

16-2. Java Corporation is operating at 80% of capacity, which means it produces 16,000 units. Variable cost is $110 per unit. Wholesaler A offers to buy 4,000 units at $126 per unit. Wholesaler B proposes to buy 3,000 units at $135 per unit. Which offer, if any, should the Java Corporation accept?

</td></tr>
<tr><td>

Decide which
company can bid
lowest
(L.O. 2)

</td><td>

16-3. Two companies, Zeus, Inc., and Titan Company, are competitors. Zeus, Inc., has just installed the latest automated equipment so that its fixed costs are $225,000. Titan Company operates an inefficient plant with only $112,500 of fixed costs. Both companies have $380,000 in sales and gross margins of 20%. Which company can bid lower on a special order to regain lost sales? Why?

</td></tr>
<tr><td>

Decide whether to
retain a product
line
(L.O. 2)

</td><td>

16-4. Analysis of product Z reveals that it is losing $6,000 annually. Five thousand units of product Z are sold at a price of $11 per unit each year. If variable cost is $10.00 per unit, what would be the increase (decrease) in company net income before taxes if product Z were eliminated?

</td></tr>
<tr><td>

Decide whether to
keep or eliminate
a department
(L.O. 2)

</td><td>

16-5. Department 2 of Rufus Company has revenues of $120,000, variable expenses of $50,000, direct fixed expenses of $25,000 (which would be eliminated), and allocated, indirect fixed expenses of $62,500. If the department is eliminated, what will be the effect on income before income taxes?

</td></tr>
<tr><td>

Decide whether to
process joint
products further
(L.O. 2)

</td><td>

16-6. Berlin Company manufactures two joint products. At the split-off point, they have sales values of:

</td></tr>
</table>

Product 1	$8.75 per unit
Product 2	$6.25 per unit

After further processing costing $6 and $4.75, respectively, the products can be sold for $18.75 and $8.75, respectively. Should further processing be done on these products? Why?

<table>
<tr><td>

Decide whether to
make or buy a
part
(L.O. 2)

</td><td>

16-7. Sanchez Corporation currently is manufacturing 90,000 units per year of a part used in its final product. The cost of producing this part is $51.60 per unit. The variable portion of this cost consists of direct materials of $28.80, direct labor of $15.60, and manufacturing overhead of $2.40. The company could earn $94,500 per year from the space now used to manufacture this part. Assuming equal quality and availability, what is the maximum price that Sanchez Corporation should pay to buy the part rather than make it?

</td></tr>
</table>

Compare income
before taxes and
ending inventory
under absorption
and direct costing
(L.O. 4)

16–8. The following data relate to Flores Company for the year ended December 31, 1994:

Cost of production:	
Direct materials.	$168,000
Direct labor.	$252,000
Manufacturing overhead:	
Variable	$ 90,000
Fixed.	$180,000
Sales commissions (variable)	$ 44,000
Sales salaries (fixed)	$46,000
Administrative expenses (fixed)	$62,000
Units produced.	75,000
Units sold (at $18 each)	60,000

Without making any computations, would you expect income before taxes to be higher under absorption costing or under direct costing? Compute the amount of income before income taxes and ending inventory under both methods.

Compute income
before taxes under
absorption and
direct costing
(L.O. 4)

16–9. The following data are for Venice Company for the year 1994:

Sales (20,000 units)	$187,500
Direct materials used (24,000 units at $2.8125)	67,500
Direct labor cost incurred	21,500
Manufacturing overhead incurred:	
Variable	6,750
Fixed.	9,000
Selling and administrative expenses:	
Variable	12,250
Fixed.	38,500

Assume that one unit of direct materials goes into each unit of finished goods. The company has an ending inventory of finished goods of 4,000 units and no other beginning or ending work in process inventories. Compute the income before income taxes under *(a)* absorption costing and *(b)* direct costing.

Discuss how
income before
taxes under
absorption costing
would differ under
direct costing
(L.O. 4)

16–10. Given below are the costs of the finished goods inventories of Hayfork Company:

Cost Element	Beginning Inventory	Ending Inventory
Direct materials	$108,000	$11,800
Direct labor	170,000	18,720
Manufacturing overhead:		
Variable	72,000	7,200
Fixed	54,000	8,200

Assume that Hayfork Company uses absorption costing and the company had no work in process inventories at the beginning or end of the year. State by how much Hayfork Company's income before income taxes for the year would have differed if direct costing had been used.

PROBLEMS

Analyze the different costs and benefits and decide on the best product choice (L.O. 1)

16–1. Rousky Enterprises renovated an old school into gymnasium space, office space, and restaurants. If all of the school was used for gymnasium space, the estimated revenue and variable costs per year to Rousky would be $860,000 and $30,000, respectively. If all of the school was used for office space, the estimated revenue and variable costs per year would be $882,800 and $60,000, respectively. If all of the space was used for restaurants, the estimated revenue and variable costs would be $1,001,100 and $85,000, respectively. Fixed costs per year would be $500,000 regardless of the alternative chosen.

Required:

What should Rousky Enterprises do? Give supporting computations.

Decide whether to keep or eliminate a product line (L.O. 2)

16–2. Following are sales and other operating data for the three products made and sold by Jade Company:

	Product			
	A	B	C	Total
Sales	$240,000	$150,000	$90,000	$480,000
Manufacturing costs:				
Fixed	$ 30,000	$ 15,000	$27,000	$ 72,000
Variable	144,000	120,000	36,000	300,000
Total	$174,000	$135,000	$63,000	$372,000
Gross margin	$ 66,000	$ 15,000	$27,000	$108,000
Selling expenses:				
Fixed	$ 3,000	$ 2,000	$ 4,000	$ 9,000
Variable	9,000	7,000	14,000	30,000
Administrative expenses:				
Fixed	3,000	1,800	7,200	12,000
Variable	6,000	1,800	4,200	12,000
Total selling and administrative expenses	$ 21,000	$ 12,600	$29,400	$ 63,000
Income (loss) before income taxes	$ 45,000	$ 2,400	$ (2,400)	$ 45,000

In view of the net loss shown above for product C, the company's management is considering dropping that product. All variable costs are direct costs and would be eliminated if product C were dropped; all fixed costs are indirect costs and would not be eliminated. Assume that the space used to produce product C would be left idle.

Required:

Would you recommend the elimination of product C? Give supporting computations.

Decide whether to accept or reject a special order (L.O. 2)

16–3. Sunlight, Inc., has the capacity to produce 4,000 units per year. Its predicted operations for the year are as follows:

Sales (3,000 units @ $70)	$210,000
Manufacturing costs:	
Variable.	48 per unit
Fixed	22,000
Marketing and administrative costs:	
Variable.	4 per unit
Fixed	6,000

Required:

a. Should the company accept a special order for 500 units at a selling price of $65? Variable marketing and administrative costs for this special order will be zero, and regular sales will not be changed.

b. What is the effect of the decision on the company's operating profit?

Decide whether to accept or reject a special order (L.O. 2)

16–4. Anticipating unusually high sales for October, Formula 500, a manufacturer of baby formula, plans to produce 40,000 pounds of formula, using all available capacity. Formula 500 anticipates production and marketing costs for October as follows:

Unit manufacturing costs per pound:		
Variable direct materials cost.	$0.15	
Variable labor	0.02	
Variable overhead	0.03	
Fixed overhead	0.10	
Total manufacturing costs		$0.30
Unit marketing costs per pound:		
Variable.	$0.03	
Fixed	0.20	
Total marketing costs		0.23
Total unit costs		$0.53
Selling price per pound		$0.82

On September 30, Formula 500 received a contract offer from Feed the Children (FTC), a nonprofit agency, to supply 5,000 pounds of formula for delivery by October 31. The FTC offer would reimburse the agency's share of manufacturing costs plus a fixed fee of $2,000. Variable marketing costs will be zero for this order; fixed costs will not change.

Required:

Should Formula 500 accept the offer? Why or why not?

Decide whether to make or buy a product (L.O. 2)

16–5. Saddle Express, a saddle manufacturer, is currently operating at 70% of capacity and producing about 10,000 saddles a year containing two stirrups per saddle. To use more capacity, the manager has been considering the research and development department's suggestion that Saddle Express manufacture its own stirrups. Currently, the company purchases stirrups from a supplier at a unit price (a unit equals one pair of stirrups) of $0.30. Estimates show that Saddle Express can manufacture its own stirrups at $0.11 per unit direct materials costs and $0.09 direct labor cost. The factory overhead is $2 per direct labor dollar, of which 20% is variable.

Required:

a. Should Saddle Express make or buy the stirrups?
b. Suppose that Saddle Express could rent out the currently unused part of the factory for $100 a month. How would this affect the decision in (a)?

Determine the most profitable price-quantity combination (L.O. 2)

16–6. Newton Company is introducing a new product and must decide what price should be set. An estimated demand schedule for the product follows:

Price	Quantity Demanded (in units)
$10.	40,000
12.	36,000
14.	28,000
16.	24,000
18.	18,000
20.	15,000

Estimated costs follow:

Variable manufacturing costs	$ 4 per unit
Fixed manufacturing costs	35,000 per year
Variable selling and administrative costs. . . .	2 per unit
Fixed selling and administrative costs	20,000 per year

Required:

a. Prepare a schedule showing the total revenue, total cost, and total profit or loss for each selling price.
b. Which price should Newton select? Explain?

Decide whether to process or sell joint products (L.O. 2)

16–7. Boots, Inc., manufactures western boots. Invariably, some of the treated leather used for the boots is left over, and Boots has been selling this leather to Leather Works, which makes leather belts. Boots receives $30 per pound for the treated leather. Boots' president, Cal West, thinks that it may be more lucrative for the company to keep the leftover leather and manufacture its own belts. The operations and marketing managers, Ms. Sunny and Mr. Gest, have determined that further processing of the leather into belts would cost $6 per belt, and the selling price would be $10 per belt. From one pound of leftover leather they determined that 10 belts could be made.

Required:

Would you recommend that the company keep the leftover leather and manufacture its own belts? Explain and give supporting computations.

Prepare income statements under direct and absorption costing; discuss reason for differences (L.O. 4)

16–8. Monarch Company employs an absorption cost system in accounting for the single product it manufactures. Following are selected data for the year 1995:

Sales (10,000 units).	$170,000
Direct materials used (12,000 units at $5.40)	64,800
Direct labor cost incurred.	21,600
Variable manufacturing overhead	6,480
Fixed manufacturing overhead	8,640
Variable selling and administrative expenses	10,800
Fixed selling and administrative expenses	36,000

One unit of direct material goes into each unit of finished goods. Overhead rates are based on a capacity of 12,000 units and are $0.54 and $0.72 per unit for variable and fixed overhead, respectively. The only beginning or ending inventory is the 2,000 units of finished goods on hand at the end of 1995.

Required:

a. Prepare an income statement for 1995 under direct costing (ignore income taxes).
b. Prepare an income statement for 1995 under absorption costing (ignore income taxes).
c. Explain the reason for the difference in net income between *(a)* and *(b)*.

Prepare income statements under direct and absorption costing; discuss reason for differences (L.O. 4)

16–9. The following data are for Bristol Company for the year 1995:

Sales (20,000 units).	$385,000
Direct materials used (24,000 units at $5.625). . . .	135,000
Direct labor cost incurred.	45,000
Variable manufacturing overhead incurred	13,500
Fixed manufacturing overhead incurred	18,000
Variable selling and administrative expenses	22,500
Fixed selling and administrative expenses	65,000

One unit of direct materials goes into each unit of finished goods. The only beginning or ending inventory is the 4,000 units of finished goods on hand at the end of 1995. Variable and fixed overhead rates (based on 100% of capacity of 24,000 units) are $0.5625 and $0.75, respectively.

Required:

a. Prepare an income statement for 1995 under direct costing (ignore income taxes).
b. Prepare an income statement for 1995 under absorption costing (ignore income taxes).
c. Explain the reason for the difference in net income between *(a)* and *(b)*.

BUSINESS DECISION PROBLEMS

Prepare income
statement under
both absorption
costing and direct
costing; explain
why net income
before taxes
differs; settle
debate between
general manager
and controller
(L.O. 4)

16–1. The general manager of the Eureka Division of Unitab Company submitted the company's income statement for the year ended June 30, 1995 (prepared under absorption costing), with the comment that the division was at least profitable. The report showed that sales amounted to 160,000 units at $48 per unit and that the following costs had been incurred:

Direct materials	$2,090,000
Direct labor	912,000
Manufacturing overhead	2,736,000
Selling and administrative expenses	2,700,000

A total of 220,000 units was put into process during the year. Regarding the 60,000 units in the June 30, 1995, inventory, all materials costs had been incurred, but the units were only 50% complete as to processing. No other beginning or ending finished goods or work in process inventories existed.

The Eureka Division's production process is highly automated, and its costs are largely fixed: $2,280,000 of the manufacturing overhead costs and $960,000 of the selling and administrative costs are fixed.

On receipt of the division's income statement, the company's controller made a few quick calculations and commented that the division actually operated at a loss. The general manager of the division took exception to this statement, causing a long argument.

Required:

a. Prepare the division's income statement under absorption costing. Include a schedule showing the computation of the cost of ending work in process inventory. Assume that fixed overhead is absorbed under expected activity and that expected activity equaled actual activity for the year.

b. Repeat *(a)* under direct costing.

c. State exactly what caused the difference in net income between *(a)* and *(b)*.

d. Who is right in this debate? Explain.

16–2. Prior to 1995, Calgan Wholesalers Company had not kept department income statements. To achieve better management control, the company decided to install department-by-department accounts. At the end of 1995, the new accounts showed that although the business as a whole was profitable, the canning department had shown a substantial loss. The income statement for the canning department, shown here, reports on operations for 1995.

CALGAN WHOLESALERS COMPANY
Canning Department
Partial Income Statement for 1995

Sales.	$550,000	
Cost of goods sold	375,000	
Gross margin.		$175,000
Costs:		
Payroll, direct labor, and supervision.	$ 73,000	
Commissions of sales staff[a]	33,000	
Rent[b].	26,000	
State taxes[c].	3,000	
Insurance on inventory	4,000	
Depreciation[d]	7,000	
Administration and general office[e]	32,000	
Interest for inventory carrying costs[f]	5,000	
Total costs		183,000
Loss before allocation of income taxes.		$ (8,000)

[a] All sales staff compensated on straight commission, at a uniform 6% of all sales.

[b] Rent charged to departments on a square-foot basis. The company rents an entire building, and the canning department occupies 15% of the building.

[c] Assessed annually on the basis of average inventory on hand each month.

[d] Eight and one-half percent of cost of departmental equipment.

[e] Allocated on basis of departmental sales as a fraction of total company sales.

[f] Based on average inventory quantity multiplied by the company's borrowing rate for three-month loans.

Analysis of these results has led management to suggest that it close the canning department. Members of the management team agree that keeping the canning department is not essential to maintaining good customer relations and supporting the rest of the company's business. In other words, eliminating the canning department is expected to have no effect on the amount of business done by the other departments.

Required:

What action do you recommend to management of Calgan Wholesalers Company? Why?

ANSWERS TO SELF-TEST

True-False

1. *False.*   Opportunity costs are based on transactions that have not occurred. However, opportunity costs are relevant costs in many decision problems because they represent real sacrifices that come about because one alternative is chosen instead of another.

2. *True.*   Public relations expense would be considered a discretionary fixed cost because management can control this cost from year to year.

3. *True.*   The contribution margin is often more valuable to management because it is needed to calculate the break-even point and make decisions regarding special order pricing.

4. *True.*   *All* fixed manufacturing overhead costs are charged off during the period.

5. *True.*   Variable selling and administrative expenses are *not* part of product costs under either method.

Multiple-Choice

1. *b.* Differential analysis estimates future revenues and costs that differ depending on the course of action selected.

2. *d.* The expected volume of sales, the price that will result in the greatest total profit, and determining the alternative for which future revenues exceed future costs by the greatest amount are all decisions made in selecting a price using differential analysis.

3. *a.* Income before taxes will be less under direct costing if production units exceeded sales units because absorption costing inventoried some of the period's fixed manufacturing costs.

4. *d.* Direct costing is acceptable for internal company reports.

5. *c.* Distribution cost analysis involves determining the costs of performing each distribution activity, arranging costs into meaningful groups, analyzing results, and taking corrective action if necessary.

17 BUDGETING FOR PLANNING AND CONTROL

LEARNING OBJECTIVES

After studying this chapter, you should be able to:

1. Define a budget and name several kinds of budgets.
2. List several benefits of a budget.
3. List five general principles of budgeting.
4. Prepare a planned operating budget and its supporting budgets, such as the sales budget, production and purchases budgets, and other expense budgets.
5. Prepare flexible operating budgets.
6. Prepare a financial budget and its supporting budgets.

In planning the management of your personal finances, you may have only a general idea of your yearly cash inflows and outflows. If your outflows exceed your inflows, you may have to borrow to cover the difference. However, if the inflows exceed the outflows, you may have excess cash to place in a bank or to invest.

At times, especially if you find that your cash position is tight, you may be tempted to prepare a written plan detailing your anticipated cash flows to better control your finances. Such a written plan is a budget.

Companies usually prepare budgets to plan for and then control their revenues (inflows) and expenses (outflows). Failure to prepare a budget could lead to significant cash flow problems or even financial disaster for a company. In fact, one of the leading causes of failure in small businesses is failing to plan and control operations through the use of budgets.

This chapter first provides a conceptual foundation for budgeting. Then we describe and illustrate a master budget. The chapter concludes with special topics relating to budgeting.

THE BUDGET—FOR PLANNING AND CONTROL

Objective 1
Define a budget
and name several
kinds of budgets

A **budget** is a *plan* showing the company's objectives and how management intends to acquire and use resources to attain those objectives. Companies, nonprofit organizations, and governmental units use many different types of budgets. *Responsibility budgets,* discussed in Chapter 19, are designed to judge the performance of an individual segment or manager. *Capital budgets,* discussed in Chapter 20, evaluate long-term capital projects such as the addition of equipment or the relocation of a plant. This chapter examines the **master budget,** which consists of a *planned operating budget* and a *financial budget.* The **planned operating budget** helps to plan future earnings and results in a projected income statement. The **financial budget** helps management plan the financing of assets and results in a projected balance sheet.

Purposes of Budgets

The budgeting process involves planning for future profitability. Earning a reasonable return on resources used is a primary company objective. A company must devise some method to deal with the uncertainty of the future. If a company does no planning whatsoever, then it chooses to deal with the future by default and can only react to events as they occur. Most businesses, however, devise a blueprint for the actions they will take, given the foreseeable events that may occur.

Objective 2
List several bene-
fits of a budget

A budget (1) shows management's operating plans for the coming period(s); (2) formalizes management's plans in quantitative terms; (3) forces all levels of management to think ahead, anticipate results, and take action to remedy possible poor results; and (4) may also be used to *motivate* individuals so that they strive to achieve stated goals.

Companies can use budget-to-actual comparisons to evaluate individual performance. For instance, the expected variable cost of producing a personal computer at IBM can be a budget figure. This figure can be compared with the actual variable cost of producing a personal computer to help evaluate employee performance.

Many other benefits result from the preparation and use of budgets. For example, (1) businesses better *coordinate their activities;* (2) managers *become aware of other managers' plans;* (3) employees become more *cost conscious* and try to *conserve* resources; (4) managers *review* the company's organizational plan and make changes where necessary; and (5) managers foster a *vision* of the company's future that they might not otherwise develop.

The planning process that results in a formal budget provides an opportunity for various levels of management to think through and commit future plans to writing. In addition, a properly prepared budget allows management to follow the management-by-exception principle by devoting attention to activities that deviate significantly from planned levels. For all these reasons, a budget must clearly reflect the expected results.

Considerations in Preparing a Budget

Failing to budget because of the uncertainty of the future is a poor excuse. In fact, the less stable the conditions, the more necessary and desirable it is to budget, although the process becomes more difficult. Obviously, stable operating conditions permit greater reliance on past experience as a basis for budgeting.

A budget should include management's assumptions relating to (1) the state of the economy over the planning horizon; (2) plans for adding, deleting, or changing product lines; (3) the nature of the industry's competition; and (4) the effects of existing or possible government regulations.

Budgets are quantitative plans for the future. However, they are based mainly on past experience adjusted for future expectations. Thus, accounting data related to the past play an important part in budget preparation. The accounting system and the budget are closely related. The accounts must be designed to assist in preparing the budget, financial statements, and interim financial reports used to facilitate operational control.

Management should frequently compare actual results with budgeted projections during the budget period and investigate any differences. Budgeting, however, is not a substitute for good management. Instead, the budget is an important tool of managerial control.

The period covered by a budget varies according to the nature of the specific activity involved. Cash budgets may cover a week or a month; sales and production budgets may cover a month, a quarter, or a year; and general operating budgets may cover a quarter or a year.

Some General Principles of Budgeting

Budgeting involves the coordination of financial and nonfinancial planning to satisfy organizational goals and objectives. No foolproof method exists for preparing an effective budget. However, budget preparers should carefully consider the factors that follow.

Objective 3
List five general principles of budgeting

Top-Management Support.   All management levels must be aware of the budget's importance to the company and must know that the budget has top-management support. Top management, then, must clearly state long-range goals and broad objectives. These goals and objectives must be communicated throughout the organization. Long-range goals include the expected quality of products or services, growth rates in sales and earnings, and percentage-of-market targets. Overemphasis on the mechanics of the budget process should be avoided.

Participation in Goal Setting.   Management uses budgets to show how it intends to acquire and use resources to achieve the company's long-range goals. Employees are more likely to strive toward organizational goals if they participate in setting them and in preparing budgets. Often, employees have significant information that could help in preparing a meaningful budget. Also, employees may be motivated to perform their own functions within budget constraints if they are committed to achieving organizational goals.

Communicating Results. People should be promptly and clearly informed of their progress. Effective communication implies (1) timeliness, (2) reasonable accuracy, and (3) understandability. Managers should effectively communicate results so employees can make any necessary adjustments in their performance.

Flexibility. If significant basic assumptions underlying the budget change during the year, the planned operating budget should be restated. For control purposes, after the actual level of operations is known, the actual revenues and expenses can be compared to expected performance at that level of operations.

Follow-up. Budget follow-up and data feedback are part of the control aspect of the budget process. Since the budgets are dealing with projections and estimates for future operating results and financial positions, managers must frequently check their budgets and correct them if necessary. Often management uses performance reports as a follow-up tool to compare actual results with budgeted results.

Behavioral Implications of Budgets

The term *budget* has negative connotations for many employees who feel they are *subjected* to a budget. Often in the past, management has *imposed* a budget from the top without considering the opinions and feelings of the personnel affected. Such a dictatorial process may result in resistance to the budget. A number of reasons may underlie such resistance, including lack of understanding of the program, concern for acceptance by their co-workers, and an expectation of increased pressure to perform. Employees may believe that the performance evaluation method is unfair or that the goals are unrealistic and unattainable. They may lack confidence in the way accounting figures are generated or may prefer a less formal communication and evaluation system. Often these fears are completely unfounded, but if an employee believes these problems exist, the objectives of budgeting will be difficult to accomplish.

Problems encountered with such *imposed* budgets have led accountants and management to adopt participatory budgeting. **Participatory budgeting** means that all levels of management responsible for actual performance actively participate in setting operating goals for the coming period. Managers (and other employees) are more likely to understand, accept, and pursue goals if they are involved in formulating them.

Where do accountants fit into a participatory budgeting process? Accountants should be *compilers* or coordinators of the budget, not *preparers*. They should be on hand during the preparation process to present and explain significant financial data. Accountants must identify the relevant cost data that will enable management's objectives to be quantified in dollars, and accountants are responsible for designing meaningful budget reports. Also, accountants must continually strive to make the accounting system more responsive to managerial needs. That responsiveness, in turn, will increase confidence in the accounting system.

Although many companies have used budget participation successfully, it does not always work. Studies have shown that in many organizations budget participation failed to make employees more motivated to achieve budgeted goals. Whether or not participation works depends on management's leadership style, on the attitudes of employees, and on the organization's size and structure. Participation is not the answer to all the problems of budget preparation. However, participation is one way to achieve better results in organizations that are receptive to the philosophy of participation.

THE MASTER BUDGET CONCEPT

A **master budget** consists of a projected income statement (planned operating budget) and a projected balance sheet (financial budget) showing the organization's objectives and proposed ways of attaining them. Illustration 17.1 shows a flowchart of the financial planning process that you can use as an overview of the elements in a master budget. In the remainder of this chapter, you will learn how a company prepares a master budget. We emphasize the master budget because of its prime importance to financial planning and control in a business entity.

The budgeting process starts with management's plans and objectives for the next period. These plans result in various policy decisions concerning selling price, distribution network, advertising expenditures, and environmental influences from which the company forecasts its sales for the period (in units by product or product line). Managers arrive at the **sales budget** in dollars by multiplying sales units times sales price per unit. These managers use expected production, sales volume, and inventory policy to project cost of goods sold. Next, managers project operating expenses such as selling and administrative expenses.

This chapter cannot cover all areas of budgeting in detail—entire books have been written on budgeting. However, the following presentation provides an overview of a budgeting procedure that many successful companies

Illustration 17.1
A FLOWCHART OF THE FINANCIAL PLANNING PROCESS

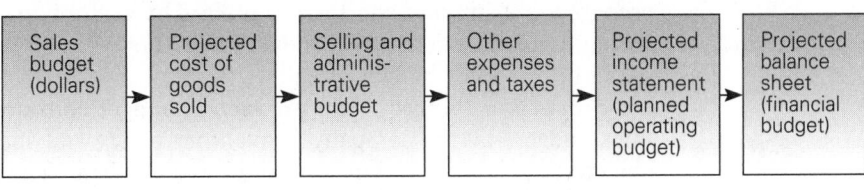

have used. We begin by discussing the planned operating budget (or projected income statement).

Preparing the Planned Operating Budget at the Expected Level of Operations

The projected balance sheet, or **financial budget,** depends on many items in the projected income statement. Thus, the logical starting point in preparing a master budget is the projected income statement, or **planned operating budget.** However, since the planned operating budget shows only the net effect of many interrelated activities, management must prepare several supporting budgets (sales, production, and purchases, to name a few) before preparing the planned operating budget. The process begins with the *sales budget.*

Objective 4
Prepare a planned operating budget and its supporting budgets, such as the sales budget, production and purchases budgets, and other expense budgets

Sales Budget.   The cornerstone of the budgeting process is the **sales budget** because the usefulness of the entire operating budget depends on it. The sales budget involves estimating or forecasting how much demand exists for a company's goods and then determining if a realistic, attainable profit can be achieved based on this demand. Sales forecasting can involve either formal or informal techniques, or both.

Formal sales forecasting techniques involve the use of statistical tools. For example, to predict sales for the coming period, management may use economic indicators (or variables) such as the gross national product or personal income and other variables such as population growth, per capita income, new construction, and population migration.

To use economic indicators to forecast sales, a relationship must exist between the indicators (called *independent variables*) and the sales that are being forecast (called the *dependent variable*). Then management can use statistical techniques to predict sales based on the economic indicators.

Management often supplements formal techniques with informal sales forecasting techniques such as intuition or judgment. In some instances, sales projections based on formal techniques are modified based on other changes in the environment. Examples include the effect on sales of any changes in the expected level of advertising expenditures; the entry of new competitors; and/or the addition or deletion of products or sales territories. In other instances, companies do not use any formal techniques. Instead, sales managers and salespersons estimate how much they can sell. Managers then total the estimates to arrive at total estimated sales for the period.

Usually, the sales manager is responsible for the sales budget, which is prepared first in units and then in dollars by multiplying the units by their selling price. The remaining budgets that support the operating budget are based on the sales budget in units.

Production Budget.   The **production budget** considers the units in the sales budget and the company's inventory policy and shows the number of units to be produced and the cost of producing them. The production budget is first developed in units, then in costs. Determining production volume is an important task. Companies should schedule production carefully to maintain certain minimum quantities of inventory on hand while avoiding excessive inventory accumulation. **The principal objective of the production budget is to coordinate (in terms of time and quantity) the production and sale of goods.**

Companies using a just-in-time (JIT) production system, which we discussed in Chapter 12, need to be particularly careful in making their schedules because they must closely coordinate purchasing, sales, and production. In general, maintaining high inventory levels allows for more flexibility in coordinating purchasing, sales, and production; however, the cost of carrying inventory is high and includes such costs as storage costs and the opportunity cost of funds tied up in inventory.

The production budget is often subdivided into budgets for materials, labor, and manufacturing overhead. Usually materials, labor, and some elements of manufacturing overhead will vary directly with production within a given relevant range of production. Fixed manufacturing overhead costs do not vary directly with production but are constant in total within a relevant range of production. For example, fixed manufacturing overhead costs may be $150,000 when production ranges from 60,000 to 80,000 units. However, when production is 80,001 to 95,000 units, the fixed manufacturing overhead costs might be $250,000. To determine fixed manufacturing overhead costs accurately, management must determine the "relevant range of production."

Selling, Administrative, and Other Expense Budgets (Schedules).   The costs of selling the product are closely related to the sales forecast. Generally, the higher the forecast, the higher the selling expenses. Administrative expenses are likely to be less dependent on the sales forecast since many of the items are fixed costs (e.g., salaries of administrative personnel and depreciation of administrative buildings and office equipment). Managers must also estimate other expenses such as interest expense, income tax expense, and research and development expenses.

Once management has prepared the planned operating budget, the next task is to prepare the *financial budget* (or projected balance sheet).

Preparing the Financial Budget

Preparing a projected balance sheet, or financial budget, involves analyzing every balance sheet account. The beginning balance for each account is the amount shown on the balance sheet prepared at the end of the preceding period. Then, the effects of any planned activities on each account are considered. Many accounts will be affected by items appearing in the operating budget and by either cash inflows or outflows. Cash inflows and outflows are usually shown in a cash budget, which will be discussed later in the chapter.

The complexities encountered in preparing the financial budget often require the preparation of detailed schedules. These schedules analyze such things as planned accounts receivable collections and balances, planned materials purchases, planned inventories, changes in all accounts affected by operating costs, and the amount of income taxes payable. Dividend policy, inventory policy, financing policy and constraints, credit policy, and planned capital expenditures also affect the amounts shown in the financial budget.

We have just covered the conceptual aspect of the master budget. In the next section, you will see how a *master budget* is prepared.

THE MASTER BUDGET ILLUSTRATED

The first part of this chapter discussed general concepts relating to the preparation of a master budget. This section illustrates step by step how to prepare the 1995 master budget for Leed Company, which manufactures running shoes.

Preparing the Planned Operating Budget in Units for Leed Company

A company develops its planned operating budget first in units rather than dollars. Since revenues and many expenses vary with volume, they can be forecasted more easily after the company estimates sales and production quantities.

To illustrate this step, assume that Leed's management forecasts sales for the year 1995 at 100,000 units. Quarterly sales are expected to be 20,000, 35,000, 20,000, and 25,000 units (each pair of shoes is one unit), reflecting higher demand for shoes in the late spring and again around the December holidays.

We assume the company's policy is to stabilize production so it will produce 100,000 units uniformly throughout the year. Therefore, production will be 25,000 units per quarter (100,000 units/four quarters). To simplify our example, assume the company has no beginning or ending work in process inventories (although we could also assume that work in process inventories would remain at a constant amount throughout the year). Finished goods inventory on January 1, 1995, is 10,000 units. From these data we can prepare the schedule of budgeted sales and production for the first two quarters of 1995, as shown in Illustration 17.2.

Notice that if Leed wants to maintain a stable production of running shoes, it must allow the above ending inventory to fluctuate if sales vary. Thus, the finished goods inventory is affected by the difference between production and sales. When establishing inventory policy, Leed's management has decided that it is less costly to deal with fluctuating inventories than with fluctuating production.

Illustration 17.2
LEED COMPANY'S PLANNED PRODUCTION AND SALES FOR THE FIRST TWO QUARTERS OF 1995

LEED COMPANY
Planned Production and Sales (in units)

	Quarter Ending	
	March 31, 1995	June 30, 1995
Beginning finished goods inventory	10,000*	15,000
Add: Planned production	25,000	25,000
Units available for sale	35,000	40,000
Less: Sales forecast.	20,000	35,000
Ending finished goods inventory.	15,000	5,000

* Actual on January 1.

Sometimes we are given sales forecasts and ending inventory targets (described as a certain percentage of the next period's sales), and we must calculate the required level of production. Suppose Leed wishes to have ending inventory equal to 50% of the next quarter's sales in units, which are forecasted to be 30,000 units for this example. If so, the following format may be used to calculate planned production:

Sales forecast (units)—current quarter	20,000
Add: Planned ending finished goods inventory	15,000*
Total units required for the period	35,000
Deduct: Beginning finished goods inventory	10,000
Planned production (units).	25,000

* 50% × 30,000.

Remember that to obtain a finished goods ending inventory that is a specified percentage of future sales, the company cannot maintain a constant production policy unless the amount of sales in each period is constant.

Preparing the Planned Operating Budget in Dollars

Next, Leed's management must introduce dollars into the analysis. To accomplish this task, management must forecast the expected selling prices and costs. Illustration 17.3 shows Leed's forecasted selling price and costs. Note that Leed's management classifies costs into variable or fixed categories and budgets these costs accordingly. As noted earlier, **variable costs** vary in total directly with production or sales. **Fixed costs** are unaffected in total by the relative level of production or sales.

Illustration 17.3
BUDGET ESTIMATE OF SELLING PRICE AND COSTS

LEED COMPANY
Budget Estimates of Selling Price and Costs
For Quarters Ending March 31 and June 30, 1995

Forecasted selling price	$ 20
Manufacturing costs:	
Variable (per unit manufactured):	
Direct materials	2
Direct labor	6
Manufacturing overhead	1
Fixed overhead (total each quarter)	75,000
Selling and administrative expenses:	
Variable (per unit sold)	2
Fixed (total each quarter)	100,000

Management now prepares a schedule to forecast cost of goods sold, the next major amount in the planned operating budget. Illustration 17.4 shows this schedule. Notice that the beginning finished goods inventory amount for the quarter ending March 31 is the amount shown on the December 31, 1994, year-end balance sheet (see Illustration 17.9 later in this chapter). Cost of goods manufactured is calculated using the variable manufacturing costs from Illustration 17.3 plus fixed manufacturing overhead. The amount of

Illustration 17.4
SCHEDULE OF PLANNED COST OF GOODS SOLD

LEED COMPANY
Planned Cost of Goods Sold

	Quarter Ending March 31, 1995	Quarter Ending June 30, 1995
Beginning finished goods inventory	$130,000*	$180,000
Cost of goods manufactured:		
Direct materials (25,000 × $2)	$ 50,000	$ 50,000
Direct labor (25,000 × $6)	150,000	150,000
Variable manufacturing overhead (25,000 × $1)	25,000	25,000
Fixed manufacturing overhead (per Illustration 17.3)	75,000	75,000
Cost of goods manufactured (25,000 units at $12)	$300,000	$300,000
Cost of goods available for sale	$430,000	$480,000
Ending finished goods inventory:		
(15,000 at $12)†	180,000	
(5,000 at $12)		60,000
Cost of goods sold	$250,000	$420,000

---

* Actual on January 1 (10,000 at $13); see balance sheet Illustration 17.9.
† First-in, first-out procedure assumed.

ending finished goods inventory is the number of units determined to be in ending inventory (from Illustration 17.2) times the cost per unit manufactured during the period.

After managers forecast cost of goods sold, they prepare a separate budget for all selling and administrative expenses. Several supporting schedules may be involved for items such as advertising expense, office expense, and payroll department expense. The schedules to support budgeted selling and administrative expenses are not illustrated here, but the total selling and administrative expenses for each of the first two quarters are entered into the planned operating budget in Illustration 17.5.

Planned Operating Budget Illustrated

Illustration 17.5 shows Leed's planned operating budget. All of the items appearing in the planned operating budget except the income tax accrual have been discussed and explained. Income taxes are budgeted for Leed at an assumed rate of 40% of income before income taxes.

If the planned operating budget does not show the desired net income, new operating plans will have to be formulated, and a new budget will be developed. The purpose of preparing a planned operating budget is to gain some knowledge of the results of a period's activities before they actually occur.

A company seldom operates at the level of operations assumed in pre-

Illustration 17.5
PLANNED OPERATING BUDGET

LEED COMPANY
Planned Operating Budget

	Quarter Ending	
	March 31, 1995	June 30, 1995
Forecasted sales (20,000 and 35,000 at $20, per Illustration 17.3)	$400,000	$700,000
Cost of goods sold (per Illustration 17.4).	250,000	420,000
Gross margin.	$150,000	$280,000
Selling and administrative expenses:		
Variable (20,000 and 35,000 at $2, per Illustration 17.3)	$ 40,000	$ 70,000
Fixed (per Illustration 17.3)	100,000	100,000
Total selling and administrative expenses	$140,000	$170,000
Income before income taxes	$ 10,000	$110,000
Deduct: Estimated income taxes (assumed to be 40%)	4,000	44,000
Net income.	$ 6,000	$ 66,000

paring the planned operating budget. After the company knows the results of actual operations, management compares actual expenses with budgeted expenses *at the actual level of operations*. To facilitate adjusting the budgeted items to the actual level of operations, management sometimes prepares in advance flexible budgets for the entire operating budget or for certain expenses. The next section discusses these flexible operating budgets and shows how companies prepare budget variances.

Flexible Operating Budgets

Objective 5
Prepare flexible
operating budgets

Early in the chapter, you learned that a budget should be adjusted for changes in assumptions or variations in the level of operations. A technique known as *flexible budgeting* is used to deal with budgetary adjustments. A **flexible operating budget** is a special kind of budget that provides detailed information about budgeted expenses (and revenues) at various levels of output.

Illustration 17.6 shows a flexible budget for Leed's manufacturing overhead costs at various levels of output. To keep the example simple, we will assume that the first four costs are strictly variable, starting at zero and increasing by a constant amount each time production increases by 10% of capacity. (In actual practice, some of these costs may be mixed or step costs.) Depreciation and supervision are completely fixed costs in this example because they are assumed to be constant over the entire relevant range of activity.

Leed's management could prepare a similar flexible budget for selling and administrative expenses with supporting schedules for each expense item. Using flexible budgeting, a company calculates variable expenses for various levels of sales volume, while fixed costs remain constant within the relevant range.

Illustration 17.6
FLEXIBLE BUDGET FOR MANUFACTURING OVERHEAD

LEED COMPANY
Flexible Budget for Manufacturing Overhead

Element of Manufacturing Overhead	*Volume (percent of capacity)*				
	70%	80%	90%	100%	
Units	**17,500**	**20,000**	**22,500**	**25,000**	
Supplies	$ 1,400	$ 1,600	$ 1,800	$ 2,000	Variable portion is $25,000
Power	7,000	8,000	9,000	10,000	
Insurance.	4,200	4,800	5,400	6,000	
Maintenance	4,900	5,600	6,300	7,000	
Depreciation	18,000	18,000	18,000	18,000	Fixed portion is $75,000
Supervision.	57,000	57,000	57,000	57,000	
	$92,500	$95,000	$97,500	$100,000	

* Capacity is 25,000 units per three-month period.

A BROADER PERSPECTIVE

BUDGETING IN MULTINATIONAL COMPANIES

Budgeting in a multinational company requires understanding the particular characteristics of the markets being served. It would be naive for managers to assume that market conditions in foreign countries are the same as in the United States.

For example, a company doing business in several parts of the world considered the following market characteristics in preparing its sales budget [see the accompanying table].

The company's budget would reflect management's knowledge of the local situation. For example, a budget for operations in Germany could be based on three different scenarios:

1. Smooth German unification takes place, resulting in unhampered product distribution.
2. Problems occur in the unification process resulting in extra product distribution expenses for the new areas because of limited distribution capabilities.

REGION OR COUNTRY	DISTINCTIVE MARKET CHARACTERISTIC
Canada.	U.S.–Canada Free Trade Agreement
Eastern Europe	Recent move to free enterprise system. Uncertain trade restrictions. Weak local currencies.
Germany	German reunification.
France	Price controls.

3. German unification progresses very slowly, resulting in little or no new market development during the first three quarters of the fiscal year [p. 41].

SOURCE: Based on the article by Paul Mannino and Ken Milani, "Budgeting for an International Business," *Management Accounting,* February 1992, pp. 36–41.

Budget Variances.   When management uses a flexible budget to appraise a department's performance, the evaluation is based on the amounts budgeted for the level of activity actually experienced. The difference between actual costs incurred and the budgeted amount for that *same level of operations* is called a **budget variance.** Budget variances can indicate a department's or company's degree of efficiency, since they result from a comparison of "what was" with "what should have been."

To illustrate the computation of budget variances, assume that Leed's management prepared an overhead budget for a three-month period based on an expected volume of 100% or 25,000 units. At this level of production, the budgeted amount for supplies is $2,000. By the end of the period, Leed has used $1,900 of supplies. Our first impression is that a favorable variance of $100 exists. However, if Leed's actual production for the period was only 22,500 units (90% of capacity), the company actually has an unfavorable variance of $100. Why? Because at 90% of capacity, according to the flexible operating budget, only $1,800 of supplies *should* have been used. Consequently, Leed may have used supplies inefficiently.

To give another example using the data in Illustration 17.6, Leed's management may have budgeted maintenance at $5,600 for a given period assuming the company planned to produce 20,000 units (80% of operating capacity). However, Leed's actual maintenance costs may have been $6,200 for the period. This result does not necessarily mean that Leed had an unfavorable variance of $600. The variance depends on *actual production volume*.

Assume once again that Leed actually produced 22,500 units during the period and budgeted maintenance costs at $6,300 for that level of production. Therefore, maintenance would have a favorable variance of $100 ($6,300 − $6,200).

Flexible budgets often show budgeted amounts for every 10% change in the level of operations, such as the 70%, 80%, 90%, and 100% levels of capacity. However, actual production may fall between the levels shown in the flexible budget. The company may have some mixed costs (partly fixed and partly variable). If so, the company can find the budgeted amounts for these mixed costs at that level of operations using the following formula:

$$\begin{array}{c} \text{Budgeted} \\ \text{amount} \end{array} = \begin{array}{c} \text{Fixed portion} \\ \text{of costs} \end{array} + \left(\begin{array}{c} \text{Variable portion} \\ \text{of cost per unit} \end{array} \times \begin{array}{c} \text{Units of} \\ \text{output} \end{array} \right)$$

Flexible Operating Budget and Budget Variances Illustrated. As stated above, a flexible operating budget provides detailed information about budgeted expenses at various levels of activity. The main advantage of using a flexible operating budget along with a planned operating budget is that management can appraise performance on two levels. First, management can compare the actual results with the *planned* operating budget; this comparison enables management to analyze the deviation of actual output and sales from expected output and sales. Second, given the actual level of operations, management can compare actual costs at actual volume with budgeted costs at actual volume. The use of flexible operating budgets gives a valid basis for expense control when actual production or sales volume differs from expectations.

Using the cost and sales price data from Illustration 17.3, Illustrations 17.7 and 17.8 present Leed's detailed planned operating budget and flexible operating budget for the quarter ended March 31, 1995. The planned operating budget was based on a sales forecast of 20,000 units and a production forecast of 25,000 units. However, Illustrations 17.7 and 17.8 show actual sales of 19,000 units and actual production of 25,000 units. The actual selling price was $20 per unit, the same price that management had forecast.

Illustration 17.7 shows the comparison of the actual results with the planned operating budget. Comparison of actual results with the planned operating budget gives useful information because it shows where actual performance deviated from planned performance. For example, sales were 1,000 units lower than expected, sales revenue was $20,000 less than expected, gross margin was $12,500 less than expected, and net income was $2,400 more than expected.

Illustration 17.7
COMPARISON OF PLANNED OPERATING BUDGET AND ACTUAL RESULTS

LEED COMPANY
Comparison of Planned Operating Budget and Actual Results
For Quarter Ended March 31, 1995

	Planned Budget	Actual
Sales (budgeted 20,000 units, actual 19,000 units)	$400,000	$380,000
Cost of goods sold:		
Beginning finished goods inventory.	$130,000	$130,000
Cost of goods manufactured (25,000 units):		
Direct materials	$ 50,000	$ 62,500
Direct labor	150,000	143,750
Variable manufacturing overhead	25,000	31,250
Fixed manufacturing overhead	75,000	75,000
Cost of goods manufactured	$300,000	$312,500
Cost of goods available for sale.	$430,000	$442,500
Ending finished goods inventory	180,000	200,000
Cost of goods sold.	$250,000	$242,500
Gross margin	$150,000	$137,500
Selling and administrative expenses:		
Variable.	$ 40,000	$ 28,500
Fixed	100,000	95,000
Total selling and administrative expenses	$140,000	$123,500
Income before income taxes	$ 10,000	$ 14,000
Deduct: Estimated income taxes (40%)	4,000	5,600
Net income	$ 6,000	$ 8,400

The comparison of actual results with the planned operating budget does not provide a basis for evaluating whether or not management performed efficiently at the actual level of operations. For example, Illustration 17.7 shows that cost of goods sold was $7,500 less than expected. The meaning of this difference is not clear, however, because the actual cost of goods sold relates to the 19,000 units actually sold, while the planned cost of goods sold relates to the 20,000 units that were expected to be sold. The planned operating budget projected sales revenue, cost of goods sold, and selling and administrative expenses that were based on a sales forecast of 20,000 units; however, Leed only sold 19,000 units. The levels of activity are not the same, so the comparisons do not give valid information for expense control.

Managers can make a better analysis for expense control purposes by comparing actual results with a flexible operating budget based on the same levels of sales and production that actually occurred. Illustration 17.8 shows the comparison of Leed's flexible operating budget with the actual results. Note that the flexible budget shown in Illustration 17.8 is made up of several

Illustration 17.8
COMPARISON OF FLEXIBLE OPERATING BUDGET AND ACTUAL RESULTS

LEED COMPANY
Comparison of Flexible Operating Budget and Actual Results
For Quarter Ended March 31, 1995

	Flexible Budget	Actual	Budget Variance Over (Under)
Sales (19,000) units	$380,000	$380,000	$ –0–
Cost of goods sold:			
Beginning finished goods inventory	$130,000	$130,000	$ –0–
Cost of goods manufactured (25,000 units):			
Direct materials	$ 50,000	$ 62,500	$ 12,500
Direct labor	150,000	143,750	(6,250)
Variable manufacturing overhead.	25,000	31,250	6,250
Fixed manufacturing overhead	75,000	75,000	–0–
Cost of goods manufactured	$300,000	$312,500	$ 12,500
Cost of goods available for sale	$430,000	$442,500	$ 12,500
Ending finished goods inventory	192,000	200,000	8,000
Cost of goods sold (19,000 units)	$238,000	$242,500	$ 4,500
Gross margin	$142,000	$137,500	$ (4,500)
Selling and administrative expenses:			
Variable.	$ 38,000	$ 28,500	$ (9,500)
Fixed	100,000	95,000	(5,000)
Total selling and administrative expenses . . .	$138,000	$123,500	$(14,500)
Income before income taxes	$ 4,000	$ 14,000	$ 10,000
Deduct: Estimated income taxes (40%)	1,600	5,600	4,000
Net income	$ 2,400	$ 8,400	$ 6,000

pieces. The flexible budget amounts for sales revenue and selling and administrative expenses are based on 19,000 units of sales.

The flexible budget amounts for production costs are based on 25,000 units of production. Since the actual level of production (25,000 units) in this case was the same as the planned level, the production costs in the planned operating budget and the flexible operating budget are the same.

In comparisons such as these, if the number of units produced is equal to the number sold, companies often do not show their beginning and ending inventories in their flexible operating budgets. Instead, the flexible operating budget may show the number of units actually sold multiplied by the budgeted unit cost of direct materials, direct labor, and manufacturing overhead. The actual costs for direct materials, direct labor, and manufacturing overhead are also shown for the number of units sold.

Comparing the actual results to the flexible operating budget (Illustration 17.8) reveals variances for cost items. For instance, direct materials cost was $12,500 more than expected. Direct labor cost was $6,250 less than expected. Variable overhead was $6,250 more than expected.

Net income was $6,000 more than expected at a sales level of 19,000 units. The main reason for the increase in net income was the lower than expected amounts of selling and administrative expenses.

Now that Leed's management has prepared the operating budget (or projected income statement), it will prepare its financial budget. Remember that the financial budget is a projected balance sheet.

Preparing the Financial Budget for Leed Company

Objective 6
Prepare a financial budget and its supporting budgets

To prepare a projected balance sheet, Leed's management must analyze each balance sheet account. First, the beginning balance is taken from the balance sheet at the end of the preceding period. Illustration 17.9 shows Leed's balance sheet as of December 31, 1994. Management must consider the effects of planned activities on these balances. Many accounts will be affected by items shown in the planned operating budget, by cash inflows and outflows, and by policy decisions. Management will use the planned operating budget shown in Illustration 17.5 and the other illustrations previously given to prepare Leed's financial budget for the first two quarters of 1995.

Accounts Receivable. Leed must make several new schedules to prepare a financial budget. The first of these schedules is the accounts receivable schedule shown in Illustration 17.10. We will assume that Leed will collect 60% of the current quarter's sales in that quarter, and all of the remaining amount will be collected in the following quarter. Thus, collections for the first quarter will be $440,000. The $440,000 equals 60% of budgeted sales of $400,000 for the first quarter plus the $200,000 uncollected sales of the previous quarter, or [(0.6 × $400,000) + $200,000]. Second quarter collections will be $580,000 calculated as follows: (0.6 × $700,000) + the $160,000 not collected in the first quarter. We have simplified the illustration by assuming all sales are on credit, and there are no sales returns or allowances, no discounts, and no uncollectible accounts.

Inventories. Leed's management must prepare a schedule of planned materials purchases and inventories. Planned usage and cost per unit of materials are from the planned cost of goods sold schedule (Illustration 17.4). We assume no work in process inventories to simplify the illustration; there will be only materials and finished goods inventories.

Illustration 17.11 shows Leed's schedule of planned purchases and inventories of materials. Leed normally maintains materials inventory at a level of one half of next quarter's planned materials usage. The $40,000 beginning inventory was greater than normal because of a strike threat in the supplier company. This threat has now passed, and the materials inventory will be reduced at the end of the first quarter to the normal planned level.

Illustration 17.9
BALANCE SHEET AT BEGINNING OF PERIOD

LEED COMPANY
Balance Sheet
December 31, 1994

Assets

Current assets:

Cash		$ 130,000
Accounts receivable		200,000
Inventories:		
Materials	$ 40,000	
Finished goods	130,000	170,000
Prepaid expenses		20,000
Total current assets		$ 520,000

Property, plant, and equipment:

Land		$ 60,000
Buildings	$1,000,000	
Less: Accumulated depreciation	400,000	600,000
Equipment	$ 600,000	
Less: Accumulated depreciation	180,000	420,000
Total property, plant, and equipment		$1,080,000
Total assets		$1,600,000

Liabilities and Stockholders' Equity

Current liabilities:

Accounts payable	$ 80,000
Accrued liabilities payable	160,000
Income taxes payable	100,000
Total current liabilities	$ 340,000

Stockholders' equity:

Capital stock (100,000 shares of $10 par value)	$1,000,000
Retained earnings	260,000
Total stockholders' equity	$1,260,000
Total liabilities and stockholders' equity	$1,600,000

Illustration 17.10
PLANNED ACCOUNTS RECEIVABLE COLLECTIONS AND BALANCES

LEED COMPANY
Planned Accounts Receivable Collections and Balances

	Quarter Ending	
	March 31, 1995	June 30, 1995
Planned balance at beginning of quarter	$200,000*	$160,000
Planned sales for period (per Illustration 17.5)	400,000	700,000
Total	$600,000	$860,000
Projected collections during quarter (per discussion in text)	440,000	580,000
Planned balance at end of quarter	$160,000	$280,000

* Actual on January 1.

Illustration 17.11
PLANNED MATERIALS PURCHASES AND INVENTORIES

LEED COMPANY
Planned Materials Purchases and Inventories

	Quarter Ending	
	March 31, 1995	June 30, 1995
Planned usage (25,000 × $2) (per Illustration 17.4)	$50,000	$50,000
Planned ending inventory (½ × 25,000 × $2) (per discussion in text)	25,000	25,000
Planned materials available for use	$75,000	$75,000
Inventory at beginning of quarter	40,000*	25,000
Planned purchases for the quarter.	$35,000	$50,000

* Actual on January 1.

Illustration 17.4 contained the calculation of planned ending finished goods inventories.

Accounts Affected by Operating Costs. Leed's management would probably prepare individual schedules for each of the accounts affected by operating costs. For illustrative purposes, however, we prepared a schedule that combines all the accounts affected by materials purchases or operating costs.

The following assumptions are made:

1. All purchases of materials are made on account.
2. Direct labor incurred is credited to accrued liabilities payable.
3. Manufacturing overhead incurred is credited to the following accounts:

	Quarter Ending	
	March 31	June 30
Accounts Payable	$ 16,000	$ 13,000
Accrued Liabilities Payable	60,000	64,000
Prepaid Expenses	6,000	5,000
Accumulated Depreciation—Building	5,000	5,000
Accumulated Depreciation—Equipment . . .	13,000	13,000
Total.	$100,000	$100,000

4. Selling and administrative expenses incurred are credited to the following accounts:

	Quarter Ending	
	March 31	June 30
Accounts Payable	$ 5,000	$ 10,000
Accrued Liabilities Payable	130,000	154,000
Prepaid Expenses	2,000	3,000
Accumulated Depreciation—Building	1,000	1,000
Accumulated Depreciation—Equipment . . .	2,000	2,000
Total.	$140,000	$170,000

5.   Planned cash payments are as follows:

	Quarter Ending	
	March 31	June 30
Accounts Payable	$ 80,000	$ 56,000
Accrued Liabilities Payable	330,000	354,000
Prepaid Expenses	–0–	10,000
Total.	$410,000	$420,000

Illustration 17.12 shows analyses of the accounts credited as a result of the above data. The illustration provides a considerable amount of information needed in constructing financial budgets for the quarters ended March 31, 1995, and June 30, 1995. The balances on both dates for Accounts Payable, Accrued Liabilities Payable, Prepaid Expenses (the only debit balance account shown), Accumulated Depreciation—Building, and Accumulated Depreciation—Equipment are computed in the schedule.

Income Taxes Payable.   A separate schedule could be prepared showing the changes in the Income Taxes Payable account, but in this example, a brief discussion will suffice. Balances reported in the financial budgets assume that Leed pays one half of the $100,000 liability shown in the December 31, 1994, balance sheet in each of the first two quarters of 1995 (shown in Illustration 17.15 later in the chapter). The accrual for the current quarter is added (Illustration 17.5). Thus, the balance on March 31, 1995, is $54,000, calculated as $100,000 − $50,000 + $4,000. The balance on June 30, 1995, is $48,000, calculated to date as $54,000 − $50,000 + $44,000. On June 30, the balance equals the accrual to date for the current year, $4,000 for the first quarter and $44,000 for the second quarter.

Cash Budget.   After the above analyses have been prepared, sufficient information is available to prepare the cash budget and compute the balance in the Cash account on March 31 and June 30, 1995. To prepare a cash budget, information about cash receipts and cash disbursements is required.

Cash Receipts.   We can prepare the cash receipts schedule from the information used to compute the accounts receivable schedule (Illustration

Illustration 17.12
ANALYSES OF ACCOUNTS CREDITED FOR MATERIALS PURCHASES AND OPERATING COSTS

LEED COMPANY
Analyses of Accounts Credited for Materials Purchases and Operating Costs
For Quarters Ending March 31 and June 30, 1995

	Total Debits	Accounts Payable	Accrued Liabilities Payable	Prepaid Expenses	Accumulated Depreciation	
					Building	Equipment
Beginning balances, January 1 (per Illustration 17.9)		$ 80,000	$160,000	$20,000*	$400,000	$180,000
Purchases or operating costs, quarter ending March 31 (credits made to accounts shown at right):						
Direct materials (per Illustration 17.11).	$ 35,000*	$ 35,000				
Direct labor (per Illustration 17.4).	150,000*		$150,000			
Manufacturing overhead (per Illustration 17.4)	100,000*	16,000	60,000	$ 6,000	$ 5,000	$ 13,000
Selling and administrative expenses (per Illustration 17.5).	140,000*	5,000	130,000	2,000	1,000	2,000
Total	$425,000	$ 56,000	$340,000	$ 8,000	$ 6,000	$ 15,000
Total including January 1 balances		$136,000	$500,000	$12,000*	$406,000	$195,000
Planned cash payments (debits made to accounts shown). .		80,000*	330,000*			
Planned balances, March 31 . .		$ 56,000	$170,000	$12,000*	$406,000	$195,000
Purchases or operating costs, quarter ending June 30 (credits made to accounts shown at right):						
Direct materials (per Illustration 17.11).	$ 50,000*	$ 50,000				
Direct labor (per Illustration 17.4).	150,000*		$150,000			
Manufacturing overhead (per Illustration 17.4)	100,000*	13,000	64,000	$ 5,000	$ 5,000	$ 13,000
Selling and administrative expenses (per Illustration 17.5).	170,000*	10,000	154,000	3,000	1,000	2,000
Total	$470,000	$ 73,000	$368,000	$ 8,000	$ 6,000	$ 15,000
Total including March 31 balances		$129,000	$538,000	$ 4,000*	$412,000	$210,000
Planned cash payments (debits made to accounts shown). .		56,000*	354,000*	10,000*		
Planned balances, June 30 . . .		$ 73,000	$184,000	$14,000*	$412,000	$210,000

* Debit balance or debit to account.

Illustration 17.13
PLANNED CASH RECEIPTS

LEED COMPANY
Planned Cash Receipts

	Quarter Ending	
	March 31, 1995	June 30, 1995
Collections on accounts receivable:		
From preceding quarter's sales	$200,000	$160,000 (0.4 × $400,000)
From current quarter's sales	240,000 (0.6 × $400,000)	420,000 (0.6 × $700,000)
Total cash receipts (per Illustration 17.10)	$440,000	$580,000

17.10). Leed's schedule of planned cash receipts is shown in Illustration 17.13.

Cash Disbursements. Companies need cash to pay for purchases, wages, rent, interest, income taxes, cash dividends, and most other expenses. We can obtain the amount of each cash disbursement from other budgets or schedules. Illustration 17.14 shows Leed's cash disbursements schedule. The illustration shows where the information came from, except for the payment of income taxes and dividends. Income taxes, discussed earlier, are assumed to be paid at $50,000 per quarter. We assumed that $20,000 of dividends will be paid in the first quarter and $40,000 in the second quarter.

Once cash receipts and disbursements have been determined, we can prepare Leed's *cash budget* as shown in Illustration 17.15. The **cash budget** is a plan indicating expected inflows (receipts) and outflows (disbursements) of cash. This cash budget helps management to decide whether enough cash

Illustration 17.14
PLANNED CASH DISBURSEMENTS

LEED COMPANY
Planned Cash Disbursements

	Quarter Ending	
	March 31, 1995	June 30, 1995
Payment of accounts payable (per Illustration 17.12)	$ 80,000	$ 56,000
Payment of accrued liabilities payable (per Illustration 17.12) . .	330,000	354,000
Payment of income tax liability	50,000	50,000
Payment of dividends.	20,000	40,000
Expenses prepaid (per Illustration 17.12).	–0–	10,000
Total cash disbursements	$480,000	$510,000

Illustration 17.15
PLANNED CASH FLOWS AND CASH BALANCES

LEED COMPANY
Planned Cash Flows and Cash Balances

	Quarter Ending	
	March 31, 1995	June 30, 1995
Planned balance at beginning of quarter	$130,000*	$ 90,000
Planned cash receipts:		
Collections of accounts receivable (per Illustration 17.13). . .	440,000	580,000
	$570,000	$670,000
Planned cash disbursements:		
Payment of accounts payable (per Illustration 17.12)	$ 80,000	$ 56,000
Payment of accrued liabilities payable (per Illustration 17.12)	330,000	354,000
Payment of income tax liability	50,000	50,000
Payment of dividends.	20,000	40,000
Expenses prepaid (per Illustration 17.12).	–0–	10,000
Total cash disbursements.	$480,000	$510,000
Planned balance at end of quarter	$ 90,000	$160,000

* Actual on January 1.

will be available for short-term needs. If a company's cash budget indicates a cash shortage at a certain date, the company may need to borrow money on a short-term basis. If the company's cash budget indicates a cash excess, the company may wish to invest the extra funds for short periods to earn interest rather than leave the cash idle. Knowing in advance that a possible cash shortage or excess may occur allows management sufficient time to plan for such occurrences and avoid a cash crisis.

The Financial Budget Illustrated

The preparation of Leed's financial budget for the quarters ending March 31 and June 30 (Illustration 17.16) completes the master budget. Management now has information to help appraise the policies it has adopted before implementing them. If the master budget shows the results of these policies to be unsatisfactory, the policies can be changed before serious problems arise.

For example, Leed's management had a policy of stable production each period. The master budget shows that production can be stabilized even though sales fluctuate widely. However, the planned ending inventory at June 30 may be considered somewhat low in view of the fluctuations in sales. Management now recognizes this problem in advance and can take corrective action if necessary.

Illustration 17.16
PROJECTED BALANCE SHEET

LEED COMPANY
Projected Balance Sheet
As of March 31 and June 30, 1995

	March 31, 1995	June 30, 1995
Assets		
Current assets:		
Cash (per Illustration 17.15)	$ 90,000	$ 160,000
Accounts receivable (per Illustration 17.10).	160,000	280,000
Inventories:		
Materials (per Illustration 17.11)	25,000	25,000
Finished goods (per Illustration 17.4)	180,000	60,000
Prepaid expenses (per Illustration 17.12).	12,000	14,000
Total current assets.	$ 467,000	$ 539,000
Property, plant, and equipment:		
Land (per Illustration 17.9)	$ 60,000	$ 60,000
Buildings ($1,000,000 less accumulated depreciation of $406,000 and $412,000) (per Illustrations 17.9 and 17.12)	594,000	588,000
Equipment ($600,000 less accumulated depreciation of $195,000 and $210,000) (per Illustrations 17.9 and 17.12)	405,000	390,000
Total property, plant, and equipment	$1,059,000	$1,038,000
Total assets	$1,526,000	$1,577,000
Liabilities and Stockholders' Equity		
Current liabilities:		
Accounts payable (per Illustration 17.12).	$ 56,000	$ 73,000
Accrued liabilities payable (per Illustration 17.12).	170,000	184,000
Income taxes payable (per discussion on page 860)	54,000	48,000
Total current liabilities	$ 280,000	$ 305,000
Stockholders' equity:		
Capital stock (100,000 shares of $10 par value) (per Illustration 17.9)	$1,000,000	$1,000,000
Retained earnings (see below).	246,000*	272,000†
Total stockholders' equity.	$1,246,000	$1,272,000
Total liabilities and stockholders' equity	$1,526,000	$1,577,000

* $260,000 (per Illustration 17.9) + Income of $6,000 (per Illustration 17.5) − Dividends of $20,000.
† $246,000 + Income of $66,000 − Dividends of $40,000.

BUDGETING IN MERCHANDISING COMPANIES

Budget preparation for merchandising companies and service companies is quite similar to budgeting for manufacturing companies. This section discusses budgeting in these other two types of companies.

Purchases Budget for a Merchandising Company

Throughout this chapter, we have focused on budgeting in a *manufacturing company*. Suppose a *retail merchandising* business, such as a dress shop or

Illustration 17.17
SALES BUDGET

STROBEL FURNITURE COMPANY
Sales Budget
For Quarters Ending March 31, 1995, through March 31, 1996

March 31, 1995	June 30, 1995	September 30, 1995	December 31, 1995	March 31, 1996
$30,000	$80,000	$50,000	$90,000	$40,000

Illustration 17.18
PURCHASES BUDGET

STROBEL FURNITURE COMPANY
Purchases Budget
For Quarters Ending March 31 through December 31, 1995

	March 31, 1995	June 30, 1995	September 30, 1995	December 31, 1995
Ending inventory desired*	$22,000	$13,750	$24,750	$11,000
Cost of goods sold (55% of sales)	16,500	44,000	27,500	49,500
Total	$38,500	$57,750	$52,250	$60,500
Less: Beginning inventory	8,250	22,000	13,750	24,750
Purchases required	$30,250	$35,750	$38,500	$35,750

* Next period's sales × 55% × 50%.

a furniture store, prepares a budget. In this case, the company prepares a
purchases budget instead of a production budget. To compute the purchases
for each quarter, management must estimate the cost of the goods to be sold
during the quarter and the inventory required at the end of the quarter.

Using Strobel Furniture Company as an example, suppose Strobel prepared a sales budget like the one shown in Illustration 17.17. Assume that the
company likes to maintain sufficient inventory to cover one half of the next
quarter's sales. Cost of goods sold is 55% of sales. The ending inventory on
December 31, 1994, was $8,250. The purchases budget can now be prepared,
as shown in Illustration 17.18. For the first quarter of 1995, notice that the
ending inventory is one half of the second quarter's cost of goods sold [0.5 ×
(55% of $80,000) = $22,000].

Strobel can now use the information in its purchases budget to prepare the
cost of goods sold section of the operating budget, to prepare cash disbursements schedules, and to prepare the inventory and accounts payable
amounts in the financial budget.

BUDGETING IN SERVICE COMPANIES

The concepts discussed in this chapter are equally applicable to service
companies. Obviously, these firms do not generally sell goods, but they do

have service revenues and operating expenses that must be budgeted. Projected income statements and balance sheets can be prepared for service companies using the techniques described in this chapter.

ADDITIONAL CONCEPTS RELATED TO BUDGETING

Two concepts that affect budgeting are being used in industry. These concepts are a just-in-time (JIT) production system and zero-base budgeting.

Just-in-Time Production System

Chapter 12 described the *just-in-time (JIT) production system*. Recall that the **just-in-time (JIT) production system** provides that materials are bought just in time to be put into the manufacturing process; small parts, or subparts, are purchased just in time to be assembled into a final product; and goods are produced just in time to be sold.

The overall purpose of the JIT system is to decrease, or in some cases eliminate, inventories in a company. By eliminating inventories, companies reduce the buffer stock between purchasing, production, and sales. Consequently, companies using a JIT system must budget purchasing and production with each other and with sales. Materials will be purchased just in time for production, and goods will be produced just in time for sales.

Zero-Base Budgeting

Zero-base budgeting is a concept that became popular in the 1970s but has since received less attention. Under **zero-base budgeting,** managers in a company start each year with zero budget levels and must justify every dollar that will appear in the budget. No costs in the budget are viewed as automatically ongoing or continuous. Decision packages are prepared by each unit in the organization. These packages describe the nature and cost of tasks that can be performed by that unit and the consequences of not performing each task. The decision packages are ranked, and only the most worthy are approved for inclusion in the budget.

This type of budgeting is not exactly a new method of budgeting, for it has been used in not-for-profit organizations, governmental entities, and service-type organizations. For instance, President Jimmy Carter used it both in the state of Georgia and in the federal government. One drawback to the use of this concept is the massive amounts of paperwork and time needed to prepare and rank decision packages, especially in large organizations.

COMPUTER SPREADSHEET APPLICATIONS

Managers find computer spreadsheets useful in budgeting. Participants in the budgeting process ask a lot of "what-if" questions. For example, the man-

ETHICS   A CLOSER LOOK

Greenhaven County was facing large budget deficits because several lumber mills had temporarily closed. Meanwhile, administrators in a particular school district were looking for ways to spend the money that had been budgeted for the district. The school district was entering the last three months of the fiscal year with excess funds because of low enrollment in several of the district's schools. The low enrollment was due to families leaving the district to find work elsewhere. However, the lumber mill executives recently announced that the mills would be opening in two months' time.

At a budget meeting, one official commented, "You know what will happen if we don't spend all of our budget. The county will claim we don't need as much money next year, and now, with the mills reopening, enrollment is going to increase and we'll need every cent we can get!"

The district's accounting manager commented, "We are legally entitled to spend all of the money this year that has been budgeted to us. However, we have received a memorandum requesting that we cut expenditures wherever possible to help reduce the county's deficit."

The first official responded, "Let's not give the county any reason to cut our budget next year. You know schools always get the biggest budget cuts anyway. I say let's spend all our budget this year."

Required
Should the school district spend all of the money that had been budgeted to it? Discuss.

ager of the western region of Delta Airlines might ask what would happen to budgeted costs, revenues, cash flows, and other amounts if an oil embargo or a Mideast war limited oil supplies and increased airplane fuel costs.

You can assume that the first budget managers prepare for a period will not be their last. Budgets require considerable input and rework to be useful planning tools. Computer spreadsheets enhance the input, speed up the process, and make budgeting more fun.

The general concepts of budgeting were discussed in this chapter. In Chapter 20, capital budgeting will be discussed. All businesses must establish long-range goals and make wise capital budgeting decisions to be successful.

Chapter 18 discusses the introduction of standard costs into a job order or process cost system to increase control over production costs. Actual costs are compared with standard costs to identify problem areas.

UNDERSTANDING THE LEARNING OBJECTIVES

1. Define a budget and name several kinds of budgets.
   - A budget is a plan showing the company's objectives and how management intends to acquire and use resources to attain those objectives.
   - Several kinds of budgets are: responsibility, capital, master, planned operating, and financial.

2. List several benefits of a budget.
   - A budget (1) shows management's operating plans for the coming period(s); (2) formalizes management's plans in quantitative terms; (3) forces all levels of management to think ahead, anticipate results, and take corrective action to remedy possible poor results; and (4) may also be used to motivate individuals so that they strive to achieve stated goals.
   - Business activities are better coordinated; managers become aware of other managers' plans; employees may become cost conscious and try to conserve resources; the organizational plan of the company may be reviewed more often and changed where necessary; and a breadth of vision, which might not otherwise be developed, is fostered.
3. List five general principles of budgeting.
   - *Top-management support.* All management levels must be aware of the budget's importance to the company and must know that the budget has top management's support.
   - *Participation in goal setting.* Employees are more likely to strive toward organizational goals if they participate in setting them.
   - *Communicating results.* Effective communication implies (1) timeliness, (2) reasonable accuracy, and (3) understandability.
   - *Flexibility.* The planned operating budget should be restated if the basic assumptions underlying the budget change during the year. For expense control purposes, after the actual level of operations is known, the actual revenues and expenses should be compared to expected performance at that level of operations.
   - *Follow-up.* Budgets should be checked continuously and corrected whenever necessary, since they deal with projections and estimates for future operating results and financial positions.
4. Prepare a planned operating budget and its supporting budgets, such as the sales budget, production and purchases budgets, and other expense budgets.
   - A planned operating budget is developed first in units rather than dollars. A schedule of budgeted sales and production in units is prepared to forecast sales for the year.
   - Next, dollars must be introduced into the analysis. A forecast of expected selling prices must be made, and costs must be analyzed.
   - Management must now also prepare a schedule to forecast cost of goods sold, another major amount on the planned operating budget.
   - After the cost of goods sold has been forecast, a separate budget is prepared for all selling and administrative expenses. Several supporting schedules may be involved for various other expenses.
   - The totals on the separate budgets are combined to form the planned operating budget, which shows the budgeted income after income taxes for a certain period of time.

5. Prepare flexible operating budgets.
    - A flexible operating budget is a special kind of budget that provides detailed information about budgeted expenses (and revenues) at various levels of output.
    - This budget shows the effect that different volume changes have on the expenses (and revenues) of a company.
6. Prepare a financial budget and its supporting budgets.
    - Preparing a financial budget involves analyzing every balance sheet account in light of the planned activities expressed in the operating budget.
    - A separate cash budget is usually prepared to show sources of, uses of, and net changes in cash for the period.
    - Supporting budgets may also be developed for accounts receivable, inventories, accounts affected by operating costs, and income taxes payable.

DEMONSTRATION PROBLEM

During January 1995, Esteban Company plans to sell 40,000 units of its product at a price of $30 per unit. Selling expenses are estimated to be $120,000 plus 2% of sales revenue. Administrative expenses are estimated to be $90,000 plus 1% of sales revenue. Income tax expense is estimated to be 40% of income before income taxes.

Esteban plans to produce 50,000 units during January with estimated variable costs per unit as follows: $3 for material, $7.50 for labor, and $4.50 for variable overhead. The fixed overhead cost is estimated at $60,000 per month. The finished goods inventory at January 1, 1995, is 8,000 units with a cost per unit of $15. The company uses FIFO inventory procedure.

Required:

Prepare a projected income statement for January 1995.

Solution to demonstration problem

ESTEBAN COMPANY
Projected Income Statement
For January 1995

Sales (40,000 × $30)		$1,200,000
Cost of goods sold (see schedule 1)		638,400
Gross margin.		$ 561,600
Selling expenses:		
Fixed	$120,000	
Variable (0.02 × $1,200,000)	24,000	
Administrative expenses:		
Fixed	90,000	
Variable (0.01 × $1,200,000)	12,000	246,000
Income before income taxes.		$ 315,600
Deduct: Income tax expense (40%)		126,240
Net income.		$ 189,360

ESTEBAN COMPANY
Planned Cost of Goods Sold
Schedule 1

Beginning finished goods inventory (8,000 × $15)		$120,000
Cost of goods manufactured:		
Direct materials (50,000 × $3)	$150,000	
Direct labor (50,000 × $7.50)	375,000	
Variable manufacturing overhead (50,000 × $4.50)	225,000	
Fixed manufacturing overhead	60,000	
Cost of goods manufactured (50,000 × $16.20)*		810,000
Cost of goods available for sale		$930,000
Ending finished goods inventory (18,000 × $16.20).		291,600
Cost of goods sold		$638,400

* The $16.20 is determined as $810,000 ÷ 50,000 units.

NEW TERMS*

Budget A plan showing a company's objectives and how management intends to acquire and use resources to attain those objectives. Major types of budgets are (1) master budget, (2) responsibility budget, and (3) capital budget. *842*

Budgeting The coordination of financial and nonfinancial planning to satisfy an organization's goals. *843*

---

* Some terms defined in earlier chapters are repeated here for your convenience.

Budget variance The difference between an actual cost incurred (or revenue earned) at a certain level of operations and the budgeted amount for the same level of operations. *853*

Cash budget A plan indicating expected inflows (receipts) and outflows (disbursements) of cash; it helps management decide whether enough cash will be available for short-term needs. *862*

Financial budget The projected balance sheet portion of a master budget. *842, 846*

Fixed costs Costs that are unaffected in total by the relative level of production or sales. *849*

Flexible operating budget Provides detailed information about budgeted expenses (and revenues) at various levels of output. *852*

Just-in-time (JIT) production system Provides that materials are received just when needed and goods are produced just in time to be sold. *866*

Master budget The projected income statement and projected balance sheet showing the organization's objectives and proposed ways of attaining them; includes supporting budgets for various items in the master budget; also called *master profit plan*. The master budget is the overall plan of the enterprise and ideally consists of all of the various segmental budgets. *842, 845*

Participatory budgeting A method of preparing the budget that includes the participation of all levels of management responsible for actual performance. *844*

Planned operating budget The projected income statement portion of a master budget. *842, 846*

Production budget Takes into account the units in the sales budget and the company's inventory policy and shows the number of units to be produced and the cost of producing them. *846*

Sales budget Arrived at by multiplying projected sales units times sales price per unit. Sales forecasting can involve either formal or informal techniques, or both. *845, 846*

Variable costs Costs that vary in total directly with production or sales and are a constant dollar amount per unit of output over different levels of output or sales. *849*

Zero-base budgeting Managers in a company start each year with zero budget levels and must justify every dollar that will appear in the budget. *866*

SELF-TEST

True-False

Indicate whether each of the following statements is true or false.

1. Budgets are oriented to the future.
2. The master budget consists of a projected income statement and a projected balance sheet.
3. The sales and production budgets are developed first in dollars, then in units.
4. A valid analysis for expense control purposes is made based on comparing actual results with a flexible budget prepared for the planned level of activity.
5. Computer spreadsheets are not useful in budgeting.

Multiple-Choice

Select the best answer for each of the following questions.

1. Which of the following statements does not describe some of the benefits related to the preparation and use of budgets:
   a. Operating units in a company coordinate their activities better.
   b. Managers become aware of other managers' plans.
   c. Employees may become cost conscious and try to conserve resources.
   d. Managers review the company's organizational plan and make changes if necessary.
   e. Foolproof methods exist for preparing effective budgets.

2. When preparing a projected income statement, which of the following budgets is prepared first?
   a. Sales budget.
   b. Selling and administrative budget.
   c. Projected cost of goods sold budget.
   d. Financial budget.

3. When preparing a financial budget, the first schedule to be prepared is:
   a. Projected balance sheet.
   b. Cash budget.
   c. Cash receipts.
   d. Accounts receivable and collections.

4. Fixed costs are $70,000, and variable cost per unit is $1.20. Determine the budgeted amount to produce 200,000 units.
   a. $300,000.
   b. $310,000.
   c. $240,000.
   d. $276,000.

5. Manufacturing costs (including $40,000 of fixed costs) are budgeted at $140,000 for an expected output of 100,000 units. Actual output was 90,000 units, while actual costs were $142,500. What is the budget variance? Is it favorable or unfavorable?
   a. $10,000 unfavorable.
   b. $12,500 favorable.
   c. $12,500 unfavorable.
   d. $10,000 unfavorable.

Now turn to page 881 to check your answers.

QUESTIONS

1. What are three purposes of budgeting?

2. What are the purposes of a planned operating budget and financial budget?

3. How does the concept of a variance relate to budgeting?

4. What are five basic principles which, if followed, should improve the possibility of preparing a meaningful budget? Why is each principle important?

5. What is the difference between an imposed budget and a participatory budget?

6. Define and explain a budget variance.

7. What are the two major budgets in the master budget? Which should be prepared first? Why?

8. Distinguish between a master budget and a responsibility budget.

9. The budget established at the beginning of a given period carried an item for supplies expense in the amount of $40,000. At the end of the period, the supplies used amounted to $44,000. Can management conclude from these data that supplies were used inefficiently or that care was not exercised in purchasing the supplies?

10. Management must make certain assumptions about the business environment when preparing a budget. Which areas should be considered?

11. Why is budgeted performance better than past performance as a basis for judging actual results?

12. Describe the concepts of a JIT production system and zero-base budgeting.

13. *Real-world question*   Your college bookstore is trying to estimate the level of textbook sales for the next academic year. The store's management wants your advice about sources of information. What would you tell them?

The Coca-Cola Company

14. *Real-world question*   Refer to Appendix C at the end of this text. The Coca-Cola Company is trying to estimate long-run sales for the years 1995–99. What factors should it consider?

THE LIMITED, INC.

15. *Real-world question*   Refer to Appendix C at the end of this text. The Limited, Inc., wants to estimate long-run sales for the period 1995–99. What factors should it consider?

EXERCISES

Prepare a schedule of planned sales and production (L.O. 4)

17–1.   Bicycle Apparel has decided to produce 72,000 spandex shorts at a uniform rate throughout 1995. The sales department of Bicycle Apparel has estimated sales for 1995 according to the following schedule:

	Sales in Units
First quarter	19,200
Second quarter	15,600
Third quarter	18,000
Fourth quarter	25,200
Total for 1995	78,000

Assume the December 31, 1994, inventory is estimated to be 9,000 pairs of shorts. Prepare a schedule of planned sales and production (in units) for the first two quarters of 1995.

Prepare a schedule of planned sales and production (L.O. 4)

17–2.   Buckeroo Boots, Inc., had decided to produce 96,000 pairs of boots at a uniform rate in 1995. The sales department has estimated sales for 1995 according to the following schedule:

	Sales in Units
First quarter	26,400
Second quarter	22,800
Third quarter	21,600
Fourth quarter	33,600
Total for 1995	104,400

If the December 31, 1994, inventory is estimated to be 11,800 pairs of boots, prepare a schedule of planned sales and production (in units) for the first two quarters of 1995.

Compute the budgeted income (L.O. 4)

17–3. Blinker Company projects sales of 60,000 units during May at $6 per unit. Production costs are $1.80 per unit. Variable selling and administrative expenses are $0.60 per unit; fixed selling and administrative expenses are $114,000. Compute the budgeted income before income taxes.

Prepare budgeted net income (L.O. 4)

17–4. Ski Jackets, Inc., expects to sell 90,000 units during the next quarter at a price of $54 per unit. Production costs are $18 per unit. Selling and administrative expenses are: variable, $8 per unit; and fixed, $420,000. What amount is budgeted net income? (Do not consider income taxes.)

Prepare an operating budget (L.O. 4)

17–5. Koala Company plans to sell 45,000 units of deadbolt locks next quarter at a price of $19 per unit. Production costs are $7.20 per unit. Selling and administrative expenses are: variable, $3.60 per unit; and fixed, $151,200 per quarter. What amount is the budgeted net income before income taxes?

Prepare a flexible production budget (L.O. 5)

17–6. Materials and labor of Jesse Corporation are considered to be completely variable costs. Expected production for the year is 150,000 units. At that level of production, direct materials cost is budgeted at $300,000, and direct labor cost is budgeted at $675,000. Prepare a flexible budget for materials and labor for possible production levels of 105,000, 120,000, and 135,000 units of product.

Compute budget variances (L.O. 5)

17–7. Assume that in Exercise 17–6 actual production was 120,000 units, materials cost was $242,000, and labor cost was $480,000. What are the budget variances?

Compute the budget variance for operations (L.O. 5)

17–8. Fixed production costs for Beechwood Company are budgeted at $288,000, assuming 80,000 units of production. Actual sales for the period were 70,000 units, while actual production was 80,000 units. Actual fixed costs used in computing cost of goods sold amounted to $252,000. What is the budget variance?

Prepare a purchases budget (L.O. 6)

17–9. The cosmetics department of Harlequin Department Store has prepared a sales budget for April calling for a sales volume of $120,000. The department expects to begin in April with a $100,000 inventory and to end the month with a $97,000 inventory. Its cost of goods sold averages 70% of sales.

Prepare a purchases budget for the department showing the amount of goods to be purchased during April.

PROBLEMS

Determine budgeted cost of goods sold; prepare operating budgets (L.O. 4)

17–1. Thoroughbred Corporation prepares monthly operating and financial budgets. The operating budgets for June and July are based on the following data:

	Units Produced	Units Sold
June	200,000	180,000
July	180,000	200,000

All sales are at $30 per unit. Direct materials, direct labor, and variable manufacturing overhead are estimated at $3, $6, and $3 per unit, respectively; while total fixed manufacturing overhead is budgeted at $540,000 per month. Operating expenses are budgeted at $600,000 plus 10% of sales, while income taxes are budgeted at 40% of income before income taxes. The inventory at June 1 consists of 100,000 units with a cost of $16.00 each.

Required:

a. Prepare monthly budget estimates of cost of goods sold assuming that FIFO inventory procedure is used.

b. Prepare planned operating budgets for June and July. (Use a single amount for cost of goods sold—as derived in part a.)

Prepare a flexible operating budget (L.O. 5)

17–2. The computation of operating income for Benedictine Company for 1994 follows:

Sales ($1 per unit)		$1,800,000
Cost of goods manufactured and sold:		
Direct materials.	$340,000	
Direct labor.	240,000	
Variable manufacturing overhead	120,000	
Fixed manufacturing overhead.	240,000	940,000
Gross margin.		$ 860,000
Selling expenses:		
Variable	$112,000	
Fixed.	168,000	280,000
		$ 580,000
Administrative expenses:		
Variable	$136,000	
Fixed.	192,000	328,000
Net operating income		$ 252,000

An operating budget is prepared for 1995 with sales forecasted at a 25% increase in volume, and sales price forecasted at $1 per unit. Direct materials, direct labor, and all costs labeled above as variable are completely variable. Fixed costs are expected to continue as above except for a $24,000 increase in fixed administrative costs.

Actual operating data for 1995 are given below:

Sales ($1 per unit)	$2,160,000
Direct materials	424,000
Direct labor	288,000
Variable manufacturing overhead	148,800
Fixed manufacturing overhead	246,000
Variable selling expenses	166,000
Fixed selling expenses	157,200
Variable administrative expenses	178,000
Fixed administrative expenses.	218,400

Required:

a. Prepare a budget report comparing the 1995 planned operating budget with actual 1995 data.

b. Prepare a budget report that would be useful in appraising the performance of the various persons charged with responsibility to provide satisfactory income. (Hint: Prepare a flexible operating budget.)

c. Comment on the differences revealed by the two reports.

Prepare a planned
operating budget
and a flexible
operating budget
(L.O. 4, 5)

17–3. a. The following data are to be used in preparing a planned operating budget for Skye Company:

Plant capacity.	50,000 units
Expected sales volume	45,000 units
Expected production	45,000 units
Forecasted selling price.	$12.00 per unit
Manufacturing costs:	
Variable (per unit):	
Direct materials.	$3.60
Direct labor.	$1.50
Manufacturing overhead.	$2.25
Fixed manufacturing overhead.	$44,000
Selling and administrative expenses:	
Variable (per unit).	$1.20
Fixed.	$35,000

Assume no beginning or ending inventory. Income taxes are budgeted at 40% of income before income taxes.

b. The actual operating data for Skye Company for the year ending December 31, 1995, are given below. (Note: The actual selling price per unit was $13.50. Actual units produced equaled expected production.)

Sales		$540,000
Cost of goods sold:		
Direct materials	$168,750	
Direct labor	67,500	
Variable manufacturing overhead	101,250	
Fixed manufacturing overhead	44,000	
Total	$381,500	
Less: Ending inventory ($381,500 × 5⁄45)	42,389	339,111
Gross margin		$200,889
Selling expenses:		
Variable	$ 51,000	
Fixed	36,000	87,000
Income before income taxes		$113,889
Deduct: Income taxes at 40%		45,556
Net income		$ 68,333

Required:

a. For (a), prepare a planned operating budget for the year ended December 31, 1995.

b. For (b), using a flexible operating budget, analyze the efficiency of operations and comment on Skye Company's performance.

Prepare a flexible budget for selling and administrative expenses (L.O. 5)

17–4. La Rue Company wants you to prepare a flexible budget for selling and administrative expenses. The general manager and the sales manager have met with all the department heads, and they have provided you with the following information regarding selling and administrative expenses:

1. The company presently employs 30 full-time salespersons with a base salary of $900 each per month plus commissions and 10 full-time salespersons with a base salary of $1,500 each per month plus commissions. In addition, the company employs nine regional sales managers with a salary of $5,400 per month, none of whom is entitled to any commissions.
2. If sales volume exceeds $20 million per year, the company will need to hire four more salespersons, each at a base salary of $900 per month plus commissions.
3. Sales commissions are either 10% or 5% of the selling price, depending on the product sold. Typically, a 10% commission applies on 60% of sales, and a 5% commission applies on the remaining 40% of sales.
4. Salespersons' travel allowances average $400 per month per salesperson (excluding managers).
5. Advertising expenses average $37,500 per month plus 3% of sales.
6. Selling supplies expense is estimated at 1% of sales.
7. Administrative salaries are $65,000 per month.
8. Other administrative expenses include the following:
     Rent—$11,000 per month
     Office supplies—2% of sales
     Other administrative expenses (telephone, etc.)—$4,000 per month

Required:

Prepare a flexible budget for selling and administrative expenses for sales volumes of $18 million, $24 million, and $30 million per year.

Prepare a schedule of planned cost of goods sold (L.O. 4)

17–5. Bisbee Company wants to prepare a schedule of planned cost of goods sold and ending inventory for the quarters ending September 30, 1995, and December 31, 1995. The following data relate to the expected activity for the two quarters.

1. Expected sales for the next three quarters are $720,000 for the quarter ending September 30, 1995; $900,000 for the quarter ending December 31, 1995; and $489,600 for the quarter ending March 31, 1996.
2. The selling price is $36 per unit.
3. Due to demand, the company wishes to carry an end-of-the-period inventory equal to 25% of the following quarter's expected requirements.
4. Inventory of finished goods on June 30, 1995, is 5,000 units at $28.80 per unit.

5. Cost of production is estimated at:

Direct materials	$4.70 per unit
Direct labor	$9.60 per unit
Variable manufacturing overhead	$2.40 per unit
Fixed manufacturing overhead	$230,000 per quarter

6. No work in process inventory existed at the beginning or end of either period.
7. The company computes inventory on a FIFO basis.

Required:

Prepare a schedule of planned cost of goods sold for the quarters ending September 30, 1995, and December 31, 1995. (Hint: Prepare production schedules in units first.)

Prepare a cash receipts schedule and a purchases budget (L.O. 6)

17–6. Brighton Company purchases and sells bathroom fixtures. Estimated sales for the next three months are:

September 1995	$ 730,000
October 1995.	1,080,000
November 1995.	840,000

Sales for August were $788,000. All sales are on account. Brighton Company estimates that 60% of the accounts receivable are collected in the month of sale with the remaining 40% collected the following month. The units sell for $30 each. The cash balance for September 1, 1995, is $163,200.

Generally, 60% of purchases are due and payable in the month of purchase with the remainder due the following month. Purchase cost per unit for materials is $18. The company maintains an end-of-the-month inventory of 2,000 units plus 10% of next month's unit sales.

Required:

Prepare a cash receipts schedule for September and October and a purchases budget for August, September, and October.

Prepare a cash budget (L.O. 6)

17–7. Refer to Problem 17–6. In addition to the information given, selling and administrative expenses paid in cash are $250,000 per month.

Required:

Prepare a monthly cash budget for September and October for Brighton Company.

Prepare a cash
budget
(L.O. 6)

17–8. Solitude Company has gathered the following budget estimates for the quarter ending March 31, 1995:

Sales	$216,000
Purchases	180,000
Salaries and wages	68,000
Rent	3,600
Supplies	3,400
Insurance	620
Other cash expenses	5,180

A cash balance of $14,400 is planned for January 1. Accounts receivable are expected to be $24,000 on January 1. All but one half of 1% of the January 1 balance of accounts receivable will be collected in the quarter ending March 31. The company's sales collection pattern is 95% in the quarter of sale and 5% in the quarter after sale. Accounts payable will be $12,000 on January 1 and will be paid during the coming quarter. The company's purchases payment pattern is 75% in the quarter of purchase and 25% in the quarter after purchase. Expenses are paid in the quarter of incurrence.

Required:

Prepare a cash budget for the quarter ending March 31, 1995.

BUSINESS DECISION PROBLEMS

Prepare a cash
budget
(L.O. 6)

17–1. Compton Company has applied at a local bank for a short-term loan of $300,000 starting on October 1, 1995. The bank's loan officer has requested a cash budget from the company for the quarter ending December 31, 1995. The following information is needed to prepare the cash budget for that quarter:

Sales	$1,296,000
Purchases	720,000
Salaries and wages to be paid	252,000
Rent payments	13,400
Supplies (payments for)	8,000
Insurance payments	2,600
Other cash payments	54,400

A cash balance of $48,000 is planned for October 1. Accounts receivable are expected to be $96,000 on October 1. All of these accounts will be collected in the quarter ending December 31. In general, sales are collected as follows: 90% in the quarter of sale, and 10% in the quarter after sale. Accounts payable will be $960,000 on October 1 and will be paid during the quarter ending December 31. All purchases are paid in the quarter after purchase.

Required:

a. Prepare a cash budget for the quarter ending December 31, 1995. Assume that the $300,000 loan will be made on October 1 and will be repaid with interest at 10% on December 31.

b. Will the company be able to repay the loan on December 31? If the company desires a minimum cash balance of $36,000, will the company be able to repay the loan as planned?

Prepare a master budget (a comprehensive budgeting problem) (L.O. 6)

17–2. Faulkner Corporation, a retail company, prepares annual budgets by quarters for its fiscal year ending June 30. Given below is its post-closing trial balance at December 31, 1994:

	Debits	Credits
Cash	$138,000	
Accounts Receivable	370,000	
Allowance for Uncollectible Accounts		$ 12,000
Inventories.	166,000	
Prepaid Expenses	12,000	
Furniture and Equipment	180,000	
Accumulated Depreciation—Furniture and Equipment . .		12,000
Accounts Payable		130,000
Accrued Liabilities Payable		46,000
Notes Payable, 5% (due 1999)		480,000
Capital Stock		300,000
Retained Earnings (deficit)	114,000	
	$980,000	$980,000

All of the capital stock of Faulkner Corporation was recently acquired by Heidi Wolf after the corporation had suffered losses for a number of years. After the purchase, Wolf loaned substantial sums of money to the corporation, which still owes her $480,000 on a 5% note. Because of these past losses, no accrued income taxes payable exist, but future earnings will be subject to taxation.

Wolf is anxious to withdraw $120,000 from the corporation (as a payment on the note payable to her) but will not do so if the withdrawal would reduce the corporation's cash balance below $120,000. Thus, she is quite interested in the budgets for the quarter ending March 31, 1995.

Additional data:

1. Sales for the quarter ending March 31, 1995, are forecasted at $1,200,000; for the following quarter they are forecasted at $1,500,000. All sales are priced to yield a gross margin of 40%. Inventory of $190,000 is to be on hand on March 31, 1995. All sales are on account, and 95% of the December 31, 1994, receivables plus 70% of the current quarter's sales will be collected during the quarter ending March 31, 1995.

2. Selling expenses are budgeted at $48,000 plus 6% of sales; $24,000 will be incurred on account, $66,000 will be accrued, $27,000 will result from expired prepaid expenses, and $3,000 will result from allocated depreciation.

3. Purchasing expenses are budgeted at $34,800 plus 5% of purchases for the quarter; $9,000 will be incurred on account, $48,000 will be accrued, $13,800 will result from expired prepaid expenses, and $1,200 will result from allocated depreciation.

4. Administrative expenses are budgeted at $42,000 plus 2% of sales; $3,000 will be incurred on account, $36,000 will be accrued, $13,200 will result from expired prepaid expenses, 1% of sales are estimated to be uncollectible, and $1,800 will result from allocated depreciation.

5. Interest accrues at 5% annually on the notes payable and is credited to Accrued Liabilities Payable.

6. All of the beginning balances in Accounts Payable and Accrued Liabilities Payable, plus 80% of the current credits to Accounts Payable, and all but $30,000 of the current accrued liabilities will be paid during the quarter. An $18,000 insurance premium is to be paid prior to March 31, and a full year's rent of $144,000 is due on January 2.

7. Income taxes are budgeted at 40% of the income before income taxes. The taxes should be accrued separately, and no payments are due in the first quarter.

Required:

a. Prepare a planned operating budget for the quarter ending March 31, 1995, including supporting schedules for planned purchases and operating expenses.

b. Prepare a financial budget as of March 31, 1995. Supporting schedules should be included that (1) analyze accounts credited for purchases and operating expenses, (2) show planned accounts receivable collections and balance, and (3) show planned cash flows and cash balance.

c. Will Wolf be able to collect the $120,000 on her note?

ANSWERS TO SELF-TEST

True-False

1. *True*. Budgets are estimates of the future and should take future plans and conditions into account.

2. *True*. A master budget does consist of a projected income statement (planned operating budget) and a projected balance sheet (financial budget).

3. *False*. These budgets start with units and then are converted to dollars.

4. *False*. The flexible budget for the *actual* level of activity must be used to achieve a valid analysis for expense control purposes.

5. *False*. Computer spreadsheets are very useful in budgeting. The spreadsheets allow budget participants to immediately see the effects of changed assumptions.

Multiple-Choice

1. *e.* No foolproof methods exist for preparing effective budgets.

2. *a.* The sales budget precedes the other budgets.

3. *d.* The first schedule is the schedule of accounts receivable and collections.

4. *b.*

$$\text{Budgeted amount} = \text{Fixed portion of costs} + \left(\begin{array}{c} \text{Variable portion of cost per unit} \times \text{Units of output} \end{array} \right)$$

$$= \$70,000 + (\$1.20 \times 200,000)$$
$$= \$70,000 + \$240,000$$
$$= \$310,000 \text{ budgeted amount}$$

5. *c.* $\$140,000 - \$40,000 = \$100,000$ variable cost

$\$100,000/100,000 = \$1.00$ per unit variable cost

Budgeted costs at 90,000 units:

90,000 × $1.00	$ 90,000
Fixed costs	40,000
	$130,000
Actual costs	142,500
Unfavorable budget variance	$ 12,500

18 CONTROL THROUGH STANDARD COSTS

After studying this chapter, you should be able to:

1. Discuss the nature of standard costs, including how standards are set.
2. Define budgets and discuss how budgets are used in a standard cost system.
3. Discuss the advantages and disadvantages of using standard costs.
4. Calculate the six variances from standard and determine if the variance is favorable or unfavorable.
5. Discuss what each of the six variance accounts shows and prepare journal entries to record the variance.
6. Discuss the three selection guidelines used to investigate variances from standard.
7. Discuss the theoretical and practical methods for disposing of variances from standard.
8. Demonstrate the difference between just-in-time and traditional standard cost flows through accounts.
9. Discuss nonfinancial performance measures.
10. Discuss how standard costs are applied in both job order and process cost systems (appendix).

You will recall that the job order and process cost systems discussed in Chapters 13 and 14 are based on actual historical cost data. These data say little about how efficiently operations were conducted. Many companies find that introducing standard costs into their cost systems is helpful. Companies can use standard costs in both job order and process cost systems, as we discuss in the appendix to this chapter.

Standard and actual cost systems differ in that an actual cost system collects *actual* costs for materials, labor, and manufacturing overhead, while a standard cost system gathers both actual costs and *standard* costs for these elements of production. The standard costs flow through the accounting system to determine a standard, or "normal," cost for finished goods inventory. Actual costs incurred during the period are then compared with standard costs to assist management in decision making to determine whether proper control is being maintained over production costs.

This chapter discusses the uses of standard costs, the advantages and disadvantages of using standard costs, and how to compute the difference between an actual cost and a standard cost, which is called a *variance*. The variances discussed are materials variances, labor variances, and overhead variances. This chapter will show you how companies control costs by investigating variances and taking corrective action, if necessary.

USES OF STANDARD COSTS

You have probably set goals for yourself that you want to achieve. You could have called these goals *standards*. Periodically, you might measure your actual performance against these standards and analyze the differences. Similarly, management sets goals, such as standard costs, and compares actual costs with these goals to identify possible problems.

This section begins with a discussion on the nature of standard costs. The second topic of this section discusses how companies use standard costs to establish budgets. Next, you will learn how management uses the process of *management by exception* to investigate variances from standard. In setting standards, management must decide whether it will use ideal standards or practical standards, the fourth topic in this section. The section closes with a discussion of other uses of standard costs.

Nature of Standard Costs

*Objective 1
Discuss the nature of standard costs, including how standards are set*

A **standard cost** is a carefully predetermined measure of what a cost *should be* under stated conditions. Standard costs are not only estimates of what costs should be, but they are goals to be achieved. The achievement of properly set standards represents a reasonably efficient level of performance.

Although standards are set in many ways, the most useful standards are those that are more than estimates determined by extending historical trends into the future. Usually, effective standards are the result of engineering studies and of time and motion studies. Companies undertake these studies to determine the amounts of materials, labor, and other services required to produce a product. In setting standards, a manufacturing company must also consider general economic conditions because they affect the costs of materials and other services that the company must purchase.

Manufacturing companies determine the standard cost of each unit of product by establishing the standard costs of direct materials, direct labor, and manufacturing overhead necessary to produce that unit. Determining the standard costs of direct materials and direct labor is less complicated than determining the standard cost of manufacturing overhead.

The standard direct materials cost per unit of a product consists of the standard amount of material required to produce the unit multiplied by the standard price of the material. You must distinguish between the terms *standard price* and *standard cost*.

Standard price usually refers to the price per unit of inputs into the production process. For example, the price per pound of raw materials is a standard price. Standard cost, however, is the standard quantity of an input required per unit of output times the standard price per unit of that input. For example, if the standard price of cloth is $3 per yard and the standard quantity of material required to produce a dress is 3 yards, then the standard direct materials cost of the dress is 3 yards × $3 per yard = $9. Similarly, the standard direct labor cost per unit for a product is the standard number of hours needed to produce one unit multiplied by the standard labor or wage rate per hour.

To find the standard manufacturing overhead cost of a unit, use the following steps. First, determine the expected level of output for the year. This level of output is called the **standard level of output.** Next, determine the total budgeted manufacturing overhead cost at the standard level of output. The total budgeted overhead cost includes both fixed and variable components. Total fixed cost is the same at every level of output within a relevant range. Total variable overhead cost varies in direct proportion to the number of units produced.

Finally, compute the standard manufacturing overhead cost per unit by dividing the budgeted manufacturing overhead cost by the standard level of output. The result is an overhead cost (or rate) per unit of output.

The formula to compute the standard overhead cost per unit is:

$$\text{Standard overhead cost (or rate)} = \frac{\text{Total budgeted overhead cost at standard level of output}}{\text{Standard level of output}}$$

Sometimes accountants find the standard overhead cost (or rate) per direct labor-hour instead of per unit. To find the cost per unit, merely multiply the direct labor-hours per unit times the standard overhead cost per direct labor-hour. For instance, if the standard overhead cost per direct labor-hour is $5 and the standard number of direct labor-hours is two hours per unit, the standard overhead cost per unit is $5 × 2 hours = $10.

Use of Standard Costs in Developing Budgets

Objective 2
Define budgets
and discuss how

As discussed in Chapter 17, the management of a business is responsible for conducting operations in an efficient and effective manner. To help meet this

budgets are used in a standard cost system

responsibility, management develops budgets as a planning and control tool. **Budgets** are formal written plans that represent management's planned actions in the future and the impacts of these actions on the business. These planned actions represent the costs (expenses) that the business expects to incur, and the impacts of these actions represent the revenues the business expects to receive as a result of the planned actions. Management uses standard costs to develop the expected costs relating to materials, labor, and overhead contained in a budget. Standard costs can also have an impact on budgeted revenues by influencing the selling price(s) set for goods to be sold.

As a business incurs actual expenses and revenues, management controls operations by comparing the actual and budgeted amounts, investigating differences, and taking corrective action when necessary.

Management by Exception

When management compares actual expenses and revenues with budgeted expenses and revenues at the actual level of operations, differences—called *variances*—are likely to occur. The responsibility of management is to investigate these variances. When companies are large, management directs its attention only to those variances that are unusually favorable or unfavorable. Obviously, management must determine when a variance is unusually favorable or unfavorable. This process of focusing on only the most significant variances is called **management by exception.** The process of management by exception enables management to concentrate its efforts on those variances that could have a material effect on the company, ignoring those variances that are not significant to the company as a whole.

Ideal versus Practical Standards

In developing standards, management must consider the assumed conditions under which these standards can be met. Standards generally fall into two groups—ideal and practical.

Ideal standards make no allowances for machinery breakdowns and maintenance or for worker rest periods or some inefficiency. Thus, ideal standards are virtually impossible to attain over long periods of time. Workers subjected to ideal standards can become demoralized rather than highly motivated. For this reason, management generally does not use ideal standards in planning.

Practical standards make allowances for machinery breakdowns and maintenance and for worker rest periods and some worker inefficiency. These standards can be attained by workers if they are reasonably efficient at their work. Practical standards can serve to motivate workers because these standards are attainable. For this reason, management generally uses practical standards in planning. However, even when practical standards are used, management must decide how "tight or loose" to make those standards.

How Tight Should Practical Standards Be?

Managers may set practical standards for performance loosely so the standards can be met a high percentage of the time, or managers may set practical standards tightly so they are met only a certain percentage of the time. Researchers find that employees generally underperform when standards are set too loosely. When managers introduce a moderate level of tension with moderately tight standards, employees tend to be more highly motivated and perform better.

Other Uses of Standard Costs

In addition to their use in developing budgets, standard costs are useful in evaluating management's performance, evaluating workers' performances, and setting appropriate selling prices.

Management's and workers' performances can be evaluated through the use of a budget. When management compares actual results with standard amounts, it can see how well it is performing its own duties in managing its employees. Management can also evaluate workers based on how well they performed relative to the budgeted amounts pertaining to the activities they performed.

Standard costs are also useful in setting selling prices. The budget shows the expected expenses incurred by the business. By considering these expenses, management can determine how much to charge for a product so as to produce the desired net income. Then, as the business actually incurs these expenses, management can determine if the selling prices set are still reasonable and, if necessary, can consider some price adjustments.

ADVANTAGES AND DISADVANTAGES OF USING STANDARD COSTS

This section discusses advantages and disadvantages of using standard costs.

Advantages of Using Standard Costs

*Objective 3
Discuss the advantages and disadvantages of using standard costs*

A number of benefits result from the use of a standard cost system. These benefits include:

1. Improved cost control.
2. More useful information for managerial planning and decision making.
3. More reasonable inventory measurements.
4. Cost savings in record-keeping.
5. Possible reductions in production costs incurred.

Improved Cost Control.   Companies control their costs by setting standards for each type of cost incurred and then highlighting *exceptions,* or variances—instances where things are not going as planned. Variances provide a starting point for judging the effectiveness of managers in controlling the costs for which they are held responsible.

Assume, for example, that in a certain Pizza Hut restaurant, actual direct materials costs for pizza dough and ingredients were $52,015 and exceeded standard cost by $6,015. Knowing that actual direct materials cost exceeded standard cost by $6,015 is more useful than merely knowing that actual direct materials cost amounted to $52,015. Now Pizza Hut's management knows to investigate the cause of the excess of actual cost over standard cost and take corrective action. Further investigation will show whether the exception (variance) was caused by inefficient use of pizza dough and ingredients or was the result of higher prices. In either case, the standard cost system has served as an early warning system by highlighting a potential hazard for management.

More Useful Information for Managerial Planning and Decision Making. When management develops appropriate cost standards and succeeds in controlling production costs, then future actual costs should be fairly close to standard. As a result, management can use standard costs in preparing more accurate budgets and in estimating costs for bidding on jobs. A standard cost system can be valuable for top management in planning and decision making.

More Reasonable Inventory Measurements. A standard cost system provides a more logical inventory valuation than does an actual cost system. Under an actual cost system, unit costs for batches of identical products may differ widely because of a machine malfunction during the production of a given batch that resulted in more labor and overhead being charged to that batch. Under a standard cost system, such costs would not be included in inventory. Rather, these excess costs would be charged to variance accounts after comparing actual costs to standard costs. Thus, in a standard cost system, all units of a given product are carried in inventory at the same unit cost. Logically, identical physical units produced in a given time period should be recorded at the same cost.

Cost Savings in Record-Keeping. Although a standard cost system may seem to require more detailed record-keeping during the accounting period than an actual cost system, the reverse is true. For example, in a job order system accumulating only actual costs, the cost flows between inventory accounts and eventually into cost of goods sold are recorded at *varying* amounts of actual unit costs, which must be calculated during the period. In a standard cost system, the cost flows between inventory accounts and into cost of goods sold are shown at *consistent* standard amounts during the period. No special calculations are needed to determine unit costs during the period. Instead, standard cost sheets may be printed in advance showing standard quantities and standard unit costs for the materials, labor, and overhead needed to produce a given amount of a certain product.

A BROADER PERSPECTIVE

EXPANDING VARIANCE ANALYSIS TO QUALITY MEASURES

Traditional standard cost systems have focused on two variances for variable costs—price variances and efficiency variances. While these variances help managers assess how well their companies are doing in managing costs and productivity, they fall short in measuring quality. Managers focusing on price and efficiency may have incentives to minimize quality which could have disastrous effects in the marketplace. Many successful American companies have found their products did not compete on quality, even though price and efficiency variances were minimal.

"Quality variances indicate the production costs of defective units. They focus attention on the resources invested in units that must be reworked, scrapped or sold as seconds" [p. 58].

Many companies are developing new measurement systems to detect quality variances. Quality variances can be detected on the production line by measuring defects at each stage of the production process. Quality can also be measured with customer satisfaction surveys.

New concerns about quality do not require companies to dismantle their standard cost systems that have traditionally focused on price and efficiency variances. However, managers concerned about quality need to understand that traditional systems should be supplemented by quality performance measures.

SOURCE: Based on the article by Carole Cheatham, "Updating Standard Cost Systems," *Journal of Accountancy*, December 1990, pp. 57–60.

Possible Reductions in Production Costs Incurred. A standard cost system may lead to cost savings. The use of standard costs may cause employees to become more cost conscious and seek improved methods of completing their tasks. Only when employees become active in reducing costs can companies really become successful at cost control.

Disadvantages of Using Standard Costs

Three important disadvantages of using standard costs exist. They include:

1. Controversial materiality limits for variances.
2. Nonreporting of certain variances.
3. Low morale for some workers.

Controversial Materiality Limits for Variances. Determining materiality limits for the variances may be controversial. The management of each business has the responsibility for determining what constitutes a material or unusual variance. Since materiality involves individual judgment, many problems or conflicts may arise among individuals in setting materiality limits.

Nonreporting of Certain Variances. Workers do not always report all exceptions (variances). Because workers are evaluated through the use of budgets and management only investigates unusual variances, workers may not report negative exceptions to the budget or may try to minimize these exceptions in an effort to conceal inefficiency. If workers succeed in hiding variances, they diminish the effectiveness of budgeting.

Low Morale for Some Workers.   The management by exception technique focuses on the unusual variances. The purpose of this technique is to investigate significant differences. Thus, workers who stay within the budget's constraints may be overlooked and not praised for their efforts. Other workers may attract attention because of material unfavorable variances resulting from their work. As a result, the morale of both types of workers could suffer.

COMPUTING VARIANCES

Objective 4
Calculate the six
variances from
standard and
determine if the
variance is favor-
able or unfavor-
able

As stated earlier, standard costs represent *goals*. Standard cost is the amount that a cost should be under a given set of circumstances. The accounting records also contain information about *actual* costs. The amount by which actual cost differs from standard cost is called a **variance.** A variance is designated as favorable when actual costs are less than standard; it is unfavorable when actual costs exceed standard. However, favorable and unfavorable variances should not necessarily be equated with good and bad. As you will see, such an appraisal should only be made after the causes of the variance are known.

Objective 5
Discuss what each
of the six variance
accounts shows
and prepare jour-
nal entries to
record the vari-
ance

The following example explains how to compute the dollar amount of variances, a process called *isolating variances,* using data for Beta Company. Beta manufactures and sells computer desks that have special places for the keyboard, terminal, printer, and paper. Vanessa Smith, the owner-manager of Beta, has developed the following standard costs for each desk:

Materials—15 board feet at $2 per board foot	$30
Direct labor—2 hours at $10 per hour	20
Manufacturing overhead—2 machine-hours at $5 per hour	10
Total standard cost per desk	$60

Additional data about the production activities of the company will be presented as needed.

Materials Variances in Manufacturing Organizations

The standard materials cost of any product is simply the standard *quantity* of materials that should be used to produce the product multiplied by the *standard price* that should be paid for those materials. Actual costs may differ from standard costs for materials because the *price* paid for the materials and/or the *quantity* of materials used varied from the standard amounts management had set. We can account for these two factors by isolating two variances for materials—a *price variance* and a *usage variance*.

Accountants isolate two materials variances for three reasons. First, different individuals may be responsible for each variance—a purchasing agent for the price variance and a production manager for the usage variance. Second, a company might not purchase and use materials in the same period. The variance associated with the purchase should be isolated in the period of purchase, and the variance associated with usage should be isolated in the period of use. As a general rule, the sooner a variance can be isolated, the greater is its value in cost control.

Finally, the probability is low that a single materials variance—the difference between the standard cost and the actual cost of the materials used—would be of any real value to management for effective cost control. A single variance would not show management what *caused* the difference. One variance might simply offset another and make the total difference appear to be immaterial.

Materials Price Variance.   The purchasing and accounting departments usually set the standard price for materials. They consider factors such as market conditions, product quality, vendors' quoted prices, and the optimum size of a purchase order when setting a standard price. The **materials price variance (MPV)** is caused by paying a higher or lower price than the standard price set for materials. The materials price variance (MPV) is the difference between the actual price paid (AP) and the standard price allowed (SP) multiplied by the actual quantity of materials purchased (AQ). In equation form, the materials price variance is:

$$\text{Materials price variance} = \left(\begin{array}{c}\text{Actual} \\ \text{price}\end{array} - \begin{array}{c}\text{Standard} \\ \text{price}\end{array}\right) \times \begin{array}{c}\text{Actual quantity} \\ \text{purchased}\end{array}$$

To illustrate, assume that a new supplier entered the market and Beta was able to purchase 180,000 board feet of material from this supplier at a price of $1.90 each. (One board foot is a piece of wood 12 inches by 12 inches and 1 inch thick.) Since the standard price set by Ms. Smith is $2 per board foot, the materials price variance is computed as:

$$\begin{aligned}\text{Materials price variance} &= \left(\begin{array}{c}\text{Actual} \\ \text{price}\end{array} - \begin{array}{c}\text{Standard} \\ \text{price}\end{array}\right) \times \begin{array}{c}\text{Actual quantity} \\ \text{purchased}\end{array} \\ &= (\$1.90 - \$2.00) \times 180{,}000 \\ &= \${-}0.10 \times 180{,}000 \\ &= \${-}18{,}000 \text{ (favorable)}\end{aligned}$$

Beta considers the materials price variance of $-18,000 to be favorable because the materials were acquired for a price less than standard. If the actual price had exceeded the standard price, the variance would be unfavorable because Beta would have incurred more costs than allowed by the standard.

In T-account form, the entry to record the purchase of the materials is:

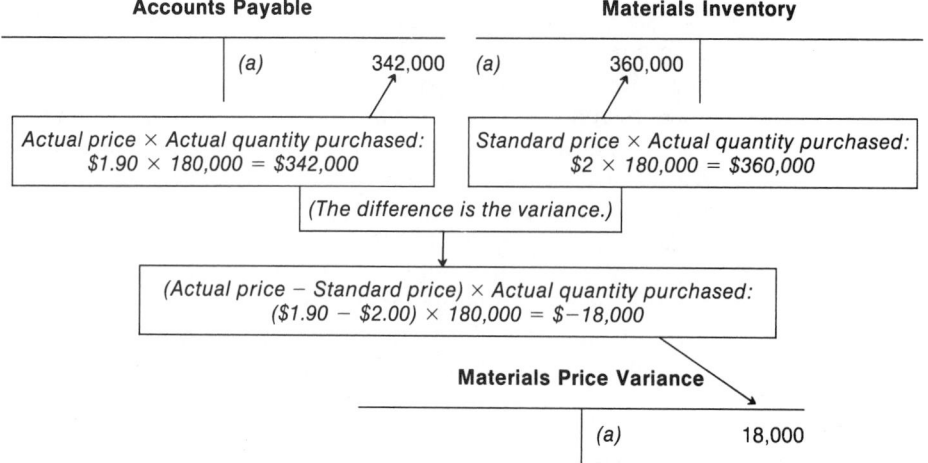

The general journal entry to record the purchase of materials is:

(a) Materials Inventory 360,000
          Materials Price Variance.   18,000
          Accounts Payable   342,000
     To record the purchase of materials at less than
     standard cost.

Note that the Accounts Payable account shows the actual debt owed to suppliers, while the Materials Inventory account shows the *standard* price of the actual quantity of materials *purchased*. The Materials Price Variance account shows the difference between the actual price and standard price multiplied by the actual quantity purchased.

Materials Usage Variance. The engineering department usually sets the standard *quantity* of materials to be used in making a product because it is largely a matter of physical requirements or product specifications. However, if the *quality* of materials used varies with price, the accounting and purchasing departments may take part in special studies to find the "right" quality.

The **materials usage variance (MUV)** is caused by using more or less than the standard amount of materials to produce a product or complete a process. **This variance shows only differences from standard caused by the quantity of materials used; it does not include any effect of variances in price.** Thus, the materials usage variance (MUV) is equal to actual quantity used (AQ) minus standard quantity allowed (SQ) multiplied by standard price (SP):

$$\text{Materials usage variance} = \left(\begin{array}{c}\text{Actual quantity}\\\text{used}\end{array} - \begin{array}{c}\text{Standard}\\\text{quantity}\\\text{allowed}\end{array}\right) \times \begin{array}{c}\text{Standard}\\\text{price}\end{array}$$

To illustrate, assume that Beta used 180,000 board feet of material to produce 11,000 desks. The standard quantity allowed for that level of production would be 165,000 board feet (15 × 11,000). The standard price of the material is $2 per board foot, so the materials usage variance is $30,000, computed as follows:

$$\text{Materials usage variance} = \left(\begin{array}{c} \text{Actual quantity} \\ \text{used} \end{array} - \begin{array}{c} \text{Standard} \\ \text{quantity} \\ \text{allowed} \end{array} \right) \times \begin{array}{c} \text{Standard} \\ \text{price} \end{array}$$

$$= (180,000 - 165,000) \times \$2$$
$$= 15,000 \times \$2$$
$$= \$30,000 \text{ (unfavorable)}$$

The variance is unfavorable because Beta used more materials than the standard amount allowed to complete the job. If the standard quantity allowed had exceeded the quantity actually used, the materials usage variance would have been favorable.

The following T-accounts record the use of the materials:

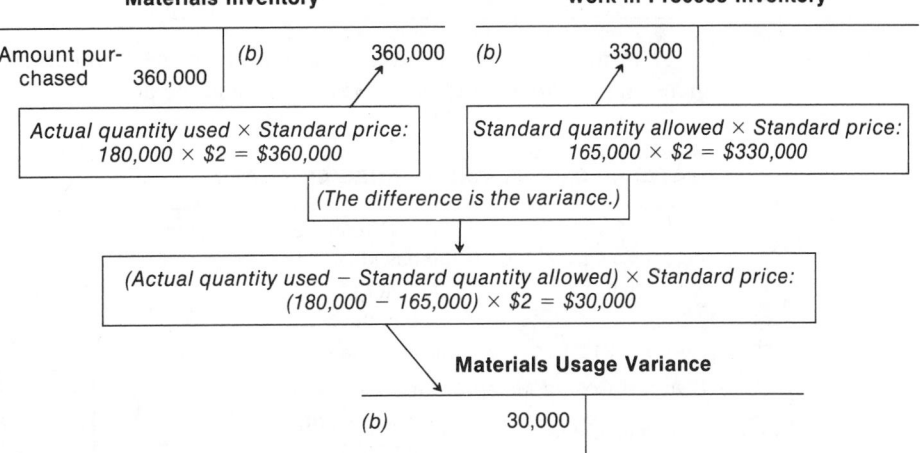

The general journal entry to record the use of the materials is:

(b)   Work in Process Inventory.   330,000
     Materials Usage Variance   30,000
        Materials Inventory   360,000
        To record the use of materials and to establish the
materials usage variance.

The Materials Usage Variance shows the standard cost of the excess materials *used*. Note also that the Work in Process Inventory account contains both standard quantity and standard prices.

The equations for both the above materials variances were expressed so that positive amounts were unfavorable variances and negative amounts were favorable variances. Unfavorable variances are debits in variance accounts because they add to the costs incurred, which are recorded as debits. Similarly, favorable variances are shown as negative amounts because they are reductions in costs. Thus, favorable variances are recorded in variance accounts as credits.

We use this format in this text, but a word of caution is in order. You will achieve far greater understanding if a variance is determined to be favorable or unfavorable by relying on reason or logic. If more materials were used than standard, or if a price greater than standard was paid, logic says the variance is unfavorable. If the reverse is true, the variance is favorable.

Analysis of Materials Variances.   Illustration 18.1 should help you understand the relationships among actual costs, standard costs, and variances. Illustration 18.1 uses the following data for Beta:

Standard price per board foot of material.	$2.00
Actual price per board foot of material	$1.90
Number of board feet of material purchased and used.	180,000
Standard number of board feet of material per desk produced.	15
Number of desks produced in the period	11,000

The materials price variance is based on the number of board feet of material *purchased* and is favorable because the actual price paid per board

Illustration 18.1
MATERIALS PRICE AND USAGE VARIANCES

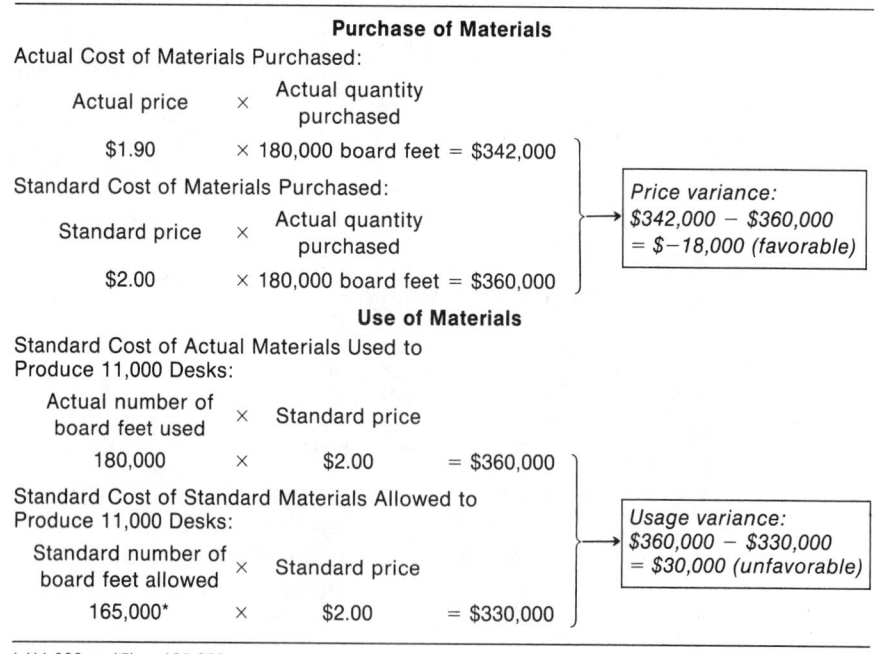

Purchase of Materials

Actual Cost of Materials Purchased:

Actual price   ×   Actual quantity purchased

$1.90   × 180,000 board feet = $342,000

Standard Cost of Materials Purchased:

Standard price   ×   Actual quantity purchased

$2.00   × 180,000 board feet = $360,000

Price variance:
$342,000 − $360,000
= $−18,000 (favorable)

Use of Materials

Standard Cost of Actual Materials Used to Produce 11,000 Desks:

Actual number of board feet used   ×   Standard price

180,000   × $2.00   = $360,000

Standard Cost of Standard Materials Allowed to Produce 11,000 Desks:

Standard number of board feet allowed   ×   Standard price

165,000*   × $2.00   = $330,000

Usage variance:
$360,000 − $330,000
= $30,000 (unfavorable)

* (11,000 × 15) = 165,000.

foot was less than the standard price. The materials usage variance is based on the number of board feet of material *used* and is unfavorable because the actual number of board feet used exceeded the standard quantity allowed to make 11,000 desks. In our example, the number of board feet of material purchased equals the number of board feet used. However, these quantities are not always equal.

Materials Variances in Nonmanufacturing Organizations

Many nonmanufacturing organizations have significant materials costs. McDonald's, for example, pays close attention to its food costs. Hospitals have become increasingly concerned about the cost of medical and surgical supplies. An example of materials cost variances for a particular restaurant at a national pizza chain follows:

Standard cost per pound of pizza dough	$1.50
Actual price paid	$1.60
Number of pounds purchased	1,200
Standard number of pounds per pizza	1
Number of pizzas made and sold in November	1,300
Number of pounds of pizza dough used	1,200

The materials price and usage variance would be computed as follows:

$$\text{Materials price variance} = \left(\begin{array}{c} \text{Actual} \\ \text{price} \end{array} - \begin{array}{c} \text{Standard} \\ \text{price} \end{array} \right) \times \begin{array}{c} \text{Actual quantity} \\ \text{purchased} \end{array}$$
$$= (\$1.60 - \$1.50) \times 1,200 \text{ pounds}$$
$$= \$0.10 \times 1,200 \text{ pounds}$$
$$= \$120 \text{ (unfavorable)}$$

$$\text{Materials usage variance} = \left(\begin{array}{c} \text{Actual} \\ \text{quantity} \\ \text{used} \end{array} - \begin{array}{c} \text{Standard} \\ \text{quantity} \\ \text{allowed} \end{array} \right) \times \begin{array}{c} \text{Standard} \\ \text{price} \end{array}$$

$$\text{Standard quantity allowed} = 1 \text{ pound per pizza} \times 1,300 \text{ pizzas produced}$$
$$= 1,300 \text{ pounds of pizza dough}$$

$$\text{Materials usage variance} = (1,200 \text{ pounds} - 1,300 \text{ pounds}) \times \$1.50$$
$$= -100 \text{ pounds} \times \$1.50$$
$$= \$-150 \text{ (favorable)}$$

Labor Variances in Manufacturing Organizations

The standard labor cost of any product is equal to the standard quantity of labor time allowed multiplied by the wage rate that should be paid for this time. Here again, the actual labor cost may differ from the standard labor cost because of the *rate* of wages paid for labor, or the *quantity* of labor used, or both. Thus, two labor variances exist—a rate variance and an efficiency variance.

Labor Rate Variance. The **labor rate variance (LRV)** is caused by paying a higher or lower average rate of pay than standard to produce a product or complete a process. The labor rate variance is similar to the materials price variance.

To compute the labor rate variance (LRV), we multiply the difference between the actual direct labor-hour rate paid (AR) and the standard direct labor-hour rate allowed (SR) by the actual direct labor-hours worked (AH):

$$\text{Labor rate variance} = \left(\begin{matrix}\text{Actual} \\ \text{rate}\end{matrix} - \begin{matrix}\text{Standard} \\ \text{rate}\end{matrix}\right) \times \begin{matrix}\text{Actual} \\ \text{hours}\end{matrix}$$

To continue the Beta example, assume that the direct labor payroll of the company consisted of 22,200 hours at a total cost of $233,100 (an average actual hourly rate of $10.50). Management has set a standard direct labor-hour rate of $10 per hour, so the labor rate variance is:

$$
\begin{aligned}
\text{Labor rate variance} &= \left(\begin{matrix}\text{Actual} \\ \text{rate}\end{matrix} - \begin{matrix}\text{Standard} \\ \text{rate}\end{matrix}\right) \times \begin{matrix}\text{Actual} \\ \text{hours}\end{matrix} \\
&= (\$10.50 - \$10.00) \times 22{,}200 \\
&= \$0.50 \times 22{,}200 \\
&= \$11{,}100 \text{ (unfavorable)}
\end{aligned}
$$

The variance is positive and unfavorable because the actual rate paid exceeded the standard rate allowed. If the reverse were true, the variance would be favorable.

Labor Efficiency Variance. The company's engineering department usually sets the standard amount of direct labor time (hours or minutes) needed to complete a product. The direct labor time standard may be based on time and motion studies, or it may be the subject of bargaining with the employees' union. The **labor efficiency variance (LEV)** is caused by using more or less than the standard amount of direct labor-hours to produce a product or complete a process. The labor efficiency variance is similar to the materials usage variance.

The labor efficiency variance (LEV) is computed by multiplying the difference between the actual direct labor-hours worked (AH) and the standard direct labor-hours allowed (SH) by the standard direct labor-hour rate per hour (SR):

$$\text{Labor efficiency variance} = \left(\begin{matrix}\text{Actual} \\ \text{hours}\end{matrix} - \begin{matrix}\text{Standard} \\ \text{hours}\end{matrix}\right) \times \begin{matrix}\text{Standard} \\ \text{rate}\end{matrix}$$

To illustrate, assume that the 22,200 hours of direct labor time worked by Beta employees resulted in 11,000 units of production. These 11,000 units have a standard direct labor time of 22,000 hours (11,000 units at 2 hours per unit). Since the standard direct labor rate is $10 per hour, the labor efficiency variance is $2,000, computed as follows:

$$\text{Labor efficiency variance} = \left(\begin{array}{c}\text{Actual} \\ \text{hours}\end{array} - \begin{array}{c}\text{Standard} \\ \text{hours}\end{array}\right) \times \begin{array}{c}\text{Standard} \\ \text{rate}\end{array}$$

$$= (22{,}200 - 22{,}000) \times \$10$$
$$= 200 \times \$10$$
$$= \$2{,}000 \text{ (unfavorable)}$$

The variance is unfavorable because Beta required more hours than standard to complete the period's production. If the reverse were true, the variance would be favorable.

The following T-accounts show how to charge Work in Process Inventory with direct labor cost and the two labor variances for Beta.

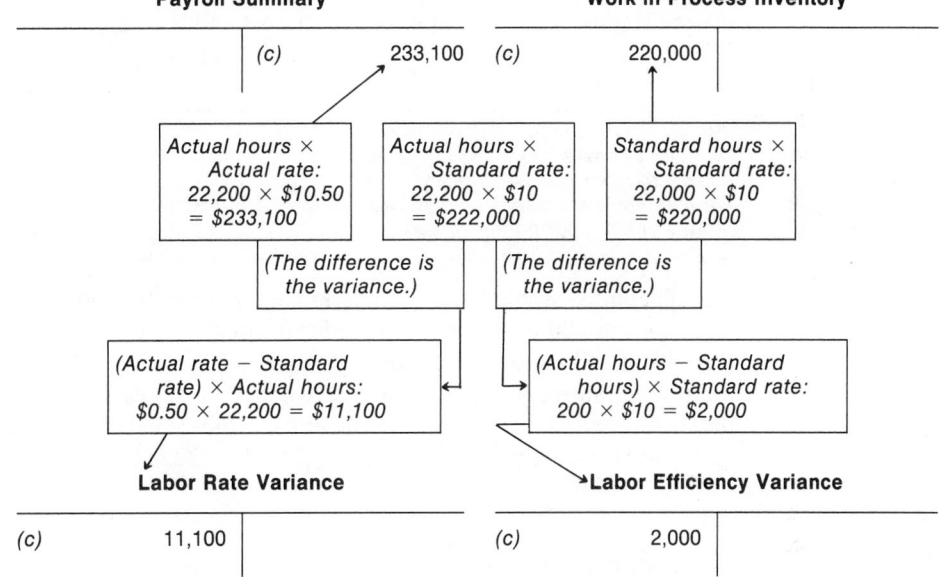

The standard direct labor time allowed for the period's output is 22,000 hours (11,000 units at 2 hours per unit). The standard direct labor cost is $10 per hour; therefore, the standard direct labor cost for the output achieved is assigned to inventory, regardless of the actual direct labor cost.

The general journal entry to charge the direct labor cost to Work in Process Inventory is:

```
(c)  Work in Process Inventory. . . . . . . . . . . . . .   220,000
     Labor Rate Variance  . . . . . . . . . . . . . . .    11,100
     Labor Efficiency Variance . . . . . . . . . . . . .    2,000
        Payroll Summary . . . . . . . . . . . . . . . .              233,100
     To charge work in process with direct labor and to
     establish the two labor variances.
```

With the above entry, gross wages earned by direct-production employees ($233,100) are distributed as follows: $220,000 (the standard labor cost of production) to Work in Process Inventory and the balance to the two labor variance accounts. The unfavorable labor rate variance is not necessarily caused by paying employees more wages than they are entitled to receive. A more probable reason is either that more highly skilled employees (with higher wage rates) worked on production than originally anticipated, or that employee wage rates increased after the standard was developed and the standard was not revised. Favorable rate variances, on the other hand, could be caused by using less skilled (cheaper) labor in the production process. Typically, the hours of labor employed are more likely to be under management's control than the rates that are paid. For this reason, labor efficiency variances are generally watched more closely than labor rate variances.

Analysis of Labor Variances.   Illustration 18.2 shows the relation between standard and actual direct labor cost and the computation of the labor variances. The illustration is based on the following data for Beta:

Standard direct labor time per desk	2 hours
Number of desks produced in the period	11,000 units
Standard labor rate per direct labor-hour	$10
Total direct labor wages paid (at average rate of $10.50 per hour)	$233,100
Actual direct labor-hours worked	22,200 hours

The unfavorable labor rate variance includes the above-standard wages paid on the 200 extra (above-standard) direct labor-hours used to produce the desks. This variation from standard is actually caused by both extra hours and above-standard wages. However, as shown, it is included in the labor rate variance. The labor efficiency variance is the standard cost of the extra hours of direct labor required [(22,200 − 22,000) × $10 = $2,000]. This

Illustration 18.2
LABOR RATE AND EFFICIENCY VARIANCES

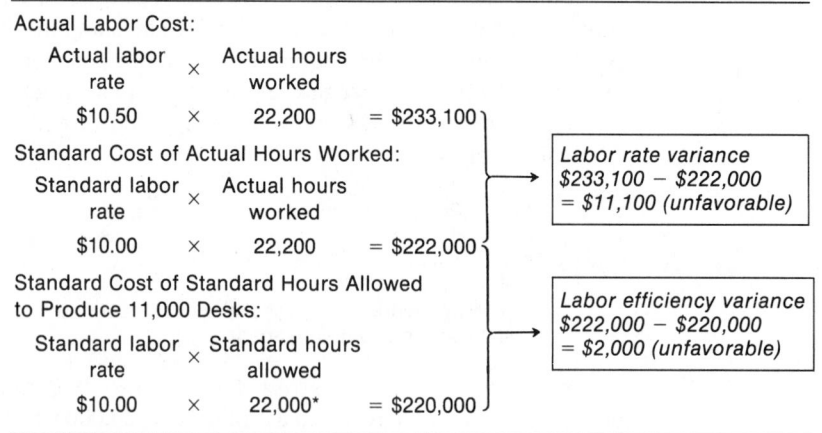

* 2 hours × 11,000 desks = 22,000.

variance is unfavorable because Beta used more hours of direct labor than allowed by the standard.

Summary of Labor Variances.   We can check the accuracy of the two labor variances by comparing their sum with the difference between actual and standard labor cost for a period. In the Beta illustration, this difference was:

Actual labor cost incurred (22,200 hours × $10.50).	$233,100
Standard labor cost allowed (22,000 hours × $10)	220,000
Total labor variance (unfavorable).	$ 13,100

This $13,100 is made up of two labor variances, both unfavorable:

Labor rate variance (22,200 × $0.50)	$11,100
Labor efficiency variance (200 × $10)	2,000
Total labor variance (unfavorable)	$13,100

Labor Variances in Nonmanufacturing Organizations

Labor costs are typically a major cost in service organizations. Banks, public accounting firms, law firms, hospitals, and parking enforcement agencies are just a few organizations that monitor labor costs closely. The following standards were developed for a university's parking enforcement people. (The university's officials explained that they do not have ticket quotas, but they expect their parking ticket writers "to be enforcing parking laws, not hanging out at the coffee house.")

Assume the university officials developed the following standard costs:

Standard direct labor time per ticket	12 minutes
Number of tickets written in March	2,000 tickets
Standard labor rate per hour	$14
Total labor costs for ticket writing (at an average rate	
of $13.50 per hour).	$5,670
Actual ticket writing hours worked	420 hours

The university would have calculated labor rate and efficiency variances as follows:

$$\text{Labor rate variance} = \left(\begin{array}{c}\text{Actual} \\ \text{rate}\end{array} - \begin{array}{c}\text{Standard} \\ \text{rate}\end{array}\right) \times \begin{array}{c}\text{Actual} \\ \text{hours}\end{array}$$

$$= (\$13.50 - \$14.00) \times 420 \text{ hours}$$

$$= \$-0.50 \times 420 \text{ hours}$$

$$= \$-210.00 \text{ (favorable)}$$

$$\text{Labor efficiency variance} = \begin{pmatrix} \text{Actual} \\ \text{hours} \end{pmatrix} - \begin{matrix} \text{Standard} \\ \text{hours} \end{matrix} \Bigg) \times \begin{matrix} \text{Standard} \\ \text{rate} \end{matrix}$$

$$\begin{aligned} \text{Standard hours} &= 12 \text{ minutes}/60 \text{ minutes} \times 2{,}000 \text{ tickets} \\ &= 0.2 \text{ hours} \times 2{,}000 \text{ tickets} \\ &= 400 \text{ hours} \end{aligned}$$

$$\begin{aligned} \text{Labor efficiency variance} &= (420 \text{ hours} - 400 \text{ hours}) \times \$14 \\ &= 20 \text{ hours} \times \$14 \\ &= \$280 \text{ (unfavorable)} \end{aligned}$$

Overhead Variances in Manufacturing Organizations

In a standard cost system, accountants apply manufacturing overhead to the goods produced using a standard overhead rate. The rate is set prior to the start of the period by dividing the budgeted manufacturing overhead cost by a standard level of output or activity. Total budgeted manufacturing overhead will vary at different levels of standard output, but since some overhead costs are fixed, total budgeted manufacturing overhead will not vary in direct proportion with output.

Companies use a **flexible budget** to isolate overhead variances and set the standard overhead rate. Flexible budgets show the budgeted amount of manufacturing overhead for various levels of output.

The flexible budget for Beta for the period is shown in Illustration 18.3. Note that Beta's flexible budget shows the variable and fixed manufacturing overhead costs expected to be incurred at three levels of activity: 90%, 100%, and 110% of capacity. For product costing purposes, the expected level of activity must be estimated in advance and a predetermined overhead rate set based on that level.

The activity level chosen is called *the standard volume of output*. This standard volume of output (or activity) may be expressed in terms of any of the activity bases that can be used in setting overhead rates. These activity bases include percentage of capacity, units of output, machine-hours, and direct labor-hours, among others. In our example, standard volume is assumed to be 100% of capacity. At this level of operation, Beta expects to produce 10,000 units and expects machines to operate for 20,000 hours. Assume that Beta applies manufacturing overhead to Work in Process Inventory using a rate based on machine-hours. According to the flexible manufacturing overhead budget, the expected manufacturing overhead cost at the standard volume (20,000 machine-hours) is $100,000, so the standard overhead rate is $5 per machine-hour ($100,000 ÷ 20,000 hours).

Knowing the separate rates for variable and fixed overhead is sometimes useful. The variable overhead rate is $2 per hour ($40,000 ÷ 20,000 hours), and the fixed overhead rate is $3 per hour ($60,000 ÷ 20,000 hours). If the expected volume had been 18,000 hours (90% of capacity), the standard overhead rate would have been $5.33 per hour ($96,000 ÷ 18,000 hours). The

Illustration 18.3
FLEXIBLE MANUFACTURING OVERHEAD BUDGET

	BETA COMPANY		
Flexible Manufacturing Overhead Budget			
Percent of capacity	90%	100%	110%
Machine-hours	18,000	20,000	22,000
Units of output	9,000	10,000	11,000
Variable overhead:			
Indirect materials	$ 7,200	$ 8,000	$ 8,800
Power	9,000	10,000	11,000
Royalties	1,800	2,000	2,200
Other	18,000	20,000	22,000
Total variable overhead	$36,000	$ 40,000	$ 44,000
Fixed overhead:			
Insurance	$ 4,000	$ 4,000	$ 4,000
Property taxes	6,000	6,000	6,000
Depreciation	20,000	20,000	20,000
Other	30,000	30,000	30,000
Total fixed overhead	$60,000	$ 60,000	$ 60,000
Total manufacturing overhead	$96,000	$100,000	$104,000
Standard overhead rate used to apply manufacturing overhead to Work in Process Inventory ($100,000 ÷ 20,000 hours)		$5	

variable overhead rate would be $2 per hour ($36,000 ÷ 18,000 hours), and the fixed overhead rate would be $3.33 per hour ($60,000 ÷ 18,000 hours). If the standard volume had been 22,000 direct labor-hours (110% of capacity), the standard overhead rate would have been $4.73 per hour ($104,000 ÷ 22,000 hours). The variable overhead rate would be $2 per hour ($44,000 ÷ 22,000 hours), and the fixed overhead rate would be $2.73 per hour ($60,000 ÷ 22,000 hours). Note that the difference in rates is due solely to dividing fixed overhead by a different number of machine-hours. That is, the variable overhead rate per unit stays constant ($2 per machine-hour) regardless of the number of units expected to be produced, and only the fixed overhead rate per unit changes.

Continuing with the Beta illustration, assume that the company incurred $108,000 of actual manufacturing overhead costs in a period during which 11,000 units of product were produced. The actual costs would be debited to Manufacturing Overhead and credited to a variety of accounts such as Accounts Payable, Accumulated Depreciation, Prepaid Insurance, and Property Taxes Payable. According to the flexible budget, the standard number of machine-hours allowed for 11,000 units of production is 22,000 hours. Therefore, $110,000 of manufacturing overhead is applied to production ($5 per machine-hour times 22,000 hours) by debiting Work in Process Inventory and crediting Manufacturing Overhead for $110,000.

In T-account form, the entry to record the application of $110,000 of manufacturing overhead to production (22,000 hours at $5 per hour) would be:

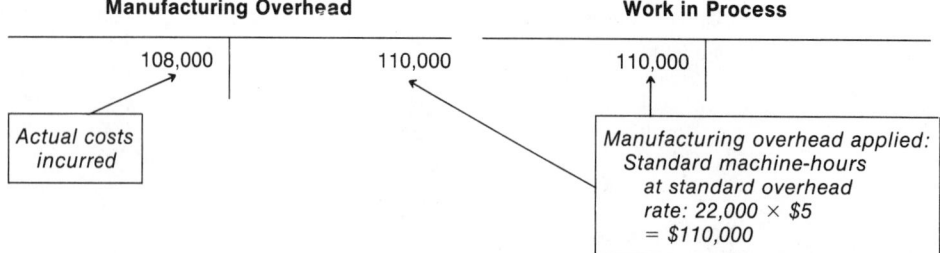

The general journal entry to apply manufacturing overhead to production would be:

Work in Process Inventory 110,000
　　Manufacturing Overhead. . . . . 　　　　110,000
　　To apply manufacturing overhead to production (22,000
　　hours at $5 per hour).

The above accounts show that manufacturing overhead has been overapplied to production by the $2,000 credit balance in the Manufacturing Overhead account. Because of its fixed component, manufacturing overhead will tend to be overapplied when actual production is greater than standard production.

The rate of $5 (which is based on output of 10,000 units) was used to apply manufacturing overhead to Work in Process Inventory when actual output was 11,000 units. The $5 is a *predetermined* rate set at the beginning of the year, when management *expected* to produce 10,000 units. Beta will not know its actual production until year-end.

Although various complex computations can be made for overhead variances, a simple approach will be used in this text. In this approach, known as the *two-variance approach to overhead variances,* only two variances are calculated—an overhead budget variance and an overhead volume variance.

Overhead Budget Variance. The **overhead budget variance (OBV)** shows in one amount how economically overhead services were purchased and how efficiently they were used. This overhead variance is similar to a combined price and usage variance for materials or labor. The overhead budget variance (OBV) is equal to the difference between total actual overhead costs (actual OH) and total budgeted overhead costs (BOH) for the *actual output attained.*

Total budgeted overhead costs are calculated as the variable overhead rate times the *standard machine-hours allowed for production achieved,* plus the constant amount of fixed overhead. For Beta, this calculation would be \$2 variable overhead times 22,000 hours, or \$44,000 variable overhead, plus \$60,000 of fixed overhead—a total of \$104,000. Since the total actual overhead was \$108,000 and the total budgeted overhead was \$104,000, the overhead budget variance is computed as follows:

$$
\begin{aligned}
\text{Overhead budget variance} &= \text{Actual overhead} - \text{Budgeted overhead} \\
&= \$108{,}000 - \$104{,}000 \\
&= \$4{,}000 \text{ (unfavorable)}
\end{aligned}
$$

The variance is unfavorable because actual overhead costs were \$108,000, while according to the flexible budget, they should have been \$104,000.

Overhead Volume Variance.   The **overhead volume variance (OVV)** is caused by producing at a level other than that used in setting the standard manufacturing overhead application rate. The OVV shows whether plant assets produced more or fewer goods than expected. Since fixed overhead is not constant on a per unit basis, any deviation from planned production will cause the overhead application rate to be incorrect. The OVV is the difference between the budgeted amount of overhead for the *actual volume achieved* (budgeted OH) and the applied overhead (applied OH):

Overhead volume variance = Budgeted overhead − Applied overhead

In the Beta example, the 11,000 units produced in the period have a standard machine-hour allowance of 22,000 hours. Budgeted overhead was calculated when we computed the overhead budget variance. The flexible budget in Illustration 18.3 shows that the budgeted overhead for 22,000 machine-hours is \$104,000. Overhead is applied to work in process on the basis of standard hours allowed for a particular amount of production, in this case 22,000 hours at \$5 per hour. The overhead volume variance then is:

$$
\begin{aligned}
\text{Overhead volume variance} &= \text{Budgeted overhead} - \text{Applied overhead} \\
&= \$104{,}000 - \$110{,}000 \\
&= \$-6{,}000 \text{ (favorable)}
\end{aligned}
$$

Note that the amount of the overhead volume variance is related solely to fixed overhead. As Illustration 18.3 shows, fixed overhead at all levels of activity is \$60,000. Since Beta used 100% of capacity, or 20,000 machine-hours, as its standard, the fixed overhead rate is \$3 per machine-hour. Beta worked 2,000 more hours (22,000 − 20,000) than was expected. The overhead volume variance can also be calculated as follows:

$$
\left(
\begin{array}{c}
\text{Number of hours} \\
\text{used in setting} \\
\text{predetermined} \\
\text{overhead rates}
\end{array}
-
\begin{array}{c}
\text{Number of standard} \\
\text{hours allowed} \\
\text{for production} \\
\text{level achieved}
\end{array}
\right)
\times
\begin{array}{c}
\text{Fixed overhead} \\
\text{rate per hour}
\end{array}
=
\begin{array}{c}
\text{Overhead} \\
\text{volume} \\
\text{variance}
\end{array}
$$

$$
(20{,}000 \quad - \quad 22{,}000) \quad \times \quad \$3 \quad = \quad \$-6{,}000 \text{ (favorable)}
$$

The variance is favorable since the company achieved a higher level of production than was expected.

Recording Manufacturing Overhead Variances. Formal entries are made in the accounts showing the two parts of the $2,000 net overhead variance. The T-account entry for Beta would be as follows (the variances are recorded in entry [*f*]):

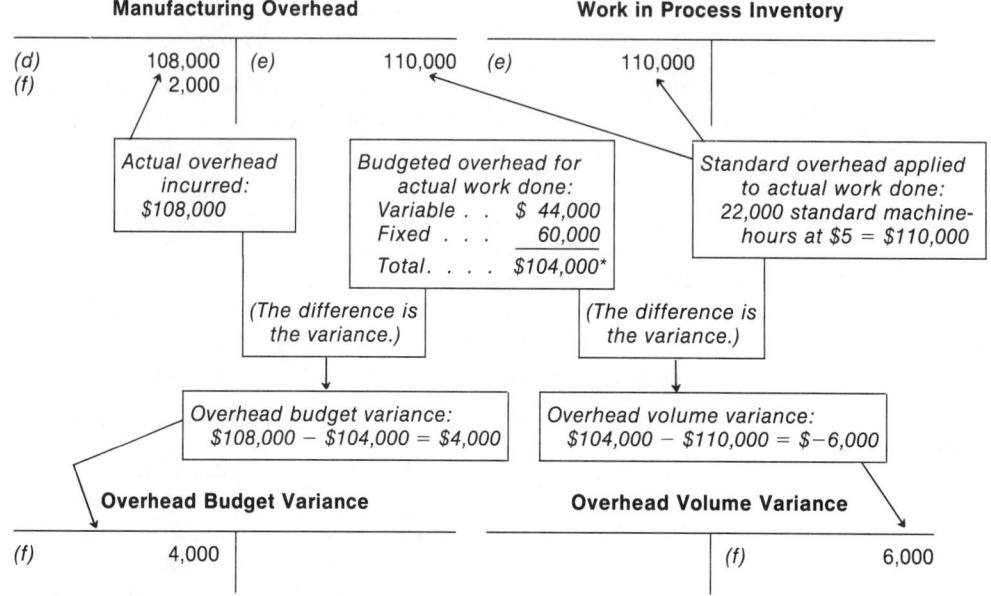

* From flexible budget. See Illustration 18.3.

The general journal entries related to overhead are as follows:

(*d*) Manufacturing Overhead   108,000
            Various accounts   108,000
        To record actual manufacturing overhead.

(*e*) Work in Process Inventory.   110,000
            Manufacturing Overhead   110,000
        To record the application of manufacturing overhead
        to work in process inventory.

(*f*) Manufacturing Overhead   2,000
        Overhead Budget Variance   4,000
            Overhead Volume Variance   6,000
        To record the variances related to overhead and close
        the Manufacturing Overhead account.

The first entry records Beta's actual manufacturing overhead costs incurred during the period. The second entry applies manufacturing overhead to Work in Process Inventory at the rate of $5 per standard machine-hour (22,000). The final entry reduces the Manufacturing Overhead account balance to zero and recognizes the two variances calculated for overhead. These two variance accounts analyze the causes of the overapplied manufacturing overhead for the period.

Summary of Overhead Variances.   The accuracy of the two overhead variances can be easily determined by comparing the sum of the budget and volume variances with the difference between the costs of actual manufacturing overhead and applied manufacturing overhead (the amount of over- or underapplied overhead). For Beta, the difference between actual and applied manufacturing overhead was:

Actual manufacturing overhead incurred	$108,000
Standard manufacturing overhead allowed (22,000 machine-hours × $5 per hour)	110,000
Total overhead variance (favorable)	$ −2,000

This difference is made up of the two overhead variances:

Overhead budget variance—unfavorable ($108,000 − $104,000)	$ 4,000
Overhead volume variance—favorable [$104,000 − (22,000 × $5)]	−6,000
Total overhead variance (favorable)	$−2,000

Illustration 18.4 provides a summary of the six variances from standard discussed in this chapter.

Overhead Variances in Nonmanufacturing Organizations

Overhead costs are a large component of costs in service organizations. Overhead in service companies, unlike the manufacturing company examples, typically includes general administrative costs in the cost of the "product."

The following example is based on a limousine service that operates between a college town and the local airport. (Although this company refers

Illustration 18.4
SUMMARY OF VARIANCES FROM STANDARD

Materials price variance = (Actual price − Standard price) × Actual quantity purchased

Materials usage variance = (Actual quantity used − Standard quantity allowed) × Standard price

Labor rate variance = (Actual rate − Standard rate) × Actual hours

Labor efficiency variance = (Actual hours − Standard hours) × Standard rate

Overhead budget variance = Actual overhead − Budgeted overhead

Overhead volume variance = Budgeted overhead − Applied overhead

to itself as a "limousine" service, all of its vehicles are vans.) First, the company estimated three levels of service, roughly corresponding to (1) peak periods such as school holidays, (2) normal periods, and (3) slow periods such as summer. Second, most overhead costs were made up of fuel and other van operating costs, so management used miles driven as the activity base (also known as a *cost driver*).

The company's estimates for the year were as follows:

	Flexible Overhead Budget per Month		
	Slow Periods	Normal Periods	Peak Periods
Cost per month:			
Variable overhead costs.	$ 6,000	$ 8,000	$10,000
Fixed overhead costs	8,000	8,000	8,000
Total overhead	$14,000	$16,000	$18,000
Miles driven per month	30,000	40,000	50,000
Number of trips.	1,000	1,333	1,667
Miles per trip	30	30	30
Variable overhead cost per mile	$0.20	$0.20	$0.20
Total overhead cost per mile (total overhead/miles) . . .	$0.467	$0.40	$0.36

For October, which the company considered to be a normal month, the actual and standard costs were:

Actual overhead incurred	$17,000
Number of trips	1,400
Standard miles allowed for 1,400 trips (30 miles × 1,400 trips)	42,000

Flexible budgeted overhead costs = ($0.20 variable overhead cost per mile × 42,000 miles allowed for 1,400 trips) + $8,000 fixed overhead cost = $8,400 + $8,000 = $16,400.

$$\text{Overhead budget variance} = \frac{\text{Actual}}{\text{overhead}} - \frac{\text{Budgeted}}{\text{overhead}}$$
$$= \$17,000 \quad - \quad \$16,400$$
$$= \$600 \text{ (unfavorable)}$$

$$\text{Overhead volume variance} = \frac{\text{Budgeted}}{\text{overhead}} - \frac{\text{Applied}}{\text{overhead}}$$
$$= \$16,400 - (\$0.40 \times 42,000 \text{ standard miles allowed})$$
$$= \$16,400 - \$16,800$$
$$= \$-400 \text{ (favorable)}$$

GOODS COMPLETED AND SOLD

To complete the standard cost system example using Beta, assume that Beta completed 11,000 units, transferred them to finished goods, and sold 10,000 units on account at a price of $96 per desk. Beta had no beginning or ending work in process inventories and no finished goods beginning inventory. In the following T-accounts, entry *(g)* shows the transfer of the standard cost of the units completed, $11,000 \times \$60 = \$660,000$, from Work in Process Inventory to Finished Goods Inventory. Entry *(h)* records the sales for the period, $\$96 \times 10,000 = \$960,000$. Entry *(i)* records the cost of goods sold, $10,000 \times \$60 = \$600,000$.

Work in Process Inventory

(b)	Materials	330,000	*(g)*	Completed	660,000
(c)	Labor	220,000			
(e)	Manufacturing overhead	110,000			

Finished Goods Inventory

(g)	Completed	660,000	*(i)*	Sold	600,000

Accounts Receivable

(h) 960,000	

Cost of Goods Sold

(i) Sold 600,000	

Sales

	(h) 960,000

In journal entry form, entries *(g), (h),* and *(i)* are:

(g)	Finished Goods Inventory 660,000	
	Work in Process Inventory.	660,000
	To record the transfer of completed units to finished goods inventory.	
(h)	Accounts Receivable 960,000	
	Sales.	960,000
	To record sales for the period.	
(i)	Cost of Goods Sold 600,000	
	Finished Goods Inventory	600,000
	To record cost of goods sold for the period.	

Work in Process Inventory has been debited with the standard costs of materials, labor, and manufacturing overhead for units put into production. Therefore, the entry recording the transfer of the standard cost of the completed units, $11,000 \times \$60 = \$660,000$, reduces Work in Process Inventory to a zero balance. Note that Finished Goods Inventory is debited with the standard cost of goods completed and credited with the standard cost of goods sold. Thus, ending finished goods inventory consists of the units actually on hand (1,000) at their standard cost of $60 each, or $60,000. Sales for the period amount to 10,000 units at $96 each.

INVESTIGATING VARIANCES FROM STANDARD

Objective 6
Discuss the three selection guidelines used to investigate variances from standard

Once all variances have been computed, management must decide which variances should be investigated further. Since numerous variances will occur, not all of them can be investigated. Management needs some selection guidelines. Possible guidelines include the (1) amount of the variance; (2) size of the variance relative to the cost incurred; and (3) controllability of the cost associated with the variance—that is, whether it is considered controllable or noncontrollable. Statistical analysis may also be used in deciding which variances to investigate. For instance, the average value of actual costs could be determined for a period of time so that only those variances deviating from the average by more than a certain amount or percentage would be investigated. To decide which selection guidelines are most useful, management should seek the opinions of knowledgeable operating personnel.

Any analysis of variances is likely to disclose some variances that are controllable within the company and others that are not. For instance, quantities used are generally controllable internally. Prices paid for materials purchased may or may not be controllable. Management may discover that the purchasing agent is not getting competitive bids; therefore, the price paid for materials would have been more controllable by seeking competitive bids. On the other hand, a raw materials shortage may exist that drives the price upward, and the price paid may be beyond the buyer's control.

Another point to remember about the analysis of variances is that separate variances are not necessarily independent. For example, an unfavorable labor rate variance may result from using higher paid employees for a certain task. However, higher paid employees may be more productive, resulting in a favorable labor efficiency variance. These employees may also be more highly skilled and may waste less materials, resulting in a favorable materials usage variance. Therefore, significant variances, whether favorable or unfavorable, should be investigated.

Performance Reports

At the end of a certain period of time (monthly, quarterly, and so on), management may develop performance reports that compare the actual results and costs with budgeted results and costs. These reports enable management to determine how well they and their workers were able to perform within the budget. At the bottom of the report, space is left for the supervisor or manager responsible for the elements mentioned in the report to give reasons for any variances. Management then investigates any variance that is not supported by an acceptable reason.

DISPOSING OF VARIANCES FROM STANDARD

Objective 7
Discuss the theoretical and practical methods for disposing of variances from standard

At the end of the year, variances from standard must be disposed of in the accounting records. The variances may be (1) viewed as gains or losses and closed to Income Summary; (2) allocated as adjustments to the recorded cost of Work in Process Inventory, Finished Goods Inventory, and Cost of Goods Sold; or (3) closed to Cost of Goods Sold. Theoretically, the alternative chosen should depend on whether the standards set were reasonably attainable and whether the variances were controllable by company employees. For instance, an unfavorable materials usage or labor efficiency variance caused by carelessness or inefficiency may be considered a loss and closed to Income Summary because the standard was attainable and the variance was controllable. An unfavorable materials price variance caused by an unexpected price change may be considered an added cost and allocated to the inventory accounts and Cost of Goods Sold because the standard was unattainable and the variance was uncontrollable. As a practical matter, and especially if variances are small, they are usually closed to the Cost of Goods Sold account rather than allocated to the inventory accounts and to Cost of Goods Sold.

Entry *(j)* in the T-accounts in Illustration 18.5 reflects this practical disposition of the variances for Beta.

Illustration 18.5
DISPOSITION OF VARIANCES

Materials Price Variance				Labor Rate Variance				Overhead Budget Variance			
(j)	18,000	*(a)*	18,000	*(c)*	11,100	*(j)*	11,100	*(f)*	4,000	*(j)*	4,000

Materials Usage Variance				Labor Efficiency Variance				Overhead Volume Variance			
(b)	30,000	*(j)*	30,000	*(c)*	2,000	*(j)*	2,000	*(j)*	6,000	*(f)*	6,000

Cost of Goods Sold		
(i)	600,000	
(j)	23,100	

In general journal entry form, entry *(j)* is:

(j)	Materials Price Variance.	18,000	
	Overhead Volume Variance	6,000	
	Cost of Goods Sold	23,100	
	Materials Usage Variance		30,000
	Labor Rate Variance		11,100
	Labor Efficiency Variance		2,000
	Overhead Budget Variance		4,000
	To close the variance accounts.		

Accountants do not report variances separately in financial statements released to the public, but they include them in the reported cost of goods sold amount. In reports prepared for internal use, accountants may list the variances separately after cost of goods sold is shown at standard cost.

JUST-IN-TIME AND TRADITIONAL STANDARD COST FLOWS

Objective 8 Demonstrate the difference between just-in-time and traditional standard cost flows through accounts

We have noted the trend toward a just-in-time (JIT) production system in earlier chapters. Companies using JIT strive to have low inventory levels or even no inventory. The use of JIT would not necessarily affect the way companies compute variances from standard costs, but it would affect the way costs flow through the accounts.

Using a JIT production system and standard costs, all manufacturing costs would be debited to Cost of Goods Sold at standard cost. Any ending inventories would be credited to Cost of Goods Sold and debited to the appropriate inventory account(s) at the end of the period. Variances for the period could be debited (for unfavorable variances) or credited (for favorable variances) to Cost of Goods Sold at the end of the period.

How would cost flows using JIT compare to traditional standard costing methods? We have already seen traditional standard cost flows in the Beta Company example, so we simply summarize it in the top section of Illustration 18.6. Assume all beginning inventory balances are zero. Ending inventory in Finished Goods Inventory is $60,000 for the 1,000 units remaining unsold. Recall that we computed six different cost variances. The illustration would be too detailed and tedious to read if we included each variance account, so we summarize the six variances in one account called Cost Variances. In actual practice, each variance would be reported in a separate account as shown earlier.

The bottom section of Illustration 18.6 shows the flow of costs using JIT. Standard costs are debited to Cost of Goods Sold when units are produced. Actual amounts are debited or credited to appropriate accounts (for example, credit to Accounts Payable) when costs are incurred. Variances are computed when standard and actual costs are known. At the end of the period, the standard costs of inventories are "backed out" or credited to Cost of Goods Sold and debited to the appropriate inventory account(s).

Illustration 18.6 COMPARISON OF JUST-IN-TIME (JIT) TO TRADITIONAL STANDARD COSTING METHODS FOR BETA COMPANY

TRADITIONAL STANDARD COST FLOWS

Accounts Payable			Materials Inventory		
	342,000	Beg. bal.	-0- 360,000	360,000
		Ending bal.	-0-	

Work in Process Inventory			Finished Goods Inventory		
Beg. bal.	-0-		Beg. bal.	-0-	
Materials	330,000				
Labor	220,000				
Overhead	110,000	660,000		660,000	600,000
Ending bal.	-0-		Ending bal.	60,000	

Manufacturing Overhead			Payroll Summary	
Actual		*Applied*		233,100
Actual	108,000	110,000		
Variances	2,000			

Cost of Goods Sold			Cost Variances		
	600,000		Net variances	23,100	23,100 (close to Cost of Goods Sold)
Variances	23,100				
	623,100				

JUST-IN-TIME STANDARD COST FLOWS

Accounts Payable			Cost of Goods Sold		
	342,000	Materials	330,000	60,000
		Labor	220,000	
		Overhead	110,000	
		Variances	23,100	
			623,100	

Manufacturing Overhead			Payroll Summary	
Actual		*Applied*		233,100
	108,000	110,000		
Variances	2,000			

Finished Goods Inventory			Cost Variances		
Beg. bal.	-0- 60,000		Net variances	23,100	23,100 (close to Cost of Goods Sold)
Ending bal.	60,000				

NONFINANCIAL PERFORMANCE MEASURES

Impact of Automation

*Objective 9
Discuss nonfinan-
cial performance
measures*

Standard costs are widely used in manufacturing, service, and not-for-profit organizations. The list of companies using standards as a method for controlling costs and measuring performance continues to grow. Managers in automated environments are developing a wide range of new performance measures.

In an automated environment, labor is a smaller proportion of product cost, often less than 5%. Thus, traditional labor variances are of little value to management. Also, the manufacturing process is more reliable in an automated environment, and the traditional variances tend to be minimal.

Types of Nonfinancial Measures

The new performance measures tend to be nonfinancial and more subjective than standard costs. Illustration 18.7 presents five sets of **nonfinancial performance measures.** The first two, *quality control* and *delivery performance*, are customer oriented. These are useful performance measures in all organizations, particularly service organizations in which the focus is on services, not goods.

The next three performance measures are production oriented. Reducing *material waste*, *inventory*, and *machine downtime* have been shown to improve quality and efficiency. These nonfinancial performance measures and measures of performance using standard costs are not mutually exclusive, of course. Reducing materials waste would eliminate an unfavorable materials usage variance, for example.

**Illustration 18.7
NONFINANCIAL PERFORMANCE MEASURES**

	Objective
1. Quality control:	
Number of customer complaints	Reduce complaints
Number of defects.	Reduce defects
2. Delivery performance:	
Percentage of on-time deliveries	Increase on-time deliveries
3. Materials waste:	
Scrap and waste as a percentage of total cost	Decrease scrap and waste
4. Inventory:	
Inventory levels	Reduce inventory levels
Number of inventoried items	Decrease number of different items
5. Machine downtime:	
Percentage of machine downtime	Decrease downtime

ETHICS   A CLOSER LOOK

The district manager of Fix-it Car Service, a nationwide chain of automotive service and repair shops, gave the following warning to the local shop managers during their monthly meeting: "The shops in this district have consistently shown the highest profits for the past year. We have worked very hard to develop the most efficiently run shops by treating our employees well to reduce turnover and training, and by computerizing operations to increase the number of repairs and services performed. Because of our hard work, we show consistently favorable labor variances, which have provided us with some nice bonuses."

The manager continued, "Last Monday, I received a tip from a friend at corporate headquarters. I learned that headquarters is sending a team of efficiency experts into your shops next week. Their job is to set standards for the standard costing system. My guess is," the district manager looked worried, "corporate is going to tighten our standards to eliminate the favorable variances and wipe out our bonuses."

"What do you mean by 'tighten our standards'?" Asked Jeff, one of the managers.

"I mean our standard costs for labor and the standard times allowed for performing many repairs and services would be lowered," the district manager replied. "I don't intend to let that happen, so here's the plan. During the next week, I want you to give your less efficient workers more hours and perform fewer services and repairs by lengthening the time it takes to do them. Now, remember, don't do anything obvious, be very subtle about these changes."

Jeff came away from the meeting feeling worried and uncertain that the district manager's plan was the way to go.

Required
What should Jeff do?

By using standard costs to control actual costs, management assumes responsibility for reducing the production costs of its products. In Chapter 19, you will learn about responsibility accounting in a broader sense. Successful companies rely heavily on responsibility accounting to make their business operations profitable.

UNDERSTANDING THE LEARNING OBJECTIVES

1. Discuss the nature of standard costs, including how standards are set.
    - A standard cost is a carefully predetermined measure of what a cost should be under stated conditions. Standard costs are not only estimates of what costs should be but they are goals to be achieved.
    - Standards are set in many ways, but the most useful standards are those that are more than estimates determined by extending historical trends into the future.
    - Engineering studies and time and motion studies are undertaken to

determine the amounts of materials, labor, and other services required to produce a product.
- General economic conditions should also be considered when setting standards.

2. Define budgets and discuss how budgets are used in a standard cost system.
   - Budgets are formal written plans that represent management's planned actions in the future and the impact of these actions on the business.
   - Standard costs are used in preparing budgets.
   - As actual costs are incurred, they are compared to the budgeted amounts. Any significant differences between the actual and budgeted amounts are then investigated by management.
   - Comparison of actual amounts to budgeted amounts also allows management to evaluate its own performance and that of its workers.

3. Discuss the advantages and disadvantages of using standard costs.
   - Advantages of using standard costs include improved cost control, more useful information for managerial planning and decision making, more reasonable inventory measurements, cost savings in record-keeping, and possible reductions in production costs incurred.
   - Disadvantages of using standard costs include controversial materiality limits for variances, nonreporting of certain variances, and low morale for some workers.

4. Calculate the six variances from standard and determine if the variance is favorable or unfavorable.
   - *Materials price variance:*
     1. (Actual price − Standard price) × Actual quantity purchased.
     2. The variance is favorable if the actual price was less than the standard price.
     3. The variance is unfavorable if the actual price exceeded the standard price.
   - *Materials usage variance:*
     1. (Actual quantity used − Standard quantity allowed) × Standard price.
     2. The variance is favorable if the actual quantity used was less than the standard quantity.
     3. The variance is unfavorable if the actual quantity used exceeded the standard quantity.
   - *Labor rate variance:*
     1. (Actual rate − Standard rate) × Actual hours.
     2. The variance is favorable if the actual rate was less than the standard rate.

3. The variance is unfavorable if the actual rate exceeded the standard rate.
- *Labor efficiency variance:*
    1. (Actual hours − Standard hours) × Standard rate.
    2. The variance is favorable if the actual hours were less than the standard hours.
    3. The variance is unfavorable if the actual hours exceeded the standard hours.
- *Overhead budget variance:*
    1. Actual overhead − Budgeted overhead.
    2. The variance is favorable if the actual overhead was less than the budgeted overhead.
    3. The variance is unfavorable if the actual overhead exceeded the budgeted overhead.
- *Overhead volume variance:*
    1. Budgeted overhead − Applied overhead.
    2. The variance is favorable if applied overhead was greater than the budgeted overhead.
    3. The variance is unfavorable if the budgeted overhead exceeded the applied overhead.

5. Discuss what each of the six variance accounts shows, and prepare journal entries to record the variance.
- The *materials price variance* shows whether the price paid for materials purchased was higher or lower than standard. The journal entry to record the purchase of materials is:

```
Materials Inventory . . . . . . . . . . . . . . . . . . .  XXXX
    Materials Price Variance . . . . . . . . . . . . .          XX
    Accounts Payable. . . . . . . . . . . . . . . . .          XXXX
```

The Materials Price Variance will be debited if the variance is unfavorable and credited if the variance is favorable.
- The *materials usage variance* shows whether the actual quantity of materials used was higher or lower than the standard. The journal entry to record materials usage is:

```
Work in Process Inventory . . . . . . . . . . . . . .  XXXX
    Materials Usage Variance . . . . . . . . . . . . .          XX
    Materials Inventory . . . . . . . . . . . . . . . .          XXXX
```

The Materials Usage Variance will be debited if the variance is unfavorable and credited if the variance is favorable.
- The *labor rate variance* shows whether the actual direct labor-hour rate paid is higher or lower than standard.

- The *labor efficiency variance* shows whether the actual direct labor-hours worked were greater or less than standard. The journal entry to charge the direct labor cost to Work in Process Inventory is:

```
Work in Process Inventory . . . . . . . . . . . . . .  XXXX
Labor Rate Variance . . . . . . . . . . . . . . . .      XX
Labor Efficiency Variance . . . . . . . . . . . . . .    XX
        Payroll Summary . . . . . . . . . . . . . .            XXXX
```

The Labor Rate Variance will be debited if the variance is unfavorable and credited if the variance is favorable. The Labor Efficiency Variance will be debited if the variance is unfavorable and credited if the variance is favorable.

- The *overhead budget variance* shows the difference between total actual overhead costs and total budgeted overhead costs.
- The *overhead volume variance* shows the difference between the budgeted amount of overhead for the actual volume achieved and the applied overhead. The journal entry to record the overhead variances and close the Manufacturing Overhead account is:

```
Manufacturing Overhead . . . . . . . . . . . . . .      XX
Overhead Budget Variance . . . . . . . . . . . . .      XX
        Overhead Volume Variance . . . . . . . . . . .        XXX
```

The Overhead Budget Variance is debited if the variance is unfavorable and credited if the variance is favorable. The Overhead Volume Variance is debited if the variance is unfavorable and credited if the variance is favorable.

6. Discuss the three selection guidelines used to investigate variances from standard.
    - Three possible selection guidelines are (1) amount of variance, (2) size of the variance relative to the cost incurred, and (3) controllability of the cost associated with the variance.
    - Significant variances, both favorable and unfavorable, should be investigated.

7. Discuss the theoretical and practical methods for disposing of variances from standard.
    - Variances may be viewed as gains or losses and closed to Income Summary; allocated as adjustments to the recorded cost of Work in Process Inventory, Finished Goods Inventory, and Cost of Goods Sold; or closed to Cost of Goods Sold.
    - Theoretically, the alternative chosen should depend on whether the standards set were reasonably attainable and whether the variances were controllable by company employees.
    - Practically, variances are usually closed to the Cost of Goods Sold

account rather than allocated to the inventory accounts and to cost of goods sold.

8. Demonstrate the difference between just-in-time and traditional standard cost flows through accounts.
   - The use of JIT does not necessarily affect the way companies compute variances from standard costs, but it does affect the way costs flow through the accounts.
   - The difference between JIT and traditional standard cost flows through accounts is that in the case of JIT, all manufacturing costs are debited to Cost of Goods Sold at standard cost. Any ending inventories are credited to Cost of Goods Sold and debited to the appropriate inventory account(s) at the end of the period. Variances are computed when standard and actual costs are known.

9. Discuss nonfinancial performance measures.
   - The new performance measures tend to be nonfinancial and more subjective than standard costs. Five sets of nonfinancial performance measures exist. The first two, *quality control* and *delivery performance,* are customer oriented. The next three nonfinancial performance measures are production oriented. Reducing *material waste, inventory,* and *machine downtime* have been shown to improve quality and efficiency.

10. Discuss how standard costs are applied in both job order and process cost systems (Appendix).
    - *Job order cost system:*
      1. Management usually does not know the exact amount of standard costs to charge to jobs that are incomplete. However, management can usually make reasonable estimates of these costs as production progresses.
      2. Typically, the overhead variances and the materials and labor variances are summarized in a report prepared periodically for internal management called *Summary of Variances from Standard.*
    - *Process cost system:*
      1. In a process cost system, the accountant can charge Work in Process Inventory with actual quantities and actual costs rather than standard quantities and standard costs and can calculate variances and place them in variance accounts at the end of the month.
      2. Alternatively, the materials price variance could be recorded when materials are purchased, and the labor rate variance could be recorded when direct labor is charged to Work in Process Inventory.
      3. As in job order costing, a report entitled *Summary of Variances from Standard* could be prepared.

APPENDIX

APPLYING STANDARD COSTS IN JOB ORDER AND PROCESS COST SYSTEMS

Standard Costs in a Job Order Cost System

*Objective 10
Discuss how
standard costs are
applied in both
job order and
process cost
systems*

In a job order cost system, management usually does not know the exact amount of standard costs to apply to the jobs that are incomplete. However, management can make reasonable estimates of these costs as production progresses. Thus, some variances can be isolated during the month.

Assume that Company A accounts for the manufacture of its products in a job order cost system using standard costs. Its flexible budget shows that at the standard level of output, variable overhead is $24,000 and fixed overhead is $16,000 per month. At the standard activity level of 4,000 direct labor-hours, these figures yield a standard overhead rate of $10 per direct labor-hour. The variable portion of this rate is $24,000 ÷ 4,000 hours = $6, and the fixed portion is $16,000 ÷ 4,000 = $4.

Company A had no work in process inventory as of June 1. The standard specifications for the two jobs started during June are as follows:

	Job 101	Job 102
Direct materials.	$20,000	$50,000
Direct labor:		
1,000 hours at $8	8,000	
2,500 hours at $8		20,000
Overhead:		
1,000 hours at $10	10,000	
2,500 hours at $10		25,000
Total standard cost	$38,000	$95,000

Company A's activities for June 1995 are summarized as follows:

a. Materials with a standard cost of $79,500 were purchased on account at an actual price of $80,150.
b. Standard direct materials were issued for both jobs. In addition, excess materials were requisitioned: Job No. 101, $400; and Job No. 102, $700.
c. Analysis of the factory payrolls debited to Payroll Summary shows they consisted of $10,000 of indirect labor ($4,000 variable and $6,000 fixed), and 3,000 hours of direct labor (Job No. 101, 990 hours; and Job No. 102, 2,010 hours) at a cost of $24,600. Job No. 101 was completed.
d. Various overhead costs were incurred: variable, $14,500; and fixed, $10,200.
e. Standard overhead was assigned to production: Job No. 101, $10,000 (1,000 hours at $10 per hour); and Job No. 102, $20,100 (2,010 hours at

$10 per hour). Even though Job No. 102 was incomplete at the end of the month, overhead needs to be assigned to this job for proper valuation of Work in Process Inventory on the balance sheet.

f. Job No. 101 was completed and transferred to the finished goods storeroom.

g. Sales for the month were all units in Job No. 101 at the total price of $60,000.

The entries to record the above information and isolate the variances follow:

(a) Materials Inventory 79,500
   Materials Price Variance. 650
     Accounts Payable   80,150
   To record purchase of materials and to isolate materials price variance.

(b) Work in Process Inventory. 70,000
   Materials Usage Variance 1,100
     Materials Inventory   71,100
   To charge standard materials to production and to charge excess materials requisitioned to a variance account.

(c) Work in Process Inventory. 24,080
   Manufacturing Overhead 10,000
   Labor Rate Variance. 600
     Labor Efficiency Variance   80
     Payroll Summary   34,600
   To distribute labor costs and to isolate labor variances:

    Job No. 101 (1,000 hours at $8) . . . . . . $ 8,000
    Job No. 102 (2,010 hours at $8)   16,080

    Total labor to Work in Process Inventory . $24,080

   Labor efficiency variance on Job No. 101: (990 actual hours − 1,000 standard hours) × $8 = $−80 (favorable). Labor rate variance: ($8.20 actual wage rate − $8.00 standard rate) × 3,000 hours = $600 (unfavorable).

(d) Manufacturing Overhead 24,700
     Accounts Payable (and various other accounts) . . .   24,700
   To record incurrence of overhead costs.

(e) Work in Process Inventory. 30,100
     Manufacturing Overhead   30,100
   To apply standard overhead to production: Job No. 101—$10,000 (standard amount, job completed); Job No. 102—2,010 hours at $10 = $20,100 (based on standard labor, job incomplete).

(f) Finished Goods Inventory 38,000
     Work in Process Inventory.   38,000
   To record transfer of completed Job No. 101 at standard.

(g) Accounts Receivable   60,000
      Sales   60,000
    To record sales for the month.

Cost of Goods Sold   38,000
      Finished Goods Inventory   38,000
    To record cost of goods sold (Job No. 101, $38,000).

Note that in the above entries we isolated the materials and labor variances as production progressed. However, we compute the overhead variances at the end of the month, when all of the actual overhead costs are known. For Company A, the overhead variances are computed as follows:

Overhead budget variance:
  Actual overhead (entries *[c]* and *[d]* above) $34,700
  Budgeted overhead (from flexible budget) (3,010* standard hours
    at $6 variable overhead + $16,000 fixed overhead)   34,060
Overhead budget variance (unfavorable) . . . . $ 640

Overhead volume variance:
  Budgeted overhead [(3,010* hours × $6) + $16,000] $34,060
  Standard overhead applied to production (3,010* hours at $10) . .   30,100
    Overhead volume variance (unfavorable)   3,960
Total unfavorable overhead variance $4,600

---

* 3,010 hours are used in the calculations because standard hours allowed for Job No. 101 are 1,000 and standard hours allowed this far on Job No. 202 are 2,010 for a total of 3,010 hours.

The following entry isolates the two overhead variances in the accounts:

Overhead Budget Variance   640
Overhead Volume Variance   3,960
    Manufacturing Overhead   4,600
    To set up separate overhead variance accounts.

Note that the credit to Manufacturing Overhead of $4,600 reduces that account to a zero balance (for previous entries to the account, see entries *[c]*, *[d]*, and *[e]* above), thus proving the accuracy of the computations.

Typically, a company summarizes the overhead variances and the materials and labor variances in a report prepared periodically for internal management. Such a report could be called a *Summary of Variances from Standard*.

Standard Costs in a Process Cost System

To provide a brief illustration of one way in which a company may incorporate standard costs into a process cost system, assume that Company P manufactures a product for which the standard specifications are:

Materials—2 pounds at $2 per pound.	$4.00
Direct labor—0.5 hours at $8 per hour	4.00
Overhead—0.5 hours at $3 per hour	1.50
Total standard cost	$9.50

The fixed overhead included in the standard cost is based on a monthly flexible budget that shows budgeted variable overhead of $120,000 and budgeted fixed overhead of $60,000 at a standard activity level of 60,000 standard direct labor-hours. Thus, the variable overhead rate is $2 per direct labor-hour ($120,000 ÷ 60,000 hours). The fixed overhead rate is $1 per direct labor-hour ($60,000 ÷ 60,000 hours). Since each unit only requires one-half hour to produce, total overhead assignable per unit is $1.50 ($3 per hour × ½ hour).

This example makes one change in the standard cost system illustrated earlier in the chapter. Work in Process Inventory will be charged with actual quantities and actual costs rather than standard quantities and standard costs, as shown previously. The variances will be calculated and placed in variance accounts at the end of the month. Alternatively, the materials price variance could be recorded when materials are purchased, and the labor rate variance could be recorded when direct labor is charged to Work in Process Inventory.

The entries to the Work in Process Inventory account for May are summarized below:

Direct materials (180,500 pounds at $2.02)	$364,610
Direct labor (40,100 hours at $7.90).	316,790
Actual fixed overhead	58,700
Actual variable overhead.	80,500
Total cost put into production	$820,600
Standard cost of units completed and transferred	
(70,000 units at $9.50)	−665,000
Balance, May 31, 1995.	$155,600

Production records show that Company P completed and transferred 70,000 units and that 20,000 units of the product remain in process at the end of the month. These units are complete as to materials and 50% complete as to conversion. From this information, the equivalent production for the period in terms of standard units of product can be computed as follows:

	Materials	Labor and Overhead (conversion)
Units started and finished	70,000	70,000
Equivalent units in ending inventory	20,000	10,000
Equivalent production	90,000	80,000

We now have enough information to calculate all of the variances presented in the *Summary of Variances from Standard* shown in Illustration 18.8.

Since the actual price paid for materials was $0.02 per pound above standard, the materials price variance is the actual usage of 180,500 pounds multiplied by $0.02 = $3,610. Since the standard materials allowed for 90,000 equivalent units is 90,000 × 2 = 180,000 pounds, the materials usage variance is 500 pounds × $2 = $1,000. Both variances are unfavorable.

The average wage rate paid employees was $0.10 less than standard. When this $0.10 difference is multiplied times 40,100 actual hours, the result is a $4,010 favorable rate variance. The 40,000 standard labor-hours allowed for the production of the period (80,000 × 0.5 hours) is 100 hours less than the actual direct labor-hours used (40,100). Hence, Company P experienced an unfavorable labor efficiency variance of $800.

Actual fixed overhead costs of $58,700 were $1,300 less than their budgeted amount of $60,000, while variable overhead costs of $80,500 exceeded their *budgeted amount* of $80,000 for the actual production in May by $500. Together, these costs yield a net favorable budget variance of $800. Since the standard overhead applied to production of $120,000 (equal to 40,000 standard direct labor-hours × $3) is less than the budgeted overhead for the month of $140,000 (equal to [40,000 standard direct-labor hours × $2] + $60,000), an unfavorable volume variance of $20,000 results. These variances amount to a net unfavorable overhead variance of $19,200. Added together, the materials, labor, and overhead variances amount to $20,600, the net variance (unfavorable) from standard for the month.

Illustration 18.8
SUMMARY OF VARIANCES FROM STANDARD

COMPANY P
Summary of Variances from Standard
Month Ended May 31, 1995

Materials:		
Price variance (180,500 pounds × $0.02)	$ 3,610	
Usage variance (500 pounds × $2)	1,000	
Total unfavorable materials variance		$ 4,610
Labor:		
Rate variance (40,100 hours × $−0.10)	$−4,010	
Efficiency variance (100 hours × $8)	800	
Net favorable labor variance		−3,210
Overhead:		
Budget variance [fixed ($58,700 − $60,000) + variable		
($80,500 − $80,000*)]	$ −800	
Volume variance ($140,000 − $120,000)	20,000	
Net unfavorable overhead variance.		19,200
Net variance from standard for the month		$20,600

* (40,000 hours × $2).

The variances shown in Illustration 18.8 can be formally recorded in the accounts by the following entry, thus removing the month's variances from Work in Process Inventory:

Materials Price Variance	3,610	
Materials Usage Variance	1,000	
Labor Efficiency Variance	800	
Overhead Volume Variance.	20,000	
Labor Rate Variance.		4,010
Overhead Budget Variance.		800
Work in Process Inventory		20,600
To set up variances from standard for the month.		

Subtracting the $20,600 from the previously given balance of $155,600 in the Work in Process Inventory account leaves a balance of $135,000, which is equal to the standard cost of the ending inventory. The standard cost of the ending inventory can be separately computed as follows:

Direct materials (20,000 units, 100% complete, unit cost $4)	$ 80,000
Direct labor (20,000 units, 50% complete, unit cost $4).	40,000
Overhead (20,000 units, 50% complete, unit cost $1.50)	15,000
Total standard cost of ending inventory.	$135,000

DEMONSTRATION PROBLEM

Gaylord's Boards, Inc., manufactures kitchen cutting boards. The standard cost of each cutting board is:

Direct materials:		
Three blocks of wood at $0.24	$0.72	
Direct labor (1 hour at $6)	6.00	
Overhead:		
Fixed ($21,600 ÷ 60,000 units)	0.36	
Variable	0.48	
	$7.56	

The standard overhead rate is based on a volume of 60,000 units per month. In May, 50,000 units were manufactured. Detailed data relative to production are summarized below.

Materials purchased:	
160,000 blocks of wood at $0.26	
Materials used:	
152,000 blocks of wood	
Direct labor: 49,000 hours at $6.12	
Fixed manufacturing overhead	$21,840
Variable manufacturing overhead	24,420

Required:

From the above data, compute the six variances from standard for the month.

Solution to demonstration problem

Materials price variance:		
($0.26 − $0.24) × 160,000.	$3,200 (unfavorable)	
Materials usage variance:		
(152,000 − 150,000*) × $0.24	480 (unfavorable)	
Total materials variance		$3,680 (unfavorable)
Labor rate variance:		
($6.12 − $6.00) × 49,000	$5,880 (unfavorable)	
Labor efficiency variance:		
(49,000 − 50,000) × $6.00.	−6,000 (favorable)	
Net labor variance		−120 (favorable)
Overhead budget variance:		
Actual ($21,840 + $24,420) $46,260		
Budgeted [$21,600 + (50,000 × $0.48)] 45,600		
Overhead budget variance	$ 660 (unfavorable)	
Overhead volume variance:		
Budget − Applied [$45,600 − (50,000 × $0.84)] . .	3,600 (unfavorable)	
Total overhead variance		4,260 (unfavorable)
Total variance for month		$7,820 (unfavorable)

* 50,000 units × 3 blocks per unit.

NEW TERMS

Budgets   Formal written plans that represent management's planned actions in the future and the impact of these actions on the business. *886*

Flexible budget   A budget that shows the budgeted amount of manufacturing overhead for various levels of output; used in isolating overhead variances and setting standard overhead rates. *900*

Ideal standards   Standards that make no allowances for machinery breakdowns and maintenance or for worker rest periods or some inefficiency. These unrealistic standards are virtually impossible to attain over long periods. *886*

Labor efficiency variance (LEV)   A variance from standard caused by using more or less than the standard amount of direct labor-hours to produce a product or complete a process; computed as (Actual direct labor-hours − Standard direct labor-hours) × Standard rate per hour. *896*

Labor rate variance (LRV)   A variance from standard caused by paying a higher or lower average rate of pay than standard to produce a product or complete a process; computed as (Actual rate per direct labor-hour − Standard rate per direct labor-hour) × Actual direct labor-hours worked. *896*

Management by exception   The process where management only investigates those variances that are unusually favorable or unfavorable or that have a material effect on the company. *886*

Materials price variance (MPV)   A variance from standard caused by paying a higher or lower price than standard for materials purchased; computed as (Actual price − Standard price) × Actual quantity purchased. *891*

Materials usage variance (MUV)   A variance from standard caused by using more or less than the standard amount of materials to produce a product or complete a process; computed as (Actual quantity used − Standard quantity allowed) × Standard price. *892*

Nonfinancial performance measures   The chapter discusses five sets of nonfinancial performance measures. The first two, *quality control* and *delivery performance*, are customer oriented. The next three nonfinancial performance measures are production oriented. Reducing *material waste*, *inventory*, and *machine downtime* have been shown to improve quality and efficiency. *912*

Overhead budget variance (OBV)   A variance from standard caused by incurring more or less than the standard manufacturing overhead for the actual production volume achieved, as shown by a flexible budget; computed as Actual overhead − Budgeted overhead at actual production volume level. *902*

Overhead volume variance (OVV)   A variance from standard caused by producing at a level other than that used in setting the standard overhead rates; computed as Budgeted overhead − Applied overhead. *903*

Practical standards   Standards that make allowances for machinery breakdowns and maintenance and for worker rest periods and some worker inefficiency. These attainable standards are generally used in planning. *886*

Standard cost   A carefully predetermined measure of what a cost should be under stated conditions. *884*

Standard level (volume) of output   A carefully predetermined measure of what the expected level of output should be for a specified period of time, usually one year. *885, 990*

Variance   A deviation of actual costs from standard costs; may be favorable or unfavorable. That is, actual costs may be less than or more than standard costs. Variances may relate to materials, labor, or manufacturing overhead. *890*

SELF-TEST

True-False

Indicate whether each of the following statements is true or false.

1. Standard cost usually refers to the price per unit of inputs into the production process.
2. Standard costs are useful in setting selling prices.
3. Under a standard cost system, all units of a given product produced during a particular month are carried in inventory at the actual unit cost.
4. The general journal entry to record the use of materials and establish an unfavorable materials usage variance is: debit Income Summary and Materials Usage Variance; credit Materials Inventory.
5. Unfavorable variances are shown in variance accounts as credits.

Multiple-Choice

Select the best answer for each of the following questions.

1. What guidelines should management follow when investigating a variance?
   a. Look at the amount of the variance.
   b. Look at the size of the variance relative to cost incurred.
   c. Decide if the variance is controllable or noncontrollable.
   d. All of the above.

2. Determine the materials usage variance and materials price variance from the following data:

Materials purchased	30,000 units
Price per unit purchased . . .	$4.00 per unit
Standard price	$4.10 per unit
Materials used	35,000 units
Standard quantity allowed . .	32,000 units

   a. $12,300 unfavorable (MUV)
      $−3,000 favorable (MPV)
   b. $−12,300 favorable (MUV)
      $3,000 unfavorable (MPV)
   c. $12,000 unfavorable (MUV)
      $−2,200 favorable (MPV)
   d. $−8,200 favorable (MUV)
      $2,500 unfavorable (MPV)

3. Which of the following journal entries might you find in a company's records for closing out the variance accounts to Cost of Goods Sold?
   a. Work in Process Inventory
      Materials Usage Variance
      Labor Rate Variance
          Materials Price Variance
          Overhead Volume Variance
          Labor Efficiency Variance
          Overhead Budget Variance

   b. Materials Price Variance
      Overhead Volume Variance
      Finished Goods Inventory
          Materials Usage Variance
          Labor Rate Variance
          Labor Efficiency Variance
          Overhead Budget Variance

   c. Materials Price Variance
      Overhead Volume Variance
      Cost of Goods Sold
          Materials Usage Variance
          Labor Rate Variance
          Labor Efficiency Variance
          Overhead Budget Variance

   d. None of the above.

4. What account would an unfavorable materials usage or labor efficiency variance caused by carelessness or inefficiency be closed to?
   a. Cost of Goods Sold.
   b. Finished Goods Inventory.
   c. Work in Process.
   d. Income Summary.

5. *(Based on the Appendix)* Which of the following choices best describes how standard costs are applied in a process cost system?
   a. Materials and labor variances are not computed.
   b. Standard costs are not used in process costing systems.
   c. Actual quantities and actual costs are charged to Work in Process Inventory and variances are separated at the end of the period.
   d. All of the above.

Now turn to page 934 to check your answers.

QUESTIONS

1. Is a standard cost an estimated cost? What is the primary objective of employing standard costs in a cost system?

2. What is a budget?

3. What is the difference between ideal and practical standards? Which standard is generally used in planning?

4. What is meant by the term *management by exception*?

5. What are some advantages of using standard costs? What are some disadvantages?

6. Describe how the materials price and usage variances would be computed from the following data:

   Standard—1 unit of material at $20 per unit.
   Purchased —1,200 units of material at $20.30;
       used—990 units.
   Production—1,000 units of finished goods.

7. When might a given company have a substantial favorable materials price variance and a substantial unfavorable materials usage variance?

8. What is the usual cause of a favorable or unfavorable labor rate variance? What other labor variance is isolated in a standard cost system? Of the two variances, which is more likely to be under the control of management? Explain.

9. Identify the type of variance indicated by each situation below and indicate whether the variance is favorable or unfavorable.

   a. The cutting department of a company during the week ending July 15 cut 12 size-S cogged wheels out of three sheets of 12-inch high-tempered steel. Usually three wheels of such size are cut out of each sheet.

   b. A company purchased and installed an expensive new cutting machine to handle expanding orders. This purchase and the related depreciation had not been anticipated when the overhead rate was set.

   c. Edwards, the band saw operator, was on vacation last week. Lands took his place for the normal 40-hour week. Edwards' wage rate is $12 per hour, while Lands' is $10 per hour. Production was at capacity last week and the week before.

10. Theoretically, how should an accountant dispose of variances from standard? How does an accountant typically dispose of variances?

11. Why are variances typically isolated as soon as possible?

12. Should favorable variances always be considered desirable? Explain.

13. Why is it said that the use of standard costs permits the application of the principle of management by exception?

14. How do standards help in controlling production costs?

15. How do standard cost flows using JIT differ from those using a traditional costing system?

16. Name two nonfinancial performance measures related to customer service.

17. Name three nonfinancial performance measures related to production.

18. *Real-world question*   Federal Express guarantees next day delivery "positively and absolutely" by 10:30 A.M. Domino's Pizza guarantees delivery within 30 minutes. What nonfinancial performance measures would be very important to these companies?

The Coca-Cola Company

19. *Real-world question*   Refer to Appendix C at the end of this text. Assume The Coca-Cola Company disposes of manufacturing cost variances by closing them to Cost of Goods Sold. Further, assume that 98% of the Cost of Goods Sold amount for 1991 was standard cost and the remaining 2% was the net unfavorable variance. (That is, after considering all favorable and unfavorable variances, the net result was 2% of Cost of Goods Sold.) Now suppose Coca-Cola had been able to reduce costs so the net variances were exactly zero. What would be the dollar and percentage effect of this swing from 2% unfavorable to no net variance on the 1991 operating income reported on the income statement?

20. *Real-world question*   Suppose a McDonald's restaurant has unfavorable purchase price variances for materials (that is, food costs), but gets favorable reviews from its customers about the quality of its food. Should management try to eliminate the unfavorable purchase price variances? What if buying cheaper food reduces customer satisfaction?

EXERCISES

Compute materials variances
(L.O. 4)

18–1. During July, the cutting department of Grabel Cabinets completed 2,000 units of a product that had a standard materials cost of 2 square feet per unit at $2.50 per square foot. The actual material purchased consisted of 4,200 square feet at $2.20 per square foot, for a total cost of $9,240. The actual material used this period was 4,040 square feet. Compute the materials price and usage variances, indicating whether each is favorable or unfavorable.

Compute materials variances; comment on possible causes
(L.O. 4)

18–2. Windows, Inc., produces window panes from recycled glass. A unit equals 100 panes and has the following standard costs:

Direct materials—5 pounds of glass at $10 per pound	$ 50
Direct labor—3 hours at $12 per hour	36
Manufacturing overhead—150% of direct labor	54
	$140

Windows' purchasing agent took advantage of a special offer from one of its suppliers to purchase 45,000 pounds of material at $8.40 per pound. Assume 5,500 units were produced and 35,100 pounds of material were used. Compute the variances for materials. Comment on the purchasing agent's decision to take the special offer.

Compute labor variances
(L.O. 4)

18–3. Compute the labor variances in the following situation:

Actual direct labor payroll (26,800 hours at $9)	$241,200
Standard direct labor allowed per unit, 4.20 hours at $9.50 . . .	$39.90
Production for month (in units)	6,500

Compute labor variances for two departments (L.O. 4)

18–4. During July, 150 units of a certain product were produced. This product has a standard direct labor cost of two hours per unit at $12.50 per hour in Department A and one hour per unit at $18 per hour in Department B. Department A paid $3,335.00 for 290 direct labor-hours, and Department B incurred a cost of $3,213 for 170 direct labor-hours. Compute the labor variances for each department.

Compute labor variances: evaluate labor (L.O. 4)

18–5. Forty-Niners Company manufactures footballs that have a standard direct labor cost of 0.5 hours per football at $12 per hour. In producing 6,500 units, the foreman used different workers than usual, which resulted in a total labor cost of $36,000 for 2,400 hours. Compute the labor variances and comment on the foreman's decision to use different workers.

Compute overhead volume and budget variances (L.O. 4)

18–6. The following data relate to the activities of Witchita Shades, which produces sunscreens for cars, for the first quarter of 1995:

Standard activity (in units)	30,000
Actual production (in units).	24,000
Budgeted fixed manufacturing overhead.	$18,000
Variable overhead rate (per unit)	$ 2.50
Actual fixed manufacturing overhead	$18,500
Actual variable manufacturing overhead.	$55,500

Compute the overhead budget variance and the overhead volume variance.

Compute overhead volume variance (L.O. 4)

18–7. Assume that the actual production in Exercise 18–6 was 26,000 units rather than 24,000. What was the overhead volume variance?

Close all variance accounts (L.O. 5)

18–8. The standard cost variance accounts of Gotcha Footwear, Inc., at the end of its fiscal year had the following balances:

Materials price variance (unfavorable)	$5,500
Materials usage variance (unfavorable).	4,600
Labor rate variance (favorable)	3,700
Labor efficiency variance (unfavorable)	8,900
Overhead budget variance (favorable)	800
Overhead volume variance (unfavorable).	6,400

Set up T-accounts for these variances, and enter the balances given above in the accounts. Then prepare one entry to record the closing of the variance accounts in the most practical manner.

Compute labor variances (L.O. 4)

18–9. Compute the labor variances for Stephanie's Pasta Palace in the following circumstances:

Actual direct labor payroll (9,900 hours)	$81,180
Standard labor allowed per unit, 0.2 hours at $7.90.	$ 1.58
Equivalent production for the month (in units)	50,000

Compute labor
variances
(L.O. 4)

18–10. During April, 100 units of a given product were produced. These units have a standard labor cost in process A of one hour at $12 per hour and two hours in process B at $10.50 per hour. Assume that Oshimo worked 90 hours on process A during the month for which she earned $1,188 and that Wong worked 205 hours on process B for which she earned $2,091. Compute the labor cost variances for each process.

PROBLEMS

Compute materials
variances
(L.O. 4)

18–1. A certain product has a standard materials usage and cost of 2 pounds per unit at $3.50 per pound. During the month, 1,300 pounds of materials were purchased at $3.65 per pound. Production for the month totaled 560 units, which required 1,050 pounds of materials.

Required:

Compute the materials variances.

Prepare entries in
T-accounts for
materials
variances
(L.O. 5)

18–2. During November, a department completed 2,500 units of a product that has a standard materials usage and cost of 1.2 square feet per unit at $0.25 per square foot. The actual material used consisted of 3,050 square feet at an actual cost of $1,332.24. The actual purchase of this material amounted to 4,500 square feet at a total cost of $2,250.00.

Required:

Using T-accounts, prepare entries (*a*) for the purchase of the materials and (*b*) for the issuance of materials to production.

Compute labor
variances
(L.O. 4)

18–3. Bottle Mania manufactures bottles out of recycled glass. One unit, which equals 500 bottles, requires two hours of direct labor at an hourly rate of $6. The company produced 220,000 units of bottles using 418,000 hours of direct labor at a total cost of $2,299,000.

Required:

Compute the labor variances.

Compute labor
variances; prepare
journal entries
(L.O. 5)

18–4. The finishing department of Cross and Blackwell Company produced 25,000 units during December. The standard number of direct labor-hours per unit is two hours. The standard rate per hour is $18.90. During the month, 52,250 direct labor-hours were worked at a cost of $940,500.

Required:

a. Record the labor data in a journal entry and post the entry to T-accounts.
b. Record the journal entry to dispose of any variances and post the entry to the T-accounts.

Compute
overhead
variances under
two assumptions
(L.O. 4)

18–5. The standard amount of output for the New Orleans plant of Cajun Company is 50,000 units per month. Overhead is applied based on units produced. The flexible budget for the month for manufacturing overhead allows $90,000 for fixed overhead and $2.50 per unit of output for variable overhead. Actual overhead for the month consisted of $90,720 of fixed overhead with actual variable overhead given below.

Required:

Compute the overhead budget variance and the overhead volume variance assuming actual production in units and actual variable overhead in dollars were:

a. 37,500 and $91,200.

b. 55,000 and $135,240.

Compute
overhead
variances
(L.O. 4)

18–6. Wilde Company manufactures desks for sale to various high schools and colleges. The expected volume of activity is 22,500 units. Standard direct labor is 1.5 hours per unit. At the 22,500 unit level of output, fixed manufacturing overhead is budgeted at $54,000, while variable manufacturing overhead is budgeted at $0.66 per direct labor-hour. Overhead is applied based on standard direct labor-hours.

In March, 33,750 direct labor-hours were worked to achieve the standard level of output of 22,500 units. Actual manufacturing overhead for March consisted of $57,700 of fixed overhead and $28,500 of variable overhead.

Required:

Compute the two overhead variances.

Compute
materials, labor,
and overhead
variances
(L.O. 4)

18–7. Based on a standard volume of output of 96,000 units per month, the standard cost of the product manufactured by Lilly Company consists of:

Direct materials (0.20 pounds)	$1.00
Direct labor (0.5 hours)	3.70
Variable manufacturing overhead.	3.50
Fixed manufacturing overhead ($144,000)	1.50
Total	$9.70

A total of 25,200 pounds of materials was purchased at $4.20 per pound. During May, 98,400 units were produced with the following costs:

Direct materials used (24,780 pounds at $4.20)	$104,076
Direct labor (48,000 hours at $7.80)	374,400
Variable manufacturing overhead	310,600
Fixed manufacturing overhead	151,248

Required:

Compute the materials price and usage variances, the labor rate and efficiency variances, and the overhead budget and volume variances. (Overhead is applied based on units produced.)

Prepare journal
entries under a
job order standard
cost accounting

18–8. Berle Manufacturing Company employs a job order standard cost accounting system. The standard cost of the materials used is $1.93 per square foot, while the standard direct labor cost is $9.62 per hour. Manufacturing overhead is assigned to jobs at a rate of $3.62 per standard direct labor-hour. Based on a standard volume of activity of 180,000 direct labor-hours, the flexible budget allows $216,000 of fixed overhead and $2.42 of variable overhead per standard direct labor-hour for the month of September 1995. The company uses only one Work in Process account.

Work in process is charged with standard quantities and standard prices. On August 1, 1995, one job (No. 10) was in process, with the following standard costs already assigned:

Materials (2,500 square feet)	$ 4,825
Labor (800 direct labor-hours)	7,696
Manufacturing overhead ($3.60 per standard direct labor-hour)	2,880
Total	$15,401

The standard quantities for completed Job No. 10 are 7,000 square feet of materials and 1,100 hours of direct labor.

During August 1995, the following transactions and events occurred:

1. Purchased 1,800,000 square feet of materials at $1.872 per square foot.
2. Materials issued:

Job No.	Actual Quantity (square feet)	Standard Quantity (square feet)
10	4,800	4,500
All others	1,260,000	1,263,600
	1,264,800	1,268,100

3. The direct labor costs and hours for the month were:

Incurred on—	Actual Hours	Standard Hours	Actual Cost
Job No. 10	312	300	$ 3,124.80
All other jobs	153,288	153,000	1,490,155.20
	153,600	153,300	$1,493,280.00

4. The appropriate amount of overhead was assigned to the jobs.
5. Actual overhead incurred during the month was $558,000.
6. Job No. 10 was completed during the month. Other production also completed during the month had a standard cost of $1,872,000.

Required:

a. Prepare general journal entries for each of the numbered transactions given above.
b. Compute the overhead budget variance and the overhead volume variance for the month, and prepare the general journal entry(ies) to record them.

Prepare journal
entries under a
process standard
cost system;
compute variances
(based on the
Appendix)
(L.O. 10)

18–9. Wellington Company employs a process cost system with standard costs to
account for the product it manufactures in a two-step process through Departments M and N. The standard cost of this product in Department M consists
of:

Direct materials (10 units at $9.40).	$ 94.00
Direct labor (5 hours at $7.10).	35.50
Variable manufacturing overhead (5 hours	
at $4.80)	24.00
Fixed manufacturing overhead (5 hours	
at $2.40)	12.00
	$165.50

The flexible overhead budget, based on 30,000 direct labor-hours as a
standard volume of activity, allows $72,000 of fixed overhead plus $4.80 per
direct labor-hour for variable overhead.

Materials price variances are isolated at the time of purchase. Labor rate
variances are isolated when direct labor is charged to Work in Process Inventory. Materials usage and labor efficiency variances are isolated at the end of
the month when production is known. Standard overhead is assigned to production, and overhead variances are isolated at the end of the month when
production and actual costs are known.

No work in process inventory existed as of January 1, 1995, in Department M. Summarized data for the month are:

1. Purchased 62,500 units of materials for $578,125.
2. Direct materials requisitioned by Department M, 55,290 units.
3. Of the payroll costs for the month, 24,950 direct labor-hours with a total
   cost of $179,856 are chargeable to Department M.
4. Total manufacturing overhead costs incurred by the department for the
   month consist of $72,540 of fixed overhead and $120,660 of variable overhead.
5. A total of 4,500 units was completed during the month; 1,000 units remain
   in process, 100% complete as to materials, and 50% complete as to labor
   and overhead.
6. Manufacturing overhead is assigned to production on the basis of standard
   direct labor-hours.

Required:

a. Prepare journal entries to record the above summarized data. (In Illustration 18.8
in the appendix, all variances were isolated at the end of the period. Use logic to
isolate them as required in this problem.)
b. Compute the materials usage variance and the labor efficiency variance, and
prepare the journal entry to isolate them from work in process inventory.
c. Compute the overhead budget variance and the overhead volume variance, and
prepare journal entries to record them.
d. Assuming that the variances isolated are for the month ending January 31, 1995,
prepare an entry that represents a practical disposition of these variances.

BUSINESS DECISION PROBLEMS

Discuss possible
causes for
variances
(L.O. 6)

18–1. Turn to Exercise 18–8 in this chapter. For each of the variances listed, give a possible reason for its existence.

Analyze situation
where actual costs
differ from
standard costs;
evaluate the two
managers involved
(L.O. 2)

18–2. Randolph Hershy, the president of the Swank Company, has a problem that does not involve substantial dollar amounts but does involve the important question of responsibility for variances from standard costs. He has just received the following report:

Standard materials at standard price for the actual production in May .	$ 9,000
Unfavorable materials price variance ($3.50 − $3.00) × 3,550 pounds .	1,775
Unfavorable materials usage variance (3,550 − 3,000 pounds) × $3 . .	1,650
Total actual materials cost for May (3,550 pounds at $3.50 per pound) .	$12,425

Randolph has discussed the unfavorable price variance with Niki Raitte, the purchasing officer. She agrees that under the circumstances she should be held responsible for most of the materials price variance. She objects, however, to the inclusion of $275 (550 pounds of excess materials used at $0.50 per pound). This amount, she argues, is the responsibility of the production department. If it had not been so inefficient in the use of materials, she would not have had to purchase the extra 550 pounds. On the other hand, Bradley Hyatt, the production manager, agrees that he is basically responsible for the excess quantity of materials used. However, he does not agree that the above materials usage variance should be revised to include the $275 of unfavorable price variance on the excess materials used. "That's Niki's responsibility," he says.

Randolph now turns to you for help. Specifically, he wants you to tell him:

a. Who is responsible for the $275 in dispute?

b. If the responsibility cannot be clearly assigned, in which materials variance should the accounting department include the variance? Why?

c. Are other circumstances likely to exist where materials variances cannot be considered the responsibility of the manager most closely involved with them? Explain.

Required:

Prepare written answers to the three questions asked by Randolph.

ANSWERS TO SELF-TEST

True-False

1. *False.* Standard cost is the standard quantity of an input required per unit of output times the standard price per unit of that

input. **Standard price** refers to the price per unit of inputs into the production process.

2. *True.* Standard costs are useful in setting

selling prices, but other factors (such as prices charged by competitors) also must be considered.

3. *False.* Under a standard cost system, all units of a given product are carried in inventory at standard cost.

4. *False.* The general journal entry to record the use of materials and establish an unfavorable materials usage variance is: debit Work in Process Inventory and Materials Usage Variance; credit Materials Inventory.

5. *False.* Unfavorable variances are shown in variance accounts as debits.

Multiple-Choice

1. *d.* Management should consider the amount, size relative to cost, and controllability of a variance when investigating why the variance has occurred.

2. *a.*

$$\begin{array}{l} \text{Materials} \\ \text{usage} \\ \text{variance} \end{array} = \left(\begin{array}{cc} \text{Actual} & \text{Standard} \\ \text{quantity} - & \text{quantity} \\ \text{used} & \text{allowed} \end{array} \right)$$
$$\times \begin{array}{l} \text{Standard} \\ \text{price} \end{array}$$
$$= (35{,}000 - 32{,}000) \times \$4.10$$
$$= 3{,}000 \times \$4.10$$
$$= \$12{,}300 \text{ (unfavorable)}$$

$$\begin{array}{l} \text{Materials} \\ \text{price} \\ \text{variance} \end{array} = \left(\begin{array}{cc} \text{Actual} & \text{Standard} \\ \text{price} - & \text{price} \end{array} \right)$$
$$\times \begin{array}{l} \text{Actual quantity} \\ \text{purchased} \end{array}$$
$$= (\$4.00 - \$4.10) \times 30{,}000$$
$$= \$-0.10 \times 30{,}000$$
$$= \$-3{,}000 \text{ (favorable)}$$

3. *c.* This choice is the correct answer. Answer (*a*) incorrectly closes the variances to Work in Process Inventory; answer (*b*) incorrectly closes the variances to Finished Goods Inventory.

4. *d.* An unfavorable materials usage or labor efficiency variance caused by carelessness or inefficiency may be considered a loss and closed to Income Summary because the standard was attainable and the variance was controllable.

5. *c.* Actual quantities and actual costs are charged to Work in Process Inventory, and variances are separated at the end of the period.

19 RESPONSIBILITY ACCOUNTING: SEGMENTAL ANALYSIS

LEARNING OBJECTIVES

After studying this chapter, you should be able to:

1. Explain responsibility accounting and its use in a business entity.
2. Prepare responsibility accounting reports.
3. Prepare a segmental income statement using the contribution margin format.
4. Calculate return on investment, margin, and turnover for a segment.
5. Calculate the residual income of a segment.
6. Allocate costs from service departments to operating departments (appendix).

When a business is small, the owner usually directly supervises many different activities. As a business grows, the owner must give responsibility for some of these activities to other persons. Obviously, the success of a business depends to a great extent on the people responsible for these activities.

In this chapter, you will learn about delegating authority to lower-level managers for managing various business activities and holding these managers responsible for the activities under their control. You will also learn how to assess the performance of these managers.

A company that uses responsibility accounting groups its activities into responsibility centers. The manager in charge of each center is responsible for controlling certain expenses. Sometimes this manager also has some control over revenues. The company measures each manager's performance in terms of the revenue and expense items over which that manager has control.

We discuss and illustrate various types of responsibility centers in this chapter. The chapter ends with a discussion of return on investment, which directly relates to the profitability of a company.

RESPONSIBILITY ACCOUNTING

Objective 1
Explain responsi-
bility accounting
and its use in a
business entity

The term **responsibility accounting** refers to an accounting system that collects, summarizes, and reports accounting data relating to the responsibilities of individual managers. A responsibility accounting system provides information to evaluate each manager on revenue and expense items over which that manager has primary control (authority to influence).

A responsibility accounting report identifies items the company expects managers to control. If, however, the report includes both controllable *and uncontrollable* items, it should clearly separate these categories. The identification of controllable items is a fundamental task in responsibility accounting and reporting.

To implement responsibility accounting, a company's plan of organization must allow individual managers to have responsibility for certain activities. The company should be able to clearly identify its various managers and define their lines of authority (and the resulting levels of responsibility). The organization chart in Illustration 19.1 demonstrates lines of authority and responsibility that a department store could use as a basis for responsibility reporting. If a company cannot determine lines of authority and resulting levels of responsibility, it probably cannot effectively implement responsibility accounting.

To identify the items over which each manager has control, the lines of authority should follow a specified path. For example, Illustration 19.1 shows that a department manager may report to a store manager, who reports to a vice president of operations, who reports to the president. The president is ultimately responsible to stockholders or their elected representatives, the board of directors. In a sense, the president is responsible for all revenue and expense items of the company, since at the presidential level all items are controllable over some period of time. The president cannot delegate responsibility to avoid personal responsibility. However, the president usually delegates authority to lower-level managers since the president cannot keep fully informed of the day-to-day operating details of all areas of the business.

The manager's level in the organization also affects identification of the items over which that manager has control. The president is usually considered a first-level manager. Managers (usually vice presidents) who report directly to the president are second-level managers. Notice on the organization chart in Illustration 19.1 that individuals at a specific management level are on a horizontal line across the chart. However, not all managers at that level necessarily have equal authority and responsibility. The degree of a manager's authority and responsibility will vary from company to company.

While the president may delegate decision-making power, some revenue and expense items remain exclusively under the president's control. For example, in some companies, only the president can approve large capital (plant and equipment) expenditures. Depreciation, property taxes, and other related expenses should not, therefore, be designated as a store manager's

Illustration 19.1
**A CORPORATE FUNCTIONAL ORGANIZATION CHART INCLUDING FOUR
LEVELS OF MANAGEMENT**

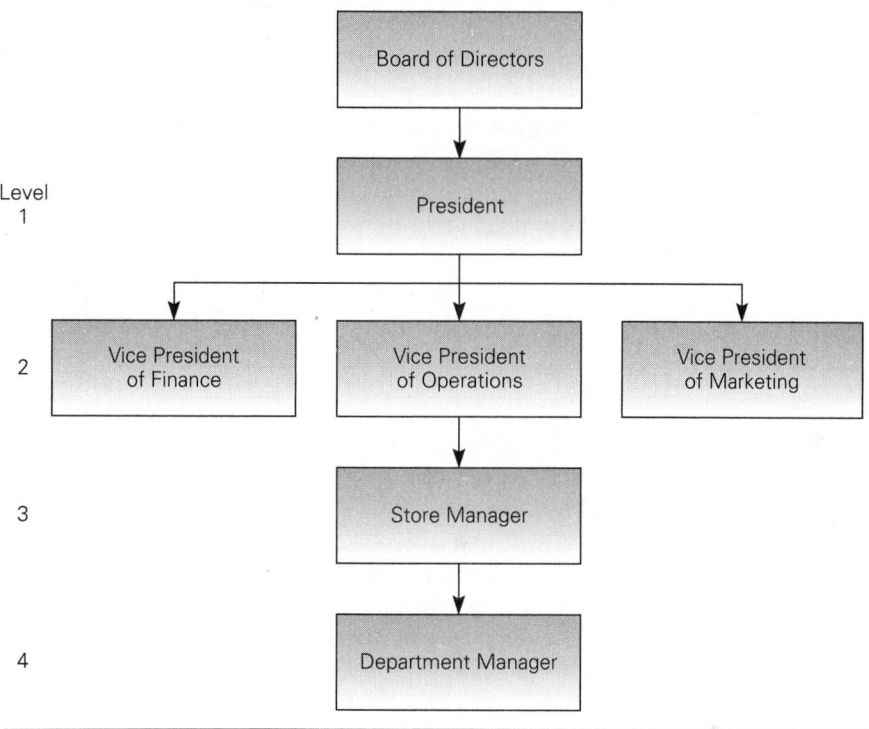

responsibility, since these costs are not primarily under that manager's
control.

The controllability criterion affects the content of performance reports
for each manager. For example, at the department manager level, perhaps
only inventory, supplies, and labor cost control are appropriate for measuring performance. A store manager, however, has the authority to make
decisions regarding many other costs that are not controllable at the department manager level (such as salaries of department managers); these other
costs would be included in the performance evaluation of the store manager,
but not the department manager.

RESPONSIBILITY REPORTS

Objective 2
*Prepare responsi-
bility accounting
reports*

A responsibility accounting system provides reports to different levels of
management. The amount of detail varies depending on the manager's level
in the organization. A performance report to a department manager of a

retail store such as Macy's would include actual and budgeted dollar amounts of all revenue and expense items under that manager's control. The report issued to the store manager would show only totals from all the department managers' performance reports and any additional items under the store manager's control, such as the store's administrative expenses. The report to the company's president includes summary totals of the vice presidents' performance reports plus any additional items under the president's control. In effect, the president's report should include *all* revenue and expense items in summary form since the president is responsible for controlling the profitability of the entire company.

The **management-by-exception** principle states that upper-level management does not need to examine operating details at lower levels unless a problem exists. As companies become increasingly complex, accountants must filter and condense accounting data so that management can analyze these data quickly. Most executives do not have time to study detailed accounting reports and search for problem areas. Reporting only summary totals highlights those areas that need attention so that the executive can make more efficient use of available time.

Responsibility accounting justifies the condensation of data that occurs in successive levels of management reports on the basis that the appropriate manager will take the necessary corrective action. Thus, department managers do not need to report specific performance details to superiors. For example, if a particular department has excessively high sales personnel costs, that department manager should seek to find and correct the cause of the problem. Then, when the store manager questions the unfavorable budget variance of that department, the department manager can inform the store manager that corrective action has been taken. Hence, reporting to any higher authority that this particular department is not operating satisfactorily will not be necessary, since the matter has already been resolved. Alternatively, if a manager's entire store has been performing poorly, summary totals reported to the vice president of operations will disclose this situation, and an investigation of the store manager's problems may be warranted.

In preparing responsibility accounting reports, accountants use two basic methods to handle revenue and expense items. In the first approach, they include in the responsibility report for a particular management level only those items over which the manager has direct control. This responsibility report does not include revenue and expense items that the manager cannot directly control. In the second approach, accountants include all revenue and expense items that can be traced directly or allocated indirectly to a particular manager, whether or not these items are controllable. This second method represents a full-cost approach, which means that a single report discloses *all* costs of a given area. When a company uses the second approach, it must be careful to separate controllable from noncontrollable items to differentiate those items for which a manager can and should be held responsible.

Features of Responsibility Reports

For maximum benefit, accounting reports must be *timely*. That is, accountants should prepare reports as soon as possible after the end of the performance measurement period. Timely reporting allows management to take prompt corrective action. Reports that are delayed excessively lose their effectiveness as control devices. For example, a report on the previous month's operations that management does not receive until the end of the current month is virtually useless for analyzing poor performance areas and taking corrective action.

Accountants should also issue reports *regularly* so that management can spot trends. Then, management can initiate the appropriate action before major problems occur. Regularity is important so that managers will rely on the reports and become familiar with their contents.

The format of responsibility reports should be relatively simple and easy to read. Accountants should avoid confusing terminology. The reports should express results in physical units where appropriate, since these units may be more familiar and understandable to some managers.

To assist management in quickly spotting budget variances, accountants should report both budgeted (expected) and actual amounts. A **budget variance** is the difference between the budgeted and actual amounts of an item. Because variances highlight problem areas (exceptions), they are helpful in applying the management-by-exception principle. To help management evaluate performance to date, responsibility reports often include both a current period and year-to-date analysis.

Illustration of Responsibility Reports

Illustration 19.2 shows how Macy's Corporation could interrelate some of its responsibility accounting reports. Assume that Macy's has four management levels, as shown in Illustration 19.2. The representative managers we will focus on are the president, vice president of operations, store manager, and department manager. Macy's has many stores and store managers. To keep our example simple, we show only one store manager in the illustrations. Illustration 19.3 shows that a responsibility report will be prepared for each management level.

In Illustration 19.4, you can see the detailed information included in the responsibility reports for each manager. (This information is assumed for illustrative purposes only.) These reports contain *only* the individual manager's controllable expenses. Notice that the store manager's report contains only *totals* from the men's clothing department manager's report. In turn, the report to the vice president of operations includes only totals from the store manager's report, and so on. In this way, accountants summarize (condense) and report detailed data from the lower levels at the next higher level. You can see that at each level, more and more costs become controllable. Also, controllable costs that were not included on lower-level reports

Illustration 19.2
ORGANIZATION CHART—MACY'S CORPORATION

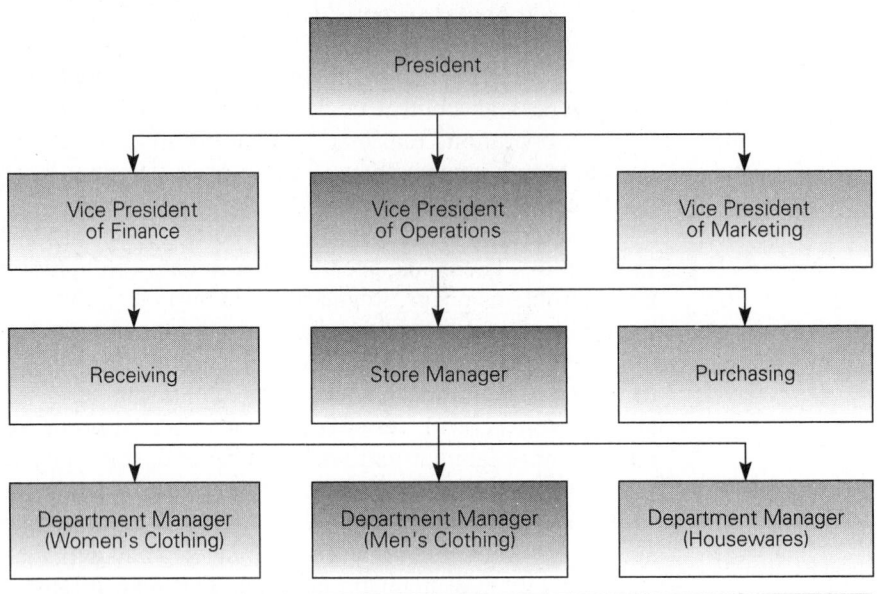

Illustration 19.3
RESPONSIBILITY REPORTS
FOR MACY'S CORPORATION

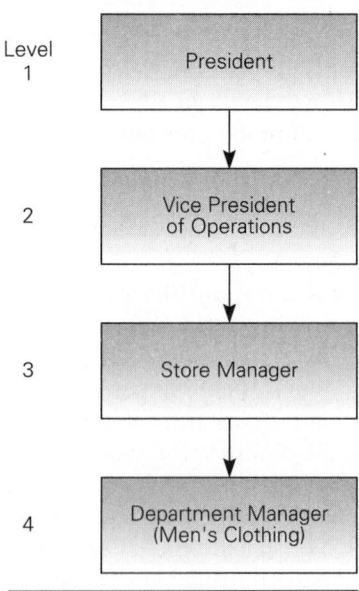

Illustration 19.4
RESPONSIBILITY REPORTS FOR MACY'S CORPORATION

First Level

MACY'S CORPORATION
President

Controllable Expenses	Amount		Over or (Under) Budget	
	This Month	Year to Date	This Month	Year to Date
President's office expense	$ 11,000	$ 55,000	$ 1,000	$ 2,000
Vice president of operations	**128,720**	**700,000**	**6,000**	**8,000** ←
Vice president of marketing	18,700	119,000	4,000	8,000
Vice president of finance	14,000	115,000	8,000	9,000
Vice presidents' salaries	29,000	145,000	–0–	–0–
Total	$201,420	$1,134,000	$19,000	$27,000

Second Level

MACY'S CORPORATION
Vice President of Operations

Controllable Expenses	Amount		Over or (Under) Budget	
	This Month	Year to Date	This Month	Year to Date
Vice president's office expense	$ 2,840	$ 9,500	$ (500)	$(8,000)
Store manager*	**88,800**	**490,000**	**2,500**	**5,000** ←
Purchasing	5,380	32,500	1,000	2,000
Receiving	4,700	33,000	3,000	9,000
Salaries of store managers and heads of purchasing and receiving	27,000	135,000	–0–	–0–
Total (include in report for next higher level)	$128,720	$700,000	$6,000	$ 8,000 ┘

Third Level

MACY'S CORPORATION
Store Manager

Controllable Expenses	Amount		Over or (Under) Budget	
	This Month	Year to Date	This Month	Year to Date
Store manager's office expense	$ 8,000	$ 91,000	$ (500)	$(1,000)
Men's clothing department	**16,800**	**86,000**	**1,600**	**2,300** ←
Housewares department	10,000	50,000	800	1,300
Women's clothing department	4,000	13,000	600	2,400
Salaries of department managers	50,000	250,000	–0–	–0–
Total (include in report for next higher level)	$88,800	$490,000	$2,500	$ 5,000 ┘

Fourth Level

MACY'S CORPORATION
Manager, Men's Clothing Department

Controllable Expenses	Amount		Over or (Under) Budget	
	This Month	Year to Date	This Month	Year to Date
Inventory losses	$ 2,000	$10,000	$ 100	$ 400
Supplies	1,800	8,500	800	950
Salaries	11,000	53,000	(100)	810
Overtime	2,000	14,500	800	140
Total (include in report for next higher level)	$16,800	$86,000	$1,600	$2,300 ┘

* If all store managers had been reported in our example, each one would be reported separately in this report.

are introduced into the reports for levels 3, 2, and 1. The only store cost not included at the store manager's level is the store manager's salary because it is noncontrollable by that store manager. This cost, however, is controllable by the store manager's supervisor (the vice president of operations), and it is included at that level of responsibility reporting.

Based on an analysis of these reports, the men's clothing department manager probably would take immediate action to see why supplies and overtime were significantly over budget this month. The store manager may ask the department manager what the problems were and whether they are now under control. The vice president may ask the same question of the store manager. The president may ask each vice president why the budget was exceeded this month and what corrective action has been taken.

RESPONSIBILITY CENTERS

A **segment** is a fairly autonomous unit or division of a company defined according to function or product line. Traditionally, companies have been organized along functional lines. In this type of organization, the segments or departments perform a specified function (e.g., marketing, finance, purchasing, production, or shipping). Recently, large companies have tended to organize segments according to product lines (e.g., electrical products division, shoe department, or food division).

A **responsibility center** is a segment of an organization for which a particular executive is responsible. The three types of responsibility centers are expense (or cost) centers, profit centers, and investment centers. In designing a responsibility accounting system, management should examine the characteristics of each segment and the extent of the responsible manager's authority. Care must be taken to ensure that the basis for evaluating performance (i.e., expense center, profit center, or investment center) matches the characteristics of the segment and the authority of the segment's manager. The following sections of the chapter will discuss the characteristics of each of these types of centers and the appropriate basis for evaluating the performance of each type.

Expense Centers

An **expense center** is a responsibility center incurring only expense items and producing no direct revenue from the sale of goods or services. Examples of expense centers are service centers (e.g., the maintenance department or accounting department) or intermediate production facilities that produce parts for assembly into a finished product. **Managers of expense centers are responsible only for specified expense items.**

The appropriate goal of an expense center is the *long-run* minimization of expenses. Short-run minimization of expenses may not be appropriate. For example, a production supervisor could eliminate maintenance costs for a short period of time, but in the long run, total costs might be higher due to more frequent machine breakdowns.

Profit Centers

A **profit center** is a responsibility center having both revenues and expenses. Since segmental earnings are usually defined as segmental revenues minus related expenses, the manager must be able to *control* both of these categories. The manager must have the authority to control selling price, sales volume, and all reported expense items. The manager's authority over all of these measured items is essential to proper performance evaluation. **Controllable profits of a segment** are shown when expenses under a manager's control are deducted from revenues under that manager's control.

Investment Centers

Closely related to the profit center concept is an *investment center*. An **investment center** is a responsibility center that has revenues, expenses, and an appropriate investment base. Companies evaluate an investment center according to the rate of return that it can earn on its investment base. To compute an investment center's **return on investment (ROI),** also called rate of return, the segmental income is divided by the appropriate investment base. For example, if a segment earns $500,000 on an investment base of $5,000,000, its ROI is 10%.

Determining the investment base that the accountant will use in the ROI calculation can be difficult. Normally, the assets available for use by the division make up its investment base. However, accountants disagree about whether they should include depreciable assets in the ROI calculation at original cost, original cost less accumulated depreciation, or current replacement cost. **Original cost** is the price paid to acquire the assets. **Original cost less accumulated depreciation** is the book value of the assets—the amount paid less total depreciation taken. **Current replacement cost** is the cost of replacing the present assets with similar assets in the same condition as those now in use. A different rate of return results from each of these measures. Therefore, management must select and agree on an appropriate measure of investment base before making ROI calculations or interdivision comparisons.

Even after the company defines its investment base, problems may still remain since many segment managers have limited control over some of the items included in the investment base of their segment. For instance, top management often makes capital expenditure decisions regarding major store assets. Therefore, the store manager may have little control over the store assets. Another problem area may exist if the company has a centralized credit and collection department. In this case, the store manager may have little or no control over the amount of accounts receivable included as segment assets since the manager cannot change the credit-granting or collection policies of the company.

Usually the above problems are overcome by realizing that if a company treats all segments in the same manner, the inclusion of noncontrollable items in the investment base may have negligible effects. Comparisons of the

ROI for all segments will then be based on a consistent treatment of items. The segment managers should agree to this treatment to avoid adverse reactions or decreased motivation.

Companies prefer to evaluate segments as investment centers because the ROI criterion facilitates comparisons of performance between segments. Segments with more resources should produce more profits than segments with fewer resources, so the performance of segments of different sizes should not be compared on the basis of profits alone. However, when using ROI as a performance measure, comparisons of performance take into account the differences in the sizes of the segments. The segment with the highest percentage ROI is presumably the most effective in using its resources.

Typical investment centers are large, autonomous segments of large companies. The centers are often separated from one another by location, types of products, functions, and/or necessary management skills. Segments such as these often seem to be separate companies to an outside observer. However, the investment center concept can be applied even in relatively small companies in which the segment managers have control over the revenues, expenses, and assets of their segments.

TRANSFER PRICES

Profit centers frequently exchange products with each other. The Pontiac, Buick, and other divisions of General Motors buy products from and sell products to each other, for example. Since no market exchange has taken place, the company uses a transfer price to record the revenue to one division and the cost to the other.

A **transfer price** is an artificial price assigned to goods or services transferred from one segment to another segment within the same company. The transfer price is recorded as a revenue of the producing segment and as a cost, or expense, of the receiving segment. In using transfer prices, cash does not necessarily change hands between the segments. Accountants may simply record the transfer price as an internal accounting transaction.

Divisions are generally evaluated based on some measure of profitability that includes these transfer-price-based costs and revenues. The transfer price can have an impact on the reported performance measures and, hence, on the performance evaluation of each division. For example, the higher the transfer price, the more profitable the selling division (from higher revenues) and the less profitable the buying division, all other things equal.

Recording a Transfer

The Frames Division of High-Rider Company makes a bicycle frame that is purchased by the Assembly Division, which manufactures bicycles. When the frames are transferred, their cost becomes a part of the cost of goods sold for the Assembly Division. If they are sold to an outside buyer, the amount received for the frames becomes revenue to the Frames Division. Likewise, if the Frames Division transfers frames to Assembly, the transfer will be recognized on the books of both the Assembly and Frames Divisions. If the frames are transferred at cost, then the Frames Division would obtain no profit from the transfer. In a decentralized organization, the internal transfer is often priced at the market value of the goods transferred.

For example, let's assume the Frames Division can either sell the frames or transfer them to Assembly at a price of $50 per frame. The manufacturing cost of the frame is $40 each. The transfer of 1,000 frames from the Frames Division to Assembly would be recorded on the books as:

Receivable from Assembly Division	50,000	
Sales Revenue.		50,000
Cost of Goods Sold	40,000	
Finished Goods Inventory		40,000

With this entry, the Frames Division would have recorded a gross margin of $10,000 from the transfer of frames to Assembly.

On the Assembly Division's books, the receipt of the 1,000 frames from the Frames Division would be recorded as:

Direct Materials Inventory	50,000	
Payable to Frames Division.		50,000

For evaluating the performance of each individual division, these costs and revenues would be used as the basis for profit measurement. However, for external financial reporting purposes, any interdivisional profits are eliminated to avoid double counting in the financial statements.

Companies generally use either cost-based or market-based transfer prices. The transfer between the Frames Division and the Assembly Division in the previous example used market prices. Since such a market price might not be available, companies often determine transfer prices on a cost-plus-profit-margin basis. Sometimes the two segments involved will negotiate their transfer prices, possibly with the help of an internal arbitration board.

If the transfer in the previous example had been at the cost of $40 per frame, the transfer of 1,000 frames would have been recorded on Frame's books as follows:

Receivable from Assembly Division	40,000	
Sales Revenue.		40,000
Cost of Goods Sold	40,000	
Finished Goods Inventory		40,000

On Assembly's books, the transaction would be recorded as:

Direct Materials Inventory	40,000	
Payable to Frames Division.		40,000

Using cost as the transfer price would eliminate the Frames Division's gross margin and reduce the cost to Assembly. In practice, if market prices are not available, these divisions would probably negotiate a cost-plus-profit-margin that would result in a price greater than $40, but less than $50 per frame. Ideally, the transfer price provides incentives for managers to make decisions that are both in their own best interests and in the best interests of the company.

USE OF SEGMENTAL ANALYSIS

So far, this chapter has described only the fundamentals of responsibility accounting. This section focuses specifically on segmental analysis.

Decentralization is the dispersion of decision-making authority among individuals at lower levels of the organization. The extent of decentralization is the degree of control that segment managers have over the revenues, expenses, and assets of their segments. When a segment manager has control over these elements, the investment center concept can be applied to the segment. Thus, the more decentralized the decision making is in an organization, the more applicable is the investment center concept to the segments of the company. The more centralized the decision making is, the more likely one is to find responsibility centers established as expense centers.

Some of the advantages of decentralized decision making are:

1. Increased control over their segments trains managers for high-level positions in the company. The added authority and responsibility also represent *job enlargement* and often increase job satisfaction and motivation.
2. Top management can be more removed from day-to-day decision making at lower levels of the company and can manage by exception. Top management that is not involved with routine problem solving can devote more time to long-range planning and to the company's most significant problem areas.
3. Decisions can be made at the point where problems arise. Often members of top management have difficulty making appropriate decisions on a timely basis when they are not intimately involved with the problem they are trying to solve.
4. Since decentralization permits use of the investment center concept, a company can use performance evaluation criteria such as ROI and residual income (to be explained later).

CONCEPTS USED IN SEGMENTAL ANALYSIS

Segmental analysis uses the concepts of variable cost, fixed cost, direct cost, indirect cost, net income, and contribution margin. This section describes each concept, except for variable cost and fixed cost, which we discussed in Chapter 12.

Direct Cost and Indirect Cost

Costs may be either directly or indirectly related to a particular cost objective. A **cost objective** is a segment, product, or other item for which costs may be accumulated. A cost is not *direct* or *indirect* in and of itself. A cost is only *direct* or *indirect* in relation to a given cost objective.

A **direct cost (expense)** is specifically traceable to a given cost objective. An **indirect cost (expense)** is not traceable to a given cost objective but has been allocated to it. A particular cost (expense) can only be designated as direct or indirect by reference to a given cost objective, and a cost that is direct to one cost objective may be indirect to another. For instance, the salary of a segment manager may be a direct cost of a given manufacturing segment but an indirect cost of one of the products manufactured by that segment. In this example, the segment and the product are two distinct cost objectives.

Since a direct cost is traceable to a cost objective, the cost is likely to be eliminated if the cost objective is eliminated. For instance, if a company closes down the plastics segment of a business, the salary of the manager of that segment probably will be eliminated.

An indirect cost is not traceable to a particular cost objective; therefore, it only becomes an expense of the cost objective through an allocation process. For example, consider the depreciation expense on the company headquarters building that is allocated to each of the segments of the company. The depreciation expense is a direct cost for the company headquarters, but it is an indirect cost to each segment. If a segment of the company is eliminated, the indirect cost for depreciation assigned to that segment will not disappear. The company will simply allocate the cost among the remaining segments. However, in some situations, an indirect cost might be eliminated if the cost objective were eliminated.

Since a segment's direct costs are clearly identified with that segment, the segment manager can often control these costs. Indirect costs become segment costs only through allocation, so the segment manager cannot control most indirect costs. However, care must be taken not to equate direct costs with controllable costs. For example, the salary of a segment supervisor may be direct to that segment and yet noncontrollable by that supervisor because supervisors cannot specify their own salaries.

Net Income of a Segment—Evaluation Criteria for a Profit Center

*Objective 3
Prepare a segmental income statement using the contribution margin format*

When preparing internal reports on the performance of a company's segments, management often finds that classifying expenses as fixed or variable and as direct or indirect to the segment is important. These classifications may be more useful to management than the traditional classifications of cost of goods sold, operating expenses, and nonoperating expenses that companies use for external reporting in their financial statements. As a result, many companies prepare (for internal use) income statements with the formats shown in Illustration 19.5.

Illustration 19.5
CONTRIBUTION MARGIN FORMAT INCOME STATEMENTS

A. All Expenses Allocated to Segments

	Segment A	Segment B	Total
Sales	$2,500,000	$1,500,000	$4,000,000
Less: Variable expenses			
(all of which are direct expenses)	700,000	650,000	1,350,000
Contribution margin	**$1,800,000**	**$ 850,000**	**$2,650,000**
Less: Direct fixed expenses	450,000	550,000	1,000,000
Contribution to indirect expenses	**$1,350,000**	**$ 300,000**	**$1,650,000**
Less: Indirect fixed expenses	270,000	330,000	600,000
Net income	**$1,080,000**	**$ (30,000)**	**$1,050,000**

B. Indirect Expenses Not Allocated to Segments

	Segment A	Segment B	Total
Sales	$2,500,000	$1,500,000	$4,000,000
Less: Variable expenses	700,000	650,000	1,350,000
Contribution margin	**$1,800,000**	**$ 850,000**	**$2,650,000**
Less: Direct fixed expenses	450,000	550,000	1,000,000
Contribution to indirect expenses	**$1,350,000**	**$ 300,000**	**$1,650,000**
Less: Indirect fixed expenses			600,000
Net income			**$1,050,000**

The income statements in Illustration 19.5 are called **contribution margin format** income statements because they show the contribution margin. **Contribution margin** is defined as sales revenue less variable expenses. In Part A, notice that all variable expenses are direct expenses of the segment. The second subtotal shown in the contribution margin format income statement is the segment's contribution to indirect expenses. The **contribution to indirect expenses** is sales revenue less all direct expenses of the segment (both variable direct expenses and fixed direct expenses). The final total in the income statement is **segmental net income,** defined as segmental revenues less all expenses (direct expenses and allocated indirect expenses).

Earlier we stated that the performance of a profit center is evaluated on the basis of the segment's profits. Using segmental net income to make this evaluation is tempting since total net income is used to evaluate the performance of the entire company. The problem with using segmental net income to evaluate performance is that segmental net income includes certain indirect expenses that have been allocated to the segment but are not directly related to it or its operations. Because segmental contribution to indirect expenses includes only revenues and expenses that are directly related to the segment, this amount is often more appropriate for evaluation purposes.

Using the facts in Part A of Illustration 19.5, if management relied on segmental net income to judge segmental performance, management might conclude that Segment B should be eliminated since it shows a loss of $30,000. However, this action would reduce overall company income by $300,000, as shown below:

Reduction in corporate revenues		$1,500,000
Reduction in corporate expenses:		
Variable expenses	$650,000	
Direct fixed expenses.	550,000	1,200,000
Reduction in corporate income		$ 300,000

Notice that the elimination of Segment B would not eliminate the $330,000 of allocated fixed costs. The company would allocate these costs to Segment A if Segment B no longer existed.

To stress the importance of a segment's contribution to indirect expenses, many companies prefer the contribution margin format income statement presented in Part B of Illustration 19.5 rather than the statement used in Part A. The difference is that the company did not allocate indirect fixed costs to individual segments. Indirect fixed expenses are only shown in the total column for the computation of net income for the entire company. The computation for each segment stops with the segment's contribution to indirect expenses, which is the appropriate figure to use for evaluating the earnings performance of a segment. Only for the company as a whole is net income (revenues minus *all* expenses) computed; net income is, of course, the appropriate figure to use for evaluating the company as a whole.

Arbitrary Allocations of Indirect Fixed Expenses. As stated above, companies can only allocate indirect fixed expenses, such as depreciation on the corporate administration building or on the computer facility maintained at company headquarters, to segments on some arbitrary basis. The basic guidelines for allocating indirect fixed expenses are (1) by the benefit received and (2) by the responsibility for incurrence of the expense.

Companies can allocate certain indirect expenses on the basis of benefit received. For instance, assume an entire company uses a corporate computer for a total of 10,000 hours. If Segment K used the computer for 4,000 hours, the company could allocate 40% of the computer's depreciation for the period to Segment K, since it received 40% of the total benefits for the period.

For certain other indirect expenses, companies can base allocation on responsibility for incurrence. For instance, assume that Segment M contracts with a magazine to run an advertisement that will benefit Segment M and various other segments of the company. Some companies would allocate the entire cost of the advertisement to Segment M, since it was responsible for incurring the advertising expense.

To further illustrate the allocation of indirect expenses based on a measure of benefit or responsibility for incurrence, assume that Daily Company operates two segments, X and Y. It allocates the following indirect expenses to its two segments using the designated allocation bases:

Expense	Allocation Base
Administrative office building occupancy expense, $50,000	Net sales
Insurance expense, $35,000	Cost of segmental plant assets
General administrative expenses, $40,000	Number of employees

The following additional data are provided:

	Segment X	Segment Y	Total
Net sales	$400,000	$500,000	$900,000
Segmental plant assets	$250,000	$400,000	$650,000
Number of employees	50	80	130

The allocation of indirect expenses is as shown in the following expense allocation schedule:

	Segment X	Segment Y	Total
Administrative office building occupancy expense .	$22,222^a	$27,778^b	$50,000
Insurance expense	13,462^c	21,538^d	35,000
General administrative expenses	15,385^e	24,615^f	40,000

^{a} $\frac{\$400,000}{\$900,000} \times \$50,000 = \$22,222.$ ^{d} $\frac{\$400,000}{\$650,000} \times \$35,000 = \$21,538.$

^{b} $\frac{\$500,000}{\$900,000} \times \$50,000 = \$27,778.$ ^{e} $\frac{50}{130} \times \$40,000 = \$15,385.$

^{c} $\frac{\$250,000}{\$650,000} \times \$35,000 = \$13,462.$ ^{f} $\frac{80}{130} \times \$40,000 = \$24,615.$

When a company uses neither *benefit* nor *responsibility* to allocate indirect fixed expenses, it must find some other reasonable, but arbitrary, basis. Often, for lack of a better approach, companies use net sales as a base for indirect expenses. For instance, if Segment X's net sales were 60% of total company sales, then 60% of the indirect expenses would be allocated to Segment X. Accountants do not recommend allocating expenses based on sales because this method of allocation reduces the segment manager's incentive to increase sales.

Now that we have discussed some basic concepts essential to segmental analysis, we present some specific procedures for performance evaluation.

INVESTMENT CENTER ANALYSIS

*Objective 4
Calculate return on investment, margin, and turnover for a segment*

The segmental analysis discussion so far has concentrated on the contribution to indirect expenses and segmental net income approaches. Now we will introduce the investment base concept into the analysis. Two evaluation bases that include the concept of investment base in the analysis are ROI (return on investment) and RI (residual income).

Illustration 19.6
COMPUTATION OF RETURN ON INVESTMENT (ROI)

		Segment A	Segment B	Segment C	Total
(a)	Income	$ 250,000	$1,000,000	$ 500,000	$1,750,000
(b)	Investment	2,500,000	5,000,000	2,000,000	9,500,000
	Return on investment (a) ÷ (b)	10%	20%	25%	18.42%

Return on Investment (ROI)

A segment that has a large amount of assets usually earns more in an absolute sense than a segment that has a small amount of assets. Therefore, a company cannot use absolute amounts of segmental income to compare the performance of different segments. To measure the relative effectiveness of segments, a company might use **return on investment (ROI),** which calculates the return (income) as a percentage of the assets employed (investment). The formula for ROI is:

$$\text{ROI} = \frac{\text{Income}}{\text{Investment}}$$

To illustrate the difference between using absolute amounts and using percentages in evaluating a segment's performance, consider the data shown in Illustration 19.6 for a company with three segments. If the company uses absolute dollars of income to evaluate performance, Segment B appears to be doing twice as well as Segment C. However, suppose the company uses ROI for evaluating the segments. This ROI measure indicates that Segment C is performing the best (25%), Segment B is next (20%), and Segment A is performing the worst (10%). ROI is therefore a more useful indicator of the relative performance of segments than is absolute income.

Although ROI appears to be a simple and straightforward computation, several alternative methods exist for making the calculation. These alternatives focus on what is meant by *income* and *investment*. Illustration 19.7 shows various definitions and applicable situations for each type of computation.

As discussed earlier in the chapter, alternative investment valuation bases include original cost, cost less accumulated depreciation, and current replacement cost. Each of the valuation bases has merits and drawbacks, as you will now see.

Cost less accumulated depreciation is probably the most widely used valuation base and is easily determined. However, since many different depreciation methods may be used, comparisons between segments or companies may be difficult. Also, as book value decreases, a constant income results in a steadily increasing ROI even though the segment's performance is unchanged. The use of original cost eliminates the problem of decreasing book value but has its own drawback. The investment in (cost of) old assets

Illustration 19.7
POSSIBLE DEFINITIONS OF INCOME AND INVESTMENT

Situation	Definition of Income	Definition of Investment
1. Evaluation of the earning power of the company. Do not use for segments or segment managers due to inclusion of noncontrollable expenses.	Net income of the company.*	Total assets of the company.†
2. Evaluation of rate of income contribution of segment. Do not use for segment managers due to inclusion of noncontrollable expenses.	Contribution to indirect expenses.	Assets directly used by and identified with the segment.
3. Evaluation of income performance of segment manager.	*Controllable* income. Begin with contribution to indirect expenses and eliminate any revenues and direct expenses not under the control of the segment manager.	Assets under the control of the segment manager.

* Often *net operating income* is used; this term is defined as income before interest and taxes.
† *Operating assets* are often used in the calculation. This definition excludes assets not used in normal operations.

will be much less than an investment in new assets, so a segment with old assets can earn less than a segment with new assets; yet it will realize a higher ROI. Current replacement cost is difficult to use because replacement cost figures often are not available, but this base does eliminate some of the problems caused by the other two methods. Whichever valuation basis a company adopts, it should consistently use the same valuation basis for comparative purposes.

Expanded Form of ROI Computation. The ROI formula can be broken into the following two parts:

$$\text{ROI} = \frac{\text{Income}}{\text{Sales}} \times \frac{\text{Sales}}{\text{Investment}}$$

The first part of the formula, Income/Sales, is called *margin* or *return on sales*. The **margin** refers to the percentage relationship of income or profits to sales. This percentage shows the number of cents of profit that are generated by each dollar of sales. The second part of the formula, Sales/Investment, is called *turnover*. **Turnover** shows the number of dollars of sales generated by each dollar of investment. Turnover measures how effectively segments use each dollar of assets.

ROI can be increased as follows:

1. A manager can concentrate on increasing profit margin while holding turnover constant. Pursuing this strategy means keeping selling prices constant and making every effort to increase efficiency and thereby reduce expenses.
2. A manager can concentrate on increasing turnover by reducing the investment in assets while holding income and sales constant. For example, working capital could be decreased, thereby reducing the investment in assets.
3. A manager can take actions that affect both margin and turnover. For example, disposing of nonproductive depreciable assets would decrease investment while also increasing income (through the reduction of depreciation expense). Thus, both margin and turnover would increase. An advertising campaign might increase sales and income. In this case, turnover would increase, and margin might increase or decrease depending on the relative amounts of the increases in income and sales.

Illustration 19.8 shows possible outcomes of some of these strategies to increase ROI.

Residual Income

Objective 5
Calculate the
residual income of
a segment

When a company uses ROI to evaluate performance, managers have incentives to focus on the average returns from their segment's assets. However, the company's best interest is served if managers also focus on the marginal returns.

To illustrate, assume the manager of Segment 3 in Illustration 19.9 has an opportunity to take on a project involving an investment of $100,000 that is estimated to return $22,000, or 22%, on the investment. Since the segment's ROI is currently 25%, the manager may decide to reject the project because accepting the project will cause the segment's ROI to decline. Suppose however, from the company's point of view, all projects earning greater than a 10% return should be accepted, even if they are lower than a particular segment's ROI.

This rejection by a segment manager of a project that exceeds the 10% desired minimum return is an example of *suboptimization*. **Suboptimization** occurs when a segment manager takes an action that is in the segment's best interest, but not in the best interest of the company as a whole.

To deal with this type of suboptimization, companies sometimes use the concept of *residual income*. **Residual income (RI)** is defined as the amount of income a segment has in excess of a desired minimum ROI. Each company sets its minimum ROI based on many factors, including expected

Illustration 19.8
STRATEGIES FOR INCREASING RETURN ON INVESTMENT (ROI)

Past year's return on investment:

$$ROI = Margin \times Turnover$$

$$ROI = \frac{Income}{Sales} \times \frac{Sales}{Investment}$$

$$ROI = \frac{\$100,000}{\$2,000,000} \times \frac{\$2,000,000}{\$1,000,000}$$

$$ROI = 5\% \times 2\ times$$

$$ROI = 10\%$$

1. Increase margin through reducing expenses by $40,000; no effect on sales or investment.

$$ROI = \frac{\$140,000}{\$2,000,000} \times \frac{\$2,000,000}{\$1,000,000}$$

$$ROI = 7\% \times 2\ times$$

$$ROI = 14\%$$

2. Increase turnover through reducing investment in assets by $200,000; no effect on sales or income.

$$ROI = \frac{\$100,000}{\$2,000,000} \times \frac{\$2,000,000}{\$800,000}$$

$$ROI = 5\% \times 2.5\ times$$

$$ROI = 12.5\%$$

3(a). Increase margin and turnover by disposing of nonproductive depreciable assets; income increased by $10,000; investment decreased by $200,000.

$$ROI = \frac{\$110,000}{\$2,000,000} \times \frac{\$2,000,000}{\$800,000}$$

$$ROI = 5.5\% \times 2.5\ times$$

$$ROI = 13.75\%$$

3(b). Increase margin and turnover through increased advertising; sales increased by $500,000 and income by $50,000; no effect on investment.

$$ROI = \frac{\$150,000}{\$2,500,000} \times \frac{\$2,500,000}{\$1,000,000}$$

$$ROI = 6\% \times 2.5\ times$$

$$ROI = 15\%$$

3(c). Increase turnover through increased advertising; sales increased by $500,000 and income by $12,500; no effect on investment.

$$ROI = \frac{\$112,500}{\$2,500,000} \times \frac{\$2,500,000}{\$1,000,000}$$

$$ROI = 4.5\% \times 2.5\ times$$

$$ROI = 11.25\%$$

Illustration 19.9
COMPUTATION OF RESIDUAL INCOME (RI)

Before acceptance of the project by Segment 3, the amounts are as follows:

		Segment 1	Segment 2	Segment 3	Total Company
a.	Income	$ 100,000	$ 500,000	$ 250,000	$ 850,000
b.	Investment	1,000,000	2,500,000	1,000,000	4,500,000
c.	**Rate of return on investment (ROI)**	10%	20%	25%	**18.89%**
d.	Desired minimum ROI (10%) . .	$ 100,000	$ 250,000	$ 100,000	*
e.	**Residual income (RI)**	–0–	250,000	150,000	*

With acceptance of the project by Segment 3, the amounts would be as follows:

		Segment 1	Segment 2	Segment 3	Total Company
a.	Income	$ 100,000	$ 500,000	$ 272,000†	$ 872,000
b.	Investment	1,000,000	2,500,000	1,100,000‡	4,600,000
c.	**Rate of return on investment (ROI)**	10%	20%	24.7%	**18.96%**
d.	Desired minimum ROI (10%) . .	$ 100,000	$ 250,000	$ 110,000	*
e.	**Residual income (RI)**	–0–	250,000	162,000	*

* The RI concept is generally not used for evaluating an entire company, since the problem of suboptimization, by definition, does not exist for the company as a whole.
† $250,000 + (22% of $100,000).
‡ $1,000,000 original investment + $100,000 new investment.

growth rate, debt coverage, industry technology, and desired returns to stockholders. The formula for residual income (RI) is:

$$RI = Income - (Investment \times Minimum \ ROI)$$

When a company uses RI to evaluate performance, the segment rated as the best is the segment with the greatest amount of RI rather than the one with the highest ROI.

Returning to our example, the project opportunity for Segment 3 could earn in excess of the desired minimum ROI of 10%. In fact, Segment 3 has RI on that project of $12,000, calculated as ($22,000 − [10% × $100,000]). If RI were applied as the basis for evaluating segmental performance, the manager of Segment 3 would accept the project because doing so would improve his or her segment's performance. That choice would also be beneficial to the entire company.

Critics of the RI method complain that larger segments are likely to have the highest RI. In a given situation, it may be advisable to look at both ROI and RI in assessing performance.

A manager will tend to make choices that improve his or her segment's performance. The challenge is to select evaluation bases for segments that will result in managers making choices that benefit the entire company.

PERFORMANCE EVALUATION OF STRATEGIC PROJECTS

Caterpillar, Inc., is investing $1.5 billion in a world-wide factory modernization program. Caterpillar's management realizes it must continually monitor the performance of this modernization if the project is to realize its potential.

At Caterpillar, the projects are grouped into "bundles" of related projects. For example, all of the new assets used for a new product would be bundled together. "Each bundle is monitored every six months at Caterpillar, although a few key characteristics of some bundles are monitored monthly" [p. 32]. Characteristics used in monitoring performance include the amount of money projected versus the amount actually spent on the projects, the number of people ex-

pected to be used on the projects versus the number actually used, and the estimated reduction in product cost versus the reduction in product cost actually achieved.

Many firms believe their evaluation of project performance leaves much to be desired. Caterpillar's idea of "bundling" similar projects should be helpful to other firms that are making significant changes in their production processes and product lines.

SOURCE: Based on the article by James A. Hendricks, Robert C. Bastian, and Thomas L. Sexton, "Bundle Monitoring of Strategic Projects," *Management Accounting,* February 1992, pp. 31–35.

When performance is evaluated using RI, choices that improve a segment's performance are more likely to also improve the entire company's performance.

When calculating RI for a *segment*, the income and investment definitions are *contribution to indirect expenses* and *assets directly used by and identified with the segment*. When calculating RI for a *manager* of a segment, the income and investment definitions should be *income controllable by the manager* and *assets under the control of the segment manager*.

Using Judgment in Performance Evaluation

In evaluating the performance of a segment or a segment manager, comparisons should be made with (1) the current budget, (2) other segments or managers within the company, (3) past performance of that segment or manager, and (4) similar segments or managers in other companies. Consideration must be given to general economic conditions, market conditions for the product being produced, and so on. A superior segment in Company A may be considered superior because it is earning a return of 12%, which is above similar segments in other companies but below other segments in Company A. However, segments in Company A may be more profitable because of market conditions and the nature of the company's products rather than because of the performance of the segment managers. Top management must use careful judgment whenever performance is evaluated.

ETHICS   A CLOSER LOOK

Jerome Lastly faced a very tough choice. He had an opportunity to increase his research laboratory space by more than 50% if he could decrease his division's fixed costs by 20%. This directive came down from Jerome's department chairman. Jerome desperately needed laboratory space to accommodate two new machines he had recently purchased.

The fixed costs in Jerome's division were primarily salaries. The only employee Jerome could lay off was Rieza, the science writer. However, Jerome needed her expertise to help him write his grants and articles, especially as he had been very successful at getting his grants funded and his articles published since having Rieza's help.

Jerome devised a scheme to pay Rieza's salary from a training grant as a postgraduate researcher. This grant was to be used to train students in the area of toxic waste reduction methods.

The scheme worked well. Fixed costs were decreased by more than 20%, laboratory space was increased to accommodate the new machinery, and the department chairman was so pleased with Jerome's success that Jerome was promoted to vice chairman of research.

Six months later, the department accountant discovered the scheme when putting together the department's annual financial report. He noticed that for the first six months of the year Rieza had a salaried position as a science writer, then the following six months she was classified as a postgraduate researcher with a stipend to bring her salary equal to a science writer's salary. When the accountant presented his findings to his supervisor, the supervisor said, "This practice is unfortunate and is against university policy, but what is done is done. Don't worry about last year's financial statements. Just be sure it doesn't happen again."

Required
What should the accountant do?

SEGMENTAL REPORTING IN EXTERNAL FINANCIAL STATEMENTS

Before 1976, accountants typically reported segmental information only to management for internal decision-making purposes. In December 1976, the Financial Accounting Standards Board issued *Statement of Financial Accounting Standards No. 14,* "Financial Reporting for Segments of a Business Enterprise." This *Statement* requires that publicly held companies publish certain segmental information in their annual financial statements. Thus, external users of financial statements now have segmental information to aid them in their decisions regarding these companies. However, these external statements present fewer details than do reports intended for management.

In this chapter you learned about responsibility accounting and segmental analysis. In Chapter 20, we discuss capital budgeting and long-term planning.

UNDERSTANDING THE LEARNING OBJECTIVES

1. Explain responsibility accounting and its use in a business entity.
    *   Responsibility accounting refers to an accounting system that col-

lects, summarizes, and reports accounting data relating to the responsibilities of individual managers.

- A responsibility accounting system provides information to evaluate each manager on revenue and expense items over which that manager has primary control (authority to influence).

2. Prepare responsibility accounting reports.
   - A varying amount of detail is included in the responsibility reports that are issued to different levels of management.
   - Although the amount of detail varies, reports issued under a responsibility accounting system are interrelated. Totals from the report on one level of management are carried forward to the report for the management level immediately above.
   - The reports have the feature of condensing data as information flows upward to increasingly higher levels of management.
   - In effect, the president's report should include all revenue and expense items in summary form since the president is responsible for controlling the profitability of the entire company.

3. Prepare a segmental income statement using the contribution margin format.
   - The contribution margin format for the income statement shows the contribution margin for the segment.
   - Contribution margin is defined as sales revenue less variable expenses. All variable expenses are direct expenses of the segment.
   - Contribution to indirect expenses is defined as sales revenue less all direct expenses of the segment.
   - The final total in the income statement is segmental net income, defined as segmental revenues less all segmental expenses (direct expenses and allocated indirect expenses).

4. Calculate return on investment, margin, and turnover for a segment.
   - Return on investment measures the relative effectiveness of segments. The formula for ROI is:

$$\text{ROI} = \frac{\text{Income}}{\text{Investment}}$$

   - Alternatively, the formula for ROI can be broken into two components as follows:

$$\text{ROI} = \frac{\text{Income}}{\text{Sales}} \times \frac{\text{Sales}}{\text{Investment}}$$

   - Margin refers to the percentage relationship of income or profits to sales. This percentage shows the number of cents of profit that are generated by each dollar of sales. The formula for margin can be expressed as:

$$\text{Margin} = \frac{\text{Income}}{\text{Sales}}$$

- Turnover shows the number of dollars of sales generated by each dollar of investment. Turnover measures how effectively each dollar of assets was used. The formula for turnover can be expressed as:

$$\text{Turnover} = \frac{\text{Sales}}{\text{Investment}}$$

5. Calculate the residual income of a segment.
   - Residual income is defined as the amount of income a segment has in excess of a desired minimum ROI.
   - Each company sets its minimum ROI based on many factors, including expected growth rate, debt coverage, industry technology, and desired returns to stockholders.
   - The formula for residual income is:

$$\text{RI} = \text{Income} - (\text{Investment} \times \text{Minimum ROI})$$

6. Allocate costs from service departments to operating departments (appendix).
   - A company must allocate service department costs to the operating departments so that the costs of conducting business in the operating departments are clearly and accurately reflected.
   - Two basic methods exist for allocating service department costs: (1) the direct method and (2) the step method.

APPENDIX

ALLOCATION OF SERVICE DEPARTMENT COSTS

*Objective 6
Allocate costs
from service de-
partments to
operating depart-
ments*

Throughout this text, cost allocations have been emphasized only in the operating departments of a company. These operating departments perform the primary purpose of the company—to produce goods and services that will be made available to consumers. Examples of operating departments are the assembly departments of a manufacturing firm and the departments in hotels that take and confirm reservations.

Eventually, companies allocate the costs of service departments to the operating departments because the purpose of service departments is to aid the operating departments. Examples of service departments are maintenance, administration, cafeterias, laundries, and receiving. Service departments aid multiple production departments at the same time, and a company must allocate and account for all of these service department costs. A company must allocate these service department costs to the operating departments so that the costs of conducting business in the operating departments are clearly and accurately reflected.

To allocate service department costs, a company must use some type of base. When companies are in the process of choosing bases to use, they consider such criteria as the types of services provided, the benefits that are received, and the fairness of the allocation method. Examples of types of bases used to allocate service department costs are number of employees, machine-hours, direct labor-hours, square footage, and electricity usage.

The two basic methods for allocating service department costs are: (1) the direct method and (2) the step method. The direct method is the simplest of the two methods. Under the direct method, a company allocates costs of each of the service departments to each operating department based on that department's share of the allocation base. The company ignores services used by other service departments. For example, if Service Department A uses some of Service Department B's services, the cost allocation process would ignore these services. Since these services are not allocated to other service departments, some accountants believe the direct method is not accurate.

Under the step method of allocating service department costs, a company allocates service costs to the other service departments and operating departments in a sequential process. The sequence of allocation generally starts with the service department that has incurred the greatest costs. After allocating this department's costs, the company allocates the costs of the service department with the next highest costs, and so forth, until the costs of the service department with the least costs are allocated. Costs are not allocated back to a department that has already had all of its costs allocated.

The following data will be used to illustrate the direct method and the step method:

	Service Departments		Operating Departments	
	Maintenance	Administration	1	2
Costs	$8,000	$4,000	$32,000	$36,000
Machine-hours used	1,000	2,000	1,500	2,500
Number of employees	100	200	250	150

The costs of the maintenance department are allocated on the basis of machine-hours used. The costs of the administration department are allocated on the basis of number of employees.

Direct Method

Using the preceding data, an example of the direct method follows:

	Service Departments		Operating Departments	
	Maintenance	*Administration*	*1*	*2*
Costs.	$ 8,000	$ 4,000	$32,000	$36,000
Allocation of maintenance department's costs*.	(8,000)		3,000	5,000
	$ –0–			
Allocation of administration department's costs†.		(4,000)	2,500	1,500
		$ –0–	$37,500	$42,500

* Department 1's fraction is 1,500/4,000; Department 2's fraction is 2,500/4,000.
† Department 1's fraction is 250/400; Department 2's fraction is 150/400.

Step Method

Using the same data as above, an example of the step method follows:

	Service Departments		Operating Departments	
	Maintenance	*Administration*	*1*	*2*
Costs.	$ 8,000	$ 4,000	$32,000	$36,000
Allocation of maintenance department's costs*.	(8,000)	2,667	2,000	3,333
	$ –0–			
Allocation of administration department's costs†.		(6,667)	4,167	2,500
		$ –0–	$38,167	$41,833

* Administration's fraction: 2,000/6,000; Department 1's fraction: 1,500/6,000; Department 2's fraction is 2,500/6,000.
† Department 1's fraction is 250/400; Department 2's fraction is 150/400.

Note that in the above examples, the maintenance department costs were not allocated to the administration department under the direct method but were allocated under the step method. Also, to eliminate the administration department's costs, under the step method those costs that were allocated to the administration department from the maintenance department must be allocated to the operating departments as part of the total administration department's costs.

DEMONSTRATION PROBLEM

Wynett Company has two segments. Results of operations for 1995 follow:

	Segment 1	Segment 2	Total
Sales	$90,000	$135,000	$225,000
Variable expenses	63,000	81,000	144,000
Fixed expenses:			
Direct	9,000	25,200	34,200
Indirect			12,600

The company has total operating assets of $315,000; $288,000 of these assets are identified with particular segments as follows:

	Segment 1	Segment 2
Assets directly used by and identified with the segment	$108,000	$180,000

Required:

a. Prepare a statement showing the contribution margin, contribution to indirect expenses for each segment, and the total income for Wynett Company.
b. Determine the ROI for each segment and then for the entire company.
c. Comment on the results of *(a)* and *(b)*.

Solution to demonstration problem

a.

WYNETT COMPANY
Income Statement Showing Segmental Contribution to Indirect Expenses
For the Year Ended December 31, 1995

	Segment 1	Segment 2	Total
Sales	$90,000	$135,000	$225,000
Less: Variable expenses	63,000	81,000	144,000
Contribution margin	$27,000	$ 54,000	$ 81,000
Less: Direct fixed expenses	9,000	25,200	34,200
Contribution to indirect expenses	$18,000	$ 28,800	$ 46,800
Less: Indirect fixed expenses			12,600
Net income			$ 34,200

b. 1.

$$\text{ROI} = \frac{\text{Contribution to indirect expenses}}{\text{Assets directly used by and identified with the segment}}$$

Segment 1

$$\text{ROI} = \frac{\$18,000}{\$108,000} = 16.67\%$$

Segment 2

$$\text{ROI} = \frac{\$28,800}{\$180,000} = 16\%$$

2. $$\text{ROI} = \frac{\text{Net operating income}}{\text{Operating assets}} = \frac{\$34,200}{\$315,000} = 10.86\%$$

c. In *(a)*, Segment 2 showed a higher contribution to indirect expenses. In *(b)*, Segment 1 showed a higher ROI. The difference between these calculations shows that when a segment is evaluated as a profit center, the center with the highest investment base will usually show the best results. However, when the segment is evaluated as an investment center, the segment with the highest investment base will not necessarily show the highest return. The computations in *(b)* also demonstrate that the ROI for the company as a whole will be lower than the ROIs for the segments because of the higher investment base.

NEW TERMS*

Budget variance   The difference between the budgeted and actual amounts of a revenue or expense item. *941*

Contribution margin   Sales revenues less variable expenses. *950*

Contribution margin format   An income statement format that shows the contribution margin (Sales − Variable expenses) for a segment. *950*

Contribution to indirect expenses   Sales revenues less all direct expenses of the segment (both variable direct expenses and fixed direct expenses). *950*

Controllable profits of a segment   Profits of a segment when expenses under a manager's control are deducted from revenues under that manager's control. *945*

Cost objective   A segment, product, or other item for which costs may be accumulated. *949*

Current replacement cost   The cost of replacing the present assets with similar assets in the same condition as those assets now in use. *945*

Decentralization   The dispersion of decision-making authority among individuals at lower levels of the organization. *948*

Direct cost (expense)   A cost that is traceable to a given cost objective. *949*

Expense center   A responsibility center incurring only expense items and producing no direct revenues from the sale of goods or services. Examples include the accounting department and the maintenance department. *944*

Indirect cost (expense)   A cost that is not traceable to a given cost objective but has been allocated to it. *949*

Investment center   A responsibility center having revenues, expenses, and an appropriate investment base. *945*

Management by exception   The principle that upper-level management does not need to examine operating details at lower levels unless a problem (an exception) appears to exist. *940*

Margin (as used in ROI)   The percentage relationship of income or profits to sales. *954*

$$\text{Margin} = \frac{\text{Income}}{\text{Sales}}$$

---

* Some terms listed in earlier chapters are repeated here for your convenience.

Original cost   The price paid to acquire an asset. *945*

Original cost less accumulated depreciation   The book value of an asset—the amount paid less total depreciation taken. *945*

Profit center   A responsibility center having both revenues and expenses. *945*

Residual income (RI)   The amount of income a segment has in excess of a desired minimum ROI. Residual income is equal to Income − (Investment × Minimum ROI). *955*

Responsibility accounting   Refers to an accounting system that collects, summarizes, and reports accounting data relating to the responsibility of the individual managers. A responsibility accounting system provides information to evaluate each manager on revenue and expense items over which that manager has primary control. *938*

Responsibility center   A segment of an organization for which a particular executive is responsible. *944*

Return on investment (ROI)   Calculate the return (income) as a percentage of the assets employed (investment). *945, 953*

$$ROI = \frac{Income}{Investment} \text{ or } \frac{Income}{Sales} \times \frac{Sales}{Investment}$$

Segment   A fairly autonomous unit or division of a company defined according to function or product line. *944*

Segmental net income   Final total in the income statement; segmental revenues less all segmental expenses (direct expenses and allocated indirect expenses). *950*

Suboptimization   A situation that occurs when a segment manager takes an action that is in the segment's best interest but not in the best interest of the company as a whole. *955*

Transfer price   An artificial price used when goods or services are transferred from one segment to another segment within the same company. *946*

Turnover (as used in ROI)   The number of dollars of sales generated by each dollar of investment. *954*

$$Turnover = \frac{Sales}{Investment}$$

SELF-TEST

True-False

Indicate whether each of the following statements is true or false.

1. When using the full-cost approach, a responsibility report includes only items over which a particular management level has direct control.

2. The objective of an expense center is the short-run minimization of expenses.

3. The salary of a segment supervisor would be considered a direct cost as well as a noncontrollable cost to that segment.

4. Segments should be evaluated using only their revenue figures.

5. When calculating RI for a segment, the income and investment definitions are—contribution to indirect expenses, and assets directly used by and identified with the segment.

Multiple-Choice

Select the best answer for each of the following questions.

1. The investment base used when determining the ROI calculation could be which of the following?
    a. Current replacement cost.
    b. Original cost.
    c. Original cost less accumulated depreciation.
    d. Any of the above.

2. Which of the following actions would increase ROI?
    a. Increase sales, with no change in income or assets.
    b. Increase investment in assets, with no change in income.
    c. Reduce operating expenses, with no effect on sales or assets.
    d. None of the above.

3. Calculate ROI using the expanded form (margin times turnover) from the following data:

Sales	$600,000
Investment	300,000
Income	60,000

    a. 20%.
    b. 10%.
    c. 15%.
    d. None of the above.

4. In evaluating the performance of a segment or manager, comparisons should be made with:

    a. Other segments or managers within the company and in other companies and past performance of segment or manager.
    b. Performance reports on segment personnel.
    c. Previous budgets.
    d. All of the above.

5. Calculate the ROI and RI for each segment below and determine if a segment should be dropped based on RI.

	Segment 1	Segment 2	Segment 3
Income	$ 100,000	$ 750,000	$ 400,000
Investment . .	2,000,000	5,000,000	2,000,000
ROI	?	?	?
Desired minimum ROI (10%) .	200,000	500,000	200,000
RI	?	?	?

    a. 5%, 15%, 20%.
        $0, $250,000, $200,000.
        Consider dropping Segment 1.
    b. 10%, 10%, 20%.
        $100,000, $500,000, $200,000.
        Do not drop any segment.
    c. 10%, 20%, 25%.
        $0, $500,000, $400,000.
        Consider dropping Segment 1.
    d. 5%, 15%, 20%.
        ($100,000), $250,000, $200,000.
        Consider dropping Segment 1.

Now turn to page 977 to check your answers.

QUESTIONS

1. What is the fundamental principle of responsibility accounting?

2. List some important factors that should be considered in designing reports for a responsibility accounting system.

3. How soon should accounting reports be prepared after the end of the performance measurement period? Explain.

4. Name and describe three types of responsibility centers.

5. Describe a segment of a business enterprise that is best treated as an expense center. List four indirect expenses that may be allocated to such an expense center.

6. Compare and contrast an expense center and an investment center.

7. What purpose is served by setting transfer prices?

8. What is the advantage of using investment centers as a basis for performance evaluation?

9. Which categories of items must a segment manager have control over for the investment center concept to be applicable?

10. What is the connection between the extent of decentralization and the investment center concept?

11. Give some of the advantages of decentralization.

12. Differentiate between a direct cost and an indirect cost of a segment. What happens to these categories if the segment to which they are related is eliminated?

13. Can a cost be *direct* to one cost objective and *indirect* to another cost objective? Explain.

14. Describe some of the methods by which indirect expenses are allocated to a segment.

15. Give the general formula for return on investment (ROI). What are its two components?

16. Give the three sets of definitions for income and investment that can be used in ROI calculations, and explain when each set is applicable.

17. Give the various valuation bases that can be used for plant assets in investment center calculations. Discuss some of the advantages and disadvantages of these methods.

18. In what way is the use of the residual income (RI) concept superior to the use of ROI?

19. How is RI determined?

20. If the RI for segment manager A is $50,000 while the RI for segment manager B is $100,000, does this difference necessarily mean that B is a better manager than A? Explain.

The Coca-Cola Company

21. *Real-world question*   Refer to Appendix C at the end of this text. Compare the performance of The Coca-Cola Company's three lines of business: (1) Soft Drinks—United States, (2) Soft Drinks—International, and (3) Foods. (See footnote 18 called "Lines of Business.") Which business line had the most profits? Which business performed better in 1991 using ROI, profit margin, and asset turnover as the performance measures? Use end-of-year identifiable operating amounts in Appendix C to measure assets, operating income amounts to measure profits, and net operating revenues to measure sales.

The Coca-Cola Company

22. *Real-world question* Refer to Appendix C at the end of the text. Which of Coca-Cola's geographic areas had the highest ROI in 1991? To compute the answer, use "Operating Income" for the profit measure and end-of-year "Identifiable Operating Assets" for the measure of assets. (See footnote 19 of Coca-Cola's annual report.)

23. *(Based on Appendix)* Briefly discuss the two methods of allocating service department costs.

EXERCISES

Prepare a responsibility report for a given management level (L.O. 2)

19–1. The following information refers to a department in a plant of The Lakers Company for May:

	Amount	Over or (Under) Budget
Supplies	$ 35,000	$ (3,200)
Repairs and maintenance	185,000	10,400
Overtime	71,000	7,200
Salary of supervisor	21,600	(3,600)
Salary of plant manager	28,800	–0–
Allocation of company accounting costs	21,600	7,200
Allocation of depreciation	14,400	(3,600)

Using the above information, prepare a responsibility report for the supervisor of the department for May.

Prepare an income statement for a segment in a contribution margin format (L.O. 3)

19–2. Present the following information for Segment Q in the contribution margin format with indirect fixed expenses not allocated:

Sales	$2,700,000
Variable selling and administrative expenses	200,000
Fixed direct manufacturing expenses	75,000
Fixed indirect manufacturing expenses	110,000
Variable manufacturing expenses	840,000
Fixed direct selling and administrative expenses	350,000
Fixed indirect selling and administrative expenses	55,000

Prepare an income statement for a segment using the contribution margin format; determine effect of elimination of a segment on company income (L.O. 3)

19–3. Given the following data, prepare a schedule that shows contribution margin, contribution to indirect expenses, and net income of the Stitching Department at Parachutes, Inc.

Direct fixed expenses	$109,000
Indirect fixed expenses	86,000
Sales	750,000
Variable expenses	518,400

What would be the effect on the company income if the segment were eliminated?

Allocate expenses
to various
segments using a
specified
allocation base
(L.O. 3)

19–4. Three segments (X, Y, and Z) of Canine Dental Care Company have net sales of $600,000, $360,000, and $120,000, respectively. A decision is made to allocate the pool of $60,000 of administrative expenses of the central administration to the segments, using net sales as the basis for allocation.

a. How much of the $60,000 should be allocated to each segment?

b. If Segment Z is eliminated, how much will be allocated to X and Y?

Calculate ROI,
margin, and
turnover for a
segment
(L.O. 4)

19–5. Two segments (hardware and software) showed the following data for the most recent year:

	Hardware	Software
Contribution to indirect expenses	$ 850,000	$ 600,000
Assets directly used by and identified with the segment	2,500,000	3,000,000
Sales	6,800,000	12,000,000

a. Calculate ROI for each segment in the most direct manner.

b. Calculate ROI using the margin and turnover components.

Determine the
effect on margin,
turnover, and ROI
when the variables
are altered
(L.O. 4)

19–6. Determine the effect of each of the following transactions on the margin, turnover, and ROI of the hardware segment in Exercise 19–5. Consider each change independently of the others.

a. Direct variable expenses were reduced by $33,600. Sales and assets were unaffected.

b. Assets used by the segment were reduced by $504,000, while income and sales were unaffected.

c. An advertising campaign increased sales by $672,000 and income by $168,000. Assets directly used by the segment were unaffected.

Calculate the ROI
in evaluating the
income
performance of a
segment manager
and the rate of
income
contribution of a
segment
(L.O. 5)

19–7. The following data are available for the mortgage department of Save-it Savings & Loan.

Net income of the segment	$ 24,000
Contribution to indirect expenses	65,000
Controllable income	36,000
Total assets related to the segment	300,000
Assets directly used by the segment	180,000
Assets under the *control* of the segment manager	118,750

Determine the ROI for evaluating *(a)* the income performance of the manager of the mortgage department and *(b)* the rate of income contribution of the segment.

Determine RI in
evaluating
segments
(L.O. 5)

19–8. Mobility Inc., manufactures wheelchairs and has three segments: Adults' Wheelchairs, Children's Wheelchairs, and Electric Wheelchairs. Data concerning income and investment follow:

	Adults' Wheelchairs	Children's Wheelchairs	Electric Wheelchairs
Contribution to indirect expenses .	$ 86,000	$ 172,000	$ 230,000
Assets directly used by and identified with the segment . . .	576,000	1,152,000	2,592,000

Assuming that the minimum desired ROI is 10%, calculate the RI of each of the segments. Do the results indicate that any of the segments should be eliminated?

Calculate ROI and RI in evaluating a manager (L.O. 4)

19–9. Assume that for Adults' Wheelchairs in Exercise 19–8, $28,800 of the direct expenses and $72,000 of the segmental assets are not under the control of the segment manager. Top management wishes to evaluate the segment manager's income performance. Calculate the manager's ROI and RI. (Since certain expenses and assets are not controllable by the segment manager, the minimum desired ROI is 15%.)

Compute ROI, margin, and turnover for a segment (L.O. 4)

19–10. Two segments (shovels and wheelbarrows) showed the following data for the most recent year:

	Shovels	Wheelbarrows
Contribution to indirect expenses	$ 120,000	$ 360,000
Assets directly used by and identified with the segment	500,000	1,440,000
Sales	2,400,000	4,320,000

a. Calculate ROI for each segment in the most direct manner.
b. Calculate ROI utilizing the margin and turnover components.

Prepare an income statement for a segment using the contribution margin format; determine effect of elimination of a segment on company income (L.O. 5)

19–11. Given the following data, prepare a schedule that shows contribution margin, contribution to indirect costs, and net income of the segment:

Direct fixed expenses	$ 82,000
Indirect fixed expenses	60,000
Sales	500,000
Variable expenses	308,000

What would be the effect on company earnings if the segment were eliminated?

PROBLEMS

Prepare responsibility reports for various levels of management (L.O. 2)

19–1. You are given the following information relevant to Bogart Company for the year ended December 31, 1995. The company is organized according to functions.

Controllable Expenses	Plant Manager		Vice President of Manufacturing		President	
	Budget	Actual	Budget	Actual	Budget	Actual
Office expense	$ 6,200	$ 9,600	$12,000	$15,800	$ 23,000	$ 16,800
Printing shop.	4,800	4,800				
Iron shop	2,400	2,000				
Toaster shop	18,200	16,800				
Purchasing.			24,000	26,400		
Receiving			12,000	14,400		
Inspection			18,200	16,800		
Vice president of marketing					182,000	168,000
Controller					144,000	120,000
Treasurer					96,000	72,000
Vice president of personnel					48,000	62,000

Required:

Prepare the responsibility accounting reports for the three levels of management—plant manager, vice president of manufacturing, and president.

Evaluate responsibility centers as profit centers and investment centers (L.O. 2)

19–2. Linne Corporation has three production plants (R, S, and T). These plants are treated as responsibility centers. Following is a summary of the results for May 1995:

Plant	Revenues	Expenses	Investment Base (gross assets)
R	$ 450,000	$200,000	$ 4,500,000
S	900,000	300,000	6,750,000
T	1,350,000	500,000	14,400,000

Required:

a. If the plants are treated as profit centers, which plant manager appears to have done the best job?
b. If the plants are treated as investment centers, which plant manager appears to have done the best job? (Assume the plant managers are evaluated in terms of ROI on gross assets.)
c. Do the results of profit center analysis and investment center analysis give different findings? If so, why?

Allocate indirect expenses to illustrate the arbitrary nature of expense allocation (L.O. 3)

19–3. Ski The 90s Fashions allocates all of its administrative expenses to its two segments, Ski Jackets and Ski Pants. Following are selected expense account balances and additional data on which allocations are based:

Expenses (allocation bases)	
Administrative building expense (net sales).	$48,400
Buying expense (net purchases).	43,600
Uncollectible accounts (net sales)	4,000
Depreciation of administrative equipment (net sales)	10,560
Advertising expense (indirect, allocated on basis of relative	
amounts of direct advertising).	43,200
Insurance expense (relative amounts of equipment plus	
average inventory in department)	12,000

Additional data:

	Ski Pants Segment	Ski Jackets Segment	Total
Purchases, net	$121,600	$38,400	$160,000
Sales, net	256,000	64,000	320,000
Equipment, cost	48,000	32,000	80,000
Advertising, cost	12,800	6,400	19,200
Average inventory.	80,000	32,000	112,000

Required:

a. Prepare a schedule showing the amounts of each type of expense allocable to Ski Pants and Ski Jackets using the above data and the bases of allocation.

b. Evaluate and criticize these allocation bases.

Prepare a schedule showing contribution margin and contribution to indirect expenses using contribution margin format; prepare segmental income statements (L.O. 3)

19–4. Clinton, Inc., is a company with two segments, Rice and Wheat. Its revenues and expenses for 1995 follow:

	Rice Segment	Wheat Segment	Total
Net sales	$192,000	$288,000	$480,000
Direct expenses:*			
Cost of goods sold	90,000	198,000	288,000
Selling	27,360	14,400	41,760
Administrative:			
Uncollectible accounts.	6,000	3,600	9,600
Insurance	4,700	2,300	7,000
Interest	960	480	1,440
Indirect expenses (all fixed):			
Selling			36,000
Administrative.			40,400

* All the direct expenses are variable except insurance and interest, which are fixed.

Required:

a. Prepare a schedule showing the contribution margin, the contribution to indirect expenses of each segment, and net income for the company as a whole. Do not allocate indirect expenses to the segments.

b. Assume that indirect selling expenses are to be allocated on the basis of net sales and that indirect administrative expenses are to be allocated on the basis of direct administrative expenses. Prepare a statement (starting with the contribution to indirect expenses) that shows the net income of each segment.

c. Comment on the appropriateness of the *income* amounts shown in *(a)* and *(b)* for determining the income contribution of the segments.

Prepare an income statement for two segments using the contribution margin format; calculate the ROI for (1) the entire company, (2) each segment, and (3) each manager (L.O. 3, 4)

19–5. The following data pertain to the operating revenues and expenses for Odessa Company for 1995:

	Segment Q	Segment R	Total
Sales.	$720,000	$360,000	$1,080,000
Variable expenses.	480,000	192,000	672,000
Direct fixed expenses	50,000	38,000	88,000
Indirect fixed expenses			154,000

Of the direct fixed expenses, $12,000 of those shown for Segment Q and $10,800 of those shown for Segment R were not under the control of that segment's manager.

Regarding the company's total operating assets of $1,800,000, the following facts exist:

	Segment Q	Segment R
Assets directly used by and identified with the segment	$720,000	$360,000
Assets under the control of the segment manager . .	600,000	300,000

Required:

a. Prepare a statement showing the contribution margin of each segment, the contribution to indirect expenses of each segment, and the total income of Odessa Company.

b. Determine the ROI for evaluating (1) the earning power of the entire company, (2) the rate of income contribution of each segment, and (3) the income performance of each segment manager.

c. Comment on the results of *(b)*.

Calculate ROI and RI for each segment and segment manager (L.O. 4, 5)

19–6. Polynesian Adventures, Inc., operates with three segments, Tahiti Adventure, Easter Isle Voyage, and Hawaii Enchantment. Data regarding these segments follow:

	Tahiti Adventure	Easter Isle Voyage	Hawaii Enchantment
Contribution to indirect expenses	$ 324,000	$ 180,000	$144,000
Income controllable by the manager	450,000	270,000	230,400
Assets directly used by and identified with the segment	1,620,000	1,200,000	576,000
Assets under the control of the segment manager	1,584,000	1,100,000	500,000

Required:

a. Calculate the ROI for each segment and each segment manager. Rank the segments and segment managers from highest to lowest.

b. Assume the minimum desired rates of return are 12% for a segment and 20% for a segment manager. Calculate RI for each manager. Rank the segments and segment managers from highest to lowest.

c. Repeat *(b)*, but assume the desired minimum rates of return are 17% for a segment and 25% for a segment manager. Rank the segments and segment managers from highest to lowest.

d. Comment on the rankings achieved.

Determine margin, turnover, and ROI for a segment and the effect on each when the variables are changed (L.O. 4)

19–7. The manager of the Pet Food segment of Condor Corporation is faced with the following data for the year 1995:

Contribution to indirect expenses	$ 1,500,000
Assets directly used by and identified with the segment.	20,000,000
Sales	30,000,000

Required:

a. Determine the margin, turnover, and ROI for the segment in 1995.

b. Determine the effect on margin, turnover, and ROI of the segment in 1996 if each of the following changes were to occur. Consider each one separately, and assume that any items not specifically mentioned remain the same as in 1995:

1. A campaign to control costs resulted in $360,000 of reduced expenses.
2. Certain nonproductive assets were eliminated. As a result, investment decreased by $1,800,000, and expenses decreased by $144,000.
3. An advertising campaign resulted in increasing sales by $7,200,000, cost of goods sold by $5,400,000, and advertising expense by $1,080,000.
4. An investment was made in productive assets costing $1,800,000. As a result, sales increased by $720,000, and expenses increased by $108,000.

Evaluate the desirability of adopting a new project using ROI, margin, and turnover (L.O. 4)

19–8. For the year ended December 31, 1995, Glamorous Bathrooms, Inc., reported the following information for the company as a whole and for one of its segments:

	Glamorous Bathrooms, Inc.	Bathroom Segment		
		Tile Project	*Floor Project*	*Total*
Sales	$6,000,000	$600,000	$300,000	$ 900,000
Income	900,000	300,000	39,000	339,000
Investment . . .	3,000,000	900,000	100,000	1,000,000

Glamorous Bathrooms, Inc., anticipates that the above relationships (ROI, margin, and turnover) will hold true for the upcoming year. The bathroom segment is faced with the possibility of adding a new project in 1996, with the following projected data:

	Jacuzzi Project
Sales	$225,000
Income	58,000
Investment.	187,500

Required:

a. Determine the ROI for Glamorous Bathrooms, the bathroom segment, and for the two projects (tile and floor) separately for the year ended December 31, 1995.

b. Using the above information, determine if the manager of the bathroom segment should add the jacuzzi project if ROI is a deciding factor. What problem may be encountered?

Evaluate the desirability of adopting a new project using RI (L.O. 5)

19–9. Using the data provided in Problem 19–8, determine the RI (1) for each of the three projects and (2) for the bathroom segment with and without the jacuzzi project if the desired ROI is 25% (the return on investment for the company as a whole). Should the jacuzzi project be added if RI is a deciding factor?

BUSINESS DECISION PROBLEM

Allocate unusual expenses to departments; determine controllable and noncontrollable expenses (L.O. 2)

Respond to each of the following situations:

a. The Christmas Factory manufactures Christmas decorations. The company's business is seasonal, and, between January and August, 10 skilled manufacturing employees were laid off. To improve morale, the financial vice president suggested that these 10 employees not be laid off in the future. Instead, the financial vice president suggested that they work in general labor from January to August but still be paid their manufacturing wages of $10 per hour. General labor personnel earn $6.80 per hour. What are the implications of this plan for the assignment of costs to the various segments of the business?

b. Blankenship Company builds sail boats. Willie is in charge of the construction department. Among other responsibilities, Willie hires and supervises the carpenters and other workers who build the boats. Blankenship Company does not do its own paint work. The painting is done by subcontractors hired by Wayland of the procurement department.

Twenty boats have been completed and are ready to be painted. Wayland hired Nelson Company to paint the boats. On the day the painting was to begin, Nelson Company went out of business. Consequently, the painting was delayed six weeks while Wayland hired a new subcontractor. Which department should be charged with the cost of the delay in the painting? Why?

c. James Jones is supervisor of Department 007 of Bond Company. The annual budget for the department is as follows:

Annual Budget for Department 007	
Small tools	$ 7,750
Set up	8,500
Direct labor	8,250
Direct materials	15,000
Supplies	4,750
Supervision	32,500
Property taxes	3,750
Property insurance	650
Depreciation, machinery	1,500
Depreciation, building	1,500
Total	$84,150

Jones's salary of $20,000 is included in supervision. The remaining $12,500 in supervision is the salary of the assistant supervisor who is directly responsible to Jones. Identify the budget items that are controllable by Jones.

ANSWERS TO SELF-TEST

True-False

1. *False.* The full-cost approach includes all revenues and expense items that can be traced directly or allocated indirectly to a particular manager.

2. *False.* An appropriate goal of an expense center is the *long-run* minimization of expenses.

3. *True.* The supervisor's salary would be a direct cost of the segment but not controllable at that level.

4. *False.* Segments should be evaluated using their revenues and *direct* expenses.

5. *True.* The income and investment definitions when calculating RI for a segment are contribution to indirect expenses and assets directly used by and identified with the segment.

Multiple-Choice

1. *d.* Any of these bases—current replacement cost, original cost, or original cost less accumulated depreciation—could be used.

2. *c.* ROI would increase if operating expenses were reduced, all other things remaining constant.

3. *a.*

$$\text{ROI} = \frac{\text{Income}}{\text{Sales}} \times \frac{\text{Sales}}{\text{Investment}}$$

$$= \frac{\$60,000}{\$600,000} \times \frac{\$600,000}{\$300,000}$$

$$= 0.10 \times 2$$

$$= 20\%$$

4. *a.* Comparison with other segments and managers, comparison with past performance, and comparison with the current budget are used to evaluate the performance of a segment manager.

5. *d.*

	Segment 1	Segment 2	Segment 3
Income	$ 100,000	$ 750,000	$ 400,000
Investment . .	2,000,000	5,000,000	2,000,000
ROI	5%	15%	20%
Desired minimum ROI (10%) .	200,000	500,000	200,000
RI	$ (100,000)	$ 250,000	$ 200,000

Consider dropping Segment 1 because RI is below minimum desired RI of 10%.

20 CAPITAL BUDGETING: LONG-RANGE PLANNING

LEARNING OBJECTIVES

After studying this chapter, you should be able to:

1. Define capital budgeting and explain the effects of making poor capital budgeting decisions.
2. Determine the net cash inflows, after taxes, for both an asset addition and an asset replacement.
3. Evaluate projects using the payback period.
4. Evaluate projects using the unadjusted rate of return.
5. Evaluate projects using the net present value.
6. Evaluate projects using the profitability index.
7. Evaluate projects using the time-adjusted rate of return.
8. Determine, for project evaluation, the effect of an investment in working capital.

In your personal life, you make many short-run decisions (such as where to go on vacation this year) and some long-run decisions (such as whether to buy a home). The quality of these decisions determines to a large extent the success of your life. Businesses also face short-run and long-run decisions.

In Chapters 15 and 16, you studied how accountants help managers make short-run decisions, such as what prices to charge for their products this year. Accountants also play an important role in advising management on long-range decisions, such as investing in new buildings and equipment, that will benefit the company for many years. Long-run decisions have a great impact on the long-run success of a company. Incorrect long-run decisions can threaten the survival of a company.

Whereas short-run decisions involve items such as selling prices, costs, volume, and profits in the current year, long-run decisions involve investments in capital assets, such as buildings and equipment, affecting the current year and many future years. Planning for these investments is called *capital budgeting*.

This chapter first discusses the general concepts behind capital budgeting. Then, the chapter discusses and illustrates four different methods for selecting the best alternatives among capital projects. Two of these methods involve the use of present value concepts. Finally, the chapter stresses the importance of the postaudit review of capital project decisions.

CAPITAL BUDGETING DEFINED

Objective 1
Define capital budgeting and explain the effects of making poor capital budgeting decisions

Capital budgeting is the process of considering alternative capital projects and selecting those alternatives that provide the most profitable return on available funds, within the framework of company goals and objectives. A **capital project** is any available alternative to purchase, build, lease, or renovate buildings, equipment, or other long-range major items of property. The alternative selected usually involves large sums of money and results in a large increase in fixed assets for several years. Once a company builds a plant or undertakes some other capital expenditure, the company becomes less flexible regarding future plans.

Poor capital-budgeting decisions can be costly because of the large sums of money and relatively long time periods involved. A company that implements a poor capital-budgeting decision can lose all or part of the funds originally invested in the project and not realize the expected benefits. In addition, if the company has to stop a project, it wastes time and resources spent in selecting and implementing a new course of action. Poor capital-budgeting decisions may also harm the company's competitive position because the company will not have the most efficient productive assets needed to compete in world markets.

Investing funds in a poor alternative can also create other problems. Workers who were hired for the project might be laid off if the project fails, thus creating unemployment and morale problems. Many of the fixed costs will still remain even if a plant is closed or is not producing. The company will have wasted its advertising efforts. Stock prices could be affected by the decline in income.

On the other hand, failure to invest enough funds in a good project can also be costly. Ford's Mustang is an excellent example of such an error. If Ford had correctly projected the Mustang's popularity at the time of the original capital-budgeting decision, the company would have expended more funds on the project. Because the company did not commit enough funds, Ford found itself short on production capacity. This shortage caused lost and postponed sales of the automobile.

Finally, the amount of funds available for investment is limited. Thus, once a capital investment decision is made, alternative investment opportunities are normally lost. The income (net benefits) lost by rejecting the best alternative investment is the **opportunity cost** of a given project.

For all these reasons, companies must be very careful in their analysis of capital projects. Capital expenditures do not occur as often as ordinary expenditures (such as payroll or inventory purchases), but they involve substantial sums of money that are then committed for a long period of time. Therefore, companies use more formal methods to evaluate capital expenditure decisions than are necessary for ordinary purchase decisions.

PROJECT SELECTION: A GENERAL VIEW

Making capital-budgeting decisions involves analyzing cash inflows and outflows. This section shows you how to calculate the benefits and costs of capital-budgeting decisions. Since money has time value, these benefits and costs are adjusted for time under the last two methods covered in the chapter.

Time Value of Money

Money received today is worth more than the same amount of money received at a future date, such as a year from now. This statement is true because of the *time value of money*. Money has time value because of investment opportunities, not because of inflation. For example, $100 today is worth more than $100 to be received one year from today because the $100 received today may be invested and will grow to some amount greater than $100 in one year. Future value and present value concepts are extremely important in assessing the desirability of long-term investments (capital budgeting).

Net Cash Inflow

Objective 2
Determine the net cash inflows, after taxes, for both an asset addition and an asset replacement

The **net cash inflow** (as used in capital budgeting) is the net cash benefit expected from a project in a period. The net cash inflow is the difference between the cash inflows and cash outflows during each period for a proposed project.

Asset Acquisition.   Assume, for example, that a company is considering the purchase of new equipment for $120,000. The equipment is expected (1) to have a useful life of 15 years and no salvage value, and (2) to produce cash inflows (revenues) of $75,000 per year and cash outflows (costs) of $50,000 per year. Ignoring depreciation and taxes, the annual net cash inflow is:

Cash inflows	$75,000
Cash outflows	50,000
Net cash inflow	$25,000

Depreciation and Taxes.   The computation of the net cash inflow usually includes the effects of depreciation and taxes. Although depreciation does not involve a cash outflow, it is deductible in arriving at taxable income. Thus, depreciation reduces the amount of cash outflow for income taxes. This reduction is a tax savings made possible by a depreciation *tax shield*. A **tax shield** is the total amount by which a company reduces taxable income due to the deductibility of an item. Thus, if depreciation is $8,000, the tax shield is $8,000. To simplify the illustration, we assume the use of straight-line depreciation for tax purposes throughout the chapter. Straight-line depreciation can be elected for tax purposes, even under the new tax law.

The tax shield results in a tax savings. The amount of the tax savings can be found by multiplying the tax rate by the amount of the depreciation tax shield. The formula is:

$$\text{Tax rate} \times \text{Depreciation tax shield} = \text{Tax savings}$$

Using the data in the previous example and assuming straight-line depreciation of $8,000 per year and a 40% tax rate, the amount of the tax savings is $3,200 (40% × $8,000 depreciation tax shield). Now, considering taxes and depreciation, the annual net cash inflow from the $120,000 of equipment is computed as follows:

	Change in Net Income	Change in Cash Flow
Cash inflows	$75,000	$75,000
Cash outflows	50,000	50,000
Net cash inflow before taxes	$25,000	$25,000
Depreciation	8,000	
Income before income taxes	$17,000	
Deduct: Income tax at 40%	6,800	6,800
Net income after taxes	$10,200	
Net cash inflow (after taxes).		$18,200

If the company had no depreciation tax shield, income tax expense would have been $10,000 ($25,000 × 40%), and the net after-tax cash inflow from the investment would have been $15,000 ($25,000 − $10,000), or $25,000 × (1 − 40%). The depreciation tax shield, however, reduces income tax expense by $3,200 ($8,000 × 40%) and increases the investment's after-tax net cash inflow by the same amount. Therefore, the following formula can also be used to determine the after-tax net cash inflow from an investment:

$$\begin{array}{c} \text{Net cash} \\ \text{inflow} \\ \text{after taxes} \end{array} = \left[\begin{array}{c} \text{Net cash} \\ \text{inflow} \\ \text{before taxes} \end{array} \times \left(1 - \frac{\text{Tax}}{\text{rate}} \right) \right] + \left[\begin{array}{c} \text{Depreciation} \\ \text{expense} \end{array} \times \frac{\text{Tax}}{\text{rate}} \right]$$

Net cash inflow after taxes (ignoring depreciation)	Tax savings attributable to depreciation tax shield

$$= [\$25,000 \times (1 - .4)] + [\$8,000 \times .4] = \$18,200$$

Asset Replacement.   Sometimes a company must decide whether or not it should replace existing plant assets. Such replacement decisions often occur when faster and more efficient machinery and equipment appear on the market.

The computation of the net cash inflow is more complex for a replacement decision than for an acquisition decision because the company must consider cash inflows and outflows for *two* items—the asset being replaced and the new asset. To illustrate, assume that a company operates two machines it purchased four years ago at a cost of $18,000 each. The estimated useful life of each machine was 12 years (with no salvage value). Each machine will produce 40,000 units of product per year. The annual cash operating expenses (labor, repairs, etc.) for the two machines together total $14,000.

After the company has used the old machines for four years, a new machine becomes available. The company can buy the new machine for $28,000. The machine has an estimated useful life of eight years (with no salvage value). The new machine will produce 80,000 units annually and will cause annual cash operating expenses of $10,000. The $4,000 reduction in operating expenses ($14,000 for the old machines − $10,000 for the new machine) is treated as a $4,000 increase in net cash inflow (savings) before taxes.

To acquire the new machine, the company must pay a $28,000 cash outflow in the first year. In addition to this initial outlay, the annual net cash inflow from replacement is computed as follows:

$$\begin{array}{c} \text{Net cash} \\ \text{inflow} \\ \text{after taxes} \end{array} = \left[\begin{array}{c} \text{Annual net cash} \\ \text{inflows (savings)} \\ \text{before taxes} \end{array} \times \left(1 - \frac{\text{Tax}}{\text{rate}} \right) \right] + \left[\begin{array}{c} \text{Additional} \\ \text{annual} \\ \text{depreciation} \\ \text{expense} \end{array} \times \frac{\text{Tax}}{\text{rate}} \right]$$

Using the data given above, the following table shows how you can use this formula to find the net cash flow after taxes:

Annual cash operating expenses:		
Old machines		$14,000
New machine		10,000
Annual net cash inflow (savings) before taxes		$ 4,000
1 − Tax rate.		×60%
Annual net cash inflow (savings)* after taxes ignoring depreciation (1).		$ 2,400
Annual depreciation expense:		
Old machines	$3,000	
New machine	3,500	
Additional annual depreciation expense.	$ 500	
Tax rate.	×40%	
Tax savings from additional depreciation (2)		200
Net cash inflow after taxes (1) + (2)		$ 2,600

* Cash savings are considered to be cash inflows.

In formula format, the calculation is:

$$\frac{\text{Net cash inflow}}{\text{after taxes}} = [\$4,000 \times (1 - .4)] + [\$500 \times .4] = \$2,600$$

Notice that the above figures concentrated only on the differences in costs for each of the two alternatives. Two other items are also relevant to the decision. First, the purchase of the new machine would create a $28,000 cash outflow immediately after acquisition. Second, if the two old machines could be sold, the selling price or salvage value of the old machines will create a cash inflow in the period of disposal. Also, the above example used straight-line depreciation. Compared to straight-line depreciation, tax laws generally allow larger amounts of depreciation in earlier years and smaller amounts in the later years of the asset's life. In view of the time value of money, taxpayers prefer to have larger deductions earlier and smaller deductions later, compared to equal deductions throughout the depreciation period.

Out-of-Pocket and Sunk Costs.   We should distinguish between out-of-pocket costs and sunk costs for capital-budgeting decisions. An **out-of-pocket cost** is a cost requiring a future outlay of resources, usually cash. A company can avoid or change the amount of out-of-pocket costs. Future labor and repair costs are examples of out-of-pocket costs.

Sunk costs are costs that have already been incurred. Nothing can be done about sunk costs at the present time; they cannot be avoided or changed in amount. As soon as you purchase an automobile, the price paid for the car becomes a sunk cost. (Before that moment it was an out-of-pocket cost.) The amount of that past outlay cannot be changed regardless of whether the machine is scrapped or used. Thus, depreciation is a sunk cost because it represents a past cash outlay. Depletion and amortization of assets such as ore deposits and patents are also sunk costs.

A sunk cost is a past cost, while an out-of-pocket cost is a future cost. Only the out-of-pocket costs (the future cash outlays) are relevant to capital-budgeting decisions. Sunk costs are not relevant, except for any effect they have on the cash outflow for taxes.

Initial Cost and Salvage Value.   Any cash outflows necessary to acquire an asset and place it in a position and condition for use are part of the **initial cost of the asset.** If an investment has a salvage value, a company should treat that value as a cash inflow in the year of the asset's disposal.

The Cost of Capital.   The cost of capital is important in project selection. Certainly, any acceptable proposal should offer a return that exceeds the cost of the funds used to finance it. **Cost of capital,** usually expressed as a rate, is the cost of all sources of capital (debt and equity) employed by a company. For convenience, most current liabilities, such as accounts payable and income taxes payable, are treated as having no cost. Every other item on the right (equity) side of the balance sheet has a cost. The subject of determining the cost of capital is a controversial topic in the literature of accounting and finance and will not be discussed here. The chapter gives assumed rates for the cost of capital.

The next four sections of this chapter examine specific techniques used to evaluate capital projects. The first of these techniques is the payback period.

PROJECT SELECTION: PAYBACK PERIOD

Objective 3
Evaluate projects
using the payback
period

The **payback period** is the period of time it takes for the cumulative sum of the annual net cash inflows from a project to equal the initial cash outlay. In effect, the payback period answers the question: How long will the capital project take to recover, or pay back, the initial investment? If the net cash inflows each year are a constant amount, the formula for the payback period is:

$$\text{Payback period} = \frac{\text{Initial cash outlay}}{\substack{\text{Annual net cash inflow} \\ \text{(or benefit) after taxes}}}$$

The payback period for the two assets discussed previously can be computed as follows. The outlay of $120,000 for the purchase of equipment discussed previously will create an annual net cash inflow after taxes of $18,200, so the payback period is 6.6 years, computed as follows:

$$\text{Payback period} = \frac{\$120,000}{\$18,200} = 6.6 \text{ years}$$

The payback period for the replacement machine mentioned above, with a $28,000 cash outflow in the first year and an annual net cash inflow of $2,600, is 10.8 years, computed as follows:

$$\text{Payback period} = \frac{\$28,000}{\$2,600} = 10.8 \text{ years}$$

The initial cash outlay should be net of any cash inflow from disposing of the old machines. The two old replaced machines are assumed to have no salvage value, so the initial cash outlay is the $28,000 paid for the new machine.

Remember that the payback period indicates how long the machine will take to pay for itself. The replacement machine being considered has a payback period of 10.8 years, but a useful life of only 8 years. Therefore, since the investment cannot pay for itself within its useful life, the machine should *not* be purchased to replace the two old machines.

In each of the two examples above, the projected net cash inflow per year was uniform. When the annual returns are uneven, a cumulative calculation must be used to determine payback period, as shown in the following situation.

Neil Company is considering a capital investment project that costs $40,000 and is expected to last 10 years. The projected annual net cash inflows are:

Year	Investment	Annual Net Cash Inflow	Cumulative Net Cash Inflows
0	$40,000	—	—
1	—	$8,000	$ 8,000
2	—	6,000	14,000
3	—	7,000	21,000
4	—	5,000	26,000
5	—	8,000	34,000
6	—	6,000	**40,000**
7	—	3,000	43,000
8	—	2,000	45,000
9	—	3,000	48,000
10	—	1,000	49,000

The payback period in this example is six years—the time it takes to recover the $40,000 original investment.

When management uses the payback period analysis to evaluate investment proposals, it may use one of the following rules to decide on project selection:

1. Select the investments with the shortest payback periods.
2. Select only those investments that have a payback period of less than a specified number of years.

Both decision rules focus on the rapid return of invested capital. If capital can be recovered rapidly, it can be invested in other projects, thereby generating more cash inflows or profits.

Companies use payback period analysis extensively in capital-budgeting decisions due to its simplicity and because cash flow is critical in many businesses. However, this type of analysis has two important limitations:

1. Payback period analysis ignores the time period beyond the payback period. For example, assume Allen Company is considering two alternative investments; each requires an initial outlay of $30,000. Proposal Y will return $6,000 per year for five years, while proposal Z will return $5,000 per year for eight years. The payback period for Y is five years ($30,000/$6,000) and for Z is six years ($30,000/$5,000). However, if the company's goal is to maximize income, it should select proposal Z rather than proposal Y, even though Z has a longer payback period. Proposal Z will return a total of $40,000, while Y simply will recover the initial $30,000 outlay.

2. Payback analysis also ignores the time value of money. For example, assume the following net cash inflows are expected in the first three years from two capital projects:

	Net Cash Inflows	
	Project A	Project B
First year	$15,000	$ 9,000
Second year	12,000	12,000
Third year	9,000	15,000
Total	$36,000	$36,000

Assume that both projects have the same net cash inflow each year beyond the third year. If the cost of each project is $36,000, then each has a payback period of three years. However, common sense indicates that the projects are not equal because money has time value and can be reinvested to increase income. The company receives cash sooner under project A, so it is the preferable project.

PROJECT SELECTION: UNADJUSTED RATE OF RETURN

Objective 4
Evaluate projects using the unadjusted rate of return

Another method sometimes used in evaluating investment projects is the **unadjusted rate of return,** which is an approximation of the rate of return on investment of a capital project. The unadjusted rate of return is computed by dividing the average annual income after taxes by the average amount of investment in the project. The average annual net income after taxes is equal to the sum of the annual net income after taxes for each year divided by the number of years of the project. The **average investment** is the (Beginning balance + Ending balance)/2. The beginning balance is the original investment, and the ending balance is the salvage value. The formula for the unadjusted rate of return is:

$$\frac{\text{Unadjusted}}{\text{rate of return}} = \frac{\text{Average annual income after taxes}}{\text{Average amount of investment}}$$

Notice that the calculation uses the annual *income* rather than net cash inflow.[1]

To illustrate the use of the unadjusted rate of return, assume Thomas Company is considering two capital project proposals; both have useful lives of three years. The company does not have enough funds to undertake both projects. Information relating to the projects is shown below:

Proposal	Initial Cost	Salvage Value	Average Annual Before-Tax Net Cash Inflow	Average Annual Depreciation
1	$76,000	$4,000	$45,000	$24,000
2	95,000	5,000	55,000	30,000

Assuming a 40% tax rate, we can determine the unadjusted rate of return for each project as:

		Proposal 1	Proposal 2
Average investment:			
(original outlay + salvage value) ÷ 2 . . . . (1)		$40,000	$50,000
Annual net cash inflow (before income taxes).		$45,000	$55,000
Annual depreciation.		24,000	30,000
Annual income (before income taxes)		$21,000	$25,000
Deduct: Income taxes at 40%		8,400	10,000
Average annual net income from investment . . . . . . (2)		$12,600	$15,000
Rate of return (2) ÷ (1)		31.5%	30%

From these calculations, if Thomas Company makes an investment decision solely on the basis of unadjusted rate of return, proposal 1 would be selected since it has a higher rate of return.

The unadjusted rate of return can also be computed with the following formula:

$$\frac{\text{Rate of}}{\text{return}} = \frac{\left(\begin{array}{c}\text{Average annual before-}\\\text{tax net cash inflow}\end{array} - \begin{array}{c}\text{Average annual}\\\text{depreciation}\end{array}\right) \times \left(1 - \begin{array}{c}\text{Tax}\\\text{rate}\end{array}\right)}{\text{Average investment}}$$

For proposal 1 above, the computation is as follows:

---

[1] Some formulas use the initial investment as the denominator instead of the average investment. However, since the investment funds are consumed in producing revenues, the average investment should be used.

$$\text{Rate of return} = \frac{(\$45,000 - \$24,000) \times (1 - 0.4)}{[(\$76,000 + \$4,000)/2]} = \frac{(\$21,000) \times (0.6)}{\$40,000}$$

$$= \frac{\$12,600}{\$40,000} = 31.5\%$$

For proposal 2, the computation is as follows:

$$\text{Rate of return} = \frac{(\$55,000 - \$30,000) \times (1 - 0.4)}{[(\$95,000 + \$5,000)/2]} = \frac{(\$25,000) \times (0.6)}{\$50,000}$$

$$= \frac{\$15,000}{\$50,000} = 30\%$$

Sometimes information is provided on the average annual after-tax net cash inflow. Average annual after-tax net cash inflow is equal to average annual before-tax cash inflow minus taxes. Given this information, the depreciation can be deducted to arrive at average net income. For instance, for proposal 2 above, average net income would be computed as follows:

After-tax net cash inflow ($55,000 − $10,000)	$45,000
Less: Depreciation.	30,000
Average net income	$15,000

The unadjusted rate of return, like payback period analysis, has several limitations:

1. The rate of return does not consider the length of time over which the return will be earned.
2. The rate allows a sunk cost, depreciation, to enter into the calculation. Since depreciation can be calculated in so many different ways, the rate of return can be manipulated by simply changing the method of depreciation used for the project.
3. The analysis does not consider the timing of cash flows. Thus, the time value of money is ignored.

Unlike the two project selection methods just illustrated—payback and unadjusted rate of return—the remaining two methods—net present value and time-adjusted rate of return—take into account the time value of money in the analysis. In both of these methods, we assume that all net cash inflows occur at the end of the year. This assumption is often used in capital-budgeting analysis and makes the calculation of present values less complicated than if we assume the cash flows occurred at some other time.

PROJECT SELECTION: NET PRESENT VALUE METHOD AND THE PROFITABILITY INDEX

In this section, you will first learn to calculate the net present value of capital projects. Then you will learn how companies can use the profitability index to evaluate projects with different initial outlays. Thus, the profitability index is a refinement of the net present value method.

Net Present Value Method

Objective 5
Evaluate projects
using the net
present value

The *net present value* method uses the company's required minimum rate of return as a discount rate and discounts all expected after-tax cash inflows and outflows from the proposed investment back to their present values. The **net present value** of the proposed investment is the difference between the present value of the annual net cash inflows and the present value of the required cash outflows.

In many projects, the only cash outflow is the initial investment, and since it occurs immediately, the initial investment does not need to be discounted. Therefore, in such projects, a company may compute the net present value of the proposed project as the present value of the annual net cash inflows minus the initial investment. Other types of projects require that additional investments, like a major repair, be made at later dates in the life of the project. In those cases, the company must discount the cash outflows to their present value before comparing them to the present value of the net cash inflows.

A major issue in acknowledging the time value of money in the net present value method is determining an appropriate discount rate to use in computing the present value of cash flows. Management requires some minimum rate of return on its investments. This rate should be the company's cost of capital, but that rate is difficult to determine. Therefore, under the net present value method, management often selects a target rate that it believes to be at or above the company's cost of capital, and then that rate is used as a basis for present value calculations.

To illustrate the net present value method, assume that Morris Company is considering a capital investment project that will cost $25,000. Morris expects net cash inflows after taxes for the next four years to be $8,000, $7,500, $8,000, and $7,500, respectively. Management requires a minimum rate of return of 14% and wants to know if the project is acceptable. The analysis at the top of the next page is developed using the tables in Appendix E at the end of this text.

Since the present value of the net cash inflows, $22,630, is less than the initial outlay of $25,000, the project is not acceptable. The net present value for the project is equal to the present value of its net cash inflows less the present value of its cost (the investment amount), which in this instance is −$2,370, calculated as ($22,630 − $25,000).

When a company uses the net present value method to screen alternative

	Annual Net Cash Inflow (after taxes)	Present Value of $1 at 14% (from Table E.3)	Total Present Value
First year	$8,000	0.87719	$ 7,018
Second year.	7,500	0.76947	5,771
Third year	8,000	0.67497	5,400
Fourth year	7,500	0.59208	4,441
Present value of net cash inflows			$22,630
Cost of investment.			25,000
Net present value			($ 2,370)

projects, it considers the project with the higher net present value to be more desirable. In general, a proposed capital investment is acceptable if it has a positive net present value. In the previous example, if the expected net cash inflows from the investment had been $10,000 per year for four years, the present value of the benefits would have been (from Table E.4 in Appendix E):

$$\$10,000 \times 2.91371 = \$29,137$$

This calculation yields a net present value of $4,137, or ($29,137 − $25,000). Since the net present value is positive, the investment proposal is acceptable. However, a competing project may have an even higher net present value.

When comparing investment projects costing different amounts, the net present value method does not provide a valid means by which to rank the projects in order of desirability assuming limited financial resources. A profitability index provides this additional information to management.

Profitability Index

Objective 6 Evaluate projects using the profitability index

A **profitability index** is the ratio of the present value of the expected net cash benefits (after taxes) divided by the initial cash outlay (or present value of cash outlays if future outlays are required). The profitability index formula is:

$$\frac{\text{Profitability}}{\text{index}} = \frac{\text{Present value of net cash inflows after taxes}}{\text{Initial outlay (or present value of cash outlays if future outlays are required)}}$$

Management should only consider those proposals having a profitability index greater than or equal to 1.00. Proposals with a profitability index of less than 1.00 will not yield the minimum rate of return because the present value of the projected cash inflows will be less than the initial outlay (or present value of cash outlays).

To illustrate use of the profitability index, assume that a company is considering two alternative capital outlay proposals that have the following initial outlays and expected net cash inflows after taxes:

	Proposal X	Proposal Y
Initial outlay	$7,000	$9,500
Expected net cash inflow (after taxes):		
Year 1.	$5,000	$9,000
Year 2.	4,000	6,000
Year 3.	6,000	3,000

Management's minimum desired rate of return is 20%.

The net present values and profitability indexes can be computed as follows (using Table E.3 in Appendix E):

	Present Value	
	Proposal X	Proposal Y
Year 1 (net cash inflow in year 1 × 0.83333) . . .	$ 4,167	$ 7,500
Year 2 (net cash inflow in year 2 × 0.69444) . . .	2,778	4,167
Year 3 (net cash inflow in year 3 × 0.57870) . . .	3,472	1,736
Present value of net cash inflows	$10,417	$13,403
Initial outlay	7,000	9,500
Net present value.	$ 3,417	$ 3,903

	Proposal X	Proposal Y
Profitability index.	$\frac{\$10,417}{\$7,000} = 1.49$	$\frac{\$13,403}{\$9,500} = 1.41$

When comparing net present values, proposal Y appears to be more favorable than proposal X because its net present value is higher. However, after computing the profitability indexes, proposal X is a more desirable investment because it has a higher profitability index. The higher the profitability index, the more profitable the project per dollar of investment. Proposal X is earning a higher rate of return on a smaller investment than proposal Y.

Another technique for evaluating capital projects that accounts for the time value of money is the time-adjusted rate of return method. The next section discusses this method.

PROJECT SELECTION: THE TIME-ADJUSTED RATE OF RETURN (OR INTERNAL RATE OF RETURN)

Objective 7
Evaluate projects using the time-adjusted rate of return

The **time-adjusted rate of return,** also called the **internal rate of return,** equates the present value of expected after-tax net cash inflows from an investment with the cost of the investment by finding the rate at which the net present value of the project is zero. If the time-adjusted rate of return

USES OF CAPITAL BUDGETING PRACTICES

Studies of capital budgeting practices show an increasing use of discounted cash flow methods in making decisions to invest in corporate assets.

A recent survey asked company managers which methods they used for several categories of investment decisions, including replacement of existing assets, expansion into new operations, investment in high technology projects, and investment in socially desirable projects. The techniques were discounted cash flow analysis (which includes both the net present value method and the time-adjusted rate of return method), unadjusted rate of return, payback and "urgency" of the need for investment.

Many companies use multiple methods, but only the primary method for each investment category was reported by the authors. Finally, respondents were asked to indicate which technique they used in each of the years 1980, 1984, and 1988.

The table at the right shows the percentage response for the 100 companies providing usable responses.

These results show an increasing use of discounted cash flow analysis. For investing in socially desirable projects, urgency of the need, not discounted cash flow is the primary method for determining in which projects to invest.

SOURCE: Based on the article by Thomas Klammer, Bruce Koch, and Neil Wilner, "Capital Budgeting Practices—A Survey of Corporate Use," *Journal of Management Accounting Research*, Fall 1991, pp. 113–30.

	1988	1984	1980
Category of investment:			
Replacement of existing assets:			
Discounted cash flow analysis	60%	57%	47%
Unadjusted rate of return	4	2	7
Payback	5	9	10
Urgency	23	21	24
Other or project not analyzed	8	11	12
	100%	100%	100%
Expansion—new operations:			
Discounted cash flow analysis	87%	81%	70%
Unadjusted rate of return	4	5	10
Payback	4	6	9
Urgency	1	2	5
Other or project not analyzed	4	6	6
	100%	100%	100%
Investment in high technology projects:			
Discounted cash flow analysis	75%	68%	60%
Unadjusted rate of return	1	1	4
Payback	8	11	14
Urgency	10	11	11
Other or project not analyzed	6	9	11
	100%	100%	100%
Investment in socially desirable projects:			
Discounted cash flow analysis	16%	13%	14%
Unadjusted rate of return	1	1	2
Payback	2	2	2
Urgency	54	55	54
Other or project not analyzed	27	29	28
	100%	100%	100%

equals or exceeds the cost of capital or target rate of return, then the investment should be considered further. However, if the proposal's time-adjusted
rate of return is less than the minimum rate, the company should reject the
proposal. **Ignoring other considerations, the higher the time-adjusted rate of
return, the more desirable the project.**

Calculators, computers, spreadsheets, or present value tables can be
used to compute the time-adjusted rate of return. To illustrate the use of
present value tables, assume Young Company is considering a $90,000 in-
vestment that is expected to last 25 years with no salvage value. The investment will yield a $15,000 annual after-tax net cash inflow. This $15,000 is
called an **annuity,** which is a series of equal cash inflows or outflows.

The first step in computing the rate of return is to determine the payback
period. In this case, the payback period is six years ($90,000 ÷ $15,000).
Next, examine Table E.4 in Appendix E (present value of an annuity) to find
the present value factor that is nearest in amount to the payback period of 6.
Since the investment is expected to yield returns for 25 years, look at that
row in the table. In that row, the factor nearest to 6 is 5.92745, which appears
under the 16.5% interest column. If the annual return of $15,000 is multiplied
by the 5.92745 factor, the result is $88,912, which is just below the $90,000
cost of the project. Thus, the actual rate of return is slightly less than 16.5%.
The rate of return is less than 16.5% but more than 16% because as interest
rates increase, present values decrease since less investment is needed to
generate the same income.

The above example involves uniform net cash inflows from year to year.
But what happens when net cash inflows are not uniform? In such instances,
a trial and error procedure is necessary if present value tables are used. For
example, assume that a company is considering a $200,000 project that will
last four years and will yield the following returns:

Year	Net Cash Inflow (after taxes)
1	$ 20,000
2	40,000
3	80,000
4	150,000
Total	$290,000

The average annual cash inflow is $290,000 ÷ 4 = $72,500. Based on this
average net cash inflow, the payback period is $200,000 ÷ $72,500 = 2.76
years. Looking in the four-year row of Table E.4 in Appendix E, we find that
the factor 2.77048 is nearest to the payback period of 2.76. In this case,
however, cash flows are not uniform. The largest returns will occur in the
later years of the asset's life. Since the early returns have the largest present
value, the rate of return is likely to be less than the 16.5% rate that corre-

sponds to the present value factor 2.77048. If the returns had been greater during the earlier years of the asset's life, the correct rate of return would have been higher than 16.5%. To find the specific discount rate that yields a present value closest to the initial outlay of $200,000, several interest rates less than 16% are tried out. The rate of return is found by trial and error. The following computation reveals the rate to be slightly higher than 12%:

Year	Return	Present Value Factor at 12%	Present Value of Net Cash Inflows
1	$ 20,000	0.89286	$ 17,857
2	40,000	0.79719	31,888
3	80,000	0.71178	56,942
4	150,000	0.63553	95,330
			$202,017

Since the cost of capital is not a precise percentage, some financial theorists argue that the time-adjusted rate of return method is preferable to the net present value method. Under the time-adjusted rate of return method, the cost of capital is used only as a *cutoff point* in deciding which projects are acceptable for more consideration.

No matter which time value of money concept is considered "better," these methods are both theoretically superior to the payback period and unadjusted rate of return methods. However, the time value of money methods are more difficult to compute unless you use a business calculator or a microcomputer spreadsheet program. In reality, no single method should be used by itself to make capital-budgeting decisions. Managers should consider all aspects of the investment, including such nonquantitative factors as employee morale (layoff of workers due to higher efficiency of a new machine) and company flexibility (versatility of production of one machine over another). The company commits itself to its investment in a capital project for a long period of time and should use the best selection techniques and judgment available.

Too often, in capital project selection decisions, investments in working capital are ignored. The next section shows how to incorporate this factor into the analysis.

INVESTMENTS IN WORKING CAPITAL

*Objective 8
Determine, for
project evaluation,
the effect of an
investment in
working capital*

An investment in a capital asset usually must be supported by an investment in working capital, such as accounts receivable and inventory. For example, a company often expects an investment in a capital project to increase sales. Increased sales usually bring about an increase in accounts receivable from customers and an increase in inventory to support the higher sales level. The increases in current assets—accounts receivable and inventory—are investments in working capital that the company usually recovers in full at the end of a capital project's life. Companies should consider such working capital investments in capital-budgeting decisions.

To illustrate, assume that a company is considering a capital project that will involve a $50,000 investment in machinery and a $40,000 investment in working capital. The machine, which will be used to produce a new product, has a useful life of eight years and no salvage value. The company estimates the annual cash inflows (before taxes) at $25,000, with annual cash outflows (before taxes) of $5,000. The annual net cash inflow from the project is computed (assuming straight-line depreciation and a 40% tax rate):

Cash inflows.	$25,000
Cash outflows	5,000
Net cash inflow before taxes	$20,000
1 − Tax rate	×60%
Net cash inflow after taxes (ignoring depreciation) (1)	$12,000
Depreciation tax shield ($50,000 ÷ 8 years)	$6,250
Income tax rate	×40%
Depreciation tax savings (2)	$ 2,500
Annual net cash inflow, years 1–8 (1) + (2)	$14,500

The annual net cash inflow from the machine is $14,500 each year for eight years. However, we must consider the working capital investment. First, the investment of $40,000 in working capital at the start of the project is an additional outlay that must be made when the project is started. The $40,000 will be tied up every year until the project is finished, or in this case, until the end of the life of the machine. At that point, the working capital will be released, and the $40,000 can be used for other investments. Therefore, the $40,000 is a cash outlay at the start of the project and a cash inflow at the end of the project.

The net present value of the project is computed as follows (assuming a 14% minimum desired rate of return):

Net cash inflow, years 1–8 ($14,500 × 4.63886)	$67,263
Recovery of investment in working capital ($40,000 × 0.35056)	14,022
Present value of net cash inflows.	$81,285
Initial cash outlay ($50,000 + $40,000)	90,000
Net present value	$ (8,715)

The discount factor for the cash inflows, 4.63886, comes from Table E.4 in Appendix E, since the cash inflows in this example are a series of equal payments—an annuity. The recovery of the investment in working capital is assumed to represent a single lump sum that is received at the end of the project's life of eight years. As such, it is discounted using a factor (0.35056) that comes from Table E.3 (the eight-period row and the 14% column) in Appendix E.

The investment is not acceptable because it has a negative net present value. If the working capital investment had been ignored, the proposal would have had a rather large positive net present value of $17,263 ($67,263 − $50,000). Thus, investments in working capital must be considered if correct capital-budgeting decisions are to be made.

The last topic discussed in this chapter is the postaudit. This important step improves the chances that future capital project selection decisions will be based on realistic projections of benefits and costs.

THE POSTAUDIT

The last step in the capital-budgeting process is a postaudit review that should be performed by a person not involved in the capital-budgeting, decision-making process. Such a person can provide an impartial judgment on the project's worthiness. A company should perform this step early in the project's life, but should allow enough time to work out any operational "bugs." Actual operating costs and revenues should be determined and compared with the costs and revenues estimated when the project was originally reviewed and accepted.

The postaudit review performs these functions:

1. Informs management about the accuracy of projections and whether the particular project is performing as expected regarding cash inflows and outflows.
2. May identify additional factors for management to consider in upcoming capital-budgeting decisions, such as cash outflows that were forgotten in a particular project.
3. Provides a review of the capital-budgeting process to determine how effectively and efficiently that process is working. The postaudit provides information that allows management to compare the actual results of decisions with the expectations it had during the planning and selection phases of the capital-budgeting process.

INVESTING IN HIGH TECHNOLOGY PROJECTS

Many companies have found it hard to justify high technology investments when they use the discounted cash flow methods illustrated in this chapter. A U.S. auto manufacturer, for example, found it difficult to justify investing in a new computer-based flexible manufacturing system because its cost savings occurred so far in the future. When discounted, the present value of these savings did not justify the initial outlay. The president of the company was convinced, however, that the new system had benefits that were not

ETHICS   A CLOSER LOOK

Terence Farley, the accountant for Communication Ventures, a public relations company, is looking into computer options for the company. He favors the idea of having lap-top computers as opposed to desk-top computers. Terence and many of the account executives are enthusiastic about lap-top computers because they are portable and would open up the possibility of working at home. Terence sees the advantages of working at home as a way to improve morale and therefore productivity and creativity. However, the company's investment review committee has a reputation for only looking at the bottom line, the dollar amount, and lap-top computers would cost 20% more than desk-top computers.

Terence was talking to one of the account executives about his concern that the review committee would reject his recommendation to buy lap-top computers based on the cost and not consider the long-term benefits. The account executive said, "One of the companies we have as an account recently bought lap-top computers and they swear by them. Come to think of it, they started showing profits not long after they purchased the computers. We even have data from this company that you could present to the committee."

Terence thought about the suggestion. He knew that in the long term the company would benefit. He also discovered that the company the account executive was talking about had increased its profits because of a new product introduction rather than from use of the lap-top computers.

Required
What should Terence do?

quantified in the cash flow estimates, so he approved the investment even though it had a negative net present value.

Companies have difficulty in justifying an investment in high technology projects for several reasons. First, often several years pass before companies see the cash inflows from the investment. Even if the cash inflows are high, their net present value is low if they come several years in the future.

Second, management has difficulty identifying and measuring all of the benefits of new technology. When personal computers replaced typewriters, for example, people learned many new ways of creating and storing documents by using the computer. These benefits occurred because people used computers and experimented with them. These benefits would have been difficult to predict, much less measure, back when companies were trying to justify investments in personal computers. Sometimes managers believe they just have to have faith that the investment is a good one, even though they cannot justify it on quantifiable economic grounds.

CAPITAL BUDGETING IN NOT-FOR-PROFIT ORGANIZATIONS

The concepts discussed in this chapter can also be applied to not-for-profit organizations, such as universities, school districts, cities, and not-for-profit hospitals. Since these organizations are not subject to as many taxes as profit-making organizations, the cash flows related to taxes are usually zero or near zero.

UNDERSTANDING THE LEARNING OBJECTIVES

1. Define capital budgeting and explain the effects of making poor capital budgeting decisions.
   - Capital budgeting is the process of considering alternative capital projects and selecting those alternatives that provide the most profitable return on available funds, within the framework of company goals and objectives.
   - Poor capital budgeting decisions can be costly for the following reasons:
     1. The company may lose all or part of the funds originally invested in the project.
     2. The company may lose its competitive position.
     3. The company may lose the benefits of investing in a profitable alternative project (opportunity cost).
2. Determine the net cash inflows, after taxes, for both an asset addition and an asset replacement.
   - Asset addition:

$$\begin{array}{c}\text{Net cash}\\ \text{inflow}\\ \text{after taxes}\end{array} = \left[\begin{array}{c}\text{Net cash}\\ \text{inflow}\\ \text{before taxes}\end{array} \times \left(1 - \frac{\text{Tax}}{\text{rate}}\right)\right] + \left[\begin{array}{c}\text{Depreciation}\\ \text{expense}\end{array} \times \frac{\text{Tax}}{\text{rate}}\right]$$

   - Asset replacement:

$$\begin{array}{c}\text{Net cash}\\ \text{inflow}\\ \text{after taxes}\end{array} = \left[\begin{array}{c}\text{Annual net cash}\\ \text{inflows (savings)}\\ \text{before taxes}\end{array} \times \left(1 - \frac{\text{Tax}}{\text{rate}}\right)\right] + \left[\begin{array}{c}\text{Additional}\\ \text{annual}\\ \text{depreciation}\\ \text{expense}\end{array} \times \frac{\text{Tax}}{\text{rate}}\right]$$

3. Evaluate projects using the payback period.

$$\text{Payback period} = \frac{\text{Initial cash outlay}}{\begin{array}{c}\text{Annual net cash inflows}\\ \text{(or benefits) after taxes}\end{array}}$$

4. Evaluate projects using the unadjusted rate of return.

$$\begin{array}{c}\text{Unadjusted}\\ \text{rate of return}\end{array} = \frac{\text{Average annual income after taxes}}{\text{Average amount of investment}}$$

5. Evaluate projects using the net present value.
   - All expected after-tax cash inflows and outflows from the proposed investment are discounted to their present values using the company's required minimum rate of return as a discount rate. The net present value of the proposed investment is the difference between

the present value of the annual net cash inflows and the present value of the required cash outflows.

6. Evaluate projects using the profitability index.

$$\text{Profitability index} = \frac{\text{Present value of net cash inflows after taxes}}{\text{Initial outlay (or present value of cash outlays if future outlays are required)}}$$

7. Evaluate projects using the time-adjusted rate of return.
   • The time-adjusted rate of return equates the present value of expected after-tax net cash inflows and outflows from an investment by finding the rate at which the net present value of the project is zero. If the time-adjusted rate of return equals or exceeds the cost of capital or the target rate of return, the project should be considered further. If the rate is less than the minimum rate, the project should be rejected.

8. Determine, for project evaluation, the effect of an investment in working capital.
   • The investment in working capital will cause the net present value to be lower than it would be if the working capital investment is ignored. Therefore, the required return of a project must be higher to account for the investment in working capital.

DEMONSTRATION PROBLEM

Barkley Company is considering three different investments. Listed below are some data related to these investments:

Investment	Initial Cash Outlay	Expected Before-Tax Net Cash Inflow per Year	Expected After-Tax Net Cash Inflow per Year	Expected Life of Proposals*
A	$50,000	$13,333	$10,000	10 years
B	60,000	12,000	8,800	15
C	75,000	15,000	10,500	20

* No estimated salvage value. Use straight-line depreciation.

The income tax rate is 40%. The salvage value of each investment is zero. Management requires a minimum return on investments of 14%.

Required:

Rank these proposals using the following selection techniques:
a. Payback period.
b. Unadjusted rate of return.
c. Profitability index.
d. Time-adjusted rate of return.

Solution to demonstration problem

a. Payback period:

Proposal	(a) Investment	(b) Annual After-Tax Cash Inflow	(a) ÷ (b) Payback Period
A.	$50,000	$10,000	5.00 years
B.	60,000	8,800	6.82
C.	75,000	10,500	7.14

The proposals in order of desirability are A, B, and C.

b. Unadjusted rate of return:

Proposal	(a) Average Investment	(b) Average Annual Before-Tax Net Cash Inflow	(c) Average Depreciation	(d) = [(b − c) × (1 − .4)] Average Annual Income	(d) ÷ (a) Rate of Return
A . . .	$25,000	$13,333	$5,000	$5,000	20%
B . . .	30,000	12,000	4,000	4,800	16
C . . .	37,500	15,000	3,750	6,750	18

The proposals in order of desirability are A, C, and B.

c. Profitability index:

Proposal	(a) Annual After-Tax Net Cash Inflow	(b) Present Value Factor at 14%	(c) = (a) × (b) Present Value of Annual Net Cash Flow	(d) Initial Cash Outlay	(c) ÷ (d) Profitability Index
A.	$10,000*	5.21612	$52,161	$50,000	1.04
B.	8,800	6.14217	54,051	60,000	0.90
C.	10,500	6.62313	69,543	75,000	0.93

* This amount was given. However, the amount can also be calculated as follows:

Expected before-tax net cash inflow	$13,333
Less depreciation	5,000
Taxable income	$ 8,333
1 − Tax rate.	× 60%
After-tax annual income	$ 5,000
Add back depreciation	5,000
Annual after-tax net cash inflow	$10,000

The proposals in order of desirability are A, C, and B. (But neither B nor C should be considered acceptable since each has a profitability index of less than one.)

d. Time-adjusted rate of return:

Proposal	Rate	How Found
A.	15% (slightly above)	($50,000/$10,000) = Factor of 5 in 10 period row
B.	12 (slightly below)	($60,000/$8,800) = Factor of 6.82 in 15 period row
C.	13 (slightly below)	($75,000/$10,500) = Factor of 7.14 in 20 period row

The proposals in order of desirability are A, C, and B. (But neither B nor C earns the minimum rate of return.)

NEW TERMS*

Annuity   A series of equal cash inflows or outflows. *994*

Average investment   (Beginning balance + Ending balance)/2. The beginning balance is the original investment, and the ending balance is the salvage value. *987*

Capital budgeting   Process of considering alternative capital projects and selecting those alternatives that provide the most profitable return on available funds, within the framework of company goals and objectives. *980*

Capital project   Any available alternative to purchase, build, lease, or renovate buildings, equipment, or other long-range major items of property. *980*

Cost of capital   The cost of all sources of capital (debt and equity) employed by a company. *985*

Initial cost of an asset   Any cash outflows necessary to acquire an asset and place it in a position and condition for its intended use. *985*

Net cash inflow   The periodic cash inflows from a project less the periodic cash outflows related to the project. *981*

Net present value   A project selection technique that uses the company's required minimum rate of return as a discount rate and discounts all expected after-tax cash inflows and outflows from the proposed investment. If the amount obtained by this process exceeds or equals the investment amount, the proposal is considered acceptable for further consideration. *990*

Opportunity cost   The benefits or returns lost by rejecting the best alternative investment. *980*

Out-of-pocket cost   A cost requiring a future outlay of resources, usually cash. *984*

Payback period   The period of time it takes for the cumulative sum of the annual net cash inflows from a project to equal the initial cash outlay. *985*

Profitability index   The ratio of the present value of the expected net cash benefits (after taxes) divided by the initial cash outlay (or present value of cash outlays if future outlays are required). *991*

Sunk costs   Costs that have already been incurred. Nothing can be done about sunk costs at the present time; they cannot be avoided or changed in amount. *984*

Tax shield   The total amount by which a company reduces taxable income due to the deductibility of an item. *982*

Time-adjusted rate of return   (also called the **internal rate of return**) A project selection technique that finds a rate of return that will equate the present value of expected after-tax net cash inflows from an investment with the cost of the investment. *992*

Unadjusted rate of return   The unadjusted rate of return is computed by dividing the average annual income after taxes from a project by the average amount of the investment. *987*

* Some terms listed in earlier chapters are repeated here for your convenience.

SELF-TEST

True-False

Indicate whether each of the following statements is true or false.

1. Once a company undertakes a capital project, the company becomes more flexible regarding future actions.
2. The price a company has already paid for a machine is a sunk cost.
3. Sunk costs and out-of-pocket costs are both relevant to capital-budgeting decisions.
4. A formula for the profitability index is as follows:

$$\text{Profitability index} = \frac{\text{Present value of net cash inflows}}{\text{Initial outlay (or present value of cash outlays if future outlays are required)}}$$

5. When investment projects costing different amounts are being compared, the net present value provides a valid means by which to rank projects in order of contribution to income or desirability under limited financial resources.

Multiple-Choice

Select the best answer for each of the following questions.

1. Which of the following choices is incorrect?
   a. Payback period ignores the time period beyond the payback period.
   b. When using payback analysis for investment decisions, one rule is to select the longest payback period investment.
   c. The formula for the payback period is:

$$\text{Payback period} = \frac{\text{Initial cash outlay}}{\text{Annual net cash inflow (or benefit) after taxes}}$$

   d. Payback analysis ignores the time value of money.
2. When making capital budgeting decisions, all aspects of the investment should be considered, including which of the following?
   a. Employee productivity.
   b. The results of more than one capital budgeting method.
   c. Company flexibility.
   d. All of the above.
3. Which of the following statements describe(s) the limitations when using the unadjusted rate of return?
   a. Timing of cash flows is not considered.
   b. It allows a sunk cost, depreciation, to enter into the calculation.

   c. The length of time over which the return will be earned is not considered.
   d. All of the above.
4. Which of the following statements is (are) true for the profitability index?
   a. Only proposals with profitability indexes of less than 1.00 should be considered further.
   b. Only proposals with profitability indexes equal to or greater than 1.00 should be considered further.
   c. The profitability index is the ratio of initial cash outlay divided by present value of cash benefits (before taxes).
   d. *(b)* and *(c)*.
5. Which of the following statements is (are) true regarding the net present value method?
   a. A company's cost of capital is difficult to calculate.
   b. With projects that require an initial outlay plus an additional investment at a later date, management must discount the latter cash outflow to its present value before the cash outflows are compared to the present value of cash inflows.
   c. The payback method and the net present value methods give identical results.
   d. *(a)* and *(b)*.

Now turn to page 1011 to check your answers.

QUESTIONS

1. How do capital expenditures differ from ordinary expenditures?

2. What effects can capital-budgeting decisions have on a company?

3. What effect does depreciation have on cash flow?

4. Give an example of an out-of-pocket cost and a sunk cost by describing a situation in which both are encountered.

5. A machine is being considered for purchase. The salesperson attempting to sell the machine says that it will pay for itself in five years. What is meant by this statement?

6. Discuss the limitations of the payback period method.

7. What is the profitability index, and of what value is it?

8. Describe the time-adjusted rate of return method.

9. What role does the cost of capital play in the time-adjusted rate of return method and in the net present value method?

10. What is the purpose of a postaudit? When should a postaudit be performed?

The Coca-Cola Company

11. *Real-world question* Refer to Appendix C at the end of the text. What were The Coca-Cola Company's capital expenditures for each line of business and in total for 1991? Which line of business had the greatest capital expenditure? (Hint: Look for the "Lines of Business" note under "Notes to Consolidated Financial Statements.")

12. *Real-world question* A friend is considering investing in a house for rental to students. He knows nothing about the concepts in this chapter and also has a short attention span. In just a few words, what would you tell your friend to think about in making this decision or any other investment decision?

EXERCISES

Determine estimated income and net cash inflow for an asset addition (L.O. 2)

20–1. Farmington Company is considering investing $300,000 in some new farm equipment with an estimated useful life of 10 years and no salvage value. The equipment is expected to produce $120,000 in cash inflows and $70,000 in cash outflows annually. Straight-line depreciation is used by the company, and an assumed 40% tax rate applies. Determine the annual estimated income and net cash inflow.

Determine additional cash inflow for an asset replacement (L.O. 2)

20–2. Del Oro Manufacturing Company is considering replacing a four-year-old machine with a new, advanced model. The old machine was purchased for $30,000, has an estimated useful life of 10 years with no salvage value, and has annual maintenance costs of $6,500. The new machine would cost $23,500 and would produce the same output as the old machine. However, annual maintenance costs would be only $3,000. The new machine would have a useful life of 10 years with no salvage value. Using straight-line depreciation and an assumed 40% tax rate, compute the additional annual cash inflow if the old machine is replaced.

Compute payback
period for a new
machine
(L.O. 3)

20–3. Given the following annual costs, compute the payback period for the new machine if its initial cost is $420,000. (Ignore income taxes.)

	Old Machine	New Machine
Depreciation	$ 36,000	$ 84,000
Labor	134,000	126,000
Repairs.	42,000	8,000
Other costs.	23,000	7,200
	$235,000	$225,200

Compute
unadjusted rate of
return for a new
machine
(L.O. 4)

20–4. Prince Company is considering investing $9,250 in a new machine. The machine is expected to last five years and to have a $2,000 salvage value. Average annual before-tax net cash inflow from the machine is expected to be $1,800. The income tax rate is 40%. Calculate the unadjusted rate of return.

Compute
profitability index
for two projects
and rank projects
(L.O. 6)

20–5. Compute the profitability index for each of the following two proposals assuming the desired minimum rate of return is 20%. Based on the profitability indexes, which proposal is better?

	Proposal M	Proposal N
Initial cash outlay	$16,000	$20,600
Net cash inflow (after taxes):		
First year	10,000	11,000
Second year.	9,000	10,000
Third year.	5,000	9,000
Fourth year	–0–	5,000

Rank projects
using payback
(L.O. 3)

20–6. Lillian Company is considering three alternative investment proposals. Using the information presented below, rank the proposals in order of desirability using the payback period method.

	Q	R	S
Initial outlay	$380,000	$380,000	$380,000
Net cash inflow (after taxes):			
First year.	$ –0–	$ 90,000	$100,000
Second year	190,000	290,000	120,000
Third year	190,000	90,000	260,000
Fourth year.	90,000	180,000	450,000
	$470,000	$650,000	$930,000

Determine
acceptability of a
project using net
present value
(L.O. 5)

20–7. Michelle Company is considering the purchase of a new machine costing $45,000. The machine is expected to save $9,500 cash (after taxes) per year for 10 years, has an estimated useful life of 10 years, and no salvage value. Management will not make any investment unless at least an 18% rate of return can be earned.

Using the net present value method, determine whether or not the proposal is acceptable.

Compute
time-adjusted rate
of return
(L.O. 7)

20–8. Refer to the data in Exercise 20–7. Calculate the time-adjusted rate of return.

Rank projects
using payback, net
present value, and
time-adjusted rate
of return
(L.O. 3, 5, 7)

20–9. Rank the following investments in order of their desirability using the *(a)* payback period method, *(b)* net present value method, and *(c)* time-adjusted rate of return method. Management requires a minimum rate of return of 14%.

Investment	Initial Cash Outlay	Expected After-Tax Net Cash Inflow per Year	Expected Life of Proposal
X	$130,000	$18,000	8 years
Y	160,000	26,000	20
Z	250,000	48,000	10

PROBLEMS

Determine net
cash inflow and
payback period for
an asset addition
(L.O. 2, 3)

20–1. The Jester Company is considering the purchase of a new machine that would cost $200,000 and would have a useful life of 10 years with no salvage value. The new machine is expected to have annual cash inflows of $120,000 and annual cash outflows of $40,000. The machine will be depreciated using straight-line depreciation, and the assumed tax rate is 40%.

Required:

a. Determine the net after-tax cash inflow for the new machine.
b. Determine the payback period for the new machine.

Determine
additional cash
inflow for an asset
replacement
(L.O. 2)

20–2. Tyson Company currently uses four machines to produce 400,000 units annually. The machines were bought three years ago for $60,000 each and have a useful life of 10 years with no salvage value. These machines cost a total of $26,000 per year to repair and maintain.

The company is considering replacing the four machines with one technologically superior machine that is capable of producing the 400,000 units annually by itself. The machine would cost $168,000 and have a useful life of seven years with no salvage value. Annual repair and maintenance costs are estimated at $14,000.

Required:

Assuming straight-line depreciation and a 40% tax rate, determine the annual additional after-tax net cash inflow if the new machine is acquired.

Evaluate asset
replacement using
payback and net
present value
(L.O. 3, 5)

20–3. Metro Manufacturing Company owns five welding machines that it uses in its manufacturing operations. Each of the machines was purchased four years ago at a cost of $120,000. Each machine has an estimated useful life of 10 years with no expected salvage value. A new machine has become available. One new machine has the same productive capacity as the five old machines combined; it can produce 800,000 units each year. The new machine will cost $648,000, is estimated to last six years, and will have a salvage value of $72,000. A trade-in allowance of $24,000 is available for each of the old machines.

Operating costs per unit are compared below.

	Five Old Machines	New Machines
Repairs	$0.6796	$0.0856
Depreciation	0.1500	0.2400
Power	0.2890	0.2036
Other operating costs.	0.2620	0.0696
Operating costs per unit . . .	$1.3806	$0.5988

Required:

Ignore income taxes. Use the payback period method for *(a)* and *(b)*.

a. Do you recommend replacing the old machines? Support your answer with computations. Disregard all factors except those reflected in the data given above.

b. If the old machines were already fully depreciated, would your answer be different? Why?

c. Using the net present value method with a discount rate of 20%, present a schedule showing whether or not the new machine should be acquired.

Calculate
time-adjusted rate
of return for new
equipment;
determine effect
of altering useful
life and net cash
inflows
(L.O. 7)

20–4. Vandicamp Canning Company has used a particular canning machine for several years. The machine has a zero salvage value. The company is considering buying a technologically improved machine at a cost of $222,000. The new machine will save $50,000 per year after taxes in cash operating costs. If the company decides not to buy the new machine, it can use the old machine for an indefinite period of time by incurring heavy repair costs. The new machine will have a useful life of eight years.

Required:

a. Compute the time-adjusted rate of return for the new machine.

b. Management thinks the estimated useful life of the new machine may be more or less than eight years. Compute the time-adjusted rate of return for the new machine if its useful life is (1) 5 years and (2) 12 years, instead of 8 years.

c. Suppose the new machine's useful life is eight years, but the annual after-tax cost savings are only $40,000. Compute the time-adjusted rate of return.

d. Assume the annual after-tax cost savings from the new machine will be $44,000 and its useful life will be 10 years. Compute the time-adjusted rate of return.

Rank proposals using payback, unadjusted rate of return, profitability index, and time-adjusted rate of return
(L.O. 3, 4, 6, 7)

20–5. Sergio, Inc., is considering three different investments involving depreciable assets with no salvage value. Listed below are some data related to these investments:

Investment	Initial Cash Outlay	Expected Before-Tax Net Cash Inflow per Year	Expected After-Tax Net Cash Inflow per Year	Expected Life of Proposal
1. . . .	$130,000	$37,333	$27,600	10 years
2. . . .	230,000	72,000	47,800	20
3. . . .	350,000	89,333	67,600	10

The income tax rate is 40%. Management requires a minimum return on investment of 12%.

Required:

Rank these proposals using the following selection techniques.

a. Payback period.
b. Unadjusted rate of return.
c. Profitability index.
d. Time-adjusted rate of return.

Make capital-budgeting decision using net present value
(L.O. 5)

20–6. Emelio Company has decided to computerize its accounting system. The company has two alternatives—it can lease a computer under a three-year contract, or it can purchase a computer outright.

If the computer is leased, the lease payment will be $4,400 each year. The first lease payment will be due on the day the lease contract is signed. The other two payments will be due at the end of the first and second years. All repairs and maintenance will be provided by the lessor.

If the computer is purchased outright, the following costs will be incurred:

Acquisition cost	$10,500
Repairs and maintenance:	
First year	500
Second year.	350
Third year	550

The computer is expected to have only a three-year useful life because of obsolescence and technological advancements. The computer will have no salvage value. Ignore income taxes. Emelio Company's cost of capital is 16%.

Required:

a. Using the net present value method, calculate the out-of-pocket costs for the lease alternative.
b. Using the net present value method, calculate the out-of-pocket costs for the purchase alternative.
c. Do you recommend that the company purchase or lease the machine?

Make
capital-budgeting
decision using net
present value
(L.O. 5)

20–7. Bjorn Sports Company is trying to decide whether or not to add tennis equipment to its existing line of football, baseball, and basketball equipment. Market research studies and cost analyses have provided the following information:

1. Additional machinery and equipment will be needed to manufacture the tennis equipment. The machines and equipment will cost $450,000, have a 10-year useful life, and have a $10,000 salvage value.
2. Sales of tennis equipment for the next 10 years have been projected as follows:

Years	Sales in Dollars
1	$ 65,000
2	102,500
3	158,750
4	177,500
5	206,250
6–10 (each year).	225,000

3. Variable costs are 60% of selling price, and fixed costs (including straight-line depreciation) will total $88,500 per year.
4. The company will need to advertise its new product line to gain rapid entry into the market. Its advertising campaign costs will be:

Years	Advertising Cost
1–3	$75,000 (each year)
4–10	38,500 (each year)

5. The company requires a 14% minimum rate of return on investments.

Required:

Using the net present value method, decide whether or not Bjorn Sports Company should add the tennis equipment to its line of products. (Ignore income taxes.) Round to the nearest dollar.

Evaluate
investment
proposal using net
present value
(L.O. 5)

20–8. Wight Company is considering purchasing new equipment that will cost $1,700,000. The estimated useful life of the equipment is five years, and the estimated salvage value is $600,000. The company uses straight-line depreciation. The new equipment is expected to have a net cash inflow (before taxes) of $258,000 annually. Assume that the tax rate is 40% and that management requires a minimum return of 14%.

Required:

Using the net present value method, determine whether the equipment is an acceptable investment.

Decision to sell
equipment using
net present value
(L.O. 5)

20–9. Mailer Company has an opportunity to sell some equipment for $40,000. Such a sale will result in a tax-deductible loss of $4,000. If the equipment is not sold, it is expected to produce net annual cash inflows after taxes of $14,000 for the next 10 years. After 10 years, the equipment can be sold for its book value of $4,000. Assume a 40% income tax rate.

Required:

Management currently has other opportunities that will yield 18%. Using the net present value method, show whether the company should sell the equipment. Prepare a schedule to support your conclusion.

BUSINESS DECISION PROBLEMS

Compute net
present value of
several proposals;
rank proposals in
order of
acceptability
(L.O. 5)

20–1. China Company wishes to invest $750,000 in capital projects that have a minimum expected rate of return of 14%. Five proposals are being evaluated. Acceptance of one proposal does not preclude acceptance of any of the other proposals. The company's criterion is to select proposals that meet its minimum required rate of return (14%).

The relevant information related to the five proposals is as follows.

Investment	Initial Cash Outlay	Expected After-Tax Net Cash Inflow per Year	Expected Life of Proposal
A	$155,000	$45,000	5 years
B	305,000	60,000	8
C	370,000	82,500	10
D	455,000	78,000	12
E	155,000	31,500	10

Required:

a. Compute the net present value of each of the five proposals. Round to the nearest dollar.
b. Which projects should be undertaken? Why? Rank them in order of desirability.

Evaluate
bookkeeper's
computation of
project's net
present value;
determine
acceptability of
project
(L.O. 5)

20–2. Brody Company is considering a capital project that will involve a $225,000 investment in machinery and a $39,000 investment in working capital. The machine has a useful life of 10 years and no salvage value. The annual cash inflows (before taxes) are estimated at $80,000 with annual cash outflows (before taxes) of $30,000. The company uses straight-line depreciation. Assume the income tax rate is 40%.

The company's new bookkeeper computed the net present value of the project using a minimum required rate of return of 16% (the company's cost of capital). The bookkeeper's computations are shown in the following table.

Cash inflows	$ 80,000
Cash outflows	30,000
Net cash inflow.	$ 50,000
Present value factor at 16%	×4.833
Present value of net cash inflow. . . .	$241,650
Initial cash outlay.	225,000
Net present value.	$ 16,650

Required:

a. Are the bookkeeper's computations correct? If not, compute the correct net present value. Round to the nearest dollar.

b. Is this capital project acceptable to the company? Why or why not?

ANSWERS TO SELF-TEST

True-False

1. *False.* Because capital projects usually involve large sums of money and therefore increase fixed assets for several years, the company becomes less flexible regarding future actions.

2. *True.* Once a company has paid the price, the expenditure becomes a sunk cost.

3. *False.* Only the out-of-pocket costs (the future cash outlays) are relevant to capital-budgeting decisions.

4. *True.* The formula as stated is correct.

5. *False.* The net present value method does *not* provide a valid means by which to rank the projects. The profitability index should be used to rank these projects.

Multiple-Choice

1. *b.* The statement, "the rule is to select the longest payback period investment," is incorrect.

2. *d.* Employee productivity, various capital budgeting methods, and company flexibility should all be considered when companies make capital budgeting decisions.

3. *d.* All of these choices—timing of cash flows; allowing a sunk cost, depreciation, to enter into the decision; and failure to consider the length of time over which the return will be earned—are limitations of the unadjusted rate of return method.

4. *b.* Only projects with a profitability index of 1.00 or greater should be considered further. A profitability index is the ratio of the present value of the expected net cash benefits (after taxes) divided by the initial cash outlay (or present value of cash outlays if future outlays are required).

5. *d.* Both *(a)* and *(b)* are true. Regarding *(c)*, payback and net present value do not necessarily give the same results because payback does not discount any cash flows during the payback period, and it ignores cash flows after the payback period.

VI MANAGERIAL ACCOUNTING: CASH FLOW AND FINANCIAL ANALYSIS

CHAPTER 21
STATEMENT OF CASH FLOWS

CHAPTER 22
ANALYSIS AND INTERPRETATION OF
FINANCIAL STATEMENTS

21

STATEMENT OF CASH FLOWS

LEARNING OBJECTIVES

After studying this chapter, you should be able to:

1. Explain the purposes and uses of the statement of cash flows.
2. Describe the content of the statement of cash flows and where certain items would appear on the statement.
3. Describe how to calculate cash flows from operating activities under both the direct and indirect methods.
4. Prepare a statement of cash flows under both the direct and indirect methods showing cash flows from operating activities, investing activities, and financing activities.
5. Describe the historical development from a statement of changes in financial position to a statement of cash flows.

In your study of the statement of income and retained earnings (as separate statements or combined) and the balance sheet, you may have realized that these financial statements do not answer all the questions raised by users of financial statements. Such questions include: How much cash was generated by the company's operations? How can the Cash account be overdrawn when my accountant said the business was profitable? Why is such a profitable company only able to pay such small dividends? How much was spent for new plant and equipment, and where did the company get the cash for the expenditures? How was the company able to pay a dividend when it incurred a net loss for the year?

Through 1987, a statement called the statement of changes in financial position answered these questions. In July 1988, the statement of cash flows replaced the statement of changes in financial position.

In this chapter, you will learn about the statement of cash flows. The statement of cash flows is another major required financial statement and shows important information that is not shown directly in the other financial statements.

PURPOSES OF THE STATEMENT OF CASH FLOWS

Objective 1
Explain the pur-
poses and uses of
the statement of
cash flows

In November 1987, the Financial Accounting Standards Board issued *Statement of Financial Accounting Standards No. 95,* "Statement of Cash Flows."[1] The *Statement* became effective for annual financial statements for fiscal years ending after July 15, 1988. Thus, the statement of cash flows is now one of the major financial statements issued by a company.

The main purpose of the statement of cash flows is to report on the cash receipts and cash disbursements of an entity during an accounting period. Cash is broadly defined to include both cash and "cash equivalents," such as short-term investments in Treasury bills, commercial paper, and money market funds. A secondary purpose is to report on the entity's investing and financing activities for the period. As shown in Illustration 21.1, the statement of cash flows reports the effects on cash during a period of a company's operating, investing, and financing activities. The effects of investing and financing activities that do not affect cash are shown in a schedule separate from the statement of cash flows.

USES OF THE STATEMENT OF CASH FLOWS

The **statement of cash flows** summarizes the effects on cash of the operating, investing, and financing activities of a company during an accounting period; it reports on past management decisions on such matters as issuance of capital stock or sale of long-term bonds. This information is available only in

Illustration 21.1
STATEMENT OF CASH FLOWS—BASIC CONTENT

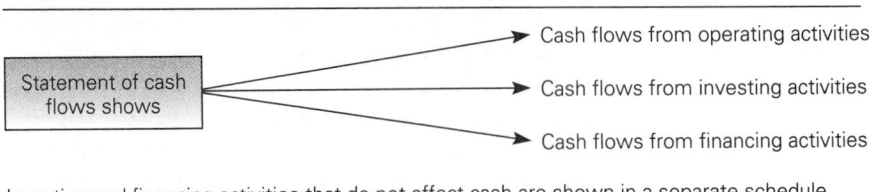

Investing and financing activities that do not affect cash are shown in a separate schedule.

---

[1] FASB, *Statement of Financial Accounting Standards No. 95,* "Statement of Cash Flows" (Stamford, Conn., 1987). Copyright by the Financial Accounting Standards Board, High Ridge Park, Stamford, Connecticut 06905. U.S.A. Quoted (or excerpted) with permission. Copies of the complete document are available from the FASB.

bits and pieces from the other financial statements. Since cash flows are vital to a company's financial health, the statement of cash flows provides useful information to management, investors, creditors, and other interested parties.

Management Uses

Since the statement of cash flows presents the effects on cash of all significant operating, investing, and financing activities, by reviewing the statement, management can see the effects of its past major policy decisions in quantitative form. The statement may show a flow of cash from operating activities large enough to finance all projected capital needs internally rather than having to incur long-term debt or issue additional stock. Or, if the company has been experiencing cash shortages, management can use the statement to determine why such shortages are occurring. Management may also use the statement to recommend to the board of directors a reduction in dividends to conserve cash.

Investor and Creditor Uses

The information in a statement of cash flows should help investors, creditors, and others to assess the following:

1. Enterprise's ability to generate positive future net cash flows.
2. Enterprise's ability to meet its obligations.
3. Enterprise's ability to pay dividends.
4. Enterprise's need for external financing.
5. Reasons for differences between net income and associated cash receipts and payments.
6. Effects on an enterprise's financial position of both its cash and noncash investing and financing transactions during the period (disclosed in a separate schedule).

INFORMATION IN THE STATEMENT OF CASH FLOWS

*Objective 2
Describe the
content of the
statement of cash
flows and where
certain items
would appear on
the statement*

The statement of cash flows classifies cash receipts and disbursements as operating, investing, and financing cash flows. Both inflows and outflows are included within each category. Illustration 21.2 shows how activities can be classified for purposes of preparing a statement of cash flows.

Operating activities *generally include the cash effects (inflows and outflows) of transactions and other events that enter into the determination of net income. Cash inflows* from operating activities affect items that appear on the income statement and include (1) cash receipts from sales of goods or services; (2) interest received from making loans; (3) dividends received from investments in equity securities; and (4) other cash receipts that do not arise from transactions defined as investing or financing activities, such as

Illustration 21.2
RULES FOR CLASSIFYING ACTIVITIES IN THE STATEMENT OF CASH FLOWS

Operating activities   Cash effects of transactions and other events that enter into the determination of net income

Cash inflows from:	Cash outflows for:
Sales of goods or services	Merchandise inventory
Interest	Salaries and wages
Dividends	Interest
Other sources not related to investing or financing activities (e.g., insurance settlements)	Other expenses
	Other items not related to investing or financing activities (e.g., contributions to charities)

Investing activities   Transactions involving the acquisition or disposal of noncurrent assets

Cash inflows from:	Cash outflows for:
Sale of property, plant, and equipment	Purchase of property, plant, and equipment
Sale of marketable securities	Purchase of marketable securities
Collection of loans	Making of loans

Financing activities   Transactions with creditors and owners

Cash inflows from:	Cash outflows for:
Issuing capital stock	Purchase of treasury stock
Issuing debt (bonds, mortgages, notes, and other short- or long-term borrowing of cash)	Payment of debt
	Cash dividends

---

amounts received to settle lawsuits, proceeds of certain insurance settlements, and refunds from suppliers.

Cash outflows for operating activities affect items that appear on the income statement and include payments (1) to acquire inventory; (2) to other suppliers and employees for other goods or services; (3) to lenders and other creditors for interest; and (4) all other cash payments that do not arise from transactions defined as investing or financing activities, such as taxes and payments to settle lawsuits, cash contributions to charities, and cash refunds to customers.

Investing activities *generally include transactions involving the acquisition or disposal of noncurrent assets.* Thus, *cash inflows* from investing activities include cash received from the sale of property, plant, and equipment; cash received from the sale of long-term marketable securities; and cash received from the collection of long-term loans made to others. *Cash outflows* for investing activities include cash paid to purchase property, plant, and equipment; cash paid to purchase long-term marketable securities; and cash paid to make long-term loans to others.

Financing activities *generally include the cash effects (inflows and outflows) of transactions and other events involving creditors and owners.* Cash *inflows* from financing activities include cash received from issuing capital stock and bonds, mortgages, notes, and from other short- or long-term borrowing. *Cash outflows* for financing activities include payments of cash dividends or other distributions to owners (including cash paid to purchase Treasury stock) and repayments of amounts borrowed. Payment of interest is not included because interest expense appears on the income statement and is therefore included in operating activities. Paying cash to settle accounts payable, wages payable, and income taxes payable are not financing activities. These payments are operating activities.

CASH FLOWS FROM OPERATING ACTIVITIES

Objective 3
Describe how to
calculate cash
flows from operat-
ing activities
under both the
direct and indirect
methods

Cash flows from operating activities show the net amount of cash received or disbursed during a given period for items that normally appear on the income statement. These cash flows can be calculated using the direct or indirect method. The **direct method** deducts from cash sales only those operating expenses that *consumed cash.* Under this method, each item on the income statement is *directly* converted to a cash basis. Alternatively, the **indirect (addback) method** starts with accrual basis net income and *indirectly* adjusts net income for items that affected reported net income but *did not involve cash.*

The FASB *encourages* use of the direct method but *permits* use of the indirect method. The indirect method is used more frequently, as shown in the table below. Whenever accountants have been given a choice between the indirect and direct methods in similar situations, the indirect method has been used almost exclusively. We will discuss and illustrate both methods.

Method of Reporting Cash Flows from Operating Activities			
	1990	*1989*	*1988*
Indirect method	585	583	526
Direct method	15	17	16
Total Companies Presenting Statement of Cash Flows	600	600	542

SOURCE: American Institute of Certified Public Accountants, *Accounting Trends & Techniques* (New York: AICPA, 1991), p. 420.

Under the direct method, each item on the income statement must be converted to a cash basis. Thus, the name *direct method* is used. For instance, assume that sales are stated at $100,000 on an accrual basis. If accounts receivable increased by $5,000, cash collections from customers would be $95,000, calculated at $100,000 − $5,000. All remaining items on the income statement are also converted to a cash basis. This process will be illustrated later.

Under the indirect method, net income is adjusted (rather than adjusting individual items in the income statement) for (1) changes in current assets (other than cash) and current liabilities, and (2) items that were included in net income but did not affect cash. Thus, the name *indirect method* is used.

The most common example of an operating expense that does not affect cash is depreciation expense. The journal entry to record depreciation debits an expense account and credits an accumulated depreciation account. This transaction has no effect on cash and therefore should not be included when measuring cash from operations. Because depreciation is deducted in arriving at net income, net income understates cash from operations. Under the indirect method, since net income is used as a starting point in measuring cash flows from operating activities, depreciation expense must be added back to net income.

Consider the following example. Company A had net income for the year of $20,000 after deducting depreciation of $10,000, yielding $30,000 of positive cash flows. Thus, Company A had $30,000 positive cash flows from operating activities. Company B had a net loss for the year of $4,000 after deducting $10,000 of depreciation. Although Company B experienced a loss, the company had $6,000 of positive cash flows from operating activities, as shown below:

	Company A	Company B
Net income (loss).	$20,000	$ (4,000)
Add depreciation expense (which did not require use of cash)	10,000	10,000
Positive cash flows from operating activities	$30,000	$ 6,000

Company B's loss would have had to exceed $10,000 for the company to have negative cash flows from operating activities.

Companies have other expenses and losses that are added back to net income because they do not actually use the company's cash; these add-backs are often called **noncash charges or expenses.** Besides depreciation, the items added back include amounts of depletion that were expensed, amortization of intangible assets such as patents and goodwill, amortization of discount on bonds payable, and losses from disposals of noncurrent assets.

To illustrate the addback of the losses from disposal of noncurrent assets, assume that Quick Company sold a piece of equipment for $6,000. The equipment had cost $10,000 and had accumulated depreciation of $3,000. The journal entry to record the sale was:

```
Cash . . . . . . . . . . . . . . . . . . . . . . . . . . . . .   6,000
Accumulated Depreciation. . . . . . . . . . . . . . . . . .   3,000
Loss on Sale of Equipment . . . . . . . . . . . . . . . . .   1,000
    Equipment . . . . . . . . . . . . . . . . . . . . . . .              10,000
To record disposal of equipment at a loss.
```

Quick would show the $6,000 inflow from the sale of the equipment as a cash inflow from investing activities on its statement of cash flows. Although Quick deducted the loss of $1,000 in calculating net income, the total $6,000 effect on cash (which reflects the $1,000 loss) has already been recognized as resulting from an investing activity. Thus, Quick must add the loss back to net income in converting net income to cash flows from operating activities to avoid double-counting the loss.

Certain revenues and gains included in arriving at net income do not provide cash; these items are called **noncash credits or revenues.** These revenues and gains must be deducted from net income to compute cash flows from operating activities. Such items include gains from disposals of noncurrent assets, income from investments carried under the equity method, and amortization of premium on bonds payable.

To illustrate why the gain on the disposal of a noncurrent asset must be deducted from net income, assume that Quick sold the equipment mentioned above for $9,000. The journal entry to record the sale is:

Cash	9,000	
Accumulated Depreciation	3,000	
Equipment		10,000
Gain on Sale of Equipment.		2,000
To record disposal of equipment at a gain.		

Quick shows the $9,000 inflow from the sale of equipment on its statement of cash flows as a cash inflow from investing activities. Thus, the total $9,000 effect on cash (including the $2,000 gain) has already been recognized as resulting from an investing activity. Since the $2,000 gain is also included in calculating net income, Quick must deduct the gain in converting net income to cash flows from operating activities to avoid double-counting the gain.

STEPS IN PREPARING STATEMENT OF CASH FLOWS

Objective 4
Prepare a statement of cash flows under both the direct and indirect methods showing cash flows from operating activities, investing activities, and financing activities

This section discusses the procedures accountants follow to prepare a statement of cash flows. These procedures are illustrated using the financial statements and additional data for Welby Company given in Illustration 21.3.

After determining the change in cash, the first step in preparing the statement of cash flows is to calculate the cash flows from operating activities, using either the direct or indirect method. The second step is to analyze all of the noncurrent accounts for changes resulting from investing and financing activities. The third step is to arrange the information gathered in steps 1 and 2 into the proper format for the statement of cash flows.

Step 1: Determining Cash Flows from Operating Activities—Direct Method

Under the direct method, the income statement must be converted from the accrual basis to the cash basis. Changes in balance sheet accounts that are related to items on the income statement must be considered. The accounts involved are all current assets or current liabilities. The following schedule shows which balance sheet accounts are related to the items on the income statement in the Welby example:

Illustration 21.3
FINANCIAL STATEMENTS AND OTHER DATA

WELBY COMPANY
Comparative Balance Sheets
December 31, 1995 and 1994

	1995	1994	Increase/ (Decrease)
Assets			
Cash	$ 21,000	$ 10,000	$11,000
Accounts receivable, net	30,000	20,000	10,000
Merchandise inventory	26,000	30,000	(4,000)
Plant assets	70,000	50,000	20,000
Accumulated depreciation	(10,000)	(5,000)	(5,000)
Total assets	$137,000	$105,000	$32,000
Liabilities and Stockholders' Equity			
Accounts payable	$ 9,000	$ 15,000	$ (6,000)
Accrued liabilities payable	2,000	–0–	2,000
Common stock ($10 par value)	90,000	60,000	30,000
Retained earnings	36,000	30,000	6,000
Total liabilities and stockholders' equity	$137,000	$105,000	$32,000

WELBY COMPANY
Income Statement
For the Year Ended December 31, 1995

Sales		$140,000
Cost of goods sold		100,000
Gross margin		$ 40,000
Operating expenses (other than depreciation)	$25,000	
Depreciation expense	5,000	30,000
Net income		$ 10,000

Additional data:
1. Plant assets purchased for cash during 1995 amounted to $20,000.
2. Common stock with a par value of $30,000 was issued at par for cash.
3. Cash dividends declared and paid in 1995 totaled $4,000.

Income Statement Items	Related Balance Sheet Accounts	Cash Flows from Operating Activities
Sales	Accounts Receivable	Cash received from customers
Cost of goods sold	Accounts Payable and Merchandise Inventory	Cash paid for merchandise
Operating expenses and taxes	Accrued Liabilities and Prepaid Expenses	Cash paid for operating expenses

For other income statement items, the relationship is often obvious. For instance, salaries payable relates to salaries expense, federal income tax payable relates to federal income tax expense, prepaid rent relates to rent expense, and so on.

The balance sheet accounts affect the income statement items as follows:

Accrual Basis		*Cash Basis (Cash Flows from Operating Activities)*
Sales	+ Decrease or − Increase in Accounts Receivable	= Cash received from customers
Cost of goods sold	+ Increase or − Decrease in Merchandise Inventory **and** + Decrease or − Increase in Accounts Payable	= Cash paid for merchandise
Operating expenses	+ Decrease or − Increase in related accrued liability **and/or** + Increase or − Decrease in related prepaid expense	= Cash paid for operating expenses

Noncash operating expenses (such as depreciation expense and amortization expense), revenues, gains, and losses are reduced to zero in the cash basis income statement.

As a general rule, an increase in a current asset (other than cash) decreases cash inflow or increases cash outflow. Thus, when accounts receivable increases, sales revenue on a cash basis decreases (some customers who bought merchandise have not yet paid for it). When inventory increases, cost of goods sold on a cash basis increases (increasing cash outflow). When a prepaid expense increases, the related operating expense on a cash basis increases (e.g., a company not only paid for insurance expense but also paid cash to increase prepaid insurance). The effect on cash flows is just the opposite for decreases in these other current assets.

An increase in a current liability increases cash inflow or decreases cash outflow. Thus, when accounts payable increases, cost of goods sold on a cash basis decreases (instead of paying cash, the purchase was made on credit). When an accrued liability (such as salaries payable) increases, the related operating expense (salaries expense) on a cash basis decreases (e.g., the company incurred more salaries than it paid). Decreases in current liabilities have just the opposite effects on cash flows.

In the Welby example, there are no prepaid expenses. The current assets and current liabilities affecting the income statement items changed as follows:

	Increase	Decrease
Accounts receivable.	$10,000	
Merchandise inventory		$4,000
Accounts payable		6,000
Accrued liabilities payable	2,000	

Illustration 21.4
WORKING PAPER TO CONVERT INCOME STATEMENT FROM ACCRUAL BASIS TO CASH BASIS

WELBY COMPANY
Working Paper to Convert Income Statement
from Accrual Basis to Cash Basis
For the Year Ended December 31, 1995

	Accrual Basis		Add	Deduct	Cash Basis (Cash Flows from Operating Activities)	
Sales		$140,000		$10,000[1]		$130,000
Cost of goods sold. . . .	$100,000		$6,000[2]	4,000[3]	$102,000	
Operating expenses . . .	25,000			2,000[4]	23,000	
Depreciation expense . .	5,000			5,000	–0–	
		130,000				125,000
Net income		$ 10,000				$ 5,000

[1] Increase in Accounts Receivable.
[2] Decrease in Accounts Payable.
[3] Decrease in Merchandise Inventory.
[4] Increase in Accrued Liabilities Payable.

Thus, the income statement for Welby can be converted to a cash basis as shown in Illustration 21.4.

Alternate Step 1: Determining Cash Flows from Operating Activities—Indirect Method

Under the indirect method, certain adjustments are necessary to convert net income to cash flows from operating activities. First, changes that occurred in current accounts other than cash must be analyzed for their effects on cash. Then, noncash items such as depreciation that affected net income but not cash must be taken into account. Welby had only one such item— depreciation expense of $5,000. Applying these adjustments to Welby's financial statements and other data in Illustration 21.3 yields the following schedule:

Cash flows from operating activities:		
Net income.	$ 10,000	
Adjustments to reconcile net income to net cash provided by operating activities:		
Increase in accounts receivable	(10,000)	
Decrease in merchandise inventory	4,000	
Decrease in accounts payable	(6,000)	
Increase in accrued liabilities payable	2,000	
Depreciation	5,000	
Net cash provided by operating activities		$5,000

Notice that both the direct and indirect methods result in $5,000 net cash provided by operating activities.

The following table can be used to make the adjustments to net income for the changes in current assets and current liabilities:

For changes in these current assets and current liabilities:	Make these adjustments to convert accrual basis net income to cash basis net income:	
	Add	Deduct
Accounts receivable	Decrease	Increase
Merchandise inventory	Decrease	Increase
Prepaid expenses	Decrease	Increase
Accounts payable	Increase	Decrease
Accrued liabilities payable	Increase	Decrease

Notice in the above summary that all changes in current asset accounts are handled in a similar manner to each other. Also, all changes in current liability accounts are handled in a similar manner, but in the opposite manner from that of the current asset changes. A more condensed table to use in making these adjustments is:

For Changes in—	Add the Changes to Net Income	Deduct the Changes from Net Income
Current assets	Decreases	Increases
Current liabilities	Increases	Decreases

In applying the rules given in the above table, a decrease in a current asset is added to net income; an increase in a current asset is deducted from net income. For current liabilities, increases are added to net income, and decreases are deducted from net income.

The complete adjustment or conversion procedure used in the comprehensive example beginning on page 1028 is summarized below:

Accrual basis net income
+ or − Changes in noncash current asset and current liability accounts
+ Expenses and losses not affecting cash
− Revenues and gains not affecting cash
= Cash flows from operating activities

Step 2: Analyzing the Noncurrent Accounts

Now that the changes in current accounts have been analyzed for their effect on cash, we will examine the noncurrent accounts. Remember that a change in a noncurrent account usually comes about because cash is received or disbursed.

In the Welby example, we must analyze four noncurrent accounts: Retained Earnings, Plant Assets, Accumulated Depreciation, and Common Stock.

1.   The analysis of the noncurrent accounts can begin with any of the noncurrent accounts, but we will begin by reviewing the Retained Earnings account. Retained Earnings is the account to which net income or loss for the period was closed. The $6,000 increase in this account consists of $10,000 of net income less $4,000 of dividends paid. The net income amount can be found in the income statement. Both net income and dividends must be entered on the statement of cash flows in Illustration 21.5, Part B. The $10,000 net income is used as the starting figure in determining cash flows from operating activities. Thus, net income of $10,000 is entered on the statement in the cash flows from operating activities section.

2.   The Plant Assets account increased by $20,000 during the year. The additional data indicate that plant assets of $20,000 were purchased during the period. A purchase of plant assets is shown as a deduction in the cash flows from investing activities section.

3.   The $5,000 increase in the Accumulated Depreciation account equals the amount of depreciation expense shown in the income statement for the period. As shown earlier, because depreciation does not affect cash, under the indirect (addback) method it must be added back to net income on the statement of cash flows to convert accrual net income to a cash basis.

4.   The $30,000 increase in common stock resulted from the issuance of stock at par value, as disclosed in the additional data (item 2) given in Illustration 21.3. An issuance of stock is shown in the statement of cash flows as a positive amount in the cash flows from financing activities section.

Step 3: Arranging Information in the Statement of Cash Flows

After we have analyzed the noncurrent accounts, we can prepare the statement of cash flows from the information generated. Part A of Illustration 21.5 presents the statement of cash flows for Welby using the direct method. Part B shows the statement of cash flows for Welby using the indirect method.

The statement of cash flows has three major sections: cash flows from operating activities, cash flows from investing activities, and cash flows from financing activities. The format in the operating activities section differs for the direct and indirect methods. The direct method adjusts each item in the income statement to a cash basis. The indirect method makes these same adjustments but to net income rather than to each item in the income statement. Both methods eliminate the effects of noncash items, such as depreciation, and also eliminate gains and losses on sales of plant assets.

Illustration 21.5
STATEMENT OF CASH FLOWS

A. Direct Method

WELBY COMPANY
Statement of Cash Flows
For the Year Ended December 31, 1995

Cash flows from operating activities:

Cash received from customers.	$ 130,000	
Cash paid for merchandise	(102,000)	
Cash paid for operating expenses	(23,000)	
Net cash provided by operating activities		$ 5,000

Cash flows from investing activities:

Purchase of plant assets.	(20,000)

Cash flows from financing activities:

Proceeds from issuing common stock	$ 30,000	
Paid cash dividends.	(4,000)	
Net cash provided by financing activities		26,000
Net increase (decrease) in cash		$ 11,000

This portion differs between the two versions

This portion is the same in both versions

B. Indirect Method

WELBY COMPANY
Statement of Cash Flows
For the Year Ended December 31, 1995

Cash flows from operating activities:

Net income.	$ 10,000	
Adjustments to reconcile net income to net cash provided by operating activities:		
Increase in accounts receivable	(10,000)	
Decrease in merchandise inventory	4,000	
Decrease in accounts payable	(6,000)	
Increase in accrued liabilities payable	2,000	
Depreciation expense	5,000	
Net cash provided by operating activities		$ 5,000

Cash flows from investing activities:

Purchase of plant assets.	(20,000)

Cash flows from financing activities:

Proceeds from issuing common stock	$ 30,000	
Paid cash dividends.	(4,000)	
Net cash provided by financing activities		26,000
Net increase (decrease) in cash		$ 11,000

The only item shown in the cash flows from investing activities section is the cash outflow of $20,000 for the purchase of plant assets. In a more complex situation, other items could be included in this category.

Two items are shown under the cash flows from financing activities section. The issuance of common stock resulted in a cash inflow of $30,000. The payment of dividends resulted in a cash outflow of $4,000.

The last line of the statement is the $11,000 increase in cash for the year. Other examples could have a decrease in cash for the year.

COMPREHENSIVE ILLUSTRATION

This section presents a more complete example of the procedures followed to prepare a statement of cash flows. A working paper (shown later in Illustration 21.8) is an aid in preparing the statement for both the direct and indirect methods. For the direct method, the information regarding cash

Illustration 21.6
STATEMENT OF INCOME AND RETAINED EARNINGS

<table>
<tr><td colspan="3">UNITED STATES CORPORATION
Statement of Income and Retained Earnings
For the Year Ended December 31, 1995</td></tr>
<tr><td>Net sales . . . .</td><td></td><td>$1,464,200</td></tr>
<tr><td>Cost of goods sold . . . .</td><td></td><td>871,150</td></tr>
<tr><td>Gross margin. . . . .</td><td></td><td>$ 593,050</td></tr>
<tr><td>Operating expenses:</td><td></td><td></td></tr>
<tr><td>Salaries expense . . . .</td><td>$215,000</td><td></td></tr>
<tr><td>Depreciation expense ($3,250, buildings; $31,050, equipment) . . . .</td><td>34,300</td><td></td></tr>
<tr><td>Supplies expense . . . .</td><td>7,320</td><td></td></tr>
<tr><td>Advertising expense . . . .</td><td>90,000</td><td></td></tr>
<tr><td>Taxes expense, payroll and property . . . .</td><td>26,000</td><td></td></tr>
<tr><td>General and administrative expenses . . . .</td><td>123,780</td><td></td></tr>
<tr><td>Total operating expenses . . . .</td><td></td><td>496,400</td></tr>
<tr><td>Income from operations. . . . .</td><td></td><td>$ 96,650</td></tr>
<tr><td>Other revenues:</td><td></td><td></td></tr>
<tr><td>Interest revenue . . . .</td><td>$ 1,950</td><td></td></tr>
<tr><td>Gain on sale of long-term investments . . . .</td><td>1,700</td><td>3,650</td></tr>
<tr><td></td><td></td><td>$ 100,300</td></tr>
<tr><td>Other expenses:</td><td></td><td></td></tr>
<tr><td>Interest expense . . . .</td><td>$ 3,800</td><td></td></tr>
<tr><td>Loss on sale of equipment . . . .</td><td>900</td><td>4,700</td></tr>
<tr><td>Income before federal income taxes . . . .</td><td></td><td>$ 95,600</td></tr>
<tr><td>Deduct: Federal income taxes . . . .</td><td></td><td>45,250</td></tr>
<tr><td>Net income. . . . .</td><td></td><td>$ 50,350</td></tr>
<tr><td>Retained earnings, January 1, 1995 . . . .</td><td></td><td>84,100</td></tr>
<tr><td>Subtotal . . . .</td><td></td><td>$ 134,450</td></tr>
<tr><td>Deduct: Dividends declared and paid . . . .</td><td></td><td>18,000</td></tr>
<tr><td>Retained earnings, December 31, 1995 . . . .</td><td></td><td>$ 116,450</td></tr>
</table>

flows from operations is used to show the reconciliation of that figure with net income. An additional working paper is used to convert the income statement to a cash basis for use in the statement of cash flows.

The basic data for the example are found in Illustrations 21.6 and 21.7, which present the United States Corporation's statement of income and retained earnings (combined) for the year ended December 31, 1995, and comparative balance sheets for the years 1995 and 1994.

Illustration 21.7
COMPARATIVE BALANCE SHEETS

UNITED STATES CORPORATION
Comparative Balance Sheets
December 31, 1995 and 1994

	1995	1994	*Increase/ (Decrease)*
Assets			
Current assets:			
Cash	$ 46,300	$ 40,900	$ 5,400
Accounts receivable, net	112,160	101,000	11,160
Merchandise inventory	130,600	115,300	15,300
Prepaid advertising	3,100	4,700	(1,600)
Total current assets	$292,160	$261,900	$30,260
Investments	$ 17,000	$ 25,000	$ (8,000)
Property, plant, and equipment:			
Land	$100,000	$ 80,000	$20,000
Buildings	175,000	130,000	45,000
Accumulated depreciation—buildings	(29,750)	(26,500)	(3,250)
Equipment	198,000	175,000	23,000
Accumulated depreciation—equipment	(57,650)	(43,100)	(14,550)
Total property, plant, and equipment	$385,600	$315,400	$70,200
Total assets	$694,760	$602,300	$92,460
Liabilities and Stockholders' Equity			
Current liabilities:			
Accounts payable	$ 91,420	$ 86,870	$ 4,550
Salaries payable	9,890	12,230	(2,340)
Federal income taxes payable	12,000	14,100	(2,100)
Total current liabilities	$113,310	$113,200	$ 110
Long-term liabilities:			
Mortgage note payable, 10% (on land and buildings)	$ 35,000	$ –0–	$35,000
Bonds payable, 8%, due 1998	40,000	40,000	–0–
Total long-term liabilities	$ 75,000	$ 40,000	$35,000
Total liabilities	$188,310	$153,200	$35,110
Stockholders' equity:			
Common stock, stated value, $50 per share	$390,000	$365,000	$25,000
Retained earnings	116,450	84,100	32,350
Total stockholders' equity	$506,450	$449,100	$57,350
Total liabilities and stockholders' equity	$694,760	$602,300	$92,460

Assume the following information about the noncurrent accounts of the United States Corporation is available:

1. No investments were made during the year. Investments that cost $8,000 were sold for $9,700.
2. Land and buildings with a cost of $65,000 ($45,000 for the buildings and $20,000 for the land) were acquired, subject to a mortgage note of $35,000.
3. During the year, the corporation sold equipment for $2,600 that had an original cost of $20,000 and accumulated depreciation of $16,500.
4. The common stock was issued for cash.

The working paper in Illustration 21.8 for United States Corporation is used to analyze the transactions and prepare the statement of cash flows. The following discussion describes the items and traces their effects in the entries made on the working paper.

The steps in preparing the working paper are described below:

1. Enter the beginning account balances of all balance sheet accounts in the first column and the ending account balances in the fourth column. Notice that the debit items are listed first, followed by the credit items.
2. Total the debits and credits in the first and fourth columns to make sure that debits equal credits in each column.
3. Write "Cash Flows from Operating Activities" immediately below the total of the credit items. Skip sufficient lines for recording adjustments to convert accrual net income to cash flows from operating activities. Then write "Cash Flows from Investing Activities" and allow enough space for those items. Finally, write "Cash Flows from Financing Activities" and allow enough space for those items.
4. Enter entries for analyzing transactions in the second and third columns. The entries serve two functions: (a) they explain the change in each account and (b) they classify the changes into operating, investing, and financing activities. These entries will be discussed individually in the next section.
5. Total the debits and credits in the second and third columns; they should be equal. You will have one pair of totals for the balance sheet items and another pair for the bottom portion of the working paper. The bottom portion of the working paper is used to prepare the statement of cash flows.

Completing the Working Paper

To complete the working paper in Illustration 21.8, we must analyze the change in each noncash balance sheet account. Remember that the focus of this working paper is on cash and that every change in cash is accompanied by a change in a noncash balance sheet account. After entries have been properly made to analyze all changes in noncash balance sheet accounts, the

Illustration 21.8
WORKING PAPER FOR STATEMENT OF CASH FLOWS

UNITED STATES CORPORATION
Working Paper for Statement of Cash Flows
For the Year Ended December 31, 1995

	Account Balances 12/31/94	Analysis of Transactions for 1994		Account Balances 12/31/95
		Debit	Credit	
Debits				
Cash	40,900	(0) 5,400		46,300
Accounts Receivable	101,000	(2) 11,160		112,160
Merchandise Inventory	115,300	(3) 15,300		130,600
Prepaid Advertising	4,700		(4) 1,600	3,100
Investments	25,000		(8) 8,000	17,000
Land	80,000	(9) 20,000		100,000
Buildings	130,000	(9) 45,000		175,000
Equipment	175,000	(11) 43,000	(10) 20,000	198,000
Totals	671,900			782,160
Credits				
Accumulated Depreciation—Buildings	26,500		(13) 3,250	29,750
Accumulated Depreciation—Equipment	43,100	(10) 16,500	(13) 31,050	57,650
Accounts Payable	86,870		(5) 4,550	91,420
Salaries Payable	12,230	(6) 2,340		9,890
Federal Income Taxes Payable	14,100	(7) 2,100		12,000
Mortgage Note Payable	–0–		(9) 35,000	35,000
Bonds Payable	40,000			40,000
Common Stock	365,000		(12) 25,000	390,000
Retained Earnings	84,100	(14) 18,000	(1) 50,350	116,450
Totals	671,900	178,800	178,800	782,160
Cash Flows from Operating Activities:				
Net Income		(1) 50,350		
Increase in Accounts Receivable			(2) 11,160	
Increase in Merchandise Inventory			(3) 15,300	
Decrease in Prepaid Advertising		(4) 1,600		
Increase in Accounts Payable		(5) 4,550		
Decrease in Salaries Payable			(6) 2,340	
Decrease in Federal Income Taxes Payable			(7) 2,100	
Gain on Sale of Investments			(8) 1,700	
Loss on Sale of Equipment		(10) 900		
Depreciation Expense—Buildings		(13) 3,250		
Depreciation Expense—Equipment		(13) 31,050		
Cash Flows from Investing Activities:				
Proceeds from Sale of Investments		(8) 9,700		
Purchase of Land and Buildings (cash portion)			(9) 30,000	
Proceeds from Sale of Equipment		(10) 2,600		
Purchase of Equipment			(11) 43,000	
Cash Flows from Financing Activities:				
Proceeds from Issuing Common Stock		(12) 25,000		
Payment of Cash Dividends			(14) 18,000	
Increase in Cash for Year			(0) 5,400	
Noncash Investing and Financing Activities:				
Mortgage Note Issued to Acquire Land and Buildings		(9) 35,000	(9) 35,000	
Totals		164,000	164,000	

working paper will show all activities affecting cash flows. The explanations below are keyed to numbers of the entries on the working paper.

Entry (0). The beginning and ending cash balances are compared to determine the change in the Cash account during the year, which is a $5,400 increase. An entry is made on the working paper debiting Cash for $5,400 and crediting Increase in Cash for Year near the bottom of the schedule. This entry is labeled *(0)* because it does not explain the change in cash but is the "target" of the analysis. The entry sets out the change in cash that the statement seeks to explain. No further attention need be paid to cash in completing the working paper.

Attention is now directed toward changes in other balance sheet accounts. These accounts can be dealt with in any order, but first we will record the net income for the period and then analyze the current assets (other than cash) and the current liabilities. Then, we will analyze the changes in the noncurrent accounts.

Entry (1). The combined statement of income and retained earnings reveals that net income for 1995 was $50,350. Entry *(1)* records the $50,350 as the starting point in measuring cash flows from operating activities and credits Retained Earnings as a partial explanation of the change in that account.

The next task is to analyze changes in current accounts other than Cash. The current accounts of United States Corporation are closely related to operations, and their changes are included in converting net income to cash flows from operating activities. The changes in the current accounts are analyzed in the manner previously discussed (pages 1024–25).

Entry (2). The $11,160 increase in accounts receivable must be deducted from net income when converting it to cash flows from operating activities. If accounts receivable increased, sales to customers exceeded cash received from customers. To convert net income to a cash basis, the $11,160 must be deducted.

The working paper technique makes the recording of these effects almost mechanical. Accounts Receivable must be debited for $11,160 to increase it from $101,000 to $112,160. If Accounts Receivable is debited, a credit must be entered for an item that can be entitled "Increase in Accounts Receivable." The increase is deducted from net income in converting it to cash flows from operating activities.

Entry (3). This is virtually a duplicate of entry *(2)*, except that it involves merchandise inventory rather than receivables.

Entry (4). Although this entry is similar to entries *(2)* and *(3)*, it has the opposite effect because prepaid advertising decreased.

Entry (5). This entry records the effect of an increase in accounts payable on net income in converting it to cash flows from operating activities.

Entries (6) and (7). These entries record the effects of decreases in two other current liability accounts (Salaries Payable and Federal Income Taxes Payable) in converting net income to cash flows from operating activities.

Next, we analyze the changes in the noncurrent balance sheet accounts.

Entry (8).   Investments is the first noncurrent account. The additional information discloses that investments were sold at a gain. The transaction was recorded in the following manner:

Cash	9,700	
Investments		8,000
Gain on Sale of Investments		1,700

The $9,700 cash resulting from the sale of investments is reported in the "Cash Flows from Investing Activities" section (entry *8*) in the lower part of Illustration 21.8. Entry *(8)* also removes the $1,700 gain on sale of investments from cash flows from operating activities because this amount is already included as part of the cash resulting from the sale of investments. If the $9,700 cash received from the sale is reported in the "Cash Flows from Investing Activities" section and the gain is not removed from cash flows from operating activities, the $1,700 gain will be counted twice. Note that the entry on the working paper is identical to the original journal entry for the sale, except for the $9,700 debit. Instead of debiting Cash, a properly described investing activity "Proceeds from Sale of Investments" is debited. The $8,000 credit accounts fully for the decrease in the Investments account balance; if this credit had not fully accounted for the change, there would have to be other transactions involving the Investments account to analyze and report.

Entry (9).   The changes in the Land and Buildings accounts resulted from the following entry:

Land	20,000	
Buildings	45,000	
Cash		30,000
Mortgage Note Payable		35,000

This transaction requires two entries on the working paper. First, Land and Buildings are debited for $20,000 and $45,000, respectively, and an item described as "Purchase of Land and Buildings" is credited for $30,000 in the investing activity section for the cash portion. Second, an entry labeled "Mortgage Note Issued to Acquire Land and Buildings" is entered at the bottom of the work sheet in both the debit and credit columns for the $35,000 noncash portion of the transaction. This item is listed on the work sheet so you will not forget to include it in a separate schedule. This transaction is an example of a significant financing and investing activity that must be included in a separate schedule even though part of it did not affect cash.

Entry (10).   The Equipment account shows a net increase of $23,000 resulting from two transactions: a $43,000 purchase (shown in entry *11* below) and a $20,000 retirement. The net change in the account must be analyzed to show both transactions.

Data relating to the $20,000 retirement were included in the additional information provided. The computation of the loss on sale can be summarized as follows using data provided in the additional information:

Cost of equipment sold (given)	$20,000[1]
Less: Accumulated depreciation (given)	16,500[2]
Book value of equipment sold	$ 3,500
Less: Cash received (given).	2,600[3]
Loss on sale (as shown in income statement)	$ 900[4]

[1] Shown as a credit to Equipment on the working paper.

[2] Shown as a debit to Accumulated Depreciation—Equipment on the working paper.

[3] Shown as proceeds from sale of equipment under "Cash Flows from Investing Activities."

[4] Shown as an addition to net income under "Cash Flows from Operating Activities."

The working paper shows cash resulting from the sale of equipment under the investing activities section and explains part of the changes in the Equipment and the Accumulated Depreciation—Equipment accounts. The loss is added back to net income because it is a noncash item that was deducted in arriving at net income. The loss has exactly the same effect as depreciation expense.

Entry (11).   This entry debits the Equipment account and credits "Purchase of Equipment" in the investing activities section for the $43,000 cash spent to acquire new equipment. The $43,000 debit to Equipment along with the $20,000 credit to Equipment in entry *(10)* fully account for the $23,000 increase in the account balance as shown below.

Equipment

Beg. bal.	175,000		
(11)	43,000	(10)	20,000
End. bal.	198,000		

Entry (12).   This entry shows the $25,000 cash received from sale of common stock as a "financing activity." The entry also explains the change in the Common Stock account. If stock had been sold for more than its stated value of $50 per share, the excess would be recorded in a separate Paid-In Capital in Excess of Stated Value account. However, the total amount of cash received from the issuance of common stock would have been reported as a single figure on the statement of cash flows. Only this total amount received is significant to creditors and other users of the financial statements trying to judge the solvency of the company.

Entry (13).   This entry adds $3,250 building depreciation and $31,050 equipment depreciation back to net income and credits the respective accumulated depreciation accounts. The depreciation expense can be found (1) on the statement of income and retained earnings, or (2) by solving for the credit needed to balance the accumulated depreciation accounts on the balance sheet. The $31,050 credit to the accumulated depreciation account for equipment less the $16,500 debit to this account in entry *(10)* explains fully the increase in this account from $43,100 to $57,650 as shown below.

Accumulated Depreciation—Equipment

		Beg. bal.	43,100
(10)	16,500	(13)	31,050
		End. bal.	57,650

Entry (14).   This entry debits Retained Earnings and credits Payment of Cash Dividends for the $18,000 dividends declared and paid. The entry also completes the explanation of the change in Retained Earnings as shown below. Notice that on the statement of cash flows, the dividends must be *paid* to be included as a cash outflow from financing activities.

Retained Earnings

		Beg. bal.	84,100
(14)	18,000	(1)	50,350
		End. bal.	116,450

If Retained Earnings had changed for reasons other than net income or cash dividends, the causes of the changes must be determined to decide whether they should be reported in the statement of cash flows. **Transactions such as stock dividends and stock splits would not be reported on the statement of cash flows or in a separate schedule because they lack significance from an analytical viewpoint and do not affect cash.** However, an entry must be made on the working paper to explain the changes caused by a stock dividend or split, even if cash was not affected. All changes in all noncash accounts must be explained to show that a change affecting cash was not overlooked.

The analysis of the noncash accounts is now complete. To be sure that a change has not been overlooked, the debits and credits in the middle two columns opposite the 1994 balances are added to or subtracted from those balances, line by line. If the working paper has been properly prepared, the results will be the 1995 balances listed in the fourth column. For the balance sheet accounts, every line must foot (total) across. For example, the $43,000 debit is added to the $175,000 beginning balance for Equipment, and the $20,000 credit is deducted to get an ending balance of $198,000.

Next, the debits and credits for the balance sheet account entries and for the statement of cash flows are added to make sure that they are equal in both sections. Note that entries made in the working paper are used only to derive cash flows into and out of the company. These entries are not entered in the company's accounting system because the transactions that caused the cash flows have already been recorded.

Preparing the Statement of Cash Flows

The data in the lower section of the working paper are now used to prepare the statement of cash flows under the indirect method shown in Illustration 21.9. Information about all material investing and financing activities of an enterprise that do not result in cash receipts or disbursements in the period are to be reported in a separate schedule, rather than in the statement of cash flows. The disclosure may be in narrative form. United States Corporation had one such transaction, the issuance of a mortgage note to acquire land and buildings. A separate schedule might appear as follows:

Schedule of noncash financing and investing activities:	
Mortgage note issued to acquire land and buildings	$35,000

If the direct method is used, the information relating to the indirect method of calculating cash flows from operating activities in the bottom part of the

Illustration 21.9
STATEMENT OF CASH FLOWS—INDIRECT METHOD

UNITED STATES CORPORATION
Statement of Cash Flows
For the Year Ended December 31, 1995

Cash flows from operating activities:		
Net income.	$ 50,350	
Adjustments to reconcile net income to net cash provided by operating activities:		
Increase in accounts receivable	(11,160)	
Increase in merchandise inventory.	(15,300)	
Decrease in prepaid advertising	1,600	
Increase in accounts payable	4,550	
Decrease in salaries payable.	(2,340)	
Decrease in federal income taxes payable	(2,100)	
Gain on sale of investment	(1,700)	
Loss on sale of equipment	900	
Depreciation expense—buildings	3,250	
Depreciation expense—equipment.	31,050	
Net cash provided by operating activities.		$ 59,100
Cash flows from investing activities:		
Proceeds from sale of investments.	$ 9,700	
Purchase of land and buildings (cash portion)	(30,000)	
Proceeds from sale of equipment	2,600	
Payment for purchase of equipment	(43,000)	
Net cash used in investing activities		(60,700)
Cash flows from financing activities:		
Proceeds from issuing common stock	$ 25,000	
Paid cash dividends.	(18,000)	
Net cash provided by financing activities.		7,000
Net increase in cash		$ 5,400

working paper (Illustration 21.8) and in the top part of Illustration 21.9 would appear in a separate supporting schedule rather than in the statement of cash flows. Also, an additional working paper is needed if the direct method is used. This working paper converts the items on the income statement to a cash basis, as shown in Illustration 21.10.

Illustration 21.10
WORKING PAPER TO CONVERT INCOME STATEMENT FROM ACCRUAL BASIS TO CASH BASIS

UNITED STATES CORPORATION
Working Paper to Convert Income Statement from
Accrual Basis to Cash Basis
For the Year Ended December 31, 1995

	Accrual Basis		Add	Deduct	Cash Basis (Cash Flows from Operating Activities)
Net sales		$1,464,200		$11,160[1]	$1,453,040
Cost of goods sold		871,150	$15,300[2]	4,550[3]	881,900
Gross margin		$ 593,050			$ 571,140
Operating expenses:					
Salaries expense	$215,000		2,340[4]		$217,340
Depreciation expense	34,300			34,300	–0–
Supplies expense	7,320				7,320
Advertising expense	90,000			1,600[5]	88,400
Taxes expense, payroll and property	26,000				26,000
General administrative expenses	123,780				123,780
Total operating expenses		496,400			462,840
Income from operations		$ 96,650			$ 108,300
Other revenues:					
Interest revenue	$ 1,950				$ 1,950
Gain on sale of long-term investment	1,700			1,700	–0–
		3,650			1,950
		$ 100,300			$ 110,250
Other expenses:					
Interest expense	$ 3,800				$ 3,800
Loss on sale of equipment	900			900	–0–
		4,700			3,800
Income before federal income taxes		$ 95,600			$ 106,450
Deduct: Federal income taxes		45,250	2,100[6]		47,350
Net income		$ 50,350			$ 59,100

[1] Increase in Accounts Receivable.
[2] Increase in Merchandise Inventory.
[3] Increase in Accounts Payable.
[4] Decrease in Salaries Payable.
[5] Decrease in Prepaid Advertising.
[6] Decrease in Federal Income Taxes Payable.

Illustration 21.11
STATEMENT OF CASH FLOWS—DIRECT METHOD

UNITED STATES CORPORATION
Statement of Cash Flows
For the Year Ended December 31, 1995

Cash flows from operating activities:

Cash received from customers.	$1,453,040	
Cash paid for merchandise for resale	(881,900)	
Cash paid to employees.	(217,340)	
Cash paid for supplies	(7,320)	
Cash paid for advertising	(88,400)	
Taxes paid, payroll and property.	(26,000)	
General administrative expenses paid	(123,780)	
Interest received	1,950	
Interest paid	(3,800)	
Federal income taxes paid	(47,350)	
Net cash provided by operating activities.		$ 59,100

Cash flows from investing activities:

Proceeds from sale of investments.	$ 9,700	
Purchase of land and buildings (cash portion)	(30,000)	
Proceeds from sale of equipment	2,600	
Payment for purchase of equipment	(43,000)	
Net cash used in investing activities		(60,700)

Cash flows from financing activities:

Proceeds from issuing common stock	$ 25,000	
Payment of cash dividends	(18,000)	
Net cash provided by financing activities.		7,000
Net increase in cash		$ 5,400

Notice that depreciation is eliminated when converting to a cash basis since it does not involve an outflow of cash in the current period. Also, the gain from sale of long-term investments and the loss on sale of equipment are eliminated since the proceeds of these transactions are reported in the cash flows from investing activities section in the statement of cash flows.

Illustration 21.11 shows the statement of cash flows under the direct method. Notice that the only difference between the direct and indirect methods is in the cash flows from operating activities section.

WORKING CAPITAL OR CASH FLOWS

*Objective 5
Describe the historical development from a statement of changes in financial position to a statement of cash flows*

Through the middle of 1988, a **statement of changes in financial position** was required to report on funds flows. This statement showed the sources and uses of funds as the two main categories rather than categorizing according to operating activities, investing activities, and financing activities. *Funds* were generally defined as either working capital or cash. **Working capital** is

A BROADER PERSPECTIVE

CASH FLOW STATEMENT ISSUED BY GASB FOR '90

Norwalk, Conn.—The Governmental Accounting Standards Board has issued a statement that will require governmental business-type entities to provide a cash-flow statement as part of a full set of financials.

GASB Statement 9 takes effect for fiscal years beginning after Dec. 15, 1989. Thus, the standard will affect 1990 calendar-year reporting.

Under Statement 9, an entity's statement of cash flows would replace the currently required statement of changes in financial position.

All proprietary and nonexpendable trust funds and governmental entities that use proprietary fund accounting would be subject to the provisions of Statement 9.

Public employee retirement systems and pension trust funds are exempted from the provisions of Statement 9 and are not currently required to provide a statement of changes in financial position. However, the GASB will address that disclosure issue in its pension plan accounting project.

According to GASB chairman James F. Antonio, Statement 9 is based on the provisions of Statement 95 of the Financial Accounting Standards Board. That document contains standards for cash flow statements issued by private-sector entities.

Antonio noted, however, that Statement 9 "takes into account the differences in environment between the public and private sectors and is therefore somewhat different from FASB Statement 95."

The new GASB standard requires that a statement of cash flows classify cash receipts and payments according to the activities they stem from—whether operations, noncapital financing, capital and related financing, or investments.

"The Board," Antonio pointed out, "is encouraging governmental entities to report cash flows from operating activities by the direct method, which shows major classes of operating cash receipts and payments. However, that statement does permit the use of the indirect, or reconciliation, method."

Antonio added that although Statement 9 applies only to proprietary and nonexpendable trust funds of government entities, there may be a need in the future for cash-flow information in governmental funds.

"Cash-flow information for all types of funds," he said, "will be addressed in the Board's project on the financial reporting model."

SOURCE: *Accounting Today,* October 9, 1989, p. 30. Reprinted with permission.

---

equal to current assets minus current liabilities. The common practice before 1983 was to define *funds* as working capital.

Accountants prepared statements based on working capital for several reasons. Accurate information was needed about the flows of liquid assets (working capital) through a company because such flows are the lifeblood of a business. Yet constant changes in accounting principles yielded net income amounts that often were not good measures of such liquid asset flows from operations. In addition, attention focused on the total amount of working capital rather than the composition of working capital, including how much of it was cash.

The Shift toward Cash Flows

Beginning in 1983, more than half of a sample of 600 companies voluntarily used the cash definition of funds. There were several reasons for this shift toward the cash definition of funds. Many companies experienced severe cash flow problems, not working capital problems. The FASB noted the importance of cash flows in the Conceptual Framework Project, stating that "the reporting of meaningful components of future cash flows is generally more useful than reporting changes in working capital."[2] Shortly after publication of this statement, the Financial Executives Institute (FEI) recommended that its members adopt the cash basis in preparing a statement of changes in financial position.[3] The FEI represents approximately 95% of the companies with securities traded on the New York Stock Exchange and the American Stock Exchange.

The shifting of attention from working capital flows to cash flows is also supported by developments in modern finance. The investment decision is seen more clearly as one in which cash outlays are compared with expected cash returns, appropriately discounted for time and risk. Management, investors, and creditors are all alike in that each "invests" cash to get future cash returns. Thus, users need information to enable them to make predictions of the amounts, timing, and uncertainty surrounding expected cash receipts. Users also need information to provide feedback on prior assessments of cash flows.

Information on prior *cash* flows provides a better basis for making predictions of future cash flows than does information on prior *working capital* flows. Cash flows often differ sharply from working capital flows. For example, a rapidly expanding business that increases its working capital by expanding inventories and accounts receivable may not have enough cash to meet current bills. Cash flow analysis, rather than working capital analysis, is required to reveal such potential problems.

The adoption of the statement of cash flows completed the shift from a working capital emphasis to a cash emphasis. The statement of cash flows seems to provide information on cash flows in a more useful and understandable format than did the old statement of changes in financial position.

In Chapter 22, you will learn how to analyze and interpret a company's financial statements so that you can better judge its solvency and profitability. Data from the statement of cash flows are used in some of the analyses.

---

[2] FASB, *Proposed Statement of Financial Accounting Concepts,* "Reporting Income, Cash Flows, and Financial Position of Business Enterprises," Exposure Draft (Stamford, Conn., 1981), p. xi.

[3] Financial Executives Institute, *Alert,* December 14, 1981.

Communix, Inc., is a medium-sized company that manufactures and sells modems for microcomputers. The company had financed a recent expansion of its facilities by borrowing $400,000 and signing a 10-year note payable. One of the terms of the note stated that, if the company showed a negative amount of cash flows from operating activities for two years in succession, the entire loan would become immediately due at that time. The statement of cash flows for 1993 reported a negative cash flow from operating activities.

In mid-December, when the accountant, Jerry Price, calculated the approximate amounts to include in the statement of cash flows for 1994, a negative cash flow from operating activities of $80,000 resulted. When Jerry showed the president the initial computations, the president was very concerned. He said that there was no way the company could repay the $400,000 at this time. He told Jerry "do something" to avoid reporting the negative amount.

Several days later, Jerry told the president that the company could avoid reporting the negative cash flow from operating activities by delaying payment of about $100,000 of accounts payable that had due dates before the end of the year. The company would miss taking about $2,000 of cash discounts and might irritate some suppliers. However, the statement of cash flows would show an increase in accounts payable of $100,000, and a positive cash flow from operating activities of $20,000.

Required
a. Is Jerry correct in believing that this action will avoid reporting a negative cash flow from operating activities?
b. Is this action legal?
c. Who could be hurt by taking this action?
d. Who could be helped by taking this action?
e. Is this action ethical?

UNDERSTANDING THE LEARNING OBJECTIVES

1. Explain the purposes and uses of the statement of cash flows.
    - The statement of cash flows summarizes the effects on cash of the operating, financing, and investing activities of a company during an accounting period.
    - Management can see the effects of its past major policy decisions in quantitative form.
    - Investors and creditors can assess the entity's ability to generate positive future net cash flows, to meet its obligations, to pay dividends, and can assess the need for external financing.
2. Describe the content of the statement of cash flows and where certain items would appear on the statement.
    - Operating activities generally include the cash effects (inflows and outflows) of transactions and other events that enter into the deter-

mination of net income. The cash flows from operating activities can be measured in two ways. The direct method deducts from cash sales only those operating expenses that consumed cash. The indirect method starts with net income and adjusts net income for items that affected reported net income but did not involve cash.

- Investing activities generally include transactions involving the acquisition or disposal of noncurrent assets.
- Financing activities generally include the cash effects (inflows and outflows) of transactions and other events with creditors and owners.

3. Describe how to calculate cash flows from operating activities under both the direct and indirect methods.
    - The direct method deducts from cash sales only those operating expenses that consumed cash.
    - The indirect method starts with accrual basis net income and indirectly adjusts net income for items that affected reported net income but did not involve cash.

4. Prepare a statement of cash flows under both the direct and indirect methods showing cash flows from operating activities, investing activities, and financing activities.
    - The first step is to determine the cash flows from operating activities. Either the direct or indirect method may be used.
    - The second step is to analyze all the noncurrent accounts for changes in cash resulting from investing and financing activities.
    - The third step is to arrange the information gathered in steps 1 and 2 into the format required for the statement of cash flows.

5. Describe the historical development from a statement of changes in financial position to a statement of cash flows.
    - Until July 1988, a statement of changes in financial position was required to report on funds flows. This statement showed the sources and uses of funds as the two main categories. Funds often meant working capital (current assets minus current liabilities).
    - In late 1987, the Financial Accounting Standards Board issued a standard requiring the substitution of a statement of cash flows for the statement of changes in financial position effective for annual financial statements for fiscal years ending after July 15, 1988.

DEMONSTRATION PROBLEM

Given below are comparative balance sheets of Dells Corporation as of June 30, 1995, and June 30, 1994. The income statement for the year ended June 30, 1995, and certain additional data are also provided.

DELLS CORPORATION
Comparative Balance Sheets
June 30, 1995 and 1994

	1995	1994	Increase (Decrease)
Assets			
Current assets:			
Cash.	$ 30,000	$ 80,000	$ (50,000)
Accounts receivable, net	160,000	100,000	60,000
Merchandise inventory	100,000	70,000	30,000
Prepaid rent	20,000	10,000	10,000
Total current assets.	$310,000	$260,000	$ 50,000
Property, plant, and equipment:			
Equipment	$400,000	$200,000	$200,000
Accumulated depreciation—equipment	(60,000)	(50,000)	(10,000)
Total property, plant, and equipment.	$340,000	$150,000	$190,000
Total assets	$650,000	$410,000	$240,000
Liabilities and Stockholders' Equity			
Current liabilities:			
Accounts payable.	$ 50,000	$ 40,000	$ 10,000
Notes payable—bank	–0–	50,000	(50,000)
Salaries payable	10,000	20,000	(10,000)
Federal income taxes payable	30,000	20,000	10,000
Total current liabilities	$ 90,000	$130,000	$(40,000)
Stockholders' equity:			
Common stock, $10 par.	$300,000	$100,000	$200,000
Paid-in capital in excess of par	50,000	–0–	50,000
Retained earnings	210,000	180,000	30,000
Total stockholders' equity.	$560,000	$280,000	$280,000
Total liabilities and stockholders' equity	$650,000	$410,000	$240,000

DELLS CORPORATION
Statement of Income and Retained Earnings
For the Year Ended June 30, 1995

Sales		$1,000,000
Cost of goods sold	$600,000	
Salaries and wages expense	200,000	
Rent expense	40,000	
Depreciation expense	20,000	
Interest expense.	3,000	
Loss on sale of equipment.	7,000	870,000
Income before federal income taxes		$ 130,000
Deduct: Federal income taxes		60,000
Net income		$ 70,000
Retained earnings, July 1, 1994		180,000
		$ 250,000
Deduct: Dividends.		40,000
Retained earnings, June 30, 1995.		$ 210,000

Additional data:

1. Equipment with a cost of $20,000, on which $10,000 of depreciation had been recorded, was sold for cash. Additional equipment was purchased.
2. Stock was issued for cash.

Required:

Using the data given for Dells Corporation:

a. Prepare a working paper for a statement of cash flows.
b. Prepare a statement of cash flows—indirect method.
c. Prepare a working paper to convert net income from an accrual basis to a cash basis. Then prepare a partial statement of cash flows—direct method, showing only the cash flows from operating activities section.

Solution to demonstration problem

a.

DELLS CORPORATION
Working Paper for Statement of Cash Flows
For the Year Ended June 30, 1995

	Account Balances 6/30/94	Analysis of Transactions for 1995		Account Balances 6/30/95
		Debit	Credit	
Debits				
Cash	80,000		(0) 50,000	30,000
Accounts Receivable	100,000	(2) 60,000		160,000
Merchandise Inventory	70,000	(3) 30,000		100,000
Prepaid Rent	10,000	(4) 10,000		20,000
Equipment	200,000	(10) 220,000	(9) 20,000	400,000
	460,000			710,000
Credits				
Accumulated Depreciation	50,000	(9) 10,000	(11) 20,000	60,000
Accounts Payable	40,000		(5) 10,000	50,000
Notes Payable—Bank	50,000	(6) 50,000		–0–
Salaries Payable	20,000	(7) 10,000		10,000
Federal Income Taxes Payable	20,000		(8) 10,000	30,000
Common Stock, $10 Par	100,000		(12) 200,000	300,000
Paid-In Capital in Excess of Par	–0–		(12) 50,000	50,000
Retained Earnings	180,000	(13) 40,000	(1) 70,000	210,000
Totals	460,000	430,000	430,000	710,000
Cash Flows from Operating Activities:				
Net Income		(1) 70,000		
Increase in Accounts Receivable			(2) 60,000	
Increase in Merchandise Inventory			(3) 30,000	
Increase in Prepaid Rent			(4) 10,000	
Increase in Accounts Payable		(5) 10,000		
Decrease in Salaries Payable			(7) 10,000	
Increase in Federal Income Taxes Payable		(8) 10,000		
Loss on Sale of Equipment		(9) 7,000		
Depreciation Expense		(11) 20,000		
Cash Flows from Investing Activities:				
Proceeds from Sale of Equipment		(9) 3,000		
Purchases of Property, Plant, and Equipment			(10) 220,000	
Cash Flows from Financing Activities:				
Repayment of Bank Note			(6) 50,000	
Proceeds from Issuing Common Stock		(12) 250,000		
Payment of Cash Dividends			(13) 40,000	
Decrease in Cash		(0) 50,000		
Totals		420,000	420,000	

b.

DELLS CORPORATION
Statement of Cash Flows—Indirect Method
For the Year Ended June 30, 1995

Cash flows from operating activities:

Net income	$ 70,000	
Adjustments to reconcile net income to net cash provided by operating activities:		
Increase in accounts receivable	(60,000)	
Increase in merchandise inventory	(30,000)	
Increase in prepaid rent	(10,000)	
Increase in accounts payable	10,000	
Decrease in salaries payable	(10,000)	
Increase in federal income taxes payable	10,000	
Loss on sale of equipment	7,000	
Depreciation expense	20,000	
Net cash provided by operating activities		$ 7,000
Cash flows from investing activities:		
Proceeds from sale of equipment	$ 3,000	
Purchases of property, plant, and equipment	(220,000)	
Net cash used by investing activities		(217,000)
Cash flows from financing activities:		
Repayment of bank note	$ (50,000)	
Proceeds from issuing common stock	250,000	
Dividends paid	(40,000)	
Net cash provided by financing activities		160,000
Net increase (decrease) in cash		$ (50,000)

c.

DELLS CORPORATION
Working Paper to Convert Income Statement
from Accrual Basis to Cash Basis
For the Year Ended June 30, 1995

	Accrual Basis		Add	Deduct	Cash Basis (Cash Flows from Operating Activities)
Sales.		$1,000,000		$60,000[1]	$940,000
Cost of goods sold	$600,000		$30,000[2]	10,000[3]	$620,000
Salaries and wages expense. . .	200,000		10,000[4]		210,000
Rent expense.	40,000		10,000[5]		50,000
Depreciation expense	20,000			20,000	–0–
Interest expense	3,000				3,000
Loss on sale of equipment . . .	7,000			7,000	–0–
Federal income taxes	60,000			10,000[6]	50,000
		930,000			933,000
Net income.		$ 70,000			$ 7,000

[1] Increase in Accounts Receivable.
[2] Increase in Merchandise Inventory.
[3] Increase in Accounts Payable.
[4] Decrease in Salaries Payable.
[5] Increase in Prepaid Rent.
[6] Increase in Federal income Taxes Payable.

DELLS CORPORATION
Partial Statement of Cash Flows—Direct Method
For the Year Ended June 30, 1995

Cash flows from operating activities:

Cash received from customers	$ 940,000
Cash paid for merchandise	(620,000)
Salaries and wages paid	(210,000)
Rent paid	(50,000)
Interest paid	(3,000)
Federal income taxes paid	(50,000)
Net cash provided by operating activities . . .	$7,000

NEW TERMS

Cash flows from operating activities   The net amount of cash received or disbursed during a given period on items that normally appear on the income statement. *1019*

Direct method   Deducts from cash sales only those operating expenses that consumed cash. *1019*

Financing activities   Generally include the cash effects of transactions and other events involving creditors and owners. Cash payments made to settle current liabilities such as accounts payable, wages payable, and income taxes payable are not financing activities. These payments are operating activities. *1018*

Indirect method   A method of determining cash flows from operating activities that starts with net income and indirectly adjusts net income for items that do not involve cash. Also called the **addback** method. *1019*

Investing activities   Generally include transactions involving the acquisition or disposal of noncurrent assets. Examples include cash received or paid from the sale or purchase of property, plant, and equipment; marketable securities; and loans made to others. *1018*

Noncash charges or expenses   Expenses and losses that are added back to net income because they do not actually use cash of the company. The items added back include amounts of depreciation on plant assets, depletion that was expensed, amortization of intangible assets such as patents and goodwill, amortization of discount on bonds payable, and losses from disposals of noncurrent assets. *1020*

Noncash credits or revenues   Revenues and gains included in arriving at net income that do not provide cash; examples include gains from disposals of noncurrent assets, income from investments carried under the equity method, and amortization of premium on bonds payable. *1021*

Operating activities   Generally include the cash effects of transactions and other events that enter into the determination of net income. *1017*

Statement of cash flows   A statement that summarizes the effects on cash of the operating, investing, and financing activities of a company during an accounting period. Both inflows and outflows are included in each category. The statement of cash flows must be prepared each time an income statement is prepared. *1016*

Statement of changes in financial position   A statement formerly required that reported the flows of cash or working capital into and out of a business in a given time period; it also showed significant financing and investing activities that did not involve cash or working capital flows. *1038*

Working capital   Equal to current assets minus current liabilities. *1038*

SELF-TEST

True-False

Indicate whether each of the following statements is true or false.

1. The requirement for a statement of cash flows was preceded by the requirement for a statement of changes in financial position.

2. The statement of cash flows is one of the major financial statements.

3. Investing activities are transactions with creditors and owners.

4. The direct method of calculating cash flows from operations is encouraged by the FASB and is the predominant method used.

5. Issuance of capital stock and the subsequent reacquisition of some of those shares would both be financing activities.

Multiple-Choice

Select the best answer for each of the following questions.

1. Which of the following statements is true?
    a. The direct method of calculating cash flows from operations starts with net income and adjusts for noncash revenues and expenses and changes in current assets and current liabilities.
    b. The indirect method of calculating cash flows from operations adjusts each item in the income statement to a cash basis.
    c. The descriptions in *(a)* and *(b)* should be reversed.
    d. The direct method is easier to use than the indirect method.

2. Investing activities include all of the following except:
    a. Payment of debt.
    b. Collection of loans.
    c. Making of loans.
    d. Sale of long-term marketable securities.

3. If sales on an accrual basis are $500,000 and accounts receivable increased by $30,000, the cash received from customers would be:
    a. $500,000.
    b. $470,000.
    c. $530,000.
    d. Cannot be determined.

4. Assume cost of goods sold on an accrual basis is $300,000, accounts payable increased by $20,000, and inventory increased by $50,000. Cash paid for merchandise is:
    a. $370,000.
    b. $230,000.
    c. $270,000.
    d. $330,000.

5. Assume net income was $200,000, depreciation expense was $10,000, accounts receivable increased by $15,000, and accounts payable increased by $5,000. The amount of cash flows from operating activities is:
    a. $200,000.
    b. $180,000.
    c. $210,000.
    d. $190,000.

Now turn to page 1060 to check your answers.

QUESTIONS

1. What are the purposes of the statement of cash flows?
2. What are some of the uses of the statement of cash flows?
3. What information is contained in the statement of cash flows?
4. Which activities are generally included in operating activities?
5. Which activities are included in investing activities?
6. Which activities are included in financing activities?
7. Where should investing and financing activities that do not involve cash flows be reported?
8. Explain the difference between the direct and indirect methods for computing cash flows from operating activities.
9. What are noncash expenses? How are they treated in computing cash flows from operating activities?
10. Describe the treatment of a gain on the sale of equipment in preparing a statement of cash flows under the indirect method.

11. Depreciation is sometimes referred to as a source of cash. Is it a source of cash? Explain.

12. Why is it unlikely that cash flows from operating activities will be equal to net income for the same period?

13. If the net income for a given period is $25,000, does this mean there is an increase in cash of the same amount? Why or why not?

14. Why might a company have positive cash flows from operating activities even though operating at a net loss?

15. Give two reasons why analysts seem to prefer cash flow statements to statements that report working capital flows.

16. Indicate the type of activity each of the following transactions represents (operating, investing, or financing) and whether it is an inflow or an outflow.
    a. Sold goods.
    b. Purchased building.
    c. Issued capital stock.
    d. Received cash dividends.
    e. Paid cash dividends.
    f. Purchased treasury stock.
    g. Sold long-term marketable securities.
    h. Made a loan.
    i. Paid interest on loan.
    j. Paid bond principal.
    k. Received proceeds of insurance settlement.
    l. Made contribution to charity.

17. *Real-world question*   Refer to "A Broader Perspective" on page 1039. What major categories (activities) will be included in the statement of cash flows for governmental business-type entities? Are the rules and recommendations regarding the direct or indirect methods for reporting cash flows from operating activities similar to or different from those contained in *FASB Statement No. 95?*

18. *Real-world question*   Refer to Appendix C at the end of this text. Of the four companies represented, which use the direct method of reporting cash flows from operating activities and which use the indirect method?

EXERCISES

Report specific
items on
statement of cash
flows
(L.O. 2, 4)

21–1. Indicate how the following data should be reported in a statement of cash flows. A company paid $240,000 cash for land. A building was acquired for $480,000 by assuming a mortgage on the building.

Report specific
items on
statement of cash
flows
(L.O. 2, 4)

21–2. The following data are from the Automobile and the Accumulated Depreciation—Automobile accounts of a certain company:

Automobile

Date			Debit	Credit	Balance
Jan.	1	Balance brought forward.			16,000
July	1	Traded for new auto		16,000	–0–
		New auto	17,600		17,600

Accumulated Depreciation—Automobile

Jan.	1	Balance brought forward.			12,000
July	1	One-half year's depreciation		2,000	14,000
		Auto traded	14,000		–0–
Dec. 31		One-half year's depreciation		2,200	2,200

The old auto was traded for a new one, with the difference in values paid in cash. The income statement for the year shows a loss on the exchange of autos of $1,200.

Indicate the dollar amounts, the descriptions of these amounts, and their exact locations in a statement of cash flows—indirect method.

Compute cash used to purchase plant assets (L.O. 2, 4)

21–3. Following are balance sheet data for Frey Corporation.

	December 31	
	1996	1995
Cash	$ 47,000	$ 26,000
Accounts receivable, net.	141,000	134,000
Merchandise inventory.	83,000	102,000
Prepaid expenses	9,000	11,000
Plant assets (net of accumulated depreciation)	235,000	230,000
Accounts payable	122,000	127,000
Accrued liabilities payable	40,000	41,000
Capital stock	300,000	300,000
Retained earnings	53,000	35,000

Assume that the depreciation recorded in 1996 was $15,000. Compute the cash spent to purchase plant assets, assuming no assets were sold or scrapped in 1996.

Prepare statement of cash flows (L.O. 4)

21–4. Use the data in Exercise 21–3. Assume the net income for 1995 was $24,000, depreciation was $15,000, and dividends declared and paid were $6,000. Prepare a statement of cash flows—indirect method.

Calculate the amount of cash paid for merchandise (L.O. 3)

21–5. Cost of goods sold in the income statement for the year ended 1995 was $628,000. The balances in Merchandise Inventory and Accounts Payable were:

	January 1, 1995	December 31, 1995
Merchandise Inventory	$320,000	$340,000
Accounts Payable.	88,000	72,000

Calculate the amount of cash paid for merchandise in 1995.

Compute cash flows from operating activities (L.O. 3)

21-6. The income statement of a company shows net income of $150,000; merchandise inventory on January 1 was $153,000 and on December 31 was $189,000; accounts payable for merchandise purchases were $114,000 on January 1 and $126,000 on December 31. Compute the cash flows from operating activities under the indirect method.

Compute cash flows from operating activities (L.O. 3)

21-7. The operating expenses and taxes (including $30,000 of depreciation) of a company for a given year were $600,000. Net income was $150,000. Prepaid insurance decreased from $9,000 to $6,000 during the year, while wages payable increased from $12,000 to $18,000 during the year. Compute the cash flows from operating activities under the indirect method.

Indicate treatment of dividend (L.O. 2, 4)

21-8. Dividends payable increased by $3,000 during a year in which total dividends declared were $60,000. What amount appears for dividends paid in the statement of cash flows?

Show effects of conversion from accrual to cash basis income (L.O. 3)

21-9. Fill in the following chart, showing how increases and decreases in these accounts affect the conversion of accrual basis income to cash basis income.

	Add	Deduct
Accounts Receivable		
Merchandise Inventory		
Prepaid Expenses		
Accounts Payable		
Accrued Liabilities Payable		

PROBLEMS

Prepare working paper to convert income statement to cash basis; prepare cash flows from operating activities under both methods (L.O. 2, 3)

21-1. The income statement and other data of Kelly Corporation are given below.

KELLY CORPORATION
Income Statement
For the Year Ended December 31, 1995

Sales		$720,000
Cost of goods sold		380,000
Gross margin.		$340,000
Operating expenses (other than depreciation) . . .	$140,000	
Depreciation expense.	40,000	180,000
Net income.		$160,000

Changes in current assets (other than cash) and current liabilities during the year were:

	Increase	Decrease
Accounts receivable		$20,000
Merchandise inventory	$12,000	
Prepaid insurance	8,000	
Accounts payable	24,000	
Accrued liabilities payable	4,000	

Depreciation was the only noncash item affecting net income.

Required:

a. Prepare a working paper to calculate cash flows from operating activities under the *direct method*.

b. Prepare the cash flows from operating activities section of the statement of cash flows under the *direct method*.

c. Prove that the same cash flows amount will be obtained under the indirect method by preparing the cash flows from operating activities section of the statement of cash flows under the *indirect method*. You need not prepare a working paper.

Prepare statement
of cash flows
under the indirect
method
(L.O. 4)

21–2. Following are Lucky Company's comparative balance sheets at May 31, 1996, and 1995, and a statement of retained earnings for the year ended May 31, 1996:

LUCKY COMPANY
Comparative Balance Sheets
May 31, 1996 and 1995

	1996	1995
Assets		
Cash	$ 379,000	$ 240,000
Accounts receivable, net	378,000	432,000
Merchandise inventory	360,000	300,000
Investment in subsidiary	285,000	240,000
Land	210,000	150,000
Equipment	1,299,000	1,140,000
Accumulated depreciation—equipment	(234,000)	(180,000)
Patents	33,000	48,000
Total assets	$2,710,000	$2,370,000
Liabilities and Stockholders' Equity		
Accounts payable	$ 390,000	$ 192,000
Taxes payable	28,000	36,000
Bonds payable.	600,000	600,000
Common stock—$100 par	1,200,000	1,200,000
Retained earnings	492,000	342,000
Total liabilities and stockholders' equity.	$2,710,000	$2,370,000

LUCKY COMPANY
Statement of Retained Earnings
For the Year Ended May 31, 1996

Balance, June 1, 1995	$342,000
Net income	200,000
	$542,000
Dividends (declared and paid)	50,000
Balance, May 31, 1996	$492,000

Additional data:

1. A tract of land adjacent to land owned was purchased for cash during the year.

2. New equipment with a cost of $195,000 was purchased for cash during the

year, while fully depreciated equipment with a cost of $36,000 was discarded.

3. Depreciation of $90,000 and patent amortization of $15,000 were charged to expense during the year.

4. Additional shares of stock of the subsidiary company were acquired for cash.

Required:

Prepare a statement of cash flows under the indirect method. Try to do so without preparing a working paper. Also show any information that should be reported in a separate schedule.

Prepare working paper and statement of cash flows under the indirect method (L.O. 4)

21–3. Given below are comparative balance sheets and other data of Telly, Inc.:

TELLY, INC.
Comparative Balance Sheets
December 31, 1996 and 1995

	1996	1995
Assets		
Cash	$ 66,105	$ 21,000
Accounts receivable, net.	26,075	24,250
Merchandise inventory	30,000	35,000
Supplies on hand	1,750	2,550
Prepaid insurance.	1,400	1,200
Land	180,000	142,500
Equipment	270,000	300,000
Accumulated depreciation—equipment.	(75,000)	(67,500)
Total assets.	$500,330	$459,000
Liabilities and Stockholders' Equity		
Accounts payable	$ 35,330	$ 46,300
Salaries payable	4,000	2,000
Accrued liabilities payable	2,000	8,250
Long-term note payable	150,000	150,000
Common stock ($5 par)	185,000	165,000
Paid-in capital in excess of par	32,500	–0–
Retained earnings.	91,500	87,450
Total liabilities and stockholders' equity	$500,330	$459,000

Additional data:

1. Land was bought for cash.
2. Equipment costing $50,000 with accumulated depreciation of $30,000 was sold for a gain of $3,500, and equipment costing $20,000 was purchased for cash.
3. Depreciation expense for the year was $37,500.
4. Common stock was issued for cash.
5. Dividends declared and paid in 1996 totaled $52,950.

Required:

a. Prepare a working paper for a statement of cash flows.

b. Prepare a statement of cash flows under the indirect method.

Prepare working
paper and
statement of cash
flows under the
indirect method
(L.O. 4)

21–4. Given below are comparative balance sheets and other data of Ruiz Corporation:

RUIZ CORPORATION
Comparative Balance Sheets
June 30, 1996 and 1995

	1996	1995
Assets		
Cash.	$ 241,000	$ 132,000
Accounts receivable, net	750,750	432,900
Merchandise inventory	819,000	850,200
Prepaid insurance	3,900	5,850
Land.	312,000	351,000
Buildings.	2,184,000	1,209,000
Machinery and tools	858,000	468,000
Accumulated depreciation—machinery and tools. .	(809,250)	(510,900)
Total assets	$4,359,400	$2,938,050
Liabilities and Stockholders' Equity		
Accounts payable.	$ 126,750	$ 175,500
Accrued liabilities payable.	85,000	11,100
Bank loans (due in 1998)	56,550	66,300
Mortgage bonds payable	382,200	185,250
Common stock—$200 par.	1,755,000	585,000
Paid-in capital in excess of par	58,500	–0–
Retained earnings	1,895,400	1,914,900
Total liabilities and stockholders' equity	$4,359,400	$2,938,050

Additional data:

1. Net income for the year was $78,000.
2. Depreciation for the year was $356,850.
3. There was a gain of $7,800 on the sale of land.
4. The additional mortgage bonds were issued at face value as partial payment for a building valued at $975,000.
5. Machinery and tools were purchased for $448,500 cash.
6. Fully depreciated machinery with a cost of $58,500 was scrapped and written off.
7. Additional common stock was issued at $210 per share.
8. Dividends declared and paid were $97,600.

Required:

a. Prepare a working paper for a statement of cash flows.
b. Prepare a statement of cash flows under the indirect method. Prepare a separate schedule of noncash investing and financing activities.

Prepare working
paper and
statement of cash
flows under both
methods
(L.O. 4)

21–5. The income statement for Roberts Company for the year ended December 31, 1996, shows:

Net sales		$1,800,000
Cost of goods sold	$1,050,000	
Operating expenses.	280,000*	
Major repairs expense	140,000	
Interest expense	42,000	
Loss on sale of equipment	22,400	1,534,400
Income before federal income taxes		$ 265,600
Deduct: Federal income taxes		134,400
Net income.		$ 131,200

* Including $56,000 of depreciation expense.

Comparative balance sheets for the company show:

ROBERTS COMPANY
Comparative Balance Sheets
December 31, 1996 and 1995

	1996	1995
Assets		
Current assets:		
Cash	$ 134,400	$ 112,000
Accounts receivable, net	271,600	212,800
Merchandise inventory	588,000	504,000
Prepaid expenses	44,800	16,800
Total current assets	$1,038,800	$ 845,600
Property, plant, and equipment:		
Buildings	$ 280,000	$ 280,000
Accumulated depreciation—buildings	(154,000)	(140,000)
Equipment	518,000	364,000
Accumulated depreciation—equipment	(176,400)	(168,000)
Total property, plant, and equipment	$ 467,600	$ 336,000
Total assets	$1,506,400	$1,181,600
Liabilities and Stockholders' Equity		
Current liabilities:		
Accounts payable	$ 158,200	$ 231,000
Accrued liabilities payable	46,200	40,600
Federal income taxes payable	134,400	126,000
Total current liabilities	$ 338,800	$ 397,600
Long-term liabilities:		
Bonds payable, 15%, due 2000	280,000	280,000
Total liabilities	$ 618,800	$ 677,600
Stockholders' equity:		
Capital stock—common, $100 par	$ 700,000	$ 420,000
Paid-in capital in excess of par	70,000	–0–
Retained earnings	117,600	84,000
Total stockholders' equity	$ 887,600	$ 504,000
Total liabilities and stockholders' equity	$1,506,400	$1,181,600

Additional data:

1. Accrued expenses payable and prepaid expenses relate solely to operating expenses.
2. Equipment sold had an original cost of $84,000. Depreciation on equipment for the year amounted to $42,000.
3. Capital stock was issued for cash.
4. Dividends declared and paid during the year totaled $97,600.

Required:

a. Prepare a working paper for a statement of cash flows.
b. Prepare a statement of cash flows under the indirect method.
c. Prepare a working paper to convert the income statement to a cash basis.
d. Prepare a statement of cash flows under the direct method.

BUSINESS DECISION PROBLEMS

Prepare a
statement of cash
flows using the
indirect method
and answer
owner's questions
(L.O. 1, 2, 4)

21–1. Bentley, Inc., is a sports equipment center owned and operated by William Bentley. During 1996, the company replaced $72,000 of the center's fully depreciated equipment with new equipment costing $92,000. Although a mid-year dividend of $20,000 was paid, William found it necessary to borrow $20,000 from his bank on a two-year note. He feels further borrowing may be needed since the Cash account is dangerously low at year-end.

Given below are the income statement and the cash flow statement, as William's accountant calls them, for 1996.

BENTLEY, INC.
Income Statement
For the Year Ended December 31, 1996

Sales		$820,000
Cost of goods sold.	$560,000	
Operating expenses and taxes	198,800	758,800
Net income		$ 61,200

BENTLEY, INC.
Cash Flow Statement
For the Year Ended December 31, 1996

Cash received:		
From operations:		
Net income.		$ 61,200
Depreciation		20,000
Total cash from operations		$ 81,200
Note issued to bank.		20,000
Mortgage note issued.		64,000
Total funds provided		$165,200
Cash paid:		
New equipment.	$92,000	
Dividends	20,000	112,000
Increase in cash		$ 53,200

William is concerned about what he sees in the above statements and how they relate to what he knows has actually happened. He turns to you for help. Specifically, he wants to know why the cash flow statement shows an increase in cash when he knows the cash balance decreased from $44,000 to $26,000 during the year. Also, why is depreciation shown as providing cash?

You believe you can answer William's questions. You ask for and receive the following condensed balance sheet data:

BENTLEY, INC.
Comparative Balance Sheets
December 31, 1996 and 1995

	1996	1995
Assets		
Current assets:		
Cash	$ 26,000	$ 44,000
Accounts receivable, net.	71,200	52,800
Merchandise inventory	114,000	70,000
Prepaid expenses	2,800	1,200
Total current assets	$214,000	$168,000
Property, plant, and equipment:		
Equipment	$160,000	$140,000
Accumulated depreciation—equipment.	(44,000)	(96,000)
Total property, plant, and equipment	$116,000	$ 44,000
Total assets.	$330,000	$212,000
Liabilities and Stockholders' Equity		
Current liabilities:		
Accounts payable	$ 34,800	$ 40,000
Accrued liabilities payable	2,400	4,400
Total current liabilities.	$ 37,200	$ 44,400
Long-term liabilities:		
Notes payable.	20,000	–0–
Mortgage note payable	64,000	–0–
Total liabilities	$121,200	$ 44,400
Stockholders' equity:		
Common stock	$160,000	$160,000
Retained earnings.	48,800	7,600
Total stockholders' equity	$208,800	$167,600
Total liabilities and stockholders' equity	$330,000	$212,000

Required:

Prepare a correct statement of cash flows using the indirect method that will show why Bentley, Inc., is having such a difficult time keeping sufficient cash on hand. Also, answer William's questions.

Prepare a schedule showing cash flows from operating activities under the indirect method and decide whether certain goals can be met
(L.O. 4)

21–2. Following are comparative balance sheets for Martin Company:

MARTIN COMPANY
Comparative Balance Sheets
December 31, 1996 and 1995

	1996	1995
Assets		
Cash	$ 60,000	$ 37,500
Accounts receivable, net.	50,000	45,000
Merchandise inventory	100,000	52,500
Land	67,500	60,000
Buildings.	90,000	90,000
Accumulated depreciation—buildings	(30,000)	(27,000)
Equipment	285,000	225,000
Accumulated depreciation—equipment.	(52,500)	(48,000)
Goodwill	120,000	150,000
Total assets.	$690,000	$585,000
Liabilities and Stockholders' Equity		
Accounts payable	$ 75,000	$ 45,000
Accrued liabilities payable	30,000	22,500
Capital stock	315,000	300,000
Paid-in capital—stock dividends	75,000	67,500
Paid-in capital—land donations	15,000	–0–
Retained earnings.	180,000	150,000
Total liabilities and stockholders' equity	$690,000	$585,000

An analysis of the Retained Earnings account for the year reveals the following:

Balance, January 1, 1996		$150,000
Add: Net income for the year		90,000
		$240,000
Less: Cash dividends.	$37,500	
Stock dividends	22,500	60,000
Balance, December 31, 1996		$180,000

Additional data:

a. Equipment with a cost of $30,000 on which $27,000 of depreciation had been accumulated was sold during the year at a loss of $1,500. Included in net income is a gain on the sale of land of $9,000.

b. The president of Martin Company has set two goals for 1997: (1) increase cash by $40,000 and (2) increase cash dividends by $45,000. The company's activities in 1997 are expected to be quite similar to those of 1996, and no new fixed assets will be acquired.

Required:

Prepare a schedule showing cash flows from operating activities under the indirect method for 1996. Can the company meet its president's goals for 1997? Explain.

Decide whether
four real
companies can
maintain their
current dividends
(real-world
problem)
(L.O. 1)

21–3. Refer to Appendix C at the end of the text. Evaluate the ease with which each of the four companies represented will be able to maintain their dividend payments in the future at 1991 amounts. (Hint: Compare current dividend amounts with cash flows from operating activities.) Rank the companies in terms of their ability to maintain their dividend payments by dividing their cash flows from operating activities by their dividends paid.

ANSWERS TO SELF-TEST

True-False

1. *True.* Before July 1988, the statement of changes in financial position was required. This statement often emphasized changes in working capital rather than changes in cash.

2. *True.* The statement of cash flows must be published every time an income statement is published.

3. *False.* Investing activities are transactions involving the acquisition or disposal of non-current assets. Transactions with creditors and owners are financing activities.

4. *False.* While the direct method is the method encouraged by the FASB, it is not the predominant method in use. In a recent study, only about 3% of the companies surveyed used the direct method.

5. *True.* Both of these transactions are with owners and therefore would be financing activities.

Multiple-Choice

1. *c.* The descriptions in *(a)* and *(b)* would be correct if they were reversed. The indirect method is easier to use, and this characteristic is probably the main reason why it is used by most companies.

2. *a.* Payment of debt is a financing activity because it is a transaction with creditors. All of the others are investing activities because they are transactions involving the acquisition or disposal of noncurrent assets.

3. *b.* Sales of $500,000 minus the increase in accounts receivable of $30,000 = $470,000.

4. *d.* Cost of goods sold of $300,000, less increase in accounts payable of $20,000, plus increase in inventory of $50,000 = $330,000.

5. *a.* Net income of $200,000, plus depreciation of $10,000, less increase in accounts receivable of $15,000, plus increase in accounts payable of $5,000 = $200,000.

22 ANALYSIS AND INTERPRETATION OF FINANCIAL STATEMENTS

LEARNING OBJECTIVES

After studying this chapter, you should be able to:

1. Describe and explain the objectives of financial statement analysis.
2. Describe the sources of information for financial statement analysis.
3. Calculate and explain changes in financial statements using horizontal analysis, vertical analysis, and trend analysis.
4. Perform ratio analysis on financial statements using liquidity ratios, long-term solvency ratios, profitability tests, and market tests.
5. Describe the considerations used in financial statement analysis.

OBJECTIVES OF FINANCIAL STATEMENT ANALYSIS

*Objective 1
Describe and
explain the objec-
tives of financial
statement analysis*

As you may recall, the two primary objectives of every business are solvency and profitability. Solvency is the ability of a company to pay debts as they come due; it is reflected on the company's balance sheet. Profitability is the ability of a company to generate income; it is reflected on the company's income statement. Generally, all those interested in the affairs of a company are especially interested in its solvency and profitability.

This chapter discusses several common methods used to analyze and relate to one another the data in financial statements and, as a result, gain a clear picture of the solvency and profitability of a company. A company's financial statements are analyzed internally by management and externally by investors, creditors, and regulatory agencies. Although these users have different, immediate goals, their overall objective in financial statement analysis is the same—to make predictions about an organization as an aid in decision making.

Management's analysis of financial statements primarily relates to *parts* of the company. This approach enables management to plan, evaluate, and control operations within the company. Management can obtain any information it wants about the company's operations since it has the ability to request special-purpose reports. This information may be used to make difficult decisions, such as which employees to lay off and when to expand operations. Our primary focus in this chapter, however, is not on the special reports accountants prepare for management. Rather, it is on the analysis of published financial statements.

Investors, creditors, and regulatory agencies generally focus their analysis of financial statements on the company as a *whole*. Since they cannot request special-purpose reports, external users must rely on the general-purpose financial statements that companies publish. They include a balance sheet, an income statement, a statement of stockholders' equity, a statement of cash flows, and the explanatory notes that accompany these financial statements.

Management is also very interested in the published financial statements because of their effect on how persons outside the company will perceive the solvency and profitability of the company. These perceptions by outsiders affect the company's stock price and future access to credit and equity sources of additional capital. Therefore, management accountants also perform the analyses described in this chapter. Management accountants advise management as to how decisions currently being considered by management will affect the analyses performed on future financial statements and thus affect the future perceptions of persons outside the firm.

FINANCIAL STATEMENT ANALYSIS

Financial statement analysis consists of applying analytical tools and techniques to financial statements and other relevant data to obtain useful information. This information is shown as significant relationships between data and trends in those data that assess the company's *past performance* and *current financial position*. The information shows the results or consequences of prior management decisions. In addition, the information is used to *make predictions* that may have a direct effect on decisions made by management and users of financial statements.

Present investors and potential investors are both interested in the future ability of a company to earn profits—its profitability. These investors wish to predict future dividends and changes in the market price of the company's common stock. Since both dividends and price changes are likely to be influenced by earnings, investors may seek to predict earnings. The company's past earnings record is the logical starting point in predicting future earnings.

Sometimes outside parties, such as creditors, are interested in predicting a company's solvency rather than its profitability. The liquidity of the company affects its short-term solvency. The company's **liquidity** is its state of possessing liquid assets, such as (1) cash and (2) other assets that will soon be converted to cash. Since companies must pay short-term debts soon, liquid assets must be available for their payment. For example, a bank that is asked to extend a 90-day loan to a company would want to know the company's projected short-term liquidity. Of course, the company's predicted ability to repay the 90-day loan is likely to be based at least partially on proven past ability to pay off debts.

Long-term creditors are interested in a company's long-term solvency, which is usually determined by the relationship of a company's assets to its liabilities. Generally, a company is considered solvent when its assets exceed its liabilities so that the company has a positive stockholders' equity. The larger the assets are in relation to the liabilities, the greater the long-term solvency of the company, since the company's assets could shrink significantly before its liabilities would exceed its assets and destroy the company's solvency.

Several types of analyses can be performed on a company's financial statements. All of these analyses rely on comparisons or relationships of data because comparisons and relationships enhance the utility or practical value of accounting information. For example, knowing that a company's net income last year was $100,000 may or may not, by itself, be useful information. Some usefulness is added when we know that the prior year's net income was $25,000. And even more useful information is gained if we know the amounts of sales and assets of the company. Such comparisons or relationships may be expressed as:

1. Absolute increases and decreases for an item from one period to the next.
2. Percentage increases and decreases for an item from one period to the next.
3. Trend percentages.
4. Percentages of single items to an aggregate total.
5. Ratios.

Items 1 and 2 make use of comparative financial statements. **Comparative financial statements** present the same company's financial statements for two or more successive periods in side-by-side columns. Illustrations 22.1 and 22.2 show comparative financial statements of Knight Corporation for the years ended December 31, 1995, and 1994. The calculation of dollar changes (column 3 of Illustration 22.1 and column 9 of Illustration 22.2) or percentage changes (column 4 of Illustration 22.1 and column 10 of Illustration 22.2) in the statement items or totals is known as **horizontal analysis.** This type of analysis helps detect changes in a company's performance and highlights trends.

Trend percentages (item 3) are similar to horizontal analysis except that a base year or period is selected, and comparisons are made to the base year or period. Trend percentages are useful for comparing financial statements

Illustration 22.1
COMPARATIVE BALANCE SHEETS

KNIGHT CORPORATION
Comparative Balance Sheets
December 31, 1995 and 1994

	December 31		Increase or (Decrease) 1995 over 1994		Percent of Total Assets December 31	
	(1) 1995	(2) 1994	(3) Dollars*	(4) Percent*	(5) 1995	(6) 1994
Assets						
Current assets:						
Cash	$ 80,200	$ 55,000	$25,200	45.8	12.6	10.0
Accounts receivable, net	124,200	132,600	(8,400)	(6.3)	19.6	24.1
Notes receivable	55,000	50,000	5,000	10.0	8.7	9.1
Merchandise inventory	110,800	94,500	16,300	17.2	17.4	17.1
Prepaid expenses	3,600	4,700	(1,100)	(23.4)	0.6	0.9
Total current assets	$373,800	$336,800	$37,000	11.0	58.8†	61.1†
Property, plant, and equipment:						
Land	$ 21,000	$ 21,000	$ –0–	–0–	3.3	3.8
Building	205,000	160,000	45,000	28.1	32.3	29.0
Less: Accumulated depreciation	(27,000)	(22,400)	(4,600)	20.5	(4.3)	(4.1)
Furniture and fixtures	83,200	69,800	13,400	19.2	13.1	12.7
Less: Accumulated depreciation	(20,800)	(14,100)	(6,700)	47.5	(3.3)	(2.6)
Total property, plant, and equipment .	$261,400	$214,300	$47,100	22.0	41.2†	38.9†
Total assets	$635,200	$551,100	$84,100	15.3	100.0	100.0
Liabilities and Stockholders' Equity						
Current liabilities:						
Accounts payable	$ 70,300	$ 64,600	$ 5,700	8.8	11.1	11.7
Notes payable	20,000	15,100	4,900	32.5	3.1	2.7
Taxes accrued	36,800	30,200	6,600	21.9	5.8	5.5
Total current liabilities	$127,100	$109,900	$17,200	15.7	20.0	20.0†
Long-term liabilities:						
Mortgage notes payable, land and building, 12%, 1997	43,600	60,800	(17,200)	(28.3)	6.9	11.0
Total liabilities	$170,700	$170,700	$ –0–	0.0	26.9	31.0
Stockholders' equity:						
Common stock, par value $10 per share . .	$240,000	$200,000	$40,000	20.0	37.8	36.3
Retained earnings	224,500	180,400	44,100	24.4	35.3	32.7
Total stockholders' equity	$464,500	$380,400	$84,100	22.1	73.1	69.0
Total liabilities and stockholders' equity . . .	$635,200	$551,100	$84,100	15.3	100.0	100.0

* Dollars = (1) − (2); percent = (3) ÷ (2).
† Rounding difference.

Illustration 22.2
COMPARATIVE STATEMENTS OF INCOME AND RETAINED EARNINGS

KNIGHT CORPORATION
Comparative Statements of Income and Retained Earnings
For the Years Ended December 31, 1995 and 1994

	Year Ended December 31		Increase or (Decrease) 1995 over 1994		Percent of Net Sales	
	(7) *1995*	*(8)* *1994*	*(9)* *Dollars**	*(10)* *Percent**	*(11)* *1995*	*(12)* *1994*
Net sales	$986,400	$765,500	$220,900	28.9	100.0	100.0
Cost of goods sold.	623,200	500,900	122,300	24.4	63.2	65.4
Gross margin	$363,200	$264,600	$ 98,600	37.3	36.8	34.6
Operating expenses:						
Selling expenses.	$132,500	$ 84,900	$ 47,600	56.1	13.4	11.1
Administrative expenses	120,300	98,600	21,700	22.0	12.2	12.9
Total operating expenses.	$252,800	$183,500	$ 69,300	37.8	25.6	24.0
Net operating income	$110,400	$ 81,100	$ 29,300	36.1	11.2	10.6
Other expenses	3,000	2,800	200	7.1	0.3	0.4
Income before federal income taxes	$107,400	$ 78,300	$ 29,100	37.2	10.9	10.2
Deduct: Federal income taxes	48,300	31,700	16,600	52.4	4.9	4.1
Net income	$ 59,100	$ 46,600	$ 12,500	26.8	6.0	6.1
Retained earnings, January 1	180,400	146,300	34,100	23.3		
	$239,500	$192,900	$ 46,600	24.2		
Dividends declared	15,000	12,500	2,500	20.0		
Retained earnings, December 31	$224,500	$180,400	$ 44,100	24.4		

* Dollars = (7) − (8); percent = (9) ÷ (8).

over *several years* because they disclose changes and trends occurring through time.

Information about a company can also be gained by the vertical analysis of the composition of a single financial statement, such as an income statement. **Vertical analysis** (item 4) consists of the study of a single financial statement in which each item is expressed as a *percentage of a significant total*. The use of vertical analysis is especially helpful in analyzing income statement data such as the percentage of cost of goods sold to sales. For example, columns 11 and 12 of Illustration 22.2 show that in 1994, cost of goods sold was 65.4% of sales and decreased to 63.2% of sales in 1995. Vertical analysis is a useful tool in analyzing intracompany data.

Financial statements that show only percentages and no absolute dollar amounts are called **common-size statements.** All percentage figures in a common-size balance sheet are expressed as percentages of total assets (columns 5 and 6 of Illustration 22.1), while all the items in a common-size income statement are expressed as percentages of net sales (columns 11 and 12 of Illustration 22.2). The use of common-size statements facilitates vertical analysis of a company's financial statements. For instance, looking at columns 11 and 12 of Illustration 22.2 gives you a better idea of the relationship of each item to sales than looking at columns 7 and 8.

Ratios (item 5) are expressions of logical relationships between certain items in the financial statements. The financial statements of a single period are generally used. Many ratios can be computed from the same set of financial statements. A ratio can show a relationship between two items on the same financial statement or between two items on different financial statements (e.g., balance sheet and income statement). The choice of ratios to be prepared is limited only by the requirement that the items used to construct a ratio have a logical relationship to one another.

SOURCES OF INFORMATION

*Objective 2
Describe the
sources of infor-
mation for finan-
cial statement
analysis*

Financial information about publicly owned corporations can come from several different sources, namely:

- Published reports.
- Government reports.
- Financial service information, newspapers, and periodicals.

Published Reports

Public corporations must publish an annual financial report. Appendix C, Consolidated Financial Statements (Annual Reports), gives such 1991 data for the Coca-Cola Company and Subsidiaries, Maytag Corporation, The Limited, Inc., and John H. Harland Company and Subsidiaries. The major sections of an annual report are:

1. *Financial statements.*   These include a balance sheet, for which two years of comparative data are given; an income statement, for which three years of comparative data are given; a statement of cash flows, for which three years of comparative data are given; and a statement of shareholders' equity. For examples of each statement, refer to those given in Appendix C.
2. *Explanatory notes.*   These notes are integral to the statements and provide essential information about items in the financial statements. For an example, see the Notes to Consolidated Financial Statements of the Coca-Cola Company and Subsidiaries in Appendix C.
3. *Letter to stockholders.*   In this letter, the CEO (chief executive officer) of the corporation reviews the past year and explains plans for the future.
4. *Report of independent accountants.*   This report gives the public accountant's opinion on the fairness of the presentations in the financial statements. For an example, refer to the Report of Independent Accountants for The Coca-Cola Company and Subsidiaries in Appendix C.

5. *Management's discussion and analysis (MDA).* This section contains management's explanations for changes in corporate operations and financial position. It enables users to gain a perspective on the long-term prospects for the company and the success of management's decision making.

Public corporations also release interim reports, which contain summarized financial reports for the most recent quarter and the year to date.

Government Reports

Publicly held companies must file detailed annual reports (Form 10-K), quarterly reports (Form 10-Q), and special events reports (Form 8-K) with the Securities and Exchange Commission. These reports are available to the public for a small charge and sometimes contain more detailed information than the published reports.

Financial Service Information

Newspapers and Periodicals. Financial statement information is often more meaningful if users can compare that information with industry norms. Two firms that provide information on individual companies and industries are Moodys' Investors Service and Standard & Poor's. Dun and Bradstreet, Inc., publishes *Key Business Ratios* and Robert Morris Associates publishes *Annual Statement Studies,* both of which provide information for specific industries. Standard and Poor's *Industry Surveys* contains background descriptions and the economic outlook for different industries.

Business publications such as *The Wall Street Journal, Barron's, Forbes,* and *Fortune* also report industry financial news. Since financial statement users must be knowledgeable about current developments in business, the information contained in financial newspapers and periodicals is valuable to them.

HORIZONTAL ANALYSIS AND VERTICAL ANALYSIS: AN ILLUSTRATION

*Objective 3
Calculate and
explain changes in
financial state-
ments using hori-
zontal analysis,
vertical analysis,
and trend analysis*

Illustrations 22.1 and 22.2 will serve as a basis for a more complete illustration of horizontal analysis and vertical analysis of a balance sheet and a statement of income and retained earnings. **Recall that horizontal analysis calculates changes in comparative statement items or totals, whereas vertical analysis consists of a comparison of items on a single financial statement.**

Analysis of a Balance Sheet

Imagine that you are a prospective investor of Knight and have acquired the comparative financial statements shown in Illustrations 22.1 and 22.2.

Columns 1, 2, and 3 in Illustration 22.1 show the absolute dollar amounts for each item for December 31, 1994, and December 31, 1995, and the change for the year. If the change between the two dates is an increase from 1994 to 1995, the change is shown as a positive figure. The percentage change is calculated by dividing the dollar change by the dollar balance of the earlier year. If the change is a decrease, it is shown in parentheses. A few of the observations you could make from your horizontal analysis of Illustration 22.1 are:

1. Total current assets have increased $37,000, consisting largely of a $25,200 increase in cash, while total current liabilities have increased only $17,200.
2. Total assets have increased $84,100, while total liabilities have remained unchanged.
3. The increase in total assets has been financed by the sale of common stock, $40,000, and by the retention of earnings, $44,100.

Next, you study column 4 in Illustration 22.1, which expresses as a percentage the dollar change in column 3. Frequently, these percentage increases and decreases are more informative than absolute amounts, as is illustrated by the current asset and current liability changes. Although the absolute amount of current assets has increased more than twice the amount of current liabilities, the percentages reveal that current assets increased 11%, while current liabilities increased 15.7%. Thus, current liabilities are increasing at a rate faster than the current assets that will be used to pay them. However, in view of the substantial amount of cash possessed, the company is not likely to fail to pay its debts as they come due.

The percentages in column 4 lead you, the analyst, to several other observations. For one thing, the 28.3% decrease in mortgage notes payable indicates that future interest charges will be lower; thus, this decrease will tend to increase net income in the future. The 24.4% increase in retained earnings and the 45.8% increase in cash may indicate that higher dividends can be paid in the future.

The vertical analysis of Knight's balance sheet discloses each account's significance relative to total assets or equities. This comparison aids in assessing the importance of the changes in each account. Columns 5 and 6 in Illustration 22.1 express the dollar amounts of each item in columns 1 and 2 as a percentage of total assets or equities. For example, although prepaid expenses declined $1,100 in 1995, a decrease of 23.4%, the account represents less than 1% of total assets and, therefore, probably does not have great significance. The vertical analysis also shows that total long-term debt financing decreased by 4.1 percentage points, from 31% of total equities (liabilities and stockholders' equity) in 1994, to 26.9% in 1995. At the same time, the percentage of stockholder financing to total assets of the company increased from 69.0% to 73.1%.

Analysis of Statement of Income and Retained Earnings

Illustration 22.2 provides the information needed to analyze Knight's comparative statements of income and retained earnings. Such a statement merely combines the income statement and the statement of retained earnings. Columns 7 and 8 in Illustration 22.2 show the dollar amounts for the years 1995 and 1994, respectively. Columns 9 and 10 show the absolute and percentage increase and decrease in each item from 1994 to 1995. The amounts and percentages in columns 11 and 12 are computed by dividing each item by net sales. Examination of the comparative statements of income and retained earnings shows the following:

1. Net sales increased 28.9% in 1995.
2. Gross margin increased 37.3% in 1995.
3. Selling expenses increased 56.1% in 1995.
4. Federal income taxes rose by 52.4% in 1995.
5. Net income increased 26.8% in 1995, while dividends increased 20.0%.
6. Net income per dollar of net sales remained virtually constant over the two years (6.1% in 1994 and 6.0% in 1995).

Considering both horizontal analysis and vertical analysis information, you would conclude that an increase in the gross margin rate from 34.6% to 36.8%, coupled with a 28.9% increase in net sales, resulted in a 37.3% increase in gross margin in 1995. The increase in net income was held to 26.8% because selling expenses increased 56.1% and federal income taxes increased 52.4%. Predicting net income for 1996 would be made easier if you, the analyst, knew whether this increase in selling expenses is expected to recur. Other expenses remained basically the same, on a percentage-of-sales basis, over the two-year period.

Having completed the horizontal analysis and vertical analysis of Knight's balance sheet and statement of income and retained earnings, you are ready to study trend percentages and ratio analysis. The last section in this chapter discusses some final considerations in financial statement analysis. Professional financial statement analysts use several tools and techniques to determine the solvency and profitability of companies.

TREND PERCENTAGES

Trend percentages are also referred to as index numbers and are used for the comparison of financial information over time to a base year or period. Trend percentages are calculated by:

1. Selecting a base year or period.
2. Assigning a weight of 100% to the amounts appearing on the base-year financial statements.
3. Expressing the corresponding amounts shown on the other years' financial statements as a percentage of base-year or period amounts. The

percentages are computed by dividing nonbase-year amounts by the corresponding base-year amounts and then multiplying the result by 100.

The following information is given to illustrate the calculation of trend percentages:

	1994	1995	1996	1997
Sales	$350,000	$367,500	$441,000	$485,000
Cost of goods sold	200,000	196,000	230,000	285,000
Gross margin	$150,000	$171,500	$211,000	$200,000
Operating expenses	145,000	169,000	200,000	192,000
Income before income taxes	$ 5,000	$ 2,500	$ 11,000	$ 8,000

If 1994 is the base year, trend percentages are calculated for each year by dividing sales by $350,000; cost of goods sold by $200,000; gross margin by $150,000; operating expenses by $145,000; and income before income taxes by $5,000. After all divisions have been made, each result is multiplied by 100, and the resulting percentages that reflect trends appear as follows:

	1994	1995	1996	1997
Sales	100%	105%	126%	139%
Cost of goods sold	100	98	115	143
Gross margin	100	114	141	133
Operating expenses	100	117	138	132
Income before income taxes	100	50	220	160

Such trend percentages indicate changes that are taking place in an organization and highlight the direction of these changes. For instance, the percentage of sales is increasing each year or period (compared to the base year or period). Income before income taxes, however, does not show the same steady increase because cost of goods sold and operating expenses have an uneven rate and direction of change. Percentages can provide clues to a user as to which items need further investigation or analysis. In reviewing trend percentages, a financial statement user should pay close attention to the trends in related items, such as the cost of goods sold in relation to sales. Trend analysis that shows a constantly declining gross margin rate may be a signal that future net income will decrease.

As useful as trend percentages are, they have one drawback. Expressing changes as percentages is usually straightforward as long as the amount in the base year or period is positive—that is, not zero or negative. A $30,000 increase in notes receivable cannot be expressed in percentages if the increase is from zero last year to $30,000 this year. Also, an increase from a loss last year of $10,000 to income this year of $20,000 cannot be expressed in percentage terms.

Proper analysis does not stop with the calculation of increases and decreases in amounts or percentages over several years. Such changes generally indicate areas worthy of further investigation and are merely clues that may lead to significant findings. Accurate predictions depend on many factors, including economic and political conditions; management's plans regarding new products, plant expansion, and promotional outlays; and the expected activities of competitors. Consideration of these factors in conjunction with horizontal analysis, vertical analysis, and trend analysis should provide a reasonable basis for predicting future performance.

RATIO ANALYSIS

Objective 4 Perform ratio analysis on financial statements using liquidity ratios, long-term solvency ratios, profitability tests, and market tests

Logical relationships exist between certain accounts or items in a company's financial statements. These accounts may appear on the same statement or they may appear on two different statements. The dollar amounts of the related accounts or items are set up in fraction form and called *ratios*. These ratios can be broadly classified as (1) liquidity ratios; (2) equity, or long-term solvency, ratios; (3) profitability tests; and (4) market tests.

Liquidity Ratios

Liquidity ratios are used to indicate a company's short-term debt-paying ability. Thus, these ratios are designed to show interested parties the company's capacity to meet maturing current liabilities.

Current, or Working Capital, Ratio.   Working capital is the excess of current assets over current liabilities. The ratio that relates current assets to current liabilities is known as the **current,** or **working capital, ratio.** The current ratio indicates the ability of a company to pay its current liabilities from current assets and, thus, shows the strength of the company's working capital position.

The current ratio is computed by dividing current assets by current liabilities:

$$\text{Current ratio} = \frac{\text{Current assets}}{\text{Current liabilities}}$$

The ratio is usually stated in terms of the number of dollars of current assets to one dollar of current liabilities (although the dollar signs usually are omitted). Thus, if current assets total \$150,000 and current liabilities total \$100,000, the ratio is expressed as 1.5:1, meaning that the company has \$1.50 of current assets for each \$1 of current liabilities.

The current ratio provides a better index of a company's ability to pay current debts than does the absolute amount of working capital. To illustrate, assume that Company A and Company B have current assets and current liabilities on December 31, 1994, as follows:

	Company A	Company B
Current assets (a)	$11,000,000	$200,000
Current liabilities (b).	10,000,000	100,000
Working capital (a − b)	$ 1,000,000	$100,000
Current ratio (a ÷ b).	1.1 : 1	2 : 1

Company A has 10 times as much working capital as Company B. Company B, however, has a superior debt-paying ability, since it has $2 of current assets for each $1 of current liabilities. Company A has only $1.10 of current assets for each $1 of current liabilities.

Short-term creditors are particularly interested in the current ratio since the conversion of inventories and accounts receivable into cash is the primary source from which the company obtains the cash to pay short-term creditors. Long-term creditors are also interested in the current ratio because a company that is unable to pay short-term debts may be forced into bankruptcy. For this reason, many bond indentures, or contracts, contain a provision requiring that the borrower maintain at least a certain minimum current ratio. A company can increase its current ratio by issuing long-term debt or capital stock or by selling noncurrent assets.

A company must also guard against a current ratio that is too high, especially if caused by idle cash, slow-paying customers, and/or slow-moving inventory. Decreased net income can result when too much capital that could be used profitably elsewhere is tied up in current assets.

Refer back to the Knight Corporation data in column 4 of Illustration 22.1 which indicate that current liabilities are increasing more rapidly than current assets. Such an observation also can be made directly using changes in the current ratio. Knight's current ratios for 1994 and 1995 follow:

	December 31		Amount of Increase
	1995	1994	
Current assets (a)	$373,800	$336,800	$37,000
Current liabilities (b).	127,100	109,900	17,200
Working capital (a − b)	$246,700	$226,900	$19,800
Current ratio (a ÷ b).	2.94 : 1	3.06 : 1	

Although Knight's working capital increased by $19,800, or 8.7%, its current ratio fell from 3.06 to 2.94, reflecting that its current liabilities increased faster on a percentage basis than its current assets.

Acid-Test (Quick) Ratio. The current ratio is not the only measure of a company's short-term debt-paying ability. Another measure, called the **acid-test (quick) ratio,** is the ratio of quick assets (cash, marketable securities, and net receivables) to current liabilities. Inventories and prepaid expenses are excluded from current assets to compute quick assets because they might not be readily convertible into cash.

The formula for the acid-test ratio is:

$$\text{Acid-test ratio} = \frac{\text{Quick assets}}{\text{Current liabilities}}$$

Short-term creditors are interested particularly in this ratio, since it relates the "pool" of cash and immediate cash inflows to immediate cash outflows. The acid-test ratios for 1994 and 1995 for Knight are:

	December 31		Amount of Increase
	1995	*1994*	
Quick assets *(a)*	$259,400	$237,600	$21,800
Current liabilities *(b)*	127,100	109,900	17,200
Net quick assets *(a − b)*	$132,300	$127,700	$ 4,600
Acid-test ratio *(a ÷ b)*	2.04 : 1	2.16 : 1	

In deciding whether the acid-test ratio is satisfactory, you must consider the *quality* of the marketable securities and receivables. An accumulation of poor-quality marketable securities or receivables, or both, could cause an acid-test ratio to appear deceptively favorable. When referring to marketable securities, poor quality means securities that are likely to generate losses when sold. Poor-quality receivables are those that may be uncollectible or not collectible until long past due. The quality of receivables depends primarily on their age, which can be assessed by preparing an aging schedule or by calculating the accounts receivable turnover. (Refer to Chapter 3 for a discussion of an accounts receivable aging schedule.)

Cash-Flow Liquidity Ratio. Another approach to measuring short-term liquidity is the **cash-flow liquidity ratio.** The numerator, as an approximation of cash resources, consists of (1) cash and marketable securities, or "liquid" current assets, and (2) cash flows from operating activities, which shows the amount of cash the company can normally generate from operations. This ratio incorporates the company's ability to sell inventory and collect accounts receivable in the coming period.

The formula for the cash-flow liquidity ratio is:

$$\frac{\begin{array}{c}\text{Cash and marketable} \\ \text{securities}\end{array} + \begin{array}{c}\text{Cash flows from} \\ \text{operating activities}\end{array}}{\text{Current liabilities}}$$

For example, if a company has $200,000 in cash, $75,000 in marketable securities, $125,000 in current liabilities, and $96,000 in cash flow from operating activities, its cash-flow liquidity ratio is:

$$\frac{\$200,000 + \$75,000 + \$96,000}{\$125,000} = 2.97 \text{ times (or } 2.97 : 1)$$

Thus, the cash and marketable securities a company has on hand plus the cash the company can generate through operations during the coming year (which is likely to be about the same as in the preceding year) can be used to pay its current liabilities.

Accounts Receivable Turnover.   **Turnover** is the relationship between the amount of an asset and some measure of its use. **Accounts receivable turnover** is the number of times per year that the average amount of receivables is collected. The ratio is calculated by dividing net credit sales by average net accounts receivable, that is, accounts receivable after deducting the allowance for uncollectible accounts:

$$\frac{\text{Accounts receivable}}{\text{turnover}} = \frac{\text{Net credit sales (or net sales)}}{\text{Average net accounts receivable}}$$

When a ratio compares an income statement item (like net credit sales) with a balance sheet item (like accounts receivable), the balance sheet item should be an average. Ideally, average net accounts receivable should be computed by averaging the end-of-month balances or end-of-week balances of net accounts receivable outstanding during the period. The greater the number of observations used, the more accurate the resulting average. Often, only the beginning-of-year and end-of-year balances are averaged because this information is easily obtainable from comparative financial statements. Sometimes a formula calls for the use of an average balance, but only the year-end amount is available. Then the analyst must use the year-end amount.[1]

In theory, only net credit sales should be used in the numerator of the accounts receivable turnover ratio because those are the only sales that generate accounts receivable. However, if cash sales are relatively small or their proportion to total sales remains fairly constant, reliable results can be obtained by using total net sales. In most cases, the analyst may have to use total net sales because the separate amounts of cash sales and credit sales are not reported on the income statement.

Knight's accounts receivable turnover ratios for 1994 and 1995 are:

	1995	1994	Amount of Increase or (Decrease)
Net sales *(a)*	$986,400	$765,500	$220,900
Net accounts receivable:			
January 1	$132,600	$121,200	$ 11,400
December 31	124,200	132,600	(8,400)
Total *(b)*	$256,800	$253,800	$ 3,000
Average net accounts receivable *(c) (b ÷ 2 = c)* . .	$128,400	$126,900	
Turnover of accounts receivable *(a ÷ c)*	7.68	6.03	

---

[1] These general comments about the use of averages in a ratio apply to the other ratios involving averages discussed in this chapter.

Since beginning-of-year data for 1994 are not provided in Illustration 22.1, assume net accounts receivable on January 1, 1994, totaled $121,200.

The turnover ratio provides an indication of how quickly the receivables are being collected. For Knight in 1995, the turnover ratio indicates that accounts receivable were collected, or "turned over," slightly more than seven times per year. The ratio may be better understood and more easily compared with a company's credit terms if it is converted into a number of days, as is illustrated in the next ratio.

Number of Days' Sales in Accounts Receivable.   The **number of days' sales in accounts receivable** ratio, which also is called the *average collection period for accounts receivable*, is calculated as follows:

$$\text{Number of days' sales in accounts receivable (average collection period for accounts receivable)} = \frac{\text{Number of days in year (365)}}{\text{Accounts receivable turnover}}$$

The turnover ratios for Knight given in the preceding table show that the number of days' sales in accounts receivable decreased from about 61 days (365/6.03) in 1994 to 48 days (365/7.68) in 1995. The change means that the average collection period for the corporation's accounts receivable decreased from 61 to 48 days. Thus, the ratio measures the average liquidity of accounts receivable and gives an indication of their quality. Generally, the shorter the collection period, the higher the quality of receivables. However, the average collection period will vary by industry; for example, collection periods will be short in utility companies and much longer in some retailing companies. A comparison of the average collection period with the credit terms extended customers by the company will provide further insight into the quality of the accounts receivable. For example, receivables arising under terms of 2/10, n/30 that have an average collection period of 75 days need to be investigated further. It is important for management to determine why customers are paying their accounts much later than expected.

Inventory Turnover.   A company's inventory turnover ratio shows the number of times its average inventory is sold during a period. **Inventory turnover** is calculated as follows:

$$\text{Inventory turnover} = \frac{\text{Cost of goods sold}}{\text{Average inventory}}$$

In comparing an income statement item and a balance sheet item, both should be measured in comparable dollars. Notice that both the numerator and denominator are measured in terms of cost rather than sales dollars. (Earlier, when calculating accounts receivable turnover, both numerator and denominator were measured in sales dollars.) Inventory turnover relates a measure of sales volume to the average amount of goods on hand to produce this sales volume.

Assume that Knight's inventory on January 1, 1994, was $85,100. The following schedule shows that the inventory turnover increased slightly from 5.58 times per year in 1994 to 6.07 times per year in 1995. These turnover ratios can be converted to the number of days it takes a company to sell its entire stock of inventory; this conversion is made by dividing 365 by the inventory turnover. For Knight, the average inventory was sold in about 60 days (365/6.07) in 1955 as contrasted to about 65 days (365/5.58) in 1994.

	1995	1994	Amount of Increase
Cost of goods sold *(a)*	$623,200	$500,900	$122,300
Merchandise inventory:			
January 1	$ 94,500	$ 85,100	$ 9,400
December 31	110,800	94,500	16,300
Total *(b)*	$205,300	$179,600	$ 25,700
Average inventory *(c) (b ÷ 2 = c)*	$102,650	$ 89,800	
Turnover of inventory *(a ÷ c)*	6.07	5.58	

Other things being equal, a manager who is able to maintain the highest inventory turnover ratio is considered the most efficient. Yet, other things are not always equal. For example, a company that achieves a high inventory turnover ratio by keeping extremely small inventories on hand may incur larger ordering costs, lose quantity discounts, and lose sales due to lack of adequate inventory. In attempting to earn satisfactory income, management must balance the costs of inventory storage and obsolescence and the cost of tying up funds in inventory against possible losses of sales and other costs associated with keeping too little inventory on hand.

Total Assets Turnover. **Total assets turnover** shows the relationship between the dollar volume of sales and the average total assets used in the business and is calculated as follows:

$$\text{Total assets turnover} = \frac{\text{Net sales}}{\text{Average total assets}}$$

This ratio measures the efficiency with which a company uses its assets to generate sales. The larger the total assets turnover, the larger will be the income on each dollar invested in the assets of the business.

For Knight, the total assets turnover ratios for 1994 and 1995 are shown at the top of page 1077. Assume that total assets as of January 1, 1994, were $510,200. In 1994, each dollar of total assets produced $1.44 of sales; and in 1995, each dollar of assets produced $1.66 of sales. In other words, between 1994 and 1995, Knight had an increase of $0.22 of sales per dollar of investment in assets.

	1995	1994	Amount of Increase
Net sales *(a)*	$ 986,400	$ 765,500	$220,900
Total assets:			
January 1	$ 551,100	$ 510,200	$ 40,900
December 31	635,200	551,100	84,100
Total *(b)*	$1,186,300	$1,061,300	$125,000
Average total assets *(c) (b ÷ 2 = c)*	$ 593,150	$ 530,650	
Turnover of total assets *(a ÷ c)*	1.66 : 1	1.44 : 1	

Equity, or Long-Term Solvency, Ratios

Equity, or long-term solvency, ratios show the relationship between debt and equity financing in a company.

Equity (Stockholders' Equity) Ratio. The two basic sources of assets in a business are owners (stockholders) and creditors, and the combined interests of the two groups are referred to as *total equities*. In ratio analysis, however, the term *equity* generally refers only to stockholders' equity. Thus, the **equity (stockholders' equity) ratio** indicates the proportion of total assets (or total equities) provided by stockholders (owners) on any given date. The formula for the equity ratio is:

$$\text{Equity ratio} = \frac{\text{Stockholders' equity}}{\text{Total assets (or total equities)}}$$

Knight's liabilities and stockholders' equity, taken from Illustration 22.1, are given below. Knight's equity ratio increased from 69.0% in 1994 to 73.1% in 1995. The schedule below shows that the company's stockholders increased their proportionate equity in the company's assets by making additional investments in the company's common stock and by retaining income earned during the year.

	December 31, 1995		December 31, 1994	
	Amount	Percent	Amount	Percent
Current liabilities	$127,100	20.0	$109,900	20.0
Long-term liabilities.	43,600	6.9	60,800	11.0
Total liabilities	$170,700	26.9	$170,700	31.0
Common stock	$240,000	37.8	$200,000	36.3
Retained earnings	224,500	35.3	180,400	32.7
Total stockholders' equity.	$464,500	73.1	$380,400	69.0
Total equity (equal to total assets)	$635,200	100.0	$551,100	100.0

The equity ratio must be interpreted carefully. From a creditor's point of view, a high proportion of stockholders' equity is desirable. A high equity ratio indicates the existence of a large protective buffer for creditors in the event a company suffers a loss. However, from an owner's point of view, a high proportion of stockholders' equity may or may not be desirable. If borrowed funds can be used by the business to generate income in excess of the net after-tax cost of the interest on such borrowed funds, a lower percentage of stockholders' equity may be desirable.

To illustrate the effect of higher leveraging (i.e., a larger proportion of debt), assume that Knight could have financed its present operations with $40,000 of 12% bonds instead of 4,000 shares of common stock. The effect on income for 1995 would be as follows, assuming a federal income tax rate of 40%:

Net income as presently stated (Illustration 22.2)	$59,100
Deduct additional interest on debt (0.12 × $40,000)	4,800
	$54,300
Add reduced tax due to interest deduction (0.4 × $4,800)	1,920
Adjusted net income.	$56,220

As shown, net income is reduced when leverage is increased by issuing bonds instead of common stock. However, there are also fewer shares of common stock outstanding. Assume that the company has 24,000 shares of common stock outstanding. Earnings per share (EPS) increase from $2.46 (or $59,100/24,000 shares) to $2.81 (or $56,220/20,000 shares). Since investors place heavy emphasis on EPS amounts, many companies in recent years have introduced large portions of debt into their capital structures to increase EPS.

It should be pointed out, however, that too low a percentage of stockholders' equity (too much debt) has its dangers. Financial leverage magnifies losses per share as well as EPS since there are fewer shares of stock over which to spread the losses. A period of business recession may result in operating losses and shrinkage in the value of assets, such as receivables and inventory, which in turn may lead to an inability to meet fixed payments for interest and principal on the debt. As a result, the company may be forced into liquidation, and the stockholders could lose their entire investments.

Stockholders' Equity to Debt (Debt to Equity) Ratio. The relative equities of owners and creditors may be expressed in several ways. To say that creditors hold a 26.9% interest in the assets of Knight on December 31, 1995, is equivalent to saying stockholders hold a 73.1% interest. In many cases, this relationship is expressed as a ratio—**stockholders' equity to debt ratio.**

$$\frac{\text{Stockholders' equity}}{\text{to debt ratio}} = \frac{\text{Stockholders' equity}}{\text{Total debt}}$$

Such a ratio for Knight would be 2.23 : 1 (or \$380,400/\$170,700) on December 31, 1994, and 2.72 : 1 (or \$464,500/\$170,700) on December 31, 1995. This ratio is often inverted and called the **debt to equity ratio.** Some analysts use only long-term debt rather than total debt in calculating these ratios. These analysts do not consider short-term debt to be part of the capital structure since it will be paid within one year.

Profitability Tests

Profitability is an important measure of a company's operating success. Generally, we are concerned with two areas when judging profitability: (1) relationships on the income statement that indicate a company's ability to recover costs and expenses, and (2) relationships of income to various balance sheet measures that indicate the company's relative ability to earn income on assets employed. Each of the following ratios utilizes one of these relationships.

Rate of Return on Operating Assets.   The best measure of earnings performance without regard to the sources of assets is the relationship of net operating income to operating assets, which is known as the **rate of return on operating assets.** This ratio is quite similar to the return on investment (ROI) concept discussed in Chapter 19 and is designed to show the earning power of the company as a bundle of assets. By disregarding both nonoperating assets and nonoperating income elements, the rate of return on operating assets measures the profitability of the company in carrying out its primary business functions. The ratio can be broken down into two elements—the operating margin and the turnover of operating assets.

Operating margin reflects the percentage of each dollar of net sales that becomes net operating income. Net operating income excludes **nonoperating income elements** such as extraordinary items, nonoperating revenues such as interest revenue, and nonoperating expenses such as interest expense. The formula for operating margin is:

$$\text{Operating margin} = \frac{\text{Net operating income}}{\text{Net sales}}$$

Turnover of operating assets shows the amount of sales dollars generated for each dollar invested in operating assets. **Operating assets** are all assets actively used in producing operating revenues. Year-end operating assets are typically used, even though in theory an average would be better. **Nonoperating assets** are assets owned by a company, but not used in producing operating revenues, such as land held for future use, a factory building rented to another company, and long-term bond investments.

These nonoperating assets are not used in evaluating earnings performance. Total assets also should not be used because they include nonoperating assets that do not contribute to the generation of sales. The formula for the turnover of operating assets is:

$$\frac{\text{Turnover of}}{\text{operating assets}} = \frac{\text{Net sales}}{\text{Operating assets}}$$

The rate of return on operating assets of a company is equal to its operating margin multiplied by turnover of operating assets. The more a company earns per dollar of sales and the more sales it makes per dollar invested in operating assets, the higher will be the return per dollar invested. Rate of return on operating assets is expressed by the following formulas:

$$\frac{\text{Rate of return}}{\text{on operating assets}} = \frac{\text{Operating}}{\text{margin}} \times \frac{\text{Turnover of}}{\text{operating assets}}$$

or

$$\frac{\text{Rate of return}}{\text{on operating assets}} = \frac{\text{Net operating income}}{\text{Net sales}} \times \frac{\text{Net sales}}{\text{Operating assets}}$$

Since net sales appears in both ratios (once as a numerator and once as a denominator), we can cancel it out, and the formula for rate of return on operating assets becomes:

$$\frac{\text{Rate of return on}}{\text{operating assets}} = \frac{\text{Net operating income}}{\text{Operating assets}}$$

For analytical purposes, the formula should remain in the form that shows margin and turnover separately, since it provides more information.

The rates of return on operating assets for Knight Corporation for 1994 and 1995 are calculated below.

	1995	1994	Amount of Increase
Net operating income (a)	$110,400	$ 81,100	$ 29,300
Net sales (b)	$986,400	$765,500	$220,900
Operating assets* (c)	$635,200	$551,100	$ 84,100
Operating margin (a ÷ b)	11.19%	10.59%	
Turnover of operating assets (b ÷ c)	1.55 : 1	1.39 : 1	
Rate of return on operating assets (a ÷ c)	17.38%	14.72%	

* Knight Corporation had no nonoperating assets, so total assets are used in the calculation.

Securing Desired Rate of Return on Operating Assets. Companies that are to survive in the economy must attain some minimum rate of return on operating assets. However, this minimum rate of return can be attained in many different ways. To illustrate, consider a grocery store and a jewelry store, each with a rate of return of 8% on operating assets. The grocery store normally would attain this rate of return with a low margin and a high turnover, while the jewelry store would have a high margin and a low turnover, as shown in the following table.

	Margin $\times$ Turnover =	Rate of Return on Operating Assets
Grocery store	1% $\times$ 8.0 times =	8%
Jewelry store	20 $\times$ 0.4 =	8

Net Income to Net Sales (Return on Sales) Ratio.   Another measure of a company's profitability is the **net income to net sales** ratio, calculated as follows:

$$\frac{\text{Net income}}{\text{to net sales}} = \frac{\text{Net income}}{\text{Net sales}}$$

This ratio measures the proportion of the sales dollar that remains after the deduction of all expenses. The computations for Knight are:

	1995	1994	Amount of Increase
Net income *(a)*	$ 59,100	$ 46,600	$ 12,500
Net sales *(b)*	$986,400	$765,500	$220,900
Ratio of net income to net sales *(a ÷ b)*	5.99%	6.09%	

Although the ratio of net income to net sales indicates the net amount of profit on each sales dollar, care must be exercised in the use and interpretation of this ratio. The amount of net income includes all types of nonoperating items that may occur in a particular period; therefore, net income includes the effects of such things as extraordinary items and interest charges. Thus, a period that contains the effects of an extraordinary item will not be comparable to a period that contains no extraordinary items. Also, since interest expense is deductible in the determination of net income while dividends are not, net income is affected by the methods used to finance a company's assets.

Net Income to Average Common Stockholders' Equity.   From the stockholders' point of view, an important measure of the income-producing ability of a company is the relationship of **net income to average common stockholders' equity,** also called **rate of return on average common stockholders' equity,** or simply the **return on equity (ROE).** Although stockholders are interested in the ratio of operating income to operating assets as a measure of management's efficient use of assets, they are even more interested in the return the company earns on each dollar of common stockholders' equity. The formula for net income to average common stockholders' equity is:

$$\frac{\text{Net income to average}}{\text{common stockholders' equity}} = \frac{\text{Net income}}{\begin{array}{c}\text{Average common}\\ \text{stockholders' equity}\end{array}}$$

The ratios for Knight are shown below. Assume that total common stockholders' equity on January 1, 1994, was $321,500.

	1995	1994	Amount of Increase
Net income (a)	$ 59,100	$ 46,600	$ 12,500
Total common stockholders' equity:			
January 1	$380,400	$321,500	$ 58,900
December 31	464,500	380,400	84,100
Total (b)	$844,900	$701,900	$143,000
Average common stockholders' equity (c) (b ÷ 2 = c)	$422,450	$350,950	
Ratio of net income to common stockholders' equity (a ÷ c)	13.99%	13.28%	

The increase in the ratio from 13.28% to 13.99% would be regarded favorably by stockholders. This ratio indicates that for each dollar of capital invested by a stockholder, the company earned nearly 14 cents in 1995.

Trading on the Equity.   Sometimes, two companies will have the same return on assets but will have different returns on stockholders' equity, as shown in the example below.

	Company 1	Company 2
Return on assets	12.0%	12.0%
Return on stockholders' equity.	6.4	8.0

The difference of 1.6% in Company 2's favor is the result of Company 2's use of borrowed funds, particularly long-term debt, in its capital structure. Use of these funds (or preferred stock with a fixed return) is called *trading on the equity*. When a company is trading profitably on the equity, it is generating a higher rate of return on its borrowed funds than it is paying for the use of the funds. The excess, in this case 1.6%, is accruing to the benefit of the common stockholders, because their earnings are being increased.

Magnifying the gains from this type of activity for the stockholders is sometimes called the use of *leverage*. Using leverage is a risky process because losses also can be magnified, to the disadvantage of the common stockholders. Trading on the equity and leverage were discussed earlier in this chapter and in Chapter 10.

Cash-Flow Margin.   In addition, the cash-flow margin can be used to measure overall efficiency and performance. The **cash-flow margin** measures the ability of a company to translate sales into cash. It is important to measure the amount of cash a company generates from every dollar of sales because a company needs cash to service debt, pay dividends, and invest in new capital assets.

The formula for the cash-flow margin is:

$$\frac{\text{Cash flows from operating activities}}{\text{Net sales}}$$

Thus, if a company has \$125,000 in cash flows from operating activities and \$3,000,000 in net sales, its cash-flow margin is:

$$\frac{\$125,000}{\$3,000,000} = 4.167\%$$

Earnings per Share of Common Stock. Probably the measure used most widely to appraise a company's operations is **earnings per share (EPS)** of common stock. EPS is equal to earnings available to common stockholders divided by the weighted-average number of shares of common stock outstanding. The financial press regularly publishes actual and forecasted EPS amounts for publicly traded corporations, together with period-to-period comparisons. The Accounting Principles Board noted the significance attached to EPS by requiring that such amounts be reported on the face of the income statement.[2] (Chapter 9 illustrated how earnings per share should be presented on the income statement.)

The calculation of EPS may be fairly simple or highly complex depending on a corporation's capital structure. A company has a simple capital structure if it has no outstanding securities (e.g., convertible bonds, convertible preferred stocks, warrants, or options) that can be exchanged for common stock. If a company has such securities outstanding, it has a complex capital structure.

A company with a simple capital structure reports a single EPS amount, which is calculated as follows:

$$\text{EPS of common stock} = \frac{\text{Earnings available to common stockholders}}{\text{Weighted-average number of common shares outstanding}}$$

The amount of earnings available to common stockholders is equal to net income minus the current year's preferred dividends, whether such dividends have been declared or not.

Determining the Weighted-Average Number of Shares. The denominator in the EPS fraction is the weighted-average number of common shares outstanding for the period. If the number of shares outstanding did not change during the period, the weighted-average number of shares outstanding would, of course, be the number of shares outstanding at the end of the period. The balance in the Common Stock account of Knight (Illustration 22.1) was \$200,000 on December 31, 1994. The common stock has a \$10 par

---

[2] Accounting Principles Board, *Opinion No. 15,* "Reporting Earnings per Share" (New York: AICPA, 1969), par. 12.

value. Assuming that no shares were issued or redeemed during 1994, the weighted-average number of shares outstanding would be 20,000 (or $200,000/$10 per share).

If the number of shares changed during the period, such a change increases or decreases the capital invested in the company and should affect earnings available to stockholders. To compute the weighted-average number of shares outstanding, the change in the number of shares is weighted by the portion of the year that those shares were outstanding. Shares are only considered outstanding during those periods that the related capital investment is available to produce income.

To illustrate, note that Knight's Common Stock balance increased by $40,000 (4,000 shares) during 1995. Assume that 3,000 of these shares were issued on April 1, 1995, and the other 1,000 shares were issued on October 1, 1995. The computation of the weighted-average shares outstanding would be as follows:

20,000 shares × 1 year.	20,000
3,000 shares × ¾ year (April–December)	2,250
1,000 shares × ¼ year (October–December)	250
Weighted-average number of shares outstanding	22,500

An alternate method looks at the total number of shares outstanding, weighted by the portion of the year that the number of shares was outstanding, as follows:

20,000 shares × ¼ year (January–March).	5,000
23,000 shares × ½ year (April–September)	11,500
24,000 shares × ¼ year (October–December)	6,000
Weighted-average number of shares outstanding	22,500

Another alternative method is as follows:

20,000 shares ×	3 months =	60,000	share-months
23,000 shares ×	6 months =	138,000	share-months
24,000 shares ×	3 months =	72,000	share-months
	12 months =	270,000	share-months

270,000 share-months/12 months = 22,500 shares

Note that all three methods give the same result.

Since Knight had no preferred stock outstanding in either 1994 or 1995, EPS of common stock is computed as follows:

	1995	1994	Amount of Increase
Net income (a)	$59,100	$46,600	$12,500
Average number of shares of common stock outstanding (b)	22,500	20,000	2,500
EPS of common stock (a ÷ b)	$2.63	$2.33	

The increase of approximately 13% in EPS from $2.33 to $2.63 would probably be viewed quite favorably by Knight's stockholders.

EPS and Stock Dividends or Splits. Increases in shares outstanding as a result of a stock dividend or split do not require weighting for fractional periods. Such shares do not increase the capital invested in the business and therefore do not affect income. All that is required is to restate all prior calculations of EPS using the increased number of shares. For example, assume a company reported EPS for 1994 as $1 (or $100,000/100,000 shares) and earned $150,000 in 1995. The only change in common stock over the two years was a two-for-one stock split on December 1, 1995, which doubled the shares outstanding to 200,000. EPS for 1994 would be restated as $0.50 (or $100,000/200,000 shares) and would be $0.75 ($150,000/200,000 shares) for 1995.

Primary EPS and Fully Diluted EPS. In the merger wave of the 1960s, corporations often issued securities to finance their acquisitions of other companies. Many of the securities issued were *calls on common* or possessed *equity kickers*. These terms mean that the securities were convertible to, or exchangeable for, shares of their issuers' common stock. As a result, many complex problems arose in computing EPS. *APB Opinion No. 15* provides guidelines for solving these problems. A company with a complex capital structure must present at least two EPS calculations, primary EPS and fully diluted EPS. Because of the complexities involved in the calculations, further discussion of these two EPS amounts is reserved for an intermediate accounting text.

Times Interest Earned Ratio. Creditors, especially long-term creditors, want to know whether a borrower can meet its required interest payments when these payments come due. The **times interest earned ratio,** or **interest coverage ratio,** is an indication of such an ability. It is computed as follows:

$$\text{Times interest earned ratio} = \frac{\text{Income before interest and taxes (IBIT)}}{\text{Interest expense}}$$

The ratio is a rough comparison of cash inflows from operations with cash outflows for interest expense. *Income before interest and taxes (IBIT)* is used in the numerator since there would be no income taxes if interest expense is equal to or greater than IBIT. (To find income before interest and taxes, take net income and add back the interest and taxes.) Analysts disagree on whether the denominator should be only interest on long-term debt or total interest expense. We prefer the use of total interest expense since failure to make any required interest payment is a serious matter.

Assume that a company has IBIT of $100,000 and that the interest expense for the same period is $10,000. The times interest earned ratio is 10:1. The company earned enough during the period to pay its interest expense 10 times over. Low or negative interest coverage ratios suggest that the borrower could default on required interest payments. A company is not likely to be able to continue interest payments over many periods if it fails to earn enough income to cover them. On the other hand, interest coverage of 10 to 20 times suggests that the company is not likely to default on interest payments.

Times Preferred Dividends Earned Ratio.   Preferred stockholders, like bondholders, must usually be satisfied with a fixed-dollar return on their investments. They are interested in the company's ability to make preferred dividend payments each year. This ability can be measured by computing the **times preferred dividends earned ratio,** which is computed as follows:

$$\frac{\text{Times preferred dividends}}{\text{earned ratio}} = \frac{\text{Net income}}{\text{Annual preferred dividends}}$$

Suppose a company has net income of $48,000 and has $100,000 ($100 par value) of 8% preferred stock outstanding. The number of times the annual preferred dividends are earned would be:

$$\frac{\$48,000}{\$8,000} = 6:1, \text{ or } 6 \text{ times}$$

The higher this rate, the higher is the probability that the preferred stockholders will receive their dividends each year.

Market Tests

Certain ratios are computed using information from the financial statements and information about market price of the company's stock. These tests help investors and potential investors assess the relative merits of the various stocks in the marketplace.

The **yield** on a stock investment refers to either an earnings yield or a dividends yield.

Earnings Yield on Common Stock.   A company's earnings yield per share of common stock is calculated as follows:

$$\frac{\text{Earnings yield on}}{\text{common stock}} = \frac{\text{EPS}}{\begin{array}{c}\text{Current market price per}\\ \text{share of common stock}\end{array}}$$

Suppose, for example, that a company has common stock with an EPS of $2 and that the quoted market price of the stock on the New York Stock Exchange is $30. The **earnings yield on common stock** would be:

$$\frac{\$2}{\$30} = 6\frac{2}{3}\%$$

Price-Earnings Ratio.   When inverted, the earnings yield on common stock is called the **price-earnings ratio.** In the case cited above, the price-earnings ratio is:

$$\text{Price-earnings ratio} = \frac{\begin{array}{c}\text{Current market price per}\\\text{share of common stock}\end{array}}{\text{EPS}} = \frac{\$30}{\$2} = 15:1$$

Investors would say that this stock is selling at 15 times earnings, or at a multiple of 15. These investors might have a specific multiple in mind as being the one that should be used to judge whether the stock is underpriced or overpriced. Different investors may have different estimates of the proper price-earnings ratio for a given stock and also different estimates of the future earnings prospects of the company. These different estimates may be factors that cause one investor to sell stock at a particular price and another investor to buy at that price.

Dividend Yield on Common Stock.   The dividend paid per share of common stock is also of much interest to common stockholders. When the current annual dividend per share of common stock is divided by the current market price per share, the result is called the **dividend yield on common stock.** If the company whose stock sells at $30 per share paid a $1.50 per share dividend, the dividend yield would be:

$$\begin{array}{c}\text{Dividend yield on}\\\text{common stock}\end{array} = \frac{\begin{array}{c}\text{Dividend per share}\\\text{of common stock}\end{array}}{\begin{array}{c}\text{Current market price per}\\\text{share of common stock}\end{array}} = \frac{\$1.50}{\$30.00} = 5\%$$

Payout Ratio on Common Stock.   Using dividend yield, investors can compute the payout ratio on a stock. **Payout ratio on common stock** is computed as the dividend per share of common stock divided by EPS. The payout ratio for the above stock is:

$$\begin{array}{c}\text{Payout ratio on}\\\text{common stock}\end{array} = \frac{\begin{array}{c}\text{Dividend per share}\\\text{of common stock}\end{array}}{\text{EPS}} = \frac{\$1.50}{\$2.00} = 75\%$$

A payout ratio of 75% means that the company paid out 75% of its current-year earnings in the form of dividends. Some investors are attracted by the stock of companies that pay out a large percentage of their earnings. Other investors are attracted by the stock of companies that retain and reinvest a large percentage of their earnings. The tax status of the investor has a great deal to do with this preference. Investors in high tax brackets often prefer to have the company reinvest the earnings with the expectation that this rein-vestment will result in share price appreciation.

Dividend Yield on Preferred Stock.   Preferred stockholders, as well as common stockholders, are interested in dividend yields. The computation of the **dividend yield on preferred stock** is similar to the common stock dividend yield computation. Suppose a company has 2,000 shares of $100 par value, 8% preferred stock outstanding with a current market price of $110 per share. The dividend yield on preferred stock is computed as follows:

$$\frac{\text{Dividend yield on}}{\text{preferred stock}} = \frac{\substack{\text{Dividend per share} \\ \text{of preferred stock}}}{\substack{\text{Current market price per} \\ \text{share of preferred stock}}} = \frac{\$8}{\$110} = 7.27\%$$

Through the use of dividend yield rates, different preferred stocks having different annual dividends and different market prices can be compared.

Cash Flow per Share of Common Stock. The **cash flow per share** of common stock ratio is calculated as:

$$\frac{\text{Cash flow per share}}{\text{of common stock}} = \frac{\substack{\text{Cash flows from} \\ \text{operating activities}}}{\substack{\text{Average number of shares} \\ \text{of common stock outstanding}}}$$

Currently, FASB *Statement No. 95* does not permit use of this ratio for external reporting purposes. However, some companies, like mortgage and investment banking firms, do use this ratio to judge the company's ability to pay dividends. An example of the cash flow per share of common stock ratio is shown in Illustration 22.3, which shows data that were included in the Coca-Cola Enterprises, Inc., annual report in 1987, before the FASB prohibited the publication of such data.

For a complete summary of all liquidity, long-term solvency, profitability, and market test ratios, see Illustration 22.4, a summary of financial statement analysis utilizing financial ratios.

FINAL CONSIDERATIONS IN FINANCIAL STATEMENT ANALYSIS

Objective 5
Describe the
considerations
used in financial
statement analysis

Standing alone, a single financial ratio may not be informative. Greater insight can be obtained by computing and analyzing several related ratios for a company. Illustration 22.5 summarizes the ratios presented in this chapter.

Financial analysis relies heavily on informed judgment. Percentages and ratios are guides to aid comparison and are useful in uncovering potential strengths and weaknesses. However, the financial analyst should seek the basic causes behind changes and established trends.

Need for Comparable Data

Analysts must be sure that their comparisons are valid—especially when the comparisons are of items for different periods or different companies. Con-

Illustration 22.3
CASH FLOW PER SHARE OF COMMON STOCK (in thousands except per share data)

	Fiscal Year		
	1987	1986	1985
Net Operating Revenues	$3,329,134	$1,951,008	$1,271,959
Cost of Sales (includes purchases from The Coca-Cola Company of approximately $652,800 in 1987, $392,400 in 1986, and $265,400 in 1985)	1,916,724	1,137,720	755,709
Gross Profit	$1,412,410	$ 813,288	$ 516,250
Selling, Administrative, and General Expenses	1,075,290	645,218	431,747
Operating Income	$ 337,120	$ 168,070	$ 84,503
Interest Income	11,566	6,327	4,587
Interest Expense	(171,466)	(82,526)	(31,945)
Other Income (deductions)	(4,445)	(7,101)	6,483
Income before Income Taxes	$ 172,775	$ 84,770	$ 63,628
Income Taxes	84,403	56,978	27,721
Net Income	$ 88,372	$ 27,792	$ 35,907
Net Income per Share	$ .63	$ .36	$ .52
Dividends per Share	$ .05	$ —	$ —
Average Shares Outstanding	140,036	76,705	68,600
Operating Cash Flow Data:			
Operating Income	$ 337,120	$ 168,070	$ 84,503
Depreciation	122,900	68,203	50,698
Amortization	71,633	24,095	4,785
Operating Cash Flow	$ 531,653	$ 260,368	$ 139,986
Cash Flow per Share	$ 3.80	$ 3.39	$ 2.04

SOURCE: Coca-Cola Enterprises, Inc., *1987 Annual Report*. Selected Financial Data and Consolidated Statements of Income. Coca-Cola Enterprises, Inc., Atlanta, Georgia, 1987.

sistent accounting practices must be followed if valid interperiod comparisons are to be made. Comparable intercompany comparisons are more difficult to secure. Accountants cannot do much more than disclose the fact that one company is using FIFO and another is using LIFO for inventory and cost of goods sold computations. Such a disclosure alerts analysts that intercompany comparisons of inventory turnover ratios, for example, may not be comparable.

Also, when comparing a company's ratios to industry averages provided by an external source such as Dun & Bradstreet, the analyst must calculate the company's ratios in the same manner as the reporting service. Thus, if Dun & Bradstreet uses net sales (rather than cost of goods sold) to compute inventory turnover, so should the analyst. Net sales is used because all companies do not compute and report cost of goods sold amounts in the same manner. Ratios based on net sales may lead to different conclusions

Illustration 22.4
SUMMARY OF FINANCIAL STATEMENT ANALYSIS UTILIZING FINANCIAL RATIOS

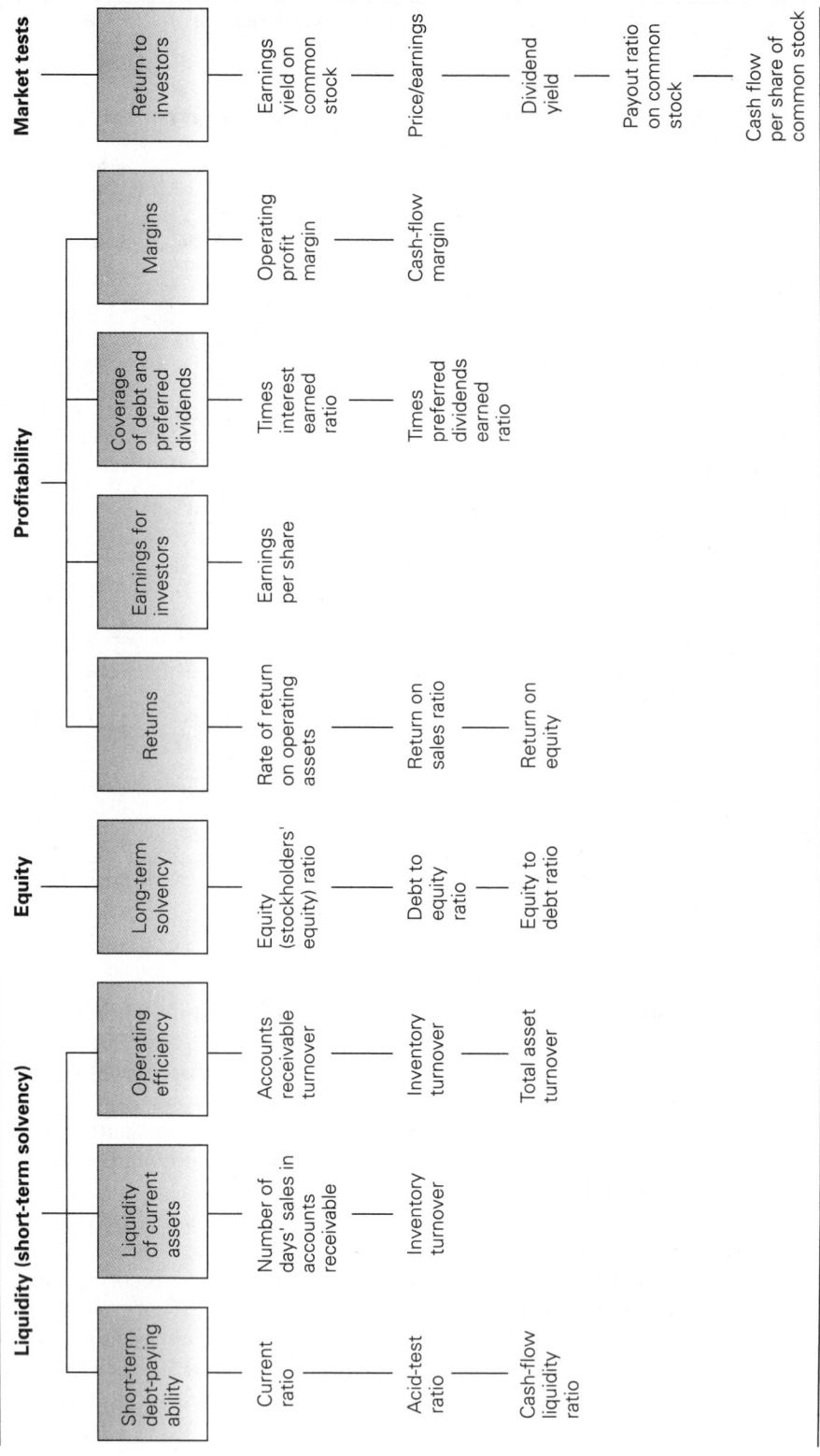

A BROADER PERSPECTIVE

BELL SOUTH CORPORATION

FINANCIAL HIGHLIGHTS
(Dollars in Millions, Except per Share Amounts)

	1990	1989	1988	1987	1986
Operating Revenues	**$ 14,345.4**	$ 13,996.3	$ 13,596.9	$ 12,229.9	$ 11,401.0
Operating Expenses	**$ 11,314.7**	$ 10,999.3	$ 10,557.2	$ 9,027.8	$ 7,957.5
Net Income	**$ 1,631.5**	$ 1,741.1	$ 1,665.5	$ 1,664.8	$ 1,588.7
Earnings per Share	**$ 3.38**	$ 3.64	$ 3.51	$ 3.46	$ 3.38
Dividends per Share	**$ 2.68**	$ 2.52	$ 2.36	$ 2.20	$ 2.04
Book Value per Share	**$ 26.28**	$ 27.21	$ 25.52	$ 24.89	$ 23.61
Weighted Average Common Shares Outstanding (millions)	**482.4**	477.7	474.9	481.2	469.5
Total Assets	**$ 30,206.8**	$ 30,049.8	$ 28,472.4	$ 27,416.5	$ 26,218.1
Capital Expenditures	**$ 3,190.7**	$ 3,22.6	$ 3,207.3	$ 3,058.6	$ 2,894.5
Return to Average Common Equity	**12.8%**	13.7%	13.8%	14.2%	14.7%
Debt Ratio	**40.7%**	38.0%	39.8%	37.3%	37.3%
Employees (end of year)	**101,945**	101,230	100,280	98,700	96,900
Telephone Employees (end of year)	**85,967**	86,728	88,801	87,560	87,700

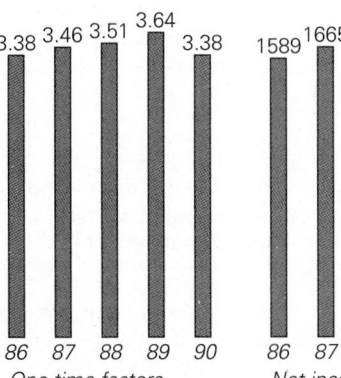

Earnings per Share
($ per share)

3.38 3.46 3.51 3.64 3.38

86 87 88 89 90

One-time factors affected reported earnings in both 1990 and 1989.

Net Income
($ in millions)

1589 1665 1666 1741 1632

86 87 88 89 90

Net income was adversely affected in 1990 by rate reductions, one-time charges, competition and a slowing of the economy.

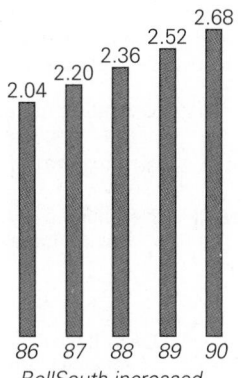

Dividends per Share
($ per share)

2.04 2.20 2.36 2.52 2.68

86 87 88 89 90

BellSouth increased the dividend in 1990 for the sixth consecutive year.

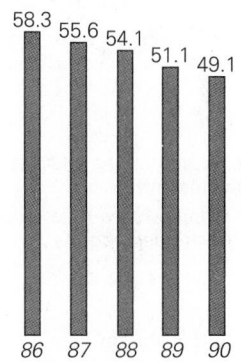

Telephone Employees per 10,000 Access Lines
(end of period)

58.3 55.6 54.1 51.1 49.1

86 87 88 89 90

BellSouth continued to improve this key measure of productivity in 1990.

Illustration 22.5
SUMMARY OF RATIOS

Ratio	Formula	Significance
Current, or working capital, ratio	Current assets ÷ Current liabilities	Test of debt-paying ability
Acid-test (quick) ratio	Quick assets (Cash + Marketable securities + Net receivables) ÷ Current liabilities	Test of immediate debt-paying ability
Cash-flow liquidity ratio	(Cash and marketable securities + cash flows from operating activities) ÷ current liabilities	Test of short-term debt-paying ability
Accounts receivable turnover	Net credit sales (or net sales) ÷ Average net accounts receivable	Test of quality of accounts receivable
Number of days' sales in accounts receivable (average collection period of accounts receivable)	Number of days in year (365) ÷ Accounts receivable turnover	Test of quality of accounts receivable
Inventory turnover	Cost of goods sold ÷ Average inventory	Test of whether or not a sufficient volume of business is being generated relative to inventory
Total assets turnover	Net sales ÷ Average total assets	Test of whether or not the volume of business generated is adequate relative to amount of capital invested in business
Equity (stockholders' equity) ratio	Stockholders' equity ÷ Total assets (or total equities)	Index of long-run solvency and safety
Stockholders' equity to debt (debt to equity) ratio	Stockholders' equity ÷ Total debt	Measure of the relative proportion of stockholders' and of creditors' equities
Rate of return on operating assets	Net operating income ÷ Operating assets or Operating margin × Turnover of operating assets	Measure of managerial effectiveness
Net income to net sales (return on sales ratio)	Net income ÷ Net sales	Indicator of the amount of net profit on each dollar of sales
Net income to average common stockholders' equity	Net income ÷ Average common stockholders' equity	Measure of what a given company earned for its stockholders from all sources as a percentage of the stockholders' investment
Cash-flow margin	Cash flows from operating activities ÷ net sales	Measure of the ability of a firm to translate sales into cash
EPS of common stock	Earnings available to common stockholders ÷ Weighted-average number of common shares outstanding	Influence on the market price per share
Times interest earned ratio	Income before interest and taxes ÷ Interest expense	Test of likelihood that creditors will continue to receive their interest payments
Times preferred dividends earned ratio	Net income ÷ Annual preferred dividends	Test of likelihood that preferred stockholders will receive their dividend each year

Illustration 22.5 *(concluded)*

Ratio	Formula	Significance
Earnings yield on common stock	EPS ÷ Current market price per share of common stock	Comparison with other common stocks
Price-earnings ratio	Current market price per share of common stock ÷ EPS	Index of whether a stock is relatively cheap or expensive based on ratio
Dividend yield on common stock	Dividend per share of common stock ÷ Current market price per share	Comparisons with other common stocks
Payout ratio on common stock	Dividend per share of common stock ÷ EPS	Index of whether company pays out a large percentage of earnings as dividends or reinvests most of its earnings
Dividend yield on preferred stock	Dividend per share of preferred stock ÷ Current market price per share of preferred stock	Comparison with other preferred stocks
Cash flow per share of common stock	Cash flows from operating activities ÷ Average number of shares of common stock outstanding	Test of ability to pay dividends

from those obtained using cost of goods sold because gross margin rates may differ. For example, Company A and Company B may both have $100 sales and $10 average inventory for an identical inventory turnover of 10 (or $100/$10) based on sales. However, if Company A's gross margin rate is 40%, its inventory turnover based on cost of goods sold is 6 [or ($100 − $40)/$10]. If Company B's gross margin rate is 30%, its cost of goods sold is $70, and its inventory turnover is 7 [or ($100 − $30)/$10].

Influence of External Factors

Facts and conditions not disclosed by the financial statements may, however, affect their interpretation. A single important event may have been largely responsible for a given relationship. For example, a new product may have been unexpectedly put on the market by competitors, making it necessary for the company under study to sell at lower prices a product suddenly rendered obsolete. Such an event would severely affect the percentage of gross margin to net sales. Yet there may be only a small chance that such an event will happen again.

General business conditions within the business or industry of the company under study must be considered. A corporation's downward trend in earnings, for example, is less alarming if the industry trend or the general economic trend is also downward.

Consideration should be given to the seasonal nature of some businesses. If the balance sheet date represents the seasonal peak in the volume of business, for example, the ratio of current assets to current liabilities may acceptably be much lower than if the balance sheet date is in a season of low activity.

Potential investors should consider the market risk associated with the prospective investment. Market risk is determined by comparing the changes in the price of a stock in relation to the changes in the average price of all stocks. For instance, when the average price went up by 8%, Company X's price increased 20% while Company Y's increased 5%. Company X's stock has a greater potential for gain than Company Y's. It also has a greater risk of loss if the average price goes down. In addition, the potential investor should realize that acquiring the ability to make informed judgments is a long process and does not occur overnight. Using ratios and percentages without considering the underlying causes may lead to incorrect conclusions.

Impact of Inflation

The usefulness of conventional financial statements has been questioned. The primary reason for this uncertainty is that financial statements fail to reveal the impact of inflation on the reporting entity. A primary rule to follow in making comparisons is to be sure that the items being compared are comparable. The old adage is that you should not add apples and oranges and call the total either apples or oranges. Yet, the accountant does exactly this when dollars of different real worth are added or subtracted as if they were the same. The worth of a dollar declines during periods of inflation.

Considerable debate has existed over the proper response by accountants to inflation. Some argue that we should change our unit of measure from the nominal, unadjusted dollar to a dollar of a constant purchasing power. Others maintain that only by adopting current cost as the attribute measured will the real effect of inflation on an entity be revealed.

Need for Standards of Comparison

Relationships between financial statement items become more meaningful when standards are available for comparison. Comparisons with standards provide a starting point for the analyst's thinking and lead to further investigation and, ultimately, to conclusions and business decisions. Such standards consist of (1) those in the analyst's own mind as a result of experience and observations, (2) those provided by the records of past performance and financial position of the business under study, and (3) those provided about other enterprises. Examples of this last type of standard are data available through trade associations, universities, research organizations (such as Dun & Bradstreet and Robert Morris Associates), and governmental units (such as the Federal Trade Commission).

In financial statement analysis, you must remember that standards for comparison vary by industry, and financial analysis must be carried out with knowledge of specific industry characteristics. For example, a wholesale grocery company would have large inventories available to be shipped to

ETHICS   A CLOSER LOOK

Since 1894, ABC Steel Company has manufactured and distributed sheet metal fabricated in its mills to many American and foreign companies. Until the mid-1970s, this family-operated company had been a very healthy and profitable operation, but the company's fortunes began to change when it faced stiff quality and price competition from foreign steel manufacturers. ABC suffered a strong decline in sales and closed several plants as a result.

During the early 1980s, ABC replaced both its aging plant equipment and its aging management team. Most of the equipment ABC once used in its manufacturing process was installed during the 1950s and had been repaired, modified, and expanded, but never replaced. By closing more than half of its existing operations, ABC concentrated on its remaining facilities and purchased $50 million of modern equipment that allowed it to successfully compete with foreign steelmakers.

The stockholders also replaced the family management team that started the company with a younger, more aggressive management team. The stockholders paid the managers competitive salaries but also realized that good managers frequently changed positions every few years. As an incentive to encourage the management's loyalty and performance, the stockholders also offered them $3 million in lucrative stock options that could be exercised when the earnings per share (EPS) first exceeded $2.00 per share, a rather sizable increase to expect at that time.

By November 1994, the company projected annual earnings of $20 million and had 11 million shares outstanding and $18 million in cash reserves for future investment. Since the 1980s and 1990s, the company's sales grew steadily to a respectable amount, but the manufacturing equipment once again began to show signs of its age. The management team was faced with a decision: Should it recommend that the company spend the $18 million in available cash on the purchase of more modern equipment or on the repurchase of 1.5 million shares of its own stock?

Required
a. What would be the consequences if the management team repurchased the stock?
b. How might this decision affect the stockholders?
c. What would you do if you were a member of the management team?

retailers and a relatively small investment in property, plant, and equipment, while an electric utility company would have no merchandise inventory (except for repair parts) and a large investment in property, plant, and equipment.

Even within an industry, variations may exist. Acceptable current ratios, gross margin percentages, debt to equity ratios, and other relationships vary widely depending on unique conditions within an industry. Therefore, it is important to know the industry to make comparisons that have real meaning.

EPILOGUE

You have now completed the last chapter in this text. Several appendixes at the end of the text contain information that may be useful to you. Appendix A covers payroll accounting and federal income taxes, Appendix B discusses accounting systems and special journals, and Appendix C shows excerpts from the 1991 annual reports of The Coca-Cola Company, Maytag Corporation, The Limited, Inc., and John H. Harland Company. These annual reports illustrate many of the concepts and financial statements presented in the text.

Appendix D presents the AICPA code of professional conduct, the IMA standards of ethical behavior for management accountants, and the FEI code of ethics. By studying these codes you can understand the high levels of personal and professional conduct expected of accountants. Appendix E contains compound interest and annuity tables.

Thank you for using our textbook. The knowledge you have gained will serve you well regardless of the career you choose.

UNDERSTANDING THE LEARNING OBJECTIVES

1. Describe and explain the objectives of financial statement analysis.
    *   A company's financial statements are analyzed internally by management, and externally by investors, creditors, and regulatory agencies.
    *   Management's analysis of financial statements primarily relates to parts of the company. Management is able to obtain specific, special-purpose reports in order to aid in decision making.
    *   External users focus their analysis of financial statements on the company as a whole. They must rely on the general-purpose financial statements that companies publish.
2. Describe the sources of information for financial statement analysis.
    *   Published reports are one source of financial information. These reports include financial statements, explanatory notes, letters to stockholders, reports of independent accountants, and management's discussion and analysis (MDA).
    *   Government reports are another source of financial information and include Forms 10-K, 10-Q, and 8-K. These reports are available to the public for a small charge.
    *   Financial service information, newspapers, and periodicals offer meaningful financial information to external users. Moody's, Standard and Poor's, Dun and Bradstreet, Inc., and Robert Morris Associates are all firms that provide useful industry information. Business publications such as *The Wall Street Journal* and *Forbes* also report industry financial news.
3. Calculate and explain changes in financial statements using horizontal analysis, vertical analysis, and trend analysis.
    *   Horizontal analysis is the calculation of dollar changes or percentage changes in comparative statement items or totals. Use of this analysis helps detect changes in a company's performance and highlights trends.
    *   Vertical analysis consists of a study of a single financial statement in which each item is expressed as a percentage of a significant total.

Use of this analysis is especially helpful in analyzing income statement data such as the percentage of cost of goods sold to sales or the percentage of gross margin to sales.

- Trend analysis is used to compare financial information over time to a base year. The analysis is calculated by:
  1. Selecting a base year or period.
  2. Assigning a weight of 100% to the amounts appearing on the base-year financial statements.
  3. Expressing the corresponding amounts shown on the other years' financial statements as a percentage of base-year amounts. The percentages are computed by dividing nonbase-year amounts by the corresponding base-year amounts and then multiplying the results by 100.

Trend analysis indicates changes that are taking place in an organization and highlights the direction of these changes.

4. Perform ratio analysis on financial statements using liquidity ratios, long-term solvency ratios, profitability tests, and market tests.
   - **Liquidity ratios** are used to indicate a company's short-term debt-paying ability. These ratios include (1) current, or working capital, ratio; (2) acid-test (quick) ratio; (3) cash-flow liquidity ratio; (4) accounts receivable turnover; (5) number of days' sales in accounts receivable; (6) inventory turnover; and (7) total assets turnover.
   - **Equity, or long-term solvency, ratios** show the relationship between debt and equity financing in a company. These ratios include (1) equity (stockholders' equity) ratio and (2) stockholders' equity to debt ratio.
   - **Profitability tests** are an important measure of a company's operating success. These tests include (1) rate of return on operating assets, (2) net income to net sales, (3) net income to average common stockholders' equity, (4) cash-flow margin, (5) earnings per share of common stock, (6) times interest earned ratio, and (7) times preferred dividends earned ratio.
   - **Market tests** help investors and potential investors assess the relative merits of the various stocks in the marketplace. These tests include (1) earnings yield on common stock, (2) price-earnings ratio, (3) dividend yield on common stock, (4) payout ratio on common stock, (5) dividend yield on preferred stock, and (6) cash flow per share of common stock.

5. Describe the considerations used in financial statement analysis.
   - **Need for comparative data:** Analysts must be sure that their comparisons are valid—especially when the comparisons are of items for different periods or different companies.
   - **Influence of external factors:** A single important event, such as the unexpected placing of a product on the market by a competitor, may affect the interpretation of the financial statements. Also, the general

business conditions and the possible seasonal nature of the business must be taken into consideration, since these factors could have an impact on the statements.

- **Impact of inflation:** Since financial statements fail to reveal the impact of inflation on the reporting entity, one must make sure that the items being compared are all comparable; that is, the impact of inflation has been taken into consideration.
- **Need for comparative standards:** It is important in financial statement analysis to remember that standards for comparison vary by industry, and financial analysis must be carried out with knowledge of specific industry characteristics.

DEMONSTRATION PROBLEM 22–A

Comparative financial statements of Amber Company for 1995 and 1994 follow:

AMBER COMPANY
Comparative Income Statements
For the Years Ended December 31, 1995 and 1994
(in thousands)

	1995	1994
Net sales	$2,200	$1,900
Cost of goods sold	1,410	1,196
Gross margin	$ 790	$ 704
Operating expenses	582	514
Income before income taxes	$ 208	$ 190
Income taxes	90	80
Net income	$ 118	$ 110

AMBER COMPANY
Comparative Balance Sheets
December 31, 1995 and 1994
(in thousands)

	1995	1994
Assets		
Cash	$ 58	$ 60
Accounts receivable, net.	134	148
Merchandise inventory.	226	182
Plant assets, net.	472	474
Total assets.	$890	$864
Liabilities and Stockholders' Equity		
Current liabilities	$156	$140
Long-term liabilities	188	188
Common stock	480	480
Retained earnings.	66	56
Total liabilities and stockholders' equity . . .	$890	$864

Required:

a. Prepare comparative common-size income statements for 1995 and 1994.
b. Perform a horizontal analysis of the comparative balance sheets.
c. Comment on the results of *(a)* and *(b)*.

Solution to demonstration problem 22–A

a.

AMBER COMPANY
Common-Size Comparative Income Statements
For the Years Ended December 31, 1995 and 1994

	Percent	
	1995	1994
Net sales	100.00	100.00
Cost of goods sold	64.09	62.95
Gross margin	35.91	37.05
Operating expenses	26.45	27.05
Income before income taxes	9.46*	10.00
Income taxes	4.09	4.21
Net income	5.37*	5.79

* Rounding difference.

b.

AMBER COMPANY
Comparative Balance Sheets
December 31, 1995 and 1994
(in thousands)

	1995	1994	Increase or Decrease 1995 over 1994 Amount	Percent
Assets				
Cash.	$ 58	$ 60	$ (2)	(3.33)
Accounts receivable, net	134	148	(14)	(9.46)
Merchandise inventory	226	182	44	24.18
Plant assets, net	472	474	(2)	(0.42)
Total assets	$890	$864	$ 26	3.01
Liabilities and Stockholders' Equity				
Current liabilities	$156	$140	$ 16	11.43
Long-term liabilities.	188	188	–0–	–0–
Common stock	480	480	–0–	–0–
Retained earnings	66	56	10	17.86
Total liabilities and stockholders' equity .	$890	$864	$ 26	3.01

c. The $300,000 increase in sales yielded only an $86,000 increase in gross margin because the gross margin rate decreased from 37.05% to 35.91%. Although operating expenses increased from $514,000 to $582,000, they declined relatively from 27.05% to 26.45% of sales. This change together with the change in gross margin combined to hold net income to an increase of $8,000, which represents a decline of 0.42% in the rate of net income to sales. The significant change in the balance sheet was the 24.18% increase in merchandise inventory that was financed by decreases in cash and accounts receivable and by increases in current liabilities and in retained earnings. The company is in a less liquid position at the end of 1995 than at the end of 1994.

DEMONSTRATION PROBLEM 22–B

The balance sheet and supplementary data for Carl Corporation are shown below.

CARL CORPORATION
Balance Sheet
December 31, 1994
Assets

Cash		$ 100,000
Marketable securities.		60,000
Accounts receivable, net		140,000
Merchandise inventory		300,000
Building	$800,000	
Less: Accumulated depreciation	200,000	600,000
Total assets		$1,200,000

Liabilities and Stockholders' Equity

Accounts payable	$ 60,000
Bank loans payable	20,000
Mortgage notes payable, due in 1997	80,000
Bonds payable, 10%, due December 31, 1999 . . .	200,000
Common stock, $100 par value	600,000
Retained earnings	240,000
Total liabilities and stockholders' equity	$1,200,000

Supplementary data:

1. 1994 net income, $120,000.
2. 1994 cost of goods sold, $1,080,000.
3. 1994 net sales, $1,800,000.
4. Merchandise inventory, January 1, 1994, $200,000.
5. Net interest expense, $30,000.
6. 1994 income before interest and taxes, $260,000.
7. Net accounts receivable on January 1, 1994, $100,000.
8. Total assets on January 1, 1994, $1,080,000.
9. No shares of stock were issued during 1994.

Required:

Compute the following ratios:

a. Current ratio.
b. Acid-test ratio.
c. Accounts receivable turnover.
d. Inventory turnover.

 e. Total assets turnover.
 f. Equity ratio.
 g. EPS of common stock.
 h. Times interest earned ratio.

Solution to demonstration problem 22–B

 a. Current ratio:

$$\frac{\text{Current assets}}{\text{Current liabilities}} = \frac{\$600,000}{\$80,000} = 7.5:1$$

 b. Acid-test ratio:

$$\frac{\text{Quick assets}}{\text{Current liabilities}} = \frac{\$300,000}{\$80,000} = 3.75:1$$

 c. Accounts receivable turnover:

$$\frac{\text{Net sales}}{\text{Average net accounts receivable}} = \frac{\$1,800,000}{\$120,000} = 15 \text{ times}$$

 d. Inventory turnover:

$$\frac{\text{Cost of goods sold}}{\text{Average inventory}} = \frac{\$1,080,000}{\$250,000} = 4.32 \text{ times}$$

 e. Total assets turnover:

$$\frac{\text{Net sales}}{\text{Average total assets}} = \frac{\$1,800,000}{\$1,140,000} = 1.58 \text{ times}$$

 f. Equity ratio:

$$\frac{\text{Stockholders' equity}}{\text{Total assets}} = \frac{\$840,000}{\$1,200,000} = 70\%$$

 g. EPS of common stock:

$$\frac{\substack{\text{Earnings available} \\ \text{to common stockholders}}}{\substack{\text{Weighted-average number of} \\ \text{common shares outstanding}}} = \frac{\$120,000}{6,000} = \$20$$

 h. Times interest earned ratio:

$$\frac{\substack{\text{Income before} \\ \text{interest and taxes}}}{\text{Interest expense}} = \frac{\$260,000}{\$30,000} = 8.67:1, \text{ or } 8.67 \text{ times}$$

NEW TERMS

Accounts receivable turnover   Net credit sales divided by average net accounts receivable. *1074*

Acid-test (quick) ratio   Ratio of quick assets (cash, marketable securities, net receivables) to current liabilities. *1072*

Cash-flow liquidity ratio   Cash and marketable securities plus cash flow from operating activities divided by current liabilities. *1073*

Cash-flow margin   Cash flow from operating activities divided by net sales. *1082*

Cash flow per share   Operating cash flow divided by the average number of shares of common stock outstanding. *1088*

Common-size statements   Show only percentages and no absolute dollar amounts. *1065*

Comparative financial statements   Present the same company's financial statements for two or more successive periods in side-by-side columns. *1063*

Current ratio   Current assets divided by current liabilities. *1071*

Debt to equity ratio   Total debt divided by stockholders' equity. *1079*

Dividend yield on common stock   Dividend per share of common stock divided by current market price per share of common stock. *1087*

Dividend yield on preferred stock   Dividend per share of preferred stock divided by current market price per share of preferred stock. *1088*

Earnings per share (EPS)   The amount of earnings available to common stockholders (which equals net income less preferred dividends) divided by weighted-average number of shares of common stock outstanding. *1083*

Earnings yield on common stock   Ratio of current EPS to current market price per share of common stock. *1086*

Equity (stockholders' equity) ratio   The ratio of stockholders' equity to total assets (or total equities). *1077*

Horizontal analysis   Analysis of a company's financial statements for two or more successive periods showing percentage and/or absolute changes from prior year. This type of analysis helps detect changes in a company's performance and highlights trends. *1063*

Inventory turnover   Cost of goods sold divided by average inventory. *1075*

Liquidity   Company's state of possessing liquid assets, such as (1) cash and (2) other assets that will soon be converted to cash. *1062*

Net income to average common stockholders' equity   Net income divided by average common stockholders' equity; often called **rate of return on average common stockholders' equity,** or simply **return on equity (ROE).** *1081*

Net income to net sales   Net income divided by net sales. *1081*

Nonoperating assets   Assets owned by a company but not used in producing operating revenues. *1079*

Nonoperating income elements   Elements that are excluded from net operating income because they are not directly related to operations; includes such elements as extraordinary items, interest revenue, and interest expense. *1079*

Number of days' sales in accounts receivable   The number of days in a year (365) divided by the accounts receivable turnover. Also called the **average collection period for accounts receivable.** *1074*

Operating assets   All assets actively used in producing operating revenues. *1079*

Operating margin   Net operating income divided by net sales. *1079*

Payout ratio on common stock   The ratio of dividends per share of common stock divided by EPS. *1087*

Price-earnings ratio   The ratio of current market price per share of common stock divided by the EPS of the stock. *1087*

Quick ratio   Same as acid-test ratio.

Rate of return on operating assets   (Net operating income ÷ Net sales) × (Net sales ÷ Operating assets). Result is equal to net operating income divided by operating assets. *1079*

Return on equity (ROE)   Net income divided by average common stockholders' equity. *1081*

Stockholders' equity to debt ratio   Stockholders' equity divided by total debt; often used in inverted form and called the **debt to equity ratio.** *1078*

Times interest earned ratio   A ratio computed by dividing income before interest and taxes by interest expense (also called **interest coverage ratio**). *1085*

Times preferred dividends earned ratio   Net income divided by annual preferred dividends. *1086*

Total assets turnover   Net sales divided by average total assets. *1076*

Trend percentages   Similar to horizontal analysis except that a base year or period is selected, and comparisons are made to the base year or period. *1063*

Turnover   The relationship between the amount of an asset and some measure of its use. See Accounts receivable turnover, Inventory turnover, and Total assets turnover. *1074*

Turnover of operating assets   Net sales divided by operating assets. *1079*

Vertical analysis   The study of a single financial statement in which each item is expressed as a percentage of a significant total; for example, percentages of sales calculations. *1065*

Working capital ratio   Same as current ratio.

Yield (on stock)   The yield on a stock investment refers to either an earnings yield or a dividend yield. Also see Earnings yield on common stock and Dividend yield on common stock and preferred stock. *1086*

SELF-TEST

True-False

Indicate whether each of the following statements is true or false.

1. An objective of financial statement analysis is to provide information about the company's past performance and current financial position.

2. Vertical analysis helps detect changes in a company's performance over several periods and highlights trends.

3. Common-size statements provide information about changes in dollar amounts relative to the previous periods.

4. Liquidity ratios show a company's capacity to pay maturing current liabilities.

5. A company that is quite profitable may find it difficult to pay its accounts payable.

6. Financial statement analysts must be sure that comparable data are used among companies to make the comparisons valid.

Multiple-Choice

Select the best answer for each of the following questions.

The following data were abstracted from the December 31, 1995, balance sheet of Max Company:

Cash	$136,000
Marketable securities	64,000
Accounts and notes receivable, net	184,000
Merchandise inventory	244,000
Prepaid expenses	12,000
Accounts and notes payable, short term. .	256,000
Accrued liabilities	64,000
Bonds payable, long term	400,000

1. The current ratio is:
    a. 1 : 2.
    b. 2 : 1.
    c. 1.2 : 1.
    d. 3 : 1.

2. The acid-test ratio is:
    a. 1 : 2.
    b. 2 : 1.
    c. 1.2 : 1.
    d. 3 : 1.

Bowman Company shows the following data on its 1995 financial statements.

Accounts receivable, January 1	$ 720,000
Accounts receivable, December 31 . . .	960,000
Merchandise inventory, January 1	900,000
Merchandise inventory, December 31 . .	1,020,000
Gross sales	4,800,000
Sales returns and allowances	180,000
Net sales	4,620,000
Cost of goods sold	3,360,000
Income before interest and taxes	720,000
Interest on bonds	192,000
Net income	384,000

3. The accounts receivable turnover is:
    a. 5.5 times per year.
    b. 5.714 times per year.
    c. 5 times per year.
    d. 6.667 times per year.

4. The inventory turnover is:
    a. 5 times per year.
    b. 4.8125 times per year.
    c. 3.5 times per year.
    d. 4 times per year.

5. The times interest earned ratio is:
    a. 4.75 times per year.
    b. 3.75 times per year.
    c. 2 times per year.
    d. 3 times per year.

Now turn to page 1117 to check your answers.

QUESTIONS

1. What are the major sources of financial information for publicly owned corporations?

2. The higher the accounts receivable turnover rate, the better off the company is. Do you agree? Why?

3. Can you think of a situation where the current ratio is very misleading as an indicator of short-term debt-paying ability? Does the acid-test ratio offer a remedy to the situation you have described? Describe a situation where the acid-test ratio will not suffice either.

4. Before the Marvin Company issued $20,000 of long-term notes (due more than a year from the date of issue) in exchange for a like amount of accounts payable, its acid-test ratio was 2 : 1. Will this transaction increase, decrease, or have no effect on the current ratio? The equity ratio?

5. Through the use of turnover rates, explain why a firm might seek to increase the volume of its sales even though such an increase can be secured only at reduced prices.

6. Indicate which of the relationships illustrated in this chapter would be best to judge:

  a. Short-term debt-paying ability of the firm.

  b. The overall efficiency of the firm without regard to the sources of assets.

  c. The return to owners of a corporation.

  d. The safety of long-term creditors' interest.

  e. The safety of preferred stockholders' dividends.

7. Indicate how each of the following ratios or measures is calculated:

  a. Payout ratio.

  b. Earnings per share of common stock.

  c. Price-earnings ratio.

  d. Yield on common stock.

  e. Yield on preferred stock.

  f. Times interest earned.

  g. Times preferred dividends earned.

  h. Return on stockholders' equity.

  i. Cash-flow margin.

8. How is the rate of return on operating assets determined? Is it possible for two companies with ''operating margins'' of 5% and 1%, respectively, to both have a rate of return of 20% on operating assets? How?

9. Cite some of the possible deficiencies in accounting information, especially regarding its use in analyzing a particular company over a 10-year period.

The Coca-Cola Company

10. *Real-world question*   From the financial highlights of The Coca-Cola Company in Appendix C, determine the percentage change in operating income from 1990 to 1991.

The Coca-Cola Company

11. *Real-world question*   From the consolidated statements of income of The Coca-Cola Company in Appendix C, determine the 1991 net income per common share.

The Coca-Cola Company

12. *Real-world question*   From the financial highlights of The Coca-Cola Company in Appendix C, determine the 1991 cash dividends per common share.

The Coca-Cola Company

13. *Real-world question*   From the financial highlights of The Coca-Cola Company in Appendix C, determine the 1991 cash-flow margin.

EXERCISES

Prepare horizontal and vertical analysis and comment
(L.O. 3)

22–1. Income statement data for Jacob Company for 1995 and 1996 are:

	1996	1995
Net sales	$3,600,000	$2,852,000
Cost of goods sold	2,200,000	1,564,000
Operating expense	720,000	668,000
Administrative expense	500,000	460,000
Income taxes	68,000	60,000

Prepare a horizontal and vertical analysis of the above income data in a form similar to that in Illustration 22.2. Comment on the results of this analysis.

Compute current ratios
(L.O. 4)

22–2. Under each of the three conditions listed below, compute the current ratio after each of the transactions described. Current assets are now $800,000. (Consider each transaction independently of the others.) The current ratio before the transactions is:

a. 1 to 1

b. 2 to 1

c. 1 to 2

Transactions:

1. Purchased $600,000 of merchandise on account.
2. Purchased $400,000 of machinery for cash.
3. Issued stock for $400,000 cash.

Compute accounts receivable ratios and comment
(L.O. 4)

22–3. Sonya Company has sales of $2,920,000 per year. Its average accounts receivable balance is $584,000.

a. What is the average number of days an accounts receivable is outstanding?

b. Assuming released funds can be invested at 10%, how much could the company earn by reducing the collection period of the accounts receivable to 30 days?

c. What assumption must you make in order for this income calculation to be correct?

Compute
cash-flow margin
(L.O. 4)

22–4. Settle Corporation had the following selected financial data for 1995:

December 31, 1995	
Net sales	$900,000
Cost of goods sold	540,000
Operating expenses	157,500
Net income	97,500
Total assets	500,000
Cash flow from operating activities	12,500

Compute the cash-flow margin.

Calculate
inventory turnover
(L.O. 4)

22–5. From the following partial income statement calculate the inventory turn-over for the period.

Net sales		$2,800,000
Cost of goods sold:		
Beginning inventory	$ 236,000	
Purchases	1,884,000	
Cost of goods available for sale	$2,120,000	
Less: Ending inventory	260,000	
Cost of goods sold		1,860,000
Gross margin		$ 940,000
Operating expenses		500,000
Net operating income		$ 440,000

Calculate earnings
per share
(L.O. 4)

22–6. The Thomas Company had 190,000 shares of common stock outstanding on January 1, 1995. On August 31, 1995, it issued 30,000 additional shares for cash. The income available for common stockholders for 1995 was $1,000,000. What amount of earnings per share of common stock should the company report?

Compute times
interest earned
ratio
(L.O. 4)

22–7. Car Company paid interest of $20,000, incurred federal income taxes of $60,000 and had net income after taxes of $120,000. How many times was the interest earned?

Calculate times
preferred
dividends earned
ratio and earnings
yield on preferred
stock
(L.O. 4)

22–8. The Red Company had 10,000 shares of $200 par value, 4%, preferred stock outstanding. Net income after taxes was $560,000. The market price per share was $128.

a. How many times were the preferred dividends earned?

b. What was the yield on the preferred stock assuming the regular preferred dividends were declared and paid?

Compute
price-earnings
ratio
(L.O. 4)

22–9. A company had 20,000 shares of $40 par value common stock outstanding. Net income was $140,000. Current market price per share is $168. Compute the price-earnings ratio.

Calculate rate of
return on
operating assets
(L.O. 4)

22–10. Bob, Inc., had net sales of $3,020,000, gross margin of $1,610,000, and operating expenses of $990,000. Total assets (all operating) were $2,480,000. Compute Bob's rate of return on operating assets.

Compute
weighted-average
number of
common shares
outstanding
(L.O. 4)

22–11. Drake Company started 1995 with 125,000 shares of common stock outstanding. On March 31, it issued 15,000 shares for cash; and on September 1, it purchased 6,000 treasury shares for cash. Compute the weighted-average number of common shares outstanding for the year.

Determine rate of
return on average
stockholders'
equity
(L.O. 4)

22–12. Britt Company started 1995 with total stockholders' equity of $2,242,000. Its net income for 1995 was $632,000, and $60,000 of dividends were declared. Compute the rate of return on average stockholders' equity for 1995.

Calculate earnings
per share and
adjusted earnings
per share
(L.O. 4)

22–13. Walter Company reported EPS of $6 ($600,000/100,000 shares) for 1995, ending the year with 100,000 shares outstanding. In 1996, the company earned net income of $903,000, issued 30,000 shares of common stock for cash on September 30, and distributed a 100% stock dividend on December 31, 1995. Compute EPS for 1996 and compute the adjusted EPS for 1995 that could be shown in the 1996 annual report.

PROBLEMS

Perform horizontal
and vertical
analysis
(L.O. 4)

22–1. Presented below are River Company's comparative balance sheets at the end of 1995 and 1996. The comparative statements of income and retained earnings for the years ended December 31, 1995, and 1996 are also given.

RIVER COMPANY Comparative Balance Sheets December 31, 1995 and 1996		
	1996	*1995*
Assets		
Current assets:		
Cash	$ 60,200	$ 32,704
Accounts receivable net	169,764	167,024
Inventory	423,808	441,504
Total current assets	$ 653,772	$ 641,232
Plant assets, net	550,228	526,768
Total assets	$1,204,000	$1,168,000

Liabilities and Stockholders' Equity	*1996*	*1995*
Current liabilities:		
Accounts payable and accruals	$ 167,356	$ 358,576
Notes payable	116,788	294,336
Total current liabilities	$ 284,144	$ 652,912
Long-term liabilities:		
Bonds payable	351,568	—0—
Total liabilities	$ 635,712	$ 652,912
Stockholders' equity:		
Common stock	$ 386,288	$ 369,088
Retained earnings	182,000	146,000
Total stockholders' equity	$ 568,288	$ 515,088
Total liabilities and stockholders' equity	$1,204,000	$1,168,000

RIVER COMPANY
Comparative Statement of Income and Retained Earnings
For the Years Ended December 31, 1995 and 1996

	1996	*1995*
Net sales	$1,664,800	$1,581,560
Cost of goods sold	1,065,472	1,028,014
Gross margin	$ 599,328	$ 553,546
Operating expenses:		
Selling	$ 241,396	$ 257,794
Administrative	224,748	205,602
Total operating expenses	$ 466,144	$ 463,396
Net operating income	$ 133,184	$ 90,150
Interest expense	41,620	20,560
Income before income taxes	$ 91,564	$ 69,590
Income taxes	41,620	28,468
Net income	$ 49,944	$ 41,122
Retained earnings, January 1	146,000	123,658
	$ 195,944	$ 164,780
Dividends	13,944	18,780
Retained earnings, December 31	$ 182,000	$ 146,000

Required:

Perform horizontal and vertical analysis of the above financial statements in a manner similar to that shown in Illustrations 22.1 and 22.2.

Prepare a
statement showing
trend percentages
and comment
(L.O. 3)

22–2.

	1995	*1996*	*1997*	*1998*
Sales	$1,400,000	$1,596,000	$1,680,000	$2,646,000
Cost of goods sold	1,000,000	1,080,000	1,300,000	2,150,000
Gross margin	$ 400,000	$ 516,000	$ 380,000	$ 496,000
Operating expenses	320,000	336,000	352,000	448,000
Net operating income . . .	$ 80,000	$ 180,000	$ 28,000	$ 48,000

Required:

a. Prepare a statement showing the trend percentages for each of the above items, using 1995 as the base year.

b. Comment on the trends noted.

Compute various
liquidity ratios
(L.O. 4)

22–3. From the following data for the Webster Company compute the (*a*) working capital; (*b*) current ratio; and (*c*) acid-test ratio, all as of both dates; (*d*) cash-flow liquidity ratio; and (*e*) comment briefly on the company's short-term financial position.

	December 31 1996	December 31 1995
Notes payable (due in 90 days)	$ 384,600	$ 330,000
Merchandise inventory.	1,560,550	1,416,400
Cash	574,800	649,000
Marketable securities	288,000	170,000
Accrued liabilities	110,000	113,200
Accounts receivable	956,050	914,720
Accounts payable	534,400	342,000
Allowance for uncollectible accounts	121,000	84,800
Bonds payable, due 2006	760,000	804,000
Prepaid expenses	34,400	36,220
Cash flows from operating activities	15,200	24,100

Determine the
effects of
transactions on
working capital
and current ratio
(L.O. 4)

22–4. On December 31, 1995, the Tyson Company's current ratio was 3 to 1. Assume that the following transactions were completed on that date and indicate (*a*) whether the amount of working capital would have been increased, decreased, or unaffected by each of the transactions; and (*b*) whether the current ratio would have been increased, decreased, or unaffected by each of the transactions. (Consider each transaction independently of all the others.)

Transactions:

1. Purchased merchandise on account.
2. Paid a cash dividend declared on November 15, 1996.
3. Sold equipment for cash.
4. Temporarily invested cash in marketable securities.
5. Sold obsolete merchandise for cash (at a loss).
6. Issued 10-year bonds for cash.
7. Amortized goodwill.
8. Paid cash for inventory.

Prepare
comparative
income statements
and balance
sheets, schedule
of each current
asset to total
current assets,
and compute
standard ratios
(L.O. 3, 4)

22–5. The following are comparative balance sheets of the Dyer Corporation on December 31, 1995, and 1996.

DYER CORPORATION
Comparative Balance Sheets
December 31, 1995 and 1996

	December 31, 1996	December 31, 1995
Assets		
Cash	$ 900,000	$1,020,000
Accounts receivable, net	780,000	900,000
Merchandise inventory	540,000	660,000
Plant assets, net	1,200,000	540,000
Total assets	$3,420,000	$3,120,000
Liabilities and Stockholders' Equity		
Accounts payable	$ 420,000	$ 300,000
Notes payable	360,000	516,000
Common stock.	1,320,000	1,320,000
Retained earnings	1,320,000	984,000
Total liabilities and stockholders' equity	$3,420,000	$3,120,000
Other Data		
Sales	$5,520,000	$4,800,000
Gross margin	2,280,000	2,040,000
Selling and administrative expenses.	1,440,000	1,320,000
Interest expense	48,000	24,000
Cash dividends.	456,000	180,000

During 1996, a note in the amount of $240,000 was given for equipment purchased at that price. Unlike the company's other notes, which are short-term, the $240,000 note matures in 2006.

Required:

a. Prepare comparative income statements that show percentage of net sales for each item.
b. Prepare comparative balance sheets that show percentage of total assets for each item.
c. Prepare a schedule that shows the percentage of each current asset to the total of current assets as of both year-end dates.
d. Compute the current ratios as of both dates.
e. Compute the acid-test ratios as of both dates.
f. Compute the percentage of stockholders' equity to total equity (or total assets) as of both dates.

Calculate various
standard ratios
(L.O. 4)

22–6. The following balance sheet and supplementary data are for the Stan Corporation for 1996.

STAN CORPORATION
Balance Sheet
December 31, 1996

Assets

Current assets:

Cash.	$ 1,200,000	
Marketable securities	640,000	
Accounts receivable, net	1,040,000	
Inventory	880,000	$ 3,760,000

Property, plant, and equipment:

Plant assets	13,600,000	
Less: Accumulated depreciation	1,000,000	12,600,000
Total assets		$16,360,000

Liabilities and Stockholders' Equity

Current liabilities:

Accounts payable	$ 680,000	
Bank loans payable	280,000	960,000

Long-term liabilities:

Mortgage notes payable, due in 2006	$ 360,000	
Bonds payable 6%, due December 31, 2006 . . .	1,720,000	2,080,000
Total liabilities		$ 3,040,000

Stockholders' equity

Common stock par value $50 per share	$ 8,800,000	
Appropriation for bond sinking fund	320,000	
Retained earnings	4,200,000	13,320,000
Total liabilities and stockholders' equity		$16,360,000

Supplementary data:

1. 1996 net income amounted to $1,200,000.
2. 1996 income before interest and taxes, $2,400,000.
3. 1996 cost of goods sold was $3,200,000.
4. 1996 net sales amounted to $6,000,000.
5. Inventory on December 31, 1995, was $600,000.
6. Interest expense for the year was $120,000 (some long-term liabilities were paid during the year).

Required:

Calculate the following ratios. Where you would normally use the average amount for an item in a ratio but the information is not available to do so, use the year-end balance. Show computations.

a. Current ratio.
b. Percentage of net income to stockholders' equity.
c. Turnover of inventory.
d. Average collection period of accounts receivable (there are 365 days in 1995).
e. Earnings per share of common stock.
f. Number of times interest was earned.

g. Stockholders' equity ratio.

h. Percentage of net income to total assets.

i. Turnover of total assets.

j. Acid-test ratio.

Calculate standard ratios and determine absolute changes (L.O. 4)

22–7. The following information is available about three companies:

	Operating Assets	Net Operating Income	Net Sales
Company 1	$ 900,000	$ 120,000	$ 1,320,000
Company 2	5,400,000	390,000	12,000,000
Company 3	24,000,000	3,150,000	22,500,000

Required:

a. Determine the operating margin, turnover of operating assets, and rate of return on operating assets for each company.

b. In the subsequent year the following changes took place (no other changes occurred):

Company 1 bought some new machinery at a cost of $150,000. Net operating income increased by $12,000 as a result of an increase in sales of $240,000.

Company 2 sold some equipment it was using that was relatively unproductive. The book value of the equipment sold was $600,000. As a result of the sale of the equipment, sales declined by $300,000 and operating income declined by $6,000.

Company 3 purchased some new retail outlets at a cost of $6,000,000. As a result, sales increased by $9,000,000 and operating income increased by $480,000.

Which company has the largest change in:

i.   Operating margin?

ii.   Turnover of operating assets?

iii. Rate of return on operating assets?

Compute various profitability ratios and comment (L.O. 4)

22–8. The following information is available for the Charlie Company:

	1996	1995
Net sales	$3,360,000	$2,080,000
Income before interest and taxes	880,000	680,000
Net income.	444,000	504,000
Interest expense	72,000	64,000
Stockholders' equity, December 31		
(on December 31, 1994, $1,600,000)	2,440,000	1,880,000
Common stock, par value $100, December 31	2,080,000	1,840,000

Additional shares of common stock were issued on January 1, 1996.

Required:

Compute the following for both 1995 and 1996:

a. Earnings per share of common stock.

b. Percentage of net income to net sales.

c. Rate of return on average stockholders' equity.

d. Number of times interest was earned.

Compare and comment.

Determine effects on ratios of change in accounting method (FIFO and LIFO) (L.O. 4)

22–9. The Fanning Company is considering switching from the FIFO method to the LIFO method of accounting for its inventory before its year-end financial statements are prepared. The January 1 inventory was $700,000. The following data are compiled from the adjusted trial balance at the end of the year.

Inventory, December 31 (FIFO)	$1,100,000
Current assets	1,700,000
Current liabilities.	850,000
Total assets (operating).	2,800,000
Net sales	6,000,000
Cost of goods sold	4,428,000
Operating expenses	872,000

If the change to LIFO takes place, the December 31 inventory would be $940,000.

Required:

a. Compute the current ratio, inventory turnover ratio, and the rate of return on operating assets using FIFO.

b. Repeat part (a) assuming the company adjusts its accounts to the LIFO inventory method.

BUSINESS DECISION PROBLEMS

Compute net income, identify reason for cash increase, state main sources of financing, and indicate further analyses needed (L.O. 3, 4)

22–1. Shown below are the comparative balance sheets of the Forrest Corporation for December 31, 1995, and 1994.

FORREST CORPORATION **Comparative Balance Sheets** **December 31, 1995 and 1994**		
	1995	*1994*
Assets		
Cash	$240,000	$ 48,000
Accounts receivable, net	43,200	57,600
Merchandise inventory	192,000	201,600
Plant and equipment, net	134,400	144,000
Total assets	$609,600	$451,200
Liabilities and Stockholders' Equity		
Accounts payable	$ 48,000	$ 48,000
Common stock.	336,000	336,000
Retained earnings	225,600	67,200
Total liabilities and stockholders' equity	$609,600	$451,200

Required:

a. What was the net income for 1995 assuming there were no dividend payments?

b. What was the primary source of the large increase in the cash balance from 1994 to 1995?

c. What are the two main sources of assets for Forrest Corporation?

d. What other comparisons and procedures would you use to complete the analysis of the balance sheet begun above?

Compute turnover ratios for four years and number of days' sales in accounts receivable; evaluate effectiveness of company's credit policy (L.O. 4)

22–2. The information below was obtained from the annual reports of Glaston Manufacturing Company.

	1992	1993	1994	1995
Net accounts receivable	$ 540,000	$1,080,000	$1,350,000	$1,800,000
Net sales	5,400,000	6,975,000	8,550,000	9,900,000

Required:

a. If cash sales account for 30% of all sales and credit terms are always 1/10, n/60, determine all turnover ratios possible and the number of days' sales in accounts receivable at all possible dates. (The number of days' sales in accounts receivable should be based on year-end accounts receivable and net credit sales.)

b. How effective is the company's credit policy?

Analyze investment alternatives (L.O. 3, 4)

22–3. Melinda Frame is interested in investing in one of three companies (A, B, or C) by buying its common stock. The companies' shares are selling at about the same price. The long-term capital structures of the companies are as follows:

	Company A	Company B	Company C
Bonds with a 10% interest rate			$1,200,000
Preferred stock with an 8% dividend rate . .		$1,200,000	
Common stock, $20 par value	$2,400,000	1,200,000	1,200,000
Retained earnings	192,000	192,000	192,000
Total long-term equity	$2,592,000	$2,592,000	$2,592,000
Number of common shares outstanding. . .	120,000	60,000	60,000

Ms. Frame has consulted two investment advisers. One adviser believes that each of the companies will earn $150,000 per year before interest and taxes. The other adviser believes that each company will earn about $480,000 per year before interest and taxes.

Required:

a. Compute each of the following, using the estimate made by the first adviser and then the one made by the second adviser.

1. Earnings available for common stockholders assuming a 40% tax rate.

2. EPS of common stock.

3. Rate of return on total stockholders' equity.

b. Which stock should Ms. Frame select if she believes the first adviser?

c. Are the stockholders as a group (common and preferred) better off with or without the use of long-term debt in the above companies?

Analyze
management's
objectives and
performance from
the viewpoints of
a creditor and an
investor
(real-world
problem)
(L.O. 3, 4)

22–4. The following selected financial data excerpted from the 1990 annual report of Maytag Corporation represents the summary information which management presented for interested parties to review:

MAYTAG CORPORATION
Selected Financial Data
(Thousands of Dollars Except Per Share Data)

	1990	1989*	1988	1987	1986
Net sales	$3,056,833	$3,088,753	$1,885,641	$1,822,106	$1,632,924
Cost of sales	2,309,138	2,312,645	1,413,627	1,318,122	1,183,377
Income taxes	60,500	75,500	79,700	105,300	97,500
Income from continuing operations	98,905	131,472	135,522	147,678	114,739
Percent of income from continuing operations to net sales.	3.2%	4.3%	7.2%	8.1%	7.0%
Income from continuing operations per share .	$ 0.94	$ 1.27	$ 1.77	$ 1.84	$ 1.32
Dividends paid per share.		0.950	0.950	0.950	0.850
Average shares outstanding (in thousands)	105,726	103,694	76,563	80,151	86,619
Working capital.	612,802	$ 650,905	$ 317,145	$ 286,124	$ 330,116
Depreciation of property, plant, and equipment .	69,279	68,077	34,454	35,277	32,659
Additions to property, plant, and equipment .		127,838	101,756	42,564	45,619
Total assets.	2,586,541	2,436,319	1,330,069	854,925	882,576
Long-term debt	857,941	876,836	518,165	140,765	46,189
Total debt to capitalization		50.6%	51.5%	28.1%	11.0%
Shareowners' equity per share.		$ 8.89	$ 6.55	$ 5.43	$ 6.53

* These amounts reflect the acquisition of Hoover on January 26, 1989.

Required:

a. As a creditor, what do you believe management's objectives should be? What information above would assist a creditor in judging management's performance?

b. As an investor, what do you believe management's objectives should be? What information above would assist an investor in judging management's performance?

c. What other information might be considered useful?

ANSWERS TO SELF-TEST

True-False

1. *True*. Financial statement analysis consists of applying analytical tools and techniques to financial statements and other relevant data to obtain useful information.
2. *False*. Horizontal analysis provides useful information about the changes in a company's performance over several periods by analyzing comparative financial statements of the same company for two or more successive periods.
3. *False*. Common-size statements show only percentage figures, such as percentages of total assets and percentages of net sales.
4. *True*. Liquidity ratios such as the current ratio and acid-test ratio indicate a company's short-term debt-paying ability.
5. *True*. The accrual net income shown on the income statement is not cash basis income and does not indicate cash flows.
6. *True*. Analysts must use comparable data when making comparisons of items for different periods or different companies.

Multiple-Choice

1. *b.* Current assets:

   $136,000 + $64,000 + $184,000
          + $244,000 + $12,000 = $640,000

   Current liabilities:

   $256,000 + $64,000 = $320,000

   Current ratio:

   $640,000/$320,000 = 2 : 1

2. *c.* Quick assets:

   $136,000 + $64,000 + $184,000 = $384,000

   Current liabilities:

   $256,000 + $64,000 = $320,000

   Acid-test ratio:

   $384,000/$320,000 = 1.2 : 1

3. *a.* Net sales:

   $4,620,000

   Average accounts receivable:

   ($720,000 + $960,000)/2 = $840,000

   Accounts receivable turnover:

   $4,620,000/$840,000 = 5.5

4. *c.* Cost of goods sold:

   $3,360,000

   Average inventory:

   ($900,000 + $1,020,000)/2 = $960,000

   Inventory turnover:

   $3,360,000/$960,000 = 3.5

5. *b.*

Income before interest and taxes	$720,000
Interest on bonds	192,000

   Times interest earned ratio:

   $720,000/$192,000 = 3.75 times

APPENDIXES

PAYROLL ACCOUNTING AND FEDERAL INCOME TAXES

INTRODUCTION

Most of you have had either a part-time or full-time job and have been paid weekly, semimonthly, or monthly. You probably were disappointed when you received your first paycheck because the deductions were greater than you expected. Payroll accounting includes the record-keeping necessary to account for employees' paychecks and deductions. Since a company's payroll costs are one of the largest expenses a company incurs, payroll accounting is an important function.

This appendix discusses the objectives of payroll accounting and the methods used to achieve these objectives. Computations of gross and net earnings and the major documents and forms used in payroll accounting are explained. Even though many businesses today use computerized payroll systems, the objectives and methods used to compute amounts and deductions are the same as for manual systems. The rates and bases used are those in effect for 1992.[1]

The appendix also describes various federal income tax provisions that affect business corporations. This discussion includes differences between net income before taxes and taxable income, tax rates, and accounting methods used for tax purposes.

Finally, this appendix provides a brief introduction to personal income tax provisions. These provisions affect all of us each year.

PAYROLL ACCOUNTING

In most business organizations, accounting for payroll is particularly important because (1) payrolls often represent the largest expense that a company incurs, (2) both federal and state governments require that detailed payroll records be maintained, and (3) companies must file regular payroll reports with both state and federal governments and make remittances of amounts withheld or otherwise due. Thus, the general objectives of payroll account-

---

[1] All estimated 1992 tax rates, exemptions, deductions, concepts, and procedures are correct as of this writing. However, all are subject to change due to the actions of Congress in 1992.

1122   Appendixes

ing are to process such data as hours worked, pay rates, and payroll deductions so that the company can:

1. Establish internal control over payroll and protect against fraud in payroll transactions.
2. Prepare and record a payroll, including gross earnings, payroll taxes and deductions, employee earnings record, and the payroll journal.
3. Pay the payroll using the payroll checking account. Also provide accurate and timely paychecks, as well as an explanation of payroll data.
4. Record employer payroll taxes, including FICA (social security) taxes, federal unemployment taxes, and state unemployment taxes.
5. Remit taxes withheld, unemployment taxes, and other deductions to the proper government agency or other organization.
6. Prepare adjusting entries for end-of-period accruals, including wages, payroll taxes, and vacation pay.

This section discusses the objectives of payroll accounting and the methods of achieving these objectives. You should be aware that even though many businesses today use more efficient computerized payroll systems, the objectives and methods used to compute amounts and deductions are the same as for manual systems.

ESTABLISHING INTERNAL CONTROL OVER PAYROLL

In small companies, the owner-manager may provide adequate internal control over payroll transactions by actually computing and preparing the payroll. Larger companies obtain internal control through application of the general principles of internal control and the more specific guides to controls over cash disbursements, as described in Chapter 6. Separation of duties is a crucial aspect of internal control over payroll transactions. Ideally, timekeeping, payroll preparation, payroll record-keeping, and payroll distribution functions should be performed by different employees.

If an employee's compensation is based on hours worked, the company must maintain an accurate record of each employee's time. In small companies, the owner may simply make notations in a notebook stating when employees report to work and leave work. Larger companies often use a time clock for hourly employees. Each day when employees report to work, every employee inserts a **timecard** into the clock, which prints the date and time on the card. Employees follow the same procedure when leaving work. Companies must safeguard against one employee punching in or out for another employee; for example, the company could station someone at the time clock to supervise the check-in and check-out procedures.

In small companies, the owner usually knows the hours each employee works. The owner, or a bookkeeper, may keep the company payroll records and compute the employees' earnings and deductions, as well as prepare, sign, and distribute the paychecks. Most large companies use the following procedure to prepare paychecks. At a regular interval before payday, the payroll department collects and verifies each employee's pay rate and hours worked to compute total (gross) pay. At this point, all legally required and authorized deductions are subtracted from the total (gross) pay, individual payroll records are updated, and payroll checks are prepared. Checks are then sent to the treasurer's office for signature. Supporting documents, such as employees' earnings statements showing earnings and deductions to date, may accompany the checks. Each check should be delivered to the employee in person or deposited directly by the employer into the employee's bank account.

Payroll Fraud

Whenever cash is disbursed, the potential for fraud exists. Some payroll fraud schemes used successfully in the past are listed below.

1. A payroll department employee pays another employee more than that employee has actually earned, and then the payroll department employee receives a kickback of part of the overpayment.
2. A payroll department employee makes out a payroll check payable to a former or fictitious employee and then cashes the check.
3. A payroll department employee prepares and cashes duplicate payroll checks.

Because of these and other schemes, companies must exercise great care to ensure payroll accuracy. Separation of duties is one way to help ensure accuracy. Fraudulent transactions are difficult to arrange and cover up when one employee's work serves as a check on another's. For example, if a payroll department employee falsifies the hours worked by a plant employee in an attempt to overpay the employee, the changed hours on the payroll record will not agree with the timecard record. Collusion by two payroll department employees would be required to commit such a fraud unless the same employee has access to timecards, other payroll records, and payroll checks.

Maintenance of accurate employment and payroll records is also crucial. As soon as possible, payroll department personnel must be informed of the hiring and termination of employees so that they know which employees currently work for the company. This information helps prevent the writing of fictitious checks. Also, current copies of documents authorizing payroll deductions should be on hand. Payroll fraud can be reduced by keeping accurate, detailed records for each employee. Companies must be alert to the possibility of payroll fraud and take steps to prevent it.

PREPARING AND RECORDING A PAYROLL

To prepare and record a payroll, you must begin by determining an employee's gross earnings. Since gross earnings are generally not the amount the employee receives, the next step is to compute the employee's payroll taxes and other payroll deductions. Using examples, the paragraphs that follow explain this phase of payroll accounting.

Computing Gross Earnings

Although the terms *wages* and *salaries* are often used interchangeably, they are not the same. The term *wages* generally refers to gross earnings of employees who are paid by the hour for only the actual hours worked. The term *salaries,* on the other hand, usually refers to gross earnings of employees who are paid a flat amount per week or month regardless of the number of hours worked in a period.

An employee's **gross earnings** are the employee's total pay or compensation, including regular pay and overtime premium. The computation of gross earnings for wage employees and salaried employees differs. Computing gross earnings for wage employees usually consists of simply multiplying the number of hours the employee worked by the employee's hourly wage rate. For example, 40 hours times $10 per hour gives gross earnings of $400 for the week. Since the gross earnings for salaried employees are usually a specified yearly amount, the annual salary is divided by the number of pay periods in the year. For example, assuming an employee is paid monthly and earns $36,000 a year, you would divide $36,000 by 12 months to determine the monthly gross earnings of $3,000. In some instances, however, the calculation of gross earnings is a little more detailed due to legal or contractual requirements.

The federal **Wages and Hours Law** (also called the **Fair Labor Standards Act**) requires that (1) most employees who are paid by the hour be paid a minimum of 1½ times their normal rate for hours worked in excess of 40 per week and (2) employees be paid at least the minimum wage. The **minimum wage** rate is set by the federal government and changes from time to time. In addition to this federal law, some union contracts also call for premium pay rates for certain hours worked, such as double time for work on Sunday. You should be aware that executive, administrative, and some professional employees are salaried and exempt from both the minimum wage and overtime pay provisions. However, lower-level nonprofessional, salaried employees are generally subject to the minimum wage and overtime pay provisions.

The payroll department must maintain detailed time records to ensure that legal and contractual requirements are being met. In the absence of valid records, assessments for overtime pay may later be made against the employer.

Three situations follow that illustrate how to compute gross earnings that include overtime premiums.

1. Mary Kennedy's basic wage rate is $9 per hour. Her overtime premium, then, is one half of $9, or $4.50 per hour. Mary's gross pay for a week in which she worked 48 hours is $468. The $468 is computed as (48 × $9) +

(8 × $4.50), or ($432 + $36) = $468. (An alternative calculation is [40 hours × $9] + [8 hours × $13.50] = $468.)

2. Grace Early's basic $18,200 annual salary is paid over 52 weeks at a guaranteed weekly minimum of $350 (40 × $8.75 per hour), even though she often only works 37.5 hours per week. She is entitled to overtime pay for hours worked in excess of 40 per week. Her gross earnings for working 42 hours in a week are computed as $350 + (2 × 1.5 × $8.75) = $376.25.

3. Dan Brown is paid $0.50 for each unit of product machined. In the current week, he worked 48 hours and completed 960 units. His gross pay before overtime premium is $480 (960 × $0.50). The $480 is divided by 48 hours to get $10 as his regular hourly rate for the week. Therefore, Dan's overtime premium is $5 per hour, and his total overtime pay is $40 (8 × $5). His gross earnings for the week are $480 + $40, or $520.

Computing Payroll Taxes and Deductions

Required **deductions from gross earnings** include withholdings for federal income taxes, state income taxes, and FICA (social security) taxes. Employees may choose to have various other deductions taken from their checks.

Federal and State Income Taxes. Wage earners in the United States are under a pay-as-you-go federal income tax system. This concept means that most employees must pay federal income taxes on wages as they are earned during the year. Employers withhold *federal income tax* when the employee's earnings are paid, and the amount of **federal income tax withheld** is noted on the employee's check stub. These federal taxes are remitted (sent) periodically by the employer to federally specified banks or to the Internal Revenue Service (IRS). Companies located in states with state income taxes also must withhold *state income tax* from employees' paychecks and remit these amounts to the revenue authority in those states. Amounts paid to independent contractors, such as outside consultants, are not subject to withholding for federal income tax and FICA tax.

The amount of income tax withheld from each employee's pay depends on the (1) amount of earnings, (2) frequency of the payroll period, and (3) the number of **withholding allowances** claimed by the employee. Withholding allowances are claimed by the employee on an **Employee's Withholding Allowance Certificate (Form W-4)** filed with the employer, usually the first day on the job. Illustration A.1 shows the W-4 form of John Hanson, who claims three withholding allowances, which usually means that he will claim three exemptions on his federal income tax return—one for himself, one for his wife, and one for his child. An exemption is a fixed amount of income ($2,150 in 1991 and an estimated $2,300 in 1992) that is not subject to taxation.

Illustration A.1
EMPLOYEE'S WITHHOLDING ALLOWANCE CERTIFICATE (FORM W-4)

Form **W-4**	**Employee's Withholding Allowance Certificate**	OMB No. 1545-0010
Department of the Treasury Internal Revenue Service	▶ **For Privacy Act and Paperwork Reduction Act Notice, see reverse.**	19**92**

1 Type or print your first name and middle initial	Last name	2 Your social security number
John R.	Hanson	253-13-2807

Home address (number and street or rural route)
325 St. George Drive

3 ☐ Single ☒ Married ☐ Married, but withhold at higher Single rate.
Note: *If married, but legally separated, or spouse is a nonresident alien, check the Single box.*

City or town, state, and ZIP code
Athens, GA 30605

4 If your last name differs from that on your social security card, check here and call 1-800-772-1213 for more information   ▶ ☐

5 Total number of allowances you are claiming (from line G above or from the Worksheets on back if they apply)   **5** | 3

6 Additional amount, if any, you want deducted from each paycheck . . . .   **6** | $

7 I claim exemption from withholding and I certify that I meet **ALL** of the following conditions for exemption:
  • Last year I had a right to a refund of **ALL** Federal income tax withheld because I had **NO** tax liability; **AND**
  • This year I expect a refund of **ALL** Federal income tax withheld because I expect to have **No** tax liability; **AND**
  • This year if my income exceeds $600 and includes nonwage income, another person cannot claim me as a dependent.

If you meet all of the above conditions, enter the year effective and "EXEMPT" here . . . ▶   **7** | 19

8 Are you a full-time student? (**Note:** *Full-time students are not automatically exempt.*) . . . .   **8** ☐ Yes ☒ No

Under penalties of perjury, I certify that I am entitled to the number of withholding allowances claimed on this certificate or entitled to claim exempt status.

Employee's signature   Date ▶   19

9 Employer's name and address (Employer: Complete 9 and 11 only if sending to the IRS)	10 Office code (optional)	11 Employer identification number
Doug's Ace Hardware 1290 Atlanta Highway, Athens, GA 30605		15-249363

A **wage bracket withholding table** (Illustration A.2) is a table provided by the Internal Revenue Service to help employers determine the amount of federal income tax to withhold from employees' paychecks. This particular table is to be used for married persons who are paid weekly. When the federal income tax laws are revised, the table amounts change. Such tables are provided for both married and single persons for various pay periods, such as weekly, biweekly, and monthly. The amount of income taxes withheld changes with the number of withholding allowances claimed.

On or before January 31, after the end of each calendar year, an employer is required to prepare for each employee a four-copy (or more) **Wage and Tax Statement (Form W-2)** for the previous calendar-year earnings. An example of a W-2 that was used in a recent year is shown in Illustration A.3. This form provides wage and tax data needed to prepare the employee's personal federal and state income tax returns. One copy is sent by the employer to the Social Security Administration, which then transmits data contained on the form to the Internal Revenue Service. The other three copies of the W-2 are given to the employee. Of these three, one copy is filed with the employee's federal income tax return, one is filed with the state income tax return (if the employee lives in a state that has a state income tax), and one is retained by the employee as a personal record. The IRS uses data from the form to determine whether the employee has reported the proper amount of earned income and taxes withheld on the tax return.

Illustration A.2
FEDERAL WAGE BRACKET WITHHOLDING TABLE

MARRIED Persons—WEEKLY Payroll Period
(For Wages Paid After February 1992)

And the wages are—		And the number of withholding allowances claimed is—										
At least	But less than	0	1	2	3	4	5	6	7	8	9	10
		The amount of income tax to be withheld shall be—										
$0	$120	$0	$0	$0	$0	$0	$0	$0	$0	$0	$0	$0
120	125	1	0	0	0	0	0	0	0	0	0	0
125	130	2	0	0	0	0	0	0	0	0	0	0
130	135	3	0	0	0	0	0	0	0	0	0	0
135	140	3	0	0	0	0	0	0	0	0	0	0
140	145	4	0	0	0	0	0	0	0	0	0	0
145	150	5	0	0	0	0	0	0	0	0	0	0
150	155	6	0	0	0	0	0	0	0	0	0	0
155	160	6	0	0	0	0	0	0	0	0	0	0
160	165	7	0	0	0	0	0	0	0	0	0	0
165	170	8	1	0	0	0	0	0	0	0	0	0
170	175	9	2	0	0	0	0	0	0	0	0	0
175	180	9	3	0	0	0	0	0	0	0	0	0
180	185	10	3	0	0	0	0	0	0	0	0	0
185	190	11	4	0	0	0	0	0	0	0	0	0
190	195	12	5	0	0	0	0	0	0	0	0	0
195	200	12	6	0	0	0	0	0	0	0	0	0
200	210	13	7	0	0	0	0	0	0	0	0	0
210	220	15	8	2	0	0	0	0	0	0	0	0
220	230	16	10	3	0	0	0	0	0	0	0	0
230	240	18	11	5	0	0	0	0	0	0	0	0
240	250	19	13	6	0	0	0	0	0	0	0	0
250	260	21	14	8	1	0	0	0	0	0	0	0
260	270	22	16	9	3	0	0	0	0	0	0	0
270	280	24	17	11	4	0	0	0	0	0	0	0
280	290	25	19	12	6	0	0	0	0	0	0	0
290	300	27	20	14	7	0	0	0	0	0	0	0
300	310	28	22	15	9	2	0	0	0	0	0	0
310	320	30	23	17	10	3	0	0	0	0	0	0
320	330	31	25	18	12	5	0	0	0	0	0	0
330	340	33	26	20	13	6	0	0	0	0	0	0
340	350	34	28	21	15	8	1	0	0	0	0	0
350	360	36	29	23	16	9	3	0	0	0	0	0
360	370	37	31	24	18	11	4	0	0	0	0	0
370	380	39	32	26	19	12	6	0	0	0	0	0
380	390	40	34	27	21	14	7	1	0	0	0	0
390	400	42	35	29	22	15	9	2	0	0	0	0
400	410	43	37	30	24	17	10	4	0	0	0	0
410	420	45	38	32	25	18	12	5	0	0	0	0
420	430	46	40	33	27	20	13	7	0	0	0	0
430	440	48	41	35	28	21	15	8	2	0	0	0
440	450	49	43	36	30	23	16	10	3	0	0	0
450	460	51	44	38	31	24	18	11	5	0	0	0
460	470	52	46	39	33	26	19	13	6	0	0	0
470	480	54	47	41	34	27	21	14	8	1	0	0
480	490	55	49	42	36	29	22	16	9	2	0	0
490	500	57	50	44	37	30	24	17	11	4	0	0
500	510	58	52	45	39	32	25	19	12	5	0	0
510	520	60	53	47	40	33	27	20	14	7	0	0
520	530	61	55	48	42	35	28	22	15	8	2	0
530	540	63	56	50	43	36	30	23	17	10	3	0
540	550	64	58	51	45	38	31	25	18	11	5	0
550	560	66	59	53	46	39	33	26	20	13	6	0
560	570	67	61	54	48	41	34	28	21	14	8	1
570	580	69	62	56	49	42	36	29	23	16	9	3
580	590	70	64	57	51	44	37	31	24	17	11	4
590	600	72	65	59	52	45	39	32	26	19	12	6
600	610	73	67	60	54	47	40	34	27	20	14	7
610	620	75	68	62	55	48	42	35	29	22	15	9
620	630	76	70	63	57	50	43	37	30	23	17	10
630	640	78	71	65	58	51	45	38	32	25	18	12
640	650	79	73	66	60	53	46	40	33	26	20	13
650	660	81	74	68	61	54	48	41	35	28	21	15
660	670	82	76	69	63	56	49	43	36	29	23	16
670	680	84	77	71	64	57	51	44	38	31	24	18
680	690	85	79	72	66	59	52	46	39	32	26	19
690	700	87	80	74	67	60	54	47	41	34	27	21
700	710	88	82	75	69	62	55	49	42	35	29	22
710	720	90	83	77	70	63	57	50	44	37	30	24
720	730	91	85	78	72	65	58	52	45	38	32	25

Illustration A.2 *(concluded)*

MARRIED Persons—WEEKLY Payroll Period
(For Wages Paid After February 1992)

And the wages are—		And the number of withholding allowances claimed is—										
At least	But less than	0	1	2	3	4	5	6	7	8	9	10
		The amount of income tax to be withheld shall be—										
$730	$740	$93	$86	$80	$73	$66	$60	$53	$47	$40	$33	$27
740	750	94	88	81	75	68	61	55	48	41	35	28
750	760	96	89	83	76	69	63	56	50	43	36	30
760	770	98	91	84	78	71	64	58	51	44	38	31
770	780	101	92	86	79	72	66	59	53	46	39	33
780	790	104	94	87	81	74	67	61	54	47	41	34
790	800	107	95	89	82	75	69	62	56	49	42	36
800	810	109	97	90	84	77	70	64	57	50	44	37
810	820	112	100	92	85	78	72	65	59	52	45	39
820	830	115	103	93	87	80	73	67	60	53	47	40
830	840	118	105	95	88	81	75	68	62	55	48	42
840	850	121	108	96	90	83	76	70	63	56	50	43
850	860	123	111	99	91	84	78	71	65	58	51	45
860	870	126	114	101	93	86	79	73	66	59	53	46
870	880	129	117	104	94	87	81	74	68	61	54	48
880	890	132	119	107	96	89	82	76	69	62	56	49
890	900	135	122	110	97	90	84	77	71	64	57	51
900	910	137	125	113	100	92	85	79	72	65	59	52
910	920	140	128	115	103	93	87	80	74	67	60	54
920	930	143	131	118	106	95	88	82	75	68	62	55
930	940	146	133	121	109	96	90	83	77	70	63	57
940	950	149	136	124	111	99	91	85	78	71	65	58
950	960	151	139	127	114	102	93	86	80	73	66	60
960	970	154	142	129	117	105	94	88	81	74	68	61
970	980	157	145	132	120	107	96	89	83	76	69	63
980	990	160	147	135	123	110	98	91	84	77	71	64
990	1,000	163	150	138	125	113	101	92	86	79	72	66
1,000	1,010	165	153	141	128	116	103	94	87	80	74	67
1,010	1,020	168	156	143	131	119	106	95	89	82	75	69
1,020	1,030	171	159	146	134	121	109	97	90	83	77	70
1,030	1,040	174	161	149	137	124	112	99	92	85	78	72
1,040	1,050	177	164	152	139	127	115	102	93	86	80	73
1,050	1,060	179	167	155	142	130	117	105	95	88	81	75
1,060	1,070	182	170	157	145	133	120	108	96	89	83	76
1,070	1,080	185	173	160	148	135	123	111	98	91	84	78
1,080	1,090	188	175	163	151	138	126	113	101	92	86	79
1,090	1,100	191	178	166	153	141	129	116	104	94	87	81
1,100	1,110	193	181	169	156	144	131	119	107	95	89	82
1,110	1,120	196	184	171	159	147	134	122	109	97	90	84
1,120	1,130	199	187	174	162	149	137	125	112	100	92	85
1,130	1,140	202	189	177	165	152	140	127	115	103	93	87
1,140	1,150	205	192	180	167	155	143	130	118	105	95	88
1,150	1,160	207	195	183	170	158	145	133	121	108	96	90
1,160	1,170	210	198	185	173	161	148	136	123	111	99	91
1,170	1,180	213	201	188	176	163	151	139	126	114	101	93
1,180	1,190	216	203	191	179	166	154	141	129	117	104	94
1,190	1,200	219	206	194	181	169	157	144	132	119	107	96
1,200	1,210	221	209	197	184	172	159	147	135	122	110	97
1,210	1,220	224	212	199	187	175	162	150	137	125	113	100
1,220	1,230	227	215	202	190	177	165	153	140	128	115	103
1,230	1,240	230	217	205	193	180	168	155	143	131	118	106
1,240	1,250	233	220	208	195	183	171	158	146	133	121	109
1,250	1,260	235	223	211	198	186	173	161	149	136	124	111
1,260	1,270	238	226	213	201	189	176	164	151	139	127	114
1,270	1,280	241	229	216	204	191	179	167	154	142	129	117
1,280	1,290	244	231	219	207	194	182	169	157	145	132	120
1,290	1,300	247	234	222	209	197	185	172	160	147	135	123
1,300	1,310	249	237	225	212	200	187	175	163	150	138	125
1,310	1,320	252	240	227	215	203	190	178	165	153	141	128
1,320	1,330	255	243	230	218	205	193	181	168	156	143	131
1,330	1,340	258	245	233	221	208	196	183	171	159	146	134
1,340	1,350	261	248	236	223	211	199	186	174	161	149	137
1,350	1,360	263	251	239	226	214	201	189	177	164	152	139
1,360	1,370	266	254	241	229	217	204	192	179	167	155	142
1,370	1,380	269	257	244	232	219	207	195	182	170	157	145

$1,380 and over   Use Table 1(b) for a **MARRIED person** on page 26. Also see the instructions on page 24.

Illustration A.3
WAGE AND TAX STATEMENT (FORM W-2)

1 Control number	22222	For Official Use Only ▶ OMB No. 1545-0008		
2 Employer's name, address, and ZIP code		6 Statutory employee ☐ Deceased ☐ Pension plan ☐ Legal rep. ☐ 942 emp. ☐ Subtotal ☐ Deferred compensation ☐ Void ☐		
		7 Allocated tips	8 Advance EIC payment	
		9 Federal income tax withheld $1,968	10 Wages, tips, other compensation $20,000	
3 Employer's identification number 15-249363	4 Employer's state I.D. number 33048	11 Social security tax withheld $1,530	12 Social security wages $20,000	
5 Employee's social security number 253-13-2807		13 Social security tips	14 Medicare wages and tips	
19a Employee's name (first, middle initial, last) John R. Hanson		15 Medicare tax withheld	18 Nonqualified plans	
325 St. George Drive Athens, GA 30605		17 See Instrs. for Form W-2	18 Other	
19b Employee's address and ZIP code				
20 /////////	21 /////////	22 Dependent care benefits	23 Benefits included in Box 10	
24 State income tax $296.44	25 State wages, tips, etc. $20,000	26 Name of state Georgia	27 Local income tax	28 Local wages, tips, etc.	29 Name of locality

Copy A For Social Security Administration   Department of the Treasury—Internal Revenue Service

Form **W-2 Wage and Tax Statement 1992**

FICA (Social Security) Taxes.   The **FICA (social security) tax** was created by passage of the Federal Insurance Contributions Act in 1935. Persons who are currently working in jobs covered by the act must pay a certain percentage of their earnings (up to a maximum specified amount) into special trust funds. Employee contributions are matched by equal payments by employers. Money paid into the trust is used to finance retirement benefits and medical benefits (Medicare) paid to persons and their families who are currently retired or disabled and who qualify for such benefits under the act. Full retirement benefits are available to workers who reach age 65; reduced benefits can be applied for at age 62. Additional voluntary medical insurance is available to persons age 65 and over.

The amount of FICA tax withheld for each employee was 7.65% of the first $53,400 of wages in 1991 and 7.65% of the first $55,500 of wages in 1992. Of this 7.65 cents per dollar, 1.45 cents is for Medicare Hospital Insurance, and 6.2 cents is for old-age, survivors, and disability insurance. The $55,500 limit only applies to the old-age, survivors, and disability portion of FICA taxes. The 1.45 cents per dollar for Medicare Hospital Insurance is deducted on all wages and self-employment income up to $130,200. Thus, the FICA rate is 7.65% on the first $55,500 and 1.45% on amounts over $55,500 up to $130,200 of earned income. The rates and bases scheduled to go into effect after 1992 continue to incorporate an inflation factor based on the change in the average covered wage in the United States during the preceding calendar year.

Other Payroll Deductions. Besides payroll deductions for taxes, companies may make other deductions from an employee's gross earnings. Some union contracts require companies to deduct union dues from gross pay as a convenience to employees and the union. The union then receives from the employer the dues withheld from the employees. Medical insurance and life insurance premiums may also be deducted from gross pay. These deductions are made most often when a company offers group life insurance plans to its employees. The amounts deducted are paid directly by the employer to the insurance companies. Employees may also authorize payroll deductions for loan repayments to, or savings in, the employees' credit union. Employee pledges to charities, such as the United Way Fund, are often collected through payroll deductions.

Other less common deductions are for pension or retirement plans, where the employee is obligated to pay at least a portion of the cost of the plan. Some businesses may allow payroll deductions to pay for merchandise purchased by the employee. Employees may purchase U.S. Savings Bonds through payroll deductions. The number and types of optional payroll deductions are determined by the company, the employment contract, and the employee.

Maintaining Employee Earnings Record

Federal law requires employers to maintain an adequate payroll record for each employee. This record is called an **employee earnings record.** As shown in Illustration A.4, an employee earnings record shows information such as name, social security number, address, phone number, date employed, date of birth, marital status, number of withholding allowances claimed, pay rate, and present job within the company. For each pay period, the record also shows the number of hours worked, gross pay, deductions, and net pay. Cumulative gross pay during the year is included to indicate when the maximum amounts have been reached for FICA tax withholdings and unemployment taxes (which will be discussed later in the chapter). The amounts shown in Illustration A.4 for federal withholding may differ from current amounts and are used for illustrative purposes only.

Preparing Payroll Journal

A business may use a **payroll journal** (Illustration A.5) to reduce the work involved in recording payroll. A payroll journal contains a debit column for

Illustration A.4
EMPLOYEE EARNINGS RECORD

Name   John R. Hanson   Social Security No. __253 13 2807__   Employee No. ____5____

Address __325 St. George Drive__   Sex: Male (x) Female ( )   Position ____Sales____

__Athens, Ga. 30605__   Single ( ) Married (x)   Hourly pay rate ___$13.00___

Date of birth __June 20, 1950__   Withholding allowances ___3___   Spouse ___Susan___

Date employed __March 12, 1972__   Date terminated _____   Telephone No. ___394-1776___

1992* Period Ended	Total Hours	Earnings			Deductions					Payment		Cumu-lative Gross Earnings
		Regular	Overtime	Gross	Federal Income Tax	FICA Tax	State Income Tax	Medical Insur-ance	Other	Net Pay	Check No.	
Feb. 5	40	520.00		520.00	48.00	39.78	6.78	24.00		401.44	673	520.00
12	40	520.00		520.00	48.00	39.78	6.78	24.00		401.44	807	1,040.00
19	45	520.00	97.50	617.50	62.00	47.24	8.06	24.00		476.20	913	1,657.50

* 1992 dates are used throughout this appendix because the tax rates used are as of 1992.

each category of salary expense, such as sales, delivery, and office. Credit columns are included for withholdings made for various taxes and other deductions and Salaries Payable. These amounts all represent liabilities that must be paid either to agencies on the employees' behalf or to the employees. Note that a Check No. column is included to show which check was used to pay the Salaries Payable liability amounts. Postings can be made directly from the payroll journal to the ledger. Alternatively, a payroll register can be used merely to collect the information so a journal entry can be made in the general journal. If the payroll shown in Illustration A.5 were recorded in the general journal, the entry would be as follows:

```
1992
Feb. 5  Sales Salaries Expense . . . . . . . . . . . . .  2,500.00
        Delivery Salaries Expense . . . . . . . . . . .    510.00
        Office Salaries Expense . . . . . . . . . . . .    520.00
            Employees' Federal Income Taxes Payable . . .              399.00
            FICA Taxes Payable . . . . . . . . . . . . .                270.06
            Employees' State Income Taxes Payable . . . .                33.49
            Employees' Medical Insurance Premiums
                Payable . . . . . . . . . . . . . . . . .                94.00
            Salaries Payable . . . . . . . . . . . . . .              2,733.45
        To record the payroll for the week ending
        February 5.
```

All accounts credited in the February 5 entry are current liabilities and will be reported on the balance sheet if not paid prior to the preparation of financial statements. When the payroll is actually paid, the payment will be recorded in the cash disbursements journal as a debit to Salaries Payable and a credit to Cash of $2,733.45.

Illustration A.5
PAYROLL JOURNAL (OR REGISTER)

PAYROLL JOURNAL (OR REGISTER)

Date Week Ended 1992	Employee	Gross Pay			Deductions				Salaries Payable (Net Pay) Cr.	Check No.
		Sales Salaries Expense Dr.	Delivery Salaries Expense Dr.	Office Salaries Expense Dr.	Employees' Federal Income Taxes Payable Cr.	FICA Taxes Payable Cr.	Employees' State Income Taxes Payable Cr.	Employees' Medical Insurance Premiums Payable Cr.		
Feb. 5	John Hanson	520.00			48.00	39.78	6.78	24.00	401.44	673
	Robert Lash		510.00		65.00	39.02	4.18	10.00	391.80	674
	Mike Miller	750.00			81.00	57.38	7.29	20.00	584.33	675
	Bill Norman	640.00			79.00	48.96	5.83	15.00	491.21	676
	Allison Wheeler	590.00			65.00	45.14	5.17	15.00	459.69	677
	Cathy Yorb			520.00	61.00	39.78	4.24	10.00	404.98	678
		2,500.00	510.00	520.00	399.00	270.06	33.49	94.00	2,733.45	

PAYING THE PAYROLL—PAYROLL CHECKING ACCOUNT

The use of a **payroll checking account**—a separate checking account maintained by the business only to pay salaries and wages—is common among companies with many employees who are paid by check. In general, a payroll checking account is used as follows: The payroll checking account is established by depositing a small amount in the account and debiting Payroll Checking and crediting Cash. Before each payday, the payroll is prepared and recorded in a routine manner. One check is drawn on the company's regular checking account for the net payroll amount. This check is deposited in the payroll checking account. The accountant debits Salaries Payable and credits Cash. Payroll checks are then drawn on the payroll checking account and issued to employees. As the payroll checks are cashed by employees and clear the bank, the payroll checking account balance approaches zero.

The use of a payroll checking account has several advantages:

1. A distinctive payroll check form may be used, with spaces provided on an attachment for gross earnings, various payroll deductions, and net cash paid. See Illustration A.6.
2. Payroll checks, identifiable as such, are easily cashed by employees.
3. The work of reconciling the bank balances can be divided among employees. Only one check is drawn on the general bank account. The hundreds or thousands of payroll checks issued each payday are drawn on the payroll bank account. Occasionally, payroll checks will be negoti-

Illustration A.6
PAYROLL CHECK AND SUPPORTING EMPLOYEE'S EARNINGS STATEMENT

Employee	Hours Worked	Rate per Hour	Regular Earnings	Extra for Overtime	Gross Earning	Fed. Inc. Tax W/H	FICA	State Inc. Tax W/H	Hosp. Ins.	Net Pay
John R. Hanson	40	13.00	520.00	0	520.00	48.00	39.78	6.78	24.00	401.44

Retain this stub for your records - Detach before cashing check

```
                    ACE                 DOUG'S ACE HARDWARE                        673
                   HARDWARE                1290 Atlanta Highway
                                         ATHENS, GEORGIA 30605
                                                                                 64-1240
                                                        February 8     19 92       611

  PAY TO THE        John R. Hanson                                      $    401.44
  ORDER OF

  Four hundred one and 44/100's ~~~~~~~~~~~~~~~~           DOLLARS

  The CITIZENS and SOUTHERN BANK
        NORTH SPRINGS OFFICE
        ATLANTA, GEORGIA
                                                      George C. Beacham
  FOR

    ⑆000673⑆ ⑈0611⑈1240⑈ 038 82 131⑆
```

ated many times or lost before clearing the bank. Including these items in the payroll reconciliation simplifies the reconciliation of the general Cash account.

4. Only one authorization is prepared, calling for one check drawn on the general bank account; therefore, payroll checks are issued without separately prepared and signed authorizations.

5. Individual payroll checks need not be entered in the regular cash disbursements record; payroll check numbers are inserted in the payroll journal; and repetition of the entering of checks is avoided.

6. The chance of fraud is reduced in a small business. Since the monthly payroll is not likely to be large, a large bogus payroll check could not clear the bank.

RECORDING EMPLOYER PAYROLL TAXES

An employer is generally obligated to pay three taxes levied on payrolls. The entry to record these taxes results in three liabilities: FICA Taxes Payable, State Unemployment Taxes Payable, and Federal Unemployment Taxes Payable.

FICA (Social Security) Taxes

An employer is required to match the amount of FICA tax withheld from each employee's pay. For example, total FICA tax in 1992 amounted to

15.3% of the first $55,500 of each employee's earnings; half (7.65%) was paid by the employee, and half (7.65%) by the employer.

Federal Unemployment Tax

The Federal Unemployment Tax Act (FUTA) requires employers to pay a federal unemployment tax based on employee salaries and wages. This tax helps finance a cooperative federal-state system of unemployment compensation. Unemployment benefits are paid to qualified unemployed persons by each of the states and territorial governments. State unemployment laws vary only in minor respects; the Federal Unemployment Tax Act sets forth certain minimum standards that must be met by each state.

The **federal unemployment tax** rate generally has varied based on the actions of Congress. In 1992, the rate was 6.2% of the first $7,000 of wages paid to each employee. This rate will be used for illustrative purposes. The Federal Unemployment Tax Act provides that employers may have a maximum credit of 5.4% against their federal unemployment tax for amounts that were paid to the state. This credit, in effect, makes the federal unemployment tax rate (6.2% − 5.4%) = 0.8% on the first $7,000 of individual employee wages.

State Unemployment Tax

The **state unemployment tax** generally is 5.4% of the first $7,000 of gross earnings per employee. This rate and base will be used for illustrative purposes in this appendix. A **merit rate** can be gained by employers to reduce the state rate to as little as 0.5% in some states and even to zero in other states. A reduced rate is earned by employers with low turnover and few layoffs. Employers with lower merit rates can still deduct a credit of 5.4% against their federal unemployment tax rate.

Payroll Tax Entry

Employer payroll taxes are usually recorded at the same time as the payroll to which they relate. For example, the employer's payroll taxes (at 1992 rates) on the amount of the February 5 payroll in Illustration A.5 are recorded as follows:

Feb. 5	Payroll Taxes Expense 488.92	
	FICA Taxes Payable.	270.06
	State Unemployment Taxes Payable	190.62
	Federal Unemployment Taxes Payable	28.24
	To record employer's payroll taxes.	

Remember that these amounts are in addition to amounts withheld from employees. This journal entry debits Payroll Taxes Expense for the total of the employer's three payroll taxes. The credit to FICA Taxes Payable is equal to the amount deducted from the employees' gross pay. Both the employer's and employees' FICA taxes can be credited to the same liability account, since both are payable at the same time to the same agency. The credits to the state and federal unemployment accounts are for 5.4% and 0.8%, respectively, of the $3,530 of gross pay for this payroll period. We assumed that no employee had been paid more than $7,000 in the current year. Any earnings in excess of $7,000 would have been excluded from the computation of unemployment taxes, since those taxes are levied only on the first $7,000 of annual income per employee.

REMITTING TAXES WITHHELD, UNEMPLOYMENT TAXES, AND OTHER DEDUCTIONS

Generally, within one month after the end of each calendar quarter, an employer must file an **Employer's Quarterly Federal Tax Return (Form 941)** with the Internal Revenue Service. This form reports the amount of FICA and income taxes withheld for the preceding quarter. The employer reports (1) total wages subject to withholding, (2) federal income taxes withheld, (3) total wages subject to FICA tax, (4) amount of FICA taxes due (from both employer and employees), and (5) combined amount of income tax withheld and FICA taxes due. A similar form is required by states with state income tax laws.

Taxes Withheld

For remittance purposes, federal income taxes withheld and both the employees' and employer's FICA taxes are combined. Generally, employers are required to deposit such taxes in a Federal Reserve Bank or an authorized commercial bank called a **federal depository bank.** When deposited, these amounts are credited by the bank to an Internal Revenue Service account. Deposit requirements are quite detailed and depend on the amount of taxes collected relative to the time elapsed since the last deposit. The more dollars of taxes that are collected, the more rapidly deposits must be made. Taxes properly deposited are considered paid.

Assuming the amount of federal income taxes withheld is $3,687 and the amount of combined FICA taxes is $2,500, the entry to record this deposit is:

```
Employees' Federal Income Taxes Payable. . . . . . . . .  3,687.00
FICA Taxes Payable. . . . . . . . . . . . . . . . . . . .  2,500.00
    Cash. . . . . . . . . . . . . . . . . . . . . . . . .             6,187.00
    To record deposit of taxes withheld and employer FICA
    taxes.
```

State and city income taxes must be withheld by employers in most states and in many cities. The procedures for withholding and the required remittances are usually modeled after federal income tax regulations. The entry for employers to record payment of these taxes debits Employees' State (City) Income Taxes Payable and credits Cash.

Illustration A.7
SUMMARY OF PAYROLL TAXES

Type of Tax	Who Pays for It	Amount of Tax
FICA (social security)	Both employer and employee pay at current rate	7.65% of first $55,500 and 1.45% on amounts over $55,500, up to $130,200, that each employee earns annually*
Income	Employee	Varies with earnings and exemptions
State unemployment	Employer (usually)	5.4% of first $7,000 each employee earns annually†
Federal unemployment	Employer	0.8% of first $7,000 each employee earns annually‡

* This rate and base are for 1992.

† Some states have a higher rate and/or base than this. Also, most states allow reduction from the basic rate to firms with low labor turnover.

‡ The federal rate varies, but in this appendix it is assumed to be 6.2%. An allowance of 5.4% is granted for amounts paid to the state, thus reducing the effective rate to 0.8%.

Unemployment Taxes

The amount of federal unemployment taxes to be deposited is determined quarterly. When a certain amount is reached, these taxes must be deposited in a federal depository bank. Assuming the amount of federal unemployment taxes is $400, the entry to record the deposit is:

Federal Unemployment Taxes Payable.	400.00	
Cash.		400.00
To record deposit of federal unemployment taxes.		

Remittance requirements for state unemployment taxes vary from state to state. Quarterly reports and payments are usually required by the end of the month following the quarter's end. The entry to record the payment is a debit to State Unemployment Taxes Payable and a credit to Cash.

Other Payroll Deductions

The remittance of other types of payroll deductions varies based on the agency or organization to which payment is to be made. Monthly payment is likely for union dues, medical insurance premiums, charitable contributions, and pension contributions.

A summary of the various payroll taxes appears in Illustration A.7.

PREPARING END-OF-PERIOD ACCRUALS

Adjusting entries are usually needed at year-end to accrue wages, employer's payroll taxes, and vacation pay.

Wages and Payroll Taxes

The matching principle requires accrued wages and employer payroll taxes on these wages to be recorded at the end of every period. To illustrate, assume that Doug's Hardware Company accrues the following salaries and payroll taxes on December 31, 1992: sales salaries, $900; delivery salaries, $160; office salaries, $210; and employer's FICA tax expense, $97.16. The required entries are:

Dec. 31	Sales Salaries Expense	900.00	
	Delivery Salaries Expense	160.00	
	Office Salaries Expense	210.00	
	Salaries Payable.		1,270.00
	To accrue salaries.		
31	Payroll Taxes Expense.	97.16	
	FICA Taxes Payable		97.16
	To accrue payroll taxes.		

Note in the first entry that credits are not entered in separate liability accounts for payroll deductions. These deductions will be recorded when the payroll is paid since they are not actually withheld from the employees until then. The second entry recorded the employer's FICA taxes on $1,270 of salaries. We assumed that no employee had reached the maximum FICA limit; therefore, all accrued salaries would be subject to FICA taxation. Accrued federal and state unemployment taxes were not included in this example because by year-end all employees' earnings should have surpassed the $7,000 maximum amount subject to taxation.

Some companies do not accrue employer's payroll taxes at year-end. The following reasons are given for this violation of the matching principle: (1) no legal liability for such taxes exists until the wages are paid, (2) such taxes do not vary much in amount from year to year, and (3) the amounts of such taxes are likely to be immaterial. A policy of not accruing payroll taxes is acceptable under these circumstances.

Vacation Pay

Most employees in this country are entitled to annual vacations of from one to four weeks at full regular pay. The compensation received while on vacation is called **vacation pay.** Thus, the employer annually pays an employee for 52 weeks but receives services for a fewer number of weeks.

How to account for vacation pay raises an important question: Should vacation pay be expensed when paid, or should it be accrued over the period in which the employee works to earn the vacation? *FASB Statement No. 43,* "Accounting for Compensated Absences," requires the accrual of a liability for vacation pay if the following conditions are met:

1. The employer is obligated to pay as a result of services already received.
2. The employee's right to vacation pay does not depend on continued performance of services.

3. It is probable the vacation pay will be paid.

4. The amount of vacation pay can be reasonably estimated.

Assume Davis Company estimates that out of every 25 workdays employees will earn 1 day of vacation pay. As a result, vacation pay is to be accrued at a rate of 4% (1 day/25 days) of gross pay. The entry to accrue vacation pay on a $3,200 payroll is:

```
Vacation Pay Expense ($3,200 × 0.04) . . . . . . . . . . .    128.00
    Estimated Vacation Pay Payable. . . . . . . . . . .                128.00
    To accrue vacation pay.
```

Accruing vacation pay in this manner records the expense over the period in which it was earned rather than when it was paid, which results in a better matching of expenses and revenues. A liability is also recorded for the vacation pay currently owed by the employer to employees. Often employees must forfeit vacation pay earned if they leave the company before some minimum length of time, such as one year. If turnover of these employees is expected, the amount of the entry to accrue vacation pay should be reduced accordingly.

When vacation pay is paid, the estimated liability account is debited, and various accounts are credited for taxes, other deductions, and cash payment. For example, an employee earning $400 per week is to be paid for two weeks' vacation. A payroll check is drawn for the net pay due and entered in the payroll journal. Using assumed deductions, the entry in general journal form would be:

```
Estimated Vacation Pay Payable. . . . . . . . . . . . .    800.00
    Employees' Federal Income Taxes Payable. . . . . . .             141.00
    FICA Taxes Payable. . . . . . . . . . . . . . . . . .              61.20
    Medical Insurance Premiums Payable . . . . . . . . .              50.00
    Employees' State Income Taxes Payable . . . . . . . .             11.00
    Cash. . . . . . . . . . . . . . . . . . . . . . . . .            536.80
    To record payment of vacation pay.
```

CONSIDERING MORE EFFICIENT METHODS OF PAYROLL ACCOUNTING

The payroll deductions described in this appendix are used effectively by many small companies. However, some of these companies use a manual system called a **pegboard system of payroll accounting** to increase efficiency. Such a system aligns the payroll check, the individual earnings record, and the payroll journal in such a way that all three are completed with one writing. Instead of having to record gross pay, deductions, and net pay three different times for each employee, the recording is done only once by using a pegboard system of payroll accounting. Of course, the forms must be designed so that they are compatible. Use of such a system can reduce clerical time dramatically. Also, many microcomputer accounting software packages used by small companies include payroll modules that can easily handle all the payroll functions described in this appendix.

Larger companies often use minicomputers or mainframe computers to perform the payroll functions. Also, many banks and service bureaus offer computerized payroll processing services.

CORPORATE FEDERAL INCOME TAXATION

Most corporations organized for profit must file a federal income tax return and pay corporate income tax on their net income. Not-for-profit organizations, specifically exempted by law, do not file an income tax return but must file an annual return of information.

INCOME BEFORE TAXES VERSUS TAXABLE INCOME

Income before federal income taxes (as shown on the income statement) and taxable income (as shown in the corporation's tax return) need not necessarily agree. Some of the reasons why they might differ are:

1. Certain items of revenue and expense included in the computation of business income are excluded from the computation of taxable income. For instance, interest earned on certain state, county, or municipal bonds is not subject to tax, although this interest is a component of business income. Additionally, the general rule is that only "ordinary" and "necessary" business expenses and "reasonable" amounts of salaries can be deducted for tax purposes. Life insurance premiums are not deductible if the corporation is the beneficiary; however, proceeds received from life insurance policies are not taxed. Costs of attempting to influence legislation are not deductible. A corporation may deduct from taxable income 80% of any dividends received from other domestic corporations. Goodwill cannot be amortized for tax purposes even though it must be for accounting purposes.
2. The timing of recognition of items of revenue and expense often varies for tax purposes from the timing used in determining business income. Interpretations of the tax code have generally held that revenue received in advance is taxable when received and that current expenses based on estimates of future costs (such as costs of performance under service contracts) are not deductible until actually incurred. Thus, taxable income is determined at least partially on a cash basis, while business income is determined on an accrual basis. The installment sales method could formerly be used for tax purposes but only rarely for accounting purposes. Under this method, revenue was recognized for tax purposes only when collections were received. Also, certain elective accounting methods may be used for tax purposes that are different from those methods used for financial statements. For instance, often a corporation

may use straight-line depreciation for book purposes and a different depreciation method for tax purposes.

For a given corporation, the reconciliation between net income before taxes and taxable income may appear as follows:

Net income before taxes per income statement		$111,000
Add:		
Life insurance premiums paid	$1,050	
Service revenue received in advance	7,500	
Estimated expenses under service contracts	1,500	10,050
		$121,050
Deduct:		
Interest on New York State bonds	$4,500	
Difference in depreciation for tax purposes ($9,000)		
and for book purposes ($6,000)	3,000	7,500
Taxable income		$113,550

Tax Rates

Once taxable income is determined, a tax rate is applied to find the amount of tax liability. As of this writing, the graduated tax rates applicable to corporations are as shown in Illustration A.8.

To illustrate, using these corporate tax rates, a corporation with taxable income of $110,000 will have a tax liability of $26,150, computed as follows:

Tax on first $50,000 (at 15%)	$ 7,500
Tax on next $25,000 (at 25%)	6,250
Tax on next $25,000 (at 34%)	8,500
Tax on remaining $10,000 (at 39%)	3,900
	$26,150

Likewise, a corporation with taxable income of $500,000 will have a tax liability of $170,000 ($500,000 × 34%).

Illustration A.8
CORPORATE TAX RATES

Corporate Taxable Income	Tax Rate
$0–$ 50,000	15%
$ 50,001–$ 75,000	25
$ 75,001–$100,000	34
$100,001–$335,000	39

A corporation with taxable income over $335,000 will pay a flat tax rate of 34% on all taxable income.

The tax law requires an alternative minimum tax to be calculated and paid by the corporation if the minimum tax is higher than the ordinary tax. The tax will be calculated at 20% of taxable income adjusted by adding back a number of the tax breaks allowed to arrive at taxable income and reduced, in some cases, by an exemption of up to $40,000.

Loss Carryback and Carryforward

A provision of the tax law allows corporations to carry losses incurred in the current year back 3 years and forward 15 years to offset past or future taxes. (Alternatively, the corporation may elect to only carry the loss forward for 15 years.) A **loss carryback** is a current loss that has been applied against taxable income of prior periods, thereby resulting in a tax refund in the current period. In applying a loss carryback, the company must apply the loss to the oldest year first, then the next oldest, and so on until the loss has been completely "used up" by offsetting it against ordinary taxable income of these years. The corporation recomputes its taxes for those previous years using the rates then in effect.

To illustrate this provision, assume the amounts of taxable income (or loss) shown below (1992 rates were used to compute taxes paid):

Year	Taxable Income (or loss)	Taxes Paid	Taxes Recovered
1991	$ 7,500	$1,125	$1,125
1992	10,000	1,500	1,500
1993	2,500	375	375
1994	(50,000)	–0–	–0–
1995	20,000	–0–	–0–
1996	5,000	–0–	–0–
1997	15,000	1,500	–0–
1998	25,000	3,750	–0–
1999	30,000	4,500	–0–

The loss of $50,000 in 1994 would first be offset against the $7,500 of taxable income in 1991, then the $10,000 in 1992, and next the $2,500 in 1993. The company would recover the taxes previously paid in those years, which total $3,000. At this point, the company would have a loss carryforward of $30,000. A **loss carryforward** is a current loss that will be applied against taxable income in future periods, thereby reducing the taxes payable of future periods. In the above example, the company would apply $20,000 of this $30,000 toward taxable income in 1995 and therefore would pay no taxes in that year. At this point, $10,000 of the carryforward remains: $5,000 of this amount would be used to offset taxable income in the next year (1996), and the other $5,000 would be applied against 1997 taxable income.

Accounting Methods Used for Tax Purposes

Accrual Method.   The method of accounting used determines when revenues and expenses are recognized. Most corporations and large businesses use the accrual method. Under this method, revenues are generally recognized when earned. The earning of revenue normally occurs when services are rendered or when goods are delivered. When payment has been received before the revenue has been earned, an exception may require recognition of income at the time payment is received.

Expenses are generally recognized when liabilities are incurred for goods or services received. Costs of assets are deferred and charged to expense in the period in which the assets are used or consumed.

Modified Cash Method.   Sole proprietorships, partnerships, and certain small corporations may use a modified cash method. This method is described as a "modified" (rather than a "pure") cash method because long-term assets cannot be charged to expense when purchased, nor can all prepaid expenses (such as a three-year insurance premium) be deducted when paid. Also, revenues must be reported when constructively received even though the cash is not yet in the possession of the business. For instance, a check received at the end of the year is considered revenue even though it has not been cashed. If inventories are a substantial factor in producing income, the company must use the accrual basis for recognizing sales, cost of goods sold, and related asset (inventory and accounts receivable) and liability (accounts payable) accounts.

Accounting for Inventories.   Accountants use several different methods to account for inventories. Each method assumes a different flow of costs and thus results in a different taxable income if used for tax purposes. In recent years many firms have adopted LIFO (last-in, first-out), in which the last goods purchased are assumed to be the first ones sold. Under this method, during periods of rising prices, the most recent *higher* costs are charged against revenues and the asset, inventory, is shown at lower earlier costs. The result is lower net income and lower taxes. The tax law generally permits a company to use the LIFO method for tax purposes only if it uses LIFO for financial statement purposes.

Depreciation Methods Used for Tax Purposes.   Tax depreciation is substantially different than depreciation used for accounting purposes. In accounting, depreciation methods are designed to match the expense of a capital investment against the revenue the investment produces. The depreciable period or useful life used for tax purposes is based on law and not on the actual useful life of the related asset; thus, no attempt is made to match revenues and expenses.

Prior to 1981, several depreciation methods were available for tax purposes, including the sum-of-the-years'-digits method and the uniform-rate-on-declining-balance method. The Economic Recovery Tax Act of 1981 introduced a new depreciation system known as the **Accelerated Cost Recovery System (ACRS).** However, effective January 1, 1987, the Tax

Illustration A.9
MODIFIED ACRS

Class of Investment	Kinds of Assets
3 years	Investments in some short-lived assets.
5 years	Automobiles, light-duty trucks, and machinery and equipment used in research and development.
7 years	All other machinery and equipment, such as dies, drills, or presses, furniture, and fixtures.
10 years	Some longer-lived equipment.
15 years	Sewage treatment plants and telephone distribution plants.
20 years	Sewer pipes and very long-lived equipment.
27.5 years	Residential rental property.
31.5 years	Nonresidential real estate.

Reform Act of 1986 substantially modified the ACRS rules. For purposes of this text, we shall refer to these rules as **modified ACRS.**

Capital assets are grouped into one of eight different classes (Illustration A.9). Each class has an assigned life over which costs of the assets (not reduced by salvage) are depreciated.

Capital assets in the 3-, 5-, 7-, and 10-year classes may be depreciated by using either the 200% declining-balance method or the straight-line method. Assets in the 15- and 20-year classes may be depreciated by using either the 150% declining-balance method or the straight-line method. Assets in the 27.5- and 31.5-year classes must be depreciated by using straight-line depreciation. The Internal Revenue Service provides tables that may be used in applying these methods. The declining-balance methods result in faster write-offs in the first few years of an investment's life. Cash saved from reduced taxes in the early years of life of the assets can be invested in new productive assets or can be applied to the replacement of the old assets when they become obsolete or worn out.

Once the asset has been classified, the depreciation schedule for the life of the asset can be completed. To illustrate a depreciation schedule, assume that Bigwig Company acquired and placed in service a depreciable asset on January 1, 1992, for $10,000. The asset falls into the five-year class. The depreciation schedule for the asset would be as follows:

Year	Recovery Percentage* ×	Original Cost =	Depreciation Expense	Total Accumulated Depreciation	Book Value
1992	20	× $10,000 =	$2,000	$ 2,000	$8,000
1993	32	× 10,000 =	3,200	5,200	4,800
1994	19	× 10,000 =	1,900	7,100	2,900
1995	15	× 10,000 =	1,500	8,600	1,400
1996	14	× 10,000 =	1,400	10,000	–0–

* These percentages are calculated by the authors using the 200% declining-balance procedure with one-half year depreciation taken in the year the asset is placed in service and switching to the straight-line method in 1995 in order to maximize depreciation. Percentages were rounded to whole numbers.

Tax depreciation is very desirable from the corporation's viewpoint since it decreases taxable income and hence the corporation's tax liability. However, when revenues are expected to be low in the early years and high in later years, taxpayers may decide to spread the depreciation more evenly over the entire life of an asset rather than taking most of it in the earlier years of asset life. For this reason, the law provides an alternative. The taxpayer may elect to use the straight-line method rather than the accelerated (table) method.

INCOME TAX ALLOCATION

Taxable income and income before federal income taxes (for simplicity, pre-tax income) for a corporation may differ sharply for a number of reasons. In fact, the tax return may show a loss, while the income statement shows positive pre-tax income. This difference raises a question about the amount of income taxes to be shown on the income statement. The answer lies in the nature of the items causing the difference between taxable income and pre-tax income. Some items create permanent differences, while others create temporary (or timing) differences. Both kinds of differences are discussed below.

Permanent Differences

Certain types of revenues and expenses included in the computation of net income for book purposes are excluded from the computation of taxable income. **Permanent differences** between taxable income and financial statement pre-tax income are caused by tax law provisions that exclude certain items of expense, revenue, gain, or loss as elements of taxable income. For instance, interest earned on certain state, county, or municipal bonds is included in book net income but is not subject to tax and therefore is not included in determining taxable income. The same is true for life insurance proceeds received by a corporation. Other items that are expensed for book purposes are not deductible for tax purposes, such as premiums paid for officers' life insurance, costs of attempting to influence legislation, and amortization of goodwill. These are only a few of the numerous items for which the tax treatment is completely different from the accounting treatment. These differences in treatment *never* change or reverse themselves. Therefore, they are called *permanent differences*. Such differences cause no accounting problem—the estimated actual amount of income tax expense for the year is shown on the income statement even if this method results in reporting only $1,000 of income tax expense on $100,000 of pre-tax income.

Temporary Differences

Other items of revenue and expense are often recognized at different times for tax purposes and for financial reporting purposes. A **temporary differ-**

ence is a difference between taxable income and financial statement pre-tax income caused by items that affect both taxable income and pre-tax income, but in different periods. For example, interpretations of the tax code generally have held that revenue received in advance is taxable when received and that current expenses based on estimates of future costs (such as costs of performance under service contracts) are not deductible until incurred. Temporary differences can also result from using accounting methods for tax purposes that are different than the ones used for financial reporting purposes. For example, a corporation may use straight-line depreciation for book purposes and modified ACRS depreciation for tax purposes. Eventually these revenues and expenses are recognized in computing both accounting income and taxable income. Therefore, these variations between taxable income and pre-tax net income are called temporary differences.

Recall the reconciliation earlier between (1) income before income taxes per the income statement and (2) taxable income per the tax return for a given corporation. We repeat that reconciliation below.

Income before income taxes per income statement		$111,000
Add:		
Life insurance premium paid	$1,050	
Service revenue received in advance	7,500	
Estimated expenses under service contracts	1,500	10,050
		$121,050
Deduct:		
Interest on New York State bonds	$4,500	
Difference in depreciation for tax purposes ($9,000)		
and for book purposes ($6,000).	3,000	7,500
Taxable income		$113,550

In the reconciliation between income before taxes and taxable income, the life insurance premiums paid (for which the corporation is beneficiary of the policy) are *never deductible* for income tax purposes, and the interest on New York State bonds is *never taxable*. These are permanent differences and therefore involve no interperiod income tax allocation. The other reconciling items are temporary differences for which interperiod income tax allocation procedures are required.

As discussed above, temporary differences include items that will be included in both taxable income and in pre-tax income, but in different periods. The items involved thus will have a tax effect. When temporary differences exist, generally accepted accounting principles require application of tax allocation procedures. Under **interperiod income tax allocation,** the tax effect of an element of expense or revenue, or loss or gain, that will affect taxable income is allocated to the period in which the item is recognized for accounting purposes, regardless of the period in which the element is recognized for tax purposes.

Illustration A.10
CALCULATION OF TAX LIABILITY

	1992	1993	1994	1995	1996	Total
Income before depreciation and income taxes	$10,000	$10,000	$10,000	$10,000	$10,000	$50,000
Depreciation for tax purposes	2,000	3,200	1,900	1,500	1,400	10,000
Taxable income	$ 8,000	$ 6,800	$ 8,100	$ 8,500	$ 8,600	$40,000
Income taxes payable (15% of taxable income)	$ 1,200	$ 1,020	$ 1,215	$ 1,275	$ 1,290	$ 6,000

Income Tax Allocation Illustrated. To illustrate the tax allocation procedure required for temporary differences, assume that:

1. A firm acquired a depreciable asset on January 1, 1992, for $10,000 that has an estimated useful life of five years with no expected scrap value.
2. The firm uses the straight-line depreciation method for financial reporting purposes and the modified ACRS method for tax purposes (the related asset falls into the five-year class for which depreciation has been previously calculated).
3. Net income before depreciation and income taxes is $10,000 for each year of the asset's life.
4. No other items cause differences between pre-tax income and taxable income.
5. The tax rate is 15% (to simplify the illustration).

The tax liability for each year would be as shown in Illustration A.10. Income tax expense for each year for financial reporting purposes would be as shown in Illustration A.11.

Note that for 1993, tax depreciation ($3,200, Illustration A.10) exceeds the book expense for depreciation ($2,000, Illustration A.11) by $1,200, but that effect is reversed during 1994 through 1996 so that depreciation at the end of 1996 is the same ($10,000) in both cases. Since the effects reverse over

Illustration A.11
EVALUATION OF TAX EXPENSE

	1992	1993	1994	1995	1996	Total
Income before depreciation and income taxes	$10,000	$10,000	$10,000	$10,000	$10,000	$50,000
Depreciation (straight-line method)	2,000	2,000	2,000	2,000	2,000	10,000
Pre-tax income	$ 8,000	$ 8,000	$ 8,000	$ 8,000	$ 8,000	$40,000
Income tax expense (15% of pre-tax income)	1,200	1,200	1,200	1,200	1,200	6,000
Net income	$ 6,800	$ 6,800	$ 6,800	$ 6,800	$ 6,800	$34,000

time, they constitute temporary differences for which deferred income taxes are provided in the books. Because tax and book depreciation happen to be the same for 1992, no deferred income tax is needed for that year. The required entries for 1992 and 1993 to record income taxes and to set up deferred income taxes for the temporary difference for the excess of tax depreciation over financial depreciation are:

	1992	1993
Federal Income Tax Expense	1,200	1,200
Federal Income Tax Payable	1,200	1,020
Deferred Federal Income Tax Payable	–0–	180
To record income tax expense.		

The required entries for 1994 through 1996 to record income taxes and to reduce the deferred income taxes as the temporary difference reverses (i.e., financial depreciation exceeds tax depreciation) are:

	1994	1995	1996
Federal Income Tax Expense.	1,200	1,200	1,200
Deferred Federal Income Tax Payable	15	75	90
Federal Income Tax Payable	1,215	1,275	1,290
To record income tax expense.			

Note again that the amount of tax expense recognized remains constant at $1,200 even though the tax liability varies from $1,020 for 1993 to $1,290 for 1996. The normalizing of the tax expense for each year is accomplished by making entries in the Deferred Federal Income Tax Payable account. The tables clearly show that the tax expense for the five years is $6,000 and that the tax payments for the five years also sum to $6,000. The only difference is that the tax expense charged to each year is not the same amount as the actual liability for the year.

In this simplified example, the Deferred Federal Income Tax Payable account has a zero balance at the end of five years. However, actual business experience has shown that once a Deferred Federal Income Tax Payable account is established, it is seldom decreased or reduced to zero. The reason is that most businesses acquire new depreciable assets, usually at higher prices. The result is that depreciation for tax purposes continues to be greater than depreciation for financial reporting purposes, and the balance in the Deferred Federal Income Tax Payable account also continues to grow. For this reason, many accountants seriously question the validity of tax allocation in circumstances such as those described above. Also, some accountants question whether a company can have a liability at a reporting date for income taxes for tax years that have not yet started. Discussion of these controversial issues must be left to more advanced texts. In the above example, the Deferred Federal Income Tax Payable account would be reported as a long-term liability on the balance sheet because the asset causing its existence is classified as a long-term asset.

THE NEED FOR TAX PLANNING

Numerous examples could be given for showing that business decisions are influenced greatly by their tax effects. With the advent of relatively high tax rates, tax planning has become an essential function of management.

The tax laws are extremely complicated and are changing constantly. Those persons who desire to stay current with the status of the law, and with the interpretations of the law made by courts, must specialize in this area.

PERSONAL FEDERAL INCOME TAXES

One of the deductions from employees' gross wages mentioned in this appendix was for federal income taxes. The purpose of this section is to give an introductory understanding of personal income taxes.

WHO MUST FILE A RETURN

In general, all U.S. citizens and resident aliens must file a federal income tax return. More specifically, the determination of who must file a return depends on filing status and income level. The income level changes frequently, so you should check the latest requirements.

Filing Status

Four basic filing statuses may be used in filing an income tax return. These are single, married filing jointly, married filing separately, and head of household. All of these statuses are self-explanatory except **head of household,** which typically is an unmarried or legally separated person who maintains a residence for a person qualifying as a dependent of the taxpayer.

GROSS INCOME

Illustration A.12 contains a general model of the determination of taxable income. The model starts with gross (total) income. **Gross income** includes all income from whatever source derived, except income specifically exempted, such as social security benefits. Gross income includes wages, interest, dividends, tips, bonuses, gambling winnings, gains from property sales, and prizes (including noncash prizes). Even income generated illegally, such as by theft, must be included in gross income. The general rule is that every income item, unless specifically exempted by law, must be included in gross income.

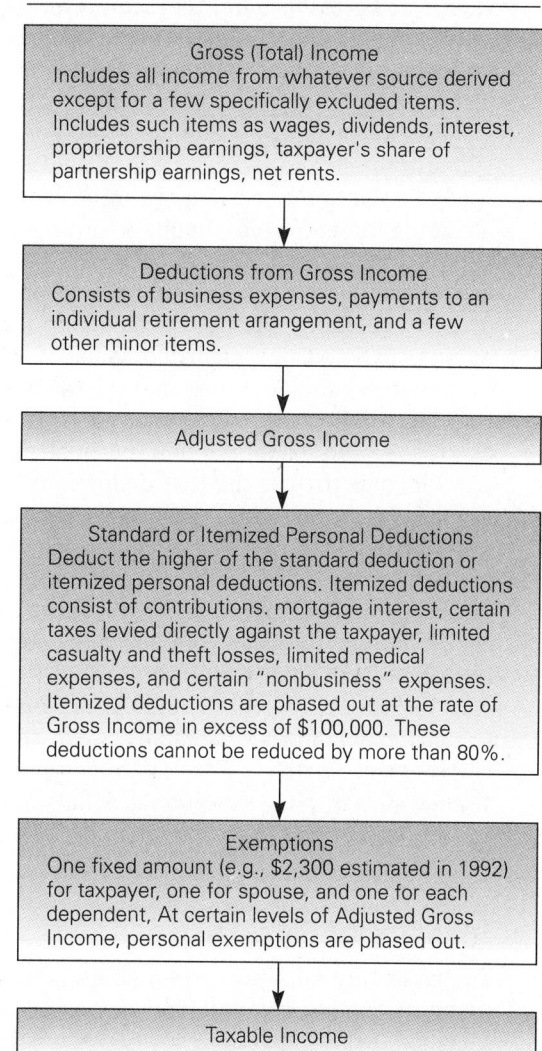

Illustration A.12
DETERMINATION OF TAXABLE INCOME FOR
AN INDIVIDUAL TAXPAYER

Gross (Total) Income
Includes all income from whatever source derived
except for a few specifically excluded items.
Includes such items as wages, dividends, interest,
proprietorship earnings, taxpayer's share of
partnership earnings, net rents.

Deductions from Gross Income
Consists of business expenses, payments to an
individual retirement arrangement, and a few
other minor items.

Adjusted Gross Income

Standard or Itemized Personal Deductions
Deduct the higher of the standard deduction or
itemized personal deductions. Itemized deductions
consist of contributions. mortgage interest, certain
taxes levied directly against the taxpayer, limited
casualty and theft losses, limited medical
expenses, and certain "nonbusiness" expenses.
Itemized deductions are phased out at the rate of
Gross Income in excess of $100,000. These
deductions cannot be reduced by more than 80%.

Exemptions
One fixed amount (e.g., $2,300 estimated in 1992)
for taxpayer, one for spouse, and one for each
dependent, At certain levels of Adjusted Gross
Income, personal exemptions are phased out.

Taxable Income

Exclusions from Gross Income

Income items specifically excluded are interest on certain state and municipal bonds, social security benefits, worker's compensation insurance benefits, and several employee "fringe" benefits, such as employer-paid health insurance premiums. Also, gifts, inheritances, certain disability benefits, scholarships, and the proceeds from life insurance policies are excluded.

ADJUSTED GROSS INCOME

Taxpayers are allowed to deduct certain items from gross income in arriving at **adjusted gross income. Deductions for adjusted gross income** include business expenses (certain limitations apply), payments by certain individuals to individual retirement accounts (IRAs) or payments to Keogh retirement plans, and alimony paid to a former spouse.

Employees may also deduct from gross income contributions to an individual retirement account (IRA) if neither the taxpayer nor the taxpayer's spouse is an active participant in an employer-sponsored retirement plan, including tax-sheltered annuities, government plans, and Keogh plans. An IRA is a retirement savings account usually set up in a bank, savings and loan association, insurance company, mutual fund, or brokerage firm. The annual deduction is limited to the lesser of 100% of earnings or $2,000 for an individual, $4,000 for a married couple if both spouses have jobs, and $2,250 for a married couple if only one spouse has earned income. Deductions can only be based on earned income, not "passive" income, such as interest and dividends. The maximum amount is phased out, however, where adjusted gross income (before the IRA deduction) is over $40,000 on a joint return or $25,000 for an unmarried individual. The deduction is eliminated when adjusted gross income reaches $50,000 on a joint return or $35,000 for an unmarried person.

Since self-employed individuals are not covered by company-established retirement plans, they are allowed to establish their own retirement plan called a Keogh plan (pronounced Key-oh). Keogh plans are available only to self-employed individuals. A self-employed individual (e.g., a consultant) may contribute annually the lesser of $30,000 or about 13% of self-employment income (20% for money-purchase arrangements) to a profit-sharing Keogh plan. Additional details concerning IRAs and Keogh plans are left to more advanced textbooks.

TAXABLE INCOME

Taxpayers are allowed certain additional deductions and exemptions in arriving at **taxable income.** The **deductions from adjusted gross income** are specified by law and consist of two categories: (1) the standard deduction or (2) itemized or personal deductions. Individuals may use either the **standard deduction amount** or the itemized deductions, whichever amount is higher. The standard deduction amount set by Congress for each type of taxpayer changes frequently. A taxpayer will itemize deductions only if such deductions exceed the standard deduction amount.

To the extent that adjusted gross income exceeds $100,000 for married persons filing jointly or single persons and $50,000 for married persons filing separately, itemized deductions are phased out. For example, a taxpayer (married filing jointly or single) with an adjusted gross income of $150,000 will lose ($150,000 − $100,000) × 3% = $1,500 of itemized deductions. These deductions cannot be reduced by more than 80%.

Itemized Deductions

The more common **itemized deductions** include:

1. *Taxes.*   Real estate taxes, personal property taxes, and state and local income taxes are deductible. License fees, state sales taxes, and federal excise taxes are not deductible.
2. *Interest.*   Interest paid on mortgages on the principal residence and the second residence is generally deductible. The interest must be attributable to loans not exceeding the original purchase price plus the cost of any house improvements (unless the excess mortgage is incurred for educational or medical expenses).
3. *Charitable contributions.*   Gifts to educational, religious, scientific, and charitable organizations are deductible to the extent they do not exceed 50% of adjusted gross income. Donations to individuals, labor unions, and organizations that seek to influence legislation are not deductible.
4. *Medical expenses.*   Within certain limits, unreimbursed hospital, medical, and dental expenses incurred by taxpayers and their dependents are deductible. Only that amount of medical costs that exceeds 7.5% of adjusted gross income is deductible. The entire cost of prescription drugs and insulin can be included in medical costs. The cost of other drugs and medicines cannot be included.

    To clarify the treatment of medical expenses, assume that in 1992, a taxpayer with an adjusted gross income of $20,000 paid $550 of health insurance premiums, incurred other medical expenses of $700, and incurred prescription drug costs of $400. The medical deduction is:

Health insurance premiums	$ 550
Other unreimbursed medical expenses	700
Medicine costs	400
	$1,650
Less: 7.5% of adjusted gross income (0.075 × $20,000)	1,500
Medical deduction	$ 150

5. *Casualty losses.*   Casualty losses are sudden and unexpected losses resulting from theft, accidents, storms, fires, and similar events. They are deductible to the extent that *each* casualty loss exceeds $100, *and* that the total of all unreimbursed casualty losses for the year exceeds 10% of adjusted gross income. Thus, to compute the deduction, subtract $100 from the dollar amount of *each* loss (ignore losses of less than $100) to obtain an adjusted casualty loss. Then, from the sum of the adjusted casualty losses, subtract 10% of adjusted gross income. The positive

difference is the casualty loss deduction. To illustrate, assume a taxpayer had adjusted gross income of $50,000 and suffered two casualty losses during the year—a fire loss of $9,000 and a theft loss of $12,000. The casualty loss deduction is computed as follows:

Adjusted fire loss ($9,000 − $100)	$ 8,900
Adjusted theft loss ($12,000 − $100)	11,900
Total	$20,800
Less: 10% of adjusted gross income	5,000
Casualty loss deduction	$15,800

6. *Other deductions.* In general, this category consists of expenses related to the taxpayer's business or profession that are not deductible from gross income. Included are the costs of professional publications and dues, union dues, safe-deposit box rentals, income tax preparer's fees, business entertainment, and job-related clothing and tools. These miscellaneous deductions are only deductible to the extent that they exceed 2% of adjusted gross income.

EXEMPTIONS

The final step to determine taxable income is to deduct exemptions. The dollar amount of exemptions is determined by multiplying the number of **exemptions** allowed the taxpayer by $2,300 (estimated) in 1992. The exemption allowance will increase in the future because of indexing for inflation. Thus, if a taxpayer has two exemptions in 1992, the dollar amount would be $4,600 ($2,300 × 2). Married persons filing jointly are both considered taxpayers and are allowed one exemption each even though only one spouse has income. An additional exemption may be taken for each dependent.

A dependent for tax purposes is a person who (1) is closely related to the taxpayer or who lived as a member of the taxpayer's family for the entire year; (2) had an income of less than $2,300; (3) received more than half of his or her support from the taxpayer; and (4) who, if married, did not file a joint return with a spouse for the taxable year. An individual eligible to be claimed as a dependent on another taxpayer's return may not deduct any amount as a personal exemption.

Personal exemptions are phased out for certain high-income taxpayers. The phase out begins at different levels of adjusted gross income, depending on the taxpayer's status. For married individuals filing a joint return this level is $150,000, for heads of households it is $100,000, and for married persons filing separately it is $75,000. The reduction is 2% for each $2,500 or fraction thereof in excess of the threshold amount.

Illustration A.13
ESTIMATED TAX RATE SCHEDULE FOR 1992

Schedule X—Single Individuals

If taxable income is:		The tax is:	of the amount
Over—	but not over—		over—
$ 0	$21,450	15%	$ 0
21,450	51,900	$ 3,217.50 plus 28%	21,450
51,900		11,743.50 plus 31%	51,900

Schedule Y-1—Married Persons, Joint Returns

If taxable income is:		The tax is:	of the amount
Over—	but not over—		over—
$ 0	$35,800	15%	$ 0
35,800	86,500	$ 5,370 plus 28%	35,800
86,500		19,566 plus 31%	86,500

Schedule Y-2—Married Persons, Separate Returns

If taxable income is:		The tax is:	of the amount
Over—	but not over—		over—
$ 0	$17,900	15%	$ 0
17,900	43,250	$ 2,685 plus 28%	17,900
43,250		9,783 plus 31%	43,250

Schedule Z—Head of Household

If taxable income is:		The tax is:	of the amount
Over—	but not over—		over—
$ 0	$28,750	15%	$ 0
28,750	74,150	$ 4,312.50 plus 28%	28,750
74,150		17,024.50 plus 31%	74,150

Note: These tax schedules were estimated by Commerce Clearing House before the IRS had issued the official figures. They include the estimated inflation adjustment for 1992.

COMPUTING TAX LIABILITY

Once taxable income has been determined, the tax liability can be computed using the rates given in Illustration A.13. The tax rates in effect for 1992 will be used unless otherwise stated.

To illustrate the use of these rates, assume Mr. and Mrs. Olson file a joint return showing taxable income of $36,280. Their tax liability is computed as follows:

$$\text{Tax} = \$5,370 + [28\% \times (\$36,280 - \$35,800)]$$
$$= \$5,370 + \$134.40$$
$$= \$5,504.40$$

Marginal and Effective Tax Rates

A quick look at the tax rate schedules in Illustration A.13 shows clearly that the rates are progressive. Progressive tax rates increase with successively higher amounts of taxable income. For example, the taxable income of a single taxpayer between $21,450 and $51,900 is taxed at a 28% rate. These percentages are called *marginal tax rates*. A **marginal tax rate** is the rate applied to the next dollar of taxable income or each incremental amount of income. Such rates are important in decision making because they show the marginal effect of a decision. For example, assume that Joe Hardy, a single taxpayer in the 28% tax bracket, could earn $400 on a plumbing job if he would work on Sunday. However, being in the 28% bracket means that Joe would have to pay $112 ($400 × 0.28) more income taxes if he takes the job, which means that he would net only $288 from the job. Joe may decide he would rather watch a football game or go fishing. This type of analysis illustrates the correct use of the marginal tax rate.

The effective tax rate rather than the marginal rate should be used as a measure of total taxes to be paid. The **effective tax rate** is the average rate of taxation of a given amount of taxable income. For example, if Joe Hardy earns $34,600 for the year, he is in the 28% marginal tax rate bracket. However, he does not pay $9,688 ($34,600 × 0.28) per year in taxes. Joe actually pays taxes at a 19.94% rate computed as follows:

$$\frac{\text{Effective}}{\text{(average) tax rate}} = \frac{\text{Total taxes paid}}{\text{Total taxable income}}$$

$$= \frac{(\$3,217.50 + [28\% \times (\$34,600 - \$21,450)])^*}{\$34,600}$$

$$= \frac{\$6,899.50}{\$34,600} = 19.94\%$$

* These rates were taken from Illustration A.13 for a single taxpayer.

CAPITAL GAINS AND LOSSES

Capital assets are all items of property other than inventories, receivables, copyrights, certain governmental obligations, and real and depreciable property used in a trade or business. Investments in capital stocks and bonds are examples of capital assets. A gain is an excess of selling price over cost.

Taxation of Capital Gains

Some capital gains escape taxation. For example, a taxpayer, age 55 or older, may exclude from gross income up to $125,000 ($62,500 on a separate return) of any gain on sale of the taxpayer's home.

All other capital gains are taxed at the same rates as ordinary income, but not to exceed 28%.

The tax law relative to net capital losses is more complex, containing certain limitations. Discussion of these losses is left for a more advanced text.

TAX CREDITS

A **tax credit** is a direct deduction from the amount of taxes to be paid, resulting largely from certain expenditures made by the taxpayer. Since tax credits reduce the amount of taxes to be paid dollar for dollar, they are much more valuable to the taxpayer than deductions. A tax credit of $100 saves $100 of cash; a $100 deduction, on the other hand, is worth only $100 times the taxpayer's marginal tax rate. The maximum value, then, of any deduction in 1992 is 31% of the amount of the deduction since the highest tax rate is 31%.

Tax credits are available for persons with low earned income levels, for the elderly, for child and dependent care expenses, for income taxes paid to foreign countries, and for wages paid in work incentive programs.

FILING THE TAX RETURN

Personal tax returns generally must be filed on or by April 15 of the year following the tax year. Extensions may be filed, but payment of any tax liability is still due by April 15. Most taxpayers are also employees; therefore, taxes are withheld by employers under our pay-as-you-go tax system. Also, taxpayers having income above a prescribed amount that is not subject to withholding must pay an **estimated tax.** This estimated tax must be paid in four installments. Underpayments may be subject to penalties and interest charges. The taxes withheld and the estimated taxes paid are entered as offsets to the total tax liability on the tax return. Any remaining unpaid taxes are paid to the Internal Revenue Service when the return is filed. In some cases, tax withholdings and estimated taxes paid may have exceeded tax liability, and the taxpayer can claim a refund.

COMPREHENSIVE ILLUSTRATION—PERSONAL INCOME TAXES

An actual tax return consists of a number of preprinted forms that are filled out by the taxpayer. Taxpayers will file either Form 1040 EZ (the easy form), Form 1040A (often called the *short form*), or Form 1040 (the *long form*). A taxpayer who intends to itemize deductions or who has taxable income of $50,000 or more may not file either Form 1040 EZ or Form 1040A. A taxpayer who uses the long form generally must attach various schedules to it. Two common schedules included in the long form are Schedule A and Schedule B. Schedule A shows the itemized deductions, while Schedule B lists all dividends and interest income when dividend and interest income exceeds a certain amount. As mentioned earlier in this appendix, one copy

Illustration A.14
JOINT TAX RETURN COMPUTATIONS

Salary		$58,000
Interest income.		4,000
Dividend income		6,000
Capital gain ($10,000) less capital loss ($1,000).		9,000
Adjusted gross income		$77,000
Itemized deductions:		
Medical expense ($5,925 − $5,775; total medical costs less 7.5% of adjusted gross income)	$ 150	
Charitable contributions	2,240	
Taxes (real estate on home, state income)	5,670	
Casualty loss ($8,250 − $7,700; total adjusted casualty losses less 10% of adjusted gross income)	550	
Miscellaneous (professional dues, subscriptions, etc.) [$1,980 − ($77,000 × 0.02)] . . .	440	
	$ 9,050	
Standard deduction amount*	$ 5,700	
Higher of itemized deductions versus standard deduction.		9,050
		$67,950
Exemptions (4 × $2,300)		9,200
Taxable income		$58,750
Income tax ($5,370 + [28% × ($58,750 − $35,800)]		$11,796
Less: Applicable tax credits		–0–
Total tax liability		$11,796
Income taxes withheld	$12,400	
Estimated taxes paid	800	13,200
Income taxes refund due		$ 1,404

* This amount was correct for 1991. The amount for 1992 was not available as of this writing.

of the taxpayer's Form W-2 is attached to the tax return. The W-2 is issued by the employer and shows wages earned and taxes withheld during the period on these wages.

Illustration A.14 shows a brief summary schedule of the tax return items for Lee and Dora Bowman, for 1992, who are married and file a joint return. Lee is chief engineer for a manufacturing company; Dora is a full-time homemaker. Both taxpayers are under age 65; they have two dependent children, ages 13 and 15. Dora owns a number of bonds and shares of stock, some of which she sold during the year, realizing $10,000 of capital gains and $1,000 of capital losses. Total income taxes withheld during the year amounted to $12,400. In addition, Lee and Dora paid estimated taxes of $800. Other information needed to compute the Bowmans' tax liability and tax payment are shown in the illustration. The income tax of $11,796 is computed using the tax rate schedule in Illustration A.13.

DEMONSTRATION PROBLEM A-1

Johnson Company employs four persons as salespersons (all are married) and pays them weekly salaries as shown below. The number of exemptions and weekly deductions for hospital insurance for each employee are also given.

	Weekly Salary	Exemptions	Hospital Insurance
Gail Dammes.	$630	2	$30.00
Christy Adams	750	4	37.50
Deidre Hart.	600	3	37.50
Don Jacobs	465	1	15.00

Each employee has 4% withheld for state income tax and 6% withheld for the retirement plan. Use the wage bracket withholding table in Illustration A.2 to determine the federal income taxes to be withheld.

Required:

a. Prepare the payroll journal for the week ending January 8, 1992, using headings that will accomplish the purpose. (The check numbers are 701–4.) Use 7.65% as the rate for FICA taxes (social security).

b. Assuming that the payroll journal is a memorandum record only, prepare the general journal entry to record the payroll.

c. Prepare the entry to transfer funds from general cash to the special payroll checking account.

d. Prepare the entry to record the employer's payroll taxes using the rates given in this chapter. (In actual practice, this entry often is made only at the end of the month.)

e. Prepare the entry to record the payment on January 11 of the federal income taxes and FICA taxes due to be paid to the federal government. (In actual practice, this entry often is made only at the end of the month or quarter, depending on the amounts involved.)

Solution to demonstration problem A-1

a.

PAYROLL JOURNAL

Date Week Ended 1992	Employee	Gross Pay— Sales Salaries Expense Dr.	Employees' Federal Income Taxes Payable Cr.	FICA Taxes Payable Cr.	Employees' State Income Taxes Payable Cr.	Employees' Medical Insurance Premiums Payable Cr.	Employees' Retirement Plan Premiums Payable Cr.	Salaries Payable (Net Pay) Cr.	Check No.
Jan. 8	Gail Dammes	630.00	71.00	48.20	25.20	30.00	37.80	417.80	701
	Christy Adams	750.00	76.00	57.38	30.00	37.50	45.00	504.12	702
	Deidre Hart	600.00	60.00	45.90	24.00	37.50	36.00	396.60	703
	Don Jacobs	465.00	52.00	35.57	18.60	15.00	27.90	315.93	704
		2,445.00	259.00	187.05	97.80	120.00	146.70	1,634.45	

b. 1992

Jan. 8   Sales Salaries Expense. 2,445.00
         Employees' Federal Income Taxes Payable . .   259.00
         FICA Taxes Payable 187.05
         Employees' State Income Taxes Payable . . .   97.80
         Employees' Medical Insurance Premiums
            Payable 120.00
         Employees' Retirement Plan Premiums
            Payable 146.70
         Salaries Payable 1,634.45
         To record the payroll for the week ending
         January 8.

c. 1992

Jan. 8   Salaries Payable 1,634.45
         Cash 1,634.45
         To record the transfer of funds to cover the
         January 8 payroll.

d. 1992

Jan. 8   Payroll Taxes Expenses 338.64
         FICA Taxes Payable 187.05
         State Unemployment Taxes Payable 132.03
         Federal Unemployment Taxes Payable 19.56
         To record payroll taxes on the January 8 payroll.

e. Jan. 11   Employees' Federal Income Taxes Payable 259.00
                 FICA Taxes Payable 374.10
                 Cash 633.10
                 To record payment of federal income taxes
                 payable and FICA taxes payable from the
                 January 8 payroll.

DEMONSTRATION PROBLEM A-2

The records of Tyler Corporation show the following for the calendar year just ended:

Sales.	$281,250
Interest earned on—	
State of New Jersey bonds	2,250
City of Miami bonds	1,125
Essex County, Ohio, School District No. 2 bonds	565
Cost of goods sold and other expenses	236,250
Allowable extra depreciation deduction under modified ACRS.	3,375
Dividends declared	11,250
Revenue received in advance, considered taxable income of this year	2,250
Contribution made to influence legislation (included in the $236,250 listed	
above)	225

Required:

a. Prepare a schedule showing the computation of taxable income.

b. Compute the amount of the corporation's tax that was payable for the current year. (Use the rates mentioned in this appendix.)

c. Prepare the adjusting entry necessary to recognize federal income taxes expense, assuming income tax allocation procedures are followed. The only permanent differences are the contribution to influence legislation and the nontaxable interest.

Solution to demonstration problem A-2

a.

TYLER CORPORATION
Computation of Taxable Income
Current Year

Sales.		$281,250
Cost of goods sold and other expenses		236,250
Operating income.		$ 45,000
Other income: Interest		3,940
Book income before taxes.		$ 48,940
Adjustments for permanent differences:		
Interest (all governmental; nontaxable).	$(3,940)	
Contribution (not deductible)	225	3,715
Income on which to compute tax expense		$ 45,225
Adjustments for temporary differences:		
Revenue received in advance	$ 2,250	
Additional depreciation	(3,375)	(1,125)
Taxable income.		$ 44,100

---

b. Computation of tax: $15\% \times \$44,100 = \$6,615$

c.

Federal Income Taxes Expense.	6,783.75*	
Federal Income Taxes Payable		6,615.00
Deferred Federal Income Taxes Payable.		168.75

  * Federal Income Taxes Expense is computed as follows:

      Computation of taxes:
      $15\% \times \$45,225 = \$6,783.75$
      Tax expense = $6,783.75
      Tax payable from *(b)* = $6,615

NEW TERMS

Accelerated Cost Recovery System (ACRS)   A tax method of depreciation that assigns depreciable assets to particular classes that have specified lives for depreciation purposes. *1142*

Adjusted gross income   Gross income minus business expenses and several other items. *1150*

Capital assets   All items of property **other than** inventories, receivables, copyrights, certain governmental obligations, and real or depreciable property used in a trade or business. Examples include investments in capital stocks and bonds. *1154*

Deductions (itemized)   Deductions from adjusted gross income for items such as contributions, interest on mortgage, certain taxes, limited casualty losses, limited medical expenses, casualty losses, and limited "nonbusiness" expenses. *1151*

Deductions for adjusted gross income   Most business expenses, payments to individual retirement plans, and certain other minor items. *1150*

Deductions from adjusted gross income   Specified by law; either standard deduction amount or itemized deductions. *1150*

Deductions from gross earnings   Required payroll deductions, such as federal and state income taxes withheld, FICA taxes withheld, and other deductions, such as medical insurance premiums and union dues. *1125*

Effective tax rate   The average rate of taxation on a given amount of taxable income. *1154*

Employee earnings record   A record maintained by an employer for each employee (see Illustration A.4) showing such details as hours worked, pay rate, gross pay, deductions, net pay, and personal biographical data. *1130*

Employee's Withholding Allowance Certificate (Form W-4)   The form (see Illustration A.1) on which an employee indicates the number of exemptions to be used in calculating federal (and state) income tax withheld. *1125*

Employer's Quarterly Federal Tax Return (Form 941)   A form used to report the amount of FICA and withholding taxes for a quarter. *1135*

Estimated tax   A tax that must be paid in four installments by persons having amounts of income above a certain level that are not subject to withholding. *1155*

Exemption   A fixed amount ($2,300 in 1992) the taxpayer may deduct from adjusted gross income for the taxpayer, the spouse, and each dependent. *1152*

Fair Labor Standards Act   See Wages and Hours Law.

Federal depository bank   A bank authorized to accept deposits of taxes by employers for credit to the Internal Revenue Service. *1135*

Federal (state) income tax withheld   The amount withheld for federal (state) income taxes deducted from employee earnings by the employer and remitted to the appropriate governmental agency under the pay-as-you-go system of government financing. *1125*

Federal unemployment tax   A tax of 6.2% levied on the first $7,000 of wages paid per employee to help finance the joint federal-state system of unemployment compensation. A credit of up to 5.4% may be taken for amounts paid to a state unemployment fund, thus reducing the rate to 0.8%. *1134*

FICA (social security) tax   The amount deducted from an employee's wages and paid into a special fund used to pay retirement and other benefits. In 1992, the rate was 7.65% on the first $55,500 of wages paid. The employer also pays a similar amount. *1129*

Gross earnings   Total pay or compensation of an employee, including regular pay and overtime premium. *1124*

Gross income   Includes all income from whatever source derived, except for a few specifically excluded items. *1148*

Head of household   An unmarried or legally separated person (and one married to a nonresident alien) who maintains a residence for a relative or a dependent. *1148*

Interperiod income tax allocation   A procedure whereby the tax effects of an element of expense or revenue, or loss or gain, that will affect taxable income are allocated to the period in which the item is recognized for accounting purposes, regardless of the period in which it is recognized for tax purposes. *1145*

Itemized deductions   See Deductions (itemized).

Loss carryback   A current loss that has been applied against taxable income of prior periods, thereby resulting in a tax refund in the current period. *1141*

Loss carryforward   A current loss that will be applied against taxable income in future periods, thereby reducing the taxes payable in future periods. *1141*

Marginal tax rate   The rate applied to the next dollar of taxable income or each incremental amount of income. *1154*

Merit rate   A reduction in the state unemployment tax rate below 5.4% as a reward for low turnover and few layoffs. *1134*

Minimum wage   Lowest hourly compensation an employer may pay an employee as required by the Wages and Hours Law. *1124*

Modified ACRS   A tax method of depreciation that assigns assets to particular groups that have specified lives for depreciation purposes. The 1986 Tax Reform Act modified the existing accelerated cost recovery system. *1143*

Payroll checking account   A separate checking account used only for payroll checks. Each payday, funds are transferred from the general Cash account to cover the amount of the payroll checks. One of the purposes is to keep the "clutter" of outstanding payroll checks from making more complex the reconciliation of the general Cash account. *1132*

Payroll journal   A formal record showing the details of each payroll, including gross pay, deductions, net pay, and check number for each employee (see Illustration A.5). It may be used as a book of original entry (in which case postings to accounts would be made from it) or it may be only a memorandum record. *1130*

Pegboard system of payroll accounting   A system that aligns the payroll check, the earnings record, and the payroll journal in such a way that all three are completed simultaneously with one writing. *1138*

Permanent differences   Differences between taxable income and pre-tax income caused by tax provisions that exclude an item of expense, revenue, gain, or loss as an element of taxable income. *1144*

Social security tax   See FICA tax.

Standard deduction amount   The standard deduction amount may be taken in lieu of itemized deductions. *1150*

State unemployment tax   A tax of 5.4% (typically) on the first $7,000 of gross earnings per employee per year to finance unemployment benefits. A **merit rate** for not laying off employees may reduce the percent below 5.4%. *1134*

Taxable income   Adjusted gross income minus deductions, minus exemptions; the amount of income on which taxes payable is computed. *1150*

Tax credit   A direct reduction of the amount of taxes payable. *1155*

Temporary (or timing) differences   Differences between taxable income and financial statement pre-tax income caused by items that affect both taxable income and pre-tax income, but in different periods. *1144*

Timecard   A form used to maintain a record of when an employee reports to and leaves work; it is used as a source document for calculating gross pay. *1122*

Vacation pay   Compensation received by employees while on vacation; it is actually earned by employees in the periods worked prior to the vacation. *1137*

Wage and Tax Statement (Form W-2)   A form that the employer must furnish to each employee after the end of the year showing gross wages, amounts withheld, and net pay (see Illustration A.3). It is used by the employee in preparing his or her personal federal income tax return. *1126*

Wage bracket withholding table   A table supplied by the IRS (see Illustration A.2) that shows the amount of federal income tax to be withheld given the wage paid and the number of withholding allowances claimed. *1126*

Wages and Hours Law (Fair Labor Standards Act)   Requires that most employees be paid at least $1\frac{1}{2}$ times their normal rate for hours worked in excess of 40 hours per week. It also requires that at least the minimum wage be paid. *1124*

Withholding allowances   A means of adjusting income taxes withheld from employee periodic earnings for exemptions that will be claimed on the income tax return. *1125*

SELF-TEST

True-False

Indicate whether each of the following is true or false.

1. FICA tax is a tax of 6.2% on the first $7,000 of wages paid per employee.

2. Gross earnings of an employee who is paid a flat amount per week or month regardless of the number of hours worked in a period are commonly referred to as wages.

3. The federal Wages and Hours Law requires that most employees who are paid by the hour be paid a minimum of one-and-one-half times their normal rate for hours worked in excess of 40 per week.

4. Income before federal income taxes as shown on the company's income statement must agree with taxable income as shown on the company's tax return.

5. Itemized deductions on an individual's tax return often include real estate taxes, interest on mortgage, and charitable contributions.

Multiple-Choice

Select the best answer for each of the following.

1. For the most effective control over payroll accounting, employees should be:
   a. Paid in cash monthly.
   b. Paid in cash weekly.
   c. Paid by check or cash, however they desire.
   d. Paid by check on a regular, established schedule.

2. A form that every employee is required to file with his or her employer reporting the number of exemptions is:
   a. W-4.
   b. W-2.

   c. Payroll register.
   d. Paycheck

3. The FICA and federal income taxes that have been withheld from the employee but not yet paid to the government are:
   a. Long-term liabilities.
   b. Current liabilities.
   c. Expenses.
   d. Revenue.

4. Permanent differences between income before taxes (per the income statement) and taxable income (per the tax return) include all of the following except:
   a. Life insurance proceeds received.

b. Costs of attempting to influence legislation.

c. Goodwill amortization expense.

d. Depreciation expense on a building.

5. All of the following filing statuses may be used in filing an income tax return except:

a. Minor.

b. Head of household.

c. Single.

d. Married filing jointly or married filing separately.

Now turn to page 1169 to check your answers.

QUESTIONS

1. Describe some of the purposes of a payroll accounting system.

2. List the various functions regarding payroll and give a method for establishing internal control over these functions.

3. Describe how the system of internal control relating to payroll works. (Begin with the recording of time and end with the issuance of the paycheck.)

4. Identify some schemes involving payroll that have been used to defraud a company.

5. Why should a distinction be made between employees and independent contractors? Give an example of each.

6. What requirements does the Wages and Hours Law place on employers? Why should accurate records be maintained as to hours worked by employees?

7. List the common deductions from gross pay.

8. What is the purpose of the Employee's Withholding Allowance Certificate (Form W-4)?

9. What purposes does the Wage and Tax Statement (Form W-2) serve?

10. Against which parties are FICA taxes levied and in what amounts?

11. What is the purpose of the Employer's Quarterly Federal Tax Return (Form 941)?

12. What are the federal and state rates for unemployment tax? What is a merit rate and what effect does it have on the credit granted by the federal government for amounts paid to the state?

13. Why should an employer maintain an individual earnings record for each employee?

14. Describe two ways in which the payroll journal might be utilized in the payroll accounting system.

15. Under what conditions would the use of a special payroll checking account be desirable? How does such an account operate?

16. What are the arguments for and against accruing employer's payroll taxes at the end of the accounting period?

17. What payroll procedures might be employed that would be more efficient than the system described in the chapter? Why are these other methods not always used in a given system?

18. A classmate states: "Why all the fuss about deferring revenues and recognizing expenses sooner for tax purposes? All net taxable income is taxed eventually anyway. It is only a matter of putting off the payment. I don't think these manipulations are worth the effort." Comment.

19. What factors might cause net income on a corporation's income statement to differ from its taxable income?

20. Classified among the long-term liabilities of A Corporation is an account entitled Deferred Federal Income Taxes Payable. Explain the nature of this account.

21. Define the term *adjusted gross income* as it is used for personal income tax purposes.

22. For what kinds of expenditures may personal deductions be taken on one's personal federal income tax return?

23. What are exemptions, and by how much does each one reduce taxable income?

EXERCISES

Note: Unless directed otherwise, use 1992 federal income tax rates for exercises involving individuals.

Determine withholding amounts for employees

A–1. Stringer Company employs four persons whose weekly wages and exemptions are as follows:

	Wage	Exemptions
Ken Thomas	$645	4
Frank Joiner	465	2
Laura Gaskin	570	3
Kathy Bowden	810	5

Assume these employees are married. Using Illustration A.2, determine the correct amount to withhold for federal income tax per week.

Compute maximum weeks of unemployment taxes

A–2. Using the data in Exercise A–1, calculate how many weeks it would take before the employer would no longer incur federal or state unemployment taxes on each individual.

Compute FICA taxes

A–3. Using the data in Exercise A–1 and assuming a rate of 7.65% on a maximum base of $55,500, how much would the employer withhold for FICA tax from each employee for the entire year? How much would the employer's FICA tax expense be for the year?

Prepare journal entry to record payroll

A–4. The January 15, 1992, gross payroll for salaries of Linker Corporation is $7,200. The total federal income tax withheld is $1,575. The employees' share of FICA taxes withheld is $550.80. What is the correct entry at the time of payment, assuming no prior recording of salaries? (Ignore federal and state unemployment taxes.)

Compute difference in payroll taxes under two alternatives	**A–5.** Donna Blake is trying to decide whether to hire four workers to perform a particular job at $54,000 each per year, or 12 workers to perform a particular job on a part-time basis at $18,000 each per year. Using the rates given in this appendix, calculate the difference in the employer's payroll tax expense under the two alternatives.
Prepare journal entry to record unemployment taxes	**A–6.** Lensey Company is in a state that has a state unemployment rate of 5.4%. Due to a record of stable employment, the company has earned a merit rate of 4.8%. Total wages on which it incurred federal and state unemployment taxes for March were $22,500. Prepare an entry to record federal and state unemployment taxes for March.
Prepare journal entries to record accrued wages and payroll taxes	**A–7.** At the end of December, Tatum Company had accrued wages of $1,500 ($750 for sales salaries, $450 for office salaries, and $300 for maintenance wages). The company makes the accrual for payroll taxes on accrued wages. Assume that no employee has earned over $55,500 (including the above wages) and that unemployment taxes still accrue only on the maintenance wages. Prepare the necessary adjusting entry to accrue the wages and payroll taxes.
Prepare journal entry to record unaccrued payroll taxes	**A–8.** Using the data in Exercise A–7, what entry would the company make if it did not follow the practice of accruing payroll taxes on accrued wages?
Compute corporate tax liability	**A–9.** *a.* Damron Corporation has taxable income of $30,000, $75,000, and $105,000 in its first three years of operations. Determine the amount of federal income taxes Damron will incur each year. *b.* Assume that in the fourth year of operations, Damron Corporation suffered a loss of $142,500. How much could it recover in back taxes?
Prepare journal entry to record income tax chargeable and tax liability for the year	**A–10.** The before-tax income reported on the income statement of Garwood Corporation for a given year amounts to $300,000, while its taxable income is only $200,000. The difference is attributable entirely to additional modified ACRS depreciation taken for tax purposes. If the current income tax rate is assumed to be 40%, give the entry to record the income tax expense for the year and the taxes payable for the year.
Determine number of exemptions allowed	**A–11.** Mark Dean is 68 years old, and his wife is 65 years old and blind. They have three sons, ages 22, 24, and 29. The son who is 22 is a full-time student in college and does not claim himself as an exemption. His parents contribute $6,000 per year toward his living expenses, which is more than one half of his support. The other two sons are self-supporting. How many exemptions are Mark and his wife entitled to on their joint return?
Compute tax liability	**A–12.** Alan Bowden has gross income of $60,000, deductions from gross income of $3,000, itemized deductions of $2,250, and six full exemptions (two personal and four dependent). He is filing a joint return with his wife, who has no income. How much is their tax liability? (Use the 1992 rates, $2,300 per exemption, and assume a $5,700 standard deduction amount.)

PROBLEMS

Compute FICA taxes, unemployment taxes, and total employer tax expense

A–1. Bridges Company has 18 employees and an annual payroll of $525,000; 4 employees earn $94,500 each per year; and 14 employees earn $10,500 each per year.

Required:

a. What is the annual FICA tax (1) for the employer and (2) for the employees? (Use rates shown for 1992.)

b. What is the amount of federal and state unemployment tax per year, assuming a federal rate of 6.2% and a state rate of 5.4% for this employer?

c. Which of the preceding items would constitute expenses on the records of Bridges Company?

Prepare journal entries to record payroll, FICA taxes, unemployment taxes, and payment of taxes

A–2. Jackson Company pays its employees once each month. The payroll data for October are as follows:

Gross payroll	$61,800	(One employee is above the $7,000 limit. Prior to October, the employee's gross salary was $55,500, and the employee's gross October salary was $6,300.)
Federal income tax withheld	$ 6,600	
FICA tax	?	
State income tax	3% of gross salary	

Required:

Prepare entries to record:

a. The October payroll.

b. The employer's FICA tax for October (use 1992 rates).

c. The employer's federal and state unemployment taxes, assuming that the federal rate is 6.2% and the state rate is 5.4%.

d. Payment of the various taxes.

Prepare payroll journal, record payroll, record employer's payroll taxes, and record transfer of funds to payroll checking account

A–3. Fraker Company employs six persons in its fast-food franchise operation. The names of the employees, weekly wages, and number of exemptions are as follows:

Employee	Weekly Wage	Number of Exemptions
Michael Frame	$900	4
Rick Buchanan	525	2
Linda Garner	510	3
Robert Lucas	675	1
Nancy Pope	555	2
Jerry Taylor	495	5

State income tax is withheld from employees at the rate of 5% on all wages paid. All of the employees are married.

Required:

a. Prepare a payroll journal with the following headings: Date Week Ended, Employee, Gross Pay—Salaries Expense Dr., Employees' Federal Income Taxes Payable Cr., FICA Taxes Payable Cr., Employees' State Income Taxes Payable Cr., Salaries Payable (Net Pay) Cr., and Check No.

b. Using the withholding table and rates given in this appendix (including 7.65% for FICA taxes using 1992 rates, 6.2% for federal unemployment, and 5.4% for state unemployment), enter the payroll data in the payroll journal for the week ending January 8, 1992. Check numbers used were 405–10.

c. Assuming the payroll journal is used as a memorandum record, prepare an entry as it would appear in the general journal to record the payroll.

d. Prepare the entry to record the employer's payroll taxes for FICA and unemployment.

e. Prepare the entry to record the transfer of funds to the special payroll checking account on January 8.

Prepare journal entries to account for accrued payroll

A–4. At the end of the year (1992), Haggard Company has $45,000 of accrued wages ($22,500 sales salaries; $13,500 delivery wages; and $9,000 office salaries). Of this total, $37,500 are subject to FICA tax, and $12,000 are subject to unemployment taxes.

Required:

a. Describe the two alternatives the company may follow in making the adjusting entry and explain why these alternatives exist.

b. Prepare the adjusting entry under the two alternatives. (Use the 7.65% rate mentioned in this appendix for FICA, 6.2% for federal unemployment, and 5.4% for state unemployment.)

Prepare schedule showing computation of taxable income; compute the tax liability

A–5. The records of Chandler Corporation show the following for the calendar year just ended:

Sales	$562,500
Nontaxable interest earned on—	
State of New York bonds	4,500
City of Detroit bonds	2,250
Howard County, Ohio, School District No. 1 bonds	564
Cost of goods sold and other expenses	472,500
Loss on sale of asset	4,500
Gain on sale of asset acquired two years ago	11,250
Allowable extra depreciation deduction for tax purposes	6,750
Dividends declared	22,500
Revenue received in advance, considered taxable income of this year .	4,500
Contribution made to influence legislation (included in the $472,500 listed above)	450

Required:

a. Present a schedule showing the computation of taxable income.

b. Compute the corporation's tax for the current year. (Use the tax rates mentioned in this appendix.)

Prepare schedule
showing
computation of
tax liability;
calculate yearly
allocation of tax
expense; prepare
journal entries;
prepare
T-accounts

A–6. Peterson Company expects to have income before depreciation and income taxes of $450,000 each year for the period 1992–95. The company acquired an asset for $540,000, which is expected to last four years and have no scrap value at the end of that period. For financial accounting purposes, the company uses the straight-line depreciation method; and for tax purposes, the property is three-year modified ACRS property. Assume that the recovery percentages are 25%, 37.5%, 18.75%, and 18.75% for each of the four years, respectively. Assume the tax rate is 40% (for the sake of simplicity) and no other items exist that cause differences between income before taxes on the income statement and taxable income.

Required:

a. Prepare a schedule showing the actual tax liability for each year.

b. Calculate the income tax expense that should be shown each year, assuming income tax allocation procedures are to be used.

c. Prepare journal entries to record the income tax expense and income tax liability for each year.

d. Show how the entries prepared in part *(c)* would be summarized in T-accounts. How would the amounts appearing in these accounts eventually be cleared from the accounts?

Calculate taxable
income

A–7. Ben Taylor was about to calculate his taxable income for 1992. He gathered together the following information:

Gross wages	$37,500
Interest received on savings account	1,800
Capital gain	19,500
Contribution to individual retirement account	
(not participant in employer pension plan)	3,375
Property taxes on residence	4,275
State income tax	5,400
Mortgage interest paid	9,450
Contributions to church	4,050

     Mr. Taylor is married and files a joint return. He has two young children who live with him and his wife. Assume a standard deduction of $5,700.

Required:

Calculate the amount of taxable income for 1992 for Mr. and Mrs. Taylor.

BUSINESS DECISION PROBLEMS

Recommend
procedures to
strengthen
internal control
over payroll

A–1. Phil Gordon operates a fine restaurant and employs 15 employees. He is interested in food preparation, supervision of servers, and customer relations. He has little aptitude for record-keeping. As a result, he hired Brian Wood to do all of the paperwork for the business. Brian's duties include preparing the payroll, keeping payroll records, signing the payroll checks, distributing the payroll checks, and reconciling the bank account. The payroll checks are written on the general Cash account rather than on a special payroll checking account.

Business seems good, but the cash position keeps getting tighter. Wages expense seems somewhat higher than Mr. Gordon believes it should be. Mr. Wood assures Mr. Gordon that all is well regarding payroll. Mr. Gordon suspects something is wrong regarding the payroll function.

Required:

a. What could be wrong?

b. What would you recommend to Mr. Gordon to correct the situation?

Determine which payroll system to use with alternative number of employees

A–2. Lisa Carr owns and runs a motel and has 10 employees. She has one opportunity to acquire a chain of five other motels (with an additional 50 employees). A second opportunity exists to acquire a second chain of 20 other motels (with an additional 200 employees). She will only consider acquiring the second chain if she acquires the first chain.

Ms. Carr is wondering about which type of payroll system to use, given the fact that she may have 10, 60, or 260 employees. Estimated costs of three alternative payroll systems are as follows:

	Clerical Cost per Employee/Week	Cost of Forms per Employee/Week	Service Charge per Week
Manual system	$2.25	$0.30	$ 0
Pegboard system	0.75	0.45	15*
Computer Service Bureau.	0.375	0.15	150

* An initial charge for pegboard equipment expressed as a weekly charge.

Required:

Calculate the cost per week of using each system for 10, 60, and 260 employees, respectively. Which system is the least costly alternative considering each possible total number of employees?

ANSWERS TO SELF-TEST

True-False

1. *False.* Federal unemployment tax is a tax of 6.2% on the first $7,000 of wages paid per employee. FICA tax is a tax on both the employee and the employer of 7.65% on the first $55,500 and 1.45% on amounts over $55,500 up to $130,200 that each employee earns annually.

2. *False.* Gross earnings of an employee who is paid a flat amount per week or month regardless of the number of hours worked in a period are commonly referred to as salary.

3. *True.* The federal Wages and Hours Law requires that most employees who are paid by the hour be paid a minimum of one-and-a-half times their normal rate for hours worked in excess of 40 worked per week.

4. *False.* These two amounts usually differ because of permanent and timing differences.

5. *True.* All of these items (and others) are included among itemized deductions.

Multiple-Choice

1. *d.* By paying by check on a regular, established schedule, effective internal control is strengthened over payroll accounting.

2. *a.* This is also known as Employee's Withholding Allowance Certificate.

3. *b.* The FICA and federal income taxes withheld but not yet paid are current liabilities to the employer.

4. *d.* Depreciation expense on a building is a timing difference.

5. *a.* "Minor" is not one of the filing statuses that may be used in filing an income tax return.

B ACCOUNTING SYSTEMS AND SPECIAL JOURNALS

INTRODUCTION

In the early part of the text you learned how to produce financial statements by processing the raw data of business transactions through the steps of the accounting cycle. The process of analyzing, recording, classifying, summarizing, and reporting business transactions is the same for all businesses. However, the speed and efficiency of the processing depend on the accounting system used.

For example, assume you decide to drive home after your accounting class. You can either go home the "long way" by using the side roads or "make time" by using the superhighway. Whichever route you take, your destination is going to be the same—home. The process of going home is the same whether you take the side roads or the superhighway—you are driving your car. However, the system you use to get to your destination—the side roads or the superhighway—is different. You probably decide to take the superhighway because it is faster. The accounting process also can be accomplished faster and more efficiently by using one particular accounting system. This chapter identifies various accounting systems and describes their features.

In this text you have used the manual accounting system with one general journal and one general ledger. This appendix introduces you to two additions to that manual system—subsidiary ledgers and special journals. Then, you will proceed to a discussion of other systems used in accounting, ending with computerized accounting systems. An understanding of the concepts contained in this appendix will enable you to process business transactions in a more efficient manner.

THE PROCESSING OF DATA—MANUAL SYSTEM

The masses of raw data generated by even a small business are not useful until processed. Businesses must routinely process these data in an orderly and efficient manner to accomplish the following:

1. Determine and report on a timely basis the results of operations (income statement) and financial position (balance sheet) of the firm.
2. Pay bills when due.

3. Send correct quantities and items of inventory to customers.
4. Conduct other aspects of business, such as sending invoices to customers and ordering merchandise, in an orderly and purposeful manner.
5. Efficiently prepare reports required by the government or regulatory agencies.

Businesses accomplish this orderly and efficient processing of accounting data by using the accounting system that best fits their needs. The basic accounting system is the manual system with one general journal and one general ledger. Usually, very small businesses use this basic system. Given an unlimited amount of time, all businesses could process their business transactions through this manual system. However, as a business grows, its number of business transactions also grows, and the company looks for ways to speed up the accounting process by streamlining its accounting system.

An accounting system can be defined as a set of records (journals, ledgers, work sheets, trial balances, and reports) plus the procedures and equipment regularly used to process business transactions. To be effective, accounting systems should:

1. Provide for the efficient processing of data at the least possible cost. (The cost of the system should be less than the value of the benefits received.)
2. Ensure a high degree of accuracy.
3. Provide for internal control to prevent theft or fraud.
4. Provide for the growth of a business.

In this appendix, you will learn first how a business begins to expand its accounting system by using control accounts in the general ledger and adding subsidiary ledgers that show the details of these control accounts. Then, you will learn about other journals (called *special journals*) that companies use along with the general journal.

CONTROL ACCOUNTS AND SUBSIDIARY LEDGERS

To process information efficiently, a business must adapt its accounting system to the type and quantity of information it needs. When a business has only a few customers and suppliers, it can set up a separate account for each customer and supplier in the general ledger. However, when a business has many customers and suppliers, it establishes a control account for accounts receivable and a control account for accounts payable in the general ledger. Also, the business adds subsidiary ledgers for receivables and payables to the accounting system to show the balances for individual customers and suppliers.

A **control account** is an account in the general ledger that shows the total balance of all the subsidiary accounts related to it. An example of a control account is the general ledger *Accounts Receivable* control account. This account summarizes all the amounts owed to the company. Since this account is a summary account, it would be impossible to send out individual customer statements showing a summary of each customer's purchases, payments, and balance due based on the summary data provided in this account.

Subsidiary ledger accounts show the details supporting the related general ledger control account balance. Companies may use the subsidiary ledger accounts for *receivables* to send out customer statements. They may use the subsidiary ledger accounts for *payables* to determine the amount payable to each supplier. Usually, companies alphabetize these accounts by the name of the customer or supplier rather than numbering the accounts. At the time a company prepares its financial statements, the sum of the balances in the subsidiary accounts in a subsidiary ledger should agree with the balance in the related general ledger control account.

A **subsidiary ledger,** then, is a group of related accounts showing the details of the balance of a general ledger control account. **Subsidiary ledgers are in a separate book or computer file from the general ledger.** Having separate subsidiary ledgers shortens the general ledger trial balance. Also, having separate subsidiary ledgers promotes a division of labor.

In T-account form, the relationship between a control account and subsidiary accounts is as follows:

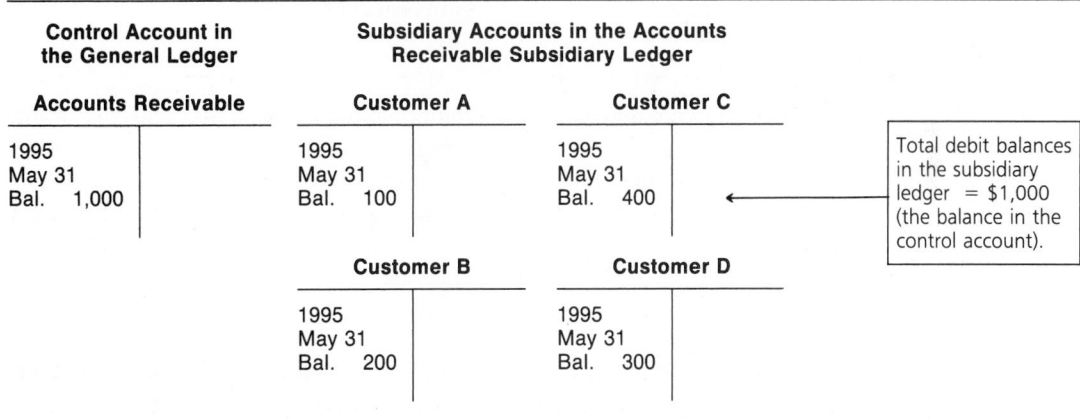

Note that the sum of all balances in the subsidiary accounts ($100 + $200 + $400 + $300) on May 31, 1995, is equal to the balance on that same date in the control account ($1,000).

When a transaction occurs that affects a control account, the transaction also affects at least one of the accounts in the subsidiary ledger. A transaction is entered in the journal before it is entered in the ledger accounts. Thus, the journal entry must indicate the subsidiary ledger account(s) affected by the transaction. Then, posting will be made to both the control account (indicated by the account number) and the subsidiary ledger account (indicated by the √). For example, if a company makes a $400 sale on July 10 to Debby Kahan on account, the journal entry would be:

```
1995
July 10   Accounts Receivable—D. Kahan . . . . . . . . .   103/√    400
               Sales . . . . . . . . . . . . . . . . . . . . . .   410              400
          To record sale of merchandise on account.
```

The amount of the sale ($400) would be posted as a debit to both the Accounts Receivable control account (103) in the general ledger and D. Kahan's account in the subsidiary ledger (indicated by the √) and as a credit to the Sales account (410) in the general ledger.

Detailed subsidiary ledgers may exist for other accounts in the general ledger in addition to the Accounts Receivable account. Some examples of accounts that frequently have detailed subsidiary ledgers are:

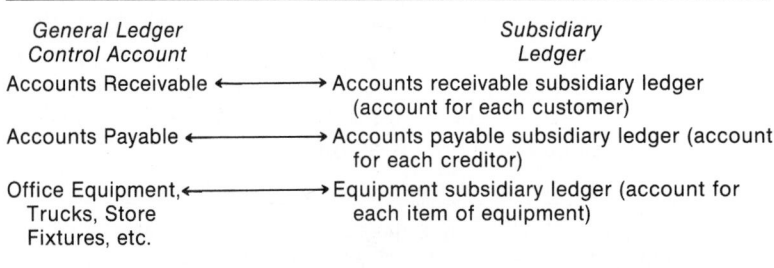

General Ledger Control Account	Subsidiary Ledger
Accounts Receivable ⟷	Accounts receivable subsidiary ledger (account for each customer)
Accounts Payable ⟷	Accounts payable subsidiary ledger (account for each creditor)
Office Equipment, Trucks, Store Fixtures, etc. ⟷	Equipment subsidiary ledger (account for each item of equipment)

The number of subsidiary ledgers maintained by a company varies according to the company's information requirements. Companies generally set up control accounts and subsidiary ledgers whenever they have many transactions in a given account and they need detailed information about these transactions on a continuing basis. This chapter focuses on the use of an accounts receivable subsidiary ledger and an accounts payable subsidiary ledger.

In the next section, you will learn about special journals. You should remember that companies may use control accounts and subsidiary ledgers even if they do not use special journals. Both subsidiary ledgers and special journals are likely to be used when companies have numerous similar transactions.

SPECIAL JOURNALS

Throughout this text only one book of original entry, the general journal, has been used to record transactions. As the transactions of a company increase, the first step in altering the manual accounting system is usually to use special journals along with the original general journal. Each **special journal** is a book of original entry that records one particular type of transaction, such as sales on account, cash receipts, purchases on account, or cash disbursements.

The advantages of using special journals are:

1. *Saves time in journalizing.* Each transaction takes only one line; a full description is usually not necessary. Special journals reduce the amount of writing because it is not necessary to repeat the account titles printed at the top of the special column or columns.
2. *Saves time in posting.* Many amounts are posted as column totals rather than individually.
3. *Eliminates detail from the general ledger.* Column totals are posted to the general ledger. The details remain in the special journals.
4. *Promotes division of labor.* Several persons can work simultaneously on the accounting records. This specialization and division of labor pinpoints responsibility and allows for more rapid location of errors.
5. *Aids in management analysis.* The journals themselves can be useful to management in analyzing classes of transactions, such as credit sales, because all similar transactions are in one place.

Special journals, then, systematize the original recording of major recurring types of transactions. The number and format of the special journals used in a company depend primarily on the nature of the company's business transactions. The special journals illustrated in this chapter are the sales, cash receipts, purchases, and cash disbursements journals.

- The **sales journal** records all sales of merchandise on account (on credit).
- The **cash receipts journal** records all inflows of cash into the business.
- The **purchases journal** records all purchases of merchandise on account (on credit). Merchandise refers to items of inventory that are available for sale to customers.
- The **cash disbursements journal** records all payments (or outflows) of cash by the business.

The use of special journals does *not* eliminate the *general journal*. The **general journal** records all transactions that cannot be entered in one of the special journals, such as adjusting entries and closing entries. All five of these journals are books of original entry. If a transaction is recorded in any one of the journals, that transaction will be posted and become part of the accounting records. Therefore, a transaction recorded in a special journal should *not* also be recorded in the general journal because the entry would then be recorded twice.

The Posting Reference column in the ledger should indicate the source of the posting. The abbreviations used in this text for the five journals are:

	Journal	Transaction	Abbreviation
Special Journals	Sales journal	Merchandise sold on account	S
	Cash receipts journal	Cash receipts from all sources	CR
	Purchases journal	Merchandise purchased on account	P
	Cash disbursements journal	Cash payments for all purposes	CD
	General journal	Any transactions that are not included in the special journals are recorded in the general journal	G

The sections that follow will show you how to use each of the four special journals. We place you in the position of "keeping the books." In other words, you are the "bookkeeper," or accounting clerk, for John Mason Company, a retail clothing store. As you study these journals, you will realize how effective they are in facilitating the recording process.

Sales Journal

Companies normally make sales either for cash or on account (on credit). They use the sales journal for sales on account and the cash receipts journal for cash sales. The simplest form of sales journal has only one money column (labeled Accounts Receivable Dr. and Sales Cr.) because every sale on account is journalized by this same debit and credit. The headings in this form of sales journal might appear as follows:

Date	Customer	Invoice No.	Accounts Receivable Dr. Sales Cr.	
			Amount	√

Variations in the sales journal will depend on the information needs of the business. For example, a company could use a separate Sales Cr. column for each department. If a company does this, it will need a separate column for Accounts Receivable Dr. because the debit will always be to Accounts Receivable regardless of which department sold the goods. The headings in a sales journal with separate columns for each department might appear as follows:

Accounts Receivable Dr.		Date	Customer	Invoice No.	Sales Cr.		
Amount	√				Dept. A	Dept. B	Dept. C

In either format, the customer's name is necessary to know which subsidiary ledger account is affected by the sales transaction. The invoice number simply provides documentation that a sale actually occurred. The column with the check mark is similar to a Posting Reference column. A check mark in that column indicates that the amount of the transaction has been posted to the customer's accounts receivable subsidiary ledger account. The column heading indicates which account(s) should be debited or credited for the column total.

Illustration B.1 on page 1178 shows a sales journal with only one money column for John Mason Company. In Illustration B.1, five credit sales transactions occurred in April. Each sale is backed up by an invoice showing the customer name and address, a description of the items sold, dollar amount, and credit terms. The invoice number for each sale is listed in the sales journal.

Posting the Sales Journal. As John Mason Company's bookkeeper, you would post the individual amounts in the money column daily to each individual customer's account in the subsidiary ledger. The daily posting shows the amount currently due from the customer. As you post each individual amount, you place a check mark, $\sqrt{}$, in the column headed $\sqrt{}$ opposite the amount. This check shows that you have posted the amount. You should also enter the posting reference of S1 in the accounts receivable subsidiary ledger accounts as each amount is posted. At the end of the month, you would post the total of the money column, $290, in the general ledger as a debit to the Accounts Receivable control account and as a credit to the Sales account. Then, you would enter the posting reference of S1 in the Accounts Receivable control account and the Sales account. Next, you would write the account numbers, 103 for Accounts Receivable and 410 for Sales in the sales journal under the total of the money column to show that you posted $290 to these accounts.

As shown in Illustration B.1, when you have completed the posting of accounts receivable, the Accounts Receivable control account in the general ledger will show a balance of $290. This $290 is equal to the sum of the balances in the accounts receivable subsidiary ledger accounts, assuming no previous balances were in the control account or the subsidiary accounts. Since the composition of the accounts receivable subsidiary ledger accounts is constantly changing, companies usually do not number these accounts but keep them in alphabetical order.

Cash Receipts Journal

Companies use the cash receipts journal for all transactions involving the receipt of cash. The most frequent types of cash receipts transactions are cash sales and collections on accounts receivable. Therefore, separate credit columns appear for those items in the cash receipts journal shown in Illustration B.2 on page 1180. Notice that three of the transactions recorded in the cash receipts journal were collections of accounts receivables that were recorded in the sales journal.

Many other types of transactions may result in the receipt of cash by the business, but these transactions involve various accounts as the credits.

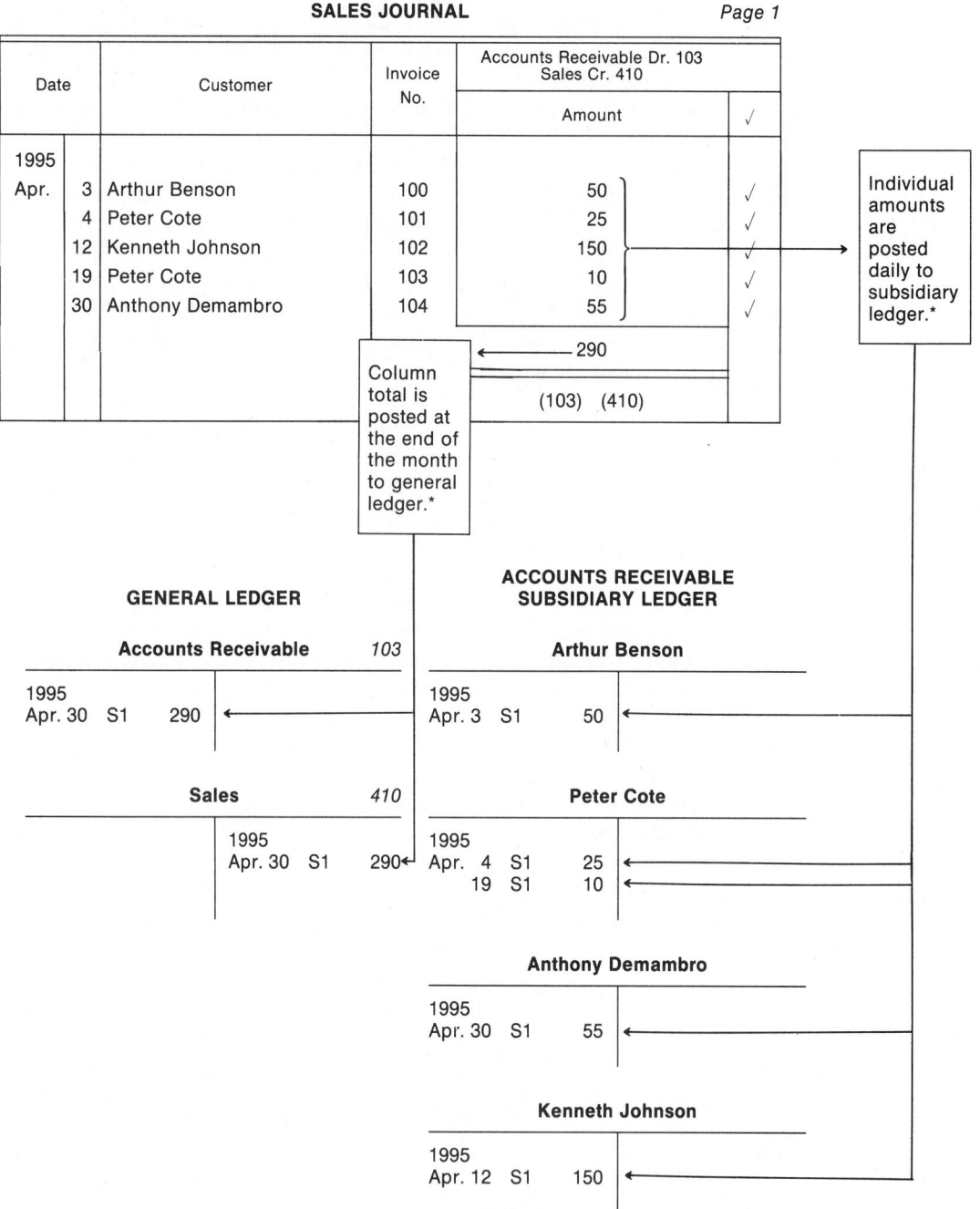

JOHN MASON COMPANY
SALES JOURNAL   *Page 1*

Date	Customer	Invoice No.	Accounts Receivable Dr. 103 Sales Cr. 410	
			Amount	√
1995				
Apr. 3	Arthur Benson	100	50	√
4	Peter Cote	101	25	√
12	Kenneth Johnson	102	150	√
19	Peter Cote	103	10	√
30	Anthony Demambro	104	55	√
			290	
			(103) (410)	

Individual amounts are posted daily to subsidiary ledger.*

Column total is posted at the end of the month to general ledger.*

GENERAL LEDGER

ACCOUNTS RECEIVABLE SUBSIDIARY LEDGER

Accounts Receivable   *103*

1995		
Apr. 30	S1	290

Arthur Benson

1995		
Apr. 3	S1	50

Sales   *410*

	1995		
	Apr. 30	S1	290

Peter Cote

1995		
Apr. 4	S1	25
19	S1	10

Anthony Demambro

1995		
Apr. 30	S1	55

Kenneth Johnson

1995		
Apr. 12	S1	150

* Subsidiary ledger accounts are posted daily to keep up-to-date balances in the subsidiary ledger. These up-to-date balances are needed in case a customer calls to ask the balance owed, for instance. The general ledger accounts will usually be posted at end-of-month or end-of-page (whichever comes first) because the balances in the control accounts are not really necessary until the end of the period for financial statement purposes.

Since these **other accounts** do not occur with enough frequency to warrant special columns, they appear in the *Other Accounts Cr.* column of the cash receipts journal. However, if after several months or periods, a certain transaction appears regularly in the Other Accounts Cr. column, the company might want to revise its format of the cash receipts journal to provide a special column for that type of transaction. For example, a company that has several rental properties may wish to provide a column for Rental Revenue Cr. in the cash receipts journal. An Other Accounts Dr. column could be included to handle transactions such as the sale of a machine (discussed in Chapter 8) where the company has a debit to at least one other account besides the Cash account. The totals of the debit columns should equal the total of the credit columns in every special journal.

Posting the Cash Receipts Journal. You would post the individual amounts in the Accounts Receivable Cr. column daily to the customers' accounts in the accounts receivable subsidiary ledger to keep the customer balances current. You would also post the items in the Other Accounts Cr. column daily to the individual accounts indicated (Accounts 130 and 420). You would post the totals of the Cash Dr., Sales Discounts Dr., Sales Cr., and Accounts Receivable Cr. columns at the end of the month to their respective general ledger accounts.

The amounts appearing in the Other Accounts Cr. column normally pertain to different accounts. Thus, you would not post the column total. You would place the letter "X" in parentheses (X) immediately below the column total. This letter "X" in parentheses indicates that you have not posted the amount shown as the column total to any account.

The ledger accounts in Illustration B.2 show only the postings of the cash receipts journal of John Mason Company.

After you have posted John Mason's sales and cash receipts journals in Illustrations B.1 and B.2, the Accounts Receivable control account in the general ledger appears as follows:

Date		Explanation	Post. Ref.	Debit	Credit	Balance
		Accounts Receivable				*Account No. 103*
1995						
Apr.	30		S1	2 9 0		2 9 0 Dr.
	30		CR5		2 2 5	6 5 Dr.

Illustration B.3 on page 1182 shows the subsidiary accounts at the same point in time.

You would prepare a **schedule of accounts receivable** at the end of the period to ensure that the total of the balances in the accounts receivable

Illustration B.2
CASH RECEIPTS JOURNAL

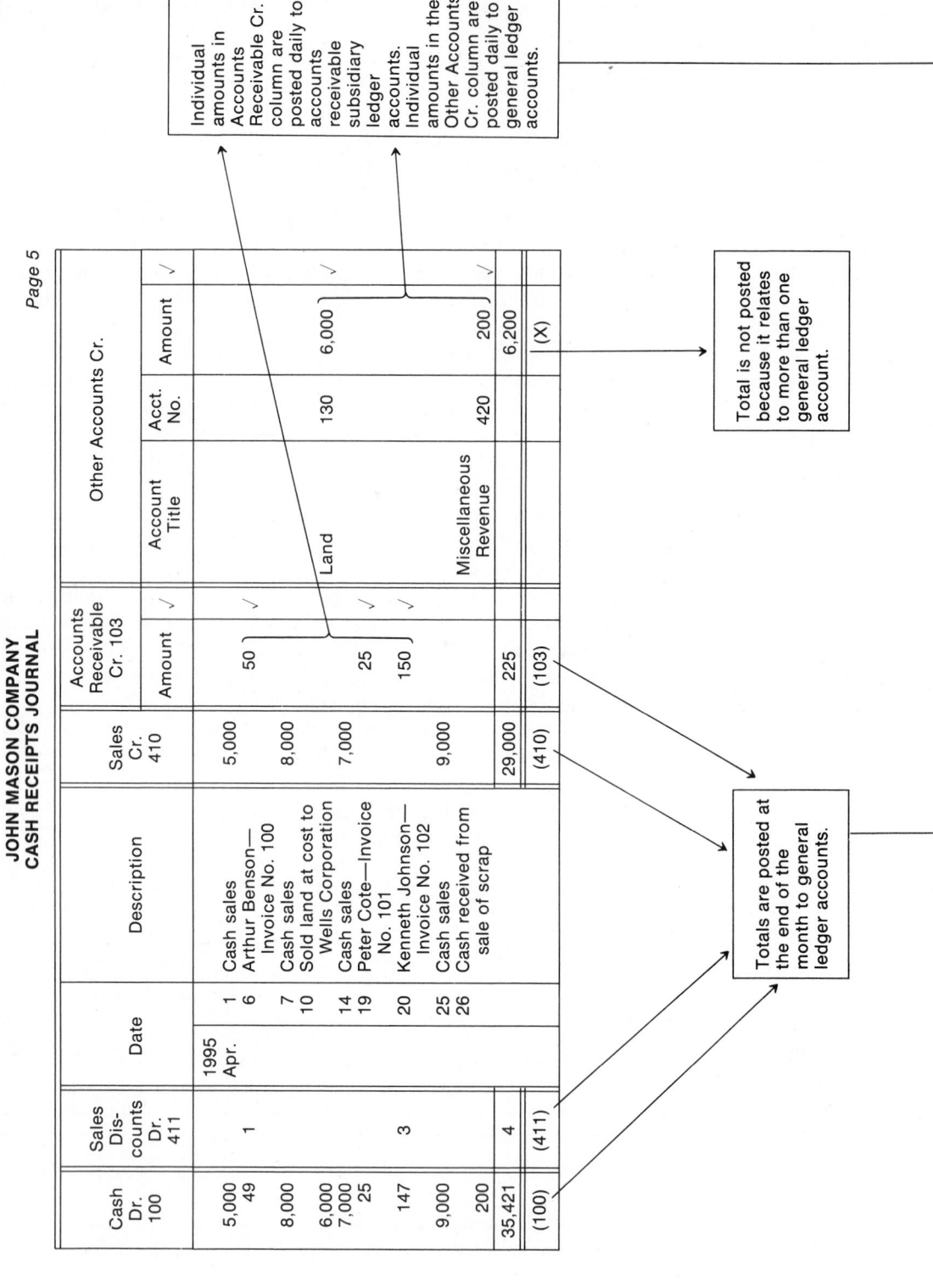

JOHN MASON COMPANY
CASH RECEIPTS JOURNAL

Page 5

Individual amounts in Accounts Receivable Cr. column are posted daily to accounts receivable subsidiary ledger accounts.

Individual amounts in the Other Accounts Cr. column are posted daily to general ledger accounts.

Total is not posted because it relates to more than one general ledger account.

Totals are posted at the end of the month to general ledger accounts.

Cash Dr. 100	Sales Discounts Dr. 411	Date	Description	Sales Cr. 410	Accounts Receivable Cr. 103 Amount	✓	Other Accounts Cr. Account Title	Acct. No.	Amount	✓
		1995 Apr.								
5,000		1	Cash sales	5,000						
49	1	6	Arthur Benson—Invoice No. 100		50	✓				
8,000		7	Cash sales	8,000						
6,000		10	Sold land at cost to Wells Corporation				Land	130	6,000	✓
7,000		14	Cash sales	7,000						
25		19	Peter Cote—Invoice No. 101		25	✓				
147	3	20	Kenneth Johnson—Invoice No. 102		150	✓				
9,000		25	Cash sales	9,000						
200		26	Cash received from sale of scrap				Miscellaneous Revenue	420	200	✓
35,421	4			29,000	225				6,200	
(100)	(411)			(410)	(103)				(X)	

1180

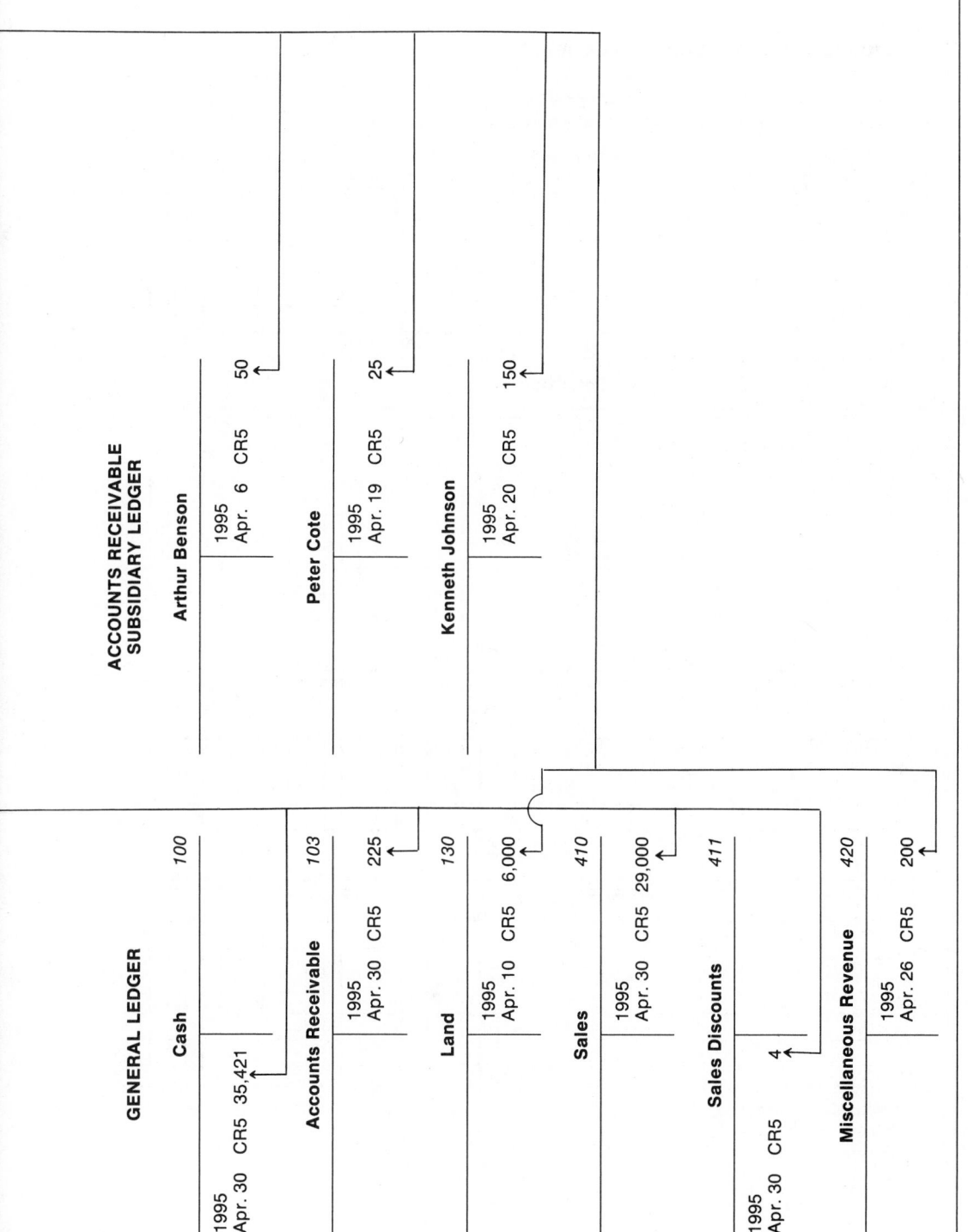

ACCOUNTS RECEIVABLE SUBSIDIARY LEDGER

Arthur Benson

1995		
Apr. 6	CR5	50

Peter Cote

1995		
Apr. 19	CR5	25

Kenneth Johnson

1995		
Apr. 20	CR5	150

GENERAL LEDGER

Cash   *100*

1995		
Apr. 30	CR5	35,421

Accounts Receivable   *103*

1995		
Apr. 30	CR5	225

Land   *130*

1995		
Apr. 10	CR5	6,000

Sales   *410*

1995		
Apr. 30	CR5	29,000

Sales Discounts   *411*

1995		
Apr. 30	CR5	4

Miscellaneous Revenue   *420*

1995		
Apr. 26	CR5	200

1181

Illustration B.3
ACCOUNTS RECEIVABLE SUBSIDIARY LEDGER

JOHN MASON COMPANY
ACCOUNTS RECEIVABLE SUBSIDIARY LEDGER
Arthur Benson

Date		Explanation	Post. Ref.	Debit	Credit	Balance
1995						
Apr.	3		S1	5 0		5 0 Dr.
	6		CR5		5 0	- 0 -

Peter Cote

Date		Explanation	Post. Ref.	Debit	Credit	Balance
1995						
Apr.	4		S1	2 5		2 5 Dr.
	19		S1	1 0		3 5 Dr.
	19		CR5		2 5	1 0 Dr.

Anthony Demambro

Date		Explanation	Post. Ref.	Debit	Credit	Balance
1995						
Apr.	30		S1	5 5		5 5 Dr.

Kenneth Johnson

Date		Explanation	Post. Ref.	Debit	Credit	Balance
1995						
Apr.	12		S1	1 5 0		1 5 0 Dr.
	20		CR5		1 5 0	- 0 -

subsidiary ledger agrees with the control account. This schedule is merely a listing of open account balances. An example of this schedule for John Mason Company follows:

JOHN MASON COMPANY
Schedule of Accounts Receivable
April 30, 1995

Peter Cote	$10
Anthony Demambro	55
Balance in the control account.	$65

Purchases Journal

Companies use the purchases journal to record all purchases of merchandise made on account. Several formats can be used for the purchases journal. One common format has only one money column headed Purchases Dr. and Accounts Payable Cr. The headings in a purchases journal with one money column might be as follows:

Date	Creditor	Terms	Invoice No.	Purchases Dr. Accounts Payable Cr.	
				Amount	√

Note that the above purchases journal has a Terms column. The sales journal discussed in the previous section did not have a Terms column because a company's terms are generally the same for each customer. However, the purchases journal uses a Terms column because various creditors often differ in the terms they offer a company. Persons responsible for paying the company's bills must know the terms offered on purchased merchandise so they can pay for the merchandise within the discount period. Cash discount terms are based on the date of the invoice. We assume that the date of purchase and the date of the invoice are the same.

Often companies make purchases for several departments. When management wants to keep the purchases of each department separate, a purchases journal could provide a separate column for the purchases of each department and a separate column headed Accounts Payable Cr. The headings in such a purchases journal might appear as follows:

Purchases Dr.			Date	Creditor	Terms	Invoice No.	Accounts Payable Cr.	
Dept. A	Dept. B	Dept. C					Amount	√

Illustration B.4 on page 1186 shows the John Mason Company purchases journal with one money column. Note that John Mason made eight purchases of merchandise on account during the month.

Posting the Purchases Journal.   You would post the individual amounts in the money column daily to the accounts payable subsidiary ledger so that the subsidiary account balances will be current at all times. Then, at the end of the month, you would post the money column total to the general ledger Purchases account as a debit and to the general ledger Accounts Payable control account as a credit.

Cash Disbursements Journal

The cash disbursements journal records all transactions that involve the payment of cash. To have an acceptable level of control over cash disbursements, most companies pay all bills by check. Therefore, the cash disbursements journal (Illustration B.5 on page 1188) contains a column in which to record the number of the check written for each disbursement.

· Payments on accounts payable constitute a major type of cash disbursement transaction. These accounts payable were initially recorded in the purchases journal when the purchases on account were made. Therefore, the cash disbursements journal provides a separate column entitled Accounts Payable Dr. Many payments on account involve a purchase discount, so this journal provides a separate column for discounts (Purchase Discounts Cr.). John Mason Company frequently purchases numerous supplies by writing a check, so its cash disbursements journal has a separate column for Supplies Expense (Supplies Expense Dr.). As with other special journals, companies adapt the cash disbursements journal to their individual needs. For instance, a company could add an Other Accounts Cr. column to record transactions such as the purchase of land by paying cash and giving a note, since the company must credit an additional account besides Cash.

Posting the Cash Disbursements Journal.   As shown in Illustration B.5, you would post individual items in the Accounts Payable Dr. column daily to accounts in the accounts payable subsidiary ledger. You would post individual items in the Other Accounts Dr. column daily to the appropriate accounts in the general ledger. Then, you would post the column totals for Accounts Payable Dr., Supplies Expense Dr., Cash Cr., and Purchase Discounts Cr. at the end of the month to accounts in the general ledger. However, you would not post the total of the Other Accounts Dr. column. Illustration B.5 shows only the amounts in the accounts from the posting of the cash disbursements journal to make it easier to trace the postings.

After you have posted both the purchases journal and cash disbursements journal, the general ledger Accounts Payable control account appears as follows:

			Accounts Payable					Account No. 200	
Date		Explanation	Post. Ref.	Debit	Credit	Balance			
1995 Apr.	30		P10		2 4 1 0 0	2 4 1 0 0	Cr.		
	30		CD7	1 8 3 0 0		5 8 0 0	Cr.		

Illustration B.6 on pages 1190–91 shows the accounts payable subsidiary ledger of John Mason Company after the posting of the purchases journal and the cash disbursements journal.

At the end of the period, a **schedule of accounts payable** is prepared to make certain that the total of the balances in the accounts payable subsidiary ledger accounts agrees with the balance in the Accounts Payable control account. The schedule for John Mason Company appears below.

JOHN MASON COMPANY
Schedule of Accounts Payable
April 30, 1995

Booth Corporation	$1,500
Mertz Company.	300
Nelson Company	4,000
Balance in the control account	$5,800

General Ledger Illustrated

After you have posted all four special journals, the general ledger appears as shown in Illustration B.7, pages 1191–94.

General Journal

As stated earlier in the chapter, each transaction that does not fit in a special journal would appear in the general journal. For example, a company could use the general journal to record the receipt of a note from a customer in settlement of an account receivable. A note would allow the company to begin earning interest on the amount due. Note the following example of such an entry:

Notes Receivable	120	2,000	
Accounts Receivable—A. Smith	103/√		2,000
To record the receipt of a 60-day, 12% note from Alex Smith in settlement of his account receivable.			

Illustration B.4
PURCHASES JOURNAL

JOHN MASON COMPANY
PURCHASES JOURNAL

Page 10

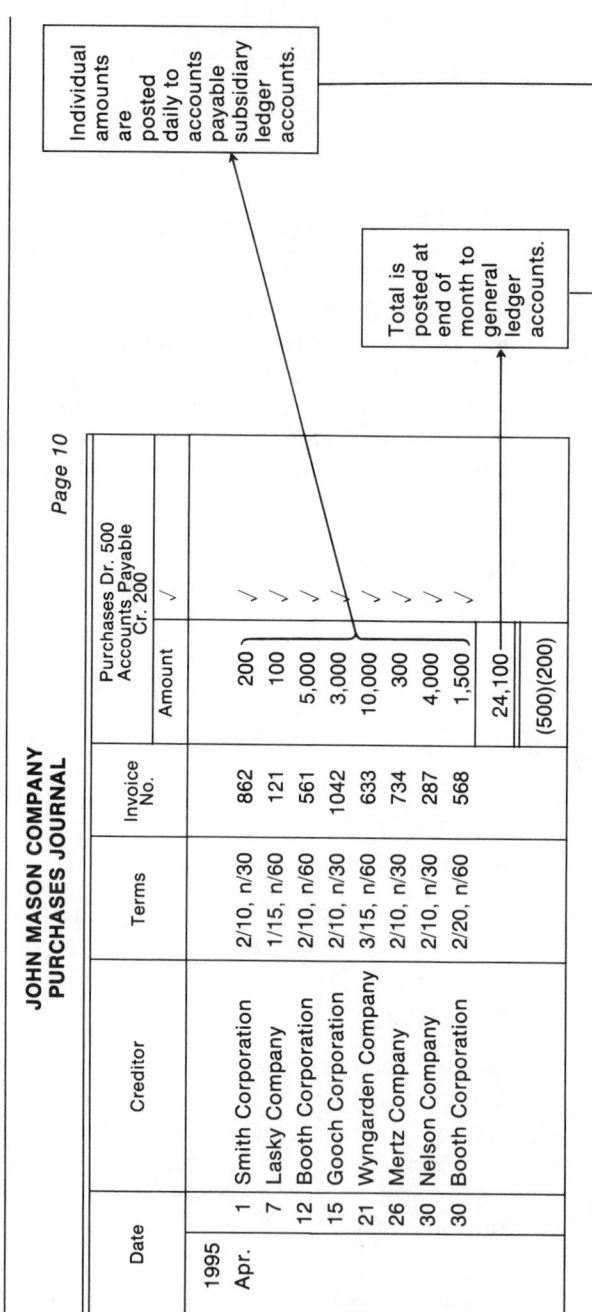

Date		Creditor	Terms	Invoice No.	Purchases Dr. 500 Accounts Payable Cr. 200	
					Amount	✓
1995						
Apr.	1	Smith Corporation	2/10, n/30	862	200	✓
	7	Lasky Company	1/15, n/60	121	100	✓
	12	Booth Corporation	2/10, n/60	561	5,000	✓
	15	Gooch Corporation	2/10, n/30	1042	3,000	✓
	21	Wyngarden Company	3/15, n/60	633	10,000	✓
	26	Mertz Company	2/10, n/30	734	300	✓
	30	Nelson Company	2/10, n/30	287	4,000	✓
	30	Booth Corporation	2/20, n/60	568	1,500	✓
					24,100	
					(500)(200)	

Individual amounts are posted daily to accounts payable subsidiary ledger accounts.

Total is posted at end of month to general ledger accounts.

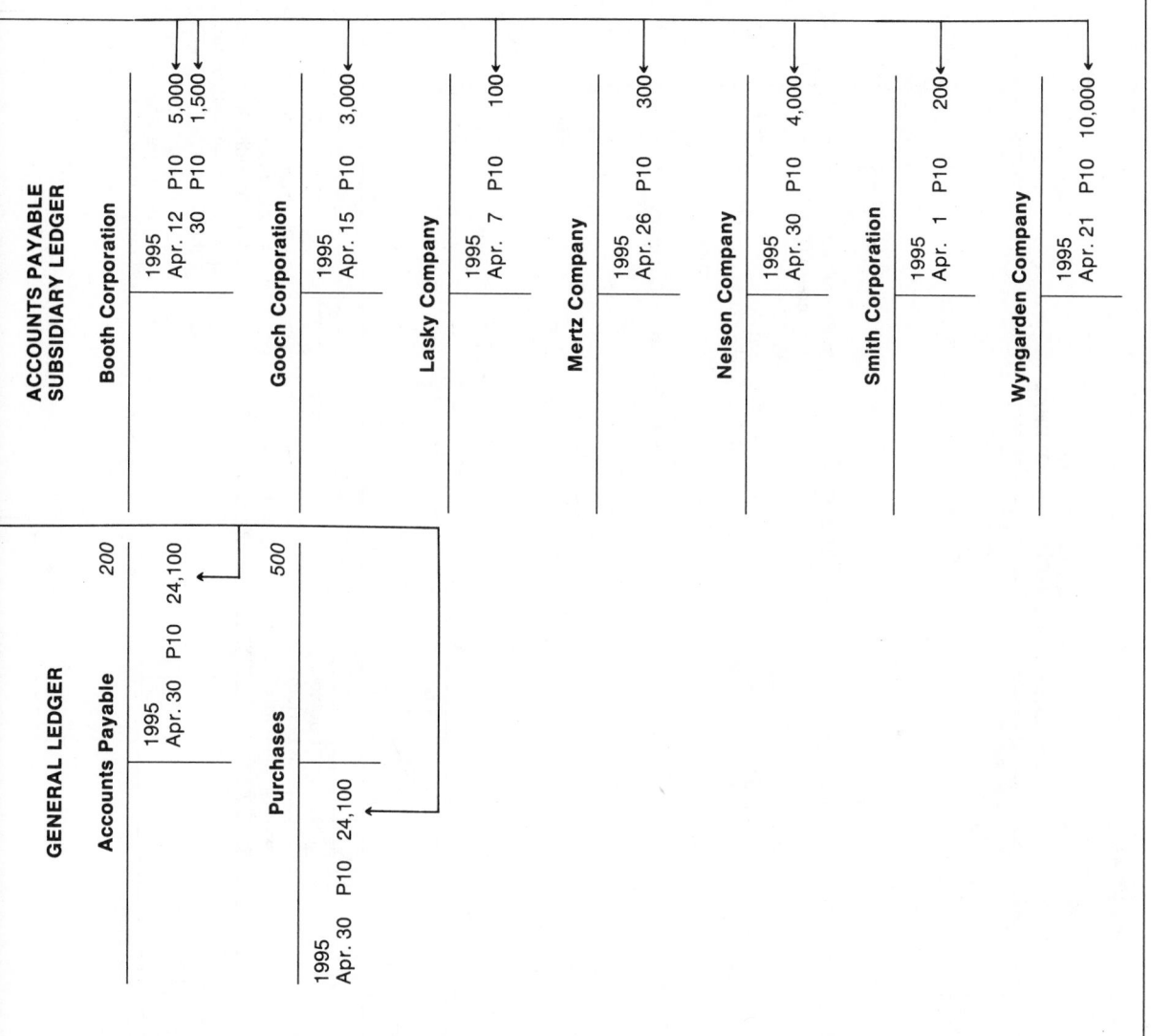

GENERAL LEDGER

Accounts Payable

				200
1995				
Apr. 30	P10	24,100		

Purchases

				500
1995				
Apr. 30	P10	24,100		

ACCOUNTS PAYABLE SUBSIDIARY LEDGER

Booth Corporation

1995		
Apr. 12	P10	5,000
30	P10	1,500

Gooch Corporation

1995		
Apr. 15	P10	3,000

Lasky Company

1995		
Apr. 7	P10	100

Mertz Company

1995		
Apr. 26	P10	300

Nelson Company

1995		
Apr. 30	P10	4,000

Smith Corporation

1995		
Apr. 1	P10	200

Wyngarden Company

1995		
Apr. 21	P10	10,000

Illustration B.5
CASH DISBURSEMENTS JOURNAL

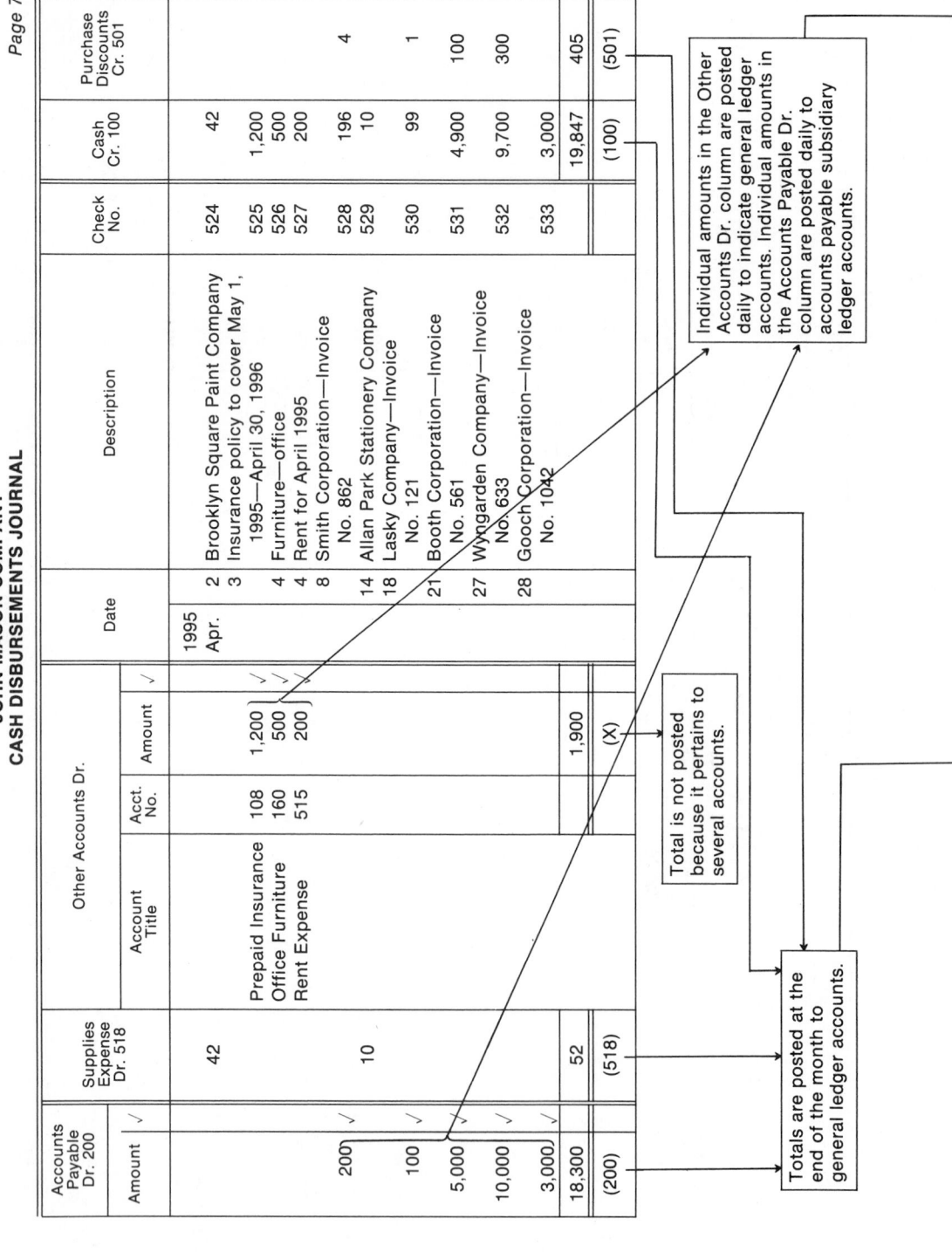

JOHN MASON COMPANY
CASH DISBURSEMENTS JOURNAL

Page 7

Accounts Payable Dr. 200		Supplies Expense Dr. 518	Other Accounts Dr.				Date	Description	Check No.	Cash Cr. 100	Purchase Discounts Cr. 501
Amount	√		Account Title	Acct. No.	Amount	√					
		42					1995 Apr.				
							2	Brooklyn Square Paint Company	524	42	
			Prepaid Insurance	108	1,200	√	3	Insurance policy to cover May 1, 1995—April 30, 1996	525	1,200	
			Office Furniture	160	500	√	4	Furniture—office	526	500	
			Rent Expense	515	200	√	4	Rent for April 1995	527	200	
200	√						8	Smith Corporation—Invoice No. 862	528	196	4
		10					14	Allan Park Stationery Company	529	10	
100	√						18	Lasky Company—Invoice No. 121	530	99	1
5,000	√						21	Booth Corporation—Invoice No. 561	531	4,900	100
10,000	√						27	Wyngarden Company—Invoice No. 633	532	9,700	300
3,000	√						28	Gooch Corporation—Invoice No. 1042	533	3,000	
18,300		52			1,900					19,847	405
(200)		(518)			(X)					(100)	(501)

Individual amounts in the Other Accounts Dr. column are posted daily to indicate general ledger accounts. Individual amounts in the Accounts Payable Dr. column are posted daily to accounts payable subsidiary ledger accounts.

Total is not posted because it pertains to several accounts.

Totals are posted at the end of the month to general ledger accounts.

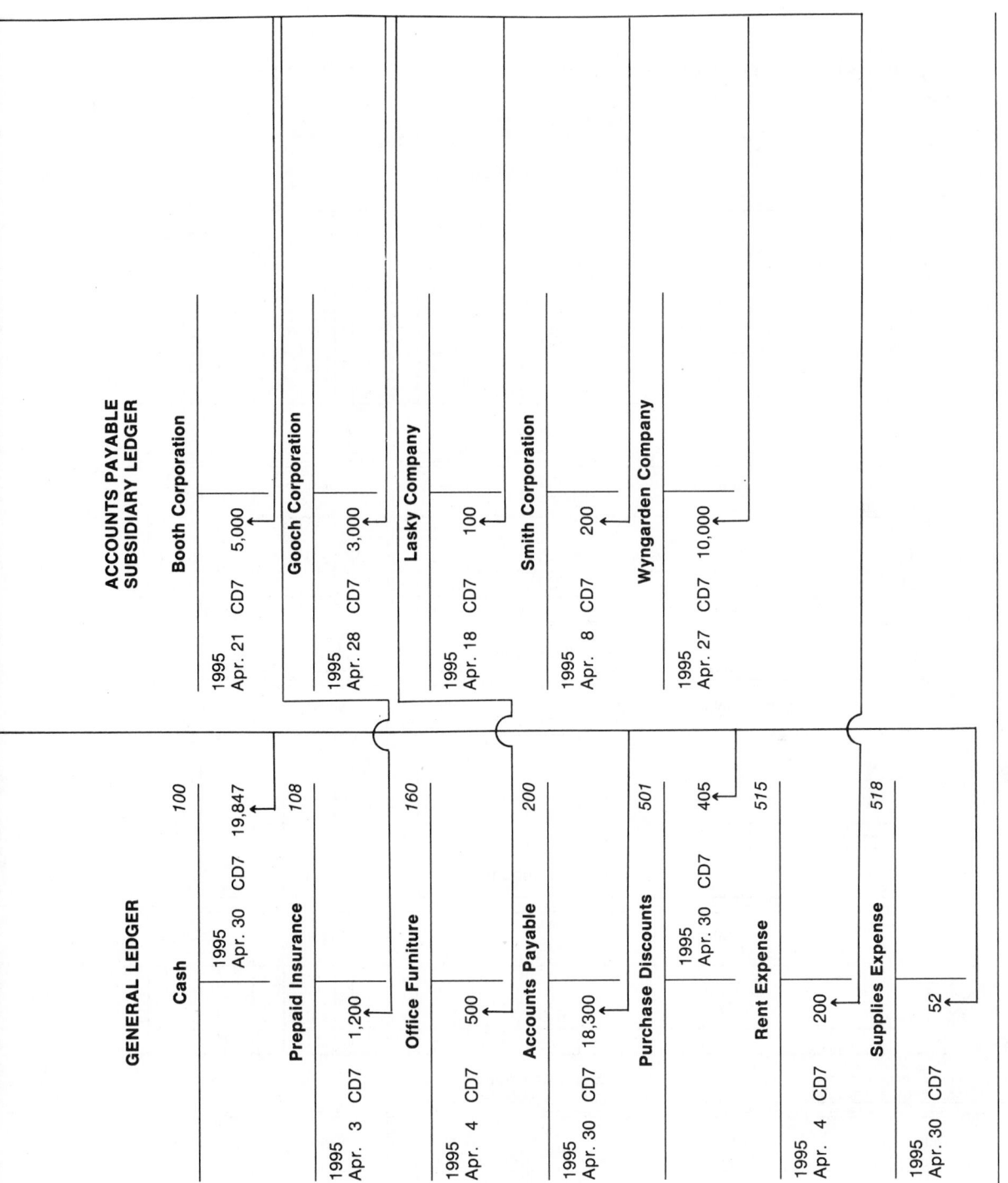

Illustration B.6
ACCOUNTS PAYABLE SUBSIDIARY LEDGER

JOHN MASON COMPANY
ACCOUNTS PAYABLE SUBSIDIARY LEDGER
Booth Corporation

Date		Explanation	Post. Ref.	Debit	Credit	Balance
1995						
Apr.	12		P10		5 0 0 0	5 0 0 0 Cr.
	21		CD7	5 0 0 0		– 0 –
	30		P10		1 5 0 0	1 5 0 0 Cr.

Gooch Corporation

Date		Explanation	Post. Ref.	Debit	Credit	Balance
1995						
Apr.	15		P10		3 0 0 0	3 0 0 0 Cr.
	28		CD7	3 0 0 0		– 0 –

Lasky Company

Date		Explanation	Post. Ref.	Debit	Credit	Balance
1995						
Apr.	7		P10		1 0 0	1 0 0 Cr.
	18		CD7	1 0 0		– 0 –

Mertz Company

Date		Explanation	Post. Ref.	Debit	Credit	Balance
1995						
Apr.	26		P10		3 0 0	3 0 0 Cr.

Nelson Company

Date		Explanation	Post. Ref.	Debit	Credit	Balance
1995						
Apr.	30		P10		4 0 0 0	4 0 0 0 Cr.

Illustration B.6 *(concluded)*

Smith Corporation

Date		Explanation	Post. Ref.	Debit	Credit	Balance
1995						
Apr.	1		P10		2 0 0	2 0 0 Cr.
	8		CD7	2 0 0		– 0 –

Wyngarden Company

Date		Explanation	Post. Ref.	Debit	Credit	Balance
1995						
Apr.	21		P10		1 0 0 0 0	1 0 0 0 0 Cr.
	27		CD7	1 0 0 0 0		– 0 –

Illustration B.7
GENERAL LEDGER

JOHN MASON COMPANY
GENERAL LEDGER

Cash   *Account No. 100*

Date		Explanation	Post. Ref.	Debit	Credit	Balance
1995						
Apr.	1	Beginning balance (assumed)				1 0 0 0 0 Dr.
	30		CR5	3 5 4 2 1		4 5 4 2 1 Dr.
	30		CD7		1 9 8 4 7	2 5 5 7 4 Dr.

Accounts Receivable   *Account No. 103*

Date		Explanation	Post. Ref.	Debit	Credit	Balance
1995						
Apr.	30		S1	2 9 0		2 9 0 Dr.
	30		CR5		2 2 5	6 5 Dr.

Illustration B.7   *(continued)*

Prepaid Insurance   *Account No. 108*

Date		Explanation	Post. Ref.	Debit	Credit	Balance
1995 Apr.	3		CD7	1 2 0 0		1 2 0 0 Dr.

Land   *Account No. 130*

Date		Explanation	Post. Ref.	Debit	Credit	Balance
1995 Apr.	1	Beginning balance (assumed)				1 8 0 0 0 Dr.
	10		CR5		6 0 0 0	1 2 0 0 0 Dr.

Office Furniture   *Account No. 160*

Date		Explanation	Post. Ref.	Debit	Credit	Balance
1995 Apr.	4		CD7	5 0 0		5 0 0 Dr.

Accounts Payable   *Account No. 200*

Date		Explanation	Post. Ref.	Debit	Credit	Balance
1995 Apr.	30		P10		2 4 1 0 0	2 4 1 0 0 Cr.
	30		CD7	1 8 3 0 0		5 8 0 0 Cr.

Capital Stock   *Account No. 300*

Date		Explanation	Post. Ref.	Debit	Credit	Balance
1994 Apr.	1	Beginning balance (assumed)				1 0 0 0 0 Cr.

Illustration B.7 *(continued)*

Retained Earnings   *Account No. 310*

Date		Explanation	Post. Ref.	Debit	Credit	Balance
1994 Apr.	1	Beginning balance (assumed)				1 8 0 0 0 Cr.

Sales   *Account No. 410*

Date		Explanation	Post. Ref.	Debit	Credit	Balance
1995 Apr.	30		S1		2 9 0	2 9 0 Cr.
	30		CR5		2 9 0 0 0	2 9 2 9 0 Cr.

Sales Discounts   *Account No. 411*

Date		Explanation	Post. Ref.	Debit	Credit	Balance
1995 Apr.	30		CR5	4		4 Dr.

Miscellaneous Revenue   *Account No. 420*

Date		Explanation	Post. Ref.	Debit	Credit	Balance
1995 Apr.	26		CR5		2 0 0	2 0 0 Cr.

Purchases   *Account No. 500*

Date		Explanation	Post. Ref.	Debit	Credit	Balance
1995 Apr.	30		P10	2 4 1 0 0		2 4 1 0 0 Dr.

Illustration B.7 *(concluded)*

Purchase Discounts   *Account No. 501*

Date	Explanation	Post. Ref.	Debit	Credit	Balance
1995 Apr. 30		CD7		4 0 5	4 0 5 Cr.

Rent Expense   *Account No. 515*

Date	Explanation	Post. Ref.	Debit	Credit	Balance
1995 Apr. 4		CD7	2 0 0		2 0 0 Dr.

Supplies Expense   *Account No. 518*

Date	Explanation	Post. Ref.	Debit	Credit	Balance
1995 Apr. 30		CD7	5 2		5 2 Dr.

The √ shows that the credit has also been posted to the accounts receivable subsidiary ledger account.

Other types of transactions that would appear in the general journal include the purchase of equipment or some other asset by giving a note, the payment of an account payable by giving a note, sales returns and allowances, and purchase returns and allowances. For instance, the entry to record a sales allowance of $100 granted to John Burke for damaged merchandise is:

```
Sales Returns and Allowances. . . . . . . . . . . . . .   412     100
      Accounts Receivable—J. Burke . . . . . . . . . .   103/√          100
      To record a sales allowance of $100 to John Burke for
      damaged merchandise.
```

All adjusting and closing entries would appear in the general journal. For instance, the general journal would be used to record an adjusting entry for depreciation expense of $1,500 on an office building as follows:

```
Depreciation Expense—Buildings . . . . . . . . . . . .   520   1,500
      Accumulated Depreciation—Buildings . . . . . . . .   141          1,500
      To record depreciation expense.
```

ALTERNATIVE METHODS OF PROCESSING DATA

The variety of equipment used in an accounting system is extensive, ranging from the hand-posted special journals of a manual system to large computers. Regardless of the accounting system a company selects, all companies use the basic steps of the accounting cycle to process their data. Also, the end result—financial statements—is the same for all companies. The selection that a company makes of one system over another depends on the company's individual situation, such as the volume of transactions, types of transactions, need for speed, resources of the company, and other cost-benefit considerations. In this section, you will study some of the alternative accounting systems available to companies.

Manual System

So far in this text, you have used the manual system. The manual system is the typical system used by some of today's smaller businesses that have one accountant and possibly one or two accounting clerks to handle their accounting function. In the manual system, accounting clerks record all accounting entries by hand. Then, they summarize the journals and post to the general ledger. Textbooks use the manual system to teach accounting because all other systems are based on it. In this appendix, you learned about the advantages of adding subsidiary ledgers and special journals to the manual system.

Manual systems called *one write* or *pegboard* systems were developed decades ago to assist small businesses to streamline their accounting tasks. By creating one document and aligning other records under it (using a pegboard), companies can record transactions more efficiently. For instance, these systems permit the writing of a check and the simultaneous recording of the check in the cash disbursements journal. Some of these systems are still in use today, but eventually computers will probably replace most of them.

During the 1950s, companies also used bookkeeping machines to supplement manual systems. These machines recorded recurring transactions such as sales on account. They posted transactions to the general ledger and subsidiary ledger accounts and computed new balances. However, with the development of computers, bookkeeping machines became obsolete. They were quite expensive, and computers easily outperformed them.

Microcomputers and Minicomputers

In this age of fast-developing computer technology with the continued lowering of computer prices, many small- and medium-sized businesses are turning to computers and off-the-shelf software to maintain their accounting records. Large businesses may use mainframe computers (described later), while small businesses might use minicomputers and/or microcomputers. **Microcomputers** are smaller than minicomputers and accommodate one person, while several persons can use a **minicomputer** at the same time. The distinction between microcomputers and minicomputers is more one of price rather than quality or capacity.

Microcomputers cost from a few hundred dollars to about $10,000. Minicomputers generally cost between $10,000 and $100,000. Microcomputers can fit on top of a desk; minicomputers are larger—about the size of a six-foot refrigerator. Divisions of large companies may use minicomputers since they can have several terminals connected to them. Companies use microcomputers for word processing, graphics, database management, and preparing spreadsheets for planning and decision making as well as for processing business transactions. Microcomputers can be networked (linked) into a system as powerful as a minicomputer. Many business executives have microcomputers on their desks and use them daily. As the price of computers continues to decline, more businesses will use computer systems. A later section describes the use of microcomputers in accounting in more detail.

Service Bureaus

Some businesses still find it economical to send certain data (e.g., payroll, inventory, and accounts receivable) to a local service bureau for processing. A **service bureau** is a large computer facility that takes data from a client, enters the data into its computer, produces required statements or reports, and returns this output to the client. Client personnel do not have to interact with the computer. Service bureaus can usually meet the specific output requirements of a business if the company does some advance planning.

Time-Sharing Terminals

Significant advances have been made in the field of computer time sharing. **Time sharing** occurs when several users utilize the same host computer to process data. In a time-sharing arrangement, client personnel interact with a computer through a remote terminal located in the client's building. The users literally share time on the host computer through remote terminals and the use of modems and telephone lines or the use of radio waves. A company employee operating a remote terminal can call up the host computer. Typical applications of time sharing enable clients to process large amounts of transactions data (e.g., printing and summarizing sales invoices, and updating inventory, accounts receivable, and accounts payable records).

Mainframe In-House Computers

Many business firms purchase their own mainframe computer to process data. The cost of these computers can be several hundred thousand dollars. Where the volume of transactions is very large, the decision to purchase a large computer is often justified. Terminals may exist throughout the company for employees to use to communicate with the mainframe computer. The next section describes the use of the microcomputer in accounting.

THE USE OF THE MICROCOMPUTER IN ACCOUNTING*

The use of the microcomputer in American business has greatly increased in recent years due to decreasing computer prices and significant technological advances in both computer hardware and software. Microcomputers now frequently cost under $5,000 and have as much power as computers that would have cost millions of dollars and filled several large rooms only a short time ago. The microcomputer is especially useful in accounting because of the great need for fast and accurate information processing when dealing with large volumes of financial data. To further your understanding of the microcomputer and its use in accounting, we will discuss the following topics: computerized accounting systems, electronic spreadsheets, database management systems, and the use of microcomputers in public accounting.

Computerized Accounting Systems

Numerous accounting system packages for microcomputers are currently available on the market, and most of them cost from just under $100 to $2,500. Two of the most popular accounting software packages are Peachtree Complete Accounting® and DacEasy Accounting®. Software companies have designed these packages for small businesses, and the packages can provide many advantages over manual accounting systems. Companies can greatly reduce the clerical work performed by their accounting staff. In addition, companies can also substantially reduce clerical errors in the financial data by changing from a manual to a computerized accounting system. Computerized systems also allow companies to gather information and produce reports much more efficiently than is possible with manual systems. The proper implementation of one of these accounting system packages can result in a company having a computerized accounting system that is both more efficient and less expensive than a manual system.

Now that you understand the potential advantages of using an accounting system package, let us examine the typical characteristics of a package on the market today. One basic characteristic of all effective systems is that some type of control exists over who can use the computer to make journal entries. Many packages have a password that a person must use to get into the accounting system. The importance of this control cannot be overstated.

Another common characteristic of most accounting packages today is that they are menu driven. The term *menu driven* means that the program user selects an option listed on the screen to access the part of the accounting system that he or she wishes to use. For example, when the user first turns on the computer and enters the proper password, a screen similar to this may appear:

---

* The remainder of this appendix was written by Gary Fayard, Partner in the Atlanta office of Ernst & Young, and Dana R. Hermanson, formerly Senior Accountant in the Atlanta office of Ernst & Young, and now a doctoral student at the University of Wisconsin.

```
                        XYZ Company
              1> General Ledger
              2> Accounts Receivable
              3> Accounts Payable
              4> Inventory Management
              5> Payroll
              6> Invoicing
              7> End Session
```

Assume the user wanted to access the Accounts Payable section of the program. Then, he or she would type a "3" into the computer and hit "ENTER." The user would now have access to the Accounts Payable section, and another menu would appear that would provide the user with several options within that section. The menu system makes accounting packages much more "user friendly."

The final characteristic to be discussed is the typical organization or format of a computerized accounting package. Most packages are divided into the modules shown on the screen above—General Ledger, Accounts Receivable, Accounts Payable, Inventory Management, Payroll, and Invoicing. Let us now briefly discuss the function of each module.

The General Ledger module contains all of a company's accounts and their balances. General journal entries are made in this module. These entries include all entries not made in one of the other system modules. For example, an entry relating to accounts receivable would be made in the Accounts Receivable module. However, an entry to record the borrowing of cash from a bank does not fit into any of the specific modules and would be made in the General Ledger module as a general journal entry. Adjusting entries would also be entered in the General Ledger module. One other function performed in the General Ledger module is the printing of a company's financial statements. Most accounting packages will automatically make all the necessary closing entries before printing out the financial statements.

The Accounts Receivable module is used to record sales on credit to various customers and amounts received from customers. The file of customers in this module serves as the accounts receivable subsidiary ledger. The Accounts Receivable control account in the General Ledger module is usually automatically updated when entries are made in the Accounts Receivable module.

The Accounts Payable module is used to record credit purchases of merchandise from various vendors and payments the company made to those vendors. The file of suppliers in this module serves as the accounts payable subsidiary ledger. The Accounts Payable control account in the General Ledger module is usually automatically updated when entries are made in the Accounts Payable module.

The Inventory Management module maintains the perpetual inventory. This module reflects all purchases and sales of inventory. The Inventory Management module interfaces with the Accounts Receivable and Accounts

Payable modules to keep track of the receivables and payables resulting from sales and purchases.

The Payroll module is used to record all the payroll entries. The totals from the Payroll module are often automatically posted to the appropriate General Ledger accounts, although this automatic posting is not always available.

The Invoicing module is simply used to print the sales invoices that are sent to customers. Sometimes this Invoicing module is combined with the Accounts Receivable module into one module.

Electronic Spreadsheets

Another type of computer program that has become extremely popular during the last decade is the electronic spreadsheet. Two of the most popular spreadsheet programs are LOTUS 1-2-3® and Microsoft Excel®. These programs have numerous applications in business and specifically in accounting. Spreadsheets are ideal for creating large schedules and performing large volumes of calculations. Their specific uses in accounting range from performing depreciation calculations to creating trial balances and other schedules. Other specific uses of spreadsheets will be discussed in the section on the use of the microcomputer in public accounting.

Let us now examine the basics of the electronic spreadsheet. An electronic spreadsheet is simply a large blank "page" on the computer screen that contains rows and columns. The spreadsheet is so large that a user can see only a very small percentage of the sheet on the screen at one time. The blocks created by the intersection of the rows and columns are called *cells*, and each cell can hold one or more words, a number, or the product of a mathematical formula. A typical blank spreadsheet appears as follows:

```
          A    B    C    D    E    F    G
    1
    2     ▨  (Cursor)
    3
    4               ▢  (Cell C4)
    5
    6
    7
    8
    9
   10
  A2>  (Type appears here)
  (Cursor location)
```

The cursor indicates the cell on the screen in which the user can enter information at a given time. For example, on the previous screen, the user can now enter one or more words, a number, or a formula into cell A2. Note that the information will appear at the bottom (on some programs, at the top) of the screen next to the cursor location until the user presses the ENTER key to transfer the information to its cell. The user can move the cursor around the screen by pressing different cursor control keys.

By going through the following example you can gain a better understanding of how the electronic spreadsheet actually works. Assume you are an accountant in Burke Company and wish to create an income statement for 1994 and a projected income statement for 1995 like those shown below:

	A	B	C	D
1	▧	BURKE CO.		
2		INCOME STATEMENT	PROJECTED	
3		YEAR ENDED 12/31/94	12/31/95	
4				
5	Sales	1,000,000	1,100,000	
6	Cost of Goods Sold	600,000	660,000	
7	Gross Profit	400,000	440,000	
8	Other Expenses	100,000	110,000	
9	Net Income	300,000	330,000	
10				

A1>

Your first step in creating these statements is to set up the proper headings. In cell B1 you would enter BURKE CO. by moving the cursor to B1, typing in the words BURKE CO., and pressing the ENTER key to transfer the words to cell B1. Likewise, you would enter the appropriate headings into cells B2, B3, C2, and C3. Your second step is to enter the income statement items in column A. You would place these items in cells A5 through A9 in the same way that you entered the other headings.

Now that you have entered all of the headings and titles, you can begin to enter the financial figures into the 1993 Income Statement. Cell B5 will contain the Sales figure of $1,000,000, and B6 will hold the $600,000 Cost of Goods Sold figure. You will enter these numbers in the same manner that you entered the headings and titles. Cell B7 will not hold a specific word or number; however, it will contain the result of a mathematical formula (B5 −

B6). By moving the cursor to B7, typing +B5 − B6, and pressing the ENTER key, you enter the result of this formula into B7. Finally, you enter $100,000 in cell B8. You will enter the result of +B7 − B8 in cell B9.

The final step in constructing this spreadsheet is to complete cells C5 through C9, which will show the projected income statement figures for 1995. Assuming that Sales, Cost of Goods Sold, and Other Expenses will increase by 10% from 1994 to 1995, you can enter the following formulas for cells C5, C6, and C8. Cell C5 will contain the number resulting from the formula +B5∗1.1. Cells C6 and C8 will show the results of +B6∗1.1 and +B8∗1.1, respectively. Finally, C7 and C9 will hold the results of +C5 − C6 and +C7 − C8, respectively. Your spreadsheet is now complete, as it presents the 1994 Income Statement for Burke Company and a projected Income Statement for 1995.

You have only used a few of the columns and rows available in a typical spreadsheet. Most spreadsheets contain many columns and rows. For instance, a recent version of LOTUS 1-2-3 contains 256 columns and 8,192 rows.

While the income statement you just constructed is a simple example of spreadsheet use, you should note several more advanced functions that spreadsheets can perform. First, when showing a current schedule and projections of that schedule far into the future, the user can play "what if" games by changing various numbers or formulas in the spreadsheet. Then, the program will recalculate all of the schedules based on the changes made. Second, many spreadsheet programs allow the user to construct various types of graphs showing the data contained in spreadsheet schedules. Finally, the user can print out on paper the schedules that appear on the computer screen for use by other people.

The computerized spreadsheet is a powerful tool, but the potential for inefficient use of spreadsheets is great. To promote better use of spreadsheets, Ernst & Young has developed the following tips for its staff:

1. Spend time on planning. Planning how to design, organize, and construct your spreadsheet can ensure that the spreadsheet meets your requirements. This planning reduces errors and makes the spreadsheet easier to use.
2. Keep the overall design simple. Spreadsheet design should aim at producing clear and concise analyses. Quality is more important than quantity.
3. Organize the spreadsheet to make it easy to understand. Separate data input areas from reports. Include instructions and a table of contents to make the spreadsheet understandable to other people.
4. Use simple formulas to make your printed output more understandable and to make errors easier to detect.
5. Use validation tests to alert you if errors occur.
6. Test the spreadsheet before use. Always check spreadsheet calculations before using the results.

7. Use graphics to highlight patterns or trends in your data and to make your spreadsheets more interesting and understandable.
8. Document the spreadsheet. Both users and reviewers need adequate documentation of spreadsheet logic and design. Proper headings and descriptions, as well as other documentation, are important for a well-designed spreadsheet.
9. Use the ''protect'' command to safeguard the spreadsheet and identify where data should be entered.
10. Make regular backups. Maintain up-to-date copies of spreadsheet files to avoid losing important data and development work.

Database Management Systems

In many accounting systems, various applications of the same data have been developed independently. As a result, although inventory, purchasing, sales, and production all use part numbers to identify inventory items, the computer would have to store each piece of information in each file for each application. The same data stored in separate files could vary as far as accuracy and timeliness. Inefficiencies (data redundancy) and inaccuracies (data inconsistency) can result. A database management system helps solve these problems by storing related data together independent of the application. Many of today's accounting systems have integrated applications through the use of a database management system. Thus, in the above example, the computer stores the inventory part number in only one file but all the applications use it.

Companies use database management software frequently on microcomputers. Two of the most popular microcomputer database management systems are D BASE® and R:BASE®. Companies can use these systems to develop integrated accounting systems. These systems are also useful for many single applications. With database software, you can easily enter data into a microcomputer and then analyze, sort, and print the information using English-like commands. The advantage of using the database management system for a single application over writing the application in a programming language (i.e., BASIC, PASCAL) is that the database management system takes care of data file access for you.

Now we will look at an example of a database application. The database file can be any organized collection of related information, such as monthly sales information. The information is kept in records, with each record consisting of a series of fields. A field is the part of a record that holds a particular item of information. An example of a record might be all information related to a salesperson. The fields in the record might include the salesperson's name, address, and ZIP code.

Suppose you are a sales manager and must maintain information about your salespersons, your customers, and your company's product. You could use a database management system to help you keep up with this information. In this case, you would probably have three database files—one for salespersons, one for customers, and one for products. However, the database management system can be instructed to match the salespersons to the customers, the customers to the products, and so on. Once you have defined this information to the database management system, you can use English-like commands to help answer such questions as: Which products have been sold? Who are the customers? What are the amounts of sales by salespersons? You would also be able to print a customer list sorted by ZIP code, alphabetical order, or salesperson.

Use of Microcomputers in Public Accounting

Microcomputers are having far-reaching effects in all areas of accounting. The following discussion explains some of the uses of microcomputers in public accounting.

Auditing.   Auditing involves performing an examination of the financial statements of a company to enable the Certified Public Accountant to express an opinion on the financial statements. The examination of the financial statements involves many different types of tests. Many times auditors use statistical sampling techniques to test the details of account balances. The microcomputer is very useful in helping both to plan and select the sample and to evaluate the results of the sample.

A typical example of microcomputer-based statistical sampling is the selection of random numbers for a test of cash disbursements. You do this by entering the sequences of the checks written during the year. Then, the statistical sampling package selects a random sample of the checks to be tested. After the checks have been tested for accuracy and source document support, the findings are entered in the statistical package to evaluate the results of the sample and to form conclusions about the entire population of cash disbursements.

The microcomputer has had a tremendous impact on the auditing profession in the areas of analytical review and trial balance/financial statement preparation. Microcomputer packages are available that enable the auditor to enter the client's general ledger information and post adjusting journal entries. These packages will print analytical review information, such as percentage changes in expense accounts as compared with the prior year. Also, such packages are useful in calculating financial ratios. They will also consolidate the financial statements of several related companies and print consolidated financial statements. Another benefit of some of these packages is that they will print the financial information in a way to facilitate income tax return preparation.

Other uses of the microcomputer in auditing are calculations of present/future values, amortization schedules for debt, depreciation schedules for fixed assets, and flowcharting of accounting systems.

Auditors use computer spreadsheets extensively both for their ease of use and the capability to quickly change and recalculate computations. Use of a computer spreadsheet to calculate the income tax provision is a typical example. This calculation can be a complicated computation, and it is subject to change if the company makes adjustments to the financial statements as a result of the audit. The use of a computer spreadsheet allows the auditor to quickly reflect the adjusted amounts and recalculate the income tax provision.

Tax.   The microcomputer has also had a dramatic impact on the tax practice of public accounting firms. Microcomputers are used to prepare tax returns, and they are used extensively in income tax and estate tax planning. In tax planning, both specialized tax programs and computer spreadsheets are used. Use of the microcomputer allows the tax professional to ask "what if" questions and quickly see the results of different tax strategies.

Another important use of the microcomputer is in the area of tax research. By using a modem, companies can access research databases over phone lines. These databases have current tax law, tax cases, and revenue rulings that can be quickly searched and the information found downloaded to the microcomputer for review and printing.

Management Consulting Services.   Management consultants, as the name implies, work with clients in a variety of areas. These areas include advising on acquisitions of computer hardware and software, implementing accounting systems, analyzing staffing needs, reviewing manufacturing procedures and cost systems, and performing financial modeling tasks.

Financial modeling is the process of taking historical financial information and projecting the results based on various scenarios. Accountants can perform financial modeling by use of a computer spreadsheet. However, accountants often use microcomputer financial modeling packages to develop most large, complicated models.

The following are examples of the uses of financial modeling.

1. A manufacturer needs help in overcoming a seasonal cash shortage. The nature of the manufacturer's business involves the annual buildup of large inventories. This buildup results in dramatic increases in payables. Using a financial model, the company is able to anticipate its cash requirements and avert an annual cash crisis.

2. A manufacturer wants to expand its business by acquiring the manufacturing capabilities of existing companies. Using a financial model, the company can develop a series of projections of the anticipated results of various acquisitions and the impact on the company's debt service and borrowing capabilities.

3. A privately held company has plans to go public. A key ingredient to a successful public offering is a well-conceived business plan that allows underwriters to make an objective initial assessment of the company's current situation and future potential. The company can use a financial model to prepare projections of its financial statements. The company would include these projected financial statements in its business plan to allow the underwriters to assess the company's future potential.

YOUR FUTURE AND THE MICROCOMPUTER

The microcomputer is now firmly established as a valuable tool in accounting. As computer technology continues to progress, accountants will find more and more ways in which to use these powerful machines.

Future applications of the computer in public accounting will involve the use of "expert systems" and artificial intelligence. Expert systems are software programs designed to duplicate the decisions of an "expert," given certain facts and circumstances. For instance, the program might be able to predict whether or not a client is a going concern with the same success rate as could an expert on this topic. These programs are extremely expensive and time consuming to develop.

Artificial intelligence is a much broader concept than expert systems. The field of artificial intelligence is devoted to making the computer think like a human being by being able to interact with humans and adapt to unstructured situations. In the distant future we may have computers that think and respond like humans.

Your success as an accountant in the future may depend greatly on your ability to use microcomputers efficiently and effectively. We hope this appendix has alerted you to the need for an understanding of the uses of the microcomputer in accounting.

DEMONSTRATION PROBLEM

The Andrews Softwarehouse uses special journals for sales, cash receipts, purchases, and cash disbursements, as well as a general journal. These journals follow the same design as those illustrated in this chapter, except that the column for Supplies Expense Dr. is omitted from the cash disbursements journal.

Transactions:

May 1 Sold Baxter Company $12,000 of computer software on account; terms 2/10, n/30; Invoice No. 94-128.

  4 Bought computer software on account from the Ace Company; Invoice No. 152; terms n/10, $8,400.

  7 Cash sales, $38,000.

  10 Rental revenue received, $1,600.

  11 Received amount due from Baxter Company for sale of May 1. The discount was taken.

  12 Paid for office equipment received today, $4,800 (Check No. 260). The equipment was for the company's own use.

  14 Paid Ace Company for purchase of May 4 (Check No. 261).

  14 Sold $8,000 of computer software on account to Mosley Company; Invoice No. 94-129; terms 2/10, n/30.

  15 Sold $2,800 of computer software on account to Wilks Company; Invoice No. 94-130; terms 2/10, n/30.

  15 Bought computer software on account from Ace Company, $3,960; Invoice No. 224; terms n/10.

  16 Bought computer merchandise on account from Carr Company, $6,000; Invoice No. 324-CD; terms 2/10, n/30.

  17 Bought office equipment today for $3,800 and gave a 30-day, 14% note in payment. The equipment was for the company's own use.

  20 Cash sales of computer supplies, $7,200.

  20 Collected $3,080 on account from Thomas Gibson.

May 22   Cash sales of computer software, $4,480.
   23   Cash sales of computer software, $1,200.
   24   Collected net amount due from Mosley Company on sale of August 14.
   25   Collected net amount due from Wilks Company on sale of August 15.
   25   Paid Ace Company on invoice of August 15 (Check No. 262).
   26   Paid Carr Company on invoice of August 16 (Check No. 263).
   27   Paid delivery expense in cash, $1,600 (Check No. 264).
   27   Paid advertising expense in cash, $3,200 (Check No. 265).
   28   Sold 10 laser printers for $14,800 on account to Wilks Company; Invoice No. 94-131; terms 2/10, n/30.
   29   Sold five microcomputers for $19,600 on account to Mosley Company; Invoice No. 94-132; terms 2/10, n/30.
   31   Bought computer software on account from Ace Company, $3,560; Invoice No. 468; terms n/10.

Required:

a.   Enter the transactions for May 1995 in the proper journals. All journal pages are to be numbered page 10.

b.   Post the individual accounts receivable and accounts payable transactions to the subsidiary ledgers. Only one customer, Thomas Gibson, owed the company a balance of $7,000 at the beginning of May. The company had one account payable to Carr Company for $4,000 at the beginning of the month. Andrews will not pay this $4,000 until a dispute over damaged merchandise is settled.

c.   Post the entries to the general ledger accounts shown below.

On May 1, 1995, the following accounts had balances:

Cash.	$20,000
Accounts Receivable	7,000
Merchandise Inventory	20,000
Accounts Payable.	4,000
Capital Stock.	30,000
Retained Earnings	13,000

d.   Prepare a trial balance as of the end of the period. General ledger accounts are:

100	Cash		407	Rental Revenue
103	Accounts Receivable		410	Sales
105	Merchandise Inventory		411	Sales Discounts
172	Office Equipment		500	Purchases
200	Accounts Payable		501	Purchase Discounts
201	Notes Payable		505	Advertising Expense
300	Capital Stock		519	Delivery Expense
310	Retained Earnings			

Solution to demonstration problem

a.

ANDREWS SOFTWAREHOUSE
SALES JOURNAL   *Page 10*

Date		Customer	Invoice No.	Accounts Receivable Dr. 103 Sales Cr. 410 Amount	√
1995					
May	1	Baxter Company	94-128	12,000	√
	14	Mosley Company	94-129	8,000	√
	15	Wilks Company	94-130	2,800	√
	28	Wilks Company	94-131	14,800	√
	29	Mosley Company	94-132	19,600	
				57,200	
				(103) (410)	

ANDREWS SOFTWAREHOUSE
CASH RECEIPTS JOURNAL   *Page 10*

Cash Dr. 100	Sales Dis-counts Dr. 411	Date	Description	Sales Cr. 410	Accounts Receivable Cr. 103 Amount	√	Other Accounts Cr. Account Title	Acct. No.	Amount	√
		1995								
38,000		May 7	Cash sales	38,000						
1,600		10	Rental revenue				Rental Reve-nue	407	1,600	√
11,760	240	11	Baxter Company—Invoice 94-128		12,000	√				
7,200		20	Cash sales	7,200						
3,080		20	Thomas Gibson		3,080	√				
4,480		22	Cash sales	4,480						
1,200		23	Cash sales	1,200						
7,840	160	24	Mosley Company—Invoice 94-129		8,000	√				
2,744	56	25	Wilks Company—Invoice 94-130		2,800	√				
77,904	456			50,880	25,880				1,600	
(100)	(411)			(410)	(103)				(√)	

ANDREWS SOFTWAREHOUSE
PURCHASES JOURNAL

Page 10

Date		Creditor	Terms	Invoice No.	Purchases Dr. 500 Accounts Payable Cr. 200 Amount	√
1995 May	4	Ace Company	n/10	152	8,400	√
	15	Ace Company	n/10	224	3,960	√
	16	Carr Company	2/10, n/30	324-CD	6,000	√
	31	Ace Company	n/10	468	3,560	√
					21,920	
					(500) (200)	

ANDREWS SOFTWAREHOUSE
CASH DISBURSEMENTS JOURNAL

Page 10

Accounts Payable Dr. 200 Amount	√	Other Accounts Dr. Account Title	Acct. No.	Amount	√	Date	Description	Check No.	Cash Cr. 100	Purchase Discounts Cr. 501
		Office Equipment	172	4,800	√	1995 May 12	Office equipment	260	4,800	
8,400	√					14	Ace Company—Invoice 152	261	8,400	
3,960	√					25	Ace Company—Invoice 224	262	3,960	
6,000	√					26	Carr Company—Invoice 324-CD	263	5,880	120
		Delivery Expense	519	1,600	√	27	Delivery expense	264	1,600	
		Advertising Expense	505	3,200	√	27	Advertising expense	265	3,200	
18,360				9,600					27,840	120
(200)				(√)					(100)	(501)

ANDREWS SOFTWAREHOUSE
GENERAL JOURNAL   *Page 10*

Date		Account Titles and Explanation	Post. Ref.	Debit	Credit
1995					
May	17	Office Equipment	172	3 8 0 0	
		Notes Payable	201		3 8 0 0
		Terms of note, 30 days, 14%.			

b.

ANDREWS SOFTWAREHOUSE
ACCOUNTS RECEIVABLE SUBSIDIARY LEDGER

Baxter Company

Date		Explanation	Post. Ref.	Debit	Credit	Balance
1995						
May	1		S10	1 2 0 0 0		1 2 0 0 0
	11		CR10		1 2 0 0 0	– 0 –

Thomas Gibson

Date		Explanation	Post. Ref.	Debit	Credit	Balance
1995						
May	1	Beginning balance				7 0 0 0
	20		CR10		3 0 8 0	3 9 2 0

Mosley Company

Date		Explanation	Post. Ref.	Debit	Credit	Balance
1995						
May	14		S10	8 0 0 0		8 0 0 0
	24		CR10		8 0 0 0	– 0 –
	29		S10	1 9 6 0 0		1 9 6 0 0

Wilks Company

Date		Explanation	Post. Ref.	Debit	Credit	Balance
1995 May	15		S10	2 8 0 0		2 8 0 0
	25		CR10		2 8 0 0	– 0 –
	28		S10	1 4 8 0 0		1 4 8 0 0

ANDREWS SOFTWAREHOUSE
ACCOUNTS PAYABLE SUBSIDIARY LEDGER

Ace Company

Date		Explanation	Post. Ref.	Debit	Credit	Balance
1995 May	4		P10		8 4 0 0	8 4 0 0
	14		CD10	8 4 0 0		– 0 –
	15		P10		3 9 6 0	3 9 6 0
	25		CD10	3 9 6 0		– 0 –
	31		P10		3 5 6 0	3 5 6 0

Carr Company

Date		Explanation	Post. Ref.	Debit	Credit	Balance
1995 May	1	Beginning balance				4 0 0 0
	16		P10		6 0 0 0	1 0 0 0 0
	26		CD10	6 0 0 0		4 0 0 0

c.

ANDREWS SOFTWAREHOUSE
GENERAL LEDGER

Cash   *Account No. 100*

Date		Explanation	Post. Ref.	Debit	Credit	Balance
1995 May	1	Beginning balance				2 0 0 0 0
	31		CR10	7 7 9 0 4		9 7 9 0 4
	31		CD10		2 7 8 4 0	7 0 0 6 4

Accounts Receivable   *Account No. 103*

Date		Explanation	Post. Ref.	Debit	Credit	Balance
1995 May	1	Beginning balance				7 0 0 0
	31		S10	5 7 2 0 0		6 4 2 0 0
	31		CR10		2 5 8 8 0	3 8 3 2 0

Merchandise Inventory   *Account No. 105*

Date		Explanation	Post. Ref.	Debit	Credit	Balance
1995 May	1	Beginning balance				2 0 0 0 0

Office Equipment   *Account No. 172*

Date		Explanation	Post. Ref.	Debit	Credit	Balance
1995 May	12		CD10	4 8 0 0		4 8 0 0
	17		G10	3 8 0 0		8 6 0 0

Accounts Payable
Account No. 200

Date		Explanation	Post. Ref.	Debit	Credit	Balance
1995 May	1	Beginning balance				4 0 0 0
	31		P10		2 1 9 2 0	2 5 9 2 0
	31		CD10	1 8 3 6 0		7 5 6 0

Notes Payable
Account No. 201

Date		Explanation	Post. Ref.	Debit	Credit	Balance
1995 May	17		G10		3 8 0 0	3 8 0 0

Capital Stock
Account No. 300

Date		Explanation	Post. Ref.	Debit	Credit	Balance
1995 May	1	Beginning balance				3 0 0 0 0

Retained Earnings
Account No. 310

Date		Explanation	Post. Ref.	Debit	Credit	Balance
1995 May	1	Beginning balance				1 3 0 0 0

Rental Revenue
Account No. 407

Date		Explanation	Post. Ref.	Debit	Credit	Balance
1995 May	10		CR10		1 6 0 0	1 6 0 0

Sales
Account No. 410

Date		Explanation	Post. Ref.	Debit	Credit	Balance
1995 May	31		S10		5 7 2 0 0	5 7 2 0 0
	31		CR10		5 0 8 8 0	1 0 8 0 8 0

Sales Discounts *Account No. 411*

Date		Explanation	Post. Ref.	Debit	Credit	Balance
1995 May	31		CR10	4 5 6		4 5 6

Purchases *Account No. 500*

Date		Explanation	Post. Ref.	Debit	Credit	Balance
1995 May	31		P10	2 1 9 2 0		2 1 9 2 0

Purchase Discounts *Account No. 501*

Date		Explanation	Post. Ref.	Debit	Credit	Balance
1995 May	31		CD10		1 2 0	1 2 0

Advertising Expense *Account No. 505*

Date		Explanation	Post. Ref.	Debit	Credit	Balance
1995 May	27		CD10	3 2 0 0		3 2 0 0

Delivery Expense *Account No. 519*

Date		Explanation	Post. Ref.	Debit	Credit	Balance
1995 May	27		CD10	1 6 0 0		1 6 0 0

d.

	ANDREWS SOFTWAREHOUSE Trial Balance May 31, 1995		
Acct. No.	Account Title	Debits	Credits
100	Cash.	$ 70,064	
103	Accounts Receivable	38,320	
105	Merchandise Inventory	20,000	
172	Office Equipment.	8,600	
200	Accounts Payable.		$ 7,560
201	Notes Payable		3,800
300	Capital Stock.		30,000
310	Retained Earnings		13,000
407	Rental Revenue.		1,600
410	Sales.		108,080
411	Sales Discounts	456	
500	Purchases	21,920	
501	Purchase Discounts.		120
505	Advertising Expense	3,200	
519	Delivery Expense	1,600	
		$164,160	$164,160

NEW TERMS

Cash disbursements journal   A special journal used to record all payments (or outflows) of cash by the company. *1175*

Cash receipts journal   A special journal used to record all transactions involving inflows of cash into the company. *1175*

Control account   An account in the general ledger that shows the total balance of all the subsidiary accounts related to it. *1172*

General journal   A general-purpose journal used to record all transactions that cannot be entered in one of the special journals. *1175*

Microcomputers   Desktop computers that can be used for word processing, graphics, database management, spreadsheets, and to maintain the accounting records for a small business; designed for use by one person. *1195*

Minicomputers   Medium-sized computers that can be used to maintain the accounting records for a small- or medium-sized business; designed for use by several persons. *1196*

Other accounts   Miscellaneous accounts. *1179*

Purchases journal   A special journal used to record all purchases of merchandise on account (on credit). *1175*

Sales journal   A special journal used to record all sales of merchandise on account (on credit). *1175*

Schedule of accounts payable   Prepared at the end of the period to make certain that the total of the balances in the accounts payable subsidiary ledger accounts agrees with the balance in the Accounts Payable control account balance. *1185*

Schedule of accounts receivable   Prepared at the end of the period to ensure that the total of the balances in the accounts receivable subsidiary ledger agrees with the Accounts Receivable control account balance. *1179*

Service bureau   A large computer facility that takes data from a client, enters the data into its computer, produces required statements or reports, and returns this output to the client. *1196*

Special journal   A book of original entry that records one particular type of transaction, such as sales on account, cash receipts, purchases on account, or cash disbursements. *1175*

Subsidiary ledger   A group of related accounts showing the details of the balance of a general ledger control account. *1173*

Subsidiary ledger accounts   Accounts in a subsidiary ledger that show the details supporting the related general ledger control account balance. *1173*

Time sharing   A system whereby several users utilize the same host computer to process data. *1196*

SELF-TEST

True-False

Indicate whether each of the following statements is true or false.

1. An accounting system is a set of records plus the procedures and equipment regularly used to process business transactions.

2. Subsidiary ledgers can only be established for accounts receivable and accounts payable.

3. When special journals are used, there is no need for a general journal.

4. The sales journal should only be used for sales of merchandise on account, and the purchases journal should only be used for purchases of merchandise on account.

5. All of the column totals in the cash receipts and cash disbursements journals should be posted to general ledger accounts at the end of the period.

6. All companies should use computers to process their data.

7. Microcomputers are used extensively in public accounting.

Multiple-Choice

Select the best answer for each of the following questions.

1. The orderly and efficient processing of data is necessary so that (select the false answer):
   a. Results of operations and financial position of the firm are reported on a timely basis.
   b. Bills are paid when due.
   c. Proper quantities and items of inventory are sent to customers.
   d. Special journals can be used.

2. Which of the following statements is true regarding control accounts and subsidiary ledgers?
   a. Subsidiary ledger accounts should be posted daily, but control accounts do not need to be posted daily.
   b. Both subsidiary ledger accounts and control accounts should be posted daily.
   c. Neither subsidiary ledger accounts nor control accounts need to be posted daily.
   d. Subsidiary ledger accounts and control

accounts can only be used when special journals are used.

3. Which of the following is true regarding the sales journal?
   a. It can only have one money column.
   b. It should be used for all sales of merchandise.
   c. Usually only the column total(s) is (are) posted.
   d. It can be used even when there are many departments for which sales need to be recorded separately.

4. When special journals are used, the general journal would be used for all of the following journal entries *except:*
   a. Adjusting entries.
   b. Closing entries.

c. Purchase allowances.
d. Purchase discounts.

5. Which of the following statements is *true* regarding alternative methods of processing data?
   a. "One write" or "pegboard" systems are no longer in use.
   b. Bookkeeping machines are no longer in general use.
   c. Minicomputers have almost completely replaced microcomputers and mainframe computers in performing accounting tasks.
   d. Service bureaus and time-sharing terminals are no longer in use.

Now turn to page 1226 to check your answers.

QUESTIONS

1. The processing of data is usually costly. Why bother with this task?

2. Is the balance of a control account equal to the total of its subsidiary accounts at all times? Explain.

3. In a manual system, the subsidiary accounts receivable and accounts payable accounts usually do not have account numbers. Why?

4. What is the definition of a special journal?

5. Describe the purpose of each of the following journals by giving the types of entries that would be recorded in each: sales, purchases, cash receipts, cash disbursements, and general.

6. Why might a sales journal or a purchases journal have more than one money column?

7. Why are some column totals in special journals posted while others are not?

8. Why does the purchases journal have a Terms column while the sales journal does not?

9. How can you tell whether a special journal has been completely posted? Describe the posting marks.

10. What is the purpose of preparing a schedule of accounts receivable and a schedule of accounts payable?

11. Of what use is the general journal when special journals are used?

12. Identify the alternative methods of processing data. What factors should a company consider in deciding which alternative to select?

13. Describe the nature of computerized accounting systems designed for the microcomputer.

14. Describe how information is entered into an electronic spreadsheet.

15. For what purposes are microcomputers used in public accounting practice?

The Coca-Cola Company

16. *Real-world question*   Refer to Note 18 in The Coca-Cola Company annual report in Appendix C at the end of the text. If you were creating the accounting system, into what lines of business would you segregate revenues and expenses?

EXERCISES

Prepare T-accounts to show Accounts Receivable control and subsidiary accounts

B–1. The correct accounts receivable subsidiary ledger account balances for a company are as follows at the end of an accounting period:

Dobbins	$1,800
Grant.	2,400
Nickel	3,600
Walters.	3,000

Using T-accounts, show how these accounts would appear and what the balance on this same date would be in the Accounts Receivable control account in the general ledger. If the balance in the control account is $12,000, what should be done?

Match transactions with journals in which they would be recorded

B–2. Match each transaction in column A with the appropriate journal in column B in which it would be recorded. Assume each of the journals listed is used as a book of original entry and is designed as illustrated in the chapter.

Column A	Column B
1. Purchased merchandise on account.	a. Sales journal.
2. Recorded depreciation expense.	b. Cash receipts journal.
3. Sold merchandise on account.	c. Purchases journal.
4. Sold merchandise for cash.	d. Cash disbursements journal.
5. Collected cash on account.	e. General journal.
6. Gave a note to a trade creditor.	
7. Received cash for services performed.	
8. Granted a sales allowance to a customer.	
9. Paid rent for the month.	
10. Received notice of a purchase allowance from a trade creditor.	
11. Paid a trade creditor.	
12. Recorded closing entries at the end of the period.	

Design sales journal for company with three selling departments

B–3. You are employed by a company that has three selling departments. You are asked to design a sales journal that will provide a departmental breakdown of credit sales. Give the column headings that you would use and describe how postings would be made.

Post data from
cash receipts
journal to
T-accounts

B–4. The column totals of a cash receipts journal are as follows:

Cash Dr.	$39,400
Sales Discounts Dr.	200
Sales Cr.	20,000
Accounts Receivable Cr..	10,000
Other Accounts Cr. (sold land at cost	
for $9,000 and sold scrap for $600).	9,600

Using T-accounts, post the amounts that appear in the cash receipts journal. How would the individual amounts in the Accounts Receivable Cr. column be posted? How would the information in the Other Accounts Cr. column be posted?

Determine
postings to
general ledger

B–5. Which of the following amounts would be posted to the general ledger?

a. The Cash Cr. column total in the cash disbursements journal.
b. The Other Accounts Dr. column total in the cash disbursements journal.
c. The individual items in the purchases journal.
d. The individual items in the sales journal.
e. The column total in the sales journal.

Indicate how
special journal
columns should
be posted

B–6. Using the following legend, indicate how the data in each special journal column should be posted:

1—Do not post the individual amounts in the column, but post the column total to general ledger account(s) at the end of the accounting period.
2—Post the individual amounts in the column to subsidiary ledger accounts during the accounting period, and post the column total to general ledger account(s) at the end of the accounting period.
3—Post the individual amounts in the column to general ledger accounts during the accounting period and do not post the column total.

Special journals:
  Sales journal:
    Accounts Receivable Dr., Sales Cr..   2

  Cash receipts journal:
    Cash Dr. . . . .   _____
    Sales Discounts Dr. . . . .   _____
    Sales Cr. . . . .   _____
    Accounts Receivable Cr. . . . .   _____
    Other Accounts Cr. . . . .   _____

  Purchases journal:
    Purchases Dr., Accounts Payable Cr.. . . . .   _____

  Cash disbursements journal:
    Accounts Payable Dr. . . . .   _____
    Supplies Expense Dr. . . . .   _____
    Other Accounts Dr. . . . .   _____
    Cash Cr. . . . .   _____
    Purchase Discounts Cr. . . . .   _____

B–7. For each of the following questions select the best answer.

1. Select the **true** statement regarding control accounts and subsidiary accounts.

    a. A control account must equal the total of the related subsidiary accounts at all times during the accounting period.

    b. The only subsidiary accounts are those for accounts receivable and accounts payable.

    c. Both control and subsidiary accounts appear in the general ledger.

    d. A company has fewer control accounts than subsidiary accounts.

2. The sales journal is:

    a. Used only to record sales on credit.

    b. Used to record all sales.

    c. Used only to record cash sales.

    d. None of the above.

3. The cash receipts journal:

    a. Cannot be used to record cash sales.

    b. Is used to record amounts received on accounts receivable.

    c. Cannot be used to record the sale of a plant asset for cash.

    d. Usually has only one money column.

4. The cash disbursements journal:

    a. Cannot be used to record purchases on account.

    b. Is used only to record the payment of accounts payable.

    c. Cannot be used to record the purchase of a plant asset for cash.

    d. Usually has only one money column.

5. Which of the following statements is **true?**

    a. The end result (financial statements) is different depending on which method of processing is used.

    b. One method of processing data is the best for all companies.

    c. Microcomputers can be used to maintain the accounting records of a small company.

    d. The purchase of a mainframe in-house computer is almost never justified.

B–8. Answer the following multiple-choice questions regarding the use of microcomputers in accounting. Select the best answer.

1. Characteristics of microcomputer accounting system packages include (select the **false** statement):

    a. Many packages have a password that must be used to get into the accounting system.

    b. These packages are usually menu driven.

    c. These packages usually cost in excess of $2,500.

    d. Modules in the packages generally include: General Ledger, Accounts Receivable, Accounts Payable, Inventory Management, Payroll, and Invoicing.

2. All but which one of the following is a characteristic of computer spreadsheets?

a. The user can play "what if" games by changing various numbers or formulas in the spreadsheet, and the program will recalculate all of the schedules automatically.

b. Many spreadsheet programs allow the user to construct various types of graphs showing the data contained in the spreadsheet schedules.

c. The schedules that appear on the user's computer screen can be printed out on paper for use by other people.

d. Because the spreadsheet packages are so well designed, it is virtually impossible to use them inefficiently.

3. A database management system (select the **true** statement):
   a. Stores related data together independent of any one application.
   b. Enables one item of information to be stored in only one file but to be used by all the applications.
   c. Uses English-like commands.
   d. All of the above.

4. Which of the following statements is **false?**
   a. Artificial intelligence is a much narrower concept than expert systems.
   b. The microcomputer is helpful in selecting statistical samples and in evaluating the results.
   c. Microcomputers are used to prepare tax returns and are used extensively in income and estate tax planning.
   d. Complicated financial modeling can be performed on microcomputers.

PROBLEMS

Record transactions in sales and purchases journals; post to T-accounts in general and subsidiary ledgers

B–1. a. K&G Clothing Store sold goods on account to the following customers on the dates indicated:

Date	Customer	Invoice No.	Amount
1995			
June 1	Simon Walls	200	$ 900
4	Mark White	201	600
12	Cassey Hanson	202	1,200
18	Marianne Burke	203	1,800
29	Roger Jones	204	1,500

Required:

Record the transactions on page 1 of a sales journal. Then, using T-accounts, post the data to accounts in the general ledger and accounts receivable subsidiary ledger. The general ledger account numbers are:

Accounts Receivable	103
Sales.	410

b. State University Book Store purchased merchandise from the following companies on the dates indicated:

Date	Creditor	Terms	Invoice No.	Amount
1995				
July 3	Able Press	2/10, n/30	240	$1,500
5	Decker, Inc.	1/15, n/30	360	750
14	Gifts & More, Inc.	2/20, n/30	142	3,000
22	Stanton Publishers, Inc.	2/20, n/60	58	3,750
30	Wells Company	2/10, n/30	410	5,250

Required:

Record the transactions on page 10 of a purchases journal. Then, using T-accounts, post the data to accounts in the general ledger and accounts payable subsidiary ledger.

The general ledger account numbers are:

Accounts Payable. 200
Purchases 500

Journalize transactions in appropriate journals; post to accounts in general and accounts receivable subsidiary ledger; prepare schedule of accounts receivable

B–2. On August 31, 1995, the Accounts Receivable control account on the books of Rigley Wholesale Furniture Store was equal to the total of the accounts in the accounts receivable subsidiary ledger. The balances were as follows: Accounts Receivable control account (Account No. 103), $45,000; Battle Corporation, $18,000; East Corporation, $12,000; and Ferguson Company, $15,000.

Transactions (ignore the fact that normally the terms to all customers are the same):

Sept. 1 Received $6,860 from Ferguson Company. A discount of $140 had been taken.

2 On this date, merchandise was sold on account for $11,000 to Olivia Company; Invoice No. 501; terms 2/20, n/30.

4 Cash sales, $25,000.

7 Received $9,000 on account from Battle Corporation. No discount was taken.

8 Received $20,000 cash for land sold at its original cost.

12 Sold merchandise on account to Ferguson Company, $9,000; Invoice No. 502; terms n/30.

15 Received payment for $5,000 of the merchandise purchased on September 2 by Olivia Company. The discount was taken on this payment.

18 Sold merchandise on account to Miles Corporation, $34,000; Invoice No. 503; terms n/30.

21 Cash sales, $57,000.

23 Allowed $1,000 credit to Miles Corporation for goods returned.

26 Sold merchandise on account to Newton Company, $10,000; Invoice No. 504; terms 2/20, n/30.

29 Received $10,000 cash from Miles Corporation to apply against the amount due on Invoice No. 503.

30 Cash sales were $39,000.

Required:

Prepare a sales journal (Illustration B.1) and cash receipts journal (Illustration B.2). Also set up a general journal. Then, using the above information:

a. Completely journalize the transactions in the appropriate journals.

b. Post only the amounts pertaining to accounts receivable to the subsidiary accounts and to the control account. You will have to prepare additional subsidiary accounts and should keep them all in alphabetical order. You will need additional accounts for Miles Corporation, Newton Company, and Olivia Company.

c. Prepare a schedule of accounts receivable at September 30, 1995, and compare it with the balance of the control account at the same date.

Journalize transactions in appropriate journal; post to general ledger and subsidiary ledger accounts; prepare schedule of accounts payable

B–3. On August 31, 1995, the Accounts Payable control account on the books of Rigley Wholesale Furniture Store was equal to the total of the accounts in the accounts payable subsidiary ledger. The balances were as follows: Accounts Payable control account (Account No. 200), $36,000; Bond Corporation, $8,000; Heizburg Company, $16,000; and Zales Corporation, $12,000.

Transactions:

Sept. 1 Purchased merchandise on account costing $15,000 from Worling Company; Invoice No. 542; terms 2/10, n/30.

3 Paid Bond Corporation $8,000 with Check No. 451. The original discount of 2% was not taken because the discount period had expired.

4 Paid rent for the month of September, $500, with Check No. 452.

5 Paid Heizburg Company $9,000 on account with Check No. 453. No discount was offered.

6 Gave Heizburg Company a $7,000, 30-day, 12% note for the balance due.

7 Purchased merchandise on account costing $8,000 from York Corporation; Invoice No. 982; terms 2/10, n/30.

8 Purchased merchandise on account costing $9,000 from Bond Corporation; Invoice No. 1522; terms 2/10, n/30.

9 Received credit from York Corporation for returning $1,000 of the $8,000 of merchandise purchased.

12 Paid Worling Company the amount due on the purchase of September 1 with Check No. 454.

15 Purchased merchandise on account costing $12,000 from New Point Corporation; Invoice No. 841; terms n/30.

17 Paid Bond Corporation the amount due on the purchase of September 8 with Check No. 455.

20 Purchased merchandise on account costing $13,000 from Bond Corporation; Invoice No. 1566; terms 2/10, n/30.

22 Purchased merchandise on account costing $7,000 from Quarter Company; Invoice No. 1910; terms n/30.

25 Paid $8,000 on account to New Point Corporation on the purchase of September 15 with Check No. 456.

29 Received $3,000 credit from Bond Corporation for returning part of the merchandise purchased on September 20.

30 Purchased merchandise on account having a cost of $5,000 from Jane Company; Invoice No. 2125; terms n/60.

Required:

Prepare a purchases journal (Illustration B.4) and cash disbursements journal (Illustration B.5). The Supplies Expense column is not needed in the cash disbursements journal. Also set up a general journal. Then using the above information:

a. Completely journalize each transaction in the appropriate journals.

b. Post only the amounts pertaining to accounts payable to the subsidiary accounts and to the control account. You will have to create some additional subsidiary accounts and arrange all subsidiary accounts in alphabetical order. Additional accounts should be created for Jane Company, New Point Corporation, Quarter Company, Worling Company, and York Corporation.

c. Prepare a schedule of accounts payable at September 30, 1995, and compare it with the balance of the control account at the same date.

Post data from journals to ledger accounts after entering beginning balances in the accounts; prepare trial balance

B–4. The post-closing trial balance of Santos Department Store as of November 30, 1995, was as follows:

SANTOS DEPARTMENT STORE
Post-Closing Trial Balance
November 30, 1995

	Debits	Credits
Cash	$ 70,000	
Accounts Receivable	48,000	
Merchandise Inventory—Men's Clothing	24,000	
Merchandise Inventory—Women's Clothing	40,000	
Merchandise Inventory—Shoes	4,000	
Merchandise Inventory—Cosmetics and Jewelry	16,000	
Merchandise Inventory—Sporting Goods	22,000	
Merchandise Inventory—Miscellaneous	5,200	
Office Equipment	20,000	
Accumulated Depreciation—Office Equipment		$ 6,800
Land	12,640	
Buildings	160,000	
Accumulated Depreciation—Buildings		38,800
Accounts Payable		40,400
Notes Payable		4,000
Capital Stock		200,000
Retained Earnings		131,840
	$421,840	$421,840

The company has five major selling departments and several minor ones. Separate general ledger accounts are maintained for sales and purchases for each of the major departments. Sales and purchases for the minor departments are grouped under Sales—Miscellaneous and Purchases—Miscellaneous.

The December transactions were recorded in the company's five journals: sales journal, cash receipts journal, purchases journal, cash disbursements journal, and general journal. At December 31, 1995, the column totals in the sales journal were as follows:

Accounts Receivable Dr.	Sales— Men's Clothing Cr.	Sales— Women's Clothing Cr.	Sales— Shoes Cr.	Sales— Cosmetics and Jewelry Cr.	Sales— Sporting Goods Cr.	Sales— Miscellaneous Cr.
162,000	40,000	50,000	16,800	16,000	31,200	8,000

The column totals of the cash receipts journal were as follows:

Cash Dr.	Sales Discounts Dr.	Sales— Men's Clothing Cr.	Sales— Women's Clothing Cr.	Sales— Shoes Cr.	Sales— Cosmetics and Jewelry Cr.	Sales— Sporting Goods Cr.	Sales— Miscel- laneous Cr.	Accounts Receivable Cr.	Other Accounts Cr.
280,400	2,240	24,000	32,000	13,200	24,000	12,800	16,000	144,000	16,640

The entries in the Other Accounts Cr. column resulted from the sale of land at cost of $12,640 (December 4) and $4,000 of revenue from the operation of a delivery service for other companies (December 31).

The column totals in the purchases journal were as follows:

Purchases— Men's Clothing Dr.	Purchases— Women's Clothing Dr.	Purchases— Shoes Dr.	Purchases— Cosmetics and Jewelry Dr.	Purchases— Sporting Goods Dr.	Purchases— Miscellaneous Dr.	Accounts Payable Cr.
56,000	76,000	24,000	30,000	55,600	16,000	257,600

The column totals of the cash disbursements journal were as follows:

Accounts Payable Dr.	Supplies Expense Dr.	Other Accounts Dr.	Cash Cr.	Purchase Discounts Cr.
234,000	38,800	31,600	298,800	5,600

The entries in the Other Accounts Dr. column resulted from the payment of $3,840 for a delivery truck (December 7) and $27,760 for the purchase of a garage (December 15).

The general journal includes the following entry at the date indicated:

Dec. 21 Buildings 34,800
               Notes Payable.   34,800

Required:

The beginning balances should be entered in the general ledger accounts. These balances are given in the November 31, 1995, trial balance. Then, post the data from the journals. Prepare a trial balance as of December 31, 1995.

Journalize
transactions; post
to general ledger
accounts; prepare
trial balance

B–5. California Microcomputer Store uses special journals for sales, cash receipts, purchases, and cash disbursements, as well as a general journal. These journals follow the same general design as those illustrated in this chapter.

Transactions:

Aug. 1 Sold Marlin, Inc., a $12,000 computer on account; terms 2/10, n/30; Invoice No. WI-A1.

3 Bought computer merchandise on account from Quark Company; Invoice No. 33-NP, terms n/10, $8,400.

5 Cash sales, $38,000.

9 Rent revenue received, $1,600.

11 Received amount due from Marlin, Inc., for sale of August 1. The discount was taken.

11 Paid for office equipment received today, $4,800 (Check No. 132). The equipment was for the company's own use.

12 Paid Quark Company for purchase of August 3 (Check No. 133).

14 Sold an $8,000 computer on account to Evans, Inc.; Invoice No. WI-A2; terms 2/10, n/30.

15 Sold a $2,800 computer on account to Brunsby Company; Invoice No. WI-A3; terms 2/10, n/30.

15 Bought computer merchandise on account from Quark Company, $3,960; Invoice No. 34-NP; terms n/10.

17 Bought computer merchandise on account from Southern Company, $6,000; Invoice No. 98-VX; terms 2/10, n/30.

18 Bought office equipment for $3,800 and gave a 30-day, 12% note in payment. The equipment was for the company's own use.

19 Cash sales of computer software, $7,200.

21 Cash sales of computer software, $4,480.

22 Cash sales of computer software, $1,200.

23 Collected net amount due from Evans, Inc., on sale of August 14.

24 Collected net amount due from Brunsby Company on sale of August 15.

25 Paid Quark Company on invoice of August 15 (Check No. 134).

26 Paid Southern Company on invoice of August 17 (Check No. 135).

27 Bought computer merchandise on account from Southern Company, $7,000; Invoice No. 120-VX; terms 2/10, n/30.

28 Paid delivery expense in cash, $1,600 (Check No. 136).

28 Paid advertising expense in cash, $3,200 (Check No. 137).

29 Sold two computers for $14,800 on account to Brunsby Company; Invoice No. WI-A4; terms 2/10, n/30.

30 Sold three computers for $19,600 on account to Evans, Inc.; Invoice No. WI-A5.

31 Bought computer merchandise on account from Quark Company, $3,560; Invoice No. 137-NP; terms n/10.

Required:

a. Enter the transactions for August 1995 in the proper journals. All journal pages are to be numbered page 5.

b. Post individual receivables and payables to the accounts receivable subsidiary ledger and accounts payable subsidiary ledger, respectively.

c. Post the entries to the general ledger accounts shown below. The following account balances existed on August 1, 1995: Cash, $20,000; Merchandise Inventory, $60,000; Capital Stock, $30,000; Retained Earnings, $50,000.

d. Prepare a trial balance as of the end of the period. General ledger accounts are:

Acct. No.	Account Title	Acct. No.	Account Title
100	Cash	407	Rental Revenue
103	Accounts Receivable	410	Sales
105	Merchandise Inventory	411	Sales Discounts
172	Office Equipment	500	Purchases
200	Accounts Payable	501	Purchase Discounts
201	Notes Payable	505	Advertising Expense
300	Capital Stock	519	Delivery Expense
310	Retained Earnings		

BUSINESS DECISION PROBLEMS

Describe and discuss special journals

B–1. Mike Stevens, the golf professional at the Green Valley Country Club, has been using a general journal to record all business transactions. The volume of business has been increasing, and now Mike seeks your assistance in devising some special journals. He wants his wife to keep track of all receipts, disbursements, and adjusting entries in her office at home. He and his assistant are to record all credit sales and purchases at the golf shop.

Sales are classified as follows: Golf Equipment, Golf Supplies, Apparel, Lessons, Cart Rental, and Miscellaneous Services. Sales are made for both cash and on account. No sales discounts are offered.

Purchases are made from many different suppliers. Items purchased include apparel, golf supplies, and golf equipment. Periodic inventory procedure is used.

Required:

a. Determine which special journals should be used.
b. Show the column headings that could be used in each of the special journals. Illustrate the use of each special journal by journalizing enough assumed transactions for 1995 so that at least one number appears in each of the columns you have designed.
c. Describe the posting of each of the special journals you have designed.

Describe important factors in deciding how to process data

B–2. Cite some of the factors that would be important in deciding whether a company should utilize a manual accounting system, a time-sharing facility, a service bureau, or a computer system installed at the firm.

ANSWERS TO SELF-TEST

True-False

1. *True.* This description of an accounting system is correct.
2. *False.* Subsidiary ledgers can be established for any account in the general ledger for which detailed information is needed. Accounts receivable and accounts payable are likely candidates.
3. *False.* A general journal is still needed to

record adjusting entries, closing entries, and any other entries that will not fit a special journal.

4. *True.* Only sales of merchandise on account are recorded in the sales journal, and only purchases on account are recorded in the purchases journal.

5. *False.* For instance, the "Other Accounts" column totals are not posted at all because they consist of entries to different accounts.

6. *False.* The costs and benefits of each alternative need to be compared. Some small businesses still do very well with a manual system.

7. *True.* Microcomputers are used in auditing, tax, and management consulting work in public accounting.

Multiple-Choice

1. *d.* Special journals are not a result of orderly and efficient processing of data; they can lead to the orderly and efficient processing of data.

2. *a.* Subsidiary ledger accounts need to be posted daily so that a company knows the details behind the control account. For instance, in case customers call and ask how much they owe on their accounts, this information needs to be up to date. The control account balance, however, is usually only needed when financial statements are to be prepared. Thus, daily posting to control accounts is not necessary and may not even be possible, since many of the postings to these accounts are monthly column totals from columns in special journals.

3. *d.* The sales journal can have one Sales column for each department. If so, it will need an Accounts Receivable debit column also.

4. *d.* Adjusting entries, closing entries, and purchase allowances would have to be recorded in the general journal because they do not fit the other journals. Purchase discounts can be recorded in the cash disbursements journal when payments of the invoices are recorded.

5. *b.* Bookkeeping machines became obsolete because computers could be purchased that cost less and would do more.

C

CONSOLIDATED FINANCIAL STATEMENTS (ANNUAL REPORTS)

Excerpts from the following 1991 annual reports are reproduced, with permission, in this appendix:

1. The Coca-Cola Company and Subsidiaries: Selected Financial Data, Consolidated Balance Sheets, Consolidated Statements of Income, Consolidated Statements of Share-Owners' Equity, Consolidated Statements of Cash Flows, Notes to Consolidated Financial Statements, and Report of Independent Auditors.

2. Maytag Corporation: Statements of Consolidated Income, Statements of Consolidated Financial Condition, and Statements of Consolidated Cash Flows.

3. The Limited, Inc.: Consolidated Statements of Income, Consolidated Balance Sheets, and Consolidated Statements of Cash Flows.

4. John H. Harland Company and Subsidiaries: Consolidated Statements of Income, Consolidated Balance Sheets, and Consolidated Statements of Cash Flows.

Selected Financial Data *The Coca-Cola Company and Subsidiaries*

Year Ended December 31, (In millions except per share data and ratios)	1991	1990	1989	1988
Summary of Operations				
Net operating revenues	$11,572	$10,236	$8,622	$8,065
Cost of goods sold	4,649	4,208	3,548	3,429
Gross profit	6,923	6,028	5,074	4,636
Selling, administrative and general expenses	4,604	4,076	3,348	3,038
Provisions for restructured operations and disinvestment	—	—	—	—
Operating income	2,319	1,952	1,726	1,598
Interest income	175	170	205	199
Interest expense	192	231	308	230
Equity income	40[1]	110	75	92
Other income (deductions)—net	41	13	66	(33)
Income from continuing operations before income taxes	2,383	2,014	1,764	1,626
Income taxes	765	632	571	537
Income from continuing operations	$ 1,618	$ 1,382	$1,193	$1,089
Net income	$ 1,618	$ 1,382	$1,724	$1,045
Preferred stock dividends	1	18	22	7
Net income available to common share owners	$ 1,617	$ 1,364	$1,702[2]	$1,038
Depreciation	$ 254	$ 236	$ 181	$ 167
Capital expenditures	$ 792	$ 593	$ 462	$ 387
Average common shares outstanding	666	669	692	729
Per Common Share Data				
Income from continuing operations	$ 2.43	$ 2.04	$ 1.69	$ 1.48
Net income	2.43	2.04	2.46[2]	1.42
Cash dividends	.96	.80	.68	.60
Market price at December 31	80.25	46.50	38.63	22.31
Balance Sheet Data				
Cash, cash equivalents and marketable securities	$ 1,117	$ 1,492	$1,182	$1,231
Property, plant and equipment—net	2,890	2,386	2,021	1,759
Total assets	10,222	9,278	8,283	7,451
Long-term debt	985	536	549	761
Total debt	2,287	2,537	1,981	2,124
Share-owners' equity	4,426	3,849	3,485	3,345
Total capital[3]	6,713	6,386	5,466	5,469
Other Key Financial Measures[3]				
Return on common equity	39.5%	39.2%	37.6%	34.7%
Return on capital	26.7%	26.0%	25.6%	21.3%
Economic profit	$ 1,043	$ 918	$ 819	$ 748
Total-debt-to-total-capital	34.1%	39.7%	36.2%	38.8%
Net-debt-to-net-capital	20.9%	22.8%	14.0%	18.9%
Dividend payout ratio	39.5%	39.2%	27.6%[2]	42.1%

[1] Equity income in 1991 includes a reduction of $44 million related to restructuring charges recorded by Coca-Cola Enterprises Inc.
[2] Net income available to common share owners in 1989 includes after-tax gains of $545 million ($.79 per common share) from the sale of the Company's equity interest in Columbia Pictures Entertainment, Inc. and the Company's bottled water business. Excluding these gains, the dividend payout ratio in 1989 was 41 percent.

1987	1986	1985	1984	1983	1982⁴	1981
$7,658	$6,977	$5,879	$5,442	$5,056	$4,760	$4,836
3,633	3,454	2,909	2,738	2,580	2,472	2,675
4,025	3,523	2,970	2,704	2,476	2,288	2,161
2,665	2,446	2,163	1,855	1,648	1,515	1,441
36	180	—	—	—	—	—
1,324	897	807	849	828	773	720
232	154	151	133	90	119	85
297	208	196	128	77	76	34
64	45	52	42	35	25	20
40	410	69	13	2	11	(20)
1,363	1,298	883	909	878	852	771
496	471	314	360	374	379	339
$ 867	$ 827	$ 569	$ 549	$ 504	$ 473	$ 432
$ 916	$ 934	$ 722	$ 629	$ 559	$ 512	$ 482
—	—	—	—	—	—	—
$ 916	$ 934	$ 722	$ 629	$ 559	$ 512	$ 482
$ 152	$ 151	$ 130	$ 119	$ 111	$ 104	$ 94
$ 304	$ 346	$ 412	$ 300	$ 324	$ 273	$ 279
755	774	787	793	817	779	742
$ 1.15	$ 1.07	$ .72	$ .69	$ .62	$ .61	$ .58
1.21	1.21	.92	.79	.68	.66	.65
.56	.52	.49	.46	.45	.41	.39
19.06	18.88	14.08	10.40	8.92	8.67	5.79
$1,489	$ 895	$ 843	$ 768	$ 559	$ 254	$ 344
1,602	1,538	1,483	1,284	1,247	1,233	1,160
8,606	7,675	6,341	5,241	4,540	4,212	3,373
909	996	801	631	428	423	132
2,995	1,848	1,280	1,310	520	493	227
3,187	3,479	2,948	2,751	2,912	2,779	2,271
6,182	5,327	4,228	4,061	3,432	3,272	2,498
26.0%	25.7%	20.0%	19.4%	17.7%	18.7%	19.9%
18.3%	20.1%	16.8%	16.7%	16.4%	17.9%	18.8%
$ 417	$ 311	$ 269	$ 268	$ 138	$ 61	$ 98
48.4%	34.7%	30.3%	32.3%	15.2%	15.1%	9.1%
15.4%	10.9%	15.6%	19.7%	5.6%	13.6%	2.9%
46.0%	43.1%	53.8%	57.9%	65.3%	62.8%	59.5%

³ See Financial Glossary on page 73.
⁴ In 1982, the Company adopted SFAS No. 52, "Foreign Currency Translation."

Consolidated Balance Sheets *The Coca-Cola Company and Subsidiaries*

December 31, *(In thousands except share data)*	1991	1990
Assets		
Current		
Cash and cash equivalents	$ 1,058,250	$1,429,555
Marketable securities, at cost (approximates market)	58,946	62,569
	1,117,196	1,492,124
Trade accounts receivable, less allowances of $34,567 in 1991 and $29,510 in 1990	933,448	913,541
Finance subsidiary—receivables	36,172	38,199
Inventories	987,764	982,313
Prepaid expenses and other assets	1,069,664	716,601
Total Current Assets	4,144,244	4,142,778
Investments and Other Assets		
Investments		
Coca-Cola Enterprises Inc. (CCE)	602,776	666,847
Coca-Cola Amatil Limited	570,774	569,057
Other, principally bottling companies	980,465	788,718
Finance subsidiary—receivables	288,471	128,119
Long-term receivables and other assets	442,135	321,977
	2,884,621	2,474,718
Property, Plant and Equipment		
Land	172,781	147,057
Buildings and improvements	1,200,672	1,059,969
Machinery and equipment	2,680,446	2,204,188
Containers	390,737	374,526
	4,444,636	3,785,740
Less allowances for depreciation	1,554,754	1,400,175
	2,889,882	2,385,565
Goodwill and Other Intangible Assets	303,681	275,126
	$10,222,428	$9,278,187

December 31,	1991	1990
Liabilities and Share-Owners' Equity		
Current		
Accounts payable and accrued expenses	$ 1,914,379	$1,576,426
Loans and notes payable	845,823	1,742,179
Finance subsidiary—notes payable	346,767	161,432
Current maturities of long-term debt	109,707	97,272
Accrued taxes	900,884	719,182
Total Current Liabilities	4,117,560	4,296,491
Long-Term Debt	985,258	535,861
Other Liabilities	493,765	332,060
Deferred Income Taxes	200,027	264,611
Share-Owners' Equity		
Preferred stock, $1 par value—		
Authorized: 100,000,000 shares; Issued: 3,000 shares of Cumulative Money		
Market Preferred Stock in 1991 and 1990; Outstanding: No shares in 1991;		
750 shares in 1990, stated at aggregate liquidation preference	—	75,000
Common stock, $.50 par value—		
Authorized: 1,400,000,000 shares; Issued: 843,675,547 shares in 1991;		
840,487,486 shares in 1990	421,838	420,244
Capital surplus	639,990	512,703
Reinvested earnings	7,425,514	6,447,576
Unearned compensation related to outstanding restricted stock	(114,909)	(67,760)
Foreign currency translation adjustment	(4,909)	4,031
	8,367,524	7,391,794
Less treasury stock, at cost (179,195,464 common shares in 1991;		
172,248,315 common shares in 1990)	3,941,706	3,542,630
	4,425,818	3,849,164
	$10,222,428	$9,278,187

See Notes to Consolidated Financial Statements.

Consolidated Statements of Income *The Coca-Cola Company and Subsidiaries*

Year Ended December 31, *(In thousands except per share data)*	**1991**	1990	1989
Net Operating Revenues	**$11,571,614**	$10,236,350	$8,622,287
Cost of goods sold	**4,648,385**	4,208,850	3,548,570
Gross Profit	**6,923,229**	6,027,500	5,073,717
Selling, administrative and general expenses	**4,604,184**	4,075,936	3,347,932
Operating Income	**2,319,045**	1,951,564	1,725,785
Interest income	**175,406**	169,985	205,035
Interest expense	**192,515**	230,979	308,034
Equity income (1991 reduced by $44 million related to restructuring charges recorded by CCE)	**39,975**	110,139	75,490
Other income—net	**41,368**	13,727	66,034
Income from Continuing Operations before Income Taxes	**2,383,279**	2,014,436	1,764,310
Income taxes	**765,277**	632,532	571,471
Income from Continuing Operations	**1,618,002**	1,381,904	1,192,839
Equity income from discontinued operation	—	—	21,537
Gain on sale of discontinued operation (net of income taxes of $421,021)	—	—	509,449
Net Income	**1,618,002**	1,381,904	1,723,825
Preferred stock dividends	**521**	18,158	21,392
Net Income Available to Common Share Owners	**$ 1,617,481**	$ 1,363,746	$1,702,433
Income per Common Share			
Continuing operations	**$ 2.43**	$ 2.04	$ 1.69
Discontinued operation	—	—	.77
Net Income per Common Share	**$ 2.43**	$ 2.04	$ 2.46
Average Common Shares Outstanding	**666,472**	668,570	691,962

See Notes to Consolidated Financial Statements.

Consolidated Statements of Share-Owners' Equity *The Coca-Cola Company and Subsidiaries*

Three Years Ended December 31, 1991 (In thousands except per share data)	Preferred Stock	Common Stock	Capital Surplus	Reinvested Earnings	Unearned Restricted Stock	Foreign Currency Translation	Treasury Stock
Balance December 31, 1988	$300,000	$417,395	$380,264	$4,385,142	$ (51,467)	$(17,010)	$(2,069,022)
Sales to employees exercising stock options	—	1,481	39,914	—	—	—	(3,804)
Tax benefit from employees' stock option and restricted stock plans	—	—	14,811	—	—	—	—
Translation adjustments (net of income taxes of $900)	—	—	—	—	—	9,804	—
Stock issued under restricted stock plans, less amortization of $7,944	—	34	2,335	—	5,575	—	—
Purchases of common stock for treasury	—	—	—	—	—	—	(1,163,137)
Net income	—	—	—	1,723,825	—	—	—
Dividends							
Preferred	—	—	—	(21,392)	—	—	—
Common (per share—$.68)	—	—	—	(469,263)	—	—	—
Balance December 31, 1989	300,000	418,910	437,324	5,618,312	(45,892)	(7,206)	(3,235,963)
Sales to employees exercising stock options	—	905	28,999	—	—	—	(2,762)
Tax benefit from employees' stock option and restricted stock plans	—	—	13,286	—	—	—	—
Translation adjustments (net of income taxes of $573)	—	—	—	—	—	11,237	—
Stock issued under restricted stock plans, less amortization of $11,655	—	429	33,094	—	(21,868)	—	—
Purchases of common stock for treasury	—	—	—	—	—	—	(303,905)
Redemption of preferred stock	(225,000)	—	—	—	—	—	—
Net income	—	—	—	1,381,904	—	—	—
Dividends							
Preferred	—	—	—	(18,158)	—	—	—
Common (per share—$.80)	—	—	—	(534,482)	—	—	—
Balance December 31, 1990	75,000	420,244	512,703	6,447,576	(67,760)	4,031	(3,542,630)
Sales to employees exercising stock options	—	972	38,422	—	—	—	(2,421)
Tax benefit from employees' stock option and restricted stock plans	—	—	20,015	—	—	—	—
Translation adjustments (net of income taxes of $958)	—	—	—	—	—	(8,940)	—
Stock issued under restricted stock plans, less amortization of $22,323	—	622	68,850	—	(47,149)	—	—
Purchases of common stock for treasury	—	—	—	—	—	—	(396,655)
Redemption of preferred stock	(75,000)	—	—	—	—	—	—
Net income	—	—	—	1,618,002	—	—	—
Dividends							
Preferred	—	—	—	(521)	—	—	—
Common (per share—$.96)	—	—	—	(639,543)	—	—	—
Balance December 31, 1991	$ —	$421,838	$639,990	$7,425,514	$(114,909)	$ (4,909)	$(3,941,706)

See Notes to Consolidated Financial Statements.

Consolidated Statements of Cash Flows *The Coca-Cola Company and Subsidiaries*

Year Ended December 31, *(In thousands)*	**1991**	1990	1989
Operating Activities			
Net income	**$1,618,002**	$1,381,904	$1,723,825
Depreciation and amortization	**261,427**	243,888	183,765
Deferred income taxes	**(66,147)**	(30,254)	37,036
Equity income, net of dividends	**(16,013)**	(93,816)	(76,088)
Foreign currency adjustments	**65,534**	(77,068)	(31,043)
Gain on sale of businesses and investments before income taxes	**(34,577)**	(60,277)	(1,006,664)
Other noncash items	**33,338**	97,752	24,360
Net change in operating assets and liabilities	**222,837**	(178,202)	279,382
Net cash provided by operating activities	**2,084,401**	1,283,927	1,134,573
Investing Activities			
Additions to finance subsidiary receivables	**(210,267)**	(31,551)	(57,006)
Collections of finance subsidiary receivables	**51,942**	58,243	188,810
Purchases of investments and other assets	**(399,183)**	(186,631)	(858,510)
Proceeds from disposals of investments and other assets	**180,058**	149,807	126,850
Proceeds from sale of businesses	**—**	—	1,680,073
Decrease (increase) in marketable securities	**2,735**	16,733	(3,889)
Purchases of property, plant and equipment	**(791,677)**	(592,971)	(462,466)
Proceeds from disposals of property, plant and equipment	**43,958**	19,208	60,665
Purchases of temporary investments and other	**(2,246)**	(113,875)	(145,009)
Proceeds from disposals of temporary investments	**—**	241,373	—
Net cash provided by (used in) investing activities	**(1,124,680)**	(439,664)	529,518
Net cash provided by operations after reinvestment	**959,721**	844,263	1,664,091
Financing Activities			
Issuances of debt	**989,926**	592,417	336,370
Payments of debt	**(1,246,664)**	(81,594)	(410,690)
Preferred stock redeemed	**(75,000)**	(225,000)	—
Common stock issued	**39,394**	29,904	41,395
Purchases of common stock for treasury	**(399,076)**	(306,667)	(1,166,941)
Dividends (common and preferred)	**(640,064)**	(552,640)	(490,655)
Net cash used in financing activities	**(1,331,484)**	(543,580)	(1,690,521)
Effect of Exchange Rate Changes on Cash **and Cash Equivalents**	**458**	32,852	(22,896)
Cash and Cash Equivalents			
Net increase (decrease) during the year	**(371,305)**	333,535	(49,326)
Balance at beginning of year	**1,429,555**	1,096,020	1,145,346
Balance at end of year	**$1,058,250**	$1,429,555	$1,096,020

See Notes to Consolidated Financial Statements.

Notes to Consolidated Financial Statements *The Coca-Cola Company and Subsidiaries*

 Accounting Policies

The significant accounting policies and practices followed by The Coca-Cola Company and subsidiaries (the Company) are as follows:

Consolidation

The consolidated financial statements include the accounts of the Company and all subsidiaries where control is not temporary. The Company's investments in companies in which it has the ability to exercise significant influence over operating and financial policies, including certain investments where there is a temporary majority interest, are accounted for by the equity method. Accordingly, the Company's share of the net earnings of these companies is included in consolidated net income. The Company's investments in other companies are carried at cost. All significant intercompany accounts and transactions are eliminated.

Certain amounts in the prior years' financial statements have been reclassified to conform to the current year presentation.

Net Income per Common Share

Net income per common share is computed by dividing net income less dividends on preferred stock by the weighted average number of common shares outstanding.

Cash Equivalents

Marketable securities that are highly liquid and have maturities of three months or less at the date of purchase are classified as cash equivalents.

Inventories

Inventories are valued at the lower of cost or market. In general, inventories are valued on the basis of average cost or first-in, first-out methods. However, certain soft drink and citrus inventories are valued on the last-in, first-out (LIFO) method. The excess of current costs over LIFO stated values amounted to approximately $27 million and $42 million at December 31, 1991 and 1990, respectively.

Property, Plant and Equipment

Property, plant and equipment are stated at cost, less allowances for depreciation. Property, plant and equipment are depreciated principally by the straight-line method over the estimated useful lives of the assets.

Goodwill and Other Intangible Assets

Goodwill and other intangible assets are stated on the basis of cost and are being amortized, principally on a straight-line basis, over the estimated future periods to be benefited (not exceeding 40 years). Accumulated amortization was approximately $16 million and $10 million at December 31, 1991 and 1990, respectively.

Income Taxes

Income tax amounts and balances have been computed in accordance with APB Opinion No. 11, "Accounting for Income Taxes."

In 1987, the Financial Accounting Standards Board (FASB) issued Statement of Financial Accounting Standards No. 96, "Accounting for Income Taxes" (SFAS 96). In 1991, the FASB issued an Exposure Draft, which would further modify accounting for income taxes. The Company's required adoption date is January 1, 1993. Based on preliminary studies and evaluations, accounting for income taxes under SFAS 96 or the Exposure Draft would not have a material impact on the Company's results of operations or financial position.

 Inventories

Inventories consist of the following (in thousands):

December 31,	1991	1990
Raw materials and supplies	$615,459	$567,694
Work in process	23,475	18,451
Finished goods	348,830	396,168
	$987,764	$982,313

 Bottling Investments

The Company invests in bottling companies to ensure the strongest and most efficient production, distribution and marketing systems possible, in order to maximize long-term growth in volume, cash flow and share-owner value of the bottler and the Company.

Notes to Consolidated Financial Statements *The Coca-Cola Company and Subsidiaries*

Coca-Cola Enterprises Inc.

Coca-Cola Enterprises Inc. (CCE) is the largest bottler of Company products in the United States. The Company owns approximately 44 percent of the outstanding common stock of CCE and, accordingly, accounts for its investment by the equity method of accounting. A summary of financial information for CCE is as follows (in thousands):

	December 31, 1991	December 28, 1990
Current assets	$ 706,298	$ 495,341
Noncurrent assets	5,970,297	4,525,255
Total assets	$6,676,595	$5,020,596
Current liabilities	$1,385,445	$1,054,791
Noncurrent liabilities	3,848,519	2,339,326
Total liabilities	$5,233,964	$3,394,117
Share-owners' equity	$1,442,631	$1,626,479
Company equity investment	$ 602,776	$ 666,847

Year Ended	December 31, 1991	December 28, 1990	December 29, 1989
Net operating revenues	$4,050,798	$4,034,043	$3,881,947
Cost of goods sold	2,380,258	2,359,267	2,313,032
Gross profit	$1,670,540	$1,674,776	$1,568,915
Operating income	$ 120,178	$ 325,548	$ 310,067
Operating cash flow[1]	$ 538,422	$ 592,391	$ 539,086
Income (loss) before income taxes	$ (91,140)	$ 184,247	$ 137,931
Net income (loss) available to common share owners	$ (91,675)	$ 77,148	$ 53,507
Company equity income (loss)	$ (39,732)	$ 34,429	$ 26,218

[1] *Excludes nonrecurring charges.*

CCE's 1991 results include pretax restructuring charges of $152 million and a pretax charge of $15 million to increase insurance reserves.

In a December 18, 1991, merger, CCE acquired Johnston Coca-Cola Bottling Group, Inc. (Johnston) for approximately $196 million and 13 million shares of CCE common stock. The Company exchanged its 22 percent ownership interest in Johnston for approximately $81 million in cash and 50,000 shares of CCE common stock, resulting in a pretax gain of $27 million to the Company. The Company's ownership interest in CCE was reduced from 49 percent to 44 percent as a result of this transaction.

Net concentrate/syrup sales to CCE were $626 million in 1991, $602 million in 1990 and $569 million in 1989. CCE purchases sweeteners through the Company under a pass-

through arrangement, and, accordingly, related collections from CCE and payments to suppliers are not included in the Company's consolidated statements of income. These transactions amounted to $185 million in 1991 and 1990 and $195 million in 1989. The Company also provides certain administrative and other services to CCE under negotiated fee arrangements.

The Company engages in a wide range of marketing programs, media advertising and other similar arrangements to promote the sale of Company products in territories in which CCE operates. The Company's direct support for certain CCE marketing activities and participation with CCE in cooperative advertising and other marketing programs, net of fees charged for services provided, amounted to approximately $199 million, $181 million and $178 million in 1991, 1990 and 1989, respectively.

During 1990, the Company sold 4 million shares of CCE common stock to CCE for $60 million under a share repurchase program.

In June 1990, the Company sold a temporary investment, Coca-Cola Holdings (Arkansas) Inc. (CCHA), to CCE for approximately $241 million and assumed indebtedness, which approximated the Company's original 1989 investment, plus carrying costs.

In June 1990, CCE recorded a pretax gain of approximately $56 million from the sale of two of its bottling subsidiaries. The purchaser of these former CCE bottling subsidiaries was Johnston, which, at the time of the sale, was 22 percent owned by the Company.

If valued at the December 31, 1991, quoted closing price of the publicly traded CCE shares, the calculated value of the Company's investment in CCE common stock would have exceeded the Company's carrying value by approximately $263 million.

Other Equity Investments

The Company owns approximately 51 percent of Coca-Cola Amatil Limited (CCA), an Australian-based bottler of Company products and manufacturer of snack foods. In August 1989, the Company acquired an initial 59.5 percent ownership interest in CCA for approximately $491 million (including certain acquisition-related costs). In separate transactions during 1990, CCA acquired an independent Australian bottler and the Company's 50 percent interest in a New Zealand bottling joint venture in exchange for consideration that included previously unissued common stock of CCA, resulting in a net reduction of the Company's owner-

Notes to Consolidated Financial Statements *The Coca-Cola Company and Subsidiaries*

ship interest to its present level. The Company intends to reduce its ownership interest in CCA to below 50 percent. Accordingly, the investment has been accounted for by the equity method of accounting.

At December 31, 1991, the excess of the Company's investment over its equity in the underlying net assets of CCA was approximately $283 million, which is being amortized primarily over 40 years. The Company recorded equity income from CCA of $15 million, $17 million and $6 million in 1991, 1990 and 1989, respectively. These amounts are net of the amortization charges discussed above.

Operating results include the Company's proportionate share of income from equity investments since the respective dates of investment. A summary of financial information for the Company's equity investments, other than CCE, is as follows (in thousands):

December 31,	1991	1990
Current assets	$1,797,396	$1,658,341
Noncurrent assets	3,794,114	4,431,810
Total assets	$5,591,510	$6,090,151
Current liabilities	$1,947,025	$1,696,796
Noncurrent liabilities	1,594,696	2,518,902
Total liabilities	$3,541,721	$4,215,698
Share-owners' equity	$2,049,789	$1,874,453
Company equity investments	$1,456,959	$1,310,209

Year Ended December 31,	1991	1990	1989
Net operating revenues	$7,876,737	$7,312,904	$5,598,946
Cost of goods sold	5,243,943	4,609,004	3,633,647
Gross profit	$2,632,794	$2,703,900	$1,965,299
Operating income	$ 559,885	$ 574,712	$ 431,915
Operating cash flow	$ 979,232	$ 940,244	$ 679,552
Income before income taxes	$ 315,231	$ 327,784	$ 199,255
Net income	$ 214,144	$ 205,436	$ 123,752
Company equity income	$ 79,707	$ 75,710	$ 49,272

Equity investments also include certain non-bottling investees.

Net sales to equity investees, other than CCE, were $1.3 billion in 1991 and $1.2 billion in 1990. The Company participates in various marketing, promotional and other activities with these investees, the majority of which are located outside the United States.

If valued at the December 31, 1991, quoted closing prices of shares actively traded on stock markets, the net calculated value of the Company's investment in publicly

traded bottlers, other than CCE, would have exceeded the Company's carrying value by approximately $189 million.

The balance sheet caption "Other, principally bottling companies" also includes various investments that are accounted for by the cost method.

▽4 Finance Subsidiary

Coca-Cola Financial Corporation (CCFC) provides loans and other forms of financing to Coca-Cola bottlers and customers for the acquisition of sales-related equipment and for other business purposes. The approximate contractual maturities of finance receivables for the five years succeeding December 31, 1991, are as follows (in thousands):

1992	$ 36,172
1993	23,325
1994	169,317
1995	10,414
1996	19,620

These amounts do not reflect possible prepayments or renewals.

In connection with the December 1991 acquisition of Sunbelt Coca-Cola Bottling Company, Inc. by Coca-Cola Bottling Co. Consolidated (Consolidated), CCFC purchased 25,000 shares of Consolidated preferred stock for $50 million, provided to Consolidated a $153 million bridge loan and issued a $77 million letter of credit on Consolidated's behalf. The Company beneficially owns a 30 percent economic interest and a 23 percent voting interest in Consolidated.

Finance receivables also include amounts due from CCE (substantially all of which were assumed by CCE upon its acquisition of Johnston) of $68 million and $56 million at December 31, 1991 and 1990, respectively.

▽5 Short-Term Borrowings and Credit Arrangements

Loans and notes payable consist primarily of commercial paper issued in the United States. At December 31, 1991, the Company had $753 million in lines of credit and other short-term credit facilities contractually available, under which $111 million was outstanding. The lines included $505 million designated to support commercial paper and other borrowings, of which no amounts were outstanding at December 31,1991. These facilities are subject to normal banking terms and conditions. Some of the financial arrangements require compensating balances, none of which are presently significant to the Company.

Notes to Consolidated Financial Statements *The Coca-Cola Company and Subsidiaries*

⑥ Accrued Taxes

Accrued taxes consist of the following (in thousands):

December 31,	1991	1990
Income taxes	$789,632	$618,590
Sales, payroll and miscellaneous taxes	111,252	100,592
	$900,884	$719,182

⑦ Long-Term Debt

Long-term debt consists of the following (in thousands):

December 31,	1991	1990
9 7/8% U.S. dollar notes due 1992	$ 89,565	$ 59,667
7 3/4% U.S. dollar notes due 1996	249,890	—
5 3/4% Japanese yen notes due 1996[1]	239,987	222,977
5 3/4% German mark notes due 1998[1]	165,206	166,953
7 7/8% U.S. dollar notes due 1998	249,372	—
11 3/8% U.S. dollar notes due 1991	—	85,675
Other, due 1992 to 2013[2]	100,945	97,861
	1,094,965	633,133
Less current portion	109,707	97,272
	$ 985,258	$535,861

[1] *Portions of these notes have been swapped for liabilities denominated in other currencies.*
[2] *Interest on a portion of this debt varies with the changes in the prime rate, and the weighted average interest rate applicable to the remainder is approximately 12.3 percent.*

Maturities of long-term debt for the five years succeeding December 31, 1991, are as follows (in thousands):

1992	$109,707
1993	28,396
1994	17,601
1995	7,932
1996	494,264

The above notes include various restrictions, none of which are presently significant to the Company.

Interest paid was approximately $160 million, $233 million and $319 million in 1991, 1990 and 1989, respectively.

⑧ Financial Instruments

The Company has entered into foreign currency hedging transactions to reduce its exposure to adverse fluctuations in foreign exchange rates. While the hedging instruments are subject to the risk of loss from changes in exchange rates, these losses would generally be offset by gains on the exposures being hedged. The Company had $2.6 billion and $1.4 billion of foreign currency hedging instruments out-standing at December 31, 1991 and 1990, respectively. The contracts are transacted with creditworthy financial institutions and generally mature within one year.

At December 31, 1991, the Company is contingently liable for guarantees of indebtedness owed by third parties of $117 million, of which $54 million is related to independent bottling licensees.

⑨ Preferred Stock

In February 1991, the Company completed the redemption of the remaining $75 million of its initial $300 million of Cumulative Money Market Preferred Stock (MMP). The Company redeemed $225 million of the MMP in 1990. Prior to redemption, the weighted average dividend rate (per annum) for the MMP was approximately 6 percent in 1991 and 1990.

⑩ Common Stock

Common shares outstanding and related changes for the three years ended December 31, 1991, are as follows (in thousands):

	1991	1990	1989
Outstanding at January 1,	668,239	674,030	709,578
Issued to employees exercising stock options	1,943	1,810	2,962
Issued under restricted stock plans	1,245	858	68
Purchases of common stock for treasury	(6,947)	(8,459)	(38,578)
Outstanding at December 31,	664,480	668,239	674,030

⑪ Restricted Stock, Stock Options and Other Stock Plans

The Company sponsors restricted stock award plans, stock option plans, Incentive Unit Agreements and Performance Unit Agreements.

Under the amended 1989 Restricted Stock Award Plan and the amended 1983 Restricted Stock Award Plan (the Plans), 10 million and 6 million shares of restricted common stock, respectively, may be granted to certain officers and key employees of the Company.

In 1991, 1990 and 1989, 1,245,000 shares, 858,000 shares and 68,000 shares, respectively, were granted under the Plans. At December 31, 1991, 8.7 million shares were available for grant under the Plans. The participant is entitled to vote and receive dividends on the shares, and, under the

Notes to Consolidated Financial Statements *The Coca-Cola Company and Subsidiaries*

1983 Restricted Stock Award Plan, the participant is reimbursed by the Company for income taxes imposed on the award. The shares are subject to certain transfer restrictions and may be forfeited if the participant leaves the Company for reasons other than retirement, disability or death, absent a change in control of the Company. On July 18, 1991, the Plans were amended to specify age 62 as the minimum retirement age. In addition, the 1983 Restricted Stock Award Plan was further amended to conform to the terms of the 1989 Restricted Stock Award Plan by requiring a minimum of five years of service prior to retirement. The amendments affect shares granted subsequent to July 18, 1991.

Under the Company's 1991 Stock Option Plan (the Option Plan), a maximum of 30 million shares of the Company's common stock may be issued or transferred to certain officers and employees pursuant to stock options and stock appreciation rights granted under the Option Plan. The stock appreciation rights permit the holder, upon surrendering all or part of the related stock option, to receive cash, common stock or a combination thereof, in an amount up to 100 percent of the difference between the market price and the option price. No stock appreciation rights have been granted since April 1990, and the Company does not presently intend to grant additional stock appreciation rights in the future. Options outstanding at December 31, 1991, also include various options granted under previous plans. Further information relating to options is as follows (in thousands, except per share amounts):

	1991	1990	1989
Outstanding at January 1,	16,532	13,504	17,315
Granted	3,996	5,196	32
Exercised	(1,943)	(1,810)	(2,962)
Canceled	(394)	(358)	(881)
Outstanding at December 31,	18,191	16,532	13,504
Exercisable at December 31,	12,026	9,569	8,561
Shares available at December 31, for options that may be granted	27,689	1,559	6,643
Prices per share			
Exercised	$6–$56	$5–$39	$5–$23
Unexercised at December 31,	$8–$59	$6–$48	$5–$24

In 1988, the Company entered into Incentive Unit Agreements, whereby certain officers will be granted cash awards based on the market value of 600,000 shares of the Company's common stock at the measurement dates. The Incentive Unit Agreements provide for a cash payment for income taxes when the value of the units is paid.

In 1985, the Company entered into Performance Unit Agreements, whereby certain officers will be granted cash awards based on the difference in the market value of approximately 1.1 million shares of the Company's common stock at the measurement dates and the base price of $10.31, the market value as of January 2, 1985.

12 Pensions and Other Postretirement Benefits

In the United States, the Company sponsors and/or contributes to pension plans covering substantially all U.S. employees and certain employees in international locations. The benefits are primarily based on years of service and the employees' compensation for certain periods during the last years of employment. Pension costs are generally funded currently, subject to regulatory funding limitations. The Company also sponsors nonqualified, unfunded defined benefit plans for certain officers and other employees. In addition, the Company and its subsidiaries have various pension plans and other forms of postretirement arrangements outside the United States.

Total pension expense amounted to approximately $42 million in 1991, $30 million in 1990 and $23 million in 1989. Net periodic pension cost for the Company's defined benefit plans in 1991, 1990 and 1989 consists of the following (in thousands):

Notes to Consolidated Financial Statements *The Coca-Cola Company and Subsidiaries*

	U.S. Plans			International Plans		
Year Ended December 31,	**1991**	1990	1989	**1991**	1990	1989
Service cost—benefits earned during the period	**$ 12,475**	$ 10,684	$ 9,830	**$ 15,894**	$ 12,902	$ 12,133
Interest cost on projected benefit obligation	**45,860**	41,786	35,393	**18,523**	14,720	12,539
Actual return on plan assets	**(112,530)**	(9,121)	(95,254)	**(17,498)**	(3,811)	(16,108)
Net amortization and deferral	**71,090**	(31,168)	56,548	**555**	(11,273)	2,240
Net periodic pension cost	**$ 16,895**	$ 12,181	$ 6,517	**$ 17,474**	$ 12,538	$ 10,804

The following table sets forth the funded status for the Company's defined benefit plans at December 31, 1991 and 1990 (in thousands):

	U.S. Plans				International Plans			
	Assets Exceed Accumulated Benefits		Accumulated Benefits Exceed Assets		Assets Exceed Accumulated Benefits		Accumulated Benefits Exceed Assets	
December 31,	**1991**	1990	**1991**	1990	**1991**	1990	**1991**	1990
Actuarial present value of benefit obligations								
Vested benefit obligation	**$359,857**	$340,598	**$ 66,907**	$ 53,386	**$ 96,074**	$ 84,890	**$ 81,609**	$ 70,044
Accumulated benefit obligation	**$383,972**	$362,724	**$ 72,610**	$ 57,372	**$106,286**	$ 89,263	**$ 91,208**	$ 72,938
Projected benefit obligation	**$455,357**	$424,118	**$ 82,251**	$ 65,703	**$145,435**	$129,435	**$144,245**	$113,842
Plan assets at fair value[1]	**583,819**	508,267	**—**	811	**175,392**	160,945	**74,640**	62,335
Plan assets in excess of (less than) projected benefit obligation	**128,462**	84,149	**(82,251)**[2]	(64,892)[2]	**29,957**	31,510	**(69,605)**	(51,507)
Unrecognized net (asset) liability at transition	**(40,764)**	(44,317)	**21,292**	23,416	**(29,229)**	(32,076)	**40,908**	38,121
Unrecognized prior service cost	**25,756**	28,302	**2,795**	1,175	**105**	2,017	**5,243**	—
Unrecognized net (gain) loss	**(114,934)**	(64,617)	**14,506**	5,647	**10,265**	5,171	**(1,672)**	58
Adjustment required to recognize minimum liability	**—**	—	**(28,952)**	(21,941)	**—**	—	**(453)**	(167)
Accrued pension asset (liability) included in the consolidated balance sheet	**$ (1,480)**	$ 3,517	**$(72,610)**	$(56,595)	**$ 11,098**	$ 6,622	**$ (25,579)**	$ (13,495)

[1] Primarily listed stocks, bonds and government securities.
[2] Substantially all of this amount relates to nonqualified, unfunded defined benefit plans.

The assumptions used in computing the above information are as follows:

	U.S. Plans			International Plans (weighted average rates)		
	1991	1990	1989	**1991**	1990	1989
Discount rates	**9%**	9%	9%	**7½%**	8%	7%
Rates of increase in compensation levels	**6%**	6%	6%	**6%**	6%	4%
Expected long-term rates of return on assets	**9½%**	9½%	9%	**7½%**	8%	8%

Notes to Consolidated Financial Statements *The Coca-Cola Company and Subsidiaries*

The Company also has plans that provide postretirement health care and life insurance benefits to substantially all U.S. employees and certain international employees who retire with a minimum of five years of service. The annual cash cost of these benefits is not significant. In 1990, the FASB issued Statement of Financial Accounting Standards No. 106, "Employers' Accounting for Postretirement Benefits Other than Pensions" (SFAS 106). SFAS 106 will require companies to accrue the cost of postretirement health care and life insurance benefits within employees' active service periods. The Company's required adoption date for SFAS 106 is January 1, 1993.

SFAS 106 allows companies to either recognize their full accumulated postretirement benefit obligation at the date of adoption or amortize it as a component of postretirement benefits expense over a period of up to twenty years. The Company is currently evaluating these options.

Based on preliminary studies and evaluations, the Company's accumulated postretirement benefit obligation at January 1, 1993, will be approximately $200 million, before related income tax benefits. The increase in annual pretax postretirement benefits expense after adoption of SFAS 106 is expected to be in the range of $20 million to $30 million.

¹³ Income Taxes

The components of income before income taxes for both continuing and discontinued operations consist of the following (in thousands):

Year Ended December 31,	1991	1990	1989
United States	$ 648,471	$ 494,544	$1,459,213
International	1,734,808	1,519,892	1,257,104
	$2,383,279	$2,014,436	$2,716,317

Income taxes for continuing and discontinued operations consist of the following (in thousands):

Year Ended December 31,	United States	State & Local	International	Total
1991				
Current	$204,781	$30,981	$595,662	$831,424
Deferred	(61,229)	(5,267)	349	(66,147)
1990				
Current	$134,973	$26,515	$501,298	$662,786
Deferred	(49,387)	(2,596)	21,729	(30,254)
1989				
Current	$478,004	$84,072	$393,380	$955,456
Deferred	(8,025)	160	44,901	37,036

The Company made income tax payments of approximately $672 million, $803 million and $537 million in 1991, 1990 and 1989, respectively.

A reconciliation of the statutory U.S. federal rate and effective rates for continuing operations is as follows:

Year Ended December 31,	1991	1990	1989
Statutory U.S. federal rate	**34.0%**	34.0%	34.0%
State income taxes—net of federal benefit	**1.0**	1.0	1.0
Earnings in jurisdictions taxed at rates different from the statutory U.S. federal rate	**(3.1)**	(2.6)	(1.6)
Equity income	**(.6)**	(1.8)	(1.5)
Other—net	**.8**	.8	.5
	32.1%	31.4%	32.4%

Deferred taxes are provided principally for depreciation, certain employee compensation-related expenses and certain capital transactions that are recognized in different years for financial statement and income tax purposes. The Company has manufacturing facilities in Puerto Rico that operate under a negotiated exemption grant that expires December 31, 2009.

Appropriate U.S. and international taxes have been provided for earnings of subsidiary companies that are expected to be remitted to the parent company. Accumulated unremitted earnings of international subsidiaries that are expected to be required for use in the international operations were approximately $373 million at December 31, 1991, exclusive of amounts that, if remitted, would result in little or no tax.

Notes to Consolidated Financial Statements *The Coca-Cola Company and Subsidiaries*

▽14 Net Change in Operating Assets and Liabilities

The changes in operating assets and liabilities, net of effects of acquisitions and divestitures of businesses and unrealized exchange gains/losses, are as follows (in thousands):

Year Ended December 31,	1991	1990	1989
Increase in trade accounts receivable	$ (31,826)	$ (87,749)	$ (99,496)
Increase in inventories	(3,020)	(169,442)	(34,709)
Increase in prepaid expenses and other assets	(325,595)	(65,758)	(204,222)
Increase in accounts payable and accrued expenses	266,684	198,631	88,940
Increase (decrease) in accrued taxes	215,877	(111,014)	456,544
Increase in other liabilities	100,717	57,130	72,325
	$222,837	$(178,202)	$279,382

The net change in operating assets and liabilities in 1990 reflects estimated tax payments of approximately $300 million related to the 1989 gain on the sale of Columbia Pictures Entertainment, Inc. stock.

▽15 Acquisitions and Divestitures

The Company periodically engages in the acquisition and/or divestiture of bottling and other related companies. Significant transactions are discussed below.

In August 1989, the Company acquired all of the Coca-Cola bottling operations of Pernod Ricard. Pernod Ricard had operated the Coca-Cola bottling, canning and distribution business in six major territories in France. The fair values of assets acquired and liabilities assumed were $285 million and $145 million, respectively. The $140 million acquisition was accounted for by the purchase method. Operating results have been included in the consolidated statements of income from the date of acquisition.

In August 1989, the Company sold Belmont Springs Water Co., Inc., a bottled water operation, which resulted in a pretax gain of approximately $61 million.

See Note 3 for discussions of the equity investment in CCA, which was acquired in August 1989, and the temporary investment in CCHA, which was acquired in July 1989 and sold in June 1990. See Note 17 for a discussion of the sale of Columbia Pictures Entertainment, Inc. stock.

▽16 Other Nonrecurring Items

"Other income—net" in 1991 includes a $69 million pretax gain on the sale of property no longer required as a result of a consolidation of concentrate operations in Japan and a $27 million pretax gain on the sale of the Company's 22 percent ownership interest in Johnston to CCE. "Selling, administrative and general expenses" and "Interest expense" include 1991 pretax charges of $13 million and $8 million, respectively, for potential future costs related to bottler litigation. In addition, 1991 equity income has been reduced by $44 million related to restructuring charges recorded by CCE.

"Other income—net" in 1990 includes a pretax gain of $52 million on the Company's investment in BCI Securities L.P. (BCI) resulting from BCI's sale of Beatrice Company stock. "Selling, administrative and general expenses" in 1990 include nonrecurring pretax charges of $49 million related to the Company's United States soft drink business. These charges reflect accelerated amortization of certain software costs due to management plans to upgrade and standardize information systems and adjustments to the carrying value of certain fountain equipment and marketing-related items to amounts estimated to be recoverable in future periods.

▽17 Discontinued Operation

In 1989, the Company sold its entire equity interest in Columbia Pictures Entertainment, Inc. (CPE) for approximately $1.6 billion in cash. The equity interest consisted of approximately 49 percent of the outstanding common shares of CPE and 1,000 shares of preferred stock. The sale resulted in a pretax gain of approximately $930 million. On an after-tax basis, the gain was approximately $509 million or $.74 per common share. The effective tax rate of 45 percent on the gain on the sale of CPE stock differs from the statutory U.S. federal rate of 34 percent due primarily to differences between the book basis and tax basis of the Company's investment in CPE.

CPE has been reported as a discontinued operation, and, accordingly, the gain from the sale of CPE stock and the Company's equity income from CPE have been reported separately from continuing operations.

Notes to Consolidated Financial Statements *The Coca-Cola Company and Subsidiaries*

18 Lines of Business

The Company operates in two major lines of business: soft drinks and foods (principally juice and juice-drink products). Information concerning operations in these businesses at December 31, 1991, 1990 and 1989, and for the years then ended, is presented below (in millions):

1991	Soft Drinks United States	International	Foods	Corporate	Consolidated
Net operating revenues	$2,645.2	$7,244.8	$1,635.7	$ 45.9	$11,571.6
Operating income	468.7	2,141.1	103.7	(394.5)	2,319.0
Identifiable operating assets	1,447.0	4,742.3	755.0	1,124.1[3]	8,068.4
Equity income				40.0[1]	40.0
Investments (principally bottling companies)				2,154.0	2,154.0
Capital expenditures	131.1	546.3	57.1	57.2	791.7
Depreciation and amortization	81.9	111.9	30.8	36.8	261.4

1990	Soft Drinks United States	International	Foods	Corporate	Consolidated
Net operating revenues	$2,461.3	$6,125.4	$1,604.9	$ 44.8	$10,236.4
Operating income	358.1[2]	1,801.4	93.5	(301.4)	1,951.6
Identifiable operating assets	1,691.0	3,672.2	759.2	1,131.2[3]	7,253.6
Equity income				110.1	110.1
Investments (principally bottling companies)				2,024.6	2,024.6
Capital expenditures	138.4	321.4	68.2	65.0	593.0
Depreciation and amortization	88.5	94.4	28.3	32.7	243.9

1989	Soft Drinks United States	International	Foods	Corporate	Consolidated
Net operating revenues	$2,222.2	$4,759.2	$1,583.3	$ 57.6	$ 8,622.3
Operating income	390.6	1,517.6	87.4	(269.8)	1,725.8
Identifiable operating assets	1,814.4	2,806.0	695.3	1,036.4[3]	6,352.1
Equity income				75.5	75.5
Investments (principally bottling companies)				1,930.4	1,930.4
Capital expenditures	136.3	215.6	61.6	49.0	462.5
Depreciation and amortization	73.9	48.4	30.7	30.8	183.8

Intercompany transfers between sectors are not material.

[1] *Reduced by $44 million related to restructuring charges recorded by CCE.*
[2] *Includes nonrecurring charges of $49 million.*
[3] *Corporate identifiable operating assets are composed principally of marketable securities and fixed assets.*

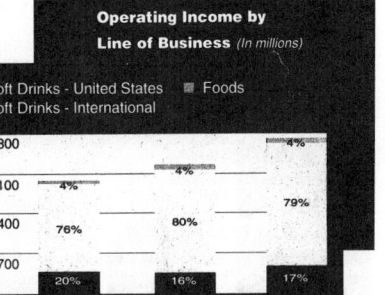

Operating Income by Line of Business *(In millions)*

Soft Drinks - United States   Foods
Soft Drinks - International

Net Operating Revenues by Line of Business *(In millions)*

Notes to Consolidated Financial Statements *The Coca-Cola Company and Subsidiaries*

19. Operations in Geographic Areas

Information about the Company's operations in different geographic areas at December 31, 1991, 1990 and 1989, and for the years then ended, is presented below (in millions):

1991	United States	Latin America	European Community	Northeast Europe/ Africa	Pacific and Canada	Corporate	Consolidated
Net operating revenues	$4,124.8	$1,103.2	$3,338.3	$613.6	$2,345.8	$ 45.9	$11,571.6
Operating income	560.2	404.6	767.3	204.1	777.3	(394.5)	2,319.0
Identifiable operating assets	2,160.9	814.6	2,558.0	423.5	987.3	1,124.1[3]	8,068.4
Equity income						40.0[1]	40.0
Investments (principally bottling companies)						2,154.0	2,154.0
Capital expenditures	184.8	105.5	330.6	61.3	52.3	57.2	791.7
Depreciation and amortization	111.3	23.3	65.8	9.7	14.5	36.8	261.4

1990	United States	Latin America	European Community	Northeast Europe/ Africa	Pacific and Canada	Corporate	Consolidated
Net operating revenues	$3,931.0	$ 813.0	$2,804.8	$562.8	$2,080.0	$ 44.8	$10,236.4
Operating income	440.4[2]	300.2	666.5	174.2	671.7	(301.4)	1,951.6
Identifiable operating assets	2,414.2	640.3	1,818.8	400.1	849.0	1,131.2[3]	7,253.6
Equity income						110.1	110.1
Investments (principally bottling companies)						2,024.6	2,024.6
Capital expenditures	204.0	59.7	203.5	38.8	22.0	65.0	593.0
Depreciation and amortization	115.6	18.0	54.5	7.6	15.5	32.7	243.9

1989	United States	Latin America	European Community	Northeast Europe/ Africa	Pacific and Canada	Corporate	Consolidated
Net operating revenues	$3,678.7	$ 646.2	$1,855.1	$425.2	$1,959.5	$ 57.6	$ 8,622.3
Operating income	468.2	226.7	540.6	147.3	612.8	(269.8)	1,725.8
Identifiable operating assets	2,476.0	515.4	1,342.8	328.8	652.7	1,036.4[3]	6,352.1
Equity income						75.5	75.5
Investments (principally bottling companies)						1,930.4	1,930.4
Capital expenditures	196.4	30.7	133.9	24.6	27.9	49.0	462.5
Depreciation and amortization	103.5	11.8	18.0	4.9	14.8	30.8	183.8

Intercompany transfers between geographic areas are not material.
Identifiable liabilities of operations outside the United States amounted to approximately $1.7 billion, $1.5 billion and $1.1 billion at December 31, 1991, 1990 and 1989, respectively.

[1] Reduced by $44 million related to restructuring charges recorded by CCE.
[2] Includes nonrecurring charges of $49 million.
[3] Corporate identifiable operating assets are composed principally of marketable securities and fixed assets.

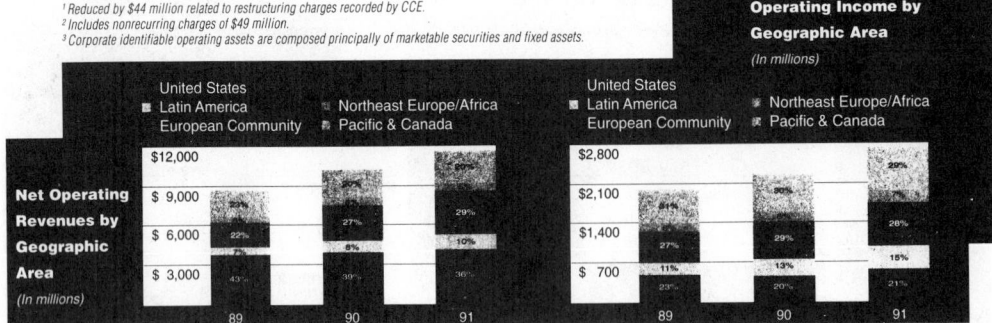

Net Operating Revenues by Geographic Area (In millions)

Operating Income by Geographic Area (In millions)

United States / Latin America / European Community / Northeast Europe/Africa / Pacific & Canada

Report of Independent Auditors

Board of Directors and Share Owners
The Coca-Cola Company

We have audited the accompanying consolidated balance sheets of The Coca-Cola Company and subsidiaries as of December 31, 1991 and 1990, and the related consolidated statements of income, share-owners' equity and cash flows for each of the three years in the period ended December 31, 1991. These financial statements are the responsibility of the Company's management. Our responsibility is to express an opinion on these financial statements based on our audits.

We conducted our audits in accordance with generally accepted auditing standards. Those standards require that we plan and perform the audit to obtain reasonable assurance about whether the financial statements are free of material misstatement. An audit includes examining, on a test basis, evidence supporting the amounts and disclosures in the financial statements. An audit also includes assessing the accounting principles used and significant estimates made by management, as well as evaluating the overall financial statement presentation. We believe that our audits provide a reasonable basis for our opinion.

In our opinion, the financial statements referred to above present fairly, in all material respects, the consolidated financial position of The Coca-Cola Company and subsidiaries at December 31, 1991 and 1990, and the consolidated results of their operations and their cash flows for each of the three years in the period ended December 31, 1991, in conformity with generally accepted accounting principles.

Ernst & Young

Atlanta, Georgia
January 24, 1992

STATEMENTS OF CONSOLIDATED INCOME
Thousands of Dollars Except Per Share Data

MAYTAG
CORPORATION

	Year ended December 31		
	1991	1990	1989
Net sales	**$2,970,626**	$ 3,056,833	$ 3,088,753
Cost of sales	**2,254,221**	2,309,138	2,312,645
GROSS PROFIT	**716,405**	747,695	776,108
Selling, general and administrative expenses	**524,898**	517,088	496,165
OPERATING INCOME	**191,507**	230,607	279,943
Interest expense	**(75,159)**	(81,966)	(83,398)
Other – net	**7,069**	10,764	10,427
INCOME BEFORE INCOME TAXES	**123,417**	159,405	206,972
Income taxes	**44,400**	60,500	75,500
NET INCOME	**$ 79,017**	$ 98,905	$ 131,472
Income per average share of Common stock	**$ 0.75**	$ 0.94	$ 1.27

See notes to consolidated financial statements.

MAYTAG
CORPORATION

STATEMENTS OF CONSOLIDATED FINANCIAL CONDITION
Thousands of Dollars

	December 31	
ASSETS	**1991**	1990
CURRENT ASSETS		
Cash and cash equivalents	$ 48,752	$ 69,587
Accounts receivable, less allowance –		
(1991 – $14,119; 1990 – $17,600)	457,773	487,726
Inventories	489,082	535,787
Deferred income taxes	24,858	22,937
Other current assets	56,168	52,484
Total current assets	1,076,633	1,168,521
OTHER ASSETS		
Pension investments	232,231	235,264
Intangibles, less allowance for amortization –		
(1991 – $28,295; 1990 – $18,980)	338,275	347,090
Miscellaneous	52,436	45,209
Total other assets	622,942	627,563
PROPERTY, PLANT AND EQUIPMENT		
Land	51,147	50,613
Buildings and improvements	296,684	282,828
Machinery and equipment	895,025	828,464
Construction in progress	92,954	61,775
	1,335,810	1,223,680
Less allowances for depreciation	500,317	433,223
Total property, plant and equipment	835,493	790,457
TOTAL ASSETS	$2,535,068	$ 2,586,541

See notes to consolidated financial statements.

MAYTAG
CORPORATION

	December 31	
LIABILITIES AND SHAREOWNERS' EQUITY	**1991**	1990
CURRENT LIABILITIES		
Notes payable	$ **23,504**	$ 56,601
Accounts payable	**273,731**	266,190
Compensation to employees	**63,845**	53,753
Accrued liabilities	**165,384**	154,369
Income taxes payable	**17,574**	13,736
Current maturities of long-term debt	**23,570**	11,070
Total current liabilities	**567,608**	555,719
DEFERRED INCOME TAXES	**75,210**	71,548
LONG-TERM DEBT	**809,480**	857,941
OTHER NONCURRENT LIABILITIES	**72,185**	86,602
SHAREOWNERS' EQUITY		
Common stock:		
Authorized – 200,000,000 shares (par value $1.25)		
Issued – 117,150,593 shares, including shares in treasury	**146,438**	146,438
Additional paid-in capital	**479,833**	487,034
Retained earnings	**696,745**	670,878
Cost of Common stock in treasury at cost		
(1991 – 10,808,116 shares; 1990 – 11,424,154 shares)	**(240,848)**	(254,576)
Employee stock plans	**(66,711)**	(63,590)
Foreign currency translation	**(4,872)**	28,547
Total shareowners' equity	**1,010,585**	1,014,731
TOTAL LIABILITIES AND SHAREOWNERS' EQUITY	**$2,535,068**	$ 2,586,541

MAYTAG
CORPORATION

STATEMENTS OF CONSOLIDATED CASH FLOWS
Thousands of Dollars

	Year ended December 31		
	1991	1990	1989
OPERATING ACTIVITIES			
Net income	**$ 79,017**	$ 98,905	$ 131,472
Adjustments to reconcile income to net cash provided by			
(used in) operating activities:			
Depreciation and amortization	**92,667**	86,079	76,994
Deferred income taxes	**1,700**	22,800	9,000
Changes in selected working capital items:			
Inventories	**37,075**	29,911	(79,401)
Receivables and other current assets	**12,867**	9,462	(34,272)
Current liabilities	**46,623**	64,322	(94,037)
Net change in pension investments	**(10,012)**	(22,506)	(7,566)
Other – net	**(25,267)**	7,803	(6,118)
NET CASH PROVIDED BY (USED IN)			
OPERATIONS	**234,670**	296,776	(3,928)
INVESTING ACTIVITIES			
Capital expenditures – net	**(138,100)**	(136,751)	(110,563)
Cash of acquired company			23,515
Proceeds from sale of furniture companies			196,780
Proceeds from reversion of excess pension investments			17,875
TOTAL INVESTING ACTIVITIES	**(138,100)**	(136,751)	127,607
FINANCING ACTIVITIES			
Proceeds from credit agreements and long-term borrowings	**57,900**	230,000	317,500
Reduction in long-term debt and notes payable	**(123,855)**	(269,921)	(264,101)
Stock options exercised and other Common stock transactions	**3,421**	6,862	19,495
Treasury stock purchases		(832)	(64,161)
Dividends	**(53,150)**	(100,386)	(99,932)
TOTAL FINANCING ACTIVITIES	**(115,684)**	(134,277)	(91,199)
Effect of exchange rates on cash	**(1,721)**	4,578	(3,722)
INCREASE (DECREASE) IN CASH AND			
CASH EQUIVALENTS	**(20,835)**	30,326	28,758
Cash and cash equivalents at beginning of year	**69,587**	39,261	10,503
CASH AND CASH EQUIVALENTS			
AT END OF YEAR	**$ 48,752**	$ 69,587	$ 39,261

See notes to consolidated financial statements.

Consolidated Statements of Income

(thousands except per share amounts)

The Limited, Inc.

	1991	1990	1989
Net Sales	**$6,149,218**	$5,253,509	$4,647,916
Costs of Goods Sold, Occupancy, and Buying Costs	**4,355,675**	3,623,070	3,201,281
Gross Income	**1,793,543**	1,630,439	1,446,635
General, Administrative, and Store Operating Expenses	**1,080,843**	932,902	821,381
Operating Income	**712,700**	697,537	625,254
Interest Expense	**(63,927)**	(56,609)	(58,059)
Other Income, net	**11,529**	12,510	6,731
Income Before Income Taxes	**660,302**	653,438	573,926
Provision for Income Taxes	**257,000**	255,000	227,000
Net Income	**$ 403,302**	$ 398,438	$ 346,926
Net Income Per Share	**$ 1.11**	$ 1.10	$ .96

The accompanying Notes are an integral part of these Consolidated Financial Statements.

Net Income

(in millions)
CAGR 34% (Compound Annual Growth Rate, last ten years)

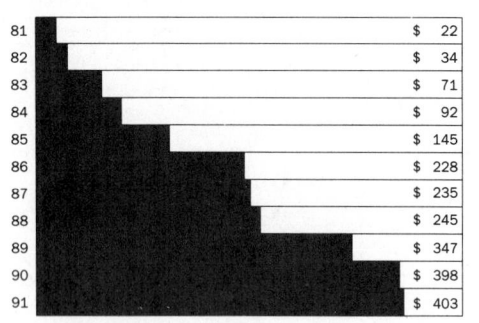

81	$ 22
82	$ 34
83	$ 71
84	$ 92
85	$ 145
86	$ 228
87	$ 235
88	$ 245
89	$ 347
90	$ 398
91	$ 403

Net Income Per Share

CAGR 32%

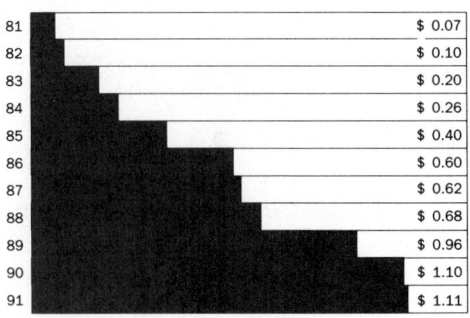

81	$ 0.07
82	$ 0.10
83	$ 0.20
84	$ 0.26
85	$ 0.40
86	$ 0.60
87	$ 0.62
88	$ 0.68
89	$ 0.96
90	$ 1.10
91	$ 1.11

Consolidated Balance Sheets

(thousands)

The Limited, Inc.

Assets	Feb. 1, 1992	Feb. 2, 1991
Current Assets		
Cash and Equivalents	$ 33,735	$ 13,180
Accounts Receivable	735,832	670,296
Inventories	730,050	585,166
Other	104,708	96,319
Total Current Assets	1,604,325	1,364,961
Property and Equipment, net	1,657,084	1,395,073
Other Assets	157,447	111,844
Total Assets	$3,418,856	$2,871,878
Liabilities and Shareholders' Equity		
Current Liabilities		
Accounts Payable	$ 199,756	$ 200,078
Accrued Expenses	265,267	256,153
Income Taxes	55,097	24,726
Total Current Liabilities	520,120	480,957
Long-Term Debt	713,758	540,446
Deferred Income Taxes	267,315	254,304
Other Long-Term Liabilities	40,871	36,119
Shareholders' Equity		
Common Stock	189,727	189,727
Paid-in Capital	100,929	99,237
Retained Earnings	1,783,027	1,480,866
	2,073,683	1,769,830
Less Treasury Stock, at cost	(196,891)	(209,778)
Total Shareholders' Equity	1,876,792	1,560,052
Total Liabilities and Shareholders' Equity	$3,418,856	$2,871,878

The accompanying Notes are an integral part of these Consolidated Financial Statements.

Consolidated Statements of Cash Flows   The Limited, Inc.
(thousands)

	1991	1990	1989
Cash Flows from Operating Activities			
Net Income	**$403,302**	$398,438	$346,926
Impact of Other Operating Activities on Cash Flows:			
Depreciation and Amortization	**222,695**	184,385	164,713
Change in Assets and Liabilities:			
Accounts Receivable	**(65,536)**	(73,791)	(65,742)
Inventories	**(144,884)**	(101,832)	(101,580)
Accounts Payable and Accrued Expenses	**8,792**	38,964	59,764
Income Taxes	**30,371**	(38,254)	(14,212)
Other Assets and Liabilities	**20,897**	16,561	14,370
Net Cash Provided by Operating Activities	475,637	424,471	404,239
Investing Activities			
Capital Expenditures	**(523,082)**	(428,844)	(318,427)
Subsidiaries (Acquired) Disposed	**(18,750)**	(10,987)	34,098
Other	**—**	(9,126)	11,505
Cash Used for Investing Activities	**(541,832)**	(448,957)	(272,824)
Financing Activities			
Net Borrowings (Repayments) of Long-Term Debt	**173,312**	(205,228)	(322,278)
Proceeds from Issuance of Unsecured Notes	**—**	300,000	250,000
Dividends Paid	**(101,141)**	(86,414)	(57,470)
Stock Options and Other	**14,579**	7,574	4,791
Net Cash Provided (Used) by Financing Activities	**86,750**	15,932	(124,957)
Net Increase (Decrease) in Cash and Equivalents	**20,555**	(8,554)	6,458
Cash and Equivalents, Beginning of Year	**13,180**	21,734	15,276
Cash and Equivalents, End of Year	**$ 33,735**	$ 13,180	$ 21,734

The accompanying Notes are an integral part of these Consolidated Financial Statements.

JOHN H. HARLAND COMPANY AND SUBSIDIARIES

CONSOLIDATED STATEMENTS OF INCOME

Year Ended December 31

(In thousands except per share amounts)	1991	1990	1989
		(Note 2)	
NET SALES	$378,659	$366,834	$ 344,734
COSTS AND EXPENSES:			
Cost of sales	189,835	188,254	172,386
Selling, general and administrative expenses	94,060	85,538	78,110
Employees' profit sharing	8,105	8,039	7,978
Restructuring charge	12,191		
Total	304,191	281,831	258,474
INCOME FROM OPERATIONS	74,468	85,003	86,260
INTEREST AND OTHER INCOME-NET	5,234	5,495	5,518
INCOME BEFORE INCOME TAXES AND CUMULATIVE EFFECT OF CHANGE IN ACCOUNTING PRINCIPLE	79,702	90,498	91,778
INCOME TAXES	29,882	33,331	33,726
INCOME BEFORE CUMULATIVE EFFECT OF CHANGE IN ACCOUNTING PRINCIPLE	49,820	57,167	58,052
CUMULATIVE EFFECT OF CHANGE IN ACCOUNTING PRINCIPLE	2,385		
NET INCOME	$ 47,435	$ 57,167	$ 58,052
PER COMMON SHARE:			
Income before cumulative effect of change in accounting principle	$ 1.33	$ 1.52	$ 1.54
Net Income	$ 1.27	$ 1.52	$ 1.54

See Significant Accounting Policies and Notes to Consolidated Financial Statements.

CONSOLIDATED BALANCE SHEETS

(In thousands except share and per share amounts)

	December 31 1991	1990 (Note 2)
ASSETS		
CURRENT ASSETS:		
Cash and cash equivalents	$ 18,923	$ 22,154
Short-term investments	52,500	20,035
Accounts receivable from customers, less allowance		
for doubtful accounts of $1,348 and $916	47,956	55,761
Inventories	24,234	23,700
Other	6,776	9,120
Total current assets	150,389	130,770
INVESTMENTS AND OTHER ASSETS:		
Investments	54,806	62,113
Other	6,232	3,037
Total investments and other assets	61,038	65,150
PROPERTY, PLANT AND EQUIPMENT	251,693	257,527
Less accumulated depreciation and amortization	111,566	106,342
Property, plant and equipment - net	140,127	151,185
TOTAL	$ 351,554	$ 347,105

See Significant Accounting Policies and Notes to Consolidated Financial Statements.

JOHN H. HARLAND COMPANY AND SUBSIDIARIES

	December 31	
	1991	**1990**
		(Note 2)
LIABILITIES AND SHAREHOLDERS' EQUITY		
CURRENT LIABILITIES:		
Accounts payable - trade	$ 7,513	$ 5,552
Industrial revenue bond - demand	4,000	4,000
Accrued liabilities:		
Salaries, wages and employee benefits	10,646	8,759
Taxes	8,382	3,499
Other	4,512	3,627
Total current liabilities	35,053	25,437
LONG-TERM LIABILITIES:		
Long-term debt	11,661	11,304
Deferred income taxes	4,122	9,889
Other	8,455	4,789
Total long-term liabilities	24,238	25,982
Total liabilities	59,291	51,419
SHAREHOLDERS' EQUITY:		
Common stock, authorized 144,000,000 shares of $1.00 par		
value, 37,907,497 shares issued	37,907	37,907
Additional paid-in capital	4,693	5,661
Foreign currency translation adjustment	306	503
Retained earnings	278,699	263,460
Total shareholders' equity	321,605	307,531
Less 1,337,544 and 553,234 shares in treasury, at cost	29,342	11,845
Shareholders' equity - net	292,263	295,686
TOTAL	*$ 351,554*	*$ 347,105*

CONSOLIDATED STATEMENTS OF CASH FLOWS

(In thousands)	1991	Year Ended December 31 1990	1989
		(Note 2)	
OPERATING ACTIVITIES:			
Net Income	$ 47,435	$ 57,167	$ 58,052
Adjustments to reconcile net income to			
net cash provided by operating activities:			
Depreciation and amortization	22,684	20,777	18,042
Deferred income taxes	(5,767)	132	3,576
Provision for restructuring charges	12,191		
Provision for postretirement benefits	4,285		
Other	1,915	525	871
Change in assets and liabilities:			
Accounts receivable	6,740	(2,145)	(1,570)
Inventories and other current assets	(1,398)	(2,713)	(2,583)
Accounts payable and accrued expenses	5,502	2,488	(4,582)
Short-term investments - net	(32,465)	(2,127)	(9,658)
Other - net	(367)	(501)	(2,017)
Net cash provided by operating activities	60,755	73,603	60,131
INVESTING ACTIVITIES:			
Purchases of property, plant and equipment	(16,899)	(28,890)	(28,707)
Proceeds from sale of property, plant and equipment	1,059	983	377
Long-term investments and other assets - net	1,989	(50,442)	9,399
Net cash used in investing activities	(13,851)	(78,349)	(18,931)
FINANCING ACTIVITIES:			
Sales of common stock	4,061	3,859	4,812
Dividends paid	(32,196)	(29,276)	(25,628)
Purchases of treasury stock	(22,806)	(9,105)	(9,413)
Other - net	806	474	451
Net cash used in financing activities	(50,135)	(34,048)	(29,778)
Increase (decrease) in cash and cash equivalents	(3,231)	(38,794)	11,422
Cash and cash equivalents at beginning of year	22,154	60,948	49,526
Cash and cash equivalents at end of year	$ 18,923	$ 22,154	$ 60,948
Cash paid during the year for:			
Interest	$ 1,115	$ 1,307	$ 1,964
Income taxes	$ 31,972	$ 32,074	$ 31,535

See Significant Accounting Policies and Notes to Consolidated Financial Statements.

D AICPA CODE OF PROFESSIONAL CONDUCT, IMA STANDARDS OF ETHICAL BEHAVIOR FOR MANAGEMENT ACCOUNTANTS, AND CODE OF ETHICS OF THE FEI

INTRODUCTION

This appendix contains the codes of ethics for members of three important accounting organizations—the American Institute of Certified Public Accountants (AICPA), the Institute of Management Accountants (IMA) and the Financial Executives Institute (FEI). By reading these codes, you can begin to understand the high standards of conduct that are expected of accountants. Being subjected to a code of ethics will not necessarily cause a dishonest person to behave honestly. However, an honest person will learn what behavior is expected and is likely to abide by the code.

AMERICAN INSTITUTE OF CERTIFIED PUBLIC ACCOUNTANTS
CODE OF PROFESSIONAL CONDUCT[1]

COMPOSITION, APPLICABILITY, AND COMPLIANCE

The Code of Professional Conduct of the American Institute of Certified Public Accountants consists of two sections—(1) the Principles and (2) the Rules. The Principles provide the framework for the Rules, which govern the performance of professional services by members. The Council of the American Institute of Certified Public Accountants is authorized to designate bodies to promulgate technical standards under the Rules, and the bylaws require adherence to those Rules and standards.

The Code of Professional Conduct was adopted by the membership to provide guidance and rules to all members—those in public practice, in industry, in government, and in education—in the performance of their professional responsibilities.

Compliance with the Code of Professional Conduct, as with all standards in an open society, depends primarily on members' understanding and voluntary actions, secondarily on reinforcement by peers and public opinion, and ultimately on disciplinary proceedings, when necessary, against members who fail to comply with the Rules.

SECTION I—PRINCIPLES

Preamble

Membership in the American Institute of Certified Public Accountants is voluntary. By accepting membership, a certified public accountant assumes an obligation of self-discipline above and beyond the requirements of laws and regulations.

These Principles of the Code of Professional Conduct of the American Institute of Certified Public Accountants express the profession's recognition of its responsibilities to the public, to clients, and to colleagues. They guide members in the performance of their professional responsibilities and express the basic tenets of ethical and professional conduct. The Principles call for an unswerving commitment to honorable behavior, even at the sacrifice of personal advantage.

Article I: Responsibilities

In carrying out their responsibilities as professionals, members should exercise sensitive professional and moral judgments in all their activities.

As professionals, certified public accountants perform an essential role in

---

[1] As revised June 30, 1992.

society. Consistent with that role, members of the American Institute of Certified Public Accountants have responsibilities to all those who use their professional services. Members also have a continuing responsibility to co-operate with each other to improve the art of accounting, maintain the public's confidence, and carry out the profession's special responsibilities for self-governance. The collective efforts of all members are required to maintain and enhance the traditions of the profession.

Article II: The Public Interest

Members should accept the obligation to act in a way that will serve the public interest, honor the public trust, and demonstrate commitment to professionalism.

A distinguishing mark of a profession is acceptance of its responsibility to the public. The accounting profession's public consists of clients, credit grantors, governments, employers, investors, the business and financial community, and others who rely on the objectivity and integrity of certified public accountants to maintain the orderly functioning of commerce. This reliance imposes a public interest responsibility on certified public accountants. The public interest is defined as the collective well-being of the community of people and institutions the profession serves.

In discharging their professional responsibilities, members may encounter conflicting pressures from among each of those groups. In resolving those conflicts, members should act with integrity, guided by the precept that when members fulfill their responsibility to the public, clients' and employers' interests are best served.

Those who rely on certified public accountants expect them to discharge their responsibilities with integrity, objectivity, due professional care, and a genuine interest in serving the public. They are expected to provide quality services, enter into fee arrangements, and offer a range of services—all in a manner that demonstrates a level of professionalism consistent with these Principles of the Code of Professional Conduct.

All who accept membership in the American Institute of Certified Public Accountants commit themselves to honor the public trust. In return for the faith that the public reposes in them, members should seek continually to demonstrate their dedication to professional excellence.

Article III: Integrity

To maintain and broaden public confidence, members should perform all professional responsibilities with the highest sense of integrity.

Integrity is an element of character fundamental to professional recognition. It is the quality from which the public trust derives and the benchmark against which a member must ultimately test all decisions.

Integrity requires a member to be, among other things, honest and candid within the constraints of client confidentiality. Service and the public trust should not be subordinated to personal gain and advantage. Integrity can accommodate the inadvertent error and the honest difference of opinion; it cannot accommodate deceit or subordination of principle.

Integrity is measured in terms of what is right and just. In the absence of specific rules, standards, or guidance, or in the face of conflicting opinions, a member should test decisions and deeds by asking: "Am I doing what a person of integrity would do? Have I retained my integrity?" Integrity requires a member to observe both the form and the spirit of technical and ethical standards; circumvention of those standards constitutes subordination of judgment.

Integrity also requires a member to observe the principles of objectivity and independence and of due care.

Article IV: Objectivity and Independence

A member should maintain objectivity and be free of conflicts of interest in discharging professional responsibilities. A member in public practice should be independent in fact and appearance when providing auditing and other attestation services.

Objectivity is a state of mind, a quality that lends value to a member's services. It is a distinguishing feature of the profession. The principle of objectivity imposes the obligation to be impartial, intellectually honest, and free of conflicts of interest. Independence precludes relationships that may appear to impair a member's objectivity in rendering attestation services.

Members often serve multiple interests in many different capacities and must demonstrate their objectivity in varying circumstances. Members in public practice render attest, tax, and management advisory services. Other members prepare financial statements in the employment of others, perform internal auditing services, and serve in financial and management capacities in industry, education, and government. They also educate and train those who aspire to admission into the profession. Regardless of service or capacity, members should protect the integrity of their work, maintain objectivity, and avoid any subordination of their judgment.

For a member in public practice, the maintenance of objectivity and independence requires a continuing assessment of client relationships and public responsibility. Such a member who provides auditing and other attestation services should be independent in fact and appearance. In providing all other services, a member should maintain objectivity and avoid conflicts of interest.

Although members not in public practice cannot maintain the appearance of independence, they nevertheless have the responsibility to maintain objectivity in rendering professional services. Members employed by others to prepare financial statements or to perform auditing, tax, or consulting services are charged with the same responsibility for objectivity as members in public practice and must be scrupulous in their application of generally accepted accounting principles and candid in all their dealings with members in public practice.

Article V: Due Care

A member should observe the profession's technical and ethical standards, strive continually to improve competence and the quality of services, and discharge professional responsibility to the best of the member's ability.

The quest for excellence is the essence of due care. Due care requires a member to discharge professional responsibilities with competence and diligence. It imposes the obligation to perform professional services to the best of a member's ability with concern for the best interest of those for whom the services are performed and consistent with the profession's responsibility to the public.

Competence is derived from a synthesis of education and experience. It begins with a mastery of the common body of knowledge required for designation as a certified public accountant. The maintenance of competence requires a commitment to learning and professional improvement that must continue throughout a member's professional life. It is a member's individual responsibility. In all engagements and in all responsibilities, each member should undertake to achieve a level of competence that will assure that the quality of the member's services meets the high level of professionalism required by these Principles.

Competence represents the attainment and maintenance of a level of understanding and knowledge that enables a member to render services with facility and acumen. It also establishes the limitations of a member's capabilities by dictating that consultation or referral may be required when a professional engagement exceeds the personal competence of a member or a member's firm. Each member is responsible for assessing his or her own competence—of evaluating whether education, experience, and judgment are adequate for the responsibility to be assumed.

Members should be diligent in discharging responsibilities to clients, employers, and the public. Diligence imposes the responsibility to render services promptly and carefully, to be thorough, and to observe applicable technical and ethical standards.

Due care requires a member to plan and supervise adequately any professional activity for which he or she is responsible.

Article VI: Scope and Nature of Services

A member in public practice should observe the Principles of the Code of Professional Conduct in determining the scope and nature of services to be provided.

The public interest aspect of certified public accountants' services requires that such services be consistent with acceptable professional behavior for certified public accountants. Integrity requires that service and the public trust not be subordinated to personal gain and advantage. Objectivity and independence require that members be free from conflicts of interest in discharging professional responsibilities. Due care requires that services be provided with competence and diligence.

Each of these Principles should be considered by members in determining whether or not to provide specific services in individual circumstances. In some instances, they may represent an overall constraint on the nonaudit services that might be offered to a specific client. No hard-and-fast rules can be developed to help members reach these judgments, but they must be satisfied that they are meeting the spirit of the Principles in this regard.

In order to accomplish this, members should

- Practice in firms that have in place internal quality-control procedures to ensure that services are competently delivered and adequately supervised.
- Determine, in their individual judgments, whether the scope and nature of other services provided to an audit client would create a conflict of interest in the performance of the audit function for that client.
- Assess, in their individual judgments, whether an activity is consistent with their role as professionals. (For example, is such activity a reasonable extension or variation of existing services offered by the members or others in the profession?)

SECTION II—RULES

Applicability

The bylaws of the American Institute of Certified Public Accountants require that members adhere to the Rules of the Code of Professional Conduct. Members must be prepared to justify departures from these Rules.

Interpretation Addressing the Applicability of the AICPA Code of Professional Conduct

For purposes of the Applicability Section of the Code, a "member" is a member or international associate of the American Institute of CPAs.

1. The Rules of Conduct that follow apply to all professional services performed except (a) where the wording of the rule indicates otherwise and (b) that a member who is practicing outside the United States will not be subject to discipline for departing from any of the rules stated herein as long as the member's conduct is in accord with the rules of the organized accounting profession in the country in which he or she is practicing. However, where a member's name is associated with financial statements under circumstances that would entitle the reader to assume that United States practices were followed, the member must comply with the requirements of Rules 202 and 203.

2. A member may be held responsible for compliance with the rules by all persons associated with him or her in the practice of public accounting who are either under the member's supervision or are the member's partners or shareholders in the practice.
3. A member shall not permit others to carry out on his or her behalf, either with or without compensation, acts, which if carried out by the member, would place the member in violation of the rules.

Client

A client is any person or entity, other than the member's employer, that engages a member or a member's firm to perform professional services or a person or entity with respect to which professional services are performed. The term "employer" for these purposes does not include those entities engaged in the practice of public accounting.

Council

The Council of the American Institute of Certified Public Accountants.

Enterprise

For purposes of the Code, the term "enterprise" is synonymous with the term "client."

Financial Statements

Statements and footnotes related thereto that purport to show financial position which relates to a point in time or changes in financial position which relate to a period of time, and statements which use a cash or other incomplete basis of accounting. Balance sheets, statements of income, statements of retained earnings, statements of changes in financial position [now called statement of cash flows], and statements of changes in owner's equity are financial statements.

Incidental financial data included in management advisory services reports to support recommendations to a client and tax returns and supporting schedules do not, for this purpose, constitute financial statements; and the statement, affidavit, or signature of preparers required on tax returns neither constitutes an opinion on financial statements nor requires a disclaimer of such opinion.

Firm

A proprietorship, partnership, or professional corporation or association engaged in the practice of public accounting, including individual partners or shareholders thereof.

Institute

The American Institute of Certified Public Accountants.

Interpretation of Rules of Conduct

Pronouncements issued by the division of professional ethics to provide guidelines concerning the scope and application of the rules of conduct.

Member

A member, associate member, or international associate of the American Institute of Certified Public Accountants.

Practice of Public Accounting

The practice of public accounting consists of the performance for a client, by a member or a member's firm, while holding out as CPA(s), of the professional services of accounting, tax, personal financial planning, litigation support services, and those professional services for which standards are promulgated by bodies designated by Council, such as Statements of Financial Accounting Standards, Statements on Auditing Standards, Statements on Standards for Accounting and Review Services, Statements on Standards for Management Advisory Services, Statements of Governmental Accounting Standards, Statement on Standards for Attestation Engagements, and Statement on Standards for Accountants' Services on Prospective Financial Information.

However, a member or a member's firm, while holding out as CPA(s), is not considered to be in the practice of public accounting if the member or the member's firm does not perform, for any client, any of the professional services described in the preceding paragraph.

Professional Services

Professional services include all services performed by a member while holding out as a CPA.

Holding Out

In general, any action initiated by a member that informs others of his or her status as a CPA or AICPA-accredited specialist constitutes holding out as a CPA. This would include, for example, any oral or written representation to another regarding CPA status, use of the CPA designation on business cards or letterhead, the display of a certificate evidencing a member's CPA designation, or listing as a CPA in local telephone directories.

Rules

Rule 101   Independence

A member in public practice shall be independent in the performance of professional services as required by standards promulgated by bodies designated by Council.

Interpretation of Rule 101

Interpretation 101-1. Independence shall be considered to be impaired if, for example, a member had any of the following transactions, interests, or relationships:

A. During the period of a professional engagement or at the time of expressing an opinion, a member or a member's firm
   1. Had or was committed to acquire any direct or material indirect financial interest in the enterprise.
   2. Was a trustee of any trust or executor or administrator of any estate if such trust or estate had or was committed to acquire any direct or material indirect financial interest in the enterprise.
   3. Had any joint, closely held business investment with the enterprise or with any officer, director, or principal stockholders thereof that was material in relation to the member's net worth or to the net worth of the member's firm.
   4. Had any loan to or from the enterprise or any officer, director, or principal stockholder of the enterprise except as specifically permitted in Interpretation 101-5.
B. During the period covered by the financial statements, during the period of the professional engagement, or at the time of expressing an opinion, a member or a member's firm
   1. Was connected with the enterprise as a promoter, underwriter or voting trustee, as a director or officer, or in any capacity equivalent to that of a member of management or of an employee.
   2. Was a trustee for any pension or profit-sharing trust of the enterprise.

The above examples are not intended to be all-inclusive.

Rule 102   Integrity and Objectivity

In the performance of any professional service, a member shall maintain objectivity and integrity, shall be free of conflicts of interest, and shall not knowingly misrepresent facts or subordinate his or her judgment to others.

Rule 201   General Standards

A member shall comply with the following standards and with any interpretations thereof by bodies designated by Council.

A. *Professional Competence.* Undertake only those professional services that the member or the member's firm can reasonably expect to be completed with professional competence.

B. *Due Professional Care.* Exercise due professional care in the performance of professional services.

C. *Planning and Supervision.* Adequately plan and supervise the performance of professional services.

D. *Sufficient Relevant Data.* Obtain sufficient relevant data to afford a reasonable basis for conclusions or recommendations in relation to any professional services performed.

Rule 202 Compliance with Standards

A member who performs auditing, review, compilation, management advisory, tax, or other professional services shall comply with standards promulgated by bodies designated by Council.

Rule 203 Accounting Principles

A member shall not (1) express an opinion or state affirmatively that the financial statements or other financial data of any entity are presented in confirmity with generally accepted accounting principles or (2) state that he or she is not aware of any material modifications that should be made to such statements or data in order for them to be in conformity with generally accepted accounting principles, if such statements or data contain any departure from an accounting principle promulgated by bodies designated by Council to establish such principles that has a material effect on the statements or data taken as a whole. If, however, the statements or data contain such a departure and the member can demonstrate that due to unusual circumstances the financial statements or data would otherwise have been misleading, the member can comply with the rule by describing the departure, its approximate effects, if practicable, and the reasons why compliance with the principle would result in a misleading statement.

Rule 301 Confidential Client Information

A member in public practice shall not disclose any confidential client information without the specific consent of the client.

This rule shall not be construed (1) to relieve a member of his or her professional obligations under rules 202 and 203, (2) to affect in any way the member's obligation to comply with a validly issued and enforceable subpoena or summons, or to prohibit a member's compliance with applicable laws and government regulations, (3) to prohibit review of a member's professional practice under AICPA or state CPA society or Board of Accountancy authorization, or (4) to preclude a member from initiating a complaint with, or responding to any inquiry made by, the ethics division or trial board of the Institute or a duly constituted investigative or disciplinary body of a state CPA society or Board of Accountancy.

Members of any of the bodies identified in (4) above and members involved with professional practice reviews identified in (3) above shall not use to their own advantage or disclose any member's confidential client information that comes to their attention in carrying out those activities. This prohibition shall not restrict members' exchange of information in connection with the investigative or disciplinary proceedings described in (4) above or the professional practice reviews described in (3) above.

Rule 302 Contingent Fees

A member in public practice shall not perform for a contingent fee any professional services for, or receive such a fee from, a client for whom the member or member's firm also performs:

(a) an audit or review of a financial statement; or

(b) a compilation of a financial statement when the member expects, or reasonably might expect, that a third party will use the financial statement and the member's compilation report does not disclose a lack of independence; or

(c) an examination of prospective financial information.

This prohibition applies during the period in which the member or the member's firm is engaged to perform any of the services listed above and the period covered by any historical financial statements involved in any such listed services.

For purposes of this rule, a contingent fee is a fee established for the performance of any service pursuant to an arrangement in which no fee will be charged unless a specific finding or result is attained, or in which the amount of the fee is otherwise dependent upon the finding or result of such service.

A member's fees may vary depending, for example, on the complexity of services rendered. Fees are not regarded as being contingent if fixed by courts or other public authorities, or, in tax matters, if determined based on the results of judicial proceedings or the findings of governmental agencies.

Rule 401 *[There are currently no rules in the 400 series.]*

Rule 501 Acts Discreditable

A member shall not commit an act discreditable to the profession.

Rule 502 Advertising and Other Forms of Solicitation

A member in public practice shall not seek to obtain clients by advertising or other forms of solicitation in a manner that is false, misleading, or deceptive. Solicitation by the use of coercion, over-reaching, or harassing conduct is prohibited.

Rule 503 Commissions and Referral Fees

A. Prohibited commissions
A member in public practice shall not for a commission recommend or refer to a client any product or service, or for a commission recommend or refer

any product or service to be supplied by a client, or receive a commission, when the member or the member's firm also performs for that client:

(a) an audit or review of a financial statement; or

(b) a compilation of a financial statement when the member expects, or reasonably might expect, that a third party will use the financial statement and the member's compilation report does not disclose a lack of independence; or

(c) an examination of prospective financial information.

This prohibition applies during the period in which the member is engaged to perform any of the services listed above and the period covered by any historical financial statements involved in such listed services.

B.   Disclosure of permitted commissions

A member in public practice who is not prohibited by this rule from performing services for or receiving a commission and who is paid or expects to be paid a commission shall disclose that fact to any person or entity to whom the member recommends or refers a product or service to which the commission relates.

C.   Referral fees

Any member who accepts a referral fee or recommending or referring any service of a CPA to any person or entity or who pays a referral fee to obtain a client shall disclose such acceptance or payment to the client.

Rule 504   *[There is currently no rule 504.]*

Rule 505   Form of Organization and Name

A member may practice public accounting only in a form of organization permitted by state law or regulation whose characteristics conform to resolutions of Council.

A member shall not practice public accounting under a firm name that is misleading. Names of one or more past owners may be included in the firm name or a successor organization. Also, an owner surviving the death or withdrawal of all other owners may continue to practice under a name which includes the name of past owners for up to two years after becoming a sole practitioner.

A firm may not designate itself as "Members of the American Institute of Certified Public Accountants" unless all of its owners are members of the Institute.

INSTITUTE OF MANAGEMENT ACCOUNTANTS
STANDARDS OF ETHICAL BEHAVIOR FOR MANAGEMENT ACCOUNTANTS

Management accountants have an obligation to the organizations they serve, their profession, the public, and themselves to maintain the highest standards of ethical conduct. In recognition of this obligation, the Institute of

Management Accountants has promulgated the following standards of ethical conduct for management accountants. Adherence to these standards is integral to achieving the *Objectives of Management Accounting*.[2] Management accountants shall not commit acts contrary to these standards nor shall they condone the commission of such acts by others within their organizations.

COMPETENCE

Management accountants have a responsibility to:

- Maintain an appropriate level of professional competence by ongoing development of their knowledge and skills.
- Perform their professional duties in accordance with relevant laws, regulations, and technical standards.
- Prepare complete and clear reports and recommendations after appropriate analyses of relevant and reliable information.

CONFIDENTIALITY

Management accountants have a responsibility to:

- Refrain from disclosing confidential information acquired in the course of their work except when authorized, unless legally obligated to do so.
- Inform subordinates as appropriate regarding the confidentiality of information acquired in the course of their work and monitor their activities to assure the maintenance of that confidentiality.
- Refrain from using or appearing to use confidential information acquired in the course of their work for unethical or illegal advantage either personally or through third parties.

INTEGRITY

Management accountants have a responsibility to:

- Avoid actual or apparent conflicts of interest and advise all appropriate parties of any potential conflict.
- Refrain from engaging in any activity that would prejudice their ability to carry out their duties ethically.
- Refuse any gift, favor, or hospitality that would influence or would appear to influence their actions.

---

[2] National Association of Accountants (now Institute of Management Accountants), *Statements on Management Accounting: Objectives of Management Accounting*, Statement No. 1C, New York, N.Y., June 1, 1983.

- Refrain from either actively or passively subverting the attainment of the organization's legitimate and ethical objectives.
- Recognize and communicate professional limitations or other constraints that would preclude responsible judgment or successful performance of an activity.
- Communicate unfavorable as well as favorable information and professional judgments or opinions.
- Refrain from engaging in or supporting any activity that would discredit the profession.

OBJECTIVITY

Management accountants have a responsibility to:

- Communicate information fairly and objectively.
- Disclose fully all relevant information that could reasonably be expected to influence an intended user's understanding of the reports, comments, and recommendations presented.

RESOLUTION OF ETHICAL CONFLICT

In applying the standards of ethical conduct, management accountants may encounter problems in identifying unethical behavior or in resolving an ethical conflict. When faced with significant ethical issues, management accountants should follow the established policies of the organization bearing on the resolution of such conflict. If these policies do not resolve the ethical conflict, management accountants should consider the following courses of action:

- Discuss such problems with the immediate superior except when it appears that the superior is involved, in which case the problem should be presented initially to the next higher managerial level. If satisfactory resolution cannot be achieved when the problem is initially presented, submit the issues to the next higher managerial level.

  If the immediate superior is the chief executive officer, or equivalent, the acceptable reviewing authority may be a group such as the audit committee, executive committee, board of directors, board of trustees, or owners. Contact with levels above the immediate superior should be initiated only with the superior's knowledge, assuming the superior is not involved.
- Clarify relevant concepts by confidential discussion with an objective advisor to obtain an understanding of possible courses of action.
- If the ethical conflict still exists after exhausting all levels of internal review, the management accountant may have no other recourse on significant matters than to resign from the organization and to submit an

informative memorandum to an appropriate representative of the organization.

Except where legally prescribed, communication of such problems to authorization or individuals not employed or engaged by the organization is not considered appropriate.

FINANCIAL EXECUTIVES INSTITUTE
CODE OF ETHICS[3]

As a member of Financial Executives Institute, I will:

- Conduct my business and personal affairs at all times with honesty and integrity.
- Provide complete, appropriate, and relevant information in an objective manner when reporting to management, stockholders, employees, government agencies, other institutions, and the public.
- Comply with rules and regulations of federal, state, provincial, and local governments, and other appropriate private and public regulatory agencies.
- Discharge duties and responsibilities to my employer to the best of my ability, including complete communication on all matters within my jurisdiction.
- Maintain the confidentiality of information acquired in the course of my work except when authorized or otherwise legally obligated to disclose. Confidential information acquired in the course of my work will not be used for my personal advantage.
- Maintain an appropriate level of professional competence through continuing development of my knowledge and skills.
- Refrain from committing acts discreditable to myself, my employer, FEI, or fellow members of the Institute.

---

[3] Adopted by the Board of Directors of the Financial Executives Institute, October 13, 1985.

E

COMPOUND INTEREST AND ANNUITY TABLES

The following tables are included in this appendix:

Table E.1
FUTURE VALUE OF $1 AT COMPOUND INTEREST: 0.5%—10% $F_{in} = (1 + i)^n$

Period	.5%	1%	1.5%	2%	2.5%	3%	3.5%	4%	4.5%	5%
1	1.00500	1.01000	1.01500	1.02000	1.02500	1.03000	1.03500	1.04000	1.04500	1.05000
2	1.01003	1.02010	1.03023	1.04040	1.05063	1.06090	1.07123	1.08160	1.09203	1.10250
3	1.01508	1.03030	1.04568	1.06121	1.07689	1.09273	1.10872	1.12486	1.14117	1.15762
4	1.02015	1.04060	1.06136	1.08243	1.10381	1.12551	1.14752	1.16986	1.19252	1.21551
5	1.02525	1.05101	1.07728	1.10408	1.13141	1.15927	1.18769	1.21665	1.24618	1.27628
6	1.03038	1.06152	1.09344	1.12616	1.15969	1.19405	1.22926	1.26532	1.30226	1.34010
7	1.03553	1.07214	1.10984	1.14869	1.18869	1.22987	1.27228	1.31593	1.36086	1.40710
8	1.04071	1.08286	1.12649	1.17166	1.21840	1.26677	1.31681	1.36857	1.42210	1.47746
9	1.04591	1.09369	1.14339	1.19509	1.24886	1.30477	1.36290	1.42331	1.48610	1.55133
10	1.05114	1.10462	1.16054	1.21899	1.28008	1.34392	1.41060	1.48024	1.55297	1.62889
11	1.05640	1.11567	1.17795	1.24337	1.31209	1.38423	1.45997	1.53945	1.62285	1.71034
12	1.06168	1.12683	1.19562	1.26824	1.34489	1.42576	1.51107	1.60103	1.69588	1.79586
13	1.06699	1.13809	1.21355	1.29361	1.37851	1.46853	1.56396	1.66507	1.77220	1.88565
14	1.07232	1.14947	1.23176	1.31948	1.41297	1.51259	1.61869	1.73168	1.85194	1.97993
15	1.07768	1.16097	1.25023	1.34587	1.44830	1.55797	1.67535	1.80094	1.93528	2.07893
16	1.08307	1.17258	1.26899	1.37279	1.48451	1.60471	1.73399	1.87298	2.02237	2.18287
17	1.08849	1.18430	1.28802	1.40024	1.52162	1.65285	1.79468	1.94790	2.11338	2.29202
18	1.09393	1.19615	1.30734	1.42825	1.55966	1.70243	1.85749	2.02582	2.20848	2.40662
19	1.09940	1.20811	1.32695	1.45681	1.59865	1.75351	1.92250	2.10685	2.30786	2.52695
20	1.10490	1.22019	1.34686	1.48595	1.63862	1.80611	1.98979	2.19112	2.41171	2.65330
21	1.11042	1.23239	1.36706	1.51567	1.67958	1.86029	2.05943	2.27877	2.52024	2.78596
22	1.11597	1.24472	1.38756	1.54598	1.72157	1.91610	2.13151	2.36992	2.63365	2.92526
23	1.12155	1.25716	1.40838	1.57690	1.76461	1.97359	2.20611	2.46472	2.75217	3.07152
24	1.12716	1.26973	1.42950	1.60844	1.80873	2.03279	2.28333	2.56330	2.87601	3.22510
25	1.13280	1.28243	1.45095	1.64061	1.85394	2.09378	2.36324	2.66584	3.00543	3.38635
26	1.13846	1.29526	1.47271	1.67342	1.90029	2.15659	2.44596	2.77247	3.14068	3.55567
27	1.14415	1.30821	1.49480	1.70689	1.94780	2.22129	2.53157	2.88337	3.28201	3.73346
28	1.14987	1.32129	1.51722	1.74102	1.99650	2.28793	2.62017	2.99870	3.42970	3.92013
29	1.15562	1.33450	1.53998	1.77584	2.04641	2.35657	2.71188	3.11865	3.58404	4.11614
30	1.16140	1.34785	1.56308	1.81136	2.09757	2.42726	2.80679	3.24340	3.74532	4.32194

5.5%	6%	6.5%	7%	7.5%	8%	8.5%	9%	9.5%	10%
1.05500	1.06000	1.06500	1.07000	1.07500	1.08000	1.08500	1.09000	1.09500	1.10000
1.11303	1.12360	1.13423	1.14490	1.15563	1.16640	1.17723	1.18810	1.19903	1.21000
1.17424	1.19102	1.20795	1.22504	1.24230	1.25971	1.27729	1.29503	1.31293	1.33100
1.23882	1.26248	1.28647	1.31080	1.33547	1.36049	1.38586	1.41158	1.43766	1.46410
1.30696	1.33823	1.37009	1.40255	1.43563	1.46933	1.50366	1.53862	1.57424	1.61051
1.37884	1.41852	1.45914	1.50073	1.54330	1.58687	1.63147	1.67710	1.72379	1.77156
1.45468	1.50363	1.55399	1.60578	1.65905	1.71382	1.77014	1.82804	1.88755	1.94872
1.53469	1.59385	1.65500	1.71819	1.78348	1.85093	1.92060	1.99256	2.06687	2.14359
1.61909	1.68948	1.76257	1.83846	1.91724	1.99900	2.08386	2.17189	2.26322	2.35795
1.70814	1.79085	1.87714	1.96715	2.06103	2.15892	2.26098	2.36736	2.47823	2.59374
1.80209	1.89830	1.99915	2.10485	2.21561	2.33164	2.45317	2.58043	2.71366	2.85312
1.90121	2.01220	2.12910	2.25219	2.38178	2.51817	2.66169	2.81266	2.97146	3.13843
2.00577	2.13293	2.26749	2.40985	2.56041	2.71962	2.88793	3.06580	3.25375	3.45227
2.11609	2.26090	2.41487	2.57853	2.75244	2.93719	3.13340	3.34173	3.56285	3.79750
2.23248	2.39656	2.57184	2.75903	2.95888	3.17217	3.39974	3.64248	3.90132	4.17725
2.35526	2.54035	2.73901	2.95216	3.18079	3.42594	3.68872	3.97031	4.27195	4.59497
2.48480	2.69277	2.91705	3.15882	3.41935	3.70002	4.00226	4.32763	4.67778	5.05447
2.62147	2.85434	3.10665	3.37993	3.67580	3.99602	4.34245	4.71712	5.12217	5.55992
2.76565	3.02560	3.30859	3.61653	3.95149	4.31570	4.71156	5.14166	5.60878	6.11591
2.91776	3.20714	3.52365	3.86968	4.24785	4.66096	5.11205	5.60441	6.14161	6.72750
3.07823	3.39956	3.75268	4.14056	4.56644	5.03383	5.54657	6.10881	6.72507	7.40025
3.24754	3.60354	3.99661	4.43040	4.90892	5.43654	6.01803	6.65860	7.36395	8.14027
3.42615	3.81975	4.25639	4.74053	5.27709	5.87146	6.52956	7.25787	8.06352	8.95430
3.61459	4.04893	4.53305	5.07237	5.67287	6.34118	7.08457	7.91108	8.82956	9.84973
3.81339	4.29187	4.82770	5.42743	6.09834	6.84848	7.68676	8.62308	9.66836	10.83471
4.02313	4.54938	5.14150	5.80735	6.55572	7.39635	8.34014	9.39916	10.58686	11.91818
4.24440	4.82235	5.47570	6.21387	7.04739	7.98806	9.04905	10.24508	11.59261	13.10999
4.47784	5.11169	5.83162	6.64884	7.57595	8.62711	9.81822	11.16714	12.69391	14.42099
4.72412	5.41839	6.21067	7.11426	8.14414	9.31727	10.65277	12.17218	13.89983	15.86309
4.98395	5.74349	6.61437	7.61226	8.75496	10.06266	11.55825	13.26768	15.22031	17.44940

Table E.1 *(concluded)*
FUTURE VALUE OF $1 AT COMPOUND INTEREST: 10.5%–20%

Period	10.5%	11%	11.5%	12%	12.5%	13%	13.5%	14%	14.5%	15%
1	1.10500	1.11000	1.11500	1.12000	1.12500	1.13000	1.13500	1.14000	1.14500	1.15000
2	1.22103	1.23210	1.24323	1.25440	1.26563	1.27690	1.28822	1.29960	1.31102	1.32250
3	1.34923	1.36763	1.38620	1.40493	1.42383	1.44290	1.46214	1.48154	1.50112	1.52088
4	1.49090	1.51807	1.54561	1.57352	1.60181	1.63047	1.65952	1.68896	1.71879	1.74901
5	1.64745	1.68506	1.72335	1.76234	1.80203	1.84244	1.88356	1.92541	1.96801	2.01136
6	1.82043	1.87041	1.92154	1.97382	2.02729	2.08195	2.13784	2.19497	2.25337	2.31306
7	2.01157	2.07616	2.14252	2.21068	2.28070	2.35261	2.42645	2.50227	2.58011	2.66002
8	2.22279	2.30454	2.38891	2.47596	2.56578	2.65844	2.75402	2.85259	2.95423	3.05902
9	2.45618	2.55804	2.66363	2.77308	2.88651	3.00404	3.12581	3.25195	3.38259	3.51788
10	2.71408	2.83942	2.96995	3.10585	3.24732	3.39457	3.54780	3.70722	3.87307	4.04556
11	2.99906	3.15176	3.31149	3.47855	3.65324	3.83586	4.02675	4.22623	4.43466	4.65239
12	3.31396	3.49845	3.69231	3.89598	4.10989	4.33452	4.57036	4.81790	5.07769	5.35025
13	3.66193	3.88328	4.11693	4.36349	4.62363	4.89801	5.18736	5.49241	5.81395	6.15279
14	4.04643	4.31044	4.59037	4.88711	5.20158	5.53475	5.88765	6.26135	6.65697	7.07571
15	4.47130	4.78459	5.11827	5.47357	5.85178	6.25427	6.68248	7.13794	7.62223	8.13706
16	4.94079	5.31089	5.70687	6.13039	6.58325	7.06733	7.58462	8.13725	8.72746	9.35762
17	5.45957	5.89509	6.36316	6.86604	7.40616	7.98608	8.60854	9.27646	9.99294	10.76126
18	6.03283	6.54355	7.09492	7.68997	8.33193	9.02427	9.77070	10.57517	11.44192	12.37545
19	6.66628	7.26334	7.91084	8.61276	9.37342	10.19742	11.08974	12.05569	13.10039	14.23177
20	7.36623	8.06231	8.82058	9.64629	10.54509	11.52309	12.58686	13.74349	15.00064	16.36654
21	8.13969	8.94917	9.83495	10.80385	11.86323	13.02109	14.28608	15.66758	17.17573	18.82152
22	8.99436	9.93357	10.96597	12.10031	13.34613	14.71383	16.21470	17.86104	19.66621	21.64475
23	9.93876	11.02627	12.22706	13.55235	15.01440	16.62663	18.40369	20.36158	22.51781	24.89146
24	10.98233	12.23916	13.63317	15.17863	16.89120	18.78809	20.88818	23.21221	25.78290	28.62518
25	12.13548	13.58546	15.20098	17.00006	19.00260	21.23054	23.70809	26.46192	29.52141	32.91895
26	13.40971	15.07986	16.94910	19.04007	21.37793	23.99051	26.90868	30.16658	33.80202	37.85680
27	14.81772	16.73865	18.89824	21.32488	24.05017	27.10928	30.54135	34.38991	38.70331	43.53531
28	16.37359	18.57990	21.07154	23.88387	27.05644	30.63349	34.66443	39.20449	44.31529	50.06561
29	18.09281	20.62369	23.49477	26.74993	30.43849	34.61584	39.34413	44.69312	50.74101	57.57545
30	19.99256	22.89230	26.19667	29.95992	34.24330	39.11590	44.65559	50.95016	58.09846	66.21177

15.5%	16%	16.5%	17%	17.5%	18%	18.5%	19%	19.5%	20%
1.15500	1.16000	1.16500	1.17000	1.17500	1.18000	1.18500	1.19000	1.19500	1.20000
1.33402	1.34560	1.35722	1.36890	1.38063	1.39240	1.40422	1.41610	1.42802	1.44000
1.54080	1.56090	1.58117	1.60161	1.62223	1.64303	1.66401	1.68516	1.70649	1.72800
1.77962	1.81064	1.84206	1.87389	1.90613	1.93878	1.97185	2.00534	2.03926	2.07360
2.05546	2.10034	2.14600	2.19245	2.23970	2.28776	2.33664	2.38635	2.43691	2.48832
2.37406	2.43640	2.50009	2.56516	2.63164	2.69955	2.76892	2.83976	2.91211	2.98598
2.74204	2.82622	2.91260	3.00124	3.09218	3.18547	3.28117	3.37932	3.47997	3.58318
3.16706	3.27841	3.39318	3.51145	3.63331	3.75886	3.88818	4.02139	4.15856	4.29982
3.65795	3.80296	3.95306	4.10840	4.26914	4.43545	4.60750	4.78545	4.96948	5.15978
4.22493	4.41144	4.60531	4.80683	5.01624	5.23384	5.45989	5.69468	5.93853	6.19174
4.87980	5.11726	5.36519	5.62399	5.89409	6.17593	6.46996	6.77667	7.09654	7.43008
5.63617	5.93603	6.25045	6.58007	6.92555	7.28759	7.66691	8.06424	8.48037	8.91610
6.50977	6.88579	7.28177	7.69868	8.13752	8.59936	9.08528	9.59645	10.13404	10.69932
7.51879	7.98752	8.48326	9.00745	9.56159	10.14724	10.76606	11.41977	12.11018	12.83918
8.68420	9.26552	9.88300	10.53872	11.23487	11.97375	12.75778	13.58953	14.47167	15.40702
10.03025	10.74800	11.51370	12.33030	13.20097	14.12902	15.11797	16.17154	17.29364	18.48843
11.58494	12.46768	13.41346	14.42646	15.51114	16.67225	17.91480	19.24413	20.66590	22.18611
13.38060	14.46251	15.62668	16.87895	18.22559	19.67325	21.22904	22.90052	24.69575	26.62333
15.45460	16.77652	18.20508	19.74838	21.41507	23.21444	25.15641	27.25162	29.51143	31.94800
17.85006	19.46076	21.20892	23.10560	25.16271	27.39303	29.81035	32.42942	35.26615	38.33760
20.61682	22.57448	24.70839	27.03355	29.56618	32.32378	35.32526	38.59101	42.14305	46.00512
23.81243	26.18640	28.78527	31.62925	34.74026	38.14206	41.86043	45.92331	50.36095	55.20614
27.50335	30.37622	33.53484	37.00623	40.81981	45.00763	49.60461	54.64873	60.18134	66.24737
31.76637	35.23642	39.06809	43.29729	47.96327	53.10901	58.78147	65.03199	71.91670	79.49685
36.69016	40.87424	45.51433	50.65783	56.35684	62.66863	69.65604	77.38807	85.94045	95.39622
42.37713	47.41412	53.02419	59.26966	66.21929	73.94898	82.54240	92.09181	102.69884	114.47546
48.94559	55.00038	61.77318	69.34550	77.80767	87.25980	97.81275	109.58925	122.72511	137.37055
56.53216	63.80044	71.96576	81.13423	91.42401	102.96656	115.90811	130.41121	146.65651	164.84466
65.29464	74.00851	83.84011	94.92705	107.42321	121.50054	137.35111	155.18934	175.25453	197.81359
75.41531	85.84988	97.67373	111.06465	126.22227	143.37064	162.76106	184.67531	209.42916	237.37631

1280   Appendix E

Table E.2
FUTURE VALUE OF AN ORDINARY ANNUITY OF $1 PER PERIOD: 0.5%–10% $F_{A_{in}} = \dfrac{(1 + i)^n - 1}{i}$

Period	.5%	1%	1.5%	2%	2.5%	3%	3.5%	4%	4.5%	5%
1	1.00000	1.00000	1.00000	1.00000	1.00000	1.00000	1.00000	1.00000	1.00000	1.00000
2	2.00500	2.01000	2.01500	2.02000	2.02500	2.03000	2.03500	2.04000	2.04500	2.05000
3	3.01502	3.03010	3.04522	3.06040	3.07562	3.09090	3.10622	3.12160	3.13702	3.15250
4	4.03010	4.06040	4.09090	4.12161	4.15252	4.18363	4.21494	4.24646	4.27819	4.31012
5	5.05025	5.10101	5.15227	5.20404	5.25633	5.30914	5.36247	5.41632	5.47071	5.52563
6	6.07550	6.15202	6.22955	6.30812	6.38774	6.46841	6.55015	6.63298	6.71689	6.80191
7	7.10588	7.21354	7.32299	7.43428	7.54743	7.66246	7.77941	7.89829	8.01915	8.14201
8	8.14141	8.28567	8.43284	8.58297	8.73612	8.89234	9.05169	9.21423	9.38001	9.54911
9	9.18212	9.36853	9.55933	9.75463	9.95452	10.15911	10.36850	10.58280	10.80211	11.02656
10	10.22803	10.46221	10.70272	10.94972	11.20338	11.46388	11.73139	12.00611	12.28821	12.57789
11	11.27917	11.56683	11.86326	12.16872	12.48347	12.80780	13.14199	13.48635	13.84118	14.20679
12	12.33556	12.68250	13.04121	13.41209	13.79555	14.19203	14.60196	15.02581	15.46403	15.91713
13	13.39724	13.80933	14.23683	14.68033	15.14044	15.61779	16.11303	16.62684	17.15991	17.71298
14	14.46423	14.94742	15.45038	15.97394	16.51895	17.08632	17.67699	18.29191	18.93211	19.59863
15	15.53655	16.09690	16.68214	17.29342	17.93193	18.59891	19.29568	20.02359	20.78405	21.57856
16	16.61423	17.25786	17.93237	18.63929	19.38022	20.15688	20.97103	21.82453	22.71934	23.65749
17	17.69730	18.43044	19.20136	20.01207	20.86473	21.76159	22.70502	23.69751	24.74171	25.84037
18	18.78579	19.61475	20.48938	21.41231	22.38635	23.41444	24.49969	25.64541	26.85508	28.13238
19	19.87972	20.81090	21.79672	22.84056	23.94601	25.11687	26.35718	27.67123	29.06356	30.53900
20	20.97912	22.01900	23.12367	24.29737	25.54466	26.87037	28.27968	29.77808	31.37142	33.06595
21	22.08401	23.23919	24.47052	25.78332	27.18327	28.67649	30.26947	31.96920	33.78314	35.71925
22	23.19443	24.47159	25.83758	27.29898	28.86286	30.53678	32.32890	34.24797	36.30338	38.50521
23	24.31040	25.71630	27.22514	28.84496	30.58443	32.45288	34.46041	36.61789	38.93703	41.43048
24	25.43196	26.97346	28.63352	30.42186	32.34904	34.42647	36.66653	39.08260	41.68920	44.50200
25	26.55912	28.24320	30.06302	32.03030	34.15776	36.45926	38.94986	41.64591	44.56521	47.72710
26	27.69191	29.52563	31.51397	33.67091	36.01171	38.55304	41.31310	44.31174	47.57064	51.11345
27	28.83037	30.82089	32.98668	35.34432	37.91200	40.70963	43.75906	47.08421	50.71132	54.66913
28	29.97452	32.12910	34.48148	37.05121	39.85980	42.93092	46.29063	49.96758	53.99333	58.40258
29 ...	31.12439	33.45039	35.99870	38.79223	41.85630	45.21885	48.91080	52.96629	57.42303	62.32271
30	32.28002	34.78489	37.53868	40.56808	43.90270	47.57542	51.62268	56.08494	61.00707	66.43885

5.5%	6%	6.5%	7%	7.5%	8%	8.5%	9%	9.5%	10%
1.00000	1.00000	1.00000	1.00000	1.00000	1.00000	1.00000	1.00000	1.00000	1.00000
2.05500	2.06000	2.06500	2.07000	2.07500	2.08000	2.08500	2.09000	2.09500	2.10000
3.16802	3.18360	3.19922	3.21490	3.23062	3.24640	3.26222	3.27810	3.29402	3.31000
4.34227	4.37462	4.40717	4.43994	4.47292	4.50611	4.53951	4.57313	4.60696	4.64100
5.58109	5.63709	5.69364	5.75074	5.80839	5.86660	5.92537	5.98471	6.04462	6.10510
6.88805	6.97532	7.06373	7.15329	7.24402	7.33593	7.42903	7.52333	7.61886	7.71561
8.26689	8.39384	8.52287	8.65402	8.78732	8.92280	9.06050	9.20043	9.34265	9.48717
9.72157	9.89747	10.07686	10.25980	10.44637	10.63663	10.83064	11.02847	11.23020	11.43589
11.25626	11.49132	11.73185	11.97799	12.22985	12.48756	12.75124	13.02104	13.29707	13.57948
12.87535	13.18079	13.49442	13.81645	14.14709	14.48656	14.83510	15.19293	15.56029	15.93742
14.58350	14.97164	15.37156	15.78360	16.20812	16.64549	17.09608	17.56029	18.03852	18.53117
16.38559	16.86994	17.37071	17.88845	18.42373	18.97713	19.54925	20.14072	20.75218	21.38428
18.28680	18.88214	19.49981	20.14064	20.80551	21.49530	22.21094	22.95338	23.72363	24.52271
20.29257	21.01507	21.76730	22.55049	23.36592	24.21492	25.09887	26.01919	26.97738	27.97498
22.40866	23.27597	24.18217	25.12902	26.11836	27.15211	28.23227	29.36092	30.54023	31.77248
24.64114	25.67253	26.75401	27.88805	29.07724	30.32428	31.63201	33.00340	34.44155	35.94973
26.99640	28.21288	29.49302	30.84022	32.25804	33.75023	35.32073	36.97370	38.71350	40.54470
29.48120	30.90565	32.41007	33.99903	35.67739	37.45024	39.32300	41.30134	43.39128	45.59917
32.10267	33.75999	35.51672	37.37896	39.35319	41.44626	43.66545	46.01846	48.51345	51.15909
34.86832	36.78559	38.82531	40.99549	43.30468	45.76196	48.37701	51.16012	54.12223	57.27500
37.78608	39.99273	42.34895	44.86518	47.55253	50.42292	53.48906	56.76453	60.26384	64.00250
40.86431	43.39229	46.10164	49.00574	52.11897	55.45676	59.03563	62.87334	66.98891	71.40275
44.11185	46.99583	50.09824	53.43614	57.02790	60.89330	65.05366	69.53194	74.35286	79.54302
47.53800	50.81558	54.35463	58.17667	62.30499	66.76476	71.58322	76.78981	82.41638	88.49733
51.15259	54.86451	58.88768	63.24904	67.97786	73.10594	78.66779	84.70090	91.24593	98.34706
54.96598	59.15638	63.71538	68.67647	74.07620	79.95442	86.35455	93.32398	100.91430	109.18177
58.98911	63.70577	68.85688	74.48382	80.63192	87.35077	94.69469	102.72313	111.50116	121.09994
63.23351	68.52811	74.33257	80.69769	87.67931	95.33883	103.74374	112.96822	123.09377	134.20994
67.71135	73.63980	80.16419	87.34653	95.25526	103.96594	113.56196	124.13536	135.78767	148.63093
72.43548	79.05819	86.37486	94.46079	103.39940	113.28321	124.21473	136.30754	149.68750	164.49402

Table E.2   *(concluded)*
FUTURE VALUE OF AN ORDINARY ANNUITY OF $1 PER PERIOD: 10.5%–20%

Period	10.5%	11%	11.5%	12%	12.5%	13%	13.5%	14%	14.5%	15%
1 ...	1.00000	1.00000	1.00000	1.00000	1.00000	1.00000	1.00000	1.00000	1.00000	1.00000
2 ...	2.10500	2.11000	2.11500	2.12000	2.12500	2.13000	2.13500	2.14000	2.14500	2.15000
3 ...	3.32602	3.34210	3.35822	3.37440	3.39062	3.40690	3.42322	3.43960	3.45602	3.47250
4 ...	4.67526	4.70973	4.74442	4.77933	4.81445	4.84980	4.88536	4.92114	4.95715	4.99337
5 ...	6.16616	6.22780	6.29003	6.35285	6.41626	6.48027	6.54488	6.61010	6.67594	6.74238
6 ...	7.81361	7.91286	8.01338	8.11519	8.21829	8.32271	8.42844	8.53552	8.64395	8.75374
7 ...	9.63404	9.78327	9.93492	10.08901	10.24558	10.40466	10.56628	10.73049	10.89732	11.06680
8 ...	11.64561	11.85943	12.07744	12.29969	12.52628	12.75726	12.99273	13.23276	13.47743	13.72682
9 ...	13.86840	14.16397	14.46634	14.77566	15.09206	15.41571	15.74675	16.08535	16.43166	16.78584
10 ...	16.32458	16.72201	17.12997	17.54874	17.97857	18.41975	18.87256	19.33730	19.81425	20.30372
11 ...	19.03866	19.56143	20.09992	20.65458	21.22589	21.81432	22.42036	23.04452	23.68731	24.34928
12 ...	22.03772	22.71319	23.41141	24.13313	24.87913	25.65018	26.44711	27.27075	28.12197	29.00167
13 ...	25.35168	26.21164	27.10372	28.02911	28.98902	29.98470	31.01746	32.08865	33.19966	34.35192
14 ...	29.01361	30.09492	31.22065	32.39260	33.61264	34.88271	36.20482	37.58107	39.01361	40.50471
15 ...	33.06004	34.40536	35.81102	37.27971	38.81422	40.41746	42.09247	43.84241	45.67058	47.58041
16 ...	37.53134	39.18995	40.92929	42.75328	44.66600	46.67173	48.77496	50.98035	53.29282	55.71747
17 ...	42.47213	44.50084	46.63616	48.88367	51.24925	53.73906	56.35958	59.11760	62.02027	65.07509
18 ...	47.93170	50.39594	52.99932	55.74971	58.65541	61.72514	64.96812	68.39407	72.01321	75.83636
19 ...	53.96453	56.93949	60.09424	63.43968	66.98733	70.74941	74.73882	78.96923	83.45513	88.21181
20 ...	60.63081	64.20283	68.00508	72.05244	76.36075	80.94683	85.82856	91.02493	96.55612	102.44358
21 ...	67.99704	72.26514	76.82566	81.69874	86.90584	92.46992	98.41541	104.76842	111.55676	118.81012
22 ...	76.13673	81.21431	86.66062	92.50258	98.76908	105.49101	112.70149	120.43600	128.73249	137.63164
23 ...	85.13109	91.14788	97.62659	104.60289	112.11521	120.20484	128.91619	138.29704	148.39871	159.27638
24 ...	95.06985	102.17415	109.85364	118.15524	127.12961	136.83147	147.31988	158.65862	170.91652	184.16784
25 ...	106.05219	114.41331	123.48681	133.33387	144.02081	155.61956	168.20806	181.87083	196.69941	212.79302
26 ...	118.18767	127.99877	138.68780	150.33393	163.02341	176.85010	191.91615	208.33274	226.22083	245.71197
27 ...	131.59737	143.07864	155.63689	169.37401	184.40134	200.84061	218.82483	238.49933	260.02285	283.56877
28 ...	146.41510	159.81729	174.53513	190.69889	208.45151	227.94989	249.36618	272.88923	298.72616	327.10408
29 ...	162.78868	178.39719	195.60668	214.58275	235.50795	258.58338	284.03062	312.09373	343.04145	377.16969
30 ...	180.88149	199.02088	219.10144	241.33268	265.94644	293.19922	323.37475	356.78685	393.78246	434.74515

15.5%	16%	16.5%	17%	17.5%	18%	18.5%	19%	19.5%	20%
1.00000	1.00000	1.00000	1.00000	1.00000	1.00000	1.00000	1.00000	1.00000	1.00000
2.15500	2.16000	2.16500	2.17000	2.17500	2.18000	2.18500	2.19000	2.19500	2.20000
3.48902	3.50560	3.52222	3.53890	3.55562	3.57240	3.58922	3.60610	3.62302	3.64000
5.02982	5.06650	5.10339	5.14051	5.17786	5.21543	5.25323	5.29126	5.32951	5.36800
6.80945	6.87714	6.94545	7.01440	7.08398	7.15421	7.22508	7.29660	7.36877	7.44160
8.86491	8.97748	9.09145	9.20685	9.32368	9.44197	9.56172	9.68295	9.80568	9.92992
11.23897	11.41387	11.59154	11.77201	11.95533	12.14152	12.33064	12.52271	12.71779	12.91590
13.98101	14.24009	14.50415	14.77325	15.04751	15.32700	15.61181	15.90203	16.19776	16.49908
17.14807	17.51851	17.89733	18.28471	18.68082	19.08585	19.49999	19.92341	20.35632	20.79890
20.80602	21.32147	21.85039	22.39311	22.94997	23.52131	24.10749	24.70886	25.32580	25.95868
25.03095	25.73290	26.45570	27.19994	27.96621	28.75514	29.56737	30.40355	31.26433	32.15042
29.91075	30.85017	31.82089	32.82393	33.86030	34.93107	36.03734	37.18022	38.36088	39.58050
35.54692	36.78620	38.07134	39.40399	40.78585	42.21866	43.70424	45.24446	46.84125	48.49660
42.05669	43.67199	45.35311	47.10267	48.92337	50.81802	52.78953	54.84091	56.97529	59.19592
49.57548	51.65951	53.83638	56.11013	58.48496	60.96527	63.55559	66.26068	69.08547	72.03511
58.25968	60.92503	63.71938	66.64885	69.71983	72.93901	76.31338	79.85021	83.55714	87.44213
68.28993	71.67303	75.23307	78.97915	82.92080	87.06804	91.43135	96.02175	100.85079	105.93056
79.87486	84.14072	88.64653	93.40561	98.43194	103.74028	109.34615	115.26588	121.51669	128.11667
93.25547	98.60323	104.27321	110.28456	116.65753	123.41353	130.57519	138.16640	146.21244	154.74000
108.71007	115.37975	122.47829	130.03294	138.07260	146.62797	155.73160	165.41802	175.72387	186.68800
126.56013	134.84051	143.68721	153.13854	163.23531	174.02100	185.54194	197.84744	210.99002	225.02560
147.17695	157.41499	168.39560	180.17209	192.80149	206.34479	220.86720	236.43846	253.13308	271.03072
170.98937	183.60138	197.18087	211.80134	227.54175	244.48685	262.72763	282.36176	303.49403	326.23686
198.49272	213.97761	230.71571	248.80757	268.36155	289.49448	312.33225	337.01050	363.67536	392.48424
230.25910	249.21402	269.78381	292.10486	316.32482	342.60349	371.11371	402.04249	435.59206	471.98108
266.94926	290.08827	315.29813	342.76268	372.68167	405.27211	440.76975	479.43056	521.53251	567.37730
309.32639	337.50239	368.32233	402.03234	438.90096	479.22109	523.31215	571.52237	624.23135	681.85276
358.27198	392.50277	430.09551	471.37783	516.70863	566.48089	621.12490	681.11162	746.95647	819.22331
414.80414	456.30322	502.06127	552.51207	608.13264	669.44745	737.03300	811.52283	893.61298	984.06797
480.09878	530.31173	585.90138	647.43912	715.55585	790.94799	874.38411	966.71217	1068.86751	1181.88157

Table E.3
PRESENT VALUE of $1 AT COMPOUND INTEREST: 0.5%–7%

$$P_{i,n} = \frac{1}{(1 + i)^n}$$

Period	.5%	1%	1.5%	2%	2.5%	3%	3.5%	4%	4.5%	5%	5.5%	6%	6.5%	7%
1	0.99502	0.99010	0.98522	0.98039	0.97561	0.97087	0.96618	0.96154	0.95694	0.95238	0.94787	0.94340	0.93897	0.93458
2	0.99007	0.98030	0.97066	0.96117	0.95181	0.94260	0.93351	0.92456	0.91573	0.90703	0.89845	0.89000	0.88166	0.87344
3	0.98515	0.97059	0.95632	0.94232	0.92860	0.91514	0.90194	0.88900	0.87630	0.86384	0.85161	0.83962	0.82785	0.81630
4	0.98025	0.96098	0.94218	0.92385	0.90595	0.88849	0.87144	0.85480	0.83856	0.82270	0.80722	0.79209	0.77732	0.76290
5	0.97537	0.95147	0.92826	0.90573	0.88385	0.86261	0.84197	0.82193	0.80245	0.78353	0.76513	0.74726	0.72988	0.71299
6	0.97052	0.94205	0.91454	0.88797	0.86230	0.83748	0.81350	0.79031	0.76790	0.74622	0.72525	0.70496	0.68533	0.66634
7	0.96569	0.93272	0.90103	0.87056	0.84127	0.81309	0.78599	0.75992	0.73483	0.71068	0.68744	0.66506	0.64351	0.62275
8	0.96089	0.92348	0.88771	0.85349	0.82075	0.78941	0.75941	0.73069	0.70319	0.67684	0.65160	0.62741	0.60423	0.58201
9	0.95610	0.91434	0.87459	0.83676	0.80073	0.76642	0.73373	0.70259	0.67290	0.64461	0.61763	0.59190	0.56735	0.54393
10	0.95135	0.90529	0.86167	0.82035	0.78120	0.74409	0.70892	0.67556	0.64393	0.61391	0.58543	0.55839	0.53273	0.50835
11	0.94661	0.89632	0.84893	0.80426	0.76214	0.72242	0.68495	0.64958	0.61620	0.58468	0.55491	0.52679	0.50021	0.47509
12	0.94191	0.88745	0.83639	0.78849	0.74356	0.70138	0.66178	0.62460	0.58966	0.55684	0.52598	0.49697	0.46968	0.44401
13	0.93722	0.87866	0.82403	0.77303	0.72542	0.68095	0.63940	0.60057	0.56427	0.53032	0.49856	0.46884	0.44102	0.41496
14	0.93256	0.86996	0.81185	0.75788	0.70773	0.66112	0.61778	0.57748	0.53997	0.50507	0.47257	0.44230	0.41410	0.38782
15	0.92792	0.86135	0.79985	0.74301	0.69047	0.64186	0.59689	0.55526	0.51672	0.48102	0.44793	0.41727	0.38883	0.36245
16	0.92330	0.85282	0.78803	0.72845	0.67362	0.62317	0.57671	0.53391	0.49447	0.45811	0.42458	0.39365	0.36510	0.33873
17	0.91871	0.84438	0.77639	0.71416	0.65720	0.60502	0.55720	0.51337	0.47318	0.43630	0.40245	0.37136	0.34281	0.31657
18	0.91414	0.83602	0.76491	0.70016	0.64117	0.58739	0.53836	0.49363	0.45280	0.41552	0.38147	0.35034	0.32189	0.29586
19	0.90959	0.82774	0.75361	0.68643	0.62553	0.57029	0.52016	0.47464	0.43330	0.39573	0.36158	0.33051	0.30224	0.27651
20	0.90506	0.81954	0.74247	0.67297	0.61027	0.55368	0.50257	0.45639	0.41464	0.37689	0.34273	0.31180	0.28380	0.25842
21	0.90056	0.81143	0.73150	0.65978	0.59539	0.53755	0.48557	0.43883	0.39679	0.35894	0.32486	0.29416	0.26648	0.24151
22	0.89608	0.80340	0.72069	0.64684	0.58086	0.52189	0.46915	0.42196	0.37970	0.34185	0.30793	0.27751	0.25021	0.22571
23	0.89162	0.79544	0.71004	0.63416	0.56670	0.50669	0.45329	0.40573	0.36335	0.32557	0.29187	0.26180	0.23494	0.21095
24	0.88719	0.78757	0.69954	0.62172	0.55288	0.49193	0.43796	0.39012	0.34770	0.31007	0.27666	0.24698	0.22060	0.19715
25	0.88277	0.77977	0.68921	0.60953	0.53939	0.47761	0.42315	0.37512	0.33273	0.29530	0.26223	0.23300	0.20714	0.18425
26	0.87838	0.77205	0.67902	0.59758	0.52623	0.46369	0.40884	0.36069	0.31840	0.28124	0.24856	0.21981	0.19450	0.17220
27	0.87401	0.76440	0.66899	0.58586	0.51340	0.45019	0.39501	0.34682	0.30469	0.26785	0.23560	0.20737	0.18263	0.16093
28	0.86966	0.75684	0.65910	0.57437	0.50088	0.43708	0.38165	0.33348	0.29157	0.25509	0.22332	0.19563	0.17148	0.15040
29	0.86533	0.74934	0.64936	0.56311	0.48866	0.42435	0.36875	0.32065	0.27902	0.24295	0.21168	0.18456	0.16101	0.14056
30	0.86103	0.74192	0.63976	0.55207	0.47674	0.41199	0.35628	0.30832	0.26700	0.23138	0.20064	0.17411	0.15119	0.13137
31	0.85675	0.73458	0.63031	0.54125	0.46511	0.39999	0.34423	0.29646	0.25550	0.22036	0.19018	0.16425	0.14196	0.12277
32	0.85248	0.72730	0.62099	0.53063	0.45377	0.38834	0.33259	0.28506	0.24450	0.20987	0.18027	0.15496	0.13329	0.11474
33	0.84824	0.72010	0.61182	0.52023	0.44270	0.37703	0.32134	0.27409	0.23397	0.19987	0.17087	0.14619	0.12516	0.10723
34	0.84402	0.71297	0.60277	0.51003	0.43191	0.36604	0.31048	0.26355	0.22390	0.19035	0.16196	0.13791	0.11752	0.10022
35	0.83982	0.70591	0.59387	0.50003	0.42137	0.35538	0.29998	0.25342	0.21425	0.18129	0.15352	0.13011	0.11035	0.09366
36	0.83564	0.69892	0.58509	0.49022	0.41109	0.34503	0.28983	0.24367	0.20503	0.17266	0.14552	0.12274	0.10361	0.08754
37	0.83149	0.69200	0.57644	0.48061	0.40107	0.33498	0.28003	0.23430	0.19620	0.16444	0.13793	0.11579	0.09729	0.08181
38	0.82735	0.68515	0.56792	0.47119	0.39128	0.32523	0.27056	0.22529	0.18775	0.15661	0.13074	0.10924	0.09135	0.07646
39	0.82323	0.67837	0.55953	0.46195	0.38174	0.31575	0.26141	0.21662	0.17967	0.14915	0.12392	0.10306	0.08578	0.07146
40	0.81914	0.67165	0.55126	0.45289	0.37243	0.30656	0.25257	0.20829	0.17193	0.14205	0.11746	0.09722	0.08054	0.06678
41	0.81506	0.66500	0.54312	0.44401	0.36335	0.29763	0.24403	0.20028	0.16453	0.13528	0.11134	0.09172	0.07563	0.06241
42	0.81101	0.65842	0.53509	0.43530	0.35448	0.28896	0.23578	0.19257	0.15744	0.12884	0.10554	0.08653	0.07101	0.05833
43	0.80697	0.65190	0.52718	0.42677	0.34584	0.28054	0.22781	0.18517	0.15066	0.12270	0.10003	0.08163	0.06668	0.05451
44	0.80296	0.64545	0.51939	0.41840	0.33740	0.27237	0.22010	0.17805	0.14417	0.11686	0.09482	0.07701	0.06261	0.05095
45	0.79896	0.63905	0.51171	0.41020	0.32917	0.26444	0.21266	0.17120	0.13796	0.11130	0.08988	0.07265	0.05879	0.04761
46	0.79499	0.63273	0.50415	0.40215	0.32115	0.25674	0.20547	0.16461	0.13202	0.10600	0.08519	0.06854	0.05520	0.04450
47	0.79103	0.62646	0.49670	0.39427	0.31331	0.24926	0.19852	0.15828	0.12634	0.10095	0.08075	0.06466	0.05183	0.04159
48	0.78710	0.62026	0.48936	0.38654	0.30567	0.24200	0.19181	0.15219	0.12090	0.09614	0.07654	0.06100	0.04867	0.03887
49	0.78318	0.61412	0.48213	0.37896	0.29822	0.23495	0.18532	0.14634	0.11569	0.09156	0.07255	0.05755	0.04570	0.03632
50	0.77929	0.60804	0.47500	0.37153	0.29094	0.22811	0.17905	0.14071	0.11071	0.08720	0.06877	0.05429	0.04291	0.03395
51	0.77541	0.60202	0.46798	0.36424	0.28385	0.22146	0.17300	0.13530	0.10594	0.08305	0.06518	0.05122	0.04029	0.03173
52	0.77155	0.59606	0.46107	0.35710	0.27692	0.21501	0.16715	0.13010	0.10138	0.07910	0.06178	0.04832	0.03783	0.02965
53	0.76771	0.59016	0.45426	0.35010	0.27017	0.20875	0.16150	0.12509	0.09701	0.07533	0.05856	0.04558	0.03552	0.02771
54	0.76389	0.58431	0.44754	0.34323	0.26358	0.20267	0.15603	0.12028	0.09284	0.07174	0.05551	0.04300	0.03335	0.02590
55	0.76009	0.57853	0.44093	0.33650	0.25715	0.19677	0.15076	0.11566	0.08884	0.06833	0.05262	0.04057	0.03132	0.02420
56	0.75631	0.57280	0.43441	0.32991	0.25088	0.19104	0.14566	0.11121	0.08501	0.06507	0.04987	0.03827	0.02941	0.02262
57	0.75255	0.56713	0.42799	0.32344	0.24476	0.18547	0.14073	0.10693	0.08135	0.06197	0.04727	0.03610	0.02761	0.02114
58	0.74880	0.56151	0.42167	0.31710	0.23879	0.18007	0.13598	0.10282	0.07785	0.05902	0.04481	0.03406	0.02593	0.01976
59	0.74508	0.55595	0.41544	0.31088	0.23297	0.17483	0.13138	0.09886	0.07450	0.05621	0.04247	0.03213	0.02434	0.01847
60	0.74137	0.55045	0.40930	0.30478	0.22728	0.16973	0.12693	0.09506	0.07129	0.05354	0.04026	0.03031	0.02286	0.01726

Period	.5%	1%	1.5%	2%	2.5%	3%	3.5%	4%	4.5%	5%	5.5%	6%	6.5%	7%
61 ..	0.73768	0.54500	0.40325	0.29881	0.22174	0.16479	0.12264	0.09140	0.06822	0.05099	0.03816	0.02860	0.02146	0.01613
62 ..	0.73401	0.53960	0.39729	0.29295	0.21633	0.15999	0.11849	0.08789	0.06528	0.04856	0.03617	0.02698	0.02015	0.01507
63 ..	0.73036	0.53426	0.39142	0.28720	0.21106	0.15533	0.11449	0.08451	0.06247	0.04625	0.03428	0.02545	0.01892	0.01409
64 ..	0.72673	0.52897	0.38563	0.28157	0.20591	0.15081	0.11062	0.08126	0.05978	0.04404	0.03250	0.02401	0.01777	0.01317
65 ..	0.72311	0.52373	0.37993	0.27605	0.20089	0.14641	0.10688	0.07813	0.05721	0.04195	0.03080	0.02265	0.01668	0.01230
66 ..	0.71952	0.51855	0.37432	0.27064	0.19599	0.14215	0.10326	0.07513	0.05474	0.03995	0.02920	0.02137	0.01566	0.01150
67 ..	0.71594	0.51341	0.36879	0.26533	0.19121	0.13801	0.09977	0.07224	0.05239	0.03805	0.02767	0.02016	0.01471	0.01075
68 ..	0.71237	0.50833	0.36334	0.26013	0.18654	0.13399	0.09640	0.06946	0.05013	0.03623	0.02623	0.01902	0.01381	0.01004
69 ..	0.70883	0.50330	0.35797	0.25503	0.18199	0.13009	0.09314	0.06679	0.04797	0.03451	0.02486	0.01794	0.01297	0.00939
70 ..	0.70530	0.49831	0.35268	0.25003	0.17755	0.12630	0.08999	0.06422	0.04590	0.03287	0.02357	0.01693	0.01218	0.00877
71 ..	0.70179	0.49338	0.34746	0.24513	0.17322	0.12262	0.08694	0.06175	0.04393	0.03130	0.02234	0.01597	0.01143	0.00820
72 ..	0.69830	0.48850	0.34233	0.24032	0.16900	0.11905	0.08400	0.05937	0.04204	0.02981	0.02117	0.01507	0.01074	0.00766
73 ..	0.69483	0.48366	0.33727	0.23561	0.16488	0.11558	0.08116	0.05709	0.04023	0.02839	0.02007	0.01421	0.01008	0.00716
74 ..	0.69137	0.47887	0.33229	0.23099	0.16085	0.11221	0.07842	0.05490	0.03849	0.02704	0.01902	0.01341	0.00947	0.00669
75 ..	0.68793	0.47413	0.32738	0.22646	0.15693	0.10895	0.07577	0.05278	0.03684	0.02575	0.01803	0.01265	0.00889	0.00625
76 ..	0.68451	0.46944	0.32254	0.22202	0.15310	0.10577	0.07320	0.05075	0.03525	0.02453	0.01709	0.01193	0.00835	0.00585
77 ..	0.68110	0.46479	0.31777	0.21766	0.14937	0.10269	0.07073	0.04880	0.03373	0.02336	0.01620	0.01126	0.00784	0.00546
78 ..	0.67772	0.46019	0.31308	0.21340	0.14573	0.09970	0.06834	0.04692	0.03228	0.02225	0.01536	0.01062	0.00736	0.00511
79 ..	0.67434	0.45563	0.30845	0.20921	0.14217	0.09680	0.06603	0.04512	0.03089	0.02119	0.01456	0.01002	0.00691	0.00477
80 ..	0.67099	0.45112	0.30389	0.20511	0.13870	0.09398	0.06379	0.04338	0.02956	0.02018	0.01380	0.00945	0.00649	0.00446
81 ..	0.66765	0.44665	0.29940	0.20109	0.13532	0.09124	0.06164	0.04172	0.02829	0.01922	0.01308	0.00892	0.00609	0.00417
82 ..	0.66433	0.44223	0.29497	0.19715	0.13202	0.08858	0.05955	0.04011	0.02707	0.01830	0.01240	0.00841	0.00572	0.00390
83 ..	0.66102	0.43785	0.29062	0.19328	0.12880	0.08600	0.05754	0.03857	0.02590	0.01743	0.01175	0.00794	0.00537	0.00364
84 ..	0.65773	0.43352	0.28632	0.18949	0.12566	0.08350	0.05559	0.03709	0.02479	0.01660	0.01114	0.00749	0.00504	0.00340
85 ..	0.65446	0.42922	0.28209	0.18577	0.12259	0.08107	0.05371	0.03566	0.02372	0.01581	0.01056	0.00706	0.00473	0.00318
86 ..	0.65121	0.42497	0.27792	0.18213	0.11960	0.07870	0.05189	0.03429	0.02270	0.01506	0.01001	0.00666	0.00445	0.00297
87 ..	0.64797	0.42077	0.27381	0.17856	0.11669	0.07641	0.05014	0.03297	0.02172	0.01434	0.00948	0.00629	0.00417	0.00278
88 ..	0.64474	0.41660	0.26977	0.17506	0.11384	0.07419	0.04845	0.03170	0.02079	0.01366	0.00899	0.00593	0.00392	0.00260
89 ..	0.64154	0.41248	0.26578	0.17163	0.11106	0.07203	0.04681	0.03048	0.01989	0.01301	0.00852	0.00559	0.00368	0.00243
90 ..	0.63834	0.40839	0.26185	0.16826	0.10836	0.06993	0.04522	0.02931	0.01903	0.01239	0.00808	0.00528	0.00346	0.00227
91 ..	0.63517	0.40435	0.25798	0.16496	0.10571	0.06789	0.04369	0.02818	0.01821	0.01180	0.00766	0.00498	0.00324	0.00212
92 ..	0.63201	0.40034	0.25417	0.16173	0.10313	0.06591	0.04222	0.02710	0.01743	0.01124	0.00726	0.00470	0.00305	0.00198
93 ..	0.62886	0.39638	0.25041	0.15856	0.10062	0.06399	0.04079	0.02606	0.01668	0.01070	0.00688	0.00443	0.00286	0.00185
94 ..	0.62573	0.39246	0.24671	0.15545	0.09816	0.06213	0.03941	0.02505	0.01596	0.01019	0.00652	0.00418	0.00269	0.00173
95 ..	0.62262	0.38857	0.24307	0.15240	0.09577	0.06032	0.03808	0.02409	0.01527	0.00971	0.00618	0.00394	0.00252	0.00162
96 ..	0.61952	0.38472	0.23947	0.14941	0.09343	0.05856	0.03679	0.02316	0.01462	0.00924	0.00586	0.00372	0.00237	0.00151
97 ..	0.61644	0.38091	0.23594	0.14648	0.09116	0.05686	0.03555	0.02227	0.01399	0.00880	0.00555	0.00351	0.00222	0.00141
98 ..	0.61337	0.37714	0.23245	0.14361	0.08893	0.05520	0.03434	0.02142	0.01338	0.00838	0.00526	0.00331	0.00209	0.00132
99 ..	0.61032	0.37341	0.22901	0.14079	0.08676	0.05359	0.03318	0.02059	0.01281	0.00798	0.00499	0.00312	0.00196	0.00123
100 ..	0.60729	0.36971	0.22563	0.13803	0.08465	0.05203	0.03026	0.01980	0.01226	0.00760	0.00473	0.00295	0.00184	0.00115
101 ..	0.60427	0.36605	0.22230	0.13533	0.08258	0.05052	0.03098	0.01904	0.01173	0.00724	0.00448	0.00278	0.00173	0.00108
102 ..	0.60126	0.36243	0.21901	0.13267	0.08057	0.04905	0.02993	0.01831	0.01122	0.00690	0.00425	0.00262	0.00162	0.00101
103 ..	0.59827	0.35884	0.21577	0.13007	0.07860	0.04762	0.02892	0.01760	0.01074	0.00657	0.00403	0.00247	0.00152	0.00094
104 ..	0.59529	0.35529	0.21258	0.12752	0.07669	0.04623	0.02794	0.01693	0.01028	0.00626	0.00382	0.00233	0.00143	0.00088
105 ..	0.59233	0.35177	0.20944	0.12502	0.07482	0.04488	0.02699	0.01627	0.00984	0.00596	0.00362	0.00220	0.00134	0.00082
106 ..	0.58938	0.34828	0.20635	0.12257	0.07299	0.04358	0.02608	0.01565	0.00941	0.00567	0.00343	0.00208	0.00126	0.00077
107 ..	0.58645	0.34484	0.20330	0.12017	0.07121	0.04231	0.02520	0.01505	0.00901	0.00540	0.00325	0.00196	0.00118	0.00072
108 ..	0.58353	0.34142	0.20029	0.11781	0.06947	0.04108	0.02435	0.01447	0.00862	0.00515	0.00308	0.00185	0.00111	0.00067
109 ..	0.58063	0.33804	0.19733	0.11550	0.06778	0.03988	0.02352	0.01391	0.00825	0.00490	0.00292	0.00174	0.00104	0.00063
110 ..	0.57774	0.33469	0.19442	0.11324	0.06613	0.03872	0.02273	0.01338	0.00789	0.00467	0.00277	0.00165	0.00098	0.00059
111 ..	0.57487	0.33138	0.19154	0.11101	0.06451	0.03759	0.02196	0.01286	0.00755	0.00445	0.00262	0.00155	0.00092	0.00055
112 ..	0.57201	0.32810	0.18871	0.10884	0.06294	0.03649	0.02122	0.01237	0.00723	0.00423	0.00249	0.00146	0.00086	0.00051
113 ..	0.56916	0.32485	0.18592	0.10670	0.06140	0.03543	0.02050	0.01189	0.00692	0.00403	0.00236	0.00138	0.00081	0.00048
114 ..	0.56633	0.32164	0.18318	0.10461	0.05991	0.03440	0.01981	0.01143	0.00662	0.00384	0.00223	0.00130	0.00076	0.00045
115 ..	0.56351	0.31845	0.18047	0.10256	0.05845	0.03340	0.01914	0.01099	0.00633	0.00366	0.00212	0.00123	0.00072	0.00042
116 ..	0.56071	0.31530	0.17780	0.10055	0.05702	0.03243	0.01849	0.01057	0.00606	0.00348	0.00201	0.00116	0.00067	0.00039
117 ..	0.55792	0.31218	0.17518	0.09858	0.05563	0.03148	0.01786	0.01016	0.00580	0.00332	0.00190	0.00109	0.00063	0.00036
118 ..	0.55514	0.30908	0.17259	0.09665	0.05427	0.03056	0.01726	0.00977	0.00555	0.00316	0.00180	0.00103	0.00059	0.00034
119 ..	0.55238	0.30602	0.17004	0.09475	0.05295	0.02967	0.01668	0.00940	0.00531	0.00301	0.00171	0.00097	0.00056	0.00032
120 ..	0.54963	0.30299	0.16752	0.09289	0.05166	0.02881	0.01611	0.00904	0.00508	0.00287	0.00162	0.00092	0.00052	0.00030

Table E.3 (continued)
PRESENT VALUE OF $1 AT COMPOUND INTEREST: 7.5%–14%

Period	7.5%	8%	8.5%	9%	9.5%	10%	10.5%	11%	11.5%	12%	12.5%	13%	13.5%	14%
1 ...	0.93023	0.92593	0.92166	0.91743	0.91324	0.90909	0.90498	0.90090	0.89686	0.89286	0.88889	0.88496	0.88106	0.87719
2 ...	0.86533	0.85734	0.84946	0.84168	0.83401	0.82645	0.81898	0.81162	0.80436	0.79719	0.79012	0.78315	0.77626	0.76947
3 ...	0.80496	0.79383	0.78291	0.77218	0.76165	0.75131	0.74116	0.73119	0.72140	0.71178	0.70233	0.69305	0.68393	0.67497
4 ...	0.74880	0.73503	0.72157	0.70843	0.69557	0.68301	0.67073	0.65873	0.64699	0.63553	0.62430	0.61332	0.60258	0.59208
5 ...	0.69656	0.68058	0.66505	0.64993	0.63523	0.62092	0.60700	0.59345	0.58026	0.56743	0.55493	0.54276	0.53091	0.51937
6 ...	0.64796	0.63017	0.61295	0.59627	0.58012	0.56447	0.54932	0.53464	0.52042	0.50663	0.49327	0.48032	0.46776	0.45559
7 ...	0.60275	0.58349	0.56493	0.54703	0.52979	0.51316	0.49712	0.48166	0.46674	0.45235	0.43846	0.42506	0.41213	0.39964
8 ...	0.56070	0.54027	0.52067	0.50187	0.48382	0.46651	0.44989	0.43393	0.41860	0.40388	0.38974	0.37616	0.36311	0.35056
9 ...	0.52158	0.50025	0.47988	0.46043	0.44185	0.42410	0.40714	0.39092	0.37543	0.36061	0.34644	0.33288	0.31992	0.30751
10 ...	0.48519	0.46319	0.44229	0.42241	0.40351	0.38554	0.36845	0.35218	0.33671	0.32197	0.30795	0.29459	0.28187	0.26974
11 ...	0.45134	0.42888	0.40764	0.38753	0.36851	0.35049	0.33344	0.31728	0.30198	0.28748	0.27373	0.26070	0.24834	0.23662
12 ...	0.41985	0.39711	0.37570	0.35553	0.33654	0.31863	0.30175	0.28584	0.27083	0.25668	0.24332	0.23071	0.21880	0.20756
13 ...	0.39056	0.36770	0.34627	0.32618	0.30734	0.28966	0.27308	0.25751	0.24290	0.22917	0.21628	0.20416	0.19278	0.18207
14 ...	0.36331	0.34046	0.31914	0.29925	0.28067	0.26333	0.24713	0.23199	0.21785	0.20462	0.19225	0.18068	0.16985	0.15971
15 ...	0.33797	0.31524	0.29414	0.27454	0.25632	0.23939	0.22365	0.20900	0.19538	0.18270	0.17089	0.15989	0.14964	0.14010
16 ...	0.31439	0.29189	0.27110	0.25187	0.23409	0.21763	0.20240	0.18829	0.17523	0.16312	0.15190	0.14150	0.13185	0.12289
17 ...	0.29245	0.27027	0.24986	0.23107	0.21378	0.19784	0.18316	0.16963	0.15715	0.14564	0.13502	0.12522	0.11616	0.10780
18 ...	0.27205	0.25025	0.23028	0.21199	0.19523	0.17986	0.16576	0.15282	0.14095	0.13004	0.12002	0.11081	0.10235	0.09456
19 ...	0.25307	0.23171	0.21224	0.19449	0.17829	0.16351	0.15001	0.13768	0.12641	0.11611	0.10668	0.09806	0.09017	0.08295
20 ...	0.23541	0.21455	0.19562	0.17843	0.16282	0.14864	0.13575	0.12403	0.11337	0.10367	0.09483	0.08678	0.07945	0.07276
21 ...	0.21899	0.19866	0.18029	0.16370	0.14870	0.13513	0.12285	0.11174	0.10168	0.09256	0.08429	0.07680	0.07000	0.06383
22 ...	0.20371	0.18394	0.16617	0.15018	0.13580	0.12285	0.11118	0.10067	0.09119	0.08264	0.07493	0.06796	0.06167	0.05599
23 ...	0.18950	0.17032	0.15315	0.13778	0.12402	0.11168	0.10062	0.09069	0.08179	0.07379	0.06660	0.06014	0.05434	0.04911
24 ...	0.17628	0.15770	0.14115	0.12640	0.11326	0.10153	0.09106	0.08170	0.07335	0.06588	0.05920	0.05323	0.04787	0.04308
25 ...	0.16398	0.14602	0.13009	0.11597	0.10343	0.09230	0.08240	0.07361	0.06579	0.05882	0.05262	0.04710	0.04218	0.03779
26 ...	0.15254	0.13520	0.11990	0.10639	0.09446	0.08391	0.07457	0.06631	0.05900	0.05252	0.04678	0.04168	0.03716	0.03315
27 ...	0.14190	0.12519	0.11051	0.09761	0.08626	0.07628	0.06749	0.05974	0.05291	0.04689	0.04158	0.03689	0.03274	0.02908
28 ...	0.13200	0.11591	0.10185	0.08955	0.07878	0.06934	0.06107	0.05382	0.04746	0.04187	0.03696	0.03264	0.02885	0.02551
29 ...	0.12279	0.10733	0.09387	0.08215	0.07194	0.06304	0.05527	0.04849	0.04256	0.03738	0.03285	0.02889	0.02542	0.02237
30 ...	0.11422	0.09938	0.08652	0.07537	0.06570	0.05731	0.05002	0.04368	0.03817	0.03338	0.02920	0.02557	0.02239	0.01963
31 ...	0.10625	0.09202	0.07974	0.06915	0.06000	0.05210	0.04527	0.03935	0.03424	0.02980	0.02596	0.02262	0.01973	0.01722
32 ...	0.09884	0.08520	0.07349	0.06344	0.05480	0.04736	0.04096	0.03545	0.03070	0.02661	0.02307	0.02002	0.01738	0.01510
33 ...	0.09194	0.07889	0.06774	0.05820	0.05004	0.04306	0.03707	0.03194	0.02754	0.02376	0.02051	0.01772	0.01532	0.01325
34 ...	0.08553	0.07305	0.06243	0.05339	0.04570	0.03914	0.03355	0.02878	0.02470	0.02121	0.01823	0.01568	0.01349	0.01162
35 ...	0.07956	0.06763	0.05754	0.04899	0.04174	0.03558	0.03036	0.02592	0.02215	0.01894	0.01621	0.01388	0.01189	0.01019
36 ...	0.07401	0.06262	0.05303	0.04494	0.03811	0.03235	0.02748	0.02335	0.01987	0.01691	0.01440	0.01228	0.01047	0.00894
37 ...	0.06885	0.05799	0.04888	0.04123	0.03481	0.02941	0.02487	0.02104	0.01782	0.01510	0.01280	0.01087	0.00923	0.00784
38 ...	0.06404	0.05369	0.04505	0.03783	0.03179	0.02673	0.02250	0.01896	0.01599	0.01348	0.01138	0.00962	0.00813	0.00688
39 ...	0.05958	0.04971	0.04152	0.03470	0.02903	0.02430	0.02036	0.01708	0.01433	0.01204	0.01012	0.00851	0.00716	0.00604
40 ...	0.05542	0.04603	0.03827	0.03184	0.02651	0.02209	0.01843	0.01538	0.01285	0.01075	0.00899	0.00753	0.00631	0.00529
41 ...	0.05155	0.04262	0.03527	0.02921	0.02421	0.02009	0.01668	0.01386	0.01153	0.00960	0.00799	0.00666	0.00556	0.00464
42 ...	0.04796	0.03946	0.03251	0.02680	0.02211	0.01826	0.01509	0.01249	0.01034	0.00857	0.00711	0.00590	0.00490	0.00407
43 ...	0.04461	0.03654	0.02996	0.02458	0.02019	0.01660	0.01366	0.01125	0.00927	0.00765	0.00632	0.00522	0.00432	0.00357
44 ...	0.04150	0.03383	0.02761	0.02255	0.01844	0.01509	0.01236	0.01013	0.00832	0.00683	0.00561	0.00462	0.00380	0.00313
45 ...	0.03860	0.03133	0.02545	0.02069	0.01684	0.01372	0.01119	0.00913	0.00746	0.00610	0.00499	0.00409	0.00335	0.00275
46 ...	0.03591	0.02901	0.02345	0.01898	0.01538	0.01247	0.01012	0.00823	0.00669	0.00544	0.00444	0.00362	0.00295	0.00241
47 ...	0.03340	0.02686	0.02162	0.01742	0.01405	0.01134	0.00916	0.00741	0.00600	0.00486	0.00394	0.00320	0.00260	0.00212
48 ...	0.03107	0.02487	0.01992	0.01598	0.01283	0.01031	0.00829	0.00668	0.00538	0.00434	0.00350	0.00283	0.00229	0.00186
49 ...	0.02891	0.02303	0.01836	0.01466	0.01171	0.00937	0.00750	0.00601	0.00483	0.00388	0.00312	0.00251	0.00202	0.00163
50 ...	0.02689	0.02132	0.01692	0.01345	0.01070	0.00852	0.00679	0.00542	0.00433	0.00346	0.00277	0.00222	0.00178	0.00143
51 ...	0.02501	0.01974	0.01560	0.01234	0.00977	0.00774	0.00615	0.00488	0.00388	0.00309	0.00246	0.00196	0.00157	0.00125
52 ...	0.02327	0.01828	0.01438	0.01132	0.00892	0.00704	0.00556	0.00440	0.00348	0.00276	0.00219	0.00174	0.00138	0.00110
53 ...	0.02164	0.01693	0.01325	0.01038	0.00815	0.00640	0.00503	0.00396	0.00312	0.00246	0.00194	0.00154	0.00122	0.00096
54 ...	0.02013	0.01567	0.01221	0.00953	0.00744	0.00582	0.00455	0.00357	0.00280	0.00220	0.00173	0.00136	0.00107	0.00085
55 ...	0.01873	0.01451	0.01126	0.00874	0.00680	0.00529	0.00412	0.00322	0.00251	0.00196	0.00154	0.00120	0.00094	0.00074
56 ...	0.01742	0.01344	0.01037	0.00802	0.00621	0.00481	0.00373	0.00290	0.00225	0.00175	0.00137	0.00107	0.00083	0.00065
57 ...	0.01621	0.01244	0.00956	0.00736	0.00567	0.00437	0.00338	0.00261	0.00202	0.00157	0.00121	0.00094	0.00073	0.00057
58 ...	0.01508	0.01152	0.00881	0.00675	0.00518	0.00397	0.00305	0.00235	0.00181	0.00140	0.00108	0.00083	0.00065	0.00050
59 ...	0.01402	0.01067	0.00812	0.00619	0.00473	0.00361	0.00276	0.00212	0.00162	0.00125	0.00096	0.00074	0.00057	0.00044
60 ...	0.01305	0.00988	0.00749	0.00568	0.00432	0.00328	0.00250	0.00191	0.00146	0.00111	0.00085	0.00065	0.00050	0.00039

Period	7.5%	8%	8.5%	9%	9.5%	10%	10.5%	11%	11.5%	12%	12.5%	13%	13.5%	14%
61 ..	0.01214	0.00914	0.00690	0.00521	0.00394	0.00299	0.00226	0.00172	0.00131	0.00099	0.00076	0.00058	0.00044	0.00034
62 ..	0.01129	0.00847	0.00636	0.00478	0.00360	0.00271	0.00205	0.00155	0.00117	0.00089	0.00067	0.00051	0.00039	0.00030
63 ..	0.01050	0.00784	0.00586	0.00439	0.00329	0.00247	0.00185	0.00140	0.00105	0.00079	0.00060	0.00045	0.00034	0.00026
64 ..	0.00977	0.00726	0.00540	0.00402	0.00300	0.00224	0.00168	0.00126	0.00094	0.00071	0.00053	0.00040	0.00030	0.00023
65 ..	0.00909	0.00672	0.00498	0.00369	0.00274	0.00204	0.00152	0.00113	0.00085	0.00063	0.00047	0.00035	0.00027	0.00020
66 ..	0.00845	0.00622	0.00459	0.00339	0.00250	0.00185	0.00137	0.00102	0.00076	0.00056	0.00042	0.00031	0.00023	0.00018
67 ..	0.00786	0.00576	0.00423	0.00311	0.00229	0.00169	0.00124	0.00092	0.00068	0.00050	0.00037	0.00028	0.00021	0.00015
68 ..	0.00732	0.00534	0.00390	0.00285	0.00209	0.00153	0.00113	0.00083	0.00061	0.00045	0.00033	0.00025	0.00018	0.00014
69 ..	0.00680	0.00494	0.00359	0.00262	0.00191	0.00139	0.00102	0.00075	0.00055	0.00040	0.00030	0.00022	0.00016	0.00012
70 ..	0.00633	0.00457	0.00331	0.00240	0.00174	0.00127	0.00092	0.00067	0.00049	0.00036	0.00026	0.00019	0.00014	0.00010
71 ..	0.00589	0.00424	0.00305	0.00220	0.00159	0.00115	0.00083	0.00061	0.00044	0.00032	0.00023	0.00017	0.00012	0.00009
72 ..	0.00548	0.00392	0.00281	0.00202	0.00145	0.00105	0.00075	0.00055	0.00039	0.00029	0.00021	0.00015	0.00011	0.00008
73 ..	0.00510	0.00363	0.00259	0.00185	0.00133	0.00095	0.00068	0.00049	0.00035	0.00026	0.00018	0.00013	0.00010	0.00007
74 ..	0.00474	0.00336	0.00239	0.00170	0.00121	0.00086	0.00062	0.00044	0.00032	0.00023	0.00016	0.00012	0.00009	0.00006
75 ..	0.00441	0.00311	0.00220	0.00156	0.00111	0.00079	0.00056	0.00040	0.00028	0.00020	0.00015	0.00010	0.00008	0.00005
76 ..	0.00410	0.00288	0.00203	0.00143	0.00101	0.00071	0.00051	0.00036	0.00026	0.00018	0.00013	0.00009	0.00007	0.00005
77 ..	0.00382	0.00267	0.00187	0.00131	0.00092	0.00065	0.00046	0.00032	0.00023	0.00016	0.00012	0.00008	0.00006	0.00004
78 ..	0.00355	0.00247	0.00172	0.00120	0.00084	0.00059	0.00041	0.00029	0.00021	0.00014	0.00010	0.00007	0.00005	0.00004
79 ..	0.00330	0.00229	0.00159	0.00110	0.00077	0.00054	0.00038	0.00026	0.00018	0.00013	0.00009	0.00006	0.00005	0.00003
80 ..	0.00307	0.00212	0.00146	0.00101	0.00070	0.00049	0.00034	0.00024	0.00017	0.00012	0.00008	0.00006	0.00004	0.00003
81 ..	0.00286	0.00196	0.00135	0.00093	0.00064	0.00044	0.00031	0.00021	0.00015	0.00010	0.00007	0.00005	0.00004	0.00002
82 ..	0.00266	0.00182	0.00124	0.00085	0.00059	0.00040	0.00028	0.00019	0.00013	0.00009	0.00006	0.00004	0.00003	0.00002
83 ..	0.00247	0.00168	0.00115	0.00078	0.00054	0.00037	0.00025	0.00017	0.00012	0.00008	0.00006	0.00004	0.00003	0.00002
84 ..	0.00230	0.00156	0.00106	0.00072	0.00049	0.00033	0.00023	0.00016	0.00011	0.00007	0.00005	0.00003	0.00002	0.00002
85 ..	0.00214	0.00144	0.00097	0.00066	0.00045	0.00030	0.00021	0.00014	0.00010	0.00007	0.00004	0.00003	0.00002	0.00001
86 ..	0.00199	0.00134	0.00090	0.00060	0.00041	0.00028	0.00019	0.00013	0.00009	0.00006	0.00004	0.00003	0.00002	0.00001
87 ..	0.00185	0.00124	0.00083	0.00055	0.00037	0.00025	0.00017	0.00011	0.00008	0.00005	0.00004	0.00002	0.00002	0.00001
88 ..	0.00172	0.00114	0.00076	0.00051	0.00034	0.00023	0.00015	0.00010	0.00007	0.00005	0.00003	0.00002	0.00001	0.00001
89 ..	0.00160	0.00106	0.00070	0.00047	0.00031	0.00021	0.00014	0.00009	0.00006	0.00004	0.00003	0.00002	0.00001	0.00001
90 ..	0.00149	0.00098	0.00065	0.00043	0.00028	0.00019	0.00013	0.00008	0.00006	0.00004	0.00002	0.00002	0.00001	0.00001
91 ..	0.00139	0.00091	0.00060	0.00039	0.00026	0.00017	0.00011	0.00008	0.00005	0.00003	0.00002	0.00001	0.00001	0.00001
92 ..	0.00129	0.00084	0.00055	0.00036	0.00024	0.00016	0.00010	0.00007	0.00004	0.00003	0.00002	0.00001	0.00001	0.00001
93 ..	0.00120	0.00078	0.00051	0.00033	0.00022	0.00014	0.00009	0.00006	0.00004	0.00003	0.00002	0.00001	0.00001	0.00001
94 ..	0.00112	0.00072	0.00047	0.00030	0.00020	0.00013	0.00008	0.00005	0.00004	0.00002	0.00002	0.00001	0.00001	0.00000
95 ..	0.00104	0.00067	0.00043	0.00028	0.00018	0.00012	0.00008	0.00005	0.00003	0.00002	0.00001	0.00001	0.00001	0.00000
96 ..	0.00097	0.00062	0.00040	0.00026	0.00016	0.00011	0.00007	0.00004	0.00003	0.00002	0.00001	0.00001	0.00001	0.00000
97 ..	0.00090	0.00057	0.00037	0.00023	0.00015	0.00010	0.00006	0.00004	0.00003	0.00002	0.00001	0.00001	0.00000	0.00000
98 ..	0.00084	0.00053	0.00034	0.00021	0.00014	0.00009	0.00006	0.00004	0.00002	0.00002	0.00001	0.00001	0.00000	0.00000
99 ..	0.00078	0.00049	0.00031	0.00020	0.00013	0.00008	0.00005	0.00003	0.00002	0.00001	0.00001	0.00001	0.00000	0.00000
100 ..	0.00072	0.00045	0.00029	0.00018	0.00011	0.00007	0.00005	0.00003	0.00002	0.00001	0.00001	0.00000	0.00000	0.00000
101 ..	0.00067	0.00042	0.00026	0.00017	0.00010	0.00007	0.00004	0.00003	0.00002	0.00001	0.00001	0.00000	0.00000	0.00000
102 ..	0.00063	0.00039	0.00024	0.00015	0.00010	0.00006	0.00004	0.00002	0.00002	0.00001	0.00001	0.00000	0.00000	0.00000
103 ..	0.00058	0.00036	0.00022	0.00014	0.00009	0.00005	0.00003	0.00002	0.00001	0.00001	0.00001	0.00000	0.00000	0.00000
104 ..	0.00054	0.00033	0.00021	0.00013	0.00008	0.00005	0.00003	0.00002	0.00001	0.00001	0.00000	0.00000	0.00000	0.00000
105 ..	0.00050	0.00031	0.00019	0.00012	0.00007	0.00005	0.00003	0.00002	0.00001	0.00001	0.00000	0.00000	0.00000	0.00000
106 ..	0.00047	0.00029	0.00018	0.00011	0.00007	0.00004	0.00003	0.00002	0.00001	0.00001	0.00000	0.00000	0.00000	0.00000
107 ..	0.00044	0.00027	0.00016	0.00010	0.00006	0.00004	0.00002	0.00001	0.00001	0.00001	0.00000	0.00000	0.00000	0.00000
108 ..	0.00041	0.00025	0.00015	0.00009	0.00006	0.00003	0.00002	0.00001	0.00001	0.00000	0.00000	0.00000	0.00000	0.00000
109 ..	0.00038	0.00023	0.00014	0.00008	0.00005	0.00003	0.00002	0.00001	0.00001	0.00000	0.00000	0.00000	0.00000	0.00000
110 ..	0.00035	0.00021	0.00013	0.00008	0.00005	0.00003	0.00002	0.00001	0.00001	0.00000	0.00000	0.00000	0.00000	0.00000
111 ..	0.00033	0.00019	0.00012	0.00007	0.00004	0.00003	0.00002	0.00001	0.00001	0.00000	0.00000	0.00000	0.00000	0.00000
112 ..	0.00030	0.00018	0.00011	0.00006	0.00004	0.00002	0.00001	0.00001	0.00001	0.00000	0.00000	0.00000	0.00000	0.00000
113 ..	0.00028	0.00017	0.00010	0.00006	0.00004	0.00002	0.00001	0.00001	0.00000	0.00000	0.00000	0.00000	0.00000	0.00000
114 ..	0.00026	0.00015	0.00009	0.00005	0.00003	0.00002	0.00001	0.00001	0.00000	0.00000	0.00000	0.00000	0.00000	0.00000
115 ..	0.00024	0.00014	0.00008	0.00005	0.00003	0.00002	0.00001	0.00001	0.00000	0.00000	0.00000	0.00000	0.00000	0.00000
116 ..	0.00023	0.00013	0.00008	0.00005	0.00003	0.00002	0.00001	0.00001	0.00000	0.00000	0.00000	0.00000	0.00000	0.00000
117 ..	0.00021	0.00012	0.00007	0.00004	0.00002	0.00001	0.00001	0.00000	0.00000	0.00000	0.00000	0.00000	0.00000	0.00000
118 ..	0.00020	0.00011	0.00007	0.00004	0.00002	0.00001	0.00001	0.00000	0.00000	0.00000	0.00000	0.00000	0.00000	0.00000
119 ..	0.00018	0.00011	0.00006	0.00004	0.00002	0.00001	0.00001	0.00000	0.00000	0.00000	0.00000	0.00000	0.00000	0.00000
120 ..	0.00017	0.00010	0.00006	0.00003	0.00002	0.00001	0.00001	0.00000	0.00000	0.00000	0.00000	0.00000	0.00000	0.00000

Table E.3 *(concluded)*
PRESENT VALUE OF $1 AT COMPOUND INTEREST: 14.5%–20%

Period	14.5%	15%	15.5%	16%	16.5%	17%	17.5%	18%	18.5%	19%	19.5%	20%
1	0.87336	0.86957	0.86580	0.86207	0.85837	0.85470	0.85106	0.84746	0.84388	0.84034	0.83682	0.83333
2	0.76276	0.75614	0.74961	0.74316	0.73680	0.73051	0.72431	0.71818	0.71214	0.70616	0.70027	0.69444
3	0.66617	0.65752	0.64901	0.64066	0.63244	0.62437	0.61643	0.60863	0.60096	0.59342	0.58600	0.57870
4	0.58181	0.57175	0.56192	0.55229	0.54287	0.53365	0.52462	0.51579	0.50714	0.49867	0.49038	0.48225
5	0.50813	0.49718	0.48651	0.47611	0.46598	0.45611	0.44649	0.43711	0.42796	0.41905	0.41036	0.40188
6	0.44378	0.43233	0.42122	0.41044	0.39999	0.38984	0.37999	0.37043	0.36115	0.35214	0.34339	0.33490
7	0.38758	0.37594	0.36469	0.35383	0.34334	0.33320	0.32340	0.31393	0.30477	0.29592	0.28736	0.27908
8	0.33850	0.32690	0.31575	0.30503	0.29471	0.28478	0.27523	0.26604	0.25719	0.24867	0.24047	0.23257
9	0.29563	0.28426	0.27338	0.26295	0.25297	0.24340	0.23424	0.22546	0.21704	0.20897	0.20123	0.19381
10	0.25819	0.24718	0.23669	0.22668	0.21714	0.20804	0.19935	0.19106	0.18315	0.17560	0.16839	0.16151
11	0.22550	0.21494	0.20493	0.19542	0.18639	0.17781	0.16966	0.16192	0.15456	0.14757	0.14091	0.13459
12	0.19694	0.18691	0.17743	0.16846	0.15999	0.15197	0.14439	0.13722	0.13043	0.12400	0.11792	0.11216
13	0.17200	0.16253	0.15362	0.14523	0.13733	0.12989	0.12289	0.11629	0.11007	0.10421	0.09868	0.09346
14	0.15022	0.14133	0.13300	0.12520	0.11788	0.11102	0.10459	0.09855	0.09288	0.08757	0.08258	0.07789
15	0.13120	0.12289	0.11515	0.10793	0.10118	0.09489	0.08901	0.08352	0.07838	0.07359	0.06910	0.06491
16	0.11458	0.10686	0.09970	0.09304	0.08685	0.08110	0.07575	0.07078	0.06615	0.06184	0.05782	0.05409
17	0.10007	0.09293	0.08632	0.08021	0.07455	0.06932	0.06447	0.05998	0.05582	0.05196	0.04839	0.04507
18	0.08740	0.04081	0.07474	0.06914	0.06399	0.05925	0.05487	0.05083	0.04711	0.04367	0.04049	0.03756
19	0.07633	0.07027	0.06471	0.05961	0.05493	0.05064	0.04670	0.04308	0.03975	0.03670	0.03389	0.03130
20	0.06666	0.06110	0.05602	0.05139	0.04715	0.04328	0.03974	0.03651	0.03355	0.03084	0.02836	0.02608
21	0.05822	0.05313	0.04850	0.04430	0.04047	0.03699	0.03382	0.03094	0.02831	0.02591	0.02373	0.02174
22	0.05085	0.04620	0.04199	0.03819	0.03474	0.03162	0.02879	0.02622	0.02389	0.02178	0.01986	0.01811
23	0.04441	0.04017	0.03636	0.03292	0.02982	0.02702	0.02450	0.02222	0.02016	0.01830	0.01662	0.01509
24	0.03879	0.03493	0.03148	0.02838	0.02560	0.02310	0.02085	0.01883	0.01701	0.01538	0.01390	0.01258
25	0.03387	0.03038	0.02726	0.02447	0.02197	0.01974	0.01774	0.01596	0.01436	0.01292	0.01164	0.01048
26	0.02958	0.02642	0.02360	0.02109	0.01886	0.01687	0.01510	0.01352	0.01211	0.01086	0.00974	0.00874
27	0.02584	0.02297	0.02043	0.01818	0.01619	0.01442	0.01285	0.01146	0.01022	0.00912	0.00815	0.00728
28	0.02257	0.01997	0.01769	0.01567	0.01390	0.01233	0.01094	0.00971	0.00863	0.00767	0.00682	0.00607
29	0.01971	0.01737	0.01532	0.01351	0.01193	0.01053	0.00931	0.00823	0.00728	0.00644	0.00571	0.00506
30	0.01721	0.01510	0.01326	0.01165	0.01024	0.00900	0.00792	0.00697	0.00614	0.00541	0.00477	0.00421
31	0.01503	0.01313	0.01148	0.01004	0.00879	0.00770	0.00674	0.00591	0.00518	0.00455	0.00400	0.00351
32	0.01313	0.01142	0.00994	0.00866	0.00754	0.00658	0.00574	0.00501	0.00438	0.00382	0.00334	0.00293
33	0.01147	0.00993	0.00861	0.00746	0.00648	0.00562	0.00488	0.00425	0.00369	0.00321	0.00280	0.00244
34	0.01001	0.00864	0.00745	0.00643	0.00556	0.00480	0.00416	0.00360	0.00312	0.00270	0.00234	0.00203
35	0.00875	0.00751	0.00645	0.00555	0.00477	0.00411	0.00354	0.00305	0.00263	0.00227	0.00196	0.00169
36	0.00764	0.00653	0.00559	0.00478	0.00410	0.00351	0.00301	0.00258	0.00222	0.00191	0.00164	0.00141
37	0.00667	0.00568	0.00484	0.00412	0.00352	0.00300	0.00256	0.00219	0.00187	0.00160	0.00137	0.00118
38	0.00583	0.00494	0.00419	0.00355	0.00302	0.00256	0.00218	0.00186	0.00158	0.00135	0.00115	0.00098
39	0.00509	0.00429	0.00362	0.00306	0.00259	0.00219	0.00186	0.00157	0.00133	0.00113	0.00096	0.00082
40	0.00444	0.00373	0.00314	0.00264	0.00222	0.00187	0.00158	0.00133	0.00113	0.00095	0.00080	0.00068
41	0.00388	0.00325	0.00272	0.00228	0.00191	0.00160	0.00134	0.00113	0.00095	0.00080	0.00067	0.00057
42	0.00339	0.00282	0.00235	0.00196	0.00164	0.00137	0.00114	0.00096	0.00080	0.00067	0.00056	0.00047
43	0.00296	0.00245	0.00204	0.00169	0.00141	0.00117	0.00097	0.00081	0.00068	0.00056	0.00047	0.00039
44	0.00259	0.00213	0.00176	0.00146	0.00121	0.00100	0.00083	0.00069	0.00057	0.00047	0.00039	0.00033
45	0.00226	0.00186	0.00153	0.00126	0.00104	0.00085	0.00071	0.00058	0.00048	0.00040	0.00033	0.00027
46	0.00197	0.00161	0.00132	0.00108	0.00089	0.00073	0.00060	0.00049	0.00041	0.00033	0.00028	0.00023
47	0.00172	0.00140	0.00114	0.00093	0.00076	0.00062	0.00051	0.00042	0.00034	0.00028	0.00023	0.00019
48	0.00150	0.00122	0.00099	0.00081	0.00066	0.00053	0.00043	0.00035	0.00029	0.00024	0.00019	0.00016
49	0.00131	0.00106	0.00086	0.00069	0.00056	0.00046	0.00037	0.00030	0.00024	0.00020	0.00016	0.00013
50	0.00115	0.00092	0.00074	0.00060	0.00048	0.00039	0.00031	0.00025	0.00021	0.00017	0.00014	0.00011
51	0.00100	0.00080	0.00064	0.00052	0.00041	0.00033	0.00027	0.00022	0.00017	0.00014	0.00011	0.00009
52	0.00088	0.00070	0.00056	0.00044	0.00036	0.00028	0.00023	0.00018	0.00015	0.00012	0.00009	0.00008
53	0.00076	0.00061	0.00048	0.00038	0.00031	0.00024	0.00019	0.00015	0.00012	0.00010	0.00008	0.00006
54	0.00067	0.00053	0.0C042	0.00033	0.00026	0.00021	0.00017	0.00013	0.00010	0.00008	0.00007	0.00005
55	0.00058	0.00046	0.00036	0.00028	0.00022	0.00018	0.00014	0.00011	0.00009	0.00007	0.00006	0.00004
56	0.00051	0.00040	0.00031	0.00025	0.00019	0.00015	0.00012	0.00009	0.00007	0.00006	0.00005	0.00004
57	0.00044	0.00035	0.00027	0.00021	0.00017	0.00013	0.00010	0.00008	0.00006	0.00005	0.00004	0.00003
58	0.00039	0.00030	0.00023	0.00018	0.00014	0.00011	0.00009	0.00007	0.00005	0.00004	0.00003	0.00003
59	0.00034	0.00026	0.00020	0.00016	0.00012	0.00009	0.00007	0.00006	0.00004	0.00003	0.00003	0.00002
60	0.00030	0.00023	0.00018	0.00014	0.00010	0.00008	0.00006	0.00005	0.00004	0.00003	0.00002	0.00002

Period	14.5%	15%	15.5%	16%	16.5%	17%	17.5%	18%	18.5%	19%	19.5%	20%
61	0.00026	0.00020	0.00015	0.00012	0.00009	0.00007	0.00005	0.00004	0.00003	0.00002	0.00002	0.00001
62	0.00023	0.00017	0.00013	0.00010	0.00008	0.00006	0.00005	0.00003	0.00003	0.00002	0.00002	0.00001
63	0.00020	0.00015	0.00011	0.00009	0.00007	0.00005	0.00004	0.00003	0.00002	0.00002	0.00001	0.00001
64	0.00017	0.00013	0.00010	0.00007	0.00006	0.00004	0.00003	0.00003	0.00002	0.00001	0.00001	0.00001
65	0.00015	0.00011	0.00009	0.00006	0.00005	0.00004	0.00003	0.00002	0.00002	0.00001	0.00001	0.00001
66	0.00013	0.00010	0.00007	0.00006	0.00004	0.00003	0.00002	0.00002	0.00001	0.00001	0.00001	0.00001
67	0.00011	0.00009	0.00006	0.00005	0.00004	0.00003	0.00002	0.00002	0.00001	0.00001	0.00001	0.00000
68	0.00010	0.00007	0.00006	0.00004	0.00003	0.00002	0.00002	0.00001	0.00001	0.00001	0.00001	0.00000
69	0.00009	0.00006	0.00005	0.00004	0.00003	0.00002	0.00001	0.00001	0.00001	0.00001	0.00000	0.00000
70	0.00008	0.00006	0.00004	0.00003	0.00002	0.00002	0.00001	0.00001	0.00001	0.00001	0.00000	0.00000
71	0.00007	0.00005	0.00004	0.00003	0.00002	0.00001	0.00001	0.00001	0.00001	0.00000	0.00000	0.00000
72	0.00006	0.00004	0.00003	0.00002	0.00002	0.00001	0.00001	0.00001	0.00000	0.00000	0.00000	0.00000
73	0.00005	0.00004	0.00003	0.00002	0.00001	0.00001	0.00001	0.00001	0.00000	0.00000	0.00000	0.00000
74	0.00004	0.00003	0.00002	0.00002	0.00001	0.00001	0.00001	0.00000	0.00000	0.00000	0.00000	0.00000
75	0.00004	0.00003	0.00002	0.00001	0.00001	0.00001	0.00001	0.00000	0.00000	0.00000	0.00000	0.00000
76	0.00003	0.00002	0.00002	0.00001	0.00001	0.00001	0.00000	0.00000	0.00000	0.00000	0.00000	0.00000
77	0.00003	0.00002	0.00002	0.00001	0.00001	0.00001	0.00000	0.00000	0.00000	0.00000	0.00000	0.00000
78	0.00003	0.00002	0.00001	0.00001	0.00001	0.00000	0.00000	0.00000	0.00000	0.00000	0.00000	0.00000
79	0.00002	0.00002	0.00001	0.00001	0.00001	0.00000	0.00000	0.00000	0.00000	0.00000	0.00000	0.00000
80	0.00002	0.00001	0.00001	0.00001	0.00000	0.00000	0.00000	0.00000	0.00000	0.00000	0.00000	0.00000
81	0.00002	0.00001	0.00001	0.00001	0.00000	0.00000	0.00000	0.00000	0.00000	0.00000	0.00000	0.00000
82	0.00002	0.00001	0.00001	0.00001	0.00000	0.00000	0.00000	0.00000	0.00000	0.00000	0.00000	0.00000
83	0.00001	0.00001	0.00001	0.00000	0.00000	0.00000	0.00000	0.00000	0.00000	0.00000	0.00000	0.00000
84	0.00001	0.00001	0.00001	0.00000	0.00000	0.00000	0.00000	0.00000	0.00000	0.00000	0.00000	0.00000
85	0.00001	0.00001	0.00000	0.00000	0.00000	0.00000	0.00000	0.00000	0.00000	0.00000	0.00000	0.00000
86	0.00001	0.00001	0.00000	0.00000	0.00000	0.00000	0.00000	0.00000	0.00000	0.00000	0.00000	0.00000
87	0.00001	0.00001	0.00000	0.00000	0.00000	0.00000	0.00000	0.00000	0.00000	0.00000	0.00000	0.00000
88	0.00001	0.00000	0.00000	0.00000	0.00000	0.00000	0.00000	0.00000	0.00000	0.00000	0.00000	0.00000
89	0.00001	0.00000	0.00000	0.00000	0.00000	0.00000	0.00000	0.00000	0.00000	0.00000	0.00000	0.00000
90	0.00001	0.00000	0.00000	0.00000	0.00000	0.00000	0.00000	0.00000	0.00000	0.00000	0.00000	0.00000
91	0.00000	0.00000	0.00000	0.00000	0.00000	0.00000	0.00000	0.00000	0.00000	0.00000	0.00000	0.00000
92	0.00000	0.00000	0.00000	0.00000	0.00000	0.00000	0.00000	0.00000	0.00000	0.00000	0.00000	0.00000
93	0.00000	0.00000	0.00000	0.00000	0.00000	0.00000	0.00000	0.00000	0.00000	0.00000	0.00000	0.00000
94	0.00000	0.00000	0.00000	0.00000	0.00000	0.00000	0.00000	0.00000	0.00000	0.00000	0.00000	0.00000
95	0.00000	0.00000	0.00000	0.00000	0.00000	0.00000	0.00000	0.00000	0.00000	0.00000	0.00000	0.00000
96	0.00000	0.00000	0.00000	0.00000	0.00000	0.00000	0.00000	0.00000	0.00000	0.00000	0.00000	0.00000
97	0.00000	0.00000	0.00000	0.00000	0.00000	0.00000	0.00000	0.00000	0.00000	0.00000	0.00000	0.00000
98	0.00000	0.00000	0.00000	0.00000	0.00000	0.00000	0.00000	0.00000	0.00000	0.00000	0.00000	0.00000
99	0.00000	0.00000	0.00000	0.00000	0.00000	0.00000	0.00000	0.00000	0.00000	0.00000	0.00000	0.00000
100	0.00000	0.00000	0.00000	0.00000	0.00000	0.00000	0.00000	0.00000	0.00000	0.00000	0.00000	0.00000
101	0.00000	0.00000	0.00000	0.00000	0.00000	0.00000	0.00000	0.00000	0.00000	0.00000	0.00000	0.00000
102	0.00000	0.00000	0.00000	0.00000	0.00000	0.00000	0.00000	0.00000	0.00000	0.00000	0.00000	0.00000
103	0.00000	0.00000	0.00000	0.00000	0.00000	0.00000	0.00000	0.00000	0.00000	0.00000	0.00000	0.00000
104	0.00000	0.00000	0.00000	0.00000	0.00000	0.00000	0.00000	0.00000	0.00000	0.00000	0.00000	0.00000
105	0.00000	0.00000	0.00000	0.00000	0.00000	0.00000	0.00000	0.00000	0.00000	0.00000	0.00000	0.00000
106	0.00000	0.00000	0.00000	0.00000	0.00000	0.00000	0.00000	0.00000	0.00000	0.00000	0.00000	0.00000
107	0.00000	0.00000	0.00000	0.00000	0.00000	0.00000	0.00000	0.00000	0.00000	0.00000	0.00000	0.00000
108	0.00000	0.00000	0.00000	0.00000	0.00000	0.00000	0.00000	0.00000	0.00000	0.00000	0.00000	0.00000
109	0.00000	0.00000	0.00000	0.00000	0.00000	0.00000	0.00000	0.00000	0.00000	0.00000	0.00000	0.00000
110	0.00000	0.00000	0.00000	0.00000	0.00000	0.00000	0.00000	0.00000	0.00000	0.00000	0.00000	0.00000
111	0.00000	0.00000	0.00000	0.00000	0.00000	0.00000	0.00000	0.00000	0.00000	0.00000	0.00000	0.00000
112	0.00000	0.00000	0.00000	0.00000	0.00000	0.00000	0.00000	0.00000	0.00000	0.00000	0.00000	0.00000
113	0.00000	0.00000	0.00000	0.00000	0.00000	0.00000	0.00000	0.00000	0.00000	0.00000	0.00000	0.00000
114	0.00000	0.00000	0.00000	0.00000	0.00000	0.00000	0.00000	0.00000	0.00000	0.00000	0.00000	0.00000
115	0.00000	0.00000	0.00000	0.00000	0.00000	0.00000	0.00000	0.00000	0.00000	0.00000	0.00000	0.00000
116	0.00000	0.00000	0.00000	0.00000	0.00000	0.00000	0.00000	0.00000	0.00000	0.00000	0.00000	0.00000
117	0.00000	0.00000	0.00000	0.00000	0.00000	0.00000	0.00000	0.00000	0.00000	0.00000	0.00000	0.00000
118	0.00000	0.00000	0.00000	0.00000	0.00000	0.00000	0.00000	0.00000	0.00000	0.00000	0.00000	0.00000
119	0.00000	0.00000	0.00000	0.00000	0.00000	0.00000	0.00000	0.00000	0.00000	0.00000	0.00000	0.00000
120	0.00000	0.00000	0.00000	0.00000	0.00000	0.00000	0.00000	0.00000	0.00000	0.00000	0.00000	0.00000

Table E.4
PRESENT VALUE OF AN ORDINARY ANNUITY OF $1 PER PERIOD: 0.5%–7%

$$P_{A_{i,n}} = \frac{1 - \dfrac{1}{(1 + i)^n}}{i}$$

Period	.5%	1%	1.5%	2%	2.5%	3%	3.5%	4%	4.5%	5%	5.5%	6%	6.5%	7%
1	0.99502	0.99010	0.98522	0.98039	0.97561	0.97087	0.96618	0.96154	0.95694	0.95238	0.94787	0.94340	0.93897	0.93458
2	1.98510	1.97040	1.95588	1.94156	1.92742	1.91347	1.89969	1.88609	1.87267	1.85941	1.84632	1.83339	1.82063	1.80802
3	2.97025	2.94099	2.91220	2.88388	2.85602	2.82861	2.80164	2.77509	2.74896	2.72325	2.69793	2.67301	2.64848	2.62432
4	3.95050	3.90197	3.85438	3.80773	3.76197	3.71710	3.67308	3.62990	3.58753	3.54595	3.50515	3.46511	3.42580	3.38721
5	4.92587	4.85343	4.78264	4.71346	4.64583	4.57971	4.51505	4.45182	4.38998	4.32948	4.27028	4.21236	4.15568	4.10020
6	5.89638	5.79548	5.69719	5.60143	5.50813	5.41719	5.32855	5.24214	5.15787	5.07569	4.99553	4.91732	4.84101	4.76654
7	6.86207	6.72819	6.59821	6.47199	6.34939	6.23028	6.11454	6.00205	5.89270	5.78637	5.68297	5.58238	5.48452	5.38929
8	7.82296	7.65168	7.48593	7.32548	7.17014	7.01969	6.87396	6.73274	6.59589	6.46321	6.33457	6.20979	6.08875	5.97130
9	8.77906	8.56602	8.36052	8.16224	7.97087	7.78611	7.60769	7.43533	7.26879	7.10782	6.95220	6.80169	6.65610	6.51523
10	9.73041	9.47130	9.22218	8.98259	8.75206	8.53020	8.31661	8.11090	7.91272	7.72173	7.53763	7.36009	7.18883	7.02358
11	10.67703	10.36763	10.07112	9.78685	9.51421	9.25262	9.00155	8.76048	8.52892	8.30641	8.09254	7.88687	7.68904	7.49867
12	11.61893	11.25508	10.90751	10.57534	10.25776	9.95400	9.66333	9.38507	9.11858	8.86325	8.61852	8.38384	8.15873	7.94269
13	12.55615	12.13374	11.73153	11.34837	10.98318	10.63496	10.30274	9.98565	9.68285	9.39357	9.11708	8.85268	8.59974	8.35765
14	13.48871	13.00370	12.54338	12.10625	11.69091	11.29607	10.92052	10.56312	10.22283	9.89864	9.58965	9.29498	9.01384	8.74547
15	14.41662	13.86505	13.34323	12.84926	12.38138	11.93794	11.51741	11.11839	10.73955	10.37966	10.03758	9.71225	9.40267	9.10791
16	15.33993	14.71787	14.13126	13.57771	13.05500	12.56110	12.09412	11.65230	11.23402	10.83777	10.46216	10.10590	9.76776	9.44665
17	16.25863	15.56225	14.90765	14.29187	13.71220	13.16612	12.65132	12.16567	11.70719	11.27407	10.86461	10.47726	10.11058	9.76322
18	17.17277	16.39827	15.67256	14.99203	14.35336	13.75351	13.18968	12.65930	12.15999	11.68959	11.24607	10.82760	10.43247	10.05909
19	18.08236	17.22601	16.42617	15.67846	14.97889	14.32380	13.70984	13.13394	12.59329	12.08532	11.60765	11.15812	10.73471	10.33560
20	18.98742	18.04555	17.16864	16.35143	15.58916	14.87747	14.21240	13.59033	13.00794	12.46221	11.95038	11.46992	11.01851	10.59401
21	19.88798	18.85698	17.90014	17.01121	16.18455	15.41502	14.69797	14.02916	13.40472	12.82115	12.27524	11.76408	11.28498	10.83553
22	20.78406	19.66038	18.62082	17.65805	16.76541	15.93692	15.16712	14.45112	13.78442	13.16300	12.58317	12.04158	11.53520	11.06124
23	21.67568	20.45582	19.33086	18.29220	17.33211	16.44361	15.62041	14.85684	14.14777	13.48857	12.87504	12.30338	11.77014	11.27219
24	22.56287	21.24339	20.03041	18.91393	17.88499	16.93554	16.05837	15.24696	14.49548	13.79864	13.15170	12.55036	11.99074	11.46933
25	23.44564	22.02316	20.71961	19.52346	18.42438	17.41315	16.48151	15.62208	14.82821	14.09394	13.41393	12.78336	12.19788	11.65358
26	24.32402	22.79520	21.39863	20.12104	18.95061	17.87684	16.89035	15.98277	15.14661	14.37519	13.66250	13.00317	12.39237	11.82578
27	25.19803	23.55961	22.06762	20.70690	19.46401	18.32703	17.28536	16.32959	15.45130	14.64303	13.89810	13.21053	12.57500	11.98671
28	26.06769	24.31644	22.72672	21.28127	19.96489	18.76411	17.66702	16.66306	15.74287	14.89813	14.12142	13.40616	12.74648	12.13711
29	26.93302	25.06579	23.37608	21.84438	20.45355	19.18845	18.03577	16.98371	16.02189	15.14107	14.33310	13.59072	12.90749	12.27767
30	27.79405	25.80771	24.01584	22.39646	20.93029	19.60044	18.39205	17.29203	16.28889	15.37245	14.53375	13.76483	13.05868	12.40904
31	28.65080	26.54229	24.64615	22.93770	21.39541	20.00043	18.73628	17.58849	16.54439	15.59281	14.72393	13.92909	13.20063	12.53181
32	29.50328	27.26959	25.26714	23.46833	21.84918	20.38877	19.06887	17.87355	16.78889	15.80268	14.90420	14.08404	13.33393	12.64656
33	30.35153	27.98969	25.87895	23.98856	22.29188	20.76579	19.39021	18.14765	17.02286	16.00255	15.07507	14.23023	13.45909	12.75379
34	31.19555	28.70267	26.48173	24.49859	22.72379	21.13184	19.70068	18.41120	17.24676	16.19290	15.23703	14.36814	13.57661	12.85401
35	32.03537	29.40858	27.07559	24.99862	23.14516	21.48722	20.00066	18.66461	17.46101	16.37419	15.39055	14.49825	13.68696	12.94767
36	32.87102	30.10751	27.66068	25.48884	23.55625	21.83225	20.29049	18.90828	17.66604	16.54685	15.53607	14.62099	13.79057	13.03521
37	33.70250	30.79951	28.23713	25.96945	23.95732	22.16724	20.57053	19.14258	17.86224	16.71129	15.67400	14.73678	13.88786	13.11702
38	34.52985	31.48466	28.80505	26.44064	24.34860	22.49246	20.84109	19.36786	18.04999	16.86789	15.80474	14.84602	13.97921	13.19347
39	35.35309	32.16303	29.36458	26.90259	24.73034	22.80822	21.10250	19.58448	18.22966	17.01704	15.92866	14.94907	14.06499	13.26493
40	36.17223	32.83469	29.91585	27.35548	25.10278	23.11477	21.35507	19.79277	18.40158	17.15909	16.04612	15.04630	14.14553	13.33171
41	36.98729	33.49969	30.45896	27.79949	25.46612	23.41240	21.59910	19.99305	18.56611	17.29437	16.15746	15.13802	14.22115	13.39412
42	37.79830	34.15811	30.99405	28.23479	25.82061	23.70136	21.83488	20.18563	18.72355	17.42321	16.26300	15.22454	14.29216	13.45245
43	38.60527	34.81001	31.52123	28.66156	26.16645	23.98190	22.06269	20.37079	18.87421	17.54591	16.36303	15.30617	14.35884	13.50696
44	39.40823	35.45545	32.04062	29.07996	26.50385	24.25427	22.28279	20.54884	19.01838	17.66277	16.45785	15.38318	14.42144	13.55791
45	40.20720	36.09451	32.55234	29.49016	26.83302	24.51871	22.49545	20.72004	19.15635	17.77407	16.54773	15.45583	14.48023	13.60552
46	41.00219	36.72724	33.05649	29.89231	27.15417	24.77545	22.70092	20.88465	19.28837	17.88007	16.63292	15.52437	14.53543	13.65002
47	41.79322	37.35370	33.55319	30.28658	27.46748	25.02471	22.89944	21.04294	19.41471	17.98102	16.71366	15.58903	14.58725	13.69161
48	42.58032	37.97396	34.04255	30.67312	27.77315	25.26671	23.09124	21.19513	19.53561	18.07716	16.79020	15.65003	14.63592	13.73047
49	43.36350	38.58808	34.52468	31.05208	28.07137	25.50166	23.27656	21.34147	19.65130	18.16872	16.86275	15.70757	14.68161	13.76680
50	44.14279	39.19612	34.99969	31.42361	28.36231	25.72976	23.45562	21.48218	19.76201	18.25593	16.93152	15.76186	14.72452	13.80075
51	44.91820	39.79814	35.46767	31.78785	28.64616	25.95123	23.62862	21.61749	19.86795	18.33898	16.99670	15.81308	14.76481	13.83247
52	45.68975	40.39419	35.92874	32.14495	28.92308	26.16624	23.79576	21.74758	19.96933	18.41807	17.05848	15.86139	14.80264	13.86212
53	46.45746	40.98435	36.38300	32.49505	29.19325	26.37499	23.95726	21.87267	20.06634	18.49340	17.11705	15.90697	14.83816	13.88984
54	47.22135	41.56866	36.83054	32.83828	29.45683	26.57766	24.11330	21.99296	20.15918	18.56515	17.17255	15.94998	14.87151	13.91573
55	47.98145	42.14719	37.27147	33.17479	29.71398	26.77443	24.26405	22.10861	20.24802	18.63347	17.22517	15.99054	14.90282	13.93994
56	48.73776	42.71999	37.70588	33.50469	29.96486	26.96546	24.40971	22.21982	20.33303	18.69854	17.27504	16.02881	14.93223	13.96256
57	49.49031	43.28712	38.13387	33.82813	30.20962	27.15094	24.55045	22.32675	20.41439	18.76052	17.32232	16.06492	14.95984	13.98370
58	50.23911	43.84863	38.55554	34.14523	30.44841	27.33101	24.68642	22.42957	20.49224	18.81954	17.36712	16.09898	14.98577	14.00346
59	50.98419	44.40459	38.97097	34.45610	30.68137	27.50583	24.81780	22.52843	20.56673	18.87575	17.40960	16.13111	15.01011	14.02192
60	51.72556	44.95504	39.38027	34.76089	30.90866	27.67556	24.94473	22.62349	20.63802	18.92929	17.44985	16.16143	15.03297	14.03918

Period	.5%	1%	1.5%	2%	2.5%	3%	3.5%	4%	4.5%	5%	5.5%	6%	6.5%	7%
61	52.46324	45.50004	39.78352	35.05969	31.13040	27.84035	25.06738	22.71489	20.70624	18.98028	17.48801	16.19003	15.05443	14.05531
62	53.19726	46.03964	40.18080	35.35264	31.34673	28.00034	25.18587	22.80278	20.77152	19.02883	17.52418	16.21701	15.07458	14.07038
63	53.92762	46.57390	40.57222	35.63984	31.55778	28.15567	25.30036	22.88729	20.83399	19.07508	17.55847	16.24246	15.09350	14.08447
64	54.65435	47.10287	40.95785	35.92141	31.76369	28.30648	25.41097	22.96855	20.89377	19.11912	17.59096	16.26647	15.11127	14.09764
65	55.37746	47.62661	41.33779	36.19747	31.96458	28.45289	25.51785	23.04668	20.95098	19.16107	17.62177	16.28912	15.12795	14.10994
66	56.09698	48.14516	41.71210	36.46810	32.16056	28.59504	25.62111	23.12181	21.00572	19.20102	17.65096	16.31049	15.14362	14.12144
67	56.81291	48.65857	42.08089	36.73343	32.35177	28.73305	25.72088	23.19405	21.05811	19.23907	17.67864	16.33065	15.15833	14.13219
68	57.52529	49.16690	42.44423	36.99356	32.53831	28.86704	25.81727	23.26351	21.10824	19.27530	17.70487	16.34967	15.17214	14.14223
69	58.23411	49.67020	42.80219	37.24859	32.72030	28.99712	25.91041	23.33030	21.15621	19.30981	17.72974	16.36762	15.18511	14.15162
70	58.93942	50.16851	43.15487	37.49862	32.89786	29.12342	26.00040	23.39451	21.20211	19.34268	17.75330	16.38454	15.19728	14.16039
71	59.64121	50.66190	43.50234	37.74374	33.07108	29.24604	26.08734	23.45626	21.24604	19.37398	17.77564	16.40051	15.20872	14.16859
72	60.33951	51.15039	43.84467	37.98406	33.24008	29.36509	26.17134	23.51564	21.28808	19.40379	17.79682	16.41558	15.21945	14.17625
73	61.03434	51.63405	44.18194	38.21967	33.40495	29.48067	26.25251	23.57273	21.32830	19.43218	17.81689	16.42979	15.22953	14.18341
74	61.72571	52.11292	44.51422	38.45066	33.56581	29.59288	26.33092	23.62762	21.36680	19.45922	17.83591	16.44320	15.23900	14.19010
75	62.41365	52.58705	44.84160	38.67711	33.72274	29.70183	26.40669	23.68041	21.40363	19.48497	17.85395	16.45585	15.24788	14.19636
76	63.09815	53.05649	45.16414	38.89913	33.87584	29.80760	26.47989	23.73116	21.43888	19.50950	17.87104	16.46778	15.25623	14.20220
77	63.77926	53.52127	45.48191	39.11680	34.02521	29.91029	26.55062	23.77996	21.47262	19.53285	17.88724	16.47904	15.26407	14.20767
78	64.45697	53.98146	45.79498	39.33019	34.17094	30.00999	26.61896	23.82689	21.50490	19.55510	17.90260	16.48966	15.27142	14.21277
79	65.13132	54.43709	46.10343	39.53940	34.31311	30.10679	26.68498	23.87201	21.53579	19.57628	17.91716	16.49968	15.27833	14.21755
80	65.80231	54.88821	46.40732	39.74451	34.45182	30.20076	26.74878	23.91539	21.56534	19.59646	17.93095	16.50913	15.28482	14.22201
81	66.46996	55.33486	46.70672	39.94560	34.58714	30.29200	26.81041	23.95711	21.59363	19.61568	17.94403	16.51805	15.29091	14.22617
82	67.13428	55.77709	47.00170	40.14275	34.71916	30.38059	26.86996	23.99722	21.62070	19.63398	17.95643	16.52646	15.29663	14.23007
83	67.79531	56.21494	47.29231	40.33603	34.84796	30.46659	26.92750	24.03579	21.64660	19.65141	17.96818	16.53440	15.30200	14.23371
84	68.45304	56.64845	47.57863	40.52552	34.97362	30.55009	26.98309	24.07287	21.67139	19.66801	17.97932	16.54188	15.30704	14.23711
85	69.10750	57.07768	47.86072	40.71129	35.09621	30.63115	27.03680	24.10853	21.69511	19.68382	17.98987	16.54895	15.31178	14.24029
86	69.75871	57.50265	48.13864	40.89342	35.21582	30.70986	27.08870	24.14282	21.71781	19.69887	17.99988	16.55561	15.31622	14.24326
87	70.40668	57.92342	48.41246	41.07198	35.33251	30.78627	27.13884	24.17579	21.73953	19.71321	18.00936	16.56190	15.32040	14.24604
88	71.05142	58.34002	48.68222	41.24704	35.44635	30.86045	27.18728	24.20749	21.76032	19.72687	18.01835	16.56783	15.32431	14.24864
89	71.69296	58.75249	48.94800	41.41867	35.55741	30.93248	27.23409	24.23797	21.78021	19.73987	18.02688	16.57342	15.32800	14.25106
90	72.33130	59.16088	49.20985	41.58693	35.66577	31.00241	27.27932	24.26728	21.79924	19.75226	18.03495	16.57870	15.33145	14.25333
91	72.96647	59.56523	49.46784	41.75189	35.77148	31.07030	27.32301	24.29546	21.81746	19.76406	18.04261	16.58368	15.33470	14.25545
92	73.59847	59.96557	49.72201	41.91362	35.87462	31.13621	27.36523	24.32256	21.83489	19.77529	18.04987	16.58838	15.33774	14.25743
93	74.22734	60.36195	49.97242	42.07218	35.97524	31.20021	27.40602	24.34861	21.85156	19.78599	18.05675	16.59281	15.34060	14.25928
94	74.85307	60.75441	50.21913	42.22762	36.07340	31.26234	27.44543	24.37367	21.86753	19.79619	18.06327	16.59699	15.34329	14.26101
95	75.47569	61.14298	50.46220	42.38002	36.16917	31.32266	27.48350	24.39776	21.88280	19.80589	18.06945	16.60093	15.34581	14.26262
96	76.09522	61.52770	50.70168	42.52943	36.26261	31.38122	27.52029	24.42092	21.89742	19.81513	18.07531	16.60465	15.34818	14.26413
97	76.71166	61.90862	50.93761	42.67592	36.35376	31.43808	27.55584	24.44319	21.91140	19.82394	18.08086	16.60816	15.35040	14.26555
98	77.32503	62.28576	51.17006	42.81953	36.44269	31.49328	27.59018	24.46461	21.92479	19.83232	18.08612	16.61147	15.35249	14.26687
99	77.93536	62.65917	51.39907	42.96032	36.52946	31.54687	27.62337	24.48520	21.93760	19.84031	18.09111	16.61460	15.35445	14.26810
100	78.54264	63.02888	51.62470	43.09835	36.61411	31.59891	27.65543	24.50500	21.94985	19.84791	18.09584	16.61755	15.35629	14.26925
101	79.14691	63.39493	51.84700	43.23368	36.69669	31.64942	27.68640	24.52404	21.96158	19.85515	18.10032	16.62033	15.35802	14.27033
102	79.74817	63.75736	52.06601	43.36635	36.77726	31.69847	27.71633	24.54234	21.97281	19.86205	18.10457	16.62295	15.35964	14.27133
103	80.34644	64.11619	52.28178	43.49642	36.85586	31.74609	27.74525	24.55995	21.98355	19.86862	18.10860	16.62542	15.36117	14.27228
104	80.94173	64.47148	52.49437	43.62394	36.93255	31.79232	27.77318	24.57687	21.99382	19.87488	18.11241	16.62776	15.36260	14.27315
105	81.53406	64.82325	52.70381	43.74896	37.00736	31.83720	27.80018	24.59315	22.00366	19.88083	18.11603	16.62996	15.36394	14.27398
106	82.12344	65.17153	52.91016	43.87153	37.08035	31.88078	27.82626	24.60879	22.01307	19.88651	18.11946	16.63204	15.36521	14.27474
107	82.70989	65.51637	53.11046	43.99170	37.15156	31.92308	27.85146	24.62384	22.02208	19.89191	18.12271	16.63400	15.36639	14.27546
108	83.29342	65.85779	53.31375	44.10951	37.22104	31.96416	27.87581	24.63831	22.03070	19.89706	18.12579	16.63585	15.36750	14.27613
109	83.87405	66.19583	53.51108	44.22501	37.28882	32.00404	27.89933	24.65222	22.03894	19.90196	18.12872	16.63759	15.36855	14.27676
110	84.45180	66.53053	53.70550	44.33824	37.35494	32.04276	27.92206	24.66560	22.04684	19.90663	18.13148	16.63924	15.36953	14.27735
111	85.02666	66.86191	53.89704	44.44926	37.41946	32.08035	27.94402	24.67846	22.05439	19.91108	18.13411	16.64079	15.37045	14.27789
112	85.59867	67.19001	54.08576	44.55810	37.48240	32.11684	27.96523	24.69082	22.06162	19.91531	18.13659	16.64226	15.37131	14.27840
113	86.16783	67.51486	54.27168	44.66480	37.54380	32.15227	27.98573	24.70272	22.06853	19.91934	18.13895	16.64364	15.37212	14.27888
114	86.73416	67.83649	54.45486	44.76941	37.60371	32.18667	28.00554	24.71415	22.07515	19.92318	18.14119	16.64494	15.37289	14.27933
115	87.29767	68.15494	54.63533	44.87197	37.66216	32.22007	28.02467	24.72514	22.08148	19.92684	18.14331	16.64617	15.37360	14.27975
116	87.85838	68.47024	54.81313	44.97252	37.71918	32.25250	28.04316	24.73571	22.08754	19.93033	18.14531	16.64733	15.37428	14.28014
117	88.41630	68.78242	54.98831	45.07110	37.77481	32.28398	28.06103	24.74588	22.09334	19.93364	18.14722	16.64843	15.37491	14.28050
118	88.97144	69.09150	55.16089	45.16775	37.82908	32.31454	28.07829	24.75365	22.09889	19.93680	18.14902	16.64946	15.37550	14.28084
119	89.52382	69.39753	55.33093	45.26250	37.88203	32.34421	28.09496	24.76505	22.10420	19.93981	18.15073	16.65043	15.37606	14.28116
120	90.07345	69.70052	55.49845	45.35539	37.93369	32.37302	28.11108	24.77409	22.10929	19.94268	18.15235	16.65135	15.37658	14.28146

Table E.4 (continued)
PRESENT VALUE OF AN ORDINARY ANNUITY OF $1 PER PERIOD: 7.5%–14%

Period	7.5%	8%	8.5%	9%	9.5%	10%	10.5%	11%	11.5%	12%	12.5%	13%	13.5%	14%
1	0.93023	0.92593	0.92166	0.91743	0.91324	0.90909	0.90498	0.90090	0.89686	0.89286	0.88889	0.88496	0.88106	0.87719
2	1.79557	1.78326	1.77111	1.75911	1.74725	1.73554	1.72396	1.71252	1.70122	1.69005	1.67901	1.66810	1.65732	1.64666
3	2.60053	2.57710	2.55402	2.53129	2.50891	2.48685	2.46512	2.44371	2.42262	2.40183	2.38134	2.36115	2.34125	2.32163
4	3.34933	3.31213	3.27560	3.23972	3.20448	3.16987	3.13586	3.10245	3.06961	3.03735	3.00564	2.97447	2.94383	2.91371
5	4.04588	3.99271	3.94064	3.88965	3.83971	3.79079	3.74286	3.69590	3.64988	3.60478	3.56057	3.51723	3.47474	3.43308
6	4.69385	4.62288	4.55359	4.48592	4.41983	4.35526	4.29218	4.23054	4.17029	4.11141	4.05384	3.99755	3.94250	3.88867
7	5.29660	5.20637	5.11851	5.03295	4.94961	4.86842	4.78930	4.71220	4.63704	4.56376	4.49230	4.42261	4.35463	4.28830
8	5.85730	5.74664	5.63918	5.53482	5.43344	5.33493	5.23919	5.14612	5.05564	4.96764	4.88205	4.79877	4.71774	4.63886
9	6.37889	6.24689	6.11906	5.99525	5.87528	5.75902	5.64632	5.53705	5.43106	5.32825	5.22848	5.13166	5.03765	4.94637
10	6.86408	6.71008	6.56135	6.41766	6.27880	6.14457	6.01477	5.88923	5.76777	5.65022	5.53643	5.42624	5.31952	5.21612
11	7.31542	7.13896	6.96898	6.80519	6.64730	6.49506	6.34821	6.20652	6.06975	5.93770	5.81016	5.68694	5.56786	5.45273
12	7.73528	7.53608	7.34469	7.16073	6.98384	6.81369	6.64996	6.49236	6.34058	6.19437	6.05348	5.91765	5.78666	5.66029
13	8.12584	7.90378	7.69095	7.48690	7.29118	7.10336	6.92304	6.74987	6.58348	6.42355	6.26976	6.12181	5.97943	5.84236
14	8.48915	8.24424	8.01010	7.78615	7.57185	7.36669	7.17018	6.98187	6.80133	6.62817	6.46201	6.30249	6.14928	6.00207
15	8.82712	8.55948	8.30424	8.06069	7.82818	7.60608	7.39382	7.19087	6.99671	6.81086	6.63289	6.46238	6.29893	6.14217
16	9.14151	8.85137	8.57533	8.31256	8.06226	7.82371	7.59622	7.37916	7.17194	6.97399	6.78479	6.60388	6.43077	6.26506
17	9.43396	9.12164	8.82519	8.54363	8.27604	8.02155	7.77939	7.54879	7.32909	7.11963	6.91982	6.72909	6.54694	6.37286
18	9.70601	9.37189	9.05548	8.75563	8.47127	8.20141	7.94515	7.70162	7.47004	7.24967	7.03984	6.83991	6.64928	6.46742
19	9.95908	9.60360	9.26772	8.95011	8.64956	8.36492	8.09515	7.83929	7.59644	7.36578	7.14652	6.93797	6.73946	6.55037
20	10.19449	9.81815	9.46334	9.12855	8.81238	8.51356	8.23091	7.96333	7.70982	7.46944	7.24135	7.02475	6.81890	6.62313
21	10.41348	10.01680	9.64363	9.29224	8.96108	8.64869	8.35376	8.07507	7.81149	7.56200	7.32565	7.10155	6.88890	6.68696
22	10.61719	10.20074	9.80980	9.44243	9.09688	8.77154	8.46494	8.17574	7.90269	7.64465	7.40058	7.16951	6.95057	6.74294
23	10.80669	10.37106	9.96295	9.58021	9.22089	8.88322	8.56556	8.26643	7.98447	7.71843	7.46718	7.22966	7.00491	6.79206
24	10.98297	10.52876	10.10410	9.70661	9.33415	8.98474	8.65662	8.34814	8.05782	7.78432	7.52638	7.28288	7.05279	6.83514
25	11.14695	10.67478	10.23419	9.82258	9.43758	9.07704	8.73902	8.42174	8.12361	7.84314	7.57901	7.32998	7.09497	6.87293
26	11.29948	10.80998	10.35409	9.92897	9.53203	9.16095	8.81359	8.48806	8.18261	7.89566	7.62578	7.37167	7.13213	6.90608
27	11.44138	10.93516	10.46460	10.02658	9.61830	9.23722	8.88108	8.54780	8.23552	7.94255	7.66736	7.40856	7.16487	6.93515
28	11.57338	11.05108	10.56645	10.11613	9.69707	9.30657	8.94215	8.60162	8.28298	7.98442	7.70432	7.44120	7.19372	6.96066
29	11.69617	11.15841	10.66033	10.19828	9.76902	9.36961	8.99742	8.65011	8.32554	8.02181	7.73717	7.47009	7.21914	6.98304
30	11.81039	11.25778	10.74684	10.27365	9.83472	9.42691	9.04744	8.69379	8.36371	8.05518	7.76638	7.49565	7.24153	7.00266
31	11.91664	11.34980	10.82658	10.34280	9.89472	9.47901	9.09271	8.73315	8.39795	8.08499	7.79234	7.51828	7.26126	7.01988
32	12.01548	11.43500	10.90000	10.40624	9.94952	9.52638	9.13367	8.76860	8.42866	8.11159	7.81541	7.53830	7.27864	7.03498
33	12.10742	11.51389	10.96781	10.46444	9.99956	9.56943	9.17074	8.80054	8.45619	8.13535	7.83592	7.55602	7.29396	7.04823
34	12.19295	11.58693	11.03024	10.51784	10.04526	9.60857	9.20429	8.82932	8.48089	8.15656	7.85415	7.57170	7.30745	7.05985
35	12.27251	11.65457	11.08778	10.56682	10.08699	9.64416	9.23465	8.85524	8.50304	8.17550	7.87036	7.58557	7.31934	7.07005
36	12.34652	11.71719	11.14081	10.61176	10.12511	9.67651	9.26213	8.87859	8.52291	8.19241	7.88476	7.59785	7.32982	7.07899
37	12.41537	11.77518	11.18969	10.65299	10.15992	9.70592	9.28700	8.89963	8.54072	8.20751	7.89757	7.60872	7.33904	7.08683
38	12.47941	11.82887	11.23474	10.69082	10.19171	9.73265	9.30950	8.91859	8.55670	8.22099	7.90895	7.61833	7.34718	7.09371
39	12.53899	11.87858	11.27625	10.72552	10.22074	9.75696	9.32986	8.93567	8.57103	8.23303	7.91906	7.62684	7.35434	7.09975
40	12.59441	11.92461	11.31452	10.75736	10.24725	9.77905	9.34829	8.95105	8.58389	8.24378	7.92806	7.63438	7.36065	7.10504
41	12.64596	11.96723	11.34979	10.78657	10.27146	9.79914	9.36497	8.96491	8.59541	8.25337	7.93605	7.64104	7.36621	7.10969
42	12.69392	12.00670	11.38229	10.81337	10.29357	9.81740	9.38006	8.97740	8.60575	8.26194	7.94316	7.64694	7.37111	7.11376
43	12.73853	12.04324	11.41225	10.83795	10.31376	9.83400	9.39372	8.98865	8.61502	8.26959	7.94947	7.65216	7.37543	7.11733
44	12.78003	12.07707	11.43986	10.86051	10.33220	9.84909	9.40608	8.99878	8.62334	8.27642	7.95509	7.65678	7.37923	7.12047
45	12.81863	12.10840	11.46531	10.88120	10.34904	9.86281	9.41727	9.00791	8.63080	8.28252	7.96008	7.66086	7.38258	7.12322
46	12.85454	12.13741	11.48877	10.90018	10.36442	9.87528	9.42739	9.01614	8.63749	8.28796	7.96451	7.66448	7.38554	7.12563
47	12.88794	12.16427	11.51038	10.91760	10.37847	9.88662	9.43656	9.02355	8.64349	8.29282	7.96846	7.66768	7.38814	7.12774
48	12.91902	12.18914	11.53031	10.93358	10.39130	9.89693	9.44485	9.03022	8.64887	8.29716	7.97196	7.67052	7.39043	7.12960
49	12.94792	12.21216	11.54867	10.94823	10.40301	9.90630	9.45235	9.03624	8.65369	8.30104	7.97508	7.67302	7.39245	7.13123
50	12.97481	12.23348	11.56560	10.96168	10.41371	9.91481	9.45914	9.04165	8.65802	8.30450	7.97785	7.67524	7.39423	7.13266
51	12.99982	12.25323	11.58119	10.97402	10.42348	9.92256	9.46529	9.04653	8.66190	8.30759	7.98031	7.67720	7.39580	7.13391
52	13.02309	12.27151	11.59557	10.98534	10.43240	9.92960	9.47085	9.05093	8.66538	8.31035	7.98250	7.67894	7.39718	7.13501
53	13.04474	12.28843	11.60882	10.99573	10.44055	9.93600	9.47588	9.05489	8.66850	8.31281	7.98444	7.68048	7.39839	7.13597
54	13.06487	12.30410	11.62103	11.00525	10.44799	9.94182	9.48043	9.05846	8.67130	8.31501	7.98617	7.68184	7.39947	7.13682
55	13.08360	12.31861	11.63229	11.01399	10.45478	9.94711	9.48456	9.06168	8.67382	8.31697	7.98771	7.68304	7.40041	7.13756
56	13.10103	12.33205	11.64266	11.02201	10.46099	9.95191	9.48829	9.06457	8.67607	8.31872	7.98907	7.68411	7.40124	7.13821
57	13.11723	12.34449	11.65222	11.02937	10.46666	9.95629	9.49166	9.06718	8.67809	8.32029	7.99029	7.68505	7.40198	7.13878
58	13.13231	12.35601	11.66104	11.03612	10.47183	9.96026	9.49472	9.06954	8.67990	8.32169	7.99137	7.68589	7.40262	7.13928
59	13.14633	12.36668	11.66916	11.04231	10.47656	9.96387	9.49748	9.07165	8.68152	8.32294	7.99232	7.68663	7.40319	7.13972
60	13.15938	12.37655	11.67664	11.04799	10.48088	9.96716	9.49998	9.07356	8.68298	8.32405	7.99318	7.68728	7.40369	7.14011

Period	7.5%	8%	8.5%	9%	9.5%	10%	10.5%	11%	11.5%	12%	12.5%	13%	13.5%	14%
61	13.17152	12.38570	11.68354	11.05320	10.48482	9.97014	9.50225	9.07528	8.68429	8.32504	7.99394	7.68786	7.40413	7.14044
62	13.18281	12.39416	11.68990	11.05798	10.48842	9.97286	9.50430	9.07683	8.68546	8.32593	7.99461	7.68837	7.40452	7.14074
63	13.19331	12.40200	11.69576	11.06237	10.49171	9.97532	9.50615	9.07822	8.68651	8.32673	7.99521	7.68882	7.40487	7.14100
64	13.20308	12.40926	11.70116	11.06640	10.49471	9.97757	9.50783	9.07948	8.68745	8.32743	7.99574	7.68922	7.40517	7.14123
65	13.21217	12.41598	11.70614	11.07009	10.49745	9.97961	9.50935	9.08061	8.68830	8.32807	7.99621	7.68958	7.40544	7.14143
66	13.22062	12.42221	11.71073	11.07347	10.49996	9.98146	9.51072	9.08163	8.68906	8.32863	7.99663	7.68989	7.40567	7.14160
67	13.22848	12.42797	11.71496	11.07658	10.50224	9.98315	9.51196	9.08255	8.68974	8.32913	7.99701	7.69017	7.40588	7.14176
68	13.23580	12.43330	11.71885	11.07943	10.50433	9.98468	9.51309	9.08338	8.69035	8.32958	7.99734	7.69042	7.40606	7.14189
69	13.24260	12.43825	11.72245	11.08205	10.50624	9.98607	9.51411	9.08413	8.69090	8.32999	7.99764	7.69063	7.40622	7.14201
70	13.24893	12.44282	11.72576	11.08445	10.50798	9.98734	9.51503	9.08480	8.69139	8.33034	7.99790	7.69083	7.40636	7.14211
71	13.25482	12.44706	11.72881	11.08665	10.50957	9.98849	9.51586	9.08541	8.69183	8.33066	7.99813	7.69100	7.40648	7.14221
72	13.26030	12.45098	11.73162	11.08867	10.51102	9.98954	9.51662	9.08595	8.69222	8.33095	7.99834	7.69115	7.40659	7.14229
73	13.26539	12.45461	11.73421	11.09052	10.51235	9.99049	9.51730	9.08644	8.69257	8.33121	7.99852	7.69128	7.40669	7.14236
74	13.27013	12.45797	11.73660	11.09222	10.51356	9.99135	9.51792	9.08688	8.69289	8.33143	7.99869	7.69140	7.40678	7.14242
75	13.27454	12.46108	11.73880	11.09378	10.51467	9.99214	9.51848	9.08728	8.69318	8.33164	7.99883	7.69150	7.40685	7.14247
76	13.27864	12.46397	11.74083	11.09521	10.51568	9.99285	9.51899	9.08764	8.69343	8.33182	7.99896	7.69160	7.40692	7.14252
77	13.28246	12.46664	11.74270	11.09653	10.51660	9.99350	9.51945	9.08797	8.69366	8.33198	7.99908	7.69168	7.40698	7.14256
78	13.28601	12.46911	11.74443	11.09773	10.51744	9.99409	9.51986	9.08826	8.69387	8.33213	7.99918	7.69175	7.40703	7.14260
79	13.28931	12.47140	11.74601	11.09883	10.51821	9.99463	9.52024	9.08852	8.69405	8.33226	7.99927	7.69181	7.40707	7.14263
80	13.29238	12.47351	11.74748	11.09985	10.51892	9.99512	9.52057	9.08876	8.69422	8.33237	7.99935	7.69187	7.40711	7.14266
81	13.29524	12.47548	11.74883	11.10078	10.51956	9.99556	9.52088	9.08897	8.69436	8.33247	7.99942	7.69192	7.40715	7.14268
82	13.29790	12.47729	11.75007	11.10163	10.52015	9.99597	9.52116	9.08916	8.69450	8.33257	7.99949	7.69197	7.40718	7.14270
83	13.30037	12.47897	11.75122	11.10241	10.52068	9.99633	9.52141	9.08934	8.69462	8.33265	7.99955	7.69201	7.40721	7.14272
84	13.30267	12.48053	11.75228	11.10313	10.52117	9.99667	9.52164	9.08949	8.69472	8.33272	7.99960	7.69204	7.40723	7.14274
85	13.30481	12.48197	11.75325	11.10379	10.52162	9.99697	9.52185	9.08963	8.69482	8.33279	7.99964	7.69207	7.40725	7.14275
86	13.30680	12.48331	11.75415	11.10440	10.52202	9.99724	9.52203	9.08976	8.69490	8.33285	7.99968	7.69210	7.40727	7.14277
87	13.30865	12.48455	11.75497	11.10495	10.52240	9.99749	9.52220	9.08987	8.69498	8.33290	7.99972	7.69212	7.40729	7.14278
88	13.31037	12.48569	11.75574	11.10546	10.52274	9.99772	9.52235	9.08998	8.69505	8.33294	7.99975	7.69214	7.40730	7.14279
89	13.31197	12.48675	11.75644	11.10593	10.52305	9.99793	9.52249	9.09007	8.69511	8.33299	7.99978	7.69216	7.40731	7.14280
90	13.31346	12.48773	11.75709	11.10635	10.52333	9.99812	9.52262	9.09015	8.69517	8.33302	7.99980	7.69218	7.40732	7.14280
91	13.31485	12.48864	11.75768	11.10675	10.52359	9.99829	9.52273	9.09023	8.69522	8.33306	7.99982	7.69219	7.40733	7.14281
92	13.31614	12.48948	11.75823	11.10711	10.52383	9.99844	9.52283	9.09029	8.69526	8.33309	7.99984	7.69221	7.40734	7.14282
93	13.31734	12.49026	11.75874	11.10744	10.52404	9.99859	9.52293	9.09036	8.69530	8.33311	7.99986	7.69222	7.40735	7.14282
94	13.31846	12.49098	11.75921	11.10774	10.52424	9.99871	9.52301	9.09041	8.69534	8.33314	7.99988	7.69223	7.40736	7.14283
95	13.31949	12.49165	11.75964	11.10802	10.52442	9.99883	9.52309	9.09046	8.69537	8.33316	7.99989	7.69224	7.40736	7.14283
96	13.32046	12.49227	11.76004	11.10827	10.52458	9.99894	9.52315	9.09050	8.69540	8.33318	7.99990	7.69225	7.40737	7.14283
97	13.32136	12.49284	11.76040	11.10851	10.52473	9.99903	9.52322	9.09054	8.69543	8.33319	7.99991	7.69225	7.40737	7.14284
98	13.32219	12.49337	11.76074	11.10872	10.52487	9.99912	9.52327	9.09058	8.69545	8.33321	7.99992	7.69226	7.40738	7.14284
99	13.32297	12.49386	11.76105	11.10892	10.52500	9.99920	9.52332	9.09061	8.69547	8.33322	7.99993	7.69226	7.40738	7.14284
100	13.32369	12.49432	11.76134	11.10910	10.52511	9.99927	9.52337	9.09064	8.69549	8.33323	7.99994	7.69227	7.40738	7.14284
101	13.32437	12.49474	11.76160	11.10927	10.52522	9.99934	9.52341	9.09067	8.69551	8.33324	7.99995	7.69227	7.40739	7.14284
102	13.32499	12.49513	11.76184	11.10942	10.52531	9.99940	9.52345	9.09069	8.69552	8.33325	7.99995	7.69228	7.40739	7.14285
103	13.32557	12.49549	11.76207	11.10956	10.52540	9.99945	9.52348	9.09071	8.69553	8.33326	7.99996	7.69228	7.40739	7.14285
104	13.32611	12.49582	11.76227	11.10969	10.52548	9.99950	9.52351	9.09073	8.69555	8.33327	7.99996	7.69228	7.40739	7.14285
105	13.32662	12.49613	11.76246	11.10981	10.52555	9.99955	9.52354	9.09075	8.69556	8.33328	7.99997	7.69229	7.40739	7.14285
106	13.32709	12.49642	11.76264	11.10991	10.52562	9.99959	9.52357	9.09077	8.69557	8.33328	7.99997	7.69229	7.40740	7.14285
107	13.32752	12.49668	11.76280	11.11001	10.52568	9.99963	9.52359	9.09078	8.69558	8.33329	7.99997	7.69229	7.40740	7.14285
108	13.32793	12.49693	11.76295	11.11010	10.52573	9.99966	9.52361	9.09079	8.69558	8.33329	7.99998	7.69230	7.40740	7.14285
109	13.32831	12.49716	11.76309	11.11019	10.52578	9.99969	9.52363	9.09080	8.69559	8.33330	7.99998	7.69230	7.40740	7.14285
110	13.32866	12.49737	11.76322	11.11026	10.52583	9.99972	9.52365	9.09082	8.69560	8.33330	7.99998	7.69230	7.40740	7.14285
111	13.32898	12.49756	11.76333	11.11033	10.52587	9.99975	9.52366	9.09082	8.69560	8.33330	7.99998	7.69230	7.40740	7.14285
112	13.32929	12.49774	11.76344	11.11040	10.52591	9.99977	9.52368	9.09083	8.69561	8.33331	7.99999	7.69230	7.40740	7.14285
113	13.32957	12.49791	11.76354	11.11046	10.52595	9.99979	9.52369	9.09084	8.69561	8.33331	7.99999	7.69230	7.40740	7.14285
114	13.32983	12.49807	11.76363	11.11051	10.52598	9.99981	9.52370	9.09085	8.69562	8.33331	7.99999	7.69230	7.40740	7.14286
115	13.33008	12.49821	11.76371	11.11056	10.52601	9.99983	9.52371	9.09085	8.69562	8.33332	7.99999	7.69230	7.40740	7.14286
116	13.33030	12.49834	11.76379	11.11060	10.52603	9.99984	9.52372	9.09086	8.69562	8.33332	7.99999	7.69230	7.40740	7.14286
117	13.33051	12.49846	11.76386	11.11065	10.52606	9.99986	9.52373	9.09086	8.69563	8.33332	7.99999	7.69230	7.40740	7.14286
118	13.33071	12.49858	11.76393	11.11069	10.52608	9.99987	9.52374	9.09087	8.69563	8.33332	7.99999	7.69230	7.40741	7.14286
119	13.33089	12.49868	11.76399	11.11072	10.52610	9.99988	9.52374	9.09087	8.69563	8.33332	7.99999	7.69230	7.40741	7.14286
120	13.33106	12.49878	11.76405	11.11075	10.52612	9.99989	9.52375	9.09088	8.69563	8.33332	7.99999	7.69230	7.40741	7.14286

Table E.4 (concluded)
PRESENT VALUE OF AN ORDINARY ANNUITY OF $1 PER PERIOD: 14.5%–20%

Period	14.5%	15%	15.5%	16%	16.5%	17%	17.5%	18%	18.5%	19%	19.5%	20%
1	0.87336	0.86957	0.86580	0.86207	0.85837	0.85470	0.85106	0.84746	0.84388	0.84034	0.83682	0.83333
2	1.63612	1.62571	1.61541	1.60523	1.59517	1.58521	1.57537	1.56564	1.55602	1.54650	1.53709	1.52778
3	2.30229	2.28323	2.26443	2.24589	2.22761	2.20958	2.19181	2.17427	2.15698	2.13992	2.12309	2.10648
4	2.88410	2.85498	2.82634	2.79818	2.77048	2.74324	2.71643	2.69006	2.66412	2.63859	2.61346	2.58873
5	3.39223	3.35216	3.31285	3.27429	3.23646	3.19935	3.16292	3.12717	3.09208	3.05763	3.02382	2.99061
6	3.83600	3.78448	3.73407	3.68474	3.63645	3.58918	3.54291	3.49760	3.45323	3.40978	3.36721	3.32551
7	4.22358	4.16042	4.09876	4.03857	3.97979	3.92238	3.86631	3.81153	3.75800	3.70570	3.65457	3.60459
8	4.56208	4.48732	4.41451	4.34359	4.27449	4.20716	4.14154	4.07757	4.01519	3.95437	3.89504	3.83716
9	4.85771	4.77158	4.68789	4.60654	4.52746	4.45057	4.37578	3.30302	4.23223	4.16333	4.09627	4.03097
10	5.11591	5.01877	4.92458	4.83323	4.74460	4.65860	4.57513	4.49409	4.41538	4.33893	4.26466	4.19247
11	5.34140	5.23371	5.12951	5.02864	4.93099	4.83641	4.74479	4.65601	4.56994	4.48650	4.40557	4.32706
12	5.53834	5.42062	5.30693	5.19711	5.09098	4.98839	4.88918	4.79322	4.70037	4.61050	4.52349	4.43922
13	5.71034	5.58315	5.46055	5.34233	5.22831	5.11828	5.01207	4.90951	4.81044	4.71471	4.62217	4.53268
14	5.86056	5.72448	5.59355	5.46753	5.34619	5.22930	5.11666	5.00806	4.90333	4.80228	4.70474	4.61057
15	5.99176	5.84737	5.70870	5.57546	5.44747	5.32419	5.20567	5.09158	4.98171	4.87586	4.77384	4.67547
16	6.10634	5.95423	5.80840	5.66850	5.53422	5.40529	5.28142	5.16235	5.04786	4.93770	4.83167	4.72956
17	6.20641	6.04716	5.89472	5.74870	5.60878	5.47461	5.34589	5.22233	5.10368	4.98966	4.88006	4.77463
18	6.29381	6.12797	5.96945	5.81785	5.67277	5.53385	5.40075	5.27316	5.15078	5.03333	4.92055	4.81219
19	6.37014	6.19823	6.03415	5.87746	5.72770	5.58449	5.44745	5.31624	5.19053	5.07003	4.95443	4.84350
20	6.43680	6.25933	6.09018	5.92884	5.77485	5.62777	5.48719	5.35275	5.22408	5.10086	4.98279	4.86958
21	6.49502	6.31246	6.13868	5.97314	5.81532	5.66476	5.52101	5.38368	5.25239	5.12677	5.00652	4.89132
22	6.54587	6.35866	6.18068	6.01133	5.85006	5.69637	5.54980	5.40990	5.27628	5.14855	5.02638	4.90943
23	6.59028	6.39884	6.21704	6.04425	5.87988	5.72340	5.57430	5.43212	5.29644	5.16685	5.04299	4.92453
24	6.62907	6.43377	6.24852	6.07263	5.90548	5.74649	5.59515	5.45095	5.31345	5.18223	5.05690	4.93710
25	6.66294	6.46415	6.27577	6.09709	5.92745	5.76623	5.61289	5.46691	5.32780	5.19515	5.06853	4.94759
26	6.69252	6.49056	6.29937	6.11818	5.94631	5.78311	5.62799	5.48043	5.33992	5.20601	5.07827	4.95632
27	6.71836	6.51353	6.31980	6.13636	5.96250	5.79753	5.64084	5.49189	5.35014	5.21513	5.08642	4.96360
28	6.74093	6.53351	6.33749	6.15204	5.97639	5.80985	5.65178	5.50160	5.35877	5.22280	5.09324	4.96967
29	6.76064	6.55088	6.35281	6.16555	5.98832	5.82039	5.66109	5.50983	5.36605	5.22924	5.09894	4.97472
30	6.77785	6.56598	6.36607	6.17720	5.99856	5.82939	5.66901	5.51681	5.37219	5.23466	5.10372	4.97894
31	6.79288	6.57911	6.37755	6.18724	6.00734	5.83709	5.67576	5.52272	5.37738	5.23921	5.10771	4.98245
32	6.80601	6.59053	6.38749	6.19590	6.01489	5.84366	5.68150	5.52773	5.38175	5.24303	5.11106	4.98537
33	6.81747	6.60046	6.39609	6.20336	6.02136	5.84928	5.68638	5.53197	5.38545	5.24625	5.11386	4.98781
34	6.82749	6.60910	6.40354	6.20979	6.02692	5.85409	5.69054	5.53557	5.38856	5.24895	5.11620	4.98984
35	6.83623	6.61661	6.40999	6.21534	6.03169	5.85820	5.69407	5.53862	5.39119	5.25122	5.11816	4.99154
36	6.84387	6.62314	6.41558	6.22012	6.03579	5.86171	5.69708	5.54120	5.39341	5.25312	5.11980	4.99295
37	6.85054	6.62881	6.42041	6.22424	6.03930	5.86471	5.69965	5.54339	5.39528	5.25472	5.12117	4.99412
38	6.85637	6.63375	6.42460	6.22779	6.04232	5.86727	5.70183	5.54525	5.39686	5.25607	5.12232	4.99510
39	6.86146	6.63805	6.42823	6.23086	6.04491	5.86946	5.70368	5.54682	5.39820	5.25720	5.12328	4.99592
40	6.86590	6.64178	6.43136	6.23350	6.04713	5.87133	5.70526	5.54815	5.39932	5.25815	5.12408	4.99660
41	6.86978	6.64502	6.43408	6.23577	6.04904	5.87294	5.70660	5.54928	5.40027	5.25895	5.12475	4.99717
42	6.87317	6.64785	6.43643	6.23774	6.05068	5.87430	5.70775	5.55024	5.40107	5.25962	5.12532	4.99764
43	6.87613	6.65030	6.43847	6.23943	6.05208	5.87547	5.70872	5.55105	5.40175	5.26019	5.12579	4.99803
44	6.87872	6.65244	6.44024	6.24089	6.05329	5.87647	5.70955	5.55174	5.40232	5.26066	5.12618	4.99836
45	6.88098	6.65429	6.44176	6.24214	6.05432	5.87733	5.71026	5.55232	5.40280	5.26106	5.12651	4.99863
46	6.88295	6.65591	6.44308	6.24323	6.05522	5.87806	5.71086	5.55281	5.40321	5.26140	5.12679	4.99886
47	6.88467	6.65731	6.44423	6.24416	6.05598	5.87868	5.71137	5.55323	5.40355	5.26168	5.12702	4.99905
48	6.88618	6.65853	6.44522	6.24497	6.05664	5.87922	5.71180	5.55359	5.40384	5.26191	5.12721	4.99921
49	6.88749	6.65959	6.44608	6.24566	6.05720	5.87967	5.71217	5.55389	5.40409	5.26211	5.12738	4.99934
50	6.88864	6.66051	6.44682	6.24626	6.05768	5.88006	5.71249	5.55414	5.40429	5.26228	5.12751	4.99945
51	6.88964	6.66132	6.44746	6.24678	6.05809	5.88039	5.71275	5.55436	5.40447	5.26242	5.12762	4.99954
52	6.89052	6.66201	6.44802	6.24722	6.05845	5.88068	5.71298	5.55454	5.40461	5.26254	5.12772	4.99962
53	6.89128	6.66262	6.44850	6.24760	6.05876	5.88092	5.71318	5.55469	5.40474	5.26264	5.12780	4.99968
54	6.89195	6.66315	6.44892	6.24793	6.05902	5.88113	5.71334	5.55483	5.40484	5.26272	5.12786	4.99974
55	6.89253	6.66361	6.44928	6.24822	6.05924	5.88131	5.71348	5.55494	5.40493	5.26279	5.12792	4.99978
56	6.89304	6.66401	6.44959	6.24846	6.05944	5.88146	5.71360	5.55503	5.40500	5.26285	5.12797	4.99982
57	6.89348	6.66435	6.44987	6.24868	6.05960	5.88159	5.71370	5.55511	5.40507	5.26290	5.12801	4.99985
58	6.89387	6.66466	6.45010	6.24886	6.05974	5.88170	5.71379	5.55518	5.40512	5.26294	5.12804	4.99987
59	6.89421	6.66492	6.45030	6.24902	6.05987	5.88180	5.71386	5.55524	5.40516	5.26297	5.12807	4.99989
60	6.89451	6.66515	6.45048	6.24915	6.05997	5.88188	5.71393	5.55529	5.40520	5.26300	5.12809	4.99991

Period	14.5%	15%	15.5%	16%	16.5%	17%	17.5%	18%	18.5%	19%	19.5%	20%
61	6.89477	6.66534	6.45063	6.24927	6.06006	5.88195	5.71398	5.55533	5.40523	5.26303	5.12811	4.99993
62	6.89499	6.66552	6.45076	6.24937	6.06014	5.88200	5.71403	5.55536	5.40526	5.26305	5.12812	4.99994
63	6.89519	6.66567	6.45088	6.24946	6.06020	5.88206	5.71406	5.55539	5.40528	5.26307	5.12814	4.99995
64	6.89536	6.66580	6.45098	6.24953	6.06026	5.88210	5.71410	5.55542	5.40530	5.26308	5.12815	4.99996
65	6.89551	6.66591	6.45106	6.24960	6.06031	5.88214	5.71413	5.55544	5.40532	5.26309	5.12816	4.99996
66	6.89565	6.66601	6.45114	6.24965	6.06035	5.88217	5.71415	5.55546	5.40533	5.26310	5.12816	4.99997
67	6.89576	6.66609	6.45120	6.24970	6.06039	5.88219	5.71417	5.55547	5.40534	5.26311	5.12817	4.99998
68	6.89586	6.66617	6.45125	6.24974	6.06042	5.88222	5.71419	5.55548	5.40535	5.26312	5.12818	4.99998
69	6.89595	6.66623	6.45130	6.24978	6.06045	5.88224	5.71420	5.55549	5.40536	5.26313	5.12818	4.99998
70	6.89602	6.66629	6.45134	6.24981	6.06047	5.88225	5.71421	5.55550	5.40537	5.26313	5.12819	4.99999
71	6.89609	6.66634	6.45138	6.24983	6.06049	5.88227	5.71422	5.55551	5.40537	5.26314	5.12819	4.99999
72	6.89615	6.66638	6.45141	6.24986	6.06050	5.88228	5.71423	5.55552	5.40538	5.26314	5.12819	4.99999
73	6.89620	6.66642	6.45144	6.24988	6.06052	5.88229	5.71424	5.55552	5.40538	5.26314	5.12819	4.99999
74	6.89624	6.66645	6.45146	6.24989	6.06053	5.88230	5.71425	5.55553	5.40539	5.26314	5.12820	4.99999
75	6.89628	6.66648	6.45148	6.24991	6.06054	5.88231	5.71425	5.55553	5.40539	5.26315	5.12820	4.99999
76	6.89632	6.66650	6.45150	6.24992	6.06055	5.88231	5.71426	5.55554	5.40539	5.26315	5.12820	5.00000
77	6.89635	6.66653	6.45151	6.24993	6.06056	5.88232	5.71426	5.55554	5.40539	5.26315	5.12820	5.00000
78	6.89637	6.66654	6.45153	6.24994	6.06057	5.88232	5.71427	5.55554	5.40540	5.26315	5.12820	5.00000
79	6.89640	6.66656	6.45154	6.24995	6.06057	5.88233	5.71427	5.55554	5.40540	5.26315	5.12820	5.00000
80	6.89642	6.66657	6.45155	6.24996	6.06058	5.88233	5.71427	5.55555	5.40540	5.26315	5.12820	5.00000
81	6.89643	6.66659	6.45156	6.24996	6.06058	5.88234	5.71427	5.55555	5.40540	5.26315	5.12820	5.00000
82	6.89645	6.66660	6.45157	6.24997	6.06058	5.88234	5.71428	5.55555	5.40540	5.26315	5.12820	5.00000
83	6.89646	6.66661	6.45157	6.24997	6.06059	5.88234	5.71428	5.55555	5.40540	5.26316	5.12820	5.00000
84	6.89647	6.66661	6.45158	6.24998	6.06059	5.88234	5.71428	5.55555	5.40540	5.26316	5.12820	5.00000
85	6.89648	6.66662	6.45158	6.24998	6.06059	5.88234	5.71428	5.55555	5.40540	5.26316	5.12820	5.00000
86	6.89649	6.66663	6.45159	6.24998	6.06059	5.88234	5.71428	5.55555	5.40540	5.26316	5.12820	5.00000
87	6.89650	6.66663	6.45159	6.24998	6.06060	5.88235	5.71428	5.55555	5.40540	5.26316	5.12820	5.00000
88	6.89651	6.66664	6.45159	6.24999	6.06060	5.88235	5.71428	5.55555	5.40540	5.26316	5.12820	5.00000
89	6.89651	6.66664	6.45160	6.24999	6.06060	5.88235	5.71428	5.55555	5.40540	5.26316	5.12820	5.00000
90	6.89652	6.66664	6.45160	6.24999	6.06060	5.88235	5.71428	5.55555	5.40540	5.26316	5.12820	5.00000
91	6.89652	6.66665	6.45160	6.24999	6.06060	5.88235	5.71428	5.55555	5.40540	5.26316	5.12820	5.00000
92	6.89652	6.66665	6.45160	6.24999	6.06060	5.88235	5.71428	5.55555	5.40540	5.26316	5.12820	5.00000
93	6.89653	6.66665	6.45160	6.24999	6.06060	5.88235	5.71428	5.55555	5.40540	5.26316	5.12820	5.00000
94	6.89653	6.66665	6.45160	6.24999	6.06060	5.88235	5.71428	5.55555	5.40540	5.26316	5.12820	5.00000
95	6.89653	6.66666	6.45161	6.25000	6.06060	5.88235	5.71428	5.55555	5.40540	5.26316	5.12820	5.00000
96	6.89654	6.66666	6.45161	6.25000	6.06060	5.88235	5.71428	5.55555	5.40540	5.26316	5.12820	5.00000
97	6.89654	6.66666	6.45161	6.25000	6.06060	5.88235	5.71428	5.55555	5.40541	5.26316	5.12820	5.00000
98	6.89654	6.66666	6.45161	6.25000	6.06060	5.88235	5.71428	5.55556	5.40541	5.26316	5.12820	5.00000
99	6.89654	6.66666	6.45161	6.25000	6.06060	5.88235	5.71429	5.55556	5.40541	5.26316	5.12821	5.00000
100	6.89654	6.66666	6.45161	6.25000	6.06060	5.88235	5.71429	5.55556	5.40541	5.26316	5.12821	5.00000
101	6.89654	6.66666	6.45161	6.25000	6.06060	5.88235	5.71429	5.55556	5.40541	5.26316	5.12821	5.00000
102	6.89654	6.66666	6.45161	6.25000	6.06061	5.88235	5.71429	5.55556	5.40541	5.26316	5.12821	5.00000
103	6.89655	6.66666	6.45161	6.25000	6.06061	5.88235	5.71429	5.55556	5.40541	5.26316	5.12821	5.00000
104	6.89655	6.66666	6.45161	6.25000	6.06061	5.88235	5.71429	5.55556	5.40541	5.26316	5.12821	5.00000
105	6.89655	6.66666	6.45161	6.25000	6.06061	5.88235	5.71429	5.55556	5.40541	5.26316	5.12821	5.00000
106	6.89655	6.66666	6.45161	6.25000	6.06061	5.88235	5.71429	5.55556	5.40541	5.26316	5.12821	5.00000
107	6.89655	6.66666	6.45161	6.25000	6.06061	5.88235	5.71429	5.55556	5.40541	5.26316	5.12821	5.00000
108	6.89655	6.66666	6.45161	6.25000	6.06061	5.88235	5.71429	5.55556	5.40541	5.26316	5.12821	5.00000
109	6.89655	6.66667	6.45161	6.25000	6.06061	5.88235	5.71429	5.55556	5.40541	5.26316	5.12821	5.00000
110	6.89655	6.66667	6.45161	6.25000	6.06061	5.88235	5.71429	5.55556	5.40541	5.26316	5.12821	5.00000
111	6.89655	6.66667	6.45161	6.25000	6.06061	5.88235	5.71429	5.55556	5.40541	5.26316	5.12821	5.00000
112	6.89655	6.66667	6.45161	6.25000	6.06061	5.88235	5.71429	5.55556	5.40541	5.26316	5.12821	5.00000
113	6.89655	6.66667	6.45161	6.25000	6.06061	5.88235	5.71429	5.55556	5.40541	5.26316	5.12821	5.00000
114	6.89655	6.66667	6.45161	6.25000	6.06061	5.88235	5.71429	5.55556	5.40541	5.26316	5.12821	5.00000
115	6.89655	6.66667	6.45161	6.25000	6.06061	5.88235	5.71429	5.55556	5.40541	5.26316	5.12821	5.00000
116	6.89655	6.66667	6.45161	6.25000	6.06061	5.88235	5.71429	5.55556	5.40541	5.26316	5.12821	5.00000
117	6.89655	6.66667	6.45161	6.25000	6.06061	5.88235	5.71429	5.55556	5.40541	5.26316	5.12821	5.00000
118	6.89655	6.66667	6.45161	6.25000	6.06061	5.88235	5.71429	5.55556	5.40541	5.26316	5.12821	5.00000
119	6.89655	6.66667	6.45161	6.25000	6.06061	5.88235	5.71429	5.55556	5.40541	5.26316	5.12821	5.00000
120	6.89655	6.66667	6.45161	6.25000	6.06061	5.88235	5.71429	5.55556	5.40541	5.26316	5.12821	5.00000

INDEX

A

Ability to raise creditor capital, corporation, 453
Absorption costing, 819–20, 821–23, 829
Academic accountants, 11–12, 20
Accelerated Cost Recovery System (ACRS), 384
Accelerated depreciation, 377–78, 398
Account, 64–65, 102
Accounting
 accountants' ethical behavior, 16–17
 accounting standards, development of, 14–16, 584–85
 accrual basis of, 74, 102, 116–17, 159, 580
 cash basis of, 116–17, 160, 586
 defined, 5, 20
 employment opportunities in, 6–12
 financial, 12–13, 21
 functions of, 5–6
 and just-in-time production system, 664–66
 as language of business, 4
 managerial, 13–14, 21
 manufacturing overhead, 704–10
 materials, 702–3
 measurement in, 584
 public, 7–10, 21
 women in, 88
Accounting differences, merchandiser and manufacturer, 640–41
Accounting entity, 24
Accounting equation, 32–33, 48
Accounting Horizons, 15
Accounting period, 118, 159
Accounting Principles Board (APB), 14, 20
 Opinions, 15, 385, 480–85, 538
Accounting qualities, hierarchy of, 598
Accounting records' accuracy, internal control and, 311–12
Accounting Review, 15
Accounting Standards Committee, 14
Accounting systems, 308, 350, 1171–74, 1195–1205

Accounting theory
 articulation, 582
 business entity concept, 578–79, 620
 changes in assets and liabilities, measurement of, 584
 comparability and consistency, accounting information, 601, 620
 conservatism, 595, 621
 consistency, 581–82, 621
 cost-benefit consideration, 593, 621
 defined, 577, 620
 double entry, 582
 exchange-price (or cost) principle, 585, 621
 expense recognition principle, 591, 621
 FASB conceptual framework project, 595–605
 financial reporting objectives, 596–97, 621
 financial statements
  elements of, 602–3
  recognition and measurement in, 603–5
 gain and loss recognition principle, 591–92, 621
 general-purpose financial statements, 581
 going-concern (continuity) assumption, 579, 621
 legal form and economic substance, 581
 major principles summarized, 592
 matching principle, 585, 622
 materiality, 593–95, 622
 measuring assets and liabilities, 584
 modifying conventions (constraints), 593–95, 622
  summarized, 594
 money measurement, 579, 622
 periodicity (time periods) assumption, 580–81, 622
 pervasive constraints, 602
 qualitative characteristics, accounting information, 597–602, 622
 relevance, accounting information, 597–99, 623

Accounting theory—*Cont.*
 reliability, accounting information, 599–601, 623
 revenue recognition principle, 586–90, 623
 stable dollar, 579–80, 623
 underlying assumptions or concepts summarized, 582–83
Accounting year, 116, 159
Accounts, effects of transactions recording on, 74–86
Accounts, materials and other inventories, 647–48
Accounts affected by operating costs, budgeting and, 859–60
Accounts payable, 31, 48, 148, 159
Accounts receivable, 31, 48
 and budgeting, 857
 defined, 147, 159
 uncollectible, 132–35
Accounts receivable turnover, 1074, 1101
Accrual basis of accounting, 74, 102, 116-17, 159
 and periodicity, 580
Accrued expenses, 140
Accrued items, 120–21, 160
Accrued liabilities, 140–41, 159–60
Accrued revenues, 138–41, 159–60
Accumulated depreciation, 148, 161, 388–89
Accumulated depreciation account, 131, 160
Accumulating costs, job order cost system, 699–700
Acid-test ratio, 1072–73, 1102
Acquisition cost, plant assets, 367, 391
Activity-based costing, 651–52, 680, 715, 817
Actual overhead rate, 705, 725, 738
Adding or dropping products, segments, or customers, 815–16
Adjunct account, 197, 230
Adjusting entries
 cash vs. accrual basis accounting, 116–17
 classes and types of, 120–23
 defined, 119, 160
 depreciation, 129–32
 failure to prepare, effects of, 141–42

Chart of Accounts Used Consistently in the
First Eleven Chapters of This Text (concluded)

Account Number	Account Title

Revenue and Gain Accounts (concluded)

408	Commissions Revenue
409	Legal Fees Revenue
410	Sales
411	Sales Discounts
412	Sales Returns and Allowances
413	Membership and Lesson Revenue
414	Management Fee Revenue
415	Subscriptions Revenue
418	Interest Revenue
420	Miscellaneous Revenue
421	Gain on Disposal of Plant Assets
422	Other Revenue

Cost of Goods Sold, Operating Expense, and Loss Accounts

500	Purchases
501	Purchase Discounts
502	Purchase Returns and Allowances
503	Transportation-In
504	Cost of Goods Sold
505	Advertising Expense
506	Gas and Oil Expense
507	Salaries Expense (or Wages Expense)
508	Sales Salaries Expense
509	Office Salaries Expense
510	Officers' Salaries Expense
511	Utilities Expense
512	Insurance Expense
513	Feed Expense
515	Rent Expense
516	Store Supplies Expense
518	Supplies Expense
519	Delivery Expense
520	Depreciation Expense — Buildings
521	Depreciation Expense — Trucks
522	Depreciation Expense — Automobiles
523	Depreciation Expense — Office Furniture
524	Depreciation Expense — Equipment
525	Depreciation Expense — Office Equipment
526	Depreciation Expense — Store Fixtures
527	Depreciation Expense — Machinery
528	Depreciation Expense — Land Improvements
529	Depreciation Expense — Furniture and Fixtures
530	Repairs Expense
531	Entertainment Expense
532	Travel Expense
533	Property Tax Expense